principles of **PSYCHOLOGY**

EUROPEAN EDITION

principles of
PSYCHOLOGY
CONTEMPORARY PERSPECTIVES

MATT JARVIS | PAUL OKAMI

OXFORD
UNIVERSITY PRESS

OXFORD
UNIVERSITY PRESS

Great Clarendon Street, Oxford, OX2 6DP,
United Kingdom

Oxford University Press is a department of the University of Oxford.
It furthers the University's objective of excellence in research, scholarship,
and education by publishing worldwide. Oxford is a registered trade mark of
Oxford University Press in the UK and in certain other countries

© Oxford University Press 2020

The moral rights of the authors have been asserted
First Edition 2020

Impression: 1

Public sector information reproduced under Open Government Licence v3.0
(http://www.nationalarchives.gov.uk/doc/open-government-licence/open-government-licence.htm)

Published in the United States of America by Oxford University Press
198 Madison Avenue, New York, NY 10016, United States of America

British Library Cataloguing in Publication Data
Data available

ISBN 978–0–19–881315–6

Printed in Great Britain by
Bell & Bain Ltd., Glasgow

Adapted from a work originally published by Oxford University Press USA. This adapted version has been customized for the United Kingdom, Europe, and the Middle East only and is published by arrangement with Oxford University Press USA. It may not be sold elsewhere.

ABOUT THE AUTHORS

MATT JARVIS Matt Jarvis is a chartered psychologist and associate fellow of the British Psychological Society. He is best known as a leading exponent of psychology education, from GCSE to postgraduate level.

A former psychology education lecturer at Keele University and visiting lecturer at the University of Southampton's department of education, Matt has contributed widely to both psychology curriculum development and to initial and continuing teacher development, and has conducted research into teacher stress, e-learning, and effective pedagogy.

Matt also freelances as an author and trainer, and has written numerous best-selling A level and higher education psychology textbooks. He currently works as learning technology and innovation manager for Nacro: a major social justice and education charity.

PAUL OKAMI Paul Okami is Adjunct Professor of Psychology at Temple University, USA, and a member of the Association for Psychological Science. Paul has published widely, in the areas of sexuality, evolutionary psychology, and child development.

A highly regarded teacher at every level of higher education, from university to community college, Paul has had great success introducing students to contemporary perspectives in the subject.

CONTENTS

DETAILED CONTENTS

PREFACE TO THE EUROPEAN EDITION

Welcome to this European reworking of Paul Okami's classic US text *Psychology: Contemporary Perspectives*. If you are embarking on a university-level psychology course, whether it's a psychology degree or the psychology components of nursing, social work, occupational therapy, physiotherapy, or any other profession involving psychology, I hope and believe you are in for a very stimulating period of your life and a lot of fun. Studying and working in psychology has vastly enriched my life and thinking, and I hope it does the same for you.

Psychology can be defined as the scientific study of mind, brain, and behaviour. Any aspect of human thinking, emotion, experience, neurobiology, or behaviour is fair game for psychologists, as long as it can be studied in a scientific manner. Sometimes there is a trade-off between a focus on what lends itself to controlled study and what is most interesting to the layperson; hence, the subject matter of this book ranges from the mechanisms of nervous transmission and the number of digits that can be held in short-term memory, to the developmental experience of adolescent identity and the social psychology of the mosh pit. It's all real psychology—*provided we research it in a scientific manner and think critically about that research.*

The structure of this book is based around the British Psychological Society's curriculum requirements for the Graduate Basis for Chartered membership, which separates psychology into domains. For those that aren't studying on a BPS-accredited course, this structure will still be useful for arranging your learning. Any attempt to classify psychology into sections is imperfect and if you would have preferred some content to be in a different place you are probably not alone—that's just the nature of psychology! In choosing content I have tried to balance theory and research from the USA, where most psychological research has always been published, with that from the UK, mainland Europe, and the rest of world. I also have aimed to bring in a range of real-life examples and applications of psychology, not only to bring psychology to life but also to make this book as useful as possible to those studying for professional qualifications, such as nursing or social work. In a very real sense though, *what you study* in psychology is less important than you might suppose; psychology is as much a way of thinking and operating as it is a body of subject matter. Those of you who do not go on to work in psychology may remember few details of theories and studies ten or 20 years down the line. However, you should retain your *psychological literacy*, meaning that you will be able to see beyond headlines and statistics and know what questions to ask about the psychology you have seen in the media or presented in training at work.

Which brings me to my main aims in writing this book. I wanted to do more than provide an account of the subject matter of psychology and how it is studied—although, of course, those things are vitally important. I also wanted to draw on modern pedagogical research as well as my experiences of studying and teaching psychology to help you develop some study habits and ways of thinking that will enable you to make sense of psychology and begin to engage with psychological theories and studies *like a psychologist*. To do this I have included chapters at the start of the book to separately address how to study psychology, the nature of psychology, and the methods used to research psychology. Throughout each chapter I have included features designed to help you think more like a psychologist and take periodic deep dives into individual pieces of research, picking apart how studies were conducted, and why these choices were made. To gain the most from this book I recommend that you pay as much attention to these features as to the main content.

As you read this book, you will notice that there are few absolute truths in psychology. This isn't a failing—as a science, psychology strives towards establishing robust explanations—but reflects the hard-to-research nature of the human mind, brain, and behaviour. It does mean though that if you read a range of books you will see the same topics being covered in different ways; inevitably different authors will see different theories, studies, examples, and conclusions as key to your learning. This can be confusing at first but being able to critically read texts and form your own understanding of and views on issues are important skills to develop as you study psychology. Finally, I wish you the very best in your studies and I hope psychology brings you as much interest and pleasure as it has me.

ACKNOWLEDGEMENTS

This might be a good moment to thank all the anonymous reviewers from the UK and elsewhere in Europe for their input. A huge thank you to the team at OUP; in particular, Martha Bailes, Judith Lorton, and Hetty Marx, for putting their faith in me and for their editorial prowess, gentle persistence, and their encouragement at all stages of developing, writing, and producing this book.

A GUIDE TO THIS BOOK

This book aims to get you thinking like a psychologist. It will introduce you to the world of psychology, and help you develop the skills you will need throughout your degree. The learning features you will come across are specially designed to support your learning, and will help you to think critically, apply your findings, and engage with psychological research.

LEARNING OUTCOMES

By the end of this chapter you should be able to:

- Offer alternative definitions of learning and appreciate difficulties in pinning down the concept
- Understand the relationship between what is 'learnt' and 'innate'
- Distinguish between habituation and associative learning
- Outline the processes of classical conditioning, drawing on examples of studies in humans and animals
- Discuss the usefulness of classical conditioning in explaining human behaviour
- Describe the principles of operant conditioning in animals and humans
- Evaluate the importance of operant conditioning as an explanation for human

Learning objectives To learn effectively, it's a good idea to know what you're aiming for! At the start of each chapter we have the 'learning objectives' in a clear, bullet-pointed list. This gives you a guide to what you should have achieved, or should be able to do, by the end of the chapter.

Suggestibility

❭ KEY IDEAS suggestibility **Suggestibility** is a type of misattribution in which a new or distorted memory originates in suggestions made to a person by someone else.

❭ KEY IDEAS the misinformation effect The **misinformation effect** takes place when a person exposed to incorrect information about an event they have experienced later recall the event in a distorted

As we saw in Loftus' eyewitness memory experiments and vividly i Kelly Michaels earlier in this chapter, the reconstructive nature of m that it is possible to distort memories by suggesting things retrospectiv nomenon of memory **suggestibility** is a specific type of misattributio from intentional or unintentional suggestions from others. Suggestion road to the development of memory distortions, particularly false mer

Much of Loftus' work during the 1980s explored the ways in whic are exposed to incorrect information about an event they have exper recall the event in a distorted manner by incorporating the false i tendency that has come to be termed the **misinformation effect** (Frend In a classic demonstration of the misinformation effect, Loftus and t asked university students to watch a series of slides depicting an a in a hardware shop in which a screwdriver was taken in addition to viewing the slides the students read narrative reports of the crime w altered—a hammer was described as having been taken instead of a scr

Key ideas All new or unfamiliar psychological terms are defined in the text but, to help you see those definitions quickly, 'key ideas' are highlighted in marginal boxes. You will also find all of these key ideas in our glossary.

Thinking features Through questions, problems, and activities, the thinking features help you not only explore the psychological theories and material, but also analyse and apply those theories, as well as develop key skills in research design.

 THINKING CRITICALLY

Much of the publicity regarding the recent decline in electronic devices around bedtime. The suggestion is However, research in this area has serious limitation

Exercise

1 Most studies in this area have been correlati

Thinking critically Our 'thinking critically' feature is designed to encourage in-depth analytical engagement with the material to hone essential critical thinking skills.

This feature uses critical thinking toolkits and specific questions to help you pick apart psychological material, identifying its strengths and weaknesses and assessing its relative importance in psychological theory and research.

 THINKING CREATIVELY

It is notoriously difficult to gather valid data about lence varies massively by age, gender, and cultural ba and social desirability to consider.

Imagine you are going to conduct this kind of resea

1 How could you ensure a representative sample

Thinking creatively The 'thinking creatively' feature allows you to solve novel problems and develop research design skills. It requires you to come up with your own ideas about how to explain psychological phenomena, find information, and conduct psychological research.

THINKING PRACTICALLY

What advice might you give a troop of Scouts or Gu
in order to keep themselves most safe from accide
sensory adaptation, the blind spot, and the roles of r

Thinking Practically 'Thinking practically' will really get you used to applying psychological ideas, theory, and research to real world situations. It might ask you to relate the theory to your own life, a case study, or ask you to recommend interventions in an imaginary scenario.

RESEARCH IN FOCUS

Mischel, W. and Ebbesen, E.B. (1970). Attention and delay of gratificat
Personality and Social Psychology, **16**, 329–37.

Aim: The aim of the study was to investigate the role of cognitive proces
ity to delay gratification. More specifically, to test whether having sma
and larger delayed rewards in view affected children's tendency to wait
It was predicted that children would find it hardest to delay gratificat
immediate nor the delayed reward was visible.

Research in Focus and Master your methodology Our 'Research in Focus' feature supports engagement with primary sources by guiding you through classic studies and more recent research.

This feature summarises research papers according to their aims, methods, results, and conclusions. These present a clear overview of the paper, familiarising you with the structure of research papers, and providing a framework to guide your future reading.

At the end of each 'Research in Focus' feature is our 'Master your Methodology' feature, a set of questions designed to prompt you to critically assess the design of the study, the methods of data collection and analysis, and the conclusions reached.

DEBUNKING—WHY DO PEOPLE BELIEVE IN ASTROLOGY?

An awful lot of people believe in astrology. According to a review of international surveys (Gr
2016) around 20% of people in the UK believe in the influence of 'their stars', as compared
29% in the USA and close to 100% in India. Without being disrespectful to anyone's cultural
tions, we can confidently say that there is no *scientific* basis to astrology. Of course you may
additional frames of reference other than science; we are just hoping to influence your sci
development. This is not to say that it is impossible that the season of your birth may imp
your development. Whether you were one of the older or younger children in your schoo
may mean that you had slightly different social and educational experiences. It may even b
the weather in your infancy influenced gene expression at crucial points in your develop
However, this is *not* the same as saying that your personality is influenced by the stars.

Debunking Our 'Debunking' feature takes apart some commonly-held beliefs and assumptions.

This feature briefly summarises the myth, and then outlines the evidence that disproves it. It also explores the reasons for the popularity of the myth, and encourages you to apply this methodology to examples from your own life.

WHAT'S HOT? CAN 'BRAIN TRAINING' BOOST IQ?

The Internet is awash with adverts for 'brain training' programmes, pr
that claim to improve our cognitive functioning. Some of these prog
some young adults, and some older people, claiming to stave off age
nitive functions like memory. Whether or not they claim to boost mea
about changing intelligence. Brain training is big business, and a sou
sorts of people, so what does psychology have to tell us?

There is no doubt that if you practise a mental task you will tend to ge

What's Hot This feature summarises what 'everyone's' talking about. This could be the recent developments in a field, research trends, classic studies that have gained new importance, or problems and challenges for the field of psychology.

READ THIS

You can learn more about the nature of scientific psychology from pret
chology book. There may, however, be some specific things you want
read this chapter. You might like to start with Magnusson's definition
Magnusson, D. (2012). **The human being in society.** *European Psychol*

For more about pseudoscience in a psychological context we can all re
Lilienfeld, S.O., Ammirati, R., and David, M. (2012). Distinguishing scie
school psychology: Science and scientific thinking as safeguards aga
of School Psychology **50**, 7–36.

Read this As you'll see in Chapter 1, it is essential to always read around psychology and it is important to understand the strengths and weaknesses of different sources and how best to use them. Our 'read this' feature gives suggestions of what to read next, allowing you to extend or consolidate your study.

IN REVIEW

- The computational theory of mind holds that the mind fun loosely analogous to a computer.

- Cognitive scientists study mental activities involved in col storing, retrieving, and manipulating information.

- Thought is the active process of mentally manipulating or p tion to solve problems, make decisions, increase knowledge,

- Thinking involves two components: mental images and conc

- Kahneman distinguishes between two thinking systems, one

In Review Our 'in review' feature offers a clear summary of the chapter in a bullet-pointed list. This can be a powerful revision tool–allowing you to identify gaps in your knowledge, and check you have understood all of the core concepts from the chapter.

TEST YOURSELF

1 Atypical attachment is a risk factor for serious mental h False ☐

2 Infant temperament predicts some aspects of adult perso

3 Toddlers are less likely to interact with another toddler if True ☐ False ☐

4 Research has consistently shown that children who sper disadvantaged. True ☐ False ☐

Test yourself At the end of the chapter, we encourage you to check what you have learned by answering the 'test yourself' questions. These questions take a variety of formats (true/false, multiple-choice, short-answer), and cover a range of topics from across the chapter.

A GUIDE TO THE ONLINE RESOURCES

 Visit the online resources that accompany this book: **www.oup.com/uk/jarvis-okami1e**

For students:

Self-test questions

To allow you to check your progress, we've included 25 multiple-choice questions for each chapter. These can help to revisit the content, and identify areas you might need to work on.

Flashcards

Our flashcards show all the key ideas in the book. You might find these useful for checking you know all the definitions, which can also be found in our glossary.

Chapter outlines

We provide 'chapter outlines' to help you structure your notes and to use in your revision.

Concept maps

We have provided mind-maps that link together the key ideas from the chapter, designed to show you how the concepts relate to one another.

To accompany these and show you how to use them effectively, there is a concept map guide that teaches you how to map concepts themselves, and provides suggestions for how to use the concept maps provided in your own learning.

Animations

To support you in your study of biological psychology, we have animated videos on the following topics:

- Types of neurons
- Resting potentials

- Action potential
- Communication
- Neurotransmitters

Discussion topics

For each chapter, we have provided 5-13 discussion questions. These cover a range of issues, allowing you to revisit the content in new and creative ways. These can be used independently or as part of a group.

Assignments

For each chapter we have 5 assignments, which you can use as homework activities. These focus on key psychological skills such as critical thinking, and prompt you to apply the content you have learned.

Weblinks

To help you consolidate and extend your learning, as well as make connections across psychology, we have provided a list of 5 'Weblinks' per chapter. These can help consolidate your learning with podcasts, videos and interactive activities, or extend your knowledge with case studies and examples. Each link is annotated, so that you know what to look out for!

A quarterly research digest

Every three months, we'll be releasing an online update written by author Matt Jarvis. He'll be keeping you up-to-date with summaries of key developments in the field of psychology.

To support lecturers

A lecturer's guide

To help make using this book and the online resources as easy as possible, our lecturer's guide gives an overview of how you might use them in your teaching. It includes:

- a preface for lecturers, introducing the aims and approach of the book
- a guide to using the book to support students in their transition to university education
- an outline of how the book and accompanying online materials meet course needs
- suggestions on how to use the book and accompanying online materials in different teaching scenarios
- a curriculum grid, to show how the book's content maps against BPS guidelines, and can be used in different course structures

PowerPoint presentations

To make putting together your lectures easy, we have provided PowerPoint presentations for each chapter, summarising the key concepts and content from the chapter. There are 20-30 slides per chapter, which include overview and summary slides.

Test bank

Our test bank is designed to slot into your teaching in the way that suits you, so that you can set students a range of questions. For each chapter, the test bank contains 50 multiple-choice questions, 10 true/false questions, 10 fill-in-the-blank questions, and 4 essay questions.

Image bank

To allow you to fully integrate *Principles of Psychology* within your teaching, we have provided all of the images used within the book in a high-quality image bank.

PART 1

PSYCHOLOGY AS SCIENCE:
PRINCIPLES AND METHODS

STUDYING PSYCHOLOGY

CHAPTER 1

LEARNING OUTCOMES

By the end of this chapter you should be able to:

- Understand the difference between academic and popular psychology
- Think critically about media representations of psychological issues
- Begin to use the scientific method to assess some common assumptions and myths in psychology
- Identify and begin to use a range of sources of psychological literature
- Appreciate some of the differences between psychology at pre-degree level and university level and better understand the requirements of undergraduate study
- Understand the limitations of textbooks and the importance of using primary sources
- Locate key primary sources and search for examples of contemporary research
- Be aware of some different types of thinking including critical and creative thinking
- Use critical thinking toolkits to evaluate psychological theory, research, and practice
- Start to think creatively by generating hypotheses and designing studies
- Begin to think practically about psychology by means of problem-based learning

In this chapter we begin to explore psychology with a particular focus on tackling some possible preconceptions and common misconceptions about the subject. This first section is pitched towards those entirely new to psychology, but if it starts to sound familiar to you, bear with us because you will probably still gain something from the later sections of the chapter. These later sections are more concerned with upgrading your skills from pre-degree to undergraduate level and starting to think like a psychologist.

The first and most basic question you might ask as someone new to psychology is 'what is psychology?' The short answer is that psychology is the scientific study of the human mind, brain, and behaviour. If that definition sounds too simple you are of course absolutely right! We explore the longer answer on the nature of psychology in Chapter 2. As psychologists we consider ourselves scientists. If psychologists sometimes sound a bit precious about this issue it is because our scientific methods clearly differentiate us from other approaches to understanding human nature such as philosophy, religion, and, debatably, sociology, and psychoanalysis. More of this in Chapter 2. For now, the point is that when you begin to study psychology, you are taking on board not just a body of knowledge but also a way of thinking scientifically about people.

MOVING AWAY FROM LAY PSYCHOLOGY

If you have an interest in psychology but have not formally studied it before, the chances are that you will have read or at least dipped into newspapers, magazine articles, and/or popular psychology paperbacks. It is important to understand at this point that what we call 'real' psychology may look a little different to the psychology you have come across until now.

Academic and Popular Psychology

❭ KEY IDEAS* popular and academic psychology Popular psychology, or 'pop' psychology, is written for ordinary people (the layperson) and is typically intended to provide the reader with insight into their experiences and perhaps a degree of therapeutic value. There is no requirement for popular psychology to stick to scientific principles or realistic claims. Academic psychology literature on the other hand is written for psychologists and psychology students, and its aim is to provide an account of psychology based closely on referenced psychological theory and research.

*We use this 'key ideas' feature to draw out particularly important concepts and clarify and/or elaborate on them to ensure you have the understanding you need of them.

Let's start with the distinction between academic and popular psychology. Go to any high street bookshop and look for the psychology section. The books you will find there will divide up (fairly) neatly into either popular psychology or academic psychology. Unless it is a university bookshop, the popular psychology books are likely to be more populous. Some bookshops helpfully split the two into separate sections. So what is the difference? Popular psychology is not *necessarily* incorrect or inferior to academic psychology. Many (though sadly by no means all) popular psychology books are written by well-qualified psychologists and based on sound psychological principles. They are generally written with the very honourable intention of communicating psychological ideas to members of the public in order to improve their quality of life. So, we are not setting out to demean any popular psychology you might have read and found helpful in the past. However, now is the time to put such things aside. Read the *Thinking critically* feature and consider the questions about popular and academic psychology material.

FIGURE 1.1 What's the difference between academic and popular psychology books?
Source: Mikael Damkier/Shutterstock.com.

THINKING CRITICALLY*

Let us illustrate the problem with popular psychology by comparing two paragraphs, both concerned with the role of patterns of negative thinking in depression.

Paragraph 1. Popular Psychology Version

We feel whatever we think. When we think negatively we start to feel negative. Say we have a negative attitude to ourselves; that makes it hard for people to be nice to us. When someone says 'your hair looks nice' we think things like 'no it doesn't' or 'they must be after something.' That is clearly depressing! No wonder that interacting with other people makes us feel down. Negative thinking also means we pay attention to all the downsides of a situation. The glass is always half empty, never half full. Finally, if we let ourselves think negatively the future always looks gloomy. Of course we get depressed; we have nothing to look forward to!

Paragraph 2. Academic Psychology Version

Beck (1976) proposed a causal role for negative thinking in the origins of depression. He suggested a '**cognitive triad**' of automatic negative thoughts concerning the self, the world, and the future. Based on the principle of cognitive primacy, Beck suggests that the emotional experience of depression is a direct consequence of these automatic negative thoughts. One line of research that provides support for Beck's ideas looks at the extent to which negative thinking predicts later depression. For example, Grazioli and Terry (2000) found that women displaying negative thinking in pregnancy were more prone to post-natal depression.

Consider the following:

1 Both paragraphs outline a *theory* of depression, not the definitive explanation. Which paragraph makes this clearer? How does it achieve this?

2 One paragraph is focused on the everyday experience of negative thinking. The other focuses on theory and research. What sort of readership might each be aimed at?

3 Paragraph 2 contains references that allow the reader to go back to the original theory and research around it. Why is this helpful?

4 Although paragraph 2 does not generally use *longer* words than paragraph 1, it does use more *technical* terms. Why is this helpful to a psychologist or psychology student? Why might paragraph 1 not use many technical terms?

*This critical thinking feature is designed to help you pick apart psychological material and identify its strengths and weaknesses. We do this in a number of ways. In some cases we will refer to the critical thinking toolkits introduced later in this chapter. In others we will ask questions of particular relevance to the theory or study we are discussing at the time.

We won't comment on the potential therapeutic value of paragraph 1 to someone suffering from **depression**. However we do feel pretty secure in our judgement that for a psychology student it is useless! It fails to distinguish between theory and fact, does not even identify the theory being outlined, and fails to use the sort of technical terms that would allow us to describe psychological material with precision. Without any references we cannot go back to original sources to expand our understanding of the points made or evaluate their accuracy or completeness. There is also no mention of scientific evidence for the points made.

Paragraph 2 is not above criticism. It provides only a partial description of Beck's theory and its argument is unbalanced. Nonetheless, it outlines a clearly identified and referenced theory using technical terms and offers comment based on scientific research. These features of precise language, modesty of claims, and reliance on evidence are a big part of good psychology.

Academic psychology is written for a very different audience compared with popular psychology. If you are writing an assignment as a student of psychology it is essential that you can put the ideas you are discussing in context as part of a theory or study. Keep in mind that there is almost no such thing as an undisputed fact in psychology. It is therefore essential that when you present an idea you present it as part of a theory that is open to challenge. The biggest problem with drawing on popular psychology sources is that they tend to present ideas as facts, often without any indication of where these 'facts' come from. As a psychology undergraduate you cannot afford to fall into the trap of copying this style. Citing 'Men are from Mars and women are from Venus' in an undergraduate psychology essay will not do your tutors' blood pressure or your grades any good at all.

Media Representations of Psychology

If the literature of popular psychology presents psychological ideas simplistically, selectively, uncritically, and out of context, the same is often true of the way psychology is reflected in the wider media. Read the article in the *Thinking critically* feature and have a look at our questions. This article extract is a composite made up from the details of a number of real articles.

 THINKING CRITICALLY

'Working Mums Ruin Lives', 3 October 2019, *Weekly Traditionalist*, p 4

Young children who are looked after by their biological mothers until school age develop faster than those who spend time with nurseries, child minders, or relatives, a damning study has found. The *Real Mums* project, which commenced in 2004, followed 300 children from South London from six months to five years of age, at which time their development was assessed by means of telephone interviews with parents and questionnaires completed by their reception teachers. One of the study's authors, Professor Tory Nunn, said the development of babies cared for by non-maternal adults was affected significantly. Babies and toddlers who were looked after in nurseries were found to fare the worst.

Intellectual and Social Development

Teachers rated children who had enjoyed the full-time care of their biological mother until five years of age as more able. This held true when teachers were asked about children's numeracy, literacy, and overall academic ability. Teachers and extended family also judged children's social development as poorer when they had spent time in childcare, these children being rated as more aggressive, withdrawn, and compliant.

Consider the following:

1 If we took these results at face value, how would this affect our opinions of childcare?

2 Before taking these results too seriously, what further details would we want to know about the study?

3 Is there anything important that the study does not consider that we might wish to think about before making a judgement about day care?

4   Can you see any examples of information that has been presented as negative that might equally be thought of as positive?

5   What factors might bias a researcher to be pro- or anti-childcare? Who do you think might have sponsored this study? Why does this matter?

FIGURE 1.2   **Are nurseries bad for children?**
Source: suriya silsaksom © 123RF.com.

Journalists, rather like popular psychology authors, are writing with the aim of communicating psychological ideas to the public. Whilst they have an obligation to do this clearly and accurately, journalists are usually writing with a political agenda, as well as intending to entertain and generally inform their audience. They are not under the same obligations as psychologists to present balanced and critical arguments. Neither do they generally have the opportunity to develop the nuanced understanding of psychological issues we would expect from an academic psychologist. It is therefore generally not a good idea to take news reports of psychological research at face value.

Moving from Commonly Held Beliefs to Scientific Research Questions

One of the things that may frustrate you as a student new to psychology is the lack of solid facts. Psychologists tend to be good at having debates, thrashing out issues, and offering theories, but much less successful at generating simple facts and sharing them with the public. Popular psychology and stories of psychology in the media tend to present ideas as facts but often the evidence is lacking or at best mixed. A key difference between proper academic psychology and popular and media psychology is that academic psychologists are generally much more cautious about identifying 'facts'. From the article above we can see that the journalist presented the idea that nurseries are bad for children's development as a fact. Other ideas presented as facts include:

1   We learn best when using our preferred learning style

2   Murder is most common when there is a full moon

3   Those with high IQ get the best grades at school

THINKING CREATIVELY*

Take the hypothesis 'nurseries are bad for children's development'. This readily generates the research question 'are nurseries bad for children?' Your task is to think of all the sources of evidence that we could draw on in order to help answer this question. We aren't (yet!) asking you to design and carry out a study, just to think about what sort of information could help us answer the question. We will start you off with an example: data comparing reception class teachers' ratings of behaviour problems.

*We use this *Thinking creatively* feature to encourage you to develop your own ideas about how to find information, design studies, and explain psychological phenomena—in other words, to be creative in your approach to psychology.

Although you will probably come across psychologists with very strong views on all these issues (both for and against the statements), we would say that these statements are definitely *not* facts. However, that is not to say that they have no value. On the contrary, they make very good *hypotheses*. A **hypothesis** is a testable statement that forms the starting point to the process of scientific research. We can take a hypothesis like 'nurseries are bad for children's development' or 'murder is most common when there is a full moon' and carry out research designed to test it.

BEGINNING TO USE PSYCHOLOGY LITERATURE

You should now have a good idea of the limitations of popular psychology books and the general media as sources of information about psychology. If you are using this book you will also have some experience of 'proper' psychology literature, but *please* don't limit yourself to a book like this. It is essential to always read around psychology and it is important to understand the strengths and weaknesses of different sources and how best to use them.

- **General psychology texts**: in your first year of undergraduate study you may be recommended a general psychology textbook—like this one. In spite of their intimidating size, textbooks like this really just skim the surface of psychology. They are helpful for providing an overview of psychology so that you can see where particular ideas fit in, and in providing some comprehensible explanations of the basics. They should also be well referenced, so that you can follow up key ideas in more detail. However, textbooks like this tend to provide very limited detail of individual studies, and have representations and conclusions that inevitably reflect the biases of the authors (even us)! We suggest that in your first year at university you use your main text regularly but that you move away from it as your main source of information as soon as you can bear to.

- **Specialist psychology texts**: these address specific areas of psychology. They vary widely in the level at which they are written and how broad an area they cover. They might be as broad in coverage as 'cognitive psychology' or narrower; for example, addressing 'working memory'. Generally as your course progresses you will move away from general texts to more specialist ones. However, *all* books date very quickly and reflect the personal preferences of the author, both in terms of what material they cover and the conclusions they reach. By the final year of your degree, even the most respected and specialist books should just be the starting point of your reading, never the end point.

- **Review articles**: these may be published in magazines, research journals, or publications like the British Psychological Society's *The Psychologist* or the Association of Psychological Science's *Observer*, which fall somewhere between the two. Review articles are often more up to date (at the point of publication) than textbooks. The authors are often invited to contribute them because of their particular expertise, so academic standards tend to be high. We recommend review articles to give you an idea about what experts conclude about a research field, and for the criticisms the authors make of other researchers. As with textbooks, however, we recommend that you move away from relying on reviews and start using original research papers as soon as possible.

- **Research journal articles and conference papers**: these are sometimes called 'primary sources'. They are the first point at which the results and conclusions of scientific research are published. These papers generally use quite complex language and may devote considerable space to detailed statistical analysis, which may not make much sense to you at first. However, do persevere with using this sort of material, even if to start with you are dipping into papers rather than reading them in their entirety. Even when the statistics seem incomprehensible you can probably unpick more methodological detail of a study from the original paper than a second-hand account. You can also be sure that you are picking up the subtleties of what the authors are really concluding. It is easy to get a false impression of this from reading second-hand accounts of research.

- **Search engines and databases**: try googling a psychological term like 'antisocial behaviour' and you will obtain millions of hits from all sorts of websites, ranging from government ministries through academic journals to personal sites and those representing a particular interest, such as political and religious groups. Relatively few of these will be of much use to you as a psychology student. We deal with judicious use of conventional search tools and using specialist electronic databases in more detail later in this chapter. For now, however, if you do start by googling psychological topics, we suggest that you always bear in mind that anyone can set up a website. You should really only use sites with some sort of quality-assurance mechanism. These include the following:

  - **Journal sites and e-journals**: many academic journals are now available online. More often than not, abstracts are free but full text access requires registration. Your university will have access to a fair range of these (ask your librarians for help—they are highly expert at locating sources). Even when this is not the case it is well worth browsing and searching abstracts of academic papers. Some journals are available only online: these are known as e-journals. An increasing number of e-journals are now free to access. The academic quality of journals varies somewhat—ask your tutor about particular sources.

  - **Conference websites**: the organizers of many academic conferences publish abstracts or full papers. Like journal articles these are primary sources, so potentially very useful. However, like online journals they vary in quality, so again we recommend asking your tutor for advice about particular sites.

  - **Think tank and government agency websites**: good-quality research is often conducted by private research establishments, commonly known as 'think tanks'. Reports of such research may be published on the websites of the institution itself or on the site of the body that commissioned the research—such as a government agency. Although these are typically written to a high academic

❯ **KEY IDEAS** search engines and databases When you search for psychological material online, you use two technologies that may appear superficially similar. A search engine looks for items that have been tagged for particular search terms. It may search the whole Internet (like Google) or selected websites. A database will probably also have a search facility but this just searches the material held together in one place, again tagged for searching. Wikipedia is an example of a database.

standard, think tanks often attract funding by supporting a particular political agenda. Bear this in mind when evaluating their publications.

- **University websites**: sometimes the university at which research was conducted has permission to re-publish the article or articles resulting from that research. Often the university will have an introductory page explaining the aims of the project in fairly non-technical language with a link to the article itself. You can recognize university URLs by the suffix .ac.uk in the UK, or .edu in the USA. Remember that material is not *necessarily* of good quality just by virtue of its being on a university website—it may have been written by a less knowledgeable student than yourself!

MAKING THE BREAK FROM PRE-DEGREE STUDY OF PSYCHOLOGY

If you studied psychology before coming to university, you may have been surprised to hear your university tutors don't necessarily rate your previous course highly. Pre-degree study of psychology doesn't necessarily develop the sort of skills you will need at university so you may face some challenges when moving from pre-degree to undergraduate psychology. Some of these challenges are listed below. The suggestions are based on a number of sources (Banister, 2003, 2005; Tombs, 2004; Green 2005; Jarvis, 2011).

- Moving away from a single textbook to multiple sources of information
- Becoming more independent in your research and information gathering
- Writing in a more analytical and less descriptive style
- Developing your skills of evaluation
- Becoming more up to date in your understanding of psychology
- Understanding psychology as it is seen at university as opposed to how it is portrayed in pre-degree courses

We can group these difficulties into three areas: use of books and other sources of information, higher-level thinking, and developing subject understanding. We can make a start on tackling all of these in this chapter.

Because many psychology undergraduates have not have studied psychology before, the first year of the degree needs to cover a lot of basics. If you have studied psychology before, it can be tempting to 'coast' for a year on your existing knowledge and understanding. We would strongly advise you against this and instead suggest that you think of your first year as a chance to develop not just your basic subject understanding but also your skills as a student as well as your general understanding of the nature of psychology. In particular, try to get much more sophisticated in terms of what sources of information you use and how you respond to them.

Surrendering Your Pre-Degree Textbooks

The chances are that as a pre-degree psychology student you relied primarily or exclusively on a single textbook. This book will probably have been chosen for you (or at least recommended), and structured closely around a particular curriculum. Pre-degree qualifications are very intensive and you work under tremendous time pressure. This means that a textbook that tells you exactly what you need to know and is pitched at exactly the level you need to get good marks in your exams is a very precious thing!

However, regardless of the affection you may still hold for your pre-degree text, now is the time to wean yourself off it. All general psychology textbooks have their limitations, and as a university student you *must get out of the habit of relying on a single textbook*. One aspect of university study you will have to get used to is referring to multiple sources, and although you will probably have some leeway with this in your first year, the sooner it becomes second nature to read a variety of sources the better. The other reason is that as your pre-degree text was based around one curriculum, they tend to be narrow in scope. At university level, your needs are different and what you really need are resources that give you a realistic overview of the whole field of psychology.

The Importance of Using Primary Sources

One thing you'll encounter when you move from pre-degree to undergraduate study is tutors directing you to 'use primary sources' and 'go to the original paper'. Primary sources are the research journals and conference proceedings where the articles were originally published. This will definitely be something of a culture change from pre-degree study; however, it is really important that you start to at least dip into primary sources as soon as possible. By the final year of your degree you should ideally reference *only* primary sources. The following exercise should make the reasons for this clearer.

> ❯ KEY IDEAS primary sources Primary sources are where theory and research are first published, most commonly academic journals. It is essential that you begin to use primary sources and work towards relying on primary sources for your understanding of psychology.

THINKING PRACTICALLY*

1 First read our summary below of a fun little psychology experiment. This is written deliberately in slightly more detail than that you would typically find in a textbook like this one.

Parsons et al (2011) investigated whether people showed better motor skills after listening to the sound of a baby crying. Forty adults took part in the study, which involved playing 'whack-a-mole', a game requiring hitting plastic shapes as they randomly pop up. In one condition participants listened first to a baby crying. In a second condition they listened to a distressed adult and in a third they listened to a distressed bird. In both accuracy and force the participants performed better at the game after listening to the human infant.

2 Now challenge yourself by dipping into the original. You can find this at www.kringelbach. dk/papers/AP_Parsons2011.pdf. Consider the following:

● What additional details did you gain from the original paper?

● Was anything clearer after looking at the original?

Overall do you feel you have a better understanding of the study after looking at the original?

*The idea of our *Thinking practically* feature is to get you used to applying psychological ideas, theory, and research to real-world situations.

You will probably notice a number of things from this exercise. In comparing your summaries you may find that you focused on different aspects of the study or interpreted aspects of it slightly differently. In short your understanding will be different, and each reader will form a different mental representation of the study. If you want to be confident of having an accurate understanding of what the authors of a study really did and concluded, you *must* read at least some of their original work.

The other key lesson from this exercise lies in comparing the level of detail in our summary with that given in the original. By looking at the original paper—even when some of it is hard to understand without help—you should be able to extract significantly more information than you can get from a textbook. You should, for example, get a much clearer idea of why the researchers conducted a study in a particular way, and you will certainly obtain more in the way of methodological detail. It is primarily for these two reasons that your tutors will insist that you to go to primary sources for your information.

There are additional reasons not to rely too much on your general textbook. There may well be cases in which otherwise excellent textbooks report details of particular studies slightly inaccurately. Remember that authors of general textbooks will have their own specialism, and for much of the book they will be writing outside this. Some authors also have very strong views on particular issues in psychology. This is absolutely their privilege as psychologists and authors, however it is inevitable that they will present those issues in a biased way. It is important that you look critically at controversial issues and make up your own mind about where the balance of evidence lies rather than accept the view of a particular author.

THINKING CRITICALLY

This exercise requires you to deconstruct the language used by a textbook author in their discussion of Freudian theory. This is a composite based on a number of real textbook accounts:

'Although Freud's residual impact on psychology and neuroscience is slim, his notoriety continues to affect public perceptions of psychology. Freud's influence also lingers stubbornly in the fields of literary interpretation, psychiatry and pop-psychology.'

Consider the following:

1 The opening clause is a strong statement. Do you think it is justified?

2 What does the word 'notoriety' suggest?

3 In what context do we normally use the word 'linger'? What does this imply about Freud?

4 What does the author achieve by linking Freud with three other disciplines outside academic psychology?

Searching for Specialist and Primary Sources

The cultural norm for information searching is googling, normally using the first hit which is more than likely Wikipedia. In fact this is now so universal that although we will try to guide you to more specialist resources, we know that you will search for information using Google and Wikipedia as well. If we can't entirely talk you out of generic search engines like Google and generic databases like Wikipedia then at least bear in mind their limitations when it comes to finding information about psychology. Google typically finds several million hits for whatever search term you enter. You can use the advanced search features to narrow this down by, for example, eliminating sites that contain irrelevant words. Even then, however, it can be hard to find what you are looking for. Moreover, many sites have no more information than a basic textbook, and many are of dubious quality. Wikipedia *can* be a good source of links but always remember that you don't know who wrote each page and that the reviewing process used by Wikipedia favours widely held beliefs rather than cutting-edge understanding.

Your tutors will probably guide you towards particular searchable and/or browsable databases to look for electronic versions of original papers. These are set up slightly differently at different universities so we won't go into too much detail here, but you will probably have access to and be encouraged to use a range of databases, most likely through your university's ATHENS account. These will probably include a range of tools designed to search the journals published by each journal publisher—Elsevier, Taylor & Francis, Wolters-Kluwer, etc. You may also receive access to the American Psychological Society's two major databases:

- PsycARTICLES: a repository of full text articles
- PsycINFO: a much larger repository of abstracts

Although some academics disapprove of it, the *Google Scholar* search engine is also well worth a look. This is a specialist Google search tool that only searches academic material. It locates multiple copies of each article so it is useful for finding full-text papers that are available in several online locations but only in full-text format in a much smaller range of sites. You can use these databases and search engines in two main ways. First, you can find papers you already know about; for example, those in the reference list of your general textbook. Second, you can find new articles on a topic. For this purpose you may want a bigger range of studies so something like *PsycINFO* or *Google Scholar* is likely to be more useful. There are two golden rules when searching:

- When you hear about a study or theory in a lecture or textbook and want to know more, always go back to the original source.
- When you want to know more about a topic, search for contemporary papers in that area so that your understanding is up to date.

The OSCA principle

To know if you are studying the right way, just think *OSCA* (Original Sources, Contemporary Articles) and you shouldn't go too far wrong. We suggest the following exercise to get an idea of how to use databases.

 THINKING PRACTICALLY

Moving away from reproducing the material in your textbook and instead constructing your own understanding of a topic based on independent research is a major challenge when starting a psychology degree. The aim of this exercise is to give you experience of using electronic databases to locate studies in psychology, both in order to find more detail on studies covered in your textbook(s) and to find new material. Check whether you have access to *PsycINFO* and *PsycARTICLES*. If you don't, you can still carry this out using free resources.

1 Your first task is to locate a copy of Watson and Rayner's classic 1920 paper on the conditioning of a fear response in a baby. If you have *PsycARTICLES* access, either enter 'conditioned emotional reaction' or go to author search and enter 'Watson'. You can also specify the date, in this case 1920. If you don't have *PsycARTICLES* access there is a free repository of classic articles at the University of York website (http://psychclassics.yorku.ca/) which contains this paper. Locate and save the article.

>

> 2 Having obtained the original source, your second task is to find more recent research in
>   the area of classical conditioning. If you have *PsycINFO* access, enter 'classical condition-
>   ing' as a search term. If you don't have such access you can use *Google Scholar* (http://
>   scholar.google.com). This works in much the same way. Scroll down your list of hits and
>   read the abstracts. Select a few relevant and recent studies and save the abstracts.

Manual Searching

You can of course use your university library! In these days of advanced technology it can be tempting to do all your searching from the comfort of your desk. However, no database is completely up to date and comprehensive, and tagging articles so that they appear on searches is an imperfect science. The best searches are therefore done electronically *and* manually. A good tip when you start using the library is to make friends with the library staff. They will be well aware that you have new skills to learn and they will be able to offer you a variety of tips for both manual and electronic searching. When you start searching the journal stacks for articles, don't be afraid to make good use of your librarians.

The Subject Matter of Psychology at Undergraduate Level

Psychology is diverse and exists in many contexts so always be cautious when someone offers their own definition of 'real psychology'. However, in the context of undergraduate academic psychology the boundaries of what is and is not psychology are fairly clear. Bear in mind the following.

Psychology is definitely a science!

Before university, you may have debated the extent to which psychology is a 'real science'. However, in higher education there is no such debate, and psychology is regarded as a pure science. Given that psychology looks a little different to the other sciences (no Bunsen burners and relatively few lab coats) the question is begged: what do we mean by 'science'? We discuss the nature of science and scientific psychology in detail in Chapter 2.

It's not about Freud and Rogers any more

A key difference between pre-degree and undergraduate psychology lies in the weighting given to different approaches to psychology. Remember that pre-degree study of psychology provides a very general introduction and may consider approaches relevant in applied as well as academic psychology. So humanistic psychology is important in counselling and sport psychology, and psychodynamic approaches are still applied in mental health, and you may therefore study those approaches. By contrast, your psychology undergraduate programme is much more about mainstream psychological research. Humanistic and psychodynamic approaches to psychology in particular are *very* marginal in modern academic research and therefore they have a very small place in most psychology degrees. Instead you should expect a lot more cognitive and biological psychology than you encountered in any pre-degree study. Once you are past your introductory lectures you can also expect a greater emphasis on up-to-date research. You will also study research methods and statistics in depth.

There will be a lot more practical work

If you studied psychology before your degree you may have carried out some class practical work, but you probably won't have been regularly designing, running, and writing up studies throughout your course. At undergraduate level you are being trained to be a competent researcher more than anything else, so expect a lot more practical work. Through your first year you will probably engage in a number of fairly small individual and small group practicals. You may or may not get a choice in what studies you run. Having to replicate classic studies rather than design your own exciting new ones can be frustrating but bear in mind that you are perfecting your basic research skills. By the time you are let loose with your own research ideas you will have much greater freedom in how to design and carry out your research precisely because of the range of practicals you ran early on in the course.

BEGINNING TO THINK MORE LIKE A PSYCHOLOGIST

Two of the common criticisms of pre-degree psychology are that it encourages de-scription rather than analysis and that it is too easy to score marks with formulaic evaluation points like 'it lacks ecological validity' rather than being forced to think deeply about the material. This kind of evaluation doesn't sit well with your uni-versity lecturers because it can be rote-learnt and repeated back to them in assess-ments without much in-depth engagement with the subject matter. This is a problem from your tutors' perspective because the whole process of identifying the strengths, weaknesses, and implications of ideas in psychology is meant to be one of thinking deeply about the details of theories and studies. Depending on how you were previ-ously taught, you may find that one of the adjustments you have to make in order to get to grips with undergraduate psychology is to unlearn the tendency to offer throw-away evaluative comments and think more deeply about the theories and/or studies you are looking at.

So is Psychological Thinking Scientific Thinking?

Well, clearly you are learning a science and thinking scientifically about theory and research is going to be an important part of this process. However, philosopher Pat-rick McGhee (2001) says that there is far more to psychological thinking than this. McGhee suggests that a good psychologist must be able to think like a scientist but also on occasion like an anthropologist, a historian, a philosopher, and a therapist. This is worth picking apart a little.

There is no doubt that what we can call core scientific thinking is the lifeblood of psychology. So when we consider evidence for an idea, generate a hypothesis, or design a study we are operating as a scientist. However, it can also be helpful to be aware of the historical context in which ideas developed because this can sometimes reveal the reasons why evidence has been looked for in certain directions and not others. Sometimes theories and concepts in psychology have a body of supporting evidence primarily because a lot of effort has been made to look for it rather than because they are intrinsically good concepts or better than alternative theories. It helps to be a bit of a philosopher because philosophy helps us to take a step back and evaluate the importance, availability, and credibility of ideas and their evidence. Debates over mind-body duality (Chapter 4) and nature and nurture (Chapter 5) have their roots in long-standing philosophical discussions.

❯ KEY IDEAS scientific and psychological thinking Scientific thinking can be described as the logical process of thinking about how to generate and evaluate evidence for an idea, remaining as objective and unbiased as is humanly possible. Psychological thinking includes scientific thinking but is broader as psychologists can often benefit from stepping back from an immediate issue and looking at wider issues such as historical influence and practical value.

Although (counter to stereotype) most psychologists are not therapists, it helps to be able to think, sometimes, as a therapist does, about the extent to which ideas are helpful to people. Sometimes, ideas that have little supporting evidence or are just very difficult to investigate scientifically (like the meaning of dreams) are still relevant to psychology because they are inherently interesting to the layperson and potentially therapeutic.

A Model to Structure Your Psychological Thinking

American educational psychologist Robert Sternberg (1997) offers a different way of understanding higher-order thinking skills. He distinguishes between three types of psychological thinking:

- *Analytic (critical) thinking*: this involves breaking down a theory or study in order to identify its strengths and limitations. This encompasses the ideas of analysis and evaluation. Whenever you find a weakness or a strength of a study or theory, or comment about how a historical context influenced its development, you are engaged in analytical or *critical* thinking. As a psychology student and certainly as a graduate you should never again accept an explanation of a piece of data without thinking to yourself 'ah, but what about . . .'. Of course, critical thinking also involves identifying strengths as well as weaknesses, contributions as well as limitations.

- *Synthetic thinking*: this involves putting ideas together rather than picking them apart, and is closely related to the idea of creativity. We think creatively about psychology every time we generate hypotheses, design studies, suggest modifications to existing theories, and put together advice or a programme using psychological theory and research. We also think creatively every time we structure an essay and synthesize an argument from evidence.

- *Practical thinking*: this involves applying your understanding of a concept, theory, or research findings in psychology to understanding or intervening in a real-life situation.

We have found this model of psychological thinking incredibly helpful, and in fact our chapters contain *Thinking critically*, *Thinking creatively*, and *Thinking practically* features, which have been inspired by Sternberg's work.

Developing Your Thinking Skills

Perhaps the most important skills you will develop as a psychology student involve *thinking* about studies and theories in psychology. One way to develop your critical thinking skills is to internalize a set of questions you can ask yourself whenever you wish to evaluate psychological material. The following critical thinking toolkits are loosely based on those used by McGhee (2001) and Jarvis (2011b). Note that using these toolkits is both a science and an art. Applying the questions involves scientific thinking; however, the art is to know which questions are the most important when it comes to evaluating each study or theory.

To use these really effectively, don't work through the questions robotically but consider how important each is in relation to the subject matter you are looking at. For example, as you can see in the critical thinking toolkit for studies (Table 1.1), sampling considerations are much more important when researching social behaviour than a cognitive function. This is because we would expect social behaviour to vary across different demographic cultures, genders, social classes, etc., a lot more than, say, cognition. The environment in which a study is carried out is much more

TABLE 1.1 **Critical thinking toolkit for studies**

Issue	Points to consider	Cue questions
1 The sample	Consider *who* takes part in the study. A good sample should be representative of the population the study is concerned with. Also consider the extent to which results can be generalized to other populations.	• Is the overall sample size large for the type of study? • Is the sample in each condition large? • Is the sampling method likely to produce a representative sample? • Is it likely that the results generalize to other populations?
2 The environment	Consider *where* the study took place. This is important for experiments, observations, and surveys. Generally there is a trade-off between the benefits of control in a laboratory environment and of natural responses and behaviour in participants' own environment.	• Is the environment controlled? • Is the environment natural? • Is there a particular reason why it was important to conduct a study in a natural environment? For example, have all previous studies in this area been in the lab?
3 The design	Consider the design decisions that were made in planning the study. Are there flaws such as potential confounding variables, or is the design in fact particularly ingenious, allowing study of a difficult area to research? Are there limitations; for example, those of an experiment comparing two groups of people or a telephone survey?	• Is the design a particularly ingenious or original way to research an issue? • Is there a flaw in the design? • Are there general advantages to this type of design that give this study credibility? • Are there inevitable limitations to this type of design?
4 The measures	Consider how you are *measuring* the outcome of the study. If you are using psychometric tests, what do you know about their reliability and validity? If you are using behavioural measures, are these behaviours representative of those your experiment is concerned with in real life?	• Are the measures standard or constructed for this study? • Are there figures available for reliability and/or validity (see Chapter 3 for a discussion) of these measures? • If so, are they satisfactory? • If the measures are behavioural, do the behaviours correspond closely to real-life behaviours they are meant to represent?
5 Theoretical value	Consider whether this is important to psychologists in *theoretical* terms. Does it lend support or contradict a particular theory or perspective?	• Does the study lend weight to a theory? • Does it appear to contradict a theory?
6 Practical value	Consider the extent to which this study has important practical *applications* within applied psychology or other contexts.	• Is this study important because it has real-world applications? • Is it particularly significant because it shows something important *and* original?
7 Corroborating evidence	Consider the extent to which this study fits in with previous findings. A study might have more credibility if it finds similar results to past studies. However, a new way of approaching a research question that yields a different finding might be important in challenging our beliefs about a psychological phenomenon.	• Is the study credible because results confirm those of previous studies? • Is the study particularly interesting because it does not confirm previous findings? • If findings are different, what is different about the way this study was conducted?
8 Ethics and social sensitivity	Consider the ethical implications raised by the study, looking at the BPS ethical guidelines, and consider the moral consequences of conducting the study.	• What ethical issues (such as harm, distress, consent, deceit, withdrawal, and privacy) are raised? • Does the importance of the results outweigh the cost to participants? • Is the whole topic inevitably controversial because it is taboo? • Can results be misused to justify discrimination?

TABLE 1.2 **Critical thinking toolkit for theories**

Issue	Points to consider	Cue questions
1 Logical characteristics of the theory	Consider the extent to which the theory makes *logical sense* (face validity). Do different parts of the theory hang together (internal consistency)? Is the explanation the simplest available (parsimony) or is it overly complicated and contrived?	• Does the theory make intuitive sense? • Do different parts of the theory fit neatly together? • Is the explanation overly complicated? • Is there a more obvious explanation that could explain the same data?
2 Origins	Consider where the theory came from. Is it based on solid research or did it come from a weak foundation such as self-analysis or anecdote? If the latter, even if there is supporting research, this might have been based on false assumptions or a falsely narrow focus.	• Is the theory built on solid foundations such as good-quality research? • Is it founded on limited evidence or plucked out of thin air?
3 Testability	A good scientific theory generates *evidence* so that we can make judgements about its credibility. Some theories are more open to testing than others. Often, some aspects of a theory are more testable than others.	• Can all aspects of the theory be tested by psychological studies? • Are there parts of the theory that are harder to investigate by means of psychological studies?
4 Supporting evidence	The single most important factor in evaluating a theory is its *support from research*. A credible explanation should be supported by research evidence. This links to the testability issue, as sometimes there is little direct support for a theory but this is because of difficulty in testing it. Evidence is most supportive when it comes from different types of study (triangulation).	• Are there studies that support all or part of the theory? • How large is this body of supporting evidence? • Is there supporting evidence from different sources; for example, studies based in the lab and real-life situations?
5 Conflicting evidence	There may be research that appears to contradict all or part of a theory. You need to be able to balance this against the evidence supporting the theory. Consider the size of the two bodies of evidence but also the nature of the evidence. It may be, for example, that lab experiments support a particular view but that these findings are not borne out by real-world studies.	• Are there studies that suggest the basic ideas behind the theory are incorrect? • Are there studies that suggest that particular parts of a theory are incorrect? • Do most studies support or contradict the theory? • Is there a difference in the nature or quality of supportive and contradictory studies?
6 Completeness	Consider the extent to which a theory can explain all aspects of a situation. For example, a theory may explain a general tendency in behaviour but not individual differences.	• Is there anything important that the theory cannot explain?
7 Heuristic value	Sometimes the major value of a theory is in helping applied psychologists think about complex issues. Such aids to thinking are called heuristics. Some theories and ideas are retained in psychology in spite of lack of evidence because they have **heuristic value**. See, for example, Maslow's concept of self-actualization in the *Thinking critically* box below.	• Does the theory help us understand or think about something? • Is this heuristic value sufficient to justify keeping the theory in the face of a lack of supporting evidence?
8 Practical applications	Like studies, some theories have particular value because they can be applied in the real world in applied psychology or other contexts like education or policing.	• Does the theory have practical applications in the real world? • Is the importance of these applications sufficient to justify keeping the theory in the face of lack of supporting evidence?

important in an observation or experiment where behaviour is observed than in a survey study because we would expect behaviour, but not necessarily attitudes, to change in an artificial environment.

THINKING CRITICALLY

Revisit the 'whack-a-mole' study by Parsons et al earlier in this chapter (see 'The importance of using primary sources'). Work through the critical thinking toolkit for studies (Table 1.1), and use it to pick out some key strengths and weaknesses of the study. Remember that the aim is not to mechanically work through every cue question but to pick out the key issues that are critical for this study.

THINKING CRITICALLY

Locate an account of Maslow's theory of human motivation (Maslow, 1943). You can find this in full online at http://psychclassics.yorku.ca/Maslow/motivation.htm. Work through the critical thinking toolkit for theories (Table 1.2) in order to evaluate the theory. You will need to do some additional searching to find out more about where Maslow got his ideas, how they are applied, and what sort of evidence is available with which to evaluate it.

Developing your creative thinking

Examples of creative thinking in psychology are synthesizing hypotheses from theories and designing studies to test hypotheses.

THINKING CREATIVELY

The aim of this exercise is to generate hypotheses from a theory. We will use Aaron Beck's explanation of emotional disorders (Chapter 18). Briefly, Beck proposed that negative early life events lead to a set of negative beliefs about the world, the self, and the future. When difficult situations are encountered later in life, our systems of negative beliefs are activated. This affects the ways we process information, leading us to focus on the negative aspects of a situation, recall unhappy events rather than happy ones, and to see ourselves, the world, and future in a negative way.

1. What hypotheses can you synthesize from this brief summary of the theory?
2. Outline how you might gather data to cast light on this hypothesis. We aren't assuming any technical understanding of research methods at this point; just think how you might gather relevant information.

Developing your practical thinking

The third thinking skill you need to develop as a psychology student is practical thinking. This involves applying psychology to real-life situations. The technical term for tasks that require you to do this is 'Psychology Applied to Learning Scenarios' or PALS for short. The following exercise is an example of a PALS.

> ❯ **KEY IDEAS** non-obvious criteria for judging a theory There are a number of ways we can judge a theory apart from the obvious supporting and conflicting evidence:
>
> **Internal consistency** is the extent to which different elements of a complex theory hang together logically.
>
> **Parsimony** is the simplicity of a theory. The idea that parsimony is a strength of a theory is closely related to Occam's razor—the idea that an explanation that requires the fewest assumptions is most likely to be correct. This is controversial because there is an argument that we would not expect human nature to be simple!
>
> **Heuristic value** concerns the usefulness of a theory as a tool to help people think about a complex issue. For example, some psychometrics used to assess learning styles or personality have very little scientific validity but are still commonly used in certain settings, such as business training, because they have proved useful in helping people reflect on their characteristics.

THINKING PRACTICALLY

Read the following real-life scenario and answer the questions. You might like to look at Chapter 7 if you aren't yet familiar with theories of forgetting.

Scenario: It is the start of Tim's first exam of his psychology degree. He has never been in the exam hall before. He has skipped his usual coffee this morning so he isn't distracted by needing the toilet during the exam. Without his coffee he is feeling tired and rather sluggish. Tim turns over the paper and sees the first question, which concerns psychodynamic theory. Although the question looks straightforward Tim finds he cannot recall any of the material.

Tim has had a hard year. He got behind on work and has recently been revising well into the night and keeping awake by drinking large amounts of coffee.

Consider the following:

1 Suggest how Tim's experience of forgetting can be explained in terms of cue dependency. If you can, consider both state and context cues.

2 Tim has a second exam coming up. Using the idea of state cues, suggest how he might perform better in that exam compared with his first.

The art of dealing with tasks like this is to make links between the scenario and the theory and/or research you are asked to apply to it. Here, the link with memory cues is fairly straightforward. Tim is in an unfamiliar room so he can't make use of context cues such as the sight of his lecture theatre or the room where he revised. Without the coffee he relied on during his revision Tim also lacks state cues. To improve his recall in the second exam Tim might want to consider either drinking coffee before the exam or consuming something different like chewing gum, both when revising and in the exam, in order to make use of state cues to maximize his recall. Tim may also want to practise visualization techniques (such as thinking about the room where he revised) in order to reinstate context cues.

IN REVIEW

- Academic psychology is a science. Because of this it tends to look very different to the popular psychology you may have come across; for example, in the media or in popular psychology literature.

- Academic psychology is a process of thinking critically about and rigorously testing ideas. There is no uncritical acceptance of popular opinions.

- It is important to begin to use proper psychological literature and to move away from tertiary sources of information and start to use primary sources.

MOVING AWAY FROM PRE-DEGREE STUDY

- Your first year at university is an opportunity to start operating more like a psychologist. This means that you will need to abandon your pre-degree textbook and start making use of primary sources.

- If you studied psychology before your degree, bear in mind that undergraduate psychology is likely to involve more cognitive psychology, more biological psychology, and more practical work.

- As well as basic googling you will need to master some more specialist electronic search tools. You should also gain some proficiency in manual searching through journal stacks.

- Your writing needs to become less descriptive and more analytical.

THINKING MORE LIKE A PSYCHOLOGIST

- In order to study psychology you need to be able to think psychologically. This includes but is broader than core scientific thinking.

- You can begin to develop your critical thinking about psychological theory and research by internalizing our critical thinking toolkits.

- You can develop your creative thinking by practising generating predictions from theories and designing studies to test these.

- You can develop your practical thinking skills by practising applying psychology to real-life scenarios.

TEST YOURSELF

1 Psychology is a science. True ☐ False ☐

2 News reports about psychology are generally fair and accurate representations. True ☐ False ☐

3 Wikipedia articles generally represent the most cutting-edge expert views. True ☐ False ☐

4 There will be a lot of humanistic and psychodynamic psychology in your degree. True ☐ False ☐

5 Which of the following is true of popular psychology

   a) It is based on scientific principles and research

   b) It is the same as academic psychology

   c) It will be an important part of your psychology degree

   d) Its main purpose is to improve the life of the reader

6 Which of the following could be described as a primary source?

   a) A research article in a research journal

   b) The website of a learned society like the British Psychological Society

   c) This textbook

   d) A review article in a research journal

7 Which of the following distinguishes studying undergraduate psychology from pre-degree level?

   a) Using more than one source

   b) Placing more emphasis on evaluation

   c) Placing more emphasis on up-to-date information

   d) All the above

8 Putting together an argument for a position on a debate is what kind of thinking?

   a) Analytical

   b) Synthetic

   c) Practical

   d) Scientific

9 Explain what is meant by thinking like a psychologist.

10 Explain why parsimony and internal consistency are important features of psychological theories.

 Visit the online resources that accompany this book: www.oup.com/uk/jarvis-okami1e

THE SCIENCE OF PSYCHOLOGY

CHAPTER 2

LEARNING OUTCOMES

By the end of this chapter you should be able to:

- Define psychology and distinguish it from other academic disciplines that deal with human mind and behaviour
- Understand why we describe psychology as a science and begin to assess the extent to which psychology lives up to the standards of science
- Define academic psychology and applied psychology and identify the core areas of study in academic psychology and core professions of applied psychology
- Recall major historical developments in the history of psychology and identify ways in which particular schools of philosophy, religion, and psychology have influenced our modern understanding of the mind
- Appreciate the role of theory and theoretical perspectives in psychology

The word 'psychology' is made up from the Greek *psyche*, meaning the mind or spirit, and *logos*, meaning to study. Technically then psychology simply means the study of the mind. Nowadays psychology is usually defined a little more precisely as the *scientific* study of the mind and behaviour. Most of the time this means the *human* mind and behaviour; however, some psychologists are also interested in animal mind and behaviour, either for their own sake or because of what they can tell us about our own psychology.

The essence of what makes psychology distinct from other disciplines that look at aspects of human mind and/or behaviour was captured brilliantly by Magnusson (2012): 'The target of analysis for psychology as a scientific discipline is the individual as an active, intentional psychobiological and social being in continuous, dynamic interaction with his/her proximal and distal [near and far] environment' (2012: 22). This definition draws out three key characteristics of psychology. First, in contrast to other academic disciplines like philosophy, sociology, and psychoanalysis, psychology is a science (what this means is discussed in 'Psychology as science', this chapter). Second, psychology focuses on the individual, although that individual is seen in the context of interactions with other individuals, groups, and wider society. This is the dividing line with sociology, which places more emphasis on society and less on the individual. Third, psychology looks at the individual as a biological, cognitive, and social being. Particular approaches to psychology emphasize one or more of these but psychology as a whole acknowledges the importance of our nervous system, our mental processes, and our interactions with other people.

WHAT PSYCHOLOGY IS NOT!

We explored the differences between 'real' psychology, popular psychology, and psychology as it is represented in the mass media in Chapter 1. Just to reinforce the point, let's get some myths out in the open and deal firmly with them before we go any further.

1 Psychology is a touchy-feely subject closely related to counselling. Although a minority of counsellors are psychologists and vice versa, most of the time professions of psychology and counselling run in parallel. Although informed by psychological theory, counselling depends in large part on good listening skills and an intuitive understanding of clients. Psychology on the other hand is a science.

2 Psychology will teach you to read body language, spot a serial killer at 100 metres, and generally give you superpowers. As a rule it won't. Taught and studied well, psychology *will* equip you with good critical and scientific reasoning that will help you see the world in a slightly different way. Those skills are well worth having and will make you more employable, whether in psychology or not, but you won't emerge from studying psychology as a Jedi Master (Figure 2.1).

3 Because psychology is about us it must be straightforward/common sense. Actually people are pretty complicated! If you think about it that way it shouldn't be a surprise to find that psychology is not easy. Another way of thinking about why studying psychology is so challenging is that you are receiving a rigorous training as a scientist. As well as learning some very technical content this means that you are learning to leave common sense behind and think in terms of evidence. This is a challenge in itself.

FIGURE 2.1 **Studying psychology won't make you into a Jedi!**
Source: Lucasfilm/Photo 12/Alamy Stock Photo.

TABLE 2.1 **Psychology and related academic disciplines**

Discipline	Definition and scope
Psychology	The scientific study of all aspects of mind, brain, and behaviour
Psychiatry	A branch of medicine dedicated to the understanding, classification, and treatment of mental disorder
Neuroscience	The multidisciplinary study of the nervous system and the tools that measure it
Psychoanalysis	A highly theoretical approach to the study of the human mind depending on the assumption of unconscious influences, and a psychological therapy based on this theory
Sociology	The study of human society and its influence on the individual
Philosophy	The study of knowledge, reality, and existence

❭ KEY IDEAS psychology and related disciplines **Psychology** can be defined as the scientific study of human mind and behaviour. Philosophy and psychoanalysis overlap in subject matter with psychology because they also seek to explain human nature but do not share psychology's commitment to scientific principles. **Psychiatry** also overlaps with psychology in the area of mental disorder; however, psychiatrists are medical doctors and their formal training does not cover the full breadth of human mind and behaviour. Table 2.1 summarizes the difference between psychology and related disciplines.

Hopefully that won't have put you off! It may help to know that once you have your bachelor's degree, if you want to take psychology further you can specialize in a particular field, whether as a practitioner or as a researcher. At this point you will be equipped to work in counselling or criminological fields but you will be able to bring to them a particular set of skills that will mark you out from non-psychologists. While we are discussing what psychology is not, it is perhaps worth drawing out the differences between psychology and its sister discipline, psychiatry.

Psychiatry is a medical speciality concerned with the treatment of serious mental health problems (discussed in Chapters 16 and 17). Psychiatrists attend medical school, and after obtaining their medical degree, they decide to specialize in the treatment of these problems. Although psychologists and psychiatrists have overlapping knowledge in the area of mental health their core professional base is quite different. Where psychologists have a broad-based understanding of human mind and behaviour, psychiatrists have a specifically medical focus on treating people with mental health problems.

PSYCHOLOGY AS SCIENCE

We've already alluded to psychology as a science a few times. But is psychology a real science and what does that actually mean? It is probably fair to say that many physicists, chemists, and biologists do not consider psychology a 'proper science'. However, there is an unwritten but real hierarchy of scientific snobbery in which physicists and chemists tend to say biology is not a true science, physicists say the same of chemistry, and theoretical physicists have even been known to say it about experimental physics! That's perhaps a slightly parodied account, but it does illustrate how pointless it is to think in terms of how scientific a whole discipline is, particularly one as diverse as psychology. It is probably more productive to start from the point that psychology *is* a science. Certainly that is the 'official line' from the British Psychological Society, the American Psychological Association, and the Association for Psychological Science.

FIGURE 2.2 The stages of the classic scientific method

❯ **KEY IDEAS** scepticism
Scepticism is a philosophical approach or point of view based on the scientific method which proposes that compelling evidence of a claim should be presented before one comes to believe in the claim. The sceptic is not negative or cynical about new ideas but they require a high standard of evidence before they accept them.

❯ **KEY IDEAS** science Science is the study of the natural world. Scientists adopt the philosophical position that there are facts to be discovered, and the methods of testing them, including observation and making predictions, are as objective as possible. Scientists accept that our current understanding will change over time as more information is discovered and maintain an attitude of open-mindedness whilst requiring high standards of evidence.

So What Is Science?

Perhaps a better question than 'is psychology a science?' would be 'what is science?' To take it right back to basics the word 'science' comes from the Latin *scire*, meaning to know. Science is therefore the pursuit of knowledge. Not just any knowledge, but knowledge about the natural world. We might be an expert in the music of Abba or the films of Joss Whedon, but these areas will never be sciences because they are not part of the natural world.

This might sound at first like a pretty straightforward definition of science but buried in it is a particular philosophical position; namely, that there are truths there to be discovered. The task faced by scientists is to attempt to discover these truths by studying phenomena *empirically*; that is, by observing evidence consistent with their existence. They aim to do this in as *objective* a manner as possible; that is, seeing what is actually there rather than from their personal perspective. This scientific view of the world as there to be discovered empirically and objectively is very different from more constructivist positions—that is, those emphasizing the role of human thought in making sense of the world—on knowledge favoured by many in other academic disciplines such as philosophy and much of sociology.

So how do scientists go about this attempt to discover facts? The classic scientific method starts with observing a phenomenon. From this comes a suggested explanation. The scientist then suggests a testable prediction (known as an hypothesis) based on the explanation. If that hypothesis is correct, the scientist predicts what we would expect to happen in a particular situation. This prediction is tested by means of research; for example, an experiment. The results are then analysed to determine whether they support or contradict the hypothesis (see Figure 2.2).

As well as the scientific method, we need to understand something of scientific attitudes. As the astronomer Carl Sagan (1995) said, 'science is primarily a way of thinking, combining healthy **scepticism** with open-mindedness'. This means that a good scientist is open to new ideas but insists on seeing evidence before those ideas can be accepted.

We need to understand one more aspect of science at this point: the way that scientific understanding develops over time. Science never reaches an end point where ideas become proven facts or where every truth is discovered. There is always room for developing a further and better understanding of whatever phenomenon we are studying. This means that whatever we believe to be true at any point in time will be subsumed later by a more sophisticated understanding based on additional evidence. Scientific philosopher Thomas Kuhn (1970) suggested that at any point in its development a science shares a set of core beliefs called a *paradigm*. When enough evidence is accumulated to suggest that these core beliefs need to be reconsidered a *paradigm shift* occurs and the science changes.

How Well Does Psychology Conform to these Principles of Science?

Surveys suggest that the general public tend not to believe that psychologists use scientific methods and that in fact most people believe that psychology is essentially common sense (Lilienfeld, 2012). However, if we assess **academic psychology** against the description of science in the previous section it actually comes out pretty well. The human mind and behaviour are aspects of the natural world. By and large psychologists employ the scientific method, carrying out empirical research and being as objective as possible in their observations and conclusions. This comes with the proviso that it is impossible to be truly objective—objectivity is an ideal rather than a reality—but the key is that we strive for it whilst at the same time reflecting on our limitations in this regard. Psychological theory is generally subject to ongoing research and it evolves over time with the accumulation of new evidence. Good psychologists are open to developments in psychological ideas but set high standards for the quality of evidence they will accept for radical ideas.

Okay, so psychologists generally try to conduct themselves like good scientists. But what about the subject matter of psychology? In this respect views have changed over the last century. Writing 100 years ago John Watson (1913) stated that in its first 50 years or so, psychology had failed as a natural science because it involved speculation about internal processes of the mind. Watson proposed that to be a successful science, psychology should only study observable behaviour. Nowadays virtually no psychologists would agree with this extreme view, but there remains a trade-off between studying the 'big questions'—things the layperson wants from psychology but which are hard to investigate in a scientific manner—and what Reicher and Haslam (2009) call '**impeccable trivia**', phenomena that are amenable to very scientific study but which are largely irrelevant to understanding what makes us tick.

If you are currently studying psychology at degree level you may find the emphasis on impeccable trivia frustrating and yearn to get on with tackling material—whether as researcher or practitioner—that fits more neatly with your personal interests or career plans—or just seems more directly relevant to understanding human nature. The point is that the main aim of your first degree is to get you thoroughly familiar with scientific attitudes and used to applying the scientific method to psychology. Depending on where you study you are likely to get a bit more leeway to follow your heart in the final year of your degree, both in terms of optional modules and your final year project/dissertation. It will be worth waiting if this allows you to bring more research expertise and scientific discipline to your chosen subject matter.

> **KEY IDEAS** impeccable trivia Impeccable trivia are psychological phenomena that are straightforward to study in a traditional scientific manner—for example, by laboratory experimentation—but which do not help us answer important questions about human nature. This criticism has, for example, been levelled at some studies of cognition.

More Radical Positions on Psychology as Science

The vast majority of psychologists support the conventional notion of science, although we are well aware of the trade-off between studying impeccable trivia and making scientific compromises in order to study more pressing issues. There are, however, some voices within psychology that challenge the idea that psychology is a science, at least as we usually understand it. Two of these radical traditions are humanistic and critical psychologies.

Humanistic psychology (see later this chapter for a more detailed account) emerged in the 1950s, emphasizing a positive view of human nature and the need to treat people as a whole rather than reducing them to biological, cognitive, or social beings. Humanistic psychologists do not claim to reject science per se, but in practice they do reject much of the way science has worked in mainstream psychology. Mainstream psychology is inevitably *reductionist*, focusing on one aspect of the person in order to study and understand it. Although we sometimes think of reductionism as a weakness in psychology, actually it is necessary in order to practise the scientific method. Humanistic psychology rejects this philosophy and therefore effectively rejects the scientific method. In research terms, humanistic psychology is therefore something of a dead end, albeit one with practical applications and a purpose to challenge the limitations of the mainstream.

Critical psychology emerged in the 1970s but became most influential in the late 1990s and early 2000s. Critical psychology has a strong sociological flavour and is overtly political. The approach rejects the possibility of scientific objectivity. Instead, critical psychologists look at how ideas within psychology may have emerged to serve the interests of ruling elites. So, for example, intelligence testing can be seen (and has certainly been used) as a strategy to marginalize immigrant communities, and the concept of mental illness can be seen as (and indeed has been) a way to oppress women. Like humanistic psychologists, critical psychologists do not reject science entirely but they see conventionally scientific psychologists as naïve, failing to recognize the social context in which their ideas develop and the social consequences of their work. Critical psychology is an example of a **social constructionist** perspective, not to be confused with the social constructivist perspective on cognitive development (Chapter 12). We will come back to social constructionist perspectives at various points throughout this book (Chapters 14 and 18).

Pseudoscience

Pseudoscience is non-science performed for non-scientific goals, but with the surface appearance of science. Consider 'firewalking'. In the 1980s, a number of entrepreneurs were making considerable sums claiming that special psychological 'training' would enable an average person to walk on a bed of red-hot coals without injury by learning to put 'mind over matter' or to create a 'mystical energy field'. Firewalking—which dated back many centuries as an Eastern spiritual practice—became a popular activity at corporate retreats and 'personal growth' seminars. That people could in fact perform this seemingly miraculous feat after taking the course seemed quite extraordinary and inexplicable until investigators began to look into firewalking seriously.

It turns out that the sort of light and fluffy coals used in these demonstrations do not retain heat very well—the conductivity of heat from the coals to one's feet is poor. As long as a person does not stand on the coals for an extended period of time, he or she will not get burned at all. Anyone can get up tomorrow morning and walk across a bed of these hot coals without injury. It has nothing to do with mystical energy fields (Shermer, 1997). It should be emphasized, however, that pseudoscientists are not necessarily liars or scammers. They often believe strongly in their work (Lilienfeld, Lynn, and Lohr, 2003a).

Pseudoscientific claims such as these are everywhere—they not only call to you from tabloids on news stands, but also are standard fare on popular science TV channels, where programmes about UFOs, ghosts, and other supernatural or otherwise dubious phenomena abound. Pseudoscience is big business. Although the boundaries between science and pseudoscience are not always as clear as one would like (Lilienfeld et al, 2003b), there are a number of indicators that suggest an enterprise is pseudoscientific rather than truly scientific:

1 *Science is self-correcting. Pseudoscience is not.* Pseudoscientists do not correct the errors of their predecessors; instead, they perpetuate them, and pseudoscience cannot advance as science can (Shermer, 1997; Ruscio, 2006). For example, astrology appears to have changed little in the past 2,500 years (Hines, cited by Lilienfeld et al, 2003b). Astrology is further discussed in Chapter 15.

2 *Pseudoscientists rely on testimonials, anecdotes, and bold statements.* Testimonials, anecdotes, rumours, and bold statements are designed to appeal to
vulnerable emotions in human beings. Shermer (1997, p 49) reports a superb
example of the bold statement offered by the so-called science of *dianetics*
(Scientology): 'The creation of Dianetics is a milestone for man comparable to
the discovery of fire and superior to the invention of the wheel and the arch.'
When a statement like that is uttered, it is hard not to believe that at least
something must be worthwhile about dianetics.

Anecdotes (stories about individual cases) can help a researcher formulate theories
and hypotheses to test scientifically. However, pseudoscientists rely on anecdotes to
convince people of their ideas and *substitute* for evidence (Ruscio, 2006). For example, let us say that your friend Jasbinder has a bad cold. She drinks one packet of
Super-C Holistic Fizzy Stuff every four hours, and two days later she has recovered
from her cold. Although there may be a hundred reasons other than Super-C why
Jasbinder no longer has a cold, people often look for simple patterns of cause and
effect under these circumstances, in this case connecting the treatment with the
effect—even if the treatment in fact had no effect. The story of your friend's miraculous recovery becomes a testimonial and anecdote purportedly showing the effectiveness of Super-C as a treatment for the common cold. By contrast the scientific
approach to Jasbinder's experience would be to conduct an experiment to test the
hypothesis that Super-C reduces the duration of colds.

3 *Pseudoscientists reverse the burden of proof from themselves to their critics.*
In science extraordinary claims require, if not always extraordinary evidence,
at the very least *adequate* evidence before they can be accepted. However,
pseudoscientists making extraordinary claims tend to place the burden of *dis-
proof* onto others: 'Prove that aliens are *not* abducting thousands of people for
strange rituals!' However, those who do not believe that aliens are abducting
thousands annually do *not* need to prove that such abductions are not taking
place. Because the claim of mass abductions is a new, extraordinary claim, *the
burden of proof is on the claimant*, not on the rest of us.

4 *Pseudoscientific claims are untestable.* Scientific claims must be testable by
independent research in order to be absorbed into the body of scientific knowledge. Pseudoscientific claims are framed in a way that makes them untestable,
or, if they are testable, pseudoscientists only accept the findings of their own
(confirmatory) research, explaining away negative findings in various *post hoc*
('after the fact') ways; for example, 'The only reason we couldn't demonstrate
thought reading in this test was that your scepticism threw out a negative energy field that blocked transmission' (Ruscio, 2006).

❭ **KEY IDEAS** pseudoscience
Pseudoscience is non-science
performed for non-scientific goals,
but with the surface appearance
of science.

THINKING CRITICALLY

Homeopathy is a medical treatment in which patients are exposed to extremely small concentrations of naturally occurring substances. It is widely agreed that homeopathy is pseudoscience, and that any apparent benefits to patients can be explained psychologically by
the placebo effect. Looking at the keeping it real feature on pseudoscience, explain why
homeopathy is best seen as pseudoscience.

ACADEMIC AND APPLIED PSYCHOLOGY

According to the British Psychological Society and the European Federation of Psychology Associations, psychology is both an academic discipline and a professional practice. Both academic and **applied psychology** are professionally recognized as 'proper' psychology and it is possible to gain Chartered Psychologist status as either an academic or an applied psychologist. Popular psychology (see later in this chapter) exists largely outside the professions of academic and applied psychology.

Academic Psychology

If you are studying psychology at university you will be engaged in academic psychology. To complete a qualification recognized by a professional association like the British Psychological Society, you will need to study six core areas of academic psychology.

1 **Cognitive psychology**: the study of mental processes, including memory, perception, and thinking, and the ways knowledge of the world is represented in the mind.

2 **Developmental psychology**: the study of psychological change and development from childhood to older adulthood. This includes social and emotional development and the development of cognitive processes.

3 **Social psychology**: the study of interactions between the individual and other individuals, groups, and society at large. Topics include social influence, attitudes, and prejudice.

4 **Individual differences**: the study of individual differences between people, including personality, intelligence, motivation, and mental health.

5 **Biological psychology**: the study of the interface between psychology and biology, including the relationship between the nervous system (particularly the brain) and psychological functioning, the relationship between genes and behaviour, and the evolution of the human brain and behaviour.

6 **Psychological research methods**: ways of gathering data including experiments, correlations, surveys, and observations, and approaches to analysing that data, both quantitative (using numbers) and qualitative (not using numbers).

These domains, which will be found in curricula across the world, can be considered a helpful way of structuring your studies.

Working in academic psychology involves conducting and publishing research, and teaching. As an academic psychologist you will be a professional researcher and/or teacher of psychology.

Applied Psychology

As the name suggests, applied psychologists apply psychological theory, research, and techniques to particular situations. To become an applied psychologist it is necessary to undertake specialist postgraduate training. Those new to studying psychology are often surprised at the lack of applied psychology in their course; remember the emphasis in your first degree will be on learning basic psychological ideas and the basics of scientific thinking and practice. Professional bodies, such as the British Psychological Society, recognize and accredit eight branches of applied psychology.

1 **Clinical psychology** involves working with people suffering from a range of mental and physical health problems. Common mental health problems include

depression, addiction, and anxiety. Some clinical psychologists have particular specialisms; for example, in working with families, couples, or children with mental health problems or learning difficulties (Figure 2.3). Clinical psychologists are involved in assessing clients' needs and providing therapy of various kinds.

2 **Counselling psychology** involves practising counselling/therapy with people in psychological distress; for example, resulting from a mental health problem or a situation such as bereavement or abuse. What distinguishes a counselling psychologist from other counsellors is their research skills and understanding of the wider mental health field. There is overlap between clinical and counselling psychology and some roles are open to either type of psychologist.

3 **Educational psychology** involves working with children and young people facing problems with their education caused by learning difficulties and/or emotional stress caused by bullying, family problems, etc. Some work involves assessing children, most commonly for dyslexia, to trigger support in the education system, such as the provision of learning support assistants or extra time in exams. Educational psychologists are also involved in teacher training and development, in particular around special educational needs.

4 **Forensic psychology** involves working in the criminal justice system. Most forensic work takes place in prisons, and includes designing treatment and behaviour management programmes for inmates. Some forensic psychologists also work with the police force, analysing data to help with criminal profiling, and with the courts, advising on mental health and risks posed by offenders.

5 **Health psychology** involves applying psychology to work with people with physical health problems. This may involve providing counselling/therapy to patients to help them cope with the stress of illness. Health psychologists may also be involved in designing and implementing programmes to tackle unhealthy behaviour; for example, around obesity or smoking. They may also work to promote health-enhancing behaviour such as exercise.

6 **Neuropsychology** involves clinical work with patients suffering from a neurological problem; for example, resulting from stroke, traumatic brain injury, or a brain tumour. This requires both clinical skills and specialist knowledge of neuroscience. Entry to neuropsychology is currently restricted to clinical and educational psychologists. Neuropsychologists use highly specialist neurological assessment tools and specialist therapeutic ways of working.

7 **Occupational psychology** involves working to improve the functioning of organizations. This is a broad field. Some psychologists focus on reducing employee stress and improving satisfaction. Others are involved in designing workplaces and systems in order to maximize output. Some occupational psychologists are involved in personnel selection and management, advising on or devising interviews and selection tasks, choosing psychometric tests, or perhaps implementing team building.

8 **Sport and exercise psychology** involves working with athletes, coaches, referees, and others in order to improve performance and satisfaction and to reduce stress. Work can include counselling/therapy with athletes recovering from injury or performance failure, team building, and reducing stress in confrontational roles such as refereeing. Exercise psychology involves promoting exercise for its health benefits as opposed to working in the context of competitive sport.

FIGURE 2.3 Educational and clinical psychologists might find themselves working with children with mental health problems or learning difficulties.
Source: ABO PHOTOGRAPHY/Shutterstock.com.

❯ KEY IDEAS academic and applied psychology Academic psychology is the scientific study of psychology, generally carried out in a research setting like a university or think tank. Applied psychology includes a set of professions that employ psychological theory and research in order to benefit people in a particular context such as education or the workplace.

Applied psychologists are distinct from other professionals working in their fields because they work within a scientist-practitioner framework. This means that science informs their practice. The psychologist works by applying psychological theory to understand their work and uses research findings to understand what techniques are likely to be effective. In addition, applied psychologists often conduct research into the situations in which they are working.

A BRIEF HISTORY OF THE MIND

Modern psychologists are not the first humans to have been interested in questions of mental life and its connection to behaviour. Very ancient peoples undoubtedly shared these concerns. However, *psychology* as a concept did not exist in the ancient world. This is perhaps because ancient peoples tended to assume that their thoughts and feelings did not originate in their own minds but were largely spiritual in origin—the work of gods, demons, and other spiritual beings (Hunt, 1993).

The Psychology Before Psychology

An early pre-scientific system of psychology was created by the Buddha, born Gotama Siddhartha, in India approximately 2,600 years ago (shown in Figure 2.4). The Buddha believed that human suffering was largely determined by each person's own mental activity. He stressed the important effects of thought both on the thinker and on those with whom the thinker came in contact (Rahula, 1959; Ekman, Davidson, Ricard, and Wallace, 2005). He then set out a concrete 'treatment' for mental suffering known as the *noble eightfold path* that offered prescriptions for behaviour as well as thought. In a sense, we might consider the Buddha the world's first *cognitive-behaviour psychotherapist*!

As discussed in Chapter 17, cognitive-behaviour therapists who treat psychological problems such as **depression** and anxiety believe that much emotional distress

FIGURE 2.4 **The Buddha, Gotama Siddhartha. The first comprehensive pre-scientific system of psychology is attributed to this historical figure.**
Source: Bule Sky Studio/Shutterstock.com.

is caused by a person's own maladaptive patterns of thinking and behaving (eg, Beck, 2005). In fact, a recent development in psychotherapeutic treatment of mental illnesses known as *mindfulness-based cognitive therapy* (MBCT) joins techniques of cognitive therapy with the same meditation techniques and ideas about the mind first described by the Buddha (eg, Kuyken et al, 2010).

During this same time period, the Chinese were also developing new ways of considering the nature of human thought and **emotion**. Their philosophical systems acknowledged the unique **consciousness** of the individual. While not denying the importance of the spiritual element in human affairs, Chinese philosophers such as Confucius and Lao-Tze affirmed that the person played a role in the generation of his or her own internal life.

Further West, in the fifth century BC the Greek philosopher Aristotle, a pupil of Plato, created an arguably comprehensive, systematic psychology, though he did not identify it as such or arrive at his ideas through the methods of science. Aristotle studied theories of learning, memory, perception, motivation, emotion, and social interaction—topics covered extensively in this book. He was the first theorist to stress the importance of objective observation and of making logical connections between what was observed and how these observations were explained. These ideas became exceedingly important in later movements towards scientific psychology (Robinson, 1989).

Indian Buddhists and Chinese and Greek philosophers all addressed what we sometimes nowadays call the 'big questions of psychology'—questions that continue to be of critical interest to virtually all psychologists, regardless of their field of study. These questions address truly fundamental questions about what it means to be human. Among them are the following:

- Where does the mind reside? Is it in some way separate from the body?

- Are human beings primarily the product of their inherited characteristics or of the environment in which they are reared?

- Does thought arise from experience, or are we born with certain beliefs about the world?

- Is reality 'real'—or is it an illusion we all somehow agree to accept?

- What are valid ways of drawing inferences from observations? Why do so many of our beliefs and ideas about the world prove to be false?

- What is the connection between thought and emotion? Do emotions emerge as a result of the content of our thoughts, or do our thoughts arise from our emotions?

Pre-Scientific Psychology in the Age of Reason

The first important 'psychologist' of the pre-scientific modern world was the French philosopher René Descartes (1596–1650, shown in Figure 2.5). Descartes lived during the Renaissance but his work greatly influenced philosophical and scientific ideas of the Age of Reason in the next century. The Age of Reason, also called the Enlightenment, emerged in the eighteenth century, at a time when science was on the rise and an attitude of questioning was prevalent throughout Western societies—questioning customs, beliefs, authorities, and institutions. Rationality became an important value, and Descartes was the founder of the movement known as **rationalism**—the view that beliefs should be formed through close reasoning and logic similar to mathematics, rather than by relying on the pronouncements of authorities or personal experiences and biases.

Descartes came upon his most famous insight as a young man, while shut up in a small, overheated room in the dead of winter. After adopting the view that we ought to reject all beliefs that were not obtained by reason and rational thought, Descartes realized there was one thing he could accept as true without hesitation—the fact of his own existence. He reasoned that the very fact that he was thinking about such questions in the first place was all the proof he needed of this fundamental truth: *I think, therefore, I exist.* From this solidly rational observation, however, Descartes moved to a somewhat less convincing conclusion: he decided that the 'I' doing the

> **❯ KEY IDEAS** rationalism
> Rationalism is the philosophical movement founded by René Descartes which held that beliefs should be formed through the use of reason, rather than by relying upon personal experience or the pronouncements of authorities.

FIGURE 2.5 Renee Descartes (1596–1650). The founder of rationalism, Descartes is famous for his observation 'cognito, ergo sum'—I think therefore I am.
Source: Public domain.

thinking—the mind or soul—was entirely distinct from the body and might continue to exist without it. This is an example of a **dualist** perspective.

Meanwhile, across the English Channel, another philosophical movement was brewing that was to have an effect on the development of modern psychology: British **empiricism**. The English philosophers in this school rejected the mainstream dualist assumption of the time that the contents of the mind are present at birth, God-ordained, and separate from the body. Instead, they believed that the mind and its contents were unified and that they developed as a result of *experience*. Indeed, the term **empirical** means 'knowledge obtained through experience'. Thus, the principal division between the rationalists and the empiricists was that the rationalists favoured the use of logic and reasoning to acquire knowledge, whereas the empiricists favoured personal experience. You will often hear the term 'empirical' used in psychology in relation to evidence. Empirical evidence is evidence that can be experienced, most commonly seen. So when we see something happening in front of us—for example, the results of a psychological study—we can accept that it is true.

The History of Psychology as We Understand it Today

Psychology as we understand it—the scientific study of mind and behaviour—emerged as a distinct discipline in the mid-nineteenth century.

The Introspectionist Beginnings

Psychology emerged from the study of philosophy and biology in the middle of the nineteenth century. Wilhelm Wundt is credited with opening the first psychology laboratory in Germany. Wundt studied a range of topics including attention and reaction times. He pioneered the technique of **introspection**: asking participants to reflect on their mental processes in real time whilst carrying out tasks. Other notable psychologists working at this time included Herman Ebbinghaus, who had a particular interest in studying memory, and William James (Figure 2.6), who is best

> **KEY IDEAS** dualism Dualism is the view that the mind and matter (including the body) belong in separate categories and are constructed of different material.

> **KEY IDEAS** empiricism **Empiricism** was a seventeenth-century philosophical movement which held that the mind had no innate content—personal experience was responsible for the development of all thoughts, beliefs, and knowledge. The term '**empirical**' comes from the empiricists' belief in defining knowledge as that which can be experienced.

> **KEY IDEAS** introspection Introspection literally means to direct one's attention to one's own mind. In the late nineteenth century, psychologists—notably William James—used the idea of monitoring one's own thoughts and sensations whilst carrying out mental tasks as a method of research into the mind.

FIGURE 2.6 **William James, (1842–1910).**
Source: Granger Historical Picture Archive/ Alamy Stock Photo.

known for publishing *Principles of Psychology* in 1890. James had broad interests across psychology, and his *Principles of Psychology* included chapters on the brain, memory, reasoning, consciousness, attention, the self, time perception, imagination, and hypnosis. Like Wundt, James extensively used introspection as a method.

The introspectionists, as these early psychologists became known, considered psychology to be a natural science and worked in laboratory settings, attempting to be objective even when introspecting. James put it thus: 'To the psychologist then, the minds he studies are objects, in a world of other objects. Even when he introspectively analyses his own mind, and tells what he finds there, he talks about it in an objective way' (1890: 183). Interestingly, the tension in psychology between studying impeccable trivia and big-picture questions was well established by the end of the introspectionist period, with William James, a philosopher by training, being positively rude about the narrow scope of Wundt's experiments.

Highly influenced by Charles Darwin (1809–82), the British naturalist who had developed the theory of *evolution by natural selection* (see Chapter 3), James agreed that human psychology had developed over evolutionary time because it served various functions. In other words, it had *adaptive value* in promoting survival and success in reproduction. Thus, James' psychology is usually termed **functionalism**, because he believed that to understand the mind one had to understand the purposes, or functions, for which it was shaped through evolution. This aspect of James' work foreshadowed the contemporary field of **evolutionary psychology**, which is described in detail in Chapter 5, by nearly a century. However, the limitations of introspection as a scientific method were clear even to the introspectionists and this approach as mainstream psychology was replaced by another movement, behaviourism.

> **KEY IDEAS** functionalism
Functionalism is the psychological school of thought championed by William James which held that the mind could only be understood by referring to the purposes for which it was shaped through evolution.

The Behaviourist Era

John Watson (depicted in Figure 2.7) effectively killed off introspectionism in one move when he published his classic 1913 paper 'Psychology as the behaviourist views it'. Behaviourism was born of a degree of desperation among psychologists to be seen as practising a pure natural science. To this end they abandoned not only introspection, but also all talk of the mind. Instead they focused on the study of observable behaviour. To the behaviourists the basic units of behaviour were stimulus-response associations; that is, associations between an event in the environment and a response on the part of the individual. The creation of stimulus-response associations is the mechanism by which organisms, including humans, learn behaviour.

Two particular types of learning were particularly important to the behaviourists. The first half of the behaviourist era was dominated by the study of classical conditioning. Classical conditioning explains how we acquire some simple learnt responses. The classic example is Pavlov's dogs; if we associate the arrival of food (original stimulus) with the ringing of a bell (new stimulus), eventually we can trigger salivating (the reflex), without any food at all! You can read more about classical conditioning in Chapter 7.

The later part of the behaviourist era was dominated by the study of operant conditioning. This involves learning by reward and punishment. Behaviour that elicits a pleasant consequence—called reinforcement—is more likely to be repeated more frequently, whereas behaviour that leads to a bad consequence is likely to be repeated less frequently. Reinforcement can be positive, introducing a new pleasant stimulus such as food or sex, or negative, taking away an unpleasant stimulus such

FIGURE 2.7 **John B. Watson (1878–1958).**
Source: Granger Historical Picture Archive/
Alamy Stock Photo.

as pain. This kind of learning takes place in nature and it is also well suited to deliberate modification of behaviour. Classical and operant conditioning are discussed in detail in Chapter 6.

Behaviourism dominated psychology in Britain and particularly in the USA from the time of Watson's 1913 article until the 1950s. It never achieved the same dominance in mainland Europe where the study of mental processes continued. Behaviourism was helpful in establishing psychology's scientific credibility, and the processes of classical and operant conditioning are still studied in academic psychology and used in applied psychology. However, the dominance of the behaviourists ended as the emphasis in psychology shifted towards a focus on the mind and mental processes.

The Parallel Development of Psychoanalysis

While scientific psychology began with introspectionism and was overtaken by behaviourism, a very different take on studying human mind and behaviour was emerging from medicine. In the 1890s Sigmund Freud (Figure 2.8) coined the term 'psychoanalysis' to mean a theory of human mind and development, a type of psychological therapy and a system for researching the human mind. In direct contrast to the mainstream scientific methodology practised by the behaviourists, Freud and his colleagues investigated the mind by means of recording detailed self-analyses and accounts of patients in therapy. By making links between adult symptoms and early experience, psychoanalysts were able to propose theories linking early experience to the unconscious mind—mental processes of which we are not normally aware—and adult functioning.

FIGURE 2.8 Freud eschewed the scientific method and instead based his ideas on what patients told him in therapy.

Source: Akademie/Alamy Stock Photo.

You might have noticed that we have spoken of psychoanalysis both as part of psychology and as a discipline separate from psychology. In Britain and America, psychoanalysis is a body of theory, research, and practice that exists mostly outside academic and applied psychology and is developed largely in a number of private institutes—where psychoanalysis is still a flourishing discipline in its own right. The situation is slightly different in mainland Europe, where psychoanalysis is a more mainstream part of psychology.

Psychoanalytic ideas are important in some areas of applied psychology, most obviously clinical and counselling, and in related fields such as psychiatry and social work. Freud is without question the first name that comes to mind when the general public think about psychology, and (certainly up to a couple of decades ago when a count was last published) he has been the most commonly cited psychologist in both published research and textbooks (Haggbloom et al, 2002). However, Freudian ideas—and to a lesser extent other psychoanalytic ideas—are controversial in psychology. Have a read of Freud for yourself—he tends to arouse strong responses so you'll probably love him or hate him—but don't cite him uncritically in a psychology essay! We will address Freudian theory in some detail in Chapter 15, but for now in order to appreciate the influence of Freud's ideas try the following quiz:

- Do you believe that sometimes people 'forget' to do something because they don't really want to do it?

- What if there was a woman in your class named Kate, and one of your friends accidentally said, 'I'd love some Kate', instead of 'I'd love some cake'—would you wonder if your friend was secretly attracted to Kate?

- Do you think that dreams have symbolic meanings related to a person's inner psychological life?

- Do you believe that talking to a therapist about long-past events sometimes works to help people feel better?

- Do you believe that it is a bad idea to keep your feelings 'locked up', and that it is better to get in touch with your feelings and express them?

- Do you believe that people can entirely repress a memory of a traumatic event, so that they do not remember details of it or don't remember its occurrence at all?

- Do you believe that people can be 'in denial' about negative aspects of their lives?

- Do you believe that the way parents choose to rear their children has important effects on their children's personalities in adulthood?

If you answered 'yes' to any of the preceding questions, you have been influenced by Freud's thinking, at least indirectly. It is truly extraordinary that one Austrian psychologist's ideas should have had such a profound effect on Western thought and life in the twentieth century and into the twenty-first. It is difficult to imagine modern Western culture without Freud. Thus, even if Freud turns out to be the fraud some consider him to have been (eg, Crews, 2007), the simple fact is this: one can walk the halls of any number of major university psychology and psychiatry departments without finding a single lecturer who adheres to Freud's views about psychology or teaches his theories. *Outside* the field of psychology itself, however—for better or worse—Freud is still influential (Cohen, 2007)!

 THINKING CRITICALLY

Based on the brief descriptions provided here of behaviourism and psychoanalysis, compare some strengths and weaknesses of each. You might like to consider their scientific status, explanatory power, and practical value but don't limit yourself to these if you have other ideas.

Humanistic Psychology: The Third Force that Never Really Was

The tradition of humanistic psychology has already been mentioned (earlier this chapter) in relation to its position on science. Humanistic psychology emerged in America in the 1950s and 60s as a reaction against behaviourism, in which human experience was reduced to a series of stimulus-response associations, and against the complex and speculative theories of psychoanalysis that often appeared to have a negative view of human nature. Against the backdrop of psychoanalysis and behaviourism, humanistic psychologists aimed to be a third force in psychology, using a small number of straightforward principles to understand human nature and seeing human nature in a positive light, emphasizing human potential, kindness, and creativity. Humanistic psychologists, in particular Carl Rogers, stressed how human nature can be immensely positive but requires some basic needs to be loved and valued as a unique person to be met.

Regardless of whether we agree with the positive view of human nature espoused in the humanistic approach to psychology, some humanistic principles hold true. As Rogers said, self-esteem (how much we like ourselves) is crucial for mental health and it is indeed linked to childhood experiences of being loved (see, for example, Orth, 2018). However, the problem with explaining human nature in such simple terms and insisting on seeing people as whole beings rather than reducing them to patterns of behaviour was that humanistic psychologists largely ran out of new ideas—or at least ideas with widespread appeal. Although humanistic psychology remains important in counselling psychology it isn't really any sort of force in modern academic psychology.

The Cognitive Revolution

Recall Kuhn's ideas about the dramatic shifts that take place within sciences (see earlier in this chapter). Many commentators believe that mainstream academic psychology underwent the kind of paradigm shift Kuhn was talking about in the 1950s and 60s when a large number of researchers moved from thinking in behavioural terms to cognitive terms; that is, referring to mental processes like thinking and memory. Philosopher Noam Chomsky (cited in Miller, 2003), a leading critic of behaviourism, commented that defining psychology as the science of behaviour was like calling physics the science of meter-reading. In other words, behaviour is most important for what it can tell us about the mind and this is missed in the behavioural approach.

Some of the most important work developing a cognitive understanding was European in origin. For example, Otto Selz (1924) proposed an early theory of knowledge and problem-solving that fits neatly with many of our current ideas. However, such was the dominance of the USA in psychological literature that any kind of meaningful revolution required American 'buy-in'. Miller (2003) points to a 1956 conference at Massachusetts Institute of Technology as the birthplace of cognitive psychology. Here papers were delivered on computing, language development, short-term memory, and perception. Miller suggests that this fusion of linguistics, computing, and experimental psychology gave rise to cognitive psychology. By the 1970s, this shift towards the scientific study of mental processes had spread to applied psychology and psychological therapies based on cognitive understandings of mental disorder were beginning to take centre stage.

The Rise of Neuroscience

Psychology grew partly out of biology and a tradition of biological psychology has been maintained for the last 150 years. However, the last decade has seen an explosion of research into the brain and its relationship to psychological functioning. Neuroscience is both an academic discipline in its own right, and an increasingly important influence within psychology. The growth of neuroscience has been exciting, and some great advances in our understanding of the brain and its relationship to psychology have been made (see Figure 2.9). However, as we shall see in Chapter 4, there have also been a range of criticisms that call into question the value of at least some neuroscience research. Opinions about neuroscience can be quite polarized in psychology. You will no doubt begin to form your own views after reading Chapter 4.

The Rise of Evolutionary Psychology

Another perspective with its roots in biology is **evolutionary psychology**. Evolutionary psychologists explain human psychological characteristics as having developed through the mechanisms of evolution, in order that we as a species adapt to our changing environment. Thus our mating behaviour can be understood as a way to maximize the chances of successful reproduction. Social behaviours such as prejudice, gossip, and **altruism** (helping) can all be seen in evolutionary terms as having been advantageous to us as a species at one or more points in our evolution.

Evolutionary psychology is controversial. It has great explanatory power because it can be used to neatly explain a wide range of apparently illogical behaviours,

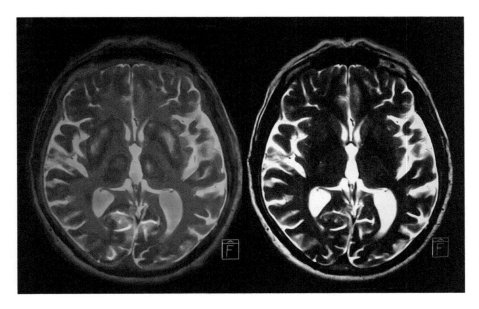

FIGURE 2.9 Developing technology over the last two decades has allowed us to learn a lot about the brain.

Source: Semnic/Shutterstock.com.

from celebrity worship to fear of the dark. However, it can also be used to explain—and some would say justify—some of the nastier aspects of human behaviour such as racism and rape (Rose and Rose, 2010; though see Winegard and Winegard, 2014, for a counterargument). To some psychologists evolutionary psychology is therefore fundamentally immoral. More of this in Chapter 5.

Psychology in International Perspective

Historically, psychology has been most studied and most influential in the USA followed by Britain and Europe. Of the academic psychology articles published worldwide between 2000 and 2009 nearly 345,000 were American, with Britain coming in second with just under 83,000. Germany, Canada, and Australia were ranked third to fifth with a combined total of around 145,000 articles between them (these figures are taken from the 2011 International Benchmarking Review of UK Psychology, conducted jointly by the European Social Research Council, the British Psychological Society, the Experimental Psychological Society, and the Association for Heads of Psychology Departments). In an analysis of authorship in leading psychology journals, Arnett (2008) reports that between 2003 and 2007, 73% of first authors were American and only around 2% were from outside the USA, Europe, Canada, and Australasia.

This situation is changing—by 2012 two Asian universities (Singapore and Tokyo) had entered the top 20 psychology departments worldwide (QS rankings). However, these figures mean that historically psychology has been dominated by American thinking. Which areas and approaches have become mainstream and which have ended up as specialist/marginal/radical have been determined largely by what has been 'in' in America and to a lesser extent Britain.

Be aware as you read this and other psychology textbooks that what you will study in psychology is largely American in origin. This is not a criticism. Given that most psychology has come from America it would be contrived to ignore or play down the importance of American theory and research. However, it can be instructive sometimes to look at how psychologists in other parts of the world have responded to American trends and to observe cultural differences between psychologies in different countries. A simple example of cultural difference is the way behaviourism dominated US psychology for half a decade, whereas it received a fairly lukewarm reception in mainland Europe. Looking at current research from America and Europe we can still see that greater value is placed on experimental methods and laboratory environments in the USA—perhaps a legacy of the behaviourist era. British psychology draws upon American and European traditions and is subject to both sets of influences.

THEORY AND PERSPECTIVE IN PSYCHOLOGY

Most published literature in psychology—and science in general—is concerned with research. However, we also need to be able to explain, understand, and think about research findings and generate ideas to research. This is the role of theory. Recall that the classic scientific method involves observing a phenomenon, explaining it, and carrying out research to test whether our explanation is supported by evidence. We can be a little more precise at this point with the term 'explanation'.

Theories and Hypotheses

When Paul Ekman predicted that members of the Fore tribe in Papua New Guinea would be able to interpret emotional facial expressions of Westerners depicted in photographs, he was creating a working hypothesis. A hypothesis is not the same as a *theory*, although the two terms are often confused. A **theory** is a set of inter-connected ideas and statements used to explain observed phenomena. The same phenomenon may be explained by two, three, or a half-dozen competing theories.

How does one decide which theory to accept? A good theory is one from which any number of testable hypotheses may be drawn (Popper, 1959). Scientists derive hypotheses from theories and submit them to testing using the scientific method. When the dust settles from a great many such hypothesis tests, the hypothesis with the strongest supporting evidence will come to be the generally accepted theory. Thus, a successful theory is one that is stated in a form that allows it to be tested and which results in a rich body of fruitful research.

The distinction between theories and hypotheses is explored further in Table 2.2.

> **KEY IDEAS** hypotheses and theories A hypothesis is a specific, testable prediction about what will happen under certain circumstances. Hypotheses are often drawn from a *theory*, which is a set of interconnected ideas and statements used to explain phenomena.

TABLE 2.2 **Theories and hypotheses**

This table shows how more than one specific hypothesis may be drawn from a more general theory.

Theory	Hypotheses
The human mind did not evolve to solve problems of abstract logical reasoning; it evolved to solve concrete problems critical to survival and reproduction.	*Hypothesis #1:* Abstract problems of logical reasoning that most people find difficult to solve will be made relatively easy when conveyed in a story about a concrete issue that would have been of importance to our evolutionary ancestors (eg, Cosmides and Tooby, 2005). *Hypothesis #2:* Seemingly foolish errors of reasoning about logical probability committed by people in psychological tests will be committed less often if the problems are framed using concrete numerical language (ie, 'How many . . .') rather than the language of abstract probability ('How probable is it that . . .', Hertwig and Gigerenzer, 1999).

THINKING CREATIVELY

The aim of this task is to help you apply the scientific method to psychology. Let's start with the observation that children from poor backgrounds tend to achieve lower grades at school than those from better-off families. One explanation for this observation is that better-off families have lower levels of stress and therefore children are better able to concentrate on study.

1 Generate a hypothesis from this explanation.

2 What sort of information could you gather in order to test this hypothesis?

Theory and Levels of Analysis

Theories differ in the point of view they take when explaining a fact, but they also differ in **level of analysis**: the *aspect* of a particular fact or set of facts they are trying to explain in the first place. Take, for example, the expression 'Guns don't kill people, people kill people'. This is a comment about level of analysis. Consider the many ways you could explain the following hypothetical fact: Uncle Albert died last night.

1 A bullet shattered his cerebellum and medulla. (*Bullets kill people*)

2 He was shot. (*Guns kill people*)

3 His girlfriend's ex-husband shot him in a fit of jealousy. (*People kill people*)

4 Despair brought on by poverty, inadequate social services, the loss of family, and a street-corner culture of violence triggered the shooting. (*Society kills people*)

5 The shooter's genetic tendency towards aggression inherited from his father's family line interacted with universal male tendencies towards sexual jealousy, cultural factors, and specific prior experiences to cause the shooting. (*Genetic, evolutionary, cultural, and experiential factors interact to kill people*)

None of these statements contradicts any of the other statements—each is addressing a different level, or aspect, of the same question. Throughout fields of psychology, theories differ in their levels of analysis.

Theoretical Perspectives on Psychology

Mao Zedong, the leader of the Chinese Revolution, famously quoted an ancient Chinese saying: 'Let a hundred flowers bloom, a hundred schools of thought contend' (Nieh, 1981, p 24). Psychologists appear to share this sentiment. For any given psychological phenomenon there may be a dozen different interpretations based on competing theories and perspectives. Psychologists working within each field do not necessarily agree on how best to explain the human behaviour they study.

Some of the more important of these current perspectives are the following:

- *Biological perspective*: Psychologists who are guided by a biological perspective believe that the keys to understanding human behaviour lie in understanding the nervous system (particularly the brain) and the genetic and environmental influences on its development. Neuroscientists and biological psychologists adopt a biological perspective almost by definition.

- *Evolutionary perspective*: Those favouring an evolutionary perspective believe that the human brain and behaviour evolved in very specific ways to adapt to conditions experienced by our ancestors over evolutionary time. These adaptations may or may not be useful in modern environments. The evolutionary perspective may be found among psychologists working in virtually any field of psychology.

- *Behavioural perspective*: Although there are few if any real behaviourists left nowadays, behaviour analysts still exist and effectively apply the principles of conditioning and observational learning to explain human behaviour, looking, for example, at how behaviours are reinforced.

- *Cognitive perspective*: Those adhering to the cognitive perspective view the human mind as an extraordinarily complex *information-processing* device, in some ways (very loosely) similar to an 'organic computer'. Again, almost by definition, those working in the field of cognitive psychology are likely to hold to this perspective, but some psychologists working in social and clinical fields also adopt a cognitive perspective.

- *Psychodynamic perspective*: Psychodynamic theorists believe that human beings are often strongly affected by unconscious conflicts and motivations that may be expressed in their behaviour and personality. They believe that these conflicts and motivations are generated from a blend of instinct and early experience, particularly in the context of family relationships.

- *Humanistic perspective*: Humanistic psychologists try to see the whole person and reject the way other perspectives reduce us to a biological or cognitive system, taking account of the full range of human needs and seeing us as capable of free will. They also see humans as innately good rather than morally neutral.

- *Positive psychology*: Those working from the positive psychology perspective use psychological science to study human strengths and positive attributes, rather than focusing primarily on human problems as is sometimes the case in branches of psychology such as clinical and counselling psychology. Positive psychologists also work towards developing programmes and techniques that promote the expression of these strengths and positive attributes.

- *Sociocultural perspective*: Sociocultural theorists emphasize the critical role played by society and culture in shaping human psychology. Many of these theorists work in the fields of social, cultural, and cross-cultural psychology.

- *Critical social psychology*: This is a radical and deliberately subversive approach to psychology that seeks to identify theories, studies, and techniques that are likely to have developed in order to serve vested interests such as the patriarchal society or the class system.

Some psychologists are fiercely loyal to a particular perspective, while others are more eclectic and draw on different perspectives when they are useful. Others do not hang their flag on any perspective at all. No one of the schools of thought just described has been consistently demonstrated to be 'better' or more productive than another across a range of contexts. The point is that each of these 'hundreds of blossoms' focuses its research energy upon a specific piece of the larger picture of human psychology.

THINKING PRACTICALLY

Jessica has developed what some people might consider to be an exercise addiction. She comes from a sporty family and has always felt that they were disappointed with her lack of athleticism. Recently she has been subscribing to various social media sites dealing with achieving a conventionally attractive thin body as well as running several miles every day. She reports experiencing a 'runner's high' and increasing satisfaction with her body shape, although friends are becoming concerned at her weight loss.

> Role models neurochemicals genetic influence social norms irrational beliefs unconscious influence

Match these factors to some of the perspectives we have identified and explain how they might have influenced Jessica's behaviour.

READ THIS

You can learn more about the nature of scientific psychology from pretty much any academic psychology book. There may, however, be some specific things you want to learn more about having read this chapter. You might like to start with Magnusson's definition of psychology.

Magnusson, D. (2012). **The human being in society**. *European Psychologist* **17**, 21–7.

For more about pseudoscience in a psychological context we can all relate to, try this:

Lilienfeld, S.O., Ammirati, R., and David, M. (2012). Distinguishing science from pseudoscience in school psychology: Science and scientific thinking as safeguards against human error. *Journal of School Psychology*, **50**, 7–36.

For a whole book on critical thinking in psychology you might like these:

Forshaw, M. (2012). *Critical Thinking for Psychology: A Student Guide*. Hoboken, NJ: John Wiley & Sons.

McGhee, P. (2001). *Thinking Psychologically*. Basingstoke: Palgrave MacMillan.

IN REVIEW

PSYCHOLOGY AS SCIENCE

- Psychology is a science—the science of mind, brain, and behaviour. This means that psychologists use the scientific method to discover and explain psychological phenomena and treat claims about human, mind, brain, and behaviour with scepticism.

- Psychologists regard themselves as scientists because they conduct and take note of research, they attempt to be objective in their observations, and they are critical of their own and others' interpretations of findings.

- There is a trade-off between the study of 'impeccable trivia', which are straightforward to study using the methods of science, and more meaningful but harder to study phenomena.

- A small minority of psychologists take more critical stances towards traditional views of science in psychology. These include humanistic and critical social psychologists.

- It is important to distinguish between science and pseudoscience in psychology. Pseudoscience is designed to appear scientific but actually lacks evidence.

ACADEMIC AND APPLIED PSYCHOLOGY

- Academic psychology involves conducting psychological research, sharing this through conferences and journals, and teaching psychology.
- Academic psychology can be divided into categories—for example, social and cognitive psychology—however, in practice there is often overlap between these categories.
- Applied psychology involves using psychological theory, research, and techniques in a range of professional settings. Branches of applied psychology include clinical and educational psychology.
- Academic and applied psychology are both 'proper' psychology and enjoy equal status in the eyes of professional bodies like the British Psychological Society and the European Federation of Psychological Associations.

A BRIEF HISTORY OF THE MIND

- The first pre-scientific systems of psychology appeared around 2,600 years ago, and are notable for the overlap of ideas with modern psychology.
- The backdrop to the existence of scientific psychology lies in European philosophers of the sixteenth century.
- Psychology emerged as a discipline in its own right from philosophy and biology in the mid-nineteenth century.
- The early scientific psychologists used introspection as their main research method but this was superseded by the behaviourists' focus on observable behaviour.
- Behaviourism, the study of learned behaviour under controlled conditions, dominated American psychology, though not so much European psychology, throughout the first half of the twentieth century.
- In parallel with behaviourism, psychoanalysis developed a more theoretical approach to psychology, based largely in European hospitals and private training institutes.
- In the 1950s, humanistic psychology was an attempt to make psychology kinder and simpler. It was briefly influential as a 'third force' in academic psychology and its principles still underlie some practice in applied psychology.
- Cognitive psychology, with its focus on mental processes, also emerged as a major force in psychology in the 1950s, dominating psychology for the rest of the twentieth century.
- Neuroscience has emerged as both a separate discipline and an approach to psychology over the last two decades, providing very exciting insights into the relationship between brain, mind, and behaviour, but there are also controversies around what some consider overblown claims.
- Evolutionary psychology is another modern biology-based approach to psychology. It has great explanatory power but is controversial for appearing to justify some immoral behaviours.

- There are cultural differences in the psychology of different countries. American psychology thus tends to be particularly experimental and mainland European psychology is typically rather more theoretical.

THEORY AND PERSPECTIVE IN PSYCHOLOGY

- Theory has an important role in psychology. A theory is a series of interconnected ideas that aims to explain a phenomenon. Theories generate hypotheses.

- An hypothesis is different from a theory, being a simple and testable statement about a phenomenon. Hypotheses are very important in formulating some kinds of psychological research.

- Different theories explaining the same phenomenon can coexist if they operate at different levels of explanation.

TEST YOURSELF

1 Psychology is another word for counselling. True ☐ False ☐

2 Most of the public see psychology as common sense. True ☐ False ☐

3 Humanistic psychology has lived up to its promise to be the 'third force' in psychology. True ☐ False ☐

4 A theory is the same as an hypothesis. True ☐ False ☐

5 Which of the following disciplines is best described as the study of the brain and nervous system?

   a) Sociology

   b) Psychology

   c) Neuroscience

   d) Psychiatry

6 What term describes the assumptions that underlie a science at any point in its development?

   a) Parador

   b) Paradise

   c) Parapsychology

   d) Paradigm

7 Which of the following is not a core component of academic psychology?

   a) Astrology

   b) Biopsychology

   c) Individual differences

   d) Research methods

8 Which approach to psychology places most emphasis on observable behaviour?

   a) Introspectionism

   b) Behaviourism

    c) Humanism

    d) Cognitivism

9 Explain what is meant by pseudoscience.

10 Explain why different approaches to psychology can be said to work at different levels of analysis.

 Visit the online resources that accompany this book: www.oup.com/uk/jarvis–okami1e

RESEARCH METHODS IN PSYCHOLOGY

CHAPTER 3

LEARNING OUTCOMES

By the end of this chapter you should be able to:

- Outline how psychologists make use of some of the major research methods, including case studies, observation, surveys, correlation, experiments, and content analysis

- Understand the particular issues arising with the use of different methods and the applications and limitations of each

- Explain the purpose of descriptive and inferential statistics and understand the role of statistical significance and effect sizes

- Distinguish between qualitative and quantitative data and clarify the relationship between qualitative data, qualitative research, and qualitative analysis

- Know and apply ethical principles and guidelines to assessing and designing psychological research with human participants

- Evaluate the arguments for and against use of animal research in psychology

Psychology is a research-based subject and if there is one competence you will acquire during a psychology degree it is to conduct and analyse research. We have already established that psychologists reject common sense, prevailing beliefs, and personal opinion. Instead we *find stuff out*. In this section we introduce you to the ways in which psychologists go about this.

When a psychological researcher wishes to conduct a research study, there are a number of possible research methods to choose from. The term *research method* is used differently in different contexts, but we use it here to mean a general strategy that one may choose to address a research problem. The basic methods can be classified as follows:

- Case study
- Observation
- Survey
- Correlation
- Experiment

❯ KEY IDEAS research methods
This term is used differently in different contexts, but it is used here to refer to general strategies that may be used for conducting research.

It is important to understand that there are many research traditions in psychology, and that some researchers have a particular commitment to one or more research methods. If you read around you will soon come across statements like these:

The preferred research method is the experiment.

Quantitative research is qualitative research done badly.

We take the view that psychological research is strengthened by its diversity, and that it is meaningless to think of globally good and bad methods. There are, of course, particularly suitable methods with which to address particular research questions. If, for example, we want to know how cats react to invasion of their territory by other cats there is no point in surveying them!

In this section we are not attempting to give you all the detail you need about research methods—there are plenty of separate books for that; for example, *Starting out in Methods and Statistics for Psychology*, by Victoria Bourne. Our aim is to give you enough detail to make sense of the research reported in this book and a sense of the limitations of each method in order to help you think critically about the research we report.

CASE STUDIES

> KEY IDEAS case study A case study is a descriptive research method in which the researcher gathers detailed information about a single individual, group, family, or organization in order to better understand a particular set of circumstances.

A descriptive study is one that attempts to *describe* some individual or group in relation to characteristics of interest to the researcher. Descriptive studies answer questions of *who*, *what*, *when*, and *how*. The most basic type of descriptive research is the **case study**. Case studies allow the researcher to gain extremely detailed information about a single individual or small group of individuals in particular circumstances. We might, for example, track the process an individual goes through as they undergo therapy for a mental disorder. This can help us understand the experience of the patient, possible causes of their disorder, and the effects of the therapy. In this book we will discuss a number of case studies and explore what they can and cannot tell us.

Case studies can be of immense value when it comes to learning about unusual circumstances or those we cannot create deliberately for ethical reasons. So if we want to know about the effects of severe early isolation on children's language development we have two problems. First, it is relatively unusual for children to be sufficiently isolated for serious effects to result and, second, we clearly cannot isolate young children for extended periods just to see the effects. Case studies of unfortunate children who have been isolated in early life are therefore an important source of information.

The problem with case study research, however, is that findings of these studies may not *generalize* to other people—they may be unique to the person or few people being studied. For example, just because it turns out that a particular person began experiencing severe anxiety following a car accident is no indication that most or even many cases of anxiety have resulted from car accidents.

THINKING CRITICALLY

Pate and Gabbard (2003) describe the case of Mr A, a police officer with adult baby syndrome. By day Mr A was a highly responsible adult but at home he dressed (and masturbated) in nappies and drank milk from a bottle. Mr A had a traumatic childhood, having been adopted and never having become close to his adoptive parents.

>

Consider the following:

1 Why are case studies such as Mr A our main source of information about adult baby syndrome?

2 A single well-documented case study is evidence that a phenomenon like adult baby syndrome exists. What is it *not* evidence for?

SURVEYS

Sometimes psychologists are interested not so much in people's behaviour or cognition but their feelings, opinions, plans, or other thoughts. The only real way to find this out is to ask them. Survey studies involve asking people things. On other occasions we are interested in behaviour that takes place in private settings or in the future so we have no option but to ask people about it. This is an important distinction because we are much better at knowing how we feel about something than we are at knowing how we will behave. Consider the kinds of questions pollsters ask voters prior to an election:

- Who is your preferred party?
- Who will you vote for?

These are superficially similar but one is asking about an opinion and the other a behaviour. Pollsters also will also tell you that answers to the second question do not necessarily correspond to behaviour come election day.

Questionnaires and Interviews

Surveys can be carried out verbally—by means of an interview—or on paper/screen by means of a questionnaire, as shown in Figure 3.1. Questionnaires are quick to complete and do not require a psychologist to be present so can be administered in

FIGURE 3.1 **A survey that is carried out on paper/screen is called a questionnaire.**

Source: Andrey_Popov/Shutterstock.com.

much larger numbers than interviews. It is not uncommon for the sample size in questionnaire surveys to run into thousands. However, response rates for questionnaires are often very low—sometimes less than 10% of questionnaires that are sent out are completed. Short questionnaires with simple titles result in better response rates (Lund and Gram, 1998). Because questionnaires are usually completed without a psychologist present to clarify questions or encourage the respondent to give full answers, they are suited to asking closed questions that have a fixed response set such as yes ❐, no ❐, or five-point agreement or *Likert* scales:

Strongly agree ❐   agree ❐   neutral ❐   disagree ❐   strongly disagree ❐

Interviews are better suited to open questions where respondents are encouraged to elaborate on their answers.

There are other issues affecting the choice between interviews and questionnaires. People may find it easier to disclose personal information using a questionnaire. This was demonstrated by Canterino et al (1999) when they surveyed pregnant women about experiences of domestic violence, using both interviews and questionnaires. Overall, 36% of respondents disclosed domestic violence, but interestingly only 60% of these disclosed in interviews whereas 85% disclosed in questionnaires. The remaining 15% only disclosed their experiences when taking part in both interviews and questionnaire conditions.

Wording Effects

In addition to issues related to questionnaire-interview choice, the way survey questions are composed can have an enormous impact on results—a problem known as **wording effects**. For example, consider how a group of people might respond to the question,

- 'Do you agree that women ought to have the right to control their own reproductive activity?' compared with the question,
- 'Do you think a woman ought to have the right to terminate the life of her unborn child?'

It is very easy for researchers with a pre-existing bias to deliberately influence the outcomes of surveys by manipulating question wordings in this way.

Sampling Issues

We can never conduct research on everyone. Instead, we select a small group who we believe to represent the population we are interested in. This is our sample. In some areas of psychology we don't expect people to vary much according to their demographics; for example, in their learning and cognition (apart from age). However, in some areas, such as social behaviour and even more so social opinions, there may be massive variation within any population. If we want to find out what a whole population thinks about an issue it is absolutely essential that the sample is representative of the people in that population; that is, the demographics and other relevant characteristics of the sample match those of the population. This can be achieved in various ways. For example, if a truly random sample, in which every member of the population has an equal chance of selection, is drawn from a population, there is a good chance that it will be representative, as long as the sample is reasonably large. Alternatively a quota sample can be drawn from the population by deliberately selecting participants that each meet some of the required characteristics. So in a population with 52% males, 30% of adults aged 20–30 people will be selected in

> ❯ KEY IDEAS survey research
> A **survey** is a descriptive research method used to obtain self-reported data about people's experiences, attitudes, feelings, and, on occasion, their behaviour in contexts where it would be impractical to observe them. A **sample** is the relatively small group of individuals selected to represent a larger group—the population from which the sample is drawn. The **population** is the larger group of interest to a researcher, from which he or she will draw a smaller sample for the purposes of conducting a research study.

those proportions. This is one reason why researchers with questionnaires in the high street sometimes approach you and sometimes not—they may be short of people with your characteristics or they may be looking for a different type of person.

A biased sample—one that in some important respect is *not* representative of the population of interest—can seriously distort research results. Think about election polls again for a moment. Imagine sampling a group of 18–21-year-old students in a single university in the North of England for an election poll and trying to extrapolate the results to the voting intentions of the whole of the UK. It would clearly be impossible because we know that voting patterns can differ hugely according to age, region, and occupation.

THINKING PRACTICALLY

Imagine you have been approached by a TV production company and asked to conduct a survey on the TV show *Dr Who*. The company have a couple of research questions in mind: first, how many people plan to watch *Dr Who* in the future, and second, what do viewers like about *Dr Who*?

They also bring examples of survey questions they want to ask, including 'do you agree that *Dr Who* should include scenes of graphic violence that might traumatize younger viewers?'

Consider the following:

1 Which research question would you recommend pursuing? Explain why this is.

2 What might be the advantages of surveying by means of a questionnaire?

3 What might be the advantages of using an interview method?

4 What advice might you give to advise them about the wording of their example survey questions?

5 Identify the target population for your survey and explain why it is important to obtain a representative sample.

OBSERVATIONS

If survey methods are best suited to answering research questions about how people think and feel, how do we answer questions about human behaviour? The most direct way to assess human behaviour is to observe it (Figure 3.2). Now, we observe behaviour in several types of study so there is a distinction between observing behaviour as a means of data collection and carrying out a pure observational study. Observational studies involve simply observing behaviour in a particular situation, without manipulating or comparing conditions. In this section we are most concerned with observational studies, but there are grey areas around the boundaries between what is an observational study and what is a natural experiment using observation.

Naturalistic and Controlled Observation

Behaviour can be observed in a natural setting or in a psychologist's laboratory. When making the choice there is a trade-off between obtaining the maximum volume of data and observing truly natural behaviour. Take the example of flirting

FIGURE 3.2 **You can assess human behaviour by observing it.**
Photographee.eu/Shutterstock.com.

behaviour. If we get two suitable people into our lab to flirt we can be sure of capturing every detail—we can have cameras zooming in from all angles and record every facial movement and postural shift, analysing it all afterwards at leisure. However, will those flirting people display the same behaviours as they would in their natural flirting environment? If not, then all the detail we have recorded and analysed may be more misleading than informative.

On the other hand, observing people flirting in a natural environment is not hassle-free; it just presents us with different problems. Romantic settings are traditionally dimly lit and flirting couples require a bit of space to themselves. These conditions do not lend themselves to capturing every nuance of facial expression and body language!

Some of the most successful controlled observations have involved babies and toddlers, who do not know or care that they are in a psychologist's laboratory. In other cases, observations have maximum credibility when the results of controlled and naturalistic observations show similar findings.

Covert and Overt Observation

Another distinction in observational research is between overt observation, in which participants are aware they are being watched, and, covert, in which they are not. Covert observations have the advantage that those being watched are more likely to behave naturally—having an observer there can be off-putting. However, covert observations can raise ethical issues. Clearly, in a laboratory setting participants will know they are there to be observed and will give consent. In a natural setting this is less clear-cut. It is generally considered to be ethically acceptable to observe people in natural settings without their knowledge, provided they are in a truly public space doing things they would be comfortable to be seen doing. In practice this can be tricky to establish.

Participant and Non-Participant Observation

A related issue concerns participant and non-participant observation. Most observation is non-participant; that is, there is a clear separation of roles between the observers and those being observed. However, sometimes observers participate in activities alongside the people they are observing. This may be covert, in which case the group being observed think the observer is one of them, or, more unusually, overt, in which case the observed group allow the researcher to hang out with them in order to observe their behaviour.

The major reason for conducting participant observation is that some social behaviour is illegal or frowned upon, and so it is conducted in private. So, for example, if we wanted to observe the pre-fight warm-up ritual in a group of football hooligans (technically called a 'firm') or learn how a sexual episode is negotiated at a swingers' club, we cannot simply go to a public place and watch. We need to be accepted as a participant, whether overtly or covertly. Infiltrating groups who don't wish to be observed raises clear ethical issues.

CORRELATION

In **correlational research**, psychologists are asking whether one variable is associated, or correlated, with another variable. A variable is any factor whose magnitude or category can vary. For example, TV watching can vary in magnitude from *no watching at all* to *watching 24/7*. **Depression** can also vary in magnitude from *not at all depressed* to *extremely depressed*. Other variables such as gender and ethnicity vary by category.

In asking whether two variables are correlated, the researcher is asking, if the value of one variable changes, does the value of the other variable also change? Either way—increase or decrease—the variables are correlated if one variable changes when the other changes. A correlational relationship is therefore a predictable relationship, because measuring one of the variables will allow us to *predict* something about the other variable.

As an example, height and weight are highly correlated—taller people tend to weigh more. Of course, this is not the case for every single individual on the planet—if that were true, the **correlation** would be said to be a *perfect correlation*. Yet the average person of 6 ft 5 inches does weigh more than the average person of 5 ft 6 inches, so knowing something about a person's height can help you predict something about their weight in a general way. In this case, as height increases so does weight. When one variable increases as the other variable increases, the correlation is said to be a positive correlation (see Figure 3.3).

A *scatterplot* is ideally suited to depicting correlations, as it represents the strength of the correlation by how closely together the data points are scattered on the graph. Each data point represents a single score. Depicted here are 'ideal' examples of six types of scatterplots. In positive correlations (A, D, and E), the data points cluster in a linear diagonal grouping from lower left to upper right. In negative correlations (B and F), the angle of the slope is reversed, from upper left to lower right. Zero correlations (C) cluster in no discernible pattern at all. Perfect correlations (A and B)—virtually unknown in psychology, and rare elsewhere—form a perfect diagonal line.

> **KEY IDEAS** correlation
> Correlational research is a method of study in which the researcher measures two or more variables to see if there is a mathematical relationship (correlation) between them. Two variables are said to be **correlated** when a change in one variable can predict change in another variable because the variables are associated in some way. However, this association between the variables may not be causal in nature.

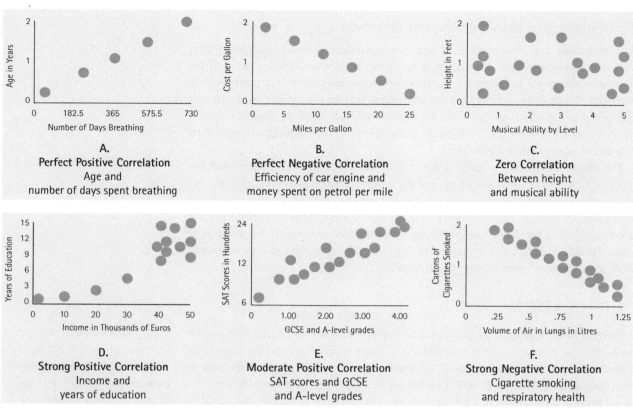

FIGURE 3.3 **Picturing correlations using a scatterplot.**

❯ **KEY IDEAS** more about correlation A positive correlation occurs when an increase in one variable is associated (correlated) with an *increase* in the other variable. Negative correlation occurs when an increase in one variable is associated (correlated) with a *decrease* in the other variable.

The correlation coefficient is a statistic which quantifies the strength and direction of correlation between two variables. The correlation coefficient ranges from −1.0 (a perfect negative correlation) to +1.0 (a perfect positive correlation). A correlation coefficient near to 0 indicates no association between the variables in question.

When one variable increases and the other variable decreases, the correlation is said to be a negative correlation. Only when one variable does not predict anything at all about another are the variables said to be *uncorrelated*. For example, weight and musical ability are likely uncorrelated. Correlation is measured with a statistic known as the **correlation coefficient**. This statistic ranges from −1.0 (a perfect negative correlation) to +1.0 (a perfect positive correlation). A coefficient at or close to 0.0 indicates no correlation at all.

Very strong correlations between different variables are rare in psychology. The strongest we can recall is the +0.9 correlation between prejudice against a range of minority groups and the social acceptability of prejudice against those groups (Crandall et al, 2002). An example of a strong negative correlation is that between the extent of a person's spiritual beliefs and the density of receptors for a neurotransmitter called serotonin—associated with mood—they have in their brain—up to −0.8 depending on the brain region (Borg et al, 2003).

Correlation and Causation

It is critically important to understand that two variables can be correlated without one causing the other. This is an example of where psychological research can reach very different conclusions from those suggested by common sense or folk beliefs. Take the common belief that musical skill is the result of practice. Time spent practising an instrument correlates fairly strongly (+0.18 to +0.36) with skill level. The obvious interpretation is that more practice leads to greater skill. However, a study by Mosing et al (2014) suggests that the relationship between practice and skill is more complex. 10,500 Swedish twin musicians took part in the study. Both practice time and skill level were more similar in identical twins than non-identical twins, suggesting they are both genetically influenced. Where identical twins differed in their practice time this was not associated with differences in skill levels, suggesting that rather than practice affecting skill, the same genetic factors affect both practice and skill. In this case genetic make-up is the **lurking variable** that affects both the variables being studied.

Having said all that, there is a world of difference between saying a single correlation coefficient does not indicate causation and saying that correlational research never tells us anything about cause and effect. There are various techniques that can suggest what variable affects what in correlations. For example, if we suspect a lurking variable is involved we can measure it and carry out a different calculation, called a partial correlation, which controls for the influence of this third variable.

We can also employ a technique called cross-lagging to get an idea of the direction of a causal relationship between two variables. Cross-lagging involves measuring variables more than once and looking at the correlations between each variable early on and the other at a later point in time. Where one of the variables measured early correlates strongly with the other later it is likely that it affects that variable.

An example of a study using both partial correlation and cross-lagging comes from Hutter et al (2013). They were interested in the causal relationship between reported quality of life in breast cancer patients and their levels of depression and anxiety. They measured these variables twice with a six-month interval and correlated depression and anxiety with quality of life measure, controlling in each calculation for the influence of each additional variable; that is, anxiety was correlated with quality of life, controlling for depression and depression was correlated with quality of life controlling for anxiety. Quality of life measured early in the study predicted later anxiety and depression whereas initial anxiety and depression did not predict later quality of life. This suggests that anxiety and depression are products of cancer patients' quality of life rather than influences on it.

> **KEY IDEAS** lurking variable
In correlational research a lurking variable is one that influences two or more measured variables, creating the false impression that there are causal relationships between them.

If this isn't quite clear yet, consider another example of the very strong negative correlation between global warming and the number of pirates in the world, as graphed in Figure 3.4. As global temperature has increased, the number of pirates has dramatically decreased. What lurking variable might be responsible for this correlation?

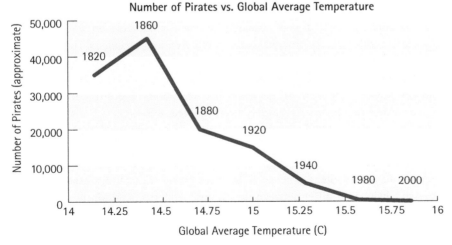

FIGURE 3.4 Correlation does *not* Equal causation. As global temperature has increased, the number of pirates has dramatically decreased. Could global warming be stopped if enough people quit their landlubber jobs and became pirates?

Source: Adapted from www.venganza.org.

❯ KEY IDEAS correlation and causation One problem in establishing cause and effect from correlations is in the possible influence of one or more lurking variables that affect both of the variables being studied we are interested in. We can control for lurking variables by means of partial correlation. There is an additional problem of establishing the direction of any causal relationship between two variables. This can be addressed by cross-lagging; correlating each variable with the other at different points in time, so that we can see which predicts the other.

❯ KEY IDEAS true experiment A true experiment is a research study where the experimenter satisfies all criteria necessary for causality to be inferred in the research results. These criteria usually include random assignment to conditions, manipulation of variables, use of control conditions, and control over confounding variables. Studies comparing two existing groups, like males and females, are not true experiments because we cannot have manipulation of variables or random allocation to conditions.

THINKING CREATIVELY

Research has consistently found a positive correlation between the outcomes of patients in psychological therapies and the quality of relationship between the patient and the therapist. The obvious interpretation is that the quality of relationship affects the outcome.

Consider the following:

1 Explain how the quality of relationship could be a product of therapeutic outcome.

2 What lurking variables might impact on both the quality of relationship and the therapeutic outcome?

EXPERIMENTS

One often hears the term *experiment* used to describe any type of scientific research study. However, in psychology, the term *experiment* actually applies only to one type of research method: *experimental* research, the purest form of which is the **true experiment**. Most research studies in many branches of psychology are not experiments at all—they are correlational studies or *quasi-experiments*: studies that fulfil some of the criteria for a true experiment, but not all of them. You can think of a quasi-experiment as a hybrid between an experiment and a correlational study. On one hand you are comparing outcomes under different conditions—like an experiment. On the other hand you know that you have not really established well-controlled conditions—so you have the same issues of lurking variables as you would in a correlational study.

So what then is a true experiment? As just explained, in a correlational study the researcher observes or measures variables as they already exist to see if they are associated. In a sense, the researcher is a passive observer. But in a true experiment, the researcher is asking: 'If I do *this*, what will happen to *that*?' More precisely, in an experiment the researcher makes some purposeful change in one variable of interest (rather than simply observing or measuring the variable) and then examines another variable of interest to see if any change has resulted.

As an example, a great deal of research has been conducted on the effects of playing violent video games on **aggression** in children and teenagers. However, the focus has been on boys and men rather than girls and women, because males spend much more time playing these games; and because males are also responsible for most of the physical violence in the world (Archer, 2004). The effect these games may have on female players has largely been ignored. Researchers Craig Anderson and Christine Murphy (2003) considered the following scenario: if they brought a sample of female introductory psychology students into their lab, and had one group of the women play a non-violent game such as *Oh No! More Lemmings* while the other group played a violent game such as *Street Fighter II*, would subsequent rates of aggressive behaviour differ between the groups? Anderson and Murphy predicted that those playing the violent games would subsequently behave more aggressively in subsequent tests.

Here the variable being purposely manipulated is the *type of video game*. This variable changes in quality from non-violent to violent depending on which group of women is playing. The type of video game is called the **independent variable (IV)** because it is free (independent) to take on any particular values the researchers decide to give it (violent or non-violent in this case). These values are called the **levels of the independent variable**.

The second variable—the one being measured to note any resulting changes—is *aggressive behaviour* and it varies by magnitude (ie, from lower to higher levels of aggression). The variable being measured is known as the **dependent variable (DV)** because changes in this variable are entirely dependent upon the researchers' manipulation of the independent variable. *Manipulation* is the technical term to describe the process of making a purposeful change in the IV.

In sum: the independent variable (IV) is what we manipulate and the dependent variable (DV) is what we measure to see if our manipulation has had any effect.

True experiments are the type of research study most likely to establish unequivocally whether one thing (eg, playing violent video games) causes another thing (eg, increased aggression). However, an experiment can only do this if we can be certain that our IV is really the only factor affecting the DV. Experimenters achieve this by making use of **controls**, which ensure that nothing else changes when the level of the IV is changed. In a true experiment, as the level of the IV changes, everything else is held constant.

To clarify this idea, what if Anderson and Murphy had allowed the women in their study to choose which game they preferred to play? Those who were already more aggressive by nature might prefer the violent game. If those who played this game later demonstrated higher levels of aggression, it might have nothing to do with playing violent video games and everything to do with their already being aggressive people. In this case, Anderson and Murphy would have allowed their research participants' *initial* level of aggressiveness to 'change' from less to more aggressive as the type of video game changed from less to more aggressive. This would not be a true experiment.

There are three specific ways to exert control in a true experiment. Without these three basic aspects of control, the study ceases to be a true experiment. These aspects are:

- random assignment to conditions;
- use of control conditions; and
- control over confounding variables.

Random Assignment

In an experiment, the groups to which participants may be assigned are known as the **conditions** of the experiment, and they represent the levels of the independent variable. In the video game experiment described earlier, there are two conditions: *violent game* and *non-violent game*. Allowing participants to choose the game they preferred to play would have been a non-random way of deciding the condition to which each participant would be assigned. The results of such a study could not be relied upon.

On the other hand, when participants are randomly assigned to conditions, each participant has an equal chance of being assigned to either of the conditions of the experiment. The purpose of random assignment is to create groups that do not differ in systematic ways prior to exposure to the independent variable. This adds to confidence that any change noted in the dependent variable is due to the manipulation of the IV, and not to any participant characteristics such as initial levels of aggression. If selection is random, it is extremely unlikely that more aggressive participants would end up in one group rather than the other strictly by chance.

❯ **KEY IDEAS** independent and dependent variable (IV, DV) The **independent variable (IV)** is the variable being manipulated in an experiment to determine the possible effects on a **dependent variable (DV)**. The independent variable is 'free' to take on any values the investigator decides to give it. These values are known as *levels* of the independent variable. The DV is the variable being measured in an experiment to determine if the manipulation of the independent variable has had any effect.

❯ **KEY IDEAS** controls In experimental design **controls** are all the ways in which experimenters work to keep all variables constant other than the independent variable(s) being manipulated. The aim is to reduce or eliminate the impact of other factors on the dependent variable(s) so that the experimenters can be reasonably certain that any variations in the dependent variable are the result of the manipulation of the independent variable.

❯ **KEY IDEAS** random assignment to conditions **Random assignment to conditions**: when each participant has an equal chance of being assigned to any of the conditions of the experiment (ie, any of the levels of the independent variable), they are said to be randomly assigned.

Control Conditions

Anderson and Murphy created two groups of female volunteers. One group played a violent video game, and the other group played a non-violent game. However, the researchers were really only interested in the effects of playing violent games. The group playing non-violent games existed only for the sake of comparison—to control for the possibility that playing any sort of video game might increase aggression. Because the only purpose for the existence of this second group is one of control, it is termed a **control group**. In contrast, the group being administered the level of the IV that is of actual interest to investigators (the 'violent' level of video game in this case) is termed the **experimental group**. Put another way, any condition of an experiment to which a control group is assigned is known as a *control condition*, and any condition of an experiment to which an experimental group is assigned is known as the *experimental condition*.

An experiment may have one or several control conditions. In this case, for example, it may be that *Street Fighter II* is not only more violent than *Oh No! More Lemmings*, but also more exciting and therefore more physically arousing. Physical arousal itself might temporarily increase aggressive responses in laboratory experiments such as this. A second control group could have been added which played a particularly exciting but non-violent game—for example, a *Wii* interactive tennis game.

Control Over Confounding Variables

What if, on the days Anderson and Murphy ran their study, the temperature outside was 94 degrees Fahrenheit (35° Celsius) and the air conditioning was malfunctioning—but only in the room in which the women assigned to *Street Fighter II* were playing their game? Research has shown that extreme temperatures can sometimes increase the risk of aggression. If the group playing *Street Fighter II* was then seen to display more aggression than the control group, the investigators might have thought they were witnessing the effects of playing a violent video game when in fact they were seeing the effects of being trapped in a stuffy room at +35° C.

> ❯ KEY IDEAS confounding variable In an experiment, any variable that exerts a measurable effect on the dependent variable without the knowledge of the experimenter is called a confounding variable or confound.

In this case, *room temperature* would constitute a confounding variable. A **confounding variable** (sometimes shortened to *confound*) is any unknown variable that changes along with changes in the level of the independent variable and exerts a measurable effect on the dependent variable (in this case, aggression) without the experimenter realizing it. (Essentially, this is identical to the *lurking variable problem* considered in the discussion of correlational research.) Such a variable receives its name because it *confounds* our ability to interpret research findings correctly. In this case, room temperature changes along with changes in the type of video game being played (the level of the IV).

Experimental research can be derailed by confounding variables if the researcher is not careful. These variables must be controlled. Random assignment to conditions and the use of control groups are two essential methods of controlling for certain types of confounding variables, but there are other hazards not addressed by these controls. Although environmental conditions (eg, broken air conditioners on hot days) can become confounding variables, this would be relatively unusual under modern research conditions. However, one type of particularly troublesome confounding variable is participant bias: the tendency for some research subjects to intuit the purpose of a research study and adjust their behaviour to match the demands of the situation—to behave as they believe they are expected to behave (Orne, 1962). The ways an experimenter communicates these demands are collectively known as **demand characteristics**. For example, an experimenter might smile more encouragingly at participants in the condition where they expect participants to perform better on a task. This might not be so bad if not for the **good subject tendency**—the well-known desire of research participants to please the experimenter (Orne, 1962; Nichols and Maner, 2008). Experimenters usually have a certain outcome in mind that they would prefer to find because they usually have a favoured hypothesis. Through their attitudes and body language, experimenters can sometimes 'push' results in their favour entirely unconsciously, by conveying in subtle ways to participants how they expect and/or want them to behave, and many research subjects are only too happy to oblige.

Because of the always-present possibility of demand characteristics and the good subject tendency, experiments are conducted in a **blind** fashion whenever possible. When studies are conducted 'blind' it means that the participants are unaware of which level of the independent variable they have received and/or are unaware of the nature of the researcher's hypothesis. For example, in the Anderson and Murphy experiment, the women were simply seated in front of the game they were assigned to play. They were not told that 'some of you will play violent games and others non-violent games'; if they had been told this, the researcher's hypothesis would have been somewhat obvious. **Double-blind experiments** take this idea a stage further by not telling the experimenters who interact with participants which condition they are administering. This means they cannot give away their expectations of outcomes by means of demand characteristics.

Alternatives to the True Experiment

Although the true experiment is the ideal method when it comes to definitively establishing causes and effects, true experiments are not always desirable or even possible to perform. For example, there is an ongoing debate in the UK over whether smacking of children is an effective means of regulating children's behaviour (psychologists are almost all against). What if you wished to compare the effects of various parenting practices such as smackings versus time-outs on children's social relationships and adjustment? You cannot very well randomly assign babies to be reared by different parents, or randomly assign some parents to smack their children and others to give time-outs. Few if any parents would agree to participate, and no university would permit such research to be conducted under its authority. It would be entirely unethical.

An alternative that would work in the above scenario is the quasi-experiment. A quasi-experiment is one that allows us to compare two conditions that constitute different levels of an IV but does not conform to all the standards of a true experiment. If we cannot randomly allocate participants to conditions, we can compare existing groups; for example, parents that already smack and those that already give time-outs. We can control for participant variables as far as possible by choosing similar parents with similar characteristics but this is only possible up to a point—there must be something fundamentally different about families that favour smacking and those opting for time-outs.

In some cases a third option is to compare the outcomes in 'before and after' conditions. We could get some insight into the effects of time-outs by comparing children's behaviour before and after families introduce time-outs as a strategy.

> **KEY IDEAS** participant bias and demand characteristics
Participant bias affects results of a study when participants realize the aim of the study and modify their behaviour accordingly. **Demand characteristics** are the cues that allow research participants to work out the aim of the study. The **good subject tendency** is the general desire of research participants to please the experimenter or give the experimenter what he or she 'wants'.

> **KEY IDEAS** blind designs
In a **blind experiment** the research participants are unaware of which level of the independent variable they have been assigned to and/or are unaware of the nature of the researcher's hypothesis. A **double-blind experiment** is one in which neither the subject *nor* those interacting directly with him or her are aware of the exact nature of the hypotheses being tested and/or to which level of the independent variable a participant has been exposed.

This kind of study is sometimes called a pre-experiment. Again, this only provides a partial picture of cause and effect because other factors may come into play in the time between the before and after conditions.

 THINKING CREATIVELY

Your task is to design a study testing the effect of a new therapy on depression. How could you carry this out as a true experiment, a quasi-experiment, and as a pre-experiment?

External Validity: The Achilles Heel of the Experimental Method

There is a subtler problem in conducting experiments. Consider again Anderson and Murphy's experimental study of the effects of playing violent video games on aggression in women. Exactly how did these researchers measure 'aggression' to determine if playing video games actually does have an effect? Aggression is an abstract concept to some extent, and people may disagree about what constitutes aggression. To study the effects of violent video games Anderson and Murphy had to come up with an **operational definition** of aggression—a precise definition fashioned in terms that could be measured in their study. All research studies, experimental or otherwise, use operational definitions of their variables, but in the case of experimental studies such as Anderson and Murphy's there is a problem. The type of aggression which Anderson and Murphy are actually concerned about in regard to violent video games is serious real-world aggression and violence. Will they be able to follow each participant in their study around for a few weeks, months, or years after the game-playing phase of the study to see if that person commits any armed robberies or axe murders, or gets into any fistfights? That is highly unlikely.

Researchers such as Anderson and Murphy who are interested in the topic of real-world aggression, but have chosen to conduct laboratory experiments, must instead create an operational definition that is an *analogue* of aggression—something that will stand in for the type of aggression they are actually interested in. In this case, Anderson and Murphy had each participant compete with a (bogus) other person on a computer purportedly set up in a separate room to see who could respond the quickest when a tone was sounded. The 'winner' of each round could blast the 'loser' with a loud noise, the intensity of which was under the player's control. Actually, the pattern of wins and losses was preset by computer program, but the participants did not know this. The intensity of the blast used by the player against her 'opponent' was the measure of aggression employed by Anderson and Murphy. As they predicted, Anderson and Murphy found that those who played *Street Fighter* were more likely than those who played *Lemmings* to administer stronger noise blasts.

However, critics of these sorts of studies point out that people who administer loud noise blasts are not necessarily also more likely than others to commit murders, muggings, rapes, spousal or child abuse, or even find themselves in more arguments than others. If they are not more likely to do these things, experiments such as Anderson's and Murphy's can be said to lack **external validity**—the quality of a study that allows the researcher to apply, or generalize, findings of the

❯ **KEY IDEAS** operational definition This is a precise definition of a variable in terms that can be utilized for a research study.

❯ **KEY IDEAS** external validity External validity is the extent to which the results of research generalize to real-world settings. This is a particular issue for experimental research where we often use an artificial measure of the real-life variable we are interested in.

research to the world outside the laboratory (Mitchell, 2012). Such experiments have value, certainly, but their value may be limited. In cases such as our proposed study of smackings versus time-outs, where external validity might pose a problem or where true experiments are unethical, impractical, or impossible to perform, investigators have no choice but to adopt correlational (or quasi-experimental) methods.

QUANTITATIVE AND QUALITATIVE DATA

The results of psychological research come in many forms, but broadly we can divide them into quantitative data and qualitative data. Quantitative data comes in the form of numbers. Any data not in the form of numbers is qualitative. Most commonly this is in the form of words, but it might be pictures or sounds, depending on the nature of the study.

Quantitative Data: The Importance of Statistics in Psychology

Research will almost always involve collecting data of some sort, whether the data is collected through the use of questionnaires, technology and equipment, or systematic observation. Once a researcher has completed the data collection phase of research, the data needs to be analysed to identify patterns to be expressed in statistics, a process that is usually done by computer. There are two basic types of statistical analysis as described in the next section: *descriptive* and *inferential*.

Both Descriptive and Inferential Statistics are Important

Descriptive statistics do exactly what you would think—they describe the data and characterize its basic 'shape'. They tell you how most participants responded, what the range of responses was like, and how participants varied one from another. Simple percentages are descriptive statistics, as are the *mean*, *median*, and *mode*. The **mean** is the numerical average, the **median** is the middle score of a data set—the score above and below which an equal number of people scored—and the **mode** is the most commonly occurring score in a data set.

Occasionally, descriptive statistics are all you need. The term 'occasionally' is appropriate here because in psychology, as compared with many other sciences, another stage is usually necessary—**inferential statistics**. Inferential statistics are generally necessary because of a (*really* annoying) factor that makes it difficult for research psychologists to draw conclusions from descriptive statistics alone. That factor is *chance*—the possibility that a study's results are not due to the effects and relationships of variables, but are strictly coincidental. Chance is always lurking behind some research bush, waiting to trip you up, and inferential statistics help to control for the possibility of chance effects.

As a fanciful example, suppose that in a study of violent video games, researchers randomly assigned one group of people to play violent games for a year, and another group to play non-violent games for a year. The researchers then spent the subsequent year monitoring their research participants' behaviour at work, home, or school. They found that those who had played violent games committed an average of 100 aggressive acts over the subsequent year, and those who played the non-violent games committed an average of two aggressive acts. Leaving aside for a moment the possibility of various confounding variables or problems with the research design, the sheer size of the difference would mean that only descriptive

> **KEY IDEAS** descriptive statistics Descriptive statistics are basic statistics which provide descriptions of a set of data, including percentage, mean, median, and mode.

The **mean** is a descriptive statistic measuring the numerical average in a set of data.

The **median** is an alternative measure of central tendency (technically only the mean should be referred to as the average) which reports the score above and below which an equal number of participants has scored—that is, the 'middle' score.

The **mode** is also a measure of central tendency representing the most frequently occurring score in a set of data.

> **KEY IDEAS** inferential statistics Inferential statistics are more advanced statistical techniques which help determine the probability that research results reflect actual relationships between variables as opposed to the effects of chance variation (significance), or which quantify the magnitude of this relationship (effect size).

statistics would be necessary to tell the 'story' of the research. It is unthinkable for such a large difference to occur strictly by chance.

However, group differences as large as these are quite rare in psychology because most internal psychological states and external behaviours are caused by many variables acting together. Even if violent video games do have any effect on aggressive behaviour (a question we address in Chapter 22), they almost certainly cannot account for the whole story—at best, they only contribute to a part in a play containing many characters. Yet most psychological studies attempt to isolate single variables that have at least some effect. As a result, in psychology, differences between groups based upon single variables (eg, whether one habitually plays violent or non-violent video games) are usually much smaller—small enough that one cannot tell merely by looking at the descriptive statistics whether the effect is a real one or the workings of chance.

Let's suppose that the score were not 100 acts versus two acts on average, but 33 versus 24 instead, perhaps a more realistic figure. Depending on several factors (eg, the size of the sample), a score like this might have resulted if the study inadvertently included a few more than the average number of people prone to being influenced by violent media. Inferential statistics would be an absolute necessity for interpreting these findings because inferential statistics can increase a researcher's confidence that his or her results did not occur merely through the workings of chance.

Statistical Significance and Effect Size: Are Results Real and Meaningful?

The inferential procedure traditionally used to determine the probability of chance factors affecting results is known as **statistical significance testing**. You may have heard this phrase used in the reporting of research (eg, 'The living individuals in our study were significantly more likely than the dead to report engaging in online gambling during the previous week'). So what exactly does statistical significance tell us? The product of an inferential stats test allows us to estimate the probability of obtaining our current data set if it were affected by chance factors alone. So when you see $p<0.05$ this means that the probability of these results (eg, the difference between two conditions or the correlation between two variables) being due to chance alone is 0.05 or 5%. These results are then said to be 'significant'; that is, the probability of their being due to something other than chance is greater than 95%.

However, a difference found between two groups on some variable is not necessarily large or meaningful merely because it is real and not due to chance (ie, significant). If enough participants are used in a study, real but tiny differences between groups may show up as statistically significant—differences that are so small that they do not have much meaning in the real world. Therefore, statistical significance is only one type of approach used by researchers today for evaluating the meaningfulness of research results. The statistic which measures the *magnitude*, or strength, of a difference found between groups on a variable is known as **effect size**. Effect size is a measure of the magnitude of a result—how meaningful the result is rather than how likely it is to be real and not due to chance. For example, what if it were found that those who eat broccoli have a 'statistically significant' reduction in blood pressure compared with those who don't eat broccoli—but this reduction, while real, is not large enough to have any real effect whatever on the person's health or likelihood of dying from hypertension? This would probably produce an exceedingly low

> **KEY IDEAS** statistical significance and effect size
> **Statistical significance** is a figure generated from inferential statistics that allows us to understand the probability that one's research results reflect actual relationships among variables and are not due to chance factors alone. **Effect size** is a different figure that provides a measure of how large and meaningful differences and correlations are.

effect size despite the statistically significant finding. For this reason, effect sizes are now routinely reported along with statistical significance.

The Importance of Statistical Literacy

Educators and policymakers often talk about the importance of functional literacy—the ability to read and write well enough to do things like read food labels and fill out a driving licence application. Financial literacy—the ability to follow a household budget, stay abreast of credit card payments, assess the pros and cons of taking out a loan, and so on—is another life skill that is hard to get along without. Another important form of literacy is statistical literacy—the ability to understand statistical data. Statistical literacy does not require extensive knowledge of formulas or mathematics—indeed, it requires little in the way of advanced education. Instead, it requires only knowledge of basic arithmetic and clear explanations of the meaning of concepts such as 'increased risk'.

Consider the following, reported by Gerd Gigerenzer and his colleagues (Gigerenzer et al, 2008, p 54): in October 1995, the Committee on Safety of Medicines in Great Britain issued a warning that the oral contraceptive pills which were new to the market at the time (known as 'third-generation' pills) increased the risk of life-threatening blood clots (thrombosis) by 100%—that is, they doubled the risk. Quite understandably, this news caused a great deal of anxiety among contraceptive pill users and their partners. A great many women stopped using these pills, and a portion of these stopped using pills altogether—resulting in a large increase in unwanted pregnancies and subsequent terminations. At the time, the rates of termination in Britain had been steadily declining, but it appears that fear over the risk of thrombosis contributed to an additional 13,000 terminations over the next five years. Moreover, for every one of these additional terminations there was at least one possibly unwanted birth, particularly among teenagers, at a cost of approximately £46 million to the British National Health System (NHS).

Gigerenzer and colleagues argue that these effects might have been avoided if one important fact had been recognized: a '100% increase in risk' only has real meaning *if the initial risk is already substantial*. As it happened, the risk of thrombosis among users of older ('second-generation') contraceptive pills was quite low—only 1 in 7,000. This meant that among the third-generation pill users, the risk was now 2 in 7,000! Yes, a 100% increase—but from what to what? The end result is a very safe third-generation oral contraceptive, at least as far as thrombosis is concerned (Gigerenzer et al, 2008).

This story points to one important point that needs to be understood as part of general statistical literacy: a statistic that 'stands alone'—that is, there is no other statistic with which to compare it—is generally meaningless or impossible to interpret. Here are two templates for common statistical claims that require comparison statistics, along with questions that need to be asked to make the stand-alone statistic meaningful:

1 *'Behaviour A carries a 100% increased risk of Condition B.'* (Ask: 'A 100% increase from what to what?') If the original risk is very small, a 100% increase in risk is often unimportant.

2 *'Group A is the fastest growing population of victims of Condition B.'* (Ask: 'How common is the condition among other groups, and exactly how fast is the condition growing among Group A members?') If the condition is quite rare,

'fastest growing' may still mean that the condition is quite rare even among the fastest growing group. This is especially true if Group A is only the 'fastest growing' because the other groups *aren't growing at all* (and the condition is actually disappearing)!

Qualitative Data, Qualitative Analysis, and Qualitative Research

We use the term 'qualitative' differently in different psychological contexts. Sometimes we will speak of qualitative *data* and sometimes we are more concerned with qualitative *research*. Just to complicate things further we also talk about qualitative *analysis*. These terms mean quite different things.

Qualitative Data

Qualitative data is data in non-numerical form. This can include what people say or write and more visual information such as pictures people draw or their facial expressions. Some studies yield qualitative data in the form of descriptions or completed tables, and we can either conduct qualitative analysis on it or transform the data into numerical form to be analysed quantitatively. More on that later.

Some studies produce purely qualitative data whilst others yield a mix of qualitative and quantitative data. This can be extremely important. Take the findings of the classic study of **destructive obedience** by Stanley Milgram (1963), described in detail in Chapter 21. Milgram's headline results were in the form of percentages of obedience—100% of participants obeyed orders and administered at least 300V to a helpless man; 65% went to 450V. This data is quantitative. If this quantitative data was all Milgram had to go on he might have concluded that people are quite happy to follow orders to hurt another person. However, Milgram also gathered qualitative data from observers, so he had details of what participants said and their facial expressions throughout the procedure, as well as their obedient behaviour to go on. Based on *all* this data Milgram was able to conclude that participants were obedient to destructive orders but that they experienced considerable distress when obeying orders that contravened their moral code.

The example of Milgram's research illustrates how we benefit from the existence of both quantitative and qualitative data. You may find that you are drawn to research that yields one or the other but we strongly recommend maintaining a healthy respect for both types of data.

Qualitative Research

The term 'qualitative research' (QR) is not always used consistently. Henwood (2014) has clarified this situation by identifying two broad definitions: literal and evocative. A literal definition describes qualitative research as 'a form of inquiry that involves collecting and analysing non-numerical data and materials' (2014, p 1612). This is straightforward and focuses on the type of data gathered. Thus Punch (2014) defines qualitative research as 'empirical research where the data are not in the form of numbers' (2014, p 3). Of course, non-numerical data can still be quantified and subject to quantitative analysis.

Evocative definitions are more conceptually difficult but capture what most psychologists mean when they speak of qualitative research, particularly European researchers. By this definition qualitative research does not simply mean collecting a particular type of data but adopting a particular view of the world. To qualitative researchers, individual human experience, embedded in **culture** and language, is the subject matter of psychology. There is an emphasis on interpretation of data rather than on the empirical attempt to uncover scientific truths. This difference can be described as ontological—**ontology** is the branch of philosophy devoted to the nature of reality. This difference in ontology has historically led to bad feeling between some qualitative and quantitative researchers. However, we recommend that you embrace both branches of research if you can be flexible enough to embrace both ontologies and switch between empirical and interpretive ways of thinking. This is hard though and most psychologists have a preference.

We will illustrate the contributions of quantitative and qualitative research by means of two studies of the experiences of gay and bisexual people (psychologists often use the term 'gay' to refer to gay men and lesbians, as well as just to refer to gay men).

Bergan-Gander and von Kurthy (2006) carried out a qualitative study exploring the experiences of gay occupational therapists at work. They conducted unstructured interviews (ie, interviews where not all participants received the same questions and those that did so did not necessarily have them in the same order) with two men and three women. Five themes emerged from the interviews, representing the difficulties gay health professionals contended with over and above those experienced by their heterosexual colleagues: difficulty in socializing with colleagues, issues of coming out at work, heterosexist assumptions at work such as service-users asking about opposite-sex partners, discrimination, and maintaining friendships with heterosexual colleagues.

In the same year, Koh and Ross (2006) published a quantitative study of stress experienced by gay people in a range of health professions. They issued questionnaires to 1,300 people asking questions about sexual orientation, out status, stress, and mental health. The headline finding was that lesbians and bisexual women experienced more stress and mental health problems than gay men. You can see that both these studies were extremely valuable to psychologists with the broad aim of understanding the stress faced by gay and bisexual people and its effects on their well-being. However, the way they were conducted was very different and they lead us to different insights. We explore this further in the *Thinking critically* feature.

> **KEY IDEAS** ontology

Ontology is the branch of philosophy devoted to the nature of reality. This is critical to qualitative research because many qualitative researchers take an interpretive view of reality in contrast to the mainstream scientific position that there is an objective reality and the aim of research is to find ways to observe this.

THINKING CRITICALLY

Look at our account of the studies by Bergan-Gander and von Kurthy and by Koh and Ross. Identify one advantage of the qualitative study; what does it tell us over and above the findings of the other study? Then consider the Koh and Ross study. What does this study tell us that the first does not? Do you have a preference for one of these studies? Why does psychology benefit from both approaches?

Analysis of Qualitative Data

Qualitative data can be analysed qualitatively. This is the norm in evocatively defined qualitative research. However, before we are accused of stating the bleeding obvious, qualitative data can also be transformed into quantitative data and analysed quantitatively. Let's have a brief look at qualitative analysis first.

❯ KEY IDEAS qualitative analysis
Qualitative analysis is the
non-statistical analysis of non-
numerical data. The simplest
form is **thematic analysis**, which
involves coding blocks of text or
transcript for themes. **Discourse
analysis** involves deconstructing
text or transcripts for examples
of how language has been used
to construct a version of reality
that suits the vested interests
of powerful groups. In **content
analysis**, qualitative data is coded
quantitatively and analysed
statistically.

The most straightforward way to conduct qualitative analysis is **thematic analysis** (TA). Thematic analysis involves coding content—for example, interviews or text—for themes. This can be by identifying key words. Typically every few sentences of a transcript or text are marked up with a theme. For example, in the study we looked at by Bergan-Gander and von Kurthy, the content to be analysed was in the form of transcripts of unstructured interviews. Once these were read the researchers were able to identify the themes represented in the interviews. In this study, five themes emerged across a number of the interviews, and from this it was concluded that these themes represented some key issues for gay people in their workplaces. Because it can be a very subjective process to look for themes it is standard practice in thematic analysis for two or more researchers to independently code the material and agree on themes.

Another form of qualitative analysis is **discourse analysis**. Whereas thematic analysis is theoretically neutral and simply a technique of analysis, discourse analysis has a particular theoretical orientation and purpose. According to McGregor (2010), discourse analysis aims to deconstruct language to uncover ideological assumptions in the ways we use language. This is an overtly political exercise. A classical example of a discourse analysis comes from Parker (1999) when he deconstructed the language on a toothpaste packet! From this apparently innocuous text Parker picked out language that defined what made a normal family and normal community, and the relationship between community and commerce in which the latter exists for the benefit of the former.

Sometimes psychologists extract quantitative data from gathered qualitative data and then extract numbers from this and subject it to quantitative analysis. For example, **content analysis** involves taking a text or transcript and counting the frequency of particular words. This can be a powerful way to show the extent of problems in text. For example, Philo et al (1994) content-analysed the coverage of mental health issues in print media and found that around two-thirds of articles linked mental ill health with acts of violence, highlighting the prejudice that existed where mental health was concerned.

ETHICAL ISSUES IN PSYCHOLOGY

Psychological research is conducted on living beings: humans and animals. As such, issues of *research ethics* are of paramount concern to psychologists and the general public. **Ethics** is the branch of philosophy concerned with morality. **Ethical codes** are sets of rules put together to make it easier to conform to standards of morally correct behaviour, particularly within a specific discipline or workplace. Because of increased concern about ethical treatment of research participants over the past few decades, preparing to perform ordinary research involving human subjects has become a complicated task for researchers.

❯ KEY IDEAS ethics **Ethics** is
technically the philosophy of
morality, but we use the term more
loosely to mean moral issues or
rules. Ethical codes are constructed
in order to help professionals like
psychologists stick to behaviour we
broadly agree to be morally correct
during research.

It was after a series of high-profile studies conducted in the 1960s that psychologists' professional bodies like the American Psychological Association and later the British Psychological Society devised ethical codes of practice that explicitly set out the principles that researchers in psychology should adhere to.

One famous example of unethical studies would be Henry Murray's (Murray, 1963) work on individuals' responses to stress. Murray subjected his participants, Harvard University undergraduates, to emotionally abusive and humiliating interrogations, which were rightly condemned for the distress they caused to the participants. One of the participants was Theodore Kaczynski, who between 1978 and 1995 was the subject of what was at the time the largest manhunt in American history. He sent bombs to universities, targeting scientists, including psychologists, and three people died and 23 were injured during this his campaign of domestic terror. As critical thinkers, we must of course avoid inferring that Kaczynski's actions were directly due to his involvement in Murray's experiments, but this case makes plain that conducting unethical research can have far-reaching implications.

Contemporary Ethical Codes

There are a number of ethical codes worldwide that psychologists are required to abide by. In Britain and Europe we are mostly concerned with the codes produced by professional bodies like the British Psychological Society. Very similar guidance is available from the European Federation of Psychologists' Associations. Note that these codes are regularly revised but that changes are usually relatively minor.

British Psychological Society's Ethical Principles

The BPS (2014) has identified four ethical principles underlying ethical conduct.

1 **Respect** for the autonomy, privacy, and dignity of individuals and communities. Thus psychologists are obliged to respect the dignity and value of every individual they work with, taking account of their rights to freedom and privacy. Participants should not experience discrimination whilst participating in psychological research.

2 **Scientific integrity.** Psychologists are responsible for ensuring that their research is of high enough quality to avoid producing misleading findings that can lead to harm or bring the profession into disrepute.

3 **Social responsibility.** Psychologists should produce research that is of benefit to both participants and the common good. In practice this means that psychologists should reflect on the impact of their work and consider its costs and benefits for society.

4 **Maximizing benefit and minimizing harm.** Psychologists are obliged to avoid harming participants' physical or mental health or general well-being. This includes avoidance of causing distress.

BPS Ethical Guidelines

• **Risk.** Risks to participants should always be considered. Mild distress or a small risk of harm may be allowable if these are outweighed by the potential value of the research. Research involving children, people without capacity (the ability to make decisions), sensitive topics or sensitive personal information, stressful situations, or risk of reduction in self-worth or value in the eyes of others such as employers should always be considered high risk.

• **Valid consent.** All research requires consent, although where data has already been collected consensually and is not sensitive, it can be used for additional research purposes. Where data is anonymized and non-sensitive it is sufficient for participants to tick a box to signify consent. However, more sensitive data requires assessment of the risk that an individual's privacy might be breached. Valid consent requires that participants are informed of any risk, that they are competent to give consent, and that there is no social pressure on them to consent. Related to consent is the right to withdraw; participants should be aware of their right *at the data collection stage of a study* to withdraw themselves or some or all of their data. Under human rights law the onus is on researchers to prove that they have consent; therefore, consent must be documented and kept.

- **Confidentiality**. Generally participants have the right to expect information to be kept confidential. If they are at risk of being personally identifiable from published studies they should be told and should give specific consent to this in advance. These rights are enshrined in data protection law; however, confidentiality can be breached if there is an exceptional reason—for example, such as believing the safety of the participant is at risk.

- **Giving advice**. There are a number of reasons why participants might ask researchers for advice. This should be anticipated where possible and referral sources identified in advance. Where advice is unexpectedly sought the researcher should exercise caution and only offer advice within their competence. Where a researcher suspects a physical or psychological problem of which participants are unaware they should inform them and make an appropriate referral.

- **Deception**. The use of deception should be carefully considered because it risks causing distress to participants and damaging the reputation of psychology as a discipline. However, it is also recognized that many studies would not be possible without a degree of deception. Deception may be acceptable but only when essential for the study and where a clear strategy has been planned to alleviate any distress caused. Note that deception means deliberately misinforming participants about the research. It is normally permissible to withhold some details of the study as long as this does not imply that the study is quite different to what it actually is. Covert gathering of data (without consent) can constitute deception, so it is usually only conducted when observing people without consent in public places doing things they would expect to be seen doing by strangers.

 THINKING CRITICALLY

Turn to Chapter 21 and read the account of Stanley Milgram's study of destructive obedience.

Consider the following:

1 What modern ethical principles and guidelines would Milgram have breached had he conducted the study today?

2 Milgram was investigated for unethical conduct by the American Psychological Association but cleared. What factors might have worked in his favour?

The Ethics of Animal Research

As you will discover while reading this book, psychologists conduct research using non-human animals as well as humans; and just as concern has been voiced over the treatment of human beings in research, concern has been voiced over treatment of non-human animals in research. Animal rights activists argue that the human attitude towards other types of animals—which leads to their slaughter for food or fun, their housing in cages in zoos, their use as pets, and mistreatment and killing in the context of scientific experiments—is not only immoral, but illogical and philosophically flawed. This argument is clearly laid out in the work of philosopher and animal rights advocate Paola Cavalieri (eg, Cavalieri, 2004, 2006).

According to Cavalieri, the central argument that human beings use to rationalize treating animals in a way that would be considered immoral if we applied it to ourselves is the notion that ethical norms should be addressed only to a particular kind of being—a *moral agent*. Moral agents are those rational beings whose behaviour can be subjected to moral/ethical evaluation. Thus, we would not hold a cat ethically responsible for killing a mouse, because cats are not moral agents. Their killing of mice is just something they do—they can't help themselves, and we should not evaluate their behaviour in a moral or ethical context.

However, Cavalieri argues that from this idea emerges the unfortunate view that, because animals are not moral agents, they should not themselves be *beneficiaries* of moral or ethical behaviour. The problem with this notion from a philosophical perspective, according to Cavalieri, is that infants and the mentally ill are not moral agents either, yet no one suggests we should kill them, eat them, or shut them in cages. To acknowledge that moral agents make morality possible does not mean that moral agents should be the only beneficiaries of moral/ethical behaviour.

Therefore, in Cavalieri's view, we treat non-human animals as we do—and feel justified in doing it—essentially because we are more powerful than they are and we can get away with it. We must realize the limits of this view in our heart of hearts, however, because we do draw the line somewhere, and we punish people for torture of animals that serves no apparent purpose. However, from the animal rights perspective, this is somewhat similar to the lines drawn by many slave owners in their treatment of slaves.

The arguments brought by animal rights advocates are compelling. However, there is another side to this story, which—unfortunately for those seeking quick and easy solutions—also has merit. This argument is less an argument of logic than a disagreement about the degree of harm caused to animals in research and a plea for recognition of the immense importance of animal research in the relief of human suffering. It is an argument that stresses pragmatism (eg, Miller, 1985; Morrison, 2001).

Those who are in favour of the use of non-human animals in research point to statistics suggesting that less than 1% of the killing of animals by humans occurs in the context of research. In fact, 96% of animals killed are killed for food (Nicholl and Russell, cited in McBurney, 2000). Second, animal testing proponents stress that only a very small portion of animal research involves pain to animals, and also point out that anaesthesia and painkillers are routinely used in animal research. These critics worry that animal rights activists, in focusing their rhetorical campaigns upon the relatively few animals who actually do experience pain during research, are ignoring the millions of humans who experience pain from diseases like arthritis—diseases that require animal research to create effective treatments (McBurney, 2000). The pro-testing group also reminds us that regulations on the housing of research animals are more stringent than those for human habitation, and that far more pain, abuse, and cruelty are inflicted upon animals by pet owners and farmers than by researchers (Miller, 1985).

Indeed, animal testing advocates believe that there are compelling reasons for the use of animals in research. For example, animal research has led to an improvement in the welfare of animals—from vaccines against feline leukaemia, rabies, and distemper, to non-lethal methods of pest control. Research on animals was also instrumental in effecting the startling improvements in health care and human longevity over the past century. According to McBurney (2000), to eliminate the use of animals for research would mean little or no further progress against diseases like AIDS, Alzheimer's disease, cancer, arthritis, birth defects, traumatic injury, mental illness, and many other conditions that cause pain and suffering to humans. Clearly, this is a difficult issue to come to grips with, and the controversy is not going away soon.

READ THIS

There is an enormous range of resources devoted to psychological research. As your first port of call we recommend our sister text:

Bourne, V. (2018). *Starting out in Methods and Statistics in Psychology*. Oxford: OUP.

One issue many people struggle with is in deciding whether qualitative or quantitative methods best suit their research idea. For a guide to working through this process and planning either type of project you might like to start with this:

Davies, M.B. and Hughes, N. (2014). *Doing a Successful Research Project: Using Qualitative or Quantitative Methods*. Basingstoke: Palgrave Macmillan.

The British Psychological Society provides a range of resources to help with ethical decision-making, including in human and animal research and in professional practice. You can find those resources here: www.bps.org.uk/psychologists/standards-and-guidelines

IN REVIEW

RESEARCH METHODS IN PSYCHOLOGY

- There are a number of ways in which psychologists can go about gathering data. There are some strong views around on the 'best' methods, but we take the view that all methods discussed here have a place in psychology.

- Case studies involve the detailed recording of information about a person, family, organization, or group in a particular circumstance. Case studies allow us to see behaviour in detail in real-life settings; however, they are not always generalizable.

- Surveys involve asking people for information via interviews or questionnaires. They are the best way to find out opinions but are less useful for predicting behaviour. Responses are affected by many factors, from the wording of questions to the sample surveyed.

- Observation allows us to systematically note how people behave in a given situation. This often raises difficult ethical issues.

- Correlational research looks at the mathematical relationships between measured variables. This allows us to predict the magnitude of one variable from another; however, it can be hard to establish cause-and-effect relationships from correlations.

- Experimental research is designed to establish cause-and-effect relationships. An experimenter manipulates one or more variables in order to see their effect on other variables. Experimental research gives the best insights into cause and effect in psychology but, in practice, experimental design is complex and imperfect because a host of variables can confound results.

QUANTITATIVE AND QUALITATIVE DATA

- Most psychological research collects at least some data in the form of numbers, which are subject to statistical analysis.

- Two statistical concepts are particularly key in psychological research. *Significance* tells us the probability that a given set of data would be expected by chance alone, in turn giving us an idea of how likely it is that we have found a real effect or correlation. *Effect size* tells us how meaningful this effect or correlation is.

- As a psychology student it is essential to acquire a degree of statistical literacy, the ability to make sense of statistical information.

- Qualitative data is information in non-numerical form. Qualitative data may be gathered as an adjunct to quantitative data or may be the sole output of qualitative research.

- There are two definitions of qualitative research. The literal definition is any research gathering non-numerical data, whether it is then analysed qualitatively or quantitatively. The evocative definition is of research that rejects numbers and adopts a more interpretive and less empirical view of the world.

- Qualitative data requires its own forms of analysis. The simplest of these is thematic analysis, whereby each line, sentence, or paragraph of text is marked up with a theme that runs throughout the text.

ETHICAL ISSUES IN PSYCHOLOGY

- Psychological research is beset with ethical issues, and there are many examples of historical research that we would now agree to be unethical.

- Following a series of ethically contentious studies in the 1960s, professional bodies put together ethical codes for researchers. The British Psychological Society, for example, has a detailed code based on the principles of respect, scientific integrity, social responsibility, and costs and benefits.

- Animal research raises its own ethical issues, and psychologists have to confront the fact that historically very inhumane things have been done to animals because researchers could get away with it. There are powerful moral arguments against the use of animals in research.

Modern animal research in psychology is heavily regulated and pro-animal research psychologists also have powerful arguments in favour of using animals in some psychological research.

TEST YOURSELF

1 Victims of domestic violence are more likely to disclose this in interviews than in questionnaires. True ❑ False ❑

2 A stratified sample has elements of random and quota samples. True ❑ False ❑

3 The boundaries between an observation and a natural experiment are always clear. True ❑ False ❑

4 Statistical significance without effect size can exaggerate the importance of effects. True ❑ False ❑

5 Which of the following is not a self-report method?

   a) Questionnaire

   b) Interview

   c) Observation

   d) Focus group

6 Which of the following groups can be best observed under controlled conditions?

   a) Football hooligans

   b) Babies

   c) Arguing couples

   d) Adolescent cliques

7 Which of the following is not a typical feature of a true experiment?

   a) Random allocation

   b) Control over confounding variables

   c) A control condition

   d) A pre-existing control group

8 Which of the following can have quantitative and qualitative elements?

   a) Discourse analysis

   b) Content analysis

   c) Thematic analysis

   d) Path analysis

9 Explain the difficulties inherent in establishing causation from correlational research.

10 What are the key differences between qualitative and quantitative analysis, and why do psychologists need to use both?

 Visit the online resources that accompany this book: www.oup.com/uk/jarvis-okami1e

BIOLOGICAL PSYCHOLOGY

CHAPTER 4

THE BIOLOGICAL BASIS OF MIND AND BEHAVIOUR

LEARNING OUTCOMES

By the end of this chapter you should be able to:

- Critically discuss evidence for alternative positions on the relationship between mind and brain, with particular reference to dualist and materialist positions
- Describe the neural basis of the nervous system, including the anatomy of neurons and different types of neuron
- Understand the physiology of neuronal functioning including the role of polarization and depolarization
- Analyse the role of various neurotransmitters and their relationship to drugs and mental life
- Know how the nervous system is organized with reference to distinctions between the central and peripheral nervous systems and between somatic and autonomic systems
- Outline the structure of the brain and consider our understanding of the relationships between brain regions and mental functions
- Explain the significance of the cerebral cortex in the human brain, with particular regard to the functions associated with the frontal, parietal, temporal, and occipital lobes
- Assess the evidence for hemispheric specialization and the implications of split brain research for our understanding of specialization
- Evaluate the case for sex differences in brain structure and function and for hemispheric dominance as an explanation for individual differences
- Discuss evidence for brain plasticity
- Describe the endocrine system and its relationship to the nervous system
- Critically discuss the relationship between brain functioning and human experience; for example, between cortical arousal and subjective sense of self, oxytocin and love, mirror neurons and empathy, and REM intrusion in near-death experiences
- Analyse the relationship between psychology and neuroscience and consider the contribution of neuroscience to psychology
- Critically consider the challenges offered to the rise of neuroscience, including methodological and philosophical issues

We live in a body, which includes a nervous system. Or, depending on your point of view we *are* the body—more on that in a moment. The structure and function of this system, in particular of the brain, is intimately connected with all aspects of our psychology, shared and individual, normal and abnormal. Take the cases of Kim Peek and Henry Molaison. Kim Peek (1952–2010) was born with significant brain abnormalities, including a malformed cerebellum, the small structure at the back of the brain involved in motor skills, and the complete lack of a corpus callosum, the strip of tissue that runs down the centre of the brain and connects the left brain to the right (see Figure 4.15 later in this chapter). Although not on the autistic spectrum, Peek inspired the film *Rain Man* because of his remarkable cognitive abilities. He memorized over 12,000 books and had an encyclopaedic knowledge of history and literature. However, Peek struggled with physical coordination and thinking about abstract concepts. At the age of 27 Henry Molaison (1926–2008) had a massive area of his **limbic system** removed to relieve severe epilepsy. From then on he was unable to acquire new memories and forever lived in the present. There are numerous cases of strokes, brain tumours, and traumatic brain injuries leading to a range of changes in psychological functioning. These can range from **depression** to personality change and memory loss. Although there are many debates around the importance of brain systems, in particular aspects of psychological functioning, there is no doubt that the brain is central to understanding the mind and behaviour.

Psychologists and others working in related fields have always been interested in understanding the workings of the brain. Until recently we have been very limited in our ability to make sense of the brain and nervous system. In the last decade technology has begun to change this, and there has been a period of massive research activity and rapid publication of findings. Neuroscience has grown into a major academic discipline in its own right, and it has also informed many issues in psychology. We return to the relationship between psychology and neuroscience later in this chapter.

WHERE IS MY MIND?

People don't usually mean this question in a literal way when they ask it, but let's take it literally for a moment and consider the nature and 'placement' of the mind. Where is it, anyway? Is it, or is it not, attached to the brain? All of us—scientists included—conduct our daily lives as though the brain and mind were in fact *dis*connected (Bloom, 2004). 'My brain is rubbish today', we might complain to our friends when struggling to complete an assignment. But where is this 'me' that can step aside from my brain and criticize it? How can I talk about '*my* brain' if 'I' *am* my brain—or at least am created by my brain?

Traditionally, there have been two basic positions on the connection between mind and the brain: *dualism* and *materialism*. Dualism, as developed by René Descartes and his followers during the seventeenth century and briefly mentioned in Chapter 2 (Pre-scientific psychology in the Age of Reason) holds that the body consists of matter, which may be objectively measured, while the mind consists of . . . *something else*. This 'something else' takes up no space and has no material existence. It is essentially a 'ghost' in the 'machinery' of the brain (Ryle, 1949).

We all may go about our business as though this were a perfectly reasonable idea. Nevertheless, as a description of reality dualism has been rejected by virtually all scientists and most modern philosophers for a few relatively simple reasons. For one thing, when you take certain substances into the body that affect the brain—drugs and alcohol, for example—these substances also affect the way you think and behave. If the brain and mind were not unified, there should be no reason why changes in brain chemistry should necessarily affect mental states. Moreover, modern neuroscientific evidence presented throughout this book demonstrates fairly conclusively that certain kinds of thoughts and actions are connected to activity in specific regions of the brain.

Finally, even Descartes realized that for a human being to function, the brain and the mind must interact somehow (Dennett, 1991). There must be a way for the 'ghost' to talk to the 'machine' and the 'machine' to talk to the 'ghost'. But how can something with *no* material existence have a physical effect on something *entirely* material? Philosopher Daniel Dennett uses the cartoon character Casper the Friendly Ghost to demonstrate this idea (Dennett, 1991, p 36). Casper can float through walls, and falling trees go right through him—yet he can catch wet clothing falling off a clothesline. Casper shouldn't be able to have it both ways—either he is immaterial or he is material. Even small children often catch this contradiction about Casper. The problem, in Dennett's words, is that 'anything that can move a physical thing is itself a physical thing' (p 35). This is why dualism is an unacceptable idea. Spirit may, of course, exist—as scientists it is probably appropriate for us to remain neutral on that question—but if so, it is hard to see how it could interact physically with matter.

In contrast to dualism, materialism holds that there is only one kind of 'stuff' responsible for mind, and that is physical matter. What may seem to be detached from the brain is in some way a material expression of properties of the brain (Harris, 2012). Scientists have provided substantial evidence in favour of the materialist view of the mind. Consider the story of Matthew Nagle. In 2001, Matthew came to the aid of a friend in a fight and was stabbed with an 8-inch blade through the neck, severing his spinal cord. As a result, Matthew was left a tetraplegic; he could not breathe without a respirator, and he could not use his arms or legs.

Matthew was undaunted, however. Mind-bogglingly, neuroscientists surgically implanted electrodes into Matthew's brain that allowed him to draw on a video monitor, pick up objects with a robotic arm, change television channels, and play video games such as *Pong—merely by thinking about performing these activities* (Hochberg, 2008). The *cyberkinetic* 'mind reading' technique used on Matthew Nagle has had only limited results, but it does provide evidence that the mind and brain are in some way unified.

Further evidence of the unity of brain and mind is provided by **functional magnetic resonance imaging (fMRI)** (see 'The basic technology of neuroscience', this chapter) studies of patients in apparent persistent vegetative states (PVS). A person in a PVS has suffered severe brain damage with coma. Although the person has technically awakened from the coma, he or she shows no signs of conscious awareness. However, some people diagnosed with PVS actually do retain some minimal awareness but are unable to communicate this awareness (Coleman et al, 2007). At least some type of minimal awareness in an apparently vegetative patient was documented by Adrian Owen and his colleagues. Among other tasks, they asked their (apparently unaware) patient to imagine she was playing tennis and walking through the rooms of her house. The regions of the patient's brain that were activated subsequent to these requests were identical to those activated in the brains of conscious patients when asked to perform the same tasks (Owen et al, 2007).

Finally, a number of experiments conducted over the last several decades have shown that the brain begins to initiate the process of performing certain actions, or making certain choices or decisions, before the person becomes aware that he or she intends to perform the action or make the choice or decision (Harris, 2012). In the first human studies in this area, Bejamin Libet and colleagues (1983) used scalp electrodes to measure electrical activity and asked participants to press a button whenever they chose. Participants monitored the time and were asked to report the moment when they felt the urge to press. The results were intriguing: electrical activity signalling the finger push began hundreds of milliseconds *before* participants experienced the urge to push. We can explore Libet et al's classic study in more detail in our *Research in focus* feature.

RESEARCH IN FOCUS

Libet, B., Gleason, C.A., Wright, E.W., and Pearl, D.K. (1983). Time of conscious intention to act in relation to onset of cerebral activity (readiness-potential) the unconscious initiation of a freely voluntary act. *Brain*, **106**, 623–42.

Aim: The aim of this study was to investigate the relationship between the conscious experience of decision-making and the physiological activity involved. More specifically, to test which came first, the conscious decision or the brain activity.

Method: Four female and two male right-handed students took part in the procedure. Each participant lay on a reclining chair and was instructed to track a light that moved around a circle in a clockwise direction at a speed of 2.56 seconds per revolution and to flex the fingers of their right hand—spontaneously rather than with pre-planning—when they felt like it. Participants were then asked to identify where the light was when they made the decision to flex their fingers, giving a measure of time from the start. EEG was used to record readiness potential (RP)—the build-up of electrical activity prior to initiating an action. Readiness potentials were divided into Type I, where participants reported planning their flex, and Type II, in which they reported flexing spontaneously. Ten training trials were followed by 40 recorded trials. The timing of the RPs was compared with that of the conscious decision to flex.

Results: In Type II cases readiness potentials preceded the conscious decision to flex by at least 150 milliseconds and an average of 350 ms. For Type I cases the disparity was greater, with RP building on average 800 ms before awareness of the decision to flex. Participants reported that they were confident that they were aware which flexes had been planned and which were spontaneous.

Conclusion: Readiness potential reliably precedes the conscious experience of making a decision, typically by several hundred milliseconds. This suggests that decision-making begins with a neural process and that the conscious experience of deciding on an action is an epiphenomenon, a by-product of the brain's activity rather than the real making of the decision itself. This in turn has implications for the dualist idea that the mind can be thought of as a separate entity distinct from the brain.

MASTER YOUR METHODOLOGY

1 The EEG method of measuring brain activity is crude by modern standards. Explain how this might affect the validity of the results. See Chapter 3 for a discussion of validity.

2 What evidence does Libet provide for the validity of the measures?

3 What would constitute stronger evidence? HINT: have a look at the next paragraph.

THINKING CRITICALLY

Look back to our critical thinking toolkit. What strengths and weaknesses can you see in relation to this study?

Conducted with 1980s technology, the Libet procedure was crude by modern standards; however, Fried et al (2011) confirmed the principle that brain activation precedes the experience of deciding to act, monitoring activation in individual neurons in the supplementary motor area whilst participants decided to press buttons. Not all the implications of these studies are clear-cut (Rowland, 2019) but they certainly suggest that the brain is deeply involved in human experiences and not a separate entity from the mind.

THE NERVOUS SYSTEM

The human *nervous system* is a complex biological system designed for communication—nearly instantaneous communication throughout the human body. Intricate and beautifully integrated communication pathways, which rival galaxies in complexity and mystery, coordinate the activity of our muscles, internal organs, and sensory systems. It is through this 'interior universe' of intricate networks that we are able to think, feel, respond to the world, and initiate action. The nervous system tells us we are hungry and then allows us to bring lasagne-laden forks to our mouths. The nervous system allows us to distinguish our cat with the injured left ear from his uninjured sister, and to walk across the room to pet him. The nervous system tells our hearts to race as we watch *Dawn of the Dead*, brings tears to our eyes when Bill Murray dies in *Zombieland* (insert your scary/weepy films of choice), and lets us switch either film off if they disappoint or disturb us. The nervous system triggers joy at the sight of a loved one and pain on separation. It does all of these things seemingly without effort.

The Cellular Basis of the Nervous System

What are the structures that make up the internal cosmos of the human nervous system? Like all structures of living beings, the nervous system is composed of *cells*, the basic units of all living matter. However, the cells of the nervous system are specialized. The cell type known as the **neuron** plays the principal role in allowing communication to take place throughout the nervous system and the bodily structures with which the nervous system communicates. The neuron receives information and transmits it to other cells. In the past it was thought that the cells of the nervous system were connected, creating a long, unbroken communication pathway. A Spanish physician named Santiago Ramón y Cajal (1852–1934)—an important founder of the field of *neuroscience*—discovered that neurons were independent entities. Although it is not possible to measure accurately the number of these entities in the nervous system, estimates given for the brain alone vary from 86 billion (Azevedeo et al, 2009) to over 100 billion (Larsen et al, 2006). This exceeds the number of stars in our galaxy! The number of possible ways these 100 billion neurons can communicate runs into the hundreds of trillions.

Although a network of millions of neurons can pass on incredibly intricate information, individual neurons do not. Like computers, which can generate multicoloured

> **KEY IDEAS** neurons
Neurons are the cell types that transmit information throughout the nervous system. They convey information by firing or not firing. This is a binary system, rather like the 1s and 0s used by computers. There are three main types of neuron: motor neurons, sensory neurons, and interneurons.

video images using binary codes containing only 1s and 0s, the neuron does its work by turning itself on (firing) or off (not firing). If a neuronal message could be translated, it would not read, 'This is an important job interview, try to appear relaxed—don't play with your hair and don't cross your arms against your body.' The messages neurons pass along to other neurons, if translated, would read only 'fire' or 'don't fire'. Yet the end effect of these communication chains is often massively complex. Three types of neurons make up the nervous system: *motor neurons*, *sensory neurons*, and *interneurons*.

Motor neurons are the main channel of communication to the muscles and organs of the body. Motor neurons carry commands for actions, actions of which you may or may not be aware. For example, when you chew your food, motor neurons convey orders to your jaw muscles. But after you swallow the chewed food, motor neurons continue—without your awareness—to help the process of digestion along as the food moves through your digestive system and is broken down by that system.

For each of your senses there are special **sensory neurons** which work to convert physical energy (or chemicals, in the case of the senses of *smell* and *taste*) into information in a form that may be transmitted along chains of neurons to the brain. Your brain is completely isolated from the physical world; sensory neurons bring the world to your brain. Sounds, sights, and sensations are all transformed into electrochemical signals—the only language your brain understands.

Motor neurons communicate with the muscles and organs, and sensory neurons relay sensory information to the brain, but **interneurons** communicate only with *other neurons* that are in a more or less adjacent position. They do not extend long distances, as do motor and sensory neurons. These neurons 'pass messages on'. Interneurons are vastly more numerous than motor and sensory neurons, however. The majority of those 100 billion total neurons in the brain are interneurons.

The Anatomy of Neurons

Although neurons come in three types and differ somewhat in appearance, with a few exceptions they share the same components as the motor neuron depicted in Figure 4.1: *dendrites*, *cell body*, *axon*, and *terminal*.

Dendrites

Dendrites (literally, 'branches') reach out from the neuron **cell body**, as depicted in Figure 4.1. The dendrites are covered with tiny openings called **synaptic receptors** which are embedded in their membranes. Synaptic receptors are designed to receive information in the form of chemical signals released from other neurons.

The cell body

The cell body, also called the *soma*, contains the *nucleus* of the cell, where most genetic information is stored. It is also here that information from the many surrounding neurons is collected and integrated, to be transmitted by electrical signal across the length of the neuron along the neuron's *axon*.

The axon

The **axon** of a neuron is a narrow extension that transmits information as *neural impulses* from the cell body to other neurons. Enclosed bundles of axons create communication channels extending from the furthest tips of our limbs deep into to the brain and spinal cord, and so axons vary in length from less than an inch to several

> **KEY IDEAS** dendrites
The branch-like projections of neurons that receive electrochemical stimulation from other neurons are called **dendrites**. **Synaptic receptors** are the openings that are embedded in the dendrites of neurons to which neurotransmitters bind during the process of neuronal communication.

> **KEY IDEAS** the cell body
The **cell body** or soma is the bulb-like end of the neuron containing the cell nucleus. Energy for the neuron is generated here, and waste is eliminated.

> **KEY IDEAS** the axon
The **axon** is a narrow extension in many neurons that transmits electrical neural impulses from cell body to terminal. A **tract** is a bundle of axons (usually enclosed in a myelin sheath) that forms a communication channel within the central nervous system (brain or spine). A **nerve** is an enclosed bundle of axons forming a communication channel within the peripheral nervous system (outside the brain or spine).

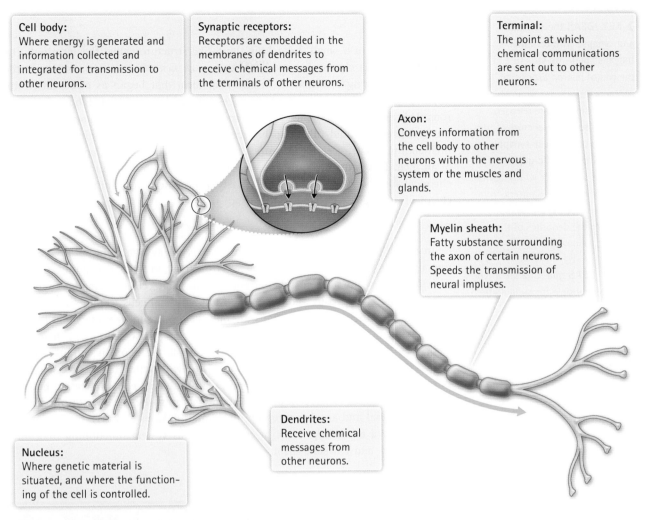

Cell body:
Where energy is generated and information collected and integrated for transmission to other neurons.

Synaptic receptors:
Receptors are embedded in the membranes of dendrites to receive chemical messages from the terminals of other neurons.

Terminal:
The point at which chemical communications are sent out to other neurons.

Axon:
Conveys information from the cell body to other neurons within the nervous system or the muscles and glands.

Myelin sheath:
Fatty substance surrounding the axon of certain neurons. Speeds the transmission of neural impulses.

Dendrites:
Receive chemical messages from other neurons.

Nucleus:
Where genetic material is situated, and where the functioning of the cell is controlled.

FIGURE 4.1 **Anatomy of a motor neuron.**

feet long. These communication channels are called **tracts** when neural communication occurs *within* the brain or spinal cord (the *central nervous system*, as described in this chapter), and **nerves** when communication occurs in points *outside* the brain or spinal cord (the *peripheral nervous system*, as described in this chapter). As an example, the bundle of axons leaving the eye to transmit visual signals to the brain is called the optic nerve. Once the axon bundle reaches within the brain, it is called the optic tract.

Not all neurons have axons—some interneurons lack them—and those that do will only have one axon. The axons of certain neurons may be wrapped in a **myelin sheath**. **Myelin** is a fatty substance that allows neural impulses to travel far more rapidly than they otherwise would. However, the myelin sheath does not cover the entire axon. The sheath has gaps of about 1 micrometre (millionth of a metre), giving the axon a 'sausage-like' appearance. The point at which a gap occurs is called the **node of Ranvier**. In the central nervous system disease *multiple sclerosis* (MS), the myelin sheaths are 'attacked' by the body's own immune defences, leading to *demyelenation*. Loss of myelin prevents effective communication between neurons, leading to a very large number of potentially debilitating physical and mental symptoms.

❯ KEY IDEAS myelin sheath
The **myelin sheath** is the layer of myelin, a fatty substance, which surrounds the axon of some neurons. Myelin increases the speed of neuronal transmission. The **node of Ranvier** is the gap between myelin sheaths of axon segments.

> **KEY IDEAS** the terminal and synapse **The terminal** is the small bulb-like structure at the end of neuron axons that contains the vesicles from which neurotransmitters are released. The **synapse** is the juncture of the pre-synaptic and post-synaptic neuron. The **synaptic gap** is the miniscule space over which neurons pass their neurotransmitters, from the terminal of the pre-synaptic neuron to the dendrites of the post-synaptic neuron.

> **KEY IDEAS** glia **Glia** are a type of cell responsible for building the myelin sheath that surrounds the axon of some neurons, and helping to develop and maintain neuron synapses.

The terminal

The axon ends in a small, branching, bulb-like structure called the **terminal**. The terminal releases chemical messengers known as *neurotransmitters*, which do the job of transmitting information in chemical form that began as electrical neural impulses. The surface of the terminal faces the dendrites of its neighbouring neurons. This point at which one sending, and one receiving, neuron meet is known as the **synapse**. The fluid-filled gap between the terminal of the sending neuron and the dendrite of the receiving neuron is unimaginably small—less than one millionth of an inch. This is the **synaptic gap**, the space over which the neurons pass on their chemical signals. We will look more closely at how neurotransmitters pass on their chemical messages a bit later in this chapter.

Glia

Neurons are not the only type of cell in the nervous system. **Glia** outnumber neurons (including interneurons) by anywhere from 10–1 to 50–1, depending on which part of the nervous system is being considered. Glial cells are smaller than neurons, and they lack axons and dendrites. Although glial cells were discovered over 100 years ago, their actual functions are only beginning to be understood (Angulo et al, 2004). In somewhat simplified terms, glial cells assist neurons in their work. First, they build the myelin sheath which surrounds the axon of certain neurons, as just described. They also help supply neurons with nutrients and oxygen, may stimulate repair of damaged neurons, and greatly promote communication between neurons by helping to develop and maintain *synapses*—the juncture of one neuron sending a signal and another receiving the signal (Pyka et al, 2011). In all, they are likely to play a much larger role in central nervous system functioning than once believed (Pack and Pawson, 2010).

THINKING CREATIVELY

Think of ways in which, subject to the necessary technology and ethical clearance, you could investigate the importance of glia. Try to come up with an experiment, a natural experiment, or an observational method.

> **KEY IDEAS** action and resting potentials An **action potential** is the electrical impulse that conveys information from one neuron to another, or from the neuron to bodily muscles and glands. The **resting potential** is the 'default' resting setting of a neuron—the setting that would be maintained if no action potentials were fired.

The Action Potential: How Neurons Work

Neural communication is electrochemical—it has electrical and chemical aspects. The electrical aspect occurs when the neuron generates ('fires') an **action potential**, an electrical impulse that travels from the point where the axon exits the cell body (the axon hillock), to the axon's terminal. This impulse conveys information from the dendrites and cell body—information that will then be transmitted by chemical messengers (neurotransmitters) to other neurons. When we speak of the 'firing of a neuron', we are talking about the firing of an action potential, and when we talk of a 'neural impulse' it is to a fired action potential that we are referring.

The action potential is an all-or-nothing process, meaning that neurons have only two settings—*on* or *off*. They are either firing or resting. The default setting of a neuron is resting, known as **resting potential**. A minimum level of intensity of stimulation from other neurons is required to successfully 'light the fuse' of an action potential—a *threshold of stimulation* that must be met to cause a neuron to fire. At any moment, a neuron may be receiving both *excitatory* (stimulating) and *inhibitory* ('anti-stimulating') messages from surrounding neurons. It sums the information it is getting, and if the 'go' signals outweigh the 'hold' signals, the neuron will generate an action potential.

Polarization and depolarization

To understand how the neuron fires an action potential, picture the neuron bathed in fluid from inside and outside the cell membrane. This fluid contains **ions**—atomic particles that may carry either negative or positive charges. At resting potential, negatively charged ions build up along the inside of the cell membrane. These negatively charged ions attract positively charged ions from outside the neuron, causing the positively charged ions to build up in the surrounding fluid. The increase in positively charged ions outside the neuron creates a resting potential balance between a somewhat higher proportion of positive charges outside, and negative charges inside the neuron. This balanced condition, known as **polarization**, is depicted in Figure 4.2.

The most important of the ions contributing to the resting potential are *potassium* (K^+) and *sodium* (Na^+). If both of these positively charged ions could move freely though the membrane of the neuron, they would change the balance of positive and negative within the neuron and disrupt polarization. As it happens, potassium ions (K^+) *do* permeate the cell membrane fairly easily through special segments along the membrane of the neuron known as *ion channels*.

❭ **KEY IDEAS** ions and polarization An **ion** is an atomic particle that carries primarily a positive or negative electrical charge. **Polarization** takes place when the resting potential balance between primarily negatively charged ions within a neuron and positively charged ions outside is altered so that the neuron contains more negative ions as compared with outside the cell.

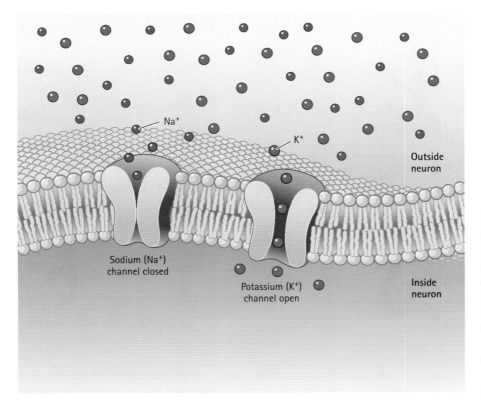

Na+

K+

Outside
neuron

Sodium (Na+)
channel closed

Potassium (K+)
channel open

Inside
neuron

FIGURE 4.2 Ions cross the neuron membrane through specialized channels. Ions enter and exit the neuron through channels specialized for each type of ion. However, the neuron membrane is *selectively permeable*—potassium (K^+) ions cross the neuron membrane relatively freely, but sodium (Na^+) ions are restricted in their passage until the moment of depolarization.

Ion channels are specialized, with one type for potassium (K⁺) and another for sodium (Na⁺). The potassium channel is highly permeable, allowing potassium (K⁺) ions to pass across the neuron membrane. The reason that polarization is not disrupted by the entry of these positively charged ions is that the membrane strongly resists the passage of sodium (Na⁺) ions through sodium channels to the inside of the neuron. Instead, most sodium ions that may exist within the cell are pumped *out* through a sodium channel that 'pumps' faster than potassium ions can enter. This maintains the balance between negative and positive charges that characterizes polarization (Huxley, 1959; see Figure 4.2).

Polarization comes to a spectacular but brief end when the neuron receives, through its dendrites, an abundance of excitatory signals from other neurons—reaching the threshold of stimulation. At that moment, the sodium ion channels closest to the *axon hillock*—the point where the axon emerges from the cell body—become open to sodium for an infinitesimal fraction of a second, allowing these positively charged ions free entry into the neuron. Sodium ions flood the neuron at the axon hillock, increasing the presence of positively charged ions dramatically. Fittingly, this event is termed **depolarization**. Depolarization begins the firing of the action potential; it is depicted in Figure 4.3.

The action potential now begins to travel down the length of the axon from the hillock. Its electrical charge triggers the opening of the next group of sodium ion

> **KEY IDEAS** depolarization
> **Depolarization** takes place when there is disruption of the resting potential balance between negatively and positively charged ions within and outside the neuron. Depolarization begins the process of the firing of an action potential.

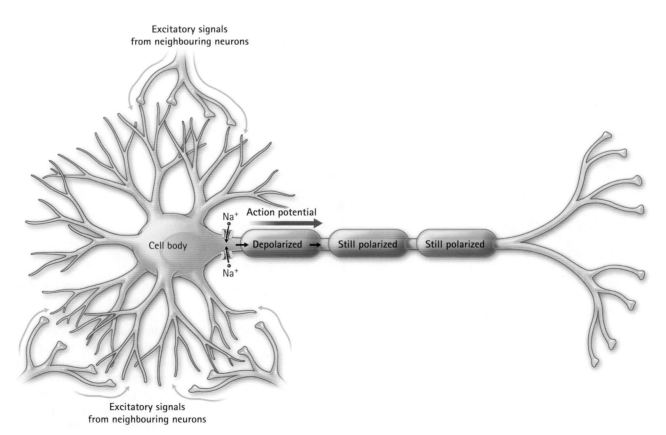

FIGURE 4.3 Depolarization of the neuron. When the neuron receives an abundance of excitatory signals from other neurons, reaching or exceeding the threshold of stimulation, depolarization occurs, firing an action potential.

channels 'down the line', allowing sodium to rush in, depolarizing the axon at this next point, and firing a new axon potential to carry on for the previous one. Thus, at each point of depolarization, a new action potential is formed by the activity of the previous one. This allows the neural message to continue rushing towards its terminal in the manner of a relay race. Once a new action potential is fired along the neuron, the previous length of neuron immediately reassumes its resting, polarized state—just like a relay runner dropping out of the race once the baton is passed to the next runner. This process is referred to as *repolarization*. Figure 4.4 depicts the triggering of action potentials along the length of the neuron.

The role of neurotransmitters

We can now look more closely at the work of **neurotransmitters**. Just below the surface of the axon's terminal are a very large number of tiny sacs (called *vesicles*) which contain neurotransmitters—the chemical substances that carry neural signals from one neuron to the next across the synapse (juncture) of two neurons. When the action potential reaches the terminal, depolarization in the action potential signals the terminal's vesicles to open, spilling neurotransmitter molecules into the synapse. Although it was once believed that the vesicles of each neuron release only one type of neurotransmitter, in fact combinations of neurotransmitters may be released (eg, Nishimaru et al, 2005).

Once they are spilled from the vesicles of the 'sending' neuron, known as the **pre-synaptic neuron**, some of the neurotransmitters will cross the (infinitesimally

> ❯ **KEY IDEAS** neurotransmitters
> A **neurotransmitter** is a chemical substance that carries neural signals from one neuron to another across a neuronal synapse. There are a number of different neurotransmitters each associated with regulating particular aspects of brain and nervous system function.

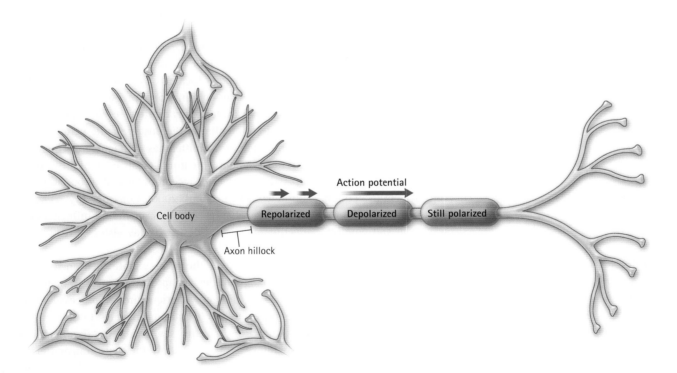

FIGURE 4.4 **The action potential generates new action potentials. The initial action potential causes new action potentials to be fired along the length of the neuron in the manner of a relay race or a series of falling dominoes. Note that as each new action potential is fired, the previous length of the neuron instantly becomes polarized once again (repolarized).**

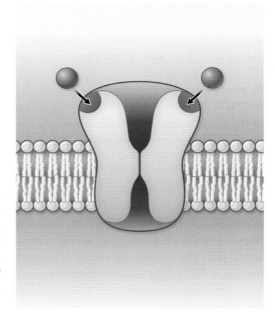

FIGURE 4.5 **Binding of neurotransmitters to receptor sites is a 'lock-and-key' event. Receptors in the dendrites of the post-synaptic neuron are specialized to receive specific neurotransmitters only. The shape of the neurotransmitter molecule precisely 'fits' that of the receptor site.**

> **KEY IDEAS** pre- and post-synaptic neurons The **pre-synaptic neuron** is the 'sending' neuron in neuronal communication. The **post-synaptic neuron** is the 'receiving' neuron in neuronal communication.

> **KEY IDEAS** reuptake After binding of the neurotransmitter to receptor sites in the post-synaptic neuron it is reabsorbed by the pre-synaptic neuron. This is called reuptake.

small) synaptic gap and *bind*, or attach themselves, to synaptic receptors in the dendrites of the 'receiving' neuron, known as the **post-synaptic neuron**. These receptors are specialized to receive specific neurotransmitters only. As depicted in Figure 4.5, this is a lock-and-key sort of event. The neurotransmitter will not bind to receptors that do not match its molecular shape.

However, each neurotransmitter may 'fit' a number of different 'locks', and its effects will differ according to the specific receptor to which it binds. When a neurotransmitter binds to certain types of receptors located at certain sites within the nervous system, the effect on the neuron may be inhibitory—preventing the neuron from firing. But when the same neurotransmitter binds to other receptors, the effect may be excitatory, generating an action potential in the post-synaptic neuron.

What this means is that the same neurotransmitter has different consequences depending on its receptor in the post-synaptic neuron. As an example, the neurotransmitter *serotonin* has *at least* 16 subtypes of receptors located throughout the nervous system (Naughton, Mulrooney, and Leonard, 2000). Consequently, as summarized in Table 4.1, serotonin has various sorts of effects, including influences on sleep, nausea and vomiting, appetite, and sexual desire. It may also be involved in the regulation of anxiety, **aggression**, and mood.

Once a neurotransmitter exerts an effect on the post-synaptic neuron, it does not remain there—this would soon clog up the synapse. Most neurotransmitter molecules are immediately reabsorbed by the pre-synaptic neuron, a process known as **reuptake**, or converted into inactive chemicals by various enzymes. Certain drugs, such as the **antidepressant** drugs known as *selective serotonin reuptake inhibitors* (SSRIs), intentionally block this reuptake process to allow the neurotransmitter to keep flooding the receptor site of the post-synaptic neuron. SSRIs are discussed in the context of mental health in Chapter 19, 'SSRIs'.

The entire process of communication between neurons through neurotransmitter activity, from the firing of an action potential to the release and reuptake of neurotransmitters, is summarized in Figure 4.6.

TABLE 4.1 A quick guide to some important neurotransmitters

This table includes some of the known (and suspected) functions of nine neurotransmitters.	
Neurotransmitter	Primary functions
Acetylcholine	Regulation of muscular activity, learning, and memory
Dopamine	Regulates how we respond to rewarding activities (the 'reward system' and experiences of pleasure); affects attention, learning, and memory processes; and helps regulate bodily movement
Endorphins	Opiate-like neurotransmitters that provide analgesia (pain relief) and a sense of well-being
GABA (gamma-aminobutyric acid)	Tends to inhibit the firing of neurons and keeps the overexcitation of neurons in check; GABA-agonist drugs induce relaxation, intoxicating effects, relief from anxiety
Glutamate	Tends to increase the speed and rate of neural transmission throughout the nervous system; increases efficiency of learning and memory
Noradrenaline	Affects attention and impulsivity, learning and memory; helps regulate involuntary responses to stress
Serotonin	Affects mood (possibly including depression), sleep, nausea/vomiting, appetite, sexual behaviour; may affect aggression
Substance P	Helps regulate the experience of pain
Oxytocin	Reduces blood pressure and other indicators of stress; may be involved in promoting maternal behaviour, bonding between mother and infant, and feelings of love (see later this chapter for more on oxytocin)

Sources: Hardman, Limbird, and Gilman, 2001; Tobler, Fiorillo, and Schultz 2005; Svenningsson et al, 2006; Ordway, Schwartz, and Frazer, 2007.

THINKING PRACTICALLY

There are various feelings that we might think of as happiness in different situations. These include love, euphoria, pain relief, and optimum arousal. Psychoactive drugs work by acting on neurotransmitter systems. If you were to design a 'wonder drug' to induce happiness, what neurotransmitters would you have it target and why?

Neurotransmitters and Drugs

Some drugs alter the effects of neurotransmitters in various ways. When a drug such as the SSRIs just described increases the effects of a neurotransmitter, the drug is known as an **agonist** for that neurotransmitter. Drugs that *decrease* the effects of a neurotransmitter are known as **antagonists**.

There are many ways in which a drug may increase or decrease neurotransmitter effects. For example, drug agonists may block the reuptake of a neurotransmitter, as is the case for the SSRI antidepressant drugs, or they may increase synthesis (production) of the neurotransmitter within the vesicles of the pre-synaptic neuron. This allows more of the neurotransmitter to be spilled out into the synapse. The stimulant *amphetamine*, described in greater detail in Chapter 11, is thought by some researchers to exert its effects in this way, in part by increasing the quantity of the neurotransmitter *dopamine* that is released into the synapse (Rothman and Baumann, 2006).

❯ KEY IDEAS agonists and antagonists An **agonist** is any substance that mimics the action of a neurotransmitter and binds to the neurotransmitter receptor. An **antagonist** on the other hand is any substance that blocks the receptors of a particular neurotransmitter, decreasing the availability and effects of the neurotransmitter.

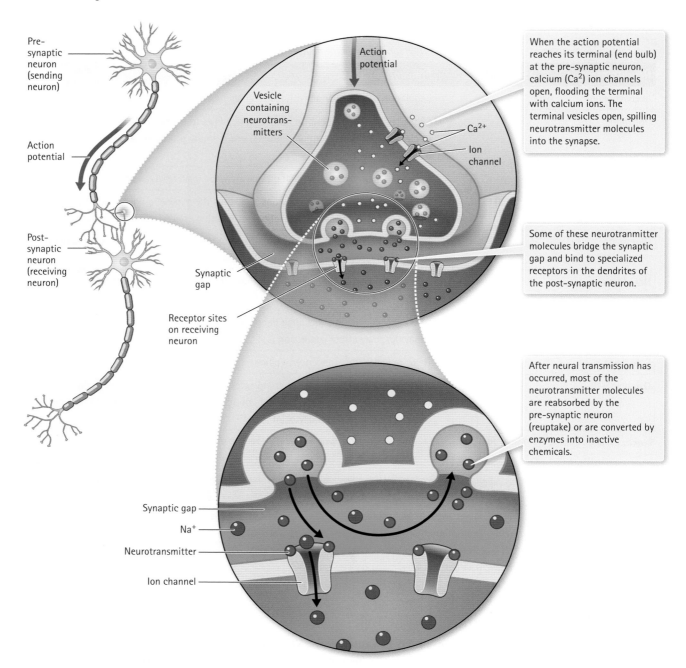

Pre-synaptic neuron (sending neuron)

Action potential

Post-synaptic neuron (receiving neuron)

Action potential

Vesicle containing neurotrans-mitters

Ca²⁺

Ion channel

When the action potential reaches its terminal (end bulb) at the pre-synaptic neuron, calcium (Ca²) ion channels open, flooding the terminal with calcium ions. The terminal vesicles open, spilling neurotransmitter molecules into the synapse.

Synaptic gap

Receptor sites on receiving neuron

Some of these neurotranmitter molecules bridge the synaptic gap and bind to specialized receptors in the dendrites of the post-synaptic neuron.

After neural transmission has occurred, most of the neurotransmitter molecules are reabsorbed by the pre-synaptic neuron (reuptake) or are converted by enzymes into inactive chemicals.

Synaptic gap

Na⁺

Neurotransmitter

Ion channel

FIGURE 4.6 Communication between two neurons. An action potential triggers neurotransmitter activity at the synapse, allowing communication to take place between a pre-synaptic and a post-synaptic neuron.

Often, an agonist drug mimics the effects of a particular neurotransmitter by binding to post-synaptic neuron receptor sites that the neurotransmitter would ordinarily occupy, directly activating the site. As an example, the *opioid* drugs *morphine* and *heroin*, which provide pain relief and a sense of euphoria, as described in Chapter 11, exert their effects in part by binding to receptor sites (*opioid receptors*).

These receptors are ordinarily occupied by a class of neurotransmitters known as endorphins, which are associated with pain relief (Pert and Snyder, 1973).

Like the agonists, neurotransmitter *antagonists* may work in a number of ways. They may block the synthesis of the neurotransmitter within the pre-synaptic neuron, block its release at the synapse, or destroy it immediately following its release. Most intriguingly, antagonists may prevent a neurotransmitter from binding to receptor sites by 'getting there first'. Consider the drug *naloxone*, an antagonist for the opioid drugs which bind to endorphin receptor sites. Naloxone occupies these receptor sites by mimicking the structure of these opioid drugs. However, while naloxone does occupy endorphin receptor sites and prevent binding by opioids, it does not activate the endorphin receptors. Naloxone molecules work a bit like someone sleeping on a park bench, thereby preventing anyone else from sitting there. Thus, naloxone is useful in treatment of **addiction** to drugs such as heroin and morphine. It blocks their effects to discourage their use. Naloxone is also used as an antidote for overdoses of these drugs (Kerr et al, 2009). See Figure 4.7 for a depiction of how agonist and antagonist drugs work.

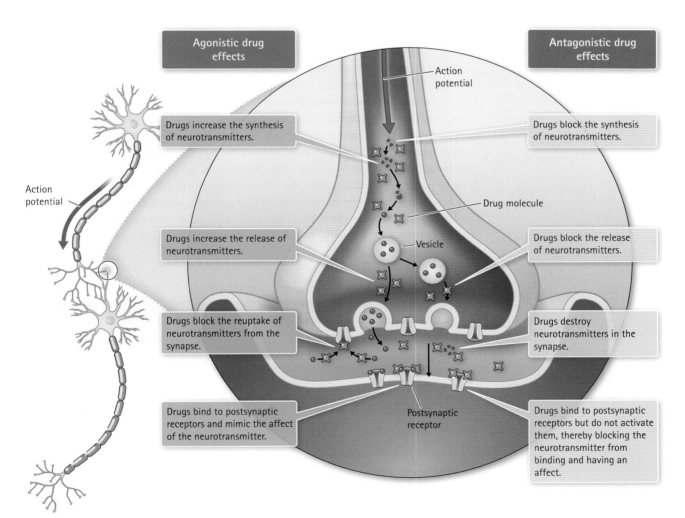

FIGURE 4.7 Neurotransmitter agonists and antagonists. Drugs that facilitate the effects of neurotransmitters are known as *agonists*. Those that decrease the effects of neurotransmitters are known as *antagonists*.

Neurotransmitters and Mental Life

Neurotransmitters have far-ranging effects on mental life. For example, as already mentioned, the neurotransmitter serotonin has a range of different effects depending on the receptor to which it binds (see Table 4.1). Another important neurotransmitter, *dopamine*, is involved in learning, memory, attention, and problem-solving. Dopamine also helps regulate muscle contraction and movement, and is an important component of our reward systems, the areas of the brain that enable us to experience pleasure. Dopamine is released when we listen to appealing music, gaze at someone we think is attractive, are presented with delicious food, or use a range of recreational drugs (Koob and Le Moal, 2008). Indeed, dopamine is agonized (promoted) directly or indirectly by almost every recreational drug, from cocaine to nicotine to ecstasy (MDMA) and LSD, opioids, and beyond (Koob and Le Moal, 2008).

The neurotransmitter GABA (*gamma-aminobutyric acid*) operates primarily by inhibiting brain neurons from firing (although it serves some excitatory functions as well). In a sense, GABA quiets brain activity. Drugs that tend to produce relaxation or sedation, such as **alcohol** or *benzodiazepines* (used for the treatment of anxiety and sleeplessness, see Chapter 19, 'Anxiolytics' for more information), are GABA agonists and bind to GABA receptor sites. Thus, psychological states such as anxiety and panic may be associated with faulty regulation of GABA neurotransmitter systems. However, this association has not been demonstrated conclusively, and even if true it would not imply that vitamin supplements purportedly containing GABA are effective treatments for anxiety. In fact they are not and their safety is questionable. GABA taken orally is unlikely ever to reach the brain because GABA does not cross the *blood-brain barrier* very well. The blood-brain barrier is formed by a group of tightly packed cells that restrict the entry of substances from the blood stream into the brain, and glial cells surrounding brain capillaries which hinder the transport of molecules to and from the brain. The inability of GABA to cross this barrier is one of the reasons that virtually all of it is produced in the brain, unlike many other neurotransmitters.

> **KEY IDEAS GABA** (*gamma-aminobutyric acid*) **GABA** is a neurotransmitter that primarily works by inhibiting synaptic transmission and so reducing brain activation. This gives GABA relaxant properties. Relaxing drugs like alcohol are GABA agonists.

THINKING CREATIVELY

In theory GABA supplements should reduce anxiety. In practice they do not appear to do so. Think of as many ways as possible to explain this paradox.

THE ORGANIZATION OF THE CENTRAL NERVOUS SYSTEM

We have seen how neurons and glia, the building blocks of the nervous system, are constructed to allow communication to occur throughout the body. But these building blocks are organized into interconnected systems and subsystems—the pathways of the nervous system. The organization of these systems and subsystems is depicted in Figure 4.8.

As you can see from Figure 4.8, the whole nervous system has two major divisions: the **central nervous system** and the *peripheral nervous system*. While the

The Nervous System

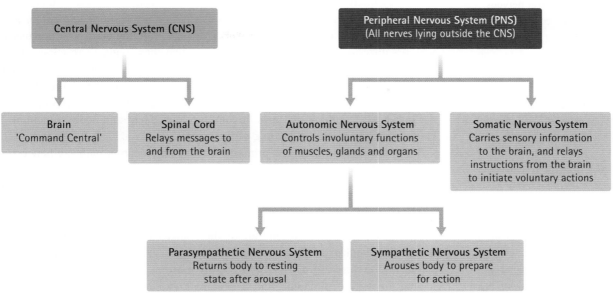

Central Nervous System (CNS)		Peripheral Nervous System (PNS) (All nerves lying outside the CNS)	
Brain 'Command Central'	**Spinal Cord** Relays messages to and from the brain	**Autonomic Nervous System** Controls involuntary functions of muscles, glands and organs	**Somatic Nervous System** Carries sensory information to the brain, and relays instructions from the brain to initiate voluntary actions

Parasympathetic Nervous System
Returns body to resting
state after arousal

Sympathetic Nervous System
Arouses body to prepare
for action

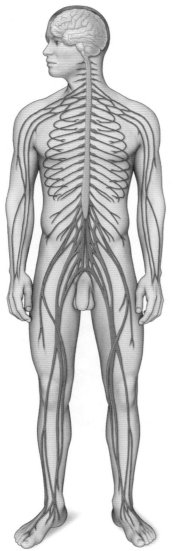

FIGURE 4.8 **The central and peripheral nervous systems. An intricate mechanism designed for nearly instantaneous communication throughout the body, the nervous system is organized into two main systems: the central nervous system (shown in yellow on the left) and the peripheral nervous system (shown in purple on the right).**

❯ KEY IDEAS the central nervous system The **central nervous system (CNS)** consists of the brain and spinal cord. It organizes and interprets the information received from the **peripheral nervous system (PNS)** and sends commands back to the PNS to take actions or make adjustments to bodily functions.

❯ KEY IDEAS the spinal cord The **spinal cord** is a thin, tubular bundle of nerve tracts contained in the vertebrae of the spinal column. It comprises **grey matter**—cell bodies, unmyelinated axons, dendrites, and glia—along with **white matter**—axons with myelin sheaths.

❯ KEY IDEAS spinal reflexes These are automatic motor actions in response to stimulation. **Spinal reflexes** bypass the brain entirely and are controlled by the spinal cord.

central and peripheral nervous systems are anatomically distinct, in actuality they are highly interdependent, and neither could do its work without the other.

The **central nervous system (CNS)**, consisting of the *brain* and *spinal cord*, is a 'command central' of sorts. It receives information from the peripheral nervous system, organizes and interprets the information, and then sends 'instructions' back to the peripheral nervous system to take actions or make adjustments to various bodily functions. The brain—to which we devote an entire section later in the chapter—is the source of all thought, emotion, memory, learning, and almost all human action. It controls all voluntary and most involuntary movement and bodily functions, including breathing and the beating of the heart.

The **spinal cord**—which acts primarily as a communication pathway between the brain and the rest of the body—is a thin, tubular bundle of nerve tracts organized in segments. These segments are protected by the *vertebrae* and *discs* of the *spinal column*, the stack of bones which runs from the base of the skull to the lower back just above the pelvis. The spinal cord is composed of two types of tissue mass. As depicted in Figure 4.9, the interior of the spinal cord consists primarily of **grey matter**—cell bodies, unmyelinated axons, dendrites, and glia. The grey matter of the spinal cord is surrounded primarily by **white matter**—axons with myelin sheaths allowing for swifter communication. Therefore, grey matter is responsible for collecting and integrating information, while white matter is responsible for transmitting that information.

The principal function of the spinal cord is to send information from the skin, organs, and muscles to the brain, and to convey motor commands back. If the spinal cord is cut at any point, the brain will no longer perceive sensation at that point and below, and the muscles and organs at that point and below will no longer respond to motor commands from the brain.

However, communication to and from the brain is not the only function of the spinal cord. The spinal cord also controls certain **spinal reflexes**—muscle contractions that result in involuntary movement and occur in response to stimulation. These motor actions are automatic and not controlled by the brain. For example, when a doctor strikes your knee with a rubber mallet and your leg kicks, that's the

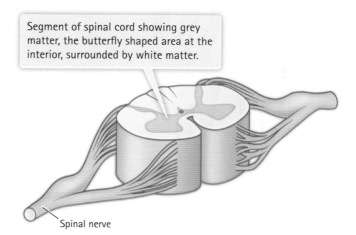

Segment of spinal cord showing grey matter, the butterfly shaped area at the interior, surrounded by white matter.

Spinal nerve

FIGURE 4.9 **A segment of the spinal cord. The spinal cord is constructed of white and grey matter.**

spinal cord *not* the brain working. The spine controls numerous other reflexes—for example, quickly withdrawing the hand from a source of pain. These and similar reflexes evolved to protect our bodies from various threats from the time of infancy.

In addition to spinal reflexes, the spine is responsible for a number of **central pattern generators**—circuits of neurons (or single neurons) that generate routine, common rhythmic movements such as moving the legs while walking (Barrière et al, 2008). Infants who are not yet able to walk will nonetheless execute walking movements if supported on a treadmill because of central pattern generators in the spine (Lamb and Yang, 2000). The point is that spinal reflexes are responses to stimulation and may result in many types of behaviours, whereas central pattern generators generate repetitive, rhythmic movements only. Figure 4.10 shows the anatomy of the spinal cord and spinal column, and helps clarify the difference between reflexes and central pattern generators.

> **KEY IDEAS** central pattern generators **Central pattern generators** are circuits of neurons that generate routine, rhythmic movements and are controlled entirely by the spine with no input from the brain.

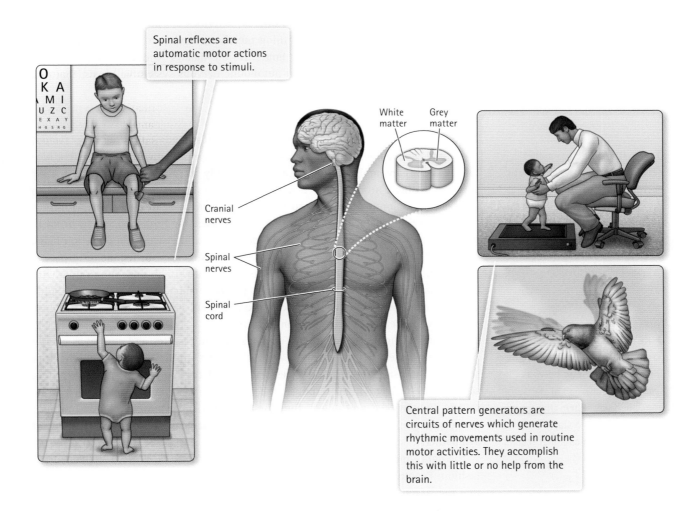

Spinal reflexes are automatic motor actions in response to stimuli.

White matter   Grey matter

Cranial nerves

Spinal nerves

Spinal cord

Central pattern generators are circuits of nerves which generate rhythmic movements used in routine motor activities. They accomplish this with little or no help from the brain.

FIGURE 4.10 Spinal reflexes and central pattern generators. Some functions of the human spine are generated by the spine itself with no help from the brain.

The Peripheral Nervous System

❯ KEY IDEAS the peripheral nervous system (PNS)
The **peripheral nervous system (PNS)** consists of cranial and spinal nerves that allow communication to take place between the brain and body. The PNS consists of two divisions: the **somatic nervous system**, which controls voluntary movement and handles sensory information, and the **autonomic nervous system**, which regulates activities that are mostly out of voluntary control.

The communication between brain and body that the spinal cord makes possible is organized by the **peripheral nervous system**. In this context 'peripheral' means 'on the outside or periphery'. It does not mean 'unimportant'. The peripheral nervous system consists of *cranial nerves*, which enter and leave the underside of the brain, and *spinal nerves*, which branch out from the sides of the spinal cord, connecting the cord to the rest of the body. The peripheral nervous system has two divisions: the *somatic* and *autonomic* nervous systems.

The **somatic nervous system** is, for the most part, in charge of regulating voluntary motor actions. Voluntary means under conscious control—you decide to catch a ball using your limbs, and these actions are controlled by the somatic nervous system receiving orders from the brain. The somatic nervous system is also responsible for relaying sensory information about the environment to the brain from your *sense organs*—eyes, ears, nose, tongue, and skin.

In contrast, the **autonomic nervous system** oversees primarily *involuntary* activities of the muscles, **glands**, and organs—activities not under conscious control. For example, you cannot stop breathing merely by saying to yourself, 'I think I'll decline to breathe for the next few hours'. If you manage to hold your breath long enough, you will pass out and your autonomic nervous system will insist that you start breathing again.

The autonomic nervous system

❯ KEY IDEAS the sympathetic nervous system The **sympathetic nervous system** is the division of the autonomic nervous system that mobilizes the body for arousal, particularly in response to a threat of some sort, but also in response to certain other conditions.

The autonomic nervous system has its own two distinct subdivisions: the *sympathetic* and *parasympathetic nervous systems*. The **sympathetic nervous system** mobilizes the organs and muscles for arousal, usually to respond to a threat of some sort. Sympathetic arousal triggers a cascade of physiological processes designed to increase the amount of oxygen to the brain and muscles to allow you to meet a threat with flight or aggression. Heart rate increases, the lungs expand to bring in more air, breathing becomes more rapid, perspiration increases, and digestion halts, causing your mouth to become dry. All of these changes are known as the *fight-or-flight* response, because they prepare a person to deal with an oncoming threat with either fists or feet—so to speak (Cannon, 1929; see Chapter 11 for more on the fight-or-flight response). The sympathetic nervous system is also activated by intense physical exercise and strong emotional states.

❯ KEY IDEAS the parasympathetic nervous system
The **parasympathetic nervous system** is the division of the autonomic nervous system that returns the body to resting state following arousal and maintains that resting state.

In contrast, the **parasympathetic nervous system** restores and conserves energy by returning the body to a resting state following arousal and maintaining that state until arousal is once again necessary. Thus, if the sympathetic nervous system supports the fight-or-flight response, the parasympathetic nervous system could be said to support 'rest and digest' functions. Paradoxically, however, genital arousal and orgasm in both males and females are associated with parasympathetic, not sympathetic, activity.

The parasympathetic and sympathetic nervous systems work in a complementary fashion. People who have escaped from life-threatening circumstances often report that the 'adrenaline rush' generated from the sympathetic system in response to the threat is followed by a feeling akin to euphoria when the danger is gone (a 'whew!' feeling). This euphoria is a sign that the parasympathetic system has taken over to restore the body's resources. Figure 4.11 depicts the complementary functions of the two divisions of the autonomic nervous system.

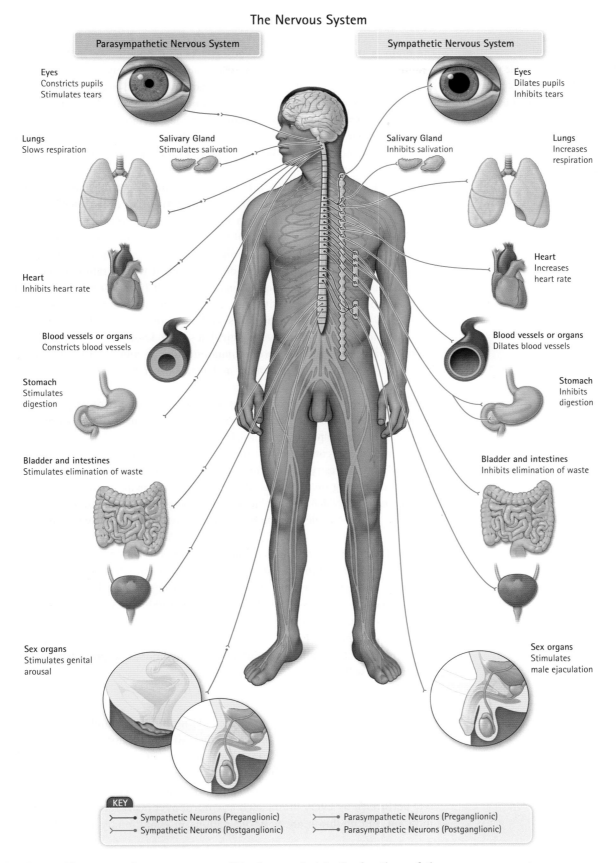

FIGURE 4.11 **The autonomic nervous system.** This diagram depicts the functions of the parasympathetic and sympathetic divisions of the autonomic nervous system.

THE BRAIN

The brain is the centre of the nervous system. But how do we look inside it? As recently as the 1980s, *brain imaging* technologies such as **magnetic resonance imaging (MRI)** were developed to enable neurologists and neuroscientists to create finely detailed images of the brain's structures and activity (Mattson and Simon, 1996). Today, brain imaging has begun to provide tentative solutions to mysteries about the human brain previously thought unlikely to be solved. One aspect of the brain these technologies have helped shed light on is its *organization*, which we will explore next.

Although the brain is often thought of as a single organ, it is perhaps more technically correct to say that it is a *system* or network of organs made up of clusters of neurons that form intricate neural circuits. However, these circuits/organs are so well integrated, and have evolved over time to work together so smoothly, that they might as well *be* a single organ. That the brain operates as a complex network of neural connections is made vividly clear when brain damage and disorders are considered. These conditions often result in a failure of brain neurons to communicate efficiently with one another. 'Failure to communicate' may be involved in psychological disorders as well as brain disorders. For example, there is some evidence that the psychological disorder known as *schizophrenia* may be accompanied by problems with communication to and from the brain's major sensory relay station, the *thalamus*, and many other brain structures (Mitelman et al, 2005).

The organization of the brain can be described in a number of ways and depicted according to different conceptual schemes. Consider a map of the world. It could stress political geography by emphasizing borders between nations and state borders within nations, or it could stress natural geography by emphasizing mountain ranges, bodies of water, forestry, and so forth. Moreover, maps can exist at numerous levels of detail, depending on the needs of the reader of the map. At the most basic level, the brain can be divided geographically into three parts: the *forebrain*, *midbrain*, and *hindbrain*. Figure 4.12 depicts the human brain divided in this way by 'geographical' region.

We will consider the divisions of the brain from the bottom up, starting with the parts that are believed to be more evolutionarily ancient (structures that were present in the most primitive animals and that perform the most basic life functions). As we move up into the higher regions of the forebrain, we will examine parts that perform tasks you will recognize as being unique to more complex animals such as birds and mammals. Figure 4.13 depicts the 'big picture' of the brain, filling in the 'contents' of the hindbrain, midbrain, and forebrain, and previewing the major structures we will consider.

The Hindbrain and Midbrain

Figure 4.14 depicts the major structures of the hindbrain and midbrain. Sometimes these structures—minus the **cerebellum** of the hindbrain, but (usually—not everyone is consistent in this) including the *thalamus* at the lower portion of the forebrain—are considered together and termed the *brainstem*. In this general region of the brain are found most of the vital 'housekeeping' functions for survival performed by every brain, such as control over heart rate and breathing. The hindbrain and midbrain are very old regions in evolutionary terms. If you were

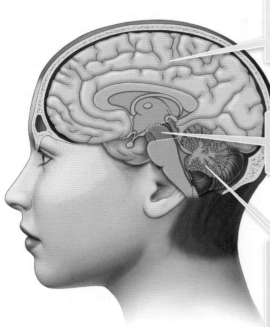

Forebrain: Perceives sensory information; controls muscular movement; is the home of thought, memory, decisions and planning, personality, and emotion.

Midbrain: Conveys visual and auditory information from the spine to the forebrain and helps coordinate movement of the head and eyes.

Hindbrain: Controls bodily functions vital to life, including heart rate and respiration, vomiting, sneezing and coughing; contributes to the regualtion of sleep/wakefulness, attention/fatigue; supports activities crucial to life including eating, sex, and waste elimination.

FIGURE 4.12 **The geography of the brain. The geographic regions of the brain include the** *forebrain, midbrain,* **and** *hindbrain.*

to crack open the skull of a fish and extract the brain, what you would see would not look radically different from Figure 4.14. The hind- and midbrain regions may be small and quite ancient, but this does not make them less important in the larger scheme of things. Injury to these areas would probably kill you, whereas various kinds of damage to the higher areas of the forebrain would make life difficult but not impossible.

Like most brain areas, one may look at structures of hindbrain and midbrain at varying levels of detail. However, the major structures include: in the **hindbrain**, the *cerebellum, medulla, pons*, and *reticular formation*; and in the **midbrain**, the *inferior* and *superior colliculi*.

The cerebellum

The **cerebellum** (literally 'little brain'), located in the hindbrain (see Figure 4.14), is the second largest individual structure in the central nervous system and, although it only contributes 10% of the brain's overall weight, it contains more neurons than the rest of the structures of the brain put together—between 50% and 70% of the total number of brain neurons (Herculano-Houzel and Lent, 2005).

The cerebellum has been considered something of a mystery since its initial description 50 years ago. It was once thought to be involved only in the control of balance and coordination. Damage to the cerebellum will result in loss of balance, and effects on the cerebellum are responsible for the staggering and clumsiness experienced after

❯ **KEY IDEAS** hindbrain and midbrain The **hindbrain** is a lower geographic area of the brain containing the cerebellum, medulla, pons, and reticular formation. The **midbrain** is a small, lower geographic area of the brain containing the inferior and superior colliculi, among other structures.

❯ **KEY IDEAS** the cerebellum The **cerebellum** ('little brain') is the second largest structure in the central nervous system, located in the hindbrain. The cerebellum coordinates sensory inputs and affects balance by assisting visual-spatial perception. It is also involved at least to some degree in attention, learning, and memory, and appropriate expression of emotion.

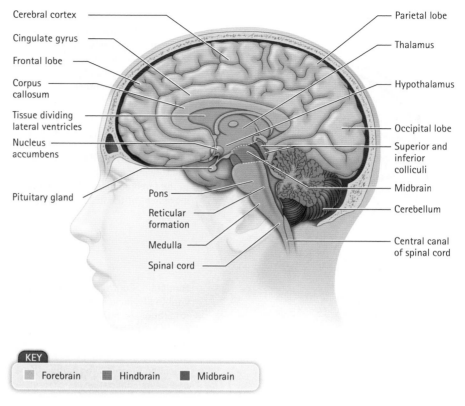

KEY

Forebrain   Hindbrain   Midbrain

FIGURE 4.13 **The major structures of the brain. This figure shows major structures of the hindbrain, midbrain, and forebrain in cross-section. Note that no single view of the brain can display *all* the important structures.**

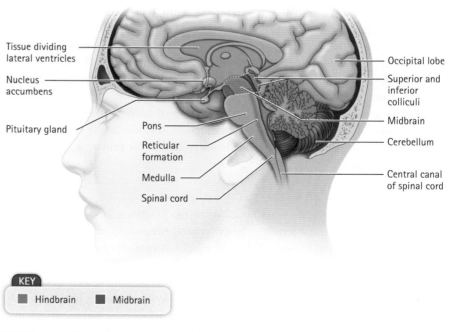

KEY

Hindbrain   Midbrain

FIGURE 4.14 **Major structures of the hindbrain and midbrain. The structures of the hindbrain and midbrain—minus the *cerebellum* but including the *thalamus* of the forebrain (not depicted)—are collectively known as the *brainstem*.**

drinking too much alcohol, for example. However, the function of the cerebellum is now known to go far beyond regulating balance as we walk or run. It appears instead primarily to coordinate the various sensory inputs we experience during waking **consciousness**, including visual inputs. The actual source of balance loss in cerebellum damage is problems with visual-spatial perception (Bower and Parsons, 2003). Cerebellum damage also can result in difficulties with processing many functions previously thought to be the exclusive domain of the cortex, including language, attention, and learning and memory—particularly learning and memory of bodily movements. Appropriate expression of emotion may also be affected (Dum and Fiez, 2009).

The medulla

The medulla, also known as the *medulla oblongata*, is a major structure originating in the hindbrain. Medulla oblongata is sometimes mentioned by those trying to impress others with their knowledge of the anatomy of the brain, especially in the context of describing intellectual function. However, the primary functions of the medulla are to control various autonomic processes, including the regulation of breathing and heartbeat. If the medulla contributes to your intellectual functioning, it is strictly because it keeps you alive so that you may think more clearly! When an individual overdoses on alcohol, tranquilizers, or opioids, the activity in the medulla can be so badly compromised that the individual stops breathing and dies.

The pons

The pons is a hindbrain structure that plays a vital role in regulating the body during sleep and in relaying information from the hindbrain to the forebrain (hence its name, meaning 'bridge' in Latin). Substructures embedded in the pons also project axons into the higher regions of the brain, making them more sensitive and responsive to sensory input under conditions of threat. You could find this extremely useful should you get into a situation where you are running or fighting for your life. These embedded structures also appear to be involved in retrieving memories associated with emotional events (Sterpenich et al, 2006).

The reticular formation

The medulla and pons include within them the reticular formation. The reticular formation is a startlingly intricate, net-like web of neurons that begins at the level of the medulla and threads upwards through the pons towards the midbrain and downwards towards the cerebellum and areas of the spinal cord involved in motor activity. This extensive structure plays a crucial role in variations of consciousness, including sleep/wakefulness, alertness/fatigue, and attention/inattention (Guillery, Feig, and Lozsádi, 1998). The reticular formation can be put 'offline'. When a boxer gets knocked out during a prize fight, chances are the blow temporarily but effectively shut down the operation of the reticular formation. More severe damage typically results in coma (Weisberg, Garcia, and Strub, 1996).

The colliculi

Whereas the hindbrain is of particular importance because it keeps us alive, the midbrain contributes the inferior colliculus and the superior colliculus. These structures are essential for conveying auditory and visual information from the cranial nerves to the forebrain areas where the information is interpreted as sounds and sights. These structures also help coordinate the movement of the eyeballs and head to allow hearing and vision to occur.

> KEY IDEAS the forebrain

The **forebrain** is the large, upper geographic area of the brain controlling the 'higher' brain functions. It consists of two cerebral hemispheres, each of which contains a limbic system, cerebral cortex, and thalamus. The forebrain is divided nearly symmetrically into left and right **cerebral hemispheres** connected by the bundle of axons known as the corpus callosum. The structures of each hemisphere correspond almost exactly to those in the opposite hemisphere, although there are also subtle, but important, differences left and right. The **corpus callosum** is the bundle of axons (white matter) that connects the right and left cerebral hemispheres.

The Forebrain

Above the hindbrain and midbrain lies the massive human **forebrain**—the seat of thought processes, emotion, personality, memory, intelligence, language, and consciousness itself. The forebrain is divided into two nearly symmetrical **cerebral hemispheres**, right and left, each with systems and structures that correspond almost exactly. Thus, there are two of each of the forebrain structures, one in each hemisphere. For reasons not yet fully understood, each hemisphere generally receives information from, and conveys commands to, the *opposite* side of the body. Thus, when a sound reaches your left ear, it is conveyed to the right hemisphere for interpretation; when your forebrain issues a command to raise your right arm, the command issues from the left hemisphere.

The hemispheres of the forebrain are connected by a bundle of over 200 million axons called the **corpus callosum**, which allows neurons from the right side of the brain to communicate with neurons on the left. The corpus callosum is the only area of the brain that may be severed, partially or entirely, without damaging critical functions—although such surgery does produce some startling effects. Figure 4.15 depicts the hemispheres of the forebrain and the connecting corpus callosum.

The major structures of each hemisphere are: the *limbic system* (composed of its own series of distinct structures and clusters of neurons), the *thalamus*, and the *cerebral cortex*.

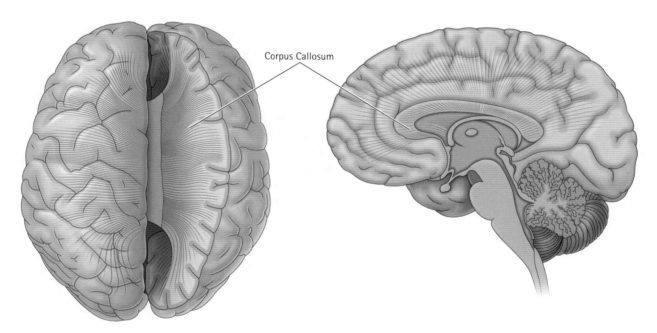

Corpus Callosum

FIGURE 4.15 Cerebral hemispheres and corpus callosum. This image of the cerebral hemispheres of the forebrain seen from the top and in cross-section depicts the neuronal fibres known as the corpus callosum that allow communication to take place between the hemispheres.

The limbic system

The **limbic system** consists of several large structures, and a number of smaller nuclei (clusters of neurons). The limbic system regulates emotions and motivations (particularly 'primal' emotions and motivations such as fear and aggression), plays

❯ KEY IDEAS the limbic system
The **limbic system** is a group of large structures and smaller nuclei that regulate mood, emotion, memory, and basic drives. It includes at least the hypothalamus, hippocampus, amygdala, basal ganglia, and nucleus accumbens.

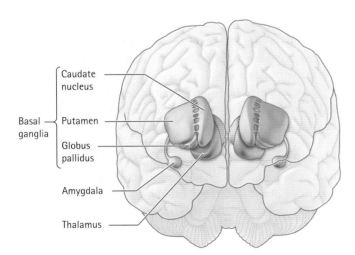

Hypothalamus: Links nervous system to endocrine system (glands and hormones); manages life-sustaining drives; plays role in aggression and sexuality.

Hippocampus: Crucial for formation of new episodic (autobiographical) memories

Nucleus accumbens: 'Reward centres' regulate effort to obtain something pleasurable

Amygdala: Helps recognize and interpret emotional messages and memories; important in the experience of fear and aggression

Caudate nucleus

Basal ganglia

Putamen

Globus pallidus

Amygdala

Thalamus

FIGURE 4.16 The limbic system. So called because it forms a border, or *limbus*, around the brainstem, the limbic system regulates emotion and motivation, is involved in formation of memory, regulates the cycle of sleep and wakefulness, and is the seat of drives such as hunger, thirst, and sex. Researchers disagree as to which structures it includes, and even on whether it should be considered a 'system'.

a part in the formation of memory, regulates the sleep/wake cycle, and is the seat of basic drives such as hunger, thirst, and sex. Figure 4.16 depicts the structures of the limbic system.

There are differences of opinion among neuroscientists as to which structures and nuclei should be considered part of the limbic system—and some contemporary researchers deny that a specific 'system' exists at all, preferring to describe the structures and their functions as part of the activity of the forebrain. However, among those who accept the limbic system idea, there would be little disagreement that the following structures should be considered among the large structures of that system: the *hypothalamus*, *hippocampus*, and *amygdala*.

The **hypothalamus** (literally 'under the thalamus') lives in two worlds. It is part of the brain's limbic system, giving it a home in the nervous system. However, it also helps to control the production of **hormones** by the **endocrine system**—the system of glands and hormones that assists in the work of the nervous system. Thus, it links the nervous system to the system of glands and hormones that support it. The hypothalamus manages our most essential life-sustaining drives—hunger, thirst, and sleep. It also plays a role in regulating sexual impulses and aggression, thus potentially contributing both to the creation and extinguishing of life. A well-known joke in neuroscience makes it easy to remember the basic jobs of the hypothalamus through the 'Four F's: Fighting, Fleeing, Feeding, and err . . . Fornicating'.

The **hippocampus** is the most crucial structure involved in the process of forming new *episodic* memories—memories associated with personal experiences (as compared with memories for facts learned from other sources (Andersen et al, 2007)). It is not an accident that the hippocampus is found in the limbic system, the seat of **emotion**. From an evolutionary standpoint, the most vital experiences to remember in our ancestral environment would have been those that directly affected survival and reproduction. Strong emotions often accompany experiences related to the sustaining of life, avoidance of death and injury, the act of mating, and the formation of important relationships. Over evolutionary time, then, an intimate connection has developed between the storage of memories of personal experiences and emotions such as fear, sadness, and joyful satisfaction.

A damaged hippocampus creates a conscious experience very much like that of the confused and harried protagonist of the 2000 film *Memento*, who was unable to create new memories, a condition known as *anterograde amnesia*. The best-known real-life case of this type of memory loss resulted from a surgical procedure that damaged a patient's hippocampus and surrounding mid-temporal lobe regions. On 23 August 1953, surgeon William Scoville performed a surgical procedure involving the removal of areas of the temporal lobe on an epilepsy patient known famously as Patient H.M. (Scoville and Milner, 1957). The outcome was unexpected: H.M. was unable to form new memories. His condition continued unabated until his death in 2008. The impairment in H.M.'s brain was entirely isolated. He simply could not register new memories for new experiences. His intelligence was not affected—if anything, his scores on standardized measures of intelligence (eg, IQ) increased following his surgery. However, his life consisted of the constant sensation of waking from a dream, with no memory of anything that had transpired just moments before (Milner, 1988, pp 254, 256).

Another important function of the hippocampus is intimately connected to its importance in forming episodic memory. The hippocampus and surrounding structures are also critical to imagination and the ability to envision future events (Buckner, 2010). Patients with damage to the hippocampus are not only unable to recall new experiences; they may find it difficult even to *imagine* new experiences. For example, when Demis Hassabis and colleagues asked patients with hippocampus damage to describe the experience of 'lying on a white sandy beach in a beautiful tropical bay' or to describe 'a possible event over the next weekend' their descriptions dramatically lacked the richness of detail provided by patients in a control group who lacked hippocampal damage. These patients could only report fragmented images and were unable to envision whole scenes 'in their mind's eye' (Hassabis et al, 2007, p 33).

The **amygdala** is an almond-shaped structure (its name means 'almond') built of neurons that work together to create an understanding of one's own emotions and those of others (LeDoux, 2007). One consequence of damage to the amygdala is the inability to recognize and interpret one's own emotions or respond to situations with appropriate emotion, and failure to pay attention to emotional messages from others (Murray, 2007). Brain imaging studies show that the amygdala may respond differently when an individual is viewing facial expressions expressing different emotions (Whalen et al, 2009).

Like the hippocampus, the amygdala is important in the formation of memory—primarily emotionally charged memory (Hamann, 2009). It plays a particularly important role in helping us to remember fear-inducing situations and in generating fearful and aggressive responses for survival and self-defence (LeDoux, 2007). It is the amygdala that gets the blood pumping and the adrenaline flowing when you are frightened or badly stressed. Rats whose normal amygdala responses have been intentionally destroyed or interfered with by researchers will cosy right up to a cat or climb all over it if the cat is sedated.

Humans suffering from anxiety and exaggerated fears have sometimes been shown to have 'hypersensitive' amygdalae, while those whose amygdalae are damaged may tend to be more trusting of others (Stein, Simmons, Feinstein, and Paulus, 2007). In an unusual study, Justin Feinstein and his colleagues tried to instil fear in a patient, SM, who had experienced damage to both her left- and right-hemisphere amygdalae. They let Patient SM handle live snakes and spiders (including pythons and tarantulas) and escorted her through a professionally designed 'haunted house', the Waverly Hills Sanatorium, USA, a closed-sanatorium now widely publicized as one of the 'most haunted' places on the planet. Every year at Halloween the sanatorium hosts a very scary tour, complete with scary scenes, noises, monsters, murderers, and ghosts. Finally, Feinstein and colleagues exposed Patient SM to ten extremely frightening film clips. Although Patient SM found the snakes and spiders fascinating, the haunted house loads of fun, and the film clips 'entertaining', she displayed little in the way of fear responses to any of these stimuli (Feinstein et al, 2011).

 THINKING CRITICALLY

Cases like that of SM are interesting sources of evidence for linking particular brain structures to particular psychological functions, in this case the amygdala and fear. However, we must always be cautious about the generalizability of case study evidence.

Questions

1 Explain why cases of brain injury like SM may not generalize well.

2 What might make this case more convincing?

Nuclei of the limbic system: basal ganglia and nucleus accumbens

In addition to the three relatively large structures listed previously, the limbic system contains some smaller 'workgroups' of nuclei that are considered 'minor' in size only—not necessarily in importance. They include *basal ganglia* and *nucleus accumbens*.

The basal ganglia are dopamine- and GABA-producing clusters of neurons surrounding the thalamus, and they play a role in the production of voluntary movement. *Parkinson's disease*, a degenerative disorder of the central nervous system, is caused by loss of dopamine within the *substantia nigra* region of the basal ganglia. Like the amygdala, the basal ganglia may also play a role in emotional communication—in understanding facial expressions and non-verbal behaviour, and in other forms of social communication (Satpute and Lieberman, 2006).

The nucleus accumbens are also dopamine-rich nuclei, receiving their dopamine primarily from various other brain structures. The dopamine released in this region accompanies feelings of excitement in the presence of pleasurable stimuli, and deep satisfaction when these stimuli are able to be consumed or enjoyed (Aron et al, 2005). Indeed, the nucleus accumbens are often referred to as 'reward centres'. If you will recall from our earlier discussion of neurotransmitters, most recreational drugs are agonists (promoters) of dopamine. Because the nucleus accumbens region is so rich in dopamine, it has been argued that suppressing nucleus accumbens activity would be an effective method of treating drug abuse and addiction, by interfering with the rewarding aspects of drug use.

However, some research challenges this view (Salamone et al, 2007). For example, Salamone and Correa (2002) have shown that the release of nucleus accumbens dopamine is not necessarily the 'cause' of feelings of wanting to engage in some rewarding behaviour such as taking drugs or eating ice cream. Instead, the nucleus accumbens dopamine regulates the amount of *effort* a person is willing to put into attempting to obtain the reward. For example, when nucleus accumbens dopamine is suppressed in caged rats, they are less willing to press bars or engage in tiring work to obtain food. However, their liking for the food and willingness to eat it is in no way diminished. This may have important implications for treatment of drug addiction, because it suggests that merely suppressing dopamine activity may not reduce the desire to take drugs, if the drugs are freely available and the cost does not exceed the perceived benefit (Salamone et al, 2007).

THINKING PRACTICALLY

It appears that the nucleus accumbens is implicated in the effort people are willing to go to in order to misuse drugs but not in the pleasure they get from the drugs. How might you use a drug that suppresses dopamine action on the nucleus accumbens in conjunction with other strategies to tackle drug misuse?

> ❯ **KEY IDEAS** the thalamus The **thalamus** is a lower forebrain structure that conveys sensory information to the cerebral cortex and receives instructions from the cortex regarding the regulation of sensory and emotional signals.

The thalamus

The **thalamus** is a hard structure to classify. Geographically it sits at the base of the forebrain, but some scientists consider it to be a part of the limbic system because it is located adjacent to the hippocampus and hypothalamus. In terms of function, however, the thalamus is generally thought of as a 'gateway' to the higher functions of the

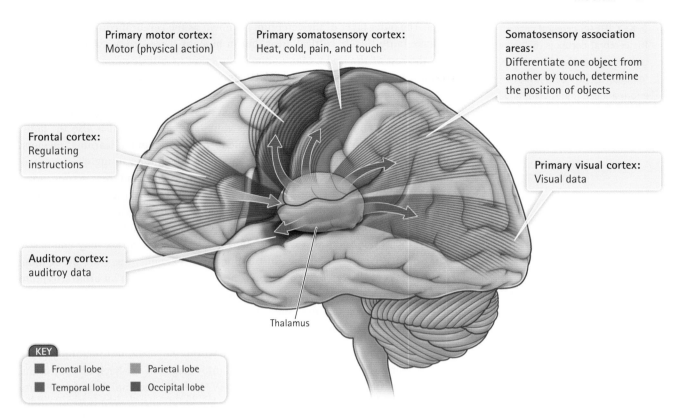

Primary motor cortex:
Motor (physical action)

Primary somatosensory cortex:
Heat, cold, pain, and touch

Somatosensory association areas:
Differentiate one object from another by touch, determine the position of objects

Frontal cortex:
Regulating instructions

Primary visual cortex:
Visual data

Auditory cortex:
auditroy data

Thalamus

KEY

■ Frontal lobe   ■ Parietal lobe
■ Temporal lobe   ■ Occipital lobe

FIGURE 4.17 The thalamus: sensory gateway to the forebrain. Sensory information passes through the thalamus and is relayed to the cerebral cortex. Information from the prefrontal cortex is also relayed back to the thalamus, regulating the amount of data from each sense that reaches the cortex.

forebrain. All types of sensory information (except that related to the sense of smell) must first pass through the thalamus before being relayed to the cerebral cortex to be interpreted and perceived (see Figure 4.17). The thalamus also limits the amount of sensory information that can reach the cerebral cortex during sleep, thus making sleep possible.

The thalamus does not act only as a relay to the cerebral cortex, however. It receives instructions back from the cortex about the type of sensory input that should be given 'free passage' and the type that should be slowed or blocked altogether. This determines how much attention one pays to any given sensory stimulus at any particular moment (Komura et al, 2001). For example, imagine yourself ravenously hungry, bringing an aromatic slice of pizza to your mouth, inhaling its aroma, and trying to manage the level of heat on your tongue by blowing on the slice. Simultaneously, someone you are romantically attracted to enters the restaurant, a siren from a fire engine or ambulance begins to blare outside, a baby starts to wail, and your favourite song begins to play on the radio. Which sights, sounds, tastes, and smells receive your attention? The cerebral cortex decides, using the thalamus as its decision tool.

The Cerebral Cortex

When 'you' think about 'your' brain (don't think about that idea for too long) your image is probably that of the most massive part—the large, wrinkly *cerebrum* that makes up the bulk of the image of the brain in the photo shown earlier in this chapter. The outer layer of the cerebrum is known as the **cerebral cortex**. Most mammals have fairly sizable cortical areas, but in humans these structures are *huge* relative to the rest of the brain. Many animals function with little more than brainstem (mid- and hindbrain) structures, and others who have fairly sizable cortical areas can still function quite well if the cortex is separated from the brainstem. However, we humans *need* our cerebral cortex. It enables us to interpret the raw information we receive from our senses, and it initiates voluntary movement. It is also the home of the higher cognitive processes—the problem-solving, planning, learning, memory, and language skills that have given us an enormous edge in the struggle for survival.

Like the spinal cord, the cerebral cortex consists of white and grey matter. However, the location of white and grey matter is exactly reversed in the cortex compared with the spinal cord—the outer layer of the cortex consists of grey matter (cell bodies, dendrites, glia), while the interior consists of white matter (myelinated axons). As with the brain as a whole, 'maps' of the cerebral cortex may emphasize one or another aspect of this part of the brain. For example, there are 50 or more identified areas of the cerebral cortex, but they can be grouped (a bit arbitrarily) into four large regions known as **lobes**. Each lobe contains neurons primarily devoted to specific sorts of tasks, but the lobes are named for the skull bones beneath which they lie. Figure 4.18 depicts the lobes of the cortex and their primary structures.

1   **Occipital lobe.** When you look out at the world, the visual information you receive through your eyes are 'translated' into images in the back of your brain, primarily in the primary visual cortex (V1) of the **occipital lobe** (see Figure 4.18). Visual information is so important for survival that well over one-third of our brain tissue is devoted to processing it. In the primary visual cortex, neural messages produced by the light receptors in our eyes arrive after being relayed by the midbrain and thalamus. The primary visual cortex analyses the information conveyed by these neural signals in very fine detail. It breaks each object down into features: elements of shape, texture, shading, angle, and so on. The specificity is so precise that individual neurons will only fire for one kind of detail—a certain angle or shading, for example.

Humans join predator birds as being perhaps the most gifted of creatures in regard to visual acuity because of our sensitivity to detail on the cortical level. For us, even a small amount of damage in visual processing areas can be highly destructive. Such damage can create devastating forms of 'selective' blindness—for example, the inability to see motion or faces (Busigny et al, 2010). Humans are very talented at working around and adapting to such obstacles, however. Neurologist Oliver Sacks (1985) described the case of 'P'—a music teacher afflicted with a degenerative disease that was destroying portions of his visual cortex. Though his deteriorating visual system caused him to misinterpret and misjudge the space around him and to fail to recognize common objects, he compensated by using sound and smell to manage his interactions with the outside world.

Analysis of visual information does not stop with the primary visual cortex. The occipital lobe also contains visual association areas which refine this analysis by comparing the visual information received with past visual information so that whatever is being viewed may be recognized. Visual information is then sent to other areas of the cerebral cortex for further processing.

An important point to remember about the flow of information to the visual cortex and visual association areas is this: as with other forebrain structures receiving

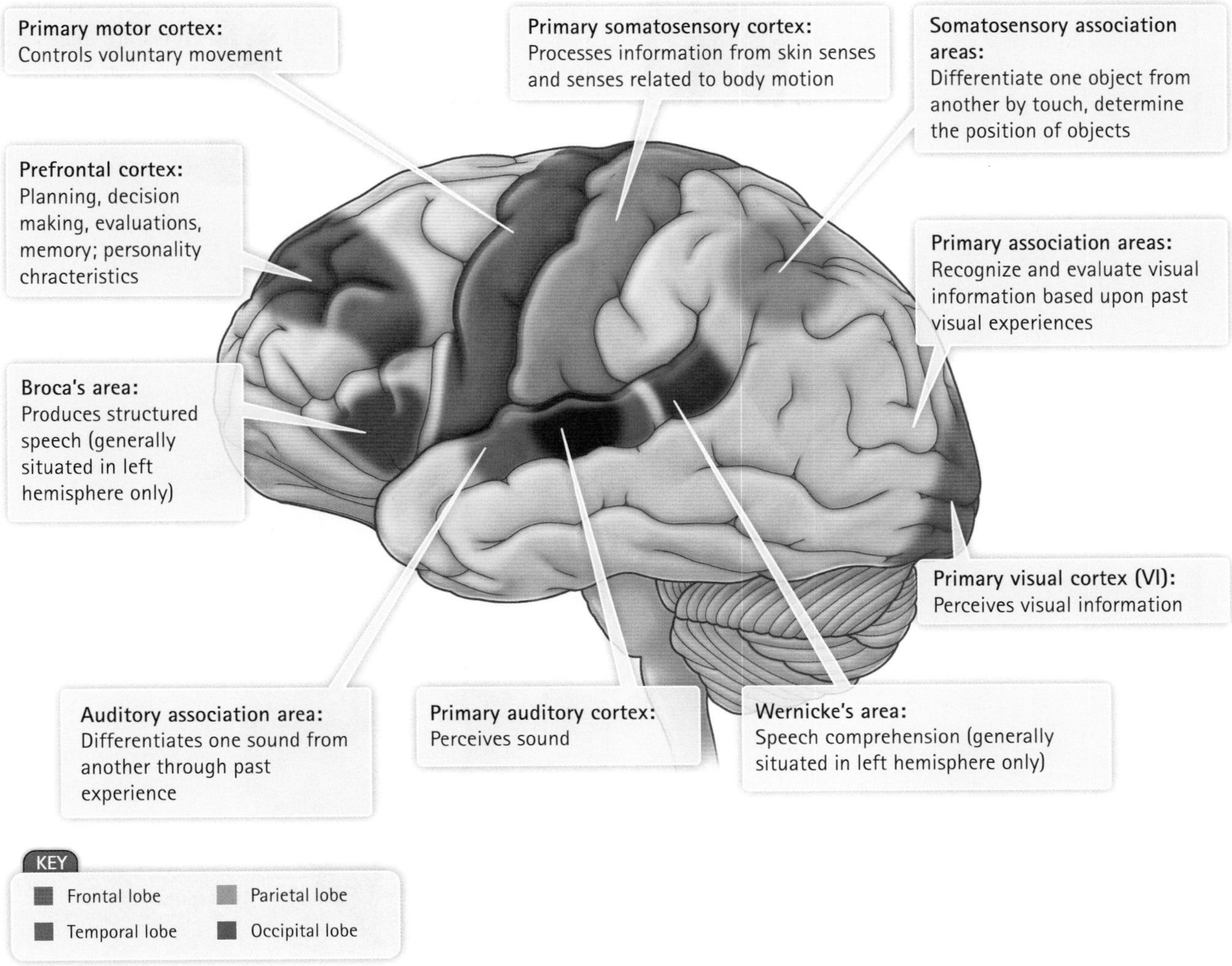

Primary motor cortex:
Controls voluntary movement

Primary somatosensory cortex:
Processes information from skin senses
and senses related to body motion

Somatosensory association
areas:
Differentiate one object from
another by touch, determine
the position of objects

Prefrontal cortex:
Planning, decision
making, evaluations,
memory; personality
chracteristics

Broca's area:
Produces structured
speech (generally
situated in left
hemisphere only)

Primary association areas:
Recognize and evaluate visual
information based upon past
visual experiences

Primary visual cortex (VI):
Perceives visual information

Auditory association area:
Differentiates one sound from
another through past
experience

Primary auditory cortex:
Perceives sound

Wernicke's area:
Speech comprehension (generally
situated in left hemisphere only)

KEY

■ Frontal lobe   ■ Parietal lobe
■ Temporal lobe   ■ Occipital lobe

FIGURE 4.18 **The four lobes of the cerebral cortex. The hemispheres of the cerebral cortex
are divided into four lobes, or regions. The principle structures of the cortex are contained
within these lobes.**

sensory signals, visual information is received by each cerebral hemisphere from
the *opposite* side—in this case, from the opposite *visual field*. However, this does *not*
mean that visual signals sent by each *eye* are conveyed to the opposite hemisphere.
Instead, *each* eye has a *right visual field* and a *left visual field*. Therefore, as depicted
in Figure 4.19, *both eyes* send signals to both hemispheres, but the signals are divided between right and left.

2 **Parietal lobe.** Immediately above and adjacent to the occipital lobe is the
parietal lobe. The primary functions of the parietal lobe are to process the
sensations of heat, cold, pain, and touch, and to inform us about the placement of our limbs and bodies in space. This is all accomplished via a strip of
tissue called the **somatosensory** cortex, which runs the whole diameter of the
parietal lobe—from the base on one side, across the top, to the bottom of the
other side (see Figure 4.18). The somatosensory cortex of each hemisphere
processes information from the opposite side of the body.

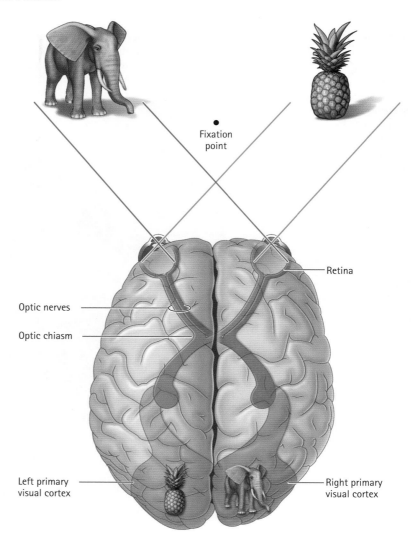

FIGURE 4.19 **Visual fields and visual processing. Each eye has a left and right visual field. Information from the right visual fields of** *both* **eyes is sent to the** *left* **visual cortex; and information from the left visual field of** *both* **eyes is sent to the** *right* **visual cortex.**

❯ KEY IDEAS the parietal lobe and somatosensory cortex
The **parietal lobe** is the lobe of the cerebral cortex containing the **somatosensory** cortex and somatosensory association areas. The somatosensory cortex processes sensory information about heat, cold, pain, and posture.

The layout of this area is a kind of topographic 'body map' known as a *homunculus.* Sensation in the face, hands, feet, limbs, and torso each corresponds to a particular area of the somatosensory cortex. In addition, each body part is allotted a certain amount of cortical tissue based not on its actual size but on the number of sensory receptors the body part contains. This number corresponds roughly to the importance of the body part in day-to-day life—and in a larger sense to survival and reproduction. Thus, the face, lips, and fingers (especially the thumb) get far more cortical tissue than the legs, torso, and arms, even though the latter are much larger in absolute size. As you might expect, the genitals get *lots* of brain tissue devoted to them—roughly equivalent to that of the lips. Figure 4.20 is an impressionistic depiction of the relative proportion of cortical tissue allotted to various body parts in the somatosensory homunculus. It also shows the placement of the somatosensory cortex within the parietal lobe.

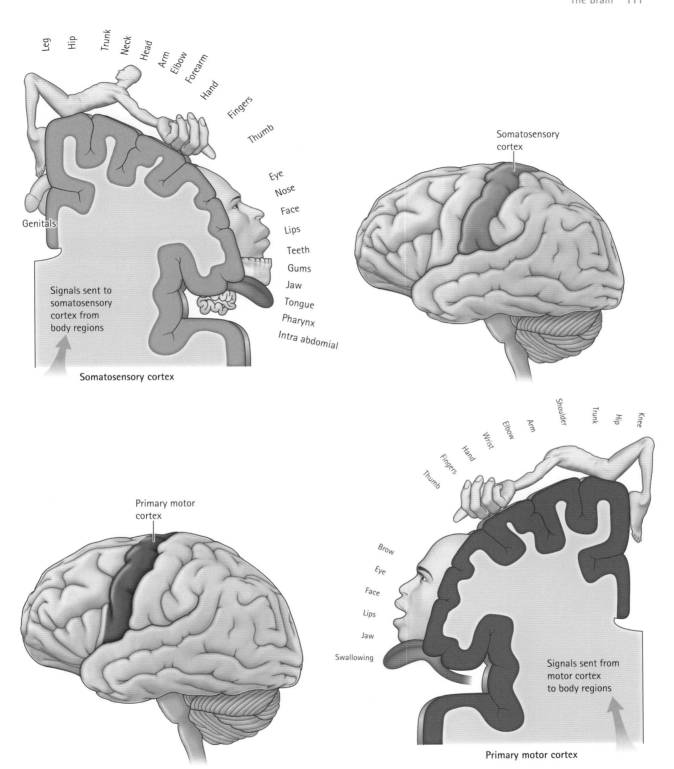

FIGURE 4.20 The somatosensory cortex homunculus and the primary motor cortex homunculus. This impressionistic depiction of the homunculus (topographical 'map') of the somatosensory cortex shows how various body parts would look if their size were proportionate to the amount of cortical tissue allotted by the somatosensory cortex. Body parts executing more complex or delicate movement receive more cortical tissue in the primary motor cortex homunculus.

Like the occipital lobe, the parietal lobe has association areas—in this case, somato-sensory association areas. These association areas allow us to determine the shape of an object or its texture through touch, as well as the placement of objects relative to one another based on memory of past experiences. Damage to these association areas from stroke or other causes can result in *neglect syndrome*, an inability to attend to events on the opposite side of the body or in an area of space opposite to the hemisphere that has sustained damage (usually the right hemisphere). A person with this condition may behave as though the opposite side of the body does not exist—shaving or applying make-up on only one side of the face, or dressing only on one side of the body, with no idea that there is anything odd about their behaviour (Coulthard, Parton, and Husain, 2007). Such people truly have 'lost' a part of their minds.

THINKING PRACTICALLY

Much of applied psychology is concerned not so much with curing psychological abnormalities but working with patients to work around their difficulties. How might you teach a patient with neglect syndrome to use a flip mirror to apply make-up and do their hair?

> **KEY IDEAS** the temporal lobe
The **temporal lobe** is the lobe of the cerebral cortex containing the auditory cortex, auditory association areas, and Wernicke's area.

3 **Temporal lobe.** The **temporal lobe**, adjacent to the occipital lobe and below and adjacent to the parietal and frontal lobes, contains the **auditory cortex**, which interprets as sound neural messages received from the ears. Like the occipital lobe, the temporal lobe has an auditory association area that allows one to recognize sounds for what they are—music, speech, natural and animal sounds, machine noise, and so forth.

Along the border of the *left* temporal lobe and the frontal lobe, sitting on the temporal lobe side, is Wernicke's area, which bears the name of its discoverer. This area has been recognized from the earliest days of brain research as being critical to speech comprehension. This area may also be involved in the comprehension and processing of music, particularly for trained musicians (Ohnishi et al, 2001).

For most people, Wernicke's areas exist in the left cerebral hemisphere only. This may be surprising given that we have characterized the left and right cerebral hemispheres as essentially symmetrical—including the same structures on each side. The placement of Wernicke's area in the left cerebral hemisphere only is an example of *hemispheric specialization*, the tendency for some differences to exist in the way the two hemispheres function.

4 **Frontal lobe.** The most noticeable difference between the brain of *Homo sapiens* and that of our close cousins in the primate family is the size of the frontal lobe. The frontal lobe makes up the bulk of the cerebral cortex and 30% of the entire human brain. The frontal lobe is so large that it is literally curled up behind our eye sockets to fit in the limited space allowed by the skull. Within the frontal lobe is the primary motor cortex, where deliberate body movements are planned and executed by sending neural commands to muscles and joints. As you might expect by now, the motor cortex in one hemisphere primarily controls movement on the opposite side of the body.

As with the somatosensory cortex, a homunculus may be mapped onto the primary motor cortex for the various parts of the body—although specific muscles do not have a specific location in the motor cortex (Graziano, Taylor, and Moore, 2002).

More motor cortex tissue is given over to muscles involved in movements that are critical to daily life, or that require greater complexity or delicacy. As with the somatosensory cortex, the extra space allotted to more important muscles is reflected in the motor cortex homunculus. For example, cortical areas devoted to the movement of fingers and hands are larger than those devoted to the movement of toes and feet. Figure 4.20 depicts the primary motor cortex homunculus.

The second major structure of the frontal lobe is the prefrontal cortex, the most complex, mysterious, and elaborate of cortical structures. Just as the frontal lobe makes up the bulk of the cerebral cortex in humans, the prefrontal cortex takes up a disproportionate area of the frontal lobe. The functions of the prefrontal cortex have long been debated. Clearly, the area receives and integrates information from all bodily systems and brain regions. It receives more neural messages than any other area of the brain—up to 23 times as many (Elston, 2003).

What, then, are the functions of the prefrontal cortex? It appears primarily to be a grand decision-maker, organizer of information, and planner of action. It allows us to weigh competing courses of action and to choose from the bewildering array of possibilities open to us in any given situation (Brass and Haggard, 2007). Consider all the information received by our sensory and motor systems—how can we sort it all out and make wise decisions about how to act? The prefrontal cortex integrates all this information and compares it against our *goals* for any given situation—pointing to appropriate behaviour to achieve those goals (Kast, 2001). Taken together, the functions of the prefrontal cortex are given the name **executive functions** because, like a business manager, they control and manage many types of cognitive and emotional activity (eg, Ramnani and Owen, 2004).

Finally, a small structure sitting at the border of the frontal and temporal lobes on the frontal lobe side is Broca's area, a kind of 'sister' structure to Wernicke's area. Just as Wernicke's area allows for speech *comprehension*, Broca's area allows a person to *produce* structured (ie, grammatical) speech.

Taken together, planning actions, monitoring emotions and behaviour, deciding between available alternatives, and communicating in the achieving of goals represent important components of our personalities—who we are as recognizable, unique individuals. In a study of 140 children with traumatic brain injury, Max et al found that almost one-fourth had experienced personality changes in the months following the injury and, further, that only injury in the prefrontal cortex was significantly associated with these personality changes (Max et al, 2005, 2006).

One of the most controversial treatments ever devised for serious psychological disorders is a *psychosurgical* procedure known as the *prefrontal lobotomy*, which involves destroying the prefrontal cortex entirely or severing it from the rest of the brain. During the early to mid-twentieth century, this procedure was used to treat a wide range of conditions including *schizophrenia* and *major depression*. It was also promoted at times as a 'cure' for those with unpopular beliefs or sexual orientations (eg, communists and gay people), or for those whose behaviour was just too disruptive to tolerate (Youngson and Schott, 1998)—although the frequency with which this occurred is probably exaggerated in some accounts (Mashour, Walker, and Martuza, 2005). Tens of thousands of people received prefrontal lobotomies at the height of its popularity, yet the procedure rarely produced the benefits purported for it. What it did often result in was a radical change in personality, characterized by apathy, memory problems, and a general lack of appropriate emotional response. For these reasons, lobotomy has fallen into disfavour over the past decades, and is rarely if ever practised in Europe or the United States.

Hemispheric Specialization

As you will recall from our brief discussion of Broca and Wernicke's areas at the border of the temporal and frontal lobes, although each of the cerebral hemispheres contains the same basic structures—*limbic system, thalamus,* and *cerebral cortex*—this symmetry is not absolute. There are some differences between the left and right hemispheres. This phenomenon has been exaggerated in the popular science literature, and there is a lot of nonsense around how some tasks are based entirely in the left or right hemispheres.

In fact, each hemisphere is specialized to respond to different kinds of information. The left hemisphere ('left brain') is 'detail oriented'. It is specialized primarily for tasks involving *sequential* (linear) processing of information. This would include spoken, written, or sign language; logical reasoning; and numerical skills. The right hemisphere ('right brain') is specialized for *integrative processing,* or 'taking in the whole picture'. Integrative processing is involved in the 'reading' of others' non-verbal emotional expressions, facial recognition, musical and other artistic experience, and visual-spatial tasks—such as imagining what an object might look like if it were rotated 90 degrees, determining the location of objects in relation to one another, or recognizing visual patterns (Gazzaniga et al, 2009). This 'division of labour' and specialization of each hemisphere of the forebrain is known as **hemispheric specialization**. Table 4.2 summarizes hemispheric specialization in the brain.

A study by Manuel Carreiras et al (2005) offers a unique demonstration of hemispheric specialization. Shepherds on the island of La Gomero in the Canary Islands use an unusual language known as *Silbo* that is composed entirely of whistling. This whistling language enables them to communicate over long distances in terrain that is difficult to traverse. Given that whistling is a musical sound, it ought to be perceived primarily by the right hemisphere. However, Silbo is also a language—the province of the left hemisphere. How then is Silbo perceived? Using brain imaging technology, Carreiras and his research team showed that *non-users* of the language perceived Silbo sounds as *music* primarily in their right hemisphere. However, those who used these sounds for communication—that is, as *language*—perceived the sounds primarily in their left hemisphere. This hemispheric 'division of labour' is further explored in Figure 4.21.

Separating the Hemispheres

Nothing demonstrates the reality of hemispheric specialization as dramatically as experiments involving epilepsy patients who have undergone a surgical procedure to sever their corpus callosum, the bundle of axons that enables communication

> **KEY IDEAS** hemispheric specialization The term **hemispheric specialization** (or **brain lateralization**) refers to the unique specializations of the two hemispheres of the cerebral cortex. The real difference between what processing takes place in the two hemispheres has been greatly exaggerated, leading to crude oversimplifications like 'you use your left brain for x function'; however, it does appear that the two hemispheres are specialized for different types of processing.

TABLE 4.2 **Differences in function of the two cerebral hemispheres (hemispheric specialization)**

Left hemisphere	Right hemisphere
Note that both hemispheres participate to some degree in all of these tasks, and that the extent of **hemispheric specialization** *varies from person to person.*	
Receives sensory signals from, and controls muscles on, right side of body	Receives sensory signals from, and controls muscles on, left side of body
Logical reasoning	Musical and artistic expression and awareness
Numerical and scientific skills	Visual-spatial skills and pattern recognition
Spoken, written, and sign-language skills	Non-verbal emotional expression recognition

Source: Adapted from Tortora and Derrickson, 2006, p 500.

Original picture

Patients with damage to the right hemisphere could remember details of the original but not the overall pattern.

Patients with damage to the left hemisphere could reproduce the global pattern but not its details.

FIGURE 4.21 Division of labour in brain hemispheres. Dean Delis and colleagues asked brain-damaged patients to view an image of the letter 'H' composed of smaller letter 'A's, as depicted here, and then redraw it. Those with damage to the right hemisphere—who therefore relied primarily on the left hemisphere for perception—typically drew randomly grouped small letter 'A's. Those with damage to the left hemisphere—who relied primarily on the right hemisphere—drew the letter 'H' with no small letter 'A's.

Source: MacNeilage, Rogers, and Vallortigara, 2009.

between the right and left hemispheres to occur. This procedure is known as **split-brain surgery**. During split-brain surgery, the patient's corpus callosum is severed. In the early procedure, known as a commissurotomy, large sections of the corpus callosum were cut, along with the thalamus. In the more modern callosotomy procedure, a smaller section of the corpus callosum is severed. This is a less drastic procedure that produces the same results, reducing epileptic seizures when medication and other techniques have failed. It works because severing the corpus callosum inhibits epileptic seizure activity from spreading from one side of the brain to the other.

Although this surgery does not result in any serious disabilities, it does have some unusual cognitive effects. Consider that in a normal brain, with the corpus callosum intact, both hemispheres are constantly interacting. They share their respective competencies to process information and produce behaviour. In a sense, 'the right hand knows what the left hand is doing' in a normal brain. In Nobel Prize-winning research conducted during the 1960s and 1970s, neuroscientist Roger Sperry (eg, Sperry, 1982) found that severing the corpus callosum resulted in the creation of two independent systems of perception, thought, memory, reasoning, and emotion—in a sense two conscious 'minds', one governed by the right and the other by the left hemisphere.

This does not mean that there is a change in the way the hemispheres of the brain control activity on the opposite side of the body. For example, signals from the left visual field of each eye continue to be processed by the brain's right opposite hemisphere, and signals from the right visual fields are processed by the left hemisphere. These neural signals are conveyed along optic nerves that are not dependent on the corpus callosum to 'cross over' (see Figure 4.19). However, in split-brain patients, the hemispheres no longer *communicate* with one another. In a sense, the right hand no longer knows what the left is doing. What happens as a result?

In Sperry's early experiments, and in those conducted subsequently by Sperry's collaborator Michael Gazzaniga (see Gazzaniga et al, 2008), split-brain patients had

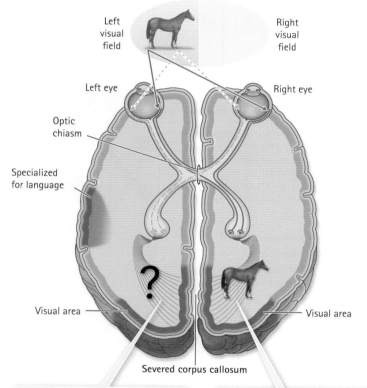
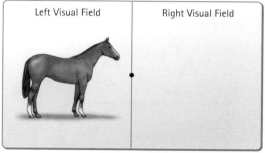

Patient can demonstrate awareness by drawing 'what goes on it' with his left hand which is controlled by his right hemisphere.

Right Hemisphere processed the image and that hemisphere has no words to describe what was seen.

FIGURE 4.22 Split-brain study #1. This split-brain patient has no awareness that a horse was flashed in his left visual field because his right hemisphere processed the image and that hemisphere has no 'words' to describe what it saw. But the patient can demonstrate awareness of the object by drawing 'what goes on it' with his left hand—the hand controlled by his right hemisphere.

Source: Gazzaniga, Ivry, and Mangun, 2002, p 414.

various sorts of images flashed either in their left or right visual fields. The results were startling. In the first study, depicted in Figure 4.22, a split-brain patient sits in front of a screen. He is asked to stare at the midpoint of the screen and is flashed an image of a horse on the left side of the screen. The image only appears in his left visual field and is therefore sent only to his *right* cerebral hemisphere for processing—the hemisphere that is inadequate for processing language. The picture is flashed too briefly for the patient to move his eyes to the left to perceive the image in his right visual field (left hemisphere).

A researcher then asks the patient to name the object he just saw, but he cannot. 'I don't know', he answers. He is then asked to name something that might 'go on top' of the object—still, he cannot do so. However, when given the opportunity to *draw* something that could 'go on it'—a right brain task—he draws a saddle with no problem. However, he uses his *left* hand to do the drawing, even though he is right-handed! Recall that motor activity of the left hand is controlled by the right hemisphere. This adds to the demonstration that only his right brain has perceived the horse (Gazzaniga et al, 2008).

In the second study, depicted in Figure 4.23, a patient is briefly shown two words in sequence: *person* and *fish*. The words appear in her left visual field (right

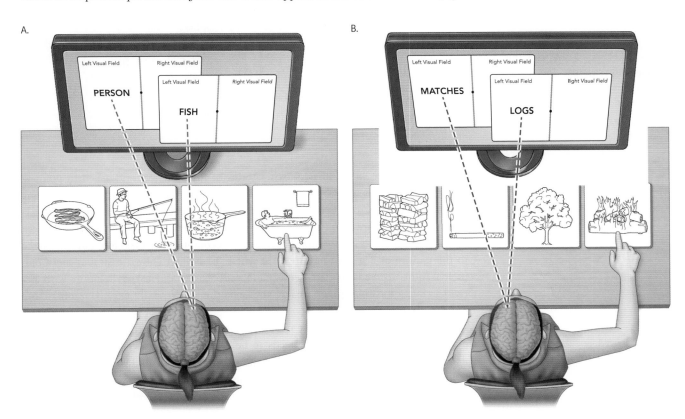

FIGURE 4.23 Split-brain study #2. When the words *person* and *fish* are presented in the left visual field to be processed in the right hemisphere, the patient cannot successfully choose an image that depicts what might happen if the words occurred together (a person fishing). This is because the left hemisphere, specialized for language, is not involved in the task of deciphering the meanings of the printed words. However, when a similar pairing of words (*matches* and *logs*) is presented in the *right* visual field—and processed in the left hemisphere—the patient finds the task extremely easy.

Source: Gazzaniga, Ivry, and Mangun, 2002, p 414.

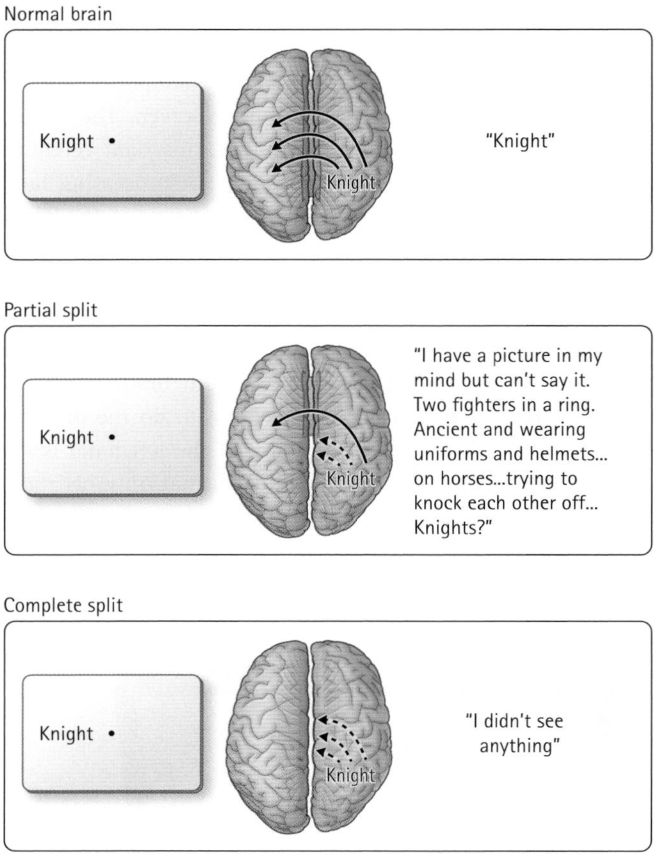

Normal brain

Knight •

"Knight"

Knight

Partial split

Knight •

Knight

"I have a picture in my mind but can't say it. Two fighters in a ring. Ancient and wearing uniforms and helmets... on horses...trying to knock each other off... Knights?"

Complete split

Knight •

Knight

"I didn't see anything"

FIGURE 4.24 When the corpus callosum is partially severed. This diagram demonstrates J.W.'s performance when his corpus callosum was partially severed and again when fully severed.

Source: Based on data from Sidtis et al, 1981, p 345.

hemisphere) only. She is then shown a series of four pictures and asked to point to the one that depicts what might happen if the two words were 'put together'. Among the images is a person fishing—that would be the correct choice. However, the patient is unable to interpret the meanings of the words *person* and *fish* in her right hemisphere in a way that would allow her to accomplish the task. She points instead to the picture of a person bathing. Yet when she is later shown a similar *word* pair in her right visual field (left-hemisphere processing) and asked to point with her right hand to the appropriate image, she finds the task trivially easy (Gazzaniga and Smylie, 1984).

Over the years surgeons have developed callosotomy procedures whereby only a portion of the corpus callosum needs to be severed to effectively treat seizures for many patients. What happens to patients' consciousness under these conditions? Some communication between the hemispheres is possible following partial severing of the corpus callosum, but it produces its own unusual effects (Sidtis et al, 1981). As depicted in Figure 4.24, for example, a patient known as J.W. is shown the word *knight* in his left visual field (right hemisphere) after only a partial severing of the corpus callosum. He struggles to find words to explain what he sees, but he does have some comprehension of the term. After time passes, he manages to think of it. But later, it was necessary to have additional surgery to sever the corpus callosum entirely. Now J.W. *claims to see nothing at all* when a word is flashed in his left visual field!

CAN LEFT AND RIGHT BRAIN DOMINANCE EXPLAIN INDIVIDUAL DIFFERENCES?

One unfortunate misinterpretation of the specialization of the cerebral hemispheres is the idea that some people are logical 'left-brained' people and others are creative 'right-brained' people—in other words, that people favour one side of their brains in their daily lives. Following Sperry's work on hemispheric specialization a *New York Times* article claimed that 'two very different persons inhabit our heads, residing in the left and right hemisphere of our brains'. From here the left-right brain theory of personality mushroomed and is now one of the most widely believed brain myths, with over 90% of UK teachers believing it to be a fact (Howard-Jones, 2014).

This idea is simply not true. Despite the reality of hemispheric specialization, for all but the simplest types of real-world tasks, both hemispheres are almost always involved (Forster and Corballis, 2000). We are dependent on both hemispheres to receive a clear and comprehensive understanding of the world.

Moreover, hemispheric specialization is not absolute. For many individuals there will be a certain amount of language processing occurring the right hemisphere and the processing of tasks typical of the right hemisphere occurring in the left. How extensively each hemisphere is used to process data for which the opposite hemisphere is specialized varies from person to person. The point is that the non-specialized hemisphere is less efficient for these tasks, and so is used to a lesser degree (Gazzaniga, Ivry, and Mangun, 2008).

WHAT'S HOT: MALE AND FEMALE BRAINS

When someone proposes that differences in some characteristic exist between men and women, many people's initial responses are suspicion and anger (Eagly, 1995; Pinker, 2002). This is justified because the history of characterizations of sex differences in psychology consists largely of pseudoscience—*sexist* ideas dressed up in scientific garb, which painted women as generally inferior to men. Such ideas have been then used to justify real discrimination against women. However, the past 30 years have seen an explosion of interest among researchers in the possible existence of real sex differences using sound scientific methods. Average sex differences have been found in a number of areas of human cognition, emotion, and motivation—although in some cases the differences are statistically significant but with tiny effect sizes. Overall these differences favour neither men nor women, but suggest that each sex has its own average strengths and weaknesses (Kimura, 2004; Halpern et al, 2007). With the advent of brain imaging technology, it is now possible to examine differences not only between male and female behaviour, but also between male and female brains.

Over the past decade, sex differences have been found within every lobe of the human forebrain—in the size and neuronal density of brain structures (see Figure 4.25), in the way structures function, in brain biochemistry, and in the way the specialization of the right and left hemispheres plays out while men and women perform various tasks (Lenroot and Giedd, 2010).

There are major limitations to the current research into sex differences in the brain. For one thing, it is not easy to find large samples of men and women who will lend you their brains

>

for detailed surgical study—even in death (and *far* fewer in life!). In the case of brain imaging studies, conducted in real time on living persons, researchers need to amass a substantial amount of funds and time, as these techniques are costly and labour-intensive. Another problem, as researcher Cordelia Fine points out, is that some people have taken fanciful leaps from real evidence of sex differences in the brain to questionable assumptions about how these brain differences might affect differences in behaviour (Fine, 2010). For example, one writer has assumed that the larger average size of men's hypothalamus (eg, Swaab et al, 2001) explains why men think about sex so much more often than women (Brizendine, 2006)! It is not that men do not think about sex more often on average than women (they do) or that the size of the hypothalamus might somehow be involved—after all, the hypothalamus is important in the regulation of sexual desire. But one cannot automatically assume that a difference in brain structure will translate into a difference in behaviour or cognition. In fact, it has already been shown that sex differences in brains often do *not* result in sex differences in behaviour (Cahill, 2006).

Take differences in the ways in which men and women use their cerebral hemispheres to perform various tasks. Hemispheric specialization—differences in the specialization of each hemisphere—exists for both sexes, as described earlier. However, the patterns are not identical for men and women. For example, although the left hemisphere is dominant for language tasks in both sexes, it appears to be more so in men than in women. When it comes to visual-spatial tasks, the opposite pattern exists: the right hemisphere is dominant for both sexes,

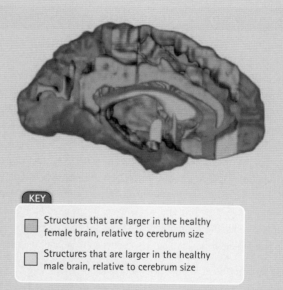

KEY

☐ Structures that are larger in the healthy female brain, relative to cerebrum size

☐ Structures that are larger in the healthy male brain, relative to cerebrum size

FIGURE 4.25 Sex differences in the size and density of brain structures. The size and neuronal density of brain structures is assumed to reflect their relative importance to the owner of the brain (Cahill, 2005).

> but more so for women than men, who experience at least some visual-spatial processing in the left hemisphere as well (Clements et al, 2006).

It is tempting to conclude that this brain sex difference is one cause (or consequence) of well-established average differences between men and women in their performances of verbal and visual-spatial tasks—differences which favour women in most verbal tasks and men in many visual-spatial tasks (Geary, 2007; Halpern et al, 2007). However, the men and women in the study who showed differences in language and visual-spatial ability were specifically selected for *equal* ability in both of these sorts of tasks—and they performed equally on their tests. Thus, brain differences may exist even where there are *no* differences in ability (see also Bell et al, 2006).

Brain Plasticity

Although neuroscientists have highlighted the specialization of brain regions and the two cerebral hemispheres, these researchers also understand that the human brain has a certain degree of **plasticity**, an important quality that enables it to adapt and be flexible in response to the environment. Brain plasticity means that the brain constantly changes throughout the life span in response to learning, practice, and sensory input (Anderson, 2011). Indeed, your brain is changing now, at the synaptic level, through your efforts to learn the information in this book.

Evidence of this type of neural plasticity comes from imaging studies of the brains of people who engage in extensive practice of some skill—professional musicians, athletes, or chess players, for example. In a series of studies of professional musicians using a brain imaging technology known as **magnetoencephalography (MEG)**, enlargements were found in specific areas of the auditory cortex devoted to processing musical tones as compared with other sounds. Not only were the enlargements correlated with the number of years the musician had been practising; they also differed in structure depending on the specific quality of sound that each instrument produced; for example, violin versus trumpet (Pantev et al, 2003).

> **KEY IDEAS** plasticity
> The term **plasticity** refers to the brain's ability to change in response to learning, practice, and sensory input; and the ability of specialized regions of the brain to adapt if necessary to perform tasks for which they are not ordinarily used; for example, following brain injury.

> **KEY IDEAS**
> magnetoencephalography (MEG) **MEG** is a brain imaging technology by which recordings are made of magnetic fields generated by neural activity.

 THINKING CRITICALLY

As discussed in Chapter 3 (see 'Correlation'), correlation is not necessarily a good indication of a particular cause-and-effect relationship. Looking at the Pantev et al (2003) study, explain why correlations between size of structures in the auditory cortex and musical experience may not mean the experience led to the increased size.

In a related study using fMRI, Fauvel et al (2014) compared young adult musicians with non-musicians and found significantly more grey matter and greater connectivity in regions of the musicians' brains associated with memory, language, and sensation-motor responses—all important in musical expertise. It is important to keep in mind that these studies were correlational in nature and may not indicate a simple cause-and-effect relationship.

However, Hyde et al monitored brain structure and behavioural changes in children with no previous musical training who had been randomly assigned either to study a keyboard instrument seriously for 15 months in weekly lessons, or simply to sit in groups on a weekly basis to sing and play bells and drums over that period of time (Hyde et al, 2009). Using MRI brain imaging technology, Hyde and her colleagues noted structural brain changes in 'musically relevant' areas of the brain only in the children who had engaged in serious musical training. These structural changes were correlated with changes in the children's motor skills and auditory experience.

There is another way in which the brain is plastic. Neural tissue generally 'assigned' to specific types of processing tasks may sometimes be used for other tasks if the need arises. The fact that some split-brain patients learn over time to produce speech from their right hemisphere is an excellent example of this type of plasticity (Gazzaniga et al, 2008). Another example of this type of plasticity is the neural changes that occur in the brains of blind people learning Braille. Areas of the visual cortex—that should not respond to tactile sensory information—are 'co-opted' in the service of reading with the fingers, and the amount of tissue of the somatosensory cortex given over to the reading fingers of Braille readers is much larger than in other individuals. In a certain respect, blind people actually do have 'eyes in their fingers' when reading Braille (Melzer and Ebner, 2008).

Danelli et al (2013) describe a particularly dramatic case of plasticity. EB had almost the entire left half of his brain removed at the age of two-and-a-half because of a very large tumour. Initially he lost all language ability but following intensive rehab this was reported to have returned to normal by the age of 5. Recent follow-up of EB at age 17 showed that he had almost normal vocabulary and grammar. However, he showed some dyslexic symptoms and poor naming of objects from pictures. This case suggests that the right half of EB's brain was able to take over most but not all the language functions normally performed by the left half.

THINKING PRACTICALLY

The idea of a 'zombie virus' has become such a feature of popular culture that the UK government now has a response plan for a zombie apocalypse. Psychiatrist Steven Schlozman has (perhaps slightly tongue-in-cheek) speculated about what areas of the brain a 'zombie virus' would have to target in order to produce zombie-like symptoms.

Task

Match the following brain structures: cerebellum, prefrontal cortex, amygdala, mirror neuron system, and hypothalamus to the following zombie symptoms: hunger, reduced intelligence, rage, lack of empathy, shambling walk.

THE ENDOCRINE SYSTEM

The nervous system does not do its vital work alone. There is a second communication system, the **endocrine system**, which partially overlaps the nervous system but is considered separate. The endocrine system is composed of bodily organs known as **glands** and the chemicals they synthesize and release into the bloodstream and tissues are termed **hormones**. Figure 4.26 shows the major glands of the endocrine system, and Table 4.3 summarizes the activity of the hormones they release.

The Relationship between the Nervous and Endocrine Systems

In a physical sense the nervous and endocrine systems overlap. Consider the **pineal** and **pituitary glands**. These glands are central 'players' in the endocrine system. The pineal gland secretes *melatonin*, a hormone critical to establishing the sleep-wake cycle. The pituitary secretes a variety of hormones and triggers other glands to secrete their hormones—helping to regulate blood pressure; body growth; aspects of pregnancy, childbirth, and lactation; and the functioning of sex and reproductive organs. Yet despite their importance in the *endocrine*

❯ **KEY IDEAS** the endocrine system The endocrine system is the collective term for the system of glands and the hormones they produce. A **gland** is a bodily organ that synthesizes and/or releases hormones. A **hormone** is a chemical synthesized and/or released by a gland.

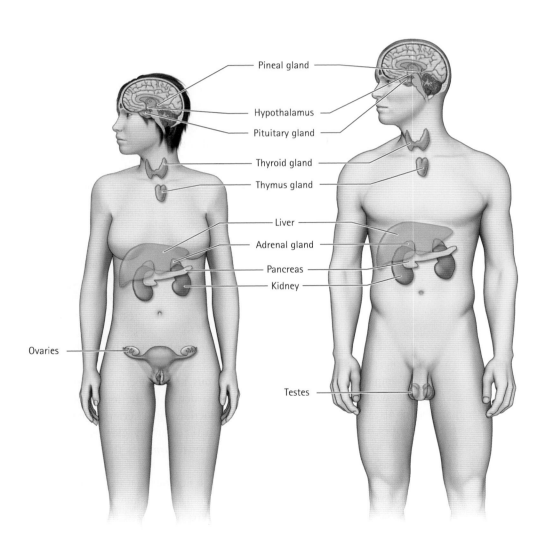

FIGURE 4.26 Major glands of the human endocrine system. The endocrine system is composed of glands and the hormones they produce.

TABLE 4.3 **Glands at a glance**

This table is a partial list of some of the major glands and the hormones they release.

Gland	Hormones	Action
Hypothalamus	Releasing hormones, including TSH-releasing hormone	Regulates hormone synthesis and release in the pituitary gland
Pituitary	Thyroid-stimulating hormone (TSH)	Stimulates thyroid
	Luteinizing hormone Follicle-stimulating hormone Prolactin	Regulates female reproductive cycle and milk production
	Growth hormone	Regulates body growth
	Oxytocin	Facilitates birth, breastfeeding, and mother-infant bonding; associated with sexual activity, possibly with romantic bonding
	Vasopressin	Helps regulate blood pressure
	ACTH	Increases production of steroids
Pineal	Melatonin	Regulates sleep-wake cycle
Thyroid	Thyroxine Triiodothyronine	Regulates metabolism and growth
Adrenal glands	Cortisol Epinephrine Norepinephrine	'Stress hormones'—increase blood pressure and blood sugar; work with parasympathetic nervous system to respond to threat or extreme stress
Testes	Androgens (eg, testosterone)	Regulate production of sperm and male sexual characteristics; associated with sexual desire in both sexes; affect immune function
Ovaries	Progesterone Oestrogens	Regulate female sexual characteristics and reproductive cycle, including pregnancy
Pancreas	Insulin Glucagon	Regulate blood sugar levels, fat storage, and conversion of fat to blood sugar

❯ **KEY IDEAS** the pineal and pituitary glands The **pineal gland**, situated in the brain, releases the hormone *melatonin*, important in regulating the sleep/wake cycle. The **pituitary gland** is also situated in the brain and secretes a variety of hormones and triggers other glands to secrete their hormones. This helps regulate blood pressure; body growth; aspects of pregnancy, childbirth and lactation; and the functioning of sex and reproductive organs.

system, as you can see in Figure 4.27, they are situated within the brain—the centre of the *nervous* system.

Another example of the overlap of the nervous and endocrine systems is the hypothalamus, which, if you recall, is a limbic structure of the forebrain. But the hypothalamus also functions as an important endocrine organ because it synthesizes certain hormones, which are then transmitted to the pituitary gland and released from there. The hypothalamus also secretes *releasing hormones* that stimulate the pituitary to release its own hormones.

A final example of the interconnectedness of the nervous and endocrine systems is the fact that the molecules that make up hormones also may operate as neurotransmitters (eg, adrenaline). If the molecules are synthesized by neurons, they will act as neurotransmitters, exerting their effects directly at specific sites, generally at brain synapses. If the molecules are synthesized by glands, they will function as hormones, and exert their effects less directly at multiple sites in the bloodstream and various body tissues.

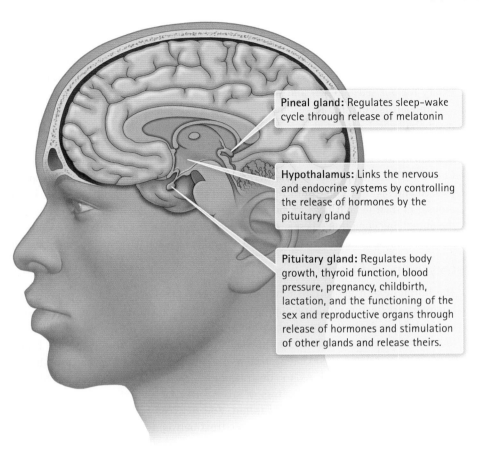

Pineal gland: Regulates sleep-wake cycle through release of melatonin

Hypothalamus: Links the nervous and endocrine systems by controlling the release of hormones by the pituitary gland

Pituitary gland: Regulates body growth, thyroid function, blood pressure, pregnancy, childbirth, lactation, and the functioning of the sex and reproductive organs through release of hormones and stimulation of other glands and release theirs.

FIGURE 4.27 The nervous and endocrine systems. Although the nervous and endocrine systems are distinct, they also overlap. The hypothalamus and the pituitary and pineal glands are all situated within the brain, but all are critical to the functioning of the endocrine system.

BRAIN FUNCTION AND HUMAN EXPERIENCE

Much of what we have discussed in this chapter is a necessary foundation for studying biological psychology; however, it is essentially biology rather than psychology. The really fascinating subject of biopsychology is concerned with the ways in which neural structure and function can be linked to psychological functioning. Some of the most exciting research in neuroscience and biopsychology has involved explaining significant human experiences with reference to brain function. There are many such experiences but we have tried to pick out some particularly interesting ones here.

Cortical Arousal and the Sense of Self

The sense of self is such a subjective experience that it defies writing about. Put simply, we just know that we are alive and conscious and that we inhabit a living body. However, sufferers of Cotard syndrome do not share this awareness. First described by Cotard (1880) this syndrome involves loss of normal sense of self so that the patient may believe they are dead or in a zombie-like undead state. Alternatively sufferers may believe that their brain or part of their body is dead. Some but not all cases are associated with **depression** or schizophrenia.

Charland-Verville et al (2013) cast light on the possible neurological basis of Cotard's when they scanned the brain of a patient who believed their brain was dead. The patient showed very low arousal across parts of the frontal and temporal lobes, a system sometimes called the default network, because it appears to represent the brain's baseline state before it engages on a mental activity (Kringlebach et al, 2009). It is believed that a certain level of arousal in these areas of the brain is necessary for our sense of self and well-being.

Although fascinating, this study is as useful as an illustration of the limitations of psychobiological case studies as it is for telling us about Cotard syndrome (Jarrett, 2013). Like all case studies this is a one-off. It is not the same as comparing cortical arousal in 100 Cotard's patients with that in 100 matched patients without signs of Cotard's. This one patient may not be typical of Cotard's patients. They were also depressed and taking a range of medication when scanned; the distinctive low patterns of arousal in their default network may have been caused by the medication rather than the underlying condition. These problems of small sample size and multiple possible influences on results have been affected the reliability of much psychobiological research.

Oxytocin and Love

The hormone and neurotransmitter oxytocin is synthesized by the hypothalamus, but released by the pituitary gland. It has long been known that as a hormone, oxytocin stimulates the muscle contractions of the uterus during labour to facilitate birth, and causes milk to be expelled from the breast during lactation. It also appears to be related to sexual arousal and is released during orgasm in both men and women (Hiller, 2005). As a neurotransmitter, oxytocin—in addition to reducing blood pressure and other indicators of stress—may be related to the formation of strong bonds between mother and infant, and between romantic partners as well (Feldman et al, 2007). Oxytocin facilitates trust between people and enhances empathic understanding—putting oneself in another person's place (Bartz et al, 2010).

Some researchers have suggested that oxytocin may turn out to be one of the most important chemical components of love itself, if not the most important (Kosfeld et al, 2005). In one group of studies of women, researchers found that those women who were in romantic relationships had greater increases in circulating oxytocin when reliving memories of love, and oxytocin levels decreased in general among the women when they relived memories of loss of a loved one (Turner et al, 2002). More recent research has shown that the release of oxytocin is associated with the display of specific non-verbal behaviours associated with feelings of closeness towards one's romantic partner—natural smiling towards the partner, leaning towards him or her, frequent head nodding while the other speaks, and a number of specific hand and arm gestures associated with feelings of wanting to be with another (Gonzaga et al, 2006).

Research suggesting a possible role for oxytocin in the bonds of romantic love has led some researchers to wonder if other sorts of bonding were also facilitated by the hormone—for example, the bond that forms between human beings and their pets. Indeed, preliminary research suggests that oxytocin levels may increase in women, but not men, during affectionate interactions with their dogs (S.C. Miller et al, 2009). Intriguingly, it seems that oxytocin levels may also rise in the pet owners' *dogs* as well (Handlin et al, 2011).

Mirror Neurons and Empathy

Empathy is the ability to perceive intentions and emotional states in others. Without empathy we would struggle to form meaningful relationships with other individuals and to live together as a social species. It appears that our ability to intuitively understand what those around us are feeling depends on a particular type of brain cell, called **mirror neurons**. Pellegrino et al (1992) first observed unusual activity in certain motor neurons in monkey brains. These cells activated both in response to the monkey grasping an object and when the monkey observed another monkey performing the same action. In other words the monkey's neurons *mirrored* the other monkey's actions.

Later studies showed that mirror neurons are present in the brains of several species, including humans, and that they only activate in response to observation of their own species (Buccino et al, 2004). Mirror neurons appear to be very important in the imitation of behaviour, but more interesting to many psychologists is the possibility that they allow us to empathize with others. Mirror neurons may account for empathy because they appear to code not so much for actions but for the intentions behind those actions (Gallese, 2001). When we observe the behaviour of others our mirror neuron system tells us *why* they are behaving that way. This process is non-verbal and automatic; therefore, when we see someone crying or smiling we intuitively understand their emotional state. We explore the roles of mirror neurons further in Chapter 11.

Near-Death Experiences

Around 3% of Americans report having had a 'near-death experience' (NDE) in which they have felt their consciousness leave their body (Mobbs and Watt, 2011). This rises to 10% in heart attack patients (Parnia and Fenwick, 2002). Often this is accompanied by euphoria and the sensation of seeing a bright light and/or dead relatives. Although biopsychology cannot prove that there is never a supernatural element to such experiences we can definitely say that they *can* be explained simply by what we know about the brain.

First let's take the sense of leaving the body—the 'out of body' (OOB) experience as it is commonly called. Blanke and Azar (2004) demonstrated that the OOBs can be produced artificially by electrical stimulation of the right brain just where the temporal and parietal lobes meet. Whilst we don't know exactly how OOBs come about outside the laboratory, this study does suggest that they are likely to be the result of something going awry in that region of the brain.

Other elements of NDE can also be explained with reference to the brain. The 'bright light' could simply be the brain's attempt to make sense of the tunnel vision that can result from both fear and oxygen starvation—both likely in a near-death situation. Nelson et al (2006) point out that REM intrusion—dream-like hallucinations in non-sleep states—are fairly common and could explain the visual elements of NDEs. Nelson et al found support for this idea when they found significantly greater frequency of REM intrusion in participants reporting NDEs with that in a control group. This explanation could account for both the 'bright light' phenomenon and visions of dead relatives.

THINKING CREATIVELY

The scientific study of NDEs raises formidable methodological challenges, especially as no reliable physiological correlates of NDEs have been found (Charland-Verville et al, 2014). Your task is to come up with a research question that could be answered by a scientific study, to operationalize your variable(s) and to propose a testable hypothesis.

NEUROSCIENCE AND PSYCHOLOGY

We have referred repeatedly during this chapter to the work of neuroscientists. Psychologists and others working in related fields have always been interested in understanding the workings of the brain. Until now, however, we have been severely limited in our ability to make sense of the brain and nervous system. In the last decade technological development has begun to change this, and there has been a period of massive research activity and rapid publication of findings. Neuroscience has grown into a major academic discipline in its own right, and it has also informed many issues in psychology.

The Relationship between Psychology and Neuroscience

It's worth saying at this point what neuroscience—or brain science as it is also called—is and is not. Neuroscience is the multidisciplinary science of the brain and nervous system. It is concerned with brain structure and function in all senses. Neuroscientists are interested in electrical and chemical activity in the brain for their own sake as much as for their implications for psychological functioning. Physics and biochemistry are just as important as foundations of neuroscience as psychology. This is important because we need to be clear that, although there is an overlap between the subject matter of biopsychology and neuroscience, the latter is a subject in its own right. It is NOT—as you might come to believe from reading some popular science literature—a new and better psychology.

Feelings about neuroscience can run quite high amongst psychologists—we are going to try to remain cautiously positive here! On the one hand, neuroscience has the potential to answer some of our most important questions. There is no denying that this is hugely exciting, and, by and large, more biologically minded psychologists have seen the growth of neuroscience as a bit of a renaissance. On the other hand some psychologists question the validity of many of the findings reported by neuroscientists and see neuroscience—at least in its current state of development—as overhyped. There is also a vague anxiety amongst some psychologists that the rapid growth of neuroscience threatens the future of psychology, potentially taking over psychology itself and eclipsing other approaches, *and* taking over *from* psychology as the 'owners' of the mind.

Behavioural and Cognitive Neuroscience

Neuroscientists study all aspects of the nervous system, and some aspects of neuroscience dovetail more closely with the subject matter of psychology than others. **Behavioural neuroscience** and **cognitive neuroscience** occupy very much the same space as true biopsychology. Behavioural neuroscientists study the anatomy, physiology, and molecular structure of the entire nervous system and apply knowledge of the nervous system to virtually any question concerning animal (including human) behaviour. These researchers conduct experimental studies, frequently using non-human animals, to shed light on the neural bases of whatever behaviour is of interest. A summary of major discoveries in cognitive and behavioural neuroscience is shown in Table 4.4.

Cognitive neuroscience earned its name in the back seat of a New York City taxi in the late 1970s. Cognitive psychologist George Miller and neuroscientist Michael Gazzaniga (whose split-brain research was described earlier in the chapter) had just emerged from a conference of scientists who were struggling to decode the ways in which the *brain* creates *mind* (Gazzaniga, Ivry, and Mangun, 2002). Gazzaniga and Miller wished to bring *cognition*—thought, memory, language, and other information-processing aspects of mental life—more clearly to the forefront of neuroscientific research. To do so, they concluded that they needed to focus on the brain itself, rather than the nervous system in its entirety. Although the focus of cognitive neuroscientists is on cognition, over the years many have added *emotion* as an important component of their field of study. Cognitive processes studied by cognitive neuroscientists include language, memory, mental imagery, and problem-solving. While cognitive neuroscientists may use non-human animals in their research, they are more likely than behavioural neuroscientists to use human subjects and include methodologies such as psychological testing and brain imaging.

The Basic Technology of Neuroscience

Neuroscience and biopsychology are in the ascendant in the twenty-first century because we finally have the technology to study the function as well as the structure of the nervous system.

Magnetic resonance imaging (MRI) works because the body consists largely of water. The MRI technique uses radio waves and protons of hydrogen atoms to obtain high-resolution photo images of the brain. The patient or research participant lies motionless within a scanner that produces a benign magnetic field. A pulse of radio waves is generated, and these momentarily alter the natural alignment of protons in the body part that is being examined. As the pulse of radio waves recedes and the protons return to their original positions, the MRI instrument receives the energy that was generated by the realignment activity of the protons. This energy results in a photo image that clearly shows grey matter, white matter, and cerebrospinal fluid (see Figure 4.28C). The procedure is safe and non-invasive, although the pulsing radio waves produce rather loud sounds (patients are often advised to wear earplugs or noise-reducing headphones during the procedure).

What do MRI images reveal? The principle use of MRI is by clinical neuroscientists to pinpoint the location of possible brain damage. However, the technology can be used in a slightly different way by cognitive neuroscientists to track blood flow to various portions of the brain while the research participant engages in various tasks and activities. This procedure results in a series of images that reveal ongoing changes in the specific portions of the brain as the person engages in the task. When the technology is used in this manner, it is called **functional magnetic resonance imaging** or **fMRI** (see Figure 4.28D).

> ❯ **KEY IDEAS** behavioural and cognitive neuroscience
> **Behavioural neuroscience** is the branch of neuroscience that studies the neural basis of behaviour. Behavioural neuroscientists study the entire nervous system and may use non-human as well as human animals for study. **Cognitive neuroscience** deals with the relationship between the nervous system and cognition and emotion.

> ❯ **KEY IDEAS** magnetic resonance imaging (MRI) MRI is a scanning technique involving creating a magnetic field around the body and using radio waves to generate an image; for example, of the brain. Traditional MRI gives us an idea of the brain's *structure*. **Functional magnetic resonance imaging (fMRI)** is the use of MRI whereby continuous images of the brain are generated while a research participant engages in specific tasks. This allows us to see changes in the brain linked to its *function*.

TABLE 4.4 Neuroscience in the twentieth century: a brief sampling

Moruzzi and Magoun (1949)	These researchers demonstrated that the reticular formation of the brainstem was essential to consciousness.
Scoville and Milner (1957)	Through their study of 'Patient H.M.', Scoville and Milner showed that damage to the hippocampus could impair or destroy the ability to form new memories—helping to establish that memory has a neural basis (see 'The limbic system' earlier in this chapter).
Penfield and Perot (1963)	By electrically stimulating various cortical regions of the brains of research participants—and noting their reactions—these researchers helped 'map' locations of the brain that correspond to specific body parts.
Hounsfield (1972)	In 1972, Godfrey Hounsfield developed *computerized tomography* (CT or 'CAT scan'), the forerunner of contemporary brain imaging technologies such as MRI and PET.
Sapolsky (1996)	In 1996, Robert Sapolsky finally demonstrated scientifically what many had suspected was true about the damaging effects of chronic stress on the brain.

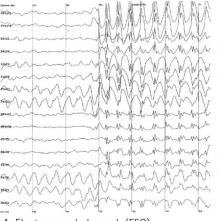

A. Electroencephalograph (EEG)

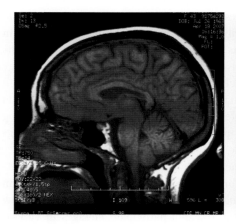

C. Magnetic Resonance Imaging
    (MRI)

B. Positron Emission Tomography (PET)

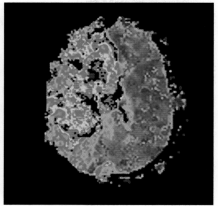

D. functional Magnetic Resonance
    Imaging (fMRI)

FIGURE 4.28 Imaging the brain. **(A) Electroencephalography (EEG)**, the oldest (and least precise) of available techniques, allows the researcher to note the general area of the brain activated during various tasks, and allows for precise measurement of the *timing* of activation. EEG is particularly useful for predicting and identifying the location of seizures (Schad et al, 2008). **(B) Positron emission tomography (PET)** depicts the brain's metabolic activity as a three-dimensional map. First, a benign radioactive substance is injected into the bloodstream of the patient or research subject, who then lies within a scanner that is highly sensitive to radiation. This produces the *tomographic*, or sectioned, map of the brain. As blood flows to various sites in the brain during the performing of a mental task, more radiation is emitted at these sites. The amount of radioactivity produced at a particular site corresponds to the activity of neurons at that site. PET technology has assisted clinical neuroscientists to describe the way the brain functions during clinical depression, anxiety, and post-traumatic stress disorder (eg, Rauch, Shin, and Wright, 2003) and is particularly good at identifying brain tumours. **(C) Magnetic resonance imaging. (D) Functional magnetic resonance imaging.**

An example of the use of fMRI was to test the hypothesis that the neural basis of *social* and *emotional* 'pain'—as might be experienced when one is excluded from a social group—is similar to the neural basis for *physical* pain (Eisenberger, Lieberman, and Williams, 2003). Researchers set up a situation in which college students were

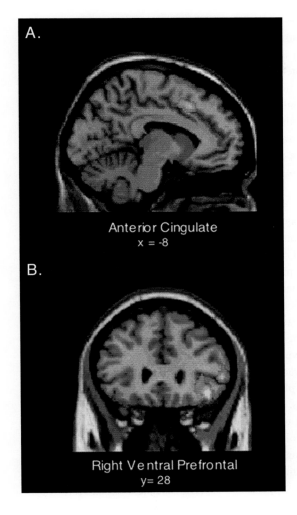

Anterior Cingulate
x = -8

Right Ventral Prefrontal
y= 28

FIGURE 4.29 Rejection really does hurt. When research participants in the fMRI study by Naomi Eisenberger and her colleagues (2003) experienced rejection in a social context, areas of the anterior cingulated cortex (ACC) ordinarily associated with the experience of physical pain (particularly emotional aspects of the experience of physical pain) were activated (image A). Following activation of the ACC, areas of the right ventral prefrontal cortex (RVPFC) were also activated (image B). These areas are associated with *inhibition* of the experience of pain and its emotionally distressing aspects. The RVPFC probably exerts this relieving effect by disrupting ACC activity.

ultimately excluded from a computerized virtual ball-tossing game. They found that during the experience of exclusion, there was activation of the *anterior cingulate cortex* (ACC), an area of the forebrain which surrounds the corpus callosum and is also activated in response to physical pain (or when a mother hears her baby cry; Eisenberger et al, 2003; see Figure 4.29). Amazingly, in a more recent study, the painkiller paracetamol reduced neural responses in brain regions associated with social rejection—and study participants taking paracetamol also reported reduced hurt feelings as compared with those taking placebos (DeWall et al, 2010)!

Challenges to the Rise of Neuroscience

There is no doubt that we have learned a lot about the brain in the last decade. Nor is there any real question that neuroscientists and biopsychologists have come up with some fascinating ideas to explain links between the brain and psychological functioning. However, brain science has been challenged from a number of angles.

Philosophical issues

One issue faced by proponents of brain science is that an emphasis on the brain is unpalatable to many because it seems to imply a decline in the importance of free will and morality. We struggle with the idea that our decisions and feelings are a product of the biological processes of our brain for two interrelated reasons. First, we like to think we have free will and dislike the idea that our decisions are determined. Second, if free will is in fact an illusion what does this say about our ideas about morality? Our ability to live together as a social species depends on the idea that we have responsibility for our actions. Yet the concept of responsibility is (arguably) redundant once we accept that individual decisions are biologically determined, and that our sense of consciously making them is something of an illusion. Pizarro (2011) argues that we are so firmly hardwired to make moral decisions and judgements that we are capable of acknowledging a degree of biological determinism and yet at the same time being 'stubbornly moralistic' in order to function socially.

Hype and scientism

Brain science is often described as 'overhyped'. By this commentators mean that the credibility and importance of findings and conclusions reported in brain science literature have been exaggerated. Not everyone is impressed with fMRI technology. Some argue that these colourful pictures greatly overstate the degree to which specific areas of the brain control specific aspects of behaviour and internal experience (Puldrack, 2010), while others merely point out that, despite the enormous investment of money and time in fMRI studies, there has been little in the way of resulting advancement in psychological theory (Coltheart, 2013).

This backlash has spawned a whole industry of neuroscience-knocking, with *Neuroskeptic*, *Neurocritic*, and *Neurobollocks* emerging as highly influential blogs.

But why the hype in the first place? One reason may be the scientific credibility the public attach to the brain as opposed to mind or behaviour. Krull and Silvera (2013) surveyed college students on their perceptions of the scientific status of the brain and other aspects of psychology. On a nine-point scale of 'scientificness' participants gave the brain an average rating of 7.86 as opposed to 5.06 for attitudes. Similarly, brain scanning techniques were rated as more scientific than questionnaires. Topics and methods that *appear* to be scientific are said to be guilty of **scientism**. The scientistic nature of the brain and the study of it seem to lend brain science a halo of credibility that may not always be justified.

Methodological issues and validity

The conclusions of any scientific research are only as valid as the research itself. Brain science is associated with some particular validity issues. Studying the brain is expensive, and this means that findings based on small sample sizes are sometimes published on the understanding that it would simply not be practical to work with larger groups. Small samples, however, do cause validity problems. An example of this comes from Redcay and Courchesne (2005) in their discussion of the possible relationship between brain size and autism. They concluded that it was very difficult to reach any kind of conclusions about this relationship because of the small sample size of much of the published research.

A related issue in brain science research crops up because of the large volume of data (in the form of three-dimensional units called voxels) from small numbers of participants input from scans to statistical analysis. This leads to a high probability of false positive results, where findings look like a significant finding, but are actually due to chance. Bennett et al (2010) demonstrated the strength of this effect by scanning the brain of a dead (in fact frozen) salmon while showing it images of people in a range of inclusive

> **KEY IDEAS** scientism
Scientism refers to the extent to which a topic conforms to stereotypes of science. Because it uses high-tech tools and deals with biology—a classic 'hard' science—brain science is stereotypically scientific and so may be judged as more scientific than it really is.

and exclusive social situations. Bizarrely the dead salmon's brain appeared to respond differently to these categories of image. As the authors put it: 'Either we have stumbled on to a rather amazing discovery in terms of post-mortem ichthyological cognition, or there is something a bit off with regard to our uncorrected statistical approach' (2010: 3). What Bennett and his colleagues have demonstrated here is the poor validity of the approach used in much published brain science research to analysing data.

The brain is not the mind

Okay, so we can set aside the fact that we might not be comfortable philosophically with the moral implications of some brain science, and just because some findings have been overhyped and others subjected to dodgy statistical analysis that doesn't mean we should throw out the baby with the bathwater. But perhaps the trickiest issue with brain science is a different one; the brain is not the same as the mind. As psychologists we are primarily concerned with the mind; the brain is (largely) interesting only in so far as it tells us about the mind.

Well, are mind and brain really so different? This is not a new debate, and we're not going to resolve it here, just remind you of it (we discussed this more fully at the start of this chapter). Briefly, the dualist position (eg, Popper and Eccles, 1977) holds that the mind is a separate entity from the brain. The alternative materialist view (Sperry, 1980) sees mind and brain as very closely linked, even synonymous. Modern research shows that altering thinking by psychological therapy alters the functioning of the brain, supporting the monist position. However, we are not yet at the point where we can understand all mental activity in terms of the brain and until that point is reached many psychologists make a clear distinction between mind and brain.

The real problem may be that while psychological events are clearly connected to physical events in the brain, they are not the *same* as physical events in the brain. Many researchers are coming to the conclusion that understanding a brain event by itself will not (and perhaps cannot) allow us to fully understand a psychological event (Gazzaniga, 2010; G.A. Miller, 2010).

READ THIS

Through most of this book we have provided a number of *Read this* features in each chapter. This chapter is an exception because this whole chapter explores brain basics so we're recommending some general reading for the whole chapter. You might like to start with these:

Purves, D., Augustine, G., Fitzpatrick, D., Hall, W., La Mantia, A., White, L., Mooney, R., and Platt, M. (2018). *Neuroscience*. Oxford: Oxford University Press.

Chandler, C. (2015). *Psychobiology*. Chichester: Wiley.

For something that explores the philosophy of mind but won't make your head hurt (too much), try this:

Gabriel, M. (2017). *I am Not a Brain: Philosophy of Mind for the 21st Century*. Chichester: Wiley.

For explorations of some myths and misunderstandings about the brain and neuroscience you might like:

Howard-Jones, P.A. (2014). Neuroscience and education: Myths and messages. *Nature Reviews Neuroscience*, **15**, 817.

Jarrett, C. (2015). *Great Myths of the Brain*. Chichester: Wiley.

IN REVIEW

WHERE IS THE MIND?

- The mind remains a somewhat mysterious entity. *Materialism* defines the mind as consisting of physical matter, whereas *dualism* maintains that it consists of something else. Brain imaging and related techniques raise intriguing questions about how the mind can function in the absence of normal brain activity or conscious awareness.

HOW IS THE NERVOUS SYSTEM BUILT?

- The human nervous system is composed of specialized cells—principally, neurons—which allow communication to take place among the various structures of the body. The nervous system also includes glia—cells that assist neurons in their work. Most neurons are composed of dendrites, cell body, axon, and terminal.

- Neurotransmitters such as serotonin, dopamine, and GABA affect many aspects of mental life. Some drugs (agonists) may increase the effects of neurotransmitters, while others (antagonists) may decrease neurotransmitter effects.

HOW IS THE NERVOUS SYSTEM ORGANIZED?

- The nervous system is organized into the central nervous system, consisting of the brain and spinal cord; and the peripheral nervous system.

- The spinal cord is a bundle of nerve tracts organized into segments that act as a communication pathway between the brain and the rest of the body. The spinal cord is composed of grey matter and white matter. The spinal cord also controls spinal reflexes and is responsible for central pattern generators.

- The peripheral nervous system, which is organized into somatic and autonomic nervous systems, makes communication possible between brain and body. The autonomic nervous system is subdivided in turn into the sympathetic and parasympathetic nervous systems.

HOW IS THE BRAIN ORGANIZED?

- The brain is a network of integrated clusters of neurons that form neural circuits. On a basic level, the brain can be divided into three parts: hindbrain, midbrain, and forebrain. The hindbrain consists of the cerebellum, medulla, pons, and reticular formation. The midbrain includes the inferior and superior colliculi.

- The forebrain is the seat of thought, emotion, personality, memory, intelligence, language, and consciousness. The forebrain is divided into two nearly symmetrical cerebral hemispheres, connected by a bundle of over 200 million axons known as the corpus callosum. The major structures of each cerebral hemisphere of the forebrain are the limbic system, the thalamus, and the cerebral cortex. The limbic system is composed of the hypothalamus, the hippocampus, the amygdalae, and clusters of nerves called nuclei—including the basal ganglia and nucleus accumbens. The cerebral cortex is the centre of higher cognitive processes, such as problem-solving, learning, memory, and language.

The areas of the cerebral cortex can be grouped into four large regions: the occipital lobe, parietal lobe, temporal lobe, and frontal lobe. The frontal lobe includes the prefrontal cortex, which appears to receive and integrate information from all bodily systems and brain regions to assist in decision-making, organizing information, and planning actions.

Experiments with patients who have undergone split-brain surgery have shown that each cerebral hemisphere is specialized to a certain extent; however, the hemispheres are also at least to some degree plastic.

WHAT IS THE ENDOCRINE SYSTEM?

The endocrine system consists of glands and the hormones they synthesize. The endocrine system partially overlaps the nervous system.

WHAT IS NEUROSCIENCE?

Neuroscience is the multidisciplinary study of the central and peripheral nervous systems. Neuroscience can be divided into sub-disciplines, including behavioural neuroscience and cognitive neuroscience. Neuroscience has advanced dramatically through the use of contemporary imaging technologies such as MRI and fMRI.

TEST YOURSELF

1 Materialism is the philosophical view that mind and body are separate entities. True ☐ False ☐

2 Some hormones are also neurotransmitters. True ☐ False ☐

3 Males are left-brained and females are right-brained. True ☐ False ☐

4 Oxytocin is involved in both orgasm and emotional bonding. True ☐ False ☐

5 Which part of the neuron contains the nucleus?

a) Soma

b) Button

c) Dendron

d) Axon

6 Which of the following is not part of the peripheral nervous system?

a) Parasympathetic system

b) Sympathetic system

c) Spinal system

d) Somatic system

7 Which brain structure is most strongly associated with the autonomic nervous system?

a) Pons

b) Amygdala

c) Medulla

d) Hippocampus

8 Which lobe contains the primary visual system?

   a) Frontal

   b) Parietal

   c) Occipital

   d) Temporal

9 Explain the relationship between the nervous and endocrine systems.

10 Explain how the biology of the brain can explain near-death experiences.

 Visit the online resources that accompany this book: www.oup.com/uk/jarvis–okami1e

CHAPTER 5

THE NATURE, NURTURE, AND EVOLUTION OF BEHAVIOUR

LEARNING OUTCOMES

By the end of this chapter you should be able to:

- Critique the traditional idea of the 'nature-nurture debate' and understand the potential role of genetic and environmental variation in shaping individual differences

- Understand the scientific principles underlying behavioural genetics, including the genome, genotype, including variation at the allele level, and phenotype as a product of genotype and environment

- Evaluate the role of natural-experimental methods including twin and adoption studies in studying the influence of genes and environment on psychological characteristics

- Critically discuss the concept of heritability with regard to its measurement, the distinction between broad and narrow sense heritability, and generalizability issues

- Distinguish between gene-environment interaction, reactive gene-environment correlation, and active gene-environment correlation

- Assess the principles of evolution, and with particular reference to the importance of natural selection and apply the concepts of adaptation and environmental mismatch to human behaviour

- Evaluate research into sex difference in sexual behaviour with particular regard to the debate over the extent to which these differences can be said to validate evolutionary psychology

- Critically consider Trivers' theory of parental investment with regard to supporting evidence and testability criteria

- Appreciate the complexity of issues around evaluating evolutionary psychology, including its theoretical basis and evidence base, and distinguish between criticism of misrepresentations and implications of evolutionary theory and the theory itself

- Discuss the 'new nature-nurture debate' between proponents of evolution and culture as influences on human behaviour and explore cultural psychology and social role theory as explanations

We often say of people 'he was just born that way' or 'she is well brought up'. These very simple statements illustrate two perspectives on the long-running discussion among scientists, philosophers, and sociologists about the importance of genetic bases and experience on human behaviour. The first statement expresses an intuitive understanding of genetic influence and the second a similar acknowledgment of the importance of experience. Traditionally, discussion of genetic and environmental influences has been framed as the 'nature-nurture debate'. However, we are going to try to move past that overly simple idea and set out some basic principles.

1 There are two potential debates around nature and nurture. One concerns the relative importance of **genes** (see 'Behavioural genetics', this chapter) and environment in determining individual differences, including psychological differences. The second, sometimes called the 'new nature-nurture debate', concerns the relative importance of evolution and **culture** on common human behaviour.

2 The first of these debates is no longer really a debate. Genes and environment always work in conjunction, never in opposition to one another, and we are now developing a sophisticated understanding of how genes and environment work together.

3 'Nature' and 'nurture' are just analogies for genes and environment, and actually both terms can be quite misleading. It is after all just as natural to have an environment as it is to have genes! Moreover some important aspects of the environment (such as physical trauma and exposure to microbes) work on a biological level and have very little to do with how we are nurtured by others. So forget the idea that nature means biology and nurture means upbringing—it's way more complicated than that.

4 Even though we now have quite a good understanding of how genes and aspects of the environment interact, and so the overarching 'nature-nurture debate' no longer really exists, there are still *'nature-nurture debates'* concerning the relative importance of genetic make-up and particular environmental influences in regard to particular psychological characteristics. An example is intelligence—see Chapter 14.

Genes and environment affect both how we differ from one another and what we have in common as a species. The first part of this chapter is concerned with **behavioural genetics**, the study of genetic and environmental influences on individual differences. The second concerns the role of evolution and culture in shaping common human behaviours.

BEHAVIOURAL GENETICS

In Chapter 4, we discussed the human nervous system and located the *mind* directly within the *brain*. But where does the brain come from? The human nervous system, including the brain, is the result of 'programming instructions' from within the **human genome**, the set of hereditary instructions that exists within every cell of every human body. Our human genome 'tells' various amino acids and the proteins they construct to build a *human* organism rather than, say, a frog or a fruit fly—both of which actually contain a great many genes in common with human beings (see Figure 5.1). Without the human genome, you might have ended up as a yeast spore. As it is, you share almost 25% of your genes with yeast spores, and between 98% and 99% with the chimpanzee.

❯ **KEY IDEAS** genes Genes are the unit of heredity. Each gene is a section of chromosome that codes for the production of a particular protein and, when activated, triggers the production of this protein.

❯ **KEY IDEAS** behavioural genetics **Behavioural genetics** is the study of the influence of genes and environments on individual differences in behaviour. Behaviour geneticists measure the differences in some trait among a sample of people and attempt to quantify the portion of these differences that is due to genes and the portion that is due to environment.

❯ **KEY IDEAS** the human genome A genome is the entire set of hereditary 'instructions', encoded in DNA, for creating an organism. The human genome, containing the necessary genetic information to build a human, exists within every cell of every human body.

		% Common with Humans
Chimpanzee 25,000 genes Just like you, chimpanzees have around 25,000 genes. But then why can't they speak? The difference could be in a single gene, FOXP2, which in the chimpanzee is missing certain sections.		98%
Mouse 30,000 genes Thanks to mice, researchers have been able to identify genes linked to skeletal development, obesity, and Parkinson's disease, to name but a few.		90%
Zebra Fish 30,000 genes 85% of the genes in these little fish are the same as yours. Researchers use them to study the role of genes linked to blood disease, such as anemia falciforme and heart disease.		85%
Fruit Fly 13,600 genes For the past 100 years, the fruit fly has been used to study the transmission of hereditary characteristics, the development of organisms, and, more recently, the study of changes in behaviour induced by the consumption of alcohol.		36%
Thale cress 25,000 genes This little plant, from the mustard family, is used as a model for the study of all flowering plants. Scientists use its genes to study hepatolenticular degeneration, a disease that causes copper to accumulate in the human liver.		26%
Yeast 6,275 genes You have certain genes in common with this organism that is used to make bread, beer, and wine. Scientists use yeast to study the metabolism of sugars, the cell division process, and other diseases such as cancer.		23%
Roundworm 19,000 genes Just like you, this worm possesses muscles, a nervous system, intestines, and sexual organs. That is why the roundworm is used to study genes linked to aging, to neurological diseases such as Alzheimer's, to cancer, and to kidney disease.		21%
Bacterium, *Escherichia coli* 4,800 genes The *E. coli* bacterium inhabits your intestines. Researchers study it to learn about basic cell functions, such as transcription and translation.		7%

FIGURE 5.1 25,000 genes and a conscience. A portion of the genes within the human genome are shared with every living organism from bacteria to broccoli to brown bears. These ancient genes likely stem from a common ancestor that lived 3.5 billion years ago. Scientists theorize that through evolution this ancestor's genome became the basis for every species living today. Pictured are estimates of the percentage of genes humans share in common with various species. These genes are so similar that, at least in some instances, the human version can be spliced into the body of an individual of another species, including a plant, worm, or fly, in place of that species' own version of the gene, with no harmful effects (Ridley, 2003).

The Gene as the Unit of Heredity

So what exactly is a gene? Most people in the industrialized world have a vague, or intuitive, understanding of the meaning of the word 'gene', but most of us would probably be hard pressed to provide a precise definition. Briefly, as explained in Chapter 4, the human body is constructed of cells. As depicted in Figure 5.2A, the *nucleus*, or inner kernel, of almost every one of these cells contains 23 pairs of **chromosomes**: rod-like bodies made up of proteins and strands of DNA. The exception to the 23-pair rule are the male and female reproductive cells, which have only 23 total chromosomes rather than 23 pairs of chromosomes. DNA (deoxyribonucleic acid) is a complex molecule with a characteristic spiralling shape. DNA contains the unique 'code' for creating every living organism, and is therefore the basis for passing on hereditary characteristics in humans (see Figure 5.2B).

> **KEY IDEAS** chromosomes, DNA **Chromosomes** are rod-like bodies, present in every human cell, made up of proteins and strands of DNA. **DNA (deoxyribonucleic acid)** is a complex molecule with a characteristic spiralling shape. DNA contains the genetic instructions for heredity in all living organisms.

Heredity is transmitted through an arrangement of functional strands of DNA grouped together along each chromosome (see Figure 5.2C). These functional units are called genes, and recent estimates suggest that there are about 20,000–25,000 of them in your body, somewhat fewer than was once thought (Human Genome

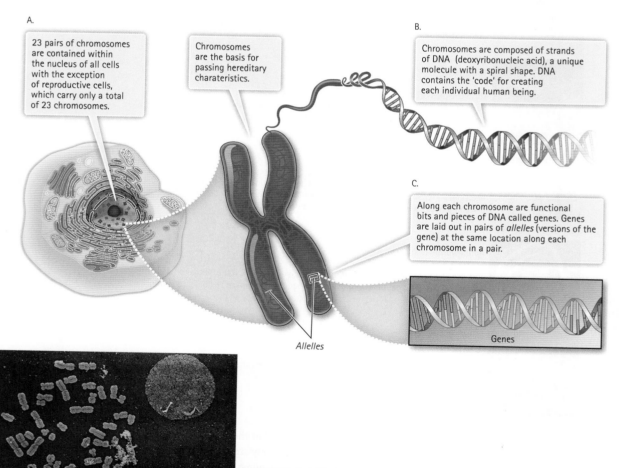

A.

23 pairs of chromosomes are contained within the nucleus of all cells with the exception of reproductive cells, which carry only a total of 23 chromosomes.

Chromosomes are the basis for passing hereditary charateristics.

B.

Chromosomes are composed of strands of DNA (deoxyribonucleic acid), a unique molecule with a spiral shape. DNA contains the 'code' for creating each individual human being.

C.

Along each chromosome are functional bits and pieces of DNA called genes. Genes are laid out in pairs of *alleles* (versions of the gene) at the same location along each chromosome in a pair.

Alleles

Genes

FIGURE 5.2 The gene is the unit of heredity. Genes store the evolutionary information about the specific species (genome) and hereditary information about the specific individual (genotypes).

Project Information, 2008). Like chromosomes, genes are laid out in pairs, and each member of a pair occupies a fixed position, or *locus*, along the chromosome.

Genes are important in psychology. As described in several chapters of this book, differences among people in personality traits (Chapter 15), and IQ scoring (Chapter 14), vulnerability to certain physical and mental disorders (Chapter 18), and many other attributes are partially due to genetic differences.

So there is no misunderstanding: all humans inherit the same basic collection of genes (the genome), but genes come in two or more different 'versions' or **alleles**. For example, the gene that determines hair colour is inherited by everyone. But one person might inherit alleles coding for blond hair and another person, alleles coding for black hair. Thus, when we talk about 'different genes' or 'genetic differences' among individual people, we are using shorthand to talk about differences in alleles. The unique collection of alleles in an individual that contributes to (or entirely determines) some trait or characteristic is known as the **genotype** for that characteristic.

> **KEY IDEAS** alleles Alleles are the different forms a particular gene might take, for example a gene might have a long or short allele. Genetic differences among people occur not because they have different genes but because people inherit unique combinations of alleles.

> **KEY IDEAS** genotype The unique collection of alleles that contribute to specific traits in living organisms is their **genotype**.

> **THINKING PRACTICALLY**

Take the following statement: 'My children have different personalities because they have different genes' and express it more scientifically using the terms 'allele' and 'genotype'.

If the human genome is the set of genetic instructions necessary to construct human beings, genotypes are sets of unique genetic instructions necessary to create a *specific* human being (or two, in the case of identical twins). Although the idea remains controversial in some circles there is overwhelming evidence collected by researchers over the past four decades to suggest that genotypes do play a part in the development of *psychological* traits just as they do in the development of *physiological* traits (Plomin et al, 2008).

Throughout history the existence of heredity—the tendency of offspring to resemble their parents in various ways—has always been taken for granted. However, it was not until the rediscovery during the twentieth century of the work of the scientist-monk Gregor Mendel (1822–84) that scientists came to understand exactly what was being inherited. Mendel realized that heredity occurs in separate 'packets' that later came to be termed *genes*. Thus, the gene is the unit of heredity.

Genes cannot ordinarily be observed. However, the effects of their activity (eg, blond hair or brown eyes) can be observed. Any potentially observable trait or characteristic of a living organism—be it physiological, anatomical, behavioural, or mental—is known as a **phenotype**. It should not be surprising that genes contribute to the development of mental and behavioural phenotypes. After all, the mind emerges in some way from the physiology and anatomy of the brain. If brains differ due to genetics—as do eyes, legs, and noses—then we might expect minds also to differ as a result of genetic differences, at least to some degree.

> **KEY IDEAS** phenotype The observable characteristics of an organism comprise its **phenotype**. Phenotype is typically the product of both genotype and environmental influences.

Functions of Genes

If the gene is the unit of heredity, how does it transmit characteristics from one generation to the next? Genes have a number of specific functions. *The first function of the gene is to create proteins*. Proteins synthesize structures in living organisms—creating everything from neurotransmitters to knee joints. Genes create proteins primarily by transmitting genetic information through RNA (**ribonucleic acid**),

> **KEY IDEAS** RNA (ribonucleic acid) **RNA** is a chemical compound found in each cell nucleus and cytoplasm. RNA carries out the job of constructing protein from 'instructions' contained in genes.

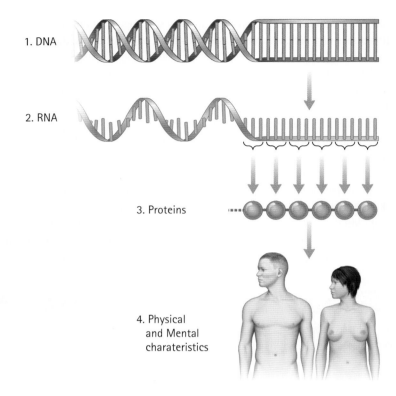

1. DNA

2. RNA

3. Proteins

4. Physical and Mental charateristics

FIGURE 5.3 RNA does the actual work of constructing proteins. Genes contained within DNA transmit hereditary information through RNA, which 'transcribes' this genetic information into a form that can be used to construct proteins. These proteins build individuals with specific physical and mental characteristics.

a chemical compound found in each cell nucleus and *cytoplasm*—the jelly-like material that fills cells. As depicted in Figure 5.3, RNA does the actual work of constructing proteins by 'transcribing' the genetic information into a form that can be used to create proteins. In this way, genes construct an entire organism according to plans laid out in the organism's DNA.

From the perspective of **evolutionary psychology** (see Chapter 2, 'The rise of evolutionary psychology') *a second function of the gene is to self-replicate*—to make as many copies of itself as it can. In the broadest sense, genes can do this by guiding the behaviour of their host organisms (the organisms in which they reside). Genes can guide the behaviour of their hosts by doing their protein-construction work in a way that will optimize the chances that the organism will survive and reproduce (Dawkins, 1989). When you jump out of the way of an oncoming car, feel revulsion at the smell of spoiled food, or experience feelings of desire in the presence of your romantic partner or tenderness in the presence of your infant children or younger siblings, you are influenced by the genes to which you are host. These genes have survived through the millennia only because they have influenced their hosts to behave in ways that allow genetic reproduction to occur.

Of course, genes can only synthesize proteins and self-replicate in an environment that is adequate. For example, without proper nutrition, the appropriate chemical and hormonal environment, and protection from toxins of various sorts, a normal brain and nervous system will not develop in a human foetus, in spite of the best efforts of the foetus's 25,000 genes. An infant whose mother drinks excessively during pregnancy may develop *foetal alcohol syndrome* even if that infant has no particular genetic vulnerability for such a condition. A human being reared in darkness during specific periods of early infancy will never develop normal vision (Maurer, Mondloch, and

Lewis, 2007). A genetically normal child deprived of human touch and the chance to play with others may develop profound cognitive and emotional problems as a result (Rutter, O'Connor, and the English and Romanian Adoptees (ERA) Study Team, 2004).

Even relatively ordinary environments can constrain or promote the effects of genes in less extreme ways. Without adequate education and access to educational materials, for example, a person with an inherited aptitude for academic learning cannot be expected to learn much; and a person genetically predisposed to develop a mental illness may never show symptoms if he or she is reared in a particularly supportive environment. Thus, certain effects of genes on behaviour may not be apparent in environments that suppress the expression of the genes—or they may be particularly apparent in environments that enhance them (Tucker-Drob, 2011).

This idea leads us to a *third* function of genes. *The gene is a 'switch' that interacts with other genes* (Ridley, 2003). If we share almost 99% of our genes with chimpanzees, why have chimps never developed pop art or punk? And why don't we spend as much time picking lice off our friends or swinging from trees as chimpanzees do?

The answer is that genes can be switched on and off—they can become active or inactive to varying degrees. If the same gene is switched on for a longer or shorter time, it may have dramatically different effects during the development of an organism and after maturity has been reached. A short period of activity might result in the development of a body with short arms relative to leg size, while a longer period might result in the opposite physique. Similarly, a short period might result in the ability to learn only a few hand signs after years of tutoring, while a longer period might result in the ability to write *1984* or *Pride, Prejudice and Zombies*. Genes switched on and off in different patterns and for different lengths of time result in different species and different individuals (Ptashne and Gann, 2002).

What does the switching? Other genes—and the proteins that help regulate them. Changes in genes and their regulating proteins promote or suppress the expression of other genes . . . and these genes may then do the same to still more genes down the line. What we have in essence is a series of genetic switches turning one another on and off—in some ways similar to the way thermostats regulate air conditioning in office buildings by automatically switching cooling or heating units on and off when the temperature drops below or moves above preset temperature points. This also explains why the same gene may have different effects in different parts of the body. As Ridley (2003, p 236) points out, these facts show why it is highly simplistic to speak of 'genes for' specific traits (eg, a 'gene for creativity' or a 'gene for homosexuality'). In one context a gene might have a certain effect, and in another context, it might have a radically different, unrelated effect.

STUDYING GENETIC AND ENVIRONMENTAL INFLUENCES

A number of methods have been used to study the importance of genetic and environmental differences on psychological characteristics, including twin studies and adoption studies.

Recall point 2 at the start of this chapter: the overarching nature-nurture debate is largely resolved and we have a good idea of how genes and environment interact to produce psychological characteristics. However, there remain many nature-nurture debates concerning how important particular genetic and environmental influences are in the development of *particular* characteristics.

Twin Studies

In 1940 identical twin boys who came to be known as Jim Lewis and Jim Springer were separated at birth. Almost four decades later, they were reunited—a highly unusual event. At the time of their reunion, each of the 'Jim twins' (Figure 5.4) was 6 feet tall and weighed 180 pounds. Each had been married twice—first to a woman named Linda, next to a woman named Betty. Jim Lewis's first-born son was named James Alan, while Jim Springer's first born was named James Allen. As children, each had owned a dog named Toy. Jim Lewis's and Jim Springer's families vacationed on the same beach in Florida, and both Jims had worked as sheriff's deputies in nearby Ohio counties (Wright, 1997).

FIGURE 5.4 The 'Jim twins'. Jim Lewis and Jim Springer were separated as infants and reunited in adulthood. At the time of their reunion they shared so many attributes in common that they remain 'poster children' for the findings of behaviour genetics. If the preceding information does not put a strain on your belief systems, consider that both men drank the same brand of beer (Miller Lite) and chain-smoked the same brand of cigarettes (Salem). Both men had woodworking shops in their garages, with Jim Lewis specializing in miniature picnic tables and Jim Springer in miniature rocking chairs. Both drove the same model of car. Both were described by their wives as romantics who left love notes around the house but who ground their teeth during their sleep and bit their nails to the quick during the day. Their personality and mental ability scores 'were all so similar that they could have been the same person'.

Source: Courtsey of Dr. Nancy L. Segal on behalf of the Jim twins.

 THINKING CRITICALLY

The case of the Jim twins sounds at first like convincing evidence for the overwhelming importance of genes in individual differences. However, before we take the case as solid evidence consider the following:

1 What similarities of their lives are probably coincidental?

2 What similarities might have been the result of similar environments?

> 3 What behavioural similarities might have been made more likely by genetically influenced physical similarities?

> 4 People are notoriously bad at judging probability. What similarities that might appear unusual are actually quite likely in any two people?

Quite aside from the difficulties of generalizing from one-off case studies like this, there are a number of arguments against the idea that the Jims' similar outcomes were determined by genetic similarity (see *Thinking critically*). Nevertheless, the Jim twins remain 'poster children' for the now well-established findings from the field of behavioural genetics that many cognitive and personality traits are influenced by a person's genetic inheritance—often substantially so (Johnson et al, 2009). Behavioural genetics is the scientific study of the influence of genes and environments on individual differences in traits and behaviour.

Behavioural geneticists begin with the understanding that for every human trait—intelligence, kindness, religious feeling and social attitudes, hostility, generosity, and so forth—there is *variation* (ie, differences) from one person to the next. This means that in any given sample, individuals will differ in their scores on measures of such traits. Behavioural geneticists attempt to *quantify* (estimate numerically) the portion of these differences that can be accounted for by genetic heredity and that portion resulting from experiences in the world (including experiences in the womb prior to birth). Behavioural geneticists accomplish this task by conducting research among groups of people—usually twins or adopted children—whose characteristics make them especially suitable to disentangling genes from the environment.

The Jim twins inaugurated the longest running study of twins reared apart, conducted by Thomas J. Bouchard and colleagues and known as the Minnesota Study of Twins Reared Apart (MISTRA; Bouchard et al, 2004). Studies of twins reared apart or together constitute what is often termed a **natural experiment**. A natural experiment is a situation that occurs naturally, but which an experimenter can utilize to create research that allows conclusions to be drawn about causation (Segal, 2010).

In research among twins reared together, nature is controlling the number of genes that pairs of twins and other types of siblings share in common. Identical (**monozygotic**) twins share 100% of their genes in common and develop from a single female egg (*monozygotic* literally means 'one egg'). Fraternal (**dizygotic**) twins share only 50% of their genes on average—no different from any other pair of siblings—and develop from two eggs (*dizygotic* means 'two eggs') (Figure 5.5). If monozygotic twins are more similar than **dizygotic twins** and other siblings on some trait, this is evidence of the influence of genes. It is the *logic* of studies of twins reared together. These studies have shown that by the time they reach adulthood, identical twins reared together are about twice as similar in personality and cognitive ability as either pairs of fraternal twins or ordinary siblings (Plomin and Spinath, 2004). This is predicted from what we know of behavioural genetics because identical twins share twice as many genes in common on average as do ordinary siblings or fraternal twins (Saudino, 2005).

> **KEY IDEAS** natural experiments A **natural experiment** is a situation that occurs naturally, but that creates conditions that represent two or more levels of the independent variable, allowing conclusions about cause and effect to be drawn. Behavioural genetics makes use of natural experiments in the form of twin and adoption studies.

> **KEY IDEAS** monozygotic and dizygotic twins **Monozygotic (MZs) or identical twins** are twins who emerge from a single ovum (egg) and share 100% of their genes in common. **Dizygotic (DZs) or fraternal twins** are twins who emerge from two ova (eggs) and share only 50% of their genes in common, on average.

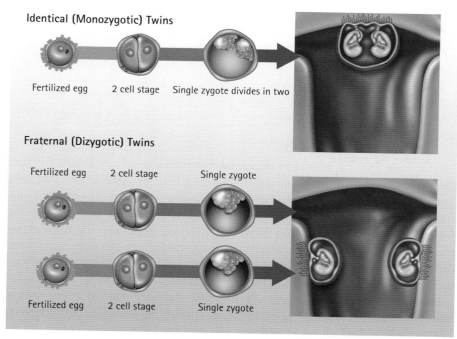

Identical (Monozygotic) Twins

Fertilized egg 2 cell stage Single zygote divides in two

Fraternal (Dizygotic) Twins

Fertilized egg 2 cell stage Single zygote

Fertilized egg 2 cell stage Single zygote

FIGURE 5.5 **Monozygotic and dizygotic twins**
Source: Gwen Shockey/Science Photo Library.

Comparing MZs and DZs twins has revealed some complex and interesting patterns of environmental and genetic influence. One of the most important lessons from this kind of research is that psychological characteristics and abilities that we commonly think of as unitary (ie, a single characteristic or ability) actually break down to smaller components with different genetic and environmental influences. An example is in literacy ability. We examine a study of the origins of reading ability in our *Research in focus* feature.

RESEARCH IN FOCUS

Byrne, B. et al (2007). Longitudinal twin study of early literacy development. Preschool through Grade 1. *Reading and Writing* 20, 77–102.

Aim: To investigate the role of genetic and environmental influences on reading ability and to see whether these were consistent in different populations. More specifically to compare the similarity of outcomes on a range of reading measures in monozygotic and dizygotic twin pairs in the USA and Australia.

Method: Participants were 92 American and 75 Australian MZ twin pairs and 105 American and 47 Australian DZ pairs. The mean ages were 88.7 months for the Americans and 83.9 months for the Australians. All the children were assessed for literacy development using a range of measures including speed-reading, comprehension, spelling, rapid naming, phonological awareness, and verbal memory. Testers worked in pairs, one assessing each twin at the same time. Testing took place in the children's homes or schools.

Results: Overall, correlations between MZ twin pairs were greater than those between DZs, suggesting there is some genetic influence on literacy. However, these differences were much more pronounced for some aspects of literacy than others. For example, in speed-reading correlations were up to 0.83 between scores for MZs as opposed to 0.42 between DZ scores. On the other hand for verbal learning correlations were 0.39 for MZs and 0.28 for DZs. When American and Australian samples were compared some differences emerged, not just in average scores but also in the MZ-DZ disparity. MZ and DZ scores were more similar in the Australian sample.

Conclusion: Genes and environment are of different relative importance in the development of different aspects of literacy. Thus speed-reading ability appears to be strongly influenced by genes but verbal memory much less so. Environmental influence appears stronger in the Australian sample, possibly reflecting the more intensive early literacy intervention in the Australian education system. This highlights the fact that genetic and environmental influences are population-specific.

MASTER YOUR METHODOLOGY

1 This kind of study can be described as a natural experiment. Explain what is meant by a natural experiment.

2 Results are in the form of correlation coefficients representing the similarity between twin pairs. What precisely is a correlation coefficient?

3 Although only a snapshot of findings is presented in this article, this analysis is part of a longitudinal study. What is a longitudinal study?

THINKING CRITICALLY

Look back to our critical thinking toolkit (see Chapter 1, 'Developing your thinking skills'). What strengths and weaknesses can you see in relation to this study?

If pairs of identical twins reared *apart* like the Jim twins are as similar to one another as identical twins reared *together*, this would present even more powerful evidence that genes play an important role in creating that similarity. MZ twins reared apart share all of their genes in common but have been reared in *different* environments. Therefore, in principal at least, similarities between the twins cannot be accounted for even in part by environmental experiences since the twins have not shared the same environment. This is the logic of studies of twins reared apart. Similarities in identical twins reared apart can be attributed to their genetic similarity.

Taken together, studies of twins reared together and apart have shown the influence of genetic differences in general cognitive ability as measured by IQ tests, personality traits, and temperament (see Chapter 14) and vulnerability to mental disorders—including *schizophrenia*, and depressive and bipolar disorders. All of these results point to the importance of genes in the development of differences in human characteristics.

Adoption studies

Identical twins reared together or apart do not provide the only natural experiments in behavioural genetics. Another source of evidence comes from adoption studies. Adopted children are usually raised in environments that do not include their biological parents. If the children end up to be more similar to their *biological* parents than to their *adoptive* parents—with whom they spend their entire lives—this also would be powerful evidence that genetic differences play an important part in development. Indeed, evidence from adoption studies is even more powerful than that derived from twin studies because (in principle at least) the *only* influences on adopted children of their genetic parents are genes (Beer, Arnold, and Loehlin, 1998)!

As it turns out, however, results of adoption studies are mixed. Most studies have shown that, by adulthood, adopted children are somewhat closer to their genetic parents than to their adoptive parents in cognitive abilities such as IQ performance and mathematical and reading ability (Petrill et al, 2004). On the other hand, the differences are much less marked in the case of personality characteristics (Beer, Arnold, and Loehlin, 1998). In general, adoption research shows a lesser contribution of genes to personality than does the twin research—a discrepancy that behavioural geneticists have not yet been able to explain fully (Petrill et al, 2004).

 THINKING CREATIVELY

Family studies are a third source of evidence that look at similarity in psychological characteristics in relation to genetic similarity between different family members. For any two relatives we can estimate their degree of genetic similarity. So, for example, siblings are more genetically similar than cousins. Explain how MZ and DZ twins, adopted children, and other family members can contribute data to family studies.

Heritability Figures and Their Limitations

> **KEY IDEAS** heritability
Heritability is a statistic that estimates the extent of genetic influence in the differences among a sample of people on a particular trait.

When behavioural geneticists conduct studies among twins or adopted children, they compute a statistic known as **heritability**, or h^2. This statistic is based on comparisons of test scores for a particular trait (eg, intelligence, shyness) among people of varying genetic relatedness (eg, identical twins, ordinary siblings) and varying environments (ie, reared together or in different homes). The heritability statistic is meant to tease apart the extent of genetic and environmental influence by computing the degree to which genes and environments contribute to the variation on some trait among people in a particular sample.

Values of the heritability statistic range from 0 to 1.0. The closer the statistic is to 1.0, the greater is the influence of genes and the less the influence of the environment. For example, if heritability is estimated to be 0.55 in a research study on intelligence, this means that 55% of the variation in intelligence among the individuals in the research study is due to genetic factors.

> **KEY IDEAS** Falconer's formula
Falconer's formula is a simple way to estimate broad sense heritability from the correlations in scores for the characteristic in MZ and DZ twin pairs. The formula is h = 2 (MZ correlation – DZ correlation). Note that this provides only a crude estimate of heritability because it measures only broad sense heritability, because it is limited by the reliability and validity of the measure being correlated and because it may not generalize well from the sample to the wider population.

There are various formulae used to calculate heritability. Perhaps the simplest is **Falconer's formula**, which makes use of the difference between correlations for measures of a characteristic in MZ and DZ twin pairs. According to Falconer's formula:

$$\text{Heritability} = 2(\text{MZ correlation} - \text{DZ correlation})$$

So if there is a 0.5 correlation between, say the symptom severity of autistic spectrum disorder in MZs and 0.25 in DZs, the heritability of autistic spectrum disorder would be estimated as 2(0.5 – 0.25), which equals 0.5.

THINKING PRACTICALLY

You can calculate heritability from MZ and DZ correlations using Falconer's formula:

Heritability = 2(MZ correlation − DZ correlation).

Taking the results of the Byrne et al study we looked at in *Research in focus* recall that the correlations between MZs and DZs for verbal learning were 0.39 and 0.28 respectively. Using Falconer's formula, calculate the heritability of verbal learning ability.

However, heritability figures can be quite misleading. Because the figure represents **broad sense heritability**, the decimal or percentage measures the entire proportion of the variance that can be attributed to genetic influence, *including gene-environment interaction*. Once heritability passes 50% it *appears* to be more important than environment but this is not necessarily the case because, although they are expressed as a decimal or percentage, heritability + environmental influence + gene-environment interaction will generally add up to more than 1.0 or 100%. A heritability figure of 0.55 does *not* mean there is only 0.45 left to attribute to other influences.

A further limitation of heritability is that any given heritability estimate applies only to the sample included in the research study, and (provided the sample is representative) to the population it represents. It cannot be assumed to apply to all people. As a particularly dramatic example of this, consider Turkheimer's study of the impact of a severely impoverished environment on the genetics of IQ (intelligence) scores (Turkheimer et al, 2003). Over the past decades, behavioural genetics researchers have demonstrated through twin and adoption studies that a substantial portion of the differences among samples of individuals in IQ scores is due to genetic differences—approximately 50% or perhaps more (Bouchard, 1996). However, most of the participants in these research studies have been of middle-class or lower-middle-class origin who have shared what Scarr (1992) describes as an **average expectable environment**. When Turkheimer and colleagues conducted a twin study using a sample of deeply impoverished and disadvantaged twins and other siblings, they found that less than 10% of the differences in IQ scoring among the individuals in this sample was due to genetic differences.

In a subsequent study comparing very young infants reared in economically advantaged homes with infants reared in disadvantaged homes, researchers found that genes accounted for about 50% of the variation in cognitive abilities, but among the disadvantaged infants the influence of genes was negligible (Tucker-Drob et al, 2011). Taken together, these findings imply that severe disadvantages may override the ordinary expression of genes—underscoring the idea that genetic programmes cannot unfold in environments that are inadequate.

Finally, bear in mind that if the results of behavioural genetics research on cognitive ability, personality traits, and social attitudes are averaged out, genetic heredity usually accounts for between 25% and 50% of the differences among most samples of people—leaving an equal or greater proportion to the environment. This average figure results from the fact that general cognitive ability often shows heritability higher than 50%, while personality characteristics and social attitudes often show

❯ **KEY IDEAS** broad sense heritability Published heritability figures, including those calculated using Falconer's formula, usually represent **broad sense heritability**, which includes both pure genetic influence and that of gene-environment interaction. This produces a higher figure than narrow sense heritability, which represents the 'pure' influence of genetic make-up alone.

❯ **KEY IDEAS** the average expectable environment Scarr (1992) used the term **average expectable environment** to mean a typical environment, variation from which exerts an influence on development. Within the average expectable environment genetic variation exerts its maximum influence but outside it environment assumes much greater importance.

heritability estimates that are much lower than 50% (Plomin et al, 2008). Because the environment often accounts for greater influence than genetic variation—for example, in personality and social attitudes—the term *behavioural genetics* itself is a bit misleading. Behavioural geneticists are as interested in estimating environmental influences as they are in estimating genetic influences.

GENE–ENVIRONMENT INTERACTION

Because most researchers consider that the case for both genetic and environmental influence on psychological characteristics has been made (Maccoby, 2002), many behavioural geneticists have moved on to more subtle questions. Some have entered the field of **molecular genetics**, where the hunt goes on for the *specific* genes responsible for various traits (Haworth and Plomin, 2010). Others have stayed within the field of behavioural genetics but have turned their attention to the ways in which genes and environments influence one another to produce traits and characteristics. These researchers have demonstrated that genes influence environments, and that environments influence how genes are expressed (Krueger et al, 2008). In other words, they have moved farther from nature *versus* nurture and closer to nature *via* nurture (Rutter, 2007). Nowhere is this more apparent than in the cases of *gene–environment correlations* and *gene–environment interactions*.

Gene–Environment Correlation

A **gene–environment correlation** occurs when a person's environment is a reflection of, or is somehow associated (correlated) with, that person's genotype—the specific arrangement of genes that contribute to the development of a particular trait. How can this correlation occur? Consider 4-year-old Lucia, who has a relatively high IQ and innate verbal ability, both resulting in part from her parents through genetic transmission. These qualities are a reflection of Lucia's genotype. Lucia is extremely curious about the world and asks endless questions. She gravitates towards books and spends hours with them each day, looking at the pictures and asking to be read to. At the age of 6, she enters school already highly educated! This is in part because of the environment in which she lives, which consists of substantial time spent with books, receiving ready answers to her many questions from adults around her, being exposed to many opportunities for learning. However, this 'bookish' environment exists as it does in part *because of Lucia's genotype*. Lucia makes certain choices (like asking to be read to and asking question after question), and these choices help shape her environment—her parents purchase more books, make them available to her, and respond to Lucia's questions with carefully considered answers. Lucia's genotype has in part determined the types of experiences she has.

Now consider Lucia's younger sister, Graciella, who asks fewer questions and is less interested in books and 'academic' matters. She enters school with a more restricted knowledge of the world than her sister. On the other hand, from a very early age, Graciella has enjoyed painting and other crafts, in part as a result of *her* genotype (her maternal grandmother and great-grandmother were artists). She asks to be taken to museums more frequently than her sister (who is bored there), and is surrounded with art supplies and people to help her learn to draw well. By the time Graciella enters school her drawing skills are far superior to those of her older sister, in spite of her being much younger. Graciella's genotype has affected the environment in which she developed and is richly correlated with that environment.

> **KEY IDEAS** molecular genetics **Molecular geneticists** attempt to identify specific genetic variations responsible for differences among people in particular traits.

> **KEY IDEAS** gene-environment correlation **Gene-environment correlation** occurs when a person's environment is correlated with his or her genotype. For example, a musically gifted child (genotype) also lives in a home where music is played frequently and where musical instruments are available.

Active, reactive, and passive gene-environment correlations

There are three types of gene-environment correlations we will consider here, as summarized in Table 5.1: *active*, *reactive*, and *passive* (Plomin, DeFries, and Loehlin, 1977). The active seeking out of certain types of environments through intentional choices—as in the case of Lucia seeking verbal, and Graciella artistic, environments—is known as an **active gene-environment correlation**.

By contrast a **reactive gene-environment correlation** occurs when individuals around a child react to the child's genotype in some way, creating a correlated environment. In other words, the child's genotype *evokes* particular kinds of behaviour from those around her. For example, some babies love to be cuddled, kissed, and held right from the beginning, while others are more restrained or stand-offish. Because parents are human, they respond to these variations—creating a warm, physically affectionate environment in the first case and one a little less so in the second. These environments in turn affect the developing child. It is a reactive *cycle* of child influencing parent, and parent influencing child in turn (Fox et al, 2007).

A particularly interesting demonstration of the importance of reactive gene-environment correlations comes from studies of children adopted at birth. Several of these studies have shown that the degree of harshness and hostility in the parenting practices of a child's *adoptive* parents can to some degree be predicted by knowing the level of aggressiveness and hostility of the child's *birth parents*—whom the infants have never known! In other words, children who have inherited aggressive tendencies from their *genetic* parents go on to elicit harshness and hostility from their *adoptive* parents in response to those inherited tendencies, through reactive gene-environment correlation (O'Connor et al, 1998).

Gene-Environment Interaction

A *gene-environment interaction* is a concept that is perhaps more intuitive and simpler to grasp than gene-environment correlation. If we consider that each person is different, it stands to reason that two different people may react to the same event in different ways (Fox et al, 2007). Suppose you go to a party with a friend. Your friend comes away glowing, and you come away mumbling. It was the same party, but it elicited radically different responses from different individuals.

Now consider two children, each of whom is mercilessly teased at school because they both have weight problems. The first child, Dylan, is high in *neuroticism*, a tendency towards negative mood states, negative thoughts, and emotionalism. Neuroticism is also highly heritable (Bouchard, 2004). Dylan takes the teasing seriously

> **KEY IDEAS** active gene-environment correlation **Active gene-environment correlation** is a correlation between environment and genotype that results from active choices made by an organism.

> **KEY IDEAS** reactive gene-environment correlation A **reactive gene-environment correlation** occurs when an organism's genotype evokes responses in others, creating an environment that shares characteristics with that genotype.

TABLE 5.1 **Two types of gene-environment correlations**

Type	Definition	Example
Active	When a person actively seeks out a particular kind of environment as a result of his or her genotype	A temperamentally timid child takes a route to school that will avoid passing by the school bullies' hangout.
Reactive	When a child's genotype-influenced behaviour helps to shape his or her environment as a result of other people's responses to the behaviour	A disagreeable child elicits annoyance or hostility from those around her. She consequently lives in a rejecting world that further reinforces her disagreeableness.
Passive	When a child's genotype and environment are related but neither influences the other	A child with aggressive parents both experiences a hostile upbringing and inherits a hostile disposition.

to heart, and its effects are traumatic—continuing to affect his personality into adulthood. The second child, Gilbert, is low in neuroticism. He finds the teasing unpleasant but brushes it off as the behaviour of 'stupid kids' who are jealous of his good grades. It has little effect on his life. Same experience, different genes. When an experience affects people differently as a result of differences in their genotypes, a **gene-environment interaction** has occurred (Dick, 2011).

READ THIS

One of the most impressive and expressive proponents of genetic influence is Robert Plomin. The following is an example of a modern paper he co-authored discussing some robust findings from behavioural genetics:

Plomin, R., DeFries, J.C., Knopik, V.S., and Neiderhiser, J.M. (2016). Top 10 replicated findings from behavioral genetics. *Perspectives on Psychological Science*, **11**, 3–23.

For a much more critical view, try this more sociological exploration of the field of behavioural genetics:

Panofsky, A. (2014). *Misbehaving Science: Controversy and the Development of Behavior Genetics*. Chicago: University of Chicago Press.

If you prefer a more hard-science as opposed to sociological critique try this:

Thapar, A. and Harold, G. (2014). Editorial perspective: Why is there such a mismatch between traditional heritability estimates and molecular genetic findings for behavioural traits? *Journal of Child Psychology and Psychiatry*, **55**, 1088–91.

EVOLUTIONARY PSYCHOLOGY

As we have seen in the preceding section, behavioural geneticists are primarily interested in the ways in which individuals differ. Why is one person more likely than another to enjoy risky activities such as riding roller coasters, driving fast, or committing crimes? Why do some people score higher than others on tests of cognitive ability? Why are some people more aggressive than others—or more compassionate? However, these questions suggest other, more basic, questions: Why do people perform risky activities at all? Where is the benefit? Why is *anyone* aggressive—where does **aggression** come from? Or compassion? Things like risky behaviour, aggression, and compassion are present in all known human societies. While individuals and entire cultures may differ in the extent to which these and many other characteristics are exhibited, such characteristics are part of what makes us recognizably human. Despite our individual and cultural differences, humans are far more similar than we are different (Buss, 2005). In contrast to the behavioural geneticists' emphasis on inherited differences, evolutionary psychology is concerned with these inherited similarities.

Evolution as a Fact and Theory

Human evolution is accepted as scientific fact by most scientists, although results are more mixed in the general public, with acceptance of evolution being closely tied up with religious beliefs and scientific literacy. According to a survey by Elsdon-Baker et al (2017), 49% of British adults endorsed the statement 'Humans and other living things evolved over time as a result of natural selection, in which God played no part'. Only 9% believed that 'Humans and other living things were created by

God and have always existed in their current form'; 22% believed in evolution as a divinely guided process and the remainder of respondents either had a different opinion or none.

Evolution remains a rather more controversial topic in the United States. As of 2009, only about 39% of Americans accept the idea that humans evolved from earlier forms of life, with the remaining 60% divided between those who reject the idea flat-out and those who are uncertain (Gallup Poll, 2009). However, acceptance or rejection of the idea of human evolution was strongly related to education. Only 21% of those with high-school educations accepted human evolution, compared with 74% of those with postgraduate degrees.

In this context the term *controversial* can be misleading as applied to the topic of evolution, because there is a difference between a *public controversy* and a *scientific controversy*. The controversy over evolution is a public controversy. There is no controversy about evolution among scientists (Larson and Witham, 1998).

If evolution is a 'fact', why do we so often hear about the 'theory' of evolution? Which is it—a *theory* or a *fact*? In truth, evolution is both theory *and* fact (Lenski, 2000). To understand how this is so, let us first define the terms. In general usage, a *fact* is something that exists—an actual happening in time and space. In science a *fact* can be defined slightly differently as an observation about the natural world that has been confirmed so frequently that it would be unreasonable to withhold acceptance, at least on a provisional basis.

Also a theory is a set of interconnected ideas or statements used *to explain* (or somehow organize) facts. Theories may be false or true—but if a theory is proved to be wrong, the facts that the theory is attempting to explain do not go away. As popular science writer Stephen Jay Gould (1981) put it, during the twentieth century Einstein's theory of gravity replaced Newton's earlier theory of gravity—but this did not change the direction in which apples fell when they left the tree.

How then does evolution qualify as both theory and fact? Here are some basic *facts* of evolution, according to biologist R.C. Lewontin (1981, p 559), accepted by the vast majority of biologists, palaeontologists, physical anthropologists, and geologists:

The earth is at least 4.5 billions of years old. Cellular life has been around for at least half of that period, and organized multicellular life is at least 1.2 billion years old.

Major life forms now on earth were not all represented in the past. For example, there were no birds or mammals (including humans) 250 million years ago.

Some major life forms of the past are no longer living. There used to be dinosaurs, but now there are none.

All current forms of life come from previous life forms that were different. Birds arose from non-birds and humans from non-humans.

These are facts of evolution that are scientifically indisputable. *Theories* of evolution—such as Charles Darwin's *theory of natural selection*, discussed below—are another matter. They continue to be debated to some extent.

Psychologists taking an evolutionary perspective propose that without a basic understanding of the facts and theories of evolution, psychological phenomena are very difficult to explain satisfactorily. For example, why do humans behave so differently in some respects from one society to the next, whereas in other respects behaviour remains remarkably similar regardless of society and culture? Why do men and women (and males and females of other animal species) differ in certain aspects of their behaviour throughout the world? Why do people in all known societies find young people with smooth skin more beautiful than older people with blemishes and wrinkles? Why do small children learn to fear snakes easily, but have a hard time learning to fear cars or electrical sockets, which pose a far greater danger (LoBue and deLoache, 2008)? There are thousands of such questions that could be asked. These are the sorts of questions addressed by *evolutionary psychologists*.

Natural Selection

The most plausible theory of how important evolutionary events occur was offered by Charles Darwin (1859/2003). It is known as the **theory of natural selection**. Because the theory of natural selection is so central to evolutionary views of psychology, it is important that we review this theory briefly before continuing. Darwin made a number of observations about the world that led him to devise the theory of natural selection. The process he eventually described is actually quite simple. Here's how it works:

1 *Darwin first considered that it is theoretically conceivable for a species to grow in numbers without limit.* Take elephants, notoriously slow reproducers. Darwin calculated that in a 60-year period of fertility with an average of six total offspring in a lifetime, the unchecked reproduction of elephants should result in a total of 15 million elephant descendants left alive on earth after only 500 years! If these aren't enough elephants for you, within a few *thousand* years—a mark that has long passed since elephants first appeared on the scene—there should have been so many elephants left alive that the earth itself ought to be little more than a ball of elephants expanding outwards into space at a rate faster than the speed of light! So where are all the elephants?

2 *In spite of the fact that species can **conceivably reproduce with unlimited numerical growth, they obviously don't***—or at least not for very long, a fact Darwin also noted. In other words, some elephants just aren't doing their job! But why? Darwin concluded that *although the potential for reproduction among species is nearly infinite, the resources needed to support individuals of any species are always finite.* There just isn't enough air, food, or water to divide among all the elephants—nor are there enough appealing or available partners for them to mate with. The need for resources among all species always outstrips the availability of resources. *And because resources are always finite, there is competition for them.*

3 *Darwin also noted that living organisms of a species varied in their characteristics*—some are taller, some stronger, some more colourful, and so on. During the twentieth century, scientists came to understand that this variability in characteristics was due to genetic diversity, but in Darwin's time it was simply acknowledged that diversity existed. Some of these characteristics increased the chances of the individual holding them of winning out in competition for resources. Thus, *those best suited to surviving and reproducing in whatever is the prevailing environment will leave the most offspring.* Some elephants have characteristics that make them better than others at locating food and shelter, avoiding predators, and finding mates.

4 *Darwin added to the fact of diversity the fact of heredity—offspring tend to resemble their parents in various characteristics more than do other members of*

the population. Therefore, the offspring of those best suited to surviving and reproducing in the current environment will be more likely than others to have inherited the very advantages in survival and reproduction that produced them. These offspring, in turn, will leave more offspring than others of their generation because they have inherited reproductive advantages. The genetic lines of individuals better adapted to their environment will continue to be represented in new generations in rapidly increasing numbers, while the genetic lines of those who are not so well adapted will die out.

5 *As a result of this natural filtering—or 'selection'—process, over many generations, small incremental changes will begin to occur in the characteristics of members of the species.* This is because the genes responsible for reproductively helpful characteristics remain in the gene pool, while genes responsible for less helpful (or overtly harmful) characteristics are filtered out. Over evolutionary time, these small changes result in the accumulation of characteristics in the species as a whole that cause members of the species to be increasingly better adapted to their environments. These accumulated characteristics are known as **adaptations.**

For example, the ability of stick insects to assume the appearance of a stick to fool predators is the result of adaptation, as is the ability of bats to navigate in the dark with *echolocation*. Beginning with only a few individuals with favourable characteristics, over hundreds and thousands of generations these advantages develop into complex adaptations that characterize virtually *all* individuals in the species to a greater or lesser extent ('greater or lesser' because of variation, see Figure 5.6).

> **KEY IDEAS** theory of natural selection The **theory of natural selection** is Charles Darwin's theory of how the most important types of evolutionary events occur. Key to natural selection is the notion of adaptations. **Adaptations** are characteristics of organisms that have evolved over evolutionary time because they confer reproductive or survival advantages. Adaptations arise as a result of small, incremental changes in the genome of organisms over many generations, and they represent solutions to specific challenges and pressures faced recurrently by the organism.

FIGURE 5.6 **Two examples of adaptation: the stick insect and the bat.**   Natural selection is not the only evolutionary process. However, it is the only one yet proposed by scientists that can account for the precision with which organisms are adapted to their environments (Williams, 1966), and for the way in which new species come into being over evolutionary time. It is also the ultimate fusion of nature and nurture, because it describes the way that life forms interact with their environments to produce change.

Sources: stick insect: Lakeview Images/Shutterstock.com; bat: anshu18/Shutterstock.com.

The Goals of Evolutionary Psychology

Now that we have reviewed the theory of natural selection, we can explore evolutionary psychology itself. Although often described as a field of psychology, **evolutionary psychology** is actually a way of looking at questions of interest to psychologists in any number of fields (Cosmides and Tooby, 2008). Evolutionary psychology is a multidisciplinary perspective with roots in evolutionary biology, cognitive science, anthropology, palaeontology, computer science, and conventional branches of psychology such as social psychology (Maner and Kenrick, 2010). In addition to its multidisciplinary origins, mainstream evolutionary psychology is characterized by adherence to a number of ideas not found in most other approaches. We will use the following terms as shorthand for two of these ideas: *psychological adaptation* and *environmental mismatch*.

Psychological Adaptation

Just as the human brain is made up of a large number of complex, evolved biological adaptations that are integrated with one another, according to evolutionary psychologists, the human mind is constructed of a large number of evolved **psychological adaptations** that work together in an integrated fashion (Tooby and Cosmides, 1992). What exactly is a psychological adaptation? Recall that natural selection results in the accumulation over evolutionary time of adaptations—characteristics that allow organisms to be well adapted to their environments. Psychological adaptations are psychological characteristics that have evolved over evolutionary time to allow individuals to be better adapted to their physical and social environments.

These psychological adaptations are somewhat analogous to miniature computer programs, each specialized to solve a specific problem faced recurrently by our ancestors and related to survival or reproduction in the environments in which they evolved. Some of these problems undoubtedly included avoiding animal predators and hostile humans, choosing nutritious food and avoiding poisons, communicating and forming alliances with other humans, selecting and retaining mates, and nurturing and protecting children (Pinker, 2002). Psychological adaptations are specialized 'solutions' to specific problems.

As examples, the emotion of fear and the capacity for aggression evolved as solutions to the problem of how to survive threats from predators and hostile humans (Barrett, 2005). The universal prohibition against mating with one's parents, children, and siblings is a solution to the problem of how to avoid **birth defects** and other health problems in infants resulting from inbreeding (Lieberman, Pillsworth, and Haselton, 2011).

According to evolutionary psychologists, the reason that we human beings are so flexible in the way we respond to the wide variety of situations in which we find ourselves daily is that our minds possess a vast number of these highly specialized psychological adaptations. As an analogy, consider the flexibility of a carpenter. A carpenter does not have one all-purpose tool that can be used in any situation—the demands of different situations are often unique. Carpenters are flexible and can accomplish many kinds of tasks because they have dozens of different tools, each of which is designed for a specific use. Evolutionary psychologists believe the same is true of the human mind. Psychological adaptations work together in a coordinated fashion, just as the carpenter's many tools complement one another, but each evolved for a specific purpose (Tooby and Cosmides, 1992). This view of the mind is known as the **modular** or *domain specific* model because it sees the mind as a

❯ KEY IDEAS evolutionary psychology **Evolutionary psychology** is a multidisciplinary approach to psychology based on evolutionary principles, including but not limited to Darwin's theory of natural selection.

❯ KEY IDEAS psychological adaptation A **psychological adaptation** is a mental characteristic that evolved through natural selection to provide solutions to specific types of problems encountered over evolutionary time by our human ancestors.

❯ KEY IDEAS the modular model **The modular model** of the mind sees it as a large collection of components (modules), each of which provides solutions only to specific types of problems.

large collection of self-contained 'modules' or components, each of which evolved to tackle problems that exist only within specific domains of existence. Not all evolutionary psychologists adhere to this view, but it does form the basis of mainstream evolutionary psychology.

Environmental Mismatch

As we have just seen, psychological adaptations evolved to solve problems related to survival and reproduction in the environments in which our ancestors evolved. These environments were vastly different in many respects from those of the modern world. Therefore, according to evolutionary psychologists, we should expect a degree of **environmental mismatch** between some psychological adaptations and life in the modern world.

> **KEY IDEAS** environmental mismatch **Environmental mismatch** occurs when a psychological adaptation is expressed in an environment different from the one in which it evolved and to which it is not suited.

For example, how is it that KFC, McDonald's, Burger King, and other fast-food chains do so well all over the world, regardless of traditions of native cuisine? Advertising is powerful, but it is not all-powerful, particularly where food preferences are concerned. It seems likely that throughout the world people have developed an evolutionary preference for foods high in fats and sugars (Rozin, 1976). This becomes a puzzle when you consider that a diet high in fats and processed sugars is extremely unhealthy. Why should we apparently have evolved to find an unhealthy diet appealing? It seems to violate the principles of natural selection, where only those characteristics helpful to survival and reproduction survive over evolutionary time.

Evolutionary psychologists answer this question in the following way: in the environments of our ancestors, calories were scarce, and humans worked hard to get them. Those individuals who avoided bitter or lean foods in favour of fatty and sweet foods had an advantage because they consumed more calories, which made them better able to survive and reproduce. Therefore, by natural selection, a taste preference for sweet and fatty foods has evolved as part of human psychology throughout the world (Buss, 1994).

However, in current industrial environments, the culture of fast-food outlets and supermarkets makes calories over-plentiful rather than scarce. In our evolutionary past, sweets and fats were primarily available only in ripe fruit and animal flesh, respectively. This is hardly the case today. The modern easy availability of calories interacts in an unfortunate way with a psychological mechanism designed for a low-calorie life in the African savannah (Wadden, Brownell, and Foster, 2002). Thus, we now have genuine epidemics of obesity in many nations throughout the world, partly as a result of the mismatch between our evolved taste preferences and our modern 'calorie-dense' environment. In effect, our *adaptation* to prefer sweet and fatty foods is no longer *adaptive* because it is not well suited to survival and reproduction in our current environment. This is a repeating theme in the work of evolutionary psychologists: we are modern humans with Stone-Age minds (Allman, 1995).

The Social Brain and Social Networks

Dunbar (1998) proposed the idea of the social brain. This is the idea that the reason primates have such large brains relative to their overall size is the processing capacity required for the large social networks and complex social interactions typical of humans. Dunbar reports a strong positive correlation between brain neocortex (the areas of cortex associated with more cognitively advanced species) and the size of social groups across primates. This calculation suggests that humans will have a social network size of around 150.

The figure of 150 (now sometimes called Dunbar's number) is consistent with community size in hunter-gatherer societies around the world today and, according to the Domesday Book, in Britain a thousand years ago. It is also the size of typical adult social networks and successful business organizations (Dunbar, 2008). Now, I hear you say, what about online social networks like *Facebook*? Studies of *Facebook* networks (eg, Long et al, 2008) typically show larger social networks than 150; however, as Dunbar points out, only a fraction of *Facebook* friends really represent stable relationships. Moreover, not all our significant people use online networking tools, or we may exclude some people from our online network so as to conceal some aspects of our lives! Therefore, online networks are not a valid tool to estimate the size of our social networks.

THINKING CREATIVELY

If Dunbar is correct and there is really an optimum group size for humans of 150, think of as many situations as possible in which we can use this knowledge to build happy, productive communities.

Psychological Sex Differences: A 'Test Case' for Evolutionary Psychology

Evolutionary psychologists believe that human beings are a single species with a single human nature. Just as we are all recognizably human in physiology despite differences such as height, skin tone, and eye colour, our psychology is very similar. This is not to deny the importance of individual differences—in fact individual differences can be explained in evolutionary terms, but the emphasis in evolutionary psychology is very much on similarities. In evolutionary terms this similarity is the result of the common environmental and social pressures acting on humans throughout our evolution. All of our ancestors needed to find food and shelter, avoid animal predators, find mates, form alliances with friendly humans, avoid attacks from hostile bands, and so forth. The same environmental and social pressures should result in the same basic adaptations, whether in physiology or psychology (Symons, 1995).

The major exception to this generalization concerns sex differences. In most cases, men and women have faced the same evolutionary pressures—and the psychological adaptations of men and women should be identical in most respects as a result. However, in certain domains of life men and women have faced quite different sorts of pressures and problems over evolutionary time. Their experiences have been different. For this reason, at least some psychological differences should be expected between men and women. According to evolutionary psychologists, it is primarily in areas related to sexuality, reproduction, and physical **aggression** that we ought to see sex differences in behaviour; and indeed, throughout the world, there are average differences between men and women in just these areas, but not in most other areas (Archer, 2009).

Because sex differences are an exception to the general evolutionary view that human nature is unified, these differences have often been used as a 'test case' by evolutionary psychologists to demonstrate the strength of their theories. Some of the most interesting (and controversial—in both public and scientific senses) research by evolutionary psychologists pertains to sexual behaviour itself.

Sex Differences in Partner Variety and Casual Sex

Most men—particularly as they age—express the desire for a long-term monogamous relationship (Mathes et al, 2002). However, men are sometimes also attracted to the idea of sex without long-term commitment (*casual sex* or, to use a technical psychology term, **short-term mating**); and by the idea of sex with a variety of partners (Petersen and Hyde, 2010). On the other hand, while many women also express interest in casual sex under certain circumstances, on average they are choosier about mating—typically women show less interest than men in casual encounters or in having sex with a variety of partners (Geary, 2010).

Note that women are *not* less interested in sex per se—they just tend to express this interest slightly differently, often in terms of a greater interest in sex as part of an ongoing relationship (termed **long-term mating**). Note the number of conditionals in the last sentence! When we speak of sex differences it is important to note that these do not preclude or override *individual* differences. It is ethically very important to emphasize that these findings are descriptive; they describe the average preferences, rather than tell us how we *should* act. There is a risk that these sort of findings can lend weight to judgemental attitudes towards individuals who act differently to the average; for example, women who choose to engage in short-term mating.

Men's average greater interest in casual sex and partner variety is evident in decades of behavioural science research (Schmitt et al, 2012). As shown in Figure 5.7 and Table 5.2, this includes research conducted among more than 200,000 individuals in 53 nations, six continents, and 13 islands (Lippa, 2009). It is also reflected in institutions such as prostitution and pornography, which cater primarily to men. Further, it is repeatedly found in folklore, fantasy, literature, art, films, and jokes. The greater tendency of males towards interest in short-term mating and sex with a variety of partners extends to most (but not all) other mammals and to numerous non-mammalian species as well (Bateman, 1948).

> **KEY IDEAS** short- and long-term mating **Short-term mating** is sexual behaviour that is casual in nature and not part of a committed relationship. By contrast **long-term mating** involves a committed, ongoing sexual relationship.

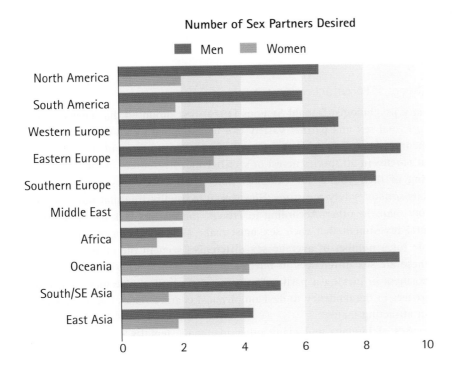

FIGURE 5.7 **Sex differences in interest in partner variety.** In his cross-national study of 52 nations, David Schmitt (2003) found that men tended to express a desire for a greater number of sex partners than women. This graph divides the world by ten major regions and summarizes the numbers of sexual partners desired by men and women 'over the next 30 years'.

Source: Schmitt, 2003, p 92.

TABLE 5.2 **Sex differences across ten world regions in the desire to have more than one sexual partner 'in the next month'**

This table summarizes the percentages of men and women from David Schmitt's (2003) sample of 16,288 to the question of whether they would choose to have more than one sexual partner over the coming month. Schmitt's sample was drawn from 52 nations on six continents and 16 islands in ten major world regions. (Source: Schmitt, 2003, p 93.)

World region	% of men wanting more than one sexual partner	% of women wanting more than one sexual partner
North America	23.1	2.9
South America	35.0	6.1
Western Europe	22.6	5.5
Eastern Europe	31.7	7.1
Southern Europe	31.0	6.0
Middle East	33.1	5.9
Africa	18.2	4.2
Oceania	25.3	5.8
South/Southeast Asia	32.4	6.4
East Asia	17.9	2.6

THINKING CREATIVELY

Evolutionary psychologists are interested in establishing cross-cultural consistent patterns of behaviour. However, for practical purposes people sometimes need to have information that is precise and specific to their particular time and cultural context. Design a study to investigate gender differences in mate preferences in your own social environment; for example, university. HINT: this could be a survey, but there are also experimental methods you could use. Don't actually carry it out without ethical approval!

Trivers' Theory of Parental Investment

> **KEY IDEAS** Trivers' theory of parental investment Robert Trivers (1972) proposed his **theory of parental investment**, an evolutionary theory which explains various sex differences in a range of species as resulting from unequal minimal levels of parental investment in reproduction between males and females.

Evolutionary psychologist Donald Symons (1979) first proposed that men's greater interest in casual sex and partner variety can be explained by an earlier and more genetic theory; Robert Trivers' (1972) theory of **parental investment**. Trivers (1972) noted that parents in all species invest or sacrifice many resources in the conception and rearing of their young—for example, time, energy, nutrients, property, care, and various sorts of safety measures. However, it is usually true that one sex must invest more than the other. According to Trivers' theory, this lack of symmetry in the parental investment that each sex must make as a minimum to reproduce is responsible for a number of average sex differences seen in the animal kingdom. Among these are sex differences in interest in short-term mating and partner variety, choosiness in picking a partner, differences in physical size and aggression, and differences in the tendency to develop physical characteristics that have no use other than attracting mates.

In the cases of humans and many other mammals, females invest much more in the entire process of reproducing than males. Consider the reproductive lives of humans throughout evolutionary history. For an ancestral woman to bring a child into the world and help the child survive during its first few years of helplessness, the mother had to invest *at least* the following:

- Nine months of uncomfortable and possibly dangerous (think about having to escape predators with a baby bump) pregnancy, during which large quantities of her generally scarce bodily nutrients were shared with her developing foetus.
- A painful and potentially life-threatening experience of labour and childbirth, lasting at least several hours and up to a day or more.
- Several years of breastfeeding following childbirth, during which time the new mother would have continued to share her bodily nutrients as well as her time and energy with her infant.

Consider also that a woman's total opportunities to reproduce are limited not only by this extraordinary effort but also by the fact that in their entire lives women experience only about 350 brief monthly windows of fertility lasting several days, as dictated by the human menstrual cycle.

Now let's look at our ancestral *fathers'* minimal possible parental investment. For these men to have reproduced, they needed only to have invested the following:

- Time spent having sex.
- Barely measurable amounts of protein and amino acids contained in an ejaculation of semen.
- Relatively few of the billions of sperm they produce in their lifetimes.

Moreover, once men reach **adolescence**, they are potentially fertile every day until they die. Their window of fertility is open as wide as can be.

Obviously, this does not mean that there are no men in the world who invest more than the minimum necessary to reproduce—and please forget any tired stereotypes you may have heard about paternal commitment in particular cultural groups. In the modern world, many men devote their entire lives and most of their earnings to their children. Human beings are unusual in the mammalian world for the extent of fathers' typical investment in their offspring. The point stressed by evolutionary psychologists is that men who invest do so *by choice*—they do not *need* to invest much of anything to reproduce.

According to Trivers, the sex that invests more in reproduction (generally females) is more valuable in reproductive terms. Members of the lesser-investing sex (generally males) compete more fiercely for the more valuable resource (ie, the attention of females). This more intense (and often violent) competition among males historically has resulted in males' greater size, upper-body strength, and physical aggressiveness. It is also the reason that, in the animal world, it is usually the male who develops various ornaments or characteristics that appear to have no use other than attracting mates—such as the peacock's tail, the songbird's call, or the bower's nest (Darwin, 1871/1874, see Figure 5.8). Males must distinguish themselves from the rest of the pack so as to be attractive to females.

Females, on the other hand, need do comparatively little to attract a male—they are attractive enough *because they are female*. As the greater-investing sex, the female is thus in the position to be more choosy than the male about which 'applicant' she allows sexual access, and under most circumstances it is in her reproductive interest to be highly selective. As was demonstrated in a series of experiments with fruit flies (Bateman, 1948), it is virtually never to the female's advantage to

FIGURE 5.8 Bird art as seduction. Apart from humans, the only animals known to spend substantial time and energy constructing a purely aesthetic display that is separate from their own bodies are male bower birds. The bower expends enormous effort and time securing the most brilliantly coloured natural objects, bringing them back to the nest, and arranging them carefully in clusters of uniform colour. The purpose? To attract a female. Once mated, the bower's nest is abandoned, and the female moves on to her own nest.
Source: Luke Shelley/Shutterstock.com.

mate indiscriminately, because mating with more males than is necessary to become pregnant does not increase her rate of reproduction (and, in fact, may expose her to unnecessary risks such as disease or violence from a jealous partner). In this way, females' rate of reproduction is limited by nature.

On the other hand, the reproductive success of the male is not limited by nature—*it is limited by females' willingness or lack of willingness to mate*. As Baumeister and Tice (2001) have stated, most acts of sexual intercourse in the mammalian world, including the human world, occur when a female changes her default position of 'no' to 'yes'. According to Trivers' theory, unlike our female ancestors, ancestral males *would* have increased their reproductive success by convincing as many females as possible to mate, and to mate with them as often as possible.

 THINKING CRITICALLY

You may find that the language evolutionary psychologists use to describe human sexual relations makes you quite uncomfortable. You would not be alone, and evolutionary psychologists are quite often criticized for 'political incorrectness'. Evolutionary psychologists might argue that they are simply applying the language of evolutionary biology to humans. Where do you stand on this?

According to evolutionary psychologists, these historical behavioural sex differences in humans shaped sex differences in psychological adaptations that persist to the present day—even among people who have no conscious interest in reproducing at all. Indeed, evolutionary psychologists emphasize that people generally have sex for reasons other than the desire to reproduce. The point made by these theorists is that those among our female ancestors who were picky about their mates and those among our male ancestors who were less picky, reproduced more successfully and left the most descendants. These descendants would have inherited a genetic make-up that predisposed them to replicating their ancestors' sexual behavioural tendencies to some degree and therefore also reproduced more successfully. Over time, then, through the process of natural selection, these aspects of sexual psychology have become widespread among humans.

Exceptions that May Prove Trivers' Rule

Trivers' theory of parental investment and sexual selection is particularly *elegant*—a term used by scientists when a theory explains a great many things with relative simplicity. The Trivers theory is elegant for three reasons. First, it applies to all sexually reproducing species, not just humans or other mammals. Second, it makes no particular predictions about *males and females*—the theory is concerned with differences between the sex that invests the most in reproduction and the one that invests the least. Third, it explains a number of sex differences in sexual and reproductive behaviour, not only interest in casual sex and partner variety.

It happens that the female is usually the greater-investing sex, and so Trivers' predictions usually do apply in the same way to males and females regardless of species. However, this is not *always* the case. In some species, these roles are reversed, and the male must invest more in reproduction than the female. What happens under such conditions?

Let's take one of the very best examples of role reversal in reproduction—the *ophidon* species of pipefish, a relative of the sea horse. Among these fish, the female deposits her eggs on male bodies, and the male carries the eggs to term, nursing them all the while—a process that is highly costly in terms of nutrients, energy, and time—and prevents the male from engaging in other reproductive opportunities. It also exposes him to grave danger from predatory fish (Berglund and Rosenqvist, 2003). Thus, the males invest much more in reproduction than the females, and the females can mate with as many males as they can find.

In accord with the Trivers theory, female *ophidon* pipefish are much larger than males due to more intense competition among females for mates. In the animal world, intense competition for mates generally involves physical combat, and in physical combat the larger individual has the advantage. Female *ophidons* also carry permanent ornamentation to attract males (blue colouring) in contrast to the males' only temporary colouration. Females also are much less choosy when it comes to mating. In short, female *ophidons* display characteristics generally associated with male animals.

So what about humans? In the Western world's recent history at least it tends to be women who seem to be more concerned about 'ornamentation' (jewellery, clothing, make-up, etc), adding that women do often compete fiercely for the attention of men. Does this contradict Trivers' idea? Humans could be seen as another exception proving Trivers' rule. Recall that humans are almost alone in the mammalian world in the extent of care that males provide. Among the vast majority of mammals, males provide *no* parental care at all (Geary, 2010). Therefore, *human* males are far more reproductively valuable than males of other mammalian species. According to Trivers' theory, we ought to expect (and we do indeed find) lesser sex differences in size and strength among humans than among most mammals, higher levels of competition among women for mates than is normally found among mammalian females, and ornamentation among human females as well as males. (It should also be noted, however, that the relative lack of ornamentation among Western men is not at all typical of more traditional societies, thus African and Native American societies generally favour ornamentation in men.)

THINKING CRITICALLY

A central idea of a good scientific theory is that it can be tested because it predicts particular research findings. Trivers' theory can be said to predict that human males will compete for females and therefore will be less concerned with appearance than females. However, it can also be said to predict that because human males invest more than males from most other species this difference will be less pronounced or even reversed. In fact both these findings can be confirmed in some human societies but not others. So to what extent is Trivers' theory testable in humans?

RESEARCH IN FOCUS

Buss, D.M. (1989). Sex differences in human mate preferences. *Behavioural & Brain Sciences*, **12**, 1–49.

Aim: To test the predictions of evolutionary psychology about sex differences in mate selection. More specifically to test the hypotheses that irrespective of cultural background women would express preferences for ambitious, hard-working, and wealthy men and that men would express more attraction towards young, chaste, and conventionally attractive women.

Method: A total of 5,446 female and 4,601 male participants were recruited from 33 countries spanning six continents. The mean age of participants was 23.05 years. In countries where the population comprised two or more distinct cultural groups these were sampled separately so a total of 37 populations were sampled. Sampling methods, sample sizes, and sample characteristics such as age varied considerably between countries. For example, the New Zealand sample were teenagers and the Estonians were marriage licence applicants while the Germans responded to newspaper adverts. Participants completed two questionnaires in their native languages. One questionnaire asked participants to rank 13 characteristics including good earning capacity and attractiveness for their importance in mate choice. The other questionnaire required participants to rate 18 characteristics for importance on a 0–3 scale.

Results: Most findings were consistent with evolutionary theory. In all 37 countries women emphasized financial prospects in a mate more than men did and in 36 of these the differences were significant. In every sample women identified an ideal mate as older than themselves. Women also placed more emphasis on ambition and work ethic in 34 of the samples. There were cultural variations, however, with men placing more emphasis on these characteristics in Spain, Colombia, and Zulu South Africa. In all 37 countries men rated attractiveness as more important than did women, and in all cultures men identified an ideal age for their mate as younger than themselves. Results concerning chastity varied more widely than any other. Although in no country did women place more importance on chastity than men, men's concern with this characteristic in a mate varied massively. In Western Europe, for example, only Irish men were bothered about a potential partner's prior sexual activity.

Conclusions: The predictions of evolutionary theory are supported. However, there are also cultural variations in the criteria for mate choice, suggesting that culture as well as evolution influences mate choice.

>

> ## MASTER YOUR METHODOLOGY

1 Comment on the sample size for this study.

2 For a study to have good population validity, its samples should reflect the characteristics of their target populations. Explain why this is a problem in this study.

3 Why was it helpful to use two measures of mate preference?

 THINKING CRITICALLY

Look back to our critical thinking toolkit (Chapter 1). What strengths and weaknesses can you see in relation to this study?

Challenges to the Evolutionary Approach

Like behavioural genetics, evolutionary psychology and similar evolution-based theories of human behaviour have been quite controversial. However, note that some evolutionary principles have become quite widely accepted by psychologists; for example, attachment theorists (Chapter 11) and modular cognitive psychologists (see Chapter 8), who do not identify as 'evolutionary psychologists' (Henrich, Heine, and Norenzayan, 2010). On one hand, given the acknowledged importance of evolution on all aspects of species development it would surely be arrogant to dismiss the possibility that processes like natural selection have influenced human mind and behaviour. On the other hand, among other things, evolutionary psychologists have been accused of the following:

- Telling stories of the origin of various human behaviours to try to rationalize patriarchal, sexist, and potentially misogynist views of human sexuality (Rose and Rose, 2000).

- Engaging in 'biological determinism'—the tendency to view all behaviour as a result of innate biology—and ignoring the importance of the environment (Gould, 1997).

- Wrongly believing that people are consciously motivated to 'spread their genes' when engaging in various behaviours, including sex (Rose and Rose, 2000).

- Wrongly attributing stereotypical 'masculine' or 'feminine' characteristics to all men and women.

- Taking a heteronormative stance on sex differences in sexual behaviour and ignoring LGBTQI people (Jackson, 2006).

Some criticisms of evolutionary psychology and other evolutionary approaches appear to result from oversimplifications of what these theorists are actually saying (Machery and Cohen, 2011), or refer to the *implications* of what they are saying rather than what they have said. For example, evolutionary psychologists do not claim that people are motivated on a conscious level to 'spread their genes'. Instead they claim that the kinds of behaviours that in the past led to increased reproductive success have become part of human nature because more and more people came to be born with these tendencies over evolutionary time, and fewer people born with opposing tendencies. Similarly, although evolutionary psychology can explain typical sex differences in preference for short- and long-term mating, and this *can* be used to justify a judgemental attitude to women who enjoy short-term mating, evolutionary psychologists do not themselves speak pejoratively of this behaviour. They take pains to emphasize that sex differences such as those just described are statistical averages only and do not apply to all men and women any more than average height differences (Buss, 2005).

However, many critics of evolutionary approaches make important points. For example:

- Some psychologists who accept the basic notion that evolution has shaped human psychology nonetheless charge that 'evolutionary psychologists' have misinterpreted Charles Darwin (Panksepp and Panksepp, 2000). If these criticisms turn out to have merit, then some of the assumptions of evolutionary psychology may ultimately prove to be wrong.

- Although evolutionary psychology may be useful in understanding the commonalities among people, evolutionary psychologists have often been unable to account very well for individual differences (Buss, 2009).

- Although, increasingly, evolutionary psychology research is cross-cultural, the bulk of it (like the bulk of all psychological research) is conducted among people in highly industrialized Western societies, primarily university students in the United States (Arnett, 2008). As we shall discover in the next section of the chapter, important truths about human psychology may not emerge from such research (Henrich et al, 2010).

Indeed, it is particularly important that research from the evolutionary perspective include samples from diverse societies and social backgrounds, because evolutionary theorists wish to make claims about the unity of human psychology (Henrich et al, 2010).

Theoretical Problems

Although the vast majority of scientists, including psychologists, accept the idea of evolution in general, this is not to say that all accept that evolutionary mechanisms are a realistic explanation for psychological characteristics. Evolution depends on the idea of the ancestral environment—the physical, social, and biological system in which our ancestors lived. Tattersall (2001) points out that actually we cannot really know what our ancestral environment was like. Actually what evolutionary psychologists do is make guesses about the ancestral environment, already knowing what sort of ancestral environment would fit with their existing ideas. This puts them at risk of bias and circular logic.

Evolution also depends on the idea that characteristics are preferentially passed on to successive generations through coding in genes. This is entirely credible when it comes to physical characteristics but not necessarily so when it comes to psychological characteristics. Ehrlich and Feldman (2003) have questioned whether the human genome contains enough genes to shape the multitude of subtle adaptations to the nervous system needed to influence behaviour. The validity of this argument depends on the mechanisms of gene-gene and gene-environment interaction, something psychologists are still getting to grips with.

Testability and Evidence

Psychologists are generally better disposed towards theories or sets of theories that can be tested; a theory or approach to psychology has a serious weakness if we cannot directly test ideas! The extent to which evolutionary psychology is testable is subject to debate. There is no shortage of studies that show results consistent with evolutionary psychology; however, there is a difference between results being *consistent* with an idea and being a direct *test* of that idea. So studies do show that women tend to be fussier about mates than men and people are indeed more likely to put themselves at risk to help those with whom they share many genes. However, evolution is not the only explanation for those findings, therefore such studies are not direct tests of evolutionary theory.

Some evolutionary ideas have been well tested and have either generated no supporting evidence or have actually found disconfirming evidence. Confer et al (2010) cite the example of the kin selection theory of male homosexuality. This theory suggests that, in line with the idea of inclusive fitness, men with little chance of reproducing themselves may 'become gay' and maximize their chances of passing on similar genes by looking after their siblings' children. However, studies comparing kin altruism in gay and straight men have consistently found no differences, strongly suggesting this explanation is without merit, even if it were possible to explain how individuals might 'become gay'. Of course, examples like this do not discredit evolutionary psychology as a whole but they do serve to illustrate that a hypothesis can be grounded in evolutionary principles yet be hopelessly wrong!

READ THIS

Although evolutionary psychology developed in psychology these early pieces from Leda Cosmides and John Tooby represent a formalization of the field:

Cosmides, L. and Tooby, J. (1987). From evolution to behavior: Evolutionary psychology as the missing link. In J. Dupre (ed), *The Latest on the Best: Essays on Evolution and Optimality*. Boston: MIT Press.

Cosmides, L., Tooby, J., and Barkow, J.H. (1992). Introduction: Evolutionary psychology and conceptual integration. In J. Barkow, L. Cosmides, and J. Tooby (eds), *The Adapted Mind: Evolutionary Psychology and the Generation of Culture*. Oxford: Oxford University Press, pp 3–15.

For a more up-to-date overview try this:

Buss, D. (2015). *Evolutionary Psychology: The New Science of the Mind*. New York: Psychology Press.

The first of these articles explores criticisms of evolutionary psychology while the second provides a solid defence against misrepresentation of the field:

Burke, D. (2014). Why isn't everyone an evolutionary psychologist? *Frontiers in Psychology*, **5**, article 910, 1–8.

Winegard, B.M. and Deaner, R.O. (2014). Misrepresentations of evolutionary psychology in sex and gender textbooks. *Evolutionary Psychology*, **12**, 474–508.

THE INFLUENCE OF CULTURE AND SOCIETY

If evolutionary psychology represents the nature side of the distinction between nature and nurture, what about the influence of 'nurture' on human similarity and difference? The relative importance of evolution and culture can be thought of as a 'new nature-nurture debate'. To complete this chapter, we now turn to those theorists whose work highlights the importance of cultural and social influence on human psychology: sociocultural theorists. As mentioned earlier, the evolutionary and sociocultural perspectives approach questions of nature and nurture in radically different ways. While evolutionary theorists highlight the unity of human psychology, sociocultural theorists highlight its diversity. As we have seen, natural selection elegantly blends nature and nurture by explaining how development and change only occur as a result of the interaction of genes and environments. However, it is undeniably true that evolutionary psychologists and behavioural geneticists tend to emphasize the 'nature' side of natural selection in their explanations for human behaviour. For example, behavioural geneticists have claimed that the unique experiences of each child—rather than overall family environment—are of crucial importance to cognitive development, but these researchers have not yet identified the specific types of unique experiences that exert important effects. Similarly, while evolutionary psychologists have accounted well for *similarities* among humans, they are more tenuous in their accounting for *differences* among individuals and entire cultures. And that is why we now turn our attention to the sociocultural perspective. Sociocultural theorists have expertly developed methods and theories that highlight psychological differences between individuals and entire cultures.

Human beings are already social creatures prior to the moment of birth. They learn to differentiate their mother's voice and language from the voices and languages of strangers while still in the womb, and they recognize the sounds of book passages that had been read to them prior to birth (Kisilevsky et al, 2009). Within hours of birth, they will respond to other people's facial expressions by attempting to imitate them (Field et al, 1989; see Chapter 11). Even innate reflexes in infants, such as the sucking reflex, will not occur unless they are triggered by physical contact with another person.

Although evolutionary psychologists have a great deal to contribute to our understanding of human psychology, as mentioned in the previous section, they generally lack detailed accounts of how society and culture influence behaviour and subjective experience. Those psychologists working from the *sociocultural perspective* focus on these influences.

Understanding Society and Culture

Society and *culture*—what do these terms mean? Unfortunately, they are often used inconsistently and interchangeably, but strictly they are not synonymous. The term **society** describes an enduring and cooperating group—anything from the Girl Scouts to rock fans, from ancient Greece to the People's Republic of China—whose members have developed institutions and organized patterns of interacting with one another.

> **KEY IDEAS** society and culture
> A **society** is an enduring and cooperating group whose members have developed institutions and organized patterns of interaction. **Culture** is the total pattern of behaviour exhibited by citizens of any given society, and the total products of a given society.

The term **culture**, on the other hand, describes the total pattern of behaviour exhibited by citizens of a given society, encompassing all of the products of that society—thought, language, actions, practices, manufactured goods, religion, and artefacts. For example, selling cookies outside supermarkets is part of Girl Scout culture; the ancient Greek language is part of ancient Greek culture; and a tendency to emphasize the welfare of the group over that of the individual is part of Chinese culture (Matsumoto and Hee Yoo, 2006). In other words, *culture* is what a *society* produces and transmits to new generations. Culture is what makes each society recognizably different from others, even those that may have somewhat similar institutions (Hofstede and McCrae, 2004).

The Sociocultural Alternative to Evolutionary Theory

What, then, is the **sociocultural perspective**? It is a general approach that attempts to describe the ways in which society and culture influence brain, mind, and behaviour. Like the evolutionary perspective, the sociocultural perspective is not a specific field—it is a perspective that can be found in fields of psychology as diverse as clinical psychology, cognitive psychology, developmental psychology, social psychology, and even neuroscience (Gelfand and Diener, 2010). However, this perspective is strongly associated with the field of **cultural psychology**—the study of psychology as it exists in different cultures (Markus and Kitayama, 1998). Cultural psychologists emphasize that different cultures are characterized by different behaviours and subjective experiences—although these psychologists do not deny that numerous similarities among cultures also exist and that certain aspects of psychology may be universal among all cultures (Norenzayan and Heine, 2005).

> **KEY IDEAS** sociocultural perspective and cultural psychology The **sociocultural perspective** is a general approach to psychology that focuses on the ways society and culture mould and influence behaviour. **Cultural psychology** is the study of psychology as it exists in different cultures.

Differences and Similarities in Cultural Perspective

Humans are not the only species with culture. For example, bands of chimpanzees living in similar kinds of environments may nonetheless differ in their patterns of behaviour and have been shown to learn these distinctive behaviours from one another through observation over the generations (Nishida, Matsusaka, and McGrew, 2009). The same is true of herds of dolphins, some of whom have been shown to transmit the use of sponges as tools from mother to daughter (Sargeant and Mann, 2009). Because these herds do not differ genetically (they are the same species), their differences in behaviour appear to demonstrate cultural differences (see Figure 5.9).

However, human culture is vibrantly unique. It pervades virtually every aspect of human thought and behaviour, and proliferates rapidly over generations (Heine and Norenzayan, 2006). Humans cooperate with one another and intentionally teach their young in ways that do not exist among other great apes such as chimpanzees or orangutans (Tomasello and Herrmann, 2010). Although cultural psychologists are interested in cultural similarities as well as differences, it is fair to say that their primary focus has been on cultural differences (Brouwers et al, 2004). Cultural

FIGURE 5.9 Culture is not limited to humans. Culture has been shown to exist in chimpanzees and dolphins. When Whiten, Horner, and de Waal (2005) taught rudimentary tool use to a group of chimpanzees, other chimps learned to use the tools through observing those who had the skills. Learning through imitation among herds of dolphins has also been experimentally demonstrated (Krützen et al, 2005).

Sources: dolphin: Yann hubert/Shutterstock.com; chimpanzee: mark higgins/Shutterstock.com.

differences are particularly informative with regard to the importance of nurture in shaping human experience and behaviour.

How do cultures differ? Clearly, cultures differ in specific ways such as language, rituals, diet, and moral beliefs. However, cultural researchers such as Geert Hofstede (eg, Hofstede and McCrae, 2004) have adopted a more sophisticated approach to understanding cultural differences. Hofstede examined responses from over 115,000 people in 72 countries with questionnaires designed to establish specific *dimensions* of behaviour along which entire cultures may typically differ. After statistical analysis, a number of essential dimensions of culture emerged. The most critical of these dimensions are the following:

1 *Individualism vs collectivism.* Individualist cultures are those, such as the United States, where the welfare and accomplishments of the individual are stressed over those of the group. Collectivist cultures, such as those found in China, Japan, and Sub-Saharan Africa, stress the importance of group effort, group membership, and group accomplishment. This cultural dimension has been of greatest interest to cultural psychologists, particularly as relates to differences between East Asian and Western cultures (Matsumoto and Hee Yoo, 2006).

2 *Power distance.* Power distance represents the degree to which the less powerful members of society accept and expect that some individuals will wield power and others will lack power. Europe, Canada, Australia, and Israel are particularly low on this dimension, while most Asian, Arab, and Latin American nations are high on power distance.

3 *Masculinity-femininity.* This dimension measures the degree to which a culture reflects what are traditionally thought of as stereotypically masculine or feminine characteristics. (Note that it does not refer to the presence or absence of patriarchal social relations in the society.) 'Masculine' cultural characteristics include competitiveness, assertiveness, ambition, and the accumulation of wealth. 'Feminine' cultural characteristics include placing greater value on quality of life, family, and relationships. According to Hofstede, Japan is an example of a strongly 'masculine' culture, and Sweden represents a highly 'feminine' culture.

4 *Uncertainty avoidance.* According to Hofstede, some societies are more likely than others to create conditions that will avoid stress, uncertainty, and risk for their citizens. These cultures have numerous rules that are stringently enforced, and they support highly structured workplaces. Employees typically remain at their jobs for long periods of time in these societies. According to Hofstede, uncertainty-avoidant cultures include Japan, Greece, Israel, and Spain, while cultures low in uncertainty avoidance include the United States, Jamaica, Sweden, and much of East Asia—with Singapore being the least uncertainty-avoidant culture studied.

Two Examples of Cultural Psychology

As you may recall, cultural psychologists have observed that most evolutionary psychology research (and most psychology research generally) is conducted among Western university students. They worry that evidence collected in such research may not always apply to people in other cultures or social circumstances. We will now look at two examples of research by cultural psychologists that illuminate cultural diversity—in one case presenting cultural differences in an aspect of life that most Westerners likely believe is truly universal.

1 The role of self-enhancement

I am the greatest.

—Muhammad Ali, boxer

Psychologists have long subscribed to the notion that humans are motivated to maintain a positive view of themselves—to *self-enhance* (Allport, 1955; and Chapter 20). Self-enhancement exists when people focus on their good qualities while downplaying the bad, when they mentally compare themselves with others and come out smelling sweet, when they underestimate the chances of bad events occurring to themselves relative to others, and so forth. However, some research indicates that self-enhancement may not be universal. Specifically, there may be substantial cultural differences in the desire to self-enhance between Westerners and those from East Asian societies. For example, in one study, when asked to choose adjectives to describe themselves, nearly all the European-Americans included the term 'special,' whereas only about 50% of Japanese students did. On the other hand, 84% of the Japanese students chose the term 'ordinary', whereas only 18% of the European-Americans did (Markus and Kitayama, 1998). Indeed, as a whole, the motivation for self-enhancement, as it appears to exist among Westerners, seems to occur relatively rarely among those who have grown up in East Asia (Norenzayan and Heine, 2005). Instead, East Asians seem more interested in assuring that *others* think well of them (as in 'saving face'), and in improving themselves as people. This idea conflicts with arguments from evolutionary psychologists that self-enhancement is a universal psychological adaptation that evolved over evolutionary time (Von Hippel and Trivers, 2011).

However, looking more closely at these cultural differences also highlights how nature and nurture may intersect. As cultural psychologist Steven Heine (2005) observes, those who are motivated by self-enhancement and self-esteem, as well as those who are motivated by maintaining 'face' and improving themselves, are equally looking to become 'good selves'—to be good examples of what is expected of a person in their respective societies. Thus, the motivation to be a 'good self' may well be a **human universal**—the result of evolutionary forces at work on human psychology—even as the specific way in which this motivation is expressed differs by culture.

Indeed, there is another way to look at East-West differences in self-enhancement. Constantine Sedikides and his colleagues have provided evidence that both Easterners and Westerners may self-enhance much to the same degree—*if* self-enhancement is understood to refer to promoting attributes that are personally important to the self-enhancer. In the case of Westerners, this would mean promoting one's personal accomplishments and individualism. In the case of Far Easterners, this would mean promoting one's dedication to the group and willingness to conform to group decisions and avoid conflict (Sedikides and Gregg, 2008).

> ❯ KEY IDEAS human universal
> A **human universal** is a human trait, custom, or sociocultural practice that can be seen or argued to exist in every known society. There is often a degree of controversy around human universals, either because they are not fully defined and testable ideas or because exceptions sometimes appear to exist.

THINKING CRITICALLY

We have previously flagged up the idea that a scientific concept needs to be clearly defined and testable. Consider to what extent the idea of a universal drive to be a good self is clear and testable.

2 Explaining the behaviour of self and others

> ❯ KEY IDEAS the fundamental attribution error The **fundamental attribution error** is the tendency to attribute another person's behaviour to his or her inner dispositions and character traits—while ignoring the possibility that situational factors are at work.

As we discuss in greater detail in Chapter 20, social psychologists have explored a bias in human thinking known as the **fundamental attribution error**. The fundamental attribution error is the tendency to attribute another person's behaviour to that person's inner dispositions and character traits—while downplaying the possibility that situational factors may have played a large role in causing the behaviour (Ross, 1977; Gilbert and Malone, 1995). For example, if you are standing in line at the supermarket and witness a woman speaking abusively to the checkout assistant, you might assume that the woman is a mean-spirited, rude, and selfish person. In fact, the woman may rarely behave this way, and her outburst may have largely resulted from a 'last straw' experience after a particularly bad week. Psychologists have always assumed that the fundamental attribution error is universal (Gilbert and Malone, 1995), but sociocultural theorists have questioned the universality of the fundamental attribution error just as they have done so with the motivation to self-enhance.

For example, some studies have suggested that people from East Asia are on the whole less vulnerable to misjudging others based on fundamental attribution errors—in other words, they are better at taking situational variables into account (Choi and Nisbett, 1998). Indeed, sociocultural research has shown that, as a general rule, East Asians may tend to do better at taking information of all sorts into account before coming to final judgements about other people's behaviour. This includes social contexts and personal histories (Markus et al, 2006).

Social Role Theory: Putting the 'Social' in Sociocultural

Recall that *society* refers to the institutions and organized patterns of interaction of a cooperating group of individuals. We have looked at the effects of *culture*—the products of society—on psychology, but what of society itself? Like culture, the influence of society pervades human psychology, and we will consider it throughout this book. Throughout the second half of this chapter we have referred to evolutionary explanations for human behaviour. Regardless of whether you found evolution a convincing explanation, it is far from the only possible interpretation of phenomena like sex differences. One of the most influential alternative accounts is offered by *social role* theorists such as Wood and Eagly (2007).

> ❯ KEY IDEAS social role theory and patriarchy **Social role theory** is a theory that proposes that people behave in highly variable ways according to differences in the type of social organization in which they live. Social organization typically involves **patriarchy,** any social organization where the large majority of the uppermost positions in political and social hierarchies are occupied by men.

Social role theory proposes that people behave in highly variable ways according to differences in the type of *social organization* in which they live. Societies differ in how they organize themselves in response to their prevailing level of technological advancement, physical environment, and social history. Social role theory, in particular, has a lot to say about sex differences—and social role theorists have been influenced by feminist insights regarding the experiences of women throughout history in *patriarchal* society. Although **patriarchy** is defined in different ways depending on the context, in general it describes any social organization where men occupy the very large majority of the uppermost positions in political and social hierarchies (Goldberg, 1993). This is somewhat different from *male dominance*, a related concept, but one less easy to define precisely. Male dominance usually refers to male authority within personal and family relationships. Although patriarchy and male dominance generally go together, this is not always the case.

Social role theorists propose that the behaviour of men and women differs according to the ways that their tasks and sex roles have been assigned in patriarchal societies. In particular, the *division of labour* under patriarchy—where women are accorded the roles of child caregiver and homemaker, and men those of warrior and breadwinner—is seen by social role theorists to be the 'engine' driving sex differences. This is because the division of labour 'summarizes' the social opportunities and constraints under which men and women live (Eagly and Wood, 1999, p 409). According to social role theorists, the division of labour evolved as it did throughout the world because males are physically larger and stronger—and therefore better suited for hunting and warfare—while females are the sex that bears and nurses children. Men and women thus accommodate themselves to whatever opportunities present themselves and whatever restrictions limit those opportunities under patriarchy.

Let's take two well-established tendencies in human mating preferences: although both men and women list qualities such as kindness and intelligence as most important in choosing a mate, men and women differ on the importance they place on certain other qualities. Women are more likely than men to prefer a mate a few years older than they are and to emphasize the importance of a prospective mate's status, dependability, and ability to acquire resources (including money). In contrast, men have a general preference for women who are young and conventionally attractive: they are usually not as interested in status and resources. This sex difference has been found in every society yet studied (Buss, 2005).

Evolutionary psychologists explain women's interest in status and resources by pointing to women's greater minimal parental investment. Ancestral women who emphasized status and resources over youth and looks in a mate would have been more reproductively successful, because a man with status and resources (who virtually always would have been older than his bride) is better able to support and protect his mate and her offspring during the long (and costly) period of pregnancy and infant care. The genetic line of women who preferred such men would have prospered, and those who did not would have died out. On the other hand, according to evolutionary psychologists, ancestral men had the problem of detecting which women in the community were most likely to be fertile. Therefore, men evolved to find young, attractive (ie, healthy) women appealing because *youth* and *health* are the most reliable cues to fertility in human females (Symons, 1995).

In contrast to this evolutionary view, social role theorists such as Eagly and Wood (1999) suggest that peoples' mate choices reflect their efforts to make the most of their available options. These options are defined by what an individual's society considers acceptable gender roles. In modern patriarchal society, a woman's preference for a man with status and wealth 'can be explained by the simple reality that . . . males monopolize ownership of productive resources' such as real estate, financial institutions, manufacturing plants, and corporate wealth (Hrdy, quoted in Eagly and Wood, 1999, p 415). From this perspective, sex differences in age preferences and interest in status and resources in a mate reflect a 'best fit' to the social roles expected of men and women. Because men have more power, they prefer younger women who, presumably, earn less money and have lower social status, education, and knowledge than same-age peers. Women, on the other hand, prefer slightly older men because older men tend to be more economically and socially successful than younger men.

With social role theory as a backdrop, we can now revisit the findings of studies showing sex differences in short- and long-term mating. Consider that men are raised with media and other role models who are sexually assertive and are rewarded for being sexually active (Oliver and Hyde, 1993). Films such as *The 40-Year-Old Virgin* (Apatow, Robertson, and Townsend, 2005), which depicts a nerdy, sexually naïve man as a hero, are extraordinarily rare in mass media of all sorts. On the other hand, girls have traditionally been raised with female role models at home and in the media who are expected to be sexually unavailable until after marriage. Although women's sexual attitudes in Western societies changed dramatically during the second half of the twentieth century—particularly as regards the acceptability of premarital sex—beliefs that women ought to be sexually reserved remain throughout most cultures around the world.

Both formal and informal punishments for women who deviate from chastity outside marriage persist in some form in many cultures. These range from informal 'slut-shaming' to execution. Although the frequency of such punishments is declining on a global scale, formal punishments continue to be allowed by law in some nations. Even where such laws are not often enforced, the very fact that they exist undoubtedly sends a clear message to girls as they grow up.

Whereas women are pressured to maintain chastity, sexually active men are seen as 'players' who are to be envied and admired rather than censured. According to social role theorists, the existence of this continued *double standard* for sexual behaviour—one that allows for men what is denied to women—ensures that women will continue to receive negative social messages for engaging in the very behaviours for which men receive positive messages (Aubrey, 2004).

There is room for both social role and evolutionary perspectives on human behaviour. While these theories often contradict one another, the contradictions are sometimes more apparent than real—resulting because the theories provide answers to different kinds of questions (van den Berghe, 2009). For example, social role theorists observe that sex differences in size and strength are partially responsible for the division of labour under patriarchy and resultant sex role differences. An evolutionary theorist would probably agree with this observation. However, evolutionary theorists are primarily interested in the question of *why* the size and strength differences exist in the first place—a question not addressed by social role theory. One way to reconcile evolutionary and social role explanations is to acknowledge that they operate at different levels of analysis. Social role theorists are primarily interested in *how* sex differences shape the lives of individuals, and evolutionary theorists are primarily interested in *why* the differences exist in the first place. But as one research team observed, knowledge of psychology would be advanced if theorists would stop arguing about whether evolved psychological adaptations or social roles cause human behaviour, and instead address the more complex question of how social and evolutionary forces interact to produce human behaviour (Kenrick and Li, 2000).

IN REVIEW

GENES

- Heredity is the tendency of offspring to resemble their parents in various ways. Genes, composed of functional strands of DNA, are units of heredity. DNA contains the unique 'code' for creating each living organism.

- Phenotypes are potentially observable traits or characteristics of an organism. The human genome is the set of hereditary instructions that programs amino acids and proteins to build a human organism.

Genes create proteins by transmitting genetic information through RNA; repli-cating; and interacting with other genes by 'switching them on and off'.

GENETIC AND ENVIRONMENTAL INFLUENCE

Behaviour genetics is the scientific study of how genes and environments in-fluence individual differences in traits and behaviour. Behaviour geneticists use studies of twins reared together, twins reared apart, and adopted children to try to estimate the proportion of individual differences on various traits in a given sample of individuals that can be attributable to genetic heredity and the pro-portion that is due to environmental influences.

A gene-environment correlation occurs when a person's environment is a reflection of, or is somehow correlated with, that person's genotype. There are two types of gene-environment correlations discussed in the chapter: an active gene-environment correlation and a reactive gene-environment correlation. A gene-environment in-teraction occurs when different individuals respond differently to the same environ-mental experience because of differences in their genotypes.

EVOLUTION

Evolution is both fact and theory. The fact of organic and geological evolution is accepted by virtually all scientists working in the life sciences. However, the-ories about how evolution occurs are often debated. Evolutionary psychology is less a field in itself than an approach to virtually any field in psychology.

Adaptations are accumulated characteristics of an organism that have resulted from natural selection as solutions to specific 'problems' over evolutionary time, and that allow the organism to be well adapted to its environment. Because these adaptations are shared by virtually all members of our species to varying degrees, evolutionary psychologists believe that humans are a single species with a single human nature.

Because psychological adaptation occurred among human ancestors over evo-lutionary time in environments in certain respects very different from modern environments, some adaptations are no longer 'adaptive'. This is known as envi-ronmental mismatch.

Evolutionary psychologists propose that in most respects men and women have faced the same evolutionary pressures over the millennia, and should be ex-pected to have the same psychological adaptations as a result. However, in the areas of sexuality, reproduction, and physical aggression men and women have faced vastly different pressures, and therefore sex differences in adaptations in these areas of life should be expected.

THE SOCIOCULTURAL PERSPECTIVE

Psychologists studying the influence of society and culture on psychology take the sociocultural perspective, which is strongly associated with the field of cul-tural psychology. Cultural psychologists emphasize that different cultures are characterized by different behaviours and subjective experiences.

Culture pervades virtually every aspect of thought and behaviour, and it pro-liferates over generations. Geert Hofstede has established specific dimensions of behaviour along which cultures typically differ, including: individualism vs collectivism, power distance, masculinity-femininity, and uncertainty avoid-ance. Although cultures differ in their ideas about morality, morality itself is a human universal.

Cultural research suggests that some characteristics believed to be universal may actually be primarily characteristics of Western peoples. These include self-enhancement, vulnerability to the fundamental attribution error (FAE), and subscribing to the idea that friendship has no negative consequences.

Social role theory proposes that people behave in highly variable ways according to differences in the type of social organization in which they live.

Theories differ in level of analysis when they address different aspects or levels of the same question, without necessarily disagreeing with one another outright. Evolutionary and social role theories of sex differences may be viewed as different levels of analysis.

TEST YOURSELF

1 Psychologists now have a good understanding of how genes and environment interact. True ❒ False ❒

2 Narrow sense heritability is normally a lower figure than broad sense heritability. True ❒ False ❒

3 More men than women in a range of cultures seek more than one sexual partner. True ❒ False ❒

4 There are cultural differences in between dolphin herds. True ❒ False ❒

5 Which of the following terms is best described as an individual's genetic make-up?

   a) Phenotype

   b) Genotype

   c) Genome

   d) Genetics

6 Studies of separated twins are examples of which research method?

   a) Experiments

   b) Field experiments

   c) Quasi-experiments

   d) Natural experiments

7 A child who inherits a gentle disposition and so elicits kind treatment from adult carers is an example of what?

   a) Reactive gene-environment correlation

   b) Active gene-environment correlation

   c) Gene-environment interaction

   d) Passive gene-environment correlation

8 Dunbar's number is

   a) 15

   b) 90

   c) 150

   d) 900

9 Contrast social role and evolutionary explanations for sex differences in behaviour.

10 Explain why evolutionary psychologists can be criticized for being 'politically incorrect'.

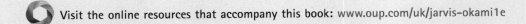 **Visit the online resources that accompany this book:** www.oup.com/uk/jarvis–okami1e

CHAPTER 6

CONSCIOUSNESS

LEARNING OUTCOMES

By the end of this chapter you should be able to:

- Appreciate the difficulties inherent in defining consciousness but offer a simple definition including the ideas of qualitativeness, subjectivity, and unity

- Assess the 'hard problem' concerning the relationship between the nature of the physical brain and the experience of consciousness

- Evaluate research into the importance of sleep and the possible influences on sleep deprivation

- Consider what we know about the physiological mechanisms regulating sleep and wakefulness including the circadian pacemaker and the sleep homeostat, and know something of the stages of sleep

- Analyse evidence for competing explanations of the functions of sleep with particular regard to memory consolidation and synaptic pruning explanations

- Understand the range of sleep mentation including sleep thinking, ordinary dreaming, and apex dreaming, and know something of the typical content of dreams and explanations thereof

- Be aware of the prevalence, symptoms, and consequences of a range of sleep disorders including insomnia, obstructive sleep apnoea, and the parasomnias

- Assess the evidence for hypnosis as an altered state of consciousness as opposed to a social phenomenon

- Consider the effects of a range of psychoactive drugs on consciousness including opiates, stimulants, depressants, and hallucinogenics and be aware of debates around non-medical use of drugs

On 16 April 1943, a chemist named Albert Hoffman was hard at work for the Sandoz pharmaceutical company attempting to synthesize various components of ergot—a fungus that grows on grain and has medicinal (and poisonous) properties. On this particular day, Hoffman was working on his twenty-fifth such synthesis; he called it LSD25 (lysergic acid diethylamide). However, as he worked with the chemical he began to experience a stream of intensely vivid and 'fantastic' images accompanied by a 'kaleidoscope-like play of colors' (Hoffman, 1970).

Hoffman realized that these symptoms must somehow be related to the LSD25, but he was unable to figure out how he could have accidentally ingested enough of the compound to have had any sort of effect at all. He decided to conduct an

FIGURE 6.1 **Blotters once contain-
ing doses of LSD.**
Source: BakalaeroZz Photography/
Shutterstock.com.

experiment on himself by ingesting what seemed to him a very small dose of the compound, only 0.25 mg. His lab notes read:

> 4:20 P.M.: 0.5 cc (0.25 mg LSD) ingested orally. The solution is tasteless.

> 4:50 P.M.: no trace of any effect.

> 5:00 P.M.: slight dizziness, unrest, difficulty in concentration, visual disturbances, marked desire to laugh. . . . (Hoffman, 1970)

At this point Hoffman's notes ended because he could no longer write!

This kind of experience constitutes an *altered state of consciousness*. But what exactly is it that is being altered? Until about two or three decades ago, scientists did not believe that it was possible to study the nature of **consciousness**, or if they thought it might be possible, they did not consider it important. Now, however, many psychologists and neuroscientists have come around to philosopher-psychologist John Searle's view that 'consciousness is the condition that makes it possible for anything at all to matter to anybody' (Searle, 1997, p xiv).

Thus, *consciousness* has recently come to be considered an important topic in psychology, and some consider it the most important topic of all. The emerging field of *consciousness studies* seeks to find solutions to what has been called the last surviving mystery of science: *what is consciousness?* In this chapter we begin by considering some proposed answers to this question. We will then review the many varieties of consciousness as they are experienced daily by people all over the world: sleep, dreaming, meditation, hypnosis, and the non-medical use of psychoactive drugs.

WHAT IS CONSCIOUSNESS?

The short answer is 'no one knows'. Blackmore (2004) put it thus: 'If you think you have found a solution to the problem of consciousness, you haven't understood the problem' (2004, p 1). Although some psychologists may consider *consciousness* the most important topic in all of psychology, those conducting consciousness research can't seem to agree on much about their topic. Unlike most other areas of psychology, these psychologists, philosophers, and neuroscientists cannot even agree on what they are studying. There is no consensus on how to define consciousness, what consciousness consists of, or how best to study it—or even if it is really possible to study it at all. And there are almost as many ideas about what *causes* consciousness as there are researchers studying it.

Indeed, in one introductory book on the topic, consciousness studies researcher Susan Blackmore begins by warning that the reader is likely to become increasingly perplexed as he or she reads, rather than increasingly enlightened (Blackmore, 2013). Why? Because we ourselves are so immersed in our own consciousness—'the condition that makes it possible for anything at all to matter'—that we generally give little thought to what consciousness really *is* or where it comes from. Once we begin to ponder such questions, it is easy to get lost in their implications—rather like questions about divine beings, the size of the universe. Nonetheless, each person's own subjective experience of himself or herself and the world—that is, *consciousness*—is too important an aspect of psychology to ignore.

A Common-Sense Definition

We have already established that there is no consensus on how to define consciousness. However, we *can* map out the general territory with which we are concerned by offering a common-sense definition of consciousness as provided by Searle: '**Consciousness** consists of inner, qualitative, subjective states and feelings or awareness' (Searle, 2000, p 559; emphasis added).

According to Searle, consciousness defined in this way exists as long as we are alive and not in a state of thoughtless, dreamless sleep, or coma. It ends only when we are in such states—or dead. In Searle's words, consciousness 'includes everything from feeling a pain, to perceiving objects visually, to states of anxiety and depression, to working out crossword puzzles, playing chess, trying to remember your aunt's phone number, arguing about politics, or to just wishing you were somewhere else' (p 559).

For Searle the three most important features of consciousness are *qualitativeness*, *subjectivity*, and *unity*. By **qualitativeness**, Searle means that something is conscious only if it 'feels like something'—in other words, consciousness involves the experience of some sort of distinctive *quality* or *qualities* (Nagel, 1974). Eating a good breakfast *feels* different from learning that you emerged as a genius on an IQ test, which in turn *feels* different from finding a rat under your bed.

Subjectivity means that consciousness can only be experienced by some sort of being and cannot exist independent of its 'owner'. Even when two people have the same experience—say, listening to the same piece of music—the experience is different because each person has her or his own consciousness (Blackmore, 2013). Subjectivity is the 'I' of consciousness.

By **unity** Searle means that consciousness is a single unified experience. As I (Matt) sit here typing, I do not just *feel* the keyboard keys under my fingertips, *see* the words form on the computer screen, *hear* the sounds of New Model Army coming from the stereo, and *think* that it's been raining for far too long. I experience all of these cognitive and sensory experiences together as consciousness (Searle, 2000, pp 561–2). To Searle, consciousness is by definition unified, and individual components such as senses, thoughts, and emotions modify consciousness in an ever-shifting, but always unified, pattern.

❯ **KEY IDEAS** consciousness
No definition of **consciousness** has been agreed upon, but John Searle's 'common-sense' definition includes three components: qualitativeness, subjectivity, and unity.

❯ **KEY IDEAS** qualitativeness
In this context **qualitativeness** describes the feature of consciousness which suggests that something is conscious only if it 'feels like something'.

❯ **KEY IDEAS** subjectivity In the context of consciousness research, **subjectivity** means that consciousness can only be experienced by an individual being and cannot exist independently of them.

❯ **KEY IDEAS** unity In consciousness studies, **unity** is the idea that consciousness is always a single, unified experience.

The 'Hard' Problem of Consciousness: From Brain to Self?

Now that we have a working, common-sense definition of consciousness (bearing in mind that there is no agreement whatever that it is the best one), what is this definition intended to help us explain? There is a basic problem about consciousness that must somehow be solved—what philosopher David Chalmers (1995) has termed the **hard problem**. It is this: how does our brain—a physical organ composed of neurons, chemicals, and electricity—produce the seemingly disembodied subjective state of consciousness? How is it that we can easily say, 'I have a brain' when we can't say for sure whether 'I' *is* our brain or is somehow *in* or *caused by* our brain? In other words, how do we get from *there* (our brain) to *here* (our 'selves')?

The hard problem of consciousness is a variation of the ancient 'mind-body' problem. If you recall from Chapter 2, *dualism*, the idea that the mind and body are separate and made up of different 'substances', has been rejected by pretty much all modern scientists and philosophers. Consciousness, like mind, is in some way a property of the brain. Rejecting dualism does not, however, solve the hard problem of consciousness. Even if we grant that consciousness is a property of the brain, we still have no idea how consciousness arises from the brain—despite the efforts of neuroscientists to identify precise neural and biochemical processes and brain sites that take us from 'there' to 'here' (Damasio, 2010).

> **KEY IDEAS** the hard problem
> In this context the **'hard' problem** is the question of how the physical human brain is able to produce the experience of consciousness. The word 'hard' does not just mean 'difficult' but also denotes hard as in hardware—the brain.

Varieties of Consciousness

Whatever consciousness may turn out to be, one thing we know for certain is that it comes in many flavours other than normal waking consciousness. Sleep, dreams,

FIGURE 6.2 Chasing altered consciousness. Throughout history and across cultures, human beings have purposely attempted to alter their consciousness in various ways. Pictured here is an attempt to do so through partial sensory deprivation in a soundproof floatation tank. Filled with Epsom salts, the density of the water makes flotation effortless. The tank is completely dark and silent. Some individuals claim to experience altered states of consciousness during such flotation sessions.

Source: Yakov Oskanov/Shutterstock.com.

hypnosis, hallucinations, meditation, and drug states are all varieties of consciousness—generally referred to as *altered states of consciousness* (ASC). Just as it is difficult to define consciousness itself, however, it is not easy to define an altered state. As Blackmore (2004) notes, we might decide to define altered states *objectively*, in terms of how the altered state was induced. For example, we could say that an altered state is one that is induced by some unusual activity, such as taking a drug or being hypnotized. Another objective way would be to define an altered state in terms of measurable changes in brain activity and physiology.

There are limitations to both of these objective definitions, however. In the first, each person's experience of taking a particular drug or being hypnotized may differ radically. What might be an altered state for one person might not be for another. The second objective approach—taking measurements—seems more promising, but with the exceptions of sleep and dreaming, researchers have not been very successful in associating altered states with specific biological measurements.

On the other hand, altered states could be defined *subjectively*—perhaps a more fruitful approach. From this perspective, **altered states of consciousness** are defined as temporary but radical changes in the overall pattern of a person's normal subjective experience (Tart, 1972). For the remainder of this chapter we will consider altered states of consciousness in all their splendour, terror, and ordinariness.

> **KEY IDEAS** altered state of consciousness An **altered state of consciousness** is a temporary but radical change in the overall pattern of a person's normal subjective experience. This can be the result of drugs, sensory deprivation, and perhaps—though this is controversial—hypnosis.

READ THIS

It is worthwhile to further explore Searle's definition of consciousness:

Searle, J.R. (2000). Consciousness, free action and the brain. *Journal of Consciousness Studies*, **7**(10), 3–22.

We also highly recommend Susan Blackmore's introductory text:

Blackmore, S. (2013). *Consciousness: An Introduction*. London: Routledge.

Specifically on the issue of the 'hard problem', this provides a nice review in the light of contemporary findings from neuroscience:

Brogaard, B. and Gatzia, D.E. (2016). What can neuroscience tell us about the hard problem of consciousness? *Frontiers in Neuroscience*, **10**, 395, np.

SLEEP

The urge to sleep is profound. After just one night of sleeplessness, human beings may risk their lives for it—falling asleep at the wheel or in wartime at a sentry post. Even if we do not fall completely asleep under such conditions, we may experience **microsleeps**—barely perceptible and involuntary periods of sleep lasting from 3 to 15 seconds (Blavivas et al, 2007). Human beings love sleep so much that they spend about one-third of their lives doing it—typically around 27 years in total. In spite of its frequency and necessity sleep remains in many respects a mystery.

> **KEY IDEAS** microsleeps **Microsleeps** are barely perceptible and involuntary periods of sleep lasting between 3 and 15 seconds. Microsleeps provide relief from fatigue but pose safety risks.

> **KEY IDEAS** total sleep deprivation **Total sleep deprivation** is defined as going entirely without sleep for 24 hours or more.

How Much Sleep?

Despite the miseries of sleeplessness, studies have shown that **total sleep deprivation**, even for a period of days, does not necessarily result in the sorts of symptoms one commonly associates with such an experience—for example, bizarre hallucinations or delusions (Gould et al, 2009). However, brief, mild hallucinations are not uncommon, and a person's motor skills and performance on memory and other cognitive tasks will suffer—sometimes severely, depending upon the task (Lim and Dinges, 2010). Decision-making—including moral decision-making—may also be impaired, and grumpiness becomes the norm during total sleep deprivation (Killgore et al, 2007).

However, unless you get into a car and try to drive, going without sleep for a period of days won't kill you. Interestingly though, sleep deprivation *will* kill a rat in about two or three weeks (Rechtschaffen, 1998). While no human being (that we know of) has attempted to remain awake that long, it may be that going without sleep for a *really* extended time actually will kill you. An exceptionally rare genetic condition known as *fatal familial insomnia* does eventually result in death, but only after a period of seven to 36 *months* of sleeplessness (Schenkein and Montagna, 2006).

In any event, human beings, in common with all other mammals, birds, reptiles, fish, and insects studied, do sleep regularly (Gilestro, Tononi, and Cirelli, 2009). If you are like the average British citizen, you probably get slightly less sleep than you'd like and slightly less than you did five years ago. Tang et al (2017) carried out a survey of over 30,000 people in the UK and found that 77% reported sleeping six to eight hours a night. Twice as many people reported a decline in sleep duration as did an increase over the four years of the study. It has been estimated (although with the proviso that it is difficult to gather accurate data so far in retrospect) that people slept around two hours longer a night 100 years ago than we do now (Hicks et al, 2001).

THINKING CRITICALLY

Much of the publicity regarding the recent decline in sleep duration has centred on the use of electronic devices around bedtime. The suggestion is that device use causes sleep disruption. However, research in this area has serious limitations.

Exercise

1 Most studies in this area have been correlational. Explain why correlations between device use and sleep duration may not show a causal relationship.

2 Why might there be a lack of validity in experiments into the effect of device use reduction?

HINT: Bartel, Scheeren, and Gradisar (2018) found a recruitment rate of 26%.

Although figures such as these have been used to argue that modern people are chronically sleep deprived (Coren, 2009), most people asked believe they are getting enough sleep (National Sleep Foundation, 2005), and some psychologists agree with them (eg, Horne, in Buysse et al, 2010). Ultimately, it is not possible to estimate accurately the number of hours an individual actually needs to sleep, so always take the advice of experts on this matter with a pinch of salt.

The situation is further complicated by the fact that some people seem to need more sleep than others. Margaret Thatcher and Donald Trump (Figure 6.3) famously reported needing relatively little sleep, but it would be impossible to extrapolate anything meaningful from two case examples.

Research into the consequences of variations in sleep duration has drawn a bewildering range of conclusions. One thing is clear from research, however: as sleep duration falls below six hours per night, the risk of health consequences increases relative to seven to eight hours per night (Buysse et al, 2010). Indeed, people who

FIGURE 6.3 Much has been made of individuals like Donald Trump, who sleeps much less than the typical person. However, we should be extremely cautious about drawing conclusions from case examples like this.

Source: Crush Rush/Shutterstock.com.

sleep less than six hours per night also have much higher mortality rates (Ferrie et al, 2007). This suggests that we need sleep. But why? In other words, what is the *function* of sleep? The answer to this question is not as straightforward as you might think, and we will consider the question of *why* we sleep a bit later. Let's begin with the simpler question of *how* we sleep.

Sleep Patterns and their Regulation

Apart from external demands such as a job or school, what determines when a person decides to go to sleep and wake up? Two basic processes interact to regulate normal human sleep: the *circadian pacemaker*, which governs each person's internal 'biological clock'; and the *sleep homeostat*, which tracks the amount of sleep you have relative to the number of hours you have been awake (Wright et al, 2005).

The circadian pacemaker

One aspect of the environment has remained constant during the evolution of all forms of life on earth: the 24-hour cycle of the earth's rotation. The sun and moon shine on protozoa, panthers, pythons, and people alike. In a variety of ways, the biology of life forms is synchronized to this 24-hour cycle of light and dark. Bacteria, plants, and animals have internal 'biological clocks' they use to regulate important physiological processes such as respiration and reproduction. Any biochemical, physiological, or behavioural cycle that adheres to a near-24-hour schedule is known as a **circadian rhythm** (Shepherd, 1988).

In human beings, sleep and wakefulness are regulated in part by the numerous circadian rhythm cycles experienced each day (body temperature, hormonal activity, mental alertness, etc). These rhythms are kept on schedule and synchronized with one another by the **circadian pacemaker**, our 'biological clock'. The pacemaker consists of a group of neurons forming the **suprachiasmatic nuclei** of the hypothalamus (Weaver, 1998; see Figure 6.4).

> **KEY IDEAS** circadian rhythm A **circadian rhythm** is any biochemical, physiological, or behavioural cycle that takes place on an approximately 24-hour schedule. The name comes from *circa* (around) and *dia* (day). We don't require accurate internal clocks to maintain circadian rhythms—they are regularly reset by environmental cues such as darkness and daylight.

> **KEY IDEAS** circadian pacemaker—the suprachiasmatic nucleus This is believed to function as a 'master control' for a person's various circadian cycles, consisting of a group of neurons forming the suprachiasmatic nuclei of the hypothalamus. The **suprachiasmatic nuclei (SCN)** is a group of neurons of the hypothalamus that constitute the circadian pacemaker.

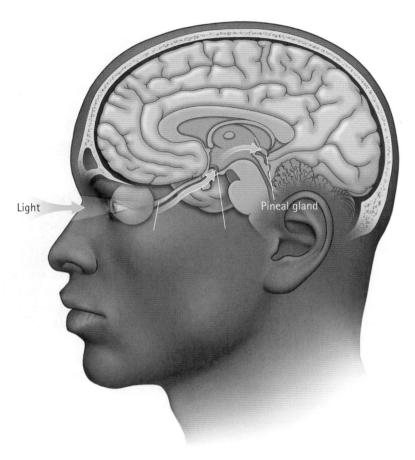

Light

Pineal gland

FIGURE 6.4 **The circadian pacemaker. The circadian pacemaker helps regulate sleep and wakefulness by keeping circadian rhythms synchronized and on schedule.**

As depicted in Figure 6.4, natural light is conducted from the retina via the optic nerve to the circadian pacemaker, conveying information about the time of day. Light does not merely 'set' the biological clock of the pacemaker, however. Once light is conducted to the pacemaker, the light affects the production of hormones. The most important of these to the sleep-wake cycle is *melatonin*, produced by the *pineal gland* deep within the brain. Melatonin production is stimulated during periods of darkness and inhibited by light. The secretion of melatonin during the cycle of darkness is strongly associated with the onset of sleep. This is because melatonin inhibits the brain's mechanisms for promoting wakefulness—allowing various other sleep-related mechanisms to do their work 'unopposed' by a drive for wakefulness (Lavie, 2001).

The net effect of regulation by the circadian pacemaker is that our best sleep is experienced at night and our most productive periods of wakefulness and activity during the day (Wright et al, 2005). Thus, night-shift workers experience sleep that is less restful and of shorter duration than those on normal schedules, and their levels of alertness and performance on the job also suffer relative to those of day workers (Oexman et al, 2002). They are fighting their circadian pacemakers. Something similar occurs in *jet lag*, the bane of frequent flyers. Jet lag happens when a flyer crosses multiple time zones in flight while moving from west to east or east to west (it's worse moving from west to east). Symptoms include difficulty concentrating, headache, insomnia, fatigue, irritability, and loss of appetite. No jet lag is experienced on flights that do not cross time zones, no matter how long they are and no matter how much *travel fatigue* occurs. Travel fatigue may result from long security lines, uncomfortable seating, inability to sleep on night flights, dehydration, and so forth (Herxheimer and Waterhouse, 2003).

 THINKING PRACTICALLY

Your friend has suffered unpleasant symptoms in the past when working shifts. She is now planning to go travelling. What advice would you offer her?

The sleep homeostat

While the circadian pacemaker is a critically important determinant of the cycle of sleep and wakefulness, it is not the only factor. The second important process regulating sleep is the **sleep homeostat**. This is a kind of internal scorekeeper made up of a number of coordinated biological functions that keep track of how much sleep (particularly deep sleep) you have had the previous night versus how long you have been awake on a given day (Dijk and Archer, 2009). The idea is to maintain a balance between sleep and waking known as **sleep homeostasis**. When the balance tips too far into the 'waking' side, the urge to sleep is increased.

What happens if you don't get enough sleep to restore sleep homeostasis? If not enough sleep occurs on a given night relative to the amount you normally require, **sleep debt** is built up, and you will feel pressure to 'make up' the lost sleep. Once asleep, you will tend to sleep longer than usual and experience more time in the deepest levels of sleep. When you sleep late on the weekends after a week of insufficient sleep during weekdays, you are experiencing the sleep homeostat's attempt to pay back sleep debt.

Falling Asleep

We all know the difference between being asleep and being awake (well, most of us do, at any rate). However, there is no precise moment when a person can definitively be said to have passed from waking into sleep. The process of falling asleep is a series of continuous, gradual changes that occur in the brain, body, and subjective experience; and changes in one of these domains (eg, changes in the brain) do not necessarily coincide with changes in another (eg, changes in subjective experience). However, eventually, all aspects of physiology, cognition, behaviour, and subjective experience are altered during the process of falling asleep (Ogilvie, 2001).

While drifting from relaxed sleepiness towards sleep, many people experience unusual auditory and visual illusions and bodily sensations known as **hypnogogia** or *hypnagogic hallucinations* (D'Agostino and Limosani, 2010). Hypnogogia is a dream-like state during which you may or may not be aware that you are experiencing hallucinations. You may hear voices, see patterns of shape and colour, or imagine yourself somewhere else. A sensation of falling is fairly typical, and it may be broken by sudden full awakening with a jerking of the limbs known as *myoclonia*. *Sleep paralysis* may also occur—the sensation of being unable to move during periods of intense and often terrifying hallucination (Cheyne, 2005). If you experience sleep

❱ KEY IDEAS sleep homeostasis
Sleep homeostasis is the relatively constant balance maintained between sleep and waking, governed by the sleep homeostat. When a person does not have enough sleep, sleep homeostasis means that they accumulate a **sleep debt**, leading to the desire to sleep. The **sleep homeostat** is the collective term for the coordinated biochemical, neural, and psychological functions that 'keep track' of the amount of sleep a person has had relative to the number of hours of waking.

❱ KEY IDEAS hypnagogia
This is a dream-like state at sleep onset during which a person may or may not be aware that he or she is experiencing hallucinations or delusions. Hypnagogia may be accompanied by sleep paralysis.

paralysis, it may be possible to emerge from it intentionally by rolling your eyes, fluttering your eyelids, or intentionally wiggling the toes and feet. On the other hand, some people enjoy the experience and learn to induce it on purpose!

Types and Stages of Sleep

There are two basic types of sleep: **rapid eye movement, or REM sleep** (sometimes called *active sleep*) and **non-rapid eye movement** or **NREM sleep** (sometimes called *slow-wave sleep*). NREM sleep occurs over the greater portion of sleep time, and is characterized by the deepest levels of relaxation and reduced brain activity. REM sleep is characterized by high levels of brain and nervous system activity, rapid movements of the eyes, and intensely vivid dreaming.

REM and NREM sleep are experienced in five **sleep stages**, the first four consisting of NREM and the fifth of REM. Because the stages of sleep are defined in part according to the particular type of **brain wave** that predominates, it will be useful first to describe these brain wave patterns. Brain wave is the term used to describe electrical activity in the brain that occurs in varying frequencies. These waves are measured by a device known as the **electroencephalograph (EEG)**.

There are four principal types of brain waves: *beta, alpha, theta,* and *delta*. During normal wakefulness, brain waves tend to be of the **beta** type—very rapid, relatively narrow oscillations. In some extremely relaxed wakeful states where eyes are closed, however (eg, meditation), lower-frequency **alpha** waves may predominate. **Theta** waves are produced under conditions of drowsiness and light sleep. **Delta** waves, which are slower and wider, are associated with the deepest levels of NREM sleep. Figure 6.5 depicts EEG patterns of the four brain wave types.

As we said earlier, each of the five sleep stages is associated with specific brain wave patterns.

1 *Stage 1 sleep.* Stage 1 represents the transition from relaxed wakefulness to the onset of sleep. In fact, it actually includes both waking and sleep states within its borders, and for this reason, some researchers do not consider Stage 1 an actual stage of sleep at all. These researchers prefer simply to refer to it

❭ **KEY IDEAS** REM and NREM sleep **Rapid eye movement (REM)**: the fifth stage of sleep characterized by high levels of brain and nervous system activity and intensely vivid, hallucinatory dreaming. **Non-rapid eye movement (NREM)**: sleep Stages 2-4, characterized by cognitive activity, ordinary dreaming, and reduced brain and nervous system activity relative to REM.

❭ **KEY IDEAS** stages of sleep There are five **stages of sleep**, including a period of sleep onset, three periods of *NREM*, and one of *REM* sleep. Each stage is associated with characteristic brain wave activity, and the stages are played out during the night in a repeating pattern (the sleep cycle). **Brain waves** are characteristic electrical brain activity of various frequencies termed *alpha, beta, theta,* and *delta*. An **electroencephalograph (EEG)** is an instrument that measures electrical activity produced by the brain.

❭ **KEY IDEAS** brain waves **Beta waves** are the brain waves that predominate in waking states and are present in REM. **Alpha waves** are the brain waves that predominate in relaxed, wakeful states while eyes are closed, and in sleep onset. **Theta waves** are the brain waves that predominate at Stage 2 and Stage 3 sleep. **Delta waves** are the slow brain waves that predominate at Stage 4 sleep.

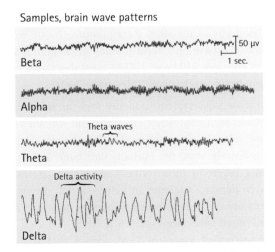

Samples, brain wave patterns

Beta   50 μv / 1 sec.

Alpha

Theta waves

Theta

Delta activity

Delta

FIGURE 6.5 **The four principal brain wave patterns. Beta, alpha, theta, and delta brain waves are associated with different stages of sleep.**

FIGURE 6.6 **Sleep spindles and K complexes.**

as *sleep onset* (eg, Yang, Han, Yang, Su, and Lane, 2010). In any case, as you experience increasing relaxation while lying in bed with your eyes closed preparing to fall asleep, more and more alpha waves are produced. As this process continues and you achieve Stage 1 sleep, theta waves come to predominate, although some alpha is still produced. During Stage 1 sleep you may be vaguely aware of your environment and you may experience hypnogogia. If awakened, you may insist that you hadn't actually fallen asleep at all. After a few minutes in Stage 1, however, you will transition to Stage 2 sleep.

2 *Stage 2 sleep.* Stage 2 is light sleep from which you can be easily awakened, but you will be unaware of the environment as you sleep. Although theta waves continue to predominate during Stage 2, there are also characteristic brain wave patterns known as *sleep spindles* and *K complexes* (see Figure 6.6). Sleep spindles are sudden, short bursts in higher voltage brain wave activity. K complexes are much sharper intermittent peaks and drops. Like Stage 1, Stage 2 sleep lasts perhaps 10 to 20 minutes, after which the sleeper passes into Stage 3.

3 *Stage 3 sleep.* Stage 3 is the first stage of deep or 'slow-wave' sleep from which it is difficult to awaken. Although theta waves continue to be produced, they are joined by the much slower delta waves.

4 *Stage 4 sleep.* Sleep deepens further during Stage 4, and delta waves now come to predominate over theta. It is very difficult to awaken from Stage 4 sleep. If someone does manage to wake you up, you may experience disorientation and not know exactly where you are.

5 *Stage 5 sleep: REM.* REM is a somewhat mysterious type of sleep about which there is some controversy, particularly in regard to dreaming (Hobson, Pace-Schott, and Stickold, 2000; Solms, 2000). In general, it is agreed that dreaming might occur during any of the sleep stages (Solms, 2000). However, it is during REM that the most intense and vivid periods of dreaming seem to occur, and most researchers consider REM and NREM mental activity to arise from different cognitive and brain mechanisms (McCarley, 2007).

During REM sleep, the nervous system suddenly revs up: heart rate, blood pressure, and respiration increase; men experience erections and women vaginal lubrication—this, however, is *not* related to sexual content in dreams—it is purely reflexive. Although the eyelids remain shut, the eyeballs dart back and forth frantically, and brain waves suddenly revert to those typical of wakeful states—with beta, alpha, and some theta waves dancing together in helter-skelter, desynchronized patterns. Among these patterns are the unique bursts known as *sawtooth waves* because they resemble the teeth of wood saws (see Figure 6.7).

Perhaps the most intriguing aspect of REM sleep is that at the same time as all this revved-up activity is occurring in the nervous system, muscle tone suddenly decreases dramatically—the sleeper is effectively paralysed. Considering that more

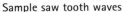

FIGURE 6.7 **Sawtooth wave patterns.**

intense, vivid, and hallucinatory dreaming tends to occur during this stage, this temporary paralysis may not be a bad thing! Imagine your body responding to a dream of being chased by zombies—especially if you are sleeping near a window and live on the twelfth floor (later in this chapter we describe a sleep disorder where exactly such an event becomes possible).

The stages of sleep (minus Stage 1, which occurs only once at sleep onset) play out in a cyclical pattern known as the **sleep cycle** throughout the night. The sleep cycle lasts between 90 and 110 minutes and is repeated between four and six times per night on average. In a normal adult, the time spent in each stage will vary as the night wears on, with REM sleep constituting only a very small amount of one's sleep in the early sleep period, but taking up more and more of the sleep cycle as the sleeper moves towards morning. Finally, the experience of NREM Stages 3 and 4 disappears altogether. When all is said and done, however, NREM still takes up about 80% of the total sleep period, and REM sleep approximately 20% (McCarley, 2007). The sleep cycle is depicted in Figure 6.8, and the five stages of sleep are summarized in Table 6.1.

❯ **KEY IDEAS** sleep cycle
The **sleep cycle** consists of the repeating pattern of Stages 2–5 sleep that recurs four to six times throughout the night following sleep onset (Stage 1).

TABLE 6.1 **The five stages of sleep**

Stage	Brain wave activity	Characteristics
1 NREM	Alpha Theta	Increasing relaxation, transition from wakefulness to very light sleep . . . You may be partially aware of the environment, and if awoken, you might not be aware that you were asleep at all.
2 NREM	Theta (sleep spindles and K complexes)	Light sleep, unaware of the environment but relatively easily awakened. Preparation to enter deeper levels of sleep.
3 NREM	Theta (over 50% of time) Delta (under 50%)	Increasingly deep 'slow wave' (delta) sleep. Difficult to awaken.
4 NREM	Delta (over 50% of time) Theta (under 50%)	Profoundly deep sleep; difficult to awaken, and if awoken, you will be disoriented.
5 REM	Beta Alpha Theta ('sawtooth' pattern)	Muscle paralysis; intense dreaming; rapid eye movements; genital arousal, increased heart rate, blood pressure and respiration; extremely difficult to awaken.

THINKING CREATIVELY

Design a study to investigate the relative importance of REM and NREM sleep. Consider how you might operationalize and manipulate the independent variable and how you could measure the dependent variable. What ethical issues should you consider and how might you respond to them?

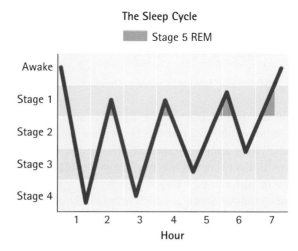

FIGURE 6.8 The sleep cycle. The five stages of sleep are played out in cycles lasting 90 to 110 minutes, repeated four to six times on average per night.

The Functions of Sleep

We noted earlier that it is not possible to determine how much sleep a person requires. This is not simply because different people need differing amounts of sleep but also because we do not have a good understanding of *why* we sleep (Cirelli and Tononi, 2008). Without understanding what sleep is supposed to accomplish, we cannot confidently address questions to which many of us would like to know the answers. How much sleep does a person really need? Do naps make up for lost night-time sleep? Do people need less sleep as they grow older? And so forth (Rechtschaffen, 2000).

Arguably the most intuitive theory of the function of sleep is the 'rest and restoration' theory. This approach suggests that we sleep because we need to rest and rejuvenate. Sleep is a quiet time, a time when we do rest, and we usually do wake feeling restored or rejuvenated. However, this does not necessarily mean that sleep evolved for this function. We often feel calm and sometimes a little sleepy after a large dinner, but the function of eating is not to make us feel calm and sleepy.

In fact, several facts argue against the 'rest and restoration' theory. Most obviously, if you lie awake in bed all day long with your eyes closed in a darkened room listening to recordings of waves lapping, you will *still* need sleep. Sleep must be doing something beyond offering a person rest.

There are many explanations for sleep. All can boast some research to support them, but research can also be found to contradict each one. However, two theories show particular promise. The first suggests that the purpose of sleep is to allow the brain to consolidate and retain memories (Rasch and Born, 2008). The second proposes that sleep regulates the strength of brain synapses, allowing unnecessary synapses to die and maintaining those that are important—in effect, to 'clean out the junk that's filling up your brain' (Gilestro et al, 2009). We will now briefly explore these ideas.

Sleep for memory consolidation

Research conducted during the first part of the twenty-first century has shown that memory processes seem to become profoundly impaired during sleep deprivation, and sleep substantially improves memory for facts and skills one has learned (Conway, and Demeter, 2010). Researchers in sleep and memory believe that this improved recall results in part from a reactivation of memories during sleep—in other words, the memories are 'replayed' during sleep and thus recalled better later on, as would be the case following a good study session (Gais, Lucas, and Bom, 2006). Sleep also appears to allow us to draw on different types of personal knowledge 'databases' to make connections between newly learned facts and facts already known (Ellenbogen et al, 2007).

Evidence shows that sleep improves memory for events one has experienced as well as for facts and skills. In particular, sleep improves memories for emotional events over those with more neutral emotional content, and specifically targets the most emotional aspects of these arousing experiences—with background details tending to fade overtime. Thus, a crime victim might recall more details about his or her assailant's gun than about his or her clothing, with memory for the clothing becoming worse over time, but memory for the gun remaining relatively strong. Sleep appears to enhance this type of effect (Payne et al, 2008).

Because emotion is often associated with important events or important aspects of events, in this way sleep appears to aid in the recall of particularly valuable memories (Payne et al, 2008). Findings such as these are prompting some researchers to speculate that gathering and replaying memories to allow for their later recall is an important function of sleep—if not its core function (Walker and Stickgold, 2006).

Sleep for synaptic pruning

The second theory, which remains controversial but is increasingly supported by convincing research, is being advanced principally by researchers Chiara Cirelli and Giulio Tononi and their colleagues (see, eg, Gilestro et al, 2009). Cirelli and Tononi recognize that sleep improves memory; however, they believe that the *ultimate function* of sleep goes beyond replaying and consolidating memories. Instead, these researchers' work with rats, humans, and fruit flies (yes, fruit flies sleep) has led them to conclude that the ultimate purpose of sleep is best understood in terms of brain synapses.

Cirelli and Tononi note that during the waking hours the number of brain synapses and the strength of their connections increase. More numerous and better-connected synapses mean a better-connected brain; however, they also take up more space and require more energy to maintain. Cirelli and Tononi believe that, in the absence of sleep, synapses would continue to become stronger, more numerous, and eventually take up too much brain space and require too much energy to maintain (Gilestro et al, 2009).

Sleep appears to prune back both the number and connectivity of synapses, allowing the strongest ones to 'scale back' to manageable size and the weaker ones to disappear altogether. This is beneficial because it allows relatively unimportant connections to disappear, saving space and energy for more important connections and helping people to perform better following a good night's sleep. This idea could explain findings cited earlier that sleep selectively improves recall of emotional events—that, presumably, have typically more value than emotionally neutral events—while allowing background details (maintained through weaker synaptic connections) to disappear.

Cirelli and Tononi present a strong case in support of their theory, derived from research conducted among members of several animal species. Unfortunately, this evidence, although strong, is essentially correlational. Indeed, theories of the ultimate function of sleep are not easy to test—and some appear virtually impossible to test (Zepelin, Siegel, and Tobler, 2005). Consequently, the function of sleep remains elusive.

THINKING CRITICALLY

Recall our discussion of psychology as science in Chapter 2. One of the common (but not uncontroversial) criteria for a good scientific theory is that it is falsifiable. Neither memory consolidation nor synaptic pruning theories of sleep can be falsified, although they are *testable* to the extent that evidence that is consistent with them can be compiled. Psychology would certainly look more of a classic science if all its theories were fully falsifiable, but we might end up leaving out some areas—like sleep—that are important to understanding our everyday (or every night!) experience of being human. Think about where you stand on this issue. There is no wrong answer—it's just good to have a view.

DREAMING

Of the many mysteries of consciousness few are quite as mysterious as the nature of dreams and dreaming. Just as there is no agreement regarding the function of sleep, there is little agreement regarding the important questions of dreaming. What *are* dreams, and what are the brain and mind mechanisms that generate them? Why do we dream at all? What do our dreams mean—if anything?

Sleep Mentation: Thinking and Levels of Dreaming

Early dream researchers believed that dreams only occurred during REM sleep (Dement and Kleitman, 1957). Indeed, REM sleep was considered virtually synonymous with dreaming. However, these beliefs are now known to be wrong (Foulkes, 1962). REM does not necessarily produce dreaming, and dreamers are not necessarily in REM when they dream (Solms, 2000). Nevertheless, dreaming is without doubt more common in REM than NREM. As many as 95% of people report dreaming during REM, as opposed to 12–25% in NREM sleep (Hobson, 2002).

THINKING CREATIVELY

We just quoted Hobson's (2002) statistic about people reporting dreams in REM and NREM sleep. But how do we arrive at such figures? Your task is to design a study to investigate the frequency of dreaming in REM and NREM sleep. Bear in mind that participants won't know what stage of sleep they are or were in at any given moment and that they probably won't remember their dreams for long once they are awake. You will need a basic methodology, such as waking participants or questioning them just after natural waking, and to consider the environment, participant design, and experimental controls.

❯ **KEY IDEAS** sleep mentation
Sleep mentation includes any and all mental activity occurring during sleep, including 'sleep thinking' and various levels of dreaming.

Because it is not always clear exactly what should or should not be considered a 'dream', researchers often use the term **sleep mentation** to describe any and all mental activity that occurs during sleep. Sleep mentation exists on a continuum that begins on one side with rational thought characteristic of waking states; and ends on the other side with bizarre, non-rational, hallucinatory experiences typical of the most memorable and intensely vivid dreaming (Fosse, Stickgold, and Hobson, 2004). Although sleep mentation exists on a continuum, it can be more easily understood by breaking it up into three categories: *cognitive activity, ordinary dreaming,* and *apex dreaming* (see Nielsen, 2000).

Sleep thinking

Have you ever become aware during a half-awakening in the middle of the night that you had been thinking during sleep about material on a test scheduled for the following day or making a list of things you needed to do over the weekend? Or perhaps you had been repeating certain images or melodies, or reflecting upon some event. This type of mentation is categorized as cognitive activity or 'sleep thinking'. Cognitive activity of this sort differs from dreaming in that it is unemotional, non-hallucinatory, and it lacks a story or dramatic progression. Rational, directed thought of this sort virtually always occurs during NREM sleep (Fosse et al, 2004). Sleep thinking can be extremely creative; in fact some of humanity's greatest scientific and artistic accomplishments have been at least partly conceived during sleep. These include Keith Richards' *I Can't Get No Satisfaction*, Crick's double-helix structure of DNA, and James Cameron's *Terminator*. Always bear in mind the scientific limitations of retrospectively gathered anecdotes like this, but these examples are *likely* to be the result of sleep thinking.

> ❯ KEY IDEAS sleep thinking (cognitive activity) This is rational, directed thought occurring during NREM sleep.

Ordinary dreaming

Although dreams are often characterized in the media and literature as irrational, bizarre, and surrealistic, this description does not apply to most dreams. The average dream contains recognizable characters engaged in relatively realistic activities that are based on the dreamer's ordinary concerns and preoccupations (Domhoff, 2010). One reason why dreams are thought to be 'stranger' than they generally are may be that bizarre dreams are more likely recalled the next day (Vogel, 2000). However, when dream research participants are awakened at various points during the night and asked to relate their dreams, they tend to report material that lacks the surrealism and irrationality attributed to dreams in general (Domhoff, 2010). The majority of dreams that occur during NREM are of the **ordinary dreaming** variety.

> ❯ KEY IDEAS ordinary dreaming The term **ordinary dreaming** describes the most common form of dreams, depicting relatively realistic activities and recognizable characters.

Apex dreaming

Apex dreams are those that are the most intense, vivid, bizarre, hallucinatory, and 'dream-like'. Nightmares and sexual dreams are good examples of apex dreams, as are dreams that are too 'beyond words' to describe, even if you recall them. While there is controversy regarding the importance of REM to the entire dream process, evidence very strongly supports the view that apex dreaming occurs primarily during REM sleep (Hobson et al, 2000).

Apex dreams are characterized by the dreamer's acceptance of wildly improbable events as being real (Hobson, 2002). However, one unusual type of apex dream in that this does not occur is known as the **lucid dream** (Voss, Holzmann, Tuin, and Hobson, 2009). Normally, one is unaware that one is dreaming. It is not even common to ask oneself the question, 'Am I dreaming?', although this occurs often in movie depictions of dreams. In a lucid dream, however, the dreamer becomes aware that he or she is dreaming. In a lucid dream there is a sense of being one's 'real self' in the dream with a consciousness similar to that of waking consciousness. Lucid dreams last about two minutes on average, but they may last as long as 50 minutes.

> ❯ KEY IDEAS apex dreams and lucid dreams **Apex dreams** are the most intense, bizarre, non-rational, and hallucinatory dreaming. Although apex dreams are uncommon they tend to be well remembered. **Lucid dreams** are a type of apex dream where the dreamer becomes aware that he or she is dreaming.

Dream Content

As studies in sleep laboratories show, we all dream, unless dreaming has been abolished by neurological damage (Hobson, 2002). Confusion on this issue probably results from the fact that some people remember dreams much better than others.

In fact, unless one is awakened during a dream, recall of dreams is actually relatively rare. But what do people dream about? Is dream content as varied as the number of people who dream? While there are substantial individual, cultural, and sex differences in the content of dreams, there are also aspects of dream content that are universal among people regardless of **culture**, or are universal for a particular sex or age group.

There is a lot of nonsense written about dream content and its significance, so here are some general conclusions of psychological research (after Hall and Van de Castle, 1966; Nielsen et al, 2003; and Domhoff, 2010).

1 *Despite major cultural changes over the second half of the twentieth century, the dream life of young adults (college students) has remained essentially unchanged.* The most common types of dreams for both young men and young women are those that contain aggression or fear. Women are somewhat more likely than men to experience nightmarish themes (Nielsen et al, 2003) including themes of social exclusion and rejection. Indeed, one of the most robust findings in the dream research is that unpleasant dreams greatly outnumber pleasant ones, with misfortune occurring in about one-third of all dreams (Domhoff, 2010). Not all dreams are unpleasant, however. Dreams of friendly interactions are common, as are dreams with sexual content. As one might expect given research suggesting that men think about sex more often than women, sexual dreams are more common for men. In addition to sexuality and friendly interactions, other highly common themes of pleasant dreams are those that depict flying or soaring through the air (Nielsen et al, 2003). Finally, college students dream about school, teachers, and studying extremely frequently.

2 *There are stable cross-cultural similarities and differences in certain aspects of dream content.* In most respects, the general picture for dream content is similar all over the world. However, dream content also varies a great deal from culture to culture, in ways that make sense given major cultural differences. For example, the appearances of animals in dreams occurs with much greater frequency in small-scale societies in which hunting plays an important part in obtaining food. In cultures where the sexes are segregated for most of the day, dreamers have fewer other-sex characters in their dreams.

3 *There is a strong continuity found between the content of people's dreams and their waking thoughts.* There are large individual differences in dream content based upon differences in people's everyday concerns and emotional lives (Domhoff, 2003). If you are concerned about your performance at school or work, or the health of a family member, you may have dreams related to such concerns. In the years following the 11 September 2001 terrorist attacks, increasing numbers of people incorporated 9/11 imagery into their dreams (Bulkeley and Kahan, 2008).

4 Finally, *sleeping environment can also affect the content of dreams.* Recently, I (Paul) dreamt that one of my daughters and I had become lost in a frozen wood. I kept struggling to find blankets to cover her but I could not. I suddenly awoke to find that the window had somehow become unlocked and had swung open—letting in blasts of frigid wintry air—and that my wife, in her sleep, had stolen all my covers!

The Meaning of Dreams

Dream researchers do not agree on what part of the brain is responsible for generating dreams or how the images of dreams are generated. There is even less agreement as to *why* the brain engages in dreaming in the first place. It should therefore come as no surprise to find that psychologists also disagree as to the meaning of particular dreams! However, there is no doubt that as personal subjective experiences for the dreamer dreams can be very powerful.

The founder of psychoanalysis, Sigmund Freud, referred to dreams as the 'royal road to the activities of the unconscious mind'. He believed that dreams expressed, in disguised and sometimes symbolic form, wishes and desires experienced by the dreamer on an unconscious level—wishes and desires that would be unacceptable or threatening if they were made conscious. Ideas like unconscious desires and their disguise have proved to be a nightmare for scientific psychology, and there is an unsurprising lack of evidence to support them; however, there is some evidence for a link between dream content and wishes. Solms (2000) has pointed to links between the loss of dreaming and of goal-directed behaviour (a proxy for wishing) in brain-injured patients and the increased frequency of dreaming about lost functions (eg, dancing and sports in paralysed patients). These findings are certainly consistent with dreaming serving a function of wish-fulfilment although they cannot be said to be a direct test.

Although Freud's wish-fulfilment model of dreams is no longer favoured by many psychologists, no consensus has emerged about what other psychological functions might be served by dreaming. Here are a few candidates:

- Dreams are the cerebral cortex's attempt to make sense out of random electrical brain activity while it is operating without the help of neurotransmitters that characterize waking cognition and rational thought. These neurotransmitter systems are lowered during NREM, but 'knocked out' during REM, explaining the preponderance of dreams (particularly apex dreams) during REM (Hobson et al, 2000).

- Dreams are the brain's attempt to solve problems during sleep or regulate mood carried over from the previous day (Cartwright, 2005).

- Dreams (especially negative or threatening dreams) evolved to allow the dreamer to 'rehearse' various sorts of responses to threatening situations and thus be better prepared to deal with actual threats (Valli et al, 2008).

Despite their many differences, each of these theories suggests an important fact: even if dreams result from nothing more than random brain activation, *dreams have meaning to the dreamer*. They consist of content drawn from the person's life history, circumstances, emotions, and subjective experience.

SLEEP DISORDERS

Sleep does not always go according to plan, with up to a third of adults experiencing some sleep disturbance (Morphy et al, 2007). As alarming as this may seem, these findings are easy to misinterpret. There is quite a difference between a 'symptom of sleep disturbance' and a true 'sleep disorder', such as *insomnia*, as defined by the medical profession. Estimates of the frequency of insomnia vary massively according to how it is assessed but is as low as 5% for formal medical diagnosis (Dewa et al, 2017).

Whilst we should not overstate the *scale* of sleep problems it is equally import-ant not to understate their seriousness. In a survey of patients with a diagnosis of insomnia conducted across ten countries (Leger et al, 2014), 21% of respondents reported an accident at home, 10% an accident at work, and 4% a vehicle accident related to sleeplessness in the previous year. Studies of the potential consequences of inadequate sleep also suggest that sleep disorders might ultimately contribute to the risk of hypertension, hormonal disturbances, heart disease, stroke, obesity, psycho-logical disorders such as depression or anxiety, and metabolic disorders including diabetes (see, eg, Bagai, 2010). Recent studies have also suggested that insomnia precedes and may have a causal relationship with psychosis (Sheaves et al, 2016).

Insomnia

> **KEY IDEAS** insomnia
Insomnia can be defined as a chronic difficulty falling asleep, staying asleep, and/or being unable to obtain restful sleep.

Insomnia is a chronic difficulty falling asleep, staying asleep, and/or being unable to obtain restful sleep (Bootzin and Epstein, 2011). Insomnia is not the same as *circadian rhythm disorder*—difficulty going to sleep and waking up at the times one would expect given the local cycle of light and dark. A person who gets into bed at 11:00 p.m., but can't fall asleep until 1:00 a.m.—but who then sleeps a restful 8 hours, waking up at 9:00 a.m.—is much more likely to have *circadian rhythm disorder* than insomnia. On the other hand, it is also true that disruption in circadian rhythms, as might be experienced in jet lag or by night-shift workers, can trigger true insomnia.

As discussed in the previous section it is hard to estimate just how common in-somnia is. We do know, however, that as a person ages, his or her likelihood of expe-riencing this disorder approximately doubles, and at all ages, almost twice as many women as men suffer from insomnia (Buysse, Germain, and Moul, 2005). Insomnia is believed to be much more common in the prison population (Dewa et al, 2017).

Insomnia impacts every aspect of a person's life, contributing to the risk of many physical and psychological disorders. Insomnia is not something that just happens to a person at night. Exhaustion, irritability, isolation, and hopelessness about the situation ever improving can pervade the sufferer's entire day (Kyle, Espie, and Morgan, 2010). As evening approaches, anxiety about what is in store for the night builds, and this anxiety contributes to perpetuating the condition. Sufferers often realize that their anxiety about sleep is working against them, but feel powerless to avoid it. Insomnia takes on a life of its own (Carey et al, 2005).

Insomnia may have long-lasting consequences. Indeed, obtaining adequate, rest-ful sleep is so important to virtually all aspects of functioning that some researchers have proposed that insomnia greatly increases the risk of a large number of physi-cal and psychological problems and disorders (Bootzin and Epstein, 2011). In other words, insomnia is a disorder that also may constitute a partial cause of numerous other disorders.

Obstructive Sleep Apnoea

> **KEY IDEAS** obstructive sleep apnoea (OSA) **OSA** is a sleep disorder caused by narrowing at various sites along the upper airway leading to repeated nightly episodes of inability to breathe.

Imagine that you are lying in bed at night, sound asleep, and someone enters the room. The intruder places one hand tightly over your mouth and pinches your nasal passages closed with the other hand so you are unable to breathe. After a few mo-ments, your body fights to awaken, but just at the point of awakening, the intruder removes both hands. You resume sleeping. Now imagine that the intruder repeats this procedure several hundred times during the night. This is essentially the expe-rience of **obstructive sleep apnoea** (OSA), a sleep disorder that results in repeated narrowing at various sites along the upper airway throughout the night, leading to complete or partial inability to breathe (Aloia et al, 2004).

OSA is likely the most common of the sleep disorders, much more common than insomnia. The elderly and the obese are at particular risk for OSA, and, unlike insomnia, men are twice as likely as women to suffer from the condition (Ram et al, 2010). Younger women are particularly unlikely to have OSA. The central problem in OSA is that repeated episodes of inability to breathe result in insufficient oxygen reaching the brain and the rest of the body. Sufferers from severe OSA who do not obtain treatment are more likely to die of cardiovascular disease than those who have been treated, and OSA patients have a unique pattern of sudden death due to heart attacks (Gami et al, 2005).

Parasomnias

Parasomnias are a group of disorders characterized by unusual or even bizarre physical behaviours, perceptions, dreams, or emotions during sleep (Schenck and Mahowald, 2010). Those who suffer from one or more of the various parasomnias may walk, talk, scream, eat, fight, urinate, grind their teeth, or have sex in their sleep; they may wake in terror or confusion, or experience repeated nightmares. They may find themselves trying to enact their dreams.

There are quite a number of parasomnias, some very rare, and some fairly common. More common parasomnias include talking in one's sleep (*somniloquy*), bed-wetting (common in children only), leg cramps during sleep, repeated nightmares, and snoring. Less common parasomnias include REM-sleep behaviour disorder, night terrors, and sleepwalking.

> **KEY IDEAS** parasomnias
> The parasomnias are a group of sleep disorders characterized by unusual or bizarre physical behaviours, perceptions, dreams, or emotions during sleep.

REM-sleep behaviour disorder

Those suffering from **REM-sleep behaviour disorder (RBD)** are missing an important component of REM sleep: the muscle paralysis that enables one to experience intense dreams without needing to respond in a physical way to the events of the dreams. RBD sufferers may find themselves enacting their dreams, sometimes with dangerous consequences. This is because the dreams RBD sufferers tend to act out are those that are violent and confrontational—dreams where one is attacked by unknown assailants, insects, or animals and is compelled to fight to protect oneself or loved ones (Schenck and Mahowald, 2010). Bed partners of RBD sufferers may find their partner 'punching, kicking, beating, biting, knocking things off the nightstand, sitting on the bed, jumping out of bed, whispering, talking, shouting, swearing, crying, laughing, and singing' (Iranzo, Santamaria, and Tolosa, 2009, p 386). Bed partners of RBD sufferers need to be careful, for they may suffer cuts, bruises, and even bone fractures as a result of their partner's unusual behaviour.

> **KEY IDEAS** REM-sleep behaviour disorder (RBD) RBD is a *parasomnia* where the sleeper is missing the muscle paralysis component of REM sleep and acts out confrontational and violent dreams.

Night terrors

Night terrors (also known as *sleep terrors*) are perhaps the most disturbing of the parasomnias. People in the grip of night terrors will suddenly sit up in bed screaming in fear, and may try to run frantically from some perceived threat. Appearing wild-eyed, with dilated pupils—although seemingly unable to see—they will experience increased heart rate and may sweat profusely. Attempts to soothe them may make things worse. The episode may last as long as a half-hour or more. Eventually, the sufferer will calm down and go back to sleep. In the morning he or she will typically not remember anything of the event (Durand, 2006).

> **KEY IDEAS** night terrors
> A **night terror** is a *parasomnia* consisting of episodes during which the sleeper may suddenly sit up in bed screaming in fear, flail, or run as though pursued by a terrifying attacker. Night terrors resemble severe nightmares but are physiologically quite different.

Unlike episodes of RBD, night terrors do not necessarily result from a nightmare or any sort of dream at all. They tend to occur during those stages of NREM sleep where dreaming is least likely to occur, and may result from sudden arousal from NREM. However, dream-like experiences may sometimes occur (Oudiette et al, 2009). Night terrors are much more common in children and adolescents than in adults, particularly older adults, and they often seem to be triggered by sleep deprivation or fever in vulnerable individuals. One child of my (Paul's) acquaintance described the experience in this way: 'It is like having my feet in two different worlds at the same time. I do recognize my parents and I hear the words of comfort that they are saying. But, I am also aware of what seems to me to be actually happening. Those events are terrifying beyond belief and equally (or more) real to me'.

Somnambulism

> **KEY IDEAS** somnambulism Commonly called sleepwalking, **somnambulism** is a *parasomnia* characterized by wandering, often aimlessly, during late-REM sleep.

In some respects, night terrors are related to **sleepwalking**—or **somnambulism.** Both disturbances are thought to result from sudden arousal from NREM (Szelenberger, Niemcewicz, and Dabrowska, 2005). Sleepwalking, however, is generally more benign. The sleepwalker—again, usually a child—may wander aimlessly, carrying and rearranging objects in the room seemingly for no particular reason. He or she may try to urinate in a cupboard or bin, or go outside for a walk, or even take an unscheduled swim in a nearby lake. The person's eyes are wide open, but they seem glassy and unfocused. You cannot generally communicate with a person while he or she is sleepwalking, although you can do so if the person is suddenly roused.

Narcolepsy

> **KEY IDEAS** narcolepsy **Narcolepsy** is a chronic disruption of the sleep homeostat and sleep cycle. Those suffering from narcolepsy may feel the irresistible urge to sleep at any time, generally falling directly into REM sleep.

Narcolepsy is a neurological illness whose sufferers fall asleep at unexpected times; for example, while speaking, playing football, or driving a car. Narcolepsy is a chronic disruption of the sleep homeostat and the sleep cycle. The narcoleptic feels the irresistible urge to sleep at unpredictable times, and during these sleeps the normal progression from NREM to REM does not occur. REM typically begins immediately at sleep onset for narcoleptics rather than following 90 minutes of NREM as would normally be the case. Thus, narcolepsy sufferers may begin to dream vividly the moment they fall asleep. Indeed, narcolepsy can be seen as a disorder where REM intrudes into a person's normal waking experience (Zuberi, 2010).

During the 1990s, researchers established that the unpredictable onset of sleep in narcolepsy was associated with a dysfunction in the ability of the brain to produce *hypocretin*, a hormone that helps to govern the sleep cycle. Later, some of these same researchers were able to establish that the dysfunction in production of hypocretin is an autoimmune response linked to a specific gene. In simple terms, the immune system of the narcoleptic interprets hypocretin-producing cells as foreign bodies, and proceeds to kill them off (Hallmayer et al, 2009).

Sleep paralysis

> **KEY IDEAS** isolated sleep paralysis Also known as a **paralysis attack,** an incident of **isolated sleep paralysis** involves paralysis and **HHEs** (hypnogogic and hypnopompic experiences), typically of the presence of a malevolent intruder, pressure on the chest, or of flying/floating. Paralysis attacks are interpreted in many cultures as alien abduction or demonic attack. Most psychologists and neuroscientists see paralysis attacks as a dysfunction of REM sleep.

Paralysis or *atonia* is a normal and necessary part of sleep—otherwise we might act out our dreams—however, sleep paralysis accompanied by vivid hallucinations—technically called hypnogogic and hypnopompic experiences or **HHEs**—can be amongst humanity's most terrifying experiences. Paralysis and HHEs occur together either whilst falling sleep (hypnogogic) or during waking (hypnopompic) and together comprise a **paralysis attack** or an incident of **isolated sleep paralysis.** Isolated sleep paralysis has been reported for thousands of years. Its basic

FIGURE 6.9 A typical dream? Although dreams are usually depicted as surrealistic, hallucinatory, and wildly improbable, such as in this image, most dreams are actually relatively realistic and logical. (Painting depicted: *The Nightmare*, 1781, by Henry Fuseli).

Source: Henry Fuseli, The Nightmare, 1781. World History Archive/Alamy Stock Photo.

elements are highly consistent across a range of cultures, although different cultures have interpreted them differently. These are as follows (Cheyne, 2005):

- Intruder: this is the experience of an evil presence so terrifying that those who have experienced it report that the emotion of fear is not an adequate descriptor. The presence has been interpreted in different cultures as an attack by a vampire, demon, witch, or alien.

- Incubus: the sensation of pressure on the chest causing difficulty in breathing. This may be accompanied by the visual hallucination of a monster or hag sitting on the victim's chest smothering them. An example is shown in Figure 6.9.

- Unusual body experience: this may be in the form of feeling grabbed or pulled by the leg or of floating or flying. In contrast to the terrifying experience of other paralysis attacks, the latter is often a positive experience, accompanied by a feeling of serenity or bliss.

Because of the commonality of HHEs it is widely believed that the hallucinations are derived from the physiology underlying the experience. This is called **experiential source hypothesis** (Hufford, 1982). Thus paralysis is the result of normal REM sleep atonia; however, unlike in normal REM sleep there is sufficient awareness of this to require interpretation, which takes place in the light of hallucinations. Thus paralysis is *experienced* as being held down by a hag or strapped to an operating table by aliens. Sleep atonia inhibits deep breathing, and the inability to breathe more deeply in response to fear might be experienced as physical compression of the chest. The sights and sounds of HHEs can be explained by activation of the limbic system, which is associated both with memory storage and retrieval and with strong emotional experiences such as terror (LeDoux, 1996).

Although paralysis attacks may have a common biological origin, they are experienced and interpreted differently in different cultural contexts. We can look in detail at one cross-cultural comparison of isolated sleep paralysis in Canadian and Japanese students in our *Research in focus* feature.

RESEARCH IN FOCUS

Fukuda, K., Ogilvie, R.D., Chilcott, L., Vendittelli, A.M., and Takeuchie, T. (1998). The prevalence of sleep paralysis among Canadian and Japanese college students. *Dreaming*, **8**, 59–66.

Aim: Prior research had suggested cultural differences in the experience of isolated sleep paralysis; however, this could have been an artefact of differing survey methodologies. The aim of this study was to directly compare experience of and beliefs about sleep paralysis attacks in Japanese and Canadian students.

Method: A bespoke questionnaire was constructed in English and translated into Japanese. This measured experiences of sleep paralysis, symptoms of narcolepsy, sleep posture, and supernatural beliefs. The questionnaire was administered to Japanese and Canadian students. In order to match the age profiles of the two groups responses from those over the age of 22 were discarded. The final sample consisted of 86 Canadian students, 23 males and 63 females; and 149 Japanese students, 88 males and 61 females.

Results: A slightly higher percentage of Canadians reported symptoms of sleep paralysis (52.3% as compared with 44.3% of Japanese respondents). The most common symptom was paralysis (87.9% of Japanese and 80% of Canadian students). Differences in the frequency of symptoms did not vary significantly between the two populations with one exception—74.2% of Japanese students reported being unable to speak as opposed to 46.7% of Canadians. The most common predictor of sleep paralysis attacks in both populations was fatigue, reported by 56.1% of Japanese and 44.4% of Canadian respondents. The most significant difference between the two groups concerned their beliefs about the origins of sleep paralysis: 55.6% of Canadians saw the experience as a type of dream as compared with 15.2% of Japanese.

Conclusions: There is no difference in the prevalence and little difference in the experience of isolated sleep paralysis among Canadian and Japanese young adults. This suggests that previously reported cultural differences may be due to variations in survey methods. However, there is a dramatic difference in cultural understandings of the experience, with Canadians much more likely to interpret sleep paralysis as a dream event.

MASTER YOUR METHODOLOGY

1 The researchers used a chi² test to analyse the significance of their results. Explain why this was a suitable test in this case.

2 Other studies have reported greater cultural differences in the prevalence of sleep paralysis attacks. Explain what a type II error is and why this is a possible explanation for the lack of statistical significance in the difference in prevalence in the two samples studied here.

3 What other variables might affect the results of this study, impacting on its validity?

HYPNOSIS: AN ALTERED STATE OF CONSCIOUSNESS?

What could be more *altered* than the state of consciousness known as *hypnosis*? Think of all the films and television programmes you have seen that depict hypnosis: people in trance-like states accurately recalling events that occurred when they were infants, allowing the hypnotist to pierce their skin with needles, displaying outrageous feats of strength, or performing behaviours a year after having being instructed to do so while under hypnosis. While such images of hypnosis are essentially mythological, if even a portion of what is commonly believed about hypnosis were true, wouldn't that qualify hypnosis as an altered state of consciousness?

Unfortunately, after 100 years of research, there still is no firm foundation upon which to answer this question, and the question itself can be interpreted in a number of ways. Indeed, there are few debates in psychology as long lasting and unlikely to be resolved in the near future as the debate over whether the experience of hypnosis represents a special, altered state of consciousness or an interesting variation on ordinary waking states (Wagstaff, 1994). Ten years after Kirsch and Lynn (1995) declared that the debate had ended in the 1990s and was now a 'myth', an entire issue of the journal *Contemporary Hypnosis* (Volume 22, number 1, 2005) was given over to articles (including one by Kirsch himself) which demonstrated that the debate was—and is—alive and well and as heated as ever.

Hypnosis as a Social Event

The term *hypnosis* was drawn from the Greek word *hypnos*, meaning sleep. **Hypnosis** has been newly redefined by the American Psychological Association (2005) in bare-bones terms as a procedure in which a person acting as a 'hypnotist' gives a variety of suggestions for 'imaginative experiences' to another person, who acts as a 'subject' (eg, 'Go ahead, try to open your eyes—you will be unable'). The suggestions given to the subject are generally preceded by an initial hypnotic *induction procedure* that corresponds to what most people would call 'being hypnotized' ('You are growing very sleepy . . .' and so forth).

Until about 40 years ago, hypnosis was thought by many psychologists and most of the public to be a special, altered state of consciousness—a *trance state*. This trance state actually defined the term *hypnosis* (Kirsch and Lynn, 1995). However, research has increasingly shown that hypnotic induction procedures are not even necessary to produce hypnotic effects, and there do not seem to be any particular criteria that can clearly distinguish a 'hypnotic state' from other states of consciousness (Spanos, 1996; Kirsch, 2005). These facts were made clear in a study conducted by Gandhi and Oakley (2005) when they subjected two groups of people to a hypnotic induction procedure, telling members of one group they would be undergoing 'hypnosis' while members of the other group were told they would be undergoing 'instructions to help you become relaxed'. The induction procedure produced only a very slight increase in suggestibility when it was labelled 'relaxation', but a substantial increase in suggestibility when it was labelled 'hypnosis'.

In fact, the hypnotic induction procedure itself can be done away with entirely as long as participants believe they are 'being hypnotized'. It appears to be the suggestions themselves, given to a willing subject in a context that he or she *believes* is hypnosis, that contain whatever power hypnosis possesses (Kirsch, Mazzoni, and Montgomery, 2007).

If that's all there is to it, what is all the fuss about? The problem is this: while hypnotic induction procedures do not appear to be the cause of hypnotic responses in people, *something* is causing these responses. Although it is likely that a certain amount of fakery is involved in hypnosis (Spanos, 1991), fakery does not account for most hypnotic phenomena. Hypnosis has been shown to be an effective treatment

> **KEY IDEAS** hypnosis
Hypnosis is an interaction between 'hypnotist' and 'subject' involving suggestions for 'imaginative experiences'. It is hard to define hypnosis any more precisely than this because there is still a debate about whether hypnosis involves an altered state or is rather a social phenomenon.

for acute pain (eg, burns, surgery, childbirth) and a useful adjunct to standard treatments for tobacco and other drug addictions (although it cannot cure these addictions alone). It can also substantially alter people's auditory and visual perceptions and beliefs about their control over their own behaviour (Gandhi and Oakley, 2005).

There is a broad spectrum of views on the question of what is actually happening during hypnosis, and the only points on which everyone seems to agree are these: (1) *imagination* and *suggestion* are somehow involved in hypnosis, and (2) hypnosis is a *social event* involving a 'subject' and a 'hypnotist'. The rest is, to one degree or another, up for grabs.

State versus non-state explanations

In general, researchers attempt to explain how hypnosis works in one of two ways, a tendency referred to as the *special state* vs *non-state* debate. Those in the *special state* camp continue to view the unusual experiences that occur under hypnosis—for example, immersing one's hand in ice water for a prolonged period yet feeling no pain—as altered states of consciousness (Spiegel, 2010). However, these researchers also acknowledge that the state a person enters following an induction procedure—'being hypnotized'—is not itself an altered state (ie, a 'trance'; Hilgard, 1986). A person may move into an altered state (eg, feeling no pain) directly from ordinary consciousness.

On the other hand, those in the *non-state* camp claim that *nothing* about hypnosis is best explained with the idea of altered states (Wagstaff et al, 2010). The most influential of the non-state group are the **sociocognitive** theorists. They take as their starting point a large literature which shows that those who have not undergone hypnotic induction procedures can produce most of the same behaviours and effects seen in hypnosis (eg, resistance to pain, amnesia, paralysis) through non-hypnotic suggestions, simple instructions designed to increase their motivation, or even through intentional attempts to pretend to be hypnotized (Spanos, 1996).

Moreover, contrary to widespread beliefs, hypnotized individuals do not have improved recall of past events, cannot 'regress' to infancy or 'past lives', can lie just as easily as at other times, and cannot achieve feats of strength or endure pain beyond their ordinary capabilities. For example, while hypnosis does increase the *number* of memories recalled, it increases the number of false memories just as it increases the number of true memories. When the amount of false information is taken into account, recall under hypnosis turns out no better than recall under normal conditions—indeed, it is worse (Mazzoni, Heap, and Scoboria, 2010).

However, it is not that sociocognitive theorists are claiming that hypnotic effects are 'not real'. Instead they are claiming that hypnosis is a bit similar to *placebo* response—where the taking of a phony medication actually brings symptomatic relief as a consequence of a person's belief that the medication is real. In both cases people experience what they *expect* to experience (Kirsch, 2005).

❯ **KEY IDEAS** sociocognitive theory of hypnosis   This is a theory that explains hypnotic effects in terms other than 'altered states'—generally emphasizing the subject's social role in the hypnotic interaction.

READ THIS

For exploration of fundamental issues around sleep you might like to read these:

Consensus Conference Panel, Watson, N.F., Badr, M.S., Belenky, G., Bliwise, D.L., Buxton, O.M. and Kushida, C. (2015). Joint consensus statement of the American Academy of Sleep Medicine and Sleep Research Society on the recommended amount of sleep for a healthy adult: Methodology and discussion. *Sleep*, **38**, 1161–83.

Buysse, D.J. (2014). Sleep health: can we define it? Does it matter? *Sleep*, **37**, 9–17.

For a neat run-down on sleep disorders try this:

Sateia, M.J. (2014). International classification of sleep disorders. *Chest*, **146**, 1387–94.

If, like me (Matt) your imagination is caught by the phenomenon of isolated sleep paralysis you might like to read David Hufford's classic ethnographic account of paralysis attacks in Newfoundland—but be prepared for a spooky read!

Hufford, D. (1989). *The Terror that Comes in the Night: An Experience-centered Study of Supernatural Assault Traditions* (Vol 7). Pennsylvania: University of Pennsylvania Press.

PSYCHOACTIVE DRUGS AND CONSCIOUSNESS

A **psychoactive drug** is any substance with properties that affect mental life or consciousness in some way. Although this would include medications used to treat psychological disorders—for example, *antidepressants*—for now we are concerned with drugs that people use without a prescription (and sometimes in violation of the law) specifically to alter their mental state or consciousness. This is termed **non-medical use of drugs**, or **recreational** drug use.

Non-medical use of psychoactive drugs is an ordinary part of most people's lives. Try to think of a single person you know who does not use at least one of the following: cigarettes, caffeine (coffee, tea, energy drinks, soft drinks), **alcohol** (including beer or wine), or illicit drugs (eg, cannabis). Although there are some people who rigorously attempt to resist all such substances for health, religious, or other reasons, the stunning enormity of the alcohol, coffee, tea, cola, tobacco, and illicit drug industries testifies that total abstainers from all mind-altering chemicals are extremely unusual. As summarized in Figure 6.10, in 2005 the World Health Organization estimated that there were 650 million smokers in the world (World Health Organization, 2005), and although the number is decreasing in the developed world, it is increasing in much of the rest of the world. Alcohol use is about four times more prevalent even than the rate of tobacco use, and alcohol use is positively dwarfed by use of caffeine.

Illegal drug use is also pervasive. As depicted in Figure 6.11, in 2008, between 155 and 250 million people (3.5% to 5.7% of the world's population aged 15–64) used an illegal substance (mostly cannabis) to alter their consciousness (United Nations Office on Drugs and Crime, 2010). In Western nations approximately one-third of all adults have used illegal drugs (again, mostly cannabis) at least once (United Nations

> **KEY IDEAS** psychoactive drug Any substance with properties that affect mental life or consciousness in some way can be termed a **psychoactive drug**. Many psychoactive substances have a **non-medical** or **recreational use**.

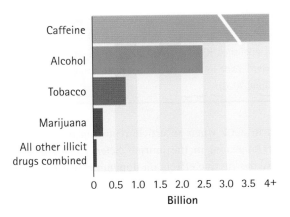

FIGURE 6.10 **Worldwide use of psychoactive drugs. This chart compares worldwide use of caffeine, alcohol, tobacco, marijuana, and other illicit drugs.**
Sources: Phillips and Lawton, 2004; World Health Organization, 2005.

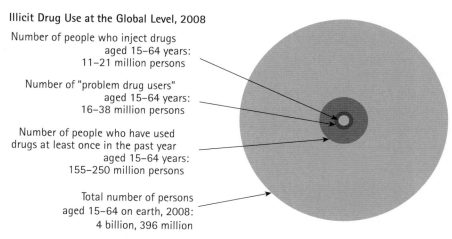

Illicit Drug Use at the Global Level, 2008

Number of people who inject drugs
aged 15–64 years:
11–21 million persons

Number of "problem drug users"
aged 15–64 years:
16–38 million persons

Number of people who have used
drugs at least once in the past year
aged 15–64 years:
155–250 million persons

Total number of persons
aged 15–64 on earth, 2008:
4 billion, 396 million

FIGURE 6.11 Illicit drug use throughout the world.
Source: United Nations Office on Drugs and Crime, 2010.

Office on Drugs and Crime, 2004). Thus, the total number of individuals using psychoactive drugs (legal and illegal) to alter their consciousness is truly staggering. This is not a recent phenomenon. Every recorded society whose natural environment supports the growing of plants has included use of psychoactive drugs as part of its culture (Siegel, 2005).

However, just because drug use is very normal this does not mean that it is good for you or that it does not pose dangers. In addition to possible medical or psychological consequences of inappropriate or abusive use of illicit drugs, in modern societies the use of these drugs can have extremely serious legal and social consequences, depriving users of their liberty, their possessions, and even their lives.

On the other hand, it is not always easy to obtain accurate information about the effects and dangers of psychoactive drugs. This is because non-medical use of drugs historically has engaged powerful emotions, moral sentiments, and social, political, legal, and economic interests (Bonnie and Whitebread, 1999). Scientists are not immune from the influence of such forces (McCook, 2005).

DEBUNKING

> KEY IDEAS ecstasy (MDMA)
MDMA is a psychedelic drug derived from *amphetamines*. It was popularized by the rave scene of the late 1980s and early 90s and remains one of the favoured recreational drugs in Western Europe.

A good example is the recent history of research on the 'club drug' **ecstasy (MDMA)**. During the late-1980s and early 1990s the public became concerned about 'rave' parties that were attracting many teenagers and featured all-night dancing and the use of various 'club drugs'—in particular, ecstasy (MDMA). In the light of the moral panic led by the popular press, pressure was put on scientists to provide evidence of the dangers of ecstasy, and researchers whose work did *not* provide such evidence had a difficult time getting published (Cole et al, 2002a). Extravagant statements that could not be supported by evidence were made in the media about brain damage and other horrors suffered by ecstasy users (Rosenbaum, 2002).

Everyone's worst fears were realized in 2002 when an article reporting research on ecstasy among non-human primates appeared in the journal *Science*. This article indicated that ecstasy had profoundly destructive effects on dopamine-related brain neurons in non-human primates, and might predispose human users to develop Parkinson's disease, a degenerative nervous system disorder characterized by severe motor disturbances resulting in difficulty walking, talking, and completing simple tasks. However, it was later revealed that these researchers had not even been using ecstasy in their research—they had been using *methamphetamine* (popularly known as 'crystal meth'). The article had to be retracted by the editors, a very unusual event for *Science*. But episodes of this sort are actually predictable given the sorts of intense pressures and incentives experienced by researchers in the field of non-medical drug use (Cole et al, 2002).

Yet, people's attitudes towards various psychoactive drugs are in part the result of historical and social forces that change with the times—they are not necessarily inherent in the nature of the drugs themselves. Consider **heroin**, one of the most socially and morally despised of all drugs. But heroin was not always despised. Indeed, it was created for Bayer Pharmaceuticals, the company that produces the world's best-selling aspirin. It was initially cheered by the medical profession for its many uses and sold over the counter as a cough suppressant and as an ingredient in tonics known as 'soothing syrups'. At the end of the nineteenth century the largest numbers of heroin addicts (by a large margin) were middle-class housewives (Acker, 2002). However, these women suffered little moral disapproval and did not necessarily lose the respect of their families or society. Instead, they were more likely pitied for having a medical problem. As the legal status of the drug changed, however, so did the groups of people most likely to use it—and so did the moral and social status of the drug (Duster, 1972). Therefore, when it comes to the non-medical use of psychoactive drugs, keep in mind that people feel passionately about this issue, a warning sign that one needs to tread carefully through the minefield of claims and counterclaims.

Now, whilst we are urging balance and a sceptical perspective on the simplistic anti-drug messages in the media, we would not wish to give the impression that MDMA is harmless. Uosukainen, Tacke, and Winstock (2015) surveyed users of a British dance music website about dependence symptoms associated with different drugs. MDMA users reported more symptoms of dependency than users of other dance drugs but were less likely to consider themselves dependent. This suggests that MDMA is more addictive than people think and should therefore be approached with caution.

RESEARCH IN FOCUS

Kirkpatrick, M.G., Lee, R., Wardle, M.C., Jacob, S., and De Wit, H. (2014). Effects of MDMA and intranasal oxytocin on social and emotional processing. *Neuropsychopharmacology* **39**, 1654–63.

Aim: MDMA is associated with increases in empathy, sociability, and interpersonal closeness. These are similar to the effects of the hormone oxytocin and it has thus been proposed that MDMA works by triggering oxytocin release. The aim of this study was to compare experimentally the effects of MDMA and oxytocin and thus test the oxytocin explanation for MDMA action.

Method: 25 female and 40 male participants with a history of light to moderate MDMA use were recruited by newspaper, online, and bulletin board advertisement. They took part in a mixed between-groups and within-groups double-blind design in which all received two doses of MDMA, one of oxytocin (one of two different doses), and one of a placebo. The dose order was randomized. Trials took place on an in-patient basis, separated by at least five days. A battery of blood, saliva, breath, and urine tests were carried out to eliminate the effects of other drug taking. During each trial participants completed a range of physiological and psychological tests, including heart rate and blood pressure, the Drug Effect Questionnaire, and computerized tests to assess emotion-recognition and social evaluation—judging faces for friendliness, attractiveness, and trustworthiness and social choices—choosing solitary or social activities.

Results: MDMA and oxytocin both increased sociability and improvements on some measures of mood. However, they also had some differing effects, oxytocin increasing emotion-recognition performance and MDMA reducing it. MDMA but not oxytocin led to increased physiological arousal and euphoria.

Conclusion: Results provided only partial support for oxytocin release as an explanation for the effects of MDMA. It is thus unlikely that MDMA effects are entirely due to oxytocin release although oxytocin release is one possible factor.

MASTER YOUR METHODOLOGY

1 This study used a double-blind design. Explain what this means and why it is important in studies like this one.

2 The study used a mixed within-groups and between-groups design, the latter separating participants taking two different doses of MDMA.

 a Explain the advantages of a within-groups design in which all participants took placebo, MDMA, and oxytocin.

 b Why might researchers have opted for a mixed design in this case? Put another way, why might they have given different participants the two MDMA doses?

Addiction

Drug **addiction** is one of the most destructive consequences of abusive non-medical use of drugs, but the term *addiction* has no accepted definition. Traditionally, *addiction* has referred to dependent and compulsive use of a drug that resulted in three outcomes:

1 **Withdrawal**: unpleasant physiological symptoms or states experienced when the body is deprived of a drug to which it has become biologically adapted as a result of habitual use. In such cases, the body experiences the removal of the drug as a harmful event.

2 **Craving**: the overpowering feeling of 'wanting' and depending upon a drug.

3 **Tolerance**: a progressive need for more and more of the drug to achieve the same effect.

This 'classical' model of addiction was based on users' physiological responses to *opium* and the various drugs derived from it, such as heroin and morphine. However, this understanding of addiction had to be revised. Consider the drug **cocaine**. While it does produce a 'crash' when its effects dissipate, it does not generally produce withdrawal symptoms in the true sense and does not necessarily result in tolerance. Therefore, cocaine is not 'physically addicting' in the sense that the opiates

> **KEY IDEAS** addiction, withdrawal, craving, and tolerance **Addiction** is a term frequently used to describe drug dependence. Originally, the term included *withdrawal*, *tolerance*, and *craving* as necessary components, but currently, *addiction* has no precise definition. **Withdrawal** involves unpleasant physiological (and psychological) symptoms experienced when the body is deprived of a drug to which it has become adapted. **Craving** means overpowering feelings of 'wanting' and depending upon a drug. **Tolerance** is a progressive need for more and more of a drug to achieve the same effect.

are addicting (Johanson et al, 1999). Yet cocaine can still produce a craving and dependence as powerful as—or in some cases more powerful than—that produced by more 'classically' addictive drugs such as heroin.

For this and other reasons, many researchers and clinicians concerned with drug problems have tended to shy away from use of the term 'addiction' in recent years (although some still use it). Many prefer to use the term *dependence* while making a point of specifying whether or not symptoms such as withdrawal, craving, or tolerance are present.

It is difficult to obtain accurate figures for illegal drug use and dependence because it is by definition something people tend to keep quiet about. However, there are estimates based on self-report and arrest. For example, in the UK 11.5% of young adults report using cannabis in the last year. Along with Ireland, France, Italy, and Portugal the UK has over 0.5% of the population admitting to using high-risk opioids like heroin (European Monitoring Centre for Drugs and Drug Addiction, 2018). According to the National Crime Survey 2017–18 19.8% of adults aged 18–59 took an illegal drug in the last year, with use of Class A drugs (judged in law to be the most 'serious' drugs) amongst 16–24-year-olds at 8.4%. Dependency is harder to estimate; around 300,000 people seek help for opiate and crack cocaine addiction in the UK each year (National Drug Treatment Monitoring System) but there is no way to know how many people suffer addiction but do not seek help.

 THINKING CRITICALLY

It is notoriously difficult to arrive at accurate figures for drug use and, in particular, addiction. Explain the limitations of each of the following sources of evidence:

a Medical statistics concerning those seeking help for addiction.

b Crime statistics concerning those caught with illegal drugs.

The term **drug misuse** is generally meant to indicate any pattern of drug use that causes personal distress or impairment in an important aspect of a person's life. However, in practice this term is often applied to *any* illegal use of a drug, and it is sometimes difficult to determine what any particular commentator means by the use of the word *abuse* in connection with illegal drug use.

Toxicity

Although some drugs are considered 'safer' and others more 'dangerous', or *toxic*, it is important to understand that, in fact, *all substances are potentially toxic*—and this includes water, which, if taken in sufficient amounts, can cause death (Riggs, Dysken, Kim, and Opsahl, 1991). Indeed, on 15 January 2007, Jennifer Lea Strange, a 28-year-old California woman, died of water intoxication after participating in a radio-station-sponsored water-drinking contest. Thus, there is no 'non-toxic' drug, which means that there is no 'safe' drug. On the other hand, technically speaking, neither is there a 'toxic' or 'dangerous' drug. Instead, there is a *dose level* for every substance above which it poses danger, and below which it produces no measurable physiological harm (Neubert, 1999).

It is for this reason that researchers use a formula based on studies with laboratory animals and humans to compute a **safety ratio** for psychoactive drugs (Gable, 2004a, 2004b). The *larger* the safety ratio, the *less* toxic the drug given the dosages normally used. For example, if a drug has a safety ratio of ten it means that ten times the ordinary 'recreational' dose of the drug would probably kill an average person. A safety ratio of 100 means that it would take approximately 100 times the ordinary recreational dose to be lethal (Gable, 2004b).

Table 6.2 lists the safety ratios of a group of drugs often used for non-medical purposes, along with a ranking of the potential for the drug to create dependence (addiction). Of course, the safety ratios are estimations that cannot be relied on to be precise because there are so many other factors that could come into play—for example, the age and health status of the person, whether a person uses several drugs at once, and so forth. The ratios should be viewed as a general picture of the *relative* toxic potential of various drugs.

Illegal use of psychoactive drugs results in many deaths per year—both directly, due to overdose, illness, or drug interaction; and indirectly due to car crashes and other accidents (Mokdad et al, 2004). This figure should be seen in the context of deaths due to *legal* non-medical and medical drug use. For example, during the same years, approximately 435,000 deaths occurred annually in the United States, directly

TABLE 6.2 Safety ratios and dependence potential of commonly misused drugs

Specific figures for the proportion of users who become dependent are given where known.		
Substance	Safety ratio	Dependence potential
Narcotics		
Codeine	20	Moderate
Morphine	15	High
Heroin	6	High (23% of users become dependent)
Depressants (Hypnotics)		
Rohypnol ('roofies')	40	Moderate
Alcohol	10	Moderate/high (13–15% of users become dependent)
GHB	10	Uncertain
Stimulants		
Caffeine	100	Low/moderate
Nicotine	50	Very high (31% of users become dependent)
Cocaine	15	Moderate/high (16% of users become dependent)
Psychedelics ('Hallucinogens')		
Cannabis	>1,000 (no verified case of death)	Low/moderate (9% of users become dependent)
LSD	1,000	Very low
Ecstasy (MDMA)	15	Low/moderate by usual criteria

Source: Adapted from data presented by Anthony, Warner, and Kessler, 1994; Gable, 2004b, 2006; Wagner and Anthony, 2002.

or indirectly, as a result of cigarette smoking (not including second-hand smoke), and 85,000 resulted from alcohol use (Mokdad et al, 2004). In Great Britain, alcohol and tobacco currently result in approximately 90% of all drug-related deaths (Nutt, King, Saulsbury, and Blakemore, 2007).

Psychoactive Drugs Classified

In general, psychoactive drugs used for non-medical purposes are placed in one of four categories: opioids (**narcotics**), which are derived from *opium* and have pain-killing and euphoric effects; **depressants** (also termed *hypnotics*), which depress the central nervous system (CNS) and produce relaxation or sleepiness; **stimulants**, which stimulate the CNS and produce alertness and energy; and **psychedelics** (also termed *hallucinogens*), which substantially alter one's perception of reality.

Opiates

Opiate drugs are drugs derived from ordinary poppy flower (*Papaver somniferum*); for example, heroin, morphine, codeine, oxycodone, and hydrocodone. **Opium**, the dried nectar of the poppy, is probably the oldest psychoactive substance known to mankind with the exception of alcohol (Booth, 1999). Opium is not a drug itself, but rather a substance containing a number of different **alkaloids** (the technical term for a compound with drug-like effects produced naturally by a plant). The most important of these alkaloids is **morphine**, one of the most powerful painkillers in existence and the drug from which heroin is derived.

Pharmaceutical drugs derived from opium—for example, morphine and codeine—are known as **opioids**. These drugs are among the most useful ever devised as treatments for pain and certain other conditions, and surprisingly, also among the safest as long as they are used properly for medical purposes (Merskey, 2004). However, these drugs are extremely dangerous when used for non-medical purposes, when they can produce a dreamy, cocoon of euphoria and well-being. When used in this way they can, and often do, result in a very serious form of drug addiction or dependence that may take a lifetime of struggle to successfully treat. The most addictive of the opioids is heroin. Approximately 23%—almost one in four—people who use heroin on a regular basis become dependent (but note that this means that over 75% of users do not become dependent; Anthony, Warner, and Kessler, 1994). Here is how William S. Burroughs, a controversial twentieth-century American novelist and infamous narcotics addict, described his life in late-addiction:

> I had not taken a bath in a year or changed my clothes or removed them except to stick a needle every hour in the fibrous grey wooden flesh of terminal addiction. I never cleaned or dusted the room. Empty ampule boxes and garbage piled up to the ceiling. Light and water had been long since turned off for non-payment. I did absolutely nothing. I could look at the end of my shoe for eight hours. I was only roused to action when the hourglass of junk [*note: heroin*] ran out. If a friend came to visit—and they rarely did since who or what was left to visit—I sat there not caring that he had entered my field of vision—a grey screen always blanker and fainter—and not caring when he walked out of it. If he had died on the spot I would have sat there looking at my shoe waiting to go through his pockets. (Burroughs, 1959, xxxvi)

Under certain circumstances opioid drugs can cause death, typically due to *respiratory depression*, a severe inhibition of the body's ability to regulate breathing.

> **KEY IDEAS** opiates, opium, morphine, and alkaloids   Opiates are a category of drug. They include: **opium**, the dried nectar of the common *Papaver somniferum* (poppy) flower containing a number of alkaloids including morphine. **Morphine** is an alkaloid of opium used as a potent painkiller. **Alkaloids** are any compounds with drug-like effects found naturally in a plant.

FIGURE 6.12 **Sid Vicious of the Sex Pistols famously died of a heroin overdose, having taken a large dose after detoxing. Although the popular explanation of drug taking amongst rock musicians is one of hedonism it may be as much a response to a stressful lifestyle (Livingston, 2017).**

Source: Marco Govel/Shutterstock.com.

> **KEY IDEAS** overdose

An **overdose** is a lethal or non-lethal but toxic dose of a drug. Real overdoses are rare—most so-called overdoses are actually the result of mixing opioids with other psychoactive drugs.

> **KEY IDEAS** cocaine, freebase, and crack **Cocaine** is an alkaloid of the coca plant in concentrated form. **Freebase** is a method of using cocaine where the active ingredient of cocaine is isolated and smoked. Unlike cocaine in powder form (cocaine hydrochloride), freebase is not soluble in water and cannot be snorted or administered through injection. **Crack** cocaine is a solid form of cocaine somewhat similar to freebase, 'cooked' from cocaine, water, and baking soda or lye. Street crack often contains other chemical components.

However, contrary to popular belief, it is not usually a particularly strong dose, or **overdose**, that produces sudden death to regular opioid users—most of whom have developed extreme levels of tolerance to the drug. Rather, it is the use of opioids simultaneously with other central nervous system (CNS) depressants such as alcohol or *benzodiazepine* drugs (eg, *Valium, Xanax, Klonopin*), which can dramatically increase the risk of 'overdose' (Brådvik et al, 2007). Although it is possible for opioid drug users to die from a particularly strong dose (Brådvik et al, 2007), this accounts for a small minority of opioid-related deaths. Particularly when heroin is involved, authorities have a tendency to apply the label 'overdose' to any sudden death of a known heroin user, even when it is unclear which drug ought to be blamed for the death (Brecher, 1972).

Stimulants

Drugs that are classified as stimulants have the effect of producing feelings of exhilaration, alertness, confidence, and mood elevation—although they can also trigger anxiety, restlessness, sleeplessness, and a number of other undesirable effects. Each stimulant is different and they produce their effects in numerous ways, but frequently stimulant effects are associated with a build-up of the neurotransmitter dopamine in the brain.

Cocaine is a concentrated form of an alkaloid of the *coca* plant, indigenous to South America. For centuries, native peoples have chewed the coca leaves for their painkilling, appetite-suppressing, and energizing effects. Cocaine is usually inhaled through the nose, but it can also be injected, or the 'base' (active ingredient) in cocaine can be isolated and smoked in **freebase**—a much more powerful, habit forming, and potentially toxic way to experience the drug. Cocaine can also be smoked as **crack**, which is similar to freebase but less expensive and easier to produce.

Cocaine users generally experience a rush of energy, elevated mood, euphoria, alertness, and feelings of well-being. However, because these effects are so short lasting (only about 10 or 15 minutes for those who snort the drug, and even less for those who freebase or use crack), users are forced to repeat dosing themselves continuously if they want the high to last. Long-term users may experience symptoms of sleeplessness, severe depression, and serious impairment in thought and perception—particularly paranoia. Cocaine-dependent individuals have lost their money, cars, homes, property, jobs, and families as a result of their cocaine habits. Approximately 16% (one in six) cocaine users eventually becomes dependent on the drug, only slightly more than the numbers of alcohol users who become dependent (Anthony et al, 1994).

Amphetamines (also collectively called 'speed', etc) include methamphetamine (crystal meth), *Dexedrine*, and *Ritalin* (used to treat ADHD). Unlike cocaine, amphetamines have long-lasting effects, and they are much less expensive. On the other hand, most amphetamines tend to be somewhat 'harsher' than cocaine as an experience and are less likely to result in feelings of euphoria and well-being. Those taking 'speed' often appear to others to be exhibiting symptoms of *mania* (see Chapter 18)—rapid speech, overconfidence, restless energy, insomnia, and bizarre attention to detailed tasks ('I think I'll clean every inch of this house tonight—and maybe my friend's mother's house too').

❯ KEY IDEAS amphetamines
Amphetamines are a family of stimulant drugs that exert their effects primarily by increasing levels of norepinephrine, serotonin, and dopamine in the brain.

Like cocaine, amphetamines can result in severe fatigue, depression, and other unpleasant symptoms when the drug wears off, and symptoms of psychosis similar to those experienced by cocaine users may also be experienced after prolonged use of amphetamines. Some evidence suggests that amphetamines may cause long-lasting changes in brain functioning and structure (Chang, Alicata, Ernst, and Volkow, 2007; Berman, O'Neill, Fears, Bartzokis, and London, 2008). Dependence upon amphetamines (especially methamphetamine) is common, but there are currently no reliable figures for risk of addiction.

Caffeine is an alkaloid found naturally in coffee, tea, and chocolate. It wards off fatigue, produces alertness, and for some people improves performance on a variety of cognitive tasks when taken in moderate doses (van Duinen, Lorist, and Zijdewind, 2005; Dagan and Doljansky, 2006). In larger doses it can produce restlessness, nervousness, insomnia, gastric and heart disturbances, and other problems. Truly excessive doses can result in serious symptoms of mental illness requiring psychiatric treatment (Hedges, Woon, and Hoopes, 2009; American Psychiatric Association, 2000).

The large majority of human beings use caffeine—either as coffee, tea, soft drinks, energy drinks, or chocolate—although some steer clear of it because it can cause insomnia or 'jitters'. However, at any given time, most people in the world are either under the influence of caffeine in some form, or soon will be (Phillips and Lawton, 2004). As I (Paul) sit here with my espresso cup filled to the brim, and I (Matt) top up my Americano with steamed milk we must admit to being an enthusiastic part of this thundering majority!

Whether or not caffeine is 'addictive' is controversial, however. Heavy caffeine users know that it can produce tolerance, and that suddenly quitting use can cause withdrawal symptoms such as severe headache, fatigue, and irritability (Juliano and Griffiths, 2004). Some caffeine users have attempted to quit or cut down and found it quite difficult, making them technically dependent on the drug. However, caffeine users generally do not display most of the other criteria that would qualify their use as dependence or addiction. These criteria would include devoting most of one's time in attempts to locate caffeine, dropping previously important activities so that caffeine can be used, frequent non-fatal overdose, and so forth.

How safe is caffeine? Periodically there are reports of health risks of caffeine, particularly in high doses, but there are also fairly numerous reports of potential benefits. Perhaps the most startling of such reports was the recent large-scale 13-year analysis of mortality data conducted by researchers from the National Institutes of Health. These researchers found that coffee drinkers were less likely to die (during the period of the study) of all causes combined (or of any specific cause) than non-coffee drinkers, after controlling for various potential **confounding variables**. More surprising still, it seemed that the more coffee a person drank—up to four to six cups daily—the stronger was the association with longevity (Freedman et al, 2012).

Of course, coffee contains more compounds than caffeine, and these correlational results certainly do not demonstrate that coffee *caused* the increases in longevity. Still, it does make one wonder. In any event, taken as a whole, caffeine seems to be a relatively safe drug that holds strong attraction for most people, but has the potential to produce a mild form of drug dependence. There is at least one exception to this 'relatively safe' judgement: so-called energy drinks. Some of these may contain many more times the amount of caffeine than in a can of cola or cup of coffee. Consumption of energy drinks has sometimes resulted in fatalities from heart attack or stroke, and more commonly can cause extremely unpleasant symptoms of caffeine intoxication (Reissig, Strain, and Griffiths, 2009). Increasingly, public concern has been raised about the use of these drinks, especially by teenagers.

Nicotine is an alkaloid found in the *nightshade* family, which includes tomatoes, green peppers, and a number of other plants including tobacco (although the fruit of these plants contains no nicotine, so there's no need to cut down on your salad intake). Nicotine produces a slight increase in alertness, and users who are dependent on it may experience a paradoxical sense of relaxation when they use the drug, probably because the experience of 'needing' a cigarette is unpleasantly arousing. Nicotine is highly addictive—more users who try a nicotine-containing product ultimately become dependent upon it than any other drug, including heroin and cocaine (Heishman, Kozlowski, and Henningfield, 1997). A meta-analysis by Birge et al (2017) concluded that between 60.9 and 76.9% of people who tried a cigarette went on to become addicted. Withdrawal is extremely unpleasant and difficult to endure; it may include headaches, anxiety, irritability, insomnia, and cognitive disturbances. Although it has not yet been demonstrated conclusively that nicotine on its own—that is, apart from its presence in tobacco—is carcinogenic (cancer-causing) in humans, some animal research suggests that it may be (Davis et al, 2009).

Cigarettes are the most deadly recreational drug available. Although heroin and cocaine are far from harmless, they do not compare to cigarettes in destructive physiological effects. Unlike heroin and cocaine, cigarette smoking negatively affects virtually every organ in the body, including the brain. For example, in addition to the many diseases caused by cigarettes, cigarette smoking *increases* stress, it does not decrease it as many smokers believe (Parrott, 1999). The illusion of decrease in stress from smoking arises because cigarette smoking decreases the discomfort of nicotine withdrawal symptoms. However, nicotine dependence/addiction is itself stressful, and those who smoke are more stressed than those who do not. When smokers quit, they report less stress.

FIGURE 6.13 Smoking cigarettes. Smoking cigarettes is perhaps the most dangerous and destructive ordinary behaviour in which a person may engage. By 'ordinary' we mean a behaviour that many people perform in the daily course of their lives. Without doubt, jumping off London Bridge, shooting oneself in the head, or spilling Tyson Fury's beer are all more dangerous than smoking cigarettes, but none of these is an ordinary behaviour.

Source: Terroa/Shutterstock.com.

According to the World Health Organization (2003), there are 1.3 billion smokers in the world, and 50% of them will die of a disease caused by tobacco before they turn age 70, losing between 16 and 21 years of life on average. Smoking causes disease in almost every organ of the body and is a risk factor for six of the eight leading causes of death in the world (World Health Organization, 2008). In addition to approximately 15 ways that smoking can kill you, there are 15 more ways it can make life miserable through non-fatal but debilitating disease. Smoking is responsible for approximately 5.4 million deaths per year, and if current smoking trends continue, one billion people will die of smoking before the end of the twenty-first century (World Health Organization, 2008). Smoking is the single most important cause of premature death in the Western world, resulting in many times—a *great* many times—more deaths than car crashes and other accidents, poisoning and drug overdose, homicide and suicide, AIDS, and alcoholic liver disease combined (Centre for Disease Control, 2005). Did we mention that it wrinkles, dries, and yellows the skin, and causes the breath and entire body to develop an unappealing odour? Put simply, there is no single behaviour in which you can engage that will increase your life expectancy more than quitting smoking or refraining from taking up the habit in the first place.

So why do people smoke? Anyone with Wi-Fi can discover what we have just told you. Given that this information is easily available, why would anyone not overtly bent on seriously harming himself or herself and causing distress to loved ones smoke cigarettes?

The answer to this question is not simple. But if a pie chart could be drawn with all probable contributing factors, the most important of these, at least in modern

Western societies, would probably be *adolescence.* It is well known that if a person has not learned to smoke in adolescence, it is highly unlikely that he or she will ever become a smoker—only about 10% of smokers begin the habit past the age of 18 (Curry, Mermelstein, and Sporer, 2009). Historically, advertisers have targeted adolescents, or even preadolescents (Curry et al, 2009). Adolescents receive these messages, which include specific product placements in film projects where 'cool' actors engage in smoking particular brands or just engage in smoking cigarettes—a benefit to the industry as a whole (Heatherton and Sargent, 2009). Because smoking is addictive and extremely difficult to stop, these adolescents will also grow up to be parents who smoke. They will have children who will learn the habit from them as well as from their own peers as they enter adolescence in turn (Chassin et al, 2002). Ultimately, advertising becomes less important in the entire process, because the habit is self-perpetuating.

Depressants

In the past, the primary medical use of depressant drugs has been to produce sleep or sleep-like states, either as a treatment for insomnia or in the context of surgical anaesthesia. However, today the drugs are just as commonly prescribed as treatments for anxiety, and their non-medical use is widespread. Alcohol is also considered a (non-medical) depressant drug, and it is without doubt the most commonly used.

> **KEY IDEAS** ethanol Commonly called *alcohol*, **ethanol** is technically just one of the alcohols, the only ingestible form. Ethanol has a powerful intoxicating effect and is the main psychoactive ingredient in alcoholic drinks.

If caffeine is the most widely used psychoactive drug in the world, then alcohol (technically, **ethanol**, the type of alcohol that is safe to ingest) is a close second. Although relatively few people drink in the Islamic world, and those following traditional Buddhist precepts also refrain from drinking, the majority of adults in Western Europe and USA report that they drink alcohol at least some of the time. In Norway and Sweden the figure is as high as 96% (Phillips and Lawton, 2004). In all, two billion people—about one-third of the earth's total population—drink alcohol (World Health Organization, 2004). Alcohol is also believed to be the oldest psychoactive substance in continuous use by human beings. Evidence of its use dates back at least 12,000 years (Fox, 2011).

Alcohol is a particularly interesting drug in terms of its effects on consciousness and behaviour for three reasons. First, effects vary greatly depending upon the person using it. The Aztec name for their alcoholic drink translates as 'four hundred rabbits' in recognition of the wide variation in responses different people have while drinking (Fox and MacAvoy, 2011). Responses to drinking alcohol might include tranquillity, joviality, sociability, aggression and violence, sexual excess, anger, melancholy, self-pity, tenderness, cheerfulness, relaxation, drowsiness, silliness, and on and on (Social Issues Research Centre, 2006). This is quite a different story from far more predictable behaviour of people under the influence of stimulants, narcotics, or even other depressants.

Second, the differing beliefs each society may hold about how alcohol typically affects a person actually affect how the average person from that society *does* respond to alcohol (Room, 2001). For example, in industrialized societies there is a strong tendency for people, including scientists, to believe that alcohol is a *disinhibitor*—a substance that reduces a person's inhibitions to perform various sorts of behaviour; in particular, of an aggressive or sexual nature. Scientists have been able to provide explanations for alcohol's disinhibiting effects: under the influence of alcohol there is a suppression of neuronal activity in centres of the brain connected to judgement and control. However, in some societies, disinhibition of aggression and sexuality are not generally expected to be part of drinking behaviour, and they do not typi-cally occur—even though alcohol has the same effect on the neurons of the brains of people everywhere (Peele and Grant, 1999).

The third aspect of the effects of alcohol on consciousness that make it so in-teresting is the importance of dose in determining effect. The effect of one drink consumed in 20 to 30 minutes is dramatically different from the effect of three or four drinks consumed during the same time period. For example, taken in small doses, alcohol tends to produce feelings of relaxation, well-being, interest in con-versation and sociability, and other positive benefits recognized for millennia in cul-tures throughout the world (Peele and Grant, 1999). However, as the dose increases, the drinker's judgement becomes increasingly impaired, as do various psychomotor, cognitive, and reaction processes. As intoxication progresses towards drunkenness, the drinker's behaviour may become radically different from his or her norm. The person who had been standing there conversing genially just an hour or two earlier may now be sobbing, fighting, or standing on the table taking off his or her clothes. Figure 6.14 summarizes effects of increasing levels of blood alcohol.

In general, a single shot of spirits (e.g. whisky, vodka) equals in alcohol content a 330 ml bottle of beer or a 125 ml glass of wine.

Blood alcohol content	Behavioural changes
0.02%	most people feel relaxed, talkative, and happy
0.03%	still talkative and happy; mild sedation; may have a flushed face
0.05%	most experience giddiness; restraint and judgement are lowered
0.06%	normal ability to make rational decisions about personal capabili-ties is affected
0.08%	muscle coordination is impaired; reaction time is slower
0.10%	speech is fuzzy; reaction time and muscle control are deteriorating
0.15%	the equivalent of half a pint of whisky in the bloodstream; balance and movement are impaired
0.20%	speech is slurred; double vision and loss of balance are likely
0.40%	usually unconscious; risk of death high even if taken to hospital
0.45%	respiration slows and can stop altogether

FIGURE 6.14 **Effects of alcohol on behaviour.** Although it would be nice to be able to report the number of drinks it takes to produce each of the behavioural changes listed in this figure, the same number of drinks will produce different behavioural changes in different people, depending on many factors. For example, women metabolize alcohol differently from men on average, and so a single drink might produce the same changes in a woman that two drinks will produce in a man. A person's size, how quickly drinks are consumed, how much food the person has taken, and genetic factors will affect the way alcohol enters the bloodstream. Therefore, Blood Alcohol Content (BAC) is used instead of number of drinks to track behavioural changes in response to alcohol.

Sources: spirits: Julia Sudnitskaya/© 123RF.com; beer: Taveesaksri/iStock.com; wine: olegdudko © 123RF.com.

Although many people can use alcohol in moderation for their entire lives without any ill effects, alcohol can also be extremely destructive. According to the World Health Organization, alcohol directly caused 1.8 million deaths in the year 2000—3.2% of the total number of global deaths (World Health Organization, 2004). Approximately 13–15% of regular users of alcohol develop alcohol dependence—a condition popularly termed *alcoholism*. Alcohol dependence is at least as difficult to treat as opioid dependence.

Alcohol differs from cigarettes in several important ways, however. First, there is no safe or beneficial way to use cigarettes, but alcohol is safe for most people to use in moderation—say one drink a day. Alcohol is also *much* less addictive than smoking, with true addiction occurring only at very high doses taken over prolonged periods.

It is much easier to understand why people might start using alcohol than start smoking. Alcohol is a liquid, and drinking any liquid has qualities in common with drinking water—an action necessary for survival. Including alcoholic drinks around meal times has a kind of logic to it. Moreover, at least in moderate doses, the effects of alcohol are experienced by most people as pleasurable right from the beginning. Few people remember their first cigarettes with pleasure. Indeed, many people's first smoked cigarette is followed by nausea, dizziness, and sometimes vomiting.

Alcohol is not only safe and enjoyable for most people in moderate doses, it may actually have certain beneficial physiological and psychological effects. For example, increasingly persuasive research suggests that moderate intake of red or white wine (and possibly even beer) is associated with a lower risk of coronary heart disease and certain forms of cancer (Brügger-Anderson et al, 2008), and many GPs recommend a glass of wine a day for their heart patients. Indeed, *moderate* alcohol consumption is associated with a lower risk of mortality from a wide variety of causes (Ferreira and Willoughby, 2008). As you may already know from personal experience, alcohol in moderation makes many people simply 'feel good', and facilitates socializing by mildly reducing inhibition and relaxing the drinker through the depression of sympathetic nervous system activity (Peele and Grant, 1999).

However—and this is a *big* 'however'—when taken at high doses, alcohol is extremely toxic to the body, particularly to the liver—hence the warning signals of nausea, vomiting, and headache. Excessive intake—known as *binge drinking* (depicted in Figure 6.15)—over a prolonged period is associated with potentially fatal liver disease, hypertension, heart disease, diabetes, stroke, preventable motor vehicle and other mechanical accidents, loss of brain functioning (particularly memory), depression and anxiety, sexually transmitted disease, and a host of violent and destructive criminal acts. Abuse of alcohol can destroy entire families as well as the lives of individuals (Taylor, Shield, and Rehm, 2011).

What constitutes binge drinking? Definitions vary but the National Health Service England defines it as drinking at least 8 units of alcohol in a single session for men and 6 units for women. The lower figure for women is in recognition of women's slower rate of gastric metabolism, which leads to higher blood alcohol levels than men for the same quantity of alcohol (Courtney and Polich, 2009).

Binge drinking is more common and problematic—in particular, amongst young people—than many people believe. However, the methodological difficulties in establishing how common it is are formidable (Kuntsche et al, 2017). In one recent Irish study it was estimated that 73% of men and 53% of women had engaged in binge drinking in the previous year (Mohamed and Aimal, 2014). This is probably lower in most mainland Western European countries but with wide national variations (ESPAD Group, 2016).

FIGURE 6.15 Binge drinking poses grave health risks. As well as the direct impact of alcohol misuse on the body, binge drinking contributes to violence and driving accidents.
Source: Photo Spirit/Shutterstock.com.

THINKING CREATIVELY

It is notoriously difficult to gather valid data about the prevalence of binge drinking. Prevalence varies massively by age, gender, and cultural background and there are issues of honesty and social desirability to consider.

Imagine you are going to conduct this kind of research and consider the following:

1 How could you ensure a representative sample?

2 How could you go about trying to minimize the impact of dishonesty, inaccurate recall, and social desirability effects?

Two other depressants, Rohypnol and GHB, have attracted particular interest in recent years for their sinister properties of inducing memory loss and lack of judgement and their resulting use as 'date rape drugs'. With the increase in use of the newer central nervous system depressant drugs in the club scene, reports of drug-related sexual assaults have increased. Not only do these drugs impair judgement and control, but also in high doses they may impair memory for events that transpired during intoxication, or even cause unconsciousness. Note, however, that in high doses alcohol can have similar properties and is by far the most common substance used to facilitate sex crimes.

Rohypnol (generic name, *flunitrazepam*; street name 'roofies') is a drug from the *benzodiazepine* group that has come into favour since the 1980s as one of several 'club drugs'. Rohypnol has legitimate medical uses, including the treatment of anxiety and insomnia. Small doses of this drug produce pleasant sensations somewhat similar to an alcohol high, but as the dose increases the experience tends to be described by users (at least in research studies) as unpleasant (Roset et al, 2001). Rohypnol is a safer drug than alcohol, most opioids, or cocaine in terms of toxicity and potential for dependence. However, once dependence does result, like addiction to all benzodiazepines, withdrawal can actually be dangerous when attempted without medical supervision and can result in death under some circumstances. Moreover, when mixed with alcohol or opioids, Rohypnol is extremely dangerous.

GHB (Gamma-hydroxybutyrate) is an unusual central nervous system depressant that initially had been marketed as a food supplement for bodybuilders until it was discovered that it was being abused as a psychoactive drug. It was then taken off the market. The experience of low doses of GHB is similar to alcohol, but at medium doses it may produce both stimulating and relaxing effects simultaneously (Gable, 2004a).

GHB is a particularly dangerous drug because the difference between a 'recreational' dose and a potentially fatal dose is not as great as with most psychoactive drugs. Thus, its safety ratio is low (10), identical to the safety ratio of alcohol (Gable, 2004a). Occasional deaths have been reported due to GHB, although most of these have occurred when the drug was used with alcohol (Kugelberg et al, 2010).

Hallucinogenic (psychedelic) drugs

Unlike the drugs described previously, psychedelic drugs (such as LSD, magic mushrooms, mescaline, and cannabis), frequently referred to as *hallucinogens*, come from a very wide variety of plant and human-made chemical sources and produce their effects in many different ways. Even more than alcohol, these effects differ dramatically according to the personal characteristics of the user and the characteristics of the setting in which the drugs are used—including the cultural context. For example, psychedelic mushrooms and the cactus peyote have been used in traditional religious ceremonies in various cultures and subcultures. A person's experience with these drugs in such religious contexts will undoubtedly differ from that of a person using the same drug at a rave in Surrey.

LSD, mescaline, and **magic mushrooms** (and their synthesized version, *psilocybin*) share in common the ability to alter perception in a dramatic way, strongly affecting one's senses of sight, hearing, smell, taste, and touch. In addition to sensory distortions and hallucinations, they may effect radical changes in thought and emotion.

The potential for dependence on these drugs is exceptionally low (if not non-existent), and their safety ratios are very high—it would be quite difficult to take enough of these drugs to cause death. The dangers posed by drugs such as LSD or peyote primarily are psychological in nature. However, because the psychological effects vary so dramatically from one person to the next, it is difficult to predict risk. Depending upon a person's innate psychology and biochemistry, the same LSD event—say, looking into a mirror and seeing a total stranger—might cause one person to react with fascination, another to laugh uproariously, a third to experience a sense of union with the divine, and a forth to endure a terrifying split from his or her sense of self. The fallout from such profoundly negative experiences might last a week, a month, a year, or a lifetime. Therefore, psychedelic drugs should be treated with a very high degree of caution.

Nevertheless, while the fallout from negative experiences can be long lasting, so can the benefit from positive experiences (J.B. Brown, 2007/2008; Griffiths, Richards, McCann, and Jesse, 2006). In a double-blind study using the psychedelic drug psilocybin with placebo controls, Roland Griffiths and his colleagues administered

> **KEY IDEAS** 'date rape drugs' 'Date rape drugs' include Rohypnol and GHB. **Rohypnol** (flunitrazapam) is a highly potent benzodiazepine drug used to treat severe insomnia (street name: 'roofies'). **GHB (Gamma-hydroxybutyrate)** is a CNS depressant drug initially marketed as a food supplement for bodybuilders. The quotation marks indicate that, although they have a bad name for their use in sex crimes, these drugs have medical and non-sinister recreational uses.

> **KEY IDEAS** hallucinogenic drugs   Hallucinogenics include **LSD (lysergic acid diethylamide)**, **magic mushrooms** (a general term used for various psilocybin-containing fungi), and **mescaline** (the refined hallucinogen from peyote seeds). In high doses cannabis can have similar properties. They share the property of inducing perceptual distortions and hallucinations.

psilocybin to volunteers. These participants frequently reported meaningful, highly positive spiritual experiences whose effects continued to be felt two months later (Griffiths et al, 2006). Fourteen months later, interviews with these participants showed that beneficial spiritual and personal aspects of these experiences had persisted (Griffiths et al, 2008). Results such as these have rekindled interest in the use of psychedelic drugs as adjuncts to psychotherapy (Brown, 2007/2008).

Cannabis or **marijuana** ('weed', 'pot', 'ganja', 'dope', 'herb', 'salmon', etc) is the leaf of the cannabis or hemp plant, formerly cultivated for making rope. Cannabis is also used in a gummy concentrate known as **hash**. Most commonly smoked, cannabis can also be eaten, often in cake or fudge. Cannabis contains a number of psychoactive substances. The most potent of these in terms of consciousness-altering properties is tetrahydrocannabol (THC). The effects of THC are tempered by those of the other main psychoactive component, cannabidiol (CBD). The ratio of THC:CBD determines the effects of cannabis and also its potential harm.

As with all psychedelics, effects of cannabis are highly dependent upon the user and the setting, but as a general rule users of cannabis at moderate doses experience a dreamy, carefree relaxation and sense of well-being, distortion in perception of time (a minute can seem like an hour), a sharpening of all the senses, a tendency to find hilarity in situations the rest of us find utterly humour-free, and increased hunger—the 'munchies'. Stronger doses can produce disruptions in emotion and thought, and as with other psychedelics, some users may experience very negative reactions that include severe anxiety, panic, and nightmarish thoughts or perceptions.

Unlike the case of ecstasy, there is an extensive research **database** on the effects of cannabis from which to paint a general portrait of its potential for harm:

1 Cannabis use *can* result in dependence. However, dependence is seen only in a small minority of users—approximately 9–10%—and this is likely to occur only after very heavy long-term recreational (not medical) use (Anthony et al, 1994).

2 Evidence that cannabis use leads to psychological disturbances and 'reduced motivation', or that it negatively impacts educational attainment because of effects on cognitive ability, is weak (Macleod et al, 2004). However, some research suggests that cannabis might have an effect on the ability to learn and remember new information and on various sorts of everyday memory tasks—at least in chronic heavy users (Cohen, 2009). And without doubt, cannabis intoxication impairs the ability to drive (Cohen, 2009).

3 On the other hand, researchers studying inflammation processes that may underlie the brain degeneration of Alzheimer's disease have produced evidence that chemical components of cannabis, including THC, may reduce this inflammation—thus also reducing memory impairment in elderly patients at risk for Alzheimer's (Cadar, 2017).

4 Cannabis smoke produces at least as many tars hazardous to the lungs as tobacco smoke (Henry, Oldfield, and Kon, 2003). However, a 20-year American longitudinal study showed no impairment in lung function even of regular cannabis use, as long as use was not truly excessive or combined with tobacco smoking (Pletcher et al, 2011). The lack of apparent harm to lung function may be because of the small volume of smoke inhaled as compared to that of cigarette smokers.

5 There is no known fatal dose of cannabis (Cohen, 2009), and the safety ratio of cannabis has been estimated as somewhere between 1,000 and 40,000, making cannabis the least-toxic psychoactive drug in existence (Gable, 2004).

> **KEY IDEAS** cannabis (marijuana) Cannabis is a mildly psychedelic drug derived from the leaves of *Cannabis sativa*, a flowering plant originally indigenous to Asia. Cannabis is usually smoked, either in powdered leaf form or in a gum called hash or hashish.

Table 6.3 summarizes the effects of the psychoactive drugs, and what is known of their potential dangers.

TABLE 6.3 **Psychoactive drugs at a glance**

Drug	Ordinary effects	Some potential dangers
Opioids (eg, opium, morphine, heroin, codeine)	Pain relief, sedation, euphoria, nausea, constipation	Extreme dependence (addiction) when used for non-medicinal purposes; death may result due to respiratory depression when mixed with other CNS depressants or when taken in an excessive dose
Cocaine	Energy, exhilaration, alertness, confidence, elevated mood, sleeplessness	Extreme dependence (addiction); nervousness, fatigue, depression, psychosis. Death may result due to respiratory failure, cerebral haemorrhage, or stroke in vulnerable individuals taking excessive doses
Amphetamines (eg, methamphetamine ritalin)	Energy, alertness, confidence, exhilaration, sleeplessness	Dependence, mania, psychosis, fatigue, depression, possible changes in brain functioning and structure
Caffeine	Energy, alertness, sleeplessness	Dependence, fatigue, nervousness. In rare cases, psychological disorder
Nicotine	Slight increase in alertness	Extreme dependence (addiction); when used in tobacco, death may result due to multiple types of disease processes
Alcohol	Effects vary greatly according to the person and dose	Easily abused drug; dependence (addiction) in those taking large doses over prolonged periods; in large doses: impaired judgement; impaired cognitive, psychomotor, and reaction processes; erratic behaviour; potential for violence in some individuals; psychological disturbance; death due to overdose or multiple disease processes in long-term abuse
Benzodiazepines (eg, Rohypnol, Valium)	Relaxation, sedation; effects may vary by dose	Extreme dependence (addiction); convulsions or psychosis if drugs are discontinued too abruptly; death may result when mixed with alcohol or other CNS depressants
GHB	Simultaneous relaxation and stimulation	Death due to overdose, particularly if used with alcohol
LSD, peyote, psychedelic mushrooms	Hallucinations, extreme alteration of perception, and subjective experience	May cause psychotic reactions or other psychological disturbances in vulnerable individuals
Ecstasy (MDMA)	Feelings of well-being, empathy, energy, reduced fear	Potential dangers sharply contested (see earlier in this chapter, 'Psychoactive drugs and consciousness')
Cannabis	Alteration of perception and subjective experience; frequent tendency towards laughter; appetite stimulation; pain relief	Potential dangers sharply contested; mild potential for dependence; the least-toxic psychoactive substance known

READ THIS

Drugs raise so many issues—biological, psychological, and social—as well as strong and varied views that it is hard to know where to start.

We recommend starting with something that considers all angles: Gossop, M. (2016). *Living with Drugs*. London: Routledge.

For some interesting recent findings regarding particular drugs and consciousness, have a read of these:

Liechti, M.E., Dolder, P.C., and Schmid, Y. (2017). Alterations of consciousness and mystical-type experiences after acute LSD in humans. *Psychopharmacology*, **234**, 1499–1510.

Barnard, G.W. (2017). Psi and psychedelics; meditation and mysticism: religion, science, and non-ordinary states of consciousness. *Religious Studies Review*, **43**, 225–33.

Ehrler, M.R., McGlade, E.C., and Yurgelun-Todd, D.A. (2015). Subjective and cognitive effects of cannabinoids in marijuana smokers. In *Cannabinoid Modulation of Emotion, Memory, and Motivation* (pp 159–81). New York: Springer.

IN REVIEW

WHAT IS CONSCIOUSNESS?

- Consciousness has been defined as consisting of inner, qualitative, subjective states and feelings or awareness.
- The 'hard problem' of consciousness is the question of how a physical organ (the brain) produces the seemingly disembodied subjective state of consciousness.
- Altered states of consciousness (ASC) include sleep, dreams, hypnosis, hallucinations, meditations, and drug states.

SLEEP

- The urge to sleep is profound, although individuals vary in the amount of sleep they need. Total sleep deprivation results in severe impairments in functioning.
- Sleep patterns are regulated by the circadian pacemaker and sleep homeostat. There are two types of sleep: REM and NREM.
- REM is characterized by high levels of nervous system activity and vivid dreaming.
- NREM, which covers the greater portion of sleep time, is characterized by the deepest levels of relaxation. Sleep is experienced in five sleep stages, which play out in a 90–110-minute repeated cycle throughout the night.
- The function of sleep is unknown, but the most often-discussed current theories are the ideas that sleep promotes memory consolidation and that sleep allows for synaptic pruning.

DREAMING

- There is little agreement as to the nature and function of sleep mentation, which can be categorized as cognitive activity, ordinary dreaming, and apex dreaming.
- Cognitive activity during sleep is often called 'sleep thinking'.

Ordinary dreaming involves recognizable characters engaged in relatively realistic activities.

Apex dreaming are the most intense, vivid, bizarre, hallucinatory dreams.

Of the numerous theories advanced regarding the purpose of dreams, none is accepted by all, but it is clear is that dreams have meaning to the dreamer, consisting of content drawn from each person's life history, circumstances, emotions, and subjective experience.

SLEEP DISORDERS

Many people have problems sleeping, but only a few experience a genuine sleep disorder.

Insomnia is a chronic difficulty falling asleep, staying asleep, and/or being unable to obtain restful sleep.

Obstructive sleep apnoea (OSA) is marked by frequent—and usually unrecognized—moments of awakening throughout the night, caused by the inability to breathe.

Parasomnias are characterized by unusual or bizarre physical behaviours, perceptions, dreams, or emotions during sleep.

Narcolepsy is characterized by abruptly falling asleep at inappropriate times and places.

HYPNOSIS: AN ALTERED STATE OF CONSCIOUSNESS?

The question of whether hypnosis is an actual ASC is known as the 'special state' vs 'non-state' debate.

State theory proposes that hypnosis is a true ASC, whereas sociocognitive theory proposes that behaviours seen under hypnosis can be produced without any special procedures.

Research suggests that a hypnotic state can be induced merely by giving suggestions when the subject believes he or she is being hypnotized. Hypnotized individuals do not have improved recall of past events, cannot 'regress' to infancy or 'past lives', can lie just as easily as at other times, and cannot achieve feats of strength or endure pain beyond their ordinary capabilities.

PSYCHOACTIVE DRUGS AND CONSCIOUSNESS

A psychoactive drug is any substance with properties that affect mental life or consciousness. Non-medical or 'recreational' drug use includes all uses specifically intended to alter consciousness.

Most humans worldwide use psychoactive drugs such as alcohol, nicotine, or caffeine.

It is difficult to obtain accurate information about non-medical drug use because powerful moral, social, economic, and political interests are involved.

Addiction was traditionally defined as dependent and compulsive use of a drug which resulted in withdrawal, craving, and tolerance. However, so-called non-addictive drugs can produce craving and dependence as powerful as addictive drugs.

All substances are potentially toxic if taken in sufficient quantities. Cannabis has the highest safety ratio of all commonly used psychoactive drugs.

The most dangerous drugs in terms of potential for death and disease are alcohol and tobacco, although when taken in moderation, alcohol is safe and may even have beneficial properties.

Psychoactive drugs can be categorized as narcotics, depressants, stimulants, and psychedelics; but some psychoactive drugs do not fit neatly into these categories. Narcotics refer generally to drugs synthesized from the dried nectar of poppy flowers. These drugs are very dangerous when used for non-medical purposes, especially when combined with other CNS depressants such as alcohol or benzodiazepines.

Stimulant drugs include cocaine, amphetamines, caffeine, and nicotine.

Cocaine produces euphoria, alertness, and feelings of well-being, but long-term users experience sleeplessness, depression, and impairment in thought and perception.

Amphetamines produce somewhat similar feelings of exhilaration, alertness, confidence, and mood elevation, but the effects are much longer lasting and 'harsh'.

Amphetamines may also cause long-lasting changes in brain structure and functioning.

Caffeine, found naturally in coffee, tea, and chocolate, wards off fatigue and produces alertness.

Nicotine produces a slight increase in alertness. It is highly addictive, and withdrawal is difficult to endure. A tobacco-containing cigarette is likely the most dangerous drug because it affects virtually every organ in the body: 50% of smokers will die of a disease caused by smoking by age 70.

Depressant drugs include alcohol, Rohypnol, and GHB. Alcohol is the oldest and most widely used psychoactive drug.

The effects of alcohol vary according to the user, the setting, beliefs about alcohol, and the dose. Like smoking, binge drinking can damage virtually every bodily organ. About one-third of the earth's population uses alcohol, and the drug directly causes nearly two million deaths per year.

Rohypnol in low doses produces sensations somewhat similar to alcohol, but high doses are very unpleasant. Rohypnol is safer than alcohol, narcotics, or cocaine, but if dependence does result, withdrawal can be dangerous.

GHB in low doses also produces alcohol-like effects, but at medium doses can produce both stimulating and relaxing effects simultaneously. GHB is particularly dangerous because it has a small difference between recreational and fatal doses.

Psychedelic drugs include LSD, peyote, psychedelic mushrooms, ecstasy (MDMA), and cannabis. These drugs produce effects that vary by individual, setting, dose, and cultural beliefs even more dramatically than is the case with alcohol.

LSD, peyote, and psychedelic mushrooms share the ability to alter perception, strongly affecting sensory experiences and effecting radical changes in thought and emotion.

MDMA produces a general sense of well-being, openness, empathy, and reduced fear. Its safety is highly controversial. MDMA is deadly if taken in excessive doses, but some evidence suggests that in its pure, 'uncut' form it may be among the safest recreational drugs.

Cannabis is the safest recreational drug commonly in use, but perhaps also the most controversial. Claims that cannabis use results in psychological disturbance, poor cognitive functioning, and reduced educational performance are not well supported. However, there may be small effects on memory, and smoking marijuana produces tars hazardous to the lungs. Marijuana has many recognized medical uses.

TEST YOURSELF

1 There is a generally agreed definition of consciousness. True ❐ False ❐

2 Synaptic pruning helps brain function by removing unnecessary connections. True ❐ False ❐

3 Hypnosis is widely believed to be a social phenomenon rather than a state of consciousness. True ❐ False ❐

4 There are no recorded deaths unequivocally due to cannabis overdose. True ❐ False ❐

5 Which of the following is not one of Searle's features of consciousness?
   a) Unity
   b) Objectivity
   c) Subjectivity
   d) Qualitativeness

6 Which of the following best describes the relationship between dreaming and REM sleep?
   a) All dreams take place in REM sleep
   b) Dreams are most commonly reported in REM sleep
   c) REM sleep always leads to dreaming
   d) There is no relationship between dreaming and REM sleep

7 Which of the following includes HHEs?
   a) Sleep paralysis
   b) Narcolepsy
   c) Night terrors
   d) Somnambulism

8 Which of the following is the most addictive drug?

   a) Caffeine

   b) Heroin

   c) Tobacco

   d) Alcohol

9 Explain what is meant by the 'hard problem' of consciousness.

10 How dangerous is MDMA?

 Visit the online resources that accompany this book: www.oup.com/uk/jarvis-okami1e

PART 3

COGNITIVE PSYCHOLOGY

LEARNING

LEARNING OUTCOMES

By the end of this chapter you should be able to:

- Offer alternative definitions of learning and appreciate difficulties in pinning down the concept
- Understand the relationship between what is 'learnt' and 'innate'
- Distinguish between habituation and associative learning
- Outline the processes of classical conditioning, drawing on examples of studies in humans and animals
- Discuss the usefulness of classical conditioning in explaining human behaviour
- Describe the principles of operant conditioning in animals and humans
- Evaluate the importance of operant conditioning as an explanation for human behaviour
- Outline observational learning, drawing on animal and human studies
- Evaluate the significance of observational learning in explaining human behaviour

Have you ever moved to a noisy house or office and gradually become used to the decibel level that at first kept you awake or prevented you concentrating on your work? Have you ever become accustomed to eating a particular food at a particular time in the day or week and found yourself craving it as that time approached? Perhaps you have admired someone's hair or dress sense and incorporated it into your own appearance. All these everyday human experiences are examples of *learning*.

For a while in the mid-twentieth century learning was the subject matter of most psychological research as the behaviourist movement held sway (most notably in the USA and to a lesser degree in Europe). Nowadays psychology is a much broader discipline, but learning is still considered a very important topic, and whilst very few modern psychologists would see themselves as behaviourists, the principles of learning discovered by the behaviourist movement are still studied and applied in contemporary psychology. This chapter is devoted to an examination of these principles of learning; a topic that could arguably sit in any of the 'parts' of this book, but which we have chosen to place within cognitive psychology.

WHAT IS LEARNING?

Learning is one of the fundamental ways that an organism changes over time. A child stops speaking loudly in the presence of her grandmother because the woman glares at her every time the girl's voice is raised; a hungry lab rat runs a maze in successively shorter times in order to reach food; a maths student solves a new equation after reviewing solutions to similar equations by famous mathematicians—all these are examples of learning. On this much psychologists can agree.

However, things get a bit trickier when we try to pinpoint more precisely what we mean by 'learning'. In fact, Lieberman (2000) has amusingly defined learning thus:

> *A term devised to embarrass learning psychologists, who tie themselves into knots trying to define it.* (2000, p 47)

A more standard definition might read more like this:

> Learning: *A relatively enduring change in behaviour as a result of specific experiences.*

However, this definition is problematic because here learning is bound up with *behaviour*. Traditionally psychologists have used changes in behaviour to measure learning because (at least until very recently) it has proved tricky to identify reliable neurological markers of learning. Historically—as pointed out by the *behaviourist* psychologists (see Chapter 2)—the only way to measure learning is to observe changes in the way a person behaves following certain experiences, and *infer* that learning has taken place: thus the pizza craving appears reliably at 7pm on Fridays and your hairstyle becomes increasingly like that of your coolest peers.

However, learning can take place without changes in behaviour. A perfectly reasonable definition of learning that makes no reference to behaviour is provided in another textbook:

> Learning: *The name we give to the psychological process (or processes) by which knowledge is acquired through experience.* (Frieman, 2002, p 5)

This definition does acknowledge that learning can take place without behaviour change—for example, you can fail an exam for any number of reasons and yet still have learned the material quite well. However, definitions that focus upon the acquisition of knowledge are equally problematic for psychologists because this cannot easily be measured. We will therefore offer the following fairly neutral definition of learning, but remember that this is a simple definition of a complex idea:

> Learning involves relatively enduring change in knowledge and/or behaviour resulting from specific experiences.

The Relationship between 'Learned' and 'Innate'

Recall the nature-nurture debate (Chapter 5). You may have come across strongly held beliefs that behaviours and characteristics such as gender roles, **aggression**, intelligence, and mental health can be seen as either 'innate' (nature) or 'learned' (nurture) by others—and that these explanations are in opposition to one another. However, *innate* and *learned* do not really operate in opposition but work together, as do *nature* and *nurture* more generally.

In order for humans to learn, the neurons of our brains must be arranged in particular ways. Brains contain innate neural circuitry that *allows* us to learn (Tooby and Cosmides, 2005). Thus, *the capacity to learn is itself innate and unlearned*, even if any given result of learning—say, the ability to speak Urdu or a love of music festivals—may be 100% cultural in origin and acquired through experience. Moreover, whilst the learning mechanisms we explore in this chapter are common to a wide range of species, every species is born prepared to learn certain things, but not other things. Thus phobias of snakes and spiders are common in humans, whereas phobias of cars, guns, and heavy machinery that are much more dangerous but have only appeared recently in our evolutionary history are comparatively rare. This phenomenon of preparedness is innate and thus we should not think of 'learned' and 'innate' as competing explanations for human behaviour. We explore the role of preparedness further in Chapter 5.

Habituation: Learning at Its Simplest

The simplest form of learning takes place when we get used to something. The technical term for this is **habituation** (see Figure 7.1). The first time we encounter blood as a nurse, gunfire as a member of the armed forces, or defiance as a teacher or police officer this will probably produce an anxiety response, probably strong enough to inhibit our performance. However, with repeated exposure such responses decline over time. Part of the learning that differentiates a 'professional' from the layperson is that through experience we have become habituated to the stressors associated with the professional role.

We also become habituated to pleasurable stimuli. Thus the first time we try a sugary dessert we may experience a powerful pleasure response; however, if we eat it regularly that pleasure response will decline. This is called *hedonic habituation*.

> **KEY IDEAS** habituation
> A simple type of non-associative learning that occurs when a stimulus comes to elicit decreasing response from an organism as a result of the organism's repeated exposure to the stimulus over time. 'I got used to it' expresses the idea of habituation.

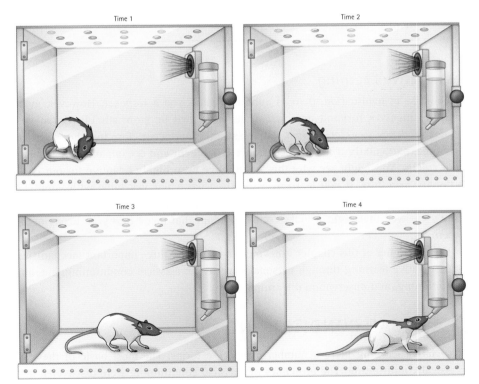

FIGURE 7.1 Habituation. At first the rat reacts with extreme alarm to the sound of a loud tone being sounded. As the tone is sounded on successive occasions, the rat responds with decreasing alarm. Finally, the rat doesn't respond to the tone at all.

This is a really good reason why we shouldn't just eat our favourite foods—we come to take that level of deliciousness for granted and it becomes harder to appreciate it.

Let us explain this in slightly more technical terms. When an organism perceives a stimulus that may signal danger or reward, it experiences a reflex response; for example, anxiety. If, over time, the stimulus turns out not to signal imminent danger or reward, the intensity of the reflex response declines. The organism has *learned* that the stimulus does not warrant its attention. When you say, 'I got used to it,' you are expressing the experience of habituation.

READ THIS

On one level habituation is a very simple form of learning. However, it is still the subject of modern research. One important line of research is concerned with its underlying neural mechanisms. To get an idea of early research in this area you might like to start with the work of Eric Kandel. These two papers represent Kandel's early and recent ideas:

Carew, T.J. and Kandel, E.R. (1973). Acquisition and retention of long-term habituation in Aplysia: Correlation of behavioural and cellular processes. *Science*, **182**, 1158–60.

Bailey, C.H., Kandel, E.R., and Harris, K.M. (2015). Structural components of synaptic plasticity and memory consolidation. *Cold Spring Harbor Perspectives in Biology*, **7**, a021758.

Understanding habituation has a range of contemporary applications. For example, in health settings habituation has been used to reduce disgust responses in patients with colostomies:

Angott, A.M., Comerford, D.A., and Ubel, P.A. (2013). Imagining life with an ostomy: Does a video intervention improve quality-of-life predictions for a medical condition that may elicit disgust? *Patient Education and Counseling*, **91**, 113–19.

Associative Learning

In the case of habituation, there is only a *stimulus* and a *response*. However, most learning involves forming *associations* between two or more stimuli. Organisms have a tendency to *associate* two or more stimuli that occur close together in space and time, particularly if this co-occurrence is frequent and accompanied by significant events. You might see why this would have been highly adaptive for our evolutionary ancestors. If you learn to associate a particular vegetable with vomiting you learn to avoid it. If on the other hand you try a new hunting tactic and your family eat well that night it makes sense to adopt that tactic into your behavioural repertoire.

The remainder of this chapter is devoted to exploring three important mechanisms of associative learning through personal experience: classical conditioning, operant conditioning, and observational learning.

CLASSICAL CONDITIONING

Associative learning takes a number of specific forms. The most basic of these is **classical conditioning**. The principles of classical conditioning were discovered accidentally by the Russian physiologist Ivan Pavlov (1849–1936; hence, *classical conditioning* is sometimes referred to as *Pavlovian conditioning*). Pavlov had no particular interest in psychology, but was investigating the digestive systems of

❯ **KEY IDEA** associative learning Changes in an organism's knowledge or behaviour that result from the association of two or more events or stimuli, or of a stimulus and a response. The most common forms of associative learning are classical conditioning, operant conditioning, and vicarious conditioning (observational learning).

❯ **KEY IDEAS** classical conditioning (Pavlovian conditioning)
A type of associative learning discovered by Ivan Pavlov (Figure 7.2). Classical conditioning occurs when an innate (or otherwise reflexive) response known as the unconditioned response (UCR) is triggered by a neutral stimulus as a result of repeated pairings of the neutral stimulus with an unconditioned stimulus (UCS). The UCS is a stimulus that would naturally trigger the reflexive response without a conditioning procedure.

mammals, work for which he received a Nobel Prize in 1904. In attempting to gather saliva from dogs by introducing food into their mouths, he noticed an odd occurrence: after undergoing this procedure a number of times, the dogs began to salivate *prior* to eating the food—indeed, they would begin to salivate at the mere sight of the food or its dish—and later, at the sight of the research assistant who placed the food in the dish! Pavlov at first considered these jumping-the-gun salivations an impediment to his research. He tried to eliminate them by various means; for example, by sneaking up behind the dogs and popping the food into their mouths.

However, it soon became clear to Pavlov that he had stumbled upon an important mechanism of learning: an innate response such as salivation, which should only occur when food is actually in the mouth, could be triggered by a **neutral stimulus**—that is, a stimulus that has no natural relationship to salivation (eg, the sight of a research assistant or a dish). However, this learning could only occur if the neutral stimulus comes to be *associated* psychologically with a stimulus that normally *would* elicit the innate response—in this case, food in the mouth. In simple terms, this is classical conditioning. Over time, Pavlov and his students trained dogs to salivate at the sound of a metronome and a tuning fork by feeding the dogs directly after making the sound until the animals began to associate the ticking/tone with eating (Anrep, 1920; Pavlov, 1927). Since Pavlov's time, many different organisms have been classically conditioned in this manner, ranging from simple life forms such as the worm to complex life forms such as human beings and other mammals.

❯ KEY IDEAS neutral stimulus
A stimulus that has no natural relationship to an innate response it nonetheless eventually comes to elicit through classical conditioning. For example, a tone has no natural relationship to the human eye-blink response, but a person can be conditioned to blink when hearing a tone if the tone has been repeatedly paired with puffs of air blown at the eye.

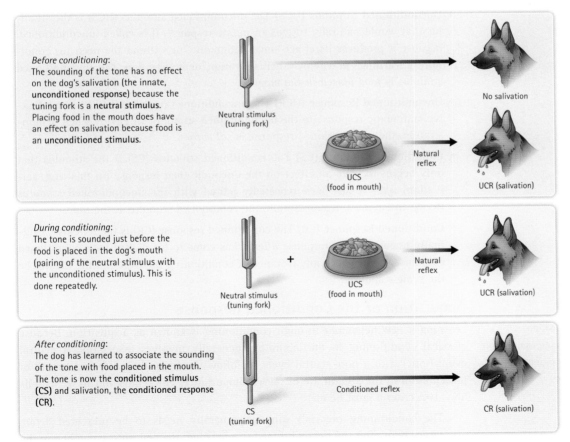

FIGURE 7.2 **Pavlov's demonstration of classical conditioning.**

Classical Conditioning Prepares an Organism to Respond to a Situation

In classical conditioning, then, the organism is learning to be *prepared* for what is to come. Thus a fox may come to associate the sounds of hunting horns and the sight of riders in red (neutral stimuli) with danger from being hunted. The fox will then become more fearful and vigilant upon hearing the sound of horns and the sight of red. While a vehicle may be considered a kind of neutral stimulus—there is no intrinsic reason for a deer to fear it unless it happens to be transporting a hunter bent on violence—throughout evolutionary history, animals have been classically conditioned when they learn to associate various naturally occurring sights, sounds, and smells with events that typically follow these stimuli (Hollis, 1997; Domjan, 2005).

In other words, classical conditioning is *functional*—its purpose is to prepare an organism for likely eventualities. According to Domjan and colleagues, our capacity to be classically conditioned has evolved because it conferred survival and reproduction advantages on those who possessed it (Matthews, Domjan, Ramsey, and Crews, 2007).

Stimulus and Response

Classical conditioning in the laboratory involves a relatively simple association between *stimulus* and *response*. Pavlov divided the stimuli and responses involved in classical conditioning into four categories:

- **Unconditioned Stimulus (UCS)** The unconditioned stimulus (UCS) is the stimulus that would naturally trigger an innate response. It is called 'unconditioned' because it produces its effect 'unconditionally', or without the need for conditioned learning. In Pavlov's bell/salivation demonstration, the unconditioned stimulus is *food placed in the mouth.*

- **Unconditioned Response (UCR)** The unconditioned response (UCR) is the reflexive, automatic response to the unconditioned stimulus. In Pavlov's bell demonstration, the unconditioned response is *salivation.*

- **Conditioned Stimulus (CS)** The conditioned stimulus (CS) is the stimulus that only begins to have an effect on the unconditioned response (in this case, salivation) *after* it has been repeatedly paired with the unconditioned stimulus (food). In Pavlov's demonstration, the conditioned stimulus is the *tone.*

- **Conditioned Response (CR)** The conditioned response (CR) is the reflexive, originally unconditioned response *after* it has come to be elicited by a conditioned stimulus. Remember in any instance of conditioning the UCR and the CR will be the same response.

Acquisition of the Conditioned Response

> **KEY IDEAS** acquisition
In classical conditioning, acquisition is the process of acquiring a conditioned response.

Learning a new behaviour through conditioning is known as **acquisition**. Because classical conditioning in the laboratory generally involves associating a neutral event (tone) with a non-neutral event to follow (feeding), the order and timing of presentation of the stimuli are of critical importance. For acquisition to occur reliably, two criteria must be met:

1 The conditioning (neutral) stimulus generally needs to be presented *before* rather than after the unconditioned stimulus (eg, the bell must come before the food; Domjan, 2002). In a series of famous demonstrations, Michael Domjan

conditioned male Japanese quail to become sexually aroused (and produce more sperm) at the sight of a red light by repeatedly pairing the light with the appearance of a female quail (see Domjan, 2002, for summary). Because the conditioning *prepared* the male quails' bodies for mating, the conditioning would not have worked had the light been flashed *after* the appearance of the female.

2 The unconditioned stimulus must follow *immediately* after the conditioning (neutral) stimulus begins to be presented—no more than a second or two at the very most—or the association between the stimuli will be weakened.

Second-order conditioning

Once a conditioned stimulus (CS) reliably begins to elicit a conditioned response (CR), that conditioned stimulus becomes powerful enough to be used to create **second-order conditioning**. Second-order conditioning involves a pairing of the CS with a completely new, neutral stimulus—almost as if the CS were an *unconditioned stimulus!* For example, let us say a dog is conditioned to salivate upon hearing a tone. What if a light were now flashed repeatedly moments before the tone is heard? The dog may now become conditioned to salivate to the light, in the complete absence of an unconditioned stimulus (food). However, the strength of the effect of second-order conditioning may be weaker than the original, first-order conditioning.

Extinction, Spontaneous Recovery, and Renewal

As already mentioned, in classical conditioning, the organism is learning to be *prepared* for what is to come. We used the example of a forest deer conditioned during hunting season to become more fearful and vigilant upon hearing the sound of a vehicle. But what if, after acquisition of a conditioned response, the conditioned stimulus (eg, sound of vehicle) continues to be presented *without* the unconditioned stimulus (hunters shooting)? Will the sound of a vehicle forever elicit fear? With repeated presentation of the conditioned stimulus without the unconditioned stimulus, the conditioned response becomes weaker until it disappears entirely, a process known as **extinction**.

However, classically conditioned responses are not truly unlearned or wiped out in the process of extinction. For example, Pavlov found that if he allowed his animals to rest for several hours following the extinction of a behaviour, the conditioned response would spontaneously appear again upon *re*-presentation of the conditioned stimulus—although in a somewhat weaker form. This phenomenon is known as **spontaneous recovery**. If new associations are formed for the conditioned stimulus over time, these may produce entirely new conditioned responses. A person conditioned in childhood to associate the taste of broccoli with the unpleasant experience of being forced to sit at the dinner table for hours until all the hated stalks are finished may grow up to be a chef who associates the taste of broccoli with the fabulous two years she spent studying Northern Italian cooking in Venice. However, once again, these new associations do not *replace* the old ones, but are instead *superimposed over* them and suppress them. Under certain circumstances the old associations may be *renewed* (Rescorla and Heth, 1975; Chan, Leung, Westbrook, and McNally, 2010).

Renewal is a resurgence of an extinguished behaviour if the animal is placed in a different *context* from the one in which extinction originally occurred (Bouton, 1991).

> **KEY IDEAS** second-order conditioning A form of classical conditioning in which an organism is first conditioned to a neutral stimulus; and then that stimulus is used to condition the organism to a new neutral stimulus. For example, a dog conditioned to salivate upon hearing a tone by pairing the tone with food, may then be conditioned to associate the tone with a new neutral stimulus—a bell. The dog will then salivate upon hearing the bell, even if the bell was never actually paired with the unconditioned stimulus of food.

> **KEY IDEAS** extinction When a learned behaviour ceases to be performed. In classical conditioning, extinction will occur when the conditioned stimulus response ceases to be exhibited following the removal of the unconditioned stimulus.

> **KEY IDEAS** spontaneous recovery and renewal **Spontaneous recovery** takes place when an extinguished behaviour re-emerges (but in a somewhat weaker form) after the organism has rested from exposure to the classically conditioned stimulus. It differs from **renewal**, where an extinguished behaviour re-emerges specifically because the organism is placed in a context different from the one in which extinction occurred.

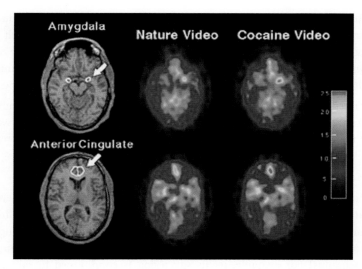

FIGURE 7.3 Renewal of craving in recovered cocaine addicts. PET scan images show increases in cerebral blood flow to areas of the limbic system associated with craving as former cocaine addicts view drug-related videos. The first image in each row represents the brain area in question prior to viewing the video. The next two images on each row contrast brain activation in the amygdala and anterior cingulate during the viewing of a nature video and viewing of a video depicting use of crack cocaine. Areas of greatest activation are shown in red.

Source: Childress, A.R. et al (1999). Limbic activation during cue-induced cocaine craving. *The American Journal of Psychiatry*, 1 Jan. https://doi.org/10.1176/ajp.156.1.11 Reprinted with permission from the *American Journal of Psychiatry*, (Copyright ©1999). American Psychiatric Association.

An excellent example of *renewal* is relapse in drug addiction. Although addiction is a complex process that cannot be explained entirely with classical conditioning, aspects of addiction may be classically conditioned. For example, addicts may come to associate drug paraphernalia (needles, pipes) or drug-taking environments (bars, certain neighbourhoods) or even certain people (stoner friends) either with effects of the drugs or with withdrawal effects and feelings of need for the drug (Childress et al, 1999).

Addicts who recover in the context of a drug treatment facility may experience a resurgence of craving for their drug of choice once they leave the facility and come into contact with people, places, or things associated with the drug. Anna Childress and her colleagues demonstrated how renewal in the context of drug addiction is reflected in brain processes (Childress et al, 1999). Previous research had shown that craving for cocaine is associated with activation of the *amygdala* and *anterior cingulate*, both structures of the limbic system that regulate emotion, motivation, and basic drives. Using positron emission tomography (PET) scans, Childress and her colleagues showed that viewing videos of crack cocaine being prepared and used activated the same areas of the limbic system. On the other hand, these brain areas were not activated in those who had never been cocaine-dependent (see Figure 7.3).

Generalization and Discrimination

Pavlov discovered that an animal might display a conditioned response when exposed to a neutral stimulus that is similar but not identical to the original conditioned stimulus. For example, a dog conditioned to salivate on hearing a particular tone generated by a tuning fork will salivate (but to a somewhat lesser extent) to a different tone. The closer the second tone is to the original tone, the stronger the response will be. This is known as **generalization**.

The capacity for generalization is one of our greatest talents. Try to imagine life without it. Let us say you were to cross the path of a snarling pit bull that attacks you viciously (fortunately the owner quickly subdues the dog or the story would probably end at this point). Now suppose the next week you were to once again cross the path of a snarling dog—but this time it's a snarling Doberman pinscher. Your capacity for generalization tells you, 'Hmm . . . maybe I'd better cross to the other side of the street' instead of, 'Oh, well, it's a completely different breed, so, no problem!'

However, just as an organism can be trained to generalize, it can also be trained to *discriminate*. **Discrimination** occurs when one neutral stimulus (eg, a tone) produces a conditioned response, but another, similar neutral stimulus (a different tone) does not. For example, animals can be trained to discriminate between tones by repeatedly pairing one tone with an unconditioned stimulus such as food, but also presenting a different tone *without* the food (Anrep, 1920). Returning to the example of the pit bull, what if, after your first experience, you felt compelled to cross the street not only whenever you saw a snarling dog but also whenever you saw *any* dog? Or cat? Or mammal? Discrimination allows us to limit our conditioned responses to appropriate situations.

An Early Study of Classical Conditioning in a Human

John B. Watson, and his student (and soon-to-be wife) Rosalie Rayner (Watson and Rayner, 1920) carried out an early demonstration of classical conditioning in a human. The study is described in detail below.

> **KEY IDEAS** generalization
> In classical conditioning, when an animal displays a conditioned response (CR) to a neutral stimulus that is similar, but not identical, to the conditioned stimulus (CS).

> **KEY IDEAS** discrimination
> In classical conditioning, when one neutral stimulus produces a conditioned response, but another, similar neutral stimulus does not. Just as generalization is essential to human survival, so is discrimination.

RESEARCH IN FOCUS

Watson, J.B. and Rayner, R. (1920). Conditioned emotional responses. *Journal of Experimental Psychology*, **3**, 1–14.

Aim: The study had four stated research questions. I. Could a fear response to an animal be created by visually presenting it and simultaneously striking a steel bar? II. If such a fear response could be learned, would it transfer to other animals or objects? III. Would a conditioned fear response decline over time? IV. Could the fear response be removed?

Method: A 9-month-old infant was selected on the basis of his emotional stability. When tested he displayed no fear towards a range of stimuli including a white rat, a rabbit, and some wooden blocks. He was afraid, however, of a loud noise made banging a steel bar with a hammer. Two months later he was shown the rat again. When he reached for it, the bar was hit with the hammer. This appeared to frighten him. This procedure of pairing the rat with the noise was repeated immediately then five times a week later. A month later the boy was tested again.

Results: The child consistently displayed fear in response to the loud noise. From the second pairing of the rat and the noise, he also appeared cautious of the rat and leaned away when the rat was nearby. At the five-day trial he cried in response to the rat and similar stimuli (ie, furry objects). These responses persisted until the final testing, seven weeks after the start of the study. The wooden blocks, which had never been paired with the noise provoked no response. After 31 days, Albert still showed fear towards the conditioned stimuli.

Conclusion: I. The child was classically conditioned to be afraid of the rat, showing that it is indeed possible to condition an emotional response. II. The conditioned response

>

>

generalized to other furry objects. III. The boy's initial strong fear of the rat and later weaker fear and greater interest in it suggests that extinction had begun to lessen his fear. IV. As he was removed from hospital it was not possible to investigate ways to tackle his learned fear.

MASTER YOUR METHODOLOGY

1   The Little Albert study is sometimes referred to as a case study and sometimes as an n = 1 experiment. Explain why each of these terms could be used to describe the study and why neither is entirely satisfactory.

2   The Little Albert study reports behaviour measured by narrative observation (ie, an observer writes what they see for later analysis). Explain the limitations of this method and outline ways in which it might have been improved.

3   Albert was selected for his emotional stability. The authors say that 'We felt that we could do him relatively little harm' (1920, p 2). What is the potential drawback to this kind of participant selection?

DEBUNKING

This may sound odd coming from two textbook writers, but one thing you need to get used to as a student of psychology is not to trust everything you read in textbooks! Coverage of the Little Albert study is a case in point. Watson and Rayner concluded in their original (1920) article that their research 'showed conclusively' (p 12) that conditioned emotional responses could persist for at least one month. As many authors have observed over the years, however, Watson and Rayner's methods and recordings of the events surrounding this experiment are flawed. Yet there is evidence for a common tendency for textbook authors to paint the study in a positive light (Harris, 2011). If, for example, you come across accounts of the experimenters' attempts to *recondition* Albert away from his fear of rats by pairing presentation of the rat with bowls of ice cream and pieces of chocolate, treat them with extreme caution—there is no evidence that this ever happened! The list of items to which Albert (falsely) has been said to have generalized his purported fear of rats is long, and includes a fur belt, his mother's fur coat, and a furry teddy bear. A painstaking historical investigation by Beck, Levinson, and Irons (2009) uncovered no evidence for several aspects of the study as it is sometimes reported.

A possible explanation for this tendency of authors to exaggerate the significance of research comes from Timothy Wilson and his colleagues (Wilson, DePaulo, Mook, and Klaaren, 1993), who have shown that the more important the topic of a piece of research is, the more likely scientists may be to overlook its flaws. For instance, they presented a different version of the same highly flawed fictitious research study to two groups of scientists. In one version they described the topic of the research as an intervention to help sufferers from anorexia. In the other version the topic was an intervention to help young people stop saying 'like' and 'you know' countless times a day. As Figure 7.4 shows, scientists were far more lenient in their critique of the 'anorexia' study. The same held true for a study topic described for one group of scientists as heart disease and for the other as heartburn, and for four additional such mock study pairs (see also Reich, Green, Brock, and Tetlock, 2007).

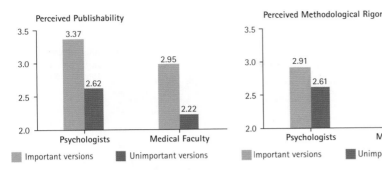

FIGURE 7.4 Scientists may be more likely to overlook flaws of a study if the study concerns an important topic. In Graph A, two groups of psychologists and medical personnel rated the 'publishability' of a study that concerned either a treatment for anorexia (the 'important' version) or an intervention to help teenagers stop saying 'like' and 'you know' (the 'unimportant' version). In Graph B, the methodological soundness of the study was rated. As you can see, higher ratings of publishability and methodological rigour were given when the study was described as being about the important topic.

Source: Wilson et al, 1993, p 324.

 THINKING CRITICALLY

Review the British Psychological Society's ethical guidelines (see Chapter 3). How do you think Watson and Raynor might fare if they were to run up against a modern ethics committee? Think of as many arguments as possible.

Later Developments in Our Understanding of Classical Conditioning

The early work on classical conditioning was conducted when psychologists had a very limited understanding of cognitive processes or **emotion**, and when the science of evolutionary biology had made little impact on psychology. Our modern understanding of classical conditioning owes much to insights from cognitive psychology, evolutionary psychology, and the experimental study of emotion. Let's examine each of these.

The role of cognition in classical conditioning

In the 1960s Robert Rescorla (1968) added the element of *cognition* to the equation of classical conditioning (see Figure 7.5). In his classic experiment, Rescorla conditioned a fear response in a group of rats to a tone by repeatedly presenting the tone just prior to administering a shock to the rats. However, for a second group of rats, Rescorla paired the tone and the shocks the same number of times, but also shocked the rats an equal number of times *without* the tone. According to the views of early behaviourists, pairing the tone with the shock should have conditioned a fear response regardless of additional shocks minus the tone. Yet, Rescorla found that only when the tone *reliably predicted* the shocks—that is, in the first group of rats—was fear conditioned. Put another way, classical conditioning depends not so much on **contiguity**, as Pavlov believed, but on *contingency*, the extent to which the unconditioned stimulus is presented only with the neutral stimulus. Rescorla proposed that the rats were engaging in cognitive activity to determine whether the tone was a

❯ KEY IDEAS contiguity and contingency **Contiguity** means how close in time two events occur. According to Pavlov it is the contiguity of the neutral and unconditioned stimulus that leads to their association. **Contingency** is the extent to which the occurrence of one stimulus is dependent (*contingent*) on the occurrence of another. To Rescorla, classical conditioning occurs when the unconditioned stimulus is contingent on the neutral stimulus.

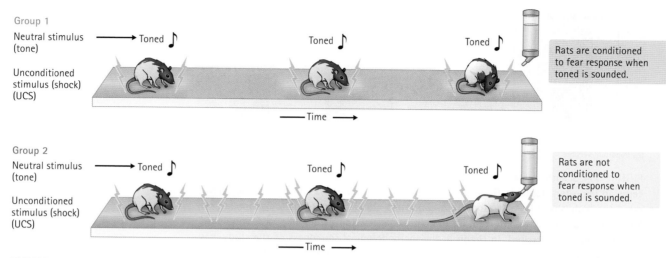

FIGURE 7.5 Robert Rescorla introduces cognition into classical conditioning.

valid predictor of a shock to follow. This insight goes a long way towards explaining why conditioning only works if the neutral stimulus is presented before the UCS. Critically, it also shows an important role for cognition in conditioning—judging a stimulus for contingency requires substantial cognitive processing, not simply the formation of a simple association.

In Rescorla's (1968) study, two groups of rats received the same number of shocks paired with a tone, but Group 2 received additional shocks that were not paired with the tone. Only the rats in Group 1, whose shocks were *reliably* paired with the tone, were conditioned with fear reactions to the tone. Rescorla concluded that rats cognitively assess whether a stimulus is a *valid predictor* of a subsequent event. This is cognitive activity—not simply the blind forming of associations.

More recent research suggests that, whilst cognitive processes are probably important in understanding classical conditioning, it does not necessarily require conscious expectation. Ohman and Soares (1998) demonstrated this when they conditioned a mild anxiety response in human participants, measured by skin conductance, pairing mild electric shocks with subliminal images of snakes and spiders. These images were presented for 30 ms and followed immediately by a 'masking' image so participants were unaware of seeing them. Nonetheless, they exhibited increased skin conductance (suggesting anxiety) in response to snakes and spiders. There is a history of inconsistent findings in this area of research and learning theorists are divided on the relative importance of contingency and contiguity.

Another line of research into the role of cognition in classical conditioning has focused on the role of conceptual categories in generalization of conditioned responses. Dunsmoor and Murphy (2014) found that fear conditioned to typical category members (eg, sparrow) generalized to atypical members (eg, penguin) better than vice versa (Figure 7.6). This suggests that classical conditioning involves information processing at the category level of mental representation and that generalization is a more complex cognitive process than simply responding to stimuli with similar superficial features to those of the conditioned stimulus.

FIGURE 7.6 A fear of sparrows will generalize to penguins in spite of their superficial differences. This shows that generalization involves information processing at the level of categories.

Source: fieldwork/Shutterstock.com.

The role of evolution in classical conditioning

As explained previously, the early behaviourists such as Watson and Pavlov saw conditioning as a process that applied equally to all organisms and to any conceivable stimuli. As long as the neutral stimulus was correctly paired with a UCS, conditioning *would* occur. Martin Seligman (1970) called this the *general process view* of classical conditioning. The inadequacy of the general process view was first demonstrated in the 1960s by theorists influenced by the new applications of evolutionary theory to animal behaviour. Put simply, some animal species are easier to condition to a particular response than others. In Seligman's (1970) terms, organisms are *biologically prepared* to form certain associations but not others.

Perhaps the most influential demonstration of **biological preparedness** was offered by John Garcia (Garcia and Koelling, 1966; Garcia, Brett, and Rusiniak, 1989). As depicted in Figure 7.7, Garcia and Robert Koelling showed that rats could easily be conditioned to avoid (fear) the neutral stimulus of sweetened water if tasting the water were paired with a nauseating dose of radiation. But the rats could *not* easily be conditioned to avoid the water if it were paired with shocks. The opposite held true for buzzes and flashes as neutral stimuli: it was much easier for rats to learn to fear buzzes and flashes that had been paired with shock than to learn to fear the buzzes and flashes when they were paired with nauseating radiation.

Thus, rats (and most other mammals, including human beings) are biologically prepared to learn to avoid foods that have toxic consequences (nausea), because of the evolutionary value of avoiding poisonous substances (Logue, 1998). Indeed, such conditioning can occur following even a single exposure. Some of you may recall a time you were sickened by eating a particular food that had gone off (or by drinking too much of a distinctively flavoured alcoholic drink) and then found

> ❯ KEY IDEAS biological preparedness **Preparedness**, sometimes called *biological preparedness*, is the evolved tendency to acquire conditioned responses to stimuli that have had survival relevance in our evolutionary past more easily than to stimuli that are irrelevant to survival or were absent until recently.

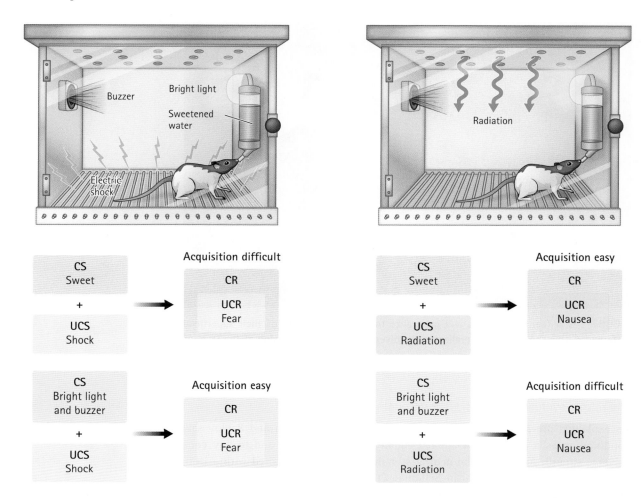

FIGURE 7.7 **Biological preparedness affects classical conditioning.** Joe Garcia found that rats easily acquired fear of sweetened water when it was paired with a nauseating stimulus. However, when he paired the sweetened water with a less salient aversive stimulus, it was very difficult to create the conditioned response.

yourself unable to face the prospect of ever having that food or drink again—even if you knew the food was fresh on subsequent encounters.

On the other hand, foods are rarely associated with physically painful consequences in the real world, making it more difficult to condition mammals to avoid food paired with shocks. The opposite is the case for unusual sights and sounds, which are frequently associated with physical pain and danger in the real world.

These findings appeared to violate the basic assumption of the general process model known as *equipotentiality*, which states that any neutral stimulus can be associated just as easily with one unconditioned stimulus as with any other. Belief in equipotentiality was so strong during the 1960s that Garcia had a very difficult time having his results published, because they were such a direct challenge to conventional learning theory (Garcia, 1981).

Much recent work in humans has supported the importance of preparedness in humans. Stussi, Brosch, and Sander (2015) demonstrated that conditioned responses to angry staring faces (achieved by pairing with a mild electric shock to the wrist) were acquired more quickly and were slower to extinguish than those conditioned to other stimuli such as averted faces, which do not have the same survival relevance.

However, this is not to say that preparedness is accepted uncritically by all psychologists. Tierney and Connolly (2013) have reviewed the evidence for preparedness for the acquisition of fear of snakes. They point out that human studies typically share methodological shortcomings and that the results of animal studies have not been consistent across species. The authors conclude that it is premature to accept that fear of snakes is prepared.

READ THIS

Look at our coverage of the Tierney and Connolly review. It is tempting to reproduce this as evaluation in an assignment. However, if you really want to get the most from this chapter, read the original study. You will then be equipped to explore what shortcomings might have characterized human studies *and* you will have enough information to form your own view on how serious they are.

THINKING CRITICALLY

Think about the central ideas of the behaviourist movement, especially as expressed by J.B. Watson (explored in detail in Chapter 3). If research into classical conditioning now suggests that it involves cognitive processing and is constrained by evolved tendencies, what does this suggest about Watson's views?

Evaluative conditioning: likes and dislikes are conditioned

Evaluative conditioning can be thought of as a related but not identical process to classical conditioning *or* you can think of it as a subtype of classical conditioning if you prefer. Either way it is a distinct phenomenon, worthy of study in its own right. Evaluative conditioning takes place when we are conditioned to like or dislike something.

Evaluative conditioning takes place when a neutral stimulus is paired with an unconditioned stimulus that already provokes a positive or negative emotional reaction (de Houwer et al, 2007). The technical term for this emotion-arousing property of a stimulus is its *valence*. The result of evaluative conditioning is that we learn to like or dislike something by associating it with something we already like or dislike.

As far back as the 1930s psychologists (eg, Allport, 1935) were pointing out that a huge amount of human behaviour can be explained by our likes and dislikes, so understanding evaluative conditioning is fundamental to understanding people. An early demonstration of evaluative conditioning came from Staats and Staats (1957), who paired nonsense words with real words carrying either positive or negative valence and found that the nonsense words quickly acquired the same valence.

Evaluative conditioning differs in some key ways to classical conditioning. Neither contingency nor contiguity appear to be as key to acquiring likes and dislikes by conditioning as they are in classical conditioning. The order of stimulus presentation seems to have less impact on learning than is the case for classical conditioning and there is no requirement for an unconditioned response—mere exposure to

> **KEY IDEAS** evaluative conditioning **Evaluative conditioning** is a type of learning in which we learn to like or dislike something after it is paired with an unconditioned stimulus that elicits a positive or negative emotional response.

the unconditioned stimulus is enough for learning to take place. In addition evaluative conditioned responses appear to be more resistant to extinction (Gawronski, Gast, and De Houwer, 2016).

Advertising makes considerable use of evaluative conditioning. When a product is paired with a positively valenced stimulus such as a popular song or the image of a likable celebrity this positive valence 'rubs off' on the product. Coca Cola are the masters of this effect.

THINKING CREATIVELY

Imagine you are designing an advertisement for your degree programme and you have decided to use evaluative conditioning as your strategy. You will need to think about an appropriate unconditioned stimulus with positive valence and an appropriate neutral stimulus linked to your degree. As scientists you want to test whether your advert successfully enhances the valence of your degree. Identify your independent and dependent variables. How might you incorporate a control condition and what is the advantage of doing so? What ethical considerations would you need to take into account were you to conduct the study?

WHAT'S HOT? THE NEURAL BASIS OF CONDITIONING

Various attempts have been made to establish what brain systems are involved in classical conditioning. At the time of writing our current understanding of this question is far from complete; however, there is a body of research casting some light. Fullana et al (2016) carried out a meta-analysis of fMRI studies looking at activation of the brain during classical conditioning of fear responses in humans. Figure 7.8 shows the brain regions reliably active in response to a conditioned stimulus but not without one.

A number of brain regions including areas of the cortex and subcortical structures appear to be involved in conditioning and the role of each is not currently clear. Moreover, this appears to be the brain's 'fear network' rather than a 'conditioning network'. It may be that relatively few elements of this neural network are involved in other conditioned responses. It does seem, however, that two subcortical structures, the hippocampus and the amygdala, are implicated in conditioned motor responses (Berry and Hoffmann, 2011) and conditioned auditory responses (Weinberger, 2011), although Weinberger is keen to assert that the auditory cortex is the 'root' of understanding such conditioning. This is important because it would be easy to confuse brain centres associated with conditioning per se with areas involved with conditioning particular responses.

There are related questions as regards the neuroanatomy of classical conditioning; for example, regarding processes like generalization and discrimination. Based on lesioning studies in animals and scanning studies in humans, Lissek (2012) has proposed a psychobiological model of fear generalization in which the hippocampus, known to have a role in memory, pattern-matches a perceived stimulus with a previously conditioned stimulus, and outputs a response to the amygdala and fear-associated part of the pre-frontal cortex. The fear response is proportional to the signal from the hippocampus which in turn depends on the extent of match to the conditioned stimulus.

❯

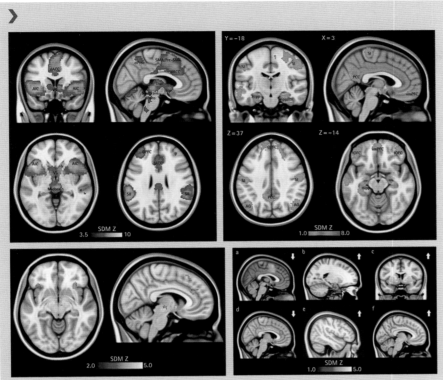

FIGURE 7.8 Active brain regions in the response to a conditioned stimulus.
Source: Reproduced with permission from Fullana, M. A., Harrison, B. J., Soriano-Mas, C., Vervliet, B., Cardoner, N., Àvila-Parcet, A., and Radua, J. Neural signatures of human fear conditioning: an updated and extended meta-analysis of fMRI studies. *Molecular Psychiatry,* **21**(4), 500. Springer Nature. Copyright © 2015.

THINKING CRITICALLY

What are the major strengths of meta-analyses, and how do they help overcome the limitations of many neuroscience studies? On the other hand, are there potential pitfalls to meta-analysis? How impressed are you by meta-analyses like the one by Fullana et al (2016)?

The Limits of Classical Conditioning

Over the past century of research in psychological science, classical conditioning has been demonstrated in a mind-boggling number of animal species and for a similarly astonishing number of stimuli and responses. Classical conditioning has been used to treat psychological disorders such as the irrational fears known as *phobias* and physiological illnesses including hypertension. In the form of evaluative conditioning it also has been used as a powerful tool of advertisers.

Classical conditioning can occur during the normal course of the day without one even being aware of it. Consider those habituated to the use of caffeine. They (all right, *we*) may begin to feel wide awake within moments of taking those first sips of coffee of the day. However, it actually takes the caffeine from coffee about 20 to 30 minutes to reach the brain. Caffeine users have been classically conditioned to associate the effects of caffeine with the taste and smell of coffee. Consequently, we may often experience at least some of these effects of the drug before the drug actually begins to take effect.

Early behaviourists like John Watson believed that classical conditioning could explain all learning, but that is now generally agreed to be impossible. The critical point to remember about classical conditioning is *that it cannot teach new behaviours to an organism*; it can only *elicit* innate or otherwise reflexive behaviours (eg, fear, physiological arousal, pleasure, salivation, and so forth) with stimuli that ordinarily would not produce these effects. Classical conditioning does this by teaching the organism new associations between events.

But is it science?

Learning theory and research is often touted as an example of psychology at its scientific best. But why exactly? Our ideas of what makes good science have changed somewhat since Watson and Skinner asserted that only the study of observable behaviour could be scientific, never the mind (see Chapter 2 for a discussion of psychology as science). So is it the emphasis on laboratory experimentation, the measurement of observable behaviour change, or the use of animals that means that the study of learning has come to exemplify good science? Some psychologists would undoubtedly say yes to all these, but for us it is a little more subtle. It is more about the way that research in this area adheres to the scientific method—the relationship between ongoing research and developing theory. Early hypotheses have been tested and largely supported. Where they have not, theories have developed. Thus modern learning theory incorporates ideas like evolution and cognition, and processes like classical conditioning are now studied by neuroscientists as well as experimental psychologists.

READ THIS

It is always worth reading the classics in their original form so we suggest you begin with something by Pavlov and Watson. These are both available free online. The Watson paper is quite brief and straightforward. Pavlov not so much . . . you might prefer to dip into that one!

Watson, J.B. and Rayner, R. (1920). Conditioned emotional reactions. *Journal of Experimental Psychology*, **3**, 1–14.

Pavlov, I.P. (1927). Conditioned reflexes: An investigation of the physiological activity of the cerebral cortex (G.V. Anrep, trans).

In view of the importance now accorded to cognition and preparedness in classical conditioning it is also worth reading what Rescorla and Seligman have to say. You might like to start with these papers:

Rescorla, R.A. (1988). Pavlovian conditioning: It's not what you think it is. *American Psychologist*, **43**, 151.

Seligman, M.E. (1971). Phobias and preparedness. *Behaviour Therapy*, **2**, 307–20.

OPERANT CONDITIONING

As we briefly mentioned earlier, classical conditioning has shown practical utility in marketing and in treating disorders of various kinds (this is explored further in Chapter 18). However, it remains a relatively limited tool, primarily because it elicits reflexive behaviours only and cannot teach new behaviours. At the turn of the century, however, a graduate student of William James named Edward Thorndike (1874–1949) discovered a principle that would later blossom into a theory of learning with broad applicability.

Thorndike (1898) was impressed with the work of evolutionist Charles Darwin. However, he was highly sceptical of evidence of advanced intelligence in animals—claims that some believed to follow logically from Darwin's theory that all forms of life originated in a single common ancestor. The logic seemed to be, if humans and other animals are related, might not non-human animals possess intelligence similar to that of humans? The aim of his research was thus essentially to show that animals are not very bright.

Thorndike placed a dish with food outside a crate (called the 'puzzle box') that held a hungry cat (see Figure 7.9). The food was visible to the cat, but the door on the crate could be opened only by means of a latch. The cat's task was to figure out how to trip the mechanism controlling the latch. Typically, the cat would stumble around, clawing and dashing back and forth until it accidentally stumbled on the correct action to open the latch. It would then be rewarded with the food.

Thorndike reasoned that if the cat truly possessed advanced intelligence, this single successful attempt would be all that was necessary for the cat to be successful on a subsequent trial. However, it was not. When Thorndike again placed the cat in the crate, the animal once more stumbled around until it accidentally tripped the latch. Thorndike found, however, that it took *less time* for this 'accident' to occur the second time around—and increasingly less time on the third and fourth attempts. Eventually, the cat had no trouble opening the door immediately.

Thorndike proposed that the cat did not improve as a result of reasoning power. Instead, the presence of *reward* strengthened actions that proved to be successful for the cat while actions that were unsuccessful became increasingly less likely to occur. Thorndike summarized his findings in his **law of effect**, which states that for any organism, those behaviours that lead to a satisfying state of affairs are 'stamped in' while those behaviours that lead to an unsatisfying or annoying state of affairs are 'stamped out' (Thorndike's words). In other words, the organism learns as a result of the consequences of his or her own actions.

While the *law of effect* remains one of the first valid laws of psychology, Thorndike did not fully envision its implications. This was accomplished by the American psychologist B.F. Skinner (1904–90). Skinner (Figure 7.10) was a solid behaviourist strongly influenced by the work of John B. Watson. Although he appreciated Thorndike's law of effect, he rejected Thorndike's use of concepts such as *satisfying*

> **KEY IDEAS** law of effect
Edward Thorndike's discovery that behaviours which lead to a satisfying state of affairs are 'stamped in', while behaviours that lead to an unsatisfying or annoying state of affairs are 'stamped out'. The law of effect formed the basis for B.F. Skinner's discoveries of operant conditioning principles.

FIGURE 7.9 **Two of Thorndike's original 'puzzle boxes'.**
Source: Robert Mearns Yerkes papers (MS 569). Manuscripts & Archives, Yale University.

FIGURE 7.10 B.F. Skinner
(1904–90) in his laboratory.
Source: Nina Leen/Getty Images.

> KEY IDEAS operant
conditioning (*operant learning,
instrumental learning*) A form
of conditioning in which the
consequences of a behaviour affect
the probability that the behaviour
will be repeated in the future.

> KEY IDEAS radical
behaviourism B.F. Skinner's version
of behaviourism, also referred to as
experimental analysis of behaviour.
Radical behaviourists propose
that all behaviour can be analysed
empirically by examining the
reinforcements and punishments
which follow the behaviour.

and *annoying* in his definition. To Skinner, *satisfying* and *annoying* implied mental states that could not be objectively observed. Recall that a central idea behind behaviourism was that only behaviour could be observed therefore only behaviour should be studied, anything else being poor science. How does one know that an animal feels emotions such as 'satisfied' or 'annoyed'?

Skinner restated Thorndike's law in terms of what he termed **operant** conditioning. According to Skinner, *operant conditioning is a type of learning in which the consequences of a behaviour affect the probability that the behaviour will be repeated in the future.* Note that this is simply a restatement of Thorndike's law, minus the emotional component.

In Operant Conditioning, the Organism Operates on the Environment

Skinner used the term *operant conditioning* to describe this type of learning because in choosing to behave in a particular manner, the organism is *operating* on his or her environment in a way that results in specific consequences. The organism then comes to associate these consequences with its behaviour. Operant conditioning is an active process entirely shaped by the organism's own behaviour, whereas classical conditioning is a passive process regulated by forces outside the control of the organism. In a sense, in operant conditioning *the organism teaches itself.* Skinner's brand of behaviourism, based in operant conditioning, became known as **radical behaviourism** (although Skinner did not favour this term) because of Skinner's insistence that psychology could *never* be a science of mind, but *only* a science of behaviour.

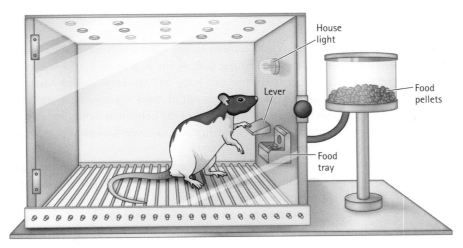

FIGURE 7.11 **Skinner's operant chamber. Skinner used a temperature-controlled, sound-proofed chamber for his experiments with rats. A house light lit the chamber, and the rat received food by pressing a lever.**

To study operant conditioning, Skinner modified the box used by Thorndike for his experiments with cats, and chose (hungry) laboratory rats as his animal subjects. Instead of using a box with a latch and placing food outside the box, Skinner placed a supply of food pellets in a container mounted to the outside of a cage. The cage was designed so that the pellets would automatically be delivered to the rat when the rat pressed down on a lever located near the food tray. To make sure that environmental conditions remained identical throughout each experiment, the cage and container were placed inside a soundproofed, ventilated chamber with controlled temperature. Skinner termed this apparatus the **operant chamber**, but it is more popularly known as the *Skinner box* (see Figure 7.11).

Reinforcement and Punishment

When the consequence of a behaviour increases the likelihood that the behaviour will be repeated—for example, when a food pellet rolls down the chute after a rat pushes the correct lever—the behaviour is said to have been reinforced, and the food pellet is a *reinforcer*. When a consequence reduces the likelihood that the behaviour will be repeated—for example, if a shock follows the pressing of the wrong lever—the behaviour has been punished, and the shock is a *punisher*.

Both **reinforcement** and **punishment** can be either *positive* or *negative*. Here the terms 'positive' and 'negative' *do not* mean 'good' and 'bad'. (What would 'good punishment' look like?) Instead, the term *positive* refers to the *addition* or presentation of something following a behaviour, and the term *negative* refers to the *removal* of something. Think of positive and negative reinforcement and punishment in terms of addition and subtraction rather than pleasantness and unpleasantness.

Positive reinforcement occurs when the frequency or probability of a behaviour is increased as a result of the addition or presentation of something following the performance of the behaviour. A bar is pressed and the rat receives food; you smile at a baby and she smiles back; you start going to sleep earlier and your grades improve—all of these consequences are positive reinforcers. They increase the likelihood of

> **KEY IDEAS** operant chamber ('Skinner box') The apparatus B.F. Skinner designed to study operant learning in rats. The operant chamber includes a container of food pellets mounted to the outside of the cage, designed so that the pellets will be delivered to the rat when the rat presses down on a lever near its food tray. The cage is placed within a soundproof, temperature-controlled, ventilated chamber.

> **KEY IDEAS** reinforcement and punishment Reinforcement takes place when the consequence of a behaviour increases the likelihood that the behaviour will continue or be repeated in the future. Punishment takes place when the consequence of a behaviour decreases the likelihood that it will continue or be repeated in the future.

the behaviour being repeated or continuing by the addition of something—generally something rewarding.

On the other hand, **negative reinforcement** occurs when a behaviour is reinforced by the removal or avoidance of something bad. A bar is pressed and shocks *stop*; you smile and make silly faces at a screaming baby and she *stops* crying; you confess to your interrogator and the beatings stop—all of these consequences are negative reinforcers. They also increase the likelihood of the behaviour being repeated (or continuing), but do so by removing or allowing one to avoid something—generally something unpleasant or aversive.

Positive punishment occurs when the consequence of a behaviour is the addition or presentation of something, generally something aversive. The wrong bar is pressed and the rat is shocked; the school bully picks on the wrong person and gets flattened; you download your final paper from an Internet website and receive an F grade for plagiarism—these are examples of positive punishers. They *decrease* the likelihood of the behaviour being repeated (or continuing) through the addition or presentation of something—generally something unpleasant or aversive.

Negative punishment occurs when the consequence of a behaviour is the removal of something. The wrong bar is pressed and the rat's food disappears down a trap door; you say something 'off message' in the office and your boss's smile fades; you stay out too late and get grounded—all these are examples of negative punishers. They also decrease the likelihood of the behaviour being repeated (or continuing), but do so through the removal of something—generally something rewarding.

One important point needs to be made about reinforcement and punishment. Although reinforcers tend to be rewarding, and punishments tend to be unpleasant or aversive, this is not always the case. A reinforcer is *anything* that increases the likelihood of a behaviour continuing or being repeated; a punisher is *anything* that decreases the likelihood of a behaviour continuing or being repeated. Yet, consider the case of a child crying out for attention from his or her mother, who generally ignores the child. Such a child might prefer anger, shouting, and even spanking to nothing at all, and may do things that elicit anger. Such a child learns to 'push his mother's buttons'. In this case, anger and shouting—which most of us would consider a punishment—may actually serve as reinforcement.

Shaping: The Building Blocks of Operant Behaviour

Now let us suppose you want to try to teach a rat to press a bar. In this case, bar pressing would be termed the **operant behaviour,** or the behaviour you are attempting to condition. If operant conditioning is to work, bar pressing must be reinforced. But suppose days go by and the rat never once presses the bar spontaneously? We could all grow old waiting for operant conditioning to occur. For this reason, operant conditioning usually involves **shaping by successive approximation**, or more simply, shaping. Shaping involves successive reinforcement of those behaviours that come increasingly closer to the behaviour you ultimately wish to reinforce. It is shaping that is responsible for the astonishing tricks that animal trainers routinely are able to teach their animals.

Suppose you wished to train your dog to play basketball. You might start by reinforcing the dog with praise and biscuits every time he walks close to the ball—the closer he comes, the more praise and biscuits. You might then *fade* or slowly discontinue reinforcement until he starts lapping or gnawing at the ball, at which time reinforcement would begin again, continuing until it seems you had got as far as you were going to get by rewarding lapping and gnawing behaviour. Luckily, reinforcing a particular response frequently has the effect of also reinforcing similar responses, a phenomenon known as *response generalization*. You might now discontinue reinforcement once more until the dog, as a result of generalization, moves from lapping to picking up the ball in its mouth. At this point, reinforcement begins again. And so forth until you have a champion basket-shooter.

Of course, actual dog training is not this simple, but this is the basic idea of shaping through successive approximation. *Chaining* is a related type of conditioning that is useful when very complex behaviours are being taught (such as doggie basketball). Rather than reinforcing behaviours that come increasingly close to the desired behaviour, behaviours are reinforced that form a chain—with each new behaviour acting as a cue for the next. In this way, sequences of behaviours are taught by reinforcing each successive element in the chain. In other words initially reinforcers follow the first behaviour, then they only follow the first two behaviours in sequence, then only the first three behaviours, etc.

Types of Reinforcer: The Premack Principle

What makes a good reinforcer for an organism? That depends on which organism we're talking about. A goldfish, a rat, and a human being undoubtedly would each find different things reinforcing. This question was addressed by David Premack (1971). Premack found that determining a good reinforcer is a simple matter of noting the length of time the individual engages in a particular behaviour when a number of behaviours are freely available. If I (Matt) spend more time at music festivals than football matches, I suppose I would press more bars (or go to more bars) to obtain a festival ticket than to get a football ticket.

Premack used this observation as the foundation for what has come to be known as the Premack principle. Simply put, the Premack principle states that high-probability behaviours—those that are freely chosen when other options are available—are good reinforcers for low-probability behaviours—those that are unlikely to be freely chosen. In other words, strong reinforcers can be used to reinforce weak reinforcers.

For example, both our kids loved watching films and hated cleaning their room (a spooky coincidence). Cleaning their room was a (way) low-probability behaviour, and watching films was a high-probability behaviour. Taking advantage of the Premack principle we could manipulate them into cleaning their rooms with the promise of a film showing.

Types of Reinforcer: Primary and Secondary Reinforcers

While different individuals find different things reinforcing, certain reinforcers automatically apply to virtually all members of a species, because they are essential for the survival or reproduction of the organism. These are known as **primary reinforcers**. For example, food, water, and sex are primary reinforcers. However, some reinforcers that are not automatically related to survival and reproductive success can nonetheless prove to be just as powerful as primary reinforcers. That is because the organism previously has been *conditioned* to associate them with primary reinforcers. These are termed **secondary reinforcers**. Money and status are excellent examples. Bits of paper and job titles have no intrinsic value as reinforcers for a human being, but many human beings have been conditioned to associate money and status with food and shelter, pleasure, romantic success, and so forth. Under many circumstances, secondary reinforcers can be just as powerful as primary reinforcers.

❯ **KEY IDEAS** primary and secondary reinforcers Primary reinforcers are intrinsically reinforcing because they are essential for the survival or reproduction of the organism (examples: food, water, sex, air, shelter, etc). A secondary reinforcer has become associated through conditioning with one or more primary reinforcers (examples: money and status).

Reinforcement Schedules

Operant conditioning depends on desired behaviours being reinforced or undesirable behaviours punished. But is it essential for the behaviour to be reinforced or punished *each time* it occurs? Not at all. Indeed, from the standpoint of conditioning, in most cases it is better that reinforcement *not* occur on a continuous basis, an important finding of operant conditioning research that we now explore.

Continuous versus partial reinforcement

Let us say you were playing a slot machine in Las Vegas and it paid a jackpot every time you inserted a quarter. In other words, your behaviour (slipping the coin into the slot) was being continuously reinforced. Now consider what you would do if the machine suddenly *stopped* paying. While the payouts were flowing, you would be highly likely to continue playing. It is hard to stop playing a machine that seems intent on paying you each time it is played. However, after a few tries with no payoff, you would likely conclude that the machine had 'gone cold' and move on. The behaviour of feeding quarters into that machine, while initially strong, would quickly have been extinguished. The term *extinguish* is used in operant conditioning theory in much the same way *extinction* is used in classical conditioning—to indicate that a learned behaviour has ceased to occur.

Now consider a slot machine that never plays *too* long without a jackpot, but does not pay off *each* time you drop in your quarter. This is the sort of machine that keeps a person glued to it until the player is stone cold broke; and, in fact, all slot machines are programmed to pay off in this way. This is because jackpots, while unpredictable, seem assured *if the person waits long enough*. 'It's got to pay off sooner or later.' **Partial reinforcement** is the term used to describe situations such as this, where reinforcement occurs only periodically. Although behaviours may be acquired very quickly using **continuous reinforcement** schedules, they are generally much more enduring and difficult to extinguish when they are conditioned with partial reinforcement. This rather counterintuitive fact is known as the **partial reinforcement effect**. There is now some fascinating evidence to show that persistent gamblers are in fact especially sensitive to partial reinforcement, although it is not yet clear whether this sensitivity is the cause of the gambling or an effect (Horsley et al, 2012).

There are reasons why most examples of operant learning—in the laboratory or the 'real world'—occur as a result of partial rather than continuous reinforcement, beyond the fact that partial reinforcement generally leads to a stronger, more enduring conditioning. Continuous reinforcement rarely occurs in the natural world, whereas partial reinforcement is everywhere. Picture a sadly common scene: a homeless man sits in a shopping precinct asking shoppers for money as they pass by. The majority do not give him cash. A few will do so and a further few may buy him food or reward his interaction in another way such as stopping for a chat. If the man required continuous reinforcement to stay motivated he would quickly become discouraged and stop asking. However, the fact that a minority will help him out is enough to reinforce the behaviour, allowing him to continue asking until he has accumulated enough money for the effort to have been worthwhile. This shows that our tendency for partial reinforcement is adaptive. The principle can be applied to any situation in which our best efforts only pay off irregularly—applying for jobs, chatting people up, trying to buy Glastonbury ticket, etc.

> **KEY IDEAS** partial and continuous reinforcement Partial reinforcement takes place when a behaviour is reinforced periodically rather than continuously. Partial reinforcement can be determined by the passage of time (an interval schedule) or the number of times an organism performs a behaviour (a ratio schedule).
>
> Continuous reinforcement takes place when a behaviour is reinforced every time it occurs.
>
> The partial reinforcement effect is the name given to research findings which show that conditioned behaviours are more enduring and difficult to extinguish when they are reinforced periodically rather than continuously.

Partial reinforcement schedules

If continuous reinforcement is difficult to find in the natural world, it is extremely difficult to *maintain* in the laboratory. Rewarding a rat with food every time it performs a behaviour can be costly and time-consuming, as Skinner found out early in his career. In experimenting with partial reinforcement to save time and money, Skinner discovered its advantages in conditioning. Skinner eventually devised four distinct partial reinforcement schedules, highlighted in Figure 7.12 (eg, Skinner, 1956).

Fixed-interval (FI) schedules provide reinforcement for the first response after a *specific interval of time* has passed (eg, after a minute, hour, or day). The number of responses has no effect on the timing of reinforcement. Therefore, the organism quickly learns exactly when reinforcement will occur, and also realizes that it does not matter if it were to press the bar one time or a thousand times unless that time interval has elapsed. Consequently, there is usually a reduction in the number of operant behaviours (bar presses) immediately following reinforcement in a fixed-interval schedule. There is an increase in the behaviour (bar presses) just before the time that reinforcement (food pellet) is scheduled to occur once again.

Variable-interval (VI) schedules provide reinforcement at *unpredictable time intervals* (eg, every 5 minutes *on average*). Here the organism is never sure exactly when reinforcement will occur, although it still realizes that the number of responses is irrelevant. Therefore, variable-interval schedules produce far more consistent and continuous responding than fixed-interval schedules, but responding is still on the slow side given that the number of repetitions does not influence the pattern of reinforcement.

Fixed-ratio (FR) schedules provide reinforcement after a *specific number of responses*. This is the logic of factory piecework, where workers are paid by the number of items produced rather than the number of hours worked. Under such conditions, the more behaviours that the organism provides, the greater the quantity of reinforcement. Therefore, organisms on fixed-ratio schedules may briefly rest following reinforcement, but then put their noses back to the grindstone and respond at a very high rate.

Variable-ratio (VR) schedules provide reinforcement after an *unpredictable number of responses*. This is the slot-machine reinforcement schedule. Here the organism is unsure of how many times it must respond for reinforcement to take place. Just as we found with fixed-ratio schedules, variable-ratio schedules are correlated with a very high response rate. However, unlike with fixed-ratio schedules, the organism does not typically pause for rest following reinforcement in variable-ratio schedules—it just continues to respond at high rates to reach the next reinforcement. This is because the organism truly has no idea when reinforcement will occur. Conditioning acquired in this way is the most difficult to extinguish.

FIGURE 7.12 Trapped by the partial reinforcement effect. Slot machines are programmed to pay out according to partial reinforcement schedules. This is what makes it so difficult to stop playing a particular machine (and slot machines generally).

Source: massimofusaro/Shutterstock.com.

> **KEY IDEAS** partial reinforcement schedules
Fixed-interval (FI) schedule A partial reinforcement schedule that provides reinforcement for the first operant behaviour after a specific interval of time has passed. **Variable-interval (VI) schedule** A partial reinforcement schedule that provides reinforcement at unpredictable time intervals. **Fixed-ratio (FR) schedule** A partial reinforcement schedule that provides reinforcement after a specific number of operant behavioural responses. **Variable-ratio (VR) schedule** A partial reinforcement schedule that provides reinforcement after an unpredictable number of behavioural responses.

THINKING PRACTICALLY

Imagine you are working with a family where a parent has recently suffered an accident at work and is unable to do as much as before around the house. It has been decided that it would be helpful if the children can help more; for example, laying the table and washing up after meals. Think about how you might use a programme of operant conditioning to encourage this behaviour. Include how you might use primary and secondary reinforcers, reinforcement schedules, and shaping to make the programme as effective as possible.

Uncontrollable Reinforcement and Superstitious Behaviour

Reinforcers can be experienced after a behaviour for any number of reasons. Some make intuitive sense; we are reinforced when we behave in a socially desirable way. Punishers follow risky behaviour and discourage us from doing silly things repeatedly. So the capacity to learn the benefits of safe sex from contracting a treatable STI might save us from a more serious condition later. However, what happens when reinforcers happen to follow a behaviour but actually have nothing to do with it? The likelihood of repeating the behaviour increases but for no good reason. Skinner demonstrated this in a classic experiment, in which he created 'superstitious' pigeons.

RESEARCH IN FOCUS

Skinner, B.F. (1948) Superstition in the pigeon. *Journal of Experimental Psychology*, **38**, 168–72.

Aim: To illustrate uncontrollable reinforcement by creating 'superstitious' behaviour in pigeons.

Method: Eight pigeons were given limited food in order to reduce their body weight and ensure that they were hungry for the duration of the experiment. Each bird was placed in a Skinner box for a few minutes each day. Here they received a food pellet every 15 seconds regardless of their behaviour. After a few days of this two independent observers recorded the birds' behaviour. The time interval between the administration of the food pellets was increased to 1 minute and the frequency of responding was recorded again. In the final phase of the study any newly learned behaviours were extinguished by placing the birds in the cage but not giving them any food pellets.

Results: Six of the eight birds developed new and distinctive repetitive behaviours, which they produced before the pellets were due. These included turning anti-clockwise, hopping, head bobbing, and swinging. Most of these new behaviours were consistently performed in the same area of the cage. When the pellets became less frequent the rate at which the new behaviours were performed increased.

Conclusion: The pigeons appeared to have learned that the delivery of food pellets depended upon whatever behaviour they were performing just before they arrived. Skinner concluded that the pigeons had learned 'superstitious' behaviour.

MASTER YOUR METHODOLOGY

1 The consistency of the two observers' observations was recorded. What is this called and why is it important?

2 There was no control condition used in this study. What is a control condition and what might a control condition have this contributed to this study? What data did researchers have available instead of a control condition?

3 There is always a potential problem in animal research of generalizing results to humans. Why might Skinner not have not been concerned by this?

> **KEY IDEAS** uncontrollable reinforcers An uncontrollable reinforcer is one which happens to occur after behaviour but which is not causally related to it. It increases the likelihood of the behaviour being repeated but not because it actually resulted from the behaviour.

Skinner believed that he had uncovered the mechanism underlying human superstition. Just as the pigeons continued to bob or hop as long as the food pellets keep coming, so humans continue to avoid stepping on the cracks in the pavement as long as their mother's back doesn't break. The pellets and the continuing integrity of one's mother's back are examples of **uncontrollable reinforcers**.

More about Punishment

Skinner (1938) believed that punishment for undesirable behaviour was in most cases a poor teacher in comparison to reward for desirable behaviour (a belief that helped spur him to oppose corporal punishment in schools). If anything, Skinner *underestimated* the usefulness of punishment. Contrary to Skinner's early beliefs, punishment *can* be an effective deterrent to behaviour—but mostly if the punishment is immediate, inevitable, and severe (Azrin, Holz, and Hake, 1963; Boe and Church, 1967; Matson and Taras, 1989; Bennett, 1998).

In real-life settings, however, these conditions are very hard to meet. Think about punishment in the criminal justice system. If you were always caught when you committed a crime, and you were punished immediately and sufficiently severely then punishment might well deter you from further criminality. The reality, however (unless you are a particularly inept criminal or do something serious enough to bring the full attention of the authorities down on you), is that you probably won't get caught and that if you are caught you will be remanded on bail then mildly punished some time in the future. On this basis it is unlikely that punishment will be effective in tackling most crime.

Punishment poses additional problems not posed by the use of positive and negative reinforcement. One problem is that many people simply consider the use of sufficiently severe punishment to be effective to be inhumane, a sentiment reflected in the lessening of social tolerance for corporal punishment of children occurring in many parts of the world (Gershoff, 2002).

Another problem is that, while punishment may alter an individual's behaviour in a desirable direction, it may simultaneously alter his or her behaviour in *undesirable* directions (Hiby, Rooney, and Bradshaw, 2004). In other words, punishment can have side effects. For example, it can engender anger and resentment, leading to revenge or retaliation. Bennett (1998) cites the example of workplace shootings by former employees who considered their supervisors to be unjustly punitive. More commonly though less dramatically, teenagers who are 'grounded' for some rule infraction may stop breaking that rule, but begin breaking other rules with a vengeance.

THINKING PRACTICALLY

Domestic violence is a huge problem in many countries including in Britain and Europe. A recent review of evidence (Dutton and Corvo, 2006) concluded that most current interventions are ineffective. Based on your understanding of effective punishment and the potential risks of punishment, design an intervention programme that uses punishment to reduce the incidence of domestic violence. You will need to consider the factors that make punishment effective and ways in which these could be achieved.

The Role of Cognition in Operant Conditioning

The first major challenge to B.F. Skinner's assertion that all behaviour could be explained by referring to reinforcement and punishment alone arrived in the work of Edward Tolman (1886–1959). Tolman was a dedicated behaviourist. However, unlike Skinner, he believed that it would be possible to use scientific methods to study the impact of *mental activity* on operant conditioning. Most of Tolman's work involved observing rats as they learned to navigate mazes to obtain food (positive reinforcement). According to radical behaviourist views, non-reinforced rats should be expected not to learn to run mazes because they receive no reinforcement for doing so. However, Tolman believed there was a crucial difference between *learning* and *performance*—that is, between the actual learning, and the behaviour which demonstrated that learning had taken place.

In a famous experiment, Tolman and Honzik (1930) placed one group of rats in a complicated maze containing a 'goal' box (see Figure 7.13). The rats were given no food reinforcement for any movement towards the goal box. As expected, these rats wandered aimlessly through the maze. With no reward of food as a goal, they had no reason to strive to locate the goal box. The researchers gave a second group of rats continuous reinforcement for locating the food box, and after 11 days, these rats learned to navigate the maze. Both of these results are predicted by operant learning theory.

But Tolman and Honzik then placed a *third* group of rats in the maze. At first, the investigators did *not* reinforce these rats, and the rats wandered as aimlessly as had those in the first non-reinforced group. However, on the eleventh day, Tolman and Honzik suddenly began to reinforce rats in the third group for finding the box. Within 1 day this group had caught up to the group that had been continuously reinforced in the speed with which they could navigate the maze. Given that Group 3 'learned' in 1 day as much as Group 2 had in 11 days, Tolman concluded that, in fact, Group 3 rats actually had been *learning* the maze all along—they merely had no motivation to *perform* maze-running until they were reinforced for doing so.

Tolman (1948) suggested that during the non-reinforcement period, the rats had been forming a **cognitive map**—a mental representation of how the maze was constructed. As soon as the rats began to be reinforced, they accessed this cognitive map to solve the puzzle of the maze. Tolman used the term **latent learning** to describe learning that takes place without reinforcement and which is not necessarily apparent in actual behaviour. Tolman's brand of behaviourism, which acknowledges the intervention of cognition in learning, came to be known as **cognitive behaviourism**.

> ❯ KEY IDEAS cognitive behaviourism **Cognitive behaviourism** is the psychological school founded by Edward Tolman. Cognitive behaviourists agree with radical behaviourists that behaviour is acquired according to a set of rules and can be analysed using concepts of reinforcement and punishment, but they disagree that this analysis must necessarily exclude cognition. Cognitive behaviourists pioneered the concepts of cognitive maps and latent learning. A cognitive map is a mental representation of the structure, location, or attributes of some phenomenon. Latent learning is learning that occurs without obvious reinforcement, and that is not apparent in behaviour.

FIGURE 7.13 **Rats can learn to run a maze. This requires cognitive processing.**
Source: Fer Gregory/Shutterstock.com.

Another line of research with implications for the role of cognition in operant conditioning comes from Mark Griffiths (eg, Griffiths, 2004). Griffiths researches gambling behaviour, notably the use of fruit machines. Griffiths (2004) points out that gambling is reinforced, not only by wins but also by near misses. Near misses do not provide tangible reinforcement in the Skinner sense (primary or secondary), nonetheless they *are* reinforcing. This suggests that, far from mindlessly responding to reinforcers, the gambler analyses them.

The role of evolution in operant conditioning

As we explained earlier, evolutionary theorists have demonstrated that the evolutionary history of an organism can have powerful effects on the way classical conditioning occurs—or does not occur. This is also true for operant conditioning, a fact that was brought home to learning psychologists in 1961 by B.F. Skinner's students Keller and Marian Breland. The Brelands had initially believed in equipotentiality—the idea that learning mechanisms were equally applicable to all types of behaviour and all forms of animal life. According to this idea, barring the physically impossible (eg, teaching a pig to fly), virtually any animal could be taught to perform virtually any behaviour, given the right reinforcement techniques and enough patience.

Breland and Breland found, however, that certain animals *would not* learn specific behaviours in spite of the fact that there appeared to be no reason why they should not. An example is their classic 'miserly raccoon' study. Breland and Breland attempted to use shaping by successive approximation to teach a raccoon to pick up coins and deposit them in a 'piggy bank' box as part of a proposed bank display for promoting thrift. The Brelands had no trouble teaching the raccoon to pick up coins by reinforcing his performance with food. They also had no trouble getting the animal to learn to slip the coins into the box's slot. However, the raccoon would *not* let the coins go, but dipped them in and out of the slot, and rubbed them together in his paws, in the Brelands' words, 'in a most miserly fashion' (Breland and Breland, 1961, p 682). The problem is that raccoons are predisposed to rub food together in their paws to remove dirt or the shells of crayfish. The raccoon had come to associate the coins with receiving food and was behaving towards the coins as if they were food.

The Brelands researchers realized that when operant conditioning is used to condition a behaviour that conflicts with an instinctive behaviour, instinct usually wins out—a phenomenon the Brelands labelled **instinctive drift**. They titled their article 'The Misbehaviour of Organisms' in an ironic tip of the hat to their mentor, B.F. Skinner who first set out the principles of operant conditioning of animals in a book titled *The Behaviour of Organisms*.

Thus, by the mid-1960s, operant conditioning theorists also had come to acknowledge that evolutionary biology places constraints on what an animal can learn through operant conditioning. There are some things that individuals of a given species cannot learn, or have great difficulty learning, because these things conflict with innate patterns of behaviour (instinct) or psychological adaptations. On the other hand, there are things that each species can learn with particular ease as a result of its evolutionary history.

Domain-specific learning

Recall from our discussion of classical conditioning that some innate responses (eg, nausea) are more easily conditioned through the use of certain neutral stimuli (spoiled food) than others (flashing lights). Something very similar holds true for

> **KEY IDEAS** instinctive drift
> **Instinctive drift** takes place when an instinctive pattern of behaviour interferes with the operant conditioning of a behaviour.

operant conditioning as well. Each species differs in the ease or difficulty with which it can be taught specific tasks through the use of specific types of reinforcements.

For example, it would be quite difficult to use operant conditioning to teach a pigeon to peck at computer keyboard keys to avoid electric shock. However, it would be a relatively simple matter to condition the pigeon to flap its wings to avoid shock. This is because wing-flapping, but not pecking, is among the pigeon's innate mechanisms for avoiding danger. On the other hand, a pigeon can easily be taught to peck at a computer keyboard using the positive reinforcement of food, because pecking is one of the pigeon's innate mechanisms for obtaining food (Bolles, 1970; Foree and LoLordo, 1973; Shettleworth, 1975).

Contemporary evolutionary psychologists studying learning generally explain such findings by suggesting that learning mechanisms are *domain specific* rather than *domain general* as behaviourists have always proposed (eg, Gallistel, 2000). If you recall from Chapter 3, by *domain specific* evolutionary theorists mean that a mechanism (in this case, a learning mechanism) evolved to help solve a *specific* problem faced recurrently by our evolutionary ancestors. This contrasts with the domain-general views of behaviourists that learning mechanisms such as classical and operant conditioning apply across the board to all species, stimuli, and reinforcements. According to the evolutionary view, the mechanism a pigeon uses when learning to escape from electric shocks is a fundamentally different mechanism from the one a rat might use in a similar situation. Thus, it may be misleading to place both of these mechanisms in the single category 'operant learning'.

Operant Conditioning in the Real World

Operant conditioning occurs on a daily basis out in the real world. Consider the small child who throws a tantrum in the middle of the supermarket when his or her parent won't buy those sweets, biscuits, etc. The child expresses such anguish, at such a loud volume, that the parent—stressed and embarrassed to the limit— eventually gives in and buys the cookies. But not always. Sometimes the parent strives valiantly to stick to his or her guns, and succeeds. Unfortunately, this lack of consistency sets up a variable-ratio (VR) schedule of reinforcement, and the child's behaviour is virtually certain to continue because he or she never knows just how much howling it will take to get the reward. The child knows only that, eventually, the reward will come. This is why, in disciplining children, consistency is critical.

Romantic partners are also using operant conditioning on a daily basis in attempts to change or control their partners. If you have ever been involved in a long-term romantic relationship, think of the many times you have attempted to use subtle (or not-so-subtle) reinforcers and punishments to alter your partner's behaviour. Much of the time, of course, these attempts are doomed to failure (Christensen and Jacobson, 2000). However, if the behaviour in question isn't too deeply ingrained, operant conditioning can work wonders.

I (Paul—Matt prefers Grunge) recall that I used to love to listen to a particular musician (John Coltrane), whom my then-girlfriend hated. Whenever she was present in the room and I happened to put on a Coltrane album (it was the years of vinyl), she wouldn't complain—she'd just quietly leave the room (negative punishment). Without consciously realizing what was happening, I began playing Coltrane less and less frequently when she was in the house until I stopped altogether. If she had come right out and said, 'I can't stand Coltrane—don't play him while I'm around', I probably would have just tried to argue her into liking the music, a foolish waste of everyone's time.

Like classical conditioning, operant conditioning has been successfully used to treat psychological distress and alter behaviour in prisons, hospitals, and other institutions. We revisit these therapeutic applications in Chapter 17. There are other interesting contemporary applications of operant conditioning, however. Poling et al (2011) trained rats to find landmines in Mozambique using operant conditioning. The rats were rewarded with mashed banana (a rat delicacy) when they stuck their heads in a hole containing TNT-contaminated soil. Shaping was employed so that initially the reinforcer followed two seconds in the hole but the rats had to build up to five seconds to keep receiving it. After this conditioning in the lab then in the field the rats were able to find landmines by the TNT smell and signal their location with remarkable success (0% mines missed and only 0.33% false positives). This study illustrates the power of operant conditioning.

READ THIS

Operant conditioning is very much the brainchild of B.F. Skinner. Skinner is often not accurately or fairly represented in secondary sources. To really get a handle on his ideas it is worth reading his original work. A search will turn up some of his papers in full and in books, either in full or in the form of substantial extracts. Papers include the superstitious pigeons study. It is also worth looking back at the work of Tolman on cognitive behaviourism—for example:

Tolman, E.C. (1948). Cognitive maps in rats and men. *Psychological Review*, **55**, 189–208.

For a more recent overview of operant conditioning research try:

Staddon, J.E. and Cerutti, D.T. (2003). Operant conditioning. *Annual Review of Psychology*, **54**, 115–44.

OBSERVATIONAL LEARNING

Early learning theorists such as Watson and Skinner tended to ignore an important fact of learning that seems quite obvious now: at least some animals—particularly but not exclusively, humans—learn certain things in the absence of conditioning, merely through observation. In 1941, Neal Miller and John Dollard first described **observational learning** (sometimes called *social learning*)—the ways in which an organism might learn by observing the experiences of *others*, rather than through his or her own experience (eg, Bandura, 1977). Theories of observational learning became more important as the influence of behaviourism waned during the 1960s and 1970s.

> KEY IDEAS observational learning Learning through the observation of others. Mechanisms of observational learning include modelling and vicarious reinforcement.

Modelling: Learning through Imitation

Observing and imitating the behaviour of others is an important part of the way human beings interact, perhaps because imitation facilitates *empathy* among people—understanding and caring about how other people feel (Iacoboni, 2009). An important type of learning through imitation is known as **modelling**. Dollard and Miller claimed that children were especially prone to imitation of the behaviours of adults they admired because of their identification with the adult and desire to be like him or her. In other words, children use favoured adults as models for their own behaviour.

The best-known series of studies based on the work of Dollard and Miller were carried out by social-cognitive learning theorist Albert Bandura and his associates. They are known by the affectionate nickname of the 'Bobo doll' experiments

> **KEY IDEAS** modelling and modelling theory **Modelling** involves demonstrating a behaviour. This may be deliberate or accidental. Observational learning takes place when an observer imitates the behaviour of an individual they admire. **Modelling theory** is an early and simple view of observational learning in which individuals acquire behaviour simply by imitating those they admire.

(Bandura, Ross, and Ross, 1961, 1963; Bandura, 1965). As depicted in Figure 7.14, in these experiments live adult models (and, in later studies, filmed ones) were used to examine the possible consequences of adult role-modelling of violent behaviours in the presence of children. In the original version, preschoolers were left in the company of an adult model who would either punch and kick an inflatable clown doll (a 'Bobo doll')—the kind with a rounded, weighted base that springs back up when knocked down—or, in the control conditions, the adult would do nothing to the doll. We can explore this study in detail.

RESEARCH IN FOCUS

Bandura, A., Ross, D., and Ross, S.A. (1961). Transmission of aggression through imitation of aggressive models. *Journal of Abnormal and Social Psychology*, **63**, 575–82.

Aim: The broad aim was to investigate whether aggression could be learned through observation of aggressive models. The impact of a number of independent variables was tested, including modelling, the sex of the model, and the congruence between sex of model and observer.

Method: 36 boys and 36 girls aged 3–6 years, all sampled from the same university nursery, were randomly assigned to a range of experimental conditions: 12 boys and 12 girls were exposed to adult models who behaved in an aggressive way, punching, kicking, sitting on, and shouting at an inflatable 'Bobo' doll. Half of these saw a male model and half a female model, so for half the model was same-sex and for the other half they were different-sex. A control group of 12 boys and 12 girls did not see any model, whilst in the non-aggressive condition, the model just assembled mechanical toys.

After ten minutes all the children were deliberately annoyed in order to increase the chances that aggressive behaviour was to be displayed. They were shown a selection of attractive toys such as a fire engine and a doll with a wardrobe, but then told that these toys were for other children. They were then moved to another play room containing a Bobo doll. The children were then observed playing.

Results: Children exposed to aggressive models imitated their aggressive behaviours and in some cases initiated new aggressive behaviours. They were overall significantly more aggressive than those in the non-aggressive modelling group or the control group. Boys were generally more aggressive and there was a greater tendency for children to imitate models of their own sex. However, girls were more likely to imitate verbal aggression from a female model.

Conclusion: Aggression can be learned through imitating the actions of a model. Same sex models are more likely to be imitated, as are gendered behaviours (thus boys imitated physical aggression more and girls verbal aggression). Overall boys are more aggressive.

MASTER YOUR METHODOLOGY

1 This is a good example of a laboratory experiment. The art of good experimental design is control of extraneous variables. Identify as many control measures in this experiment as you can.

2 The experiment used a *between groups* design (sometimes called an unrelated or **independent measures design**). What is the major limitation of this kind of design and why was it necessary in this study?

3 72 is a fairly large sample size for a laboratory experiment; however, think about the number of conditions and the number of participants in each condition. Does it seem so impressive now?

FIGURE 7.14 The 'Bobo doll' experiments. In the 'Bobo doll' experiments of Albert Bandura and his colleagues, children who observed an admired adult mistreating the inflatable doll were more likely than others to do the same when given the chance.
Source: Bandura, Ross, and Ross, 1961.

Vicarious Conditioning: Learning by Observing Consequences

Modelling theory set the stage for the development of more sophisticated theories of observational learning. Following the initial 'Bobo' studies, Bandura and his colleagues created a second series of studies where, rather than watching live displays, children watched films of adults kicking and punching the doll, whacking it with a mallet, and generally behaving in a mean way towards the doll. The other difference between these and the earlier studies was that in the films, the children were able to watch the adults experience either rewarding or punishing *consequences* for their behaviour. There was also a version in which no consequences occurred at all.

As shown in Figure 7.14, children who witnessed the punishment condition were much less likely to hit 'Bobo' than those who witnessed either the reward condition or the no-consequence condition (Bandura et al, 1963; Bandura 1965). Bandura described these results as examples of **vicarious conditioning**, where observation of rewarding or punishing consequences experienced by others serves much the same function as being rewarded or punished oneself.

Interestingly, however, almost all the children could be induced to hit and punch the Bobo doll for a real-life reward of cake and other goodies, regardless of whether they had witnessed reward, punishment, or no consequences. In Bandura's view this result was particularly alarming, demonstrating that *all* the children had acquired aggressive learning at some level, regardless of vicarious rewards or punishments (Bandura et al, 1963; Bandura, 1965). Moreover, as with the earlier experiments in modelling, boys in Bandura's studies were more vulnerable to the effects of vicarious conditioning of aggression than were girls. As Figure 7.15 shows, boys' aggressive

> **KEY IDEAS** vicarious conditioning Learning through observing the rewarding or punishing consequences of other people's behaviour. In vicarious reinforcement the model is seen being rewarded for the behaviour, in which case this behaviour is more likely to be imitated.

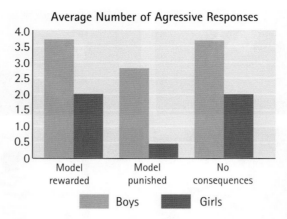

Average Number of Agressive Responses

Boys　　Girls

FIGURE 7.15 Vicarious conditioning of aggression. In later experiments with the Bobo doll, Bandura and his colleagues demonstrated that observing aggressive behaviour being punished may counter the effects of modelling and deter physical aggression in children. However, the deterrent effect of punishment was far more marked for girls than boys.

Source: Bandura, 1965; Bandura, Ross, and Ross, 1963.

behaviours increased more markedly than girls' in the reward and no consequence conditions, and boys who witnessed punishment were much less likely than girls to be deterred from aggressive behaviour. The 'Bobo' studies and Albert Bandura's early work on observational learning were instrumental in sounding an early warning alarm about the presence of violence in the mass media. Could children learn to become aggressive by watching their favourite Saturday morning cartoon show? We will consider this question in detail in Chapter 20.

The cognitive processes of observational learning

Like Edward Tolman (this chapter), Bandura worked within a broadly behaviourist approach but acknowledged the importance of cognitive processes. One of the key differences between the ideas of Bandura and Skinner is that although Bandura acknowledged the importance of reinforcement he took account of the cognitive processes leading up to it. Bandura (1977) suggested a model of observational learning involving four processes.

1 Attention to the model's behaviour

2 Retention of the observed behaviour

3 Reproduction of the observed behaviour in an appropriate situation

4 Reinforcement of the reproduced behaviour

This was the beginning of Bandura's development of social learning theory, later developed into social cognitive theory. We will revisit this in Chapter 13.

Observational learning in animals

You might imagine that with the amount of cognitive processing needed to analyse the sex and status of a model that this kind of selective observational learning is unique to humans. Actually, human beings are not the only ones who engage in observational learning. A study by Nicol and Pope (1999) illustrates selection of models by gender and status in chickens. A dominant cockerel, a dominant hen, a mid-ranking, and a subordinate hen were selected from each of 24 flocks and trained how to obtain food by pecking a pad. The trained birds from 19 of these flocks were selected for the experiment on the basis that they were well matched for performance on the pecking task. They were then observed by other hens from their flocks. The hens imitated the dominant hens more than the dominant cockerels or lower-status hens, showing that, like Bandura's human participants, they selectively attended to the behaviour of particular models.

WHAT'S HOT? MIRROR NEURONS AND OBSERVATIONAL LEARNING

Over the last decade there has been tremendous interest in the existence of mirror neurons. **Mirror neurons** have revolutionized the way we think about observational learning. So what is all the fuss about? In a groundbreaking study, Giacomo Rizzolatti and his colleagues found that in the *premotor cortex* of the monkey brain there is a network of neurons that fire either when a monkey performs a particular action or when the monkey merely *observes* another monkey or a human performing that action (Rizzolatti, Fadiga, Gallese, and Fogassi, 1996).

Rizzolatti's research team discovered these neurons by accident. One of the investigators (Fogassi) walked into the room where they had been studying neural activity in the brain of a macaque monkey as the monkey reached for various objects, including raisins from a bowl on the table. Fogassi himself casually reached for a raisin to eat, and the investigators were astonished to see that as the monkey watched Fogassi reach for the raisin, the same neurons fired that had previously fired when the monkey reached for a raisin himself (Dobbs, 2006)!

Subsequent research showed that these neurons will fire if the animal *hears the sounds* of a behaviour being performed that he or she has previously performed (Kohler et al, 2002). There also appear to be neurons in the monkey brain that are specifically dedicated to firing when the individual monkey uses a tool of some sort (eg, a stick) or when the animal observes someone else using a tool (Ferrari, Rozzi, and Fogassi, 2005).

Rizzolatti and his colleagues use the term *mirror neuron* to describe a neuron that fires when an animal performs a particular action and also when the animal observes the action performed by someone else. These researchers hypothesize that mirror neurons allow the brain to create mental 'representations' of observed behaviour, allowing such behaviour to be learned (Rizzolatti, Fadiga, Fogassi, and Gallese, 2002; Cataneo and Rizzolatti, 2009; Rizzolatti and Fabbri-Destro, 2010). In other words, at least some of the things we watch others do we mentally rehearse doing ourselves without realizing it.

Mirror neurons are important in grasping the goals and intentions of others based upon their actions (Fogassi et al, 2005; Iacoboni et al, 2005; Gallese, in Gallese et al, 2011). This skill can be critical in the process of observational learning. Observing a behaviour without comprehending the intention or goal behind the act can be a highly ambiguous experience. A person may need to understand the goals and intentions to comprehend the act itself. So a punch is by definition intended to hurt, and the concept of 'punch' is meaningless without that intentional element. Without this basic comprehension, initial *attention* to the act—a first step in observational learning as described by Bandura (1977, 1986)—may never occur. Some researchers believe that mirror neurons may hold the key to the development of *empathy* and language in human beings—as well as explaining mechanisms of observational learning and social interactions in general.

> **KEY IDEAS** mirror neurons
A neuron that fires both when an animal performs an action and when the animal observes another performing the same action.
Mirror neurons are associated with imitation of others' behaviour, and comprehension of others' thoughts, intentions, and emotions.

Mirror neurons have generated great excitement amongst psychologists, partly because of what they can tell us about observational learning but also because they may help explain empathy, language development, and perhaps some conditions like autistic spectrum disorder. However, have a read of some polemic attacks (eg, Hickock, 2014) and more cautious reviews of the evidence (eg, Milner and Lemon, 2013), and form your own opinion of the significance of mirror neurons.

IN REVIEW

- Learning takes place when the organism acquires some new knowledge or behaviour as a result of experience.
- The changes in behaviour or knowledge that occur in learning are relatively enduring.
- The capacity to learn is innate and unlearned, even if the result of some particular learning is cultural or experiential. Organisms are born 'biologically prepared' to learn certain things but not other things.

HABITUATION AND ASSOCIATIVE LEARNING

- Habituation is the simplest form of learning. Habituation occurs when a stimulus at first produces a strong response from an organism, but this response is lessened over time due to repeated exposure.
- Associative learning occurs when an organism comes to associate two or more stimuli or events that occur close together in space and time.
- Associative learning encompasses classical conditioning, operant conditioning, and observational learning.

CLASSICAL CONDITIONING

- In classical conditioning, a neutral stimulus comes to elicit an unconditioned response (UCR) after it has been repeatedly paired with an unconditioned stimulus (UCS). After conditioning, the neutral stimulus is termed the conditioned stimulus (CS) and the unconditioned response is termed the conditioned response (CR).
- In classical conditioning, the neutral stimulus must be presented before the UCS, and the UCS must follow immediately after the neutral stimulus. Second-order conditioning involves the pairing of a CS with a new neutral stimulus until the UCR is elicited when the new neutral stimulus is presented.
- Extinction occurs when a CS is repeatedly presented over time without the UCS. However, if, after the CS is presented again later (without the UCS), the UCR may once again occur; this is known as spontaneous recovery. Renewal is the resurgence of an extinguished behaviour in a different context from the one in which extinction originally occurred. Generalization has occurred when an

organism displays a CR when exposed to a neutral stimulus that is similar, but not identical, to the original CS. Discrimination occurs when one neutral stimulus produces a CR, but another similar neutral stimulus does not.

- Evaluative learning is either similar to or a subtype of classical conditioning in which a neutral stimulus becomes paired with the emotional valence of an unconditional stimulus so that it comes to elicit the same emotional response.

- Contrary to the assertions of early behaviourists it appears that classical conditioning involves cognition, and various cognitive elements must be in place for strong conditioning to occur.

- Also contrary to the assertions of early behaviourists it appears that some responses are much easier to condition than others because of their survival value in the evolutionary past.

- Classical conditioning cannot condition new behaviours; it can only elicit innate or reflexive behaviours.

OPERANT CONDITIONING

- Thorndike's law of effect provided the basis for B.F. Skinner's development of operant conditioning techniques. In operant conditioning, the organism teaches itself by coming to associate a behaviour with its consequences.

- Reinforcement of a behaviour increases the likelihood that the behaviour will continue or be repeated, while punishment decreases this likelihood. Reinforcers tend to be rewarding and punishers unpleasant or aversive, but this is not always the case.

- Operant conditioning frequently involves shaping through successive approximation.

- The Premack principle states that high-probability behaviours are good reinforcers for low-probability behaviours.

- Primary reinforcers are suitable for conditioning with virtually all members of a species because they are essential for survival or reproduction. A secondary reinforcer is not intrinsically associated with survival or reproduction, but has become associated with a primary reinforcer through conditioning.

- Reinforcement schedules affect conditioning. Continuous reinforcement is reinforcement that occurs every time a behaviour occurs. Partial reinforcement refers to situations where reinforcement occurs periodically.

- Partial reinforcement schedules include fixed-interval schedules, variable-interval schedules, fixed-ratio schedules, and variable-ratio schedules.

- Punishment can be effective in operant conditioning if it is immediate, severe, and consistent. However, it may pose ethical problems, and can result in retaliation or other negative side effects rather than conditioning. Reinforcement is generally preferable as a conditioner.

- As with classical conditioning, cognition and the evolutionary history of the organism may set limits on operant conditioning. For example, cognitive activity including latent learning can either interfere with or hasten operant behaviour, and conditioning may fail if it runs counter to an animal's instinctual patterns of behaviour.

OBSERVATIONAL LEARNING

- Observational learning describes ways in which an organism might learn by observing the experiences of others. Modelling is a type of observational learning where a child might acquire behaviours he or she observes in an admired adult.

- Other factors appear to influence the probability of a model being imitated, including their gender and social status. These effects can be seen in animals as well as humans.

- Vicarious conditioning involves learning through observing the consequences of others' behaviour.

- Mirror neurons may help explain how observational learning occurs.

TEST YOURSELF

1 What is the problem with definitions of learning that rely entirely upon the idea that learning can only be inferred from behaviour? What is the problem with definitions that refer to the acquiring of knowledge?

2 When a stimulus at first causes a strong response, but due to repeated exposure over time the response is lessened, what type of learning has occurred?

3 Describe the meanings of the following terms, and explain how they would be used in a demonstration of classical conditioning: neutral stimulus, unconditioned stimulus, unconditioned response, conditioned stimulus, conditioned response.

4 For acquisition to occur reliably, two criteria must be met. What are they?

5 When conditioning occurs because a new neutral stimulus is paired with a conditioned stimulus rather than an unconditioned stimulus, it is known as:

   a) renewal

   b) second-order conditioning

   c) spontaneous recovery

   d) vicarious conditioning

6 True or false: when a conditioned response has been extinguished, but reappears after a period of rest if the conditioned stimulus is once again presented, it is known as renewal.

7 What is the term used when an animal displays a conditioned response when exposed to a neutral stimulus that is similar but not identical to the original CS?

   a) spontaneous recovery

   b) discrimination

   c) generalization

   d) renewal

8 What is one explanation for the 'long shelf-life' of the Little Albert study?

9 How did the findings of John Garcia and his colleagues violate the assumption of equipotentiality?

10 Explain two ways in which evaluative conditioning differs from ordinary classical conditioning.

11 Operant conditioning through the removal of a (generally) unpleasant or aversive stimulus is known as:

   a) positive reinforcement

   b) negative reinforcement

   c) positive punishment

   d) negative punishment

12 Operant conditioning through the removal of a pleasant or reward stimulus is known as:

   a) positive reinforcement

   b) negative reinforcement

   c) positive punishment

   d) negative punishment

13 What is the major difference between Thorndike's law of effect and Skinner's operant conditioning?

14 Training animals to perform tricks is generally accomplished with the operant conditioning technique or techniques known as:

   a) continuous reinforcement

   b) negative reinforcement

   c) shaping through successive reinforcement or chaining

   d) partial punishment

15 Why do we say that in operant conditioning 'the organism teaches itself'?

16 Differentiate the four partial reinforcement schedules.

17 Define the terms *cognitive map* and *latent learning.*

18 If an animal refuses to learn a behaviour because it conflicts with an instinctive behavioural pattern, it is known as

   a) equipotentiality

   b) instinctive drift

   c) fixed action pattern

   d) latent learning

19 Outline modelling theory of observational learning.

20 Explain the cognitive processes that take place in observational learning.

21 Explain why psychologists interested in observational learning are excited by mirror neurons.

 Visit the online resources that accompany this book: www.oup.com/uk/jarvis-okami1e

CHAPTER 8

PERCEPTION, SENSATION, AND ATTENTION

LEARNING OUTCOMES

By the end of this chapter you should be able to:

- Define perception and related concepts, including sensation and transduction, and outline the field of psychophysics with particular reference to sensory thresholds, signal detection, and sensory adaptation

- Evaluate the nature and scope of subliminal perception in the light of research and apply this to judging the claims sometimes made of its power

- Understand the nature of light energy and how the eye works with particular regard to photoreception, transduction of visual stimuli, and the interpretive role of the visual cortex

- Analyse the role of trichromacy and opponent processes in colour perception

- Understand the nature of sound and how the ear works with particular regard to transduction of aural stimuli and the interpretive role of the auditory cortex

- Comment on the unique features of touch perception and the skin as a sense organ

- Explain gate control theory as an explanation for pain phenomena

- Understand processes of perceptual organization with particular regard to the Gestalt principles including the importance of proximity, similarity, closure, and continuity

- Critically discuss research into depth perception and draw appropriate conclusions regarding its origins

- Critically consider the likely role of evolution and culture in perception with particular regard to experience, expectation, and attention, and comment on research into cultural differences in perceptual set

- Take a position on Gibson's radical alternative to orthodox views of perception

- Evaluate the possibility of extrasensory perception, with particular regard to the disparity between positive findings of meta-analyses and the more sceptical interpretations of most psychologists

Perception can be defined formally as the processes by which we take in and make sense of information about the outside—and sometimes internal—world. The 'make sense of' is absolutely critical here. The old adage 'seeing is believing' is simply not true as far as most psychologists are concerned. Let us illustrate this with a picture I (Matt) took recently (see Figure 8.1). This is one of a sequence of pictures of an outdoor fire. There is relatively little visual information here to interpret—no clear lines or texture, few colours, and shifting soft-focus flames. Yet our brains interpret what we see and many people *perceive* a sinister figure with glowing eyes. Having been present I am pleased to say that no such figure made its presence known at the time!

So how do we know what is real and what is not? Perhaps we cannot know what is real and what is not in a way that would fully satisfy every philosophical argument. However, it is through the evidence of our senses and perceptions that we come to *believe* we know what is real and what is not. **Sensing** occurs when our sense organs receive raw physical or chemical energy from the natural world—light through the eyes; sound waves (vibrations) through the ears; chemical properties of objects through the nose and taste buds; heat, cold, and pressure through the skin. This received energy is then converted into neural signals, a process known as **transduction**. The signals are then sent to the brain where most cognitive psychologists believe it is subject to intensive interpretation. **Perception** occurs when we actually *see* the face, *hear* the sound, *taste* the sweetness, and *feel* the heat (see Figure 8.2).

Thus, to some degree, the often-used term 'sensation' can be misleading because it seems to imply an experience of some sort ('When you tickle my back I get a weird sensation' or 'I love the sensation of ice cream sliding down my throat on a hot day'). Indeed, what we often call 'sensations' in casual speech are actually perceptions. *All conscious experiences derived from physical or chemical information flowing through our sense organs are perceptions.* Without the interpretation of sensory information by the brain there is no experience of 'sensation' at all and no ability

> **KEY IDEAS** sensation, transduction, and perception **Sensation** is the receiving of raw physical or chemical energy through the sense organs. **Transduction** is the conversion of raw physical or chemical energy into sensory signals. **Perception** is the collective term for the processes by which the brain organizes and interprets these sensory signals.

FIGURE 8.1 **What do you see?** The image is of the centre of a fire. The black shape is simply a piece of wood. However, people tend to perceive a frightening shape with glowing eyes.

Source: Photo by Matt Jarvis.

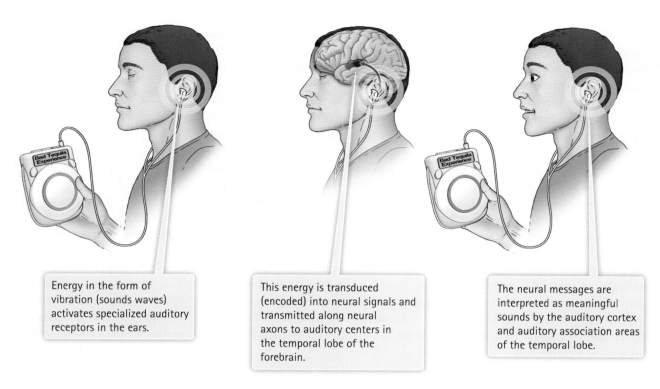

FIGURE 8.2 The road to perception.

Energy in the form of vibration (sounds waves) activates specialized auditory receptors in the ears.

This energy is transduced (encoded) into neural signals and transmitted along neural axons to auditory centers in the temporal lobe of the forebrain.

The neural messages are interpreted as meaningful sounds by the auditory cortex and auditory association areas of the temporal lobe.

to engage in activity directed towards any sort of goal—from taking a few steps in a room to completing a PhD. So remember: 'sensing' is something that happens to your sense organs and neurons; 'perception' is something that happens to *you*.

PSYCHOPHYSICS: THE RELATIONSHIP BETWEEN STIMULI AND PERCEPTION

> **KEY IDEAS** psychophysics and psychophysicists **Psychophysics** is the scientific study of the relationship between sensation and perception. **Psychophysicists** are the scientists who study sensation, perception, and the relationship between them.

In the course of ordinary experience, sensing and perception are seamlessly linked. However, it is useful to separate them for scientific purposes. The field of the relationship between physical stimuli and how they are perceived through the senses is known as **psychophysics** and those who study it are called **psychophysicists**. The distinction between sensing and perception becomes clear when one considers unusual disorders such as *motion blindness*—the inability to perceive movement, a condition which may result from brain damage to the visual cortex or certain other cortical regions (Cooper et al, 2012). In motion blindness, sensing and perception are no longer seamlessly linked—the visual *sense organs* (eyes) are working perfectly well, performing their task of receiving light and transducing visual images into electrochemical signals. However, visual *perception*—the meaning accorded these signals by the brain—is out of order. Individuals who have acquired motion blindness can see perfectly well—if everything is still. However, when something moves, it is perceived in a series of 'freeze frame' snapshots. For example, watching a single black Porsche glide down the road is watching a series of images of many black Porsches lined up behind one another. As depicted in Figure 8.3, even pouring a cup of coffee can be a daunting task for those with motion blindness.

FIGURE 8.3 In motion blindness perception is disordered, but sensing is in order. In motion blindness, the world is perceived as a sequence of 'freeze frames' or snapshots. The fluid from the tip of the coffee pot to the cup appears as a stream of coffee frozen in space. By the time a motion–blindness patient perceives the image of a full cup, the cup is already overflowing.

Even if both your sensory and perceptual systems are in working order, however, there is no guarantee that you will perceive a sensory stimulus. For one thing, a stimulus such as a sound must occur within the normal range our sense organs evolved to detect. Because dog whistles are designed to produce sound waves at *frequencies* too high for human ears to perceive, a dog whistle would not disturb us. Similarly, we would be unable to use *echolocation* to find our way around a pitch-dark cave or locate our dinner as bats do. They navigate and find prey by sending calls out and detecting the resultant sound waves bouncing off solid objects (Jones, 2005).

Another problem is one of simple *strength* rather than range. Even if a stimulus is within normal human perceptual range, it must be strong enough to be detected. In order for you to hear the couple in the flat next door to you arguing, they have to be shouting loudly enough for your ears to hear. What psychologists call an **absolute threshold** of stimulus intensity must be reached. The absolute threshold is the minimum intensity of a stimulus necessary for it to be detected by a human or non-human animal at least 50% of the time. Absolute thresholds for each sense differ from person to person, and may also differ under various sorts of psychological conditions—for example, a person's emotional state, expectations for a situation, or how much attention he or she is directing towards a particular stimulus. Thus, commonly used approximations for the absolute threshold of various senses may be misleading. For example, it is often said that the absolute threshold for vision is equivalent to 'a candle flame seen at 30 miles on a dark, clear night'. Yet, the absolute threshold for a person walking alone on a clear, dark, but unfamiliar and *scary* road is likely to be different from that for a person walking home on the same clear, dark night after a pleasant meal at a neighbour's house.

There is a different sort of threshold involved in detecting *differences* between two sensory stimuli—for example, in the lengths of two lines, brightness of two lights, or loudness of two sounds. This is known as the **just noticeable difference (JND)**. The JND was first described by an early psychophysicist, Ernst Weber (1795–1878). Weber noticed something interesting about the JND for weights. When people were

❭ KEY IDEAS the absolute threshold and just noticeable difference (JND) **The absolute threshold** of a stimulus can be defined as the minimum intensity necessary for it to be detected by the appropriate sense organ 50% of the time. The **JND** is the smallest difference between two stimuli that can be detected by the appropriate sense organ at least 50% of the time.

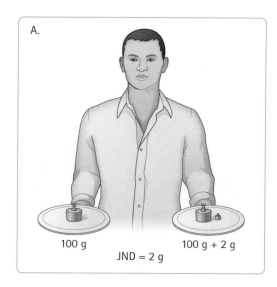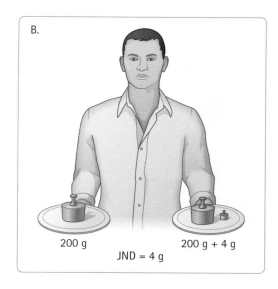

FIGURE 8.4 The just-noticeable difference (JND). In the left drawing (A) the man can detect the difference between a relatively light standard weight (100 g) and another weight just 2 g heavier. However, in the right drawing (B), the standard weight is much heavier (200 g), so the comparison weight must also be heavier for a difference to be detected. Notice, however, that the *ratio* of the JND remains constant: the comparison weight in the right must be *twice* as heavy as that in the left to be noticed when compared with a standard weight that is also *twice* as heavy.

asked to lift a particular weight (termed the *standard*) and then to lift a comparison weight that differed somewhat in heaviness, their ability to detect a difference between the two weights was highly dependent upon the weight of the standard. If the weight of the standard (the first weight) was light, people were able to detect even slight differences between the standard and a heavier comparison weight. But if the standard was heavy, a much greater difference between the two weights was necessary before a difference could be detected (see Figure 8.4).

Weber found that this relationship was true of the JND applied to the other senses. For example, the ability to notice a difference between the magnitudes of two lamp lights is proportionate to the magnitude of the first lamp (termed the *standard*). It would be easy to notice the difference between a 75-watt bulb and a 100-watt bulb, but not between a 300-watt bulb and a 325-watt bulb, even though the difference is 25 watts in both cases. If you think about it, you can see that this principle operates in many aspects of ordinary life unrelated to sensing and perceiving. For example, you might drive a mile to avoid paying an extra 10 pence a litre for petrol, but you would probably not even notice a 10p difference when buying a car. Thus, for any given stimulus, the JND is always directly proportionate to the level of the standard. Weber's colleague and the founder of psychophysics, Gustav Fechner (1801–87), expressed this idea in mathematical terms, calling it **Weber's law**.

Signal Detection Theory

The concepts of absolute threshold and JND are important contributions to understanding perception, but they do not fully explain how stimuli come to be detected. This is because Weber and Fechner failed to factor in a most important variable:

> **KEY IDEAS** Weber's law
> **Weber's law** is a mathematical expression of the idea that for any given stimulus, the just noticeable difference (JND) is always proportionate to the level of the standard stimulus.

human judgement and bias. A simple example: when in our younger days the authors (separately) trained intensively in the martial arts we could detect the sounds of footsteps of strangers walking up behind us while they were still some distance away. This is because our attention was strongly focused on the possibility of physical attack. But nowadays, since we no longer practise martial arts, you'd probably have to clear your throat loudly a half a centimetre away before we would be aware of you on the street. Thus, under certain psychological conditions, weak signals may be detected because the person judges them to be important or is biased in favour of recognizing them. Under other conditions, even strong signals may go undetected. **Signal detection theory** emerged to help understand the interaction between human judgement and bias and the detection of stimuli (Macmillan and Creelman, 2005).

Signal detection theorists have found two specific ways in which human judgement and predisposition interfere in signal detection: *noise* and *response bias*. **Noise** acknowledges that sensory stimuli do not occur in a vacuum—they occur within a specific context consisting of other, competing, sensory stimuli and various psychological states. An expected knock in a quiet hall of residence room will be much easier to detect than an unexpected knock that occurs while a loud party is going on next door.

Response bias means that for any given stimulus one may be biased in favour of detection or against detection. Bias can result from one's motivations and expectations in a given situation. If you were in your hall eagerly expecting your romantic partner to knock on the door, you might find yourself mistaking all sorts of irrelevant sounds for a knock, and the chances of your failing to hear the actual knock would approach zero. On the other hand, if you were studying hard, focused upon your work, and hoping no one would come by to bother you, you might be biased against detecting a knock and fail to respond when a knock actually occurred.

> **KEY IDEAS** signal detection theory **Signal detection theory** is a theory that attempts to explain how stimuli are detected by factoring in the variables of human judgement and bias.

> **KEY IDEAS** noise and response bias In signal detection theory, **noise** acknowledges that detection of sensory stimuli may be affected by the occurrence of other, competing stimuli, or by varying psychological states of the perceiver. In signal detection theory, **response bias** refers to the fact that a person may be biased in favour of, or against, the detection of a stimulus.

THINKING CREATIVELY

Devise a simple experiment to demonstrate the effect of 'noise' (not necessarily auditory noise, just competing stimuli) on the detection of a target stimulus. HINT: auditory noise might be the easiest to work with, so perhaps think in terms of detecting a sound with and without noise. If you are feeling confident feel free to use a different sensory modality or to run more than two conditions.

Sensory adaptation

Another influence on the detection of stimuli is **sensory adaptation**, the tendency for sensitivity to stimuli to be lessened over time during continuous exposure. I (Paul) once had a friend who used to burn a particular brand of pine-sandalwood incense in her home that I found irresistible. I bought some, hoping my home would smell as fabulous as hers did. However, it seemed that no matter how much I burned, my house never smelled of incense except for a few minutes first thing in the morning. The answer to this riddle is sensory adaptation. When visiting my friend, I walked in off the street right into the floating aroma of the incense. In my own home, however, I was drenched in the scent all day, so my perception quickly became desensitized to it. You experience sensory adaptation every time you get into a blisteringly hot bath, only to have it seem to turn cool on you within a very short time.

> **KEY IDEAS** sensory adaptation **Sensory adaptation** is the tendency for one's sensitivity to stimuli to be lessened over time during continuous exposure.

Subliminal Perception

> KEY IDEAS subliminal
perception **Subliminal perception**
occurs when a stimulus is perceived
unconsciously (implicitly). This can
occur when it is below the absolute
threshold or is presented too briefly
to reach conscious awareness.

It is sometimes possible to perceive a stimulus unconsciously, or *implicitly*, when it is either below the absolute threshold or presented too briefly to reach conscious awareness. This is known as **subliminal perception**. For example, a person may be temporarily affected by messages or images viewed on a screen even if these messages or images are flashed much too briefly to reach conscious awareness. Psychologist Morris Eagle (1959) asked research participants to judge the personality of a boy by looking at his picture. However, half the participants were first subliminally flashed an image of the boy engaged in an aggressive act (throwing a birthday cake) and the other half were flashed an image of the boy smiling and holding the cake. The group that had been flashed the subliminal image of the boy holding the cake gave a much more positive evaluation of the boy's personality.

Subliminal perception was also demonstrated by Robert B. Zajonc (pronounced *Zy*-once) and his colleagues as part of their programme of research into the **mere exposure effect**–the tendency for people to prefer something they were exposed to repeatedly over something in the same category to which they had no exposure (Monohan, Murphy, and Zajonc, 2000, discussed further in Chapter 21). Zajonc and his colleagues presented one group of non-Chinese research participants with a series of 25 Chinese ideographs (written characters) subliminally flashed only once, too quickly to be consciously perceived (five microseconds). Another group was presented with only five ideographs, each character subliminally flashed five times. When the participants subsequently viewed all the ideographs, they preferred the characters they had seen repeatedly (but subliminally) over those they had viewed only once.

The mere exposure effect is used to good advantage by advertisers in product placement campaigns, where it is not necessary to provide any information whatever about a product beyond the fact that it is being used by a character in a film, TV show, music video, or video game. Simple exposure, whether or not it is recalled later, may be enough to turn preferences in the advertiser's favour, particularly if one is already familiar with the product being placed (Matthes, Schemer, and Wirth, 2007).

DEBUNKING

In 1957, newspapers reported a startling claim: advertiser James Vicary had announced that he had used a device to subliminally subject thousands of cinema-goers to the messages 'Drink Coke' and 'Eat Popcorn' as they watched the featured film. According to Vicary, there was a subsequent 18% increase in Coke sales, and a 58% jump in popcorn sales (Pratkanis, 1992). This was the first public claim that had been made about the effects of subliminal perception. Initial outrage was followed by disappointment, however. When Vicary failed to publish his findings, pressure was put on him to release his data. Finally, he admitted that his claims of having tested 'thousands of subjects' in a six-week long study were largely concocted—a publicity stunt to reverse the fortunes of the advertising agency in which he had a share (Rogers, 1992–3).

So what can be achieved using subliminal perception techniques? There is some evidence from fMRI brain imaging techniques (see 'The basic technology of neuroscience' in Chapter 4) that subliminal messages may register in the brain (Bahrami, Lavie, and Rees, 2007), and researchers have shown that people's moods can be affected through subliminal techniques (Ruys and Stapel, 2008). However, no convincing evidence exists that subliminal *persuasion* as claimed by Vicary is even possible. Fifty years of controlled experimental studies have repeatedly shown that the most typical response to subliminal advertising messages is *no* response at all, or at best very weak, transient, and inconsistent effects (Vargas, 2008). If you are fearful that advertisers are using these techniques frequently, consider that weak, transient, and inconsistent effects are *not* what advertisers are after. Who needs subliminal advertising when effective product placement is routinely written into songs, novels, computer games, and television scripts (Chang, Newell, and Salmon, 2009)?

What about the use of subliminal techniques to further one's own personal goals rather than to sell products or political candidates to unsuspecting consumers? People spend a fortune every year on recordings that claim to use subliminal messages to improve their memory or study skills, boost self-esteem, break unwanted habits, or heal psychic traumas (Natale, cited in Pratkanis et al, 1994). But do these methods work? Controlled research repeatedly indicates that they do not (eg, Froufe and Schwartz, 2001).

In a particularly clever test of these recordings, Pratkanis et al (1994) randomly assigned a group of participants to receive either a memory improvement subliminal tape or one intended to increase self-esteem. However, without their knowledge, a subset of the memory group actually received the self-esteem tape, and a subset of the self-esteem group got the memory tape. In all, those in the self-esteem group reported that they felt better about themselves—regardless of whether they had received the memory or the self-esteem tape—and those in the memory group reported that their memories had improved, again, regardless of which tape they actually had received. However, by objective measures of memory and self-esteem that included a battery of standard tests, there were no significant improvements in any of the groups as a result of the tapes—neither in memory nor self-esteem.

READ THIS

The following are some basic introductions to psychophysics and basic perceptual processes:

Stevens, S.S. (2017). *Psychophysics: Introduction to its Perceptual, Neural and Social Prospects.* London: Routledge.

Gescheider, G.A. (2013). *Psychophysics: The Fundamentals.* Hove: Psychology Press.

VISUAL PERCEPTION

You may take for granted that there are only five human senses—sight, smell, taste, touch, and hearing—but many researchers believe the number is closer to nine or even more. For example, balance is sometimes referred to as a sense, as is pain, temperature, placement of the body in space (the 'kinaesthetic sense'), and more. One reason why an exact figure for the number of human senses cannot be given is that researchers do not agree on a precise definition of the term *sense*. Regardless of how many senses there may be, however, there are six primary areas of the body that house them: the eyes, nose, tongue, ears, skin, and the non-skeletal interior of the body—including muscles, joints, tendons, and internal organs. These are the sense organs, and in the coming pages we will investigate how they work, beginning with the eye.

Many of the sense organs perform more than one function for the body. For example, the tongue is essential for spoken language as well as housing the taste buds, and structures within the ear contribute to the sense of balance as well as hearing. But the eye has one function and one function only: *to receive light and process the images that result* so that the person may see. Light is a form of

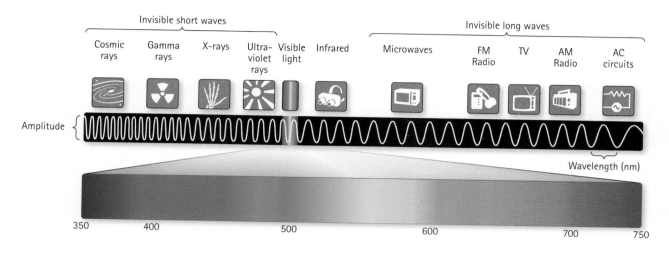

FIGURE 8.5 The electromagnetic spectrum. The earth is surrounded by a sea of electromagnetic energy, but only a very small portion is visible. Instruments such as radio, television, and X-ray radiography devices have been designed specifically to detect energy at non-visible wavelengths.

❯ **KEY IDEAS** electromagnetic radiation, wavelength, and amplitude **Electromagnetic radiation** is energy that travels around the world in waves of variable intensity (amplitude) that are separated by varying lengths known as wavelengths. **Wavelength** is a measure of the lengths between electromagnetic waves. **Amplitude** is the intensity of a sound or light output source expressed in the height of light or sound waves.

electromagnetic radiation—energy that travels around the world in waves that are separated by varying lengths, known as **wavelengths** (see Figure 8.5). All matter is electrically charged and produces radiation, but visible light exists only in a very narrow spectrum of electromagnetic wavelengths. You can see in Figure 8.5 that as the wavelength varies in the spectrum, the colour that we see also varies.

In addition to varying by wavelength, light also varies by **amplitude**. Amplitude is a measure of the *intensity* of a light source, expressed as the height of a light wave. In Figure 8.5, the light waves depicted differ by wavelength across the spectrum, but they are all of equal height and therefore of equal amplitude.

The Eye

How does light turn into visual images in our brain? In order for images to form, light reflected from an object must first pass through the cornea, a transparent window membrane which covers the eye and is probably the most important single component in the eye's ability to transmit visual imagery (see Figure 8.6). Light is *refracted* (bent) as it passes through the cornea so that it may be focused on the retina.

From the cornea the light passes through the **pupil**, a small opening in the **iris**. The iris is a muscular structure that expands and contracts, altering the size of the pupil to allow more or less light into the eye. If the available light is low, the iris expands, dilating the pupil to let more in, and if there is strong light, it contracts in order to reduce pupil size and reduce the light entering the eye.

Light is then conveyed through another transparent structure, the **lens**. Like the iris, the lens alters its shape, but it does so by flattening or thickening to create an even sharper focus of the light upon the **retina**—a light-sensitive membrane spread out across most of the eye's inner surface. It is upon the retina that an image is actually formed. However, before reaching the retina, the light must make the longest leg of its journey, through the gel-like substance known as the **vitreous humour** which fills 80% of the volume of the eye and constitutes much of what is ordinarily thought of as the eyeball.

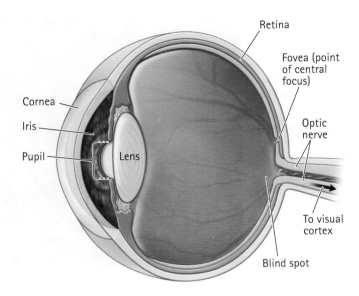

FIGURE 8.6 A cross-section of the human eye.

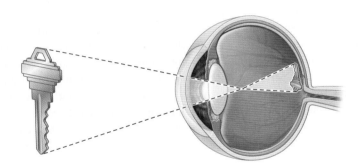

FIGURE 8.7 Images that form on the retina are inverted and reversed. As a result of the angle at which light hits the eye, images that form on the retina are inverted and left/right reversed. It is not until they are transduced into neural signals and these signals reach the brain that the images are perceived as images in their actual orientation.

When light finally reaches the retina, images are formed that are upside down and left/right reversed (see Figure 8.7). However, 'seeing' has not yet occurred. It is not until these images are transduced to electrical signals and these signals reach the brain that the process of seeing—that is, visual perception—actually begins and the retinal images are interpreted by the brain in their correct 'right side up' orientation.

Photoreceptors

The retina contains over 125 million **photoreceptors**—neurons dedicated to capturing light. Photoreceptors initiate the process of transduction, which changes light into electrical signals to be sent to the brain. There are two principal types of photoreceptors in the human eye: *rods* and *cones*, which earned their names as a result of their distinctive shapes (see Figure 8.8).

❯ KEY IDEAS photoreceptors; rods and cones **Photoreceptors** are specialized neurons dedicated to capturing light in order to initiate transduction. **Rods** are photoreceptors specialized to allow night vision and vision in low light. **Cones** are photoreceptors specialized for day vision, colour vision, and capturing fine detail. Cones are concentrated in a small region near the centre of the retina called the **fovea**; images focused here provide the clearest images and sharpest focus.

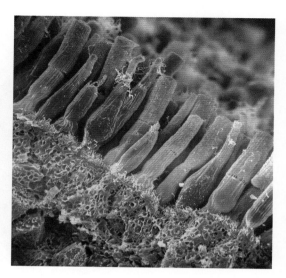

FIGURE 8.8 Rods and cones. Rods and cones magnified approximately 14,000 times. Rods (*green*) are shaped like cylinders; cones (blue) have a pear shape at the bottom and a cone shape at the top. Rods are specialized to allow night vision, but are not good at capturing colour or detail. Cones are specialized for daylight, detail, and colour, but they need more light to function.
Source: Science History Images/Alamy Stock Photo.

Rods and cones not only have different shapes, but they also perform different functions. **Rods** are specialized to allow us to see at night—they respond in low light, but are not particularly good at capturing fine detail. Moreover, their peak sensitivities for responding to light do not correspond to those necessary for human beings to perceive colour particularly well. This is why it is difficult to perceive colour at night. However, rods do not perform at their maximum efficiency immediately upon encountering darkness. A period of *dark adaptation* is necessary; it generally takes about 30 minutes for the rods to fully adapt after the lights go out or the person enters a darkened room. That is why, when you enter a darkened cinema, at first you cannot see your own hand, but within a relatively short time you can count the kernels of your neighbour's popcorn.

Cones are specialized for daylight vision and colour vision. They need more light to function than do rods, but they allow for perception of detail, and their peak sensitivities to light include those wavelengths associated with human colour vision. Although cones are scattered in various areas of the retina, there is a small region near the centre of the retina that contains a particularly large concentration of cones. This area is known as the **fovea** (see Figure 8.8). Because cones are concentrated in the fovea—and these cones are slightly thinner in shape, allowing for this concentration—we perceive images that fall on the fovea especially clearly (Medeiros, 2006).

Images seem less sharply focused the farther from the fovea they get (Levi, Klein, and Aitsebaomo, 1985). You can see this for yourself. Close your left eye and hold up both of your index fingers in front of you about 10 cm apart. Fix your gaze on your right index finger. Your left finger will seem out of focus because its image is to the side of the fovea.

The fovea contains virtually no rods. Instead, rods exist primarily in the peripheral areas of the retina. Because rods are more responsive to dim light than are cones, we actually may have superior vision at night by looking out of the corners of our eyes—a trick used by stargazers to spot dim stars (Wolfe et al, 2009).

When rods and cones receive light, they produce chemical changes that initiate transduction of light into neural signals. The signals are modified further by cells whose axons (extensions) are bundled together in a structure known as the **optic nerve**. The optic nerve carries the neural signals out from the back of each retina to the brain. Interestingly, the area where the optic nerve leaves the retina, known as the **optic disc**, has neither rods nor cones and is therefore 'blind'. Although we do not notice this **blind spot** in the normal course of our lives because the brain 'fills in' the missing information for us, based on available information (Ramachandran, 1992), you can demonstrate its existence for yourself fairly easily, as shown in Figure 8.9.

FIGURE 8.9 See your blind spot. To 'see' the blind spot caused by an absence of either rods or cones at the optic disc, close your left eye and fix your gaze on the 'F' in this image. Hold the book approximately 15 cm away, and adjust this distance backwards or forwards until the yellow dot disappears.

THINKING PRACTICALLY

What advice might you give a troop of Scouts or Guides going for a night walk in the woods in order to keep themselves most safe from accidents? HINT: you might want to consider sensory adaptation, the blind spot, and the roles of rods and cones.

The Visual Cortex

As the optic nerves exit the back of the cornea at the optic disc, each nerve includes information about the right visual field and the left visual field. (Recall from Chapter 2 that *each* eye contains a right and a left visual field.) This information passes first through the thalamus, a structure of the lower forebrain. From the thalamus, the signals are relayed to the **visual cortex**, a complex, multilayered area dense with hundreds of millions of neurons, located at the back of the brain just above the top of your neck. It is here that much of the information conveyed by the optic nerves is interpreted and perceived as visual images of the world.

It is also in the visual cortex that sensations of touch relayed from the hands and fingers are interpreted as visual images, hence blind people can still form mental images provided their blindness is the result of an eye problem rather than a brain one. This demonstrates that the sensory systems of the human brain possess at least some degree of **plasticity**.

Colour Perception

> *There is no red in a 700 nm light, just as there is no pain in the hooves of a kicking horse.*
>
> —Steven Shevell (cited by Wolfe et al, 2009, p 105)

As briefly mentioned earlier, the colour we see varies according to the wavelength of light reflected from objects. For example, a red rose absorbs all the wavelengths of light the sun or a light bulb can throw its way *except* wavelengths at between approximately 650–750 nanometres. These are the wavelengths associated with the colour red, and they are reflected off the surface of the rose to be captured by our vision system. However, *the colour red does not exist in these waves of light*. As Isaac Newton pointed out in 1704, 'The rays, properly speaking, are not themselves coloured.' In other words, colour is not a physical property of an object; instead,

❯ **KEY IDEAS** the optic nerve, optic disc, and blind spot The **optic nerve** carries neural signals from the back of the retina to the central nervous system. The **optic disc** is the area where the optic nerve leaves the retina. The **blind spot** is an area formed by the optic disc that contains neither rods nor cones.

❯ **KEY IDEAS** the visual cortex The **visual cortex** is the area at the back of the brain that receives and interprets visual neural signals from the eyes.

it is created by the brain of the animal perceiving the object. Colour results from an interaction between light and brains—just as pain results from an interaction between the hooves of a kicking horse and the brain of the unfortunate recipient of the kick.

The fact that colour is a psychological property rather than a physical one becomes even clearer when we consider that in the light of the moon the many colours that were visible just a few hours earlier vanish (Wolfe et al, 2009). Obviously, a mysterious force does not visit the world each night to drain every thing of its colour. Instead, the dim light of nighttime primarily stimulates the rods of the retina, which do not have the capacity to create colour vision alone.

Trichromacy

Although most languages have relatively few names for different colours, under good lighting conditions human beings can distinguish at least one million different shades of colour and possibly as many as ten million (Kaiser and Boynton, 1996). How are all those millions of colours formed?

During the early nineteenth century, Thomas Young proposed that any colour could be created if the light waves typically associated with three primary colours—blue, green, and red—were combined at various intensities and in various combinations— a process known as *additive colour mixture.*

> **KEY IDEAS** trichromatic theory **The trichromatic theory of colour** explains how all colours are created through the additive mixture of blue, green, and red. Trichromacy results because S-, M-, and L-cones in the retina are particularly sensitive to short, medium, or long wavelengths—which correspond to the perception of blue, green, and red. **Red–green colour blindness** takes place when M- and L-cones are equally sensitive to red and green, making differentiation of these colours impossible.

Young's idea was elaborated upon in the mid-nineteenth century by Hermann von Helmholtz and ultimately came to be known as **trichromatic theory of colour vision.** This theory has contributed importantly to our understanding of colour vision. In the days of Young and Helmholtz, the science of vision was not advanced enough to work this out. But researchers during the mid-twentieth century identified three types of cones in the vision system. As we have discussed, it is cones that best allow for the perception of detail and colour. Although the three types of cones can be stimulated by all spectrums of light, the peak sensitivity of each type of cone falls within a different spectrum: *short-, medium-,* and *long-wavelength.* Thus the cones are known generally as S-cones, M-cones, and L-cones. It happens that the three primary colours identified by Young and Helmholtz are associated with these spectrums—blue with S-cones, red with M-cones, and green with L-cones. Thus, S-, M-, and L-cones allow us to distinguish between light at different wavelengths, and to perceive different colours as a result of the additive mixture of these wavelengths of light. When a person's S-cones are working properly, but the M- or L-cones are not functioning (or are absent entirely), this gives rise to a genetic condition known as **red–green colour blindness.**

Opponent process theory

> **KEY IDEAS** opponent process theory **Opponent process theory** is the theory of colour vision that proposes that because certain wavelengths of light cannot be combined in an additive process, colours are created in colour vision by mixing in three opposing pairs: blue vs yellow, red vs green, and black vs white.

Trichromacy is not the whole story of colour vision. As Ewald Hering first observed during the late nineteenth century, certain additive combinations cannot occur in colour vision. For example, you can probably visualize combining blue and green to get a bluish green (aqua), or red and yellow to get to get a reddish yellow (orange), but you cannot create a reddish green or a bluish yellow in colour vision (Wolfe et al, 2009). From this observation Hering created a 'rival' theory to trichromacy known as the **opponent process theory** of colour vision. Hering proposed that, because some colours appeared to be 'opposed' to one another, colours actually were mixed in three opposing pairs: blue or yellow, red or green, and black or white. This contrasts with trichromacy, which states that all colours are perceived as a result of the mixture of blue, green, and red.

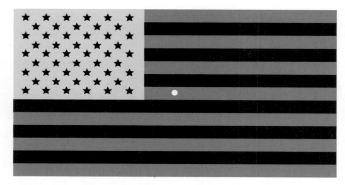

FIGURE 8.10 Opponent process theory and the negative afterimage. For 30 seconds stare at the white dot only (don't look around you). After 30 seconds have passed, look to the white space at the right. You should see a much more familiarly coloured flag. Why does this afterimage effect occur? Staring for a long time at the image of the flag causes the sensors responding at peak efficiency to black, green, and yellow to 'tire' (sensory adaptation). When you suddenly shift to a white surface, they are no longer required to function and they swing back momentarily to their opposing colour. Yellow shifts to blue, green to red, and black to white.

According to more modern views of opponent process theory emerging during the mid-twentieth century, specific *opponent neurons* in the retina and the thalamus of the brain will respond with stimulation from one part of the spectrum of light (say, the blue spectrum) while simultaneously inhibiting response to another spectrum (in this case, yellow)—creating an opponent process response pairing blue and yellow. The same occurs for the black/white and red/green pairings (Goldstein, 2010). When a colour is a mixture of the basic opponent process colours—for example, orange is a mixture of red and yellow—one of the dimensions of each opponent neurons is firing, and the other suppressed. You can see opponent processes at work in the phenomenon of the *negative afterimage* in Figure 8.10.

Although opponent process theory was at first a 'rival' theory to trichromacy, during the twentieth century research has established that trichromacy and opponent processes are both part of the colour vision system (Hubel, 1995). The retina does contain the three types of cones suggested by trichromatic theory. However, some neurons in the retina (and the brain) react only to blue but are inhibited from responding to yellow, while others respond to yellow but are inhibited from responding to blue. The same holds true for the red-green dimension (Abramov and Gordon, 1994).

AURAL PERCEPTION

Most people would probably agree that vision is the sense that contributes most importantly to functioning in daily life. However, hearing—technically, **audition**—is not very far behind. Hearing not only alerts us to potential dangers or opportunities, but it helps us express ourselves and communicate through language. For this reason, the famous humanitarian Helen Keller, who was both blind and deaf, claimed that deafness, not blindness, was her greatest handicap. She claimed that blindness cut her off from things, while deafness cut her off from people (quoted in du Feu and Fergusson, 2003, p 95).

❭ KEY IDEAS audition **Audition** is the technical term for the sense of hearing.

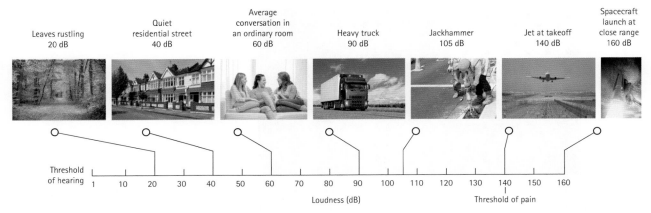

FIGURE 8.11 **Amplitude of common sounds. Long-term exposure to sound above 85 dB results in hearing loss. A decent rock or punk band amplified at close range equals approximately 140 dB, similar to a jet plane take-off. If you like a good gig it is worth keeping an eye (ear?) on your hearing and if you work regularly with live music or take children to gigs look into ear protection.**

Sources: leaves: S. Borisov/Shutterstock.com; street: Ron Ellis/Shutterstock.com; conversation: Syda Productions/Shutterstock.com; truck: Andrey Pavlov/Shutterstock.com; jackhammer: Lawrence Wee/Shutterstock.com; jet: MP_P/Shutterstock.com; spacecraft launch: Horizon International Images Limited/Alamy Stock Photo.

Sound

❯ **KEY IDEAS** frequency and pitch The **frequency** (of sound wave) represents the number of sound waves per second, expressed as Hertz units. **Pitch** is the 'highness' or 'lowness' of a sound, dependent on its frequency.

Just as the eyes do not see but instead collect and focus light, ears do not 'hear', they merely collect and amplify sound. But what exactly *is* sound? Sound is created when objects vibrate. When an object vibrates it causes vibrations in the air (or water) molecules surrounding it. In turn, these vibrations cause pressure changes in the air (or water) known as sound waves. If you recall, light waves vary by two properties, amplitude and wavelength. Sound waves also vary by two properties. The first is *amplitude*. As with light waves, sound wave amplitude refers to the intensity of the output source, expressed in the height of the wave. Amplitude is measured in units known as *decibels* (see Figure 8.11)—the higher the decibels the greater the perception of loudness.

The second property of sound is **frequency** (see Figure 8.12). Frequency refers to the rate of speed of vibration, or number of waves per second. Frequency is measured in *hertz* units, and it determines the **pitch**, or highness or lowness of the sound (eg, a flute vs a bass guitar). The faster the vibration, the greater will be the number of waves per second—and the higher will be the pitch of the sound.

The Ear

❯ **KEY IDEAS** the outer ear and the pinna **The outer ear** is the outer structure of the ear, consisting primarily of the pinna and ear canal. The **pinna** is the visible structure of the outer ear that collects sounds and orients us to the placement of their source.

The structure of the ear is divided into an *inner, middle,* and *outer ear* (see Figure 8.13). What most people call 'the ear' is actually the **pinna** of the **outer ear**. Only mammals have pinnae, and the size and shape of these structures vary considerably among different species. The pinna collects sounds and helps orient us as to the placement of their source (see Figure 8.13).

❯ **KEY IDEAS** the ear canal and tympanic membrane **The ear canal** (the ear hole) is an outer-ear structure that funnels sound to the eardrum or **tympanic membrane**. This is a membrane stretched across the end of the ear canal which vibrates in response to sound waves and marks the border between the outer and middle ear.

After sounds are collected, they are funnelled through the **ear canal**, an outer-ear structure whose primary purpose is to protect the membrane tightly stretched across it at the end. This is the **tympanic membrane** or *eardrum*. The eardrum vibrates in response to changes in air pressure (or water pressure if the sound is occurring under water). Your mother may have scared the wits out of you by warning that you'd go deaf if you pressed a cotton bud too far into your ear and

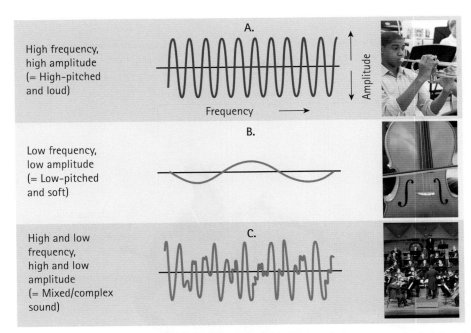

FIGURE 8.12 Frequency and amplitude of sound waves. Amplitude refers to the height of the sound wave and determines loudness. Amplitude is measured in decibels. Frequency refers to the number of waves per second and determines pitch. Frequency is measured in hertz units.

Sources: A: Monkey Business Images/Shutterstock.com; B: Minerva Studio/Shutterstock.com; C: Ted Foxx/Alamy Stock Photo.

broke the ear drum, but in fact, while this might hurt and could potentially cause serious damage through infection, a ruptured eardrum can typically heal without treatment.

The eardrum marks the border to the middle ear, which consists of three tiny bones, or **ossicles**, called the *hammer, anvil,* and *stirrup.* The vibrations of the eardrum are picked up by the ossicles, greatly magnified, and transmitted to a membrane-covered opening known as the *oval window* at the border of the middle and inner ear. From the oval window the sound waves are transferred to the **cochlea**, a small fluid-filled structure resembling a tube coiled in the shape of a snail. The cochlea is the central auditory component of the inner ear, and by the time sound vibrations reach it, they have been amplified dozens of times.

The fluid of the cochlea vibrates in response to the sound waves transmitted to the oval window, and this vibration causes rippling in the **basilar membrane**—a collection of stiff fibres within the cochlea. Embedded in the surface of these fibres are approximately 16,000 *hair cells*—specialized neurons that act as **auditory receptors**—much as rods and cones function as photoreceptors (see Figure 8.14).

It is in the hair cells that the transduction of sound from vibrations to neural signals begins. When the basilar membrane ripples in response to vibrations from the oval window, the hair cells are bent, resulting in the firing of neural signals. These signals are conveyed towards the cerebral cortex via the **auditory nerve**—collections of axons that emerge from the cochlea. This is similar to the way that visual signals are conveyed towards the brain along the optic nerve. As with visual signals, the auditory signals pass to the thalamus and ultimately reach the cortex. However,

> **KEY IDEAS** the ossicles and cochlea **Ossicles** are three tiny bones of the middle ear that amplify sound. The bones are called the hammer, anvil, and stirrup. The **cochlea** is a pea-sized, tube-like structure of the inner ear filled with fluid and curled into the shape of a snail. The cochlea is the central component of the inner ear.

> **KEY IDEAS** the basilar membrane and auditory receptors **The basilar membrane** is a collection of stiff fibres housed within the cochlea of the inner ear. The basilar membrane contains the hair cells that act as **auditory receptors**.

> **KEY IDEAS** the auditory nerve and cortex **The auditory nerve** conducts transduced auditory signals to the thalamus, to be then relayed to the **auditory cortex**, the portion of the temporal lobe responsible for interpreting transduced auditory signals.

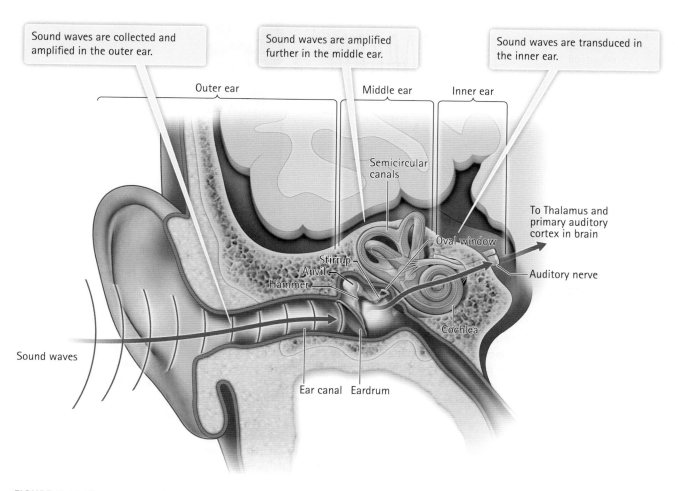

FIGURE 8.13 **The structure of the ear.**

rather than reaching the visual cortex in the occipital lobe of the forebrain as with visual signals, auditory signals reach the **auditory cortex** of the temporal lobe. It is here that they are interpreted and perceived as sound (see Figure 8.15).

Locating Sounds

As I close one eye and look at my desk, I am in no danger of thinking that the espresso cup sitting by my right hand actually sits to my left. Although we don't need two eyes to determine the location of an object in the visual field, the same cannot be said for the ears. It may be possible to locate the source of a sound with one ear, but using two ears makes this task immeasurably easier and more accurate. Why? Picture yourself in a cafe checking your social media on your phone as you wait for a friend to arrive. Suddenly, you hear your friend calling your name from just behind you as she approaches your table from the right-hand side. You turn to look over your right shoulder. But how do you know to turn to your right instead of left? First, the sound of her voice hits your right ear before it hits your left. The sound of your friend's voice is also louder in your right ear than the left. This is because the waves are partially blocked in their travel to your left ear by your head,

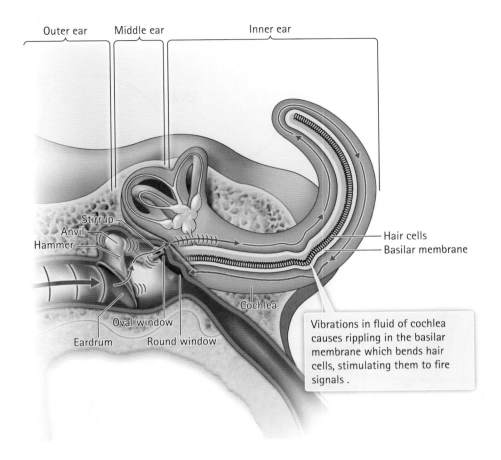

Outer ear   Middle ear   Inner ear

Stirrup
Anvil
Hammer

Hair cells
Basilar membrane

Cochlea

Oval window
Eardrum   Round window

Vibrations in fluid of cochlea causes rippling in the basilar membrane which bends hair cells, stimulating them to fire signals .

FIGURE 8.14 Magnification of portions of the inner and middle ear. This figure places the focus on the cochlea, uncoiling it slightly to demonstrate how it functions. When fluid of the cochlea vibrates in response to sound waves transferred to the oval window, rippling occurs in the basilar membrane. This rippling causes stimulation of hair cells that fire neurons to carry auditory signals to the thalamus and, ultimately, the auditory cortex.

which dampens the volume. Your brain factors in both the time of arrival (interaural time difference) and loudness differences (interaural level difference) to calculate the source of the sound of your friend's voice (see Figure 8.16).

TOUCH-RELATED PERCEPTION

You may never have thought of your skin, muscles, joints, tendons, and internal organs as 'sense organs', but they are. **Touch** is the skin's principal sense. The sense of touch can be broken down into three subdivisions: **tactition** (touching), **thermoception** (hot and cold), and **nociception** (pain). The muscles, tendons, and joints primarily contribute to the kinaesthetic sense—our awareness of where our limbs are and how we are moving. However, they may also contribute pain sensations and therefore are also part of the nociception subdivision of touch. Our internal organs also contribute to nociception when they are injured or malfunctioning.

> **KEY IDEAS** touch **Touch** is the principal sense that obtains sensory information from the skin. It is comprised of three subsenses: tactition, thermoception, and nociception. **Tactition** is literally the touch component of the sense of touch. **Thermoception** is the component of the sense of touch that registers temperature, whilst **nociception** is the component of the sense of touch that registers pain.

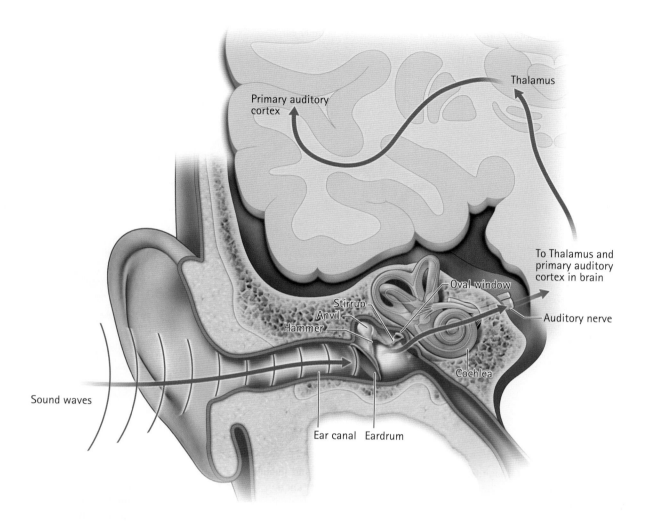

FIGURE 8.15 Auditory signals travel via the auditory nerve. Signals transduced by the hair cells of the cochlea leave the ear via the auditory nerve where they travel to the thalamus, and from there to the auditory cortex of the temporal lobe.

The Skin as Sense Organ

None of the sense organs can easily trigger the extremes of joy and misery provided by the skin. The sight of a sunset over a Greek beach or the flavour of England's finest farmhouse cheddar cheese can provide great pleasure, even joy—but it is doubtful that these experiences can compare to the joy experienced by a child receiving his mother's loving touch after waking from a nightmare, or the sensation of our first embrace and kiss from someone we have secretly loved for a long time. Similarly, listening to a song you hate (for Matt this would be anything by the Spice Girls) can involve pretty unpleasant sensations, but these cannot compare to the suffering experienced by a victim of torture whose skin is cut, shocked, or burned. *Touch* is truly the medium for the expression of love and hatred and the experience of pleasure and pain.

FIGURE 8.16 **How the brain locates the direction of sound.** Your brain locates the direction of sound by factoring in differences in the time sound waves arrive at each ear (the ITD) and differences in the level of the sound at each ear (the ILD).

Tactition

The 'touching' subdivision of the sense of touch is known as *tactition*. The possible range of tactile sensations is extraordinary. Just think about all the ways your skin has ever felt (apart from hot, cold, or pained): itchy, tickled, numb, prickly, smooth, bumpy, gooey, slimy, greasy, wet, dry, and on and on. It is through tactition that blind painters are able to 'see'. Touch is perhaps of more fundamental importance than the other senses, and is the first to emerge in the developing foetus (Ackerman, Nocera, and Bargh, 2010).

Physiologically speaking, how do we *feel* when touching? Touch receptors known as **mechanoreceptors** are embedded in the outer layer of skin (*epidermis*), the layer of skin underneath the epidermis (*dermis*), and the layer of *subcutaneous fat* below the dermis. Tactile sensations are converted into neural signals by mechanoreceptors and are then carried by trunks of nerves which travel to the spinal cord instead of directly to the brain as with other senses. The signals then travel up the spinal cord to the thalamus, and from there to the **somatosensory area** of the cortex where they are perceived as touch.

Psychologists came to appreciate the importance of tactition following the experiments of Harry Harlow (1905–81) and his colleagues during the 1950s and

❯ **KEY IDEAS** mechanoreceptors and the somatosensory area

Mechanoreceptors are sensory receptors embedded in the skin that play a role in tactition. The **somatosensory area** is a region of the cortex where tactile sensations are perceived.

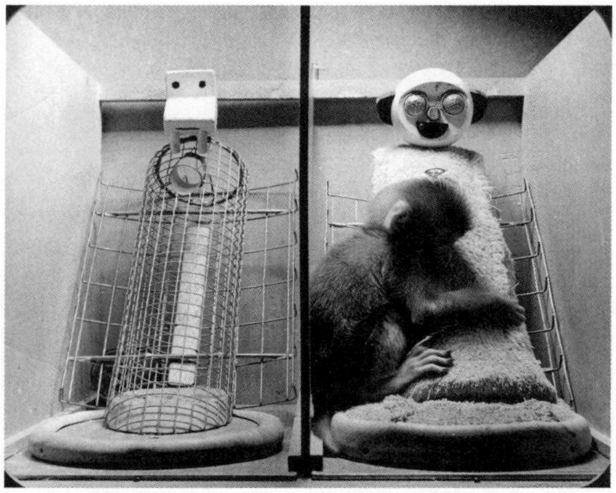

FIGURE 8.17 **One of Harry Harlow's monkeys and his 'mother'. Rhesus monkeys reared by a cloth-covered surrogate 'mother' preferred her over a surrogate made of wire cage even when the wire cage mother was the only place where the monkeys could obtain food (Harlow, 1958).**
Source: Science History Images/Alamy Stock Photo.

1960s—see Figure 8.17. In those days, most psychologists subscribed to the notion that infants came to develop strong affectional bonds with their mothers primarily because they depended upon their mothers for nourishment. However, Harlow and his colleagues created two 'surrogate mothers' to rear a group of rhesus monkeys that were taken from their mothers (Harlow, 1958). One of the surrogates was built from comfortable (and comforting) foam and terry towelling. The other was built from uncomfortable wire cage material. Half of the monkeys were fed by the terry towelling surrogate, and half by the wire surrogate. All of the monkeys strongly preferred the terry towelling mother regardless of which provided food. They all spent more time clinging to the cloth surrogate, and in particular were far more likely to run to it when they were frightened or upset. These results strongly imply that primates depend upon touch as a way of developing bonds of affection in infancy.

Touch may possess even more remarkable powers—the communication of specific emotions. Touch has always been known to have the capacity to communicate a *general* emotional tone—a warm and loving touch feels different from the touch of a person feeling pain or anger. However, preliminary research by Hertenstein et al has shown that human beings can communicate *specific* emotions through touch—disgust, love, fear, anger, even subtle emotions such as gratitude and sympathy (Hertenstein et al, 2006).

The touch of a person with whom one has a close relationship also has been shown to substantially lessen brain activation under conditions of stress and fear (Coan, Schaefer, and Davidson, 2006). James Coan and his colleagues enlisted a group of married women and subjected them to a procedure that included the threat of receiving electric shocks. The women underwent the procedure under three conditions: in one, each woman held her husband's hand during testing, in another the hand of a male stranger, and in a third, no one's hand. Brain imaging techniques (fMRI) were used to monitor the women's brains during testing. As Figure 8.18 shows, the touch of another person reduced the women's reports of agitation and unpleasant emotional responses to the experience, with the touch of the husband having a greater effect than the touch of a stranger. Interestingly, those who reported the happiest marriages showed the greatest effect in this regard (Coan et al, 2006).

Perhaps most astonishing of all, sensations of touch may activate unconscious decision-making processes and behaviours grounded in metaphor. Many metaphors make reference to sensations of touch; for example, to say someone is very *warm* is a metaphor for a person who is kind, open, affectionate, and so on.

In a series of experiments, Ackerman and his colleagues found that various experiences of touch influenced impressions and decisions due to the metaphorical implications of the touch experience (Ackerman et al, 2010). For example, passersby were asked to evaluate a job candidate on the basis of the candidate's CV. Those given the CV attached to a heavy clipboard were more likely to view the candidate as having 'more serious interest' in the job opening than those holding a light clipboard (a 'heavy' candidate vs a 'lightweight' candidate). In a separate study, negotiators sitting in hard chairs were *harder* and more *rigid* in their negotiations than those sitting in soft chairs. In a third, solving puzzles containing pieces covered with sandpaper (rough) caused puzzle solvers to rate a described social interaction as less friendly, and more adversarial ('rougher') than those solving a puzzle that contained smooth, varnished pieces. And so forth.

Thermoception

Perception of warm and cold is known as *thermoreception*. Like *mechanoreceptors*, **thermoreceptors** are embedded in the skin. There are two types—one for detecting increases in skin temperature, and one for decreases. Thermoreceptors respond when your body temperature rises or lowers in response to changes in environmental temperature or when you touch warm and cold objects.

There are a number of odd aspects to our sense of temperature. For example, if you grab a coil of two pipes, one of which contains very cold water and the other mildly warm, you will not perceive both temperatures—instead you will perceive a painfully hot sensation (see Figure 8.19). This is because 'hot' is experienced under two conditions: when receptors for rising temperatures are stimulated, or when receptors for rising *and* decreasing temperatures are stimulated simultaneously. On the other hand, cold is experienced only when receptors for decreasing temperatures are stimulated (Craig and Rollman, 1999).

Nociception

We normally think of pain as a bad thing. However, our survival would be seriously threatened without *nociception*, the sense of pain. Consider children with a rare genetic disorder known as *congenital insensitivity to pain*. Tragically, such children experience burned or severed fingers and hands, multiple fractures, and untreated infections. They often die in childhood because they do not respond to pain as a warning that something is wrong. Thus, the sense of pain is critical to survival (Nagasako, Oaklander, and Dworkin, 2003).

So pain is one of our very best friends—although certainly also an unwelcome visitor, accounting for the majority of all trips to the doctor (Edwards et al, 2009). Pain is experienced as the most purely *physical* sensation imaginable. Yet, pain is actually largely *psychological*. It is not simply the relaying of sensory signals from the site of an injury to the brain. Beliefs, emotions, motivations, prior experiences, and observations of other people's behaviour affect the pain experience (Gatchel et al, 2007). Consider that a football player might barely notice a broken ankle experienced while playing an important game, while the same broken ankle resulting from a fall after the game might cause excruciating pain. In a similar way, soldiers on the battlefield often report little pain from wounds that, in another context, would be agonizing (Keefe and France, 1999).

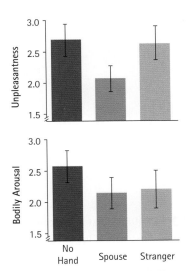

FIGURE 8.18 Lending a hand. Women threatened with electric shock by experimenters experienced less unpleasant emotion and physical agitation when they were holding the hand of another person. The effect was greatest when they held their husband's hand. These subjective reports were backed up by functional magnetic resonance imaging (fMRI) data.

Source: Coan et al, 2006, p 1036.

❯ **KEY IDEAS** thermoreceptors
Thermoreceptors are sensory receptors embedded in the skin that register temperature.

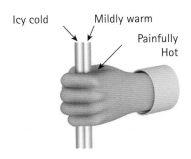

FIGURE 8.19 Warm + cold = painfully hot! When coils with icy cold water and mildly warm water are grasped together, the experience is of a painfully hot sensation.

The process of perception of pain is quite different from perception of other sensory information. There are no specific receptors designed to receive pain. *Free nerve endings* anywhere in the body can serve as nociceptors—receptors for pain sensations. The way pain messages travel to the brain is also much more complex than that for the other senses.

There are two types of pain experiences that occur when painful stimuli are experienced: *first pain* and *second pain* (Melzack and Wall, 1983). **First pain** is the initial sharp sensation one experiences at the moment of the painful stimulus—when we receive a cut, burn, or splinter, for example. As depicted in Figure 8.20, first pain is conveyed along *A-delta fibres*—myelinated (sheathed) axons that transmit neural signals very quickly. First pain alerts us that 'something bad' has happened and tells us *where* it happened and *what type* of injury we have experienced (cut, bruise, burn, etc).

However, first pain is actually less 'painful' than second pain. **Second pain** sensations are conducted along much slower unmyelinated *C-fibres*, and they arrive seconds or even minutes after first pain. Although they may be slower to arrive, they tend to be more unpleasant. Second pain is a throbbing, burning, radiating sensation that is not as localized as first pain. When you receive a splinter in the foot, for example, you may cry out in pain (or say something impolite) as you sit down and examine your foot. The initial sharp sensation when the splinter entered your foot is quickly followed by a throbbing ache that spreads out beyond the point of entry of the splinter. This is generally a more unpleasant experience—in other words, *having* a splinter is worse than *getting* a splinter. Second pain sensations tend to be more unpleasant in part because by the time they arrive we have had time to respond *emotionally* and *cognitively* to the pain (Ploner et al, 2002). Second pain highlights the psychological nature of pain.

There is an evolutionary logic to the experience of first and second pain. First pain sensations provide precise information about threats to the body so that immediate action can be taken (eg, sit down to take the pressure off your broken foot), whereas second pain, because it is generally more unpleasant, provides longer-lasting motivation to do what is necessary to promote the healing process and take steps to prevent similar injuries in the future (eg, don't rush down the slippery stairs in socks or fit a stair carpet)!

Gate control theory of pain

Melzack and Wall (1965) revolutionized the way scientists and medical doctors of the time understood pain (Yaksh, 1999). Although their theory, which came to be known as *gate control theory*, does not explain everything important about pain, no other theory has produced as much useful research on pain or stood up as well under scrutiny (Gatchel et al, 2007).

Gate control theory proposes that when *nociceptive* (pain) signals travel towards the brain, they pass through a gelatinous mass of small neurons in the outer layers of the spinal cord known as the *substantia gelatinosa* ('gelatinous substance'). These neurons act as a 'gate' for pain, because pain signals must pass through them in order to reach the brain.

According to gate control theory, only a certain amount of neural activity can occur at the pain gate at any given time. If other neural signals are dispatched to this location, they can 'close the gate' for further pain. These signals close the gate

> **KEY IDEAS** first and second pain **First pain** is the initial sharp sensations at the moment of a painful stimulus. **Second pain** is the generally longer lasting, less localized, and more unpleasant pain sensations, conducted along the slower C-fibres.

> **KEY IDEAS** gate control theory **Gate control theory** is a theory of pain perception that emphasizes the activity not only of pain signals from the injury site but also of pain blocking signals originating in the brain or elsewhere in the body.

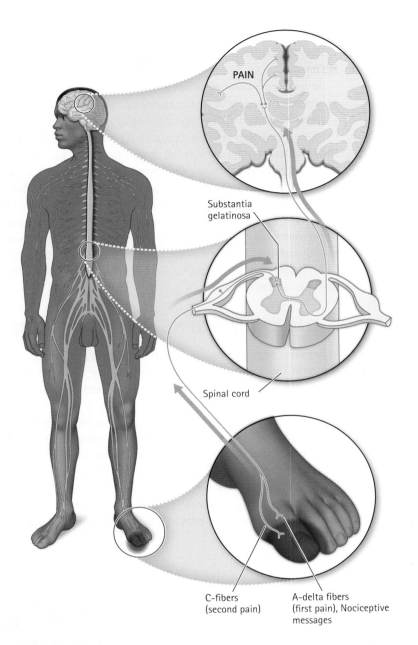

PAIN

Substantia
gelatinosa

Spinal cord

C-fibers
(second pain)

A-delta fibers
(first pain), Nociceptive
messages

FIGURE 8.20 The processes of first pain and second pain. In this figure
the pain gate is open. Nociceptive messages due to a wound travel along
A-delta (first pain) and C-fibres (second pain) through the *substantia gelatinosa* of the spine and are interpreted as pain by the brain.

by creating neural activity at the pain gate with which nociceptive messages must compete for the gate's limited 'entry space' to the brain. Because these neural signals inhibit the transmission of nociceptive signals, they are known as *anti-nociceptive* signals.

So how are anti-nociceptive messages generated? They can originate in the brain as a result of cognitive or emotional factors. For example, the soldiers and football players mentioned earlier are emotionally committed to 'soldiering on' regardless of injury, and they are also cognitively focused on the game or combat, not on their bodies. As you may recall from Chapter 4, pain-suppressing neurotransmitters known as *endorphins* are created by the body itself, and these also generate anti-nociceptive signals, as do painkilling narcotic drugs derived from opium, such as morphine and codeine. Pain-blocking signals can also originate at the site of injury. For example, massaging or gently tapping an injured area or bathing it in warm water may sometimes help relieve pain because these sensations stimulate neural activity in the area unrelated to the injury. These anti-nociceptive signals then compete with nociceptive signals at the pain gate, inhibiting the pain signals from passing to the brain.

FROM VISUAL SENSATION TO PERCEPTION

As we have seen, sensing is only the beginning of perception. For example, glance briefly at the image in Figure 8.21. If you are like most people, you will probably see bushes or branches in close-up with a series of spider webs covering them. The picture will have little depth.

Now look at the image in Figure 8.22. This image shows a forest view with substantial depth—the scene begins close to the viewer and continues into the distance. However, as you may have surmised already, both images are identical. The first version has been reversed (east to west) and inverted.

Why do we perceive these images so differently? During the course of human evolution, the only available light source was the sun—illumination came from above, and our eyes were primarily adapted to interpret visual imagery based on the

FIGURE 8.21 **What are you seeing? When most people view this photo, they see a series of thick spider webs covering some bushes or branches.**
Source: Used with permission from Aude Oliva.

FIGURE 8.22 **What do you see now? When the image is reversed and inverted, a forest view with depth emerges.**

Source: Used with permission from Aude Oliva.

'assumption' that light is coming from above (Torralba and Oliva, 2003). When the image is turned upside down, the assumption of lighting from above has been violated because the light is now coming from below. Violation of the 'light from above assumption' is the primary reason why human faces look 'spooky' when illuminated by a flashlight from underneath the chin in the dark. When you perceive spider webs in Figure 8.21 or a scary face when you shine a flashlight under someone's chin, your perceptual 'machinery' is attempting to impose order on stimuli it did not evolve to interpret.

When the sense organs receive physical or chemical stimuli, these stimuli have no inherent meaning—they merely form the basis for what will happen later in the brain. The signals are sent 'up' to the brain for further processing and interpretation. The remainder of this chapter is devoted to exploring the ways in which the machinery of perception does its everyday work, generally succeeding well, but occasionally failing in predictable ways.

Organization of Visual Images

Consider the following paragraph, which has been floating around the Internet since the early 2000s:

> Aoccdrnig to rseerach at Cmabrigde Uinervtisy, it deosn't mttaer in waht oredr the ltteers in a wrod are, the olny ipmroatnt tihng is taht the frist and lsat ltteer be at the rghit pclae. The rset can be a total mses and you can sitll raed it wouthit porbelm. Tihs is bcuseae the huamn mnid deos not raed ervey lteter by istlef, but the wrod as a wlohe. Amzanig huh?

In fact, no such research exists at Cambridge, and the trick—it is a trick—only works because the misspellings follow certain basic patterns (see if you can figure them out) and small connecting words are correctly spelled. However, if you are a native English speaker you should be able to zip through this paragraph fairly easily. As you read the misspelled paragraph you perceive whole words from what amounts to little more than alphabetic clues. Your brain 'fills in' the identity of each word and places it correctly in the context of a thought. In the same way, when you look at a television screen, you do not see a large group of glowing phosphorous dots arranged in patterns (unless you put your eyes right up against the screen). Instead, you see people, places, and things.

THINKING CREATIVELY

The above paragraph with the jumbled letters looks impressive at first but we have suggested it is something of a trick. Design a simple experiment to test how well we read a paragraph like this with whole words, jumbled-order words, and substituted letter words. You will need to decide how to operationalize the dependent variable 'how well we read' and think about how to ensure a reliable and valid procedure.

> **KEY IDEAS** the Gestalt school 'Gestalt' is German for 'whole form' or 'shape'. The **Gestalt school** was an early school of psychology that emphasized the mechanisms by which human beings create perceptions of meaningful 'wholes' from inherently fragmented and meaningless sensory signals.

At the turn of the twentieth century, Max Wertheimer (1880–1943) and his colleagues in Berlin founded a school of early scientific psychology known as the **Gestalt school** to explain how human beings made the necessary decisions to organize visual elements in a meaningful way. The term **Gestalt** is German for *whole form* or *shape*. The basic idea behind the Gestalt school is that human beings have an innate tendency to perceive meaningful 'wholes' out of inherently meaningless and fragmented sensory impressions. This idea is summed up in the expression *the whole is greater than the sum of its parts*. The most important contributions of Gestalt theory to the study of perception are the notion of *figure-ground relationships* and an explanation for the way human beings group isolated features of objects to form whole perceptions.

Figure-ground discrimination

The world is a vibrating, teeming mass of sensory signals competing for our attention. Yet we are able to focus our attention on certain pieces of information while filtering out other aspects of the environment. When you and a friend sit at a table in a restaurant, you are surrounded by people speaking, but you probably will be focusing on what your friend is saying. The dozens of dialogues around you are likely little more than background noise. Proud parents watching their daughter on the football pitch may perceive all the other players as background movement as they focus on their child's triumphs and failures. As you read this page, you focus on the words in black—not the white page the words are printed on.

> **KEY IDEAS** figure and ground In Gestalt psychology the **figure** is the aspect of a visual image upon which a person focuses, while relegating other aspects of the image to the background (ground). **Ground** refers to those aspects of a visual image relegated to the background.

Gestalt theorists proposed that every time we view a scene, we focus on certain elements while others fade into the background. The portion of the image that holds our attention is the **figure**, and the remaining portion of the image is the **ground** (Rubin, 2001). Consider Figure 8.23. Which of the shapes in Image A is reproduced in Image B? Most people choose the top shape in Image B, but the bottom shape is also a part of Image A. However, the bottom shape exists in white, created by the way the purple and red shapes are placed on the page. Most people perceive the white areas as the *ground* of Image A, and do not perceive them as shapes at all.

The inherent ambiguity of what constitutes figure and what constitutes ground is most famously presented in the two *reversible images* depicted in Figure 8.24. In Image A, you may see two human profiles in white, one on the left and one on the right—or you may see a single urn in the middle of the page in black. It all depends on whether you choose white as figure or as ground. In Image B, depending on your

A.

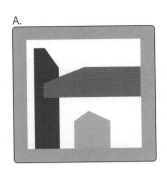

B.

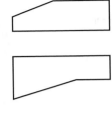

FIGURE 8.23 **Which of the shapes in Image A are reproduced in Image B?**

Source: Adapted from Rubin, 2001.

A.

choice for figure and ground, you may see a 'witch-like' image of an old woman with her chin tucked to her chest, or an elegant young woman in old-fashioned garb, gazing over her right shoulder.

Why does this form of organizing perception occur? It is important to realize that forming perceptions involves an expenditure of energy and mental resources. As Nava Rubin (2001) points out, if we were to take the coloured figure shapes from Figure 8.23 and rearrange them on the page, their shape would always remain the same, but the ground shapes would be completely transformed. Thus, ground shapes are 'accidental' outcomes of how figures are arranged. As a rule, then, it is a waste of mental resources to pay attention to the shapes of grounds.

Gestalt perceptual grouping

Gestalt psychologists also described laws governing the way we *group* specific features of objects once we have discriminated figures from grounds. Aspects of images such as shapes, sizes, colours, and so forth are transformed into meaningful wholes (Wertheimer, 1950). Some of these laws of *perceptual grouping* are apparent in the way infants as young as 3 months attend to various types of visual stimuli, while others develop as the human being gains more experience in the world (Quinn et al, 2002). Among the more important of the original laws of perceptual grouping described by Gestalt psychologists are:

B.

FIGURE 8.24 **Reversible images. Each image can be seen two different ways, depending upon which aspect of the image you choose as figure and which as ground.**

- **Proximity:** We tend to group figures together that are near one another. For example, in Figure 8.25 you probably see three sets of two horizontal lines, rather than six lines on a page.

- **Similarity:** We tend to group figures together if they are similar to one another. In Figure 8.26 you probably see three vertical rows of similar letters, rather than three horizontal rows of dissimilar letters.

- **Closure:** If there is a gap in the image of a familiar object, we will mentally fill in the missing portion to form a meaningful whole. Consider what happens if you view a car behind a pole. The pole dissects the car into two pieces, but you see a whole car, not two disconnected car halves (S.E. Palmer, 2002). Closure is also illustrated by the drawing in Figure 8.27. Although the drawing consists of disconnected lines, you are likely to have no trouble recognizing it as a horse.

- **Good continuation:** According to the law of good continuation, any visual elements that suggest a continued line will be grouped together. For example, the images in Figure 8.28 will be seen as two continuous lines. These lines could just as easily be seen as two V-shapes, but because of the law of good continuation, you have to really work hard to see it that way.

FIGURE 8.25 **Proximity. People tend to group figures together that are close to one another. This figure could be perceived as six lines on a page, but we tend to perceive them as three sets of two adjacent horizontal lines.**

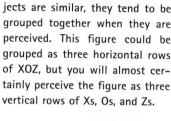

X O Z
X O Z
X O Z

FIGURE 8.26 **Similarity.** If objects are similar, they tend to be grouped together when they are perceived. This figure could be grouped as three horizontal rows of XOZ, but you will almost certainly perceive the figure as three vertical rows of Xs, Os, and Zs.

FIGURE 8.27 **Closure.** When there is a gap in a familiar object, we tend to mentally fill in the missing portion to form a meaningful whole. You will likely have no trouble recognizing a horse in this incomplete figure.

FIGURE 8.28 **Good continuation.** When visual elements suggest a line—but may be perceived in other ways as well—the tendency will be to perceive them as a line. You probably have to 'struggle' to perceive this image as two V-shapes formed by A–B and A[1]–B[1], whereas it is easy to perceive the image as two continuous lines A–A[1] and B–B[1].

Depth Perception

When an image forms on your retina, it is two-dimensional, much like the image in a photograph. Yet, we perceive the image in three dimensions, just as we perceive the image contained in a photograph to contain three dimensions even though it is printed on a two-dimensional piece of paper. Moreover, human beings and other animals acquire this talent of **depth perception**—which enables us to judge the distances of objects—extremely early in life. In a classic experiment, Gibson and Walk (1960) devised a *visual cliff*—a table with a glass top that extends out over a steep cliff-like drop at one end, and a one-inch drop at the other end. We look in detail at this study in our *Research in focus* feature but briefly, all of these infants crawled towards the mother over the apparent 1-inch drop—but only three ventured out over the steep drop. This suggests very early development of depth perception in humans.

> **KEY IDEAS** depth perception
> **Depth perception** is the collective term for the visual perceptual mechanisms that allow for the judgement of distance of objects and creates a mental '3-D' image from a 2-D retinal image

RESEARCH IN FOCUS

Gibson, E. and Walk, R. (1960). The visual cliff. *Scientific American*, **202**, 67–71.

Aim: To investigate whether depth perception is innate and intact at a very young age or has instead to be acquired by experience. More specifically researchers were interested in whether both mobile human infants and much younger mobile infants from other species would cross a glass-topped 'visual cliff', which was set up to display depth cues and so simulate a drop. The rationale was that reluctance to cross the cliff would signal intact depth perception whereas willingness to cross would suggest that depth perception is acquired later.

Method: This study was a laboratory experiment: 36 crawling human infants aged 6–14 months were placed on an opaque centre board in the middle of the visual cliff. On one side under the glass were small squares serving as visual cues for a drop (the deep side) and on the other side there were much larger squares (the shallow side). The children were then called by their mothers. In order to go to her they would have to cross the visual cliff. A range of infant animals were also placed on the centre board, including new-born chicks, goats, and sheep, all of which were mobile within 24 hours of birth or hatching. This is important because, unlike the human babies, they would have no opportunity to learn depth perception. The infant animals also underwent a condition in which the surface under the glass was lowered, simulating a sudden increase in depth. In a control condition the surface under the glass was uniform grey so that there were no depth cues.

Results: 27 of the 36 human infants crawled off the centre board. All 27 crawled on the 'shallow' side at least once whereas only three crawled on to the 'deep' side. Many crawled away from the mother when she called them from the 'deep' side. All the lambs, kids, and chicks moved on to the shallow side and none to the deep side. When the surface was lowered they froze. In the control grey surface condition no animals showed any preference for either side.

Conclusion: Whilst there is no conclusive evidence to show human infants are born with intact depth perception, results do strongly suggest intact depth perception in a number of other species and that human babies can perceive depth by the time they are mobile. This is supportive of the idea that depth perception is innate.

MASTER YOUR METHODOLOGY

1 Like many researchers Gibson and Walk used a *behavioural* measure—direction of movement off the centre board—as a measure of a *cognitive* ability—depth perception. Comment on the validity of measuring cognition by means of behaviour and explain why it was done in this case.

2 Explain the limitation of using older human infants and why this was necessary for this study.

3 How does being placed on the visual cliff differ from the real-life situations in which we perceive depth? What does this mean for the ecological validity of the study?

 THINKING CRITICALLY

Later research by Pei, Pettit, and Norcia (2007) has suggested that infants make use of crude depth cues like the squares under the visual cliff but not of more subtle cues. What does this suggest about Gibson and Walk's findings?

Depth perception does not only keep infants—or adults—from tumbling over cliffs. Without depth perception we would be unable to find our coffee cups on the table. How do our brains transform two-dimensional retinal images into three-dimensional reality? We use two types of environmental cues—**binocular cues**, which require the use of both eyes, and **monocular cues**, which only require use of only one eye.

Binocular Cues

Each of your eyes takes in a very slightly different view of the world because there is a distance of a few centimetres between the eyes, and therefore a *disparity* between the views of your left and right eyes. This **retinal disparity** in the view of each eye is the first binocular cue to depth. While the views of each eye differ slightly, however,

> **KEY IDEAS** binocular and monocular cues **Binocular cues** are cues for depth perception that necessitate both eyes—specifically retinal disparity and convergence. **Monocular cues** are those that can operate even when only one eye is available. Specifically: relative size, texture gradient, linear perspective, interposition, atmospheric influence, and position on the horizon.

they obviously also overlap, given that our eyes are not on opposite sides of the head (as are rabbits' eyes, for example). The brain makes complex calculations based upon the amount of retinal disparity and overlap to arrive at a judgement of depth. This occurs much the way stereophonic sound creates the illusion of depth by emphasizing one or another instrument in each speaker, yet allowing the instruments to overlap in both speakers as well. Visual *virtual reality* devices take advantage of retinal disparity as a binocular cue to depth by presenting two slightly different, but overlapping, images on two separate video screens, one for each eye.

A second binocular cue is **convergence**. When you focus on objects that are relatively close to your face, your ocular muscles rotate your eyes inwards, allowing them to *converge*. The brain notes the strength of the muscular signal and computes distance accordingly. You can see this by focusing on your fingertip at arm's length, and slowly moving your finger inward towards your nose. Your eyes will increasingly converge until you become 'cross-eyed'. (This is a great way to amuse small children, by the way—and, no, doing this exercise won't leave you or them cross-eyed.)

> **KEY IDEAS** retinal disparity and convergence **Convergence** is a binocular cue to depth perception based on the fact that ocular muscles rotate eyes inwards when viewing close objects. **Retinal disparity** is a second binocular cue to depth perception based on the fact that each eye takes in a slightly different, but overlapping, view.

Monocular Cues

Monocular depth cues are particularly important because binocular cues only operate at short distances. Convergence is irrelevant at long distances because the eyes do not converge at all when viewing distant objects. Neither is there significant retinal disparity when viewing distant objects—each eye sees much the same thing. There are four primary monocular cues.

1 *Relative size.* When objects are closer, their image on the retina is larger than when they are more distant. Thus, closer objects seem larger, and more distant objects smaller. Several wonderful optical illusions have been created that take advantage of our tendency to use relative size as a monocular cue to depth. Undoubtedly the most famous is known as the Ames room (after its creator, Adelbert Ames, Jr), depicted in Figure 8.29. In the photo on the left, the girl on the right is the taller of the two girls. In the photo on the right, she has shrunk, while the other girl has become giant-sized—a true Alice in Wonderland situation.

How is the Ames effect achieved? The viewer, who sees the scene only through a peephole (indicated by the black arrow in Figure 8.30), believes that the room is rectangular and therefore assumes that both girls are on the same plane, equally distant from his or her view. If this were true, then the girls really would be different sizes. But in fact, the rear wall is constructed so that it angles forward considerably on the right, making the girl on the right always much closer to the viewer. This plays on our judgements of distance based upon relative size (Sedgwick, 2001). The ceiling is also constructed at an angle so that it slopes downward, towards the girl on the right, making her head closer to the ceiling.

2 *Linear perspective.* Any parallel lines moving away from an observer—floor boards, railway tracks, motorway, and so forth—converge as they stretch out into the distance until they eventually meet at a single point, known as the *vanishing point*, as seen in Figure 8.31.

An interesting perceptual illusion that plays upon linear perspective cues to depth is known as the Ponzo illusion, depicted in Figure 8.32. Most people perceive Box A to be larger than Box B. However, both boxes are identical in size, as you can easily ascertain with a ruler. The reason Box A appears larger is because we assume any object seen towards the vanishing point of parallel lines must be farther away

FIGURE 8.29 The incredible shrinking girl. The Ames room uses the monocular cue of relative size to create the illusion that a person standing to the right is much larger than a person standing to the left.

Source: Robert K. Chin/Alamy Stock Photo.

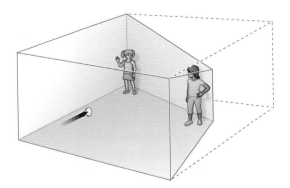

FIGURE 8.30 The true shape of the Ames room.

than an object seen towards a more parallel point in the lines. And yet, because the boxes actually *are* the same size, they will create retinal images of equal sizes. If an object that is very far away throws an image on the retina that is identical in size to a close object, the farther away object would ordinarily be much larger than the close object. Thus, we misperceive the size of the boxes.

3   *Interposition (object blocking).* When one object blocks the view of another object, we assume that the blocked object is behind the first object and therefore farther away from us, as evident in the photo of two deer in Figure 8.33.

4   *Position on the horizon.* An interesting perceptual reversal occurs depending upon whether we view objects below or above the horizon line. In general, if objects are *below* the horizon line, they are perceived as closer—and the lower in our visual field they appear, the closer they appear.

FIGURE 8.31 **Linear perspective.**
Source: iStock.com/deimagine.

FIGURE 8.32 **The Ponzo illusion.**
Which box is larger?

The opposite happens for objects *above* the horizon line. When objects are *above* the horizon line, the *lower* in your visual field they appear, the farther away they will be perceived to be. One marvellous natural illusion that may be explainable according to the position on the horizon depth cue is the *moon illusion*. When the moon is at a low point on the horizon (either rising or setting), it always looks much

FIGURE 8.33 **Interposition.**
Source: WildMedia/Shutterstock.com.

FIGURE 8.34 **The moon hanging low on the horizon.**
Source: Peter Cripps/Alamy Stock Photo.

larger than when it is high in the sky, as is evident in Figure 8.34. However, as time-lapse photography of a moon rising over Seattle, Washington, clearly shows in Figure 8.35, the moon is not larger when it is low in the sky.

Monocular cues to depth depend greatly upon mental 'assumptions' (such as the light-from-above assumption) and environmental factors that have remained relatively constant throughout human evolutionary history on earth. Artists spend

FIGURE 8.35 **The moon illusion—a genuine natural illusion. Time-lapse photography over Seattle, Washington by Shay Stephans shows that the moon actually remains the same size regardless of its place on the horizon.**
Source: Alan Dyer/VWPics/Alamy Stock Photo.

many years developing the skills necessary to utilize such earthly constants to fool the eyes into perceiving monocular cues where none exist, as spectacularly depicted in Figure 8.36.

Visual Constancy

Depth perception allows you to locate objects in your visual field. The only problem is that neither you nor objects are always standing still. If you walk towards, around, or away from an object—or the object itself moves—its image on your retinas may change size or shape, and conditions of illumination may also change. Given these possible changes, how do you continue to recognize an object as being what it is? The human ability to perceive an object as 'itself' despite changes in angle of view, distance, illumination, and so forth is known as **perceptual constancy**. There are four primary categories of perceptual constancy: *size constancy*, *shape constancy*, *brightness constancy*, and *colour constancy*.

Recall that the size of the image an object casts upon the retina changes as we change our distance from the object. **Size constancy** is the ability to perceive that an object remains the same size in the world regardless of changes in the size of its image on our retina. As we watch a friend walk away down the street, we do not scream in horror as she slowly shrinks in size. Our brains factor in both the size of an object on our retina and our *knowledge* of how distant the object is to arrive at a judgement of actual size (see Figure 8.37).

Shape constancy is the way we maintain a constant perception of an object's shape regardless of the angle from which we view it. Consider a door opening from the inside, as depicted in Figure 8.37. When the door is shut it is rectangular in shape. As the door begins to open, it loses its rectangular shape on the retina, but we still perceive it as a rectangle.

> **KEY IDEAS** perceptual constancy **Perceptual constancy** is the ability to perceive an object as itself regardless of changes in angle of viewing, distance, or illumination.

> **KEY IDEAS** size and shape constancy **Size constancy** is the facet of perceptual constancy that allows us to perceive an object as the same size regardless of the size of its image on our retina. **Shape constancy** is the facet of perceptual constancy that allows us to perceive an object as the same shape regardless of the angle from which we view it.

FIGURE 8.36 Monocular depth cues on the city streets. A particularly astonishing use of monocular depth cues is employed in a type of graphic art known as *trompe l'oeil*, which means literally 'fool the eyes'. Trompe l'oeil artists, such as Julian Beever, whose work is displayed here, create amazing three-dimensional scenes with photographic realism.

Source: RAUL ARBOLEDA/AFP/Getty Images.

FIGURE 8.37 Shape constancy. The door remains rectangular in our minds although it changes shape on the retina.

Source: akr11_ss/Shutterstock.com.

Changes in proximity to an object or changes in angle of viewing necessitate size and shape constancy. But changes in environmental conditions such as the extent or type of illumination necessitate **brightness constancy** and **colour constancy**. For example, my perception of the brightness of my (Paul's) daughter's gold locket sitting on my desk does not change because it is nighttime and the locket reflects less

❯ KEY IDEAS brightness and colour constancy **Brightness constancy** is the facet of perceptual constancy that allows us to perceive an object as the same brightness regardless of the available illumination. **Colour constancy** is the facet of perceptual constancy that allows us to perceive an object as the same colour regardless of the amount or type of illumination.

light. My mind adjusts to less reflected light by perceiving that everything around the locket is also reflecting less light than during the day. Thus, it is the *ratio* of reflected light from the locket to objects around it, rather than the *absolute* level of reflected light from the locket, that accounts for my perception of brightness. This is **brightness constancy**.

Colour constancy is trickier to maintain in changing illumination. Our colour perceptual system evolved under conditions of natural lighting—sunlight. Some of the qualities of sunlight are mimicked by various types of electric bulbs, but others are not. For example, sunlight contains about equal levels of energy at all wavelengths, but most light bulbs tend to contain more energy at longer wavelengths (Goldstein, 2010). How, then, do I perceive the pink cherry blossoms seen outside my window to be the same colour when they drift inside my home at night, illuminated only by artificial indoor lighting? This question is not easily answered—even by scientists studying sensation and perception. It is likely the result of a number of factors. Nevertheless, without colour constancy, the colour of the cherry blossoms would depend entirely on the light source and its intensity.

Sometimes, however, colour constancy breaks down if the conditions of illumination stray too far from those that mimic sunlight. Take the type of mercury vapour lighting often used in outdoor car parks, for example. Lack of colour constancy under such lighting conditions is one reason it can be hard to find your car in outdoor car parks at night where all cars appear to be of a similar colour.

EVOLUTION, CULTURE, AND PERCEPTION

Earlier we mentioned how important aspects of visual perception were shaped over evolutionary time by the fact that the sun was the only source of light for our early ancestors. Indeed, all of our sense organs and basic perceptual systems were shaped through evolutionary processes, and evolution has affected perception from A to Z. However, the effects of evolution on perception may be more specialized than previously considered. For example, there is evidence that human beings possess specific visual, neural, and cognitive tools dedicated to recognizing and distinguishing faces, and those specialized for detecting movement in living creatures—a phenomenon termed *biological motion* (Moulson et al, 2009). Some researchers consider these visual-cognitive tools to result from evolutionary psychological adaptations, as described in Chapter 5 (Slaughter, Stone, and Reed, 2004). Let us consider the phenomenon of face perception.

Face Recognition: A Specialized Tool of Perception?

Face recognition is the ability to distinguish faces from other objects or body parts, and to recognize specific familiar faces. You might think that distinguishing a human face from the back of a human head (or from a bag of *crisps for that matter*) doesn't take all that much skill, and chalk this talent up to something acquired over time through experience. However, consider the following:

- Infants as young as 3 days prefer to look at faces and patterns depicting faces than at non-face patterns—but this preference does not hold if the images of faces are upside down or the facial features are scrambled (Pascalis and Kelly,

2009); 2- to 3-day-old infants are also able to distinguish their mother's face from that of a stranger, and they prefer to gaze at it (Pascalis and Kelly, 2009).

- People are better able to recognize an image of an upside-down object than an upside-down face (Nelson, 2001).
- Damage to specific brain regions results in an inability to recognize objects or words, but may leave facial recognition processes intact (Moscovitch, Winocur, and Behrmann, 1997); damage to other brain regions does the opposite—it impairs the ability to recognize faces while leaving object and word recognition intact (Kleinschmidt and Cohen, 2006).

Although certain brain regions that become activated during face perception are also activated during a number of other tasks, Nancy Kanwisher has shown that there is a 'blueberry-sized' cortical region of the right hemisphere seemingly set aside exclusively for face perception and recognition. Kanwisher coined the term *fusiform face area* (FFA) to refer to this brain region (eg, Liu, Harris, and Kanwisher, 2010; see Figure 8.38). Several other brain regions were also identified as associated with face perception (Moulson et al, 2009).

Studies of macaque monkeys strongly support the notion that faces are 'special' to the brain. Doris Tsao and her colleagues studied a group of macaques using fMRI technology to detect brain region activity (Tsao, Freiwald, Tootell, and Livingstone, 2006). As with fMRI studies of human beings, these investigators found a specific brain region (in the case of monkeys, the *middle face patch*) that became activated

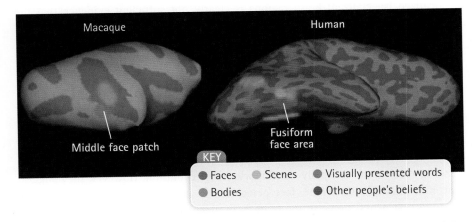

FIGURE 8.38 The face is 'special' to the brain. In the image of a human brain on the right, regions that respond to face processing tasks are highlighted in pink, with the fusiform face area (FFA) noted. Other colours represent regions activated in recognizing bodies, visual scenes, words presented visually, and when considering what other people might be thinking. On the left is a macaque monkey brain with the monkey equivalent of the FFA (*middle face patch*) noted. Tsao and colleagues (2006) were able to record the activity of neurons within the middle face patch, demonstrating conclusively that this area is used selectively to respond to faces (but not to bodies or objects). (Both brain images presented here show the back of the brain to the left side.)

Source: From Kanwisher, N. 2006. What's in a Face? *Science* 3 Feb, 311 (5761), pp 617–18. DOI: 10.1126/science.1123983.

as the monkey viewed images of faces, but not as the animals viewed images of bodies, fruits, and other objects. However, Tsao and her colleagues went a step further and implanted electrodes in the monkeys' brains to record the activity of the neurons of the middle face patch. (This technology cannot be used in human beings for safety reasons.) Tsao and her research team found that 97% of the neurons in this region fired during face recognition tasks, but not during other tasks (see Figure 8.38).

 THINKING CRITICALLY

Tsao's research involved monkeys rather than humans. Explain why this decision was made and why it limits the usefulness of the findings.

EXPERIENCE AND PERCEPTION

While it certainly is tempting to conclude that specialized visual-cognitive mechanisms—such as but not limited to face perception—evolved to assist our ancestors to survive in a world populated with other humans, the story may not be so simple. For example, there are specific brain regions that appear to respond selectively to the visual presentation of words and strings of letters; given that written language did not exist among our evolutionary ancestors, these regions could not have evolved specifically to serve the function of reading. Thus, the mere existence of localized (specialized) brain regions is clearly not sufficient evidence that the regions evolved specifically to serve the functions they apparently now do serve (Kanwisher, 2006).

But let us assume for a moment that evolution did indeed shape face perception mechanisms in the brain through natural selection. Certainly, there is a good case for this being true (Pascalis and Kelly, 2009). Evolutionary psychologists nonetheless debate whether face perception mechanisms are intact at birth. Although some researchers do believe that we are born with face perception mechanisms already in place, others argue that *experience* is critical for the development of specialized visual-cognitive mechanisms such as face perception (Turati et al, 2005). These researchers do not deny the importance of evolution. However, they suggest that, rather than being innate, face perception is an experience-expectant process, meaning that neural tissue in the brain is in place at birth that 'expects' to receive certain 'input'—in this case, visual exposure to faces over time. However, at birth, face perception mechanisms are only a *potential*. Such mechanisms cannot develop without experience. Thus, from the experience-expectant view, natural selection has not shaped face perception—it has shaped the *potential* for face perception. It is experience—repeated visual exposure to faces—that actually forms and 'fine-tunes' the mechanisms themselves.

Some evidence supports this view. Maurer et al found that specific aspects of normal face recognition ability are profoundly and permanently impaired in children who are born with cataracts that prevent ordinary early experiences of viewing faces—in spite of treatment for these cataracts within months of birth (Maurer, Mondloch, and Lewis, 2007).

THINKING CRITICALLY

Research such as that by Maurer and colleagues involving blind children raises particular ethical issues. Explain what these issues might be and why the researchers might consider it so important as to work to overcome these issues rather than conduct more straightforward research elsewhere.

The Importance of Expectation and Attention

Even if it turns out that face perception mechanisms are innate and not experience-expectant, it is beyond question that experience profoundly influences perception. One aspect of experience that is particularly influential is *expectation*. It is often said that 'people see what they want to see', but more frequently it is the case that 'people see what they *expect* to see' based on previous experiences.

For example, imagine watching the television news in which the view cuts between the newsreader and video material and remote reporters. You probably think you would notice if the newsreader had changed clothes and background each time they were on display. However, it appears that we do not notice this kind of change to what we see.

When studies such as this one are conducted, approximately 50% of participants do *not* notice the change. This has been shown to occur even when the sex and ethnicity of the person changes! The inability to detect even radical changes in a scene following a very brief distraction is known as **change blindness** (Simons and Levin, 1998). It results when our expectations for a scene block out our ability to perceive actual details of the scene.

While expectation may prevent us from noticing radical changes to objects or persons in our environment, *attention*—or, rather *in*attention—can prevent us from seeing the objects and persons at all, even when we are looking straight at them (Chabris and Simons, 2010). A famous example of this (that has ended up in numerous copycat videos on YouTube) is the 'Gorillas in Our Midst' experiment by Simons and Chabris (1999; see Figure 8.39). We can look in detail at this study in our *Research in focus* feature.

> **KEY IDEAS** change blindness
> **Change blindness** is the inability to detect changes in a scene following a brief distraction.

RESEARCH IN FOCUS

Simons, D.J. and Chabris, C.F. (1999). Gorillas in our midst: Sustained inattentional blindness for dynamic events. *Perception*, **28**, 1059–74.

Aim: To investigate the phenomenon of inattentional blindness, extending previous research to see whether inattentional blindness would take place in a complex and moving scene. Specifically researchers tested whether participants would spot either a woman with an umbrella or someone wearing a gorilla suit walking into a basketball practice session when given instructions designed to ensure they focused their attention on the basketball players.

Method: 228 observers watched a 75-second video in which two groups of basketball players, dressed in black or white, passed a basketball to one another. Their task was to count the passes by either the black-clad or white-clad team. This is an example of a primary

❯

> ❯

monitoring task. The results of 36 who lost count or recorded inaccurately were discarded, leaving 192. There were four different videos. In two videos a woman carrying an umbrella walked through the basketball players and in two a person in a gorilla suit strode into the middle of the practice, beat their chest, and walked off again. In one umbrella and one gorilla condition the video was realistic and in the other it was rendered semi-transparent in order to replicate a prior study. In an 'easy' variation participants just counted the passes, but in a 'hard' condition they had to count both bounce and aerial passes separately. The outcome was measured by the number of observers seeing the unexpected event—umbrella woman or gorilla. To establish this they were asked questions including: (i) While you were doing the counting, did you notice anything unusual on the video? (ii) Did you notice anything other than the six players? (iii) Did you see anyone else (besides the six players) appear on the video? (iv) Did you see a gorilla [or woman carrying an umbrella] walk across the screen?

Results: Overall 54% of observers noticed the umbrella woman or gorilla; 46% thus displayed inattentional blindness. There was some variation according to condition. Thus fewer noticed the unexpected event in the transparent and hard conditions. Observers were much more likely to notice the gorilla when attending to the black-clad team than the white-clad team; however, there was very little difference when it came to noticing the umbrella woman.

Conclusion: The main conclusion was that inattentional blindness is a robust phenomenon, taking place in complex, dynamic visual scenes. Around half observers fail to notice a dramatic unexpected event when their attention is focused on another aspect of the visual field. Counter to common sense the effect is greatest when the unexpected event is dissimilar to that being attended to. Thus those watching the white-clad team passing were less likely to see the gorilla than those watching the team in black.

MASTER YOUR METHODOLOGY

1 This was an example of a between-groups experimental design. Explain why this can be problematic and why it might have been chosen for this study.

2 The researchers analysed the significance of the results using a Chi^2 test. Explain why this was an appropriate choice of test.

3 Why was it important to discard data from observers who lost count?

This experiment has been repeated numerous times in different countries and under slightly different conditions, but the result is always the same—about 50% of participants miss what one would think could not be missed.

Inattentional blindness is the term used when a person is *looking* directly at an object without *seeing* the object due to that person's attention being drawn elsewhere. In this case, the viewer's attention is drawn to the task of counting ball passes, and he or she is blind to the chest-thumping gorilla. Inattentional blindness can be funny (just watch the many YouTube videos), but it is not a joke. Plane crashes, car crashes, boating accidents, and mistaken eyewitness testimony in criminal cases all have likely resulted from inattentional blindness (Chabris and Simons, 2010).

❯ **KEY IDEAS** inattentional blindness **Inattentional blindness** is the inability to see highly visible objects at which one is looking directly when attention is drawn elsewhere.

Perceptual Set

Although change blindness and inattentional blindness are complex phenomena involving vision, memory, expectation, attention, and other factors, they are also part of a much larger phenomenon known as *perceptual set*. When we view a scene,

FIGURE 8.39 Gorillas in our midst: inattentional blindness. Researchers Daniel Simons and Christopher Chabris asked volunteers to count the number of completed passes made by one team in a video of students playing basketball. Approximately 50% failed to notice a woman in full-body gorilla suit who calmly walked out in the middle of the scene, turned to the camera, and began to thump her chest. Similar results have been found in numerous studies conducted around the world.

Source: Simons, D. and Chabris, C.F. (1999). Gorillas in our midst: Sustained inattentional blindness for dynamic events. *Perception*, 28, 1059–74. Figure provided by Daniel Simons. www.theinvisiblegorilla.com.

we bring with us a lifetime of personal experiences, as well as immediate expectations—including expectations for where attention ought to be placed and what ought to be occurring at any given moment—which bias our perceptions. These expectations, biases, and predispositions are our **perceptual set.**

A simple example is displayed in Figure 8.40. If you look at these changing images, beginning with the image to your far right, by the time you reach the middle image you will still see an image of a tree. If you begin at the far left, by the time you reach the middle, you will still see a caricatured man's face. This is because you have already acquired a perceptual set by the time you reach the middle image.

The *Rorschach test*, popularly known as the 'inkblot test', is a well-known (though controversial) psychological instrument for measuring personality and psychopathology that operates on the assumption of perceptual set. In this test, a series of ambiguous inkblot cards, such as the one in Figure 8.41, are presented to a participant, who is asked to tell the researcher what he or she sees. The expectation is that the participant will 'project' aspects of his or her personality or psychopathology on to the inkblot by way of a perceptual set for interpreting the design. However, in general, the most important part of the response is not so much what the person 'sees' in the inkblot, but rather an amalgam of factors including the participant's explanation for *what* it was about the blot that gave it its designated appearance, how similar the blot *actually* looks to the identified object, how the participant organizes

> **KEY IDEAS** perceptual set
Perceptual set is the collective term for all our expectations, biases, and preconceptions that we bring to bear when making sense of a visual scene. Perceptual set means that what we perceive may differ quite starkly from what is actually there.

FIGURE 8.40 Perceptual set. If you start at the right and move inward, by the time you reach the middle image you will still see an image of a tree. If you begin at the left, you will end up viewing the middle image as a man's face (Fischer, 1968).

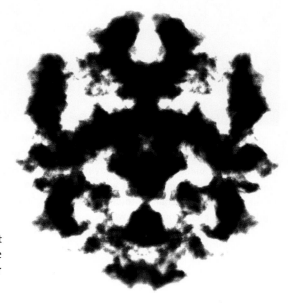

FIGURE 8.41 A Rorschach test card. What you see in this image may be determined in part by your perceptual set.

❯ KEY IDEAS the Müller–Lyer illusion The Müller–Lyer illusion is a visual illusion where two lines of identical length appear to be of unequal length.

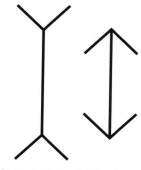

FIGURE 8.42 The Müller–Lyer illusion.

his or her responses, and so forth (Hunsley, Lee, and Wood, 2003). In this example, I (Paul) see a bat-like crab. I (Matt) just see monsters in all of them . . .

Culture and perceptual set

Now take a look at the two lines in Figure 8.42. Which line is longer? You might be surprised to learn that the lines are of identical length (use a ruler to check if you like).

There are several possible explanations for why we see these lines as different in length, a perceptual effect known as the **Müller–Lyer illusion**. Richard Gregory (1973, 1997) proposes that when we view these lines, they are reminiscent of the corners formed by the joining of two walls. The line on the right looks like two walls whose corner points towards us (outside corner), and the line on the left looks like two walls whose corner points away from us (inside corner; see Figure 8.43). In most cases, an outside corner would be closer than an inside corner. If the sizes of the images of two objects on our retinas are identical, but one of the objects is assumed to be farther away, that object will also be perceived to be larger. Therefore, the line to the left in Figure 8.42 will be perceived to be larger because—being an inside corner—we assume that it is farther away. According to Gregory, it is not necessary that we consciously perceive these lines to represent corners. This association is made below the level of awareness.

FIGURE 8.43 Gregory's (1973) explanation for the Müller–Lyer illusion. We assume that inside corners are farther away than outside corners. If an apparent inside corner throws an image on our retina of identical size to that of an outside corner, we assume that the inside corner is larger.

There is some cross-cultural evidence consistent with Gregory's explanation. Throughout the twentieth century, researchers in visual perception struggled to explain why some people living in rural, non-Western environments did not seem to be as susceptible to the Müller–Lyer illusion as Westerners. During the 1960s, cross-cultural psychologists suggested that the explanation lay in the fact that Westerners live in a 'carpentered world', filled with angular walls and structures. In contrast, many traditional non-Western structures are more often circular, and the forms of nature also tend to lack the angularity of the square and rectangular structures created by Westerners for living and working quarters. These researchers claimed that people living in 'non-carpentered worlds' would not see inside or outside corners when viewing the Müller–Lyer lines (Pedersen and Wheeler, 1983).

Studies comparing Westerners and East Asians have added evidence for the notion that **culture** may affect visual perception (Boduroglu, Shah, and Nisbett, 2009). Masuda and Nisbett (2000) began with the general observation that *context* appeared to be of greater importance in the cognitive processes of East Asians as compared with Westerners. For example, Americans are more likely than Chinese people to explain another person's behaviour in terms of stable characteristics and personality, whereas Chinese people are more likely to take into consideration the context and circumstances in which the behaviour occurs as well as the person's characteristics.

Masuda and Nisbett then used a unique method to test the hypothesis that these general cultural characteristics would have specific effects on visual perception. They had Japanese and American participants view underwater scenes that included fish prominently moving among other objects such as plants, rocks, and coral.

After viewing the scenes, Japanese participants were able to recall many more details about these background objects than Americans, while recalling an equal number of details about the fish. However, when the Japanese were asked to recognize one of the fish they had seen when it was placed in a different background context, they had far more trouble than the Americans, who were uninfluenced by the background context (Masuda and Nisbett, 2001). Thus, the Japanese showed a greater tendency to view objects embedded in their background and context, rather than isolating the object and focusing on its unique properties.

But while these results are fascinating, it is not clear exactly why they occurred. Did the Americans and Japanese differ in the way they actually *saw* the scenes, or only in the way they recalled them? Perhaps they merely differed in the way they tended to *report* their perceptions when questioned about them. To more directly test the hypothesis that Far Easterners and Westerners actually *see* things differently, Chua, Boland, and Nisbett (2005) presented Americans of European and Chinese descent with scenes of a focal object (eg, a tiger) placed in a characteristic background (eg, jungle). Using devices that precisely track eye movements, these researchers found that Americans fixed their gaze upon the focal object sooner and remained there longer than the Chinese. On the other hand, Chinese participants engaged in more rapid eye movements than the Americans from the object to the background and back again. Results like these have been used to argue that East Asians perceive objects holistically, taking in the environmental context (Chua et al, 2005).

THINKING PRACTICALLY

In Chapter 5 we discussed the role of culture and evolution as a 'new nature-nurture debate'. What do the findings of Chue, Boland, and Nisbett (2005) suggest about this question?

According to Nisbett and his colleague Miyamoto (2005), these results, and a series of others reported by cultural psychologists, suggest specific East-West differences in perception. Far Easterners focus *holistically* on the relationships among objects in context when perceptually organizing the environment, whereas Westerners focus *analytically* on the specific qualities of objects in order to categorize and organize them. This idea has been supported to some extent in subsequent research (Park and Huang, 2010).

From where does this perceptual difference emerge? To some degree, this cultural difference may reflect East-West differences in *social orientation*—with Far Easterners endorsing an *interdependent* orientation that emphasizes harmony, relatedness, and connection with others; and Westerners endorsing an *independent* orientation emphasizing individual achievement (Varnum et al, 2010).

GIBSON'S ECOLOGICAL THEORY OF PERCEPTION

Throughout this chapter we have gone along with the widely held assumption that perception involves the extensive cognitive interpretation of sensation. Before we finish the chapter, however, let us throw out there a deliberately radical and subversive alternative in the form of J.J. Gibson's (1950, 2002) theory of direct visual perception. Gibson suggests that instead of interpreting sensation, perception is a direct process of analysing the very rich information in the visual field. Visual perception is thus the process of exploring the **ambient optic array** (ie, the information in the visual field at any moment) and detecting the permanent stimuli there necessary to know what is in that visual field. Gibson's emphasis is on the richness of information in the ambient optic array, and he proposes much less cognitive processing of this information than is assumed in what Gibson called the 'orthodox' view of perception.

Ecological Optics

When Fonts Gibson speaks of information his emphasis is not on the signals sent to the brain for analysis (**afferent information**) but on the extent of information in the environment available in the form of patterns of light and captured by the retina. He calls the latter **optic array information**. This information is incredibly rich because ambient light reflects off all surfaces in all directions, revealing detail in the form of angles. The ambient optic array (ie, what we can see at any moment) consists of a 'bundle of angles' that reveal objects and surfaces. These are invariant in contour and texture regardless of angle, distance, and lighting. Movements of head, eyes, and objects in the visual field reveal these invariants, thus perception involves constant *sampling* of information. The retina thus perceives objects without a need for higher cognitive processes.

Re-Interpreting Perceptual Phenomena

It is straightforward to understand phenomena like visual constancy and depth perception in terms of theories of perception that assume a substantial degree of cognitive processing in order to make sense of the visual field. But can Gibson's theory explain them? Gibson (2002) explains depth perception by distinguishing between the perception of space and of an environment. In the latter he says there is sufficient information about the layout of objects to directly perceive relative distance and depth. Similarly there is sufficient information in the ambient optic array to see that objects remain constant in spite of changes in angle, lighting, etc.

So what about illusions? Gregory (1997) says that Gibson effectively denies the existence of illusions in his direct theory of perception. However, Gibson (1978) puts it differently, pointing out that illusions generally result when artists deliberately restrict the information available to the viewer and are thus not a fair representation of real-life perception. Where natural illusions do occur—like the Moon's apparent change in size as it nears the horizon—they are generally in situations with unusually little information available in the ambient optic array.

> **KEY IDEAS** the ambient optic array **The ambient optic array** is Gibson's term for the array of visual information available to us at any given moment as we view a scene. Gibson's theory is based on the idea that there is an enormous amount of information in this array and that this allows us to perceive objects and events without higher-level cognitive processing.

> **KEY IDEAS** afferent and optic array information **Afferent information** is what is transmitted through the sense organs (eg, from the eye through to optic nerve to the brain). This is the basis of traditional theories of perception—afferent information is processed for meaning in the brain. **Optic array information** is a quite different idea, meaning the totality of visual information in the ambient optic array. This is the basis of direct theory of perception.

THINKING CRITICALLY

Orthodox views of perception provide straightforward explanations of many aspects of perception; however, Gibson is able to argue convincingly against these phenomena as evidence. Where do you think you might stand?

THINKING PRACTICALLY

Look back to the ambiguous photograph with which we began this chapter. How might Gregory and Gibson explain it?

Affordances

Gibson (1979) suggested that an important aspect of our perception is **affordance** of how we can interact with each object in the visual field. Our understanding of affordances is dependent on the richness of information in the ambient optic array rather than prior knowledge of the functions of each object we can see. Thus a chair *affords* sitting and we tend to recognize it as a chair even if it looks nothing like any chair we have seen before (see Figure 8.44).

Understanding affordances has important real-life applications regardless of what we think of Gibson's view of perception as a whole. For example, if we want to design doors in public spaces with health and safety in mind we want people to recognize whether to pull or push. Common sense would predict that a sign saying 'push' or 'pull' should achieve this; however, this may fail if the sign does not correspond to the door's affordances (see Figure 8.45).

 THINKING PRACTICALLY

Kinchington (2006) has used the concept of affordances to explain the overuse of bullet points in presentation software. Explain this in terms of affordances and propose how the software might be designed in order to avoid this.

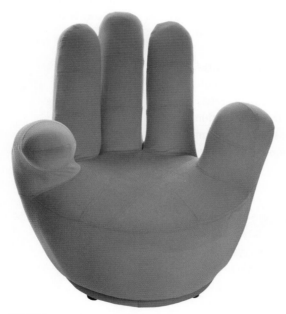

FIGURE 8.44 This chair affords sitting; therefore, we perceive it as a chair even though we have probably never seen a chair shaped like this one and its shape is of a hand rather than a chair.

Source: Brenda Carson/Shutterstock.com.

FIGURE 8.45 Most people tend to pull rather than push this door regardless of the sign because the handle affords pulling the door open.

Source: wedninth/Shutterstock.com.

THINKING CREATIVELY

A number of theorists have attempted to combine the direct and orthodox—what we might call 'top-down'—views of perception. Put together your own mini-account of perception that combines ideas from each. HINT: you could think in terms of two-stage perception, two parallel processes in perception, two types of perception operating under different circumstances, or a combination of these.

READ THIS

Highly readable accounts of approaches to perception involving higher cognitive processes can be found in the work of Richard Gregory. Here is an introductory textbook and an article:

Gregory, R.L. (2015). *Eye and Brain: The Psychology of Seeing.* Princeton: Princeton University Press.

Gregory, R.L. (1997). Knowledge in perception and illusion. *Philosophical Transactions of the Royal Society of London B: Biological Sciences,* **352**(1358), 1121–7.

It is well worth reading some original J.J. Gibson, especially as experts have expressed dissatisfaction with textbook representations (Costall and Morris, 2015). You might like to start with the following:

Gibson, J.J. (2014). *The Ecological Approach to Visual Perception: Classic Edition.* Hove: Psychology Press.

Gibson, J.J. (2002). A theory of direct visual perception. In A. Noe and E. Thompson (eds.), *Vision and Mind: Selected Readings in the Philosophy of Perception.* Cambridge, MA: MIT Press, 77–90.

For a modern rejection of Gregory's ideas of cognition affecting perception try this:

Firestone, C. and Scholl, B.J. (2016). Cognition does not affect perception: Evaluating the evidence for 'top-down' effects. *Behavioral and Brain Sciences,* **39**, 1–77.

THE INTRIGUING POSSIBILITY OF EXTRASENSORY PERCEPTION

We established at the start of this chapter that sensation and perception were quite distinct concepts. Is it possible then that we can perceive external information in the absence of input from a recognized sense organ? This would be **extrasensory perception** or ESP. Well, on a subjective level, yes! Probably most of us have had the experience of suddenly 'knowing' something in the absence of direct sensory information. Most of the time, however, this can be explained simply by our impressive abilities of **logical inference**—the ability to make connections between events—and our equally *unimpressive* ability to judge probability! Say it's 7.30pm on Thursday, the phone rings and you have a strong feeling that it's Aunt Betty. Before hypothesizing a psychic connection to Aunt Betty (this would be a form of ESP) it's worth considering more obvious explanations. For example, of all your family and friends does Aunt Betty alone consistently fail to respect your *Eastenders* time? If so then you probably did not *perceive* Betty but instead *inferred* that it was her calling. This provides a much simpler explanation for your apparent extrasensory perception.

Similarly, the not uncommon experience of dreaming about someone dying shortly before their death might appear a spookily unlikely coincidence but consider this from Susan Blackmore (1990):

> **KEY IDEAS** logical inference
Logical inference refers to the cognitive processes by which we draw conclusions from information, including apparently very limited information. Some experiences that we might attribute to ESP are actually the result of logical inference. Rather than mysteriously perceiving external information we suddenly 'know' things because we have inferred them from existing information.

There are about 55 million people in Britain and they live about 70 years each. If each has one such dream [a dream of a person dying that turned out to come true] in a lifetime there should be 2000 every night. Also about 2000 people die in each 24 hours. So there will be 4 million coincidences among 55 million people. In other words such an 'amazing' coincidence will be expected about once every two weeks. (1990, p 63)

So it seems that such coincidences are not really unlikely at all, we just misjudge their likelihood and pay more attention to them than they warrant when they take place. The study of extrasensory perception falls under the domain of **parapsychology**, the scientific study of those anomalous experiences that lend themselves to controlled experimental research. Parapsychology forms part of the wider field of **anomalistic psychology**, the study of all anomalous experiences, including those highly resistant to rigorous research such as seeing ghosts and demonic possession.

Parapsychology includes the study of extrasensory perception. Parapsychologists tend to classify the kinds of ESP that can be studied under controlled conditions into three phenomena:

- **Telepathy:** communication between two people in the absence of direct sensory contact
- **Clairvoyance:** informally this term has been used to describe a range of dubious 'experiences' from predicting the future to contacting the dead. In parapsychology it means the perception of objects and events outside the range of the known senses (strictly this is visual perception, clairaudience denoting similar auditory experiences)
- **Precognition:** perception of events that have not yet taken place

Other forms of ESP have been proposed and are deeply embedded in many people's belief systems. These include communication with the dead and perception of past events. However, these alleged phenomena are firmly outside the realm of parapsychology because of the methodological difficulties they pose. Psychologists do, however, study *beliefs* in such things.

In principle, telepathy, clairvoyance, and precognition are straightforward to study. A procedure that can be adapted to all three phenomena involves Zener cards (see Figure 8.46). These come in packs of 25 and are each marked on one side with one of five distinctive symbols. By chance we should be able to guess the next card in a sequence five times in every 25.

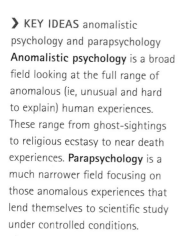

❯ KEY IDEAS anomalistic psychology and parapsychology **Anomalistic psychology** is a broad field looking at the full range of anomalous (ie, unusual and hard to explain) human experiences. These range from ghost-sightings to religious ecstasy to near death experiences. **Parapsychology** is a much narrower field focusing on those anomalous experiences that lend themselves to scientific study under controlled conditions.

THINKING CREATIVELY

To use Zener cards to study clairvoyance a pack of Zener cards is shuffled and a participant attempts to visualize each card in sequence. How might you adapt this procedure in order to study telepathy and precognition?

However, in practice ESP is extremely tricky to study because the experimental situation has to be incredibly tightly controlled to avoid sensory leakage and unconscious communication. If you try this for yourself you may well find that you identify more than one in five Zener cards. Sadly, this is probably not because

FIGURE 8.46 Zener cards are used to study ESP. By chance we would expect to identify the next card in sequence one time in every five. Reliably exceeding this may indicate ESP.

Source: Aida Servi/Shutterstock.com.

you are telepathic. Your cards might not be as opaque as you believed or you might pick up a reflection from behind them. You might also pick up cues from the person holding them, such as a slightly raised eyebrow every time you get a card right—given that you know how many of each card there is in a pack your chances of guessing correctly increase each time you can eliminate one card. The modern standard procedure for identifying Zener cards takes place under conditions of sensory deprivation in a heavily soundproofed and radio-shielded room with cards randomized and administered by a computer. This is called the **Ganzfeld procedure.**

So, the big question. Under this kind of tightly controlled conditions does the evidence support the existence of ESP? Unfortunately there is no simple answer to that. Meta-analyses, studies in which the results of previous published studies are combined and re-analysed weighting each study for sample size, have by and large found highly significant results. So a meta-analysis of clairvoyance experiments by Storm et al (2012) found that the probability of findings being explicable by chance alone was absolutely remote at $p = 2.14 \times 10^{-3}$. Based on statistics like this Cardena (2018) concludes that the available evidence cannot be explained away by methodological incompetence, fraud, or publication bias (the failure to publish negative findings, see 'The file drawer problem' in Chapter 19 for a longer discussion), and that the strength of evidence for ESP is comparable to that for most widely accepted psychological concepts.

Certainly then sceptics cannot claim that there is no evidence for ESP. However, the *quality* of this evidence is another matter altogether. Wagenmakers et al (2016) point out a number of problems with evidence including meta-analysis of flawed studies, publication bias, flawed analysis, and a lack of direct replications in the literature. Both Wagenmakers and Cardena accept that these problems exist, but they vary in their assessment of their importance.

❯ KEY IDEAS the Ganzfeld procedure The **Ganzfeld procedure** is an experimental situation designed to optimize the conditions for ESP to take place whilst reducing as far as possible the possibility of sensory leakage, demand characteristics, and fraud. A participant sits in a comfortable chair listening to white noise and wearing pingpong ball goggles on which a red light is shone—this is a mild form of sensory deprivation. The room is soundproofed and shielded against signals. The only communication is with the experimenter who, for purposes of complete avoidance of cues, may in fact be a computer.

This branch of psychological science is thus highly controversial, and is considered poor science by many psychologists. Most scientists question the point of continuing to conduct research on abilities that violate the laws of physics as we currently understand them and so are unlikely to exist (Hyman, 2010). In addition, scientific claims of evidence in favour of ESP historically are rife with out-and-out fraud (Marwick, 1978) or, more commonly, simple self-delusion and inadequate methodology on the part of experimenters (Blackmore, 2004). Nonetheless, ESP remains an intriguing possibility and its study a respectable if small and specialist field within cognitive psychology.

IN REVIEW

PSYCHOPHYSICS

- Sensing is the process by which we receive energy from the natural world; perception occurs when our brains organize and interpret sensory signals.

- An absolute threshold of stimulus intensity must be reached in order for a stimulus to be detected. The just-noticeable difference is the smallest difference between two stimuli that the appropriate sense organ can detect. Weber's law is the mathematical expression of the proportion of the standard (the original stimulus) to the JND.

- Signal detection theorists propose that noise and response bias interferes with detection of stimuli. Sensory adaptation also influences stimulus detection. Subliminal perception is the unconscious perception of a stimulus.

THE EYE

- Visible light exists in a narrow spectrum of wavelengths. Eyes allow light to be focused upon the retina where rods and cones begin transducing images into electrical signals to be conveyed to the brain, where they are perceived as visual images. Rods allow us to see at night, while cones are specialized for daylight and colour vision.

- Colour is not a physical property but rather is created by the brain. Two dominant theories of colour are trichromacy theory and opponent process theory.

THE EAR

- Sound is vibration that causes pressure changes known as sound waves. The ear collects, amplifies, and transduces sound waves into electrical signals, which pass to the brain where they are perceived as sound. Both ears are needed to locate sounds.

TOUCH-RELATED PERCEPTION

- Touch includes the subdivisions of tactition, thermoception, and nociception. The muscles, tendons, and joints primarily contribute to the kinaesthetic sense. Tactile sensations are converted into neural signals by mechanoreceptors and then carried along trunks of nerves directly to the spinal cord. The signals then travel up the spinal cord to the brain, where they are perceived as touch.

Pain is a psychological experience as much as a physiological event; there are no specific pain receptors. First pain is the initial sharp sensation at the moment of painful stimulus, whereas second pain is slower to arrive. Gate control theory has been highly influential in pain research.

VISUAL PERCEPTION

Gestalt theorists propose that human beings have an innate tendency to perceive meaningful visual 'wholes' out of inherently meaningless and fragmented sensory impressions. Among the laws of Gestalt perceptual grouping are proximity, similarity, closure, and good continuation.

Depth perception relies upon binocular and monocular cues. Binocular cues include retinal disparity and convergence. Monocular cues include relative size, linear perspective, interposition, and position on the horizon.

Perceptual constancy is the ability to perceive an object as 'itself' despite changes in angle of view, distance, and illumination. Four primary categories of perceptual constancy are size constancy, shape constancy, brightness constancy, colour constancy.

EXPERIENCE AND PERCEPTION

Human beings may have evolved specific visual and cognitive tools and brain regions set aside for the specific task of face recognition—the ability to distinguish faces from other objects and to recognize specific faces. However, this would not rule out the importance of experience in developing and fine-tuning these mechanisms.

Perception is influenced by experience and expectation. Change blindness and the Rorschach test are two examples of this fact. Expectations, biases, and predispositions that we bring to the viewing of a scene are known as perceptual set. Some researchers suggest that cultural differences exist between Westerners and East Asians in how visual scenes are perceived.

GIBSON'S DIRECT THEORY OF PERCEPTION

J.J. Gibson proposed a radical alternative to the orthodox beliefs about perception assumed throughout most of this chapter, emphasizing the ability of the eye to detect rich information in the ambient optic array without the need for cognitive interpretation of visual sensation.

Gibson has been able to argue convincingly against the traditional evidence for highly cognitive, interpretive perception such as visual illusions.

Gibson's idea of affordance is particularly influential; affordance represents the relationship between an organism and an object in terms of what the object appears to offer the organism in the way of interactions.

THE INTRIGUING POSSIBILITY OF EXTRASENSORY PERCEPTION

Most real-life instances of apparent ESP can be neatly explained as logical inference and/or poor probability judgement.

ESP phenomena of telepathy, clairvoyance, and precognition are, however, studied under tightly controlled laboratory conditions.

Most meta-analyses have supported the existence of small but consistent ESP effects; however, these analyses have been heavily criticized by more sceptical psychologists.

TEST YOURSELF

1 In signal detection theory *noise* refers to the effect of expectation and motivation on perception. True ☐ False ☐

2 Subliminal perception provides us with reliable ways to influence behaviour. True ☐ False ☐

3 First pain is more intense than second pain. True ☐ False ☐

4 We can judge distance to some extent with one eye using monocular cues. True ☐ False ☐

5 The technical term for transforming energy received by sense organs into nerve signals is called

a) Transcription

b) Transmission

c) Transduction

d) Transfiguration

6 Which of the following has a high concentration of cone cells in the retina?

a) Fovea

b) Blindspot

c) Optic disc

d) Optic nerve

7 Which colour does not have its own cones?

a) Red

b) Green

c) Blue

d) Yellow

8 Which of the following Gestalt principles involves filling in gaps in lines?

a) Proximity

b) Similarity

c) Closure

d) Good continuation

9 Explain how J.J. Gibson's notion of direct perception differs from more orthodox views.

10 To what extent does evidence support extrasensory perception?

 Visit the online resources that accompany this book: www.oup.com/uk/jarvis–okami1e

MEMORY

LEARNING OUTCOMES

By the end of this chapter you should be able to:

- Distinguish between the processes of memory encoding, storage, and retrieval
- Outline the multistore model of memory and evaluate it in the light of modern views of short- and long-term memory
- Critically discuss working memory as a model of short-term memory and the distinction between explicit and implicit long-term memory
- Outline the evidence base for separate memory stores with respect to both experimental and neuropsychological evidence
- Consider levels of processing as an alternative framework to the multiple stores framework
- Discuss a range of factors affecting retrieval, with reference to cue dependency, flashbulb memory, and depression
- Understand the reconstructive nature of memory and its reliance on schemas and scripts, and apply this understanding to the fallibility of eyewitness memory
- Evaluate research into the accuracy of eyewitness memory, including the effect of weapon focus, violence, and post-event information
- Discuss the malleability of children's memory and exemplify this with cases involving the manipulation of children's memories
- Describe and evaluate Schacter's model of memory fallibility including his evolutionary perspective
- Analyse the debate over repression in the light of experimental and clinical evidence, and understand why repression is so controversial
- Separate the debates over repression and recovered memories and critically consider the possibility of recovered memories for traumatic events

I (Matt) can still remember as a toddler being afraid of the grandfather clock in the hallway of my family house. It wasn't until many years later that I mentioned this to my siblings who were quite nonplussed. You've probably guessed it by now—there was no grandfather clock in that or any other house we ever lived in. Someone's memory—probably mine as I was so young—is mistaken! Even stranger, I can simultaneously *remember* the clock and *know* that it did not exist. Thus, memory cannot always be taken at face value as an accurate record of past events. And yet, we rely on memory in virtually everything we do. Is our faith in our memory systems misplaced? Is our memory just dodgy? We will consider this question a bit later. First, we consider what is known about the way memory works.

BASIC MEMORY PROCESSES: ENCODING, STORAGE, AND RETRIEVAL

There are two basic ways to define **memory**. First, memory can be defined in a general way as the ability to retain information about past personal experiences or facts about the world, and to utilize this information in the present. However, psychologists who study memory generally define it from an *information-processing* perspective. Looked at this way, memory is a group of mechanisms and systems that *encode, store,* and *retrieve* information (Baddeley, Eysenck, and Anderson, 2009).

What do we mean when we speak of encoding, storing, and retrieving information? The differences between these terms may quickly be grasped by thinking of a computer: as depicted in Figure 9.1, when you enter data into a computer via your keyboard, the computer *encodes* the keystrokes in the computer's memory in a way that can be processed as information. You may continue to work with the data online or *store* it in files on your hard drive, an action requiring more complex encoding processes. When you wish to access these files later to view or work on them, you are *retrieving* the data.

FIGURE 9.1 Encode, store, retrieve. Contemporary information-processing models of memory are based on the idea that memory systems encode, store, and retrieve information. Using an (imperfect) computer analogy, in Panel A, information is being encoded as keystrokes = sensory information encoded as perceptions; in Panel B, information is being saved on the hard drive = perceptions stored as memories; in Panel C, the saved file is opened once again = memories are retrieved for recall.

In a somewhat similar way, when you receive information about the world through your senses, it is encoded as perceptions (eg, meaningful sights and sounds) and either used immediately in thought ('online') or encoded more deeply as memory and stored for later retrieval (memory access). Put simply, **encoding** means getting the information into your brain, **storage** is keeping it there, and **retrieval** is finding it when you need it.

However, you shouldn't take this computer analogy too seriously. When you open a saved computer file you have retrieved an identical copy of what you have stored. As we shall see later, this is not at all true in the case of memory retrieval.

THE MULTISTORE MODEL OF MEMORY

Ideas about the processes of encoding, storage, and retrieval in memory have undergone 'near-revolutionary' change over the past 20 years (Jonides et al, 2008, p 193). However, it makes sense to start with a model of memory known as the **modal** or **multistore model**. Although this approach is no longer as popular as it was 30 years ago, it is certainly the most widely known model of memory, and many of the newer ways of looking at memory can be fitted into its general structure (Freedman and Martin, 2001).

The modal model describes three stages in the memory process, with each stage also functioning as a kind of 'storage area', or *store*, for memory (Atkinson and Shiffrin, 1968). As depicted in Figure 9.2, these stages/stores are termed *sensory memory*, *short-term memory* (STM), and *long-term memory* (LTM). They differ from one another in their specific function, the amount of information they can store, and the length of time that information can be stored within them:

Sensory Memory

According to the multistore model, new information reaches **sensory memory** first. Sensory memory very briefly stores large amounts of fleeting sensory impressions for further processing by other memory systems. As you walk down a street, drive along the road, or enter a room and look around, you perceive a great many sights and sounds, but most of what you perceive vanishes from awareness within a fraction of a second. It makes sense that most of the sensory impressions to which we are exposed during the day should leave only brief traces on the nervous system. Try to imagine the mental confusion that would result if you were to hold in your awareness every sight that passes before your eyes and every sound that reaches your ears while walking down a busy street.

Sensory memory is divided into two categories. When sensory impressions are visual in nature, they are termed *iconic store*. These traces last less than half a second. When they are auditory, they are termed *echoic store*, and may last as long as a few seconds (hence the term *echoic*; Sperling, 1960).

Sensory memory serves two functions. At the most basic level, it 'collects' sensory information and briefly holds it for possible further processing in memory. Second, it allows us to perceive the world as a continuous stream of events, rather than a disjointed series of visual and auditory 'snapshots'. For example, consider the arc formed by the gymnast's legs as she does a front walkover in Figure 9.3. In actuality, what is occurring in a walkover is a quickly moving series of disconnected sequential leg and body positions, suggested by the photo. But when we watch the movement, sensory memory retains each position very briefly, so that the position that came before is incorporated in our brain as part of the motion that brings us to the next position.

> **KEY IDEAS** encoding, storage, and retrieval **Encoding** is the process of 'translating' sensory information and thoughts into a form that can be stored as memory. **Storage** is the process whereby encoded material is retained as memory. **Retrieval** involves recognizing or recalling something from storage in memory.

> **KEY IDEAS** the multistore (modal) model **The multistore model of memory** is a traditional model of memory that views memory as consisting of three stages or stores: sensory memory, short-term memory (STM), and long-term memory (LTM).

> **KEY IDEAS** sensory memory **Sensory memory** is the memory stage that very briefly stores large amounts of fleeting sensory impressions. Sensory memory is comprised of iconic store (visual) and echoic store (auditory).

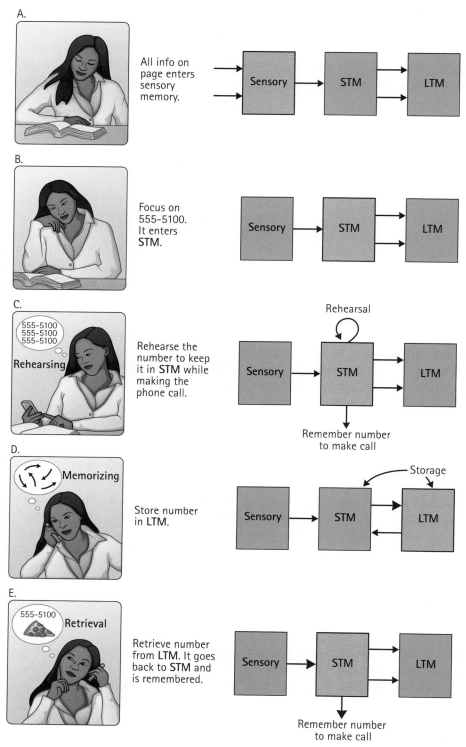

FIGURE 9.2 **The modal model of memory.**
Source: Goldstein, 2005, p 141.

FIGURE 9.3 **Sensory memory gives us motion.** Sensory memory collects sensory information for processing in memory. It also allows us to perceive the world as a continuous stream of events rather than a series of disjointed snapshots.

Source: Gustoimages/Science Photo Library.

Short-Term Memory

When you decide—consciously or unconsciously—to pay attention to a specific piece of information in sensory memory for any particular reason, the information is 'transferred' into **short-term memory**, or STM. Of the hundreds of people who pass you while walking down the street, perhaps one is particularly attractive, impressive, familiar, or otherwise distinctive. You may comment on this fact to yourself, holding in mind the image or idea of this person. As you do so, the person leaves sensory memory and enters STM. Or you pass a bar and hear a song you like. As you walk by you begin to hum the tune to yourself, transferring it to STM—while the sounds of the conversations of passersby slip forever out of sensory memory. Or you visually scan a document trying to find a particular phrase or word—you find what you are looking for and all the rest of the letters and words are gone forever. Only the phrase remains, now part of STM.

The transferring of information from sensory memory to STM is a result of further processing of the information by the brain. Any time you *pay attention* to a sight, sound, feeling, idea, or piece of information—either automatically or as a conscious decision—that information is transferred to STM. **Attention** is the force that singles out information in sensory memory for transference to STM, and it is attention that determines how long the information remains in STM.

However, short-term memory is quite brief. In general, information can remain in STM for no longer than about 20 seconds unless it is actively thought about or repeated—mental effort known as **maintenance rehearsal** (Peterson and Peterson, 1959). This is what happens when you ask a potential date for their phone

> ❯ KEY IDEAS short-term memory
> **Short-term memory (STM)** is a memory store used for attending to information in the short term. Short-term memory is limited in the length of time the memory can remain active—no longer than about 20 seconds. It is also limited in the amount of information that can be stored, to no more than about seven items or chunks of information. STM is one component of the modal model of memory.

> ❯ KEY IDEAS maintenance rehearsal **Maintenance rehearsal** involves actively repeating or thinking about information so that it remains in short-term memory.

number, but you have no phone handy to enter the information in your contacts. You repeat the number to yourself continuously while looking for a pen. Then someone else calls your name, you answer—and the number is gone, along with your future happiness!

In addition to its limited duration, STM has a limited *capacity*, which is termed **memory span**. Memory span is the amount of information that can be held in STM at any one time. For almost everyone, memory span averages seven single items or pure *chunks* of information (Cowan, 2001, 2010). What is a chunk? Consider the following list of letters:

VTYKSXILFTENCBB

Read them once slowly, then look away and try to repeat them back in order. You will almost certainly fail at this task. Now reverse the order of letters:

BBCNETFLIXSKYTV

If you watch television at all, you should have no trouble remembering the letters in order now after only a single reading. Why? Because they are no longer a series of 15 meaningless, unrelated single items. Instead, they have become a series of *four* meaningful and related chunks of information. A **chunk** is any grouping of items that are strongly associated with one another, but only weakly related (or unrelated) to items in other chunks (Gobet, 2005).

Chunking involves organizing information into manageable units. Chunking is the reason we can easily remember sentences composed of 20 words, but cannot remember 20 unrelated words in order (unless we use our own highly personal system to create chunks out of otherwise unrelated items). Chunking also allows us to remember phone numbers—the area code or mobile prefix comprises one chunk. According to the modal model, the function of STM is to allow information to be 'used online' (ie, thought about in the present) or held long enough to be transferred to long-term memory (LTM) for more permanent storage.

Encoding in short-term memory tends to be primarily acoustic, secondarily visual, and much less often semantic (Baddeley, 2007). For example, when you attempt to keep a string of words or numbers in mind, or when you read words from a page, you are likely to be encoding the information in STM by its sound by mentally 'talking to yourself' (see Figure 9.4). If you doubt this, try to read this page without reciting the words to yourself and see how far you get! And when abstract shapes, diagrams, and other stimuli that cannot easily be named are being processed in STM, visual encoding may be preferred.

THINKING CREATIVELY

We have suggested a simple demonstration of the importance of reciting words during reading. However that is quite different to providing solid evidence. Briefly explain how you could carry out an experiment to test the idea that recitation aids reading. You will need at least two conditions and to consider how to match them so that the recitation is the only variable impacting on differences in outcome between conditions.

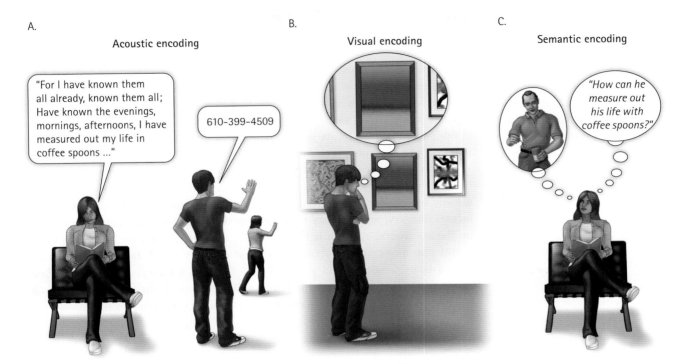

FIGURE 9.4 Most encoding in short-term memory is acoustic. Visual encoding may happen when abstract shapes or diagrams are being held in STM. Although semantic encoding may occasionally occur in STM, it is characteristic of the elaborative rehearsal used to process long-term memory.

Long-Term Memory

Encoding in short-term memory is an active process and will involve maintenance rehearsal if the 'shelf life' of information is to be extended—for example, when you continue to repeat a shopping list to yourself as you browse the grocery aisles. But repeating shopping lists or telephone numbers to oneself is not what most people are thinking of when they think of *memory*. Instead, most people are referring to *long-term memory* (LTM)—recalling the time they burned their hand on a hot iron at age 5, correctly remembering how to do prime factorization for a maths test, placing the name of that Italian actor they saw eating in a restaurant, or being able to ride a motorcycle competently ten years after last riding. If STM can be thought of as whatever appears on the screen of your computer at any given moment, then long-term memory represents the data stored in files for later retrieval. Thus, **long-term memory (LTM)** is a relatively permanent store of memory. Unlike STM, LTM has a theoretically limitless capacity (Bahrick, 2000).

So how does information get from STM to LTM? In other words, how is information *encoded* in LTM? Encoding in LTM generally relies upon the idea of *meaningfulness* of the information being encoded. Long-term memories are most effectively encoded when the information being encoded is associated meaningfully with information already known. Therefore, encoding in LTM is primarily semantic and depends upon *meaning*.

> ❯ KEY IDEAS long-term memory
> **Long-term memory (LTM)** is a theoretically unlimited memory store that contains memories for facts, autobiographical events, and learned skills. LTM is a component of the multistore model of memory.

> **KEY IDEAS** elaborative
rehearsal **Elaborative rehearsal**
means mentally encoding
information into long-term
memory in a way that is personally
meaningful and associates the new
information with information that
already exists in long-term memory.

According to the multistore model, material is most likely to be recalled at a later date if it has been encoded for LTM during **elaborative rehearsal**, which may or may not occur deliberately. Elaborative rehearsal differs from maintenance rehearsal in that it does not consist of simple repetition. Elaborative rehearsal involves processing new material in a way that is personally meaningful and which associates the new information with other information that already exists in LTM. Repeating a phone number over and over to yourself many times may help you to keep it in mind long enough to locate your mobile phone and dial, but it will not guarantee that you will remember the number ten minutes later, let alone the next year.

You are engaging in elaborative rehearsal when you study for a test successfully by, for example, perceiving the connection between new concepts and concepts already learned, or deliberately creating unique personal systems of associations, mental imagery, and memory tricks. If you recall the time you burned your hand on the hot iron at age 5, it is likely because this event was associated with meaningful sensations and emotions, awareness of the time of day, the identity and responses of people around you, and so forth. This memory may also have been further elaborated upon over the years in discussion with family members or simply by bringing the scene into consciousness and reflecting upon it.

THINKING PRACTICALLY

Research into effective revision practices has identified two particularly effective strategies: retrieval practice (ie, taking practice tests) and distributed practice (working in short spread-out periods rather than 'cramming') (Dunlowski et al, 2013). Explain why these strategies work using the concept of elaborative rehearsal.

WORKING MEMORY: A MODERN UNDERSTANDING OF SHORT-TERM MEMORY

> **KEY IDEAS** working memory
Working memory is defined
in different ways by different
theorists, and is often used
synonymously with (or in place
of) short-term memory. As used
here, the term describes 'what
happens' in short-term memory
when information is manipulated
or processed.

A number of influential concepts that move beyond the modal model have recently become part of the accepted picture of human memory. Perhaps the most important of these concepts is **working memory**, developed by Alan Baddeley (2012). Although working memory may be defined in a number of different ways by different theorists (eg, Cowan, 2005), most cognitive psychologists think of working memory as a way of looking at what happens *in* short-term memory when information is manipulated—for example, during maintenance rehearsal, during the transfer of information from STM to LTM, or during the retrieval of material from LTM back into STM for 'online' use.

Although working memory does its 'work' within the limited-capacity space and duration of short-term memory, it draws on information from long-term memory as well. For example, when adding or subtracting figures in your head, you keep the figures in mind through maintenance rehearsal, a short-term memory process, while drawing on long-term memories for how to carry out addition and subtraction. Because most of the time we actually *are* in some way manipulating and processing information while it is in short-term memory, some psychologists have come to use the term *working memory* in place of *short-term memory*. Figure 9.5 depicts a hypothetical example of working memory.

FIGURE 9.5 Working memory in an everyday task. When shopping for food you are maintaining your shopping list in working memory through short-term memory processes (eg, maintenance rehearsal), while retrieving memory for the placement of items in the supermarket from long-term memory.

EXPLICIT AND IMPLICIT MEMORY: A MODERN VIEW OF LONG-TERM MEMORY

Over the years, the notion of long-term memory (LTM) has been greatly expanded and elaborated upon. At present, it is widely believed that there are two fundamental types of LTM, as depicted in Figure 9.6: *explicit memory* and *implicit memory*.

Explicit Memory

Explicit memories are conscious memories for personal experiences or facts about the world. Explicit memories are often termed *declarative memories* because they are memories which we can 'declare'—that is, consciously recall. Tulving (1972, 2002) distinguished between two types of declarative or explicit memory.

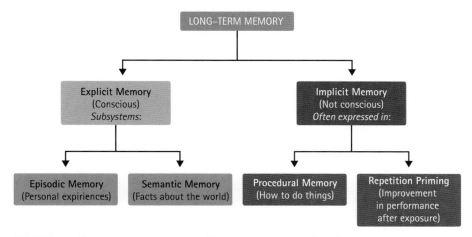

FIGURE 9.6 The component systems of long-term memory (LTM).

Episodic memories for events—they include our personal autobiographical memories. **Semantic memories** are memories for facts that we have learned such as numbers, vocabulary words, names of people and places, historical events, scientific information, concepts, and so forth.

THINKING PRACTICALLY

Which of the following memories is semantic and which is episodic?

1 I remember that in December, the daytime temperature in Rio de Janeiro rarely falls below 30° Celsius after early morning has passed.

2 I remember that when I was in Rio de Janeiro last December, the daytime temperature rarely fell below 30° Celsius.

Of course, we may recall the event of learning the fact, so for example you might recall the lecture when you first heard about different memory systems. While *episodic* and *semantic* memory are believed to be distinct systems, they are related because every new piece of semantic (factual) knowledge initially occurs in the context of a personal experience (reading, listening to someone speak, and so forth).

Anterograde amnesia

Evidence for the existence of distinct episodic and semantic memory systems comes from rare cases of **anterograde amnesia**. Patients with anterograde amnesia, which generally results from damage to the *hippocampus* and surrounding tissue of the temporal lobe, can form new semantic memories, but their ability to form new episodic memories is severely impaired (see Figure 9.7).

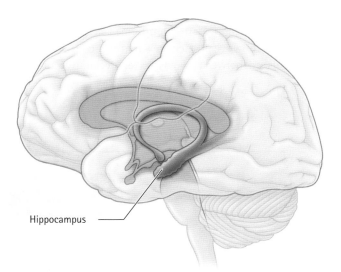

Hippocampus

FIGURE 9.7 Amnesia is associated with damage to the hippocampus. Both anterograde amnesia (inability to form new episodic memories) and retrograde amnesia (inability to access past episodic memories) may result from damage to the hippocampus and surrounding structures of the temporal lobe.

Vargha-Khadem et al (1997) report the cases of three young adults who had experienced severe hippocampal damage, in one case at birth, in another case by age 4, and in the third at age 9. In childhood, Jon, Beth, and Kate had amnesia for the episodes of daily life. They could not recall where things were located or whether they had made appointments, and they could not make any reliable account of what had happened to them during the day or whom they had seen. They lived in a continuous 'present moment'.

Given the severity of their early memory impairment, it would seem logical that they should be unable to attend school or learn much about their world. Indeed, according to earlier ideas about LTM—that it was a unitary system regulated by the hippocampus—Jon, Beth, and Kate should have ended up intellectually disabled. Such was not the case, however. These children were able to perform relatively normally in school in reading, writing, and the acquisition of general factual knowledge. They could tell you the major accomplishments of Mahatma Gandhi, identify the nation with the highest population, explain the purpose of the Koran, and define *encumber, sanctuary*, and *boast*. Yet they could not tell you if they had been to school that day and could not remember how they had acquired their factual knowledge. The semantic memories of what they learned remained, but the episodic memories of their *experience* of learning did not. Cases of amnesia that selectively target episodic memory, while leaving semantic memory functional, support the view that these systems are distinct.

However, when performance of one of these children in acquiring new semantic memories was tested against that of ordinary children, the hippocampus-damaged child did not perform as well. Thus, it seems that while semantic and episodic memory systems may be distinct, semantic memory is impaired without the support of episodic memory (Gardine et al, 2008).

THINKING CRITICALLY

Case studies of people with hippocampal damage and varying degrees of impairment to different types of memory provide evidence for the existence of separate long-term memory systems. However, as evidence they have limitations. Explain these limitations.

Implicit Memory

Implicit memory occurs when we retrieve something, but have no awareness that we are doing so (Mitchell, 2006). Because people have no recollection of implicit memories, the existence of these memories is generally demonstrated in behaviour. For example, when you get into a car and drive to work or university you are demonstrating memory for a complex and varied number of skills that once had to be learned—turning the steering wheel while glancing at the rear-view mirror, wing mirror, and through the front windscreen virtually simultaneously and also controlling the rate of acceleration. Yet you perform these actions effortlessly, without the conscious experience of recalling how to do them—and possibly while talking to a passenger in the car and drinking coffee at the same time!

Although implicit memory is not divided by subtypes, as is explicit memory, it is most frequently expressed in two ways: *procedural memory* and *repetition priming*.

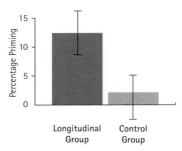

FIGURE 9.8 Is implicit memory invulnerable? Participants who had viewed intact drawings for one to three seconds were better able to identify the objects depicted in these drawings from small fragments viewed 17 years later than from a second group of fragments of drawings they had never seen. A control group of volunteers who had not been part of the original research showed no superior recognition for either group of drawings.

Source: Mitchell, 2006.

Procedural memory is implicit memory for skills involving motor coordination, such as driving a car, walking, or flipping a pancake in the pan. These are behaviours that are performed automatically. **Repetition priming** refers to the way that a person's performance of certain tasks can improve without his or her awareness merely as a result of previous exposure to the task—even if the person is unaware of the previous exposure (Goetz, Goetz, and Robinson, 2007).

In a mind-boggling demonstration of the power and long-term stability of implicit memory through repetition priming, Mitchell (2006) exposed a group of university students in 1982 to a series of black-and-white line drawings. The group only viewed the drawings for between one and three seconds. Seventeen years later, in 1999, Mitchell contacted the former students and asked them to participate in a follow-up study. He showed these participants small partial fragments of the drawings they had viewed so briefly 17 years earlier, mixed in with fragments of drawings they had never seen.

As depicted in Figure 9.8, when asked to identify the name of the object depicted in the fragment, the students were far more likely to successfully name the object from a fragment of drawing they had seen whole 17 years earlier, as compared with fragments of a second group of drawings they had never seen whole. This superior recognition ability included four individuals who could not even remember having been brought into the laboratory the first time in 1982! On the other hand, a control group of volunteers who had not been part of the original group showed no difference in ability to identify objects from either group of fragments.

Consider also a group native English-speaking adults under the age of 40 studied by Bowers, Mattys, and Gage (2009). These adults had, in early childhood, been exposed to either Hindi or Zulu languages because their parents had worked in India and Africa. After returning to England, they never heard these languages again. However, as adults in the research lab they were relatively easily able to learn subtle sounds of that childhood language—sounds that do not occur in English. This was in spite of having no explicit memory for any aspect of the language. In contrast, adults who had never been exposed to the language were unable to learn these sounds.

Like explicit memory, implicit memory is associated with specific brain regions, and may become impaired while leaving explicit memory intact (Fleishman et al, 2004). However, unlike explicit memories, which deteriorate considerably over time, implicit memories appear to have remarkable longevity.

 THINKING PRACTICALLY

Explain the saying 'It's like riding a bike' in terms of the properties of implicit memory.

Evidence for Separate Memory Stores

Before reading more about the evidence for separate memory stores, try the following experiment. Read through the list of nouns in Figure 9.9 once only, taking no more than one second with each word. Then cover the list and immediately try to remember as many of the words as you can, in any order, writing them down.

Lorry	Pencil	Doughnut	Telephone
Roof	Glass	Torch	Drawing
Book	Door	Pool	Pistol
Artichoke	Hammer	Stapler	Tree
Piano	Paper	Sink	Bread
Knife	Toaster	Chair	
Elbow	Shop	Flower	

FIGURE 9.9 **Demonstration of recency and primacy effects.**

If you compare your list of recalled words with the original list in Figure 9.9, you will probably note a peculiar pattern: you recalled more of the words presented towards the beginning of the list (termed the primacy effect) and at the end of the list (termed the recency effect). You probably had most trouble recalling the words presented in the middle of the list (Murdoch, 1962). Because both the primacy and recency effects occur at the same time, a unique U-shaped curve exists when people's memories for lists of words are graphed, as depicted in Figure 9.10. The term *serial position curve* is used to describe this curve.

Perhaps the most obvious explanation for the serial curve involves short- and long-term memory; the most recently presented words are still in STM and are thus easily accessible (the recency effect); while the originally presented words have already been transferred to LTM and are thus also accessible through retrieval (the primacy effect). On the other hand, words presented in the middle have been 'bumped out' of STM by the more recent words (recall that STM has a limited capacity), but have not had enough time to be processed deeply enough to enter LTM (Glanzer and Cunitz, 1966). They are in a 'phantom zone' for memory.

While this explanation for the serial position effect sounds reasonable, it is rejected by levels-of-processing theorists. These critics propose that primacy and recency effects might result because items presented first and items presented last are more distinctive—they just stand out from those presented in the middle because they hold distinctive positions in the list (Neath, 1993).

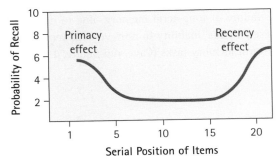

FIGURE 9.10 **The serial position curve.** As depicted in this graph, when people are asked to memorize lists of words, their recall is most reliable for words presented first (primacy effect) and words presented last (recency effect). Recall is poorest for words presented in the middle of a list.

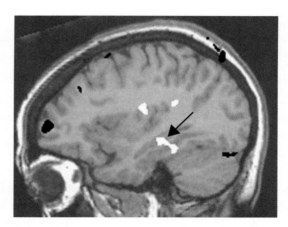

FIGURE 9.11 Imaging the serial position curve. When Talmi and her colleagues used fMRI technology to monitor the brains of participants who scanned word lists, they found that the hippocampus and surrounding areas of the mid-temporal lobe were engaged during recall of early listed items (indicated by arrow), but not during recall of late-listed items (areas in black towards the left of image). Late-listed items activated brain regions in the frontal cortex associated with short-term memory.

Source: Talmi, Deborah et al (2005). Neuroimaging the serial position curve: A test of single-store versus dual-store models. *Psychological Science*, 16(9), pp 716–23, Copyright © 2005, © SAGE Publications.

Talmi et al attempted to resolve this debate with a neuroimaging study using fMRI technology (Talmi et al, 2005). As depicted in Figure 9.11, these researchers found that items recalled from early positions in lists (primacy effect) activated brain regions associated with long-term memory processes in the hippocampus and surrounding temporal lobe regions, just as would be predicted by modal model theorists. These brain regions were not activated at all when participants recalled items in late-list positions (recency effect). In fact, when participants recalled late-list items, regions of the brain associated with short-term and working memory—such as the frontal and parietal cortexes—were activated.

This evidence is consistent with the view that the serial position curve reflects the distinction between short- and long-term memory stores. The study by Talmi and her colleagues is also consistent with earlier studies of patients who had experienced ordinary *amnesia*—failure of long-term memory—due to damage to the hippocampus. In spite of these patients' inability to retrieve long-term memories, they had no trouble with short-term memory tasks (Cave and Squire, 1992).

 THINKING CRITICALLY

The fact that primacy and recency effects are associated with activation of different brain regions is certainly *consistent* with the idea of distinct short- and long-term memory. However, is it strong evidence? How else might a psychologist or neuroscientist explain these findings? HINT: one answer lies in the section on levels-of-processing theory.

LEVELS OF PROCESSING

Not everyone agrees that the most useful way to think about memory is in terms of separate systems of storage. An alternative approach is based on the idea that memory phenomena can be interpreted in terms of information being encoded at deeper or shallower levels. This originated in the work of Craik and Lockhart (1972, 2009) and is known as the **levels-of-processing** framework.

Although the levels-of-processing framework can 'fit in' to the modal model, Craik and Lockhart did not adhere to the notion that memory is best thought of as separate stores and stages such as STM and LTM. Instead, they simply proposed that the more deeply an item is processed, the more likely it is to be recalled at a later date (Craik and Brown, 2000).

So what makes information processing deep or shallow? Craik (1973) suggested that depth of processing could be seen in terms of the extent of meaning that is extracted from the information. Information that is deeply processed (ie, a lot of meaning has been extracted from it, is likely to be remembered). Craik and Lockhart (1972) outlined three possible levels at which information is processed (see Figure 9.12).

Structural processing. Information about appearance is extracted.

Phonemic processing. Information about what something sounds like is extracted.

Semantic processing. Information about what something means is extracted.

Semantic processing is thus the *deepest* form of information processing because extracting meaning involves the most cognitive work. Semantically processed material is best remembered. Structural processing on the other hand is the *shallowest* form of information processing, involving the least processing and resulting in the least material being remembered.

Craik and Lockhart (1975) demonstrated that words which had been encoded according to their meanings (semantic encoding) rather than sound or appearance

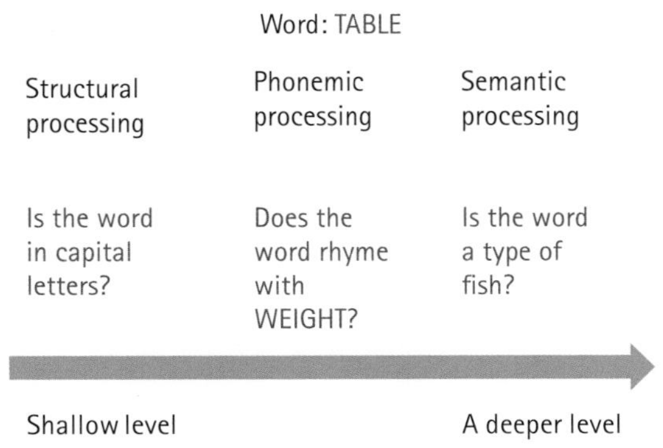

> **KEY IDEAS** levels of processing
> **Levels of processing** is the framework for understanding memory processes originated by Craik and Lockhart. Its most basic assumption is that the more deeply an item is processed, the more likely it is to be recalled.

Word: TABLE

Structural processing	Phonemic processing	Semantic processing
Is the word in capital letters?	Does the word rhyme with WEIGHT?	Is the word a type of fish?

Shallow level → A deeper level

FIGURE 9.12 Craik and Lockhart (1975) demonstrated that words which had been encoded semantically were recalled more readily than words encoded structurally or phonemically. They concluded that this was due to a deeper level of processing in semantic encoding.

Source: Adapted from Ekuni, Roberta et al (2011). Levels of processing: The evolution of a framework. *Psychology & Neuroscience*, 1 July. Copyright © 2011, American Psychological Association. DOI: 10.3922/j.psns.2011.3.006.

were recalled more readily. These researchers concluded that this was due to a deeper level of processing in semantic encoding. We can look at Craik and Lockhart's study in detail in our *Research in focus* feature.

RESEARCH IN FOCUS

Craik, F.I. and Tulving, E. (1975). Depth of processing and retention of words in episodic memory. *Journal of Experimental Psychology* **104**, 268–94.

Aim: To test the central hypothesis of levels-of-processing theory—that more deeply processed material is better remembered. More specifically to test whether words processed for meaning would be more easily retrieved than words that were processed more shallowly for information about their appearance or sound.

Method: There were several variations on the procedure. The first is reported here: 20 participants were individually presented with lists of 40 one- or two-syllable words. They were asked one of three questions, each representing a level of processing. In the first condition, to trigger structural level processing they were asked whether each word was written in capitals. In the second (phonemic processing) condition they were asked whether it rhymed with a particular word. In the third (semantic processing) condition they were asked whether they were part of a category or fitted into a gap in a sentence.

To control for how memorable each word might be, questions and words were rotated so that all possible combinations were presented to participants. Later participants were tested for either free recall of the words (participants were asked to remember as many of the words as possible) or recognition (participants chose the words from a range of options).

Results: In the above procedure (and in all the variations not described here) participants remembered the semantically processed words best. In the above procedure 96% of semantically processed words were recognized. Structurally processed words were remembered worst, thus only 18% of words were recognized following structural processing.

Conclusion: Depth of processing profoundly affects how well memories are remembered. Semantic processing involving processing words for meaning leads to most successful retrieval.

MASTER YOUR METHODOLOGY

1 The key to this study was operationalizing the independent variable: depth of processing. Explain what is meant by 'independent variable' and 'operationalization'.

2 Why was it important to control for how memorable words were? What might make a word more or less memorable?

3 Why do you think the researchers carried out a number of procedures investigating depth of processing in different ways?

They suggested that it was not necessary to hypothesize the existence of separate memory stages and stores—in understanding levels of processing, one understood the process of memory. They did not deny that short- and long-term memory phenomena existed, but they questioned the idea that they represented distinct mental stores (Craik, 2002) and disputed the idea that *stores* represented the most helpful way to think about memory *processes*.

The levels-of-processing framework has been enormously influential, not only in memory research, but in cognitive psychology generally (Roediger and Gallo, 2001). However, it has also come under a substantial degree of criticism. Perhaps the most obvious criticism is simply this: how can we know how 'deeply' a memory has been processed? We cannot view memories burrowing away into some 'deep', secret location in the brain. The only indication we have that the memory had been deeply processed is that it is recalled over time. In other words, to say that an item has been 'deeply processed' is not much different from saying that it has been remembered over time. There is a circularity to this definition (Watkins, 2002). Simply giving something a label ('deep level of processing') is not the same as explaining it.

Moreover, those who support the modal model point to a number of lines of evidence supporting the idea that memory truly has distinct stores and stages. See earlier in this chapter where we discussed evidence for separate memory stores.

THINKING CRITICALLY

What is meant by circular logic? Why is levels of processing vulnerable to such an accusation? To what extent do you agree?

READ THIS

It is worth starting with some original material on the development of the multistore model by Atkinson and Shiffrin and Murdock. These are quite readable articles:

Murdock Jr, B.B. (1967). Recent developments in short-term memory. *British Journal of Psychology*, **58**, 421–33.

Atkinson, R.C. and Shiffrin, R.M. (1971). The control of short-term memory. *Scientific American*, **225**(2), 82–91.

Working memory represents our current view of short-term memory. You can read an early and a more up-to-date account of this approach from Alan Baddeley here:

Baddeley, A. (1992). Working memory. *Science*, **255**, 556–9.

Baddeley, A.D. (2017). The concept of working memory: A view of its current state and probable future development. *Exploring Working Memory* (pp 99–106). London: Routledge.

In similar vein these are some key resources to help you understand more about long-term memory as most psychologists currently see it:

Parkin, A.J., Reid, T.K., and Russo, R. (1990). On the differential nature of implicit and explicit memory. *Memory and Cognition*, **18**, 507–14.

Tulving, E. (1972). Episodic and semantic memory. *Organization of Memory*, **1**, 381–403.

For levels of processing, once again we're going to recommend going back to the original:

Craik, F.I. and Lockhart, R.S. (1972). Levels of processing: A framework for memory research. *Journal of Verbal Learning and Verbal Behavior*, **11**, 671–84.

FACTORS AFFECTING RETRIEVAL

How is information in long-term memory accessed when we need it? Retrieval of information from LTM—that is, remembering—may happen either through *recognition* or *recall*. Recognition occurs when you are presented with something and are able to identify it—a fact you have previously learned, a person with whom you have had contact, and so forth. Recall occurs when you reproduce something from LTM either in response to cues (cued recall) or without cues (free recall).

❯ KEY IDEAS retrieval cues
Retrieval cues are any stimulus that provides a hint or association that helps one retrieve a long-term memory. Cues can be related to external context, internal state, or a semantic link.

❯ KEY IDEAS context-dependent memory **Context-dependent memory** occurs when retrieval of a memory is enhanced in contexts that were similar to the one that existed when the memory was encoded.

THINKING PRACTICALLY

Exams and tests can make use of different types of retrieval. Match the following types of question to different types of retrieval:

Multiple choice   Short answer   Essay

Cued recall   Free recall   Recognition

Retrieval Cues

Retrieval of long-term memories is greatly enhanced through **retrieval cues**. A retrieval cue is any type of hint or association that helps you sift—consciously or unconsciously—through the immense and complex store of long-term memory to select the appropriate information. These cues may be *external*, originating outside yourself (seeing books stacked on your desk reminds you that you have an assignment due); or internal, originating from within (thinking about your best friend reminds you of the time the two of you went hiking and got lost in the woods).

Context Cues

An important type of external retrieval cue is *context*. **Context-dependent memory** describes situations in which retrieval of a memory is enhanced in contexts that were similar to the one that existed when the material was encoded. For example, you might be listening to a song and recall another event that occurred when you were listening to the same music. Indeed, Godden and Baddeley (1975) (Figure 9.13) demonstrated context-dependent memory vividly when they had scuba divers memorize lists of words either underwater or on land, and later tested them for recall of these words both on land and underwater. We can look at this study in detail in *Research in focus*.

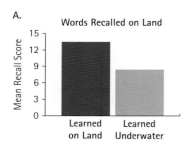

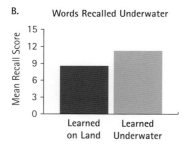

FIGURE 9.13 **Context-dependent memory on land and underwater.** Scuba divers best remembered words memorized underwater when they were underwater (Graph A), whereas words they memorized on land were best recalled on land (Graph B).

Source: Godden and Baddeley, 1975.

RESEARCH IN FOCUS

Godden, D.R. and Baddeley, A. (1975). Context-dependent memory in two natural environments: On land and underwater. *British Journal of Psychology*, **66**, 325–31.

Aim: To test the hypothesis that cues in the environment present at both encoding and retrieval aid the process of recall. Specifically, to see whether words learned on land or underwater would be better recalled when in the same environment than when recalled in the other environment.

Method: The study was experimental and carried out under natural conditions: 18 volunteer divers (13 male, 5 female) recruited from a diving club were read lists of 36 two- to three-syllable words to learn. Half the participants were read the list on land and the others underwater (through a radio) either on a beach or 15 feet under the surface of the sea; 24 hours later they were asked to recall the words without cues (a free recall task). There were four conditions:

1 Learned on land, recalled on land.

2 Learned on land, recalled underwater.

3 Learned underwater, recalled underwater.

4 Learned underwater, recalled on land.

Results: 50% more words were recalled when they were learned and recalled in the same environment as compared with when the words were recalled in a different environment. For example a mean of 13.5 words were recalled in the land–land condition as compared with 8.6 in the land–water condition.

Conclusion: Context cues enhanced recall.

MASTER YOUR METHODOLOGY

1 What was the advantage of carrying this study out in a natural environment rather than in the laboratory?

2 In spite of the natural environment this study can be criticized for its lack of realism. Explain why this might be.

3 Why was it important to test all four conditions rather than just two, say learn on land—recall on land and learn on land—recall underwater?

State cues

State-dependent memory takes place when the retrieval cue is internal (ie, a physiological state). Mood and other psychological states, including drug-induced changes in consciousness, can act as retrieval cues. Caffeine is a good example of this. Caffeine may increase performance on cognitive tasks for some people. However, the probability that it will work, say, to increase your test performance, is much increased if you also used caffeine while studying for the test (Kelemen and Creeley, 2003). Indeed, while **alcohol** and marijuana have been shown to impair memory as a rule, if you happen to learn some new information while under the influence of these drugs, the information is often better recalled when in the same condition than when sober—although this effect is seen primarily in *free-recall tasks* (eg, a fill-in-the-blank question) as compared with recognition tasks (eg, a multiple-choice question; Eich, 1989). Obviously there are good reasons not to put this to the test on your psychology degree! We'd go with the coffee idea . . .

> **KEY IDEAS** state-dependent memory **State-dependent memory** occurs when retrieval of a memory is enhanced by internal states such as mood or drug effects that were present when the memory was encoded.

THINKING PRACTICALLY

Episodic memory is impaired in Alzheimer's disease, leading to confusion and distress. However, psychologists have used cameras—rather like dashboard cams for 'life-logging' (Lee and Dey, 2007). This allows patients to record and replay key events. Explain how this benefits patients using the idea of state and context cues.

Semantic cues

Recall that the word 'semantic' refers to *meaning*. Tulving and Pearlstone (1966) demonstrated that meaning cues can improve memory just as can state and context cues. They instructed participants to memorize word lists with accompanying category headings then asked them to recall the words with or without the categories. They recalled more words with category headings, suggesting that these acted as semantic cues to trigger recall of the words.

In a follow-up study Tulving and Osler (1968) carried out a similar procedure with three conditions. As in the original study category cues present at encoding and retrieval enhanced retrieval; however, categories provided at retrieval only did not. In addition a category cue provided with each word was no more effective at enhancing recall than a single presentation of the category. This showed that it was the match between semantic category at encoding and retrieval that led to the improved recall, in turn demonstrating the effect of semantic cuing.

Flashbulb memories

A unique type of internal retrieval cue that has fascinated researchers and the public alike is the flashbulb memory (Figure 9.14). A flashbulb memory is a highly vivid and detailed remembrance of one's personal circumstances at the moment of learning of some shocking and unexpected event—the assassination of a public figure, a natural disaster, an attack by a foreign nation (Hirst et al, 2009). For example, we can both recall where we were at the moment we first heard about the 11 September 2001 attacks on the World Trade Center and the Pentagon. Neither of us has a clue what we were doing the same time on 10 or 12 September! In a sense, then, a flashbulb memory is a memory for unremarkable events, cued by memories of remarkable events.

It seems that in spite of their vividness flashbulb memories are not particularly reliable and accurate memory deteriorates substantially over the first year following the event—as researchers studying the aftermath of the September 11 attacks discovered. Among a sample of Americans drawn from seven cities and surveyed over a period of several years, there was a 20% rate of forgetting for 'flashbulb' aspects of memory for 9/11 during the first year and an additional 5–10% over the next two years. Flashbulb aspects of memory included questions such as, 'Where were you at the time?', 'What were you doing?', and 'How did you feel?' Emotional aspects of the event—how each participant felt at the time—were especially unreliably recalled (Hirst et al, 2009). The unreliability of flashbulb memories suggests an important point about memory: memory may be fragile, even for events that would seem extremely important.

THINKING CREATIVELY

The art of studying flashbulb memory is to identify a suitable event that a large number of people within a population will remember. Identify a target population and an event that is likely to be well remembered.

THINKING CRITICALLY

Flashbulb memory is notoriously hard to investigate, hence evidence for it is rather weak and mixed. Explain why this might be.

A.

B.

C.

D.

FIGURE 9.14 Flashbulb memories. Indonesia tsunami, 2004; Columbine High School Massacre, 1999; assassination of Martin Luther King, 1968; attack on World Trade Center, 2001. Flashbulb memories are intensely vivid and detailed, though not always reliable, memories for one's personal circumstances at the moment of learning about an unexpected and shocking event.

Sources: Indonesia tsunami: David Rydevik/Wikimedia Commons/Public Domain; Columbine High School: Kevin Higley/ AP/Shutterstock; Martin Luther King: AP/Shutterstock; World Trade Center: Chao Soi Cheong/AP/Shutterstock.

Depressive memory

A memory is often more accurately recalled when one is in a mood (or drug state) similar to that which existed when the memory was encoded (state-dependent memory). Research has found that those suffering from **depression** are more apt to recall unhappy memories from their past than happy ones—but this is not the case once their depression passes. On the other hand, mood can also seriously distort memories for the past. In a depressed mood, one may remember an event as primarily negative, but in a good mood, one may focus instead on positive aspects of the same event. Which memory is more realistic (McNally, 2003)?

Reconstructive Memory

Much traditional memory research has emphasized questions related to *how much* of various types of memories will 'fit' into memory stores and *how long* these memories will remain where we 'stick' them (Koriat, Goldsmith, and Pansky, 2001). However, there has recently been a shift among many researchers towards understanding how memories change over time as they go through a process of reconstruction (Brewer and Wells, 2011).

Nearly a century ago Bartlett (1932) arrived at the conclusion that memory was more of 'an imaginative reconstruction' of events (1932, p 213). This line of research has shown that the popular metaphor for memories as snapshots or videos of past events—accurate records that remain in their original condition for access at a later date—has been misguided. Instead, as Lynn and Payne (1997) propose, memories are *constructed*, not 'played back'. Retrieval of stored memories involves an active process of *reconstruction*. Whenever we try to recall an event, we actively piece it together using a range of information.

Bartlett developed the *serial reproduction* method of studying reconstructive memory. This involves one person telling a story to a second, who passes it on to a third person—and so on. This is designed to simulate under controlled conditions the social process in which information is passed from one person to another. Bartlett famously used the Native American story, *The War of the Ghosts*, in serial reproduction studies.

Bartlett found that once stories like *The War of the Ghosts* had been serially reproduced through half a dozen people it changed in particular ways. It was around half the original length, omitting details specific to Native American culture. Thus the story became increasingly like an English story.

The effect of schemas and scripts on memory

Our *expectations*, based on previous experiences of the *type* of situation being recalled—rather than specific memories—can interfere with the retrieval of accurate memory and result in distorted and false memory as in misattribution. To understand how this works, we need to discuss the workings of *schemas* and *scripts* (Figure 9.15).

A schema is an organized mental model or knowledge structure that helps to organize our experience of some type of event or situation, or our understanding of some object or concept. Once a schema is formed, we can then place within the schema new experiences and memories of that, or similar, events, situations, objects, and concepts. For example, suppose you are visiting a dentist for the first time in your life. You take in the events that occur during the visit and end up with a general idea or picture of what dentist visits are about. This becomes your schema for dentist visits. Subsequent visits may alter or refine the schema in various ways, but the schema allows you to anticipate in a general way what is likely to happen on any given visit.

Schemas are useful because they allow us to place new memories into an organizational structure that makes sense. If you were to visit the dentist and find some new piece of equipment, or a new dental hygienist replacing the old one, you would not have to start from scratch in trying to understand the nature of dental visits. You would simply fit this new information into your existing schema for dentists, which now will include the comings and goings of various assistants and pieces of equipment.

Schemas often play out in the form of scripts—structures in long-term memory that represent the typical sequence of events likely to occur in any given situation for which we have a schema—in a sense, the 'story' of the situation (Schank and Abelson, 1977). Scripts also include ideas about causes of events within a schema, and roles that different individuals are expected to take. A dentist visit script might include being greeted by a receptionist and being asked to sign various forms, a long wait in a waiting room, being ushered into a room, and given protective glasses before being lowered back on a dentists' chair, and so forth.

As useful as schemas and scripts may be in helping us respond to and interpret new situations, memory researchers have discovered some interesting ways in which they may distort memory or cause outright forgetting:

1 *People often falsely 'remember' details or events that do not actually occur because the event is strongly consistent with an existing script or schema* (Kleider et al, 2008).

2 *People are sometimes more likely to correctly recall details or objects that are* inconsistent *with script or schema expectations for some particular situation or location* (Lampinen et al, 2000).

Can you imagine why people seem to be better at recalling objects or items whose locations or appearances are inconsistent with existing schemas and scripts? It may simply be that things which stand out against their backgrounds are better remembered. Consider the following sequence of words: *apple pear orange banana television plum grapes papaya.* The word *television* is likely to stand out from this list and may therefore be more memorable. Studies such as these demonstrate the importance of the *context in which an event occurs* for subsequent accurate recall (Pezdek et al, 1989).

FIGURE 9.15 When believing is seeing. After a delay of two days, research participants who had been shown slide shows depicting men and women engaged in various activities often falsely remembered 'female-typical' actions as having been performed by women, and 'male-typical' actions as having been performed by men, even when the sex-typical actions were actually performed by a person of the other sex. Studies such as this demonstrate the powerful effects of schemas and scripts upon memory.

Source: Kleider et al, 2008, p 5.

READ THIS

The following are some of the key articles for understanding the effect of cues on retrieval:

Godden, D.R. and Baddeley, A. (1975) Context-dependent memory in two natural environments: On land and underwater. *British Journal of Psychology*, **66**, 325–31.

Tulving, E. and Pearlstone, Z. (1966). Availability versus accessibility of information in memory for words. *Journal of Verbal Learning and Verbal Behavior*, **5**, 381–91.

The original work on flashbulb memory and a recent review can be found here:

Brown, R. and Kulik, J. (1977). Flashbulb memories. *Cognition*, **5**, 73–99.

Rubin, D.C. and Talarico, J.M. (2017). Ordinary memory processes shape flashbulb memories of extraordinary events: A review of 40 years of research. In *Flashbulb Memories* (pp 89–111). Hove: Psychology Press.

Bartlett's original work on reconstructive memory is well worth a read, as is this recent review from Brady Wagoner:

Bartlett, F.C. (1932). *Remembering: A Study in Experimental and Social Psychology*. Cambridge: Cambridge University Press.

Wagoner, B. (2017). What makes memory constructive? A study in the serial reproduction of Bartlett's experiments. *Culture and Psychology*, **23**(2), 186–207.

EYEWITNESS MEMORY

A major practical application of our understanding of the fallibility of memory (this is explored in more detail later in this chapter) and, in particular, reconstructive memory is in judging and making best use of eyewitness memory in testimony. Over a century ago Hugo Munsterberg published a series of experiments demonstrating how inaccurate the memory of eyewitnesses is for witnessed events (Munsterberg, 1908; cited in Memon, Mastroberardino, and Fraser, 2008). However, his work proved controversial and throughout the last century many thousands of criminal cases all over the world have been decided on the basis of witness testimony. Of a sample of 302 Americans revealed to be innocent through DNA testing following conviction, over 80% had been wrongfully convicted on the basis of witness testimony (Innocence Project, 2013).

Our current understanding of the reconstructive nature of witness memory—and hence its unreliability—owes much to the work of American researcher Elizabeth Loftus. In a series of experiments in the 1970s and 1980s Loftus and colleagues demonstrated a range of factors affecting witness testimony. For example, Loftus and Messo (1987) demonstrated the effect of **weapon focus**. Participants watched a bank scene in which a cashier was either held up at gunpoint or paid in a cheque. They directed more attention to the gun than to the cheque and consequently recalled details of the rest of the scene less well. Similarly inclusion of scenes of violence inhibited accurate recall of details of a film for up to two minutes before the violent act (Loftus and Burns, 1982).

Perhaps most importantly Loftus demonstrated the distorting effect of post-event information on memory for an event. Loftus and Zanni (1979) found that after simply referring to *the* broken headlight as opposed to *a* broken headlight after watching a film of a car crash nearly four times as many participants falsely recalled a broken headlight (there wasn't one in the film). In similar vein, Loftus and Palmer (1974) found that people estimated different speeds after hearing that cars 'hit', 'contacted', or 'smashed into' one another.

THINKING CRITICALLY

The studies of eyewitness memory described so far in this section have been conducted under tightly controlled laboratory conditions. Explain the advantages and disadvantages of relying on this kind of evidence. What might be gained by carrying out more realistic studies and what might be the pitfalls of doing so?

Manipulation of Children's Memory

In addition to revelations of problems with eyewitness accounts, concern about memory accuracy was heightened by a series of wrongful convictions during the 1980s and early 1990s in cases of alleged sexual abuse of small children in US pre-schools (Bruck and Ceci, 1999). Children at these centres were subjected to repeated interrogation, sometimes lasting many months, by well-meaning but misguided so-cial workers, therapists, and police who believed they were 'getting at the truth'. Typically, the children at first truthfully denied that any abuse had taken place, but after questioning involving suggestion, threats, brow-beating, and/or bribes, the children ultimately made accusations involving exceedingly bizarre and unlikely forms of sexual abuse, supposedly perpetrated by people with no history of inap-propriate behaviour. Children's denials that abuse had taken place were frequently met by responses such as this from therapists interviewing preschool children in the McMartin case in California during the mid-1980s: 'Are you going to be stupid, or are you going to be smart and help us? You must be dumb' (cited by Nathan and Snedeker, 1995, p 140).

Like the fallibility of eyewitness testimony, the ease with which the memories of small children can be manipulated has been demonstrated in laboratory research. Bruck and Ceci created a series of studies showing that even under very gentle, non-coercive forms of repetitious questioning and suggestion, small children could be induced to recall with vivid detail events that never occurred, including having had their genitals penetrated violently with objects by a paediatrician during a rou-tine examination—when the paediatrician in fact had not even gone near the child's genitals (Ceci and Bruck, 1995).

What makes the studies by Bruck and Ceci particularly disturbing is that the chil-dren do not merely appear to be pressured to report an event that did not happen primarily to please their questioners—although this undoubtedly does occur in some cases (Cassell, Roebers, and Bjorklund, 1996). In many cases, this pressure seems to have convinced the children to believe that their memories are genuine. That is, their episodic memories have been 'rewritten' and they have developed **false memories** (Ceci et al, 1994).

Bruck and Ceci and their colleagues have also demonstrated this possibility in studies during which small children are induced to 'recall' memories of events that never occurred, such as going on a hot air balloon ride, falling off a tricycle, being

> **KEY IDEAS** false memory
A false memory is a memory of an event that did not actually occur. In some cases, blatantly inaccurate recollection of details of an event that did occur may also be considered a false memory.

taken to Accident and Emergency, and so forth. Many of these children continue to insist that the event actually occurred, even after being informed by parents and others that the events in fact never occurred (Bruck and Ceci, 1997, 1999).

The case of Kelly Michaels

We'd like to warn you that the case described below contains reference to child sexual assault, which is explicit and distressing to read. Please consider carefully whether for you personally the education benefits of reading it outweigh any distress. If you prefer, you can skip ahead to the next section on memory fallibility.

Twenty-three-year-old Kelly Michaels, with no record of any wrongdoing or unusual behaviour, was accused of bizarre (and in certain cases physically impossible) forms of sexual abuse of children at the Wee Care Day Nursery in Maplewood, New Jersey, on the basis of testimony of small children after coercive interviewing by police and therapists.

The following extract is from the Kelly Michaels Wee Care preschool case in New Jersey. The adult interrogator has been repeatedly trying to get the child to admit that Michaels had performed a bizarre sexual act:

> Adult: . . . Did she [touch your 'hiney']?
>
> Child: I don't know, I forgot.
>
> Adult: . . . Oh, come on, if you just answer that you can go.
>
> Child: I hate you.
>
> Adult: No you don't.
>
> Child: Yes I do.
>
> Adult: You love me I can tell. Is that all she did to you [note: the child never said that Michaels did anything to her], what did she do to your hiney?
>
> Adult #2: What did she do to your hiney? Then you can go.
>
> Child: I forgot.
>
> Adult #2: Tell me what Kelly did to your hiney and then you can go. If you tell me what she did to your hiney, we'll let you go.
>
> Child: No.
>
> Adult: Please.
>
> Child: Okay, okay, okay.
>
> Adult: Tell me now . . . what did Kelly do to your hiney?
>
> Child: I'll try to remember . . . (Nathan and Snedeker, 1995, p 141)

On the basis of children's testimony like this Michaels was convicted of 115 counts of child abuse and sentenced to 47 years in prison. After five years in prison her appeal was successful and she was released. (*Sources:* Nathan and Snedecker, 1995; Rabinowitz, 2003.)

MEMORY FALLIBILITY

We speak of memory failure rather than forgetting because although most memory failure involves forgetting—either in the form of complete loss of memories or their distortion—memory also causes problems when we remember too much or too well. Cognitive scientist Daniel Schacter has analysed processes of forgetting,

TABLE 9.1 **The seven sins of memory**

Sin	Description	Example
Transience	Decreasing accessibility of memory over time	Simple forgetting of long-past events
Absent-mindedness	Lapses of attention that result in forgetting	Forgetting location of car keys
Blocking	Information is present, but temporarily not accessible	Tip-of-the-tongue phenomenon
Misattribution	Memories are attributed to an incorrect source	Confusing a dream for a memory
Suggestibility	When memory is distorted due to suggestions implanted by others	Leading questions or misinformation can produce false memories
Bias	Current attitudes, feelings, and beliefs distort memories for the past	Recalling one's past feelings as having been more similar to current feelings than was actually the case; recalling one's past actions as having been more (or less) praiseworthy than was the case
Persistence	Unwanted memories that we cannot forget	Traumatic war memories

Source: adapted from Schacter, Chiao, and Mitchell, 2003, p 328.

the construction of distorted or false memories, and the unwanted intrusion of unpleasant memories. He characterized these processes in a list of seven memory 'sins' along the lines of the 'seven deadly sins' described by various religious traditions (Schacter, 2004; see Table 9.1). Schacter's choice of this metaphor is not meant to be flippant or disrespectful. The seven deadly sins consist of the improper use of human attributes that, when properly used, are not considered sinful at all. For example, *gluttony* is a distortion of the normal appetite for food; *lust* a distortion of normal sexual desire; *pride* a distortion of healthy self-esteem; and so forth. In the same way, according to Schacter, the seven sins of memory are not mistakes in the 'design' of memory, but rather, unfortunate 'side effects' of memory mechanisms that are in most aspects highly adaptive and without which we could not easily survive. Three of Schacter's sins pertain to forgetting, three to memory distortion, and one to the intrusion of unwanted memories. We begin with Schacter's three sins of forgetting: *transience, absent-mindedness,* and *blocking.*

Memory Transience

Transience describes the way that retrieval of memories becomes more difficult over time—that is, memories 'fade'. Transience is responsible for failing to recall how to do long division of fractions expressed as decimal numbers, failing to remember the way to your grandmother's house, failing to recall the story of a book you know you have read, and failing to remember how to play a musical piece you used to play perfectly. When people speak of 'forgetting', they are generally referring to memory transience.

Offer et al (2000) reported results of a 34-year longitudinal study of memory transience for events in **adolescence**. In 1962, the authors interviewed 73 mentally healthy 14-year-old boys about a wide range of topics. They then re-interviewed them 34 years later, at age 48. The accuracy of study participants' memory of past events was generally no better than would be expected by chance! For example, at age 14, 70% answered that religion was helpful to them, but only 26% of the

> ❯ KEY IDEAS transience
> **Transience** refers to the 'fading' of memories from long-term memory. Transience describes what most people mean when they say 'forgetting'.

men remembered having answered in this way. At age 14, 82% claimed that they received physical punishment as discipline, but at age 48, only 33% said they had been physically punished (Offer et al, 2000).

If memory for adolescence is transient, memory for childhood events prior to the age of 3 is essentially non-existent—a fact referred to as **childhood amnesia**. Although fragments of memories and isolated images of events that occur between the ages of 3 and 4 are sometimes available to adults, coherent episodic memories are not usually available for events prior to the fourth birthday (Davis, Gross, and Hayne, 2008). If you believe you can remember events before then, you are more likely than not remembering photographs, stories, or reveries about the event. In some cases a memory from childhood is mentally rehearsed and repeated throughout childhood, and in such cases you are in effect 'remembering remembering' the event—rather than remembering the event as it occurred.

One of the first attempts to study memory transience scientifically was by Hermann Ebbinghaus (1850–1909). Ebbinghaus was interested in determining how much information was lost to awareness after varying lengths of time had passed. He chose himself as his research participant and attempted to memorize as many meaningless 'nonsense syllables' as he could (Ebbinghaus, 1885/1964). Ebbinghaus tested his memory for such syllables (eg, TAK, JAV, KOP) at six time periods after having studied the words—from less than one hour to one month.

As depicted in Figure 9.16, Ebbinghaus noticed that there was a rapid loss of memory within the first hour, and within nine hours he had forgotten approximately 60% of the words. However, after that the pace of forgetting slowed markedly. One month later he had forgotten only an additional 15% of the words. Thus, most of the 'action' in forgetting occurred early on. This discovery came to be known as the **forgetting curve**, and while Ebbinghaus' methods were simple, he had discovered

> **KEY IDEAS** childhood amnesia
> **Childhood amnesia** is the term used to describe the fact that adults do not have accurate, coherent memory for events of early childhood. Theorists currently propose that coherent memories are not retained for events prior to the fourth birthday.

> **KEY IDEAS** forgetting curve
> **The forgetting curve** describes the pattern that forgetting follows over time, with most memory loss occurring rapidly, and the pace then slowing.

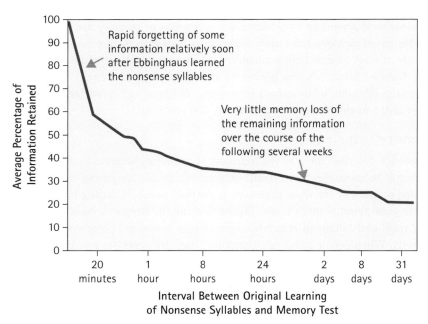

FIGURE 9.16 **The Ebbinghaus forgetting curve.** There is rapid memory loss over the first hour, and within nine hours 60% of the words are forgotten. After that, the pace of forgetting slows.

a law of memory transience that has been shown repeatedly to be valid in literally thousands of studies, for ordinary episodic memories as well as lists of words and the like (Thompson et al, 1996).

So what causes memory transience? The most obvious explanation is **trace decay**, the idea that long-term memories *decay* or fade away if they are not used, in the same way as happens with short-term memories. Early memory theorists believed that this was the case. However, this theory does not explain why some 'unused' memories appear to fade over time while others remain strong for decades or even a lifetime. It also does not explain how the ease or difficulty of retrieving memories is highly dependent upon retrieval cues, regardless of the length of time the memory has remained unused. If memories actually decay over time, then they no longer exist and should not be retrievable regardless of cue.

Instead, most modern researchers speculate that transience is explained in large part by the **interference** of one memory in the retrieval of another. Theorists have proposed two basic types of interference: *proactive* and *retroactive*. In **proactive interference**, a memory that one has formed in the past interferes with the retrieval of a new memory—particularly if the new information is in some way similar to the old (see Figure 9.17).

For example, as a young man I (Paul) worked as a cook in a Japanese restaurant, and learned something of the language, with a particular emphasis on matters pertaining to food. Years later, I tried to learn Portuguese. I did alright generally, but when I went to Brazil and tried to order food in a restaurant, Japanese words kept coming to mind and confounding my efforts. I could not recall the appropriate Portuguese words due to proactive interference. The effects of proactive interference for a memory tend to *increase* over time (Wixted, 2004).

Retroactive interference is much the same mechanism, but in reverse. In this case, the learning of new information interferes with memory for the old. For example, when you acquire a new mobile phone number and learn it, it may soon become virtually impossible to remember the old one due to *retroactive* interference (see Figure 9.17). Retroactive interference may *decrease* over time, and it is less dependent upon the new information being similar to the old (Wixted, 2004).

Absent-Mindedness

Ever walked away from a coffee shop without your coffee or, worse, from a cash machine without your money? If so you are guilty of the second memory sin, **absent-mindedness**. This is usually considered the bane of the middle-aged, but actually anyone can be afflicted.

Tatiana Cooley claims that she is so 'incredibly absent-minded' that she is forced to 'live by Post-Its' (Schacter, 2001). Without her 'to-do lists' she admits she would be lost. 'So what?' we hear you say. Well it is interesting because Tatiana Cooley is a memory champion! Using methods of elaborative rehearsal and chunking, she can recall strings of 4,000 numbers or 500 words, recite 50-line poems verbatim, and place names to faces with astounding accuracy. Nonetheless, she is very absent-minded.

Absent-mindedness can happen for two reasons: either (a) the information was encoded improperly (or not at all); or (b) it was encoded properly and is technically available, but at the moment that its retrieval is necessary it is overlooked for some reason.

We are probably all guilty of absent-mindedness. For me (Paul) I regularly fail to encode properly where I put my glasses. For me (Matt) it's my inhaler! Because we

❯ **KEY IDEAS** trace decay **Trace decay** is a theoretical explanation for memory transience, in which the physical trace of long-term memories decays on a neural level. Although trace decay is an intuitively obvious explanation it has proved difficult to provide direct supporting evidence.

❯ **KEY IDEAS** interference, proactive and retroactive **Interference** is the notion, subscribed to by most memory researchers, that problems in retrieving memories results from the interference of one memory with another. There are two types of interference: *proactive* and *retroactive*. **Proactive interference** takes place when an old memory interferes with the retrieval of a new memory. **Retroactive interference** takes place when a new memory interferes with the retrieval of an old memory.

❯ **KEY IDEAS** absent-mindedness **Absent-mindedness** involves lapses of attention that result in a failure to recall information. This can result from a failure to encode properly or lapse of attention/ preoccupation at the moment of retrieval.

FIGURE 9.17 Proactive and retroactive interference. You experience *proactive interference* when old memories interfere with the retrieval of new memories. *Retroactive interference* occurs when new memories interfere with the retrieval of old ones.

are constantly putting these essentials down wherever we are doing so has become an automatic process and so we do not pay it conscious attention. There are many more dramatic examples of absent-mindedness that have had tragic consequences. It is more common than you might think for parents to forget to drop babies off for day care and leave them in a hot car—sometimes leading to their death. This may seem unlikely but it results from the same everyday cognitive errors that lead us to lose our glasses or inhaler. People tend to leave babies in hot cars when they are in a hurry or when there is a break in routine—for example, when a parent does not usually drop the child off on their way to work. In these circumstances our tendency for automatic processing becomes a problem.

Blocking

Have you ever had a word 'on the tip of the tongue'? This is an example of blocking. **Blocking** differs from transience and absent-mindedness because the long-term memory exists but momentarily cannot be accessed. In transience, a memory fades over time or is altered by interference. In absent-mindedness a memory is not encoded properly in the first place. In blocking, a memory is encoded properly, is not subject to interference, and may even be primed by a solid retrieval cue—it *should* be recalled. It just isn't.

Blocking occurs most often with names. When you know the face but can't place the name, you are *blocking*. Name blocking is the most frequent memory complaint of the middle-aged and older people, particularly when the name seems to be on 'the tip of the tongue' but just won't complete the voyage to speech (James, 2006)!

One may completely block a name while recognizing a face. But what about those times—as just described—when you feel sure you *do* remember the name (or word), but somehow . . . somehow . . . it just won't appear in your mouth to be uttered. It's on the *tip of your tongue*. The **tip-of-the-tongue phenomenon (TOT)** is a specific type of blocking characterized by a powerful sensation that a word or name is remembered, but is somehow just out of reach (Schwartz, 2002).

Nearly everyone experiences TOT fairly regularly, generally about once per week—although, as with blocking in general, TOT occurs more frequently as one ages (James, 2006), and more frequently during times of emotional arousal (Schwartz, 2010). About half the time people are successful in resolving the TOT within about a minute (Brown, 1991), but if you find yourself in a TOT experience, you might do best to stop trying for a few moments and come back to it (Choi and Smith, 2005). In any case, most of those who persevere ultimately succeed.

Misattribution

Misattribution or **source confusion** occurs when a person attributes a memory to a source other than its actual origin. For example, many people have memories of past lives. This is probably the result of misattribution (Roe, 2018). So an adult who recalls visual scenes from being a Celt in the Boudiccan revolt against the Romans in 61AD probably saw part of a film or historical documentary as a young child. They *attribute* the scenes they can remember to a past life and so *experience* a past life but it is far more likely they are simply recalling a TV programme.

Misattribution can have dangerous consequences. Eyewitnesses have been known to identify perpetrators of crimes with confidence, only to find out later that they *had* seen the person—just not at the scene of the crime (Loftus, 1996). In what is surely the most ironic of such cases, psychologist Donald Thomson, an expert in memory distortion and false recognition, was arrested for rape on the basis of the victim's detailed reconstruction of his face. However, Thomson had an alibi—*he was being interviewed on television about false recognition at the moment the attack occurred*. The victim had been watching the programme just prior to the attack and misattributed her memory of Thomson's face to that of the rapist (Schacter, 2001).

> **KEY IDEAS** blocking **Blocking** takes place when a memory has been encoded properly and primed by a retrieval cue yet cannot be retrieved.

> **KEY IDEAS** tip-of-the-tongue phenomenon (TOT) **TOT** occurs when there is a powerful sensation that a word or name is remembered but somehow is out of reach.

> **KEY IDEAS** misattribution or source confusion **Misattribution** or **source confusion** takes place when a memory is attributed to a source other than its actual origin. Some elements of the memory can be real; however, not all.

❯ KEY IDEAS suggestibility **Suggestibility** is a type of misattribution in which a new or distorted memory originates in suggestions made to a person by someone else.

❯ KEY IDEAS the misinformation effect The **misinformation effect** takes place when a person exposed to incorrect information about an event they have experienced later recall the event in a distorted manner by incorporating the false information.

Suggestibility

As we saw in Loftus' eyewitness memory experiments and vividly in the case of Kelly Michaels earlier in this chapter, the reconstructive nature of memory means that it is possible to distort memories by suggesting things retrospectively. This phenomenon of memory **suggestibility** is a specific type of misattribution that results from intentional or unintentional suggestions from others. Suggestion is a powerful road to the development of memory distortions, particularly false memory.

Much of Loftus' work during the 1980s explored the ways in which people who are exposed to incorrect information about an event they have experienced, later recall the event in a distorted manner by incorporating the false information—a tendency that has come to be termed the **misinformation effect** (Frenda et al, 2011). In a classic demonstration of the misinformation effect, Loftus and her colleagues asked university students to watch a series of slides depicting an armed robbery in a hardware shop in which a screwdriver was taken in addition to money. After viewing the slides the students read narrative reports of the crime with one detail altered—a hammer was described as having been taken instead of a screwdriver. The students were then tested on their memories of the crime. The majority of the students quickly and confidently declared that a hammer had appeared in the depiction of the crime (Loftus et al, 1989).

The misinformation effect has been demonstrated in scores of other studies (Loftus and Bernstein, 2005). People have been fed misinformation that caused them to confuse Minnie for Mickey Mouse, substitute a Give Way sign for a Stop sign, change a white car into a blue one, and alter numerous other sorts of details in their reports of witnessed events. People may come to alter their recollection of events if they later speak to other people who have different versions of the event or if they read about the event in the mass media (Loftus, 2003).

However, as Loftus (2003) herself observes, it is one thing to change a hammer into a screwdriver or alter some other detail for an event one has actually witnessed, but quite another for the misinformation effect to create a rich and vivid memory for an event that never occurred at all. Loftus knows that such a thing is possible because she experienced it herself. When Loftus was 14, her mother died in a tragic pool-drowning accident. After that time, vague memories of the event 'haunted' her, although they were unfocused and she had no recollection of viewing the death scene itself. Loftus had always thought it had been her Aunt Pearl who had discovered the body, but 30 years after the accident, an uncle informed her that it had been Loftus herself who had discovered her mother's lifeless body. Suddenly,

> It all made sense. No wonder I was always haunted by the circumstances of my mother's death. . . . the memory had been there all along, but I just couldn't reach it. . . . Perhaps this new memory, dead and now revived, could explain my obsession with memory distortion, my compulsive workaholism, my unfulfilled yearning for security and unconditional love. (Loftus and Ketcham, 1994, p 39)

Over the coming days, Loftus was flooded with details of the event—her terror and screams, the police cars, the stretcher with the white blanket tucked around the edges of her mother's body. However, several days afterwards, Loftus received a call from her brother. It appeared that the uncle had been mistaken. It *had* been Aunt Pearl who discovered the body, a fact confirmed by numerous other relatives. A casual piece of misinformation—'It was *you* who discovered your mother's body'—triggered the construction of a **rich false memory**, a vivid false memory replete with extensive detail and emotional content.

Loftus and her colleagues began to experiment with the deliberate implanting of rich false memories using the *lost-in-the-mall* technique. In this type of study, relatives of the research participants are enlisted as **confederates** of the experimenter and asked to provide false information to the participant about a childhood event—such has having been lost in a mall, hospitalized for a serious illness or injury, attacked by an animal, or rescued from drowning by a lifeguard. These events are entirely fabricated by the investigators and the participant's relatives (Loftus and Pickrell, 1995). Typically, the participant is given descriptions of a number of childhood events, most of them true, but one of them false. The participant is asked if they remember each event and, if so, to provide details.

In most such studies, a substantial minority (approximately 30% on average but as many as 50% or as few as zero) develop rich false memories for the fictitious events. If a doctored photograph is used as supportive 'evidence' of the occurrence of the event, the development of false memories may occur in as many as two-thirds or more of participants (Lindsay et al, 2004). After completing these studies, participants are 'debriefed'—the purpose of the study is explained, and they are informed that their memories are false. In general, they tend to be astonished. As one participant put it: 'No way! I remember it! That is so weird!' (Lindsay et al, 2004, p 153).

Rich false memories have consequences in behaviour. Research participants in a study by Elke Geraerts and her colleagues were led to falsely believe they had been sickened as children from eating egg salad that had gone off. A substantial minority of these participants subsequently avoided eating egg salad for at least four months (Geraerts et al, 2008).

Memory Bias

I (Paul) shall never forget the face of my friend Nita's 6-year-old as she watched a videotape of herself at age 2½ walk calmly over to her 6-month-old brother and bop him hard on the head with a book for no particular reason at all, resulting in screams of distress from the baby. 'Why did I do that?' she asked in shamed wonderment.

The point of the story is this: that 6-year-old girl *could not believe what she was witnessing*. Being faced with undeniable evidence of less-than-admirable past behaviour violates a general memory *bias* known as the **egocentric bias**—a tendency to recall past events in a way that enhances one's current view of oneself (M. Ross and Wilson, 2003).

The *egocentric bias* is only one of a number of pervasive memory *biases*. A **bias** is any systematic distortion in perception, cognition, or memory that results from some aspect of a person's current psychology. The egocentric bias in memory is particularly interesting, because it does not necessarily cause us to remember ourselves as 'better' than we actually were—in fact, it quite often does the exact opposite. Researchers have shown that there is a tendency for people to think of themselves as having 'improved' over time (whether or not they actually have), and to exaggerate past failures or unreasonably criticize their former selves as a way of enhancing their views of their selves in the present (Wilson and Ross, 2001, 2003). The further in the past one goes, the more likely one is to distort one's memory for oneself in a negative direction.

> **KEY IDEAS** rich false memory A **rich false memory** is vivid but false memory containing rich detail and emotional content.

> **KEY IDEAS** bias **Bias** is a systematic distortion in perception, cognition, or memory as a result of some aspect of one's current psychology. An example is **egocentric bias,** the tendency to recall past events in a way that enhances one's current view of oneself.

❯ KEY IDEAS consistency bias
Consistency bias is the tendency to recall one's past attitudes, feelings, and beliefs in a way that brings them in line with one's *current* attitudes, feelings, and beliefs.

In addition to the egocentric bias, memory is distorted through the **consistency bias**, a tendency to recall one's past attitudes, feelings, and beliefs in a way that brings them in line with one's *current* attitudes, feelings, and beliefs (Cameron, Wilson, and Ross, 2004). For example, Elaine Scharfe and Kim Bartholomew (1998) asked 77 dating, cohabitating, or married couples to fill out extensive questionnaires describing their relationship 'style', closeness of the relationship, love for their partner, importance of the relationship, happiness in the relationship, how often their partner 'got on their nerves', and so forth. Eight months later the investigators asked the participants to recall how they had answered these questions. Among those participants whose feelings about their partners and their relationships had not changed, memory was highly accurate: 89% of women and 85% of men correctly recalled how they had answered the questions put to them eight months earlier. However, the picture was dramatically different for those whose feelings *had* changed: only 22% of these women and 13% of the men correctly recalled the answers they had given—with the majority of these incorrect answers bringing former feelings in line with current feelings. Those who no longer felt as loving as they originally had felt claimed that they had always felt less than happy in their relationships; those who no longer felt negatively about the relationship claimed that things had always been blissful!

WHAT'S HOT? EVOLUTIONARY PERSPECTIVES ON MEMORY FALLIBILITY

Why do we forget and distort memory? Are the memory 'sins' described earlier evidence of defects in our memory systems? Researchers such as Gary Marcus contend that our memory systems have been constructed over evolutionary history in a more or less haphazard fashion, and have survived not because they are particularly good but because they are 'good enough' (Marcus, 2008). Theorists such as Marcus view problems of distortion and forgetting primarily from a 'defect' perspective.

However, applying a different type of evolutionary view, Schacter (2001) suggests that mechanisms of forgetting serve specific adaptive functions. For example, *transience* enables us to lose information that is no longer current—where we parked our car last week, as opposed to where we parked it this morning (Figure 9.18). Memory for last week's parking location no longer needs to be rehearsed, allowing us to place our cognitive resources elsewhere. Something similar is at work in *blocking*, according to Schacter, particularly in tip-of-the-tongue (TOT) experiences. If you recall, names and words that one has not recently used are most frequently subject to TOT. TOT may represent one expression of general mechanisms that inhibit memory for items that are unlikely to be used frequently, freeing up resources for more critical memory tasks.

The principle that fewer memories may make for better memories is even more clearly apparent in *absent-mindedness*. Encoding memories at depth requires rich elaboration. Schacter asks, what if *all* events—the unimportant as well as the important—were elaborated and encoded with the same amount of rich detail? The mind would be an 'overwhelming clutter of useless details' (2001, p 190). Thus, in Schacter's view, there is a 'trade-off' in forgetting. Although forgetting can prove frustrating, on the whole it maintains the adaptive functioning of memory.

The same applies to memory distortion sins such as *misattribution* and its offspring *suggestibility*. These involve failing to maintain memory for the sources of experience or information.

❯

FIGURE 9.18 Schacter suggests that *transience* enables us to lose information that is no longer current; for example, it's more useful to remember where we parked our car this morning than where we parked it last week.

Source: James McDowall/Shutterstock.com.

Once again, however, were we to recall *all* the details of context and source for *all* memories, our minds would be excessively cluttered. Source and context details would interfere with the retention of more important information. In general, there is no need to recall many precise details of context and source unless these details are likely to be needed in the future. The important thing is to remember that water does not put out oil fires, not to recall specifically how you learned this fact. Being able to recall the *gist* of events—to benefit from knowledge without necessarily recalling its source—is a memory strength, according to Schacter, not a weakness. The 'trade-off' is the unfortunate capacity of the human mind to create distorted memories.

Is there evidence to support Schacter's view of forgetting? Kuhl and colleagues used fMRI technology to measure activity in the prefrontal cortex during memory tasks (Kuhl et al, 2007). These researchers found that better memory for details was associated with increased demands on regions of the cortex, but that these demands were reduced when competing, irrelevant memories were forgotten—just as Schacter's theory would predict.

THINKING CRITICALLY

Like all evolutionary psychology, Schacter's theory makes intuitive sense but is hard to test directly. To what extent is the study by Kuhl et al a direct test of the theory?

REPRESSION: MOTIVATED MEMORY

Repression is an explanation for memory loss and distortion that falls outside Schacter's model. Also it is so controversial that it warrants a section of its own. Indeed, it is hard to overstate the strength of feeling this topic arouses among memory researchers and among those who work therapeutically with people who recover—or appear to recover—memories of forgotten trauma and who attribute the initial memory loss to repression. Note though that although many psychologists see recovered memory and repression as closely intertwined they are *not* synonymous—there are other explanations for recovered memories (Howe et al, 2016) and not all repression involves the complete loss and recovery of memory.

So what is repression? Sigmund Freud (1894) suggested that we forget events that provoke negative emotions, hence we protect ourselves from these experiences. To Freud these memories remain in some way 'active' in the mind, triggering symptoms like anxiety. Freud identified a range of repression phenomena. At one end of the spectrum, repression involves the complete loss of traumatic memories. The classic example is childhood sexual abuse, forgotten until adolescence or early adulthood. At the other end of the spectrum is a general tendency to recall happy memories more easily than unhappy ones—we might call this mild repression. We may also recall events but repress the emotion originally attached to them.

 THINKING CRITICALLY

There is more evidence for the persistence or *hypermnesia* of traumatic memory than there is for repression. Some psychologists have used this as an argument against repression. The argument goes that if many victims of trauma struggle to stop thinking about the experience how can it be that repression also occurs? What do you think of the logic of this argument?

To cognitive psychologists repression, at least in the form of complete loss of traumatic memories, is intensely frustrating because it would be unethical to recreate that level of trauma under controlled conditions in order to study it. The accounts of therapists that they see clinical evidence for repression daily in their professional practice cut very little ice with cognitive psychologists who are acutely aware of the reconstructive nature of memory and the ease with which false memories can be generated. However, it *is* possible to run experiments that test the recall of mildly uncomfortable experiences. Unfortunately, such studies have produced mixed findings.

In one such study Koehler et al (2002) recorded participants' galvanic skin response (which uses sweat as a measure of anxiety) following the presentation of each of 50 words and tested their recall for the words. The existence of mild repression would predict that the words producing the greatest anxiety as measured by GSR responses are the least well recalled. This was indeed the case. In another study using a different method Walker et al (1997) asked participants to keep an 'emotion diary' in which daily events were rated for pleasantness/unpleasantness. When tested later they showed better recall of pleasant events than unpleasant ones. It can be argued that these studies assess the much less controversial phe-nomenon of memory bias, yet bias and milder forms of repression may be much the same thing.

On the other hand when Hadley and MacKay (2007) presented participants with taboo words (ie, those with rude connotations or are just plain rude) such as *snatch, whore*, and *prick*, and matched non-taboo words (matched for length and frequency of use) such as *snack, wheat*, and *plate*. In direct contradiction to the findings of Koehler et al, taboo words were better remembered. This is the opposite of what repression hypothesis would predict. Of course, studies like this do not show con-clusively that repression never occurs. They do, however, demonstrate how difficult even milder forms of repression are to evidence.

DEBUNKING: RECOVERED MEMORIES OF CHILDHOOD TRAUMA

Sometimes people who experience a traumatic event in childhood go through a phase in which they do not recall it and then, perhaps in adolescence or early adulthood, they appear to recover the memory. This has prompted a vigorous debate about the extent to which recovered memories of childhood trauma are genuine. This debate is tied up to some extent with the theoretical under-standing of memory. To those that believe in repression—largely but not entirely those involved in therapeutic work—the recovery of memories is likely to represent the return of a repressed memory and there is therefore an emphasis on genuine recovery of **veridical memories**.

Memory researchers tend to be more sceptical about the idea of repression and are more likely to base their understanding of recovered memory in the reconstructive nature of memory (Patihis et al, 2018). Remember from our discussion of post-event information (see 'Eyewitness memory' earlier in this chapter) that questioning following an event can help construct a distorted or even completely false memory. We have also seen that memories for childhood events seem to be particularly fallible.

Although progress has been made in resolving some of the controversies surrounding this question, it is not likely that all issues will be entirely resolved to everyone's satisfaction, at least not in the near future. The problem is that it is extremely difficult to conduct the sort of research that would unambiguously settle the most important questions. To do so, one would have to be able to determine with certainty that (a) a 'remembered' incident of abuse actually took place many years ago as described, and (b) the person actually *had* completely forgotten the abuse for all those years (McNally, 2003).

For example, several people in research studies who sincerely believed they had forgotten their abuse since the time of its occurrence, in fact had discussed it on numerous occasions with their spouses—they had simply forgotten they had remembered (Schooler, Bendiksen, and Am-badar, 1997)! Indeed, in experimental research, recovered-memory claimants have been shown to be particularly vulnerable to 'forgetting they remembered' in other contexts as well (Geraerts et al, 2006).

However, even if it could be determined that abuse actually occurred and truly had been forgotten for some period of time, it still would not be clear *why* the abuse had been forgotten. For example, the person may simply have not thought about the abuse over a period of years. Many events of childhood, pleasant as well as unpleasant, are not thought about over periods of time (McNally, 2003). Moreover, memory recovery could be the result of newly available cues—such as beginning a consensual sexual relationship in adolescence or early adulthood—to trigger the recall of related earlier events like non-consensual childhood sexual activity.

> **KEY IDEAS** veridical memories A **veridical memory** is a relatively accurate memory for a real event. If the way we recall an event corresponds to what really happened that memory is veridical.

So what do we *know* about this difficult topic? Broadly, research has identified three robust findings.

1 As we have already discussed in depth, *many cases of reported childhood sexual abuse are false memories*, reconstructed as the result of poor interviewing (and therapeutic) practice.

2 *Most people who experience traumatic events try very hard to forget these memories, but cannot.* Moreover, the more traumatic the event, the more difficult it is to forget (McHugh, 2008). Such memories are most likely to display the seventh memory 'sin' of **persistence**—the intrusion of unwanted thoughts upon a person's consciousness. In the specific case of child sexual abuse, Alexander et al used documented cases of child sexual abuse to examine victims' memory accuracy 12–21 years later for details of the abuse (Alexander et al, 2005). They found that the more traumatic the experience was for the victim, the more likely he or she was to recall details of the event accurately.

> **KEY IDEAS** persistence
Persistence takes place when an unpleasant memory intrudes upon a person's thoughts against his or her will.

This line of evidence comes with a couple of important provisos. First, trauma victims do commonly forget details of their experiences. For example, holocaust survivors may forget a particular incident that occurred while they were interned in a concentration camp as children, although they certainly do not forget having been in the camp (Schelach and Nachson, 2001, p 129). Second, logically, the existence of false recovered memories does not preclude the possibility of veridical recovered memories.

3 *It is has been conclusively demonstrated that a traumatic memory such as sexual abuse or rape* **can** *be completely forgotten for many years and later recalled* (Brenneis, 2000). For example, a 41-year-old woman in treatment for her childhood experiences of abuse (which she remembered all too vividly) was driving home from a therapy session during which her therapist had mentioned that child victims sometimes also become adult victims. All of a sudden, she recalled having been raped by a stranger, 13 years previously, at the age of 22. At that time she actually had brought charges against the man, who had been prosecuted and convicted. Astoundingly, she had completely forgotten the entire event, including the trial. The rape, the trial, and her lack of memory for both are well documented.

This kind of evidence also comes with important provisos. First, cases conclusively documented in this way are fairly rare, thus although we can be confident in saying that genuine recovery of memory does occur we cannot say how often or why. Most accounts of 'recovered memories' of sexual abuse are more dubious for a wide variety of reasons: in some cases the abuse is conclusively shown never to have taken place, the memory's origin in suggestive or coercive psychotherapy sessions is highly probable, or the events recalled are wildly implausible (or even physically impossible) (McHugh, 2008).

The controversy will no doubt continue. In an important sense, however, *all memory is false*, at least to some degree (Bernstein and Loftus, 2009). This is because all our memories are reconstructions—pieced together narratives and images which constitute our personal autobiographies. This is critical because it means we are unlikely to arrive at a reliable and valid method to distinguish between veridical and false recovered memories.

THINKING CREATIVELY

Although it is unlikely that psychologists will arrive at an objective method for distinguishing between real and false memories it may be possible to draw up guidelines for when an alleged recovered memory is particularly credible or implausible. What might you include in such guidelines? HINT: consider the nature of the memory, the circumstances in which it is recovered, and the possibility of corroborating evidence.

READ THIS

We recommend these as some of the key references around memory failure and its implications:

Loftus, E.F. (2018). Eyewitness science and the legal system. *Annual Review of Law and Social Science*, **14**, 1–10.

Davis, D. and Loftus, E.F. (2018). Eyewitness science in the 21st century: What do we know and where do we go from here? *Stevens' Handbook of Experimental Psychology and Cognitive Neuroscience*, **1**, 1–38.

Schacter, D.L. (2001). *The Seven Sins of Memory: How the Mind Forgets and Remembers*. Boston: Houghton-Mifflin.

When it comes to repression and recovered memories the vast majority of publications express very strong views. Nothing wrong with that but we suggest you might like to start with a clear and detailed account of the history, theory, and research underlying the debate. You can't do better than this for that kind of read:

Smith, S.M. and Gleaves, D.H. (2017). Recovered memories. *Handbook of Eyewitness Memory*, **1**.

IN REVIEW

BASIC MEMORY PROCESSES

- Memory is a set of cognitive systems that allow the encoding, storage, and retrieval of information.

THE MULTISTORE MODEL

- According to this model there are three memory stores: sensory store, short-term memory, and long-term memory. These differ in their capacity, encoding, and longevity.
- Short-term memory has a capacity of around seven items which are encoded acoustically or visually and can be sustained for a few seconds.
- Long-term memory is more likely to encode material semantically and has an unlimited capacity, maintaining memories indefinitely.
- Working memory is a way of looking at what happens in short-term memory when information is manipulated or processed.
- LTM has two types and two subtypes. Explicit memories are conscious memories for personal experiences or facts about the world. There are two subtypes of explicit memory: episodic memories and semantic memories. Implicit memory occurs when we recall something but have no awareness that we are doing so.

Implicit memory is most frequently expressed as either procedural memory or repetition priming.

THE LEVELS-OF-PROCESSING APPROACH

The levels-of-processing framework is an alternative way to look at memory, proposing that information can be encoded at deeper or shallower levels.

According to the LOP approach, so-called 'short-term memory' simply represents shallower levels of processing, while LTM results from deeper levels.

FACTORS AFFECTING RETRIEVAL

Retrieval depends on cues, which may be internal state cues or external context cues.

Flashbulb memories are those for major events. Their distinctive feature is that we tend to recall peripheral details remarkably well in addition to the event itself.

Most people have a bias towards remembering happy events; however, this is reversed in depression, in which people find it easier to retrieve unhappy memories.

Memories are constructed at the point of retrieval rather than played back. This process of reconstruction is influenced by schemas and scripts.

EYEWITNESS MEMORY

Because of the reconstructive nature of memory, eyewitness testimony can be surprisingly unreliable.

Witness memory is less accurate when there is violence or a weapon present, and in particular it can be distorted by post-event information

Children's memory appears particularly vulnerable to post-event questioning, and aggressive questioning has resulted in cases of wrongful convictions of adults for crimes against children.

MEMORY FALLIBILITY

The 'seven sins of memory' include sins of forgetting and sins of memory distortion. Sins of forgetting include transience, absent-mindedness, and blocking. Sins of memory distortion include misattribution, suggestibility, and bias.

A seventh sin, persistence, refers to the intrusion of unwanted memories upon consciousness. This can occur after trauma.

The fact that human memories are imperfect may reflect evolutionary 'trade-offs' which cause fewer problems than we would encounter if forgetting and memory distortions did not exist.

The notion that traumatic memories may be repressed and hidden from later recall has been highly controversial. Evidence is mixed but generally experimental evidence has only supported the existence of mild repression.

A related but conceptually separable debate concerns the recovery of forgotten memories for traumatic childhood events. It appears that there are genuine cases of recovered memory; however, there is a large body of evidence to show that many so-called recovered memories are false and result from poor therapeutic practice.

TEST YOURSELF

1 Information is lost from short-term memory by maintenance rehearsal. True ☐
   False ☐

2 Episodic memory is an example of explicit memory. True ☐ False ☐

3 Levels-of-processing theorists deny the existence of short- and long-term memory. True ☐ False ☐

4 There is plenty of evidence for both true and false recovered memories. True ☐
   False ☐

5 Which of these is not a component of the multistore model of memory?

   a) Sensory memory

   b) Working memory

   c) Short-term memory

   d) Long-term memory

6 Anterograde amnesia results from damage to which part of the brain?

   a) Amygdala

   b) Cerebellum

   c) Hippocampus

   d) Frontal lobe

7 Which of these is not a type of memory cue?

   a) Phonemic

   b) Semantic

   c) Context

   d) State

8 Which of Schachter's seven sins of memory would explain mistaking a dream
   for an episodic memory?

   a) Absent-mindedness

   b) Persistence

   c) Suggestibility

   d) Misattribution

9 Explain what is meant by the primacy-recency effect

10 Explain why repression is so controversial

 Visit the online resources that accompany this book: www.oup.com/uk/jarvis-okami1e

CHAPTER 10

THINKING AND LANGUAGE

LEARNING OUTCOMES

By the end of this chapter you should be able to:

- Explain the computational approach to understanding cognition
- Distinguish between thinking and cognition and between mental imagery and concepts
- Discuss Kahneman's distinction between System I and System 2 processes
- Evaluate a range of problem-solving strategies including trial and error, algorithms, insight, and heuristics
- Understand the particular influence of a range of heuristics on thinking
- Appreciate the role of bias in decision-making with particular reference to the importance of confirmation bias
- Explain the key characteristics of language as an open-ended code, including recursion, displacement, and generativity
- Critically discuss the notion of language as a mental organ as posited by Chomsky, with reference to the critical period and universal grammar
- Understand critiques of Chomsky's ideas including the connectionist perspective
- Appreciate that many grammatical rules in English represent social rules and do not represent universal grammar
- Evaluate the notions of linguistic determinism and linguistic relativity with regard to the examples of cross-cultural variations and universals in concepts
- Critically consider the notion of animal communication as language

We are constantly thinking about something. In fact, although we are sometimes very critical of the *quality* of each other's thinking the *constancy* of our thinking is one of our distinguishing features as a species. We think so much that we have developed techniques from yoga to meditation to mindfulness in order to *reduce* our thinking. So what is thinking?

In the late 1960s, philosopher Jerry Fodor (1968, 1983) and several others developed an idea that had been floating around philosophy circles since the 1950s, and in so doing changed the entire direction of many branches of psychology. Fodor and those who had been working along the same lines made the claim that the mind functioned in a manner loosely analogous to a computer—that is, that the mind was designed to process and manipulate *information*. This idea has come to be known as the **computational theory of mind (CTM)**, and it has formed the basis of much of *cognitive science*. **Cognitive science** is the term used to describe those branches of science that study mental activities and attributes that are involved in collecting, processing, storing, retrieving, and manipulating information. In addition to psychologists, cognitive scientists include among their number philosophers, neuroscientists, computer scientists, and linguists.

Of course, Fodor and other early cognitive scientists did not mean that the mind was designed like a PC, Mac, or other commercially available computer, or that people went about their business like robots or androids. Instead, these theorists meant that the mind operates according to sets of largely universal rules and principles for processing and manipulating information—much the way computer programs process and manipulate whatever data is entered into them. In other words, mental activity is *lawful*, and the best way to describe its laws is to invoke the metaphor of computation.

As you might expect, there are many disagreements among cognitive scientists about the nature of the mental computations that make up cognition, and there are those who reject the computational model entirely. Nonetheless, the computer metaphor popularized by Fodor is pervasive throughout cognitive psychology and has been responsible for many of the important insights described in the discussions of *thinking, language,* and *intelligence* to follow.

> **KEY IDEAS** computational theory and cognitive science
> **Computational theory of mind (CTM)** refers to the idea that the mind functions as an information processor in a manner loosely like a computer. **Cognitive science** is a multidisciplinary branch of science that studies mental activities and attributes involved in collecting, processing, storing, retrieving, and manipulating information. Cognitive scientists may come from disciplines as varied as psychology, linguistics, philosophy, neuroscience, and computer science.

THINKING CRITICALLY

Think about the computational model of cognition. In what ways do you think the mind is really like a computer and in what way does it differ?

THINKING AND COGNITION

Although people often use the terms *thinking* and *cognition* interchangeably, they are not synonymous. Cognition encompasses all mental activities and attributes concerned with information. In addition to thinking, cognition includes learning and memory, language, intelligence, and perception. Thus, we might say that thinking is a subset of cognition. But what *is* thinking? **Thought** is the active process of mentally manipulating or 'working with' information to solve problems, make decisions, increase knowledge, or just fantasize. Thinking is composed of two primary components: *mental images* and *concepts*.

> **KEY IDEAS** thought **Thought** is the active process of mentally manipulating information in order to solve problems, make decisions, increase knowledge, or fantasize. Thought consists of mental images and concepts.

Mental Images

How many shelves are in your refrigerator? How many vegetables can you name that are not green? How would you describe your sixth-form psychology teacher's hairstyle? As Pinker (1997) observes, when asked questions such as these, most people respond by creating mental visualizations for inspection by the 'mind's eye', rather than reeling off recalled facts. Such visualizations are known as **mental images**, and they are a type of thought. These pictures—images of people, places, and things that occur to us countless times a day—are *representations* of information in visual form. When you read a story and form mental images of the events about which you are reading, when you hear the front door open and picture your flatmate coming

> **KEY IDEAS** mental images
> **Mental images** are a type of thought in which objects are represented in picture form.

through the doorway, when you feel hungry and imagine a hamburger or an organic sprout salad with avocados, you are representing information in picture form.

The term *mental image* is apt. When research participants engage in tasks that require the construction of mental images, they utilize areas of the *occipital cortex* normally associated with vision (Kosslyn, Thompson, and Ganis, 2006). Moreover, a meta-analysis of studies of neural activity whilst thinking of abstract and concrete ideas (the latter but not the former can be imaged) by Wang et al (2010) revealed reliable differences in brain areas involved—with concrete ideas being associated with greater activation of the perceptual system.

More interestingly, as depicted in Figure 10.1, areas of the brain that are activated during visual perception differ according to the *content* of what is being viewed— whether it is a face or place—and the same differences are found for brain activation during the formation of *mental* imagery of faces and places. Simply by looking at fMRI brain scans, researchers are able to tell whether a person is imagining a face or a place (Liu, Harris, and Kanwisher, 2010).

Figure 10.1 depicts brain-slice fMRI data for four research participants in the study by O'Craven and Kanwisher (2000). The arrows in the images on the top two rows show activation in the FFA for these participants as they viewed images of faces or imagined viewing faces. The top row shows activation while participants actually viewed faces, and the row below that shows activation while participants imagined viewing faces. Similarly, the bottom two rows show perception and

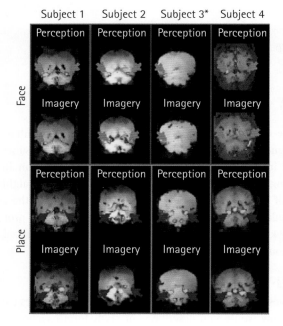

FIGURE 10.1 Mental images. fMRI data from four participants shows that the same area of the brain, the *fusiform face area* (FFA), activates when either seeing or imagining faces. Likewise the *parahippocampal place area* (PPA) activates when either seeing, or imagining places.

Source: Reproduced with Permission from K.M. O'Craven and N. Kanwisher (2000). Mental Imagery of Faces and Places Activates Corresponding Stimulus-Specific Brain Regions. *Journal of Cognitive Neuroscience*, November, 12(6), pp. 1013-23. © 2000 by the Massachusetts Institute of Technology.

imagination tasks for the viewing of places, with corresponding activation of the PPA as participants actually viewed images of places, or imagined viewing places.

Perhaps the most interesting question around mental imagery concerns how mental images are used. According to Kosslyn (eg, Moulton and Kosslyn, 2009) mental images are not simply a way to represent objects and situations but they also serve as simulations of possible scenarios, allowing us to answer 'what if' questions by visualizing different situations. Note though that others, notably Pylyshyn (eg, Pylyshyn, 2002) are critical over the quality of evidence to support this. To Pylyshyn mental images are epiphenomena, bi-products of thinking about objects. From this perspective mental images have much less psychological significance than they do according to Kosslyn's approach.

THINKING CREATIVELY

Kosslyn has proposed that mental images are an aid to thinking because they allow us to visualize scenarios. Design a study to test the hypothesis that being able to use a mental image enhances our thinking ability. You will need to decide on a way to measure thinking, such as a mathematical or logical problem (success on this will be the dependent variable), and a way to activate/inhibit mental imagery (the independent variable).

Concepts

Pictures may sometimes be worth a thousand words, but not always. What sort of mental image can you conjure up for 'ambivalence'? Is it colourful? Does 'fatigue' have jagged or smooth edges? Of course, you might be able to conjure up an image of a person you believe to be ambivalent on some issue, or an activity you find particularly fatiguing. But what of the innumerable examples of *ambivalence* and *fatigue* that are not covered in these specific images? To think usefully about such matters, we need more than mental images: We need **concepts**.

Concepts are mental categories or groupings into which we can place people, places, things, events, and ideas that share certain characteristics and qualities in common (even though they may also differ substantially). For example, the concept 'food' lets us recognize edible substances (Figure 10.2). Without this concept it would be meaningless to say, 'Let's get something to eat' or 'I have to buy some things for dinner'. We would have to stipulate every single item we intended to purchase, because there would be no obvious relationship between 'cucumbers' and 'tortilla chips'. Thus, concepts provide us with the most information with the least mental effort, and they reduce the need to be endlessly learning new facts. When we utilize concepts in our thinking, the similarities between the things that are contained within the concept are emphasized, while the differences are played down or ignored.

Fuzzy boundaries

Concepts have features or attributes that define them. Sometimes these features are precise and strictly defined in physical terms. For example, a shape with three straight sides is a *triangle*, and that's all there is to it. There is no three-sided shape that is *not* a triangle, and no shape that has fewer or greater than three sides that *is* a triangle. Concepts such as *triangle*, *oxygen*, or *water* have formal rules that cannot be violated— an item is either part of the concept or not. Such concepts have *clear boundaries*.

❯ **KEY IDEAS** concepts **Concepts** are mental categories into which we can place people, places, things, events, or ideas that share common characteristics. In creating concepts, the similarities between phenomena placed in the mental category are emphasized, and the differences are ignored.

FIGURE 10.2 **Food concepts.** Food is a type of concept of which *vegetable* is an example and a concept in its own right. In turn, *broccoli* is an example of the *vegetable* concept and is also a concept on its own. Concepts are often arranged in hierarchies in this way.

Sources: food: Hurst Photo/Shutterstock.com; vegetables: Ana Blazic Pavlovic/Shutterstock.com; broccoli: s_derevianko/Shutterstock.com.

❯ **KEY IDEAS** fuzzy boundaries
Fuzzy boundaries are a feature of most concepts, occurring when it is not precisely clear where a concept begins and ends, or what does or does not belong in the concept.

❯ **KEY IDEAS** prototypes **A prototype** is an example of a concept or category that is thought to be particularly typical or representative.

However, there are relatively few concepts in existence that have clear boundaries. Most concepts have **fuzzy boundaries**—you cannot always say exactly where the concept begins and ends or what should or should not be included in it. Take the concepts *life* and *death*. You might think that a person is either alive or dead, and that there would be no argument about it. But the exact moment when a person has died is not always clear, even to scientists and medical professionals. And some patients have been 'brought back to life' after they have 'died' (ie, after their heart has stopped, electrical activity has ceased in the brain, and other signs of death have occurred). People also do not agree as to when 'life' begins—hence the debate over abortion. Life and death have fuzzy boundaries.

An item thought to be a particularly ideal representative of any given concept is known as a **prototype** of the concept. For example, for people living in Europe, the United States, or Latin America, *trumpet* and *piano* are good prototypes of the concept *musical instrument*, whereas *mbira* and *sitar* are probably not, at least for most of us. On the other hand, in Eastern or Southern Africa, the *mbira* is an excellent prototype of a musical instrument, and throughout Southern India the same could be said for the *sitar*. The more closely some item matches a person's prototype of a concept, the more likely the person is to see the 'family resemblance' and include it as part of the concept.

 THINKING CREATIVELY

Identify some examples of prototypes and non-prototypes for the following concepts: 1. Pets. 2. Sports. 3. Footwear.

KAHNEMAN'S TWO-SYSTEM THEORY OF THINKING

Time for some audience participation: take a look at Figure 10.3.

Did you have any trouble immediately grasping that these children were having a good time? Probably not. Now answer the problem 1 + 1 = ? How long did it take? Less than a half-second, I would hope—about the same length of time it should take for you to complete the phrase 'bread and _____'.

FIGURE 10.3 Did you have any trouble immediately grasping that these children were having a good time?

Source: Bojan Milinkov/Shutterstock.com.

Now consider this problem:

A bat and ball cost £1.10.

The bat costs £1 more than the ball.

How much does the ball cost?

An answer likely came to your mind almost as easily and rapidly as the solution to the 1 + 1 problem. Unfortunately, in this case, haste makes waste. If you answered 10p you were wrong. Think for a moment: if the bat costs £1 more than the ball, and the ball costs 10p, then the bat would cost £1.10 and the bat and ball together would cost £1.20, not £1.10. Give this problem your full attention for just a moment more, and you'll be able to come up with the correct answer.

Where are we going with this? Nobel Prize-winner Daniel Kahneman (2011) has proposed a *dual-system theory* of thinking that explains why it is so easy to add 1 + 1 instantly, to automatically come up with 'butter' to complete the phrase 'bread and butter', and to grasp immediately that the children in the preceding photo are happy—but to drop the ball entirely (along with the bat) on the computational problem.

Building on earlier 'dual-process' theories of cognition and many decades of research (his own and others'), Kahneman proposes that there exist two entirely separate, but interacting, *systems* of thought. *System 1* is rapid, intuitive, effortless, and automatic. It is generally not under voluntary control. It allows us to recognize a happy, frightened, or angry face; drive 'on autopilot' on a familiar route during hours when traffic is light; sense the direction of a sudden loud sound; judge which of two lines is the longer; solve very simple arithmetic (1 + 1) instantly; and understand simple sentences in our native language. Unfortunately, because it is effortless and automatic, we may often employ System 1 thought at times when what we *really* need is System 2.

System 2 is slower, effortful, and demands concentration and attention. It is also lazier than System 1: it would rather not be brought into play at all if it can be avoided. This is why so many of us get the ball-and-bat problem wrong at first. Because of its misleading wording, we sense (wrongly) that the problem can be solved easily with intuitive System 1 thought.

System 2 comes into play when we try to write an assignment or article, judge whether or not a logical argument has merit, solve maths problems involving double or triple digits, try to pick a friend's face out of a crowded lecture theatre, or decide whom to invite to a party with an eye towards avoiding conflict among the guests. System 2 pays attention, chooses, weighs evidence, and considers. Intense System 2 thinking burns calories (really!) and needs blood glucose to run properly. (*Don't* take important exams on an empty stomach.) System 2 thought also dilates the pupils of the eyes so reliably that by observing changes in pupil dilation researchers can tell when a person has finished working on a difficult mental task (Badmatz and Ozturk 2008).

However, there are limits to what we can do while System 2 is in gear. It demands most of the limited resource of attention we have to spend at any given time. As Kahneman states, if you are on a jog or brisk walk with a friend and you turn to her and ask her to solve a double-digit multiplication problem in her head right then and there, the first thing she is likely to do (if she agrees to the task) is to abruptly stop running or walking in order to do the mental work. It is exceedingly difficult to pay attention both to the movements of your body and the cognitive demands of a maths problem at the same time.

Similarly, you may find driving on a familiar, deserted road an effortless matter. You may be able to do so quite easily while having an intense conversation with a passenger, singing at the top of your lungs if there are no passengers (or very tolerant ones), or following a conversation closely on the radio. But try doing any of this while manoeuvring to park in a tight spot on a crowded city street or trying to locate an unfamiliar address on a dark road at night in pouring rain while cars are backed up behind you. There just isn't enough System 2 attention to go around. But don't worry—System 2 will likely prevent you from conversing, singing, or listening closely to the radio. It will focus your attention on the more important task at hand.

When System 2 is fully engaged and attention focused on a task, one may become literally blind to events outside the domain of the task, a phenomenon known as *inattentional blindness*. We described one example of this in Chapter 8—remember the gorilla in the midst of the group of basketball players?

Although Kahneman distinguishes System 1 from System 2, he emphasizes that the systems evolved to work together. In general, most of us bumble along during the day in System 1 mode, responding relatively automatically and effortlessly, opening and closing doors, eating, brushing teeth, walking up and down stairs, answering the phone, daydreaming, driving familiar routes. System 2 is brought into play only when a question or problem occurs that is beyond the reach of the intuitive System 1: What is the square root of 17? How should I help my brother make up with dad? Is that an animal in the middle of the road up ahead or just a paper bag? When System 2's work is done, it sits back and relaxes.

System 1, on the other hand, because it is effortless and needs little energy to run, can afford to remain engaged at all times. Indeed, it cannot be turned off at will. Kahneman uses the Müller–Lyer illusion we discussed in Chapter 8 to demonstrate this idea. Take another look at the image, reproduced here in Figure 10.4.

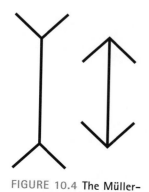

FIGURE 10.4 **The Müller–Lyer illusion.**

If you studied Chapter 8 you already know that both lines are equal in length. Yet, unless you are very unusual, you will still *see* the line on the left as longer than the line on the right. That's System 1 talking (Kahneman, 2011). System 2 has no problem judging which of two lines is longer—in most cases. But here, due to the unusual construction of the diagram which plays upon biases in perception, System 1 is unable to cope and you are advised not to listen to the messages it is sending. It's time to take out a ruler and allow System 2 to do its work.

THINKING PRACTICALLY

This maths problem is commonly shared on social media: 6/2(1+2) = ? First try to work this out as fast as possible. Now go back and apply BODMAS (brackets, of, divide, multiply, add, subtract). Most people get a different answer. Explain this difference in terms of System 1 and System 2 thinking.

The notion that two distinct systems of thought exist did not begin with Kahneman (eg, Stanovich and West, 2000), and there are commentators who do not believe it is productive to 'think about thinking' in this way (eg, Newstead, 2000). Kahneman himself, after introducing the two systems, calls them 'fictions'—shortcuts for describing cognitive events that occur automatically versus those that involve effort, are associated with pupil dilation, focused attention, and nervous system arousal. He does not propose that these systems exist in particular brain locations or anywhere else in the material world. Instead, like many such psychological constructions, they are convenient metaphors—relatively simple ways to describe enormously complex processes.

READ THIS

This is one of the most conceptually tricky areas in psychology, and it is worth beginning with the work of Michael Eysenck, who has a unique ability to make cognitive psychology accessible:

Eysenck, M.W. and Keane, M.T. (2013). *Cognitive Psychology: A Student's Handbook.* Hove: Psychology press.

Particularly interesting though quite high-level debate about the nature and role of mental imagery can be found in the work of Kosslyn and Pylyshyn. You might like to start with these papers:

Pylyshyn, Z.W. (2002). Mental imagery: In search of a theory. *Behavioral and Brain Sciences,* **25**(2), 157–82.

Moulton, S.T. and Kosslyn, S.M. (2009). Imagining predictions: Mental imagery as mental emulation. *Philosophical Transactions of the Royal Society B: Biological Sciences,* **364**(1521), 1273–80.

PROBLEM-SOLVING

Problems are obstacles that stand in the way of achieving some goal. *Problem-solving* is the process by which people use thought to find a way to remove these obstacles—to move from a situation that *actually* exists now to a situation that is desired but does not yet exist. When confronted with a problem, people generally choose a particular strategy. These choices are not necessarily made consciously—they may be made automatically and below the level of awareness. However, they are often very well suited to the problem at hand. In this section of the chapter we will briefly examine four such strategies: *trial and error, algorithms, heuristics,* and *insight.* We will then consider *creativity*—a unique way to create problems as well as solve them!

Trial and Error

❯ KEY IDEAS trial and error
Trial and error represents the most basic problem-solving strategy, where solutions are tried out and eliminated one at a time.

Trial and error is the most basic problem-solving strategy. It involves a conscious decision to eliminate one solution at a time until a solution that works is found. When finding a 'workaround' to avoid problems caused by a bug in a piece of software, computer users often employ trial and error—trying one method, then another, until they stumble upon a solution that works. If you desperately needed to get your wallet out of a friend's locker and you didn't know the combination for the lock, you might fiddle with it for a while, hoping eventually to hit upon the right numbers.

When a problem has relatively few possible (or available) solutions, slugging it out with trial and error can be effective. However, the greater the number of possible solutions, the less efficient trial and error will be. For example, trying to open your friend's combination lock using trial and error could keep you busy for a bit longer than you probably would want to sit in one place. Nonetheless, sometimes there is no viable alternative to trial and error.

Algorithms

❯ KEY IDEAS algorithms
Algorithms are step-by-step sets of computational instructions to correctly solve a specific type of problem. Algorithms have a specified beginning and ending and can be applied identically to any problem of the type they were designed to solve.

An **algorithm** is a step-by-step series of systematic 'instructions' that can be used to solve any problem of some given type. The procedure always remains the same, and you can 'plug in' whatever variables you like—as long as what you are 'inputting' consists of data in the form the algorithm is designed to compute. For example, simple arithmetic, complex mathematical formulas, and methods for converting one type of measurement into another (eg, inches to millimetres, feet to metres) are all algorithms. They work every time, but the algorithm for converting feet to metres will not work if you 'plug in' inches instead of feet; and the algorithm for adding whole numbers will not work if one of the numbers is a fraction.

Computers use algorithms to make computations and to solve problems that are not overly complex. If you have ever been involved in computer programming you will have written algorithms.

Heuristics

❯ KEY IDEAS
heuristics **Heuristics** are mental problem-solving shortcuts or 'rules of thumb'. Heuristics are very fast and often accurate, but they are not always accurate, and relying upon them can result in numerous erroneous assumptions.

When faced with having to make choices or decisions relatively quickly where the number of possible alternatives is uncertain, we sometimes fall back on *heuristics.* A **heuristic** is a problem-solving 'rule of thumb'—a mental shortcut designed to help us make judgements and decisions when all the facts are not known. We generally apply heuristics automatically, without consciously deciding to use them. They are a perfect example of Kahneman's System 1 as described earlier, and Kahneman—along with his late colleague Amos Tversky—is, not coincidentally, the most influential researcher and theorist on the topic of heuristics (eg, Tversky and Kahneman, 1973).

❯ KEY IDEAS the availability heuristic The **availability heuristic** is an heuristic that biases people towards using mental information that is more easily 'accessible' or mentally available. The availability heuristic is used when coming to a judgement about how often something occurs or how likely it is to occur in the future.

The availability heuristic

A good example of the use of heuristics is the **availability heuristic**, which helps us to judge how often something occurs or how likely it is to occur in the future. This heuristic works by biasing us towards mental information, memories, or images that are more easily 'accessible' to our consciousness—that is, those that come to mind easily. The more easily an event comes to mind, the more common and likely to occur in the future we generally believe it to be (Tversky and Kahneman, 1973).

As it happens, things tend to come to mind more easily if they have occurred recently, if they have strong negative emotional content, or both. For example, my (Paul's) neighbour's 3-year-old, Skye, was recently stung multiple times by a wasp at a particular location in the woods near our house. My wife's and my immediate response was to assume that he probably would not be the last to be attacked in this way. We became hesitant to allow our own children to play in that location, and announced to friends that this particular patch of woods was 'full of wasps'—even though, for all we knew, Skye's attacker was the only wasp for miles.

Of course, over the balance of history, a wasp nest is probably more likely to exist near a location where someone has been stung than in some other, random location. So the availability heuristic often serves a purpose. However, it can also cause problems. As an example, researchers have found that students often believe that tens of thousands, or even millions, of children are kidnapped by strangers each year. In fact the number of people under age 18 kidnapped by strangers each year is tiny.

Another example, provided by American statistician Nate Silver, concerns airborne terrorism—something that worries many people each time they board a flight. Based upon the number of acts of terrorism on commercial aircraft over an eight-year period, Silver calculates that there has been one terrorist incident per 16,553,385 departures, or one incident per 11,569,297,667 miles flown (that's 1,459,664 trips around the earth). Based upon these statistics (and a few others we won't saddle you with), according to Silver the odds of being on an airplane subject to a terrorist incident would be one in 10,408,947 (Silver, 2009). You are more likely to die as a result of eating pasta salad that's been left out too long.

Why are so many people's intuitive estimates of the number of child kidnappings and terrorist attacks wildly off the mark? Because these crimes are particularly horrific, and, as such, they linger unpleasantly in our minds. The tendency for people to remember them in detail is also stimulated by the fact that *each* of these events is reported nationally—precisely *because* they are both unusual and horrific. Legislation has even been passed as a result of publicity over a single child kidnapping. Media coverage and legislation increase the cognitive accessibility of child kidnappings and terrorist attacks, and the availability heuristic then inflates our estimates of how frequently they happen (Lichtenstein et al, 1978; see also Figure 10.5).

The representativeness heuristic

When people are confronted with an example of a person or thing that they do not know how to categorize or explain, they often use the **representativeness heuristic** (Tversky and Kahneman, 1974). This heuristic works in tandem with prototypes; recall that a prototype is a particularly good example of a concept or category. Using the representativeness heuristic involves making instantaneous comparisons of the new person or thing with prototypes of various categories until a 'match' is found. As an example, consider the following description (based on Nisbett and Ross, 1980):

> Lawrence Batson is 5′ 6″ tall, quite slim, and not particularly muscular. He likes to read mid-nineteenth-century British poetry and the published correspondence of great authors with their friends and spouses.

Would you say it is more likely that Lawrence is a professor of psychology or a lorry driver? If you guessed 'lecturer' you were using the *representativeness* heuristic

❯ KEY IDEAS representativeness heuristic The **representativeness heuristic** is used when people are confronted with an example of a person or thing that they do not know how to categorize or explain, they may compare the new person or thing to *prototypes* of various categories until a 'match' is found.

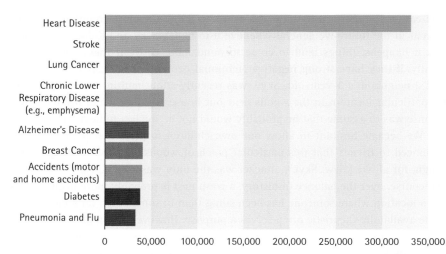

FIGURE 10.5 **The availability heuristic and perceptions of women's health risks.** Because of the publicity surrounding breast cancer, and the high degree of negative emotion generated by thoughts of this disease, actual mortality rates due to breast cancer are often overestimated by the average person. Heart disease, stroke, lung cancer, chronic lower respiratory disease, and Alzheimer's disease all claim many more female lives than breast cancer. Breast cancer mortality is approximately equalled by rates of death due to home and vehicle accidents, and diabetes.

Sources: US CDC National Vital Statistics Report, 2007, Vol 56. Retrieved from http://www.cdc.gov/nchs/data/nvsr/nvsr56/nvsr56_05.pdf on 17 November 2008; American Cancer Society Breast Cancer Facts 2007–2008 retrieved from http://www.cancer.org/downloads/STT/BCFF-Final.pdf on 17 November 2008.

> ❯ KEY IDEAS base rate **The base rate** is the basic probability of something occurring in a population, expressed as a percentage. Can also be understood as an indication of how prevalent something is in a population.

to match the description of 'Lawrence' to your prototypes of professors and lorry drivers, and deciding which made a better match (Nisbett and Ross, 1980). However, by now you might be able to see the problem with heuristics in general. Although they are fast and often accurate, they are not always accurate and can be highly misleading. 'Lawrence' might well turn out to be a lorry driver after all. In point of fact, Lawrence is *much* more likely to be a lorry driver than a professor! Why? To understand this, we must consider the important question of *base rates*.

A **base rate** is a probability figure, expressed in percentage, that indicates how prevalent something is in a population or how frequently it occurs. For example, if 5% of Europeans suffer from depression, then the base rate of depression in Europe would be 5%. To estimate the likelihood that Lawrence is a professor rather than a lorry driver, we have to take into account two important base rates: the base rates of professors and that of lorry drivers. How many of them are there?

Considering that there are only a few hundred universities in Britain and Europe, that psychology staff make up a small proportion their staff, and that even amongst the psychologists only a minority are professors it should be easy to see that there are no more than a few thousand psychology professors at large. Furthermore, it is likely that relatively few are slim and 5′ 6″ tall. 'Slim, relatively short psychology professor' is a good example of a category of people with *low base rate* status. On the other hand, there are many many more lorry drivers in Europe. Even if a large majority of psychology professors—say, 75%—enjoy reading mid-nineteenth-century British poetry (almost certainly an overestimate), and only a tiny percentage of truck drivers fit this description—say, 0.5%—that would still amount to many more lorry drivers who enjoy mid-nineteenth-century British poetry than psychology professors.

Perhaps you can now see that in spite of the fact that Lawrence might not sound like a truck driver to you, unless we had specific information about the man such as 'he works at Keele University', we would be far better off to guess that he is a lorry driver if given the choice between these two occupations. The probability is much higher that Lawrence is a lorry driver because it is highly unlikely that virtually *any* specific individual is a professor of psychology, regardless of their personal characteristics (Nisbett and Ross, 1980).

Unfortunately, most people do not take base rate information into account when they make judgements of the likelihood of some event—for example, the likelihood that a person has some disease given that they have particular symptoms, or the likelihood that a person belongs in some category (eg, lorry driver/professor) given that they have certain characteristics (eg, love of English literature; Tversky and Kahneman, 1973). In such cases, the representativeness heuristic may lead us astray.

Thus, the moral of the representativeness heuristic and base rate problem is this: if it looks like a duck and walks like a duck—and the base rate of ducks is low—it is probably a goose! (See Table 10.1 for a summary of the uses and misuses of the heuristics described in this section.)

Insight

> KEY IDEAS insight and impasse
>
> **Insight** is the term used to describe a situation where the solution to a problem appears suddenly 'as if from nowhere' after an impasse had been reached and it seemed that the problem was not solvable. An **impasse** occurs when a person has made repeated unsuccessful attempts to solve a problem yet possesses the mental ability to solve the problem.

The problem is not finding [musical ideas], it's—when getting up in the morning and getting out of bed—not stepping on them.

—Johann Sebastian Bach (cited by Myers, 2002, p 61)

Writing a textbook like this—or any other literary work—is a lengthy process. It takes time and one comes across numerous difficulties. However, we have repeatedly had the experience of struggling all day to solve one of these problems, falling asleep, and waking the next day with the solution seemingly pouring from our fingertips to the computer keyboard. This is the process of **insight**. Insight begins when a person is unable to see how a problem can be solved in spite of numerous (sometimes seemingly endless) attempts. He or she is at an **impasse**. Then, suddenly—'*Aha!*' A solution appears with ease as if from nowhere (Jones, 2003). It is often accompanied

TABLE 10.1 Uses and misuses of heuristics: two mental 'rules of thumb'

Heuristic	Description	Uses	Misuses
Availability (Tversky and Kahneman, 1973)	Things that are cognitively accessible more easily are thought to recur more frequently.	This heuristic can help us make quick decisions about the likelihood of something occurring.	Sometimes things are easily accessible for reasons other than their frequent recurrence (eg, a fictitious or unrepresentative story or picture is often more easily accessible than factual and statistical information).
Representativeness (Tversky and Kahneman, 1974)	'If it looks like a duck, quacks like a duck and walks like a duck, it probably is a duck'. Comparing a new object or person to our idea of a 'typical' member of the group to which it belongs.	Quickly determining the category or group to which a new object or person belongs.	May encourage the failure to take base rates into account; may increase prejudice and inappropriate stereotyping; contributes to failures in reasoning such as the gambler's fallacy (discussed later in this chapter).

> KEY IDEAS fixation **Fixation** involves being 'stuck' in a specific way of mentally representing a problem. Fixation may occur when one applies previously successful problem-solving strategies to new problems that may or may not best be solved with these strategies.

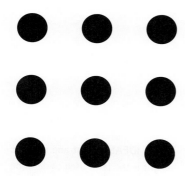

FIGURE 10.6 **The nine-dot problem. Connect all nine dots with four straight lines** *without* **lifting your pencil from the paper.**

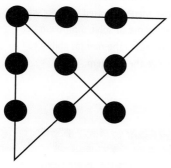

FIGURE 10.7 **The nine-dot problem solution: think outside the box! People have a very difficult time solving this puzzle because they are usually fixated on the idea that the lines of the pencil must fall within the boundaries of the outer dots—even though instructions to the puzzle do not limit where lines may be drawn (only that the pencil must not leave the paper). Three of the four lines must extend beyond the boundaries formed by the dots.**

by feelings of pleasure and confidence that one has truly solved the problem (Topolinski and Reber, 2010). Insight occurs in the context of general problem-solving, in creative and artistic work, when trying to retrieve an elusive memory, or when trying to understand what a foreign-language speaker or toddler is trying to tell you. It also can occur when you are struggling to define some sort of sensory perception that seems mysterious ('What on earth *is* that sound?'; Kounios and Beeman, 2009).

A person who solves a problem through insight is by definition already able to solve that problem. He or she has all the information or experience necessary and the cognitive ability to use this information and experience—otherwise, the problem would not be solved! This is one limitation of insight: it cannot occur if the solution does not already lie somewhere in one's consciousness. But if you are able to solve a problem, why is a point reached where you feel *unable* to solve the problem? That is, why do you reach an impasse? Knoblich and colleagues propose that impasses in solving problems often result from the fact that people begin their attempts to solve new problems using approaches that have proved successful in solving previous problems (Knoblich et al, 1999). In a sense, our successful experiences with old problems *bias* the way we structure and conceptualize new problems by constraining, or limiting, the number of options we can imagine in finding a solution to the new problem (Storm and Angello, 2010).

Being 'stuck' in a specific way of mentally representing a problem is known as **fixation**. The *nine-dot problem* (Burnham and Davis, 1969) depicted in Figure 10.6 is an excellent example of a problem that typically results in impasse due to fixation. This problem has caused many otherwise stable people to begin to tear their hair out.

How and why does insight occur after impasses are reached? According to Knoblich and his colleagues, insight occurs when we *change the way we mentally represent the problem* (Knoblich et al, 1999). In a sense, we are no longer trying to solve the same problem, but a different one. For example, should you find yourself in a locked room, you may at first assume that you must solve the problem of how to break the door down. After many failed attempts, it may suddenly occur to you that the room is only on the second floor and it might be possible to break the window and climb down. The problem is now a completely new one: how to tie enough material together to form a rope that will hold your weight.

This re-representation of the nature of the problem may activate aspects of your memory and knowledge base (the knot-tying you learnt in primary school, for example) not touched by the previous representation—expanding the number of options and possibilities to be considered. The solution can then come quite rapidly if it is 'contained' within the new mental spaces that have opened up. The solution to the nine-dot problem is depicted in Figure 10.7.

Neuroscientists have shown that brain wave activity and the sites of brain activation differ in research participants as they solve problems with insight as compared with non-insight strategies (Kounios et al, 2006). For example, using fMRI brain imaging, Mark Jung-Beeman and his colleagues found higher levels of activation in the *anterior superior temporal gyrus* (aSTG) of the right hemisphere around the moment of insight solution of verbal problems—but not while verbal problems were solved with non-insight methods. Among its many functions, aSTG is a brain region associated with making connections between distantly related pieces of information (Kounios and Beeman, 2009).

As depicted in Figure 10.8, using EEG imaging these researchers also found that approximately three-tenths of a second prior to the experience of insight

A.

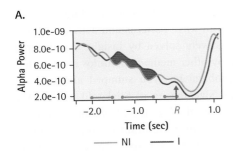

Alpha wave activity just prior to the burst of gamma wave activity. As you can see in the graph above, alpha power increases in insight solutions (purple line) versus non-insight solutions (blue line) beginning about 1.5 seconds before the insight solution (indicated by the green R and arrow). As a solution grows nearer, alpha power decreases.

B.

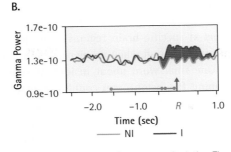

Gamma wave activity at the moment of solution. The graph above shows that beginning about 3/10ths of a second prior to solution, there is a sudden burst in gamma wave power in insight solutions (purple line), but no such increase in non-insight solutions.

C.

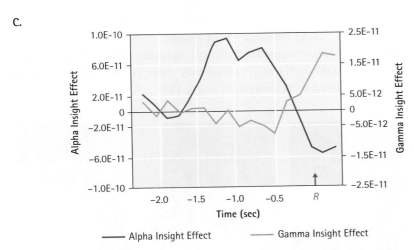

The comparison graph above demonstrates the increase in alpha (purple line) at 1.5 second prior to solution and its decrease as gamma waves shoot up beginning 3/10ths of a second prior to solution.

FIGURE 10.8 A picture of insight: brain wave activity during insight problem-solving.
Source: Jung-Beeman et al, 2004.

there are distinctive bursts of brain wave activities in the right temporal area and parietal-occipital area. These patterns were not found when non-insight solutions were reached. Jung-Beeman and colleagues concluded from these results that insight is characterized first by unconscious glimmerings of a solution—indirectly affecting alpha wave activity—leading to sudden awareness of the solution, reflected in the burst of *gamma* wave activity.

Can a person's method of solving a problem—insight vs non-insight—be predicted? In other words, can a given mental state *prepare* a person to use insight over a non-insight method? Kounis and his colleagues studied a group of participants as they prepared to solve, and then solved, a large series of verbal problems. The participants' subjective reports of the way each problem was solved, by insight or non-insight methods, was compared against fMRI and EEG brain imaging scans of brain activity as they *prepared* to solve each problem. As with the earlier study by Jung-Beeman and his colleagues, these researchers found brain wave patterns and activity of neurons at specific brain regions when problems were solved by insight that differed from that found when problems were solved by other methods (Kounios et al, 2006).

One final word about insight: if some problem has you stumped and you are hoping for insight, you could do worse than 'sleeping on it'. Stickgold and Walker (2004) found that a good night's sleep more than doubles the likelihood of discovering an insightful solution. Whether this is because the brain continues to work on the problem during sleep or whether we simply think better after a good rest is open to question.

Creativity: Finding Problems and Solving Them

Creativity has been defined in different and often conflicting ways, but one thing is clear: it is an important engine that drives cultural change and helps society to advance (Hennessey and Amabile, 2010). Creativity is more than writing great novels, painting masterpieces, making magnificent music, solving unsolvable equations, or devising unique software applications; it is an important force in human life that encompasses aspects of cognition, skill, personality, motivation, and various environmental variables—including the workings of chance.

Creative individuals solve problems. But creativity is much more than problem-solving. Indeed, as depicted in Figure 10.9, creative people may spend just as much time *finding* problems to solve as solving them (Csikszentmihályi, 1990).

A.

B.

FIGURE 10.9 Finding and solving musical problems. Creative people find problems as well as solving them. The composer Béla Bartók (A) decided that the folk melodies of his native Hungary were beautiful and important enough to be incorporated into serious art ('classical') music. He then masterfully solved the problem of how to do this. The composer–pianist Thelonious Monk (B) decided that the rhythms and 'feel' of traditional jazz stride piano could be brought forwards and wedded to rigorously modern harmonic and melodic innovation. He set about to do just that in his own thoroughly unique style. The problems of incorporating Hungarian folk melodies into classical music, or creating a modern musical style from the foundation of traditional stride piano, did not exist before Bartók and Monk 'found' them—and solved them.

Sources: Béla Bartók: Popperfoto/Getty Images' Thelonius Monk: CBS Photo Archive/Getty Images.

As we said, there is no universal definition of creativity, but we can think of it as a kind of syndrome or complex set of behaviours that include at least the following:

- *Originality.* Creative people are able to think 'outside the box'. Their thinking and the products of their work diverge in some way from what has come before, and their work represents new ideas or understandings (Mumford and Gustafson, 1988).

- *Utility.* The output or work of creative individuals is considered useful or valuable—particularly by those who are knowledgeable in the area in which the work has been accomplished (Paulus and Nijstad, 2003; Hennessey and Amabile 2010).

In addition, creativity usually involves flexibility—creative individuals are generally open to new ideas, and are able stay attuned to technological and other changes in the environments in which they work (Diedrich et al, 2017).

DECISION-MAKING

Although there is no doubt that human beings can be clear-thinking decision-makers, our discussion of heuristics has also shown that human beings are not always rational when making judgements and decisions when some uncertainty is involved (Tversky and Kahneman, 2005). Of the universities that offer me a place, which should I accept? Should I go to Accident and Emergency or just wait until Monday and call the doctor? Is the guy behind me following me, or is it just a coincidence that he's been behind me for five minutes?

How many questions like these do you suppose you've asked yourself over the course of your life? Seemingly, we do not always consider the risks and benefits of various alternatives open to us in a logical manner, and our perceptions of reality can be biased. In fact, we systematically violate principles of rational decision-making in predictable ways in certain types of situations. These tendencies are known as **cognitive biases**—systematic distortions in thinking, memory, and perception. In Chapter 8 we described the consistency bias and the egocentric bias as they apply to memory. We will now discuss one predictable bias as it applies to decision-making: the *confirmation bias*.

> **KEY IDEAS** cognitive bias
> **Cognitive bias** is any tendency towards systematic violation of principles of rational decision-making, judgement, or memory.

Confirmation Bias

The **confirmation bias** may be the single most prevalent and potentially destructive of all problems with human reasoning (Lilienfeld, Ammirati, and Landfield, 2009). Cognitive psychologist Raymond Nickerson (1998) wonders if this bias, 'by itself, might account for a significant fraction of the disputes, altercations, and misunderstandings that occur among individuals, groups, and nations' (p 175). Although the confirmation bias has many facets, in essence the term refers to the tendency to pay more attention and accord more weight to evidence that *confirms* what we already believe—or even to seek such evidence out—while ignoring evidence that would *disconfirm* our beliefs. Thus, when gathering evidence, people are often simply 'building a case' for what they already believe rather than actively attempting to discover the truth.

A good example of the confirmation bias at work is astrology. People who believe in astrology may vividly recall and pay attention to those traits and behaviours that conform to stereotypes of a person's zodiac sign—while ignoring or playing down all the traits and behaviours that flatly contradict characteristics of the sign and are much more typical of other signs.

> **KEY IDEAS** confirmation bias
> **Confirmation bias** is the tendency to pay more attention and accord more weight to evidence that confirms what we already believe—or even to seek such evidence out—while ignoring evidence that would disconfirm our beliefs.

Prejudice and harmful stereotyping are also strongly reinforced by the confirmation bias. This bias may cause a person to pay attention to and recall only those experiences with members of disliked groups that confirm prior negative beliefs about those groups (eg, 'That's just been my experience with those people'). Thus, the confirmation bias 'tells us what we want to hear' by confirming pet beliefs and theories to which we are emotionally or intellectually attached.

THINKING PRACTICALLY

Once an argument is well established and people have taken sides it can be remarkably difficult to get opponents to compromise or give credence to the other position. A UK example of this that is very topical at the time of writing is in the Brexit debate. Explain how confirmation bias has contributed to the depth of divisions over Brexit.

Belief persistence

> **KEY IDEAS** belief persistence **Belief persistence** is the phenomenon whereby once a belief is formed and confirmed it tends to be highly resistant to change, even when disconfirming evidence is inescapable.

What happens when people are faced with disconfirming evidence they cannot ignore? Once a belief is formed, it can be highly resistant to change—a related bias known as **belief persistence** (C.A. Anderson, 2008). When faced with clearly disconfirming evidence, a person may engage in mental gymnastics to play down its relevance or credibility ('Oh, they can do anything they want with statistics!'). If this fails, the person might struggle to find ways to fit the disconfirming evidence into a mental framework that does not threaten the belief—in a sense, to 'quarantine' the evidence. For example, when faced with a member of a disliked group who does not display the supposed negative characteristics of that group, someone experiencing belief persistence may say, 'Oh, well, he/she is one of the good ones'.

Of course, people do change their beliefs and biases. The point is only that, because of confirmation bias and **belief persistence**, this change may often take more time and more evidence than might be considered 'reasonable' by an objective observer.

The Gambler's Fallacy

> **KEY IDEAS** the gambler's fallacy The **gambler's fallacy** is the misperception of randomness that causes a person to believe that the likelihood of a random event is affected by events that precede it. For example, people often incorrectly assume that the likelihood of tails occurring in a fair coin toss will increase according to the number of times heads has come up in succession—see Figure 10.11.

An excellent example of human cognitive biases is the *gambler's fallacy*. Let us say you toss a coin and it comes up heads five times in a row. What would you say the likelihood would be that the next toss would be tails? What if it turned out to be heads yet again? Would the *next* toss be *even more* likely to be tails? The answer is no. Even if a coin were to turn up heads ten times in a row, each and every time you toss it (if the toss is fair) the odds are always exactly the same: 50/50. The odds of tails coming up do not 'accumulate' with each toss. As much as it *feels* as though the odds are stronger with each new toss of heads that the next toss will be tails, this is an illusion, known as the **gambler's fallacy**.

The gambler's fallacy keeps slot machine players feeding coins into the same machine over and over, certain that the odds of a jackpot increase with each play ('This thing is *due* to pay out —I can't leave now!'). Unfortunately, the odds of the machine paying out stay exactly the same with each new button press or handle pull.

Where does the gambler's fallacy come from? The first problem is a simple misunderstanding of the way probability odds work. The chances of tossing heads five times in a row are rather low—1 in 32. However, these odds only exist *prior* to the coin toss. So it would be a good bet when starting out that five straight heads will not show up over the next five tosses. But if you actually *do* manage to flip five heads in a row (which will definitely happen sooner or later if you keep tossing coins all day), you cannot then presume that the odds of another head coming up on the next toss are very small. *Chance does not have a memory*, and the likelihood of a random event occurring (eg, tails coming up) is not affected by events that have preceded it (eg, heads coming up five times). The odds for each single new toss are always 50/50.

Probability theory is extremely difficult for the average person to grasp—even highly educated people have trouble with it (Gigerenze et al, 2008). Therefore, the representativeness heuristic creates still more fertile soil for the gambler's fallacy to take hold. Consider the two series of 25 coin tosses depicted in Figure 10.10.

Which chart seems more typical of fair coin tosses at a 50/50 level of chance, Chart A or Chart B? Looking at Chart A, if you were to start paying attention on toss number two, there will be a seemingly unlikely streak of eight heads broken only by three tails. However, this is the normal operation of chance (randomness) at odds of 50/50. Ultimately—in the long run—an approximately equal number of heads and

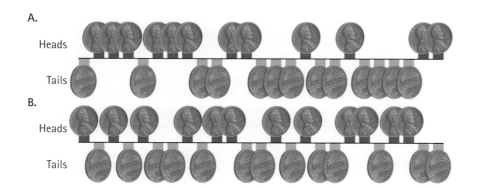

FIGURE 10.10 Which chart seems more typical of fair coin tosses at a 50/50 level of chance, Chart A or Chart B?

FIGURE 10.11 The gambler's fallacy. It might seem that the more times the roulette wheel spins without hitting your number (or colour), the more likely the next spin will be to do so. But, in fact, the odds of the table paying out stay exactly the same with each turn of the wheel: they do *not* 'accumulate'. The likelihood of a random event is not affected by events that precede it.

Source: iStock.com/mbbirdy.

tails will be tossed. However, cutting out a small segment of the 'long run' can produce remarkable streaks of unlikely events (Gilovich, Vallone, and Tversky, 1985). As statistician Robert P. Abelson (1995) put it, 'chance is lumpy'. Because Chart B *seems* more random, the representativeness heuristic prompts us to believe that it *is* more representative of randomness. In fact, Chart B is not at all typical of a string of random coin tosses.

READ THIS

Our understanding of heuristics owes much to the early work of Simon and Newell, whilst our contemporary understanding is particularly influenced by Tversky and Kahneman. You might like to start with these papers:

Simon, H.A. and Newell, A. (1958). Heuristic problem solving: The next advance in operations research. *Operations Research*, **6**(1), 1–10.

Tversky, A. and Kahneman, D. (1983). Extensional versus intuitive reasoning: The conjunction fallacy in probability judgment. *Psychological Review*, **90**, 293–315.

Understanding the issue of confirmation bias will be of great practical value. Have a read of these key papers:

Nickerson, R.S. (1998). Confirmation bias: A ubiquitous phenomenon in many guises. *Review of General Psychology*, **2**(2), 175–220.

Talluri, B.C., Urai, A.E., Tsetsos, K., Usher, M., and Donner, T.H. (2018). Confirmation bias through selective overweighting of choice-consistent evidence. *Current Biology*, **28**(19), 3128–35.

LANGUAGE

As Pinker (1994) suggested in his influential book *The Language Instinct* (1994, p 15), each human being has a most extraordinary ability: by marking symbols on a sheet of paper, signing with the hands, or making noises with vocal cords and mouth, each of us, with 'exquisite precision', can cause an entirely new idea to form inside the mind of another person. This happens, not through telepathy or any other metaphysical process, but through the use of language.

Take the following description from Raymond Chandler (1940/1992), an American mystery author noted for his descriptive prose:

> He was a big man but not more than six feet five inches tall and not wider than a beer truck. . . . He wore a shaggy borsalino hat, a rough gray sports coat with white golf balls on it for buttons, a brown shirt, a yellow tie, pleated gray flannel slacks and alligator shoes with white explosions on the toes. From his outer breast pocket cascaded a show handkerchief of the same brilliant yellow as his tie. There were a couple of colored feathers tucked into the band of his hat, but he didn't really need them. Even on Central Avenue, not the quietest dressed street in the world, he looked about as inconspicuous as a tarantula on a slice of angel food. (pp 3–4)

We suspect that a man who stands out like 'a tarantula on a slice of angel food' is a man who has never existed in your mind before just now. Chandler's descriptive language causes an entirely new idea (a mental image) to form in the mind of the reader.

Language as Open-Ended Code

The term *language* has distinct meanings that differ according to context. In the first, most obvious sense, language is any of the human systems of communication and personal expression (eg, Chinese, English, Arabic, Swahili) which have been built upon symbols or *representations*. By representations we mean that words (or gestures in the case of sign language) 'stand in' for the things they are intended to represent. To put it another way, languages are *codes*. According to linguistics, the scientific study of language, there are at least three important properties that characterize a human language: *generativity, recursion*, and *displacement*.

Generativity

Generativity is the quality of language that allows a person to use the relatively small number of words and grammatical structures of a language to compose a theoretically infinite number of sentences expressing an infinite number of new thoughts and ideas. Moreover, any one of these thoughts and ideas may often be expressed using different words, word orders, and phrases (Chomsky 1965, 1972). In describing the man who was 'no wider than a beer truck' and 'as inconspicuous as a tarantula on a slice of angel food', Raymond Chandler took advantage of generativity to create entirely new ideas from a unique arrangement of words. But he might have conveyed much the same idea had he described the man as 'no broader than a steamroller' and noted that he was about as inconspicuous as 'a cluster of 10-carat diamonds on a slab of black tar'.

The generativity of language demonstrates that language is *open-ended*, unlike other animal communication systems. Honeybees have a dance-like system of communication (see Figure 10.12) that may be used to alert others to the presence of succulent flowers and direct one another to the flowers' exact location (Esch et al, 2001).

> ❯ KEY IDEAS generativity
> **Generativity** is the quality of language that allows a speaker to use a relatively small number of words and grammatical structures to compose a theoretically infinite number of sentences and new ideas.

FIGURE 10.12 Honeybees have a unique system of 'dance language' to communicate distance and location of food sources and nesting sites (Esch et al, 2001). However, this system of communication is closed-ended, and can only convey very limited types of information—unlike human languages.

Source: iStock.com/RonBailey.

However, they cannot combine various elements in this dance system to communicate the arrival of Asian hornets (a major predator) or to describe places best avoided for other reasons (Wynne, 2004). Their system of communication is *closed-ended*.

THINKING PRACTICALLY

Take any sentence in this book, even the simplest—say, 'The term *language* has distinct meanings that differ according to context'. Encase the sentence in quotation marks and google it (the quotation marks are essential for the engine to search for the exact word order). In spite of the fact that there are billions of pages on the World Wide Web, it is highly unlikely that you will find this sentence anywhere in cyberspace.

Recursion

One way that generativity occurs is through recursion. In linguistics, *recursion* means that any sentence can be extended indefinitely by embedding clauses or phrases within or following it. For example, the sentence

Maya was watching a programme that featured the Nigerian actor.

can become:

Maya was watching a programme that featured the Nigerian actor whom she met last week.

which can become:

Joel told me this morning that Maya, the woman who just moved next door, was watching a programme that featured the Nigerian actor whom she had met last week.

which can become:

Joel, who rarely gossips, told me this morning that Maya, the woman who just moved next door into the flat that was left empty last month, was watching a programme that featured the Nigerian actor she had met last week—right after she had decided to stop watching the kind of programmes that . . .

You get the idea. Some linguists believe that the capacity for recursion is the single most important factor separating the evolution of human language from that of other animal communication systems (Hauser, Chomsky, and Fitch, 2002).

Displacement

> **KEY IDEAS** displacement
> **Displacement** is the quality of language that allows one to converse about things that do not exist, exist in other places, or are abstractions.

Displacement means that people can converse about things that do not exist at all, things that exist in places other than that where the conversation takes place, or about complete abstractions—feelings, beliefs, opinions, and so on. We can talk about things that occurred in the past, will occur in the future, or that we wish or fear might happen. Imagine for a moment how impoverished your thoughts and conversations would be without displacement!

Language as a 'Mental Organ'

To come to know a human language would be an extraordinary intellectual achievement for a creature not specifically designed to accomplish this task.

—Noam Chomsky (1975, p 4)

The term *language* has a second meaning for many cognitive scientists and linguists. It refers to a hypothesized **internal language faculty**. The language faculty includes innate, partly specialized neural circuitry ('hardwiring') in the brain and cognitive structures of the mind designed to acquire language in early childhood and to use language for thought, expression, and communication (Hauser et al, 2002). From this perspective, children acquire language not only because of their human intelligence and powers of observation and learning (which certainly play an important part), but also because they possess brain and mind mechanisms specifically *dedicated* to acquiring and using language (Chomsky, 1975; Pinker and Jackendoff, 2009).

According to this view, all languages possess a **universal grammar**—a basic structure or set of intrinsic 'rules' that all languages share in common. Obviously, this does not refer to ordinary rules of grammar that are famously and amazingly diverse among languages. It means that in spite of variance in correct word orders, use of tenses, and so forth, there exist certain commonalities that do not vary. Usually, universal grammar 'rules' are expressed by linguists in this way: 'If a language has X (eg, some particular way of placing a verb), it will also have Y (some way of utilizing nouns)'. Or 'If a language has a word for X (eg, the colour red), it will also have a word for Y (the colour purple)'. However, proposed rules of universal grammar are actually scientific hypotheses that only hold weight until a language is discovered that violates the rule—something that has been known to occur for numerous proposed universal grammar rules (Evans and Levinson, 2009).

Knowledge of universal grammar is considered by its advocates to be innate in human beings, and it is universal grammar that forms the internal language faculty. It enables children to easily assimilate the language of their parents and community, and second languages if need be, by automatically applying the rules of *universal* grammar to the *specific* grammar they are attempting to learn (Thomas, 2004).

No one claims that the internal language faculty resides in some specific anatomical location of the brain; instead, numerous areas are no doubt involved. But many cognitive scientists do conceive of this faculty as a kind of mental 'organ', much as the heart, kidneys, and lungs are anatomical organs. According to this view, rather than speaking of language as something that one 'learns', it may be more accurate to refer to it as something that 'grows' (S.R. Anderson and Lightfoot, 1999, p 698). The optimal 'growing period' for this organ—technically known as its *critical period* for development—is in early childhood, when language seems to be acquired effortlessly. Indeed, in those unusual cases where children have not been exposed to any language until puberty, they are generally unable to acquire language at all, or are only able to learn language in a very rudimentary way after rigorous training (Newport, 2002).

The hypothesis that all languages are united by a universal grammar is not new; indeed, it originated several centuries ago. However, the modern scientific version of this idea originated in the work of linguist, cognitive scientist, philosopher, and political activist Noam Chomsky (1980), who initially referred to the internal language faculty as a *language acquisition device* or LAD. Chomsky first noted a puzzle about language development in children: when one considers the number of words, word orders, phrases, and sentences that could conceivably be spoken in any language, it is clear that any given child is exposed only to an exceedingly small sample. Moreover, the *actual* speech to which children are exposed is choppy and often lacking in coherence (set up an audio recorder when you and your friends get together and just let it run for an hour—you'll be amazed at the results). As Chomsky

> **KEY IDEAS** internal language faculty The **internal language faculty** is the notion, initially proposed by Noam Chomsky and originally termed the *language acquisition device* (LAD), that human beings possess innate, specialized cognitive structures dedicated to acquiring and using language.

> **KEY IDEAS** universal grammar **Universal grammar** is the concept originated by Noam Chomsky to describe a basic internal structure or set of intrinsic rules that languages share in common.

put it, the *stimulus* to which children are exposed for learning language by imitation is *impoverished*. Yet, within a few years of infancy children have developed an extraordinarily rich ability to construct sentences that are theoretically infinite in number—expressing an infinite number of thoughts.

How children are able to do this is a puzzle. Constructing sentences is not a matter of simply stringing words together. The rules governing the construction of grammatically intelligible and meaningful sentences in each language are complex. The number of *incorrect* possibilities for ordering words is limitless. These rules are never taught, and yet children acquire them effortlessly. No English-speaking toddler ever says, 'Bottle I my want' instead of 'I want my bottle'—not even once as a 'test'. This is in spite of never receiving instruction in the correct word placement for such sentences. Moreover, when children are corrected for mistakenly saying 'badder' instead of 'worse' or 'taked' instead of 'took', they frequently *resist* correction—because in English, *badder* and *taked* are grammatically logical and *ought* to be correct. Children seem to be applying the rules of universal grammar to instances of weird English grammar!

On a more subtle level, consider the word *is*: contractions of this word are perfectly acceptable when saying something like 'Dylan's here' instead of 'Dylan *is* here'. However, there are some occasions when the word *is* can never be contracted, for example, 'I wonder where the book *is* that was on top of the table this morning'. No one ever tells a child they are not supposed to say, 'I wonder where the book's that was on top of the table'. They *just know*—'as if by magic' (Anderson and Lightfoot, 1999, pp 699–700).

When it comes to language, then, children seem to 'know more than they learn', to use Anderson and Lightfoot's (1999) phrase. Children learn language effortlessly—and this is the case whether the language they are exposed to is spoken or signed. Children learn without effort even if they are rarely spoken to directly at all, except for the occasional command or scolding, as is the case in traditional Samoa (Ochs and Schieffelin, 1984). Thus, Chomsky concluded that a child who speaks or signs cannot have developed this talent only through learning and imitation. Some recent research supports this view: researchers have shown that infants prefer the sounds of spoken language to other similar sorts of sounds from birth, and can more easily extract abstract rules about patterns of sounds from listening to speech than listening to other types of sounds (eg, musical sounds; Marcus, Fernandes, and Johnson, 2007). Additionally, specific genes appear to be involved in the acquisition and use of language (see, for example, Enard et al, 2002 and Vargha-Khadem et al, 2005).

Objections to Chomsky

Chomsky met an onslaught of opposition to his ideas at first, but it is probably fair to say that the majority of cognitive scientists and linguists now agree with his basic insight that language acquisition reflects—at least in part—innate cognitive structures and mechanisms. Yet there remain radical disagreements over the precise nature of these structures and mechanisms, whether they evolved by natural selection or some other means, and whether they exist within specific brain sites. As we will discuss in the next section of the chapter, researchers also debate whether or not certain aspects of these mechanisms are shared with non-human animals.

Moreover, in spite of the widespread acceptance of the notion of an innate language faculty, some theorists and researchers continue to flatly reject such ideas. One theory that denies the existence of an innate language faculty is known as connectionism (McClelland et al, 2010). Connectionists argue that the mechanisms of the mind are 'plastic' in the sense of being highly flexible and adaptable, and that many neural structures of the brain as well as mental mechanisms could be adapted for the learning of language. This is a view of the mind that sees mental mechanisms as *domain general* rather than *domain specific* or *modular*.

Is There 'Good' and 'Bad' Grammar?

We are often picked up for the use of incorrect grammar. In fact if we had wished to write this book in informal language that ignored grammatical conventions we would have never got away with it. *However you would still have been able to follow what we were saying.* Language is about communication and expression, and people communicate and express themselves just fine in spite of grammatical errors. From the perspective of *linguistics*—the science of human language—so-called grammatical errors are not *errors* at all. This is because grammatical rules are arbitrary conventions of language usage that are constantly changing with the times. In fact, from the linguistics perspective, there really is no such thing as 'bad grammar' in English. If you say 'innit' to mean 'is that not so?' you may not get a job with the BBC but don't let grammar snobs put you down! You are simply using a contemporary expression. Phrases that aren't intuitively comprehensible tend not to catch on.

There certainly are grammatical practices known as *prescriptive grammar* that are currently considered to reflect standard forms of languages, and one is obviously well advised to learn them in order to sound educated and function well on the job and in society generally. Without doubt, those who do not use standard forms of language are at a very strong disadvantage in the workplace, as writers, at school, and in numerous social settings, some of which may be important to one's personal goals.

However, these are social rules rather than linguistic ones, and it might surprise you to learn that the rules of standard English originated not from learned studies by linguistic scholars, but primarily from two books written in the late 1700s—one by an English bishop, Robert Lowth, and the other by an American lawyer, Lindley Murray. These books have had an incalculable influence upon what is considered to be correct English grammar for the past 200 years. However, as linguist John McWhorter (1998) recounts, these men were not linguists and knew virtually nothing about the history of the English language. On the other hand, they did know something about the grammars of Latin and ancient Greek. In essence, these authors 'decided' that English ought to follow standard rules of Latin and Greek—languages revered by classical scholars, but with roots completely unrelated to those of English!

Consider the 'rule' some of us may have learned in school that it is incorrect to end sentences with prepositions ('Which table did you put my book on?' instead of 'On which table did you put my book?'). In Latin, ending sentences with prepositions makes no sense. But in English, ending sentences with prepositions takes nothing whatever away from meaning, and may sometimes improve clarity. In fact, if people really followed this rule strictly it would make for some very strange sentences—a problem about which Winston Churchill was famously said to have quipped, 'This is the sort of pedantry up with which I shall not put!' (This quote is rendered somewhat differently in different sources.)

McWhorter (1998) lists several insights about language derived from the science of linguistics that helps to put prescriptions for English grammar, pronunciation, and usage into perspective. Among them are the following three (partially paraphrased):

> **KEY IDEAS** connectionism
Connectionism is the belief that the mind is constructed of complex networks of interconnected units similar to the neural networks of the brain. Connectionism is a domain-general theory of how the mind works, in contrast to domain-specific or modular theories.

1   *Any language is always on its way to changing into a new one.* Many of the word meanings and pronunciations, and grammatical patterns we now characterize as 'sloppy' and 'incorrect' are the very things that will be considered 'proper' language in the future. McWhorter provides an excellent example of this occurring over the past 125 years. At the end of the nineteenth century, it was considered sloppy and vulgar to say, 'The house is being built across the street' rather than, 'The house is building across the street' (sometimes spoken as 'The house is a-building'). Anyone who uttered this last sentence today would receive some very strange looks.

2   *Because a language changes in different random directions among different groups, any language is actually a bundle of dialects.* A *dialect* is a unique variety of language specific to a particular group or locale. Typically, the dialect that ends up being considered 'standard' is simply the one used by those at the seat of political power. In other words, a standard language is 'a dialect with an army and a navy' (Max Weinrich, cited by S.R. Anderson, 2004). There is no reason that dialects which diverge from the standard one can logically be seen as 'degraded' or inferior, because they all arise from the same process of gradual—and unstoppable—change.

3   *No language has ever changed in a way that contradicts basic logic*, and what looks 'illogical' in one dialect—for example, the double negative in the English sentence 'I don't know nothing'—inevitably turns up as correct in the most elevated standard speech in some other language—as in the Spanish '*Yo no se nada*' or the French '*Je ne sais rien*', which translates literally as 'I not know nothing' (Pinker, 1994).

LANGUAGE AND THINKING

During the 1930s, a fire prevention engineer and inspector for an insurance company named Benjamin Lee Whorf constructed a linguistic hypothesis that continues to exert influence on the way scientists think about language. Based upon earlier observations by the famed anthropologist Eduard Sapir, with whom he had briefly studied, Whorf proposed that the ways in which each language is grammatically constructed determines the ways in which those who speak the language construct their reality. This idea came to be known as the **Sapir-Whorf hypothesis** or **linguistic determinism**. Whorf and his followers made a number of now-famous claims to support their hypothesis, among them:

> **KEY IDEAS** linguistic determinism (the Sapir-Whorf hypothesis) Also known as the **Sapir-Whorf hypothesis**, **linguistic determinism** is the notion that the way we construe reality is determined by the way our particular language is constructed.

- The Hopi are a people with no words indicating past or future, or referring in other ways to time—therefore they have little concern with hours and minutes, the days of the week, calendars, chronology, and so forth.

- Inuit (Eskimo) languages have many more different words to describe various kinds of *snow* than do Western languages such as English, expressing the importance of snow in the Inuit world (Figure 10.13). Although Whorf himself put the number of words for snow at seven, subsequent accounts incrementally upped this figure until it reached the now commonly repeated 'several dozen' or even 'several hundred' in some reports.

- Languages differ in the colour categories they contain. People whose language contains no word for a given colour are unable to differentiate that colour, and those whose languages have only words for dark or light colour see no specific colours at all.

FIGURE 10.13 Dozens of words for 'snow'? Followers of Benjamin Lee Whorf have made a number of unsubstantiated claims, among them that Inuit (Eskimo) languages contain dozens or hundreds of words for 'snow'. In fact, English probably contains more words to describe snow than Inuit languages (eg, Pullum, 1991).

Source: iStock.com/sodar99.

On the face of it, these claims seem to defy common sense, and for good reason—they are all either factually incorrect or greatly exaggerated. Inuktitut (the Eskimo language of the Inuit) does not have more words for snow than English (Pullum, 1991). In fact, it probably has fewer, although an exact count is impossible due to differences in Inuktitut dialects. Whorf's claims about Hopi conception of time are even more puzzling. In a detailed analysis of Hopi linguistics, Ekkehart Malotki (1983) demonstrated that the Hopi language contains the same time references that are contained in any other language.

What about those **cultures** with only two colour words in their languages? The languages of some cultures do not contain specific words to differentiate colours. However, members of those cultures do differentiate one colour from the next by sight—that is, they know how to distinguish colours, they just do not refer to them in speech (Rosch-Heider, 1972). Moreover, substantial research among Japanese, Chinese, and English speakers provides little or no evidence that language differences result in fundamental differences in the way objects are perceived (Barner, Li, and Snedeker, 2010).

As increasing evidence was collected debunking the more excessive claims of Whorf and his followers, by the 1970s the Sapir-Whorf hypothesis began to lose favour in psychology (I.R.L. Davies et al, 1998). However, while language may not *determine* the way people construe reality, this does not mean that language has no *effect* on the way we think and perceive—and some researchers have continued to explore Whorf's hypothesis in a modified form generally known as the **linguistic relativity hypothesis** (Pilling and Davies, 2004). According to this hypothesis, language is one of many factors affecting the way people construe reality.

For example, language does affect the way people notice and categorize aspects of their world (Boroditsky, 2009). In a particularly interesting series of studies

❯ KEY IDEAS linguistic relativity hypothesis **Linguistic relativity hypothesis** is the modified 'weak form' of the Sapir-Whorf hypothesis (linguistic determinism). Linguistic relativity theory proposes that the way we construct reality is affected, but not necessarily determined, by our language.

demonstrating this idea, cognitive linguists Susan Hespos and Elizabeth Spelke (2004) took as their starting point the observation that the Korean language, but not the English language, uses entirely different verbs to describe whether an object fits loosely or tightly inside or on top of another. On the other hand, the English language, but not the Korean language, uses entirely different words to indicate whether an object is *in* or *on* another object.

Hespos and Spelke showed that when native Korean speakers are presented with a series of images of objects placed loosely or tightly inside other objects, or fitted loosely or tightly on top of other objects, the Korean speakers will intuitively rate the images as being similar or dissimilar based only upon the looseness or tightness of the way the objects fit together—not on whether one object is inside or on top of the other. Native English speakers, on the other hand, perform very differently in this task. They intuitively rate images as similar or dissimilar based on whether one object is *in* or *on* the other, but not according to looseness or tightness of fit. This supports the idea that language influences perception.

However, in the same series of experiments, Hespos and Spelke demonstrated that language does not *determine* perception, as Whorf contended. Hespos and Spelke used experimental techniques based upon the tendency of small infants to stare noticeably longer at images that they perceive to be dissimilar to images they have been exposed to previously—a variation on the learning mechanism of *habituation* as described in Chapter 7 (Aslin, 2007). In Hespos and Spelke's studies, 5-month-old infants stared longer at objects fitting tightly inside other objects after first being exposed to objects fitting loosely—and vice versa. This demonstrates that even very small infants are able to notice the difference between tight and loose fits. According to the Sapir-Whorf hypothesis, perception of the distinction between 'tight' and 'loose' should not be present at all in very small infants, because infants have not yet learned to distinguish tight from loose in language. Hespos and Spelke's research suggests that at least some categories exist in the human mind prior to language. They may represent innate natural human concepts not dependent upon language for their perception.

THINKING PRACTICALLY

Linguistic relativity may be particularly useful when it comes to abstract concepts that don't generalize terribly well across cultures and are therefore hard to translate. What are the nearest equivalent concepts in English to the Japanese *giri* and the Hindu and Bhuddist concept of *Karma*? These may not be familiar terms or you may well have been using them incorrectly so research them before you answer. How meaningful are these terms in your cultural context?

DO NON-HUMAN ANIMALS HAVE LANGUAGE?

If a lion could talk we would not understand him.

—Ludwig Wittgenstein

On 27 April 1998, Koko, a gorilla trained in American Sign Language (ASL) for the past quarter-century by developmental psychologist Francine ('Penny') Patterson, became the first non-human to conduct a live Internet chat session. Here is one of the conversational exchanges, verbatim from the transcript of the chat session:

Moderator: Storm1004 [e-mail address] asks: Dear Koko . . . I've watched you for years now . . . your gentle spirit is an inspiration for many. . . . I'd like to know what you'd like for your birthday.

Koko: Birthday. Food and smokes.

Moderator: SMOKES?

Dr Patterson: You have to understand. . . . Smoke is the name of her kitten.

(Complete transcript available at https://www.fi.edu/blog/koko)

Koko can clearly communicate using English but does research indicate that Koko has learned language? Without doubt, animals communicate. While some of this communication is extremely minimal and limited to maintaining group solidarity or conveying one's mood or personal identity, some animal communication is *referential* (Wynne 2004). This means that different signals *refer* to specific things. In addition to the dances of honeybees described earlier—which can refer to distance, direction, and quality of food sources—vervet monkeys can communicate specific information about external events using bark-like calls. For example, they can 'say' something like 'There's another group of monkeys coming' or 'It's a leopard, watch out!' rather than just emitting a general warning signal like 'Get out of the way!' (Seyfarth and Cheney, 2003). Wild Campbell and Diana monkeys also produce referential calls (Zuberbüler, 2003), and certain birds—particularly chickens—have this ability (C.S. Evans and Evans, 1999).

However, even these referential forms of communication are *closed-ended.* They may refer to specific situations, but they cannot be recombined to refer to other situations (Nowak, Plotkin, and Jansen, 2000). In contrast, human words can be combined to refer to a potentially infinite number of situations. Human words can also be combined to refer to people, places, and things that do not currently exist, or that only exist elsewhere—a characteristic absent from animal communication systems. Indeed, even 12-month-old infants who do not yet use language will point to locations where a desired object had previously been placed by an experimenter as a way of requesting the object (a toy); however, in the same experimental set-up, chimpanzees will only point to a location to request a desired object (food) if the food is currently there (Liszkowski et al, 2009).

Animal communication systems do not contain the properties of *generativity, recursion,* and *displacement* described earlier, and therefore they are not languages. Not only are non-human communication systems unable to express an infinite number of new thoughts and ideas and refer to non-existent entities, they are unable to express very many things at all. Interestingly, one species that thus far has *not* been shown to possess referential communication systems is the chimpanzee, whose vocal utterances are quite limited (Wynne, 2004). Yet it is to the chimpanzee that researchers have looked in the hope that non-human animals could be taught human language.

Washoe, Nim, and Kanzi: Conversationalists or Trained Chimps?

By 1970, more linguists and cognitive scientists were starting to come around to Noam Chomsky's view that language was unique to humans and required specific brain and cognitive mechanisms to exist. However, certain theorists, notably *behaviourists* such as B.F. Skinner, strongly opposed this idea. Skinner and the behaviourists argued instead that language was a behaviour like any other and that it was learned like other behaviours through reinforcement, as described in Chapter 7. From this perspective, even though chimpanzees might not communicate among themselves with natural language, there was no reason to assume that they could not be *taught* to communicate with language. Because chimpanzees are genetically very close to human beings, they were considered to be the best candidates among non-human animals for learning language.

Attempts to teach chimpanzees actually to *speak* have always been unsuccessful due to the way the chimpanzee larynx and throat are structured. However, during the late 1960s, Allen and Beatrice Gardner hit upon the idea of teaching a chimpanzee named Washoe to sign, using American Sign Language (ASL) (Figure 10.15). The Gardners successfully taught Washoe to produce more than 130 signs. In a particularly famous utterance, Washoe saw a swan while out in a boat on a lake and signed 'water bird'. Although it is not clear whether Washoe was giving a name to the swan by combining 'water' and 'bird', or simply observing a bird on the water, it is a startling achievement nonetheless. We can look at the Washoe study in detail in our *Research in focus* feature.

RESEARCH IN FOCUS

Gardner, R.A. and Gardner, B.T. (1969). Teaching sign language to a chimpanzee. *Science*, **165**, 664–72.

Aim: To investigate the possibility than non-human species can acquire human language. More specifically, to test the idea that a chimpanzee can acquire sign language. This is in the context of previous studies showing that chimps cannot acquire human speech because of the limitations of their vocal apparatus.

Method: A female infant chimpanzee called Washoe took part in the study over a period of 32 months. A chimp was chosen because of their intelligence, sociability, and capacity to form human-like attachments. American Sign Language (ASL) was chosen as the sign language because it has a grammatical structure similar to that of English.

Washoe was a wild-born chimp, aged somewhere between 8 and 14 months when she arrived to be cared for by the Gardners. All the staff working with Washoe were taught ASL. Washoe was given opportunities to learn ASL by imitation, and reinforcement was provided in the form of praise and tickling whenever Washoe successfully used a sign. For some signs the Gardners had to help Washoe form the hand shapes. For a sign to be recorded as having been learned successfully it had to be noted by three observers in an appropriate context every day for 15 days.

Results: After 22 months Washoe had acquired 30 signs according to the strict criteria detailed above. Washoe also showed displacement by referring to ideas not physically present and she combined signs such as 'come-gimme', 'please', 'hurry', and 'more' with others such as 'tickle'. These were usually but not always used in the grammatically correct order. Some signs appeared to be learned after a delay, thus 'flower' appeared spontaneously months after it had been demonstrated.

Conclusion: American Sign Language is an appropriate medium for teaching chimps human language, and chimps can learn to communicate using ASL. As to whether Washoe really

❯

acquired language the authors were cautious in their conclusions, pointing out that from their perspective there is no scientific criterion for distinguishing between language and communication.

MASTER YOUR METHODOLOGY

1   Explain why it was important for the observers to use such strict criteria to define the acquisition of a sign.

2   What ambiguity in results was revealed by the fact that sign combinations were usually but not always used in the correct order?

3   What advantages would there have been in teaching ASL to several chimps?

 ## THINKING CRITICALLY

What ethical issues are raised by this kind of study with non-human primates?

The Washoe project led to other, similar attempts to teach language to non-human primates, including Koko the gorilla. One such non-human primate was a chimpanzee named Nim Chimpsky (a joking reference to Noam Chomsky), trained by Herbert Terrace (Terrace, 1987). Terrace was a behaviourist, who, like Skinner, rejected Chomsky's views and believed strongly that chimpanzees could learn language given enough time and appropriate methods. Terrace succeeded in teaching Nim about the same number of signs as Washoe had learned. Unfortunately, Terrace's funding ran out, and he had to give Nim away.

Because Terrace was no longer working with Nim, he had a chance to carefully examine the videotapes of his training sessions. What he found startled and disappointed him. Terrace concluded that what Nim had accomplished was not language, but simple operant learning—not much different from that of a rat learning to press a bar to obtain food or a dog learning that the sounds 'Do you want to go out?' meant that he or she was about to go for a walk. Terrace claimed that Nim and chimps such as Washoe had learned that when they made certain signs, certain things happened—notably, they obtained things they wanted such as food. This is the method used to train animals to do all sorts of amazing things. Take Wanpen—a Thai elephant trained to paint in Chinese style by the artist Chaowalit (see Figure 10.14).

Terrace's revelations—in fact, stinging critiques of his own research—caused a storm of controversy. He and other researchers noted a series of problems with the claims of those teaching language to apes. For example, after decades of intense daily training, chimpanzees do not appear to be capable of learning more than a few hundred signs. Even toddlers frequently have vocabularies exceeding those of chimps trained for decades. Thus, critics, including Chomsky, charged that to claim that these chimps use language is equivalent to a claim that people can learn to fly because pole vaulters, divers, and ballet dancers sail through the air.

In addition, Terrace and other researchers have noted that there is sometimes a discrepancy between what researchers who work with apes claim the ape is 'saying' and what videotapes show the chimp is *actually* signing. Wynne (2004, p 123)

FIGURE 10.14 But is it art? The Thai elephant Wanpen creates paintings.
Source: iStock.com/kowit sitthi.

FIGURE 10.15 Training primates to use sign language. Pictured from left to right are Washoe, Nim Chimpsky, and Kanzi. Claims and counterclaims have been made regarding the ability of non-human primates to learn human language, and research with these chimpanzees has been at the heart of many of the controversies. The primary question is this: are these chimpanzees learning rudimentary, but genuine, language—or are they simply being trained to do linguistic 'tricks'?

Sources: Washoe: Gary Stewart/AP/Shutterstock; Nim Chimpsky:Susan Kuklin/Science Photo Library; Kanzi: Photo © William H. Calvin, PhD (CC BY-SA 4.0).

provides the following example of a short conversation between a *bonobo* ('pygmy chimp') named Kanzi and his trainer:

Kanzi: Want milk. Milk.

Human: You want some milk? I know, you always want some milk when you're planning to be good.

Kanzi: Key. Matata. Good.

Human: Oh, you want the key to Matata, and you're going to be good. Well, I'm glad to hear that.

Wynne points out that the utterances of Kanzi are abrupt and largely meaningless apart from a demand for milk. He does not say he wants the key to Matata (Kanzi's bonobo companion) and plans to be good—indeed, he says nothing at all about planning to be good. It is the trainer who supplies this meaning.

While these criticisms are important, some evidence suggests that this is not the whole story, and criticisms of ape language research may be overly harsh (Shanker, Savage-Rumbaugh, and Taylor, 1999). First, Zuberbüler (2003) has shown that the meaning of wild Campbell monkeys' referential calls changes according to the order in which they occur. Thus, something similar to *syntax*—the ordering of words in sentences—is at least possible in non-human primates.

More dramatically, some evidence collected by Sue Savage-Rumbaugh, the trainer of the bonobo Kanzi 'quoted' in the previous dialogue, suggests that not all chimpanzee accomplishments in learning human language are an illusion (Savage-Rumbaugh, Shanker, and Taylor, 1998). For example, Savage-Rumbaugh claims that Kanzi has shown evidence of understanding (but not using) grammar. She tested this ability by giving commands to Kanzi that are grammatically 'reversible'. For example, if Kanzi had no understanding of grammar, the sentence 'put the banana on the plate' could just as easily be understood by him as 'put the plate on the banana' because the words *plate, on, banana*, and *put* have radically different meanings depending on how they are ordered. When Savage-Rumbaugh did present Kanzi with a group of such reversible commands, the bonobo scored enough of them correctly to rule out the probability that the results were strictly due to chance (Wynne, 2004).

However, even if the critics are overly harsh and Savage-Rumbaugh's claims are accurate, there is no denying that the linguistic accomplishments of even an extraordinary ape such as Kanzi after decades of training differ dramatically from those of almost any healthy 2- or 3-year-old human child—including a child who is not spoken to very often by adults. Therefore, it is worth contemplating the significance of findings that an ape can be trained over decades to learn a few hundred signs and develop rudimentary comprehension of simple syntax.

For example, Povinelli and Bering (2002) argue that in trying to avoid the trap of thinking of human beings as 'special' and 'higher' than other animals, some scientists are instead struggling to make non-human animals fit a human mould—to see them as 'watered-down human beings' (p 170). Instead of looking for signs of humanness in non-human animals, Povinelli and Bering argue that we should be listening to these animals tell their own unique stories—radically different from human stories, but no less valuable.

The 'stories' animals may have to tell may need to be understood more through gestures than vocalizations, however—at least in the cases of our nearest evolutionary relatives, the bonobo and the chimpanzee. Amy Pollick and Frans de Waal catalogued 31 gestures and 18 facial/vocal signals among groups of bonobos and chimpanzees (Pollick and de Waal, 2007). As depicted in Figure 10.16, Pollick and de Waal found that the facial and vocal signals were highly limited in their 'meaning'— they were applied in relatively specific situations, and were used identically in both species. Conversely, the arm and hand gestures were flexible in their content. Bonobos used them differently from chimpanzees, and the contexts in which the gestures were used also differed among individual bonobos and chimps.

This research provides evidence in favour of one hypothesis about how language developed—that it emerged from hand and arm gestures, not vocalizations. Recall that vocalizations and facial signals were the same for both the bonobos and the chimps— but the hand and arm gestures were not. This suggests that, among apes, gestures may be freer to take on different meanings depending upon context. In comparison, vocalizations and facial signals are 'frozen' as to their meanings. As a result, gestures might be more easily adapted to symbolic communication, as in language. Pollick and

FIGURE 10.16 For Bonobos and chimpanzees, a gesture may be worth a thousand words. Among chimpanzees and bonobos, facial expressions and vocalizations are tied to specific and limited contexts. Their 'meanings' are frozen. Conversely, arm and hand gestures are more flexible modes of communication. These findings have been used to support arguments that language may have evolved through gesture, not vocalization.

Source: Rahmo/ Shutterstock.com.

de Waal also point out that monkeys do not use gestures to communicate—and monkeys are evolutionarily older than bonobos, chimpanzees, or humans. Because vocal language evolved recently with human beings, the evolutionary 'youth' of bonobo and chimpanzee communication through gesture adds more weight to the notion that language may have evolved initially through gestures rather than vocalizations.

READ THIS

For a general overview of language try this:

Yule, G. (2016). *The Study of Language.* Cambridge: Cambridge University Press.

For recent versions of Chomsky's ideas try these:

Yang, C., Crain, S., Berwick, R.C., Chomsky, N., and Bolhuis, J.J. (2017). The growth of language: Universal Grammar, experience, and principles of computation. *Neuroscience and Biobehavioral Reviews,* **81**, 103–19.

Berwick, R.C. and Chomsky, N. (2016). *Why Only Us: Language and Evolution.* Cambridge, MA: MIT Press.

Moro, A. and Chomsky, N. (2015). *The Boundaries of Babel: The Brain and the Enigma of Impossible Languages.* Cambridge, MA: MIT Press.

For a contemporary overview of the animal language debate try this:

Pepperberg, I.M. (2017). Animal language studies: What happened? *Psychonomic Bulletin and Review,* **24**(1), 181–5.

IN REVIEW

- The computational theory of mind holds that the mind functions in a manner loosely analogous to a computer.
- Cognitive scientists study mental activities involved in collecting, processing, storing, retrieving, and manipulating information.
- Thought is the active process of mentally manipulating or processing information to solve problems, make decisions, increase knowledge, or fantasize.
- Thinking involves two components: mental images and concepts.
- Kahneman distinguishes between two thinking systems, one being intuitive and effortless, the other being conscious and effortful.

PROBLEM-SOLVING

- Problems are obstacles that stand in the way of achieving a goal, and we use thought to solve them. Four strategies for problem solving are: trial and error, algorithms, heuristics, and insight.
- Trial and error works well if the options for possible solutions of a problem are relatively few.
- Algorithms are step-by-step 'recipes' that can solve any problem of a specific type.
- Heuristics, including the availability heuristic and the representativeness heuristic, are mental shortcuts that are used automatically under conditions of uncertainty. The representativeness heuristic is misleading if base rates are not taken into consideration. A base rate is a percentage probability figure indicating the prevalence of something, or how frequently it occurs.
- Insight occurs when a person has reached an impasse in attempts to solve a problem and then suddenly and effortlessly arrives at a solution. Creativity is a complex set of behaviours generally involving originality, flexibility, and utility; it includes *finding* problems as well as solving them.

DECISION-MAKING

- Cognitive biases are systematic distortions in thinking, memory, and perception.
- The confirmation bias is often considered the most prevalent and destructive of all problems with human reasoning. The confirmation bias is primarily seen in the tendency to pay more attention to evidence that confirms what we already believe.
- Belief persistence, a related bias, allows a person to resist changing a belief by discounting disconfirming evidence. The gambler's fallacy is a misperception of randomness.

LANGUAGE

- At least three principles characterize human language: generativity, recursion, and displacement.
- Languages may influence the way we think, but they do not determine the way we think.
- Many researchers believe that the capacity for language is a special internal faculty comprising innate, specialized neural and cognitive structures and 'wiring'. From this view, all languages possess a 'universal grammar'.

• The internal language faculty allows children to learn language effortlessly, even though they are exposed to only a few of the words and constructions possible in the language.

DO NON-HUMAN ANIMALS HAVE LANGUAGE?

• Animals communicate, but they do not have language. Unlike human language, animal communication systems are closed-ended rather than open-ended.

• Extensive efforts to teach language to chimpanzees have resulted only in the teaching of limited vocabularies and virtually no grammatical structures.

• Research among primates suggests that language may have evolved from gestures rather than vocal utterances.

TEST YOURSELF

1 Thought can be defined as the manipulation of information. True ☐ False ☐

2 Belief in astrology can be explained by confirmation bias. True ☐ False ☐

3 Connectionism is a domain-specific theory of cognition. True ☐ False ☐

4 Linguistic relativity can be described as a weak form of linguistic determinism. True ☐ False ☐

5 Which two of the following concepts have fuzzy boundaries?

  a) Psychology

  b) Neuron

  c) Yellow

  d) Justice

6 Which of the following tasks would require System 2 thought?

  a) Face recognition

  b) Cycling

  c) Political debate

  d) Simple subtraction

7 Which of the following is not a problem-solving strategy?

  a) Common sense

  b) Algorithm

  c) Heuristic

  d) Trial and error

8 Which of the following is not a necessary characteristic of language?

  a) Generativity

  b) Vocalization

  c) Recursion

  d) Displacement

9 Explain how Kosslyn's and Pylyshyn's views of mental imagery differ.

10 What have we learned from primate studies of language?

 Visit the online resources that accompany this book: www.oup.com/uk/jarvis-okami1e

DEVELOPMENTAL PSYCHOLOGY

CHAPTER 11

SOCIAL–EMOTIONAL DEVELOPMENT IN CHILDHOOD

LEARNING OUTCOMES

By the end of this chapter you should be able to:

- Assess the range of factors affecting early social-emotional development
- Evaluate the nature and significance of temperament in affecting social-emotional development
- Describe and evaluate attachment theory as an explanation of the relationship between early childhood and later development, including reference to its pre-quelae and sequelae
- Discuss research into the alleged effects of short-term separation events in infancy such as day care, and take a view on critical perspectives (eg, feminist) on this research
- Apply data from follow-up studies of children adopted from Romanian orphanages in the 1990s to understand the impact of early institutionalization on development
- Understand the significance and development of peer relationships in childhood, and assess research into factors affecting childhood popularity

There are few questions in psychology quite as personal or sensitive as why our children end up as they are. At one extreme, no one likes to hear that they ruined their child's life by being slow or grumpy when responding to them at 4am when they were 3 months old. At the other extreme, no exhausted parent wants to hear that all their sacrifice and hard work was for nothing and that their child's nature was predetermined all along by their genetic make-up. Obviously, these are extreme and (slightly) parodied accounts but they illustrate the sometimes-angry split between developmental psychologists who emphasize the role of temperament (nature) and **attachment** (nurture) in early social-emotional development.

TEMPERAMENT

As every parent of multiple children will tell you, all babies are different, right from the start. The term **temperament** refers to the initial tendency to act in relatively consistent ways when it comes to certain general qualities and ways of responding to the world (A.H. Buss and Plomin, 1984; Kagan, 2003) (Figure 11.1). We can think

> **KEY IDEAS** temperament
> **Temperament** refers to each infant's relatively consistent behavioural characteristics, characterized by Mary Rothbart within three dimensions: effortful control, negative emotionality, and extraversion. Temperament emerges as a result of genetic and other biological factors as well as environmental factors, but most theorists stress the importance of biology.

FIGURE 11.1 **Babies are social animals. Babies are social from the moment of their birth. As they grow, they develop characteristic ways of interacting with others. These characteristics are in part a result of temperament—relatively predictable aspects of emotional response, activity level, and sociability displayed by each infant from the earliest moments of life.**
Source: iStock.com/Rawpixel.

> **KEY IDEAS** Effortful control **Effortful control** is the dimension of temperament that describes the extent to which an infant or child is able to focus or shift attention, inhibit inappropriate behaviour, and plan actions constructively; similar to executive functions in adults. **Negative emotionality** is the dimension of temperament that describes the degree to which an infant or child is easily frustrated, fearful, uncomfortable, sad, or difficult to soothe. In temperament theory **extraversion** is the dimension of temperament that describes the degree to which an infant or child lacks shyness, is highly active, anticipates pleasurable activities, laughs and smiles frequently, and desires closeness with others.

of temperament as infant personality. For example, some babies are fussy, while others are calm; some are curious about everything, outgoing, and highly active, while others are shy and less active. Extensive quantitative research conducted by Mary Rothbart and her colleagues has confirmed the idea, first proposed in a somewhat different form by personality psychologist Arnold Buss and behaviour geneticist Robert Plomin (1984), that temperament can be summarized along three dimensions of behaviour. These are: *effortful control, negative emotionality*, and *extraversion* (eg, Rothbart and Bates, 2006; Rothbart, Ahadi, Hershey, and Fisher, 2001):

- **Effortful control.** This refers to the extent to which an infant or child is able to focus or shift attention as needed; inhibit behaviour that is inappropriate; and plan actions constructively.

- **Negative emotionality.** An infant or child high in this dimension is easily frustrated, fearful, uncomfortable, sad, or difficult to soothe.

- **Extraversion.** In general usage, an *extraverted* person is outgoing, assertive, self-confident, and enjoys socializing with others. As used by Rothbart and her colleagues to describe temperament, an infant or child high in extraversion lacks shyness, is highly active, experiences anticipation for pleasurable activities, laughs and smiles frequently, and desires closeness with others.

According to Rothbart, some aspects of temperament are apparent even in the foetus, and develop rapidly in the newborn (Rothbart, 2007). Temperament tends to be stable at least through the toddler years (Lemery et al, 1999) and may persist until **adolescence** (Kagan, 1994). There are sex differences in typical temperament as well: infant girls tend to score higher than boys in measures of effortful control, while boys score higher on average in extraversion (Else-Quest et al, 2006).

Infant temperament may also be apparent in some adult behaviour. One longitudinal study tracked a sample of men and women from early childhood into adulthood. The researchers found that those children who lacked sociability (ie, they tended to seek and enjoy social contact less than most) at age 3 years were correspondingly shy and unassertive as young adults. Those children who were impulsive and lacked the ability to regulate **emotion** (eg, they had tantrums) at age 3 were impulsive and easily upset as adults; indeed, by age 32, these children were approximately twice as likely to have compulsive gambling problems. Finally, those who were sociable and emotionally even-tempered as toddlers remained so to adulthood (Slutske et al, 2012).

The Origins of Temperament

Although brothers and sisters tend to have slight resemblances in temperament, this resemblance is often not much greater than the resemblance between two strangers picked at random. Indeed, adopted children reared in the same home do not resemble one another in temperament any more than two strangers would (Plomin and deFries, 1985).

On the other hand, repeated research has demonstrated that identical twins strongly resemble each other in temperament regardless of whether they are reared together or apart. The resemblance is far from perfect, but it is clear that genes play a substantial role in the development of temperament in infants (Plomin, DeFries, Craig, and McGuffin, 2003). Indeed, specific genes have been tentatively identified as contributing to the development of certain aspects of temperament (Posner, Rothbart, and Sheese, 2007). The prenatal biological environment of the womb (eg, the presence of toxins, maternal stress, and nutritional deficiencies) may also play a role in determining aspects of temperament that are present in an infant from birth. Thus, numerous researchers believe that temperament is essentially a biologically based phenomenon.

 THINKING CREATIVELY

Biological factors appear to be overwhelmingly important when it comes to the development of *temperament*. Yet, as we shall see later in this chapter, there are also very important factors in the child's psychological environment that impact on their development. Consider as many ways as you can to resolve this apparent paradox. HINT: one explanation would be that temperament and attachment exert separate influences on development.

However, it is unlikely that genes and prenatal environments alone account for the entire story of infant temperament. If they did, identical twins would be truly *identical* in temperament because they share 100% of their genes and virtually all aspects of the prenatal environment. As identical twins are not identical in temperament, there must be something strictly environmental at work that occurs *after* the infant is conceived. Yet, as already mentioned, being reared in the same home does not make children more similar in temperament.

Which 'strictly environmental' variables *do* contribute to infant temperament, if not those shared by all siblings in the home (socioeconomic status of the family, ethnic background, parents' child-rearing styles and beliefs, general parental warmth and expressiveness, parents' education level, and so forth)? It appears to be the *unique experiences of each infant* rather than shared family influences

> **KEY IDEAS** the non-shared environment This is the term given to the unique biological and psychological environmental factors and experiences encountered by each developing child but not encountered by other children in the home. For example, a childhood illness, a traumatic experience, a different set of friends, and so forth.

that contribute the most to the environmental portion of temperament (Plomin et al, 2003; Saudino, 2005). Such unique experiences are part of what is termed **non-shared environment**. What might these unique, non-shared experiences be? They could include chance adverse events such as trauma or infection in infancy, differences in the way that parents and other important adults treat each sibling (eg, being stricter with one than the other), differences in nutrition (one sibling eats well, the other does not), and any number of chance events, both positive and negative.

READ THIS

Anything by Jerome Kagan concerning temperament is worth reading. The first paper below is an excellent overview of the temperament field and the second describes a study of anxiety responses and their relationship to temperament.

Kagan, J. (1989). Temperamental contributions to social behaviour. *American Psychologist*, **44**, 668–74.

Kagan, J. (1997). Temperament and the reactions to unfamiliarity. *Child Development*, **68**, 139–43.

ATTACHMENT AND ATTACHMENT THEORY

> **KEY IDEAS** attachment **Attachment** is a two-way emotional bond between two people characterized by proximity-seeking, separation distress, and reunion pleasure. **Attachment theory** is a broad collection of ideas from different psychologists, sharing the idea that the qualities of the child's first attachment relationship are stable and generalize to later attachments.

In the course of our lives we develop emotional bonds directed towards many different people—and for that matter pets, places, inanimate objects like mobile phones, and (if we have a religion) to our deity or deities. We can broadly think of all these bonds as attachments. To developmental psychologists, the term **attachment** has a more precise meaning and has its roots in the unique, intimate bond that develops between infant and caregivers, beginning when the infant is about 6 months old. In its precise sense, an attachment is a two-way relationship with three main characteristics:

- Proximity-seeking: both individuals are motivated to remain physically close to each other
- Separation distress
- Pleasure at reunion

Attachment theory is probably the most influential of modern theories of early infant social and emotional development. It explains the development of the first attachment relationship, between an infant and its primary carer, and the consequences of this relationship. Attachment theory was initially formulated by psychoanalyst John Bowlby and his colleague Mary Ainsworth as an unusual blending of evolutionary theory of primate development with psychoanalytic theory of child development (Bowlby, 1968; Ainsworth et al, 1978).

According to Bowlby and Ainsworth, the first attachment relationship is generally formed with the primary caregiver, most commonly the biological mother. The infant comes to prefer her and does everything possible to remain in close proximity to her—displaying distress when separated and joy on reunion. This is the relationship that the infant turns to when under stress. After the initial attachment relationship becomes firm, the infant may then develop secondary attachment relationships with others, such as their father, grandparents, or siblings.

FIGURE 11.2 **Is this child's happiness a product of attachment, temperament, or both?**
Source: iStock.com/digitalskillet.

The Evolutionary Roots of Attachment

Bowlby in particular was strongly influenced by the work of Konrad Lorenz, an important early figure in the evolutionary study of animal behaviour. Lorenz identified a critical period in the development of the relationship between newly hatched geese (goslings) and their mothers. A gosling becomes permanently **imprinted** with the image of whatever moving object—the animal—it sees on hatching. It will subsequently follow this animal and attempt to remain in close proximity to it. Given that a mother goose hatches the gosling, the imprinted animal is virtually always the gosling's mother. However, Lorenz (1937) showed that goslings would become imprinted with the image of Lorenz himself if he, and not the mother goose, were present during the critical post-hatching imprinting period. Indeed, the Lorenz-imprinted goslings ignored their actual mothers and followed Lorenz on land or water. See Figure 11.3.

Bowlby did not suggest that human infants become imprinted with the image of their mothers as goslings do. However, he did suggest that the years of infancy and toddlerhood constitute a critical period in the development of infant attachment relations. He also believed that, just as imprinting has survival value because it leads goslings to remain close to a protective adult, so does attachment in mammals. He proposed that if such a relationship—with the mother or with another caregiver—did not develop successfully, consequences could be severe and persist throughout the person's life.

The Internal Working Model

Why should first attachment relationships be of such critical importance to a person throughout their life span? Bowlby (1969) suggested that an infant develops an **internal working model** of the social world based largely on their early relationships. The internal working model is a metaphor for the way the child develops an understanding of his or her place in the world and arrives at expectations about the likely

> **KEY IDEAS**
imprinting **Imprinting** is a form of learning that occurs rapidly during a critical period and which the animal is biologically prepared to acquire. Specifically, in birds, imprinting occurs when a chick hatches and imprints on the first moving object it sees.

> **KEY IDEAS** the internal working model The **internal working model** is a notion by attachment theorists that a child's understanding of his or her place in the world, and his or her expectations about the behaviour of others, is modelled on, or reflects, attachment relations experienced in infancy.

FIGURE 11.3 **Konrad Lorenz and friends.** Newly hatched goslings become indelibly imprinted with the image of the animal they see first on hatching. They will then prefer that animal—including a human—to their own mother.

Source: The LIFE Picture Collection/Getty Images.

behaviour of other people (Dykas and Cassidy, 2011). If an infant has a competent caregiver who provides consistently and predictably kind and responsive treatment, he or she should develop a working model that suggests that the social world is a safe place, that other people are to be trusted, and that he or she is a lovable and worthy person. On the other hand, if the early attachment relationship forms with an unkind, unpredictable, or incompetent caregiver, the child may come to view the world as a dangerous place, and its inhabitants untrustworthy. The child may also come to see himself or herself as unlovable and unworthy.

Attachment Styles and the Strange Situation

In the example of the internal working model, we referred to an infant becoming attached to an unkind and incompetent caregiver. You might think that an infant is unlikely to become attached to such a person. However, according to attachment theorists, *some* form of attachment will occur for all infants as long as an individual caregiver is consistently present in their life during the critical period.

Mary Ainsworth (Ainsworth et al, 1978) developed a controlled observation procedure called the **Strange Situation** to measure individual differences in the quality of infants' attachment relations with their primary caregivers (in this case, their mothers)—shown in Figure 11.4. In the Strange Situation, which lasts about 20 minutes, the mother and her infant play alone in a room, and a stranger enters. The stranger converses with the mother, and the mother then leaves unobtrusively so that the infant is alone with the stranger. The mother then returns. Next, the mother leaves again so that the infant is alone. The stranger re-enters the room and interacts with the infant. The mother then returns.

Ainsworth originally identified and named three 'styles' of response to the Strange Situation reflecting three styles of attachment relations: *secure, avoidant,* and *insecure-ambivalent.*

> **KEY IDEAS** the Strange Situation The **Strange Situation** is a controlled observation procedure designed to create mild anxiety in order to measure the key elements of attachment: proximity-seeking, separation distress (and stranger anxiety), and response to reunion. Based on infant behaviour in the Strange Situation, mobile babies and toddlers can be classified with an attachment type.

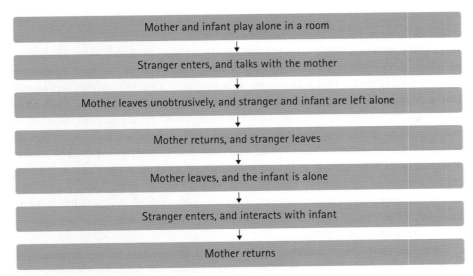

FIGURE 11.4 **The Strange Situation, as developed by Mary Ainsworth.**

1 *Secure attachment (type B).* Securely attached infants are active and curious when placed in a strange room as long as the mother is present. If the mother leaves, the infant may become quite upset, but will react with joy on the mother's return. Securely attached infants show friendliness towards strangers if the mother is present, but wariness if the mother is absent.

2 *Avoidant attachment (type A).* Avoidant attachment is characterized by less interest in exploration and curiosity in the Strange Situation, even when the mother is present. However, the avoidant infant also shows little distress when the mother leaves, and he or she generally ignores the mother on her return. The assumption among many attachment theorists is that avoidant infants have arrived at this place of 'not caring' as a result of having learned that their emotional needs will not be met (Silverman, 2011).

3 *Insecure-ambivalent attachment (type C).* Unlike avoidant infants, who 'shut down', insecure-ambivalent infants are on 'high alert'. They do not easily venture away from the safety of their mothers to play, may fearfully cling to her, and become even more upset than securely attached infants when she leaves. When the mother returns, the insecure-ambivalent infant may rush back to her, but is equally likely to resist her attempts at soothing, or may even strike her in anger, as though to punish her for having left. Insecure-ambivalent infants are wary of strangers whether or not the mother is present.

 THINKING CREATIVELY

The Strange Situation is used to measure attachment security in young children by assessing their proximity-seeking, separation and stranger anxiety, and reunion response. Based on these aspects of attachment, design a tool to measure attachment type in adults. This could be in the form of a questionnaire, interview, or controlled observation procedure. You will need to decide to whom the attachment is that you are measuring. This could be a retrospective attachment to primary caregiver(s), partner, or even to a fictional character.

Atypical attachments and attachment disorders

If we think of Ainsworth's three attachment types as typical variations in attachment style, 85–90% of children fall fairly neatly into one of the three categories (Main and Solomon, 1990). However, a minority of children display behaviour in the Strange Situation which falls outside these normal categories. Such children may, for example, alternate between type A and type C behaviour or they may maintain proximity but resist contact. They may also freeze and display fear towards the primary carer. Main and Solomon (1986) have called this type of attachment behaviour type D or **atypical attachment**. It is also known as **disorganized attachment**. Note that in your wider reading (hint!) you may come across the term 'type AC attachment'. There is some debate over whether type D and type AC are equivalents but they describe a broadly similar set of attachment behaviours (Teti et al, 1995).

Since the 1980s, some patterns of atypical attachment have been recognized in major systems of psychiatric classification (see Chapter 18 for a discussion) as **attachment disorders**, although the distinction between an attachment type and a mental disorder of attachment is controversial (Richters and Volkmar, 1994). The current major psychiatric classification systems—DSM-5 and ICD-11—recognize two attachment disorders:

- **Reactive attachment disorder**: characterized by lack of comfort-seeking, minimal positive emotion, minimal social contact, and unexplained fear or sadness during interaction with adults. This takes place in the context of neglect or institutional/foster care with multiple changes of carer.

- **Disinhibited social engagement disorder** (sometimes called disinhibited attachment): characterized by lack of the usual inhibitions in interacting with strangers, so that the child actively approaches and interacts with strangers indiscriminately. This takes place most commonly in the context of institutional care.

> ❯ **KEY IDEAS** atypical attachment and attachment disorders There is no clear distinction between an atypical attachment and an attachment disorder. Both are patterns of attachment behaviour that fall outside the range of normal variations in attachment. Atypical attachment, also called type D or disorganized attachment, results when an infant has no set strategy for dealing with separation in the way type As have avoidance and type Cs have control. Two patterns of attachment behaviour falling outside the norm, reactive attachment disorder and disinhibited social engagement disorder have been recognized as mental disorders.

Explaining Attachment Security: Maternal Sensitivity Hypothesis

Ainsworth suggested that the principal factor underlying variations in attachment security is the behaviour of the mother or primary carer towards the child in the first few months of life. Specifically, high levels of **sensitive responsiveness** are associated with secure attachment. Sensitive responsiveness is the ability of the primary carer to detect and respond to the non-verbal cues with which the infant signals its needs. According to Ainsworth, carers who are skilled at interpreting and responding to the child's signals tend to parent type B children.

The corollary of this is that types A and C attachment are the consequences of *insensitive* parenting. Types A and C patterns of behaviour in the Strange Situation represent different coping strategies for dealing with the anxiety of the situation, developed in response to insensitive parenting styles. Thus type A children cope with anxiety by avoiding adults in order to maintain emotional distance and not suffer disappointment. Type C children on the other hand use anger and control as their main coping strategies. They maintain very close proximity to their primary carer in order to keep them 'on a short leash' and display considerable anger when abandoned and when reunited (Figure 11.5).

FIGURE 11.5 **A child having a tantrum. It's normal for all children to express anger and frustration at times, but type C children may do this more frequently to control their caregivers.**
Source: iStock.com/Lokibaho.

Considering Attachment Theory

Infants undeniably create important bonds with their caregivers early in life, and if no such relationships are formed, the consequences can be serious—see the section later in this chapter on research into the large number of Romanian orphans rescued following the collapse of the Ceaușescu regime in 1989 (see 'The effects of early separation', this chapter). A large number of the orphans who remained in the orphanages during the early attachment period displayed maladaptive patterns of social behaviour throughout early childhood. Cross-cultural studies of attachment have also provided support for attachment theorists' claims that forming attachment relationships in infancy is a universal human tendency (Reebye, Ross, and Jamieson, 1999), and infants do seem to form expectations of the typical behaviour of their caregivers as described in attachment theory (Johnson et al, 2007).

But what of the specifics of attachment theory? One of the major challenges in considering attachment theory as a whole is that it is a broad, multifaceted theory and, although its parts hang together coherently as a single theory, different parts of the theory can be supported or challenged independently of one another. So let's break it down and see what we have to evaluate. First, let's take the evolutionary basis of attachment. Evolution as an underlying 'why' factor is always controversial in psychology because, whilst evolutionary explanations tend to have excellent face validity and explanatory power, they tend not to generate testable hypotheses. That said, evolutionary principles do predict that children growing up in high-mortality environments are less likely to form secure attachments with their parents and later with others because the emotional investment needed for a secure attachment is not adaptive in that context where either party is likely to experience the death of the other (Belsky 1999; Keller 2013).

THINKING CRITICALLY

One criterion for evaluating a theory is its **internal consistency**. This means the extent to which different elements of the theory fit neatly with one another. The more complex a theory, the more important internal consistency becomes. Would you say attachment theory has good internal consistency? How important a strength is this relative to other evaluation criteria?

Research into prequelae and sequelae of attachment

❯ KEY IDEAS prequelae **Prequelae** are things that precede something. In the case of attachment formation, prequelae include maternal sensitivity, but also probably genetic predisposition and social context.

❯ KEY IDEAS sequelae **Sequelae** are things that come after something; for example, psychological characteristics developing after the development of an attachment type in infancy. Because the causal relationships between events and their sequelae are unclear it is preferable to say 'sequelae' rather than 'consequences'.

Note the terms '**prequelae**' and '**sequelae**'. They mean 'what comes before' and 'what comes after' respectively (think film prequels and sequels). Psychologists prefer this to more loaded terms like 'causes' and 'consequences' because prequelae and sequelae do not imply simple causal relationships between parenting, attachment security, and later outcomes for children.

Maternal sensitivity—the 'how' of attachment theory—is controversial for both empirical and political reasons. Contemporary research has supported a role for sensitive responsiveness in the formation of secure attachments, but only as one factor amongst several. Fuertes et al (2006) followed up 48 infant–mother dyads from birth to 1 year and found that both maternal sensitivity at 9 months and temperament at 1 and 3 months predicted attachment type at 1 year.

It also appears that contextual factors like poverty are important (Rabey et al, 2015), with caregivers who are preoccupied with immediate survival priorities like where the next meal is coming from are more likely to struggle to maintain sensitive responsiveness towards their children. Effects may be particularly strong in relation to gross insensitivity and type D *disorganized* attachment (Lyons-Ruth, 2003). Even though most psychologists no longer favour sensitive responsiveness as a complete explanation for attachment security, it appears to be important enough to explain some real-life effects. So Jacobsen et al (2013) and Gabler et al (2016) have found that more sensitive foster carers were more likely to alter foster-children's attachment type to secure than their less sensitive peers. This has a clear practical application in training and selecting foster carers.

THINKING PRACTICALLY

Based on what you know about sensitive responsiveness, consider how you might train foster carers prior to deploying them to work with insecurely attached babies. You might want to read up on attachment training.

The most researched question regarding attachment theory concerns the sequelae of infant attachment. The most basic question here is whether infant attachment type predicts later attachment type. Evidence for attachment stability, sometimes called continuity hypothesis, is mixed. A meta-analysis by Pinqart, Feubner, and

Ahnert (2013) analysed continuity in 21,000 children at various time intervals and found an overall correlation of 0.39 between measurements over time. This shows reasonably high levels of continuity of attachment type through childhood; however, no evidence emerged of continuity over periods beyond 15 years.

So what about the advantages of secure attachment in infancy? Here the evidence for attachment theory is strong. Secure attachment is associated with lower rates of delinquency in adolescence (Hoeve et al, 2012), though the effect was much stronger in early adolescence than late. Secure attachment also predicts good peer relations throughout childhood (Groh et al, 2014). There may be a number of reasons for this. Sharp et al (2016) found that insecure attachment is associated with hypermentalizing (excessive rumination on a problem from a single perspective), inability to self-regulate emotions, and borderline personality, a mental disorder characterized by relationship difficulties, self-sabotaging behaviour, and self-harm. These all make social interaction more difficult. This social disadvantage appears to last into adulthood.

Banse (2004) examined the relationship between attachment type and marital satisfaction in 333 German couples. Satisfaction of each partner was positively related to secure attachment both in self and partner. So where both partners had secure attachment status satisfaction was greatest. Scores of secure attachment correlated strongly (r = 0.43 for wives and 0.37 for husbands) with marital satisfaction. Scores for each of the insecure attachment types correlated negatively with marital satisfaction.

There is also a wealth of evidence linking insecure—and, in particular, disorganized—attachment with increased vulnerability to mental health problems. Insecure attachment is a risk factor for depression (Gilbert et al, 2014), personality disorder (Sharp et al, 2016), eating disorders (Tasca and Balfour, 2014), and psychosis (Harder, 2014). However, studies have employed a range of methods and attachment measures and, in many cases, attachment has been assessed retrospectively once a patient's cognitions are affected by their condition. There is a much smaller body of **prospective studies** that have followed up children of different attachment statuses and looked for associations with mental health problems (Gumley et al, 2014).

> **KEY IDEAS** prospective studies
Most studies linking early events and their sequelae are carried out retrospectively (ie, looking back after the sequelae are apparent). An alternative is to carry out **prospective studies**. These involve following people up after a significant early event like developing an attachment type and seeing how they develop.

THINKING CRITICALLY

Most of the evidence linking attachment status to mental health problems has been gathered retrospectively. Consider the following:

1 Why is this a problem?

2 Why might there be so few prospective studies of attachment and mental health?

The feminist critique

In spite of its empirical support and practical applications, attachment theory has attracted the ire of some feminist commentators. As Burman (2016) points out, the very fact that a question about children's development has become one of evaluating *parents*' choices reflects the use of psychology to interrogate and regulate the behaviour of families, in particular mothers.

The issue is that, although many contemporary attachment researchers are at pains to emphasize that the primary carer need not be the biological mother or indeed female, in practice most primary carers are mothers, and mothers are thus the subject of blame. Some feminists have described attachment theory as 'profoundly conservative' and 'a pretext deployed by clinicians and social care professionals for constructing mothers as solely responsible for infants and then for policing this caregiving' (Duschinsky, Greco and Solomon, 2015, p 174). In addition, attachment theory has effectively sidelined fathers as significant influences on children's development and justified discrimination against working mothers (Hewitt, 2013). This is an example of an area where critical social psychologists have clashed with more mainstream psychological scientists.

 THINKING CRITICALLY

We (and probably your tutors) have spent a lot of time talking about psychology as a science, with the emphasis on evidence. How can we reconcile this with the importance of feminist critiques that focus on moral and political issues rather than empirical evidence?

READ THIS

There is an enormous volume of research devoted to attachment theory. There is also a lot of over-simplification around it so it is essential to read some original material by Bowlby and Ainsworth. These should get you started:

Ainsworth, M.S. and Bowlby, J. (1991). An ethological approach to personality development. *American Psychologist*, **46**, 333.

Bowlby, J. (2005). *A Secure Base: Clinical Applications of Attachment Theory* (Vol 393). Taylor and Francis.

Ainsworth, M.S. (1979). Infant–mother attachment. *American Psychologist*, **34**, 932.

To pick up on the social context of attachment theory's development you might like to read this:

LeVine, R.A. (2014). Attachment theory as cultural ideology: Different faces of attachment. In Otto, H. and Keller, H. (eds), *Cultural Variations on a Universal Human Need*. Cambridge: Cambridge University Press, 50–65.

For a contemporary understanding of the implications of attachment type try this:

Belsky, J. (2015). Beyond vulnerability: attachment, adversity, gene-environment interaction, and implications for intervention. *Journal of Developmental and Behavioral Pediatrics*, **36**, 464–6.

THE EFFECTS OF EARLY SEPARATION EXPERIENCES

Of course, in real life, young children do not spend all their time in a one-to-one relationship with their primary caregiver. They experience separation under a range of circumstances, ranging from short term to permanent.

Day Care

> KEY IDEAS day care **Day care** is a broad term meaning all non-parental care in childhood, including that provided by relatives, nurseries, and childminders. Psychologists are particularly interested in day care for babies and toddlers and there is a lively debate about the possible positive and negative effects of day care on their development.

According to the Department for Education (2017) there are just over 3,000,000 registered child care places in the UK (Figure 11.6). This includes pre-school provision and before-and after-school clubs. 53% of places are provided by a school, 39% by nurseries, and 9% by childminders. The school-based places take older children, so nurseries and childminders account for the bulk of very young children in **day care**.

FIGURE 11.6 **Many very young children attend nursery school, play school, or kindergarten.**
Source: riopatuca/Shutterstock.com.

The debate presented here mostly concerns these very young children. The evidence for the benefits of pre-school is overwhelming and not really controversial (Taggart et al, 2015).

A brief look at the literature on the alleged effects of day care on young children quickly reveals a split between research suggesting positive effects for children in day care and research suggesting negative effects. This split is so dramatic that psychologists sometimes speak of research in this area as the 'child care wars'! It is tempting to look for a simple answer: is day care good or bad for children? Indeed, many researchers have presented their conclusions in this simplistic form. In reality, however, studies have been conducted by so many researchers focused on different outcomes (social, educational, etc) for so many children in different circumstances whose parents use child care for a variety of reasons, that it is incredibly difficult to extract a simple 'right or wrong' answer as to whether day care is good for children or not.

Some researchers, for example Jay Belsky (2001, 2009), have argued that extensive experience of day care outside the home, particularly in the first few years of life, leads to insecure attachments between parent and child, and increases child aggressiveness and behaviour problems. Others counter that high-quality day care may provide cognitive and intellectual development not easily obtainable for infants and toddlers reared in the home. Andersson (1996) followed up 128 Swedish children who had experienced day care in early childhood and assessed them on their intellectual and social-emotional development at 13 years. Their development was compared with that of a matched group with full-time maternal care. Children who had spent time in day care scored higher in both educational achievement and social skills.

The longitudinal study conducted in ten US cities by the National Institute of Child Health and Development (NICHD) Early Child Care Research Network (ECCRN, 2010) provides the largest scale evidence available of the effects of early child care on later development. This is because the NICHD study was able to control for variables such as parenting quality, day care quality, the amount of time spent in day care, and the specific type of day care situation (eg, centre care vs home care).

The good news for parents is that the NICHD study showed that the relationship between infant and mother *at home* was the best predictor of mother-child attachment and that, in general, parenting quality (and parents' genetic contributions to their children) had a far greater impact on the child than any aspect of the day care experience. Moreover, there was an increase in cognitive and language skills in children who spent more hours in day care regardless of their family backgrounds. Children who experienced high-quality day care (but not low-quality care) showed higher levels of academic achievement scores on standardized tests in maths, reading, and memory at 8–9 years.

The news is not all good, however. More hours spent in child care (regardless of its quality) was consistently associated with lower teacher ratings of the child's social skills and work habits through the third year at school, higher levels of conflict with parents and other adults, and higher levels of aggressive 'acting-out' behaviour– although negative effects are much more pronounced in the case of low-quality day care. Thus, high-quality day care appears to be good for very young children's cognitive-intellectual development, but day care as a whole does not appear in such a good light when it comes to social and emotional development (NICHD ECCRN, 2010).

 THINKING CRITICALLY

Overall, there is a much larger body of research showing negative effects of day care than there is for positive effects. However, as in all things, size isn't everything.

Consider the following:

1 What sort of families are most accessible to researchers and how might this have skewed findings?

2 What sort of political agendas do you think might have affected research and its funding?

We can see from this very mixed picture of findings that there is no single answer as to whether day care is good or a bad for children. Instead, it may be more productive to look at what factors affect whether it provides a positive or negative influence. Edward Melhuish and colleagues deserve great credit for asking the alternative and perhaps better question: what makes good child care?

RESEARCH IN FOCUS

Melhuish, E.C., Mooney, A., Martin, S., and Lloyd, E. (1990a). Type of childcare at 18 months I: Differences in interactional experience. *Journal of Child Psychology and Psychiatry*, **31**, 849–59.

Melhuish, E.C., Lloyd, E., Martin, S., and Mooney, A. (1990b). Type of childcare at 18 months II: Relations with cognitive and language development. *Journal of Child Psychology and Psychiatry*, **31**, 861–70.

❯

Aim: The aim of the study was to compare the social-emotional and intellectual development of children in full-time maternal care with those who experienced a range of day care environments. A secondary aim was to investigate what factors differed between alternative forms of day care and how these might have contributed to any differences in the development of the children.

Method: The study was a natural experiment comparing children in four conditions: full-time maternal care; nursery care; childminder care; and care by a relative. The participants were 255 first-born children from two-parent families in which all the mothers worked full-time before having a child: 25% of these remained full-time mothers for their child's first 18 months. Of the children in day care, 30% were cared for by a relative, 50% by a childminder, and 20% at a nursery.

At 18 months of age, the four groups of children were assessed on their social-emotional development using several measures including the *Strange Situation* (see 'Attachment and attachment theory', this chapter) and observation measures such as time spent crying. Observation and interviews with carers were used to assess their intellectual and language development. Day care environments were also assessed for a range of potentially relevant variables, including the adult:child ratio; stimulating environment; age, training, and experience of the carers.

Results: Some outcome measurements did not vary across the four conditions, including the amount of crying, playing, and maintaining physical contact with adults. No differences were observed in the proportion of children showing secure attachments to their mothers in the four groups. However, there were some significant differences in the children's behaviour. The amount of vocalization at 18 months was greatest in maternal care, followed by relative care, less with a childminder, and lowest in nurseries. Children in nurseries came out as most aggressive, with those in maternal care least. The reverse effect was observed for affection, this being greatest with mothers and least in nurseries. At 3 years of age, the children in maternal care showed the most affection but those in nurseries showed the best social skills.

Substantial variations in the quality of care were noted, with nurseries coming out badly. The nurseries looked at in the study were characterized by a low level of responsiveness to children's communications and a high child:adult ratio (mean = 4.6:1). Nursery staff tended to be younger than the carers in the other conditions and much less likely to have experience with their own children. The nurseries also tended to have a higher turnover of staff than in other settings, meaning that children lacked consistency in the adults that cared for them.

Conclusions: On most (but not all) measures of development, the children in nurseries did less well than others. This can be understood in terms of the common characteristics of nurseries in this study, which detracted from the quality of their care.

MASTER YOUR METHODOLOGY

1 This study is a natural experiment, in which existing conditions representing different levels of the independent variable are compared. Why was it not possible to conduct this study as a true experiment with random allocation to conditions?

2 In a study of this type it must be assumed that the families in the four groups were comparable and that differences in the dependent variables are due to the main four being studied. What confounds might exist in the four conditions?

3 The findings of this study could point to bad outcomes for all nurseries, or it may be that the nurseries in this study were of low quality. How might you carry out a follow-up study to investigate whether good-quality nurseries would experience similar problems?

THINKING CREATIVELY

There are likely to be other variables that impact on the positive/negative effects of day care on children's development. Brainstorm as many of these as possible. You might like to think about aspects of the child's home life, the child's individual differences, and further aspects of the care.

THINKING PRACTICALLY

Based on what you have read in this chapter, what advice might you give someone thinking about using day care? Why would it be crucial to be cautious with your recommendations?

Growing Up in Institutional Care

> **KEY IDEAS**
>
> institutionalization We use the term 'institutionalization' to mean slightly different things in different contexts, but we most commonly use it to refer to the effects of living full time in an institution like a hospital or orphanage. When talking about young children the institution concerned is a hospital or orphanage.

Institutional care takes place when children grow up entirely outside their families, living instead in orphanages or care homes. Here, the degree of separation is much greater than that experienced in day care and the effects are correspondingly greater. The research question considered by psychologists is not so much whether the experience has harmful effects (it does) but whether they can be reversed with good later care.

A fascinating opportunity to study the effects of early institutional care comes from the severely deprived Romanian orphans of the 1990s (Figure 11.7). As the Communist government of Romania collapsed in 1989, a heartbreakingly large number of impoverished infants and small children were abandoned in orphanages. Conditions in these institutions were often horrific. With no more than one attendant for every 10–20 children, the malnourished children were packed into small rooms where they received little in the way of human contact, play, or learning—and often with no access whatever to natural light (Fisher, Ames, Chisholm, and Savoie, 1997; McGeown, 2005).

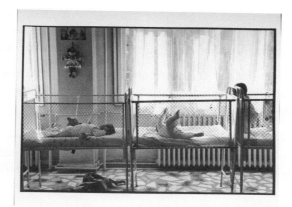

FIGURE 11.7 Children in cots. When Michael Rutter and his colleagues tracked the development of Romanian orphans who had experienced severe deprivation in infancy, they found evidence that some aspects of normal cognitive, emotional, and social development required specific types of experiences during critical periods.

Source: Taro Yamasaki/Getty Images.

Many of these children were fortunate enough to have been adopted subsequently into high-functioning homes in Britain and the USA. Michael Rutter and his colleagues recruited a sample of these adopted orphans, and followed their development into early adolescence (Rutter et al, 2004; Kreppner et al, 2007) in the English and Romanian Adoption (ERA) study. Rutter and his research team found that the majority of the orphans experienced profound and lasting effects on their cognitive development, probably as a result of actual brain damage and/or a lack of exposure to normal stimulation, human contact, and play during critical periods. The longer the period of **institutionalization**, the greater was the extent of impairment—particularly if institutionalization extended beyond the first six months of life. Although there was remarkable recovery from the initial extremely low level of functioning for some of these children, most of this recovery was complete within two years of adoption, and the rest by age 6. Between age 6 and 11 little additional recovery was seen, regardless of the quality of the new home life. These findings strongly support the idea that there are critical periods for normal cognitive development in humans and limits to the corrective effects of beneficial environments.

Earlier in this chapter we mentioned disinhibited social engagement disorder (sometimes called disinhibited attachment). This is a common consequence of early institutional care. In one study, part of the Bucharest Early Intervention Project, Zeanah et al (2005) found that 44% of 12–31-month-olds who remained in institutional care and 20% of those who had spent significant time there as a baby but who had later been adopted in Romania exhibited disinhibited attachment.

However, this is not the whole story. For reasons not well understood, a portion of the orphans in the ERA and Bucharest Early Intervention Project showed no impairment at all—neither in infancy, nor early childhood, nor early adolescence—in spite of having had the same experiences as many who were severely impaired (Kreppner et al, 2007). As Figure 11.8 shows, the large majority of children who showed few or no ill effects from their experience ended their institutional life prior to the age of 6 months. Six months appeared to be a 'cutoff' threshold for the children, beyond which the likelihood of severe impairment dramatically increased.

 THINKING CRITICALLY

There is a potential flaw in studies comparing adopted orphans with those remaining in care. Either they are naturally occurring groups or they are randomly allocated to adoption or further institutional care.

Consider the following:

1   What is the problem with comparing naturally occurring groups of adopted and non-adopted children who experienced early institutional care?

2   What is the problem with randomly allocating children to adoption/non-adoption conditions?

Experiences of severely deprived Romanian orphans demonstrate both the importance of critical or sensitive periods of brain development and also the plasticity of brain development. Figure 11.8A shows that orphans whose experiences of deprivation ended prior to the sixth month of life were actually more likely to show few ill effects of their experiences. Moreover, although not apparent in the graph, only

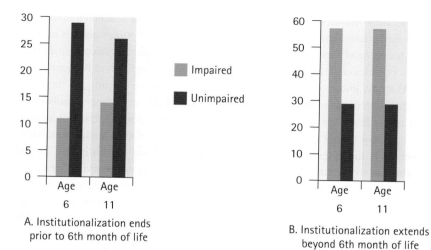

FIGURE 11.8 Experiences of deprivation after the first six months create more lasting damage.

Source: Kreppner, Jana M. et al, (2007). Normality and impairment following profound early institutional deprivation: A longitudinal follow–up into early adolescence. *Developmental Psychology*, 1 July. Copyright © 2007, American Psychological Association.

three of these children who seemed to be unimpaired at age 6 ended up showing impairment at age 11. Figure 11.8B shows a very different pattern. The large majority of children whose experiences of deprivation extended beyond the first six months of life showed severe impairment.

READ THIS

The paper that ignited the controversy over day care is:

Belsky, J. and Steinberg, L.D. (1978). The effects of day care: A critical review. *Child Development,* **49**(4), 929–49.

Here is a recent update of the largest ongoing research programme on day care. You'll notice that Jay Belsky is in there too!

Vandell, D.L., Belsky, J., Burchinal, M., Steinberg, L., and Vandergrift, N. (2010). Do effects of early child care extend to age 15 years? Results from the NICHD study of early child care and youth development. *Child Development,* **81**, 737–56.

To learn more about the effects of institutionalization, the research from the ERA project are excellent sources.

Rutter, M. and Sonuga-Barke, E.J. (2010). X. Conclusions: Overview of findings from the era study, inferences, and research implications. *Monographs of the Society for Research in Child Development,* **75**, 212–29.

THE DEVELOPMENT OF PEER RELATIONS IN CHILDREN

In the early part of childhood, the most significant relationships are those with family members, initially the primary carer, then the wider family. However, the importance of peer relationships increases throughout childhood and by mid-adolescence most young people tend to share greater intimacy with and accord more importance to friends than family and are significantly influenced by them. In Chapter 12 we consider the ideas of Judith Rich Harris, who proposed that peers are more important than family as an influence on social development, in more depth (Chapter 12).

Friendship with peers appears to have potential benefits for children (Erwin, 1998). Early friendships serve as a 'sand box' where social skills like conflict resolution can be learnt. Friendships also have the potential to allow children the chance to develop sensitivity to other people's needs, find sources of social comparison in order to develop socially typical behaviour, and provide sources of emotional support. It *may* be that the experience of friendship can compensate for poor family relationships, although this is made trickier in practice by the fact that children with insecure attachments find it harder to form and maintain friendships (Groh and Fearon, 2014).

 THINKING CRITICALLY AND CREATIVELY

There is a strong relationship between the quality of children's peer relations and later benefits, such as reduced incidence of loneliness and depression (Burk and Laursen, 2005) and victimization (McDonald et al, 2010). However these correlations do not necessarily indicate a simple causal relationship.

Consider the following:

1 What variables might be at work here?

2 Explain how you could use techniques like cross-lagging and partial correlation to try to establish whether there is a causal relationship between quality of childhood peer relations and adult characteristics like depression.

Development of Peer Relations

Children as young as 6 months appear to show interest in their peers. If two infants are given the opportunity to interact they will typically touch, smile, and vocalize at each other (Vandell et al, 1980). By 18 months they help each other; for example, reaching for objects that another toddler cannot reach (Hepah, Kante, and Tomasello, 2016). A counterintuitive finding is that toddlers are more likely to interact with another toddler if that toddler is interacting with an adult (Tremblay-Leveau and Nadel, 1996). However, most toddlers do not show much preference for one peer over another so it is misleading to speak of 'friends' at this age.

In younger children we can only define friendship using observable behaviour. One such behavioural definition comes from Hinde et al (1985) who defined friends as children who choose to play together more than 33% of the time. By this criterion 20% of 18-month-olds and over 50% of 4-year-olds in their sample had stable friendships. It seems then that friendship tends to develop around the 4-year age mark, but with wide individual differences.

There appears to be an important role for adults in structuring and intervening in early peer interactions (Figure 11.9). Williams, Mastergeorge, and Ontai (2010) observed children in a nursery setting and recorded the ways in which adults regulated peer interactions. Strategies included arranging, preventing, and terminating peer interactions, direct instruction, setting rules, and modelling socially appropriate behaviour.

FIGURE 11.9 **Adults can have a great impact on child-to-child interactions, particularly if they are in a caregiving role.**
Source: Robert Kneschke/Shutterstock.com.

This is particularly interesting given findings, for example, by Melhuish et al ('The effects of early separation', this chapter) that inexperienced and unqualified adults in nursery settings were associated with poorer social development.

Older children and adolescents tend to be researched by means of survey methods rather than observation. In one study, O'Brien and Bierman (1988) asked American children and adolescents aged 9, 13, and 16 to describe the nature of friendship groups. The younger participants tended to define friendship groups behaviourally—as those who engaged in activities together. By adolescence the criterion for belonging to a friendship group had shifted to shared values and appearance.

 THINKING CRITICALLY

Studies of friendship in young children tend to make use of behavioural measures whilst those focused on older children tend to use self-reported measures. Why might this be and how does it limit research in this area?

Individual Differences in Children's Sociometric Status

Some children have more friends than others, and this would be the simplest way to define popularity. However, the picture is actually more complicated. What about children that are largely ignored? They are different to those who are actively disliked and those 'marmite children' that attract strong opinions split between like and dislike. Coie and Dodge (1983) have sought to clarify this confusing picture by identifying five categories of **sociometric status** or popularity type. They asked children to categorize their peers as 'liked most' or 'liked least' and every child was categorized accordingly. This yielded five popularity types.

> ❯ **KEY IDEAS** sociometric status Crudely, **sociometric status** means popularity. However, this is not as simple as describing a child as popular or unpopular. Children can also be neglected, controversial, or average in popularity.

- **Popular:** often 'liked most' and seldom 'liked least'.
- **Average:** moderately and equally likely to be 'liked most' or 'liked least'.
- **Controversial:** frequently categorized both as 'liked most' and 'liked least'.
- **Neglected:** rarely categorized as 'liked most' or 'liked least'.
- **Rejected:** frequently categorized as 'liked least' and rarely as 'liked most'.

Factors affecting sociometric status

These are very much as anyone who has been through the school system would expect! Children who behave conventionally and conform to group norms tend to have higher status than those displaying greater individuality (Kraus et al, 2014). This extends to gender norms, with aggression predicting popularity in boys but not girls (Zwaan, Dikstra, and Veestra, 2013).

Conventional attractiveness also conveys advantages in the popularity stakes. Coie et al (1982) rated children for attractiveness, then asked peer groups to rate each other as 'most liked' and 'most disliked'. A strong positive correlation emerged, with the children rated highest for attractiveness being those most likely to be categorized as 'most liked' and vice versa. Cash (1995) reported that disfigurement interferes with non-verbal communication and so makes the affected child more difficult to interact with. This in turn has a negative impact on their popularity status.

READ THIS

For a general introduction to children's friendships you might look at these books:

Dunn, J. (2004). *Children's Friendships: The Beginnings of Intimacy*. Oxford: Blackwell Publishing.

Erwin, P. (2013). *Friendship in Childhood and Adolescence*. London: Routledge.

And for sociometric status:

Cillessen, A.H., Schwartz, D., and Marks, P E. (eds) (2011). *Popularity in the Peer System*. New York: Guilford Press.

IN REVIEW

TEMPERAMENT

- There is a divide between psychologists emphasizing the importance of temperament and those emphasizing the importance of attachment. This is a nature-nurture debate.

- Temperament is the infant personality, influenced primarily by genetic make-up. Three robust factors of temperament have emerged: effortful control, negative emotionality, and extroversion.

- There appears to be reasonable continuity between infant temperament and adult personality.

ATTACHMENT

- Attachment quality is also a major influence on infant development. Attachment theory proposes an evolved innate tendency for attachment formation and a set of environmental prequelae that lead to secure attachment, most importantly maternal sensitivity.

- Attachment theory also posits a set of sequelae of secure and insecure attachment, with secure attachment conferring a set of advantages on the developing child.

- Attachment security in infants can be measured using a controlled observation called the Strange Situation, which produces mild anxiety then tests proximity-seeking, separation and stranger anxiety, and response to reunion.

- The Strange Situation classifies children into secure and a range of insecure attachment types.

- Research supports the advantages of secure attachment for infant development and partially supports the importance of maternal sensitivity. The evolutionary roots of attachment are fairly resistant to empirical study.

SEPARATION EXPERIENCES

- Day care has generated heated debates amongst developmental psychologists, with research showing both positive and negative effects.

- Institutional care in infancy is associated with more serious effects including attachment disorders, although early adoption reverses these effects in many cases.

PEER RELATIONS

- Children demonstrate an early interest in peers but friendships usually do not form for some years. Adults scaffold early peer interactions.

- Children's popularity status can be classified into a range of types based on peer ratings. Children with high-popularity status tend to be attractive and conventional.

TEST YOURSELF

1 Atypical attachment is a risk factor for serious mental health problems. True ❒ False ❒

2 Infant temperament predicts some aspects of adult personality. True ❒ False ❒

3 Toddlers are less likely to interact with another toddler if they are with an adult. True ❒ False ❒

4 Research has consistently shown that children who spend time in day care are disadvantaged. True ❒ False ❒

5 Which of the following is not a sign of attachment?

a) Proximity-seeking

b) Separation distress

c) Imprinting

d) Reunion pleasure

6 What did Ainsworth consider the major factor in affecting attachment security?

a) Poverty

b) Time spent with primary caregiver

c) Temperament

d) Sensitive responsiveness

7 In the UK, which is the most common form of registered child care?

   a) Relative

   b) School

   c) Childminder

   d) Nursery

8 Which of these popularity types is least popular?

   a) Rejected

   b) Neglected

   c) Average

   d) Controversial

9 Explain feminist concerns with attachment theory.

10 Explain the relationship between temperament and attachment.

 Visit the online resources that accompany this book: www.oup.com/uk/jarvis–okami1e

CHAPTER 12

COGNITIVE DEVELOPMENT

LEARNING OUTCOMES

By the end of this chapter you should be able to:

- Critically consider research into infant perceptual development and innate knowledge of the physical world
- Describe Piaget's constructivist theory of cognitive development with particular reference to schemas and stages
- Evaluate the current status of Piaget's theory in the light of more recent research
- Outline and evaluate the social constructivist Vygotsky–Bruner model of cognitive development
- Contrast domain-general theories of cognitive development with research into specific domains of development
- Assess theories of and research into moral development with particular reference to the work of Kohlberg and Haidt
- Discuss research into the development of theory of mind

> **KEY IDEAS** qualitative and quantitative age-related change Developing individuals clearly undergo **quantitative change** in their cognition. In other words they start to know and understand more as time passes. Nothing controversial there but more interesting is the idea that we also become capable of understanding *different* things as opposed to simply *more* things at different ages. This is **qualitative change**.

> **KEY IDEAS** domains of development There are many cognitive abilities that require development. Each of these is a **domain** of cognitive development. To theorists like Piaget, cognitive development is a single process and all domains develop together. However, some research focuses on one particular domain; for example, perception, moral judgement, or theory of mind. Typically such research does not make the same assumption of domain-generality.

At what point in our development do we understand what is going on around us, and how does this understanding change with age? Prior to the twentieth century, the newborn infant was viewed as an utterly helpless organism that perceived the world, in the famous words of William James, as a 'blooming, buzzing confusion'. However, once a child was walking and talking, they were not seen as much different in their abilities to a small, inexperienced adult. In modern developmental psychology there are very healthy debates about how well developed infant cognition is and how this changes qualitatively as well as quantitatively with age.

Another important tension to keep in mind when reading this chapter is between the study of specific **domains** of cognitive development and that of domain-general cognitive development. When we are discussing infant perceptual abilities, moral development, and theory of mind development, we are focused on specific *domains* or aspects of cognitive development. However, when we look at broad, overarching views of cognitive development like that by Jean Piaget, we are trying to understand general processes underlying *all* cognitive development.

INFANT COGNITION

Historically there has been a common assumption that babies are born with very little in the way of cognitive abilities. However, contemporary research has challenged this view and identified some surprisingly advanced perceptual abilities and innate knowledge of the world.

Infant Perceptual Abilities

Thanks to newly developed methods of research, we now know that infants have perceptual competencies that were never suspected as recently as two or three decades ago. For example, within hours of birth newborn infants prefer to gaze at, and will increase their sucking behaviour in response to, images of their mother's face compared with images of other female faces (Pascalis and Kelly, 2009). Newborns who are breastfed will be able to recognize and prefer their own mother's scent over that of other women (Nishitani et al, 2009). The hearing of newborns is acute enough to recognize subtle patterns of sound, including the sounds of spoken language, and this acuity develops well before the infant is born. From at least three months prior to birth, foetuses respond to changes in sound from the outside world (Fernald, 2004). Indeed, foetuses can distinguish their mother's voice from that of an unfamiliar woman, and the language spoken by their mother from a foreign language (Lagercrantz and Kuhl, 2013).

You might well ask how researchers could possibly know this. As there is no way to directly measure recognition in a foetus the researchers had to find a proxy physiological measure—in this case foetal heart rate. They monitored foetal heart rate as they placed a speaker directly above the mother's stomach and alternately played tape recordings of the infant's mother and a strange female speaking, or their mother's language versus a foreign language. Foetal heart rate consistently increased when the mother's voice or the mother's language was heard and decreased when the stranger's voice (or a foreign language) was heard. This strongly suggests that the foetus distinguished both familiar speaker and language. As another example, when DeCasper and Spence (1986) had mothers recite portions of the Dr Seuss book *The Cat in the Hat* repeatedly during the last few weeks of their pregnancies, their newborn infants increased their sucking behaviour when these passages were read to them, but other passages had no effect.

Infant Knowledge

Bloom (2004) summarizes evidence gathered in recent studies by Renee Baillargeon, Elizabeth Spelke, and their colleagues showing that infants make the same fundamental assumptions about the physical attributes of objects made by adults everywhere. For example, babies, like adults, apparently believe that:

- *Objects are solid.* Babies look longer at set-ups that appear to violate the solidity of objects, such as a screen placed in front of an object tilting all the way back without hitting the object (Baillargeon, Spelke, and Wasserman, 1985). (In such experiments, the object has fallen through a hidden trap door.) Infants also look longer at images of structurally impossible objects, such as a cube where one side is simultaneously in front of, and behind, another (Shuwairi, Albert, and Johnson, 2007). Further, infants expect different behaviours from solids and liquids (Hespos, Ferry, and Rips, 2009).

- *Objects only move through contact.* The example given by Bloom is a ball on a pool table—it will not move unless something touches it. Babies are surprised if objects move without being touched (Spelke, Phillips, and Woodward, 1995).

- *Objects travel through space in a continuous path.* Objects in motion do not suddenly disappear and then reappear somewhere down the line. Babies are surprised at demonstrations where this rule is apparently violated (Spelke et al, 1995).

THINKING CRITICALLY AND CREATIVELY

We rather glibly just said that babies 'were surprised'. Why is this actually quite hard to establish? How might researchers go about finding appropriate measures of surprise in preverbal infants? You might like to do some research before answering. You might like to start with this paper: Baillargeon, R (1994). How do infants learn about the physical world? *Current Directions in Psychological Science*, 3(5), pp 133–40. http://journals.sagepub.com/doi/abs/10.1111/1467-8721.ep10770614?journalCode=cdpa

What else do infants know? Would you believe that they can add and subtract? Developmental psychologist Karen Wynn thought they could, and she provided evidence of the ability of small infants to understand basic addition and subtraction. Wynn (1992) presented 5-month-old infants with a shallow, empty case on a small stage-like area (see Figure 12.1). A hand emerges from the side holding a Mickey Mouse doll and places it in the case. A screen slides up obscuring the case from view. The hand emerges into the infant's view once again to place another doll beside the first one, out of sight behind the screen. We would be very surprised if the screen should be lifted and only one doll is left standing—and so were Wynn's 5-month-old infants. They stared longer when the screen fell to display one doll than when two dolls were shown. The same results were found for a subtraction task, also depicted in Figure 12.1. These studies proved quite startling, because it was not believed that infants 'should' have a concept of number.

Not everyone was convinced, however (Cohen and Marks, 2002), so cognitive neuroscientists Andrea Berger and her colleagues devised more stringent tests of infants' maths perceptions (Berger, Tzur, and Posner, 2006). Berger and her colleagues repeated Wynn's addition and subtraction procedure with a group of 6–9-month-old infants while monitoring the infants' brains, using EEG technology (see Figure 12.2). These researchers found that the infants' **brainwave** activity while viewing impossible solutions was similar to brainwave activity previously identified in studies of adults as they detected various errors and violations of expectations. This research provides even stronger support for Wynn's views of infant abilities.

Thus, infants can do many things they 'should not' be able to do. As you might imagine, because some of this evidence goes against our intuitions about what an infant is capable of accomplishing, it has been challenged (Uller, Carey, Huntley-Fenner, and Klatt, 1999; Newcombe, 2002). But there is another reason it has often been challenged, as you might also have surmised: it appears to suggest that humans come into the world with certain knowledge already in place. This is an example of a *nature-nurture* debate, often referred to in developmental psychology as *nativism vs empiricism* (Spelke, 1998; Newcombe, 2002). **Nativism** is the view that we come into the world with some number of innate abilities or tendencies, while **empiricism**, as described in Chapter 1, is the view that most (or all) mental characteristics are acquired through experience.

Finally, evidence of infant competence in cognition such as that provided in the research like that of Renee Baillargeon described in the last few paragraphs has also been particularly difficult for many developmental psychologists to accept. These findings appear to contradict much of the work of Jean Piaget (1896–1980)—the most important theorist in the history of developmental psychology of cognition, and one of the greatest of all pioneers in psychology.

> **KEY IDEAS** nativism and empiricism **Nativism** is the view that at least some human abilities and tendencies are innate. It is often contrasted with empiricism in 'nature-nurture' debates. **Empiricism** is the philosophical tradition that emphasizes the importance of experience in acquiring knowledge. In the 'nature-nurture' debate in psychology, empiricism is contrasted with nativism.

Sequence of events 1+1 = 1 or 2

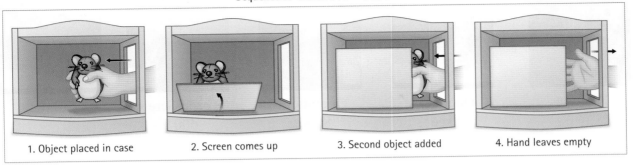

1. Object placed in case   2. Screen comes up   3. Second object added   4. Hand leaves empty

Then either: possible outcome

Or: impossible outcome

5. Screen drops...   ...revealing 2 objects

5. Screen drops...   ...revealing 1 object

Sequence of events 2−1 = 1 or 2

1. Objects placed in case   2. Screen comes up   3. Empty hand enters   4. One object removed

Then either: possible outcome

Or: impossible outcome

5. Screen drops...   ...revealing 1 object

5. Screen drops...   ...revealing 2 objects

FIGURE 12.1 Addition and subtraction in 5-month-old infants. Karen Wynn (1992) presented correct and incorrect (impossible) 'solutions' to addition and subtraction 'problems' to a group of 5-month-old infants. The infants stared longer at the impossible solutions.

Source: Adapted from Wynn, 1992.

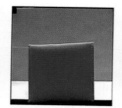

Fixation   Operand   Operation   Frozen Screen   Solution
4 sec   8 sec   600 ms

Sound Track

Time

FIGURE 12.2 **2 + 1 equals . . . 1?** Brain-imaging infant addition. Andrea Berger and her colleagues repeated Karen Wynn's 'doll arithmetic' procedures with a group of infants whose brains were monitored using EEG technology. They found that the infants looked longer at impossible than correct arithmetic solutions. When viewing impossible solutions, infants simultaneously showed brain activity similar to that in adults whose expectations had been violated or who were in the process of detecting errors.

Source: Copyright (2006) National Academy of Sciences, U.S.A.

READ THIS

Much of the most innovative work in the area of infant knowledge has been conducted by Renee Baillargeon and colleagues, so a good place to start would be with one of her classic papers, plus a more recent review:

Baillargeon, R. (1987). Object permanence in 3½- and 4½-month-old infants. *Developmental Psychology, 23*, 655–64.

Baillargeon, R. (2002). The acquisition of physical knowledge in infancy: A summary in eight lessons. In U. Goswami (ed), *Blackwell Handbooks of Developmental Psychology. Blackwell Handbook of Childhood Cognitive Development* (pp 47–83). Oxford: Blackwell.

For infant perception the following is an excellent starting point:

Cohen, L.B. and Salapatek, P. (eds) (2013). *Infant Perception: from Sensation to Cognition: Basic Visual Processes, Volume 1.* New York: Academic Press.

PIAGET'S CONSTRUCTIVIST THEORY OF COGNITIVE DEVELOPMENT

The Swiss psychologist Jean Piaget stands out in the history of psychology not only for the extent of his contributions, but also for their longevity. Although we now believe that Piaget was mistaken about some aspects of cognitive development, as we shall see, a surprising number of his insights have remained firmly established in contemporary thinking (Flavell, 1996; T.L. Rose and Fischer, 2009).

Piaget (1952, 1954) did not believe that human beings came into the world 'pre-equipped' with certain knowledge as the nativists proposed, nor did he believe that the human being was the passive 'blank slate' to be 'written on' by the environment as portrayed in some empiricist accounts (eg, behaviourism). Piaget suggested instead that each infant and child actively 'constructs' an understanding of the world based on his or her experience, always pushing for an understanding that is more advanced than the one previously held (Siegler and Ellis, 1996). Accordingly, Piaget's theory is known as **constructivism**.

Three important concepts underlie Piaget's theory of cognitive development: agency, schemas, and **developmental stages**.

Agency

Perhaps the single most distinctive concept in Piaget's theory is that of **agency**. In the context of Piagetian theory, agency referred to the internal and individual motivation to master understanding. Put another way, we are the agents of our own learning and cognitive development. Piaget noted that even very young children are very inquisitive, both about their own abilities and the external world. Agency is the reason why learning and cognitive development are such active processes. Children explore the world and construct an internal representation of it based on what they discover in their explorations. These representations become successively more complex with development.

Schemas

Schemas are cognitive models that people construct of the world and how it works—they are a way to make meaningful sense out of experience. While adults and children both use schemas, Piaget insisted that children possess age-specific schemas. Children's schemas develop and become more realistic over time as a result of biological and psychological maturation, not just experience and learning.

Children use the processes of **assimilation** and **accommodation** to construct increasingly accurate and advanced schemas. Assimilation describes the way a child fits a new experience into a pre-existing schema. When my (Paul's) daughter Anisa was about 11 months old, she had just learned the word 'ball'. It happened that the moon was spectacularly full one night, and after seeing it, she delightedly observed, 'Ball!' She was attempting to *assimilate* the new experience of observing a full moon into her schema for round objects ('round objects are "balls" ').

Eventually, Anisa began to notice the many differences between the moon and rubber balls, so she began to *alter* her schema for round objects to include, or accommodate, the moon ('round objects can have many names that refer to various things other than balls'). Children's schemas are constantly being altered according to the push-and-pull of assimilation and accommodation.

Piaget's Developmental Stages

Piaget believed that children passed through four distinct stages of development that were invariant—that is, *everyone* passed through them, and they *always* occurred in the same order. However, there is substantial variation in the length of time each individual remains in a given stage. The stages reflect *qualitatively* different ways of thinking and processing information, not just *quantitative* differences in the amount of knowledge acquired. A qualitative difference is a difference *in kind*. For example, when a caterpillar passes into the butterfly stage, it has not simply grown older, larger, and faster moving (quantitative difference). It is a different creature altogether (qualitative difference).

> **KEY IDEAS** constructivism
> **Constructivism** is the stage theory of child development devised by Jean Piaget. Constructivism holds that each child actively constructs an understanding of the world based on experience and his or her stage of psychological and biological maturation.

> **KEY IDEAS** Schemas
> **Schemas** are mental structures or cognitive models that represent some aspect of the world and how it works.

> **KEY IDEAS** assimilation and accommodation **Assimilation** is Piaget's term to describe the process whereby a person processes a new experience by fitting it into a pre-existing schema. **Accommodation** is Piaget's term for the process whereby a person significantly alters his or her schema to incorporate new information or experiences. This may involve the creation of a new schema.

> **KEY IDEAS** stages
> **Developmental stages** are age-related periods of development with distinct boundaries, and that reflect qualitatively different types of cognitive activity.

> **KEY IDEAS** sensorimotor stage
The **sensorimotor stage** is Piaget's
first developmental stage lasting
from birth to approximately age 2.
It is characterized by unthinking
responses to internal and external
stimuli and events.

> **KEY IDEAS** object permanence
Object permanence is the child's
understanding that objects
continue to exist even if they are
no longer in view.

> **KEY IDEAS** the preoperational
stage The **preoperational stage** is
Piaget's developmental stage lasting
from approximately age 2 to 7. It
is characterized by development
of the symbolic capacity of the
child's mind. At this stage the child
is **egocentric**: they lack the ability
to see things from the perspective
of another person. They also
struggle with **conservation**: the
understanding that an object
may retain its identity even if its
appearance has changed.

The sensorimotor stage

The first stage of development according to Piaget is the **sensorimotor stage** (birth to approximately age 2). Piaget did not believe that small infants possessed the sophisticated skills and understandings of the world reflected in some of the current research described earlier in this chapter. According to Piaget, small infants learn about the world through basic reflexes such as sucking, senses of hearing and vision, increasing motor development, and the ability to grasp and manipulate objects. Babies in the sensorimotor period lack the capacity to *think*—they merely respond to internal and external events. According to Piaget, only towards the end of the sensorimotor stage, when infants are able to use words and images to *represent* objects, ideas, and experiences, does the capacity for thought develop.

One of the principal cognitive skills Piaget claimed the infant acquires during the sensorimotor period is **object permanence**, which he suggested develops at about the eighth or ninth month of life. As depicted in Figure 12.3, object permanence is the understanding that objects continue to exist when they are no longer in view. For example, Piaget noted that if a blanket is thrown over a toy, an infant who has not yet achieved object permanence will not even attempt to reach for the toy. Piaget concluded that the infant literally believes that the toy no longer exists. However, recent research (including some of the research already described) has shown that infants as young as 2½ months have at least some understanding of object permanence (Wang, Baillargeon, and Brueckner, 2004).

The preoperational stage

The second stage of development is the **preoperational stage** (approximately age 2 to 6 or 7). This is a time of intense development of the symbolic capacity of the child's mind. Imaginative play, intense language development, and the ability to

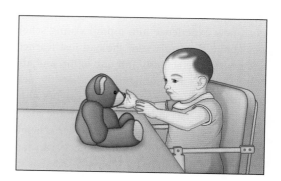

FIGURE 12.3 Object permanence. Piaget believed that infants younger than 8 or 9 months did not possess an understanding that objects continue to exist when they are no longer in view. However, recent research suggests that infants as young as 2½ months possess a basic understanding of object permanence.

FIGURE 12.4 Demonstrating lack of conservation in preoperational child. Two beakers holding identical amounts of water are shown to a 4- or 5-year-old boy. While the boy watches, one beaker (sealed at the top) is turned upside down. The water level now appears much higher in the upturned beaker. The child is then asked, 'Do these glasses have the same amount of water, or a different amount?' In spite of the fact that the boy 'should' know that the glasses still hold an identical amount of water, he claims that the beaker on the left holds more. However, as was the case with the sensorimotor period, Piaget appears to have overstated the limitations of preoperational thought and underestimated the abilities of these children. To some degree, this was a result of the way he constructed tasks for children to perform (Gelman, 1972). Moreover, although very young preoperational children are clearly egocentric in their thinking, focusing on the egocentrism of these children ignores one of the most impressive feats of overcoming egocentrism that occurs during these years: the development of a *theory of mind* (Callaghan et al, 2005). We examine theory of mind in detail later in this chapter

consider the past and possible futures are important new developments that open up a world of possibilities to the preschool age child. Contrary to the concerns of some parents, the creation of imaginary playmates and other seemingly outlandish flights of fancy in children of this age are associated with strong social, imaginative, and cognitive skills, not emotional problems (Taylor, Hulette, and Dishion, 2010).

According to Piaget, however, the child is constrained in development during this period by several factors. First, preoperational children are **egocentric**. This term does not mean that babies are 'conceited'—it means that they lack the ability to see things from the perspective of another person. When a parent says, 'Put yourself in [my, her, his] place—how would *you* feel if someone did that to you?', preoperational children may literally be unable to do so, according to Piaget.

The preoperational child may also have difficulty performing mental operations requiring logic. The classic example of this involves lack of **conservation** in preoperational children. Conservation is the understanding that an object may retain its identity even if its appearance is changed for some reason (see Figure 12.4).

The stage of concrete operations

The third stage of development is the **stage of concrete operations** (approximately age 7 to 11 or 12). During this stage, the child begins to master tasks involving the application of logic. Tasks that eluded the preoperational child are performed easily.

> **KEY IDEAS** stage of concrete operations The **stage of concrete operations** is Piaget's developmental stage lasting from approximately age 7 to 11 or 12. It is characterized by mastery of tasks involving the application of logic.

When I (Paul) offered the water conservation task to my preoperational daughter Anisa, she failed predictably. When I gave the same task to her concrete operational sister Naima, and asked her if the beakers contained different amounts of water—she looked at me as though I were a bit odd.

The concrete operational child performs abstract mathematical computations, classifies objects in multiple ways (eg, human beings are *primates* which are a type of *mammal* which is a type of *animal*), and has a strongly developed theory of mind. As any parent learns, this last development is a mixed blessing, because a theory of mind makes the child a far more accomplished liar! Their egocentrism has diminished, and they can now 'read minds'.

The stage of formal operations

> **KEY IDEAS** stage of formal operations The **stage of formal operations** is Piaget's developmental stage beginning at age 11 or 12, and characterized by the ability to apply systematic logic to abstract concepts and to think hypothetically and sceptically.

The fourth and final stage of development is the **stage of formal operations** (approximately age 11 or 12 into adulthood). According to Piaget, formal operations mark the onset of **adolescence**. Where the concrete operational child can perform logical operations on *objects* using arithmetic and classification, the formal operational adolescent can perform logical operations on abstract *concepts*. He or she can juggle ideas, think hypothetically and sceptically, and apply logical reasoning in a systematic manner. For example, the formal operational child can understand and explain why the following statement is false: 'All men are fools; Lucinda is a fool; therefore, Lucinda is a man.'

THINKING PRACTICALLY

How might Piaget's theory be applied to education? You could consider the idea of agency and active learning and the links between Piaget's stages and the curriculum.

The formal operations stage is perhaps the most controversial of Piaget's ideas. Some evidence suggests that many supposedly concrete-operational children can perform characteristically formal operational tasks (Ennis, 1975). On the other hand, consistent research also shows that not only do a great many adolescents *lack* the ability to use formal operations (or, at least, do not use them consistently), but also unfortunately, so do a great many adults (Klaczynski and Narasimham, 1998; Klaczynski, 2001; Gilovich, Griffin, and Kahneman, 2002). Moreover, the degree to which a person is capable of formal operations is in part dependent on **culture**, schooling, and other external variables (Flieller, 1999). As Kuhn (2006, p 60) forcefully puts it, very few, if any, contemporary researchers support the idea of a sudden emergence in adolescence of distinct cognitive abilities similar to those described by Piaget as formal operations.

Table 12.1 summarizes Piaget's developmental stages.

Considering Piaget

As we have seen, Piaget often underestimated the abilities of infants and children (and in some cases *over*estimated their abilities). However, this in itself is not a particularly damning criticism of his work. The research technologies and methodologies available in Piaget's time (1896–1980) were primitive compared with those

TABLE 12.1 **Piaget's developmental stages**

Ages	Stage	Principal characteristics according to piaget
Birth–2	*Sensorimotor*	Development proceeds as a result of reflexive, sensory, and motor experiences; object permanence is achieved.
2–6/7	*Preoperational*	Child displays symbolic thought; language and imaginative play develop; thinking is egocentric; child lacks conservation.
6/7–11/12	*Concrete operations*	Child learns to apply logic to tasks involving objects and concrete situations; can use arithmetic and multiple classification; diminished egocentrism and developed theory of mind.
11/12–adult	*Formal operations*	Adolescent learns abstract reasoning and systematic application of logic to ideas and concepts; may develop moral and philosophical concerns.

accessible to modern researchers. In any case, Piaget's primary concern was not identifying with precision the ages at which certain cognitive changes take place. Rather, his central concern was to establish that children are active participants in their own development, that changes in development proceed in an orderly fashion, and that the order of developmental changes does not vary. That is, children do not develop formal operations in primary school, only to abandon them in favour of concrete operations in adolescence! The case for these assertions has been well made (Flavell, Miller, and Miller, 1993).

However, theories undergo revision as a result of research, and more substantial criticisms of Piaget's theory have been made over the past few decades that go beyond observing that he under- or overestimated the capabilities of children at specific ages. Here are a few of these objections:

1 *Piaget overemphasized the notion of stages.* Researchers adhering to information-processing models of development have suggested that cognitive development is often *continuous* rather than occurring in discontinuous stages, and highly dependent on the nature of the specific task at hand (Siegler and Ellis, 1996; Fischer and Bidell, 1998). This idea helps to explain why many children who 'should' be able to pass certain Piagetian tasks don't, while others who 'shouldn't' be able to pass, do.

2 *Piaget did not sufficiently take into account social and cultural influences on development.* While Piaget did not ignore social and cultural influences on the child (Matusov and Hayes, 2000), it is fair to say that he was vague on the subject in comparison to certain other theorists. The most prominent *sociocultural* theorist of Piaget's generation was Lev Vygotsky (1896–1934). Vygotsky (1929) emphasized that cognitive growth in the child is highly variable and dependent on the individual child's social and cultural experiences as well as the broader sociocultural context, as expressed in phenomena such as language. Therefore, development differs not only from child to child but also from society to society. Vygotsky's theory readily explains findings that in certain societies, formal operational thought does not appear to exist (Neimark, 1975).

3 *Piaget's theory describes development, but does not explain it.* Psychologists working from the evolutionary perspective complain that much of psychology *describes* behaviour but does not *explain* it (Buss, 2005). This criticism has been levelled at Piaget. In other words, it is not enough merely to predict that children's cognitive development proceeds in a certain orderly fashion. The question remains, *why* does it do so? *Why* are preschool children unable to understand conservation, and *why* do formal operations develop less predictably than concrete operations?

RESEARCH IN FOCUS

McGarrigle, J. and Donaldson, M. (1974) Conservation accidents. *Cognition*, **3**, 341–50.

Aim: One alternative explanation for Piaget's findings in conservation experiments is that children were responding to the social cue of the adult deliberately changing the appearance of the set-up. The aim of this study was to test this idea by creating number and length conservation conditions in which the counters appeared to move accidentally rather than being deliberately moved by the experimenter.

Method: The design was a within-groups experiment carried out under laboratory conditions—80 children aged 4–6 years took part in two conditions: intentional transformation and accidental transformation. In the control condition, participants undertook the same tasks as those in Piaget's experiments. In the first experiment, an adult experimenter presented them with two rows of counters, asked them about the number in each row, then pushed the counters in one row closer. The second experiment was a length conservation task involving a straight piece of string being presented and then repositioned into a curve. Finally, the experimenters questioned the children about the numbers and lengths again.

The experimental condition simulated was an accidental alteration of the rows and strings. They achieved this by means of a 'naughty teddy' which ran across the table and 'accidentally' knocked the counters in one row closer together or knocked the string into a curve. The children were then asked whether the number of counters in each row was the same, and if the strings were the same length.

Results: In the control Piagetian condition, only 13 of the 80 children (16%) correctly conserved following the change in appearance. In the experimental condition, however, 50 participants (62%) answered correctly.

Conclusion: Piaget's findings as regards number and length conservation in preoperational children were an artefact of his procedure, and in fact most 4–6-year-olds are capable of conservation.

MASTER YOUR METHODOLOGY

1 A **within-groups design** was used for this study. Explain the major advantage of this choice compared with a **between-groups design**.

2 What is counterbalancing and why was it used in this study?

3 Like many developmental researchers, Piaget tended to use participants from a university nursery. McGarrigle and Donaldson took half their participants from a university nursery and half from a local primary school. Why was this sensible?

❯ **KEY IDEAS** within-groups and between-groups designs In experiments, participants may either take part in all conditions or just one. The former is called a **within-groups design** (also called a related design or repeated measures design) and the latter a **between-groups design** (or unrelated design or independent measures design).

READ THIS

It is always worth starting with the original. This lecture summarizes the theory and is one of Piaget's easier reads:

Piaget, J. (1997). Development and learning. In: Gauvain, M. and Cole, G.M. (eds), *Readings on the Development of Children*, 2nd edn. New York: W.H. Freeman, 19–28.

Originally published as: Piaget, J. (1964). Development and learning. In R.E. Ripple and V.N. Rockcastle (eds), *Piaget Rediscovered*. Ithaca, NY: Cornell University Press, 7–20.

This book captures Piaget's core ideas very well; however, it is not a particularly easy read. Be warned!

Piaget, J. (1954). *The Construction of Reality in the Child*. London: Routledge.

There is an enormous literature evaluating Piaget's theory. Anything by Margaret Donaldson will provide a good critical account. For a quite advanced defence of Piaget's position try this:

Lourenço, O. and Machado, A. (1996). In defense of Piaget's theory: A reply to 10 common criticisms. *Psychological Review*, **103**(1), 143–64.

THE VYGOTSKY–BRUNER SOCIAL CONSTRUCTIVIST THEORY

Lev Vygotsky was a Russian contemporary of Piaget. Vygotsky was influenced by Piaget and the two agreed on many issues. Both believed that cognitive development takes place in stages, each of which is characterized by qualitatively different cognitive capabilities. However, Vygotsky had a different take on constructivism. Instead of seeing children as individually motivated by a need to understand the world, Vygotsky saw them as primarily social beings, with learning primarily taking place through interaction with more expert others. For this reason his approach is sometimes called **social constructivism**. He also differed from Piaget in viewing language as absolutely central to cognitive development.

The Cultural Nature of Cognitive Development

Vygotsky noted that children growing up in different cultural contexts master different cognitive abilities that correspond to the requirements of their physical and cultural environment. He proposed that, whilst all children are born with some common basic mental abilities such as selective attention, higher mental functions such as thinking and problem-solving can only be acquired through interaction. These 'mental tools' are specific to the child's culture, and are transmitted by older, more expert individuals through guided learning experiences. These can be formal, such as interactions with teachers at school, or informal, such as interactions with other children during play. Cultural tools are as diverse as human cultural activities, ranging from spear fishing to computer programming!

During the process of transmission, cultural tools initially exist on an **intermental plane** (ie, between people) but become internalized to form part of the child's own mental representation of the world—the **intramental plane**. This is in sharp contrast to Piaget's view, in which the child's individual explorations form their mental representation of the world.

> **KEY IDEAS** social constructivism
Social constructivism is the Vygotsky–Bruner model of cognitive development in which a child constructs an increasingly complex mental representation of the world with the help of expert others through a process of interaction.

> **KEY IDEAS** intermental and intramental planes In Vygotskian theory, understand ing at first exists *between* the child and their instructor on the **intermental plane**. Later it also exists in the mind of the child on an **intramental plane**.

THINKING PRACTICALLY

The current generation of older people has seen massive cultural change within their lifetimes. Identify aspects of the modern world that older people sometimes struggle with. Explain why this should be from a Vygotskian perspective.

The Zone of Proximal Development and Scaffolding

Consistent with his own collectivist cultural roots as a Russian, Vygotsky put tremendous emphasis on the role of social interaction in learning. He believed that children can develop their understanding of a situation more quickly through interacting with others than they can through individual discovery. Development of higher mental functions, such as formal and scientific reasoning, could not be acquired through discovery alone but requires learning from others.

The gap between what a child can understand alone and what they have the potential to understand after interaction with others is known as the Zone of Proximal Development (or ZPD). Instruction by an expert allows children to cross the ZPD and understand as much of a subject or situation as they are capable.

The processes by which an expert assists the child through the ZPD have been retrospectively termed 'scaffolding' by Jerome Bruner and colleagues (eg, Wood et al, 1976). As a child charts a course across a ZPD, the level of scaffolding required declines. Explicit instructions need to be provided initially, but prompts subsequently become sufficient for the child to progress. As intervention becomes more minimal, the level of interaction by the expert becomes more contingent (ie, dependent) on the success of the learner at each point (Conner and Cross, 2003).

> **KEY IDEAS** the ZPD and scaffolding The **ZPD** is the conceptual gap between the complexity of learning that a learner can master on their own and the complexity of learning which they can potentially master with the help of an expert instructor. The processes by which the expert instructor provides assistance are collectively called **scaffolding**.

The Importance of Language

A key difference in the approaches taken by Piaget and Vygotsky is in their views on the role of language in development, the latter placing far more emphasis on its importance. For Piaget, cognitive development was a completely domain-general process, and, like all cognitive abilities, language developed in line with the individual's cognitive development. For Vygotsky, however, language was a uniquely important cultural tool that developed through interaction with experts. Vygotsky believed that language and thought develop independently, with language initially used purely as a tool for communication. Later in development, the child internalizes language and begins to use it as a mental tool to aid thinking.

Considering Vygotsky

The key idea that distinguishes Vygotsky's theory from others is the central role of interaction with experts in learning. Numerous studies appear to support this principle by demonstrating that children master novel situations quicker and more thoroughly with others than alone (Roazzi and Bryant, 1998). However, this phenomenon could also be explained in other ways. A study by Howe (1992) casts doubt on the idea that interactions equate to transmission. Howe placed 9–12-year-olds in groups of four and asked them to analyse the movements of objects on a sloping surface together. At the end of the discussion all of the children displayed greater understanding, *but* each child's understanding was highly individual. This is more consistent with Piaget's position than Vygotsky's.

THINKING PRACTICALLY

How might Vygotsky's ideas about learning and cognitive psychology be applied in an educational context? You might like to consider the importance of language and social interaction.

THINKING CREATIVELY

The finding that children tend to learn more in the presence of others is consistent with Vygotsky's theory. However, there may be other explanations.

1 Think of as many possible explanations for the effect of presence of others on learning.

2 Consider how you might design studies to test one or more of these explanations.

READ THIS

Vygotsky's classic book is widely believed to be *Mind in Society*. This version has a useful contextualizing introduction:

Vygotsky, L.S. (1980). *Mind in Society*. Boston: Harvard University Press.

For dipping into more of Vygotksy's work you might like to try this:

Van de Veer, R. and Valsiner, J. (eds) (1994). *The Vygotsky Reader*. Oxford: Blackwell.

Many of the contemporary reviews of Vygotsky are in the context of education, where Vygotsky's ideas have proved particularly influential. For a general review in educational contexts try this:

Scott, S. and Palincsar, A. (2012). *Sociocultural Theory*. Education.com.

THE DEVELOPMENT OF MORAL JUDGEMENT

Morality is defined differently in different contexts, but generally describes personal or social beliefs, feelings, and behaviour regarding what is right or wrong. Morality is studied in various academic disciplines, including philosophy and religious studies. In psychology we are not usually concerned with defining what is right and wrong, more with understanding how we make moral decisions. In developmental psychology this largely means understanding how moral understanding and decision-making becomes more sophisticated with age.

Kohlberg's Theory

Like Piaget's theory of constructivism, Kohlberg's **cognitive-developmental theory of moral reasoning** describes moral development as occurring in a series of universal, invariant stages. As in Piaget's theory, each stage of moral development builds on the previous one and reflects a child or adolescent's increasingly sophisticated ways of thinking about moral issues and choices. Kohlberg was not as interested in what people considered to be right or wrong behaviour at various stages of development as he was in the *reasons they gave* for arriving at their judgements. For example, as depicted in Figure 12.5, children of any age might agree that 'stealing is wrong', but they may hold this belief for very different reasons.

> **KEY IDEAS** types of morality
According to Lawrence Kohlberg, **preconventional morality** is moral judgement based on the prospect of reward or punishment. **Conventional morality** is moral judgement of school-age children and young adolescents, based on respect for law, social norms, and rules set by authorities. **Postconventional morality** is moral judgement based on abstract principles and personal beliefs.

A poor man's wife is dying of a rare disease. Only a special medicine can save her, and in this town only one pharmacy carries the medicine. But the pharmacist is greedy—he knows he can charge what he wants for it, and he is charging many thousands of dollars—much more than the drug is worth. The man goes to the pharmacist and begs him to sell him the medicine for cheaper, but the pharmacist refuses. The man knows his wife will die if he doesn't get the medicine. Late that night, he breaks into the pharmacy and steals the medicine.

Was the man right or wrong in what he did? If he was right, why was he right? If he was wrong, why was he wrong?

Preconventional Morality
(Stages 1 and 2: preschool and younger school age)

"The man was *right* because then his wife would be happy and her parents would thank him and he would be a hero."
Or
"The man would be *wrong* because he would get in trouble with the police."

Conventional Morality
(Stages 3 and 4: older school age, young adolescents)

"The man was *right* because the pharmacist was overcharging, which is against the law anyway—so the man was just righting a wrong."
Or
"The man was *wrong* because stealing is against the law, and in order for society to function properly, people need to obey the law. The man should have found another way, like taking out a loan or something."

Postconventional Morality
(Stages 5 and 6: older adolescents and adults)

"Whether he was right or wrong may depend on the specific circumstances which aren't really that clear from the story. For example, the pharmacist was price-gouging—crazy price gouging. But you obviously can't use other people's lawbreaking to excuse your own. On the other hand, human life is more precious than property and justifies property crime. But it could have been the case that the man might have been able to find the drug within a reasonable driving trip or bus ride, and avoided all this. It's just not clear."

FIGURE 12.5 Kohlberg's three levels of moral development.
Sources: top: Romrodphoto/Shutterstock.com; middle: wavebreakmedia/Shutterstock.com; bottom: goodluz©123RF.com.

Lawrence Kohlberg divided moral development in children and adolescents into six stages, grouped in three levels, with two stages per level. Children's specific stage and level are determined by the answers to moral problems such as the one depicted here. The important thing is not whether the child believes that something is right or wrong, but rather, the reasons the child gives to explain his or her judgement. To clarify this, Kohlberg identified six specific stages of moral development and divided them into three broad levels, with two stages per level. The three broad levels are **preconventional morality, conventional morality,** and **postconventional morality**.

According to Kohlberg, the *preconventional level*, generally characteristic of younger school-age children (most under-9s), describes moral judgements based on the prospect of reward or punishment. The *conventional level*, characteristic of older school-age children and many adolescents and adults, is based on respect for law, social norms, and rules set by parents and other authorities. The *postconventional level*, characteristic of some older adolescents and adults, involves more complex personal judgements based on abstract principles, such as fairness or justice. According to Kohlberg, each level is more 'adequate' than the level that came before it.

Considering Kohlberg

As was the case with Piaget, certain aspects of Kohlberg's theory have stood the test of time. For example, children do seem to move 'forwards' in a general way on moral reasoning tasks devised by Kohlberg, from preconventional reasoning to conventional reasoning. And some people (only a minority, however) do move from conventional reasoning to postconventional in adolescence or adulthood. As people progress, they do not return to an earlier stage (Krebs, 2005).

However, very strong criticisms of Kohlberg's theory have been offered over the years, and views of moral development have changed considerably, even among those who adhere to many of the foundations of the cognitive-developmental approach (Dawson, 2002). The most important of the criticisms levelled at Kohlberg's work is this: *tests of moral reasoning do not capture actual moral reasoning in children and adolescents and may not predict moral behaviour.* As depicted in Figure 12.6, Kohlbergian tests present research participants with short *hypothetical* descriptions of moral dilemmas and record participants' explanations for the moral judgements they give in response. However, there appear to be differences between the way children respond to these stories and how they respond when faced with *real-life* moral dilemmas (eg, seeing one classmate hit another; Nucci, 2001). As we shall see in the next section, one problem may be that people often do not make moral decisions based on *reasoning* at all.

An Alternative Approach from Positive Psychology

Consider the following scenario:

> You are a passenger on a train whose driver has fainted. On the main track ahead are five people. The main track has a side track leading off to the left, and you could turn the train onto it. There is one person on the left-hand track. You could turn the train to the left, killing the one; or you could refrain from turning the train, letting five die. Is it morally permissible to turn the train to the left, killing one to save five?

After you have made up your mind, now read the following alternative scenario:

> You are on a footbridge over train tracks. You see a train approaching the bridge, out of control. There are five people on the track. You know that the only way to stop the train is to drop a heavy weight into its path. But the only available, sufficiently heavy weight is a very large man, also watching the train from the bridge. You could shove the man onto the track in the path of the train, killing him; or you can refrain from doing this, letting the five die. Is it morally permissible to shove the man onto the track? (Scenarios adapted from Hauser, Cushman, Young, Jin, and Mikhail, 2007, p 6)

As depicted in Figure 12.6, if you are like the overwhelming majority of the 5,000 English-speaking men and women of varied income levels, nationalities, ethnicities, education levels, and ages tested by Marc Hauser and his colleagues, you will

Scenario	Image	Description	% "Yes"
1	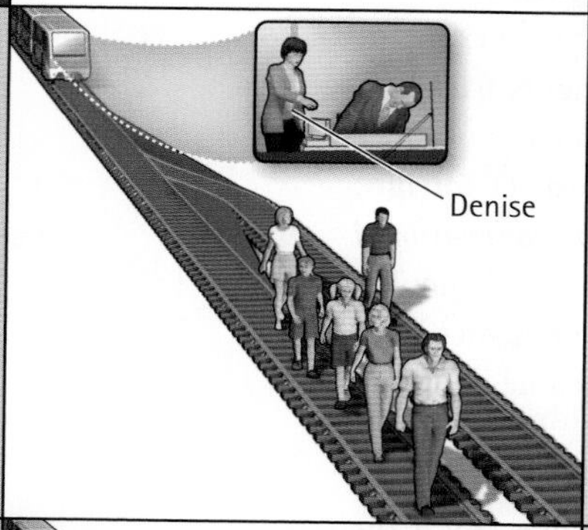	Denise is a passenger on a train whose driver has fainted. On the main track ahead are 5 people. The main track has a side track leading off to the left, Denise can turn the train on to it. There is 1 person on the left hand track. Denise can turn the train, killing 1; or she can refrain from turning the train, letting the 5 die.	Is it morally permissible for Denise to turn the train? 85%
2		Frank is on a footbridge over the train tracks. He sees a train approaching the bridge out of control. There are 5 people on the track. Frank knows that the only way to stop the train is to drop a heavy weight into its path. But the only available, sufficiently heavy weight is 1 large man, also watching the train from the foot bridge. Frank can shove the 1 man onto the tracks in the path of the train, killing him; or he can refrain from doing this, letting the 5 die.	Is it morally permissible for Frank to shove the man? 12%

FIGURE 12.6 Moral dumbfoundedness: when is it okay to kill one to save five? When Marc Hauser and his colleagues presented these scenarios to 5,000 men and women of varying ages, ethnicities, nationalities, incomes, and education levels, the overwhelming majority approved of killing one to save five in the first scenario described, but rejected this choice in the second scenario. When asked to explain their judgements they could not do so coherently—they were 'morally dumbfounded'. Hauser and his colleagues hypothesize that moral intuitions differ between dilemmas that invoke social emotions and those that are relatively impersonal.

> KEY IDEAS social intuitionism
Social intuitionism is a term from positive psychologist Jonathan Haidt's theory of moral judgement. The theory proposes that moral judgements are more often than not the result of intuition and emotion rather than reasoning. Reasoning tends to occur after the fact to explain to oneself or others why one has arrived at a particular moral judgement.

overwhelmingly approve of killing one person to save five in the first scenario, but reject that action in the second (Hauser et al, 2007). In addition, if you are like the majority of the participants in the study, you will find it difficult to explain your choices: why is killing one to save five permissible in the first, but not the second scenario? To use positive psychologist Jonathan Haidt's term, you will be *morally dumbfounded*—convinced that something is wrong but unable to explain why in a coherent fashion (Haidt, 2008; Haidt and Bjorklund, 2008). Similar results were obtained when research participants were presented with scenarios involving (protected, consensual) sex between adult siblings. They insisted that the behaviour was wrong but could not adequately explain why.

According to Haidt (2001), although we often do use reason to arrive at moral judgements, more often than not we arrive at these judgements largely intuitively and often instantaneously in the absence of reasoning. We may *then* engage in a reasoning process—but only to explain to ourselves (and perhaps to others) why we have made the choices we've made. Haidt calls his theory of moral systems **social intuitionism** because it proposes that moral judgements are frequently intuitive and emotional rather than rational.

But where do these moral intuitions come from? Every culture has its own moral system. Moral systems are universal, even though the specifics of what each culture considers moral or immoral behaviour may vary (Bloom, 2010). Because of the universality of moral systems and their obvious importance to survival and reproduction, positive psychologists and evolutionary psychologists have proposed that the capacity for morality is the result of evolutionary psychological adaptations (Haidt, 2007). These adaptations constitute a kind of *moral sense*, or instinct (Haidt and Bjorklund, 2008). If you recall from Chapter 2, positive psychologists focus on studying human strengths, including moral development and behaviour. According to Haidt and several other positive and evolutionary psychologists, the moral sense—like many other psychological adaptations—frequently taps into **emotion** first and reason second. This is the explanation for moral dumbfoundeness: we make moral decisions based on intuition and emotion, and attempt to explain our decisions with logic after the fact.

There is some neuroscientific evidence to support the view that moral judgements may often be arrived at much too rapidly for deliberate reasoning to take place. When faced with morally objectionable statements, participants in the study by Jos Van Berkum and his colleagues showed instantaneous changes in their brainwave patterns within 200–250 microseconds after the utterance of the first word signalling a morally objectionable idea (Van Berkum et al, 2009).

Five foundations of morality

Consider now the following acts: are they morally wrong?

- A family's dog is killed by a car in front of their house. The family has heard that dog meat is delicious, so they cut up the dog's body and cook and eat it for dinner.
- On her deathbed, a mother asks her son to promise to visit her grave each week. The son promises, but even though he loved his mother, after she dies he doesn't visit her grave because he is 'too busy'.
- A man buys a dead chicken from a supermarket each week and has sex with it. Afterwards, he cooks the chicken and eats it.

The preceding acts share two things in common: each is upsetting or disgusting to most people, but no apparent harm results to anyone as a result of the acts and no one has been treated unfairly. When scenarios such as these were presented to high-socioeconomic-status (high-SES) college students at elite universities in the United States, judgements tended to reflect the idea that these acts were offensive but not *morally wrong*. The reasons given by these students for their judgements reflected a view that because no one has been treated unfairly, and no real harm has been done to anyone (the dog, man's mother, and the chicken were dead and could not suffer), acts such as these boil down to personal decisions.

On the other hand, among those with lesser income and education, particularly those participants who resided in a nation with less industrialization and development (Brazil), these acts were generally seen as both morally wrong *and* personally disturbing. Building on earlier work conducted by anthropologist Richard Shweder, Haidt (2007) proposes that there are *five psychological foundations* on which all moral systems are built. However, individuals, social classes, and entire cultures may vary in the importance they place on each of these foundations and the way they are expressed in specific moral codes.

The five foundations are:

- Caring for others and avoiding causing harm
- Fairness and justice

- Loyalty to one's group
- Respect for authority
- Purity and sanctity

Examples of each foundation are given in Table 11.2.

Haidt proposes that educated Westerners are primarily concerned with only the first two foundations of moral systems: *caring for others and avoiding harm* and *fairness and justice*. Consequently, most psychological and social science research on morality focuses on these two aspects of moral systems (Haidt and Kesebir, 2010).

However, cross-cultural research and research among various social classes and political ideologies in the West show that there may be more to morality than care/harm and fairness/justice. In particular, traditional and tribal cultures and subcultures of lower-SES groups often include the last three foundations in their moral systems to a degree equal—or nearly equal—to the first two (Haidt and Graham, 2007).

The notion that universal moral foundations include more than harm/care and fairness/justice is not universally accepted (Turiel, Killen, and Helwig, 1987). For example, Turiel and colleagues argued that many of the factors that were subsequently incorporated in Haidt's final three foundations (Table 11.2) are actually social conventions; for example, rules about food preparation, sex, and nudity. Turiel also proposed that some cultural practices that appear unrelated to harm/care may actually be strongly related to it if the practices are understood from that culture's perspective. For example, some cultures have strict rules forbidding women to prepare food when they are menstruating. Is this a moral proscription related to purity/sanctity, or is it that members of such cultures truly believe that preparing food during menstruation is harmful to others (harm/care)?

TABLE 11.2 Jonathan Haidt's five psychological foundations of morality (Haidt, 2007)

Foundation	Examples
Care/harm	Stopping to help a person stranded at the side of the road Refraining from killing, stealing, or lying
Fairness/justice	Civil rights for minorities Overturning wrongful criminal convictions
Loyalty to one's group	Uniting to fight an occupying army Ethnic solidarity Participating in family feuds
Respect for authority	Speaking respectfully of your leaders even if you disagree with their policies Revering teachers and the elderly Ancestor worship
Purity and sanctity	Rules about which sexual acts and partners are permissible Rules about which foods may be eaten and how they may be prepared Rules about menstruation Rules about toileting and nudity

WHAT'S HOT? THE NEUROSCIENCE OF MORALITY

Research in neuroscience may provide a partial framework for understanding the neural basis of moral behaviour displayed by very young children in real-life situations. This research shows that when human beings—including children—perceive pain in others, the same brain circuits are activated as when the person himself or herself experiences pain (Decety, Michalska, and Akitsuki, 2008). This may constitute a 'building block' for the important human quality of *empathy*. Empathy is the ability to understand another person's experience or state of mind—to 'put yourself in another person's shoes'. Empathy in turn is an important component of *compassion*—'feeling another person's pain' and wanting to do something to alleviate it. Empathy at least (and perhaps compassion as well) is thought by many to underlie the ability to develop moral reasoning and behaviour. For example, those diagnosed with antisocial personality disorder—characterized in part by exploitative behaviour towards others and a lack of guilt or remorse over wrongdoing—appear to lack empathy as well as compassion (Decety et al, 2008).

To test the connection between empathy and morality in children from a neuroscientific perspective, Jean Decety and his colleagues extended previous fMRI studies of human brain responses

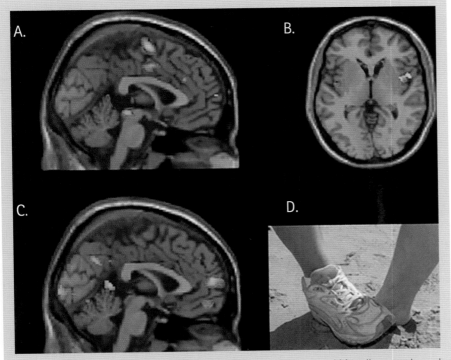

FIGURE 12.7 Morality in the children's brains? When Jean Decety and his colleagues showed a group of (female) children images of other people accidentally in pain (A and B), areas of the insula involved in experiencing pain first-hand 'lit up'. When the images showed intentionally inflicted pain (D), additional areas at the border of the temporal and parietal lobes, the frontal cortex, amygdala, and paracingulate also became involved (C). These areas thus appear to be associated with brain response to social interaction and moral behaviour.

❯

> to images of pain experienced by others (Decety et al, 2008). First, the researchers found the expected 'mirroring' of pain-related brain circuits in children's brain scans. The perception of other people's pain was associated with increased activity in the children's brain circuits involved in experiencing pain first-hand. However, the researchers took this finding a step further. They showed the children images of people experiencing pain accidentally, and also showed images of people *intentionally* inflicting pain on others—a moral violation. As Figure 12.7 shows, the researchers found that when viewing the images of pain intentionally inflicted by another person, additional areas of the brain 'lit up'—those areas that previously have been shown to be engaged when considering social interactions and moral behaviour or violations of moral behaviour.

READ THIS

The classic work in this area is still Lawrence Kohlberg's. A nice summary can be found here:

Keith, K.D. (ed) (2013). *The Encyclopedia of Cross-Cultural Psychology.* New York: Wiley, pp 891–7.

For some original Kohlberg, try this:

Kohlberg, L. (1963). The development of children's orientations towards a moral order. *Vita Humana*, **6**, 11–33.

For something more recent:

Haidt, J. (2008). Morality. *Perspectives on Psychological Science*, **3**, 65–72.

> **KEY IDEAS** theory of mind
Theory of mind is the cognitive ability to 'mind read'. We all develop some ability to understand or predict what people around us are thinking, feeling, and planning. This is important in social interaction.

THEORY OF MIND

'Theory of mind' is *not* a theory. This can be confusing! **Theory of mind** or ToM is the cognitive ability to interpret what is going on in the minds of others. We are said to have a theory of mind when we hold a belief (ie, a theory) about what thoughts, feelings, and intentions are going on in someone else's mind. We can think of this as mind reading.

Different teams of researchers have studied theory of mind in different ways in children of different age groups, so there is a range of views concerning the age at which children acquire theory of mind. For example, children become capable of some theory of mind tasks at around 4 years of age so some researchers see this as the age when ToM appears. Others see theory of mind developing more gradually.

False Belief Tasks and the Four-Year Shift

It seems that a major shift in children's theory of mind takes place at around 4 years of age. Evidence for this shift comes from **false belief tasks**. Wimmer and Perner (1983) developed the first false belief task: a story in which a boy called Maxi left some chocolate in a green container in the kitchen. When Maxi was out of the room his mother used some of the chocolate for cooking and put the leftovers in a blue container. The participant's task is to state which container Maxi will look in on his return. Understanding that Maxi could not know that the chocolate was not where he left it demonstrates an understanding of Maxi's false belief about where the chocolate would be. Most 4-year-olds but very few 3-year-olds succeeded in this task.

Baron-Cohen, Leslie, and Frith (1985) developed an alternative false belief task known as the Sally-Anne task (Figure 12.8). Children are told a story about two dolls, Sally and Anne. Sally has a basket and Anne a box. Sally puts a marble in her basket, but when Sally is not looking Anne moves it to her box. Participants' task is to identify where Sally will look for her marble. The correct answer is of course her basket. Understanding this, however, requires the understanding that Sally has a false belief about the marble's location. Most 4-year-olds proved capable of this understanding but not most 3-year-olds, supporting the idea of the four-year shift in theory of mind. Interestingly, children on the autistic spectrum appear to struggle with false belief tasks, suggesting a deficit in their theory of mind.

RESEARCH IN FOCUS

Baron-Cohen S., Leslie, A.M., and Frith, U. (1985). Does the autistic child have a theory of mind? *Cognition*, **21**, 37–46.

Aim: The authors proposed that a deficit in theory of mind would account for the difficulties that people on the autistic spectrum have in social interactions, and the observation that some people on the spectrum appear to treat people and inanimate objects alike. The aim of the study was to investigate ToM deficits in autism, testing the hypothesis that even high-functioning children on the spectrum (ie, those with an IQ of over 70 have particular difficulty in false belief tasks).

Procedure: 20 high-functioning children with a diagnosis of autism aged 6–16.5 years formed the experimental group; 14 children with Down's syndrome aged 6.25–17 years and 27 children without a diagnosis (age range 3.4–5.75 years) constituted the control conditions. The two clinical groups (those with a diagnosis) were administered an IQ test, scoring means of 82 (autism group) and 64 (Down's syndrome group). All children were individually administered the Sally Anne task (see Figure 12.8). Participants' general understanding of the story was assessed by means of two control questions concerning the original and final locations of the marbles.

Findings: All the participants successfully answered the control questions; however, there were dramatic differences in the belief question 'where will Sally look for her marble?': 85% of the non-diagnosis group and 86% of those with Down's syndrome answered the question correctly that Sally would look in her basket. However, only 20% of children in the autism group answered the belief question correctly. Results were not accounted for by IQ—the 20% of children in the autism group that answered the question successfully were not those with the highest IQ.

Conclusion: Children on the autistic spectrum find false belief tasks very difficult, suggesting that they suffer a deficit in theory of mind. The fact that the Down's syndrome group did well on the task strongly suggests that development of theory of mind is independent of general cognitive development.

MASTER YOUR METHODOLOGY

1 Explain why it was important to have a control group of children with Down's syndrome as well as a non-clinical control group.

2 The three groups were not particularly closely matched. Explain why this is less of a problem in this study than it might be in others.

3 Variables need to be operationalized. How were the independent and dependent variables operationalized in this study?

Sally puts her marble in the red box.

Sally goes away.

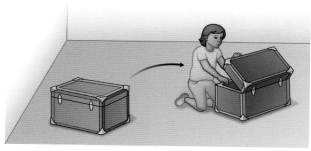

Anne moves the marble.

"Where will Sally look for her marble?"

FIGURE 12.8 **The Sally Anne task used by Baron–Cohen, Leslie, and Frith (1985).**

Intentional Reasoning in Toddlers

The theory of mind researchers that rely on false belief tasks to assess theory of mind tend to place great emphasis on the four-year shift in theory of mind ability. However, other research groups have found that much younger children appear to demonstrate some understanding of the reasoning underlying adult behaviour. This is known as **intentional reasoning**, and can be considered an aspect of theory of mind.

In a classic demonstration of intentional reasoning by Meltzoff (1988), 18-month-old toddlers observed adults performing a range of tasks including placing beads in a container. In a control condition, the adult successfully placed beads in the container but in an experimental condition they failed, dropping the beads. The toddlers were then given beads and a container, so they had an opportunity to recreate the procedure. In both conditions the children attempted to place the beads in the container. This strongly suggests that they must have understood the adult's intention to place the beads in the container regardless of their success in doing so. This appears to demonstrate a theory of mind ability at a much earlier age than that at which false belief tasks become possible.

Theories of Theory of Mind

There are Piagetian and Vygotskian perspectives on how theory of mind develops. Recall that to Piaget, cognitive development was a single domain-general process in which all cognitive abilities develop in tandem when the mind achieves a certain general level of sophistication. Perner et al (2002) explained theory of mind from a Piagetian perspective, suggesting that theory of mind and other abilities develop together. They tested this idea, giving 48 3–5-year-old children a false belief task and an additional task identifying similar meanings in word pairs. They found that performance across the two tasks was very similar, supporting the idea that theory of mind develops alongside other cognitive abilities.

 THINKING CRITICALLY

Looking at the studies of theory of mind already discussed in this chapter, can you see anything that Perner's explanation for theory of mind cannot easily explain?

Remember that Vygotsky placed his emphasis on the role of social interaction in driving cognitive development. Astington (1998) applied this principle to explaining the development of theory of mind. Astington suggested that children internalize theory of mind as a mental tool during early social contact with others, notably their primary carer. There is support for this explanation from research showing that children with high-quality interactions with their primary carer tend to have the best theory of mind abilities (Symons and Clark, 2000).

 THINKING CREATIVELY

Recap on the rest of Vygotsky's theory of cognitive development (earlier this chapter). What other hypotheses can you develop from his theory that might lend support for a Vygotskian explanation for theory of mind?

A domain-specific alternative

A radical alternative to the ideas of Piaget and Vygotsky comes from Leslie (1994). Leslie takes an **innatist modular** approach to explaining the development of theory of mind. The innatist modular approach is a departure from constructivist perspectives on cognitive development. The underlying precept is that each cognitive function depends on a brain system or *module*. Each module becomes active at a particular age as the brain matures.

Leslie (1994) proposed that at least two modules underlie theory of mind development. One is active from an early age and facilitates intentional reasoning. The second activates at around 4 years of age and allows the child to understand false beliefs. The major support for this innatist modular approach comes from the study of atypical development. In autism, for example, children may develop some advanced cognitive abilities but *not* theory of mind. In **Williams syndrome** on the other hand, around half of children show normal theory of mind development and others typically have theory of mind as one of their stronger cognitive abilities (Tager-Flusberg, Boshart, and Baron-Cohen, 1998). The idea of a theory of mind module that fails to activate in autism but activates in Williams syndrome despite the absence of other modules needed for strong general cognitive development is a very neat explanation for atypical development.

> **KEY IDEAS** Williams syndrome
> **Williams** is a less well-known condition characterized by rich verbal and social interaction but low scores on non-verbal IQ.

THINKING CREATIVELY

Try to synthesize a theory of your own to explain the development of theory of mind that draws upon the ideas of Perner, Astington, and Leslie. You might like to start by explaining how cognitive development can be both domain-general and domain-specific.

READ THIS

For a review of theory of mind research you might like to start with this:

Flavell, J.H. (2004). Theory of mind development: Retrospect and prospect. *Merrill-Palmer Quarterly*, **50**, 274–90.

This text is written by some of the leading experts in the field:

Baron-Cohen, S., Tager-Flusberg, H., and Lombardo, M.V. (eds) (2013). *Understanding Other Minds*. Oxford: Oxford University Press.

For a recent paper revisiting theory of mind in autism try this paper:

Baron-Cohen, S., Bowen, D.C., Allison, C., Auyeung, B., Smith, P., and Lai, Meng-Chuan (2015). The 'reading the mind in the eyes' test: Complete absence of typical sex difference in ~400 men and women with autism. *PLOS One*, **10**, np.

IN REVIEW

INFANT PERCEPTUAL ABILITIES AND INNATE KNOWLEDGE

- From a few hours after birth, babies appear to distinguish their mother's face and voice from others. This cannot be directly tested; however, there are physiological markers for it such as increased heart rate.

- Rule violation studies show that infants appear to be aware of some key attributes of the physical world, including properties of solid objects and basic numerical understanding.

- The extent of infant knowledge and perception is part of the nature-nurture debate, with the nativist position holding that these abilities are present at birth and the empiricist position that they are acquired through experience.

PIAGET'S CONSTRUCTIVIST THEORY OF DEVELOPMENT

- Piaget believed that we are agents of our own cognitive development in the sense that we are motivated to understand the world and actively explore it in order to construct our own understanding.

- Understanding exists in mental structures called schemas. Schemas become more sophisticated with age and experience by processes of assimilation and accommodation.

- Piaget proposed a set of developmental stages, each of which is characterized by particular reasoning abilities.

- In the sensorimotor stage, children learn through reflexes and acquire understandings like object permanence.

- In the preoperational stage, children are mobile and verbal but lack much reasoning ability. Thus they cannot conserve and are egocentric.

- In the stage of concrete operations, children can conserve and decentre; however, they struggle with more abstract and scientific reasoning.

- In the stage of formal operations children and adolescents (over the age of 11) acquire abstract and scientific reasoning.

- Later researchers have supported Piaget's principle that children become capable of increasingly sophisticated reasoning with age; however, it is now widely believed that Piaget underestimated younger children and overestimated older children. Thus, the extent of cognitive change in childhood is perhaps not as dramatic as Piaget believed.

SOCIAL CONSTRUCTIVIST THEORY

- Lev Vygotsky, and later Jerome Bruner, proposed a social constructivist alternative to Piaget's theory in which social interaction rather than personal exploration is the main influence on cognitive development.

- Mental tools are transmitted from more expert individuals to less expert individuals through social processes. Cultural transmission means that different mental abilities are more or less well developed in different cultures.

- Learning takes place when children cross zones of proximal development, the gap between what they can achieve alone and with expert help, with scaffolding from the expert.

- Language is more important in social constructivist theory, becoming internalized and used as a tool for thinking.

THE DEVELOPMENT OF MORAL JUDGEMENT

- Kohlberg produced a stage theory of moral development in which children pass through three levels of development. In the first *preconventional* level, children are motivated to access rewards and avoid punishment.

- In the second *conventional* level, children have a respect for social norms, rules, and laws.

- In the third *postconventional* level, adolescents begin to prioritize more abstract ideas like justice and fairness as opposed to rules.

- Kohlberg's essential principle that people advance through levels of increasingly sophisticated moral reasoning holds true; however, his tests of moral reasoning are not predictive of moral behaviour in real-life contexts.

- Haidt offers an alternative perspective on moral development based on the idea of moral dumbfoundedness; we can find some decisions morally repugnant but be unable to reason why this is so.

- Social intuitionism is the term used to describe the spontaneous moral response to a scenario. To Haidt, conscious moral reasoning comes after this instant response.

- There is support from neuroscience for the idea that our first responses to moral dilemmas are too fast to be reasoned; therefore, our initial responses do seem to be intuitive.

THEORY OF MIND

- Theory of mind is the cognitive ability to mind-read (ie, to perceive the thoughts, emotions, and intentions of other people).

- False belief tasks like the Sally Anne story are used to study theory of mind abilities. A significant shift in theory of mind abilities appears to take place at around 4 years of age when children become capable of false belief tasks.

- Children on the autistic spectrum have difficulty with theory of mind and lag several years behind others in false belief tasks.

- Another line of research has investigated intentional reasoning in much younger children. Research has found that toddlers can imitate intended adult behaviours even when the adults fail at them.

- There are several competing explanations for the development of theory of mind, including Piagetian and Vygotskian perspectives and the more recent innatist modular approach.

TEST YOURSELF

1 Babies less than a day old appear to recognize their mother. True ☐ False ☐

2 There is evidence to show that babies can add and subtract. True ☐ False ☐

3 Piaget appears to have overestimated the abilities of younger children. True ☐ False ☐

4 The innatist modular approach to cognitive development is an example of a domain-general theory. True ☐ False ☐

5 At which of Piaget's stages would you expect a child to become capable of abstract thinking?

a) Sensorimotor stage

b) Preoperational stage

c) Stage of concrete operations

d) Stage of formal operations

6 Which term best describes the gap between what a child can learn alone and with help?

a) Intermental plane

b) Intramental plane

c) Zone of Proximal Development

d) Scaffolding

7 According to Kohlberg which type of morality is based on respect for rules and conventions?

a) Preconventional

b) Conventional

c) Postconventional

d) Unconventional

8 Under which of Haidt's foundations of morality would you expect to find rules
   about sex and toileting?

   a) Purity and sanctity

   b) Respect for authority

   c) Fairness and justice

   d) Care and harm

9 Explain why theories like Piaget's and Vygotsky's are described as 'domain-general'.

10 Explain the evidence for a deficit of theory of mind in autism.

 Visit the online resources that accompany this book: wwww.oup.com/uk/jarvis-okami1e

CHAPTER 13

LIFESPAN DEVELOPMENT

LEARNING OUTCOMES

By the end of this chapter you should be able to:

- Appreciate the place of the lifespan approach to the study of developmental psychology
- Assess prenatal development and the range of influences upon it
- Describe and evaluate Erikson's overarching theory of lifespan development
- Understand psychological development in adolescence
- Outline the main features of early and mid-adulthood
- Discuss psychological issues around older adulthood and dying

❯ KEY IDEAS lifespan perspective
The **lifespan perspective** is the perspective in developmental psychology that emphasizes the importance of studying human development throughout life, rather than focusing exclusively on infancy and childhood (as has often been the case in developmental psychology).

Have you ever wondered when your development will be over and you will finally be the 'real' or 'complete' you? It sounds like a slightly silly idea, but most developmental psychology, with its focus on infancy and childhood, makes the implicit assumption that early development has an end point. So, for attachment theorists, relationship patterns are fairly stable throughout adult life, and for cognitive-developmental theorists, the mind reaches a stage of maturity when we become capable of adult thinking. **Lifespan** developmental psychology takes a radically different view, seeing developmental change as occurring from 'womb to tomb'.

Baltes (2006) has crystallized the assumptions of the lifespan developmental approach as:

1. *Development is a lifelong process.* Development begins at conception and continues until death.

2. *Development involves constant loss as well as gain.* Development involves both decline and growth. Individuals may gain in wisdom as they age, but may also experience reduced memory functioning. Children may increase their verbal and mathematical reasoning ability as they go through school, but simultaneously lose the vivid imagination that characterizes early childhood.

3. *Development is determined by a multiplicity of causes.* Development is rooted in the interactions between genes and other biological factors, environments, cultures, lifespan periods, and historical contexts.

4. *Development is characterized by plasticity throughout the lifespan.* Although each period of the lifespan can be characterized by a typical set of abilities and concerns, the course of development can be altered as a result of experience and personal decisions made throughout the lifespan. See Table 13.1 for a summary of these periods.

TABLE 13.1 **Periods of the lifespan**

Period	Age range (approximate)
Prenatal period	Fertilization to birth
Infancy	Birth to age 1
Toddlerhood	1–3 years
Preschool period	3–5 years
School-age period	6–12 years
Adolescence	12–age when adult roles are assumed (approximately 20)
Early adulthood	20–40 years
Middle adulthood	40–65 years
Late adulthood	Over 65

PRENATAL DEVELOPMENT

The processes of conception, prenatal growth of the foetus, and childbirth cannot help but inspire awe no matter how often they are encountered. The star players in the drama of human reproduction are the woman's secondary oocyte (mature female reproductive cell), often somewhat incorrectly termed the ovum, and the man's reproductive cell, known as the sperm. Hundreds of millions of sperm are released in a male ejaculation, but only about 100 of them actually get anywhere close to the woman's secondary oocyte. If one of these 100 sperm manages to pass the oocyte's protective layers of cells and arrive at the interior of the oocyte, a hardened shell forms around the oocyte that will not yield to any other sperm's attempts at penetration.

At this point, the oocyte divides into two cells: the ovum (egg), the term now given to the female reproductive cell, and the second polar body, which is little more than a collection of discarded chromosomes. The nuclei of the sperm and ovum fuse, producing a single nucleus that contains the genetic contributions of each parent. Fertilization (also termed conception) has now occurred. This fused nucleus—the first stage of development of the human organism—is known as the zygote.

At about 24 hours after fertilization, rapid cell division begins to occur in the zygote, and after about five days the zygote attaches itself to the endometrium, the lining of the woman's uterus (womb), where it will grow over the coming months. After another week of remarkably rapid cell division, the zygote enters the embryonic stage, and is now referred to as an embryo. However, the zygote is extremely vulnerable; a large number do not survive to become embryos and are miscarried, usually before the woman knows she was pregnant.

An embryo that survives undergoes major transformations. It is now dependent on the placenta for nutrition and oxygen, and the placenta in turn absorbs waste products from the embryo. The placenta is connected to the uterus on one side and to the embryo on the other by the umbilical cord (the eventual source of the baby's navel). The placenta also screens out toxins and transfers some of the mother's antibodies to the embryo, giving it immunity against some diseases. Within 6–7 weeks, the embryonic heart begins to beat.

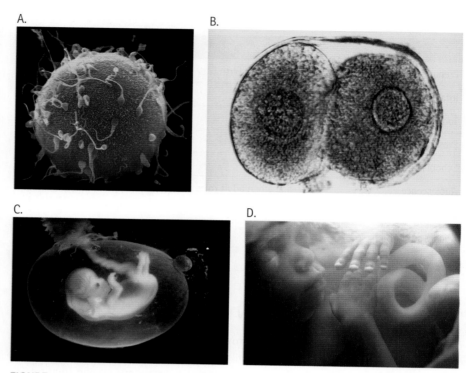

FIGURE 13.1 Prenatal development from fertilization to foetus. At A, a single sperm penetrates the secondary oocyte's protective layer. At B, cell division begins in the zygote. At C, the embryo has formed and by 6 weeks, the developing heart had begun to beat. At D is the foetus at 4 months.

Sources: A: D. Phillips/Science Photo Library; B: Omikron/Science Photo Library; C: Dr G. Moscoso/Science Photo Library; D: Neil Bromhall/Science Photo Library.

❯ KEY IDEAS congenital malformation (birth defect) A congenital malformation (birth defect) is any physical abnormality or defect present at birth. Congenital malformations may result from genetic causes or prenatal events, including exposure to radiation, drugs and alcohol, or maternal illness. A teratogen is any harmful substance, bacteria, or virus that can be transferred through the placenta to the developing foetus.

At about 8–9 weeks after conception, the embryonic stage has passed, and the developing organism is known as a foetus. At this point, the foetus is only about 3–4 cm long and weighs only about 15 g, but all human organs have formed and, as you can see in Figure 13.1, it has taken on a distinctly human appearance. If the pregnancy progresses well, approximately 30 weeks later, the newborn infant will emerge into the world.

Although the embryo and foetus are not as vulnerable as the zygote, they also face challenges as they develop. The placenta acts as a screen for toxins, but it is not always successful. Harmful bacteria, viruses, and substances such as drugs or alcohol can be transferred to the developing foetus and result in **congenital malformations**, physical defects or abnormalities present at birth (often termed *birth defects*). The harmful agents that cause birth defects are termed **teratogens**. Approximately 15% of infants are born with minor problems resulting from teratogens, and 5% experience severe problems (Sadler, 2004).

In terms of the numbers of infants affected, the most damaging preventable teratogens are cigarettes and **alcohol**. Maternal prenatal cigarette smoking results in increased rates of miscarriage, premature birth, and low birth weight. The more cigarettes the mother smokes, the worse the effects (Law et al, 2003; Espy et al, 2011). More than half of infants whose mothers smoked one pack or more per day during pregnancy experience neurological problems requiring intensive care (Habek et al, 2002).

Prenatal tobacco exposure also increases the odds of *sudden infant death syndrome* (SIDS) (DiFranza, Aligne, and Weitzman, 2004).

As damaging to the foetus as cigarettes may be, alcohol is even more dangerous because alcohol crosses the placental barrier more easily. Alcohol remains one of the leading causes of preventable congenital disorders and malformations, intellectual disability, and developmental disorders. The effects of alcohol are particularly harmful early in pregnancy, often before the mother realizes that she is pregnant—one reason for a woman to eliminate alcohol use if she is attempting to become pregnant.

The most serious outcome of maternal prenatal alcohol use is **foetal alcohol syndrome (FAS)**. Children with FAS have characteristically small heads and weight, and specific types of facial abnormalities. They show signs of damage to the central nervous system and score below normal on IQ tests (Floyd, O'Connor, Sokol, Bertrand, and Cordero, 2005). Currently, *no* amount of alcohol ingestion during pregnancy is considered safe (Ikonomidou et al, 2000), although controversy exists about exactly how much alcohol actually poses a danger. One reason so many health care workers and medical researchers advocate complete abstention from alcohol during pregnancy is the existence of milder forms of FAS known as *foetal alcohol effects* or FAE. The symptoms of FAE are the same as FAS, although somewhat less severe. However, like FAE, these symptoms are lifelong and irreversible.

> ❯ **KEY IDEAS** foetal alcohol syndrome (FAS) Foetal alcohol syndrome (FAS) is a congenital disorder resulting from prenatal maternal alcohol use. FAS symptoms include low IQ as well as physical abnormalities such as a small head.

DEBUNKING

During the 1980s, a new way to deliver cocaine to the body was discovered in the form of **crack**, a smokable substance similar to purified cocaine (freebase). As the use of crack spread rapidly in inner cities (initially in the USA and later and to a lesser extent in Europe) and brought with it devastation in the form of increased crime, violence, drug abuse, and child neglect, a tidal wave of public opinion rose up against crack and cocaine in general—which, during the previous decade, had been seen as a rather benign, non-addictive party drug for the well-to-do (Coles, 1993). At that time, reports began to surface of babies born to crack-addicted mothers who appeared to have suffered severe birth defects or lasting developmental damage. These findings were seized on by the media, and the idea of the 'crack baby' was born. It was said of these infants that the part of their brains that 'makes us human beings, capable of discussion or reflection' had been 'wiped out' (Howard, cited by Greider, 1995). The babies were reported to shriek, tremble, and be incapable of bonding with anyone. It was stated confidently in the media that their mothers' use of cocaine had marked the infants indelibly for a life of misery and addiction to cocaine.

Although the babies of crack-smoking mothers often *did* show developmental problems, and some showed birth defects, there was a problem with the research that had created the concept of the 'crack baby': women who smoked crack during pregnancy also used alcohol, cigarettes, and other drugs. Moreover, because crack use was characteristic of poor, inner-city communities, pregnant women who smoked crack often lacked access to proper nutrition, prenatal care, and education about pregnancy and health (including information about sexually transmitted infections), and were at increased risk of violence in the home (Rose-Jacobs, Cabral, Posner, Epstein, and Frank, 2002). Normally, efforts would be made to separate the effects of all these variables prior to coming to conclusions about the effects of another factor such as the use of crack. However, in the rush to judgement about cocaine, these other variables were ignored or poorly controlled in research studies (Coles, 1993).

As more careful research was conducted over time, it was discovered that while cocaine is clearly a dangerous drug for many reasons, causing birth defects and developmental disabilities in foetuses does not seem to be one of its dangers (eg, Messinger et al, 2004). It seems that the crack baby is mythological. Babies of cocaine-using mothers are *not* born addicted to cocaine, and there is little evidence that they suffer intellectual impairment, developmental disability, permanent motor impairment, or other severe problems when the effects of other variables are controlled (Frank et al, 2005; Okie, 2009).

The most important lesson to be learned from this episode for our purposes is this: even sincere and competent researchers work in a context where popular opinion, media coverage, and the demands that come with funding can have an impact. It is for this reason that when dealing with highly controversial topics, about which passionate opinions abound, you must remember to consider the source and the evidence carefully.

READ THIS

For more on prenatal development you might like this:

Walker, S.P., Wachs, T.D., Grantham-McGregor, S., Black, M.M., Nelson, C.A., Huffman, S.L., ... and Gardner, J.M.M. (2011). Inequality in early childhood: Risk and protective factors for early child development. *The Lancet*, **378**, 1325–38.

ERIKSON'S THEORY OF LIFESPAN DEVELOPMENT

Erik Erikson was a Freudian psychoanalyst, and we can see the influence of Freud's ideas about development (see Chapter 15 for a discussion) in Erikson's invariant stages, each of which has consequences for later development. Erikson's stages are summarized in Table 13.2. Each stage is characterized by a particular developmental conflict. Successful resolution of each developmental conflict aids the development of what Erikson called a **basic virtue**, a positive personality characteristic.

The Oral-Sensory Stage

Erikson saw the task of the infant in its first year as achieving *basic trust* or 'trust borne of care' (1963, p 225). Where the primary carer manages to create a secure, reliable, and comfortable environment, this creates trust and becomes generalized to the rest of the social world. Poor care on the other hand risks developing mistrust in both themselves and others that will affect its later development. Successful negotiation of the conflict between basic trust and mistrust leads the developing child to acquire the basic virtue of hope.

The Muscular-Anal Stage

By the end of their first year a child has a full sense of self and sufficient muscular development to enact holding on and letting go; for example, of urine and faeces. This physical maturity brings with it the challenge to assert the child's *autonomy* while simultaneously maintaining a close emotional relationship with its parents. Successful negotiation of this stage facilitates the successful development of *will*. The child who struggles to negotiate this conflict tends to lack assertiveness, becoming excessively inhibited or uninhibited.

> **KEY IDEAS** basic virtue
A basic virtue is a positive personality characteristic. In Erikson's theory there are eight basic virtues, each acquired at a particular age as the result of successfully managing a developmental stage.

TABLE 13.2 Erikson's psychosocial stages. Adapted from Jarvis (2004)

Age	Name of stage	Developmental conflict	a) Primary issues to be resolved	b) Developing basic virtue
0–1	Oral-sensory	Basic trust vs mistrust	Can the world—and its inhabitants—be trusted?	Hope
1–3	Muscular-anal	Autonomy vs shame and doubt	Am I an individual who can make my own decisions and control my own behaviour?	Will
3–5	Locomotor-genital	Initiative vs guilt	Can I carry out my plans, accomplish new things, and learn from my mistakes? Will I be punished if I do not succeed?	Purpose
6–11	Latency	Industry vs inferiority	Can I work alongside others competently?	Competence
12–18	Adolescence	Identity vs role confusion	Who am I?	Fidelity
19–24	Young adulthood	Intimacy vs isolation	Can I make a lasting commitment to another person in a loving relationship, or will feelings of insecurity isolate me from others?	Love
25–64	Adulthood	Generativity vs stagnation	Have I accomplished anything of value to pass on to the next generation?	Care
65+	Maturity	Ego integrity vs despair	Have I lived a meaningful life?	Wisdom

 THINKING CRITICALLY

A good scientific theory generates predictions that can be tested by research. Consider Erikson's idea that problems during the muscular-anal stage can lead to *either* inhibition *or* disinhibition. Does this lend itself to testable predictions? What does this say about the scientific status of Erikson's theory?

The Locomotor-Genital Stage

From the age of 3–5 years the child develops rapidly both physically and intellectually and is motivated to explore both the physical world and their own abilities. This motivation for exploration and problem-solving is for Erikson the root of the child's sense of purpose. Curiosity at this stage frequently encompasses exploration of adult anatomy and sexuality, both through physical examination and fantasy play. Such fantasy play can include taking the place of the child's same-sex parent in the relationship with the opposite-sex parent. This is analogous to Freud's idea of the Oedipus complex (Chapter 15). Failure to manage this stage of curiosity and exploration—for example, by being too controlling of exploration or private about personal information—can prevent the development of initiative and leave the child with a sense of guilt instead.

THINKING CRITICALLY

If you have not already done so, turn to Chapter 15 and read about Freud's Oedipus complex. Erikson's explanation of Oedipal fantasy is perhaps more popular than that of Freud because it explains why children play 'mummies and daddies' without reference to the unpalatable idea of incest fantasy. Consider the following:

1 Is palatability a good reason for a scientist to favour one theory over another?

2 Does Erikson's theory have other advantages over Freud's? You might like to consider Occam's razor here (Chapter 1).

The Latency Stage

Where the first three stages of development are centred around family relations, by the age of around 6 the child's developmental focus shifts to the wider world as they establish the skills needed for productivity as a worker. To Erikson all **cultures** have the equivalent of school where the child can learn the key practical and technological skills valued in the adult world of that particular culture. In this context 'technological' means the use of tools, which can vary from hunting or farming tools to computers, depending on the cultural context. Relationships with peers and a wider circle of adults outside the family also become important at this stage. The child that succeeds in mastering cultural technology and forming extrafamilar relationships achieves the basic virtue of *competence*, defined by Erikson as the capacity to be productive. Failure to achieve competence leaves the child feeling inferior.

Adolescence According to Erikson

In the teenage years, a combination of rapid physical development and changing social demands means that a child can no longer effectively maintain his or her childhood identity, the subjective self of who he or she is. However, the child does not initially have an adult identity to grow into. This induces a state of confusion where the young person sees the range of life choices to be made but does not have a good grasp on how to choose. In the face of this overwhelming choice the task of the adolescent is to maintain a stable identity. A solid relationship with parents is critical to achieving this; however, this is made harder by the growing influence of peers throughout **adolescence**. Erikson believed that failure to maintain good family relations and hence a stable identity leads to a state of identity diffusion which manifests as delinquency, identification with subcultures and political movements, and even psychosis. If this identity diffusion continues into adulthood it can result in role confusion, the inability to commit to relationships or a career, and perhaps to subscribe to extremist ideologies.

THINKING PRACTICALLY

There is considerable concern in Britain and Europe at the time of writing about adolescents being drawn into extremist political ideologies. What would Erikson's theory predict to be some risk factors for this? Conduct secondary research and find out whether the literature does indeed support these as fact risk factors. What does this tell us about Erikson's views of adolescence?

Young Adulthood

Having achieved a stable adult identity in adolescence, for Erikson the next developmental task of a young adult is to achieve intimacy with other adults by means of platonic, romantic, and erotic relationships. Failure to achieve intimacy leads to isolation. Erikson particularly emphasized the importance of sexual relationships; however, he also applied the same principles to adult relationships with friends and family members. The basic virtue achieved through intimacy in early adulthood is love. Although Erikson's concept of love included platonic and familial love, he believed that sexual love was particularly important and he listed six characteristics of 'utopian' sex—see Table 13.3.

Having read Erikson's characteristics of utopian sex you may be outraged! Certainly by modern standards of morality some of Erikson's views on sex are at best overly conservative. However, pathologizing anything other than monogamous heterosexual sex was very typical of the time when Erikson was developing his ideas.

 THINKING CREATIVELY

Erikson's views on young adulthood are rooted in the culture of the 1950s when he was writing. What might his young adulthood stage look like if it were written now? Have a go, and feel free to include some more modern standards of utopian sex!

Adulthood According to Erikson

What Erikson called adulthood is what most psychologists now refer to as *middle* adulthood. For Erikson the developmental task in middle age was to maintain generativity—the capacity to keep one's interest in the next generation. This is manifested in interest for work, family, and the wider world but particularly in children and in anything which will affect future generations. A failure in generativity or *stagnation* leads to loss of the will to maintain a successful working life and poor relationships. Critically, Erikson did not say that parenthood leads to generativity or that non-parenthood dooms us to stagnation. Generativity could be also expressed in creative and altruistic ways, such as working or volunteering with children and young people.

TABLE 13.3 **Erikson's characteristics of 'utopian' sex**

1.	Both partners achieve orgasm.
2.	Sex is with a loved partner.
3.	The loved partner is of the opposite sex.
4.	There is mutual trust with the partner.
5.	There is sharing and cooperation between partners in matters other than sex; for example, in work and leisure.
6.	Sex leads to the procreation of children.

Maturity

Erikson's final stage is maturity: 65 years and over. As our working life ends, or at least starts to wind down, opportunities for new achievements are reduced and we become increasingly aware of our mortality. At this point a conflict begins between ego integrity and despair and disgust. If we achieved generativity in the previous stage, we can accept our circumstances and successes and achieve ego integrity, a sense of order and meaning that leads in turn to the basic virtue of wisdom. Wisdom is associated with a balanced perspective on what is important, meaning an increase in social responsibility and a decline in selfishness. If ego integrity is not achieved, the older person despairs at their failures and missed opportunities. They may show disgust at their lack of achievement and may become bitter and critical of others.

Whilst some aspects of Erikson's work are clearly rooted in his historical period and hard to reconcile with current moral values, his central principles that different ages are associated with particular conflicts and that success in managing one stage is often the key to managing the next have some support. However, research supporting lifespan changes in personality is at odds with research by personality trait theorists who emphasize the stability of personality throughout life (Whitbourne, Sneed, and Sayer, 2009).

Exploration of subjective experience like identity lends itself to qualitative research, and qualitative studies of identity at particular ages broadly support Erikson's ideas. For example, Hoogland (2014) held three focus groups with 18 adults aged 62–85 divided by age. Discussions focused on beliefs and values were subjected to thematic analysis. It was found that ageing was associated with greater acceptance, non-judgemental attitudes, focus on others, and reduced fear of death. Large-scale quantitative studies have also supported some predictions derived from Erikson's theory. For example, Freund and Blanchard-Fields (2013) analysed data from 1,241 Swiss respondents to the World Values Survey and found that desire for wealth declined through middle and older adulthood whilst concern over environmental issues increased.

Erikson's Theory of Lifespan Development: Is It Science?

Erikson was primarily concerned with the lifespan changes in the subjective experience of identity. This kind of experience is tricky at best to study and certainly harder-nosed scientists like many lab-based experimentalists would reject it entirely as respectable psychology. This illustrates the dilemma in psychology between confining research to impeccable trivia and compromising on scientific rigour to explore important human experiences. That said, Erikson's theory has generated some testable hypotheses and has partial research support (eg, Whitbourne, Sneed and Sayer, 2009; Hoogland, 2014) so not all psychologists would criticize its scientific status.

READ THIS

For an easy introduction to Erikson's theory try this:

Jarvis, M. (2004). *Psychodynamic psychology: Classical theory and contemporary research.* London: Cengage Learning EMEA.

For some original material you might like to start with these:

Erikson, E.H. and Erikson, J.M. (1998). *The Life Cycle Completed* (extended version). New York: WW Norton and Company.

Erikson, E.H. (1993). *Childhood and Society.* New York: WW Norton and Company.

ADOLESCENCE

Adolescence—literally, 'becoming adult'—has existed throughout all of known human history and in all known societies (Weisfeld, 1999). However, the nature and length of adolescence differs from culture to culture (see Figure 13.2). In most traditional societies, adolescence ends for women in the early to mid-teens, and for men in their late teens (Schlegel and Barry, 1991). In modern industrial societies adolescence is generally thought to end at about age 20 or even beyond, into the mid-20s (Baumrind, 1987). Clearly, the term *adolescent*, while including a biological dimension (the ability to reproduce), also includes very strong social and cultural components. The end of adolescence relies entirely on the particular society's conception of what it means to be 'adult'.

Although it has been thought of as an event that occurs in adolescence, puberty is actually a process that begins in childhood with the onset of steroid hormone production in the adrenal glands. Adrenal maturation culminates at about age 10—the age at which most people recall experiencing their first real feelings of romantic and/or sexual attraction.

The transition from childhood to adolescence is momentous—perhaps only at birth does another change as radical as this occur (Weisfeld, 1999). However, adolescence is not something that happens to a child overnight. Even the clearest marker of

> **KEY IDEAS** adolescence
> **Adolescence** literally means 'becoming adult'. Adolescence includes cultural as well as biological dimensions. Adolescence begins at age 10, according to the World Health Organization, but the end of adolescence is highly dependent on sociocultural factors.

FIGURE 13.2 The length of adolescence varies by culture—especially for girls. When girls of traditional Maasai societies of Kenya begin to experience bodily changes associated with adolescence at about age 10 or 11, they are free to take lovers among the warriors, as long as they do not become pregnant. However, when they reach the ages of 13–15, like the girl pictured on the right, they undergo a ceremony of ritual genital circumcision (what we would generally call female genital mutilation or FGM), after which they are considered to be adult women (*Esiankiki*) and eligible for marriage and the responsibilities of adulthood (Finke, 2003). Thus, their adolescence lasts only a very few years. Although European and American girls (such as those on the left) enter adolescence at the same time as the Maasai, they are not permitted to engage in sexual behaviour for at least another five to seven years (although they often do so anyway), and are not expected to assume adult responsibilities for at least another eight to ten years (although they often do *not* do so for considerably longer than that).

Sources: left: iStock.com/Bartosz Hadyniak; right: pikselstock/Shutterstock.com.

adolescence, *puberty*, is a process that begins at about age 6 or 7, when the adrenal glands first produce steroid hormones (most prominently testosterone) in both females and males (Remer et al, 2005). This hormone production peaks with the full maturation of the adrenal glands at about age 10, an event known as **adrenarche** (Palmert et al, 2001).

Traditionally, the onset of puberty was thought to be marked by **gonadarche**, the maturation of the sexual organs several years later. However, it is adrenarche that is associated with the onset of the romantic and sexual feelings ordinarily associated with puberty and adolescence (McClintock and Herdt, 1996; Herdt and McClintock, 2000). For this reason, and because adrenarche is necessary for many of the physical changes of puberty to occur, most researchers are reframing puberty as a *process* beginning in middle childhood rather than an *event* marking the end of childhood.

Of course, adolescence is not only about puberty—other events of adolescence are equally continuous. Brain development continues unabated from infancy. What began as *temperament* in infancy and the preschool years evolves into *personality* (see Chapter 15) and undergoes further maturation (Klimstra, Hale, Raaijmakers, Branje, and Meeus, 2009). Where judgements of right or wrong were previously largely dependent on what parents, teachers, and other authorities said was 'bad' or 'good', a sense of personal morality often begins to develop that incorporates greater complexity and perspective (Kohlberg, 1963). Relationships with parents change, but the direction these changes take are related to all that has transpired between parent and child since infancy. Relationships with peers take on greater intimacy and urgency.

The Adolescent Brain

Until the 1990s it was thought that brain development was essentially complete by adolescence, and that the adolescent was equipped with an adult brain. It was then recognized that adolescents were different in their behaviour, but this was largely ascribed to social factors and hormonal factors—primarily massive increases in the production and availability of the steroidal hormones testosterone and oestrogen.

The development of brain imaging technologies such as magnetic resonance imaging (MRI) has changed this view. Researchers are now able to chart the development of the human brain through adolescence in detail, and what they have found is 'explosive change' throughout the teen years. Simplifying what is in fact quite a complicated picture, as depicted in the quantity of *white matter*—myelinated axons—increases dramatically during adolescence, creating faster and more efficient neuronal transmissions and allowing information from multiple sources to be combined more effectively. At the same time, *grey matter*—the slower, unmyelinated axons—generally decreases in density (Giedd, 2008)—see Figure 13.3. The development of white matter and loss of grey matter in the *prefrontal cortex*—the brain region associated with planning, weighing consequences, self-control, and judgement—occurs relatively late and is still 'under construction' until adulthood (Gogtay et al, 2004). On the other hand, regions in and around the limbic system, associated with social and emotional experiences (particularly those involving reward and gratification), are under rapid myelinization early in adolescence (Steinberg, 2007). Support for the idea that neural development is associated with changes in decision-making comes from Blakemore et al (2007), who compared decision-making in adolescents (12–18 years) and adults (22–38 years) under fMRI (see Chapter 4 for a discussion of fMRI).

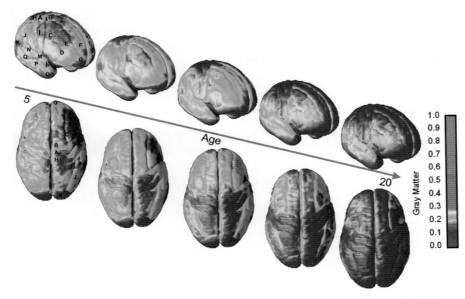

FIGURE 13.3 Loss of grey matter from ages 5 to 20. A research team from the National Institute of Mental Health, led by Nitin Gogtay, took MRI scans of a group of 13 children on a yearly basis, beginning when the children were 5 and ending at age 20. They were able to produce a 'time-lapse' series of images of the thinning of grey matter in the cerebral cortex, the area associated with higher mental functions. This figure shows lateral views of the right cerebral cortex and views of the top of the brain. The thinning of grey matter is represented by the colour blue. It proceeds from the back of the cortex to the front, with the prefrontal cortex area maturing last.

Source: Nitin Gogtay, Jan N. et al (2004). Dynamic Mapping of human cortical development during childhood through early adulthood. *PNAS*, 25 May, 101(21), 8174–9; https://doi.org/10.1073/pnas.0402680101. Copyright (2004) National Academy of Sciences, U.S.A.

There were significant differences in the cortical regions active in the two groups while making decisions about events involving physical causality and intention and causality. This suggests that in the absence of brain maturity adolescents use sub-optimal neural strategies.

A further issue with adolescent brain development concerns cerebral blood flow. Satterthwaite et al (2014) found that cerebral blood flow—the flow of blood to the cerebral cortex—declines in boys (though not in girls) in key brain regions during the teens. This may impair boys' judgements with regard to risk.

You can probably see where we are going with this! If brain systems associated with emotion, reward, and gratification are functioning well quite early in adolescence, but systems associated with judgement, weighing consequences, and self-control are still 'under construction', and with reduced blood flow to decision-making centres in boys, certain problems are likely to result! For example, one of the most robust findings of researchers in adolescence (and well known to parents of teenagers) is that adolescents are risk-takers and sensation seekers who have a tendency to engage in reckless behaviour (Gardner and Steinberg, 2005). At least 50% of Western adolescents drive drunk, use illegal drugs, have sex without protection, or commit minor crimes. Reckless behaviour of all sorts is an ordinary part of normal adolescent development, at least in the West (Arnett, 1992). As Moffitt (1993) observes, it is statistically abnormal to refrain from *all* such behaviour.

THINKING PRACTICALLY

Sixteen-year-old Kevin has been caught racing stolen cars. His parents are shocked as he was a sensible child and as his older sister sailed through her teens without difficulty. How might you explain Kevin's behaviour and provide his parents with some reassurance?

THINKING CREATIVELY

Adolescent risk-taking has been studied in the laboratory but, interestingly, individual adolescents in an artificial environment actually tend to be quite risk averse (Albert, Chein, and Steinberg, 2013).

Consider the following:

1 Explain why this might be. Try to come up with more than one explanation—there may be more than one factor at work.

2 How might you design a study of real adolescent risk-taking?

Critical periods in adolescent brain development

Perhaps of greater concern is evidence that adolescence may represent a second *critical period* in brain development (Kuhn, 2006). At about age 10–12, there is a burst in synaptic production similar to that which occurs in infancy, although not as massive. As in infancy, following this new 'overproduction' of synapses, there is synaptic pruning, a reduction in the number of synapses. By mid- to late adolescence, then, as the result of pruning and the increased volume of white matter (myelinated axons, see 'The axon', Chapter 4) described earlier, teenagers have fewer but more selective, faster, and stronger neural connections (Kuhn, 2006).

However, it is the *experiences* of adolescents that *shape* this selectivity of neuronal connections. Experience dictates *which kinds* of synapses remain and become strengthened, and which are lost to pruning (Luna, Garver, Urban, Lazar, and Sweeney, 2004). By engaging in chosen activities, then, adolescents are getting better at what they choose to do—and losing the opportunity to excel at things left unpractised. *Adolescents shape their own brain development by their behaviour.* Therefore, some researchers believe strongly that it is important for adolescents to consider carefully how they are spending their time. As neuroscientist Jay Giedd (in Brownlee, 2005, p 21) puts it: 'You are hard-wiring your brain in adolescence. Do you want to hardwire it for sports and playing music and doing mathematics—or for lying on the couch in front of the television?'

The Role of Parents and Peers in Adolescence

There is a paradox in adolescence that, whilst part of adolescence is the establishment of independence in both identity and behaviour, relationships with parents also continue to be important.

Conflict with parents

The stereotypical adolescent is moody and withdrawn and has frequent conflict with parents—perhaps because we all had those moments in adolescence and their emotional intensity makes the memories particularly vivid. But is adolescence as a whole really such a time of conflict? Squabbling and day-to-day disagreements do tend to increase from early adolescence onwards (Smetana, 2011). Adolescents also experience more unstable moods even when unaffected by stress or mental health problems (Larsen, Csikszentmihalyi, and Graef, 2014).

However, as strong as the evidence of modest increases in conflict in early adolescence is, the evidence is equally strong that the stereotype of adolescence as a time of severe 'storm and stress', alienation from parents, rejection of adult values and authority, and rebellion is inaccurate (Smetana et al, 2006). Only 5–15% of adolescents experience extreme personal problems and conflict with their parents, and of those who do, the origins can often be traced to conditions that existed prior to adolescence (Smetana et al, 2006).

 THINKING CREATIVELY

An Eriksonian interpretation of *Buffy the Vampire Slayer* (after Schlozman, 2000; Jarvis, 2004)

At the time of writing, *Buffy the Vampire Slayer* is still regularly shown on UK television, having been originally broadcast from 1997 to 2003. It remains one of the most innovative and successful television series ever and, unusually, it spawned its own academic journal and annual conference.

The story: Buffy, a teenage girl from California has, very much against her will, been granted superhuman powers and a duty to perform as a 'Slayer'—to battle the vampires and other monsters that congregate in her hometown, inconveniently sited over a 'Hellmouth', a portal to demonic dimensions. Buffy is accompanied in her struggle by a cast of archetypal characters known as the Slayerettes. Her school librarian, Rupert Giles, is a middle-aged English 'fuddy-duddy' member of a centuries' old secret society dedicated to supporting and controlling the activities of Slayers. Buffy's key ally of her own age is Willow, a quiet, bookish girl who later achieves power and status as a witch. Buffy's boyfriend, Angel, is a vampire whose soul has been reinserted by a Romany curse so that he can feel guilt for his depredations.

Consider what themes associated with adolescence are played out in *Buffy the Vampire Slayer*. Can you see the influence of Erikson's theory?

The growing importance of peer relations

Despite our different ages and nationalities, when we think back on secondary school, college, and university, with a few exceptions both of us have recollections consisting mostly of time with friends. Our friends shared our leisure, music, and social activities. Not since the years of adolescence have we experienced peer friendships of such burning emotional *intensity*—relationships that seemed absolutely essential for continued existence. Considering their subjective importance, functional adolescent friendships are an under-researched area in psychology.

Romantic relationships fare even worse in the psychology literature. These relationships are among the most under-researched topics in all of developmental psychology, and yet they are among the most characteristic aspects of the entire adolescent experience—happening at least once to the majority of adolescents by the time they are in their mid-teens (Steinberg and Morris, 2001). Once again, the large majority of the (very few) psychology articles on adolescent romance focus on the negative aspects of these relationships; for example, risky sexual behaviour, rejection, body image problems in females, and physical and sexual aggression.

Adolescents in the Western world spend more time talking to their friends than performing any activity other than schoolwork (defined as actual classwork and homework), and adolescents report that they are happiest when talking to peers. These relationships are critical to developing important social skills and learning to become an adult (Harris, 2006). As children become adolescents, their friendships become more intimate and supportive, with increased disclosure of personal information between friends (Brown and Klute, 2006).

Group socialization theory

Harris (1995) proposed the highly radical idea that parents are a much weaker influence on the development of children and adolescents than previously thought and that in fact peers are the most important single influence on development. Harris explained away the apparent influence of parents by two factors:

1 *Parents pass on genes to their children as well as child-rearing style.* Similarity in personality of parents and children could be more about shared genes than provided environment.

2 *The parents' child-rearing style may result from the type of child they have—not vice versa.* The type of child parents have has been shown to affect the way parents treat the child and may also elicit a certain type of parenting style.

So how do Harris's views about the importance of peers versus parents hold up? Harris attracts strong views on both sides of the debate but, for our purposes, she is on target for criticizing most traditional research on the effects of parenting for neglecting to control for the effects of genes and **child-to-parent effects**. However, even if parents' child-rearing style is in part a response to a child's behaviour, this does not necessarily mean that the child-rearing style has no effect. For example, an aggressive and hostile child may elicit an aggressive, authoritarian style of parenting. But the child may then react to her parents' aggressive authoritarianism with even worse behaviour and problematic personality development in a spiralling, interactive cycle (Maccoby, 2002). Thus, the picture of parent-to-child effects and child-to-parent effects is complex.

Harris is also correct that the importance of peers in the socialization of children has been underestimated in the past. Nevertheless, parents' child-rearing approaches can affect children's choice of peers (Collins et al, 2000). If peers are highly influential—and they are although group socialization theory is quite vague on how this influence takes place (Reitz et al, 2014)—then parents may have an influence on their children's personality and social development indirectly through their influence on choice of peers.

An example of this is in teenage smoking and drinking. Although adolescents who do not smoke are *much* more likely to begin smoking if their friends smoke, it is not always clear if it is *peer pressure* or *peer selection* that is at work. An adolescent might develop a desire to smoke for any number of non-peer-related reasons, and that adolescent might then *select* friends who already smoke and will therefore be supportive. Recent research suggests that both peer influence and peer selection take place. For example, Leung et al (2016) found evidence for a role for peer selection and influence in the drinking behaviour of 11–14-year-olds in Australia and the USA. It seems then that Harris has rightly identified peer influence as an underestimated factor in adolescent development but that she is incorrect to discount the importance of parental influence.

> KEY IDEAS the nurture assumption **The nurture assumption** is the term used by Judith Rich Harris to refer to widespread beliefs that parents are the primary socializers of children and that the behaviour of parents has a profound impact on the personalities and behaviour of their children as adolescents and adults.

> KEY IDEAS child-to-parent effects **Child–to–parent effects** occur when the behaviour of a child alters the way the parent behaves towards the child—including the parent's overall parenting style (eg, authoritative, authoritarian, or permissive).

<u>**READ THIS**</u>

For a very comprehensive and up-to-date set of data concerning British adolescence, this is well worth reading:

Hagell, A., Coleman, J., and Brooks, F. (2017). *Key Data on Adolescence 2013*. London: Association for Young People's Health. You might find chapter 6, which deals with well-being and mental health, particularly interesting in the light of the notion of adolescence as a time of storm and stress.

An exciting area of research is concerns the adolescent brain. For a run-down of the history of research in this area you might like to begin with this:

Blakemore, S.J. (2012). Imaging brain development: The adolescent brain. *Neuroimage*, **61**, 397–406.

ADULTHOOD

Unlike societies that practice specific coming-of-age rituals, adolescence in Western societies moves relatively seamlessly into **early adulthood** without a clear cut-off point. For example, in Europe and the United States, first-year university students who are 17–19 years old are generally considered adolescents. But by the time a student graduates from university, he or she will likely be a *young adult*. However, although European 18-year-olds are technically adults for purposes of voting, drinking, marrying, and so on, many university graduates remain under the care and protection of their parents. Therefore, they may lack the respect and resources accorded to a 'real' adult by the outside world (Arnett, 2010). If you are visibly identifiable as a student you may have noticed this lack of respect. Pub landlords, for example, may struggle with the idea that as a student you have earned a beer by the end of the day in the same way as a full-time worker!

So what is a 'real' adult? In the mid-twentieth century, most people defined adulthood in terms of five factors: *finishing school*, *leaving home*, *becoming financially independent*, *marrying*, and *parenthood*—all of which tended to occur for most people in their early 20s and often earlier (Furstenberg et al, 2004). These criteria are no longer really appropriate because now many people are postponing marriage and parenthood or opting out of one or both altogether (Dye, 2008). Furthermore, in the economy of the twenty-first century, employment does not always pay enough to result in financial independence, as it once did. Moreover, the amount of schooling and training necessary to find the sort of employment that *does* result in financial independence has increased dramatically (Smeeding and Phillips, 2002). Thus, a vast number of young people are stuck in a netherworld where they are considered neither adolescents nor adults.

There are several possible side effects of the emergence of this new stage of life. According to developmental psychologist Jeffrey Arnett, the emergence of early adulthood as a new stage is responsible for a widespread belief that, in comparison with previous generations, those born during the 1970s and after are generally more selfish and self-focused ('narcissistic'), less content with their lives and more likely to be emotionally disturbed, lazier, more materialistic, less concerned with the welfare of others, and less trusting—qualities captured in the epithet 'Generation Me' (Arnett, 2010). Arnett argues that because aspects of adolescent life have been extended into adulthood, ordinary adolescent experiences such as identity exploration, choosing career paths, developmentally appropriate focus on the self, and

❯ **KEY IDEAS** early adulthood
Early adulthood is a term for the developmental stage between adolescence and what many would regard as true adulthood.

youthful optimism have been misinterpreted as suffering, slacking, selfishness, and narcissistic grandiosity.

More recent research conducted in Europe with Millennials (those born around the year 2000) has challenged this negative view of young people. Maxwell and Broadbridge (2016) conducted a series of focus groups with UK university students and found that, whilst the students had high expectations of their future employment status and life satisfaction, they also had a strong work ethic and a positive outlook, with no evidence of narcissism.

Although major changes have occurred over the past half-century in the ages at which people approach various events and tasks traditionally defining adulthood, factors such as work, marriage, and parenthood continue to be important elements defining adult stages of life.

THINKING CRITICALLY

Research into the values and expectations of adolescents and young adults can be conducted using quantitative or qualitative methods. Suggest ways in which qualitative research can add to our understanding. Can you see any advantages to supplementing this with quantitative research?

Work

Most adults work. In 2017, 75% of people in the UK aged 16–64 worked full or part time (Office of National Statistics, 2017). By late adolescence, most people have made an effort to narrow their available options for adult work and a career by weighing their interests, skills, and values against the amount of training necessary for various careers, their probable financial rewards and status, working conditions, likelihood of getting a job, and other factors.

Choosing a career has become an increasingly complex task, and researchers have found changes over time in how students are making career decisions as well as gender and cultural differences in how these decisions are made. For example, research has shown that men and women differ in their career-related values. A ten-year study of over 30,000 men and women in their first year of university showed that men place higher importance on 'extrinsic' rewards, such as high salaries, and are attracted to careers that are high in prestige. Women are more attracted to careers that reflect their intrinsic interests and desire to work with others and be socially useful (Duffy and Sedlacek, 2007) (see Chapter 16 for a discussion of intrinsic and extrinsic motives). There were changes over time as well—between the mid-1990s and mid-2000s, students as a whole became more concerned with intrinsic rather than extrinsic career rewards and less concerned about careers in general.

The lottery question

So why do we work and what do we get out of it? Common sense would predict that people would give up work if they no longer needed the income. However, many people who become unexpectedly rich report remaining in their jobs. The question of how people respond to unexpected wealth in terms of their employment has become known as 'the **lottery question**'.

❯ **KEY IDEAS** the lottery question The lottery question is a research paradigm used to investigate motives for working, in which people are asked whether they would continue to work if they won the lottery and no longer needed to work for financial security.

There are no figures available from the UK National lottery about how many jackpot winners gave up work, nor has a UK survey of winners or potential winners been published for some decades. However, in a survey of US winners (Arvey, Harpaz, and Liao, 2004) only 17% gave up work altogether after winning the jackpot, which would generally have enabled them to give up work and live comfortably; 63% continued to work full time in the same job. Interestingly, although surveys are often a poor predictor of actual behaviour, surveys of intention to quit work tend to produce fairly similar findings to the Arvey et al survey. Paulson (2008) reviewed 15 lottery question surveys conducted in a range of countries and found that 60–93% of people reported an intention to continue working in the event of a jackpot win. Clearly this is one of those areas where common sense lets us down!

Psychological reasons for working

The obvious answer to why we work is of course financial, but in fact the picture is much more complex because there are intrinsic and extrinsic motives at work. Money is an example of an extrinsic motive because it comes from outside the individual. Gagne et al (2010) define **extrinsic motivation** to work as for 'instrumental reasons' (2010, p 629), including but not limited to financial considerations. **Intrinsic motivation** can be defined as 'doing something for its own sake because it is interesting and enjoyable' (p 629).

Clearly work can be both interesting and enjoyable. Work has the potential to provide social and intellectual stimulation along with a sense of achievement and belonging. However, if surveys are to be believed, work often fails to live up to this promise. A Gallup poll of 213,000 workers in 142 countries reported in Schwartz (2015) revealed that 63% of employees reported that they were not engaged by their work and that 90% reported more frustration than satisfaction as a result of their work. So it appears that neither straightforward extrinsic or intrinsic motives are sufficient to explain motivation to work.

THINKING CREATIVELY

You have a free hand to design your own study of work motivation or satisfaction. You could focus for example on the lottery question or intrinsic and extrinsic motivation at work. Decide on a research question and choose a quantitative or qualitative method appropriate to your research question. Think carefully about what sample you would choose.

Romantic Relationships and Parenthood

We examine romantic relationships in their own right in Chapter 22. In this chapter we are concerned specifically with the place that long-term relationships and reproduction have in adult development. It is conventional to speak of 'marriage' at this point but formal marriage—in particular, religious heterosexual marriage—is in decline. In 1974, just under 8% of men in England and Wales tied the knot. In 2014 this fell to just over 2%. Church weddings have declined in particular. By 2014, only 28% of opposite sex weddings and 0.5% of same-sex weddings were religious (Office of National Statistics). People are also marrying much later so it is no longer appropriate to think of marriage as a rite of young adult passage as was once the case. That said, the majority of young adults still enter long-term monogamous relationships, and the majority of couples that marry have already cohabited (Office of National Statistics, 2014).

Interpreting all these statistics can be tricky, however. Do they mean that marriage is dying out? Probably not, because statistics collected per year or by age group are affected by the increase in age at the point of marriage. Also, most people still list a happy marriage as one of their major life goals, with the exception of those that are separated or divorced (Taylor, 2010). So, debates about the traditional institution of marriage aside, we can definitely think of entering one or more permanent or semi-permanent relationships—perhaps including marriage—as a part of typical development.

As we've seen, marriage/cohabiting is very much the norm in adult relationships. But does it make us happy? Woody Allen once described marriage as the 'death of hope'. Clearly, not every marrying couple throughout the world is delighted with the event. People may marry for reasons other than love; for example, out of a sense of familial responsibility, at parental insistence, for financial security, or for other reasons. Nonetheless, marriage and cohabitation remain important parts of the lives and aspirations of the large majority of adults. Surveys report that marital happiness contributes more to an individual's overall happiness than financial status or satisfaction with work and friendships (Kiecolt-Glaser and Newton, 2001).

So if marriage and/or cohabitation is high on so many people's priorities, what benefits does it confer? Living together carries the promise of companionship, security, reliable social support, intimacy, and regular emotionally committed sex. Although none of these things are guaranteed, research does by-and-large support the benefits of both marriage and cohabiting. Thus, married and cohabiting people have better mental health and are happier than single people (Amato, 2015). Interestingly, in direct comparisons of different relationship statuses, married couples appear to have additional advantages over and above cohabiting couples. This may be, as Amato suggests, because marriage confers additional advantages in terms of social norms and status. However, it may also be that direct comparisons between single, cohabiting, and married people are misleading because we are not really comparing like with like—people who choose to marry, cohabit, or neither may be different in the first place. For example, religious people and those living in religious contexts are more likely to marry and to benefit additionally from conforming to the religious approval of marriage (Lee and Ono, 2012).

In addition we should consider the direction of causality. At least to some extent it is likely that healthier, more financially secure, and happier people are more appealing as mates and are more likely to get someone to marry or at least live with them and less likely to divorce (Koball et al, 2010). On the other hand, it would be difficult to argue that people with lower blood pressure (suggesting lower stress levels) are more likely to marry, yet in at least one study, happily married people did show consistently lower blood pressure relative to happy singles with broad networks of social support (Holt-Lunstad, Birmingham, and Jones, 2008). Therefore, there may be something unique to marriage that produces specific beneficial effects. Some of this may be related to the reduced financial strain that often comes with marriage, increased networks of social support, and improvement in health behaviours (particularly among men; Koball et al, 2010). There has been a much smaller body of research into non-married cohabiting couples but the evidence suggests that cohabiting has similar benefits to those of marriage (Umberson, Crosnoe, and Reczek, 2010).

FIGURE 13.4 Miserable long-term relationships make us miserable.
Source: iStock.com/PeopleImages.

Whether marriage/cohabitation leads to happiness or happiness leads to forming a long-term monogamous relationship, the association between marriage/cohabitation and positive health and emotional outcomes is substantially lessened—or reversed—in the case of long-term unhappy relationships. Severe long-term marital distress can be as damaging to health and well-being as relative marital harmony can be protective (Hawkins and Booth, 2005). It seems then that just establishing a long-term co-living relationship is something of a gamble; it may have a positive or negative impact.

Parenthood

It is difficult to prepare psychologically for parenthood, because when it arrives it is almost always different from what you expected. The research literature on parenting can be confusing: 'costs' and 'benefits' of parenting are usually weighed against one another, with some studies stressing the costs, and others, the benefits. However, whether the transition to parenting is experienced primarily as a joy or a pain, and whether it improves or detracts from the parents' feelings of well-being or relationship with each other, may depend on a great many factors, including the way the study has been conducted (Doss et al, 2009). Factors that may (or may not) influence a new parent's experience of parenthood include the following:

- Marital status (married, never-married, cohabiting, separated/divorced) (Angeles, 2009)
- Initial level of mental health and expectations for parenthood
- Family history of divorce
- Social status, social support, financial resources, and employment status
- Quality of the relationship between the parents
- Gender of the parent (mothers tend to get both the best and the worst of it)

- Gender of the child (new parents with daughters do not fare as well as new parents with sons, perhaps because fathers may tend to be more involved in parenting sons (Doss et al, 2009))
- Temperament of the baby (a 'difficult' baby can create a difficult experience for the parents)

New parents face radical changes in their lifestyles. Sleep deprivation is a common problem, particularly for new mothers, but also for those fathers who share responsibility for feeding and comforting the newborn. One problem in evaluating research on the effects of parenthood on new parents is that the type of sample used, survey questions asked, and statistical analysis chosen can make a very big difference (Nelson et al, 2013).

Three recent studies by Katherine Nelson and her colleagues investigated whether a nationally representative sample of American parents: (1) were happier overall than non-parents; (2) were happier on a moment-to-moment basis than non-parents; and (3) derived more positive feelings from taking care of their children than from other activities (Nelson et al, 2013). The researchers' results persuasively came down on the 'parenthood is positive as a general rule' side: parents in their studies were happier overall than non-parents, happier moment to moment, and they enjoyed caring for their children on average more than their other daily activities. However, the effect sizes—the *degree* to which parents were happier than non-parents—were not very large, and the primary beneficiaries in the happiness department were fathers, not mothers, who tend to do the lion's share of the day-to-day hands-on labour of parenthood.

Whether parenting increases or decreases the parent's quality of life, however, only a small number of young people without children are adamant that they do not want them in the future. In the Pew Research Center poll published in 2010, 95% of 18–29-year-olds were either certain they wanted to have children (76%) or were 'not sure' (19%) (see Figure 13.5). Moreover, consider that the death of a child

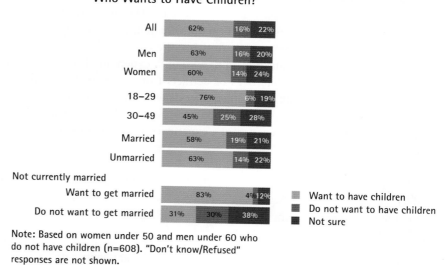

Note: Based on women under 50 and men under 60 who do not have children (n=608). "Don't know/Refused" responses are not shown.

FIGURE 13.5 Who wants to have children?

Source: Taylor, 2010.

is considered to be the worst tragedy that can befall an individual in virtually all cultures (Lyubomirsky and Boehm, 2010). This suggests at least the possibility that measures of happiness used in studies of parenting may not always be tapping into levels of profound happiness and satisfaction offered by the experience of parenting and may instead be focusing on day-to-day experiences of *pleasure* (Lyubomirsky and Boehm, 2010). Although enduring sleepless nights, repetitive cycles of infant crying, and the loss of freedom to do as one pleases are obviously unpleasant, one wonders how many parents enduring such discomforts would accept an offer to have their new babies 'taken back'.

AGEING

Exactly how we develop physically in adulthood is in part genetically determined and in part dependent on our activity level, nutrition, psychological state, and various socioeconomic factors. However, there comes a point in the life of virtually everyone in their 30s when they realize that changes are beginning to occur that signal the onset of ageing. Interesting new lines appear on the face. Somehow, it's just a bit more difficult to complete that last mile on the morning run. Although overall weight may or may not have changed, that favourite cut of jeans just doesn't fit right anymore because things have *shifted* somehow.

Although there is a general slowing down of nervous system activity as a person ages—and consequent overall slowing down in movement—the degree to which this occurs is in part dependent on personal choices made by the ageing individual. To some extent, age is not as good a predictor of vitality and endurance as *activity level*. The 'slowing down' of ageing is also represented in positive and negative emotions. Where there was once joyful excitement there is now serenity. Where once there was anxiety and anger there may now be lethargy and **depression**

FIGURE 13.6 **Old punks never die; they just stand at the back. Some music fans that have moshed since the early 1980s are now starting to struggle.**

Source: Rene Oonk/Shutterstock.com.

(Ross and Mirowsky, 2008). It may also be true that a person's own stereotypes and beliefs about what it means to age and what an older person 'is like' may influence the physiological (and psychological) changes of ageing.

Physical Changes Associated with Ageing

For men and women, entering older adulthood is broadly associated with a decline in strength and agility, although there are wide individual differences. This is accompanied by a reduction in skin elasticity and loss or greying of hair. These factors contribute to a decline in conventional attractiveness. Self-esteem tends to decline in old age (Orth, Trzesniewski, and Robins, 2010), and this may be linked to physical decline.

For most women, the most significant physical change occurring in later adulthood is the **menopause**, the cessation of menstrual cycles. Menopause is the culminating event of the *perimenopause*—the series of gradual physiological changes lasting about five years on average, beginning sometime in the mid-40s. The perimenopause represents the woman's natural transition from fertility to infertility. Menopause itself usually occurs somewhere between the late 40s and early 50s, but individuals may vary as a result of genetic, environmental, socioeconomic, and lifestyle factors. For example, earlier menopause is associated with cigarette smoking (Pokoradi, Iversen, and Hannaford, 2011).

During the perimenopause, menstrual periods become shorter or longer, and may become unpredictable in their onset and quality of the menstrual flow. During menopause, the woman ceases to menstruate, and the ovaries cease production of the hormones oestrogen and progesterone. This can precipitate various unpleasant symptoms including sweating, 'hot flushes', headaches, sleep disturbances, joint pain, mood changes, and skin problems (Cray, Woods, and Mitchell, 2010).

Despite the commonness of the symptoms just described, many women experience menopause and the perimenopause as a period of relief from menstrual symptoms, the need to use birth control, and concerns about fertility in general. In fact, cross-cultural research has demonstrated that, while some menopausal symptoms are experienced by women around the globe, the majority of women experience menopause without severe physical or psychological symptoms (Avis et al, 2001).

Cognitive Changes Associated with Ageing

Cognitive functioning in areas such as memory, reasoning about spatial relations of objects, and perceptual speed begins to decline very gradually in the late 20s or early 30s, and more rapidly from around the age of 50. However, in areas involving the accumulation of factual knowledge such as vocabulary and verbal memory, cognitive ability actually peaks at age 50 or 60 and then begins to decline (eg, Salthouse, 2006).

Nevertheless, the cognitive changes associated with ageing generally occur gradually and do not generally lead to actual cognitive impairment in middle age (Willis and Schaie, 1999). While the middle-aged complain bitterly about 'senior moments' and other cognitive crises, objective studies show that such declines are not occurring to the extent that their subjective experience suggests. The memory of a healthy 60-year-old adult is likely to be closer to that of a 20- or 30-year-old than to that of a 75- or 80-year-old (Cregger and Rogers, 1998).

Moreover, researchers have noted a discrepancy between the cognitive declines of ageing adults as measured in laboratory studies and the actual functioning of ageing adults in real-world settings, such as employment and family life. As just one example, CEOs of major corporations tend to be in their late 50s or even early 60s, not

> **KEY IDEAS** menopause and perimenopause **Menopause** is the cessation of a woman's menstrual cycles. The **perimenopause** is the period leading up to the menopause when menopausal symptoms begin.

their 20s or 30s, when most cognitive capabilities peak, as measured in laboratory tests (Salthouse, 2011).

Finally, not all cognitive changes associated with ageing are unwelcome. Regardless of declining memory capacity, studies show that as a person ages, he or she pays more attention to positive than to negative stimuli. Indeed, older adults tend to report higher levels of positive mood and well-being, at least until extremely advanced age. They are the happiest of all age groups studied, contrary to stereotypes of 'grumpy old men and women' (Stone et al, 2010). On the other hand, throughout the world, middle age is associated with the highest levels of *unhappiness*, with the currently middle-aged baby-boomer generation being less happy than most previous middle-aged generations (Blanchflower and Oswald, 2008).

Dementia

Although cognitive differences exist between healthy adults in their 80s and those in their 20s, an even greater difference exists between the performance of healthy adults in their 80s and that of a person of any age with dementia. **Dementia** is a brain syndrome that involves serious memory loss, confusion, problems with speech and comprehension, and problems negotiating normal activities of daily life. Psychiatric symptoms and apparent personality changes may also appear (Salmon and Bondi, 2009).

Contrary to some stereotypes of older people, dementia does not normally occur alongside ageing. Rates of dementia vary somewhat throughout the world, but even in North America—which has the highest rates of dementia in the world—it is found in no more than around 5% at most of adults by age 79. By age 89, however, the figure rises to about 24%, and around 37% of adults that are 90 or older have some form of dementia (Plassman et al, 2007).

While dementia can result from a number of different diseases and conditions, by far the most common type of dementia is **Alzheimer's disease**, first identified a century ago by neuropathologist Alois Alzheimer and his colleague, psychiatrist Emil Kraepelin. Conducting a postmortem examination following the premature death of a housewife who had shown severe symptoms of dementia before she died, Alzheimer and Kraepelin found that the woman's brain was covered with clumps of plaque and that brain neurons themselves were infused with unusual tangles of protein. The discoverers agreed to call this pattern of memory loss and brain scarring Alzheimer's disease (Shurkin, 2009). Like other forms of dementia, the likelihood of developing Alzheimer's disease increases as a person ages. A list of common symptoms of Alzheimer's disease is given in Table 13.4.

Once Alzheimer's begins to progress, the symptoms become more severe. Forgetfulness starts to interfere with daily functions. Alzheimer's patients may forget how to tie their shoes or brush their teeth. Their thinking becomes confused, and they may not recognize members of their own family. They start to have great difficulty speaking or comprehending speech. Eventually, they need 24-hour care (National Institute on Aging, 2006).

However, cognitive problems other than memory loss may predate and possibly contribute to memory problems in the early stages of Alzheimer's disease. In particular, there may be deterioration in *executive functions* (Storandt, 2008). **Executive functions** is a cognitive psychology term used to describe the way the brain manages attentional processes, remains flexible in responding to situations, and plans constructive actions while inhibiting inappropriate actions.

❯ KEY IDEAS dementia
Dementia is caused by biological deterioration of the brain that most commonly occurs in older people. Symptoms include progressive cognitive decline, severe memory loss, confusion, problems with speech and comprehending others, and difficulty with self-care. There are different causes of dementia and they are associated with variations in symptoms.

❯ KEY IDEAS Alzheimer's disease
Alzheimer's disease is a neurodegenerative disease characterized by increasingly severe memory loss, confusion, difficulty speaking or comprehending speech, and difficulty with self-care. Alzheimer's disease is the most common type of dementia.

❯ KEY IDEAS executive functions
Executive functions are those cognitive functions involved in managing attention, planning constructive action, inhibiting inappropriate action, and remaining flexible in responding to situations.

TABLE 13.4 **Common symptoms of Alzheimer's disease**

Alzheimer's disease shows itself in different ways, depending on the person and the stage of development of the disease. However, the most common symptoms of Alzheimer's disease are:
• Asking the same questions repeatedly. • Repeating the same story multiple times, word for word. • Forgetting how to do basic tasks that the person once performed easily, such as cooking, making repairs, and playing cards. • Problems paying bills or balancing a checkbook (assuming these tasks were not previously difficult). • Getting lost in familiar places. • Neglecting personal hygiene habits such as bathing or dressing in clean clothes while insisting on having taken a bath or put on a new outfit. • Relying on someone else to make decisions—such as what to buy at a supermarket or where to go next—that were easily handled in the past.
As with other psychological disorders, bear in mind that no single symptom—alone or in combination—necessarily means that an individual has the disease. Medical examination is essential for an accurate diagnosis.

Source: Scientific American Mind, November/December, 2009, p 60.

There is no cure for Alzheimer's disease, and its causes are not known with certainty, although it is likely a function of interactions between genes and environmental experience. This interaction may include *epigenetic* effects (the effects of the environment on the way genes are expressed in development, behaviour, disease processes, and so forth; Mastroeni et al, 2011). Thus, identical twins share identical DNA, but each co-twin may be more or less vulnerable to the effects of degenerative brain disease over time as a result of environmental experiences. Clearly, then, while ageing does not cause Alzheimer's, something about the ageing process does involve brain changes that provide 'fertile ground' for the development of Alzheimer's, given genetic vulnerability.

Can cognitive decline be slowed?

There is some controversy as to whether the undesirable cognitive effects of ageing can be slowed. One difficulty is that much of the research is correlational. Most research does suggest that older adults who maintain an active, intellectually stimulating life suffer less cognitive decline (Hertzog et al, 2009). Yet, who *are* the adults who lead active, intellectually stimulating lives? Those whose cognitive structures are active and well functioning! This may have more to do with genes, early environmental experiences, and nutrition than current activity levels. In other words, it may merely be the case that adults who suffer low levels of cognitive impairment . . . suffer low levels of cognitive impairment!

 THINKING CREATIVELY

Active, well-stimulated adults tend to age better cognitively. However, there is a problem with establishing causality. There may also be lurking variables like physical health. How could you try to control for lurking variables and establish causality? HINT: read 'Correlational research', Chapter 3.

Social-Emotional Changes in Older Adulthood

At the outset of this chapter we considered that one key assumption of the lifespan developmental perspective is that development involves gain as well as loss. This is evident in the social and emotional lives of those in the middle and later years. Typical losses of middle to late-middle adulthood may (or may not) include the following:

- The exit of grown children from the home
- Reduced health, physical vitality, cognitive ability, and sexual attractiveness
- Loss of employment status and income
- Loss of networks of friendships due to death, geographical relocation, or reduced motivation to attend social events
- The realization that some of the dreams of one's youth are truly unlikely ever to come to pass. (A personal example of this final item: this morning I [Paul] awoke for the first time with the *certain knowledge* that I would *never* become a film director!)

Gains may (or may not) include the following:

- Increased leisure time
- Increased quality of relationships with one's spouse/partner and children
- Entry of grandchildren into one's life
- Less unpredictability in emotional life, and less frequent negative emotions generally (until extremely advanced age)
- Achievement of long-term career goals with increased income (in some professions this may be more likely than the loss of status and income that can occur in other careers)
- A calmer perspective on achievement, success, and matters of romance and sexuality
- Decreased aggression in men and an end to reproductive concerns in women
- Increased feelings of freedom, control, and wisdom

As Margie Lachman (2004) emphasizes in her review of development in midlife, how all of this plays out is highly dependent on historical and social factors, gender, ethnicity, social class, and personality variables. Researchers have isolated three variables that appear to contribute most importantly to the quality of life for older adults, and there are no surprises here: well-being in older adults is highly dependent on having sufficient financial resources to meet one's basic needs, enjoying good health, and experiencing a sense of meaning and purpose in life (Low and Molzahn, 2007).

DEATH AND DYING

No one can pinpoint with certainty the moment that life begins. Even if one believes that life begins at conception, conception is still a process rather than a specific moment. No one can specify the instant that it has occurred. And if one believes that life begins at birth, it is still the case that birth is a process, not a specific moment. At some point all reasonable people will agree that a person has been born and is alive, but there will be disagreements as to the precise moment that the person began to exist.

It is the same with death. All reasonable people will agree that a person buried for several months is dead (hopefully anyway), but differences of opinion are possible as to the precise moment that death occurred. This is because various bodily systems cease to function at different rates, and whether the cessation in functioning is permanent is sometimes an open question. People are occasionally brought 'back to life' after one or more of these systems has apparently 'died'. Such issues are at the core of contemporary debates and legal cases involving the right to die (Berger, 1993).

Kübler-Ross's Model of Dying

The psychological experience of dying is also a process. For those who die in their sleep or who die instantaneously, the dying process may not be a difficult one. But for those of us who suspect (or know) we are dying of an illness, the process of dying is a challenge. In 1969, Swiss psychiatrist Elisabeth Kübler-Ross contributed substantially to our understanding of the experience of dying in her book *On Death and Dying*. Kübler-Ross outlined a series of stages she believed invariably occur during the process of dying: (1) *denial* ('This can't be happening'); (2) *anger* ('Why is this happening to *me*?'); (3) *bargaining* ('Please God, I'll stop drinking—just give me a few more years'); (4) *depression* ('I don't want to see anyone—I'm losing everything that is important to me'); and (5) *acceptance* that death is an inevitable outcome. At this final stage, the person may achieve a measure of peace prior to dying. However, throughout all the stages, according to Kübler-Ross, runs a thread of hope.

Kübler-Ross's model has been highly influential, and her work sensitized the medical and mental health professions to the importance of understanding the subjective experience of dying. Ultimately, her stage theory was applied to all experiences of grief; for example, the death of a loved one (rather than one's own impending death). However, most theorists no longer accept the idea that grief over one's impending death or that of a loved one occurs in invariant stages (Kastenbaum, 2000). In fact, the first genuinely empirical attempt to validate Kübler-Ross's model failed to do so (Maciejewski et al, 2007). Indeed, in this longitudinal study, the initial grief response was most typically acceptance rather than denial and anger, and the level of acceptance grew over time. Although the person dying may often experience the emotions described by Kübler-Ross, the notion that these emotions invariably occur, and do so in sequence, has been abandoned.

Dying in Cultural Perspective

As shown in Figure 13.7, social, economic, and cultural factors affect life expectancy around the world. Culture and socioeconomic realities also shape the experience of dying in a great many ways. A cross-cultural look at funerals and wakes makes this abundantly clear. As Metcalf and Huntington (cited by Sigelman and Rider, 2006, p 487) observe: 'funerals are the occasion for avoiding people or holding parties, for fighting or having sexual orgies, for weeping or laughing, in a thousand different combinations'.

Scott Murray and his colleagues conducted extensive interviews with patients dying of cancer in Scotland and Kenya (Murray, Grant, Grant, and Kendall, 2003). They found profound differences in the subjective experiences of patients in the two countries. In Scotland, a nation with universal health care and social security

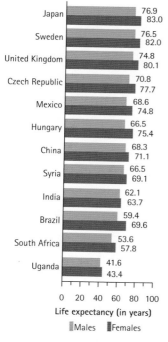

FIGURE 13.7 **Life expectancy for men and women in 12 nations.**

Source for data: Kinsella and Gist, 1998, cited in Sigelman and Rider, 2006, p 488.

benefits, patients and their caregivers were primarily concerned with the prospect of imminent death. As one patient explained, 'You're wondering if you're going to see tomorrow. When I first was told, that was the first thing that went through my head: How long?' (p 369). The Scottish patients, all of whom had access to potent pain medication, found themselves battling worries about their families and feelings of isolation and personal despair rather than personal discomfort. They did not feel that their spiritual needs were being met.

In Kenya, a nation with no universal health care system or social security, few benefits for patients, no affordable pain medication, and a lack of easily available specialist or home care, patients were far more worried about bearing the pain of life than they were about their impending death. The pain was 'constant and unbearable' for many (p 370). As one patient put it, 'There are times when the pain is so severe that I feel like hanging myself in the house to die.'

Unlike the Scottish patients, who often experienced anger about their condition, the Kenyan patients tended to accept their fate ('There is nothing that being angry can achieve' (p 370)). Also in contrast to the Scottish patients, the Kenyan patients felt well supported by their families and communities, and by their religion. These patients did feel that their emotional and spiritual needs were being met. It was their medical needs that were grossly underserved.

READ THIS

The following are useful accounts of adult development (you will notice some Erikson influence):

Specht, J., Bleidorn, W., Denissen, J.J., Hennecke, M., Hutteman, R., Kandler, C., . . ., and Zimmermann, J. (2014). What drives adult personality development? A comparison of theoretical perspectives and empirical evidence. *European Journal of Personality*, **28**, 216–30.

Hutteman, R., Hennecke, M., Orth, U., Reitz, A.K., and Specht, J. (2014). Developmental tasks as a framework to study personality development in adulthood and old age. *European Journal of Personality*, **28**, 267–78.

IN REVIEW

LIFESPAN DEVELOPMENT

- Development is a lifelong process affected by multiple factors. Historically this perspective has been neglected by many developmental psychologists.
- Development begins prenatally, with environmental factors like teratogens affecting foetal development.
- Some myths have grown up around prenatal development, most critically the myth of the 'crack baby'.

ERIK ERIKSON'S THEORY

- Erik Erikson produced an influential overarching theory of lifespan development. He identified eight stages of development, each of which has a developmental task and, if successful, leads to the development of a positive personality characteristic.

Erikson's theory has been helpful in thinking about adolescent and adult development and some aspects are testable and have empirical support.

Because Erikson focuses on subjective experiences like identity it has proved tricky to investigate his theory with scientific rigour.

ADOLESCENCE

Adolescence is the stage of development between childhood and adulthood. It is characterized by rapid physical changes to the brain and body and in social role and personal identity.

Mood swings, some conflict with parents, and increased risk-taking are characteristics of adolescence; however, the stereotype of adolescence as a time of storm and stress is generally exaggerated.

Recent developments in neuroscience have cast light on the biological underpinnings of distinctive adolescent behaviours. Decision-making centres develop late and, in boys at least, have reduced blood flow during adolescence. This can help explain the poor impulse control and risk-taking that characterize adolescence.

Peers assume greater and growing influence throughout adolescence, and one influential approach—group socialization theory—attributes adolescent peer relations as the biggest single influence on development.

Group socialization theory is widely credited with challenging assumptions about development and identifying peers as an important influence; however, most psychologists do not accept it in its entirety.

ADULTHOOD

The timescales of adulthood vary culturally. Interestingly, some psychologists now identify a stage of early adulthood between adolescence and true adulthood.

Traditionally adulthood has been seen as characterized by full-time work and an early and permanent heterosexual marriage and children. However, adult lifestyles have become increasingly diverse and many adults no longer fall into these stereotypes.

Work conveys psychological benefits and most people continue to work even if they achieve permanent financial security although, paradoxically, most people report dissatisfaction with their working lives.

Most adults engage in one or more long-term monogamous relationship involving marriage or cohabiting. Happy relationships convey considerable physical and psychological benefits.

Most adults aspire to parenthood. How positive an experience this turns out to be depends on numerous factors.

Middle adulthood is associated with a decline in strength and conventional attractiveness. This may impact on hobbies and on self-esteem. The current middle-aged generation report being less happy than at other life stages and compared with previous generations at their age.

Although many middle-aged people report 'senior moments', actually cognitive decline usually begins much later and is less severe than many people believe unless the individual suffers from dementia.

AGEING

- The nature of individual ageing varies widely amongst individuals and is affected by many factors, including the physical and the psychological. Although active, stimulated adults age better, there is a problem of establishing direction of causality.

- A particularly unpleasant aspect of ageing for some people is dementia, the physical degeneration of the brain. However, counter to stereotypes most older people do not suffer from it.

- Unless we die suddenly and prematurely we all have a psychological experience of the dying process. Kübler-Ross's influential stage model of adaptation to dying has not generally been supported by research.

- There are wide cultural differences in perceptions of imminent death and dying, with people in Western cultures expressing anger and being more focused on isolation than experiences of pain.

TEST YOURSELF

1 The idea of the 'crack baby' is largely a media invention. True ☐ False ☐

2 The developmental task of Erikson's oral-sensory stage is to acquire autonomy. True ☐ False ☐

3 Most people continue in their job after a big lottery win. True ☐ False ☐

4 Less than half of young adults now aspire to a monogamous permanent or semi-permanent romantic relationship? True ☐ False ☐

5 Which of the following stages from Erikson's theory does not have an equivalent in Freudian theory?

   a) Muscular-anal

   b) Locomotor-genital

   c) Latency

   d) Young adulthood

6 Which term best describes the maturation of the sex organs?

   a) Adrenarche

   b) Gonadarche

   c) Puberty

   d) Adolescence

7 In group socialization theory, what term best describes the ways in which children elicit parenting behaviours?

   a) Group socialization

   b) The nurture assumption

   c) Child-parent effects

   d) Temperament

8 Which of the following is *not* a typical gain in older age?

a) Self-esteem

b) Leisure time

c) Grandchildren

d) Mood

9 Explain the parallels between Erikson's oral-sensory stage and attachment theory.

10 Explain why Erikson's characteristics of utopian sex are so controversial.

 Visit the online resources that accompany this book: www.oup.com/uk/jarvis-okami1e

INDIVIDUAL DIFFERENCES

INTELLIGENCE

CHAPTER 14

LEARNING OUTCOMES

By the end of this chapter you should be able to:

- Recall definitions of intelligence and understand the difficulties in pinning down the concept
- Critically consider g and the psychometric approach to intelligence
- Understand IQ tests and explain the psychometric issues around IQ testing, including reliability and validity
- Discuss other issues in testing with particular reference to the importance of norms and risks of cultural bias
- Outline alternative views of intelligence, with particular reference to Gardner's multiple intelligences theory, Sternberg's triarchic theory, and Carroll's three-stratum theory
- Critically discuss evidence for genetic and environmental influences on intelligence and for related concepts including brain training
- Take a view on broader debates around the concept of intelligence, in particular whether intelligence is a real psychological entity or a social construct

Intelligence is one of those concepts of which we all have some intuitive understanding, and yet is very tricky to pin down precisely and explain in words. It is also harder than it might first appear to classify individuals according to their intelligence. Of course, there are those people who are always top of the class through school, get high grades, and head off to university and a high-flying job. It is tempting to conclude that they are highly intelligent while the rest of us are less so. However, psychology is always more complicated and nuanced than that!

When I (Matt) was a child my parents had my IQ tested and it revealed something rather strange. My verbal intelligence turned out to be in the top 1% of the population. However, my **practical intelligence**—what we might call common sense—was extremely low, in the borderline region for what was in those days called retardation. So did that test identify me as intelligent? There is no simple answer.

And what about those highly successful people we remember from school. Were they really brighter than the rest of us or were they simply very motivated, organized, and conformist? Those qualities can get you a long way in the education system. So, you get the idea that intelligence isn't a straightforward topic. Let us explore the most basic question: what is intelligence?

> **KEY IDEAS** verbal and practical intelligence **Verbal intelligence** is a measure of our cognitive abilities concerned with handling words. **Practical intelligence** is a concept hypothesized by Sternberg to describe the ability to come up with efficient solutions to everyday problems. It is roughly equivalent to the idea of 'common sense' (see Figure 14.1).

FIGURE 14.1 Verbal and practical intelligence.

Sources: left: Dmitriy Shironosov © 123RF.com; right: Radachynskyi Serhii/Shutterstock.com.

DEFINING INTELLIGENCE

To Jean Piaget (Chapter 12 for a detailed discussion), intelligence was all about being able to adapt to the environment. Watch a pet rabbit try to nudge open the unlocked door to their hutch and you'll soon conclude that they aren't terribly bright. Doors don't exist in their natural environment and bunnies just don't have the cognitive flexibility to adapt to such a novel feature in their physical world. Humans on the other hand are brilliant at adapting; whether it's to something obvious like a different physical environment or the subtleties of changing office dynamics we quickly work out how to adapt to new situations. Piaget's approach is appealing and explains human success as a species. However, it falls down logically; by his definition '*Rocks are smarter than cats because rocks have the sense to go away when you kick them*' (cognitive scientist Zenon Pylyshyn, paraphrased by Pinker, 1997, p 61).

After 100 years of really, really trying, experts have not been able to agree on a universally acceptable definition of intelligence (Deary, Weiss, and Batty, 2010). Indeed, as intelligence researcher Ian Deary remarked, 'Intelligence is rarely discussed for long before the word "controversial" appears' (Deary, 2012, p 454). However, most people have a common-sense understanding of what intelligence means, and they often know it when they see it—or, perhaps more accurately, when they *hear* it. A number of studies have shown that people are quite accurate in judging a stranger's intelligence (as measured by formal intelligence tests) after even very brief exposure to the sound of the person reading a few short sentences or speaking for 20 seconds (Borkenau et al, 2004).

What are people listening for in making these judgements? Although the researchers conducting these studies attempted to isolate certain factors on which people were basing their decisions (such as the speed and clarity of the target person's speech or the number of words he or she used), such simple cues do not convey what people mean when they call another person 'intelligent'. For one thing, people sometimes differentiate between *types* of intelligence, captured in the American expressions 'book smarts' and 'street smarts'.

You can think of intelligence as individual differences in the developing ability to think and reason. We have included it in the individual differences section of the book, but we could equally have put it in cognitive psychology, in which we discussed thinking, or in developmental psychology where we discussed cognitive development. What does this tell us about the way the discipline of psychology is structured?

Two General Meanings of the Word 'Intelligence'

In this sense, the word *intelligence* can be used in two general ways. Intelligence can simply mean rational 'humanlike' thought, as in the question 'Is there intelligent life in the universe?' (Pinker, 1997). This type of intelligence includes the ability to overcome obstacles, solve problems, and make decisions by means of rational (reality-based) considerations. Such a meaning of intelligence corresponds loosely to common sense or what intelligence researcher Robert Sternberg calls practical intelligence—the ability to come up with efficient solutions to the problems of everyday life, at home or on the job (Sternberg, 2003c; Grigorenko, Sternberg, and Strauss, 2006). A hunter with no education, but who can devise intricate traps to outwit clever animals, might be thought to possess this type of intelligence—even if they cannot read, write, or do arithmetic.

However, it is academic achievement that probably best captures the average person's idea of the concept 'intelligence' (Carroll, 1997; Jensen, 1998). Yet, intelligence researchers themselves are often widely divided as to what 'book smarts' actually means and whether it is the most appropriate indication of intelligence.

General Intelligence (*G*)

General intelligence, or *g*, is the technical term to describe what is popularly understood as intelligence; cleverness, academic excellence, or *book smarts*. General intelligence (*g*) describes a person's underlying general capacity to process complex information—to perform well on a wide variety of mental and even manual tasks. The most frequently administered intelligence tests (eg, the **Stanford-Binet Intelligence Scale** and the **Wechsler Adult Intelligence Scale [WAIS®-III]**) are thought to measure individual differences in *g*, and reflect the ease and speed with which a person should be expected to be able to learn new information (Spearman, 1904; Johnson, te Nijenhuis, and Bouchard, 2008). However, batteries of physical and psychological tests correlated with *g* may include measures of manual dexterity and perceptual speed as well as ability to juggle mental concepts and demonstrate proficiency in mathematical and verbal tasks (Deary, Weiss, and Batty, 2010).

❯ **KEY IDEAS** general intelligence (*g*) A way of referring to a person's underlying general capacity to process complex information—to perform well on a variety of mental tasks. General intelligence, or *g*, was initially hypothesized by Charles Spearman. *G* is measured by general IQ tests such as the Wechsler Adult Intelligence Scale and Stanford-Binet Intelligence Scale.

The Psychometric Approach to Intelligence

It was Charles Spearman (1927) who first proposed the existence of *g*. In examining groups of test scores of cognitive ability using a complex statistical procedure known as *factor analysis*, Spearman noted that there were correlations between the way individuals scored on one aspect of cognitive ability—say, numerical ability—and their scoring on other aspects of cognitive ability, such as verbal ability or visual-spatial reasoning. Although it was certainly possible to score exceptionally well on

❯ KEY IDEAS theorem of the indifference of the indicator This is Spearman's idea that you can take a person's score on any test of mental ability and use it in a general way to predict their score on a test of any other mental ability.

❯ KEY IDEAS IQ (intelligence quotient) IQ is a statistical measure of performance on intelligence tests based upon comparisons of a person's score with the average scores of others of their age. IQ was originally conceived as a measure of children's performance. When tests began to be administered to adults, new computational formulas had to be devised. Two IQ tests are the Wechsler Adult Intelligence Scale and the Stanford-Binet Intelligence Scale.

Stanford–Binet Intelligence Scale—the first version of the IQ test created by Alfred Binet. The purpose of the test was to predict academic performance so that children of deficient ability could be identified and placed in special remedial programmes. The test has been revised four times over its 100-year history.

Wechsler Adult Intelligence Scale (WAIS®-III)—a standardized test of intelligence designed by David G. Wechsler. This was the first IQ test to include testing of adults.

tests of one ability, and less well or even poorly on tests of another, Spearman found that this was the exception rather than the rule. More commonly, Spearman found that he could predict in a general way how a person would score in one type of task just by knowing that person's score on any other type of task. This suggested to Spearman that there was some sort of underlying factor uniting all the abilities. The fact that a person's score on virtually any of the tests he administered could be used to predict that person's score on any of the other tests was termed by Spearman the **theorem of the indifference of the indicator**. This general tendency for those scoring high on tests of one type of cognitive ability also to score relatively high on tests of other abilities is the rationale for hypothesizing the existence of *g*, a general intelligence factor that runs like a current through all mental abilities (Johnson et al, 2008).

Spearman's research initiated the modern psychometric tradition, which has long been the dominant one in the field of intelligence research. The psychometric tradition relies upon objective measurement by means of various standardized tests (eg, *IQ* tests). What do we mean by *standardized*? The absolute number of correct answers in a test is not the key to IQ. Instead, it is how a person scores in relation to the way large groups of similar individuals have scored in the past. These are groups of people presumably representative of the population for which the test has been designed. The scores produced by these larger groups are known as *norms* for the test, and administering the test to these large groups is called *norming* the test.

IQ (INTELLIGENCE QUOTIENT)

IQ (intelligence quotient) is the most common statistic used to describe *g*. This statistic was originally developed in the first part of the twentieth century by intelligence researcher Lewis Terman to interpret students' scores on a mental abilities test known as the *Stanford-Binet Intelligence Scale*. The Stanford-Binet was the most common standardized intelligence test for children prior to the creation of the first version of the Wechsler Intelligence Scale for Children (WISC®-IV), and it is still in widespread use. Although IQ is firmly associated with conventional definitions of intelligence, David Wechsler, the creator of the WISC tests, actually defined intelligence in somewhat broader terms than those typically used to define either IQ or *g*. According to Wechsler, intelligence is the 'global capacity of the individual to act purposefully, to think rationally and to deal effectively with his environment' (1944, p 3). Thus, Wechsler's definition includes aspects of practical intelligence.

Technically, *IQ* in its original sense no longer really exists. The statistic was originally computed by comparing a child's scores against the scores of other children from a similar population but of different ages. Thus, if an 8-year-old scored similarly to the average 10-year-old, it would indicate an elevated IQ. If the score were similar to an average 6-year-old it would indicate low IQ. However, because intelligence tests are now given to adults as well as children, you can see that this method of computing IQ would not work very well for adults, whose mental development does not change year by year as does a child's. It wouldn't be very meaningful to say, 'I'm a genius—I'm only 25 but I read as well as a 30-year-old!' Therefore, intelligence test developers have devised new ways to compute an IQ-like score, based on placing raw scores on a population distribution—see below. These methods work

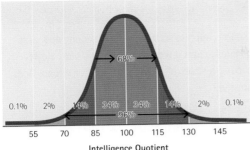

FIGURE 14.2 **The normal distribution of IQ scores. This bell-shaped curve charts the normal distribution of IQ scores. Notice that the figures add up to two-tenths of 1% greater than 100%. This is because the figures are approximations, and there is a fraction of 1% of most populations that may score higher than 145 or lower than 55.**

as well for adults as for children. Although the new methods do not really produce an IQ in the technical sense, the term *IQ* is still generally used by researchers and the public alike.

IQ and the Normal Distribution

Scores on standardized IQ tests such as the WAIS®-III, WISC®-IV, or the Stanford-Binet Intelligence Scale are designed to reflect a predictable pattern of individual differences with a mean (average) score at the centre of the distribution. This pattern is known as the **normal distribution** or, in popular terms, the *bell curve*. As Figure 14.2 shows, the pattern does form a bell shape, with 68% of scores in ordinary populations clustering between 85 and 115. This is considered the normal range of IQ scoring, with 100 being the average IQ score. An additional 28% of scores fall between 115 and 130 at the upper end and between 70 and 85 at the lower end. Scores between 115 and 130 are considered to represent 'bright' or 'superior' scoring while those between 70 and 85 are termed 'borderline' scoring.

In all, then, 96% of people's scores tend to fall between 70 and 130. The remaining 4% of individuals score either lower than 70 or higher than 130. An IQ score between about 50 and 70 (2% of the population) may reflect **intellectual disability**—a psychiatric designation for a person who has difficulty acquiring very basic academic skills, problems in social relationships, and who may need assistance in managing ordinary life tasks (American Psychiatric Association, 2013). This is what until 2013 was called retardation.

On the other hand, a score above 130 reflects *gifted* or *extremely gifted* scoring, with scores above 150 or thereabouts reflecting *profound giftedness*—a designation that applies only to a very small fraction of 1% of the population. These IQ scores and labels such as 'extremely gifted' and 'profoundly gifted' vary sometimes substantially according to who is doing the labelling and which IQ test is being used.

IQ and Real-Life Success

IQ tests are reliable. Wechsler (2014) suggests that the fourth edition of the Wechsler Adult Intelligence Scale (WAIS-IV) has inter-rater reliability of 0.9+ and test-retest reliability of 0.7–0.9 for subscales. There is also a good match between scores on the WAIS and those on other IQ tests (0.88 correlation between scores on WAIS-IV and the Stanford-Binet test). This is evidence for **concurrent validity**.

These figures for reliability and validity appear quite impressive. There is, however, a huge debate among psychologists over the extent to which IQ tests are meaningful (ie, whether they tell us anything useful about real-life success).

> **KEY IDEAS** normal distribution This is a bell-shaped pattern of scores of any human characteristic across a population, in which most scores cluster around the mean and in which very few people score very high or low.

> **KEY IDEAS** intellectual disability Formerly known as mental retardation, intellectual disability is the modern term used in psychiatry to define someone who has difficulty in managing a culturally normal life without help as a result of low intelligence—an IQ below 70.

> **KEY IDEAS** test-retest reliability and concurrent validity These are two standard ways to assess the quality of a psychological measure. Remember that reliability means consistency. **Test-retest reliability** is a way of testing this. If people take the test twice and get similar results this is indicated by a test-retest correlation coefficient of close to 1. Lower scores indicate that people's scores when they take the test twice are less consistent and hence the test is not reliable. Validity indicates the extent to which we are measuring what we seek to measure. When a test produces similar results to a *concurrent* test, an existing test believed to measure what we are interested in—indicated by a correlation of close to 1—this means that the test has good **concurrent validity**.

THINKING CRITICALLY

An inter-rater reliability figure of over 0.9 sounds impressive. If we were observing and quantifying a complex sequence of behaviour on a tally chart it would be extremely high. However, scoring an IQ test is more a process of marking a series of answers as right or wrong. Does this figure of 0.9 reliability still sound impressive?

Intelligence tests were initially designed as tools of *prediction*. Their primary job was to *predict* how well a person was likely to do in an academic setting. IQ is far from the only factor associated with a person's educational outcome—motivation and engagement with schoolwork, self-discipline and self-control, access to good schooling, personality and socioeconomic factors, and beliefs about one's own ability are also extremely important. Indeed, these factors, if combined, are responsible for the majority of the differences among people in academic achievement, and in some individuals, factors such as resilience, self-discipline, and self-control can trump IQ in predicting academic success (see, eg, Steinmayr and Spinath, 2009). However, high IQ does appear to convey some advantage. This was illustrated by Lubinski et al (2001). For ten years, these investigators followed 320 young adolescents whose average IQ scores prior to age 13 put them in the profoundly gifted range. By age 23, virtually all had graduated from college, and 56% were already pursuing PhD degrees—a figure 50 times greater than the number of expected PhDs in the general population.

THINKING CREATIVELY

The obvious interpretation of the findings of Lubinski et al is that the high IQ in the sample they followed up directly led to their high level of academic success. However, there are many other possible factors at work here. Identify as many of these as possible.

In general, European researchers have been more cautious than American psychologists in their conclusions as regards the predictive value of IQ in education. Furnham and Ritandelli-Tabaton (2011) looked at IQ and GCSE performance in an English sixth-form college. They concluded that IQ accounted for a modest 10% of the variance in GCSE performance (the correlation between GCSE score and IQ was +0.34). Interestingly the relationship was stronger for some subjects than others, with correlations with IQ ranging from maths (+0.46) to languages (+0.17). Moreover, IQ emerged as less predictive of school success than personality.

Although IQ is far from the most important predictor of how well a person does on the job (Sternberg and Wagner, 1993), IQ and similar tests of cognitive ability can predict some aspects of job hiring and performance, particularly jobs involving complex tasks (Berry and Sackett, 2009; Kuncel and Hezlett, 2010). Not surprisingly, those with higher IQ scores tend to be found more often in higher-status occupations, and their incomes are on average higher than those with lower IQs. However, researchers have not yet been able to determine if it is IQ itself that predicts higher income and status, or if it is the effect IQ has on the number of years of schooling a person experiences which produces these results (Scullin et al, 2000). This is a good example of where we should be cautious about interpreting causal relationships from simple correlation statistics.

THINKING PRACTICALLY

How much should people worry about their IQ score? You might like to think about the following:

- the impressive reliability and concurrent validity figures
- the relationship between IQ and GCSE score
- the existence of *g* but also the spiky profiles of some individuals' abilities
- the uncertainty over links between IQ and career success

One puzzling, but potentially important, fact about intelligence: it may be on the rise, at least in some populations. In most of the developed world, and beginning in portions of the developing world, average raw IQ scores have risen over the decades. While some of the more developed countries seem to have experienced a levelling off of IQ gains, in Britain and the United States average IQ scores have continued to rise at the rate of about three points per decade throughout the twentieth century and into the twenty-first (Nisbett et al, 2012). Shown in Figure 14.3 and known as the **Flynn effect** after its discoverer James Flynn, IQ gains over the years have not yet been explained adequately. Flynn himself (2009) has suggested that our increased scientific understanding and use of technology has promoted more abstract ways of thinking and problem-solving—more advanced thinking and hence higher IQ. However, this has proved very difficult to test scientifically; as social psychologist Richard Nisbett and his colleagues proclaim, 'It is easier to eliminate causes than to provide a convincing causal scenario' (2012, p 12).

> ❯ **KEY IDEAS** the Flynn effect Named after James Flynn, the Flynn effect describes the steady increase in raw scores on IQ tests that has characterized the late twentieth and early twenty-first century.

THINKING CRITICALLY

Flynn's explanation for rising IQ levels makes intuitive sense. However, it is very difficult to provide direct evidence to confirm or falsify. Explain why this is a problem. You might like to refer to our discussion of psychology as science in Chapter 2.

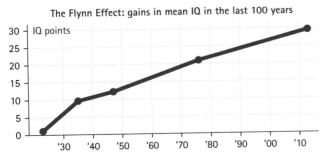

FIGURE 14.3 **The Flynn effect.**
Source: Akshat Rathi, Data: Pietschnig & Voracek (2015)/theatlas.com.

Cultural Bias in IQ Testing

IQ tests cannot directly measure the quality of processing in the mind. They can only measure performance on tasks that require particular cognitive abilities. But what if people in different cultural contexts are more or less familiar with the tasks or use different cognitive strategies to address them? We are not then comparing like with like and the tests become biased. A dramatic illustration of this is in the mathematical ability of Brazilian child street vendors.

Carraher and colleagues went into the streets of Recife, a city in north-eastern Brazil, to study the mathematical abilities of child street vendors. Carraher and her team first created maths problems stated in the context of purchase transactions (eg, 'I'll take three coconuts . . .'). After the child computed the answer, the investigators tried to tease out information about the mental processes the children used to solve the problem ('How did you get that so fast?'). The children appeared primarily to be using very rapid series of small, mentally manageable addition and multiplication operations 'chained' together. The children's average score for these initial, informal math tests was 98.2% correct. The researchers then created formal arithmetic problems using the identical numbers and operations used in the informal tests, but framing the problems with abstract symbols divorced from context ('What is 6×50?'). The children's average score was 36.8% correct (Carraher, Carraher, and Schliemann, 1985).

Are these children intelligent? They communicate well with language and can perform complex cognitive operations very rapidly. And yet they would undoubtedly score quite low on most IQ tests.

Raw scores on IQ tests tend to discriminate between people of different cultural backgrounds. This is inevitable as whatever items we put in the tests will be more or less familiar to different groups of people, and the nature and quality of schooling vary widely between different populations. In addition people in different cultural contexts learn different cognitive strategies to perform the same mental tasks, and these may not lend themselves equally well to the items in IQ tests (like the Brazilian street vendors' maths). As long as IQ tests are normed appropriately and the individuals being tested are representative of the population IQ tests can be used in non-biased ways.

On the other hand, if a person is *not* representative of the group against which the test has been normed—for example, if a person does not understand English well and is given an English version of the test—then the test most certainly *is* biased. Moreover, although IQ tests do not simply measure facts one has learned in school, a person's IQ is at least to some degree influenced by their schooling. The experience of schooling itself (regardless of the quality of schooling) plays a role in developing the cognitive skills for performing well on IQ tests, as does exposure to learning in the home—for example, exposure to vocabulary words spoken by parents (Nisbett et al, 2012).

Bigger problems arise when psychologists have attempted to use the IQ tests developed by and normed against one population to test others. In Britain Hans Eysenck (1971) and in the USA Arthur Jensen (1969) caused huge controversy by suggesting that disparities in raw scores indicate real racial differences in intelligence. Eysenck, whose family fled the Nazis, strenuously argued that he was not a racist, maintaining his 'hatred for those who suppress any sector of the community on grounds of race' (1971, p 9). By modern standards, his position would be viewed by many people as reflecting a racist mindset.

Fortunately, there is now a well-established body of solid scientific evidence to refute the idea of racial differences in intelligence—see Colman (2016) for an excellent review—so we don't have to confront Eysenck's conflict between hating racism and si-multaneously believing that science supports an idea almost everyone considers racist.

THINKING CRITICALLY

Eysenck's argument was essentially that as scientists we should look objectively at the existing evidence rather than believe what we would like to. There are perhaps three possible takes on this.

1 Accept the evidence of raw test scores at face value and disregard other interpretations and sources of evidence (Eysenck's position).

2 Look for a more sophisticated and nuanced interpretation of raw test scores and evaluate whether modern evidence supports Eysenck's position (the scientific position taken by most current intelligence researchers).

3 See psychology as a vehicle for promoting equality and social justice first and science second, and dismiss Eysenck's argument on principle.

What do you see as the strengths and weaknesses of each of these positions? Where do you stand?

The debate about population differences in intelligence has more recently been stirred up again by Richard Lynn (eg, Lynn and Hanvanen, 2006) who proposed the idea of **national IQ**. The idea is that the mean raw scores of each country are normed against British norms so that each country emerges with a score like an individual. By this measure a few countries like China and Iceland score above Britain but the vast majority score lower, some considerably so. Lynn and Meisenberg (2010) attempted to validate the idea of national IQ by identifying positive correlations with measures of national educational attainment and economic prosperity. They propose that these correlations are the result of national IQ having a direct impact on education and productivity. However, there is plenty of evidence to counter this interpretation (see, eg, the effect of migration on IQ, see later this chapter), and critics consider the idea of national IQ to be at best meaningless (Hunt and Sternberg, 2006).

❯ KEY IDEAS national IQ
National IQ is the controversial idea by Richard Lynn that there are real differences in intelligence between the populations of different countries.

THINKING CREATIVELY

It is often said that we should be extremely cautious about proposing causality based on a correlation (see 'Correlation and causation', Chapter 3, for more information). Take the correlations identified by Lynn between his measure of national intelligence and educational achievement and economic productivity. How many possible lurking variables and directions of causality can you identify in these correlations?

READ THIS

To better understand these psychometric approaches to intelligence, we recommend some classics and some more recent texts.

Wechsler, D. (1944). *The Measurement of Adult Intelligence*. Baltimore: Williams and Wilkins.

Buckhalt, J.A. (2002). A short history of g: Psychometrics' most enduring and controversial construct. *Learning and Individual Differences*, **13**(2), 101–14.

Rust, J. and Golombok, S. (2014). *Modern Psychometrics: The Science of Psychological Assessment*. London: Routledge.

Kline, P. (2013). *Intelligence: The Psychometric View*. London: Routledge.

ALTERNATIVE VIEWS OF INTELLIGENCE

Not all researchers accept the idea of a single factor (g) underlying all of intelligence, nor do all define intelligence in terms of scores on standardized IQ tests. We can look here at three theoretical approaches to understanding intelligence that step aside from the dominant psychometric model and notion of g.

Multiple Intelligences

Some hypothesize the existence of multiple forms of intelligence not captured in the idea of g and not adequately measured in intelligence tests. For example, during Spearman's time, Louis Thurstone (1938) argued that intelligence actually consisted of a set of seven distinct mental abilities—word fluency, numerical facility, analytical reasoning, and so forth—without any underlying single general factor. He suggested that a person could score very high on one of these dimensions, while quite low on another, and he believed that a person's intelligence was best described by the pattern of these variations in performance, rather than by a single underlying factor. However, research eventually showed that Thurstone's seven specific mental abilities actually *were* united by an underlying factor. To score high on some of these abilities but low on others—while possible—was relatively unusual. Thurstone himself ultimately acknowledged this (Thurstone and Thurstone, 1941; Deary, 2012).

A more modern version of the multiple intelligences (MI) idea has been proposed by Howard Gardner (1983, 2006, 2008). In Gardner's view, the entire notion of intelligence needs to be stretched to include abilities as wide-ranging as physical coordination (which he terms *bodily-kinaesthetic intelligence*), musical ability (*musical intelligence*), artistic ability (*visual intelligence*), or the ability to understand one's own and others' emotions and motivations (*interpersonal intelligence*). According to Gardner, defining intelligence in terms of IQ or g causes certain human qualities to become greatly overvalued at the expense of other, equally important qualities. On the other hand, critics have charged that some of the abilities cited by Gardner should more properly be termed talents, aptitudes, or skills rather than 'intelligences' (see Figure 14.4).

Gardner's position is very different from that of Thurstone. He does not deny the *existence* of g, rather its *usefulness*. Gardner is coming from an educational perspective where he feels that the school system places too much value on verbal and logical-mathematical intelligence at the expense of the full range of human cognitive abilities. This is as much a philosophical values system as a psychological theory of intelligence.

Gardner's influence has been greatest in education, where the idea that all sorts of cognitive strengths should be valued and nurtured—as well as the verbal and logical-mathematical abilities emphasized in standard curricula—has resonated with teachers. However, as Gardner himself has pointed out (Gardner, 1995, 2003), many of teachers' interpretations of his work have been very simplistic and

FIGURE 14.4 The heights of musical, visual, and bodily-kinaesthetic intelligence. Pictured here are musician Kurt Cobain, the work of anonymous artist Banksy, poet and actor Benjamin Zephaniah, and boxer Nicola Adams. We have no way of knowing their respective IQ scores, but Howard Gardner would likely view Cobain as high in musical intelligence, Banksy as high in visual intelligence, Zephaniah as high in verbal and interpersonal intelligence, and Adams as high in bodily-kinaesthetic intelligence.

Sources: Kurt Cobain: Pictorial Press Ltd/Alamy Stock Photo; Banksy artwork: Steve Taylor ARPS/Alamy Stock Photo; Benjamin Zephaniah: Kathy deWitt/Alamy Stock Photo; Nicola Adams: Featureflash Photo Agency/Shutterstock.com.

unlikely to benefit learners. These have included treating intelligences as learning styles and having children moving around in the hope that this will activate their bodily-kinaesthetic intelligence. A more detailed account of these blunders is shown in Table 14.1.

TABLE 14.1 Examples of 'pseudo-applications' of multiple intelligences (after Jarvis, 2005)

1	Planning contrived lessons in an attempt to apply every MI to every topic.
2	Simply stimulating the senses during lessons; for example, playing music or encouraging movements in the belief that this somehow activates different intelligences.
3	Misunderstanding the intelligences and their implications. For example, suggesting that learners high in interpersonal intelligence prefer learning with others (virtually all learners do) and that those high in intrapersonal intelligence (or self-awareness) learn best alone (this has no basis in MI theory).
4	Using MIs as memory aids. This is not to say that constructing diagrams or making up rhymes are not useful mnemonic techniques, but they are just that—memory techniques, nothing to do with using or stimulating intelligences.
5	Labelling children with a single learning style based on the MI in which they score most highly.

Sternberg's Triarchic Theory

Another influential challenge to the importance of *g* as a measure of intelligence comes from researcher Robert J. Sternberg. Sternberg is well known for his scepticism about the ability of IQ tests to measure all aspects of intelligence adequately—and about the usefulness of the notion of *g* as a single factor underlying all types of cognitive abilities. However, like Gardner, it is not that Sternberg denies the existence of *g*. He affirms its existence (Sternberg, 2003b, p 400). However, he insists that *g* only underlies certain types of mental abilities—specifically, those that involve solving problems through *analytic reasoning*. Such problems (a) are already formulated and clearly defined (eg, a test question); (b) have a single correct answer; (c) come with all the information necessary to solve them (eg, a vocabulary question or mathematical problem); (d) are detached from ordinary experience; and (e) have little intrinsic interest—that is, their sole purpose is to test a person's ability (Neisser et al, 1996).

However, life is filled with problems that do not fit this mould. For example, *practical* problems often are not well formulated or defined ('How can I best organize my schedule to balance work, studying, and a social life?'). Such problems usually do not come with all the information necessary to solve them—they require an information-gathering process (eg, Which classes require the most studying? How much money do I really need to get by?). Practical problems also often have many different possible solutions. Finally, because these problems are embedded in the context of a person's everyday life, they hold intrinsic interest for that person.

> **KEY IDEAS** triarchic theory of successful intelligence This is the full title of Sternberg's theory that intelligence consists of three distinct types: analytic intelligence, creative intelligence, and practical intelligence.

Sternberg and his colleagues have used such observations to evolve a theory of intelligence known as the **triarchic theory of successful intelligence** (Sternberg, 2000, 2003b, 2005). Sternberg uses the term *successful*, because he defines intelligence as 'one's ability to succeed according to what one values in life, within one's sociocultural context' (2003b, p 400.) The triarchic theory proposes that there are three distinct forms of intelligence that are independent of one another—that is, a person can be quite high on one and quite low on another.

1 *Analytic intelligence* is a person's ability to solve the sorts of problems one would ordinarily find in an academic setting. This type of intelligence is reflected in the idea of *g* and is measured by intelligence tests.

2 *Creative intelligence* is a person's ability to use insight and his or her existing knowledge base to solve new problems and come up with new ideas—to think 'outside the box'. According to this idea, a student may have poor IQ scores and exam results yet may excel in creative problem-solving and project design.

3 *Practical intelligence* is a person's ability to adapt to their environment effectively, solve everyday problems, and achieve personal goals. The Brazilian street vendors described earlier might be a prime example of this type of intelligence.

Evaluating the triarchic theory

The triarchic theory is appealing in many ways. Many of us have known people who are exceedingly brilliant academically, but who would probably starve to death if they found themselves stranded in the woods, and they cannot seem to find a way to translate their intellectual brilliance into a salary that can support themselves and their families. Similarly, some people may find academic work extraordinarily difficult, but are brilliant mechanics and can cleverly improvise tools out of common household objects. Moreover, as Sternberg (2000) correctly notes, many highly successful people are not known for their intellectual gifts.

The triarchic theory is also *democratic*. It suggests that there is a place at the 'intelligence table' for all. Many people hold a frank distaste for the idea that some individuals are somehow 'superior' to others in an attribute (intelligence) on which everyone seems to place so much importance. The triarchic theory is therefore philosophically attractive to many people.

And yet we are scientists and, from a scientific perspective, *truth can never be established on philosophical grounds*. This means that we cannot assume something is true because we would like it to be true. So then—how does the triarchic theory hold up to empirical testing? For this theory to be valid, two important criteria would need to be met: first, the three forms of intelligence must be independent of one another. A person's score on one type of intelligence should not predict their score on another type of intelligence. Second, scores on tests of *g* such as IQ tests should only be correlated with scores on tests of *analytic* intelligence—not with scores on tests of practical or creative intelligence. If these criteria are not met, then tests of the triarchic forms of intelligence may differ little from tests of *g*, and 'successful intelligence' may be little more than another term for *g* (Gottfredson, 2003).

Unfortunately for all those who find the triarchic theory appealing, tests of its validity conducted over its first 25 years of existence have not been very encouraging. Nathan Brody (2003a, 2003b) found that the scores on tests of the three abilities were correlated, suggesting that the abilities may not be independent. Specifically, Brody (2003a) found that analytical and creative abilities were correlated (+0.75), analytical and practical abilities were correlated (+0.66), and creative and practical abilities were correlated (+0.62). These are moderate-to-high correlations. A more serious problem for the theory is the fact that scores on tests of all the triarchic abilities—*including* creative and practical intelligence—are correlated with scores on tests of *g*, also at moderate-to-high levels. Similar results have been found for other theories of multiple intelligences, such as those of Howard Gardner discussed previously (Deary, Penke, and Johnson, 2010).

Sternberg and his colleagues acknowledge some of these problems, but they suggest that the fault lies not with the theory, but with the tests that have been used to evaluate the theory in the past (Sternberg, 2003c). In fairness, it is undoubtedly true that it is much more difficult to devise effective tests of practical and creative intelligence than to devise tests of analytic intelligence and *g*.

Most theories of intelligence incorporate the idea of *g*. Despite widespread interest in the idea of multiple intelligences and controversy over *g*, it is probably fair to say that the majority of researchers now believe that the evidence is 'overwhelming' (Carroll, 1997) that (a) *something* like *g* does exist; (b) it measures some, though probably not all, important aspects of human cognitive abilities.

Three-Stratum Theory

One compromise between *g* theories and theories of multiple intelligences is the **three-stratum theory**, depicted in Figure 14.5. In 1993, John B. Carroll undertook a mammoth reanalysis of 70 years of data involving intelligence testing—encompassing over 460 studies—in an attempt to synthesize a new theory that took into account everything then known about *g* and other aspects of the structure of intelligence. He ended up with a hierarchical model of intelligence with three *strata*, or levels, known as the three-stratum theory of cognitive abilities.

According to Carroll, *Stratum I*, at the very bottom, includes 69 highly specific, or *narrow*, abilities—everything from the ability to discriminate musical tones to general science knowledge, perceptual speed, word fluency, reading comprehension, logical reasoning, and so forth.

Stratum II, directly above Stratum I, includes *eight* broad abilities that directly determine one's success in tasks measuring the 69 narrow abilities. Among these eight broad abilities are **fluid intelligence** (*Gf*) and **crystallized intelligence** (*Gc*). These terms were borrowed from an earlier theory by Raymond B. Cattell and John

> **KEY IDEAS** three-stratum theory This is an empirically based theory of intelligence devised by John B. Carroll that blends the idea of *g* with Horn and Cattell's *Gf-Gc* theory and the idea that intelligence includes multiple cognitive abilities.

> **KEY IDEAS** fluid and crystallized intelligence **Fluid intelligence** (*Gf*) is Cattell and Horn's term used to refer to largely innate analytic skills and abstract reasoning ability. **Crystallized intelligence** (*Gc*) is Cattell and Horn's term used to refer to skills or knowledge one acquires as a result of exposure to education and culture—what one has learned.

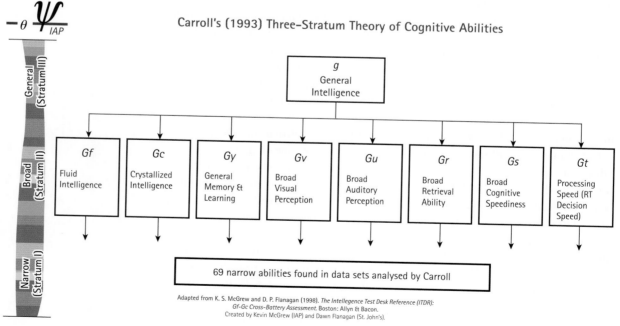

FIGURE 14.5 Carroll's three-stratum theory of cognitive abilities (1993).

Horn (Horn and Cattell, 1966; Horn, 1991). According to Horn and Cattell, two general factors—not one—constituted general intelligence (*g*) and underlay similarities in the way people scored on various tests of cognitive abilities. Fluid intelligence is a largely innate ability characterized by analytic and abstract reasoning. It is 'fluid' because it is adaptable to any situation or task and is not dependent upon previous learning, experience, education, or **culture**—in other words, what one has been able to *learn*. Crystallized intelligence on the other hand is about acquired expertise. Doing well on a vocabulary test, a foreign language test, or a test of reading musical notation would all reflect high levels of crystallized intelligence (McArdle, Ferrer-Caja, Hamagami, and Woodcock, 2002).

Finally, *Stratum III* at the very top is *g*—the underlying factor that determines success in tests of both Stratum I and Stratum II abilities.

The three-stratum theory has the advantage of being entirely *evidence-based*, unlike the triarchic theory. This means that Carroll had few preconceptions of what would happen when he analysed those 70 years of data sets. His theory emerged entirely from the picture presented in the data. Thus, it is a strongly empirical theory with a base of support in decades of scientific research, and many researchers consider it to be particularly useful as a result (Johnson and Bouchard, 2005; Deary, 2012). On the other hand, because it derives all of its data from standardized tests, possible aspects of intelligence not evaluated in such tests—for example, practical and creative problem-solving—do not play a role in his theory.

The three-stratum theory exemplifies the limits of what we can state with confidence about intelligence: in spite of its seeming reasonableness and strong evidence base, many researchers nonetheless oppose it. Instead, they favour various other approaches, including the idea that *g* is all that really matters, theories that focus primarily on crystallized and fluid intelligence, or multiple intelligence theories such as Sternberg's or Gardner's. No consensus regarding the nature of intelligence has been reached in spite of a century of data collected and analysed. Indeed, the same sets of data are sometimes given opposite interpretations depending on how the data is analysed or interpreted. Thus, nowhere more than in intelligence research is the fragility of psychological science more apparent. Even in this area—where so much research has been conducted—there are few general laws that are accepted without challenge.

 THINKING CRITICALLY

Scientists often claim to be objective in their interpretation of data. What does the disagreement about three-stratum theory, which is based entirely on data, tell us about science and psychologists as scientists?

Intelligence as a Social Construct

Most scientific psychologists take the idea of intelligence seriously and believe that the term describes something real, although we have some quite heated debates over the details of what it is, where it comes from, and how useful the idea is. However, one branch of psychology offers a radically different view, questioning the very existence of intelligence.

From a social constructionist perspective (see 'More radical positions on psychology as science', Chapter 2), debates over the fine details of what intelligence is miss the most fundamental question; whether intelligence is a real psychological entity or rather a **social construct**. Recall that a social construct is a concept derived in a particular political and historical context to serve a political purpose, generally to maintain a social status quo, and that social constructionism is a radical perspective aiming to uncover social constructs in psychology.

Social constructionism comes in various flavours, one of which is **critical psychology**. Critical psychology is concerned with uncovering and challenging the social constructs that exist within psychology. It is deliberately subversive (Parker and Burman, 2008). Coming from this perspective, Cernovsky (1997) suggests that intelligence research is a mechanism by which scientists have helped maintain social inequalities and prop up dominant groups. Think back to our discussion of how raw scores on IQ tests discriminate (in every sense!) between different populations, and how a minority of intelligence researchers have drawn on these figures to suggest racial and/or national differences in intelligence (discussed this chapter). Cernovsky (1997) proposes that this is more than a simplistic interpretation of data and rather an attempt to justify racism and limit immigration. Burman (2017) goes further and proposes that the very emergence of psychology as a major discipline in the twentieth century is closely tied to the fit between IQ testing and political agendas like individualizing social problems and establishing 'normal' patterns of development for the purposes of social control and race discrimination.

The history of intelligence research is a chequered one, and the concern expressed by critical psychologists over links between IQ testing and unpleasant political agendas carries considerable weight. Although IQ tests were developed in nineteenth-century France for educational purposes, uses thereafter were often more sinister. The eugenics movement, begun by Francis Galton (1884), advocated selective breeding of white middle-class families in order to promote higher levels of intelligence in the population. In practice this meant restricting breeding in populations deemed to be inferior, in part by means of IQ testing. In various manifestations the principles of eugenics underlay policies including the Holocaust and compulsory sterilization of people with learning disabilities still practised in some countries.

There is little doubt that, as critical psychologists have recognized, intelligence as a concept is very open to misuse, and has been misused historically for very unpleasant purposes. Some contemporary ideas in intelligence research, such as national intelligence, look quite dubious through the lens of critical psychology. However, most mainstream psychologists would argue that the idea of intelligence is scientifically robust and not inherently abusive or sinister.

READ THIS

To really get a sense of where each of the authors of the alternative views of intelligence is coming from, you ought to go back to the original material. These are some of the key sources:

Gardner, H.E. (2000). *Intelligence Reframed: Multiple Intelligences for the 21st Century.* London: Hachette UK.

Moran, S., Kornhaber, M., and Gardner, H. (2009). Orchestrating multiple intelligences. In Kevin Ryan and James M. Cooper (eds), *Kaleidoscope: Contemporary and Classic Readings in Education.* London: Houghton Mifflin, 188–92.

Sternberg, R.J. (1984). Toward a triarchic theory of human intelligence. *Behavioral and Brain Sciences,* **7**(2), 269–87.

Sternberg, R.J. (2015). Successful intelligence: A model for testing intelligence beyond IQ tests. *European Journal of Education and Psychology*, **8**(2), 76–84.

Carroll, J.B. (1997). The three-stratum theory of cognitive abilities. In D.P. Flanagan, J.L. Genshaft, and P.L. Harrison (eds), *Contemporary Intellectual Assessment: Theories, Tests, and Issues*. New York, NY: The Guilford Press, pp 122–30.

Fox, D., Prilleltensky, I., and Austin, S. (eds) (2009). *Critical Psychology: An Introduction*. London: Sage.

THE ORIGINS OF INTELLIGENCE

A person's level of general cognitive ability as measured in standardized tests of intelligence remains much the same throughout their adult lifetime, unless there is a dramatic change in circumstances. Moreover, measurements of a person's IQ taken at the age of 1 year are generally similar (although not necessarily identical) to measurements taken at age 17 or 18—and this correlation is even stronger beginning at about age 5 (Davis, Haworth, and Plomin, 2009).

For example, as shown in Figure 14.6, a 70-year-long study on a large Scottish sample found that IQ at age 11 was very highly correlated with IQ at age 80 (Deary et al, 2004). In another remarkable study, Marc Bornstein and his colleagues found far more modest, but still important, stabilities in measurable mental abilities beginning in the first months of life and continuing through age 4 (Bornstein et al, 2006).

The Argument for the Role of Genes

Findings of long-term stability of IQ scores, combined with observations of similarity in levels of cognitive ability among family members, have led to widespread interest in the genetics of intelligence. So what have researchers found? **Behavioural genetics** research over the course of three decades has demonstrated that both genes *and* environments play their part in the development and expression of cognitive abilities. Averaged out, about 50% of the differences in IQ scores among individuals in most samples are due to genetic differences, and 50% are due to environmental effects (Plomin and Spinath, 2004).

However, from the pro-genetic perspective these averages (means) don't really tell the full story of heritability of intelligence very well. This is because the contribution

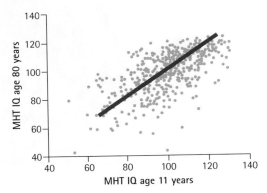

FIGURE 14.6 This scatterplot shows a strong positive, linear correlation between intelligence test scores at age 11 and scores from tests taken at about age 80. Strong linear positive correlations are shown in scatterplots when the data points group closely together and their direction can be characterized by an upward diagonal line drawn through them.

of genes to differences in scores on tests of cognitive ability appears to become much more pronounced as a child grows older (Haworth et al, 2010; Deary, 2012). In early childhood the contribution may be no greater than 20%, but this increases to around 60% at 16 years, and genes may ultimately account for as much as 80% of the differences in intelligence test scores found among 50-year-olds (Haworth et al, 2009; Plomin and Deary, 2015).

This figure of 80%, however, can be rather misleading. *It does not, for example, mean that the environment ceases to be important.* It appears that with age people increasingly seek out environments of their choice—it is these choices that are genetically influenced (see Figure 14.7). This is key because it suggests that genetic influence is not just on cognitive abilities but on personality, motivation, energy levels, etc, all of which affect our choice of environment, which continues to exert an effect. When psychologists say that genes are the most important single factor in the origins of intelligence (of course, not all psychologists *would* say this) they are *not* saying that they directly control cognitive abilities.

Twin studies (see 'Twin studies', Chapter 5) of IQ tend to find very high correlations between identical twins (monozygotic or MZ) reared together. However, the correlation of scores for identical twins separated for adoption and reared *apart* (.72) is not quite as high as that for identical twins reared together (.86), demonstrating at least some effect of the environment (Bouchard and McGue, 1981). A larger effect of the environment is apparent when we compare the scores of fraternal (dizygotic or DZ) twins reared together with those of ordinary siblings reared together. Fraternal twins share the same number of genes in common as any ordinary pair of siblings—about 50% on average. Yet the average correlation in their scores (.60) is substantially higher than that for ordinary siblings (.47). Something about the *environment* of fraternal twins causes higher correlations in their test scoring—perhaps their age similarity and the resulting likelihood of exposure to similar school, peer, and home experiences.

FIGURE 14.7 'Smart' genes? Genes don't directly control your cognitive ability, but they can lead you to seek out certain environments that might affect your intelligence.
Source: Nejron Photo/Shutterstock.com.

A recent variation on classic twin study methods has added further support for the importance of genetic influence. Jansen et al (2015) have reviewed longitudinal studies in which MZ and DZ twin pairs have been brain-scanned throughout their childhood, using both structural and functional MRI (see Chapter 4 for a discussion). The MZs had substantially more similar measures of physical brain development than the DZs. Jansen and colleagues estimate that genes account for 60–80% of the variance in brain structure and around 40% of the variance in brain function. Although we cannot be sure how closely brain development is linked to IQ these results are certainly consistent with strong genetic influence on IQ. Almost all psychologists now support the idea that genetic make-up affects intelligence. However, there remains a spectrum of opinion concerning just how strong this genetic influence is.

Limitations of the evidence for genetic influence

It is very tempting to be swayed by the impressive numbers quoted by proponents of what we might call the 'almost-entirely-genetic' view on the origins of intelligence put forward by some geneticists. To be fair, we should also acknowledge that those on the other side of the argument really want to believe in the importance of environment on philosophical grounds and so may find it hard to look objectively at heritability data. With that proviso in mind consider some of the following counterarguments:

- One reason for the very high figure of 80% for heritability of intelligence is **assortative mating**. This means that, whereas mothers and fathers are only modestly similar in most characteristics, they tend to be quite similar in measured IQ, with correlations of around 0.4 (Plomin and Deary, 2015). Assortative mating tends to inflate heritability figures by concentrating any key genetic variations in children.

- Another reason to be cautious about the almost-entirely-genetic view is a notable lack of **candidate genes** (ie, genes likely to be associated with variations in intelligence!) Once we take out candidate genes identified by one-off studies that have not been replicated successfully and genetic variations associated with intellectual disability and **dementia**, there have been very few positive results in the many attempts to identify genetic variations associated with normal variations in intelligence (Chabris et al, 2012; Arslan and Penke, 2015).

- A third reason for caution is that there is limited and conflicting data available for the effect of shared prenatal environment on the similarity of MZ twins (Beijstervel et al, 2016). It is possible, though unproven, that the very similar environment shared by monochorionic identical twins (ie, identical twins who also share a placenta) in the womb contributes to the similarity of IQ in MZs and inflates heritability figures.

- There is something *really* misleading about heritability figures themselves, and once you are aware of this they will never look quite the same again. Although they are expressed as a decimal or percentage heritability and environmental influence don't have to add up to 1.0 or 100%! A figure of 0.8 for genetic influence does *not* mean there is only 0.2 left for environment. Because the figure represents *heritability*, genetic inheritance is always listed first as a percentage number. Moreover, it is broad-sense heritability, which includes both the direct influence of genetic make-up + the influence of gene-environment interaction (this is explained in detail in Chapter 5). Once heritability passes 50% it *appears* to be more important than environment but it is not necessarily so (Bronfenbrenner and Ceci, 1994).

> **KEY IDEAS** assortative mating
This takes place when parents similar in genetically influenced characteristics tend to mate. This leads to more genetically similar children and inflates the apparent heritability of characteristics.

- And finally, heritability figures are based on traditional IQ tests which measure *g*. This is understandable as those tests are well established and claim good reliability and validity. However, when we think about cognitive abilities in real-life situations we might well be thinking of intelligence in a way more akin to that proposed by Gardner or Sternberg. It may be that *g* is highly heritable and yet this may say little or nothing about the influences on the cognitive abilities we are concerned with, particularly in education.

This is an emotive debate, and as we have identified, those on the environmental side of the debate are highly motivated by philosophical considerations. One reason why many people are philosophically uncomfortable about the highly heritable nature of intelligence is that heritability implies **constraint**. Common sense suggests that if IQ is strongly influenced by genes then it is constrained (ie, it cannot change much). In fact, intelligence is **malleable** (ie, it changes in response to environmental change). We tend to settle into a fairly constant environment and so maintain a fairly constant IQ there. However, if this environment were to change, so would our IQ. Thus studies of IQ change following migration have shown gains of up to 20 IQ points (depending on age and the degree of contrast between pre- and post-migration environments) (Sauce and Matzel, 2018).

> **KEY IDEAS** constraint and malleability Heritability appears to imply **constraint**; the idea that if IQ is genetically determined then it must be constrained (ie, relatively unchangeable). Actually IQ is quite **malleable** (ie, subject to change).

 THINKING CRITICALLY

Okay, we have given you both sides of the debate over the heritability of intelligence. The bulk of the statistical evidence is for heritability and yet critics have raised some very awkward points for the almost-entirely-genetic side to argue against.

Which side of the argument impresses you more? Reflect on whether this is more because of your politics or because of the kinds of arguments that impress you. There is no wrong answer here; we just think you might benefit from being aware of your responses to psychological theory and research.

Environmental Influences on Intelligence

A number of environmental variables have been associated with intelligence. These include **attachment** security and intellectual stimulation.

Attachment and IQ

There have been many studies linking attachment security (see 'Attachment and attachment theory', Chapter 11) to the development of cognitive ability, with moderate correlations being typical. West, Mathews, and Kerns (2013) investigated the possible reasons for this. They assessed attachment type at 15, 24, and 36 months and IQ, using a battery of tests including a short version of the Wechsler in school years 3–4. They also looked at a range of possible mediating factors (ie, reasons why attachment might be linked to IQ). A correlation of 0.23 was found between IQ and attachment security at 24 months. The most important mediating variables by far were the quality of parental assistance and the child's cooperation during interactions. In other words, securely attached parents and children had better-quality interactions and these appeared to lead to better development of cognition.

The attachment–IQ link has important implications for clinical practice; for example, in fostering. Almas et al (2016) followed up 107 fostered children from the Romanian orphanages (see Chapter 11 for a discussion), testing their IQ at age 12. They found that those who achieved secure attachment early in life were more likely to have a normal range IQ by 12. This suggests that achieving attachment security should be a priority in psychologists and social workers working with fostering.

Intellectual stimulation and IQ

If we are interested in aspects of the environment that might impact on developing intelligence perhaps the most obvious place to start is the amount of stimulation in the child's environment. There is no shortage of evidence to show that **environmental insults** like childhood neglect, which leads directly to reduced intelligence, have a serious effect on intellectual development (Peterson, Joseph, and Feit, 2013). Most evidence for this comes from retrospective studies of adults exposed to neglect early in life; however, one study which stands out is an experiment in which babies were deliberately understimulated in a failed attempt to demonstrate that infant development was simply a process of maturation and unaffected by environment.

> **KEY IDEAS** environmental insults An environmental insult is a negative event that falls outside the normal range of experiences. Environmental insults are associated with serious negative effects on development.

RESEARCH IN FOCUS

Dennis, W. (1941). Infant development under conditions of restricted practice and of minimum social stimulation. *Genetic Psychology Monographs*, **23**, 143–91.

Aim: To investigate to what extent infant behaviour is innate and how much requires stimulation and social interaction. More specifically, to test the hypothesis that infant behaviour is innate and arises spontaneously without the need for intellectual or social stimulation.

Method: Husband and wife research team Wayne and Margaret Dennis brought home two 36-day-old female DZ twins. They agreed with the twins' struggling single mother that they would provide care in exchange for studying the children. The girls lived for the next 14 months in a nursery with no pictures and minimal furniture. The window afforded a view of sky and treetops only. The girls were positioned in such a way that they could not interact with each other, and the Dennises provided as little stimulation as possible when attending to their physical care. Adult-baby contact was kept to a maximum of two hours a day. After a year the Dennises increased their interaction with the twins, particularly in the fifteenth month after which they were returned to their mother. Tests of cognitive development suitable for the age were regularly administered.

Results: Until around 7 months intellectual development appeared to be progressing relatively normally, with scores in the low-average region. However, scores declined more seriously from 7 months on and at 14 months the girls were seriously behind. They were followed up after being reunited with their mother but during the follow-up period their development did not normalize.

Conclusion: The hypothesis was not supported; normal infant development did not take place in the absence of intellectual and social stimulation. In fact understimulation in infancy has serious negative effects on cognitive development.

>

>

MASTER YOUR METHODOLOGY

1 This study took place before the advent of ethical guidelines and ethics committees. It did not attract attention from the Dennis's colleagues. What breaches of ethical codes might it have led to if carried out later?

2 Why might the decision have been made to prevent the twins from lying together?

3 It appears likely that one of the twins experienced a brain injury prior to entering the Dennis's care as she displayed hemiplegia (paralysis down one side). How might this affect the validity of the findings?

The Dennis study is a shocking example of the risks of experimenting with young children without adequate ethical scrutiny. It also illustrates effectively why the evidence for the effects of early abuse on later development *must* be largely in the form of case studies. If you ever find yourself frustrated by the lack of a clear conclusion about development because of a case-study-only evidence base think back to this and allow yourself a shudder at the alternative.

So we have a good idea that environmental insults knock cognitive development off track and lead to reduced intelligence. A trickier question concerns whether we can intervene to *promote* intelligence. American *Headstart* programmes in which enriched nursery environments are provided to poor populations, often alongside nutritional supplements and other services like parenting training, have had mixed reviews. Encouragingly though, perhaps the most sophisticated analysis of long-term outcomes by Norwegian researchers de Haan and Leuven (2016) concludes that *Headstart* leads to significant gains in educational attainment and income by the participants' early 30s.

READ THIS

For this section we recommend up-to-date sources. You will see that none of these papers are neutral; all express a definite view of the origins of intelligence so you will need to read critically and make up your own mind:

Plomin, R. and Deary, I.J. (2015). Genetics and intelligence differences: Five special findings. *Molecular Psychiatry*, **20**(1), 98.

Plomin, R. and von Stumm, S. (2018). The new genetics of intelligence. *Nature Reviews Genetics*, **19**(3), 148.

Arslan, R. and Penke, L. (2015). Zeroing in on the genetics of intelligence. *Journal of Intelligence*, **3**(2), 41–5.

Almas, A.N., Degnan, K.A., Nelson, C.A., Zeanah, C.H., and Fox, N.A. (2016). IQ at age 12 following a history of institutional care: Findings from the Bucharest Early Intervention Project. *Developmental psychology*, **52**(11), 1858.

West, K.K., Mathews, B.L., and Kerns, K.A. (2013). Mother–child attachment and cognitive performance in middle childhood: An examination of mediating mechanisms. *Early Childhood Research Quarterly*, **28**(2), 259–70.

WHAT'S HOT? CAN 'BRAIN TRAINING' BOOST IQ?

The Internet is awash with adverts for 'brain training' programmes, predominantly digital apps that claim to improve our cognitive functioning. Some of these programmes target children, some young adults, and some older people, claiming to stave off age-related decline in cognitive functions like memory. Whether or not they claim to boost measured IQ they are talking about changing intelligence. Brain training is big business, and a source of temptation for all sorts of people, so what does psychology have to tell us?

There is no doubt that if you practise a mental task you will tend to get better at it over time—brain training is no exception and one reason for its success is that people see their improving scores and believe they are seeing a real cognitive gain. The tricky question is whether this gain generalizes to cognitive activities outside the brain-training tasks. There is some limited evidence for such gains. For example, Alloway et al compared two groups of children with learning difficulties, the experimental group training on *Jungle Memory Training*.

After eight weeks there was a significant difference on one of the Wechsler subscales; however, the effect was not replicated when the procedure was repeated with a larger sample (Alloway et al, 2013).

In another study, Zinke et al (2014) showed a significant difference in scores on an IQ test called Raven's Progressive Matrices in older people who undertook a training programme targeting working memory (see 'Working memory', Chapter 9, for a discussion). The results are shown in Figure 14.8.

Unfortunately, whilst the difference in test scores post-test is significantly higher in the training group as opposed to the control group, it is only slightly higher than in the same group pre-test. The difference is not statistically significant and so this study does not produce convincing results (Redick, 2015).

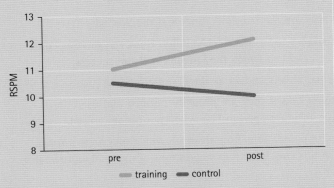

FIGURE 14.8 These results from Zinke et al (2014) appear to show significant benefits for working memory training; however, the pre–post test difference was not significant.
Adapted with permission from Zinke et al (2014). Working memory training and transfer in older adults: Effects of age, baseline performance, and training gains. *Developmental Psychology*, 1 Jan. Copyright © 2014, American Psychological Association.

> Simons et al (2016) reviewed the evidence for the success of brain training and concluded that there is very little evidence for brain-training effects generalizing to improved cognitive functioning in real-life situations. Absence of evidence is not the same as evidence of absence, however, and brain training may improve in time. Currently though—sadly—it is probably not going to do much for you.

IN REVIEW

DEFINING INTELLIGENCE

- Psychologists struggle to define intelligence, and all definitions are controversial.
- One popular definition of intelligence is the ability to adapt to one's environment. This captures the major factor in human success but fails on logical criteria.
- *g* or general intelligence describes a person's underlying general capacity to process complex information—to perform well on a wide variety of mental and even manual tasks. This approach to intelligence was proposed by Charles Spearman in the early twentieth century.
- *g* is measurable and has given rise to psychometric theories of intelligence and IQ testing.

IQ

- IQ or intelligence quotient is a measure of *g*. It is calculated by comparing the raw scores on IQ tests against population norms.
- IQ is normally distributed and the mean score for a population set at 100. Most people's IQ clusters around 100 with only around 2% scoring below 70 or above 130.
- Two commonly used IQ tests are the Stanford-Binet and the Wechsler Test.
- IQ tests are reliable and show good concurrent validity. However, there is considerable debate about the extent to which they predict real-life success.
- Scores on IQ tests are rising. This is known as the Flynn effect.
- IQ tests can be used without bias if they are properly normed and used on appropriate people. However, they are open to bias when not properly used.
- IQ tests used to test different populations from those on which they were normed are biased and their use in this way has led to suggestions of national and racial differences in intelligence.

ALTERNATIVE VIEWS OF INTELLIGENCE

- Gardner has suggested that *g* is not a useful concept and proposed multiple intelligences (MIs).
- The idea of MIs has resonated with teachers who see a range of abilities in their students and see the current system as valuing only a small selection of these.

- Sternberg has proposed a triarchic theory of intelligence, based on analytical, creative, and practical modes of intelligence.

- Triarchic theory has proved difficult to validate with psychometric tests; however, it is philosophically appealing and has important applications in education. Whether psychometric tests are appropriate to triarchic theory remains a debate.

- Carroll proposes a compromise between traditional g theories and the positions of Gardner and Sternberg.

- The three-stratum theory proposes three layers of intelligence, with g at the bottom, with a middle layer of eight broad abilities, and a top layer of 69 specific abilities.

- The critical psychology perspective sees intelligence as a social construct that has been used to justify racism and questions its existence as a real psychological entity.

THE ORIGINS OF INTELLIGENCE

- IQ is generally quite stable throughout the lifespan. This is consistent with a high level of heritability.

- Longitudinal studies suggest that genetic influence increases with age.

- Twin and adoption studies suggest that the heritability of IQ is around 80%. This is supported by neuroscience studies showing that the heritability of brain structure is similar.

- There are, however, good reasons not to accept the heritability figures produced by behavioural genetics. These range from the influence of assortative mating through the lack of clarity over the malleability of IQ to problems with the calculation of 'heritability'.

- There is a large body of research showing the effect of environmental variables such as attachment security and intellectual stimulation.

- Psychologists have successfully applied this understanding to boost IQ in vulnerable children.

- At present there is very little support, however, for the benefits of 'brain training' software.

TEST YOURSELF

1 There is a single, agreed definition of intelligence. True ❏ False ❏

2 Around two-thirds of people cluster closely around the mean IQ. True ❏ False ❏

3 Everyone with an IQ below 70 has intellectual disability disorder. True ❏ False ❏

4 Infants with secure attachments are more likely to develop high IQ than others. True ❏ False ❏

5 Which of the following is not an IQ test?

   a) The Stanford-Binet

   b) The Wechsler

   c) Spearman's Rho

   d) Raven's progressive matrices

6 What does IQ stand for?

a) Intelligence quality

b) Intelligence quotient

c) Intelligence quantity

d) Intelligence quiz score

7 What IQ would you have to have to be considered gifted?

a) 100

b) 120

c) 130

d) 150

8 Explain what is meant by bias in the use of IQ tests normed in one culture to test people from other cultures.

9 Explain one reason why we might believe that intelligence is largely inherited and one reason to question the strength of this evidence.

10 Explain what is meant by the idea of intelligence as a social construct.

 Visit the online resources that accompany this book: www.oup.com/uk/jarvis-okami1e

PERSONALITY

LEARNING OUTCOMES

By the end of this chapter you should be able to:

- Explain what is meant by personality and how a technical definition used by psychologists differs from everyday casual use of the term
- Appreciate the complexity of Freud's ideas of personality, including the structural model of the mind, stages of psychosexual development, and dynamic processes of the mind
- Outline and evaluate behaviourist and humanistic approaches to understanding personality
- Assess research into the importance of self-esteem in personality and psychological functioning
- Discuss trait theories including Eysenck's two-factor theory and Costa and McCrae's five-factor theory with reference to their links to social-emotional and occupational functioning
- Analyse the relative importance of personality and situation as determinants of behaviour and understand how the concept of trait-situation behaviour profiles helps reconcile the issue
- Assess the role of nature and nurture in the development of personality with particular reference to elements of the non-shared environment including parenting, peer influence, and random events
- Evaluate projective and objective personality tests with particular regard to their reliability and validity
- Analyse the tension between research findings indicating stability and change in personality traits across the lifespan
- Appreciate other approaches to understanding personality change including characteristic adaptations and self-narratives

Visualize for a moment any group of people with whom you spend a reasonable amount of time. They might be your friendship group or your psychology seminar group. They are clearly all individuals, but what *makes* them individual? Some will be livelier and more confident than others. Some will be serious and others happy-go-lucky. Some will be lazy and others conscientious (Figure 15.1).

FIGURE 15.1 Serious, happy-go-lucky, lazy, and conscientious: all characteristics and behaviour patterns that define us as individuals.

Sources: serious: m-imagephotography/Shutterstock.com; happy-go-lucky: Oxford University Press; lazy: photomak/Shutterstock.com; conscientious: fizkes/Shutterstock.com.

In this chapter we will explore personality—the characteristics and behaviour patterns that define us as individuals. What are we like? How did we get to be that way? Will we always stay much the same as we are now, or can we change? Do the situations in which we find ourselves determine our behaviour, or is our behaviour mostly determined by stable characteristics, either innate or acquired over time? Such questions strike to the core of each person's sense of themselves as an individual person.

WHAT IS PERSONALITY?

Ajani is a little slow, but she has a great personality.

Max is a funny dude—he has a lot of personality.

Have you ever heard someone spoken of in these ways? The term *personality* is sometimes used to describe appealing or attractive aspects of the way a person behaves. In this casual use of the term, personality is something that some of us have a lot of and some of us lack. Another casual use suggests that a person might possess the great version of personality or the terrible version.

To psychologists, however, no one has any *more* personality than anyone else, and no one's personality is *better* than anyone else's. This is not just because psychologists are fair-minded, politically correct people who don't want to leave anyone out. It is because the term *personality* has a technical meaning quite different from the casual ones just described. Unfortunately, however, personality psychologists are not in agreement as to the precise nature of this technical definition. *Personality* is an abstract concept whose definition is not universally agreed upon; however, psychologists wish to measure and study it as though it were a concrete reality.

The Characteristics of Personality

To some extent we share our behaviours with all other humans, yet we also have a unique combination of characteristics. We are also guided in our behaviour by our perceptions of what we are like and so how we should behave—what psychologists call self-narratives.

However, knowing our species-typical and distinctive characteristics and self-narratives is not enough to understand personality: we also need to understand that these qualities are *organized, integrated*, and *relatively enduring*. What does this mean?

- *Organized* means that a person's personality forms a coherent picture that might be described in words. However, in describing this coherent picture, you may need to do more than use terms that denote characteristics ('She's a kind person')—you may also need to make reference to situational factors. A person may behave one way in one context, but another way in another context ('She's very kind with children, but hard on her employees').

- *Integrated* means that the various aspects of personality are related to—and work with—one another. For example, someone who is gentle is probably also kind—someone who was physically gentle but unkind to others would leave themselves open to aggression so it makes no sense to adopt this combination of behaviours. People are not merely a random collection of traits, mental and behavioural tendencies, and self-narratives that may be described by adjectives and references to situations. Aspects of personality form a *whole* person.

- *Relatively enduring* means that personality is fairly constant over extended periods of time. Most people are not kind and outgoing six months out of the year, but hostile and shy the next six. Although certain aspects of personality are subject to change, as we shall see, most aspects are remarkably stable.

Thus, our full, workable definition of personality might be stated in this way: *personality consists of variations on common human mental and behavioural characteristics, traits, characteristic adaptations, and self-narratives. These factors are organized, integrated, and relatively enduring.*

THE 'GRAND THEORIES' OF PERSONALITY

The field of personality psychology was once dominated by what are usually termed the **grand theories** (Cervone and Shoda, 1999). The word *grand* in this context does not necessarily mean 'great', it simply means 'big'. These were theories developed by pioneers of personality psychology who worked primarily during the first 60 or 70 years of the twentieth century when *behaviourism, psychoanalysis*, and *humanistic psychology* were the dominant approaches to psychology, as we described in Chapter 2.

> **KEY IDEAS** grand theories of personality **'Grand theories'** is the term given to describe theories of personality, primarily developed during the early to mid-twentieth century, whose creators wished to address all of the important areas in the study of personality. The most prominent grand theories were those developed by psychoanalysts, behaviourists, and humanistic psychologists.

These early personality psychologists wanted their theories to address large issues in the study of personality—in certain cases, they wanted their theories to explain virtually everything there was to explain about human personality. The 'grand theorists' were usually well-read, sophisticated men and women, often steeped in philosophy as well as psychology. They each had numerous disciples, and they all were strongly influential. Although their theories are far less influential than they once were, they continue to have adherents, and certain of their insights have been incorporated into more modern theorizing about psychology. I'll begin with the work of the most influential psychologist in modern history, Sigmund Freud (1856–1939).

Freud's Psychoanalytic Theory

The first of the grand theorists is surely the most 'grand'—Sigmund Freud (Figure 15.2). As briefly discussed in Chapter 2, Freud's influence on Western **culture** has been massive, and this aspect of his influence shows no particular signs of abating, even as the presence of Freudian theory in the field of psychology has diminished quite substantially over the past several decades, having endured widespread—often quite severe—criticism (Crews, 2007).

Freud termed his work as a whole *psychoanalysis*, because it involved the analysis of conflicts which occurred within a person's own mind, or *psyche*—conflicts that were often played out below the person's level of awareness in that region of the mind Freud referred to as the unconscious.

Psychoanalysis includes a psychotherapeutic technique which we describe in Chapter 19; for now we are concerned with the theoretical aspect. Psychoanalytic theory is enormously complex—perhaps the most complex in the history of psychology. However, for our purposes, Freud's theory of personality may be divided into three central components: a **structural model of the mind**, a theory of **psychosexual development**, and theories of **dynamic processes**.

The Structural Model of the Mind

By the early 1920s, Freud (1923/1962) had come to believe that the mind consisted of a number of integrated processes or metaphorical 'structures' that eventually were called **id** ('it'), **ego** ('I'), and **superego** ('above me'). The id, ego, and superego are not organic structures—that is, Freud didn't suggest that they resided in some particular area of the brain. Instead, they are metaphors for qualities possessed by the human mind, with unknown neural origins in the brain.

According to Freud, in the beginning of human life there is nothing but id, also termed the *primary process*. The word 'id' is Latin for 'it' as in 'it just came over me'. This was intended to capture the sense of being influenced by an impulse to behave irrationally. Id functions primarily at the level of the unconscious mind and is driven by the **pleasure principle**: to seek pleasure and avoid unpleasure, in other words pain or discomfort. Id is expressed in dreams, in superstition, in uncontrolled aggressive or immoral behaviour, and in satisfaction of basic drives such as sex, hunger, and thirst. Although we are not consciously aware of our id it exerts a constant influence on us.

Just as id functions according to the pleasure principle, ego, the *secondary process*, functions according to the **reality principle**. Ego—partly conscious, partly unconscious—allows the person to survive, decision-making and mediating between the demands of the real world and the blind strivings of the id. It is primarily

> **KEY IDEAS** structural model, stages of psychosexual development, and dynamic processes Freud's **structural model** of personality encompasses the instinctive *id*, the logical *ego*, and the moral *superego*. To Freud these appear at different **stages of psychosexual development**. In the oral stage the baby operates on instinct and so is entirely id. In the anal stage the ego appears and in the phallic stage the superego forms. To Freud there are dynamic processes between elements of the mind; for example, conflict between the instinctive id and the moral superego.

FIGURE 15.2 Sigmund Freud (1856–1939). Freud's influence on modern Western culture is incalculable, but his influence on psychology has waned.
Source: World History Archive/Alamy Stock Photo.

concerned with assuring the safety and functioning of the individual. The ego allows the individual to delay striving for pleasure if delaying gratification will ultimately be beneficial. If reality demands that wishes from the id not be expressed, the ego is instrumental in controlling or *repressing* these id instincts—that is, keeping them unconscious. It includes what we sometimes call the existential self, the 'I' as opposed to the 'me'. This is the conscious and self-aware part of the self.

The ego thus serves both the demands of reality and the strivings of the id. However it has a third master as well: superego. Superego represents the conscience. It watches the work of ego and passes judgement on it. The term means 'above me' and is intended to capture the sense of being watched over from a morally higher position. Superego punishes the psyche with guilt or shame when it perceives that wrong has been done, and points the individual in the direction of ideal behaviour. Figure 15.3 presents a diagram of Freud's structural model of the mind.

THINKING CRITICALLY

Freud's structural model of personality was intended as a phenomenological account of the human experience of being pulled in different directions by logic, instinct, and morality (phenomenology is the branch of philosophy devoted to human experience). However, modern neuroscience has been able to link particular brain regions to pleasure seeking, logical thought, and inhibitory processes. Given that this was probably never Freud's aim, should we take such research as validating Freud's theory? HINT: there isn't a right answer to this, it's a matter of perspective—what is yours? Your answer might, for example, depend on whether you think phenomenology should be part of scientific psychology.

Psychosexual Development

Freud proposed that human beings are born with a fund of mental energy which he termed **libido** or life-force, which is erotic in nature. Although libido has a sexual foundation, its effects are felt far beyond simple sexual experience. Consider a small child dropped off for the first time at a **day care** centre. She may cry or just sit in a corner, refusing to play or eat. In Freud's view, this in part because a portion of the child's flow of libidinal energy has become 'attached' (a process termed *cathexis*) to the child's mental image of her mother, who has metaphorically taken the energy away with her. Since one's supply of libido is limited, the loss of some of this energy may result in lessened vitality or will to participate in life. According to this idea, the little girl is crying because, in a real sense, a part of her was taken away when the mother departed.

Understanding libido is essential to understanding what Freud referred to as the **stages of psychosexual development**, summarized in Table 15.1. All human beings, according to Freud, experience an inevitable progression through developmental periods in childhood, each of which represents a stage in psychological growth related to sexual life. If the stages are not navigated properly, **neurosis** may result in adulthood—crippling emotional illness and distortion of personality.

During each psychosexual stage, the libidinal energy of the infant or toddler is focused on a different, specific part of his or her body that is particularly sensitive to pleasurable stimulation. These sensitive body locations are referred to as erogenous zones (primarily the mouth, anus, and genitals). The stages of psychosexual development are divided as follows.

> **KEY IDEAS** id The **id** is that part of Freud's structural model which represents the irrational portion of the mind which lacks moral restraint or a conception of right and wrong, and cares only for satisfaction of its own cravings—seeking pleasure and avoiding unpleasure (such as pain) (the **pleasure principle**). The id operates primarily at the level of the unconscious mind and can be expressed in dreams, uncontrolled behaviour, and satisfaction of basic drives.

> **KEY IDEAS** ego **Ego**, also termed the secondary process, is the aspect of Freud's structural model which represents that part of the mind which operates according to the **reality principle**. Partly conscious, partly unconscious, the ego mediates between the demands of the real world, the blind strivings of the id, and the judgements of the superego. The ego is partly conscious, hence it includes the existential self.

> **KEY IDEAS** superego According to Freud's structural model, the **superego** represents the individual's conscience, and is the origin of human morality. The superego observes the work of the ego and passes judgement on it—punishing the psyche with guilt or shame for wrongdoing, and pointing in the direction of ideal behaviour. Although Freud never used the term himself, the superego's equivalent to pleasure and reality principles would be the morality principle.

> **KEY IDEAS** libido Freud proposed that human beings are born with a limited fund of psychic 'energy', or life force, which he termed **libido**. This life force has an erotic foundation, although its effects need not be explicitly sexual in nature nor bear only upon sexual life.

> **KEY IDEAS** stages of psychosexual development Freud believed that children pass through five developmental **stages of psychosexual development**. For healthy personality to develop, the child must successfully complete the tasks and resolve the conflicts which typically occur at each stage. Fixation at any particular stage may result in adult neurosis or distortion of personality. The stages are termed oral, anal, phallic (Oedipal), latency, and genital.

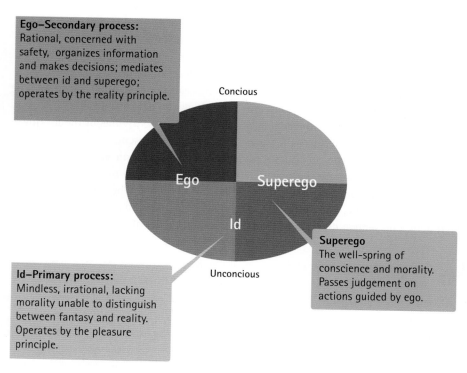

Ego–Secondary process: Rational, concerned with safety, organizes information and makes decisions; mediates between id and superego; operates by the reality principle.

Id–Primary process: Mindless, irrational, lacking morality unable to distinguish between fantasy and reality. Operates by the pleasure principle.

Superego The well-spring of conscience and morality. Passes judgement on actions guided by ego.

FIGURE 15.3 **Freud's structural model of the mind. Although many attempts have been made to create diagrams based on Freud's structural model of the mind, none are fully valid because Freud's descriptions of id, ego, and superego are not based on a map-like idea.** *Source:* Adapted from LeVay and Valente, 2002, pp 165, 187–8.

Stage one: the oral stage (birth–approximately 18 months)

Freud believed that the infant's incessant focus on the mouth as a mode of exploration during early life has an aspect of erotic gratification associated with it. However, he specified that the infant's oral eroticism is a *pregenital* sexuality, clearly devoid of the kinds of sexual emotions and meanings attributed to erotic behaviour by adults.

A degree of libido is always fixated on the erogenous zone corresponding to each **developmental stage**. This is important in normative development. However, if the developmental arc of the oral stage is somehow disturbed—if under-satisfaction or over-satisfaction of oral impulses occurs (eg, too much or too little breastfeeding), or if there is some type of psychological trauma at this stage—then the child's libidinal energy may become overly fixated and development will be **arrested**.

For example, whilst some oral fixation is essential for the person to develop the ability to have close, trusting, and mutually dependent relationships, arrest at the early part of the oral stage may result in the person developing an *oral-receptive personality* type. The oral-receptive personality is overly dependent on others; he or she likes to eat, smoke, drink, or use drugs; and tends to be a good listener—sometimes to the point of gullibility—hence the term 'sucker'. Fixation at later portions of the oral stage may result in an *oral-sadistic* personality type. Such people are sarcastic, cynical, and use words in a 'biting' manner.

Stage two: the anal stage (approximately 18 months–3)

As infants become toddlers and acquire more control over their world, according to Freud they enter the anal stage, characterized by the acquisition of new skills such as language and bowel control. If fixation occurs in the early portion of the anal stage, when the anus is the primary erogenous zone and the greatest pleasure is derived from expelling faeces, the child may grow up with an *anal-expulsive* personality. Such people care little for rules, may be disorderly or sloppy in their personal habits, and are prone to highly emotional outbursts. However, they also tend towards generosity (symbolically giving away their beloved faeces to others!).

In contrast, if fixation occurs at the later portion of the anal stage, when the greatest pleasure is being derived from retaining faeces to master bowel control, the *anal-retentive* personality type may develop. Anal-retentive types are orderly, preoccupied with rules, stingy, and stubborn.

Stage three: the phallic (Oedipal) stage (approximately 3 or 4–5 or 6)

Freud termed this stage 'phallic' because the boy child supposedly is preoccupied with his penis and the girl child with her *lack* of penis—a problem known as *penis envy*. It is during this critical phallic stage that the *Oedipus complex* arises and must be resolved for healthy personality development to occur. The **Oedipus complex** is Freud's term for his notion that children of this age experience a powerful desire to erotically possess the other-sex parent and remove the same-sex parent, who is a rival of sorts. Although interpretations vary, Freud was probably not suggesting that the child experienced sexual or murderous desires in the way some people do as adults (Jarvis, 2004).

Freud proposed that because each boy experiences jealousy towards the father and a wish for his removal, he fears the father's rage and retaliation. Specifically, the boy fears that he might be castrated by his father (castration is the removal of the testicles and/or penis). At this point, the boy—no longer fighting the father—learns to internalize the image of the father by *identifying* with him. In this way he gets to possess the mother indirectly. Critically, the father is a symbol of moral authority, and in identifying with his father and resolving the Oedipus complex the boy develops a superego.

The situation of the girl child is quite different. The girl's story begins similarly, with an 'erotic' attachment to the mother who is her primary love object. However, the girl comes to perceive her genitals as inferior to those of the male, whose penis she envies. Because the poor girl realizes that both she and her mother lack this important phallic attribute and the male authority which it symbolizes, she comes to transfer her erotic longings to her father, whom she hopes will supply her with the penis she lacks—or its substitute in the form of a baby. This is the female Oedipus complex, sometimes called the Electra complex although not by Freud.

In the absence of castration threat, the girl's motivation to resolve this problem is much less powerful than the boy's. She realizes that female qualities possessed by her mother are appealing to her father, and this begins her identification with her same-sex parent.

> **KEY IDEAS** Oedipus complex Freud's belief that children in the phallic stage (age 3 or 4 through to age 5 or 6) experience powerful erotic desires for the opposite-sex parent, while wishing to eliminate the same-sex parent who is perceived as a rival. According to Freud, the Oedipus complex arises and is resolved differently for boys and girls, with girls experiencing an incomplete resolution. According to Freud, a successful resolution of the Oedipus complex results in the development of an adequate superego.

THINKING CREATIVELY

A common criticism of Freud's ideas is the difficulty inherent in testing his ideas and their correspondingly small and inconsistent evidence base. How could you go about testing whether an unresolved Oedipus complex affects later development? Think first about what Freud would predict about the future of individuals with different experiences of the phallic stage and/or different qualities of Oedipal resolution. How could you define and measure suitable dependent and independent variables? What methodology would you use?

Later stages of development: latency and genital

> **KEY IDEAS** gonadarche
> The maturation of the sexual
> organs during puberty.

Stage four, or latency, lasts approximately from age 6 until the onset of puberty. During the latency stage, the child's sexual interests supposedly lessen in urgency as same-sex friendships assume a position of greater importance in the child's life. Stage five, or the genital stage, lasts from **gonadarche** in early **adolescence** through adulthood. In the genital stage, sex resumes its place of importance as libidinal energy is focused once again upon the genitals—this time as an expression of adult sexuality.

Dynamic Processes of the Mind

Dynamics as Freud used the term implies the idea of constant motion, energy, and conflict between component parts of the mind. His view of the mind is therefore a dynamic view because the id, ego, and superego are constantly interacting, in motion, and in conflict. Various mental processes are pressed into service by the mind in its efforts to navigate and resolve the conflicts with which it is continuously faced.

Among the most prominent of these dynamic processes are dreams. Freud believed that dreams are expressions of unconscious sexual or aggressive wishes and conflicts, expressed in symbolic form. Analysis of the latent (hidden) meanings of dreams was to Freud an important part of psychoanalysis as a therapy.

TABLE 15.1 Freud's stages of psychosocial development

Stage	Ages	Erogenous zone	Personality type if fixated
Oral	Birth–18 months	Lips, tongue, gums	Oral receptive (dependent; likes to eat, drink, and smoke; good listener but tends towards gullibility) Oral sadistic (sarcastic, cynical, 'biting' with words)
Anal	18 months through to age 3	Anus	Anal expulsive (generous, disregard for rules or order, may be sloppy and slovenly) Anal retentive (orderly, stingy, stubborn, preoccupied with rules)
Phallic (Oedipal)	Age 3 through to 5 or 6	Genitals	Failure to resolve Oedipus complex results in various neuroses
Latency	Age 6 to puberty	None	Not applicable
Genital	Puberty	Genitals	Not applicable

Ego defence mechanisms

Other dynamic processes of the mind include the **ego defence mechanisms**. These mechanisms are used by the ego to keep threatening or anxiety-provoking material from reaching awareness. Although Freud did discuss a few types of ego defences—primarily **repression**, where an unacceptable wish, thought, or memory is removed from conscious awareness—this idea was actually developed fully by his daughter, Anna Freud (1936). Table 15.2 lists some of the most important of the ego defences with a description of each.

THINKING PRACTICALLY

Match the following relationship scenarios to these defence mechanisms: displacement, sublimation, reaction.

1 A nun who believes she has suffered particularly bad fortune turns against her religion.

2 A woman who has recently experienced a painful relationship break-up finds herself in an intense rebound relationship.

3 An athlete falls in love with someone unattainable and deals with the resulting difficult feelings by training particularly hard.

❯ KEY IDEAS ego defence mechanisms and repression These are a group of psychological mechanisms described in part by Sigmund Freud but primarily by his daughter, Anna Freud. The ego uses these mechanisms to keep threatening material from reaching awareness. The defence mechanisms include repression, denial, displacement, projection, reaction formation, sublimation, and undoing. **Repression** is a particularly important and perhaps the most basic ego defence mechanism identified by Freud, where an unacceptable wish, thought, or impulse is removed from conscious awareness.

TABLE 15.2 Important ego defence mechanisms as described by Anna Freud (1936)

Defence mechanism	Description	Example
1. Denial	When events or realities that are threatening to the ego are ignored.	Parents whose son has recently died refuse to change anything in his room, keeping it exactly as it was when their child was alive.
2. Displacement	When a sexual or aggressive impulse is redirected from the actual (threatening) target to another, less threatening target.	A man who works in a shop, and is bullied by his boss throughout the day, comes home and yells at his wife instead of expressing rage to the boss.
3. Projection	When one's own unacceptable wishes or impulses are attributed to the person who was the object of the unacceptable wish or impulse.	A rowing couple are shouting at each other: 'Don't you shout at me!'
4. Reaction	When an unacceptable wish or impulse is transformed into an exaggerated version of its opposite.	A gay man adopts a homophobic attitude in response to his discomfort with his real feelings.
5. Repression	Removal from conscious awareness or memory of an unacceptable wish or impulse. Repression plays a role in most of the other defence mechanisms.	A teenager has no memory of a childhood sexual assault.
6. Sublimation	When an unacceptable wish or impulse is 'translated' into a socially acceptable behaviour.	A singer-songwriter channels their unhappiness at the end of a relationship into writing a sad song.

Criticisms of Freud

No theory in the history of psychology has generated so much controversy as Freudian psychoanalysis. This strong feeling is consistent with the extent of Freud's influence, his focus on highly emotive and taboo subjects—and that they make so many grand claims. Indeed, despite Freud's pervasive influence, the man and his theories have been under siege in many quarters (Farrell, 1996; Crews, 2007).

Critics charge that the theoretical map of the human mind devised by Freud is unsupported by conventional scientific evidence (Eysenck and Wilson, 1973). However, some of these valid criticisms have become muddled with those put forward in popular literature in which authors from other disciplines, like history, have attacked Freud's character and motives, sometimes on the basis of quite poor evidence. Our task in evaluating Freud's methods and ideas from the perspective of scientific psychology is to identify valid criticisms and not be swayed by hyperbole.

So how does Freudian psychoanalysis really fare as a theory? Well, it is highly comprehensive. In addition some of Freud's concepts—such as the Oedipus complex and penis envy—are counterintuitive to say the least. To put this criticism into context, some ideas fit very well with ordinary experience and are clearly insightful—for example, the notion that a person may displace their anger from an unacceptable target (eg, the boss) to a more 'acceptable' one (the dog) without being aware of having done so. In addition, from a scientific perspective whether something makes intuitive sense is much less important than its evidence base.

 THINKING CRITICALLY

Freud's evidence base consisted almost entirely of clinical case studies. One of the problems with his approach is the degree of interpretation involved in linking the details of his cases to his theoretical ideas. Consider the following two of Freud's classic cases.

1 **Anna O (Breuer and Freud, 1896):** Anna O was a 21-year-old middle-class woman from a well-off family with a history of mental disorder. Her symptoms developed when she was nursing her father in the early stages of a terminal illness. Her symptoms included weakness, anaemia, and loss of appetite. She was left bed-ridden, at which point she suffered a sequence of symptoms including headaches, deafness, paralysis, and loss of sensation in the limbs. Her doctor, Breuer, had her treated in a country hospital. Breuer allowed Anna to speak at length and noted that she sometimes linked her symptoms to life events, upon which that symptom would worsen then lessen in severity. For example, she discussed her hearing difficulty in relation to the shame of being caught as a child listening to her parents having sex. At this point she became completely deaf, but then the symptom disappeared altogether. Breuer and Freud believed that when Anna spoke of her symptoms she achieved catharsis, the expression of pent-up mental energy.

2 **The Wolf Man (Freud, 1918):** The Wolf Man was a 23-year-old Russian aristocrat who had suffered ill health following a bout of gonorrhoea. He became extremely reliant on carers, to the extent of being unable to have a bowel movement without an enema. Freud focused on a dream the Wolf Man reported in which he saw a number of white wolves sitting in a tree outside his bedroom window and looking at him. Freud interpreted this dream as linking to the trauma of an event in which, as an 18-month-old, he saw his parents having sex from behind (ie, 'doggy'-style'). Freud believed that this interpretation marked the beginning of the Wolf Man's return to health.

Consider the following:

1 Do clinical case studies like these form a good basis for a theory of personality? Explain your reasoning.

❯

The Anna O and Wolf Man cases illustrate more than one weakness in Freud's approach. Often, he proposed convoluted, complex explanations where a simple, ordinary one will do. When more than one plausible explanation exists for some phenomenon, scientists like to choose the simpler of the explanations. This is because simpler explanations contain fewer assumptions that might be incorrect—in a sense, they contain fewer 'parts' that can 'go wrong'. This is known as the principle of **parsimony**, or *Occam's razor*. Psychoanalysis consistently violates parsimony.

Furthermore, psychoanalysis is often unnecessarily laden with jargon that is mysterious even to professional psychologists. Because psychoanalytic principles and statements may be interpreted in so many ways, the theory is, for the most part, impossible to *disprove*. According to mainstream scientific philosophy, one criterion for a sound scientific theory is that it specifies the conditions under which it can be disproved, or falsified (Popper, 1962). Psychoanalysis rarely allows for falsification. There is sometimes an 'Alice in Wonderland' quality to psychoanalysis, where things can mean anything that one wants them to mean. This can be frustrating to those trained in methods of psychological science.

> **KEY IDEAS** parsimony The scientific principle that if there is more than one competing explanation for a phenomenon, scientists favour the simpler explanation. This is because simpler explanations contain fewer assumptions that might be incorrect. The principle of parsimony is also known as Occam's razor.

Evidence for Freud's Ideas

We have already said that some of Freud's ideas are unnecessarily complex and very difficult to test scientifically. However, it is important to be clear about what is and is not a fair criticism. Yes, Freud's ideas tend to be tricky to investigate with scientific rigour. Yes, there are some ideas for which there is a lack of supporting evidence—or mixed evidence, indicating an ongoing debate. It is not, however, correct to say that Freud's ideas have been disproved, nor that they have no supporting evidence.

Substantial support exists for more general observations initiated by Freud—for example, that early childhood experiences can affect the development of personality or that a person may feel contradictory emotions towards another person simultaneously, such as love and hate (Westen, 1998). Perhaps Freud's most basic assumption that we are influenced by unconscious sexual pleasure-seeking and unpleasure avoidance has been supported in an ingenious study by Motley (1985). We can consider this study in detail in our *Research in focus* feature.

RESEARCH IN FOCUS

Motley, M.T. (1985). Slips of the tongue. *Scientific American*, **253**, 116–27.

Aim: To test the existence of Freud's unconscious motives of sexual pleasure-seeking and pain-avoidance by recording slips of the tongue under conditions of pain-threat and sexual anxiety. The hypotheses were tested that more 'Freudian slips' would be sexual nature in the sexual condition and more would be pain-related in the pain-threat condition.

⟩

Method: The experiment was carried out under laboratory conditions. Male participants were given the task of reading word-pairs from a screen. Some of these were designed so that if transposed they would be electric shock-related (eg, 'worst cottage', transposed to 'cursed wattage'). Others were sexual when transposed (eg, 'shared boulders', which transposes to 'bared shoulders'). The dependent variables were the number of transposition errors in which phonemes from the sexual and shock-related word-pairs were swapped. In a control condition there was no cuing of particular transposition errors. In the pain-threat condition, participants were told that at some point in the procedure they would receive a painful electric shock. In the sexual anxiety condition the procedure was administered by a conventionally attractive and provocatively dressed woman.

Results: In the control condition 20% of word-pairs had transpositions, with no difference in the frequency of shock-related and sexual transpositions. In the sexual anxiety condition 35% of sex-related word-pairs were transposed as opposed to 17% of shock-related pairs. In the pain-threat condition transpositions occurred in 33% of shock-related word-pairs and 17% of sexual word-pairs.

Conclusion: Results were consistent with Freudian theory. Slips of the tongue appear to be related to sexuality and pain-avoidance.

MASTER YOUR METHODOLOGY

1 This is a good example of a laboratory experiment. Explain what constitutes a laboratory experiment and why it was important to conduct this experiment under controlled conditions.

2 Would you have carried out an experiment of this nature using a within-groups or a between-groups design? Explain your answer.

3 Suggest some potential confounds that psychologists should control for in experiments of this kind.

 THINKING CRITICALLY

Look back to our critical thinking toolkit (Chapter 1). What strengths and weaknesses can you see in relation to this study?

Empirical research has supported certain of the defence mechanisms identified by Freud and his daughter Anna and described in Table 15.2 (Baumeister, Dale, and Sommer, 1998). Freud's notion that traumatic memories are frequently repressed is an example of an ongoing (and fierce!) debate. The evidence for and against is examined in Chapter 9, which deals with memory. Moderate support does exist for some of Freud's other ideas; for example, the existence of personality types that Freud described using the terms 'anal' and 'oral' (Fisher and Greenberg, 1996).

Freud's Influence in Later Psychology

Although few contemporary academic psychologists would align themselves with Freud's vision of the human mind taken as a whole, some of his ideas live on in some key theories and areas of research. For example, in Chapter 11 we introduced

Bowlby's attachment theory. Although Bowlby is best known for introducing evolutionary principles to child psychology, he was a psychoanalyst by training and his ideas about the importance of infant experience and family life owed a lot to Freud. Whilst Bowlby focused on developing Freud's ideas about infancy, Erik Erikson (see Chapter 13) was extending Freud's notion of the developing personality through the entire lifespan.

In **applied psychology**, Freud's ideas still have significant pockets of influence; for example, in trauma-focused explanations for mental disorder and in psychodynamic therapies. Meanwhile, outside **academic psychology**, psychoanalysis still exists as an independent tradition, largely focused on the delivery of intensive and long-term psychotherapies (see Jarvis, 2004). Even some of the newest branches of psychological practice such as coaching psychology, the unconscious influences on current choices and anxieties, may be a focus of attention (Sandler, 2011).

READ THIS

It is easy to dismiss Freud's ideas about personality development as far-fetched and unpalatable. However, think back to our academic gold standards: to read the original and some up-to-date literature. There is an awful lot of rubbish written about Freud, so my (Matt's) advice is much about where *not* to look for further information. Stick to either the original material or reviews written by psychologists or psychoanalysts and avoid popular literature sources written by those from other disciplines. Freud wrote an intimidating volume of material, but for purposes of this chapter you might like to start with these:

Freud, S. (1900). *The Interpretation of Dreams.* London: Hogarth Press.

Freud, S. (1905). *Three Essays on Sexuality.* London: Hogarth Press.

Freud, S. (1914). *The Psychopathology of Everyday Life.* London: Hogarth Press.

Freud, S. (1923). *The Ego and the Id.* London: Hogarth Press.

For a summary and review of evidence, see also:

Fisher, S. and Greenberg, R.P. (1996). *Freud Scientifically Reappraised: Testing the Theories and Therapy.* New York: John Wiley and Sons.

Jarvis, M. (2004). *Psychodynamic Psychology: Classical Theory and Contemporary Research.* London: Thomson.

You probably won't read Freud's whole collection but it is worth dipping into, perhaps with the help of a 'reader' like Peter Gay's (*The Freud Reader*). Also, try an electronic search or two for reviews of the evidence for and against Freud, and read these with critical eyes. Your overall impression of Freud may not change but your understanding will become more nuanced.

THE BEHAVIOURISTS: PERSONALITY AS LEARNED THROUGH EXPERIENCE

The essence of behaviourism is learning, a topic to which we have devoted an entire chapter (Chapter 7). Thus, we will consider behaviourist approaches to personality only very briefly here. Although the behaviourists were not primarily interested in personality development, in contrast with the psychoanalysts, strict behaviourist theorists such as John B. Watson and B.F. Skinner had much to say about personality, treating it as they would any other psychological variable: by analysing behaviour according to principles of learning. Behaviours acquired through association between stimuli (classical conditioning) or experiences of reinforcement and punishment (operant conditioning) become both the definition and expression of each person's personality.

As a hypothetical example, consider a child whose mother is overly anxious about illness. At the slightest sign of a minor symptom in her son she grows concerned, paying the child an inordinate amount of attention he does not otherwise receive from her. She keeps him home from school at a mere sign of a sniffle, and he gets to do whatever he wants; play video games, drink Coca-Cola, and spend lots of time with his mother. In short, he receives a high degree of **positive reinforcement** (reward, see Chapter 7) for being sick. According to the behaviourist view, such treatment might be instrumental in shaping an adult personality that includes excessive preoccupation with matters of health and disease, constant experience of symptoms (*hypochondria*), and generalized anxiety.

Experiences of reinforcement and punishment undoubtedly exert important effects on the developing personality. However, the behaviourists' insistence that principles of learning could explain virtually all aspects of personality—or at least those aspects of personality that could be studied scientifically—lost favour during the 1960s and 1970s. During these years, cognitive and evolutionary theories of psychology began to emerge along with an extremely popular new force in psychology—humanistic psychology.

THINKING CRITICALLY

Cognitive psychology is concerned with the internal processes of the mind, whilst evolutionary psychology is concerned with the ways our evolutionary past has shaped human psychology. What ideas from each of these perspectives might have contributed to the decline in the popularity of the behaviourist view? You might like to refresh your knowledge of these perspectives using Chapters 2 and 5.

FIGURE 15.4 **Carl Rogers** (1902–87).

Source: Michael Rougier/Getty Images.

THE HUMANISTIC PSYCHOLOGY PERSPECTIVE

The founders of humanistic psychology had faith in human nature. They were unashamedly optimistic, and in this sense they are the 'spiritual forefathers and foremothers' of the more recent movement in *positive psychology*, which focuses upon human strengths rather than human weaknesses, failings, and disorders (Seligman, Linley, and Joseph, 2004). According to humanistic psychologists such as Carl Rogers (Figure 15.4) and Abraham Maslow, human beings are reasoning creatures, born with free will and innate strivings for positive goals. The humanistic psychologists believed that people face problems in a generally rational manner and try to make good decisions that will benefit themselves and others. This is in sharp contrast to Freudian psychoanalysts, who, with their melodramatic scenarios of good and evil fighting it out on the battlefield of the unconscious, held a distinctly pessimistic view of the human condition.

As briefly discussed in Chapter 2, Rogers is probably the person most often associated with personality from a humanistic psychology perspective. In certain respects Rogers, who began his career as a divinity student, was carrying forward the optimistic conception of human nature popularized by the nineteenth-century Romantic philosopher Jean-Jacques Rousseau. Like Rousseau, Rogers believed that human beings are born basically good; he maintained that each of us is designed to develop into a competent, fulfilled, and compassionate human being—what he called a fully functioning person—unless we lack a growth-promoting environment. Such an environment is one that enables each individual to develop a healthy self-concept—an intrinsic evaluation of the quality of his or her unique existence in the world. Self-concept answers the questions, 'Who and what am I really? How should my unique existence be evaluated?' For a person to develop a healthy self-concept, the environment must fulfil four interrelated conditions: **accurate empathy, congruence, unconditional positive regard,** and **positive self-regard.**

By accurate empathy, Rogers meant that those around a child during the child's formative years must truly listen and hear the child—withholding judgement and wishing only to communicate. Congruence implies that those around the growing person are genuine—they are truly being themselves and are not presenting a self which reflects others' values and wishes rather than their own.

Unconditional positive regard and positive self-regard are interdependent ideas. For a person to develop positive self-regard—feelings of self-esteem, self-worth, and being loved and accepted—they need to be treated with unconditional positive regard by others. This means that the approval and love we receive from important people in our lives are freely and fully given, regardless of flaws in our own behaviour or character. In unconditional positive regard, approval and acceptance are not based upon any conditions. As a counterexample, a young child may come to learn that she is loved and approved of only if she refrains from wetting her bed, spilling her food, or getting poor grades at school. Refraining from these behaviours then become the **conditions of worth.** Conditions of worth are conditions the child must fulfil to receive the acceptance and love she needs—a situation opposite to that of unconditional positive regard, and therefore one that will not promote positive self-regard.

Rogers was adamant that growing up in a health-promoting environment was not only a question of having loving parents and a supportive family. To a large degree it necessitated being surrounded by a culture supportive of mental health. Rogers claimed that it was cultural influences that were the major factor in evil behaviour by human beings (cited by May, 1982).

Rogers' psychotherapy techniques were firmly rooted in his view of personality and human nature in that he attempted to create a relationship between therapist and **client** based upon unconditional positive regard, empathy, and acceptance; allowing the client to receive what had been lacking in important early relationships.

❯ KEY IDEAS empathy and congruence **Accurate empathy** was Rogers' term to describe the quality of communication between two people where each person genuinely listens to the other's words, hears the words, perceives the intention accurately, and withholds judgement. **Congruence** was Rogers' term to describe an environment of development where those surrounding the developing person are genuine—that is, truly being themselves and not presenting a self that reflects the values and wishes of others.

❯ KEY IDEAS unconditional positive regard, positive self-regard, and conditions of worth **Unconditional positive regard** was Rogers' term to describe relationships where the love and approval a person receives from important others is given freely and is not dependent upon conditions. For example, if a therapist treats a client with approval, respect, and high regard when the client behaves in a way the therapist thinks is constructive—but not if the client engages in self-destructive behaviour—this is conditional rather than unconditional positive regard. **Positive self-regard** was Rogers' term to describe feelings of self-worth and self-esteem, and being loved and accepted. According to Rogers, positive self-regard is dependent upon experiences of unconditional positive regard from others. According to Rogers, **conditions of worth** are the conditions a person must fulfil to obtain love and approval from important people in his or her life. These conditions only exist within relationships which lack unconditional positive regard.

THINKING CRITICALLY

Referring back to our critical thinking toolkit for theories in Chapter 1, apply these criteria to evaluating Rogers' humanistic theory of personality. Try to ensure you identify both strengths and limitations.

❯ KEY IDEAS self-esteem—high, low, and fragile Self-esteem is a person's emotional assessment or evaluation of his or her self-worth. If we have high self-esteem we like ourselves whereas low self-esteem involves not liking ourselves so much. Self-esteem is usually thought of as consistent and global; however, self-esteem can vary according to situation. Of particular concern is fragile or defensive self-esteem. This tends to be high until challenged but is easily threatened and challenges can lead to aggression.

❯ KEY IDEAS terror management and sociometer theories These are both explanations for the importance of self-esteem. Terror management theory suggests that self-esteem buffers us against the fear of death, while sociometer theory posits that self-esteem provides us with feedback about how socially accepted we are.

Is Self-Esteem Really Important?

Humanistic psychologists such as Carl Rogers stressed the importance of **self-esteem**—each person's emotional experience of his or her own self-worth—or put more simply, how much we like ourselves. Self-esteem is of great interest to a lot of people. It is one of the most frequently studied concepts in psychology (Watson, Suls, and Haig, 2002), and interest in self-esteem doesn't end in the psychology lab. What began as a psychological concept has become a household word. To some degree, this is understandable. Self-esteem feels good, and reduced self-esteem feels bad. People with high self-esteem tend to be happier, suffer less from **depression**, and are more likely to enjoy the good things that happen to them to the fullest and more likely to help others do the same (Krueger, Vohs, and Baumeister, 2008). People will go to great lengths to maintain feelings of self-esteem (Pyszczynski et al, 2004). Why exactly does self-esteem feel so good? Several theories have been proposed. Researchers adhering to a theory known as **terror management theory** (described in greater detail in Chapter 22) suggest that self-esteem acts as a psychological buffer against the general anxiety all human beings feel when faced with the knowledge of their own inevitable death (Schmeichel et al, 2009). According to terror management theory, because we understand how vulnerable we really are, feelings of security depend upon achieving a kind of symbolic immortality through valued roles, attributes, and accomplishments. Self-esteem imparts meaning to a life that could end at any time.

Another approach, known as **sociometer theory**, focuses on the possibility that one's level of self-esteem provides important feedback about social acceptance or rejection (Leary, 2004). In other words, self-esteem is a kind of social barometer. High self-esteem is a signal that you are likely to be socially accepted and unlikely to be rejected. Regardless of the true explanation for the importance of self-esteem to human beings, however, it is beyond doubt that most people are highly motivated to maintain self-esteem. According to self-help books and media experts, self-esteem can be credited with improving school performance, success in work, interpersonal relationships, and numerous other life endeavours. And the absence of self-esteem can be blamed for criminality, prejudice, teenage pregnancy, drug and alcohol misuse, and sexual excesses. But does self-esteem really have these near-magical properties? As you might have noticed by now, the truth is always more complex and nuanced!

There are at least two areas where evidence does show benefits to self-esteem. Perhaps the most straightforward of these is eating disorders. Low self-esteem is strongly related to the development of the eating disorder **bulimia nervosa** (Baumeister et al, 2003). In addition, realistic high self-esteem—self-esteem that is not defensive and does not result from an unrealistically inflated view of the self—appears to be associated with increased prosocial behaviours; that is, helping others. However, as one study showed, those with high self-esteem are overrepresented both as bullies and as the people who stand up to bullies (Salmivalli et al, 1999).

Some areas are less straightforward; for example, **aggression** and delinquent 'acting-out' behaviour. Conclusions about the evidence here differ but Baumeister and his colleagues could find only a single methodologically sound study which suggested that low self-esteem might be associated with aggressive acting-out behaviour. More surprising is the fact that substantial evidence does point to high self-esteem as a frequent culprit in aggression (Bushman et al, 2009)! High self-esteem results from many things, and one of these is narcissism—an inflated view of the self that can lead to aggressive retaliation when pride is threatened (Thomaes et al, 2009). This type of self-esteem has been termed defensive or fragile high self-esteem (Kernis et al, 1999).

Another area believed by many to be affected by self-esteem is interpersonal relations. But while it is often said that 'loving oneself is a prerequisite for loving others', Baumeister and his research team report that high self-esteem individuals do not necessarily have superior social skills and interpersonal skills, although they often think they do. Those with high self-esteem rate themselves as more popular and socially adept than those with low self-esteem, but when rated by others (peers, teachers, co-workers) or when other, more objective measures are used, the self-assessments of high self-esteem people are not confirmed. In fact, in some cases, those with high self-esteem receive lower ratings than low self-esteem people, with the added problem that when their pride is challenged they can become angrier than those with low self-esteem. As Baumeister and his colleagues put it, '[T]he superior social skills and interpersonal successes of people with high self-esteem exist mainly in their own minds' (2003, p 20).

TRAIT APPROACHES TO PERSONALITY

In response to the focus of psychoanalysis on pathology and the unconscious, during the mid-1930s, a young psychologist named Gordon Allport devised a theory of personality based on the notion of **traits**—relatively stable personality characteristics, attributes, and motivations that can be commonly captured in adjectives such as honest, cheerful, kind, short-tempered, conscientious, and so forth. This initiated an important new movement towards a more scientific account of personality than that offered in earlier personality theories, including psychoanalysis.

To identify the number of possible personality traits in existence, Allport and a colleague extracted 17,953 adjectives from *Webster's New International Dictionary* that were in some way descriptive of personal attributes (Allport and Odbert, 1936). A portion of these words described personality characteristics, some of which were stable, and others usually temporary (eg, joyful, angry, embarrassed). The stable characteristics, of which there were about 4,500, were referred to as traits by Allport, and the temporary characteristics—often related to moods or emotions—were termed **states**.

Allport's work initiated what came to be known as the **trait perspective**. Because traits describe a person's characteristic patterns of behaviour, thought, emotion, and motivation without offering an explanation of the origins of these characteristics—as was the goal of earlier grand theories—the trait perspective was a significant change in focus for psychologists. Allport's trait theory was also the starting point for the first attempts to build truly empirical, research-based theories of personality.

Eysenck's Two-Factor Theory

Allport's work was popular because it made intuitive sense. The adjectives Allport and Odbert (1936) extracted from the dictionary were words that ordinary people use to describe their own characteristics and those of others. However, what makes intuitive sense is not necessarily true. German-born psychologist Hans Eysenck, who fled the Nazis in the 1930s and settled in Great Britain, also believed in the concept of traits. It was Eysenck's work that brought personality from the era of the grand theories into the contemporary era of research-based personality theory.

> KEY IDEAS traits and states
Traits are stable, enduring personality attributes and motives for behaviour. Traits may generally be described using adjectives (eg, extraverted, conscientious, cheerful, honest, compassionate). Traits are limited in number, and each person differs in the degree to which they display any particular trait. **States** are not stable but depend on the situation, thus we all have anxious states but only some of us are consistently anxious and are said to be high in the trait of anxiety.

> KEY IDEAS trait perspective
The trait perspective on personality is an approach to understanding personality that focuses on identifying and measuring stable personality traits in the individual.

In collaboration with his wife, Sybil, Eysenck created a new trait-based theory of personality within the framework of empirical research and revised it continuously over time as research results showed one or another aspect of the theory incorrect. According to Eysenck, Allport's 4,500 trait terms 'boiled down' statistically to two basic trait dimensions—known as **superordinate traits**—with all other trait labels being redundant of these two 'umbrella traits' and subsumed under them. A trait dimension is a trait label constructed of two opposing concepts or poles (eg, hostile–kind, dominant–submissive, shy–outgoing), where any degree of the trait may exist between the poles (Eysenck and Eysenck, 1963).

Thus, his original model is known as the two-factor model. The superordinate trait dimensions are extraversion–introversion and emotional instability–stability. Introversion–extraversion means the degree to which a person is reserved, quiet, and thoughtful, versus assertive, outgoing, and sociable. By emotional instability (often termed neuroticism), Eysenck is referring to the degree to which a person has enduring tendencies towards various types of negative emotional states (eg, anxiety, moodiness). Emotional stability indicates a very low level of such tendencies. Eysenck considered these superordinate dimensions to be primarily genetic in origin and grounded in neurophysiology.

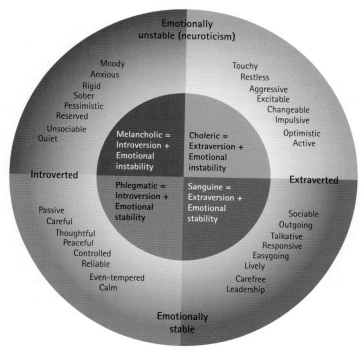

FIGURE 15.5 Hans Eysenck's two-factor model of personality. Eysenck's original two-factor model demonstrates the way that different personality characteristics result from the interaction of the two dimensions introversion–extraversion and emotional instability–emotional stability. For example, as the trait adjectives close to the introversion pole move in the direction of the emotionally unstable pole, they assume increasingly undesirable aspects of introversion—for example, anxiety. The same is true in the case of extraversion: emotionally unstable extraverts tend towards aggression and touchiness. The same holds true in reverse as the introversion or extraversion trait terms move in the direction of emotional stability.

Source: Diagram adapted from Eysenck, 1958.

As depicted in Figure 15.5, Eysenck was particularly interested in the way these two superordinate traits interacted with one another. For example, if you were high in both introversion *and* emotional instability, you would tend towards moodiness, anxiety, pessimism, and would be socially withdrawn. However, if you were high in introversion and *low* in emotional instability, you would express the more ideal form of introversion—calm and even-tempered, peaceful, thoughtful, and reliable.

As time went on, Hans and Sybil Eysenck modified this model substantially, incorporating a third dimension: psychoticism, tough-mindedness associated with antisocial behaviour and—according to Eysenck—increased vulnerability to psychotic conditions such as schizophrenia, discussed in Chapter 18. However, this third dimension has remained somewhat controversial, and it is the original two-factor model that is probably more frequently referred to by those describing Eysenck's work.

The 'Big Five' Model of Personality

Although Eysenck's model was useful, some personality researchers suspected that it may have reduced personality from too many factors to too few. A group of psychologists, among them Robert McCrae and Paul Costa, conducted research in nations throughout the world and found evidence to support a universal **five-factor model** of personality, often termed the **'Big Five'** (McCrae and Costa, 2013). Costa and McCrae's approach is based on the **lexical hypothesis**, the idea that important personality characteristics will be well represented in language and that therefore we can identify traits by looking for personality terms with equivalents across a range of languages. According to Costa and McCrae, five personality factors emerge from lexical analysis. The Big Five model is currently the most widely accepted trait model of personality.

The five factors are labelled **O**penness to experience, **C**onscientiousness, **E**xtraversion, **A**greeableness, and **N**euroticism. (An easy way to remember them is the acronym OCEAN.) Table 15.3 describes the characteristics of high and low scorers for each of the five factors.

TABLE 15.3 **The five-factor model of personality (the 'Big Five'): the five factors are summarized in the acronym OCEAN**

Factor	High scorers	Low scorers
Openness to Experience	High scorers are imaginative, curious, intellectual, creative, and artistic, and they dislike routine.	Low scorers are conventional and practical, they enjoy routine, are not oriented towards intellectual pursuits, and are 'down-to-earth'.
Conscientiousness	High scorers are careful, thorough, well organized, and responsible.	Low scorers are careless, inefficient, disorganized, and irresponsible
Extraversion	High scorers are sociable, energetic, assertive, and oriented towards others.	Low scorers are passive, reserved, quiet, and oriented towards self.
Agreeableness	High scorers are warm, kind, empathetic, compassionate, and trusting.	Low scorers are hostile, suspicious, unkind, and lacking in trust and compassion.
Neuroticism	High scorers are easily upset, anxious, emotional, and self-pitying, and they tend to worry.	Low scorers are even-tempered, comfortable with themselves, calm, and emotionally stable.

How convincing is the research in favour of the five-factor model? Actually, many psychologists are convinced. People's scores on personality inventories really do appear to cluster in a small number of factors, approximately five, although there is some difference of opinion about the exact number and how best to label them (Allik et al, 2010). Research on the Big Five has been conducted on five continents among members of at least 50 cultures, and the five factors have been shown to describe personality in all of these cultures (Allik et al, 2010).

Finally, longitudinal research has shown that the Big Five personality traits matter. They account for a portion of the differences between people in rates of divorce, educational and occupational success, and even longevity (Roberts et al, 2007). Using controlled longitudinal research, Roberts et al assessed the importance of personality traits versus the importance of IQ and socioeconomic status (SES) in predicting three outcomes: divorce, occupational success, and age of death. Figure 15.6 presents their findings. As you can see, only in the case of occupational success did a non-personality factor (IQ) produce higher correlations with eventual outcome than one or more personality trait scores.

THINKING CREATIVELY

Think of an area of adult functioning in which you are interested. This might be something already mentioned, like career success or relationship longevity, or there might be something else you find more interesting. Design a study to test the idea that this is in some way related to personality as defined by the five-factor model. Think about how to measure both personality and the variable you are interested in. Think as well about whether it is possible to assess cause and effect (ie, whether personality affects the variable you are interested in).

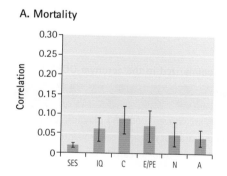

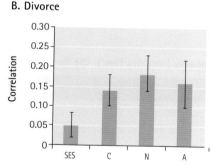

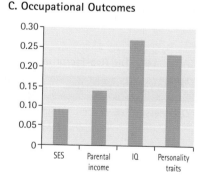

FIGURE 15.6 Traits matter. Brent Roberts and his colleagues found that, in the case of mortality (Graph A), the traits conscientiousness (high) and extraversion/positive emotion (high) were more predictive of greater longevity than either SES or IQ. In the case of divorce (Graph B), levels of conscientiousness, agreeableness, and neuroticism were all more predictive than SES variables such as education and income. (There was insufficient evidence about the effects of IQ to include it in the graph.) In the case of occupational attainment (Graph C), only IQ was more predictive of level of occupational advancement than personality traits as a whole.

In terms of stable personality traits that are moderately predictive of real-life performance and outcomes, the five-factor model is currently the most popular approach. However, there are a number of criticisms of the trait approach itself that challenge the five-factor model. We explore one of these—the impact of situation on behaviour—in detail below. Others include the following:

- Hogan and Foster (2016) suggest that the whole logical basis of trait theories is flawed. One logical issue is that a trait is defined simultaneously as a set of behaviour patterns and as an underlying mental structure—it cannot be both. Another is that traits both describe and predict. For example, someone behaves arrogantly because they are arrogant—this is circular logic.

- Some personality theorists reject the possibility of devising trait theories that capture *all* aspects of personality, and instead support the more modest aim of measuring and explaining particular aspects of personality. Such **narrow-band theories** of personality include Zuckerman's model of **sensation seeking** (Zuckerman, 2015).

- Changing social-historical contexts may reveal new aspects of personality. This poses a major challenge to the lexical hypothesis, which can only be based on snapshots of the personal characteristics represented in languages at particular moments in history. This is borne out by a study by Brick and Lewis (2014) who found that the five-factor model was only very modestly predictive of environmental attitudes and behaviours, which are becoming important aspects of individual differences.

❯ KEY IDEAS narrow band theories and sensation seeking Narrow band theories of personality are those which seek to address a particular aspect of personality rather than trying to explain personality in its entirety. An example of a narrow band personality theory is Zuckerman's sensation seeking. Sensation seeking refers to our tendency to seek out 'varied, novel, complex, and intense sensations and experiences, and the willingness to take physical, social, legal, and financial risks for the sake of such experience' (Zuckerman, 1994, p 27).

PERSONALITY VS SITUATION

In a sense, trait models of personality such as Allport's, Eysenck's, and the Big Five literally define personality as 'a set of scores along a set number of trait dimensions'. If you feel that personality is more than just a set of trait scores, there are many who would agree with you (Funder, 2009). Think about yourself for a moment. What sorts of trait adjectives would others use to describe you? Generous? Sneaky? Tender-hearted? Mean? Honest? Now think back carefully over your life and try to remember specific occasions where you behaved quite differently—perhaps even opposite—to what the trait adjective would predict. If traits are stable and enduring, and 'honesty' is one of your traits, for example, how is it then that you cheated on your maths test in secondary school and lied to your parents about where you were sleeping the night of the school graduation party? Were you 'not yourself' on those days?

In 1968, at the height of popularity of the trait theories of Allport, Eysenck, and others (but before the development of the Big Five), a little book was published that asked a very challenging question: if traits are real, stable, and enduring, why is it that people's scores on inventories of personality traits do not predict how they will actually behave on any given occasion? The book was *Personality and Assessment*, and it was written by personality theorist Walter Mischel. Mischel pointed out that the correlations between people's trait scores on personality tests and their behaviour in research studies of personality were very small. Someone who scored very high in extraversion might, for example, behave in a very reserved fashion in a mock 'party' set up by researchers to study social interaction.

❯ KEY IDEAS the person-situation controversy This is a major debate within personality psychology beginning during the 1960s in the work of Walter Mischel. The debate contrasted the views of those who believed traits were of primary importance in determining behaviour and those who believed that situations—not traits—determine behaviour.

Mischel argued that it was situations, not traits, which played the largest role in determining behaviour. People behave differently depending upon the particular situation in which they find themselves. According to this idea, the very concepts 'traits' and 'personality' are not particularly meaningful when it comes to behaviour, and in fact may be little more than illusions. The **person-situation controversy** had erupted.

Mischel's critique was devastating, and it quite literally created havoc in the field. Research and publishing in personality psychology waned quite dramatically, and a number of major graduate programmes in personality psychology closed down (Swann and Seyle, 2005).

The Trait Empire Strikes Back

Finally, in the late 1970s, personality psychologists struck back at Mischel. A researcher named Seymour Epstein took aim at Mischel's work and fired an equally devastating critique right back at him. Epstein (1979) argued that the only reason behaviour did not appear to correlate with traits in the research studies Mischel had examined was that these studies only looked at *a single slice of behaviour*—the one instance of behaviour (generally an artificial situation set up by researchers) that had been observed in the study itself.

Epstein proposed that traits did indeed predict behaviour if behaviour were examined on a number of occasions, not just one, and the results *aggregated*, or averaged. Epstein argued that traits were tendencies, and that people were not robots, behaving identically on every occasion according to their dispositions. Thus, one needed to take in the big picture and observe the person over time, because a trait would not necessarily be apparent on any given single occasion.

Who is right, Mischel or Epstein? Is it traits or situations that are the best predictors of behaviour? As we shall now see, Mischel and Epstein were both right (Funder, 2009).

Interaction of Traits and Situations

Mischel (1979) agreed that Epstein had made an important point. Single instances of behaviour cannot be used to determine whether people do or do not behave consistently according to some trait measure. However, Mischel continued to insist that how one behaves in one type of situation may not reflect how one behaves in another type of situation. A person who is consistently 'honest' in her aggregated dealings with her friends and family may be consistently 'dishonest' when she takes tests or fills out tax forms. Therefore, according to Mischel, measures which focused on traits alone were still uninformative of personality.

Take, for example, two secondary school students, Meghan and Kara. On the Big Five test, each ends up with an identical score for *extraversion*. However, each student has certain idiosyncratic aspects to her extraverted personality. Meghan is very outgoing at home and with friends, but in the classroom she is shy and never raises her hand—even when she knows the answer. Also, when she gets within 10 metres of someone she is attracted to, she becomes very shy. Kara, on the other hand, is passive and obedient at home, relatively quiet around her friends, but shines in the classroom and is very outgoing in her interactions with people she is attracted to. If one were to give each student a *separate* extraversion score for each situation, it might look like this:

	Home	Classroom	Friends	Boys
High Extraversion	Meghan	Kara	Meghan	Kara
Low Extraversion	Kara	Meghan	Kara	Meghan

If you were to connect each student's scores for all four situations by drawing separate (diagonal) lines from column to column, two entirely opposite zig-zag patterns would emerge. And yet, each student has two high scores and two low scores, potentially averaging out to an identical numeric score for extraversion. If all we knew about Meghan and Kara was that they both had the same average extraversion score on a test such as the Big Five, we would conclude that they were very similar to each other in their behaviour, but in fact they are quite dissimilar.

Does this mean that trait scores are worthless? Not at all. As two decades of research following Epstein's work has demonstrated, trait scores do reflect general tendencies, and if one looked at many more situations over time, it would undoubtedly turn out that both Meghan and Kara display more extraverted behaviour than introverted (Funder, 2001). The point of this hypothetical example is that if you truly wish to understand Kara and Meghan as individuals, trait scores are not enough. You also need to understand their unique **trait-situation behaviour profiles**—the patterns created by the intersection of their traits with the specific situations in which they find themselves (Mischel, Shoda, and Mendoza-Denton, 2002).

According to Mischel and Shoda, trait-situation behaviour profiles are organized, integrated, and relatively enduring, fulfilling our definition of personality. Thus, both Epstein and Mischel were correct: traits and situations are at the centre of personality, and they both must be considered to understand how personality is expressed in behaviour.

> **KEY IDEAS** trait-situation behaviour profile This is the unique, stable behaviour pattern created by the interaction of a person's traits with specific situations. Trait-situation behaviour profiles are like 'If . . . then . . . else' statements in computer language. For example, 'If I am at school, then I will behave politely, honestly, and conscientiously . . . else (ie, otherwise) I will do my best to avoid my responsibilities, cheat whenever possible, and use foul language.' Trait-situation behaviour profiles account for the fact that people may appear to display different traits depending upon the situation.

DEBUNKING—WHY DO PEOPLE BELIEVE IN ASTROLOGY?

An awful lot of people believe in astrology. According to a review of international surveys (Groome, 2016) around 20% of people in the UK believe in the influence of 'their stars', as compared with 29% in the USA and close to 100% in India. Without being disrespectful to anyone's cultural traditions, we can confidently say that there is no *scientific* basis to astrology. Of course you may have additional frames of reference other than science; we are just hoping to influence your scientific development. This is not to say that it is impossible that the season of your birth may impact on your development. Whether you were one of the older or younger children in your school year may mean that you had slightly different social and educational experiences. It may even be that the weather in your infancy influenced gene expression at crucial points in your development. However, this is *not* the same as saying that your personality is influenced by the stars.

The vast majority of scientists—if not all scientists—are convinced that there is no virtue to astrology, and that astrology is a good example of a pseudoscience, as described in Chapter 2. For example, astrology is not self-correcting but changes only for arbitrary reasons (eg, social fashion), if at all; it relies on testimonials, anecdotes, and bold statements; it uses jargon to obscure rather than clarify; it cannot produce scientific evidence to support its validity (indeed, virtually all such evidence denies its validity); it over interprets coincidence; it uses 'after the fact' (*post-hoc*) reasons to explain away its failures; and, perhaps most important, it simply doesn't do what it says it can do—that is, *it doesn't work*. In a classic example of a scientific evaluation of astrology

❯ **KEY IDEAS** data-proof topics Some debates inspire such strong feelings in people that they are not influenced in their views by evidence. These are described as **data-proof topics**. Astrology is one such topic.

Finally, astrology, like many belief systems, may be helpful for some people in dealing with stressful life events, negative self-concepts, and general uncertainties about living (Glick, Gottesman, and Jolton, 1989). Attempts to understand oneself and the world are important components of human nature. Although astrological information is illusory, it may nonetheless help fulfil these basic human needs (Lilqvist and Lindeman, 1998).

Voas (2007) used British census data to look at ten million marriages to test the most basic of astrological predictions—that certain sun signs would be attracted to certain other signs, and the personalities of people born under those signs would be compatible with each other. Voas found that no combination of sun signs was found among married couples more frequently than would be expected by chance.

What is perhaps most interesting about all this to psychologists is that intelligent people still believe in astrology, and those who do are generally not at all convinced by evidence or logic. In other words, astrology is a **data-proof** topic. People will believe regardless of evidence that it cannot do what believers claim that it can. Why is belief in astrology immune to evidence? This is a complex question. Attempts to explain important aspects of life in terms of the supernatural or paranormal are pervasive in all known human societies (Brown, 1991), suggesting that tendencies towards such beliefs may be part of human psychological nature. Human beings also have a tendency to mentally construct patterns from events that conceivably could be related, particularly if these events have an impact on important aspects of life. This pattern-finding skill—'putting two and two together'—likely evolved over evolutionary time because it aided in survival and reproduction. The problem is that we sometimes see patterns where none really exist, and 'over interpret' coincidence and chance occurrences (Dawes, 2001).

THINKING PRACTICALLY

What might you say to someone who is planning to use astrology as the basis of a major life decision?

NATURE AND NURTURE IN THE DEVELOPMENT OF PERSONALITY

Recall that we said that trait theories are mainly concerned with describing personality rather than explaining its origins. Nonetheless, understanding traits has allowed reliable and valid measurement of personality and this in turn has meant that we can investigate its origins.

The claim that genes play a role in personality was once highly controversial, but it has now entered the mainstream of personality and developmental psychology (Maccoby, 2002; Rutter, 2002). When one thinks about it, there should be nothing controversial about such findings. At least some genetic influence on most traits is found for all known species of life (Lynch and Walsh, 1998).

However, some personality traits appear to be more or less heritable than others, and heritability estimates usually differ somewhat from one study to the next. Various methodological limitations in most research studies on this question virtually guarantee that the estimates will not be precise (Collins et al, 2000). Nonetheless, studies have yielded fairly consistent findings. As Table 15.4 shows, studies conducted using the Big Five and Eysenck's two superordinate factors as indicators of personality suggest a heritability of around 50% (Bouchard, 2004). Note that this is broad-sense heritability, including the influence of gene-influence interactions (see Chapters 5 and 14 for discussion of narrow and broad-sense heritability). Interestingly there is also some evidence of genetic influences on trait-situation behaviour profiles (Borkenau et al, 2006).

TABLE 15.4 **Genetic and environmental influences on personality**

Heritability (h2) represents the average portion of differences among people in personality that can be explained by broad-sense genetic inheritance. Environmental influence is the sum of shared and non-shared environmental influence in the development of personality differences. As you can see, no contribution of shared environment has been found in behaviour genetic studies of the Big Five and Eysenck's two superordinate factors.

Trait	Heritability (h2) (genetic influence)	Shared environmental influence	Non-shared environmental influence
Big Five			
Extraversion	.54	None	.46
Agreeableness	.42	None	.58
Conscientiousness	.49	None	.51
Neuroticism	.48	None	.52
Openness to Experience	.57	None	.43
Eysenck's Two Superordinate Factors			
Extraversion–Introversion	.50	None	.50
Emotional Instability–Stability	.44	None	.56

Source: Adapted from Bouchard, 2004, p 150.

Given the fact that both genes and environments contribute to personality approximately equally (see Table 15.4), is it possible to determine which aspects of the environment are most important to the development of personality?

Environmental Influences

In Chapter 4 we saw that the environmental component of child temperament was contributed by the non-shared rather than the shared environment. The same appears to hold true for adolescent and adult personality. If you recall from Chapter 4, the unique experiences encountered by each developing child are known as the **non-shared environment** because these environmental factors are experienced only by the child in question and not by other children in the home. Environmental factors shared by all children living in a home—parent education, income, beliefs and attitudes, childrearing and discipline styles, and so forth—are termed the **shared environment**. Virtually all available behaviour genetics research (summarized in Table 15.4) suggests that it is the child's unique experiences in the world, rather than the shared environment to which all children living in a home are exposed, that contributes virtually all of the environmental influence on adolescent and adult personality (Saudino, 2005).

The Non-Shared Environment

But if the non-shared environment is of primary importance, what *sorts* of non-shared experiences are most critical to personality development? This is a controversial question, but three possibilities have been suggested frequently: *differing parental treatment of each child*, *peer influence*, and simple *chance*.

❯ **KEY IDEAS** shared and non-shared environments The **non-shared environment** is the unique environmental factors and experiences encountered by each developing child but not encountered by other children in the home. For example, a childhood illness, a traumatic experience, a different set of friends, and so forth. The **shared environment** on the other hand refers to the environmental factors and experiences shared by all children living in a home—for example, the parent's socioeconomic status, language and culture, beliefs and attitudes, and childrearing and discipline styles.

Research showing that the non-shared rather than the shared environment is most important in shaping personality has elicited one major objection: it implies that parenting has little or nothing to do with the way personality develops. However, one aspect of the non-shared environment that would accord a more important role to parenting in personality development is a situation where parents treat each of their children quite differently. When they do this, they are in a sense creating separate environments for each child (Vandell, 2000).

Consider a young woman we will call Kelly, whose life was consumed by her very promising career as a ballerina. Kelly's career was derailed when she accidentally became pregnant at age 22. She gave birth to a healthy baby boy, but resented her son for his part in altering the course of her ballet career. However, Kelly gradually came to accept and even enjoy her new life as a mother and part-time dance teacher. When her son was ready to start school, she had a second child; this time the pregnancy was planned, and Kelly had no reason to feel resentment towards the new baby. It was her first child, and only the first, who bore the brunt of Kelly's resentment during the child's formative years.

Differing treatment of children in a family might also result from divorce, sudden parental unemployment, and other changes in family circumstances. Such changes may occur at a critical period in the development of one sibling, but not another.

Judith Rich Harris (2006) has been the most vocal proponent of the idea that peer groups, not parents, are the primary socializers of children (see Chapter 11). According to Harris, it is mainly from peers that children learn the ways of their society and culture. Harris proposes that peers are not only primarily responsible for making us *similar* to one another, particularly to others of the same sex and age; but they also have an important role in making us *different* from one another—in shaping our personalities (Harris, 2006).

According to Harris, personality develops in large part according to the unique ways each child learns to resolve the conflict between the desire to 'fit in' with peers and the desire to 'stand out' from them. Harris refers to this as the conflict between the *socialization system*, which prompts the child to conform to the expectations of their peers; and the *status system*, which prompts the developing child to compete with others in order to establish his or her unique identity and contributions. Each child learns entirely different strategies for conforming and competing based upon prior experience, and Harris proposes that developing these strategies is the primary 'engine' driving personality development.

For example, Keiko is a 13-year-old in a school that heavily emphasizes sport performance. Try as she may to conform to the expectations of the other students, however, Keiko is hopeless at sport. Instead, she devotes time to study and reading and attains status and admiration as a high-scoring student ('standing out') who is generous sharing her gifts by tutoring her fellow students ('fitting in').

Some influences on development are actually quite random in nature: 10-year-old Gabriel is browsing in the children's room at the library, but his sister is sick at home. At the library Gabriel makes a new friend—a boy whose mother turns out to be a music teacher. Gabriel ends up taking music lessons from the mother, an event that has an impact on his personality by promoting concentration, discipline, admiration from peers and parents, and an artistic worldview. On the other hand, Gabriel's sister is never exposed to this influence. This scenario is an example of how simple *chance* is often at work as part of the non-shared environment. It is also an example of how the term 'nurture' in the nature-nurture debate is slightly misleading. In the above example it would be a harsh judgement to say that Gabriel's sister had been less well nurtured than himself.

It may be that no single chance event contributes very greatly to personality, but when many of them are taken together they represent a cumulative effect that would cause children in the same family to be substantially different in personality (Pinker, 2002). If so, it may turn out that identifying the important aspects of the non-shared environment is virtually impossible; it may be that no single variable is of very great importance in itself, and so none will stand out statistically in research (Plomin and Daniels, 1987).

CULTURE AND PERSONALITY

We have already mentioned the lexical hypothesis—the idea that the key personality traits are those which appear frequently in a range of languages. Certainly a good theory of personality should be able to apply to people in a range of cultural contexts. This is, however, not the only question raised by looking at personality through the lens of culture. We should also consider whether there are cultural differences in personality, although with caution—this is an ethical and methodological minefield!

Evaluating Personality Theories across Cultures

One criterion that any psychological theory has to meet is that it can be applied to people who live in a variety of cultural contexts. So how well do the theories of personality we have looked at in this chapter hold up under cross-cultural scrutiny?

Freudian theory has been subject to considerable criticism on this count. Freudian ideas, in particular the preoccupation with the struggle between the instinctive id and societal superego, is firmly grounded in the Judeo-Christian tradition, the id representing the idea of original sin. This view of the person is not shared across the full range of human societies. For example, central to Hinduism is the idea that human desires, far from being our innermost self (id), are merely a distraction from knowing our true self (Stevenson et al, 2017).

However, just because a theory does not fit in with a range of cultural beliefs, this does not mean that it is *wrong*. Research into the possibility of cross-cultural universals in Freudian ideas has produced mixed results. For example, a study comparing the use of defence mechanisms in populations of Americans and Thai Buddhists found remarkable similarity (Tori and Bilmes, 2002). On the other hand Xian-Li and Guang-Xing (2006) found sharp differences in the dream content of Chinese and American students, the latter being more aggressive. It is thus very difficult to assess the cross-cultural validity of Freud's theory.

THINKING CRITICALLY

Studies have found cultural differences in the content of dreams (eg, Xian-Li and Guang-Xing, 2006). One obvious interpretation of this is that the unconscious mind proposed by Freud does not apply well to people in a range of cultural contexts. However, what difficulties beset this kind of research and how else could we interpret these findings?

So what of other approaches? The behaviourist approach to personality is much less controversial in terms of culture. Anyone can learn by association and reinforcement, and the emphasis of the behavioural approach on the environment lends itself to cross-cultural comparison—we learn according to the environment fostered by culture. Humanistic theory, however, fares rather less well. The very emphasis on the self in the work of Rogers and Maslow is very hard to reconcile with the norms and values of cultures in which there is less emphasis on personal happiness and fulfilment and more on interdependence and collective responsibility (Triandis, 1986).

Cultural Differences in Personality

Clearly behaviour differs across cultures. In fact this is something of a tautology—if there were no cultural variations in behaviours then we could not really identify or differentiate between cultures. The question of whether personality *as distinct from behaviour* varies culturally is a more complex one. People in hot climates could be forgiven for displaying irritable *behaviour*, but does this mean they are more irritable *people?* To make valid cross-cultural comparisons we need to be confident that our measures of personality are really measuring personality rather than responses to current environments—this is in practice quite difficult.

On the other hand, with a small number of exceptions, people living in a wide range of cultural contexts identify the same personality traits (McCrae and Terracciano, 2005). This suggests that cross-cultural comparison of personality traits may be a worthwhile exercise because we are at least comparing characteristics that are meaningful across cultures.

We need to be careful to separate out cultural differences in personality traits from national stereotypes. Ethical concerns over harmful stereotyping meant that for some time the whole question of cultural differences in personality was ignored (Church, 2001). Trait research is, of course, not immune from this kind of concern but at least it has not supported insulting national stereotypes. For example, the English emerge as quite extravert in spite of having the reputation of being highly reserved (McCrae et al, 2010)!

 THINKING CRITICALLY

Studies that have compared trait scores across nationalities are controversial. Identify as many criticisms as possible. You might like to consider ethical issues, practical issues such as translation, confounding variables like climate and the economy, and the possible impact of cultural values on the interpretation and social acceptability of test items.

PERSONALITY MEASUREMENT

When a researcher attributes some portion of differences in a personality trait to heredity and some portion to environment, or proposes that a particular personality trait affects a person's chances of experiencing divorce, how does the researcher measure the personality trait in the first place? Tests that measure some aspect of psychology are known as *assessment instruments*. There are two basic categories of personality assessment instruments: *projective tests* and *objective tests*.

Projective Tests: Interpreting Personality

Projective tests emerged during the mid-twentieth century primarily from psycho-analysis and related theories. They are termed 'projective' because the person taking the test is said to unconsciously 'project' his or her personality or psychiatric disorder into test items that might seem quite ambiguous—that is, on their face they may be interpreted in a great many ways.

For example, the **Rorschach test** (see Figure 15.7) presents a test-taker with a standard set of ten cards, each containing symmetrical inkblots, five in colour and five in black and white. (You can create a typical Rorschach-type image yourself by pouring a small blot of ink in the middle of a piece of paper and folding the paper in half.) The psychologist administering the test asks the test-taker to view the cards and describe what he or she sees in each blot and to identify the specific areas of the blot from which the image was seen. The psychologist writes down everything the test-taker says and then interprets it, based on a standardized scoring method (Exner, 2003). The researcher or clinician then arrives at judgements about the test-taker's personality or mental health.

You might wonder how such a process can lead to an understanding of personality and mental health problems. According to those who support the use of the Rorschach, the test is meant to be an adjunct to other forms of assessment and should not be used alone to diagnose mental illness or assess personality (Merlo and Barnett, 2001). However, proponents do insist that the test can be an important measure of both personality and mental health (Viglione and Taylor, 2003).

On the other hand, the Rorschach has been sharply criticized—indeed, it is one of the most heavily criticized of all psychological tests currently in use. Critics charge, first, that the test lacks validity. A valid test is one that actually measures what it is supposed to measure. For example, if a test is supposed to measure *depression* but is actually measuring *neuroticism* or ordinary sadness, it is not a valid test of depression. Critics charge that the standards for scoring the Rorschach are not valid and may cause psychologically normal people to appear to have serious psychological disturbances (Garb et al, 2005).

Second, critics claim that the test lacks inter-rater *reliability*. The term reliability can be used in a number of different ways. In one sense, it means that if a test is intended to measure something enduring about a person, such as personality, the person ought to score much the same if taking the test on two separate occasions (this is called test-retest reliability). Reliability also means that a person should get the same test result regardless of who is doing the scoring; scoring should not be subjective and should not differ from one rater to the next. It is suggested that the Rorschach lacks inter-rater reliability because its scoring is overly subjective so different raters will produce different interpretations of the same test results. Concerns over inter-rater reliability make the Rorschach very controversial as evidence in court (Garb et al, 2005).

A reliable test is constructed so that if it is intended to measure something enduring about a person, the person will score much the same if taking the test on two or more separate occasions. A reliable test is also one which will report the same result regardless of who is doing the scoring—in other words, scoring is not subjective and will not differ from one rater to the next.

Another projective test is the **Thematic Apperception Test** (TAT; Murray, 1943). In the TAT, 31 emotionally loaded, but ambiguous, drawings are shown and the test-taker is asked to tell the 'story' of the drawing. According to proponents of the test, the test-taker, in creating the story, reveals important motives, drives, conflicts, emotions, and other psychological variables (see Figure 15.8).

> **KEY IDEAS** Rorschach test
This is a well-known projective personality and mental health test originally devised by Hermann Rorschach in 1921. The test consists of a standard set of five colour and five black-and-white symmetrical inkblots. The test-taker is asked to describe what they see in each blot and to identify the specific areas of the blot from which the image is constructed.

FIGURE 15.7 **A typical Rorschach image. The Rorschach test is a controversial projective test of personality or psychiatric illness.**
Source: Kheng Guan Toh/Shutterstock.com.

> **KEY IDEAS** reliability
You may recall from other discussions that reliability means consistency. A good personality test should measure something consistently. A reliable test should consistently give the same result if the same person is tested and retested. This is **test-retest reliability**. It should also produce the same result if more than one professional is using it to assess the same person. This is **inter-rater reliability**.

AS Thematic
...ption Test (TAT) The TAT
...s a projective personality test first
devised during the 1930s by Henry
Murray and Christiana Morgan. In
the TAT the test-taker is presented
with 31 emotionally loaded but
ambiguous drawings and asked
to tell the 'story' of the drawings.
According to proponents of the
test, in doing so the test-taker
reveals important motives, drives,
conflicts, and emotions.

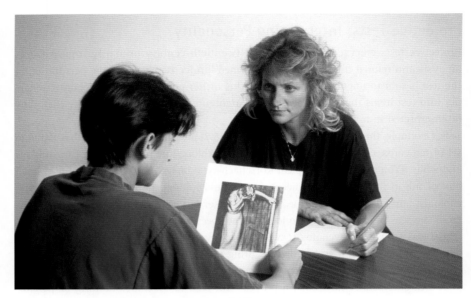

FIGURE 15.8 **Thematic Apperception Test (TAT).**
Source: Lew Merrim/Science Photo Library.

THINKING CREATIVELY

Objective tests of personality typically quote reliability figures of around 0.8. This might indicate that there was 80% agreement when two or more raters scored the same people's tests (inter-rater reliability), that someone scored using half the items then the other half would receive an 80% correspondence between the two halves (split half reliability) or 80% correspondence between the scores when the test is taken on two occasions (test-retest reliability).

Design a study to test the reliability of the TAT. Consider in particular which measure or measures of reliability you will use.

For decades a serious drawback to the TAT has been that while some standards for scoring the test did exist, only a very tiny portion of psychologists actually used these standards. Clearly, without standard scoring procedures a test cannot be said to be valid or reliable. However, in recent years the TAT has been revitalized, with a number of researchers devising workable scoring methods that have shown better validity and reliability (Woike and McAdams, 2001).

Objective Tests

❯ **KEY IDEAS** Minnesota
Multiphasic Personality Inventory
(MMPI) The MMPI is the first and
most frequently used objective
test of personality. It has shown
particular validity in distinguishing
between abnormal personality traits
indicating mental health problems,
and, to a lesser extent, validity in
distinguishing normal personality
traits.

Take a moment to respond to the following statements as either true or false about yourself: 'At times I get strong cramps in my lower intestines.' 'I like rhyming poetry.' 'Sometimes there is a feeling like something is sitting on my head.' 'I used to like to touch my toes in gymnastics lessons.' 'I would like to be a debt collector.' 'At times I feel like smashing someone's nose.'

Do you think your answers would help to objectively measure important aspects of your personality and determine whether you suffer from mental health problems? These statements are adapted from items drawn from the **Minnesota Multiphasic Personality Inventory (MMPI)**, the first, and probably still the most frequently used, objective test of personality (although a revised version called MMPI-2RF is now used). Tests such as the MMPI are referred to as 'objective' because they are constructed empirically and scored by computer, so subjectivity does not enter into their interpretation.

For example, the empirical method used to create the MMPI is known as the *criterion-key method*. This technique is based on the fact that people who have certain traits or are experiencing certain states (eg, shyness, depression, paranoia, or anxiety) tend to endorse certain statements as true about themselves while identifying other statements as false. The responses to these statements given by the test-taker can then be used to construct a person's trait or state profile (low in depression, high in anxiety, high in paranoia, moderate in shyness, etc).

In the criterion-key method, the statements to which the test-taker responds (known as test items, or simply *items*) do not need to correspond at face value to any particular personality characteristic or mental state. For example, a valid scale for shyness created by the criterion-key method need not necessarily contain items such as 'I feel embarrassed easily around others' or 'I dislike being the centre of attention'. The only criterion for inclusion of an item is that, for whatever reason—known or unknown, understood or not understood—shy people have been found by empirical testing to endorse that item. Therefore, if depressed people tended to endorse an item like 'I enjoy wearing different coloured socks, but only as long as one of them is not beige', such an item could appear on the depression scale of an empirically valid criterion-keyed test of depression (although the likelihood of this particular item appearing is rather slim).

Although some of the items on the MMPI sound comical enough to have generated numerous parodies of the test, the updated MMPI-2 has repeatedly demonstrated validity in assessing personality traits associated with different types of mental health problems (Garb, Florio, and Grove, 1998). It has also demonstrated validity in assessing normal personality traits, but to a somewhat lesser degree. The test is used in a wide variety of psychiatric and non-psychiatric settings to assess areas of personality vulnerability to psychological problems; for example, career counsellors often use it to advise their clients, and human resource officers sometimes use it when hiring new employees.

PERSONALITY CHANGE OVER TIME

For most of us, by age 30 the character has set like plaster and will never soften again.

—William James (1890/1981)

It was a clarification that came to me while I was there on that walk. I was not the same person when I came back from the walk. I don't know if I'd call it a divine intervention, or a personal, powerful insight. I'm not sure what it was. I changed.

—Research participant in C'de Baca and Wilbourne (2004, p 535)

'Am I always going to be this way?' Without doubt, every one of us has asked himself or herself this question at least once, on the heels of some characteristic but daft behaviour. There's good news for those who would like to change their behaviour. Behaviour change is entirely possible. Cigarette smokers and heroin users quit. Obsessed, jilted lovers stop calling their exes and delete their depressing *Spotify* playlist. People who characteristically fly into violent rages and get into fistfights learn to stop doing so (sometimes with age but for others with the help of therapy, religion, or the criminal justice system).

Changing your personality, however, is not the same as changing habits or behaviour. Let us return to the first part of our definition of personality:

> *Personality consists of variations on common human mental and behavioural characteristics. . . .*

'Common human mental and behavioural characteristics' cannot be done away with, unless one can find a way to change one's species. For example, you will probably have a tendency to feel at least a bit of excitement and perhaps anxiety when you are about to jump out of an aeroplane for the first time. You will probably grieve more after the death of your own child than the death of another's child. You will care what others think of you, or at least what certain specific other people think. And so on.

Trait Stability

Most available evidence suggests one basic idea about personality traits: they are pretty stable from childhood through adulthood, but they are not entirely unchangeable. Personality traits do change to some degree over the lifespan, at least until middle age (Hampson and Goldberg, 2006). However, it is also true that these changes may be relatively limited after ages 30 to 50 (Ferguson, 2010).

Evidence for stability

Let us look first at evidence of the stability of traits. It is sobering to consider that even infant and toddler temperament—active or passive, contented or 'difficult', friendly or fearful—may predict adult personality to some degree, and can be seen as evidence of long-term stability of traits. Only measures of cognitive ability are more consistent over time than personality traits (Caspi et al, 2005). For example, Hampson and Goldberg (2006) found remarkable continuities in traits between childhood and adulthood in their 40-year study of personality from elementary school through middle age. Similar results were found in a comprehensive meta-analysis of longitudinal research conducted prior to 2000 by Roberts and DelVecchio (2000). As you can see in Figure 15.9, Roberts and DelVecchio found that personality is least stable prior to age 3 (when it is measured as *temperament*—see Chapter 12), and most stable past age 50. Although personality traits are subject to change to some degree throughout life, beginning in adulthood changes in traits are relatively minimal (Ferguson, 2010). As we grow older, we do become more 'set in our ways'.

Findings of moderate long-term stability of traits are not always popular (McCrae and Costa, 1994). Many people bristle at this idea, perhaps because they interpret such findings as affronts to the power of human beings to change. However, remember that a personality trait is not the same as a habit or behaviour; the latter may always be amenable to change. Take a volatile young man with a history of violence. There is a limit to how much he can change his emotional instability—although he can take some comfort in the fact that emotions usually become less intense with age—but he *can* make a decision not to express this violently. Moreover, acceptance of one's own personality traits may represent a type of wisdom (McCrae and Costa,

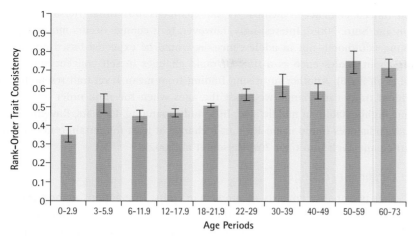

FIGURE 15.9 Personality traits become more stable over time. The average consistency of personality traits at various age ranges suggests that personality is at its most stable from age 50 through to age 73.

Source: Roberts and DelVecchio, 2000, p 15.

1994). This idea was expressed eloquently by a person who experienced a profound self-acceptance in the context of a course in meditation:

> I'd been at this month-long meditation course, and the [teacher] said that we weren't becoming different people, that we were becoming the person that we always were. Right there, at that moment was when I began the serious thought, 'I'm ready to accept that person—warts and all.' A door opened and I walked through it and the door behind me closed and I never worried about opening that door again. It was just a total opening of myself. (Cited in C'de Baca and Wilbourne, 2004, p 536)

Evidence for change

The foregoing discussion has made it clear that personality traits are relatively stable over the lifespan. However, 'relatively' stable implies that traits are not entirely stable. Indeed, personality traits are amenable to change, particularly in childhood, adolescence, and young adulthood (Specht, Egloff, and Schmukle, 2011).

Most of the evidence of stability in traits comes from research looking at the *pattern* of traits (usually, the Big Five) in each participant in a longitudinal study from one time to the next. Does a person high in extraversion but low in conscientious at age 20 look much the same at age 30? Or have they now become low in extraversion and high in conscientiousness? This type of study is therefore looking at **rank-order stability**, because stability is measured by comparing the pattern of rank order of the traits (from low to high) in each person from one time to the next.

On the other hand, most of the evidence for trait change has come from studies which look at **mean-level stability** rather than rank-order stability. In this type of analysis, investigators do not measure change in rank order for each person's pattern of Big Five trait scores. Instead they compare the average score of the *entire group* of participants on each single trait separately, to see if change has occurred over time for that trait. Thus, if the average score of the group is higher on extraversion in 2004 than in 1994 or 1984, change in the personality trait 'extraversion' has occurred, and this is evidence of *lack* of stability of that trait.

❯ KEY IDEAS rank-order stability
Rank-order stability is a measure of personality stability based upon the pattern of rank order of traits (from high to low) for each person in a sample from one measurement period to the next.

❯ KEY IDEAS mean-level stability
This is measure of personality stability based upon comparison of the mean score for each individual trait among a sample as a whole from one measurement period to the next.

And, indeed, evidence of mean-level trait change is substantial (Helson et al, 2002; Helson and Soto, 2005). Interestingly, however, trait change occurs most frequently in young adulthood—not in adolescence, as would be expected based on common beliefs about adolescence as a time of rapid changes in self-concept and identity (Caspi et al, 2005). Another surprising finding from mean-level trait research is that individual traits can change well past the ages when the rank order of traits has become highly stable (in middle age). In a study spanning 40 years, Ravenna Helson and her colleagues found mean-level trait change at least for certain traits in groups of participants well into their 70s (Helson et al, 2002).

Other personality changes

Recall that personality consists of more than traits. Interactions among traits, situations, environments, cognitions, emotions, and behaviour can produce personal characteristics that are a part of our personality and that may change—sometimes quite dramatically—over time. For example, our goals, values, beliefs, social roles, and plans for our lives may change considerably. This aspect of personality has been termed **characteristic adaptations** by personality psychologist Dan McAdams (McAdams and Olson, 2010).

However, changes in characteristic adaptations do not necessarily imply a change in traits. For example, at age 20, a person high in openness to experience on the Big Five might take up moshing whereas at age 70 the same person might get into cruises. A 20-year-old political activist committed to direct action might be more interested in standing for Parliament at 40. Same tune, different lyrics.

There is one type of personality change that may be more fundamental than changes in characteristic adaptations. According to Dan McAdams, in addition to traits, trait-situation behaviour profiles, and characteristic adaptations, there is yet a fourth level of personality: the *self-narrative*. **Self-narratives** are internal 'life stories' that evolve over time—stories and myths that we tell to ourselves about ourselves and which reflect our understandings of our place in the world. Self-narratives are about the *meanings* we give to our personalities and to our very identities (McAdams and Olson, 2010).

These stories come complete with settings, scenes, characters, plots, and themes. They are based on biographical events, but because we select which events to recall, how to recall them, and how to interpret our recollections, self-narratives are not the same as simple biography. As an example, the way a person views the 'story' of their childhood may change dramatically during an episode of clinical major depression. It is the same childhood recalled, but events previously viewed in a positive light may now take on a mournful tone. The good times will be downplayed or forgotten altogether, and unpleasant events elevated in importance.

According to McAdams (2001), the self-narrative is an aspect of personality that has assumed particular prominence in the modern industrial world. This is because issues of *identity* are not as clear-cut as they were in earlier centuries. Our self-narratives address problems of establishing and maintaining a self-concept in a world where our identities are not thrust upon us at birth and maintained throughout life, but where we are instead allowed a certain degree of choice in the matter. We can change careers repeatedly, move to new geographic locations if we choose, associate with different social groups and ethnicities, and learn a myriad new skills. Our self-narratives help us adapt to these many types of identity change.

> **KEY IDEAS** characteristic adaptations **Characteristic adaptations** are Adams' term to describe aspects of personality such as goals, values, beliefs, social roles, and plans for the future. According to Adams, characteristic adaptations change substantially over the lifespan.

> **KEY IDEAS** self-narratives **Self-narratives** can be defined as internal 'narratives of the self' which evolve through the lifespan. Self-narratives are stories and myths people tell themselves about events in their lives and personal characteristics which reflect their current understanding of their place in the world and the meaning of their life.

READ THIS

It is well worth reading some original Hans Eysenck as he wrote comprehensive and accessible books. This one sums up many of his ideas:

Eysenck, H.J. (1981). *A Model for Personality*. New York: Springer-Verlag.

Costa and McCrae's ideas about the five-factor model are explained here:

Costa Jr, P.T. and McCrae, R.R. (1990). Personality disorders and the five-factor model of personality. *Journal of Personality Disorders*, **4**, 362–71.

Their personality test, the NEO-PI, is described in detail here:

Costa, P.T. and McCrae, R.R. (1985). The NEO personality inventory. *Journal of Career Assessment*, **3**, 123–39.

We also recommend following up on Dan McAdams' work. You might like to start with this:

McAdams, D.P. (1996). Personality, modernity, and the storied self: A contemporary framework for studying persons. *Psychological Inquiry*, **7**, 295–321.

IN REVIEW

WHAT IS PERSONALITY?

- Each person is like all other persons in some ways (human attributes), like just some other persons in certain ways (differences in traits), and like no other person in other ways (unique qualities).
- Personality is the set of common human psychological characteristics and unique patterns of traits and behaviour possessed by each individual.
- These sets of traits and behaviour patterns are organized, integrated, and relatively enduring.

WHAT ARE THE 'GRAND THEORIES' OF PERSONALITY?

- The grand theories of personality include psychoanalysis, behaviourism, and humanism.
- Psychoanalysis is possibly the most complex theory in the history of psychology and also the most controversial. Three central components of the theory are the structural model of the mind, theory of psychosexual development, and theories of dynamic processes.
- The structural model of the mind includes id, ego, and superego. The five stages of psychosexual development are the oral, anal, phallic, latency, and genital.
- Freud believed that dreams contained hidden symbolic meanings that express forbidden sexual and aggressive wishes and impulses.
- Ego defences, as detailed by Freud's daughter Anna, include repression, denial, displacement, projection, reaction formation, sublimation, and undoing.
- Behaviourist theories of personality assert that personality is learned behaviour, and that one acquires personality traits through operant and classical conditioning.

The founders of humanistic psychology were optimistic, believed in free will, and had faith in human nature—believing that people generally face problems in a rational manner.

Humanistic psychologist Carl Rogers believed that each person needs a growth-promoting environment to grow into the fully functioning, competent, fulfilled human being he or she was designed to be.

For a person to develop a healthy self-concept, four conditions are necessary: accurate empathy, congruence, unconditional positive regard, and positive self-regard.

Self-esteem is a person's cognitive and emotional assessment of his or her own self-worth. People with high self-esteem are happier, suffer less from depression, and are more likely to enjoy the good things that happen to them to the fullest and help others do the same.

Two theories attempt to explain the importance of self-esteem: terror management theory, which suggests that self-esteem acts as a buffer against the anxiety we all feel when reminded of our own inevitable death; and sociometer theory, which focuses on the idea that a person's level of self-esteem gives important feedback about social acceptance or rejection.

Contrary to popular belief, evidence for the psychological benefits of high self-esteem is mixed. Low self-esteem is strongly linked to eating disorders, however, and it may be linked to aggression or antisocial behaviour in men.

HOW DO TRAITS AND SITUATIONS AFFECT PERSONALITY?

Traits are relatively stable personality characteristics, attributes, and motivations. Gordon Allport identified 4,500 possible traits. Trait psychology emphasizes description of a person's characteristic patterns of behaviour, thought, emotion, and motivation.

Hans Eysenck created the two-factor model, which views personality as having a limited number of characteristics which interact within any individual and can be measured using psychological tests. Eysenck proposed two basic trait dimensions, extraversion–introversion and emotional instability–stability (neuroticism).

Some psychologists, including Lewis Goldberg and Robert McRae, developed a five-factor model (the 'Big Five') after conducting statistical research in nations throughout the world. The five factors are Openness to experience, Conscientiousness, Extraversion, Agreeableness, and Neuroticism.

Walter Mischel argued that situations, not traits, play the largest role in determining behaviour. However, Seymour Epstein proposed that if a person were observed on a number of occasions and the person's behaviour 'aggregated' or averaged out, the effects of traits would be apparent.

Later work by Mischel and Shoda suggested that people's behaviour is best understood by looking at the patterns created by the intersection of people's traits with the various situations in which they find themselves—patterns known as trait-situation behaviour profiles.

HOW DO GENES, ENVIRONMENTS, AND CULTURE INFLUENCE PERSONALITY?

- Genes play an important role in personality development. However, some personality traits are more heritable than others, and heritability estimates may vary from study to study. On average, approximately 50% of differences among people in Big Five or Eysenck's two-factor traits is due to genetic factors.

- Non-shared environments contribute the bulk of the environmental portion of influence on personality. Non-shared environmental experiences that are likely to have the greatest effects on personality include simple chance, peer influence, and the possibility of differing parental treatment of each child.

- Rich Harris is the most vocal proponent of the idea that peer groups, not parents, are the primary socializers of children and the strongest influences upon the development of personality.

HOW IS PERSONALITY MEASURED?

- Personality assessment is the measurement of personality. Projective tests (eg, Rorschach and TAT) emerged primarily from psychoanalytic theory, and they are designed to allow a person to 'project' his or her personality unconsciously onto ambiguous test items.

- Objective tests of personality (eg, MMPI-2 and NEO PI-R) are constructed empirically and scored by computer.

DOES PERSONALITY CHANGE OVER TIME?

- Personality traits are relatively stable over time. Evidence of trait stability comes primarily from research in rank-order stability, which measures an individual's scoring on various traits over time. These studies show that temperament is stable to age 3, and personality is most stable past age 50.

- Evidence for changes over time in traits comes from research using mean-level stability. In this type of analysis, researchers compare the average score of the entire group of participants on each single trait separately, to see if change has occurred over time for that trait.

- Other aspects of personality may undergo considerable change without necessarily signalling trait change. Characteristic adaptations include goals, values, beliefs, social roles, plans for the future, and self-narratives.

TEST YOURSELF

1 In Freudian theory the superego represents the most conscious and logical element of the mind. True ❏ False ❏

2 Humanistic theories of personality like that by Carl Rogers place a lot of emphasis on self-esteem. True ❏ False ❏

3 There is evidence to support cultural differences in personality. True ❏ False ❏

4 Judith Rich Harris believed the most important aspect of the environment is parenting style. True ❏ False ❏

5 At which of Freud's stages of development does the ego first appear?

  a) Oral stage

  b) Anal stage

  c) Phallic stage

  d) Latency stage

6 How many personality traits are identified in Eysenck's theory?

  a) One

  b) Two

  c) Three

  d) Four

7 Which two of the following approaches to personality work well applied across cultures?

  a) Freudian psychoanalysis

  b) Behaviourist approach

  c) Humanistic theory

  d) Trait theory

8 Outline one criticism of Freudian theory of personality.

9 Explain one criticism of projective tests of personality.

10 Explain what is meant by self-narratives.

Visit the online resources that accompany this book: www.oup.com/uk/jarvis-okami1e

MOTIVATION

LEARNING OUTCOMES

By the end of this chapter you should be able to:

- Appreciate the complexity of defining and studying the scope of human motivation
- Outline and evaluate biological understandings of motivation including the concepts of instinct, adaptation, and drive
- Understand the distinction between intrinsic and extrinsic motivation including research into the additive principle and undermining effect
- Evaluate the concept of needs with particular regard to Maslow's hierarchy and Kenrick's fundamental needs
- Critically compare cognitive approaches to motivation including self-efficacy, goal-setting, and growth mindset
- Understand factors affecting individual differences in motivation with particular regard to personality traits and locus of control

What do you want? Why do we do things? These are fundamental questions if we want to understand human behaviour. Some of our motives might appear very straightforward—we eat because we are hungry, for example. Yet even eating behaviour is complex. The most obvious motive for eating may be hunger, but people may also eat when they are not particularly hungry—for the pure pleasure of taste, to be sociable at a dinner party, as a result of psychological distress or disorder, to foster a political alliance between families or tribes, and so forth (see Figure 16.1). Some eating-related motives are harder to understand. In 2002, Armin Meiwes advertised on the *Craigslist* website for a volunteer whom he could eat. If Meiwes' motives are hard to explain, spare a thought for the motives of the man who responded and agreed to be eaten alive—and went through with it.

It goes without saying that the range of human motives is much broader than the deceptively complex example of eating behaviour. We are motivated by a range of factors to behave in particular ways in our work, family, and romantic lives. Why is one person more ambitious than another? Why do some people seek safety and others excitement? Why do people sometimes behave in ways that, when analysed, appear to be downright irrational? These are the kind of questions addressed by research into human motivation.

FIGURE 16.1 **People are motivated to eat for many reasons: hunger, pleasure, to be sociable, to soothe themselves.**
Source: Monkey Business Images/Shutterstock.com.

DEFINING MOTIVATION

Some motivations—perhaps the more mundane ones—can be understood as evolutionary gifts to the human species from our ancestors. They enable us to survive, avoid danger, thrive, and reproduce. They direct us towards friendship, love, and belonging, and enable us to defend ourselves against aggression—as well as to use aggression to obtain our goals. They are an important part of the fabric of explanation for human behaviour.

Motivations Initiate and Direct Behaviour

We (Paul and Matt) remember the same joke from our childhoods. People would ask, 'Why did the chicken cross the road?' and answer, 'To get to the other side.' This works as a joke because we share an intuitive understanding that this is indeed the *purpose* of crossing the road but not a *motive*. **Motivations** can be defined as the mental states that cause people to engage in **purposive** behaviour. Here the term *purposive* refers to any activity directed towards achieving some goal or satisfying a need or desire—behaviour with a purpose in other words. Motivations are psychological forces that initiate actions, direct them towards the desired goal, and encourage us to sustain the effort necessary to attain that goal, whatever it may be: creating a CV, helping a lost child find his or her mother, creeping downstairs at midnight to finish a tub of ice cream, or committing a violent crime.

All motivated behaviour is purposive, even when the purpose is not obvious to the rest of us. However, not all purposive behaviour is motivated. One morning my (Paul's) daughter Anisa threw a ball at me from the side without warning, not realizing that I was not paying attention. My hands flew up to guard my face. Even though my behaviour served a purpose (self-protection) and was associated with a specific mental state (extreme alertness due to the effects of an adrenaline rush), the behaviour was not intentional. My behaviour was reflexive or automatic—like

> **KEY IDEAS** motivations and purposive behaviour **Motivations** are mental states which cause people to engage in **purposive behaviour** (ie, behaviour directed towards achieving some goal or satisfying a need or desire). Motivations initiate actions, direct them towards the desired goal, and help the person sustain the necessary effort to attain the goal.

blinking when someone blows air into your eye. Thus, motivated activities have three characteristics:

1 Purpose

2 Causes rooted in specific mental states

3 Intentionality

Purpose and cause are fairly straightforward notions, but *intention* can be tricky because, although it implies that a behaviour has been consciously chosen, this is not necessarily the case. Motivations may sometimes be *unconscious*—below a person's level of awareness (Latham, Stajkovic, and Locke, 2010).

Studying Motivation

Motivations cannot be observed directly, and for this reason behaviourists (see Chapters 2 and 7 for detailed discussions) have long argued that they are not an appropriate topic for scientific study (Skinner, 1965). However, motivations can be measured to a certain extent by looking at the *intensity* and *persistence* of a behaviour (L.V. Brown, 2007). An action has *high intensity* if it is engaged in with great physical or mental effort, or with strong application of will. Actions high in intensity tend to be highly motivated actions. For example, pulling an all-night study session (as in Figure 16.2) when you'd rather be out partying or in bed asleep is an example of intense activity in the service of a motivation (to avoid failing a test).

Persistent behaviours are those that continue over a long period of time, even in the face of adversity. The intensity of such behaviour may or may not be great, but its persistence implies the existence of strong motivation. Staying at university, even if one does not work very hard at it and does not do particularly well, is an example of persistent (but not intense) behaviour. Behaviour that is both intense and persistent is likely to be the most highly motivated type of behaviour. Obtaining a PhD in a rigorous field of study generally requires both intense and persistent behaviour and can thus be said to be highly motivated (see Figure 16.2).

FIGURE 16.2 **Studying all night for an exam is an example of a high intensity but short-term behaviour. Studying for a PhD is an example of a high intensity and persistent behaviour.**
Sources: left: Sergey Skripnikov © 123RF.com; right: iStock.com/Steve Debenport.

Unconscious Motivation

Unconscious motivation is one of those areas that can lead us to question the scientific boundaries of psychology. Everyday experience tells us that we can be unconsciously motivated. Most of us have at some point forgotten a dreaded dental appointment or to take our turn at cleaning the house, and it seems likely that we would not have forgotten similarly important but pleasant tasks.

However, because it may be difficult or impossible to demonstrate the existence of any specific unconscious motivation, some psychologists argue that the entire concept of unconscious motivation is more or less useless in explaining behaviour. Scientific research on unconscious motives is fairly rare and generally controversial because there is always a high level of inference involved in linking results to explanation. We can look at one such controversial study by Harris and Campbell in our *Research in focus* feature:

RESEARCH IN FOCUS

Harris, K. and Campbell, E.A. (1999). The plans in unplanned pregnancy: Secondary gain and the partnership. *British Journal of Medical Psychology*, **72**, 105–20.

Aim: To investigate whether women whose pregnancy was unplanned were more likely to perceive secondary gain from the pregnancy than those who had planned their pregnancy. This would suggest that unconscious motives at least partly explained becoming pregnant in spite of the lack of conscious intent.

Method: Participants were 128 women from North London. They were recruited from a hospital and a General Practice surgery. Three groups were compared: women with planned pregnancies, those with unplanned pregnancies, and a control group of non-pregnant women. A matched-groups design was used in which the three groups matched for age. The profile of socio-economic status was similar across the three groups.

Participants undertook a semi-structured interview designed to assess the secondary gains they attributed to their pregnancy. Secondary gains included improvements to their romantic relationships and to their status within their household. Written interview transcripts were blind-rated for secondary gain by other researchers.

Results: 44% of the unplanned pregnancy group were judged to believe in a high probability of secondary gain from pregnancy as opposed to 16% of the planned pregnancy group and 8% of the control group.

Conclusions: Belief in the secondary gains of pregnancy is strongly predictive of unplanned pregnancy. This is highly consistent with the idea of unconscious motivation as a factor in pregnancy.

MASTER YOUR METHODOLOGY

1 Identify the dependent and independent variables in this study.

2 Explain why this study can be described as both a survey study and a natural experiment.

3 What extraneous variables might affect a study like this, and what controls have been put in place?

 THINKING CRITICALLY

Look back to our critical thinking toolkit for studies in Chapter 1. What strengths and weaknesses can you see in relation to this study? You might like to look in particular at the ethical issues and issues of social sensitivity.

Conflicting Motives

Motives may also conflict with one another, a state known as **ambivalence**. The attempt to quit smoking is a good example. A person may wish to increase their health, lifespan, and attractiveness and therefore be motivated to quit smoking. Yet the same person might also want to avoid the extreme discomfort brought on by tobacco withdrawal and therefore be motivated *not* to quit smoking. Conflicting goals produce ambivalent motivation.

MOTIVES AS INSTINCTS

Over the past 100 years, a number of theories about the nature of motivation have emerged. But motivation is a tricky concept, and no one of these theories has been able to account for human motivation in full. However, each has made important contributions. The first coherent psychological theory of motivation was proposed by the important early psychological scientist William James (1890/1981). Heavily influenced by Darwin's theory of evolution by natural selection, James proposed that most human behaviour is motivated by *instincts*. Instincts are innate, automatic behavioural tendencies that will occur reliably in all (normally developed) members of a species in response to some sort of cue from the environment. These cues are known as *releasing stimuli* because they 'release' the instinctive behaviour.

James believed that characteristics such as aggression, sympathy, playfulness, modesty, parental love, curiosity, fear, and jealousy were all instincts that are evoked by releasing stimuli. A releasing stimulus for jealousy might consist of telephone calls received by one's partner secretively late at night or hearing that a friend had been offered a job you would have liked for yourself. A releasing stimulus for parental love might consist of a hearing one's small child uttering a particularly charming statement. Sympathy could be released by the sight of a homeless person on the street.

James and others, such as the English psychologist William McDougall (1912/2005), who further developed ideas about instinctive motivations, hypothesized that human beings had a great many highly specific instincts that served as motivators—far more than those possessed by other animal species. James did not believe, however, that human instincts were rigid and unchangeable. He saw them instead as behavioural *tendencies* that were relatively consistent but still subject to change over time through experience or as a result of differences among types of releasing stimuli.

Since James's time, scientists have come to define the concept of instinct more narrowly to include only patterns of behaviour that are entirely predictable and that will occur virtually invariably unless they are somehow blocked. Because instincts are now considered to be truly 'fixed' sequences of behaviour initiated by some releasing stimulus, the term *fixed-action pattern* was coined to replace use of the term *instinct* among most scientists. Examples of fixed-action patterns in human beings include the consequences of stroking the cheeks of newborn infants—they will respond by opening their mouths and turning their heads in the direction of the stroke. In this case, stroking is the releasing stimulus that elicits the fixed-action pattern. See Figure 16.3 for an example of a fixed-action pattern in the black-backed gull.

> ❯ **KEY IDEAS** ambivalence When a person experiences conflicting emotions or motivations—what we might call 'being in two minds' about something, they are said to be ambivalent. The word comes from *ambi*, meaning 'equal' as in *ambi*dextrous and *valence*, which refers to the strength of emotions.

> ❯ **KEY IDEAS** instinct An **instinct** is an innate, automatic behaviour tendency that will occur reliably in all normally developed members of a species in response to a releasing stimulus, or cue, from the environment. Because of past difficulties in identifying instincts, more often than not the term *fixed-action pattern* is used instead of the term *instinct*.

FIGURE 16.3 Fixed-action pattern in the black-backed gull. When a black-backed kelp gull chick views the red spot on its mother's beak, it pecks at it. This causes the mother to regurgitate food into the chick's mouth. Here the red dot is the releasing stimulus, and pecking is the fixed-action pattern.

Source: Dan Bagur/Shutterstock.com.

Fixed-action patterns are so strongly 'encoded' in the nervous system that an animal may sometimes engage in instinctive behaviours when faced with inappropriate stimuli. Tinbergen (1974) showed that cardinals who have lost their nests and offspring may end up feeding worms to minnows when the fish come to the surface of a pond looking for food. The birds are responding with a fixed-action pattern to the releasing stimulus of the opening and closing of hungry mouths in search of food.

Problems with the Concept of Instinct

Although theorizing about instinctive motivations was extremely popular for a few decades, this approach eventually ran into problems for a simple reason: rather than providing true *explanations* for motivations and behaviour, theorists were for the most part merely *describing* motivations by *labelling* them with the names of hypothetical instincts (Tolman, 1923). For example, a person who goes along with the group does so out of a 'conformity instinct', but should she oppose the group, it is out of her 'individuation instinct'. When an explanation consists merely of a label or a description, it cannot be said to be an explanation at all, and is of limited value. Such 'explanations' are *circular*, because they attempt to define a thing in terms of itself. 'He is constantly starting fights because he is very aggressive' is a circular explanation, because 'very aggressive' is little more than another way of saying 'constantly starts fights'.

It also became clear that there were no standards for distinguishing what did or did not constitute a human instinct. Various lists of instincts produced by psychologists appeared to consist primarily of guesses and opinions.

Adaption: An Evolutionary Take on Instinct

Interestingly, over the past few decades the notion of human instincts has been revived and 'rehabilitated' by evolutionary psychologists, who have reframed human instincts as *psychological adaptations* (see Chapter 5). Evolutionary psychologists propose that these adaptations evolved through natural selection to allow human beings to respond 'instinctively' to cues from the environment in ways that helped our ancestors to solve important problems they encountered repeatedly over evolutionary time (Tooby and Cosmides, 1992; Buss, 2005).

To evolutionary psychologists, motivations are part of the psychological 'architecture' of adaptations in humans. An example of a motivational adaptation is *pleasure-seeking*. Good food and drink, sex and love, friendship, meaningful work, spending time with one's children—such things are intrinsically pleasurable in most cases, and people are motivated to pursue them. They give us pleasure because, on average, finding them pleasurable promoted the survival and reproduction of our distant ancestors. They then passed on their preferences for such activities to us through psychological adaptation as part of our human genetic inheritance.

Modern evolutionary theorizing about instinct and motivation is a substantial advance over the descriptive labelling engaged in by early instinct theorists. This is because evolutionary psychologists offer *explanations*—not just labels—for how various motivations may have evolved, and they are sometimes able to test these explanations using empirical methods (Alcock, 2001).

Following the demise of early instinct theories of motivation in the 1920s and 1930s, psychologists interested in motivation began to look towards aspects of human life that held greater power of explanation. Over the years, three variables have been most frequently studied: human *drives*, *incentives*, and *needs*.

DRIVES

During the 1930s, psychologists began to wonder if motivations were mostly automatic attempts to achieve certain physiological states. The earliest of these ideas was known as **drive theory** of motivation (Hull, 1943). Drive theorists proposed that behaviour is motivated primarily by the desire to *reduce* unpleasant conditions of arousal that result from basic physiological needs. For example, a thirsty person experiences unpleasant arousal (thirst) as a result of their need for water. This drive state motivates behaviour—drinking—intended to reduce the drive. Desires to reduce unpleasant arousal states are known as **drives**. Thus, drive theory is sometimes referred to as *drive-reduction theory*.

Drive theory is based on the notion that organisms seek to maintain a steady, consistent, and balanced physiological state. This means maintaining appropriate levels of oxygen and water intake, blood sugar, body temperature, and so forth. This steady, regulated state is known as **homeostasis**, which literally means 'to stay the same'. Motivational systems such as hunger and thirst are triggered when any of our basic physiological systems is out of balance and needs attention—as when we are cold, hungry, tired, or thirsty.

Although drive theory made sense for certain motivational behaviours, particularly those related to basic drives such as hunger or thirst, it soon became clear that maintaining homeostasis was not necessarily the goal of all motivations. Human beings are sometimes motivated to *increase* arousal rather than reduce it. For example, it is difficult to imagine the biological need for which bungee-jumping produces homeostasis, yet some people will go to great lengths (ie, are highly motivated) to bungee jump. Curiosity, the enjoyment of pure sensation and stimulation, and simple boredom are all motivating forces which cause individuals to increase their levels of arousal. Thus, many theorists turned from drive theory to **optimal arousal theory**. According to this idea, people seek to maintain an optimal level of physiological arousal (Hebb, 1955; Korman, 1974). If arousal levels are too high, as when drives are activated, the organism seeks to reduce arousal (drive reduction). But if they are too low, as during periods of boredom or excessive rest, arousal is actively sought.

THINKING CRITICALLY

Optimal arousal theory suggests that we are motivated to achieve a particular level of physiological arousal. However, reversal theorists have identified two motivational states. We are said to be telic when we seek to reduce our arousal levels and paratelic when we are motivated to achieve higher arousal. We can be classified by reversal theory as one of two types. Telic-dominant people generally seek to reduce their arousal levels whilst paratelic-dominant people generally seek to increase it. What does reversal theory suggest about optimal arousal theory?

INCENTIVES

Researchers eventually also demonstrated that human beings are frequently motivated by the idea of rewards or **incentives**, rather than internal drives or arousal needs. Incentive theory suggests that while drives and needs for optimal arousal may *push* us in certain behavioural directions, incentives *pull* us. What does this

> **KEY IDEAS** drive theory Drive theory is a theory of motivation initially proposed by Clark Hull in 1943. The central idea is that behaviour is motivated primarily by the desire to reduce unpleasant conditions of arousal which have resulted from basic physiological needs.

> **KEY IDEAS** homeostasis Literally meaning 'to stay the same', the term *homeostasis* is used to describe a steady, regulated state where various physiological processes (eg, water intake, blood sugar, body temperature) are maintained at appropriate levels.

> **KEY IDEAS** optimal arousal theory This is a theory proposed in reaction to problems with drive theory. Optimal arousal theory is based on the idea that people are motivated to achieve and maintain an optimal level of arousal. This could mean reducing levels of arousal from unpleasantly high levels, as described in drive theory, but it could also mean *increasing* levels of arousal from unpleasantly low levels, as in states of boredom or excessive rest.

> **KEY IDEAS** incentives An incentive is any rewarding condition that provides a motive for some behaviour. Incentives are extrinsic. Examples of incentives include financial rewards and punishment avoidance.

push-pull distinction mean? As a result of learning over time, people come to asso-ciate certain experiences with pleasurable sensations and mental states. We are then 'pulled' (motivated) towards such states and sensations, even if no specific drive or arousal system has been activated to 'push' us there. Getting high on recreational drugs or **alcohol** is a good example of behaviour that is often incentive motivated—although it may also result from arousal needs (to alleviate boredom).

Intrinsic and Extrinsic Motivation

❯ KEY IDEAS intrinsic and extrinsic motivation **Intrinsic motivation** is a category of motivation which leads a person to engage in a behaviour because the behaviour is rewarding for its own sake, rather than providing some sort of additional external incentive or reward. **Extrinsic motivation** on the other hand is a category of motivation which compels a person to engage in a behaviour for an external reward that the behaviour might bring.

The idea that incentives, in addition to needs and drives, motivate behaviour led psychologists to distinguish between two general categories of motivation: **intrin-sic** and **extrinsic** (eg, Deci, 1975). An **intrinsic motivation** compels us to engage in some behaviour because it is rewarding for its own sake (see Figure 16.4). For example, studying hard for an exam and doing well can be intrinsically rewarding in that it brings a sense of personal accomplishment and satisfaction—regardless of any external, tangible reward. If you are motivated to study for such reasons, you are *intrinsically* motivated.

On the other hand, studying hard and doing well may also bring higher grades, the approval of your parents or teachers, chances of scholarships, and so forth. Studying hard for purposes such as these is *extrinsically* motivated behaviour because you are working towards some sort of *external* reward. Most behaviour probably occurs as a result of a combination of intrinsic and extrinsic motivations. However, educators have been particularly interested in understanding how intrinsic motivation arises, because research has shown that when students work from intrinsic motivation they

FIGURE 16.4 Intrinsic motivation. When asked why he decided to climb Mt Everest, George Mallory famously responded, 'Because it's there.' This is a classic example of in-trinsic motivation. An extrinsic motive to climb Everest—for example, because your boss wanted you to do it and would pay you a bonus to do so—would be unlikely to count for as much once you were cold, tired, and worried about falling to your death!
Source: Daniel Prudek/Shutterstock.com.

learn more efficiently, are more engaged and enthusiastic, and use more effective study strategies (Ryan and Deci, 2000).

The distinction between extrinsic and intrinsic motivations was first acknowledged in the context of animal studies, where it was noted that animals may engage in some behaviours apparently out of simple curiosity, playfulness, and sense of exploration, even in the absence of any obvious payoff or reward (Harlow, Harlow, and Meyer, 1950; Harlow, 1953; White, 1959). These early researchers discovered some surprising properties of intrinsic and extrinsic motivations.

The Additive Principle vs the Undermining Effect

It makes intuitive sense that doing something that is intrinsically interesting and satisfying in its own right might lead to a good level of motivation. However, you might equally expect that if the prospect of external rewards were added to the mix, motivation for the activity might be strengthened even further. This combination of extrinsic and intrinsic motives is known as the **additive principle**.

However, in studies among rhesus monkeys, primatologist Harry Harlow and his colleagues (Harlow et al, 1950) found that the monkeys' natural inclination to learn through exploration and play *diminished* when rewards were offered for performing the same activity (see Figure 16.5). These findings led researchers to propose that extrinsic motivation might actually undermine rather than support the learning experience in human beings, particularly if the learning experience is intrinsically interesting (Lepper, Greene, and Nisbett, 1973). This is sometimes called the **undermining effect**. As researcher Martin Covington put it, 'If someone has to pay me to do this, then it must not be worth doing for its own sake' (Covington, 2000, p 23). The end result is that if the reward is no longer available, the person loses motivation to continue performing the task.

This undermining effect can be seen in sport, where it is common for athletes to lose motivation once they have achieved elite status and become rich. However, the situation is complex (Cerasoli, Nicklin, and Ford, 2014). Some activities are not inherently fun or interesting, even when they relate to something that can inspire intrinsic motivation in some contexts. However much you enjoy a sport this does not mean that all the training activities are enjoyable. Similarly scales are not interesting for musicians and, however much you love your psychology, it is unlikely that you enjoy every activity that comes with studying it—think referencing, advanced statistics, and 9.00 a.m. lectures! Nonetheless we do these things for a blend of reasons that span the intrinsic-extrinsic divide. In practice we are probably motivated by a blend of intrinsic and extrinsic motives in most aspects of life.

To complicate things further it seems that extrinsic motives may have more impact on the *frequency* of a behaviour whilst intrinsic motives are more associated with its *quality*. So you can probably influence someone to do something more often by means of extrinsic motivation; however, you probably won't make them care more how well they do it and you may in fact lead them to care *less* (Cerasoli, Nicklin, and Ford, 2014). To return to the example of sport, you can persuade a champion boxer to keep on fighting by offering huge fees, but you can't make them *hungry* for victory as they were when chasing their first title.

Some research suggests that if extrinsic rewards such as grades are viewed as feedback to help improve one's performance, or if the reward is well earned for intrinsically interesting work successfully performed, intrinsic motivation may be increased (Covington, 2000). Specific rewards that stimulate intrinsic aspects of a

> **KEY IDEAS** the additive principle and the undermining effect These concepts have both been developed in relation to combining intrinsic and extrinsic motives in order to try to boost performance. The **additive principle** states that adding an extrinsic motive to an existing intrinsic motive will increase the overall level of motivation. The **undermining effect** takes place when in practice introducing an extrinsic motive reduces intrinsic motivation.

FIGURE 16.5 The undermining effect. Rhesus monkeys studied by Harry Harlow and his colleagues spent over ten days playing with a series of clasps and hooks, with the only reward being discovery of how the mechanisms work. When they subsequently were rewarded for their activity with food, they became less interested in the locks and clasps.

Source: Harlow Primate Laboratory/ University of Wisconsin-Madison.

learning experience—such as rewards of books for reading tasks accomplished—may also increase performance (Marinak and Gambrell, 2008). However, it seems that introducing external rewards for activities people are already enjoying is not generally a good idea.

 THINKING PRACTICALLY

Think about your study of psychology. If you are studying undergraduate psychology or psychology elements of a course, your lecturers will use elements of their practices and policies to stimulate your motivation, using both intrinsic and extrinsic strategies.

Exercise: explain how each of these strategies might make use of intrinsic and/or extrinsic motives.

a) Recording attendance at lectures and setting a minimum percentage to pass modules or avoid disciplinary action.

b) Exemplifying psychological theory and principles using real-life examples in lectures that have particular relevance for students.

c) Giving feedback that involves both grades and suggestions for how to improve essay or report-writing technique.

Interestingly, pursuing extrinsic life goals such as financial rewards, fame, and beauty may lead to more than disappointment if these goals are not achieved. More surprisingly they may lead to reduced feelings of well-being when they *are* achieved! In a study of individuals during their second year after graduating from university, Niemiec et al (2009) found that students who had set out to fulfil intrinsic goals such as 'deep, enduring relationships' or helping others to 'improve their lives', and who had fulfilled these goals in part, experienced increased feelings of contentment, well-being, connection with others, and satisfaction with life. However, those who has set out to fulfil extrinsic goals such as wealth, fame, or beauty—*and who had fulfilled their goals* at least in part—reported *reduced* feelings of well-being, increased physical symptoms of anxiety (headaches, stomach aches, fatigue), and more negative emotions such as shame and anger.

NEEDS

> **KEY IDEAS** needs A need is an internal state of physiological and/or psychological tension or discomfort that motivates a person to perform some action. This tension can be physiological, as in hunger, thirst or cold, emotional as in loneliness, or more cognitive, as in concern over future financial security.

Needs can be defined as internal states of tension that motivate a person towards some action (Kanfer, 1990). So through experiencing a need for food, we are motivated to eat. A need for the company of others can get us out of bed, into our clothes, and out into the street. Experiencing a need for security, we may be motivated to seek a career with a good salary and secure employment in the hopes that this will help resolve the inner tension produced by our security needs.

Maslow's Hierarchy of Needs

Humanistic psychologist Abraham Maslow (1970) proposed that human motivations form a hierarchy based on the urgency of the motivating need. Provided we are well fed and safe people spend considerable time and energy pursuing intellectual or social interests (Maslow would call these higher-level needs). However, these things soon become luxuries if we find ourselves in a position where we cannot take more basic needs for granted. You might for example really love psychology and look forward to spending some time in the university library following up our suggested reading (satisfying your intellectual needs). If though you were to find yourself homeless or trapped in a war zone the chances are that you would be more preoccupied with your next meal and overnight shelter—these are basic needs.

As depicted in Figure 16.6 Maslow proposed five categories of needs which form a hierarchical pyramid. Maslow later proposed that there were six categories of needs, with the sixth being 'self-transcendence'. However, the vast majority of research and writing on Maslow's ideas adheres to the five-category model. The importance of each category of needs at any given time is determined by the order in which they are fulfilled. The first (bottom) category must be satisfied before the second category of need will become important; the first and second must be satisfied before the third category becomes important, and so forth.

In the first category at the very bottom of the pyramid are immediate physiological survival needs such as food, water, and oxygen. At the top of the hierarchy is *self-actualization*—the fulfilment of a person's creative potential—which Maslow believed represented a human need. In between these two extremes are needs including safety and security, love, belonging, prestige and achievement, and so forth.

It certainly makes intuitive sense that motivations to fulfil life-sustaining needs, sometimes termed *primary motivations*, generally take precedence over *secondary motivations*—motivations to fulfil less basic needs such as the need for belonging with others or the need for achievement (discussed this chapter). Despite the common-sense nature of this idea, however, early research found relatively little evidence that Maslow's needs existed universally, particularly self-actualization needs (Wahba and Bridwell, 1976). It was also often pointed out that primary and secondary motivations cannot always be neatly separated into categories. In some

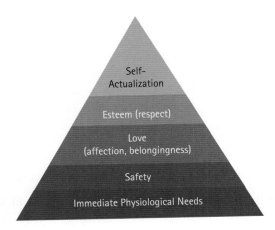

FIGURE 16.6 Maslow's hierarchy of needs. Humanistic psychologist Abraham Maslow proposed that human needs form a hierarchy, with higher-level needs becoming activated only when lower-level needs are satisfied. Maslow's levels of needs are: *physiological needs, safety needs, needs for love and belonging, needs for self-esteem and the esteem of others, and self-actualization needs.*

cases, so-called secondary motivations may be stronger than primary motivations. Consider the lives of saints, martyrs, soldiers, artists, and others who sacrifice their comfort and their very lives in the service of causes, religions, or ideas in which they believe. In spite of threats of bodily harm, loss of employment and resources, they persisted.

 THINKING CRITICALLY

Following the military response to civil unrest in Tibet in 2008, a number of Tibetans protested by means of self-immolation. This is a remarkably painful death, yet political activism motivated many Tibetans to choose this end. What are the implications of self-immolation for Maslow's theory as a universal explanation for human motivation?

Consequently, the notion of a hierarchy of needs fell into general disfavour for a time. However, beginning in the 1990s, a new round of studies was conducted using more sophisticated methods. These newer studies began to corroborate parts of Maslow's basic common sense theory of motivation (Kluger and Tikochinsky, 2001). For example, researchers provided ample evidence that throughout the world, *most* people in *most* situations do turn towards satisfaction of higher-level needs only after their basic physiological and safety needs are fulfilled (Ronen, 1994). Exceptions, such as where political activists sacrifice their lives for a cause, tend to take place in exceptional situations.

 THINKING PRACTICALLY

Homelessness is a complex social problem with many contributory factors, both societal and individual. Approaches to working to rehouse homeless people can be broadly categorized as part of one of two models: 'housing first' or 'continuum of care'. In the dominant *continuum of care* model homeless people work through stages of supported housing, only achieving permanent housing when they have stayed sober or engaged with mental health services. However, the less common *housing first* model, in which homeless people are provided with secure and reliable housing before working to tackle other problems, tends to have better outcomes (McNaughton, Nicholls, and Atherton, 2011). Explain why this might be the case using Maslow's hierarchy of needs.

Fundamental Motivations: Maslow's Hierarchy 'Renovated'

In spite of research confirming some of the intuitive aspects of Maslow's theory, Maslow's pyramid of needs itself is often considered by psychological scientists to be a 'quaint' idea without much contemporary relevance (Kenrick et al, 2010, p 292). However, recently, Kenrick and colleagues have attempted to 'renovate' Maslow's pyramid by bringing it in line with contemporary thinking in anthropology, psychology, and evolutionary science. Their goal was to preserve what is most useful in Maslow's model, while expanding its accuracy and contemporary relevance (Kenrick et al, 2010).

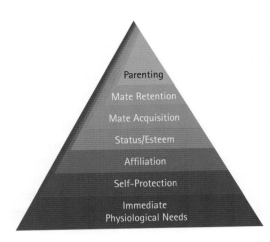

FIGURE 16.7 Maslow's hierarchy 'renovated'. In Kenrick et al needs form an overlapping pyramid according to levels of analysis: evolutionary, developmental, and cognitive.

As depicted in Figure 16.7, according to Kenrick et al, certain needs/motivations are *fundamental* in an evolutionary sense. They have arisen in human beings everywhere because they reflect the evolutionary history of our species. Kenrick and colleagues' updated pyramid of fundamental needs includes some of Maslow's original needs, specifically: *immediate physiological needs*, *safety needs* (termed *self-protection*), and *esteem/respect* (termed *status/esteem*). However, Kenrick et al contained Maslow's needs for love and self-actualization within their categories of *affiliation/belongingness*, *mate acquisition*, *mate retention*, and *parenting*.

More than simply adding some new needs and shuffling the placement of others, however, Kenrick et al view the pyramid not as a series of needs stacked on top of one another—each one brought into play only when the one below has been satisfied—but as overlapping motivational systems that must be understood according to different *levels of analysis*. If you recall from our brief discussion in Chapter 2, different levels of analysis address different aspects of the same question.

Kenrick et al use three levels of analysis to create their revised pyramid of needs: the *evolutionary* level, the *developmental* level, and the *cognitive* level. The evolutionary level examines how the various needs evolved through natural selection to help solve specific survival- or reproduction-related problems faced recurrently by our ancestors. Immediate needs for food, water, shelter, and self-protection have obvious relevance to survival and reproduction, but also important are needs to associate with other people (affiliation), enter close relationships (belongingness), obtain status or esteem in one's group, acquire and maintain mating relationships, and parent children.

The developmental level views the pyramid of needs as they play out across the life cycle in a *life history*. Different organisms mature at different rates and engage in different kinds of activities related to survival and reproduction at different points in their life cycle and for shorter or longer lengths of time. As a result, different needs may become more or less prominent, not only because more basic needs have or have not been satisfied but also due to the organism's **developmental stage** and the genetic 'programme' common to its species (the genome).

The cognitive level of analysis explores which of the motivational systems is operating to motivate a behaviour at any given time. This level looks at immediate or *proximal* causes of motivated behaviour. An example given by Kenrick et al is this: if you are having lunch with your boss, and you discover a poisonous spider crawling up your leg, self-protection goals are likely to supersede goals for satisfying hunger as well as goals for status and esteem. But if it is an ant instead of a spider, and your boss has just offered you a promotion, esteem goals are likely at the forefront (Kenrick et al, 2010, p 302).

Kenrick et al's 'renovation' of Maslow's hierarchy of needs is new and will undoubtedly undergo scrutiny from other researchers. However, various early commentaries on their work, while taking issue with certain details, have generally applauded their basic notion: that Maslow's hierarchy contains truths about human nature that should be preserved, but that the original model needs to be brought into line with contemporary thinking based upon empirical research and theory (Schaller et al, 2010).

Universal Motives

Kenrick and colleagues' 'renovation' of Maslow's hierarchy of needs raises the issue of *universality* of certain human motivations. From time to time in this chapter, one motivation or another may be referred to as *universal* or *nearly universal.* This does not mean that every individual or nearly every individual experiences a particular motivation every day, as is typically (but not always) the case with hunger. Instead, these terms refer to motivations that are *species-typical*—common to our species regardless of **culture** or historical era, and reflecting fundamental evolutionary forces that have operated on the history of the human species (Kenrick et al, 2010).

Certain motivations are clearly universal because they sustain and reproduce human life itself—motivations to breathe, eat, drink, and engage in sexual behaviour, for example. However, the story is less clear for the motivations often termed *secondary,* such as belonging and achievement. Nonetheless, both empirical evidence and theory suggest that many such secondary motivations are experienced by people all over the world and deserve the term *universal* or *fundamental* (Barkow, Cosmides, and Tooby, 1992). See Figure 16.8.

READ THIS

Some of the early theories of motivation are complex and fairly impenetrable, but you might like to *dip into* this:

Hull, C.L. (1950). Behaviour postulates and corollaries—1949. *Psychological Review,* **57,** 173.

The work of Maslow is more accessible and relevant so we'd give that a go in more detail:

Maslow, A.H. (1943). A theory of human motivation. *Psychological Review,* **50,** 370.

Maslow, A.H. (1964). *Religions, Values, and Peak-Experiences* (Vol 35). Columbus: Ohio State University Press.

For something more up to date try something by Dan Kenrick et al; for example, this:

Kenrick, D.T., Neuberg, S.L., Griskevicius, V., Becker, D.V., and Schaller, M. (2010). Goal-driven cognition and functional behavior: The fundamental-motives framework. *Current Directions in Psychological Science,* **19,** 63–7.

FIGURE 16.8 Secondary motivations may overcome primary motivations. In 1963, Mahayana Buddhist monk Thich Quang Duc immolated himself in a busy street in Saigon, South Vietnam, to protest against the oppressive policies of then-president Ngo Dinh Diem. This photograph starkly demonstrates that basic physiological and safety needs are not always primary in human motivation.

Source: Malcolm Brown/AP/Shutterstock.

COGNITIVE APPROACHES TO MOTIVATION

When it comes to explaining individual differences in motivation in **applied psychology**—including workplace, sporting, and educational settings—most of the theories and perspectives we have looked at so far are of limited use. Either they explain common motives rather than individual differences or they are just too crude to explain the subtleties of motivation in particular situations. There are exceptions—there will always, for example, be a place in applied psychology for the distinction between intrinsic and extrinsic motives—but in general applied psychology is dominated by more cognitive and social-cognitive approaches.

Self-Efficacy

Think back over your own life for a moment. How often have you wanted to learn to do something—drawing, ballet, car repair, martial arts, fiction writing, computer programming, carpentry—but did not even try to learn because 'I'm not good at that sort of thing'? On the other hand, how often have you attempted something difficult because that kind of task is in your comfort zone. Your core belief about your ability to produce change or accomplish a specific task through your own efforts is known as **self-efficacy** (Bandura, 2007). Self-efficacy is an important influence on motivation because we have a tendency to both seek out and persevere at tasks that we are confident of carrying out successfully.

According to Bandura, human beings first and foremost work to exercise *control* over the nature and quality of their lives. These efforts are channelled in part through

> ❯ **KEY IDEAS** self-efficacy This is Albert Bandura's term to describe one's core beliefs about one's ability to produce change or accomplish a specific task through one's own effort. Although some people may be higher than others in self-efficacy across many domains, perceived self-efficacy is not a trait in which a person can be globally high or low. It always refers to specific tasks, and a person high in self-efficacy on one task can be quite low on another.

---

the mechanism of perceived self-efficacy. If we do not believe that we can achieve a goal or produce a desired effect by our actions—that is, if we are low in self-efficacy for that goal or effect—we may not be motivated to continue when faced with difficulties. From Bandura's perspective, all other motivating factors, emotional or cognitive, have at their roots a core belief that we can produce change by our own actions.

Self-efficacy first influences your choice of goals—whether you enrol in that class, apply for the job, buy the art supplies or the book on computer programming in the first place. Next, it influences how much effort you put into accomplishing your chosen goals. It affects the length of time you are willing to persevere in the face of difficulties. In other words, self-efficacy affects the direction, intensity, and duration of motivated behaviour. Self-efficacy also appears to be associated with reduced or better management of anxiety; for example, in exams (Putwain, Sander, and Larkin, 2013).

A number of factors have been demonstrated to affect self-efficacy. Understanding these factors has many practical applications in the workplace, sport, and education because self-efficacy appears to be fluid rather than fixed and because high levels of self-efficacy are associated with good performance. There are strong correlations between self-efficacy and success, leading to the suggestion that success affects self-efficacy. Of course, it may simply be that self-efficacy influences success, and this is a good example of an area of research where causation has to be teased out from correlational research. Spurk and Abele (2014) measured occupational self-efficacy and career success over nine years in 600 German professionals and found evidence of a positive feedback loop—success influenced self-efficacy and self-efficacy influenced career success.

THINKING CREATIVELY

We believe that perceived success influences self-efficacy. It may therefore be possible to improve self-efficacy by changing someone's perceptions of their success. Suggest as many ways as possible to improve people's perceptions of their success. You might wish to think about a particular sporting, educational, or occupational scenario. HINT: start with the obvious—persuasion.

Self-efficacy may also be influenced by the confidence of others. This was demonstrated in a sporting setting by Jackson et al (2014) in which athlete perceptions of their peer and coach confidence in their abilities in Australian athletes including football, volleyball, basketball, and water polo players predicted their self-efficacy.

Goal Setting

Recall from the beginning of the chapter that motivated behaviour is *purposive* behaviour—defined in part as any activity directed towards achieving a goal. But how we set goals for ourselves and others has a profound impact on motivation and the performance of tasks. This is the essence of **goal-setting theory**, devised over the past several decades by Edwin Locke and Gary Latham (2006). It is among the most influential theories in all of psychology (Mitchell and Daniels, 2003).

As Locke and Latham observed, 'When people are asked to do their best, they do not do so' (2002, p 706). Locke and Latham do not mean that people are contrary by nature. They mean that motivation is increased and performance enhanced in the workplace when *specific* rather than general goals are set. 'Do your best' does not work as well as 'Please finish constructing eight of these boxes before 3:00 p.m.' This applies to goals one sets for oneself as well: 'I'm going to finish as many of these stupid boxes as I can' does not work as well as 'I'm going to finish eight of these stupid boxes before 3:00 p.m.'

However, goals must not only be specific, they must be *difficult*. Contrary to what you might think, the more difficult the goal, the higher the level of motivation and performance. Although easy goals are by definition easier to attain, people do not work as hard or as well to attain them as they do when the stated goal is difficult. Only when the goal is *impossible* are motivation and performance reduced.

Setting specific and difficult goals for yourself or others (eg, employees) increases motivation and performance in three basic ways:

- First, it directs *attention* towards activity that will help accomplish the job and away from activity that is not relevant to the job.

- Second, setting specific and difficult goals increases *effort*.

- Third, it increases *persistence*. People are more willing to work harder and longer to attain specific and difficult—but possible—goals.

> **KEY IDEAS** goal-setting theory Goal-setting theory is an important theory of motivation in applied settings devised by Edwin Locke and Gary Latham. According to goal-setting theory, work motivation and performance are enhanced when *specific* and *difficult* (but not impossible) goals are set. Setting specific and difficult goals directs attention towards appropriate activities to reach goals, increases effort to achieve goals, and increases persistence in working towards goals.

THINKING CREATIVELY

The scouting movement aims to foster physical, psychological, and spiritual development in young people by providing challenging and disciplined activities. Scout leaders require young recruits to chant 'I will do my best' (Figure 16.9). Goal-setting theory would predict that this is an ineffective motivational strategy. Based on what you know about goal setting devise your own motivational chant for the Scouts.

FIGURE 16.9 **Scouts chant 'I will do my best'.**
Source: SasinTipchai/Shutterstock.com.

> KEY IDEAS SMART and
SCRUFFY targets **SMART** targets
are highly structured targets
based on the work of Doran
(1981), designed to be maximally
motivating by being specific,
measurable, assignable, realistic,
and time-related. As a reaction
against the alleged overuse of
SMART targets, **SCRUFFY** targets
have emerged—these being
student-led, creative, unspecified,
and fun for youngsters.

DEBUNKING: ARE SMART TARGETS REALLY MORE MOTIVATING?

The idea of using specific targets or goals as ways to organize and regulate purposive behaviour
dates back at least to nineteenth-century philosophy. It is also an important application of cognitive theories of motivation—in particular, goal-setting theory. The current understanding of what
makes a motivating target owes a lot to Doran (1981), who proposed the idea of **SMART** targets.
Doran proposed that ideally targets should have five characteristics:

- **Specific:** targets should focus on something specific for improvement.
- **Measurable:** targets should identify a measure of progress.
- **Assignable:** targets should assign responsibility for a task to a named person.
- **Realistic:** they should state what results can realistically be achieved given available re-
  sources. Targets should identify what can be achieved realistically.
- **Time-related:** targets should identify a time frame in which the outcome will be achieved.

Although Doran was clear that not all targets had to have all the SMART elements, in current
education and work SMART targets have become omnipresent—and in many cases exclusive. It
has become conventional wisdom in management circles that targets are motivating if they are
SMART and not so otherwise. But is there any evidence for this?

Well, there *is* evidence to show that teaching students to plan their learning using SMART targets as a framework can lead to performance improvements (Castrillion et al, 2013; Rubin, 2015).
However, these results could equally be explained by the usefulness of simply teaching students
target setting rather than *SMART* target setting. There is a lack of more direct evidence for the
advantages of SMART targets over generic targets.

SMART targets may have a special role in contexts where the impact of specific achievements
within an identified time frame have been modelled and we have a good idea that it really matters whether x change is achieved by y time. An example is in environmental science and policy
(Watson et al, 2015). So in the 2020 Strategic Plan for Biodiversity a target has been set of 17% of
Land and 10% of Sea to have the status of Protected Areas. Environmental scientists have a good
idea of the impact of meeting or failing to meet these targets so the specificity of the percentages
and date are meaningful. This is very different to saying that a child must be able to write ten
fronted adverbials by 2.15 p.m. on Friday when there is no evidence to suggest that whether the
child can do this will have any effect on the rest of their life!

Because of the rigidity with which SMART targets are often applied there has been something of a
backlash against them. In the domain of Special Educational Needs and Disabilities (SEND) the idea
of **SCRUFFY** targets has gained considerable ground. Lacey (2011) proposed that effective targets
should be student-led, creative, unspecified, and fun for youngsters. There is a small body of evidence to show that practitioners prefer this kind of target and believe in its usefulness; however,
like SMART targets, SCRUFFY targets have very limited support from rigorous outcome research.

So in conclusion it seems that SMART targets have their uses but that there is no real evidence to
support the dogma that they are uniquely motivating, or that all targets need be SMART.

WHAT'S HOT? GROWTH MINDSET THEORY

Carol Dweck (2000) proposed what has become arguably the most talked about—and
debated—theory of motivation in current applied psychology. Dweck made the distinction
between fixed and growth **mindsets**. These mindsets are based on our **implicit theories of**

intelligence. We can be said to have a **fixed mindset** when we believe our cognitive abilities are fixed. This belief is called an **entity theory** of intelligence. By contrast a **growth mindset** is based on the belief that our intelligence is mutable (changeable) and that we can therefore significantly boost our mental abilities through effort. This belief is called the **incremental theory** of intelligence. Dweck noted that students from populations with a cultural belief that cognitive abilities are principally the result of effort showed better perseverance and resilience as compared with those (like Western Europe and the USA) who see them as largely fixed. Dweck was interested in student motivation to learn; however, her ideas have been applied in other contexts, proving highly influential in the workplace.

Dweck (2010) identified three ways in which students with fixed and growth mindsets respond differently in academic situations. First, students with fixed mindsets avoid challenge because they see it as more important to look clever than to learn, whereas those with a growth mindset relish difficulty. Second, those with a growth mindset realize that even the naturally talented need to work hard, whereas there is little incentive for those with a fixed mindset to work hard as they regard abilities as unresponsive to effort. Finally, those with a fixed mindset are easily discouraged by failure because they see it as insurmountable, as opposed to those with a growth mindset who see failure as an opportunity to develop.

Dweck (2010) proposed a set of strategies to help students develop a growth mindset:

1 *Emphasize challenge not success.* Tasks should never permit some students to succeed easily as this promotes a fixed mindset. Instead tasks should stretch and challenge students as much as possible, whilst giving them the opportunity to succeed with effort. Feedback on successful completion of tasks should emphasize effort rather than achievement.

2 *Give students a sense of progress.* Exercises and feedback should be organized so that students are aware of their increasing mastery of concepts and tasks. Praise can then be targeted to cases where effort has led to improved mastery.

3 *Grade for growth rather than raw achievement.* No student should be able to 'coast' to a top grade. Nor should anyone fail without the possibility to upgrade the result. Effort as well as achievement can be graded as long as it is clear that a real value is placed on effort.

Dweck's ideas make intuitive sense; however, evaluations of programmes designed to boost growth mindset have yielded very inconsistent findings. Donohoe, Topping, and Hannah (2012) examined the impact of Dweck's online *Brainology* programme in Scottish 13–14-year-olds. They found that initially the programme shifted mindset but that this was not sustained for long and that it had no impact on student resilience. Of course, lack of effect of an online programme does not invalidate Dweck's ideas, but it does suggest that it is much harder than it sounds to shift to and maintain a growth mindset.

Dweck (2015) has explained such failures using the concept of false growth mindset. She suggests that some practitioners endorse growth mindsets, even referring to them in class, but do not follow through with the necessary behaviours to shift fixed mindsets in students.

Dweck's theory generates a number of testable predictions; for example, that students with growth mindsets persevere and achieve better than those with fixed mindsets. So far, so good.

❯ **KEY IDEAS** mindsets and implicit theories of intelligence These are closely related ideas that form the basis of Carol Dweck's theory of motivation. Our implicit theory of intelligence is our belief in the potential for intelligence or mental abilities to be enhanced by effort and practice. We are said to have an entity theory if we believe intelligence is fixed and an incremental theory if we believe intelligence can change. Having an entity theory of intelligence leads to a fixed mindset, in which we are not motivated to master cognitive tasks. If, however, we have an incremental theory of intelligence we believe our cognitive abilities are open to change and so we will have a growth mindset and be motivated to work towards mastering abilities.

However, a number of commentators have criticized the concept of false growth mindsets as pseudoscience. The problem is that an explanation that can explain any critical argument or contradictory evidence is not really testable. If a study shows that mindset-based interventions don't have the intended effect this can be explained away by saying that those administering the intervention had a false growth mindset.

READ THIS

It would be easy to accept the intuitive appeal of Dweck's theory, but equally easy to uncritically accept the pseudoscience argument. However, the 'right' thing to do is to investigate further. Before you make up your own mind about growth mindset you might want to read Dweck's defence of her theory. You can read one such article here: Dweck, C, (2015) Carol Dweck Revisits the 'Growth Mindset', Education Week, **35**(5), pp 20—24.

 THINKING CRITICALLY

Dweck's theory was based on sound science but has received mixed reviews. Work through our evaluation toolkit for theories in Chapter 1 for Dweck's theory. How does it stand up?

PERSONALITY AND MOTIVATION

As discussed in greater detail in Chapter 15, personality is a broad concept denoting the ways in which individuals differ from one another in patterns of cognition, emotion, and behaviour.

Trait Approaches

> ❯ KEY IDEAS personality traits
> Traits are relatively stable, enduring personal characteristics. Traits are relevant to having a complete understanding of motivation because they help explain individual differences in how strongly motivated we are by different factors.

Personality traits are relatively stable, enduring personal characteristics, attributes, and motives for behaviour. Traits can generally be described using adjectives of various sorts. For example, *conscientious, honest, lazy, aggressive, sociable, shy, bad-tempered,* and *kind* are all adjectives that could be used to describe traits.

The influence of traits on motivation is complex, however, because (as discussed in Chapter 15) people may behave differently in different situations regardless of their overall traits. This is true of work situations as much as any other (Tett and Burnett, 2003). For example, in jobs with high levels of autonomy, performed without substantial reliance on others (eg, author, house cleaner, repair person, CEO, travelling sales rep), people high in the trait *conscientiousness* tend to outperform those who are less conscientious. This is presumably because they need to be able to regulate their own motivation without oversight by a boss (see Figure 16.10).

On the other hand, in jobs that depend on working effectively with other people, conscientiousness seems to have little positive effect on performance, and might even reduce job performance if the conscientious worker in question generally lacks 'people skills' and has difficulty in social situations (Witt and Ferris, 2003). In such cases conscientiousness can become a disadvantage because the motive to be

FIGURE 16.10 Authors who are conscientious tend to be more successful than those who aren't, because they are able to self-motivate.

Source: Rawpixel.com/Shutterstock.com.

thorough in the face of the complex motives affecting the people we work with can result in inflexibility.

Locus of Control

Self-efficacy is sometimes confused with a related idea—the *locus of control*, a concept pioneered in the work of Julian Rotter (1966). Locus of control refers to a person's beliefs about the causes of events in their lives. Those who are high in *internal* locus of control generally attribute their successes and failures to their own efforts and behaviours, while those low in internal locus but high in *external* locus of control tend to attribute life events to factors beyond their control—the workings of fate, circumstance, or the actions of other people.

Unlike self-efficacy, locus of control is a more general orientation to explaining events in one's life in terms of internal or external factors. It is stable across situations so, unlike self-efficacy, it can be considered an aspect of personality. Yet the constructs are clearly related, and those who are high in internal locus of control have a tendency towards high self-efficacy in many situations.

So how does locus of control impact on motivation? One answer lies in its link to **metacognition**. Metacognition is our awareness of our own mental processes. We vary in metacognitive knowledge (ie, how well we understand our own cognitions). In one recent study internal locus of control predicted the use of metacognitive knowledge which in turn predicted achievement in maths (Bishara and Kaplan, 2018). This suggests that people with an internal locus of control are more motivated to understand how to do maths—or anything else. This makes sense—if you see your own efforts as responsible for success in a task it becomes worthwhile to put effort into understanding *how* to be successful. If you see success as externally controlled there is little point in trying to understand how you can affect it.

READ THIS

The modern cognitive approaches to motivation are definitely 'where it's at'. We would therefore recommend reading some of the original material; for example:

Bandura, A. (1977). Self-efficacy: Toward a unifying theory of behavioral change. *Psychological Review*, **84**, 191–215.

Locke, E. and Latham, G. (1994). Goal-setting theory. In John B. Miner (ed), *Organizational Behavior 1: Essential Theories of Motivation and Leadership*. London: Routledge, 159–83.

Dweck, C.S., Mangels, J.A., Good, C., Dai, D.Y., and Sternberg, R.J. (2004). Motivational effects on attention, cognition, and performance. *Motivation, Emotion, and Cognition: Integrative Perspectives on Intellectual Functioning and Development*, **2**, 41–55.

Rotter, J.B. (1990). Internal versus external control of reinforcement: A case history of a variable. *American Psychologist*, **45**, 489–93.

IN REVIEW

MOTIVATION

- Motivations are mental states which lead us to engage in purposive activity.
- Some motives are unconscious and some are hard to comprehend. Motives can conflict with one another.
- As an internal state motivation is inherently difficult to study.

BIOLOGICAL APPROACHES TO MOTIVATION

- Early psychologists conceived of motives as instincts. Instincts are innate behaviour triggered by releasing stimuli.
- Instinct as it was originally conceived raises issues of circular logic; however, the ideas of fixed-action patterns and adaptation are still part of contemporary psychology.
- Hull developed the idea of drives as an alternative to instincts. Drives are desires to reduce unpleasant physiological sensations.
- Drives can explain some simple motives like hunger but not more complex motives nor individual preferences.

INCENTIVES

- We are motivated by external incentives as well as internal drives/instincts. This gives rise to the distinction between intrinsic and extrinsic motives.
- Intrinsic motives involve an action being rewarding in itself. Extrinsic motives are based on some external reward.
- The relationship between intrinsic and extrinsic motivation is complex. Under some circumstances extrinsic motives appear to undermine intrinsic motives; however, most behaviour is guided by both.
- Frequency of behaviour can be manipulated by extrinsic motives; however, its quality is usually more influenced by intrinsic motives. Fulfilling intrinsic motives is generally more satisfying.

NEEDS

- Needs differ from drives in that they can be social, cognitive, and emotional as well as physiological.

- Maslow conceived of a hierarchy of needs in which we are motivated to first satisfy physiological needs, then social needs, the cognitive needs, and finally to self-actualize.

- Most of the time people generally satisfy needs in this order of priority. There are exceptions, however.

- Kenrick et al have reconceived of Maslow's hierarchy as not a linear hierarchy but a set of three overlapping domains: evolutionary needs, developmental needs, and cognitive needs.

COGNITIVE THEORIES OF MOTIVATION

- In keeping with the dominance of the cognitive paradigm cognitive theories of motivation dominate current psychology.

- Bandura proposed self-efficacy—the idea that we are motivated to do things we believe we are capable of.

- Locke's goal-setting theory sets out the idea that we are motivated by specific and difficult-to-achieve goals.

- Doran proposed the related idea of SMART goals. SMART goals have become very popular in education and management; however, they are probably not uniquely motivating in most circumstances.

- Dweck proposed the idea of growth mindsets, in which the main determinant of motivation is belief in the mutability of intelligence.

INDIVIDUAL DIFFERENCES AND MOTIVATION

- Some personality traits, such as conscientiousness, appear to be associated with motivation.

- We also differ in locus of control. Generally an internal locus of control is associated with higher levels of motivation.

TEST YOURSELF

1 All behaviour is purposive. True ☐ False ☐

2 There is evidence for the existence of unconscious motivation. True ☐ False ☐

3 Getting high on recreational drugs is an example of an incentive motive. True ☐ False ☐

4 Which of the following is **not** one of the three most often types of motivation?

   a) Drives

   b) Needs

   c) Incentives

   d) Whims

5 Which of the following types of motive can be defined as one where we are responding to an external reward?

a) Intrinsic motive

b) Extrinsic motive

c) Achievement motive

d) Unconscious motive

6 Which of the following is the best definition of the undermining effect?

a) When a colleague deliberately undermines your work and spoils your motivation

b) When an extrinsic motive added to an intrinsic motive increases your over-all motivation

c) When an extrinsic motive added to an intrinsic motive decreases your over-all motivation

d) When your achievements are overshadowed by those of peers, decreasing your motivation

7 Which of the following is **not** an element of a SMART target?

a) It is achievable

b) It is measurable

c) It is relevant

d) It is time-bound

8 Outline one problem with the concept of instinct.

9 Distinguish between self-efficacy and growth mindset.

10 Explain how one personality trait can affect motivation.

 Visit the online resources that accompany this book: www.oup.com/uk/jarvis-okami1e

CHAPTER 17

EMOTION

LEARNING OUTCOMES

By the end of this chapter you should be able to:

- Define emotion and understand the range of basic emotions
- Appreciate the importance of human emotions in decision-making and regulating social interaction
- Evaluate different theories of emotion, including James-Lange and Cannon-Bard biological theories and cognitive theories by Schachter and Singer and Lazarus
- Recognize the concept of embodied emotion, and evaluate research into facial feedback
- Take a position on debates around anger, including the effectiveness of catharsis and forgiveness
- Critically evaluate research into happiness, with particular regard to factors affecting happiness, including genes, lifestyle, social factors, and income

Emotion has historically been seen as a kind of human flaw—an obstacle to intelligent action. This view has a long history in philosophy going back to the ancient Greeks. For much of the twentieth century psychologists tended also to adhere to this notion (Evans, 2001). It is not difficult to see why: all they had to do was look at their own lives. But would a person *without* emotion really behave more intelligently and live a more successful life? What are emotions, anyway? If they are more hindrance than help, why do we have them in the first place?

THE NATURE OF EMOTION

Like most important questions in psychology, there is disagreement about specifics of definitions of the term *emotion*, and no definition has gained wide acceptance (Izard, 2009). However, most behavioural scientists agree in a general way when it comes to certain basic facts about the characteristics of emotion: an **emotion** is a psychological state consisting of five essential components:

1 *Neural systems* dedicated to processing or producing emotion.
2 *A subjective experience* or *feeling*.
3 *Physiological changes*.
4 *Cognitive changes* associated with the emotion.
5 *Behavioural responses* which express the emotion. (Izard, 2009; Figure 17.1)

FIGURE 17.1 The five emotion characters in *Inside Out* represent five of the six basic emotions identified by Paul Ekman. The sixth, surprise, was judged too difficult to personify as a character distinct from fear.

Sources: top left: Diego Cervo/Shutterstock.com; top right: WAYHOME studio/Shutterstock.com; top middle: WAYHOME studio/Shutterstock.com; bottom left: Vikafoto33/Shutterstock.com; bottom right: paulaphoto/Shutterstock.com.

Emotion can thus be described as a psychological state consisting of subjective experience or feeling, physiological changes, and behavioural responses. Emotions tend to be intense, attributable to a potentially identifiable cause, and relatively short-lived.

As an example, *fear* is characterized by:

1 Neural pathways from the thalamus and cerebral cortex to the amygdala, insula, and other brain regions.

2 A distinct subjective feeling of alarm and the presence of danger.

3 An increase in activity of the sympathetic nervous system.

4 Fear-related changes in thinking.

5 Any number of behavioural responses, such as the appearance of characteristic facial expressions, changes in tone of voice, actions, or postures designed to protect the body from harm, and so forth.

Emotion, Mood, and Affect

Emotions are relatively intense but short-lived experiences. Consider *anger.* You may be able to recall being angry with someone 'for days', but if you think more carefully about it, you'll probably note that you slipped in and out of a genuinely angry state, perhaps reigniting angry feelings periodically with thoughts about the offender or the triggering event. Thus, emotions can be distinguished from **moods**, which are typically less intense states, but which may pervade a person's life for days, weeks, months, or possibly even years at a time. A person may be *depressed* (mood) more or less continuously on an ongoing basis, but they are not likely to remain in a state of acute *sadness* (emotion) 24 hours per day for very long. Moods and emotions differ in one other respect. The origin of a particular mood is often difficult to trace to specific events, and it might be hard to pinpoint the reasons underlying its presence. Emotions are more likely to have identifiable causes (Lazarus, 1991a, 1991b; Morris, 1999).

Affect describes the general quality of your feelings. Affect does not refer to any specific emotion or mood, and it does not differentiate between moods and emotions in general. Instead, it is the raw material from which emotions and moods are created (J.A. Russell, 2003). For example, there are many ways of feeling 'good' in affect. You could be joyous, serene, peaceful, buoyant, content, excited, and so forth—all specific emotions or moods.

As depicted in Figure 17.2, affect differs along two dimensions. The first is *valence*, the positive-negative dimension of affect. Positive affect is experienced under conditions that are pleasant, helpful, or rewarding. Negative affect is experienced under conditions that are unpleasant, hurtful, or threatening (Barett, Mesquita, Ochsner, and Gross, 2007).

As Figure 17.2 shows, affect also differs by *level of activation*, or strength of arousal. Affect can be highly activated (in either good or bad ways) or low in

> **KEY IDEAS** emotion and related constructs An **emotion** is a short-lived, intense psychological state with physiological elements and the subjective experience of a feeling. **Mood** is a feeling state that is typically less intense than an emotion, but which may last for a much longer time. **Affect** is a more general feeling state which provides the 'raw material' from which emotions and moods are created. Affect differs along two dimensions: valence (positive-negative) and activation or arousal (high-low).

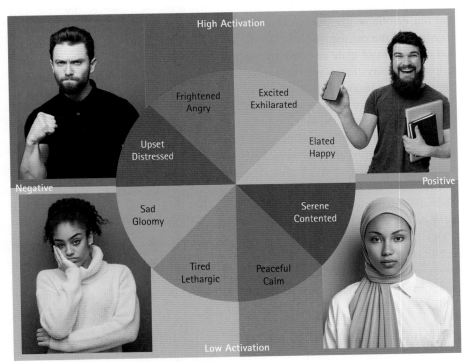

FIGURE 17.2 **The two dimensions of affect. Affect exists along two dimensions which interact: valence (negative-positive) and activation (low-high). For example, two equally pleasant states—*exhilarated* and *peaceful*—differ markedly in their levels of activation. Exhilaration is associated with an excited, high-activated state, whereas peacefulness is associated with calm and low levels of activation. Similarly, lethargy and fear are both unpleasant, but lethargy is low in activation and fear high in activation.**

Source: Adapted from Russell, 2003, p 148; Top left: F8 studio/Shutterstock.com; top right: Vulp/Shutterstock.com; bottom left: Asier Romero/Shutterstock.com; bottom right: WAYHOME studio/Shutterstock.com.

activation (also in good or bad ways; Feldman, 1995; J.A. Russell, 2003). Understanding the way affect differs from emotion or mood is important to understanding some of the ongoing debates about emotion we will attend to later.

Pleasant and Unpleasant Emotions

Although most of us prefer to experience pleasant emotions, unfortunately, the number of possible unpleasant emotional states greatly outnumbers the number of pleasant ones.

This imbalance is reflected in the statistic that in most languages there are at least twice as many words to describe negative as positive emotions. The ratio is even greater if we consider only the emotions *fear, anger, joy/happiness, disgust, interest/ surprise, contempt,* and *sadness.* These are often termed **basic emotions**, in part because they are universal and thought to form the basis for other emotions when they are blended—much like the primary colours form the basis for other colours when they are blended (see Ekman and Cordaro, 2011, for a complete discussion of basic emotions). When we consider how prevalent unpleasant emotions are, it is clear that the notion frequently advanced in pop psychology and self-help books that emotional pain is somehow 'not normal' (and therefore needs to be treated) is not well grounded in human history and experience (Horwitz and Wakefield, 2007).

Why do we experience so many different negative emotions in comparison to positive ones? There is no definitive answer to this question. However, if we consider that our emotions, like our motivations, are the products of evolutionary history, it may be that the consequences of ignoring potentially harmful situations (eg, danger and death, loss of mate or family) were greater on average during most of our evolutionary history than were the consequences of ignoring potentially helpful ones (eg, the chance to form a beneficial love relationship or friendship; Baumeister et al, 2001). Harmful situations may have commanded our attention to a greater degree than situations that were benign or helpful, and caused us to evolve more subtle distinctions in our feelings about negative events (Schrauf and Sanchez, 2004). This would have resulted in more varied types of negative emotions and the words to describe them. Some research also suggests that people have a tendency to assume that someone is expressing a negative emotion when the person's facial expression might be interpreted as either positive or negative—as in the emotion of surprise (Neta and Whalen, 2010).

This theory explains two other facts: people try harder and have more varied techniques to escape bad moods than they have to induce good moods; and they remember experiences of bad emotions better than they recall experiences of good emotions. As one group of researchers put it, 'bad is stronger than good' (Baumeister et al, 2001, p 323).

Functions of Emotions

As these ideas suggest, emotions, like motivations, were likely to have fulfilled numerous functions over human evolutionary history. These functions might have included enabling communication and social interaction with friends, family, potential mating partners, co-workers, and strangers; motivating people to avoid harmful situations or relationships and seek out beneficial ones; and providing feedback on behaviour so that a person could have altered their course of action if it had proved counterproductive (Ekman, 2003a). While there is little doubt that emotions can deceive us and lead us into ill-chosen actions, it is equally clear that their benefits greatly outweigh their risks, and if they really hindered intelligent action they would have disappeared long ago (Baumeister et al, 2007).

Decision-making

Research has demonstrated that rational decision-making is disastrously disrupted when the ability to experience emotion is lost. Antonio Damasio (1994) describes the case of 'Elliot'. Elliot suffered damage to a circuit between the prefrontal cortex and the amygdala (a brain structure associated with emotional life—see 'The limbic system', Chapter 4). Following the damage, Elliot continued to score in the normal or above-normal range on intelligence tests. However, his emotional experience was blocked. Rather than increasing the rationality of his decision-making processes, however, his condition utterly disrupted his ability to make intelligent decisions— from what would be a good menu choice when dining out to which restaurant to visit in the first place. He could not make decisions as simple as whether to use a pen with black or blue ink. Why? Because he had no particular *emotional* preference for any of the many options available to him in any given situation. He could not fathom the connection that exists between bad feelings and bad choices. Consequently, he soon lost his job, his wife, and his ability to earn a living. Elliot's lack of emotional response extended to the disastrous consequences of his injury, which he seemed to accept with icy calm. Elliot's case suggests that emotion and reasoning processes must be balanced to produce intelligent and productive action. Without emotion, we cannot truly learn from our mistakes because these mistakes would not produce punishing consequences (Bechara et al, 1997).

 THINKING CRITICALLY

Damasio's case study of Elliot is a convincing illustration of the role of emotion in decision-making. However, what are the limitations of clinical case studies like this. You should consider both the limitations of all case studies and the particular issues associated with brain injury with large lesioned brain areas.

Regulating social interaction

The ability to identify, manage, and express one's emotions constructively and to empathize with the emotions of others has been termed **emotional intelligence** by the writer Daniel Goleman (1995). As Goleman puts it, emotional intelligence is a set of abilities 'such as being able to motivate oneself and persist in the face of frustrations; to control impulse and delay gratification; to regulate one's moods and keep distress from swamping the ability to think; to empathize and to hope' (Goleman, 1995, p xii). Although psychologists continue to debate whether such talents are akin to a form of intelligence or are simply a set of skills or personality traits (see, eg, Locke, 2005), the qualities that are included under the label 'emotional intelligence' are associated with a host of positive outcomes in areas such as academic performance, personal relationships, social behaviour, and organizational leadership (Mayer et al, 2004).

❯ KEY IDEAS emotional intelligence This is the ability to identify, manage, and express one's emotions constructively and to empathize with the emotions of others. Emotional intelligence is believed to be extremely important in permitting successful social interaction.

BASIC EMOTIONS

Researcher Dylan Evans (2001) recalls the time when, at age 15, he was asked by members of a punk rock band to replace their lead singer who suffered from stage fright. Evans was delighted enough to join the band, but when one of its members told Evans that he was personally very happy Evans had joined the band, Evans reports that he experienced an intense reaction:

> A warm wave spread outwards and upwards from my stomach, rapidly enveloping the whole of my upper chest: It was a kind of joy, but unlike any moment of joy I had felt before. It was a feeling of acceptance, of belonging, of being valued by a group of people whom I was proud to call my friends. I was momentarily lost for words, shocked by the novelty of the sensation. In the years since then, the feeling has never repeated itself exactly, and I have never forgotten it. (pp 1–2)

Evans commented that there is no word in English to describe the 'oceanic feeling' he experienced that day. It was not until he heard the Japanese word *amae*, which translates loosely as 'feeling secure and comforted in the complete acceptance and benevolence of another person' that Evans believed he had found the right word. But while Japanese-speakers have a single word for this emotional experience and English-speakers do not, it is clear that many English-speakers have experienced a similar emotion (Hupka, Lenton, and Hutchison, 1999).

Numerous emotion theorists have come to the conclusion that certain emotions are experienced at some time by virtually *all* human beings, whether or not we have words for them in our language. They may be part of our evolutionary heritage—and perhaps the heritage of at least some other mammals as well (Panksepp, 2005a, 2005b). These emotions are termed **basic emotions** (Ekman and Cordaro, 2011).

According to basic emotion theorists, basic emotions are universal, entirely distinct, 'hardwired' into the human nervous system, and *primary*. Just as a vast number of colours may be derived from primary colours, a vast number of emotions may be derived from basic emotions. For example, the emotion described earlier which the Japanese refer to as *amae* is one of an uncountable number of emotions derived from the basic emotion of enjoyment/happiness. *Annoyance* and *rage* are among the emotions derived from anger; *anxiety*, *worry*, and *terror* from fear; *anguish*, *melancholy*, and *loneliness* from sadness. Emotion researcher Carroll Izard refers to emotions which are derived from basic emotions as emotion schemas (Izard, 2011), while other theorists merely refer to each basic emotion as having a large 'family' of more complex or subtle emotions (Ekman and Cordaro, 2011).

Exactly which emotions are basic, and how would one know such a thing? Not only have psychologists been unable to come to a consensus on this issue, but also the problems in coming to agreement have led some investigators to doubt that it would ever be possible to devise a definitive list. Others claim that the very concept of basic emotion is misleading and results from misinterpretation of the evidence (Barrett, 2006). Nevertheless, it is probably fair to say that the majority of psychologists affirm the existence of basic emotions.

In this book we use a relatively short list of basic emotions including only those upon which there is fairly wide (although not unanimous) agreement: *fear, anger, sadness, enjoyment/happiness, disgust, contempt,* and *surprise.* Each of these emotions is entirely distinct—a person simply cannot confuse enjoyment/happiness with

> ❯ **KEY IDEAS** basic emotions
> **Basic emotions** are those which appear to be universal, innate, and distinct. Characteristic facial expressions and/or body language are generally associated with basic emotions. It has been suggested that more complex emotions are derived from the basic emotions. Psychologists are not in agreement as to the number of basic emotions, which specific emotions are basic, or even if the concept itself is valid.

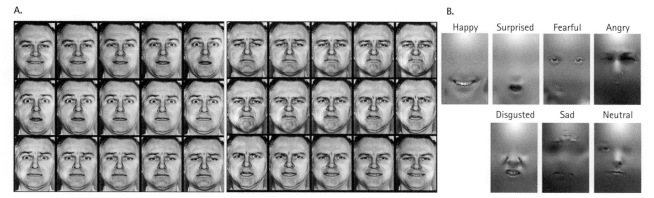

FIGURE 17.3 How much visual information do we need to identify basic emotions? In Figure A, each face depicts a 'pure' basic emotion at the far left of each row. The face is then morphed through various stages by blending it with another emotion as it moves to the right. By the time the image reaches the far right it has become a different 'pure' basic emotion. The researchers found that only the 50–50% blended image (the middle image of each row) was not reliably identified as whichever was the predominating emotion. In Figure B, researchers presented research participants with small portions of faces randomly sampled by computer. The images here represent the amount of visual information that was necessary for the participants to correctly distinguish each emotion at 75% accuracy.

Sources: (A) Reprinted from Calder, Andrew J. et al (2010). The relation between anger and different forms of disgust: Implications for emotion recognition impairments in Huntington's disease. *Neuropsychologia*, July. Copyright © 2010, Elsevier; (B) Marie L. Smith et al (2005). Transmitting and decoding facial expressions. *Psychological Science*, 3 Jan, p 187. Copyright © 2005 © SAGE Publications. DOI: 10.1111/j.0956-7976.2005.00801.

fear, sadness with disgust, or contempt with surprise (see Figure 17.3). Each is readily identified and comprehended by others and, as leading emotion researcher Paul Ekman has shown in 40 years of research, each is associated with specific facial expressions and frequently with specific body language as well (Ekman, 1994, 2003a; see Figure 17.3).

While basic emotions are distinct, it is relatively rare to experience a pure basic emotion for very long. Emotions play off one another and are often experienced in sequence. For example, we may initially feel fear, then immediately become angry because we have been made to feel afraid. We may then feel frightened by our own anger, followed by contempt at ourselves for having experienced this entire sequence. The whole thing may then make us miserably sad (Ekman, 2003).

Basic emotions may also sometimes blend. Consider the emotion described by Brazilians and Portuguese as *saudade*. *Saudade* is a dreamy, wistful, and fatalistic longing for a beloved person or place that currently is absent from one's life, but for which there is at least a possibility of reunion in the future (slim as the chance may be). This subtle and complex emotion schema is derived from a blending of sadness in the present with happiness in memories of the past and hopes for the future.

Ekman eventually discovered that specific facial muscles were involved in creating the expressions of basic emotion, and he has catalogued these muscular configurations into a coding scheme known as the **facial action coding system** (FACS; Ekman and Friesen, 1978; Ekman and Rosenberg, 2005). For example, a smile of genuine enjoyment, known as a **Duchenne smile**, can easily be distinguished from a forced or a polite smile, but not by looking at the smile itself. The key is the eyes.

❯ **KEY IDEAS** facial action coding system This is Paul Ekman's coding scheme of the facial muscle configurations which create expressions of basic emotion. An example of an expression revealed by the FACS is the **Duchenne smile**. This is a smile of genuine enjoyment or pleasure, characterized by contraction of the orbicularis oculi muscle surrounding the eye. This muscle is extremely difficult to contract at will.

A.   B.

FIGURE 17.4 Unmasking the fake smile. Photos A and B depict the 'closed' smile, with no teeth showing. However, the smile in Photo A is forced. Photo B shows the real thing—the Duchenne smile involving contraction of the *orbicularis oculi* muscle. Incidentally, the photos A and B depict Ekman himself.

Source: The Paul Ekman Group.

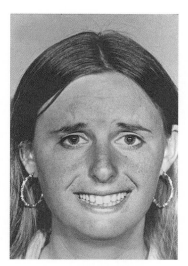

FIGURE 17.5 Happy or sad? In this photograph, a smiling mouth has been joined to a face expressing sadness in the area surrounding the eyes. Japanese observers were more likely to characterize this as a sad face, while American observers were more likely to call it happy.

Source: Reprinted from Yuki, M. et al (2007). Are the windows to the soul the same in the East and West? Cultural differences in using the eyes and mouth as cues to recognize emotions in Japan and the United States. *Journal of Experimental Social Psychology*, March. Copyright © 2006 Elsevier Inc. All rights reserved. https://doi.org/10.1016/j.jesp.2006.02.004

A true smile includes a contraction of the *orbicularis oculi* muscle which surrounds each eye. A portion of this muscle is difficult for most untrained people to contract at will, and only 10% of those studied by Ekman over the past 40 years have been able to do it. According to Ekman, actors who convincingly appear to be enjoying themselves are among those few who can voluntarily display a Duchenne smile (Ekman, 2003a; see Figure 17.4).

Basic Emotions and Culture

Human beings are particularly good at 'decoding' each other's facial expressions of basic emotion, and it is likely that this skill evolved along with the evolution of the emotions themselves (Schyns, Petro, and Smith, 2009). However, there appear to be cultural differences in how this is done; for example, in the parts of the face used to recognize emotions. Yuki et al hypothesized that, when recognizing emotion, people in a **culture** such as Japan—where emotional expression is subdued and controlled—will focus on parts of the face that are difficult to control intentionally (Yuki, Maddux, and Masuda, 2007). On the other hand, in a culture such as the United States, where emotional expression is encouraged, people may focus on the part of the face that is easiest to control. As depicted in Figure 17.5, when Yuki and his colleagues presented Japanese and American participants with images of faces which had been morphed to reflect happiness around the eyes and sadness at the mouth—or sadness around the eyes and happiness at the mouth—the American participants used the mouth to diagnose the emotion, whereas the Japanese participants tended to use the eyes (which are more difficult to control in genuine smiles and frowns).

This cultural difference is evident in differences in the computer *emoticons* used to suggest pleasure or displeasure in emails and such. In Europe and the United States the emoticon :-) suggests pleasure or happiness and :-(suggests displeasure or sadness. These emoticons focus on the up- or down-turned mouth to characterize the emotion. Japanese generally use the symbols (^_^) for happiness and (;_;) for sadness (crying), both of which focus upon on the eyes (Yuki et al, 2007).

THINKING PRACTICALLY

Modern emojis are designed to be recognizable across a range of cultures. Explain how this has been achieved in the following emojis—see Figure 17.6

FIGURE 17.6 **Modern emojis.**

Source: Roberto Scandola © 123RF.com.

Display rules

Recognizing emotion and expressing emotion may be related, but they are not identical. In addition to cultural differences in emotion recognition, the specific manner in which emotions are expressed varies across cultures as well as among individuals and between the sexes in any given society (Matsumoto, Willingham, and Olide, 2009).

Display rules are the implicit standards and expectations that regulate the way emotion is displayed in a given culture. Consider the expression of bereavement at funerals: in certain cultures or subcultures one is expected to express grief at funerals of loved ones by wailing, weeping, pounding the coffin, and so forth. In other cultures, one is expected to keep one's grief tightly contained. The emotion of grief in each case is equally profound, but the unspoken rules governing its expression differ.

The existence of display rules was discovered by Paul Ekman and his colleagues when they compared the reactions of American and Japanese participants as they watched stressful or disgusting films. The investigators observed the participants as they watched the films while sitting alone and also while in the presence of others (Ekman and Friesen, 1975). In Ekman's original study, American subjects rarely varied their reactions to the film whether they were watching alone or in the presence of others. However, Japanese subjects were much more likely to keep their reactions to a minimal smile in the presence of the experimenter—perhaps because the experimenter was perceived to be in a position of authority or it was deemed unseemly to display negative feelings too openly. On the other hand, when alone, the Japanese participants reacted with disgust and displeasure, just as the Americans had.

Display rules are complex and vary according to the emotion, the situation, the sex, and the status of those expressing and those observing emotion, as well as the general cultural setting. Ekman identified four ways in which display rules might vary:

- *Intensifying*, as at a funeral where one is expected to show a great deal of vivid grief.
- *De-intensifying*, as after a tennis match when the victor is usually expected to tone down expressions of joy while the defeated opponent is present (Friedman and Miller-Herringer, 1991).

❯ **KEY IDEAS** display rules
Display rules are the cultural norms and expectations that govern what is or is not a socially acceptable way to display emotion.

- *Masking*, as when one pretends to feel a certain emotion while actually feeling a different (probably unacceptable) one. Consider your response as you accept a disappointing gift in the presence of the gift-giver.
- *Neutralizing*, the complete hiding of emotions—as while attempting to be convincing during a lie.

Emotion and Deception

Are you a liar? We all hate to think so but consider that an online survey of 3,000 British adults conducted by the Science Museum (Serota and Levine, 2014) found an average of 2.08 lies told per day in the UK, with minor differences emerging between England, Wales, Scotland, and Northern Ireland. However, this is a good example of where means do not tell the whole story. The standard deviation, a common measure of how spread out results are around the mean, emerged as very large. This shows that there are wide individual variations in lying, with a small number of people accounting for a disproportionate number of lies.

Some researchers have investigated whether rates of lying differ according to the communication mode—face-to-face, telephone, or in computer-mediated communication such as email, texting, or instant messaging. In one study, substantial differences in rates of lying emerged: phone conversations elicited the highest rate of lies, while email elicited the lowest rate (Hancock, Thom-Santelli, and Ritchie, 2004).

Lying may be destructive and immoral, and it may get you into various degrees of trouble, but being deceptive and spotting deception in others is part of the way human beings—and other species—go about the business of their daily lives (Trivers, 2010). Evolutionary theorists such as Robert Trivers and Richard Dawkins propose that deception evolved as one tool in the struggle for survival and reproductive success.

So who do people lie to? If you are like Bella DePaulo's research participants, you will tell fewest lies to those to whom you feel closest—and you will feel more distressed at having told these lies. The exceptions to the *feel closer → tell fewer lies* rule are romantic partners (one lie in every three interactions) and mothers (one lie in every *two* interactions!) (De Paulo and Kashy, 1998). Of course, many of the lies you tell those to whom you feel close (including Mum) will be lies designed to spare the other person's feelings in some way, known as *altruistic lies*. Most of the lies you tell others will be entirely self-serving.

Without doubt, then, lying is a part of most people's lives, although some of us lie quite a bit more often than others. And, while we try hard not to be discovered in a lie, we would all very much like to be able to tell when *others* are lying. Unfortunately, research has shown that most people are unable to tell a lie from the truth when it comes to the lies of relative strangers intent on deception. On average, people can tell a truth from a lie no better than 54% of the time in research studies, which is only slightly better than chance guessing (Hartwig and Bond, 2011). If you think you can 'just tell' when a person is lying, you are probably wrong.

On the other hand, human beings evolved under conditions where attempts at deception must have been common (as they continue to be). People lie outright or withhold the truth to gain advantages of various sorts. It stands to reason that at least a modest ability to *detect* lies also ought to have evolved, in a co-evolutionary process as the talent for deception evolved (Trivers, 2010). As liars got better, it stands to reason that we should have gotten better at ferreting them out. Then why does research paint us all as terrible lie detectors?

Part of the problem may be in the research itself (von Hippel and Trivers, 2011). Most research in human lie detection involves relatively trivial lies told by strangers under laboratory conditions. However, this is not how the vast majority of lies are told. Lies are told in real life, often by people known to one another, and these lies may have important consequences—such as during police investigations. When researchers had participants keep 'lie diaries', the journal keepers reported that their lies were detected by those close to them a substantial portion of the time (DePaulo et al, 1996); and in a study of police officers evaluating statements made on video tape by actual suspects in high-stakes cases, the officers' average accuracy in detecting lies was 72%—substantially above chance and better than they themselves predicted they would perform (Vrij et al, 2006).

When people do detect the lies of others, face to face, how do they do so? There is no foolproof method of human lie detection, because cues that a person is telling a lie can be faint, and some of them appear when a person is telling the truth as well (von Hippel and Trivers, 2011). For example, although liars are often nervous in telling their lies because they are afraid of being discovered, truth tellers may be just as nervous if they are afraid of not being believed! Emotions linked to lying may be linked to truth-telling as well.

However, researchers using cognitive psychology to increase the effectiveness of face-to-face lie detection have made a simple but powerful observation about lying: telling a lie is more *demanding* on a person's cognitive resources than telling the truth—that is, lying increases *cognitive load* (Vrij et al, 2011). As Aldert Vrij and his colleagues point out, liars need, first, to make up a good, plausible story. They need to remember the details of the story to keep it consistent. They need to keep from providing inadvertent leads to the truth. They need to strictly monitor their behaviour so they appear to be honest and credible people—and they need to monitor the behaviour of the person to whom they are lying to make sure they are getting away with their lie. Liars may be preoccupied with reminding themselves to remain in the role they have created for themselves. All of this can require extreme mental effort (Vrij et al, 2011).

Vrij and colleagues note that since liars have fewer cognitive resources remaining than truth-tellers, this deficit can be exploited by those seeking to ferret out the truth. For example, the next time you believe you are being lied to, ask the suspected liar to tell his or her story *in reverse order* of its occurrence. This may increase the person's cognitive load to the point that the whole enterprise may fall apart. Another technique is to ask the person to maintain eye contact with you as he or she speaks. When people need to concentrate to tell a story—for example, when trying to remember forgotten details of a true event, or when lying—they often look away from their conversation partner to a fixed point, because maintaining eye contact can be distracting. Unfortunately, such techniques are very far from foolproof, and the holy grail of lie detection by means of facial observation is still beyond our grasp.

THEORIES OF EMOTION

As long as psychology has existed there have been debates around the nature of emotion. Early theorists were concerned by the relationship between emotional experience and physiological state. More recent theories have been concerned with the role of cognition in emotion.

Early Theories: Which Comes First, Feeling or Emotion?

William James, writing at the end of the nineteenth century, believed that the preceding sequence was an illusion. Instead, he argued that emotion exists first and foremost in a person's physiology. That is, *emotion is feeling*. He concluded that it is the physiological response which triggers the emotion, not the other way around. For James, the proper sequence is 1, 3, 2: there is a thought or event; it creates physiological changes such as an increase in autonomic nervous system activity; awareness of these physiological changes reaches the cerebral cortex; and only *then* do we feel the appropriate emotion. Thus, we are happy because we are smiling, sad because we are crying, and frightened because our hearts are racing and our palms are sweating (James, 1890).

Because this theory was independently proposed by Danish psychologist Carl Lange, it has become known as the **James–Lange theory of emotion**. Does it seem unlikely to you? It did to physiologists Walter Cannon and Phillip Bard during later decades. Cannon and Bard argued that any number of emotions, including anger, love, and fear, could be responsible for identical physiological symptoms of arousal such as racing heart, sweaty palms, and elevated blood pressure. How would a person know which emotion to feel (Cannon, 1929a)?

Cannon and Bard advanced a competing theory which has come to be known as the **Cannon–Bard theory of emotion**. According to Cannon and Bard, when some sort of emotion-laden event is perceived, the sensory impulses are relayed to the thalamus first (see 'The brain', Chapter 4). The thalamus in turn stimulates *both* the autonomic nervous system *and* the cerebral cortex at about the same time. The autonomic nervous system alters levels of physiological arousal (increasing or decreasing them through activation of the sympathetic or parasympathetic nervous systems, as the case may be) and the cerebral cortex does the work of allowing the person to feel the emotion. In contrast to James and Lange, who insisted that our levels of arousal are altered first and that we experience the emotion subsequently, Cannon and Bard argued that changes in arousal and the experience of emotion occur at the same time (Cannon, 1929b).

Although Cannon and Bard's idea may make more intuitive sense than the James–Lange theory—and the thalamus does receive most sensory signals first—a number of research findings challenge Cannon and Bard's theory. For example, as we shall discover a bit later in the chapter, although activating the nervous system by injecting adrenaline does not necessarily produce a specific emotion, assuming the facial expression associated with a given emotion may produce—at least to some extent—aspects of the emotion in question (Mori and Mori, 2009). Thus, changes in physiology may well create emotional changes, as James and Lange believed.

However, even if it turned out to be the case, as James and Lange argued, that emotions such as fear originate in feelings of arousal, exactly how does the body know to produce arousal? Wouldn't we somehow need to evaluate the implications or *meaning* of a mother smacking her child when the child asked for something to eat? That is, wouldn't we need to have a sense of the injustice of the mother's actions prior to experiencing physiological arousal and emotion? Questions such as this have been of major concern to modern researchers in the *cognitive* aspects of emotion.

> **KEY IDEAS** physiology and emotion The **James–Lange theory of emotion** states that thoughts or the perception of events trigger directly autonomic nervous system changes; awareness of these changes reaches the cerebral cortex; and only then is there an experience of emotion. The alternative **Cannon–Bard theory of emotion** states that during the perception of an event, sensory impulses are first relayed to the thalamus. From there the impulses are relayed to the autonomic nervous system and the cerebral cortex at about the same time, rather than to the autonomic nervous system first and second to the cerebral cortex, as proposed in the James–Lange theory.

Cognitive Theories of Emotion

Each of us has been in situations in which we felt afraid for what turned out to be no good reason. From my (Paul) own memories: while staying at a relatively secluded cabin in the Vermont woods as a very young man, I heard a noise in the house in the middle of the night that sounded to me like someone breaking glass. I had a vision of someone breaking a windowpane to enter the cabin. My heart began to pound, my limbs started trembling, and my mouth became dry. I tried to remember my martial arts training and plan what I would do, but my mind had gone blank. I grabbed a hatchet that I had been using to chop kindling wood, tiptoed slowly into the kitchen and found . . . a raccoon rooting around in the kitchen bin. I had been seriously *afraid*—but suddenly I was not. Yet all that had really changed was the way I *thought* about the situation—my interpretation of the noises. The raccoon was still making noise in the kitchen, but the noise was no longer frightening.

Moreover, as I had been sitting up in bed experiencing a racing heart and the other symptoms of an aroused autonomic nervous system, how did I know I was *afraid*? As Cannon and Bard complained, symptoms such as sweaty palms and thumping heart could have occurred if I were angry or even when asking someone out with whom I was seriously infatuated. But I certainly knew I was afraid, not in love. Why?

Most modern theorists of emotion acknowledge the importance of *cognition* in the experience of emotion—even those researchers primarily concerned with the neuroscience and biochemistry of emotion. Although both the James–Lange and the Cannon–Bard theories *implicitly* recognize that cognitive activity must take place in the experience of emotion, they did not *explicitly* address the nature of this activity.

The Schachter–Singer two-factor theory

The first important cognitive theory was devised by Stanley Schachter and Jerome Singer (1962) and is known as the **two-factor theory of emotion**. Schachter and Singer agreed with James and Lange that autonomic nervous system activity preceded emotion. However, they believed that the changes in arousal produced by this activity were general and not specific to any particular emotion. How then did specific emotions emerge? Schachter and Singer claimed that *only when a cognitive label is attached to arousal in order to explain it does the person experience emotion*. According to this idea, the brain needs to interpret or *appraise* the source of the physiological effects it is experiencing to 'choose' the correct emotion to feel.

From this perspective, the stimuli of the noise in the kitchen set my heart racing that night, but it was only when I interpreted the noise as having been caused by a human intruder that I experienced actual fear. As soon as my interpretation changed, my fear instantly disappeared—even though the arousal took some time to subside completely. The two-factor theory differs from the James–Lange theory in that James and Lange believed that the generation of emotion was a virtually automatic response to physiological arousal, without the necessity of 'higher order' cognitive processes intervening. Schachter and Singer demonstrated the effect of cognitive priming on the experience of emotion in a classic study. We can look at this in detail in our *Research in focus* feature:

> ❭ KEY IDEAS the two-factor theory of emotion This is the theory proposed by Stanley Schachter and Jerome Singer which states that thoughts or perceptions of events directly trigger autonomic nervous system arousal—in agreement with the James–Lange theory. However, according to the two-factor theory, emotion will emerge only after a cognitive label is attached to the arousal to explain it.

RESEARCH IN FOCUS

Schachter, S. and Singer, J. (1962). Cognitive, social and physiological determinants of emotional state. *Psychological Review*, **69**, 379–99.

Aim: To test the hypothesis that participants experiencing a high level of arousal will apply a cognitive label to this and experience it as an emotion. The researchers further proposed that this labelling process can be manipulated by providing appropriate cues. They also aimed to investigate the effects of such cueing in the absence of arousal.

Method: The procedure was experimental, conducted under controlled conditions; 185 participants were told they were taking part in a study of the effect of vitamin supplements on vision. The 184 that agreed to a vitamin injection were given either adrenaline or a placebo of salt water. Participants receiving the adrenaline were divided into three conditions. In the adrenaline-informed condition they were told to expect physiological changes including raised heart rate. In an adrenaline-ignorant condition they were not told anything about physiological effects and in the adrenaline-misinformed condition they were told to expect numbness and itching.

Half the participants in each adrenaline condition were subject to cues to suggest anger (a confederate behaved angrily in response to the procedure) or euphoria (a confederate playing happily with materials in the room). Participant emotion was then assessed by means of self-report and observation.

Results: In the adrenaline-informed conditions participants were unaffected by the euphoria and anger cues. However, in the other conditions those who received euphoria experienced and displayed signs of euphoria whilst in the anger conditions they displayed and reported anger. In the placebo condition cues did not influence behaviour or self-perception of mood.

Conclusions: Both physiological and social-cognitive cues are required for the experience of euphoria and anger. Neither physiological nor external cues are sufficient. When an ambiguous internal state of high arousal is present the experienced emotion is powerfully influenced by external cues.

MASTER YOUR METHODOLOGY

1 Why might both observation and self-report have been used to assess emotion?

2 A double-blind design was used, with those administering the injections not knowing whether they contained adrenaline. Explain why this is important.

3 Participants consented to receiving an injection but they did not know the purpose of the experiment. To what extent would this comply with the British Psychological Society's current ethical guidelines?

 THINKING CRITICALLY

Look back to our critical thinking toolkit for studies in Chapter 1 (Tables 1.1 and 1.2). What strengths and weaknesses can you see in relation to this study? You might like to look in particular at criteria relating to experimental design.

The cognitive-motivational-relational theory

Another important cognitive theory of emotion was produced by Richard Lazarus. Lazarus's theory evolved considerably during the 50 years he worked in the field of emotion and cognition, and it is known by several names, notably the **cognitive-motivational-relational theory** (Lazarus, 2000). However, the most important aspect of the theory is the notion that both an emotion and any related physiological changes occur *only* after a person interprets—or *appraises*—the meaning of the event. Unlike Schachter and Singer, to Lazarus, cognition always comes first and arousal and emotion second.

Returning for a moment to our example of disciplining children, different people hold different opinions about smacking and its appropriateness. Some of us think it appropriate under all conditions of a parent's choosing, some think it appropriate only under certain conditions, and others believe it is never appropriate. Therefore, only those in the latter two groups should be expected to experience anger at the sight of a mother smacking her child. Moreover, the second group should only experience anger after appraising the specifics of the situation and concluding that the smacking is unjust. Therefore, even if the experience of anger appears instantaneous, cognitive appraisal of the situation must occur *prior* to arousal and emotion, according to Lazarus—albeit at lightning-fast speed and below the level of conscious awareness.

Emotional experiences that bypass cognition

If cognitions cause emotions, as Lazarus, Schachter, and Singer argued, how is it that infants can be happy, sad, angry, surprised, fearful, and disgusted even though they have no language and relatively few well-developed cognitive concepts (Yirmiya et al, 1998)? And how is it that some non-human animals display the physiological arousal, behaviours, and facial expressions characteristic of human emotion (Baars, 2005)?

There is no doubt that emotion can emerge without *conscious* thought. For example, stimuli such as angry or happy faces flashed on a screen much too quickly for a person to become consciously aware of them can influence the person's mood and produce movement in the facial muscles associated with the particular emotion exhibited in the face flashed upon the screen (Dimberg, Thunberg, and Elmehed, 2000). As explained earlier, however, cognitive theorists such as Lazarus (1991a, 1991b) have insisted that even in these cases, at least *some* form of cognitive appraisal must be occurring, even if it is below the level of awareness.

Yet substantial evidence from brain imaging studies shows that certain emotions, notably *fear*, may sometimes have direct pathways from perception to emotion that bypass the cortex—and therefore, cognition—entirely. This is a perspective that Robert Zajonc argued for over a quarter of a century (Zajonc, 1984). Evidence supporting his ideas comes most importantly from the work of neuroscientist Joseph LeDoux (2000). LeDoux demonstrated that there is a pathway of neural impulses from the thalamus, which receives and processes sensory signals, to the amygdala. The amygdala is activated during many emotions, but appears to be the most important brain region responsible for fear responses (Barot et al, 2009). The amygdala in turn activates other brain structures which produce the physiological arousal associated with fear. This direct pathway to the amygdala accounts for the fact that

> **KEY IDEAS** cognitive-motivational-relational theory of emotion This is the theory proposed by Richard Lazarus. It states that autonomic nervous system arousal occurs not directly, as stated in the James–Lange and two-factor theories, but only after the thought or event has been appraised so that the meaning of the event is interpreted by the person. In this theory, cognition always comes first.

we can respond instantly with fear to the appearance of potentially threatening visual or auditory stimuli. For example, a person coming quietly into a room and then speaking suddenly while you have been concentrating on a task might sound your fear alarm. ('Oh! You scared me!')

However, the direct pathway to fear, somewhat like most smoke alarms, is highly *sensitive* but not very *specific*. Highly sensitive mechanisms produce many false alarms, technically referred to as false positives (eg, the person coming quietly into the room is just your little sister). On the other hand, highly *specific* mechanisms will only go off when they are supposed to, in the presence of the correct stimuli. But sometimes they may fail to go off at all if the stimulus isn't strong enough, creating false negatives. As you might see, the consequences of a fear mechanism not going off when it is supposed to are potentially much more severe (eg, death) than such a mechanism firing numerous false alarms (false positives).

Yet, when a seeming threat occurs that turns out to be a false alarm, how do we recover our composure so quickly? ('Oh—it's just you. Can't you knock or walk a little louder when you come into the room?') According to LeDoux's findings, there are *two* pathways to fear (see Figure 17.7). The first is the rapid, direct pathway from the thalamus to the amygdala described previously, sometimes referred to as the 'low road'. However, signals are also travelling from the thalamus to the cerebral cortex, only more slowly. It is in the cortex that the threat is evaluated and appraised. This second pathway to fear—the 'high road'—is highly *specific*, but not particularly sensitive. The results of the cortex's computations are then sent to the amygdala. If the threat is real, the amygdala continues to ring the alarm. If it is not, it shuts the fear response down.

Fear is an unusually powerful emotion. You can probably see why: not responding to fear-inducing situations could easily result in death. Thus, it seems likely

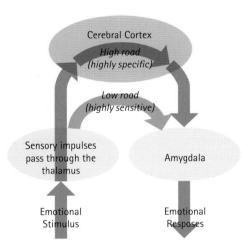

FIGURE 17.7 LeDoux's dual pathways to fear. Joseph LeDoux hypothesized that there are two pathways to fear: a 'high road' and a 'low road'. The initial fear response (low) travels directly from the sense organs (eyes, ears, etc) to the thalamus and from there to the amygdala. This pathway is highly sensitive. A secondary response occurs as the sensory impulse is relayed from the thalamus to the cortex, where it is evaluated and appraised (the 'high road'). If the stimulus is judged to be a genuinely fearful one, impulses are relayed to the amygdala and the body continues to respond in a fearful manner. Otherwise, the entire mechanism is shut down. This pathway is slower, but it is specific rather than sensitive.

that we have evolved particularly sensitive mechanisms involving fear. This fact is understood well by advertisers, politicians, and others seeking to create persuasive messages. Those seeking to persuade use fear as a tool, particularly if the audience feels vulnerable to some threat (eg, terrorism) and the message offers a coping strategy or hope for effective response to the threat (Crano and Prislin, 2006). Historically fear has been employed in the age-old practice of manipulating people into buying all kinds of useless products that allegedly protect them from a variety of ills, real and imagined, or supporting military actions, wrong-headed legislation, and all manner of social policies.

The tendency to be persuaded by fear may have its good side, however. It is now being used with some success by health psychologists and other professionals who wish to promote more constructive lifestyle choices like reducing alcohol consumption and smoking, and promoting safer driving practices (Das, deWit, and Stroebe, 2003).

Embodied Emotion: The Body Is the Mind

None of the theorists and researchers of emotion described earlier believed, as did the followers of René Descartes (see 'Pre-scientific psychology in the Age of Reason', Chapter 2), that the mind is actually separate from the body. Nonetheless, they all describe the process of emotion metaphorically as including a 'body' (physiological arousal, facial expression, posture, etc) and a 'mind' (cognitive appraisal, labelling, awareness of specific emotions, etc; Barrett and Lindquist, 2008). More recently, a group of emotion researchers have suggested that when it comes to perceiving, recognizing, or thinking about emotion, to a large extent the body *is* the mind. The theories created by this group of researchers are loosely encompassed in the category of *embodied emotion* (Barrett and Lindquist, 2008).

What does the term **embodied emotion** actually mean? Embodied emotion theories generally share a number of assumptions (Barrett and Lindquist, 2008), but most central is this: *emotions are 'captured' as body memories.* Each time an emotion is experienced, the sights, sounds, physiological processes, and patterns of body movement that occur during the experience of the emotion are encoded in clusters of neurons assigned to each of these various modalities (sight, sound, physiological responses, etc). Over time, these experiences form a conception of each particular emotion. A person returns to this conception each time he or she recognizes, recalls, or thinks about that emotion. In a sense, when thinking about or recognizing an emotion you are partially 'reliving' or 'reactivating' the original emotion as it was experienced in the various modalities of your body (Winkielman et al, 2008).

Facial and postural feedback

From an embodied emotion perspective we ought to expect a very close correspondence between one's physiology and one's emotional life. Indeed, embodied emotion theorists have found a connection between assuming specific facial expressions or bodily postures and feeling specific emotions, a finding technically known as *facial* and *postural feedback*. As already discussed, there is a very strong *link* between each basic emotion and a specific facial expression. For example, when we feel happy or hear something funny, we do tend to smile. This fact led some researchers (eg, Laird, 1984) to wonder what would happen if we forced ourselves to smile first? Might that change our emotional condition in the *direction* of happiness?

> **KEY IDEAS** embodied emotion
Embodied emotion theories assume that emotions are 'captured' as body memories. Each time an emotion is experienced, the sights, sounds, physiological processes, and patterns of motor activity that occur are encoded in clusters of neurons assigned to the various sensory and motor modalities of the body. Over time, these experiences build a conception of the particular emotion in question, which a person may reactivate by thinking about or re-experiencing the emotion.

> **KEY IDEAS** facial feedback hypothesis This is the idea that the facial expression associated with a basic emotion increases the intensity of the experience of that emotion; and that purposely activating the muscles which form a facial expression of basic emotion may actually result in a person experiencing the emotion itself— or at least experiencing a mood change in a positive or negative direction (depending on the specific expression).

As depicted in Figure 17.8 and very briefly mentioned earlier, research over four decades in this **facial feedback hypothesis** has found that activating the muscles that form facial expressions associated with basic emotions can not only increase the intensity of the corresponding emotion if one already feels it, but can sometimes actually *create* the experience of emotion or something close to it (Izard, 1990). While the effects of assuming a facial expression are not always specific to a particular basic emotion, at the very least they alter mood or emotional experience in a generally positive or negative direction, depending upon the expression. For example, smiling increases positive mood, particularly if the *orbicularis oculi* muscles are contracted. That's right—put on a happy face, and you'll feel better, just as your grandmother told you (Soussignon, 2002). In one study, simply having the muscles of the cheeks associated with smiling lifted with bandages increased happiness ratings in a group of volunteers (Mori and Mori, 2009). This works in the opposite direction as well—research participants who were instructed to assume a pained facial expression in response to burning heat sensations from a heat stimulator reported more pain than those instructed to assume a relaxed face (Salomons et al, 2008).

The body, as well as the face, offers feedback that may alter emotion. For example, research conducted during the 1990s showed that people who had been told to assume a slumped posture were more likely to report a depressed mood after receiving (bogus) information about their scores on achievement tests than were people receiving the same news in an upright posture (Stepper and Strack, 1993).

 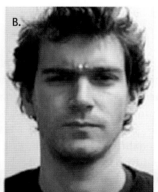 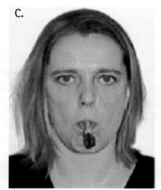 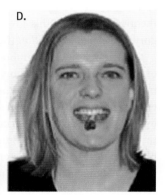

FIGURE 17.8 Put on a happy face: the facial feedback hypothesis. Researchers attached golf tees to the inside of participants' eyebrows (Photo A), and then asked the participants to bring the ends of the tees together (Photo B). This task was designed to force participants to contract their brow muscles in a manner similar to that which occurs naturally during negative emotions such as sadness. Those who furrowed their brow reported more sadness in response to disturbing photographs than those who did not engage in this exercise. In a separate study, researchers had one group of participants hold a pen between their lips, without touching their teeth to the pen, preventing the formation of a smile (Photo C). Another group held the pen between their teeth, facilitating a smile (Photo D). Those holding the pen between their teeth reported finding a series of cartoons funnier than did those holding the pen between their lips.

Sources: A and B: Reproduced with permission from Randy J. Larsen, Margaret Kasimatis, et al (1992). Facilitating the Furrowed brow: An unobtrusive test of the facial feedback hypothesis applied to unpleasant affect. *Cognition* and *Emotion*, 1 Sep. London: Taylor & Francis. Rights managed by Taylor & Francis; C and D: Reproduced with permission from Paula M. Niedenthal et al (2007). Embodying emotion. *Science*, 1 May. Copyright © 2007, The American Association for the Advancement of Science.

However, we should not exaggerate the effects of assuming a given facial expression or posture. Walking around with a broad grin on your face and your shoulders back is not likely to turn a miserable day into a sunny one. Emotion is a result of a great many factors in addition to facial expression and body posture (Duclos et al, 1989; McIntosh, 1996), and embodied emotion theorists do not rely upon facial and postural feedback as their only source of empirical support.

You may have become dizzy trying to disentangle the various claims of emotion theorists to come away with a take-home message about which theory is 'correct'. If you are looking for a take-home message, you are probably wasting your time. Each of the theories we have considered contributes a piece to the jigsaw puzzle of human emotion. Each theory looks at the problem from a slightly different perspective, stressing certain influences over others. But no single theory can unarguably be said to contribute the largest portion of the completed picture of emotion. Without doubt, physiology and cognition are both critical in the experience of emotion. In some cases, cognition may trump physiology, whereas in other cases the reverse may be true. In some cases, disentangling cognitive from physiological influences, determining which came first, or identifying the underlying neural events accompanying emotion may not be possible. Therefore, it is not necessary to become an adherent of one single theory, the way you ultimately must decide which candidate to vote for in an election. Instead it is probably best to focus on having a clear idea of the differences between these major theories of emotion.

ANGER

As we have already seen, negative emotions outnumber positive ones. An important aspect of human emotional life is coping on a day-to-day basis with these unpleasant feelings. Emotions such as *fear, anger, jealousy, envy, shame, guilt, disgust,* and *sadness* often present formidable challenges for human coping skills. We'll consider one of the most common, and without doubt the most dangerous, of the negative emotions: *anger*.

Anger is an extremely common basic emotion that most people report experiencing from several times a week to several times a day (Averill, 1982). Most people know when they are angry, but pinning down a precise definition of a complex emotion like anger can be tricky. In the broadest sense, **anger** could be defined as a feeling of hostility towards something or someone. Anger typically occurs as a reaction to an unpleasant event or idea—such as a belief that one has been harmed or threatened, or an injustice has occurred. However, anger may also exist as a character trait unrelated to any specific occurrence—a person's general tendency towards grumpiness, aggressiveness, and defensiveness.

The types of events eliciting anger—what we might call the 'triggers'—are exceptionally varied. Anger can be elicited by frustration when you are unable to realize a goal of some sort or are being interfered with in some way. Anger also results from being hurt by someone else; being insulted, denigrated, or rejected by someone important to you; or when experiencing disappointment, pain, or stress (Harmon-Jones and Harmon-Jones, 2007). Anger can range from vague annoyance to an all-consuming, fiery, homicidal rage. Although anger does not necessarily result in **aggression**—a deliberate effort to harm someone—it often does. Anger is therefore the most dangerous of all emotions. In fact, anger is defined in part as

> **KEY IDEAS** anger Anger is a hard-to-define basic emotion involving high levels of physiological arousal and a sense of antagonism towards something or someone.

an emotion 'linked associatively with an urge to injure some target' (Berkowitz and Harmon-Jones, 2004a, p 108).

However, anger may sometimes be experienced as pleasurable (eg, 'righteous anger'), and some people are more prone towards enjoying anger than others (Harmon-Jones, cited by Ekman, 2003a, p 125). Nonetheless, anger is generally extremely uncomfortable. In at least one world religion (Buddhism) it is considered one of the central causes of human suffering (Rahula, 1959), and it is also among the 'seven deadly sins' of Christianity.

Anger is difficult to avoid. Because each person's interests may not coincide with those of the next person, conflicts are bound to arise, and most people will feel unjustly treated on occasion. Anger and desire for revenge are typical human responses to such transgressions (McCullough, 2000; Pinker, 2011). The problem with anger, however, is that it often causes more suffering to the angry person than to the recipient of the anger. Although most of us usually do our best to control our anger when it arises and to look for ways to dissipate it, anger can lead to behaviour that we later regret.

Catharsis: Can We Let Anger Out?

The **phenomenology** of anger (ie, how it is subjectively experienced by the individual) is a fascinating topic in itself. One popular description of anger depicts it as a kind of liquid substance that exists within a person's mind and body ('my anger'). When cooled, the substance is not noticeable and causes no problems. But when heated, it boils, turns to steam, and strains for release. Unless the anger is expressed, it will either create an explosion ('I'm about ready to explode'), or cause our 'insides' to somehow fester ('His anger was eating him up inside'). According to this notion, you may be able to push anger around and situate it in various places in your mind, but you cannot get rid of it without expressing it.

The 'liquid substance' idea applies to other emotions as well. 'Express your feelings', we are urged, 'don't keep them bottled up' (now the liquid is in a bottle!). As a general view of emotion this idea is known as the *hydraulic model of emotion*, because in a hydraulic system liquid circulates perpetually inside a machine or device to power it. The relief one may experience by expressing emotion is termed **catharsis**, which comes from the Greek word for 'cleansing'. As suggested earlier, anger is thought to demand catharsis or else bad things will happen. Anger catharsis is popularly termed *venting*, as in 'Go ahead, let it out—you need to vent.'

In spite of the popularity of catharsis as an approach to dealing with anger the evidence for its benefits is actually pretty mixed. Punching pillows is probably a pretty ineffective strategy for dealing with anger, and there is some evidence to suggest that this kind of venting is essentially a 'rehearsal' of anger and aggression—it only serves to improve the 'performance' by keeping angry feelings and thoughts alive. This is particularly true when you *ruminate* about the events that made you angry, focusing your thoughts on the offender and the offence as you vent (Rusting and Nolen-Hoeksema, 1998). In one study Bushman (2002) first angered a group of college students by providing false but stinging criticism of an essay they had written—criticism supposedly given by another participant in the study. One group of these students was encouraged to hit a punching bag while keeping a photo of the supposed offender in view and thinking about him or her. Another group was encouraged to think about becoming physically fit as they punched the bag. Yet another group did nothing at all. Those who were encouraged

> ❯ **KEY IDEAS** catharsis Derived from the Greek word for cleansing, **catharsis** refers to the relief one may experience by expressing emotion.

to ruminate about the offender while punching the bag became the angriest, most aggressive, and reported the most negative mood later on. Those who punched the bag but thought about becoming physically fit became less aggressive and angry than the first group. Those who did nothing at all became the least angry and aggressive of all groups.

This kind of study paints a damning picture of the whole idea of catharsis; however, experimental simulations like this do not tell the whole story, and may confuse a meaningful cathartic experience with displaced aggression accompanied by unhelpful rumination. A radically different way of looking at catharsis is to study the benefits of expressed emotion in real-life contexts where anger can be expressed in a controlled and socially sanctioned manner. Elias (2008) describes moshing (a form of dance frequently practised at rock concerts) as regulated by both a set of unwritten rules and external constraints including the band and venue security, allowing the (relatively) safe and socially sanctioned expression of anger. It has a number of variations but all involve displaying ritual aggression by making hard physical contact with fellow dancers in a context where there are strict though largely unwritten rules designed to prevent serious injury. The area of a concert hall where moshing takes place is known as the 'mosh pit' or simply 'the pit' and participants are called 'moshers'. Something much more complex occurs at rock concerts than when punching a pillow. Shared responses to lyrics about personal pain and social injustice in an environment where physical expression in the form of dance is expected and sanctioned leads to massive expression of emotion that are associated with benefits to mental health (Keyes, 2002).

There may also be effective cathartic strategies that do not involve physical activity at all. If you feel the need to vent but moshing does not appeal, you might consider **scriptotherapy**. This involves writing about one's feelings. A meta-analysis by Frisina, Borod, and Lepore (2004) supports the idea that this kind of catharsis significantly benefits physical and mental health.

 THINKING CRITICALLY

The contrasting conclusions reached by experimental and field research into catharsis illustrate the complexity of conducting psychological research. Psychologists differ in the weight they accord to experimental and field research so there is no simple right or wrong answer here, but you can at least be clear on the issues. Using catharsis research as an example, identify the strengths and weaknesses of lab experiments and field studies, as described in Chapter 3.

Forgiveness: An Alternative to Catharsis

Forgiveness—which can occur through a conscious decision to forgive as well as the result of a generally forgiving disposition—is a cognitive, motivational, and emotional process that unfolds over time. As the person forgives, he or she willingly renounces the 'right' to resentful, bitter, and hostile feelings and judgements towards the offending party, abandons grudges or plans for revenge, and may also intentionally foster compassion, generosity, and other positive emotions towards the offender (Worthington et al, 2007).

Forgiveness can have powerfully positive consequences for the forgiven, the forgiver, and for their relationship. Forgiveness has been shown to have beneficial effects on Americans following the 11 September 2001 attacks; Rwandans following the catastrophic Tutsi genocide; and among former child soldiers from the Congo and Uganda (Fehr, Gel-fand, and Nag, 2010). Research even suggests that forgiveness may improve physiological health, including beneficial effects on cardiovascular disease and hypertension (Witvliet and McCullough, 2007). Thus, the point of forgiveness is not to do someone else a favour. It is to promote *your own* well-being and, if appropriate, heal relationships that you consider important. When one forgives, one may be released from the prison of one's own anger and resentment.

HAPPINESS

Clearly, not all emotions are negative. As the movement towards positive psychology has gained momentum over the past 20 years, there has been an explosion of interest in the study of human strengths and positive emotions and attributes, including happiness, life satisfaction, and subjective well-being (Lyubomirsky, Sheldon, and Schkade, 2005). A picture has begun to form of who among us is truly happy and what makes us happy, as well as what threatens happiness.

What is happiness? The larger meaning of this term has been debated by philosophers for thousands of years (Oishi, Diener, and Lucas, 2007) but there are two general senses in which *happiness* is used by psychologists. The first is to describe the basic emotion of enjoyment/happiness. Like other emotions, this form of happiness is intense, but fleeting. The other sense in which the term is used is to describe an overall subjective sense of well-being, contentment, fulfilment, and life satisfaction—the general feeling that things are going well. This is the sense in which the term is most often used by psychologists, and that's the way we will use the term in the discussion to follow.

Levels of Happiness

Happiness and its long list of variants—enjoyment, contentment, satisfaction, gladness, fulfilment, well-being, and so forth—are important goals of most people's lives, and most of us appear to be reasonably happy when we consider our lives overall. Polls and psychology research studies consistently report that, when asked, most people around the world, regardless of race, sex, or form of government—unless they are living under conditions of extreme political suppression—report that they either are very happy and satisfied with their lives or reasonably so. Relatively few report being very unhappy or unsatisfied. Interestingly though, happiness scores are not normally distributed. Brule and Veenhoven (2017) plotted the distribution of 1–10 happiness scores across 90 nations and found a bimodal distribution, with 5 and 8 being the modes. This appears to indicate that most people are either neutral—not particularly happy nor unhappy—or pretty (but not entirely) happy. This is shown in Figure 17.9.

Findings that people are at least reasonably happy and satisfied with their lives occur regardless of how these variables are measured. Although most surveys simply ask people to rate how satisfied they are with their lives overall, Daniel Kahneman and his colleagues asked a sample of 909 women to fill out a highly detailed evaluation of *each* of the activities they engaged in the day before. These researchers gave participants a choice of adjectives to describe how they felt as they performed the activity—for example, *enjoying myself, happy, warm/friendly* or *frustrated/annoyed, depressed/blue, hassled/pushed around, angry/hostile.* Kahneman and his

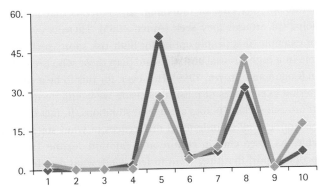

FIGURE 17.9 The distribution of 1–10 happiness scores in two international samples. Almost all scores are at least 5 out of 10; however, two clear modal scores of 5 and 8 can be seen.

Source: Brulé, G. and Veenhoven, R. (2017). *Social Indicators Research*, 131, 853. https://doi.org/10.1007/s11205-016-1265-x

research team found that, while certain activities were rated more positively than others, participants rarely chose any negative adjectives to describe how they felt (Kahneman et al, 2004).

What Makes Us Happy?

Understanding what makes us happy begins with the person's 'happiness set point', a general level of subjective well-being to which we tend to return even if we experience temporary periods of uncharacteristically higher or lower levels. There is evidence to suggest that people's typically chronic level of happiness is to some degree a result of genetic inheritance. As much as 50% of the variance in happiness set point is likely to be genetically determined (Lyubomirsky, Sheldon, and Schkade, 2005), with the 5HTT LPR gene being suggested as one mechanism for inheritance (Rotenberg, 2013).

Although it would be very tricky to come up with a formula for what would make *us* happy personally, it *is* possible to identify some typical behaviours among happy and less happy people. When Robinson and Martin (2008) examined 34 years of data collected from daily diary studies, they found that those who describe themselves as happy engage in more social activities, religious observance, and newspaper reading than those who describe themselves as unhappy. On the other hand, happy people watch *much* less television than the unhappy.

However, one's happiness set point is not set in stone, and although people do *tend* to revert to their set point following uncharacteristic changes in well-being—for example, following divorce or the loss of a loved one—they are somewhat more likely to experience lasting changes over time in happiness (or its opposite, depression and anxiety) than in various other characteristics that appear to be influenced by genes (Kendler et al, 2011).

Individual and cultural differences

One person's idea of a really good time involves surfing or moshing, while another experiences bliss sitting in a deck chair at the Cape Cod seashore watching the gentlest of waves roll in as he knits a beret for his wife.

One explanation for this kind of individual difference is that people differ in the level of physiological arousal they seek (Apter, 1985). There is evidence from sport psychology, for example, that people opting for high-risk sports such as snowboarding spend more time in a high-arousal seeking state than those who prefer low-risk sports like badminton (Cogan and Brown, 1999). However, for this to be a complete explanation of our differing experiences of musical pleasure we would need to be consistently different in our arousal seeking across a range of situations. In fact this is not the case.

There are cultural as well as individual differences in what states people consider to be pleasurable. As researcher in culture and emotion Jeanne Tsai points out, although most people report that they want to feel good, what people mean by 'feeling good' and what they do to achieve this affective state may differ from individual to individual and from culture to culture (Tsai, 2007). For example, Tsai and her colleagues have found that personality traits and innate temperament are probably far more important than culture in determining a person's *actual* affect (Tsai, 2007)— that is, how we feel *now*. However, culture is an important force in determining the type of affect each individual considers *ideal*—the affective states people value, prefer, and ideally wish to feel. Culture influences the type of affect we 'chase'.

Members of all nationalities, all cultures, and both sexes agree on the *valence* dimension of ideal affect—we all want to 'feel good' rather than 'feel bad'. But there appear to be important cultural differences in the level of *activation* or arousal we prefer. As an example, Tsai and her colleagues compared ideal affect in a sample of European Americans, Chinese Americans, and Chinese from Hong Kong (Tsai, Knutson, and Fung, 2006). In addition to taking various objective measurements of how the research participants rated various affects, Tsai came right out and asked each person, 'What is your ideal state?' A typical European American response: 'I just want to be happy. Normally for me that means I would be doing something exciting. I just want to be entertained . . . I just like excitement.' A typical Chinese Hong Kong response: 'My ideal state is to be quiet, serene, happy, and positive' (Tsai, 2007, p 244). Both the American and Chinese participants wanted to be 'happy' but, as Figure 17.10 depicts, their idea of what 'happy' looks like was somewhat different.

Because it was not clear when during human development preferences for ideal affect appear, Tsai and her colleagues also conducted studies among preschoolers in the United States and Taiwan (Tsai et al, 2007). The results they found were markedly similar: European American preschoolers wanted to be excited, while Asian children preferred the calmer variety of happiness. Regardless of the cause of development of such standards for ideal affect, they seem to occur early in life.

Lifestyle and happiness

If we want to be happy we should perhaps consider our lifestyle. Lifestyle in this context refers to behaviours like healthy eating, employment, and marital status. These are all at least partially a matter of lifestyle choice. Gschwandtner, Jewell, and Kambhampati (2016) examined this in a sample of 40,000 UK households followed from 2009 to 2015. They operationalized happiness as life satisfaction as measured by the General Health Questionnaire and a simple 1–7 rating. Lifestyle variables included diet, exercise, employment status, education level, smoking, and alcohol consumption. Other variables included marital status and number and age of children.

Some interesting gender differences emerged. Life satisfaction was associated with healthy diet in women but not men, whereas regular exercise was associated with satisfaction in men but not women. Separation was associated with greater life satisfaction

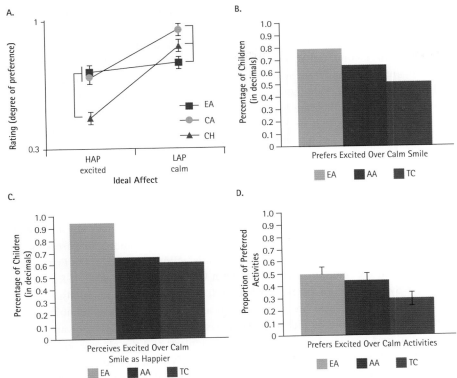

FIGURE 17.10 Chasing affect: culture affects the way we want to feel. In studies among European American (EA), Chinese American (CA), and Hong Kong Chinese (CH) adults (see Graph A), Tsai and her colleagues found that European Americans valued highly activated positive states (HAP) more than did both Chinese groups, whereas the Chinese groups valued low-activated positive states (LAP) more than the European Americans (Tsai et al, 2006). In studies among European American, Asian American, and Taiwan Chinese pre-schoolers (Graphs B, C, and D), these researchers found that European American children (EA) were more likely than either Asian Americans (AA) or Taiwanese Chinese (TC) to prefer an excited smile over a calm smile, to believe those with excited smiles to be happier, and to prefer activities that were both pleasant and exciting over those which were pleasant and calm.

Sources: Adapted from figures in Tsai, 2007, p 244; Tsai et al, 2007, p 21.

in women but lesser satisfaction in men. Having children was weakly negatively associated with life satisfaction in both men and women. Unemployment was associated with lower life satisfaction in men and women; however, retirement was associated with greater satisfaction in men but not women.

Social factors

When researchers measure the quality of various aspects of people's lives (friendships, income, work, love relationships, etc) and compare these measurements against reported levels of happiness or life satisfaction, the most important factors that emerge are *social* in nature. The same result is found if people are prompted to look at their lives overall and list those factors which *they* believe have contributed most importantly to their well-being. Research repeatedly emphasizes the primacy of social relationships in the lives of happy people (Diener et al, 2010).

As suggested earlier, social factors associated with happiness include relationships with one's friends, children, romantic partners or spouses, and other family; involvement with social networks; engaging in meaningful work; being a respected member of one's community; and contributions made to the welfare of others. People who are very happy spend less time alone than people who are not (Diener and Seligman, 2002). Although it is not clear if happier people have strong social relationships *because* they are happy, or if they are happy in part because of the relationships, it remains that strong social relationships are associated with happiness, and poor social relationships with unhappiness.

Money

People worry about money, thus most people believe that they would be happier if they had more of it (Kahneman et al, 2004). However, one of the most interesting findings in research on happiness and well-being is that money does not *necessarily* buy happiness (Diener and Seligman, 2004). In Table 17.1, a sample of *Forbes* magazine's 'richest Americans' show levels of life satisfaction identical to the Pennsylvania Amish and the Inughuit Inuit of Northern Greenland. The Maasai of Kenya and the entire Swedish nation are not far behind (Diener and Seligman, 2004).

High levels of happiness are possible even among nations whose inhabitants are quite poor. For example, as Figure 17.11 shows, Nigeria and El Salvador are among the very poorest nations, but also among the happiest; and the place whose citizens report the highest levels of happiness and life satisfaction, Puerto Rico, has a GNP (gross national product) of only approximately $10,000 per person. These figures also point to the possibility that relative wealth as distinct to absolute wealth may be a determinant of happiness. Consider the Calcutta slum dwellers with their better-than-neutral happiness scores. Most of us might consider slum dwelling to be a form of deprivation; however, these people could compare their circumstances favourably with those of the Calcutta pavement dwellers.

TABLE 17.1 **Life satisfaction compared among various groups**

Group	Rating
Forbes magazine's 'richest Americans'	5.8
Pennsylvania Amish	5.8
Inughuit Inuit people of Northern Greenland	5.8
Maasai of East Africa	5.7
Swedish representative (probability) sample	5.6
International college-student sample (47 nations, year 2000)	4.9
Illinois Amish	4.9
Calcutta slum dwellers	4.6
Fresno, California homeless	2.9
Calcutta pavement dwellers (homeless)	2.9

Source: Diener and Seligman, 2004, p 10.
Note: participants indicated their agreement with the statement 'You are satisfied with your life' using a scale from 1 (complete disagreement) to 7 (complete agreement); 4 is neutral.

Research into the relationship between happiness and relative wealth has produced very mixed results (Cheung and Lucas, 2016). However, there is no such question mark over the effects of different forms of taxation. Crudely, taxation can be progressive or regressive. Progressive taxation involves the richest people paying proportionately more than poorer people. Oishi, Kushlev, and Schimmack (2018) compared life satisfaction as measured by the American General Social Survey across years of high and low progressive taxation from 1962 to 2014. They found that in periods of highly progressive taxation the bottom 40% of earners were significantly happier whilst the top 20% were no less happy. Progressive taxation appears to be good for happiness.

However, it is also true that sometimes money *does* buy happiness . . . or at least comfort and life satisfaction (Diener et al, 2010). The relationship of money to happiness and life satisfaction is complicated. Figure 17.11 shows that while many very poor nations report high levels of happiness and life satisfaction, *all* nations whose inhabitants report the *least* happiness are also among the poorest (GNPs below $5,000). Moreover, the majority of nations scoring in the higher 'happiness' ranges have relatively high GNPs.

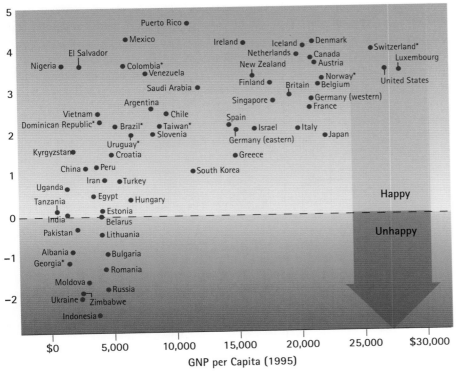

*Poll results for these countries were from 1995.

FIGURE 17.11 International comparison chart of happiness and life satisfaction. As part of the University of Michigan's World Values Survey, citizens from 81 nations were asked about their level of happiness and life satisfaction. Many countries (particularly in Latin America) with low per capita gross national products (GNPs) nonetheless report high levels of happiness and life satisfaction. On the other hand, *all* of the nations scoring in the 'unhappy' range have per capita GNPs below $5,000—and the majority of nations scoring in the highest happiness ranges are relatively wealthy.

Source: Inglehart et al, 2004.

Overall correlations between income and happiness are positive but quite modest (Apergis and Georgellis, 2015); however, this in itself does not mean that income is not important. It may, for example, be that the effects of higher income are moderated by other variables, such as greater chance of relationship breakdown, which in turn reduce happiness. It also appears that the relationship between income and happiness is not a linear one. We are all told by our bosses that if they paid us more we would not be happier, but actually this probably depends on how much they already pay us! So how much are we talking about? Figure 17.12 shows the relationship between happiness and household income. Satisfaction scores level off at a household income of around $100,000 (Layard, Mayraz, and Nickell, 2008). Allowing for inflation and exchange rates, this figure means that you can expect to reach a position where a pay rise will not make you any happier once you are bringing in a household income of around 100,000 GBP or 120,000 euros.

 THINKING CRITICALLY

We have made a rather bold statement about how much you need to earn before your happiness won't be affected by income. Never take such statements at face value! Consider how the following variables may impact on this figure: average income in your neighbourhood, average income in your occupation, size of mortgage, your age, whether you have children. There are others but you get the idea. There are always additional variables to consider.

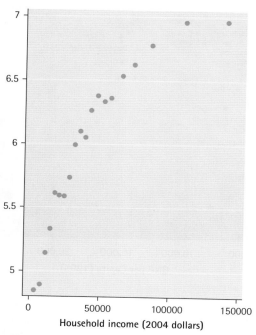

Household income (2004 dollars)

FIGURE 17.12 **The relationship between household income and happiness as measured in the 2004 US General Social Survey.**

Source: Reprinted from Layard, R., et al (2008). The marginal utility of income. *Journal of Public Economics,* August. Copyright © 2008 Elsevier B.V. All rights reserved.

The relation between money and happiness is clarified further by data from the recent Gallup World Poll (Diener et al, 2010). According to Diener, income is related to happiness primarily in terms of satisfaction with one's standard of living, pleasure derived from the ownership of luxury conveniences, and overall life evaluation; but money is only weakly related to the experience of positive feelings (and lack of negative feelings), enjoyment of life, smiles, and laughter—the *emotional* side of happiness. Emotional happiness is much more strongly related to what Diener and colleagues refer to as *social psychological prosperity*—having the freedom to do as one wishes, learning, engaging in work that utilizes one's skills, being respected in the community, and having friends and family to count on in an emergency.

So, can money ever buy *un*happiness? Films and books are filled with wealthy characters who are miserable, but what does research say? People who strongly aspire to financial success beyond that necessary for a reasonably comfortable life frequently do experience *decreases* in their feelings of well-being, directly attributable to their focusing on material gain at the expense of performing work they consider meaningful or engaging in a satisfying family life and leisure activities (Kahneman et al, 2006). Such income-focused individuals often judge their progress not by their actual wealth, but by their wealth as compared with others or as compared against some ideal standard (Boyce, Brown, and Moore, 2010). If you judge your financial status in a comparative way like this, you may be perpetually dissatisfied and unhappy (Johnson and Krueger, 2006).

Finally, although earning large sums of money may not buy much emotional happiness, *spending* money might—*if you are spending it on others*. In a series of longitudinal and experimental studies published in *Science*, the premier American journal of scientific research, Elizabeth Dunn and her colleagues showed that higher levels of happiness and subjective well-being were associated with larger percentages of a person's income spent on others as gifts or contributions to charity (Dunn, Aknin, and Norton, 2008).

READ THIS

Here are some of the key readings from this part of the chapter. For the older theories, start with this review:

Lang, P.J. (1994). The varieties of emotional experience: A meditation on James–Lange theory. *Psychological Review*, **101**, 211–21.

To get a flavour of the original writings try these:

Cannon, W.B. (1927). The James–Lange theory of emotions: A critical examination and an alternative theory. *The American Journal of Psychology*, **39**, 106–24.

Lange, C.G. and James, W. (1922). *The Emotions* (Vol 1). Philadelphia, PA: Williams and Wilkins.

For more modern research we would recommend these:

Ekman, P. (1992). An argument for basic emotions. *Cognition and Emotion*, **6**, 169–200.

Seligman, M.E., Steen, T.A., Park, N., and Peterson, C. (2005). Positive psychology progress: Empirical validation of interventions. *American Psychologist*, **60**, 410.

IN REVIEW

EMOTIONS

- Emotions are short-lived psychological states characterized by a physiological state and a characteristic subjective experience.
- The majority of emotions are negative experiences.
- Emotions serve some distinct functions. For example, they help with decision-making and they help structure our social interactions.

BASIC AND COMPLEX EMOTIONS

- According to Ekman there are a small number of basic emotions, each easily identified by ourselves and others. Basic emotions include fear, anger, pleasure, surprise, disgust, and sadness.
- Emotions are displayed in facial expressions, which can be categorized by means of the Facial Action Coding System.
- Much of the time we experience complex emotions, which are derived from the basic ones. So a blend of happy memories and current sadness can lead to the experiences of *saudade* and nostalgia.
- Although we all experience similar emotions, there are cultural differences in which emotions have a name and in how we display and read emotion from facial expression.

EMOTION AND DECEPTION

- We regulate our expression of emotion when we lie. We tend to tell altruistic lies to those with whom we are close and selfish lies to others.
- Concealing emotion when we lie creates cognitive load. This can be exploited in order to catch people out.

THEORIES OF EMOTION

- Early theories of emotion were concerned with the relationship between physiology and emotion. The earliest theory, the James–Lange theory, proposed that physiological state triggers the experience of emotion.
- The Cannon–Bard theory emerged in opposition, suggesting that the thalamus produces both physiological changes and the experience of emotion in response to emotion-provoking stimuli.
- More recent theories have been concerned with the relationship between cognition and emotion. Schachter and Singer proposed the two-factor theory; emotion is determined by physiological state and our interpretation of it.
- Lazarus suggested that in fact cognition comes first, and that we only experience the physiological state of an emotion when we have appraised the situation.
- It appears likely that some emotions can be experienced with minimal cognition; for example, fear. This has led LeDoux to propose a high road and a low road to fear, the former involving more cognition.
- An alternative view of emotion sees it as embodied; rather than seeing emotion as a cognitive experience embodied emotion theorists see it as encoded neurologically as associated with bodily sensations and experienced as such.

ANGER

- Anger involves a sense of antagonism towards others.

- Anger is often experienced as a ball of liquid or energy that requires release. This release is called catharsis. Evidence for the benefits of catharsis is very mixed.

- Forgiveness may be an effective alternative to catharsis; it has been shown to reduce physiological signs of anger like blood pressure.

HAPPINESS

- Most people describe themselves as at least reasonably happy, there being a bimodal distribution of scores.

- There appears to be a fairly strong genetic influence on individual differences in set point happiness. However, life events cause significant upward and downward change in well-being from this set point.

- There are individual and cultural differences in what state is considered happy, with some craving excitement and others tranquillity.

- Lifestyle is associated with happiness, with some notable gender differences in the lifestyle factors associated with happiness. Thus exercise, marriage, and retirement predict happiness in men, whilst healthy diet and separation appear to make women happy. Happy people of both sexes tend to spend less time alone.

- Although people spend considerable time and energy seeking wealth the relationship between wealth and happiness is complex, with absolute wealth, relative wealth, and taxation possibly exerting separate influences.

- Income correlates positively with happiness up to a certain level, whereafter increased wealth has no additional effect.

TEST YOURSELF

1 There are five basic emotions. True ❒ False ❒

2 An emotion generally lasts longer than a mood. True ❒ False ❒

3 Loss of emotion—for example, through brain injury—inhibits decision-making. True ❒ False ❒

4 A Duchenne smile signals genuine pleasure. True ❒ False ❒

5 Which of the following is **not** a core component of all emotions?

   a) A subjective experience

   b) Physiological changes

   c) Behavioural response(s)

   d) An emoji

6 What complex emotion encompasses feelings of acceptance, comfort, security, and benevolence?

   a) Ambivalence

   b) Amity

   c) *Amae*

   d) Amiability

7 Which of the following display rules involves toning down an emotional response?

a) De-intensifying

b) Intensifying

c) Masking

d) Neutralizing

8 Explain the difference between the James–Lange and Cannon–Bard theories of emotion.

9 Explain how emotion can bypass cognition.

10 Explain the conflicting evidence around the usefulness of catharsis to deal with anger.

 **Visit the online resources that accompany this book:** www.oup.com/uk/jarvis-okami1e

ISSUES IN MENTAL HEALTH

LEARNING OUTCOMES

By the end of this chapter you should be able to:

- Critically examine a range of ways in which mental health problems have been conceived historically and appreciate the diversity of current perspectives on mental health
- Understand a range of criteria by which mental health can be assessed, including statistical abnormality, deviation from norms, distress and failure to function, and appreciate the limitations of each criterion
- Recall the basics of the DSM and ICD systems for classifying and diagnosing mental disorder
- Take a view on the controversy around the diagnosis of mental disorder and contrast the medical model with alternative perspectives
- Outline symptoms of some major categories of mental disorder including anxiety, depression, psychosis, and personality disorder
- Explain biological and psychological factors affecting mental disorder and psychological distress, and the place of theoretical explanations

Among those uninitiated to the world of psychology, there is a common (and wrong) belief that most of psychology is concerned with mental illness. It isn't but we'll pause there to take a closer look at the term 'mental illness'! It is almost impossible to discuss issues around mental health without using language that represents a particular way of looking at the topic. So 'mental illness' and to a lesser extent 'mental health' are part of the language of medicine. As we shall see in this chapter, many (though by no means all) psychologists and other professionals have good reason for rejecting a rigidly medical perspective. This will become clear later but for now be aware that the use of technical terms matters because it structures our understanding of the topic. Where possible terms like 'mental disorder' are used in this chapter because this is slightly more neutral, yet plenty of clinical psychologists would still challenge the idea that it is valid or helpful to speak in terms of distinct disorders.

What are psychological disorders? Are they medical conditions, diseases in the same sense that multiple sclerosis, hepatitis, and cancer are diseases? Are they unusual patterns of thinking, behaviour, and feelings resulting from individual experience? Or are they in fact social constructs, ways in which each **culture** decides to explain unusual behaviour and states of mind (see 'More radical positions on psychology as science', Chapter 2)?

A VERY BRIEF HISTORY OF MENTAL DISORDER

This is a very brief account and we do not pretend to fairly represent the range of global traditions around mental health, just to pick up on some interesting historical themes that help us understand some contemporary debates and issues.

The Ancient Greek Traditions

As far back as ancient Greece tensions between different explanations for and attitudes to mental disorder can be seen. What is particularly fascinating about these tensions is how they echo those that exist now. To many ancient Greeks the concept of 'madness' was closely associated with criminal violence—much as it is now. You may, for example, have heard of violent criminals referred to as 'psychos' or 'nutters' whilst some of the most notorious hard men have had their names prefixed by 'Mad . . .'. At the same time Hippocrates (he of the Hippocratic Oath doctors take—to do no harm, etc) began the process of classifying sets of abnormal behaviour into illnesses such as depression and paranoia. Ultimately our modern psychiatric classifications are the extension of Hippocrates' work.

Yet others in ancient Greece saw in spiritual terms some unusual experiences that we might call abnormal. There is still very much a tension between respecting a range of religious and cultural traditions on one hand and on the other targeting psychological help to those who might benefit from it. For example, a number of spiritual traditions include the notion of direct communication by ancestors. If a member such a community presents hearing voices but interpreting them as ancestral communication this presents a dilemma for a clinician who has been trained to interpret this as a symptom of serious mental disorder but who also wishes to respect spiritual traditions other than his or her own. Some among the ancient Greeks even acknowledged the positive and creative aspects of some symptoms. Thus Socrates spoke of the link between symptoms of mental disorder and literary inspiration in similar terms to those used by modern creative geniuses from Virginia Woolf to Stephen Fry. Woolf captured this link poignantly in her classic question, 'How many times have people used a pen or paintbrush because they couldn't pull the trigger?' (Woolf, 2009).

From the Middle Ages through to the Enlightenment

In the Europe of the Middle Ages the two major strands of interpretation of unusual behaviour were medical and spiritual. Some medical traditions drew on an ancient idea (probably Greek or Roman in origin) of imbalance between the four humours (bodily fluids)—blood, phlegm, and black bile and yellow bile. Biological treatments such as blood-letting were applications of the humours model. At the same time the Christian tradition explained symptoms as demonic possession or divine punishment. Treatments derived from this understanding included prayer, fasting, and exorcism.

A number of modern theorists have tried to integrate the most useful features of different psychological and biological models to produce better explanations and treatments for mental disorder (see Chapter 19 for a discussion). This **integrative** tradition can be traced back to thirteenth-century doctor and religious reformer Arnaldus de Villa Nova who tried to hedge his medical and spiritual bets by advocating drilling holes (this process is called trepanning) in the skull to let out both blood *and* evil spirits!

The same tension between medical and spiritual traditions existed in the Islamic world in the Middle East, North Africa, and modern-day Spain and Portugal.

❯ KEY IDEAS integrative models Integrative models of mental disorder are ways of understanding and treating mental disorder that combine ideas from more than one pure model. For example, modern cognitive behavioural therapy uses techniques based on behavioural and cognitive models of mental disorder.

However, Arab and Persian scholars and doctors were generally several hundred years ahead of European Christians. For example, there are records of asylums in Syria dating back to the thirteenth century, where treatments included drugs, music therapy, and what we would now call occupational therapy.

In keeping with the European Enlightenment (a philosophical change characterized by a sense of emerging from ignorance to a scientific understanding of the world), by the eighteenth century the dominant European model of mental disorder was firmly medical. Asylums grew in number and as doctors specialized in asylum work the profession of psychiatry emerged. Early asylums generally had poor conditions. A notable exception was the Quaker-run York Retreat, established in 1796.

The Twentieth Century

By the start of the twentieth century neurology and psychiatry were firmly established as medical disciplines and a medical understanding of mental health dominated in Europe and the USA. Although psychology existed as a science by this time its involvement with mental health was limited. Nonetheless, psychological models of mental disorder were gaining ground; for example, in the form of Freudian psychoanalysis. At the same time Pavlov and Watson (see Chapter 7) were making links between conditioned responses and symptoms like anxiety. The roots of a contemporary understanding of mental health can be seen in these two traditions.

By the 1920s serious attempts were being made to bring the medical practice of **nosology**—the classification of disease—to bear on mental disorder. This was formalized in 1952 when the American Psychiatric Association published the first edition of the *Diagnostic and Statistical Manual of Mental Disorder* (DSM). From the start there was a tension in classification between nosology and **aetiology**—understanding the origins of disorder. The latest edition, DSM-5, was published in 2013. Since DSM-III classifications have become increasingly biological in orientation and a major purpose behind DSM-5 was to incorporate recent neurological research findings.

> ❯ KEY IDEAS nosology and aetiology These are both medical terms and their use reflects the medical understanding of mental health. **Nosology** is the classification of illness and disease. **Aetiology** is the cause of illness and disease.

MODERN ASSESSMENT OF ABNORMALITY

So how do psychiatrists and psychologists know when symptoms constitute psychological abnormality as opposed to being just unusual behaviour, characteristics, or experiences—or even a person's totally understandable response to extreme circumstances? A separate question concerns how they decide what—if any—disorder with which to diagnose the person but we'll come back to that in the next section.

Are people who commit cruel, violent acts and experience no remorse suffering from a disorder (we might call this *antisocial personality disorder*), or are they just engaging in bad (or evil) behaviour? Is a young man who devotes all the years of his youth to the care of his sick and aged parents at the expense of his own social life a caring person, or is he suffering from *avoidant personality disorder with dependent features*? If your first response to this latter example is that yes, this does seem abnormal, consider whether you would have responded the same way to a female carer.

These are examples of potentially abnormal *behaviour*, but we should also think about when it is helpful to judge someone's personal experiences as abnormal. A person may, for example, experience hallucinations—these may or may not impact significantly on his or her behaviour and may or may not cause him or her distress. There is a range of criteria that can be used to decide when someone has crossed the boundary between normal and abnormal but be aware that these are all imperfect.

Statistical Abnormality

If we were to ask what makes behaviour or experience 'normal', perhaps the most obvious answer is that it is something most people have, do, think, or feel. Turning this around, any unusual behaviour or experience is potentially abnormal. An example of a disorder where this criterion would be part of the assessment process is **intellectual disability disorder**. This requires an IQ (see Chapter 14) of below 70, placing the person in the bottom 2% of the population.

In practice mental health professionals do not use this criterion alone to assess someone as abnormal. Someone with an IQ of 131 is precisely as unusual as someone with one of 69 yet they clearly do not have a problem. Also, it may be that someone with an IQ of 69 can manage the tasks they need to for their chosen lifestyle and is content to do so. In such a case what would be the point in assessing them as abnormal? However, where someone is unable to meet the standards of their community in communication, social skills, independence, or work/education because of their low IQ it is likely that they would benefit from targeted psychological help. In this situation the person might well be judged to be abnormal and receive a diagnosis like intellectual disability disorder.

Psychological Dysfunction

> **KEY IDEAS** psychological dysfunction Any breakdown in mental functioning—cognitive, emotional, or behavioural. The boundaries between 'functional' and 'dysfunctional' are often fuzzy, however, and there is wide disagreement as to how to characterize these boundaries.

Psychological dysfunction is a breakdown in some aspect of normal psychological functioning. In other words, when one's behaviour, thoughts, or feelings go wrong. However, boundaries between the functional and dysfunctional may be impossible to determine with precision—they are fuzzy boundaries.

At some point, a person's emotions, cognitions, or behaviour can be clearly dysfunctional; for example, when someone is too depressed to get out of bed. However, critics of diagnostic systems point out that we are still left with the problem of who decides when a person is dysfunctional and when they are not. Who decides whether a person must feel depressed for two weeks to be dysfunctional, rather than four weeks or four days?

Diagnostic systems like the DSM make use of dysfunction as one of the major criteria for assessing someone as abnormal. However, they also recognize that to some degree its use inevitably reflects social judgements or cultural values. We cannot make objective judgements that someone's psychological state is dysfunctional in the same way as we make medical judgements of dysfunction in physical organs such as the heart or lungs (Wakefield, 2003).

THINKING PRACTICALLY

In which of the following cases would you judge that an individual is sufficiently dysfunctional in their behaviour, cognition, or emotional state to warrant being assessed as abnormal? Explain your reasoning.

1 Douglas concerns staff at the benefits office by gesturing with a stuffed lobster when he complains that his payments are late.

2 Constance experiences the unusual hallucination of seeing animals that are not there. They do not interact with her and she knows they are not real. This bothered her as a child, but as an adult she has learned to ignore them.

3 Saffi is deeply distressed because she is confused about her sexuality and she fears that her very traditional family will reject her if she comes out as bisexual or a lesbian. Saffi has begun cutting herself in an attempt to relieve her distress.

Personal Distress or Impairment

More often than not, a person with a mental disorder suffers distress. In fact some disorders like anxiety and depression are defined by the nature of distress they cause. However, there are exceptions. A person displaying the characteristics of *antisocial personality disorder* may not be at all distressed by his or her condition. Antisocial personality disorder is a condition characterized by extremely selfish and often unlawful behaviour; lying and other forms of deceit; lack of concern for the feelings, needs, or suffering of others; aggression or violence; recklessness and disregard for safety; and lack of remorse for all the foregoing. Thus, it is *the rest of us* who are generally upset by a person's antisocial personality disorder—not the 'sufferer'. The concept of **impairment in functioning** exists to cover those situations where a person has symptoms of a disorder but does not experience personal distress. Impairment in functioning refers to problems experienced in important areas of life as a result of the psychological symptoms: problems in work, school, or personal relationships, for example; or trouble with the law.

However, people frequently become severely distressed when they are not experiencing a mental disorder—just think about the last time your love life went horribly wrong. Also there are no objective standards for deciding when psychological symptoms have actually caused significant impairment in important areas of one's life. Who is to say? Thus, personal distress and/or impairment also pose logical problems as objective markers of psychological disorder.

> **KEY IDEAS** impairment in functioning The concept used for diagnosis in the DSM to cover situations where a person has symptoms of a disorder but does not experience personal distress.

Deviation from Social Norms

Sometimes we define behaviour as abnormal primarily because it deviates so far from social norms. This is highly problematic because our perceptions of social norms vary wildly between individuals of different political, religious, and subcultural persuasions, never mind between different countries or historical periods. There is, however, at least one example where there is enough broad agreement to use social norms to define abnormality. This is the case of **antisocial personality**, defined in the DSM system by 'absence of pro-social internal standards associated with failure to conform to lawful or culturally normative ethical behaviour' (2013, p 764). However, even in this apparently clear-cut case deviation from social norms is not sufficient for diagnosis—it is combined with impairment in functioning.

We should be very cautious about using deviation from social norms as a criterion for abnormality because it has a historical association with human rights abuses. In the 1850s the term **drapetomania** was coined in the United States (Cartwright, 1851) to describe the tendency of slaves to abscond. Standard treatment involved 'whipping the devil out of them' (1851, np). By labelling any person of colour who resisted the position of slave as mentally ill, this 'diagnosis' clearly facilitated racism and supported the institution of slavery. Similarly in the 1800s, the concept of **nymphomania**, characterized by the conveniently vague 'irresistible and insatiable desire, in females, for the venereal act (ie, having sex)' (Dunglison, 1856, p 604), could be invoked in response to anything seen as sexual: flirting, masturbation, or attraction to men of lower social status. This allowed the male establishment to restrict female sexuality. It is now accepted (obviously, we hope!) that these are not real mental disorders but **social constructs** designed to serve the interests of the white men in power.

> **KEY IDEAS** antisocial personality Commonly called psychopathy (although there is debate about the extent to which the two are interchangeable), antisocial personality is recognized as a mental disorder in major diagnostic systems. The antisocial personality is impulsive, irresponsible, and lacking in empathy.

> **KEY IDEAS** social constructs (mental disorders) Historically, diagnoses such as **drapetomania** and **nymphomania** were used to oppress vulnerable and minority groups, preserving white male privilege. There is still some debate about whether current diagnoses can serve the same purpose. A category of mental disorder can be described as a **social construct** if it is believed to exist for that kind of purpose.

THINKING CREATIVELY

Schizotypal personality disorder is characterized by beliefs in conspiracy theories and the supernatural. It is frequently diagnosed in family members of patients diagnosed with schizophrenia.

Explain how schizotypal disorder could be a social construct. Whose interests might be served by being able to diagnose conspiracy theorists and those who believe in the supernatural but not 'standard' religions?

The Harmful Dysfunction View: Fact *and* Social Judgement Define Disorder

❯ **KEY IDEAS** harmful dysfunction view This is a view of psychological disorder pioneered by Jerome Wakefield. According to the harmful dysfunction view, disorder exists when symptoms cause harm according to subjective social or cultural judgements, *and* there is objective evidence of dysfunction. Dysfunction is said to exist only when a psychological characteristic or mechanism is not performing the function for which it evolved through natural selection.

Wakefield (2010) proposed the **harmful dysfunction view**. He agrees with the myth of mental illness view (see later in this chapter) that judgements of the *harmful* nature of certain behaviours or states of mind are always and forever social judgements involving cultural values. For example, it is a social and cultural judgement that there is harm in hearing voices that are not there, using illegal drugs in excess, weeping for no apparent reason and feeling worthless, or being terrified of flying in an airplane.

However, Wakefield also states that the *dysfunction* aspect of psychological disorder can be treated as a matter of objective fact and need not be subject to social judgement. According to Wakefield dysfunction occurs when a psychological attribute or mechanism *fails to perform the function for which it was shaped through evolution by natural selection* (see Chapter 5).

One might well wonder how one is to know which functions a psychological attribute evolved to perform. Wakefield (2003) suggests that the function of a psychological attribute or mechanism—like the function of a physical organ, such as the heart—can be defined by looking at the effects of the mechanism and asking: do these effects help explain why the mechanism or attribute came into being in the first place?

Consider *anxiety*, for example. The *effect* of anxiety is to make us tense and wary of dangerous or potentially harmful situations. Without anxiety we might decide to take a swim in water clearly marked 'Warning—Shark Infested!' or tell the motorway police officer giving us a speeding ticket exactly what we thought of her (and her entire extended family). Although an unpleasant experience, anxiety can be something of a blessing.

Harmful dysfunction in obsessive-compulsive disorder

Obsessive-compulsive disorder (OCD) is an extremely severe disorder characterized by distressingly intrusive and anxiety-provoking thoughts, and compulsive behaviours designed to reduce the anxiety. One frequent 'theme' of OCD is pollution by disease-causing germs, and OCD sufferers sometimes engage in crippling hand-washing rituals which prevent them from leaving the house or engaging in normal activities. They may scrub their skin raw from excessive washing. This behaviour is *harmful* (a social judgement) but also demonstrates a *dysfunction* of psychological mechanisms regulating health and hygiene.

Although the harmful dysfunction view is a bold attempt to solve the problems of defining abnormality, like the other views it has its weaknesses. For one thing, our state of knowledge about the functions of *psychological* mechanisms is still quite primitive compared with our understanding of the functions of *physiological* mechanisms such as the heart. We may believe that we understand the function of anxiety clearly, but what about the functions of premenstrual symptoms, jealousy, or aggressive acting out in childhood? There may be disagreements as to their function. Without knowing their function, how can we determine whether *premenstrual dysphoric disorder*, *delusions (jealous type)*, or childhood *conduct disorder*—all of which appear in psychiatric classification systems—are valid disorders? Therefore, until our understanding of the functions of psychological mechanisms becomes more sophisticated and complete, the harmful dysfunction view, despite its promise, may not be very much more useful than more traditional approaches to defining abnormality.

CLASSIFICATION AND DIAGNOSIS OF MENTAL DISORDER

Worldwide there are a number of psychiatric classification systems. The two that you are most likely to encounter in Western Europe are the American Psychiatric Association's DSM-5 (5th edition of the *Diagnostic and Statistical Manual of Mental Disorder*) and the World Health Organization's ICD-11 (11th edition of the *International Classification of the Causes of Disease and Death*).

Although many mental health professionals use the categories and diagnostic criteria for disorders of ICD or DSM, this is not to say that they do so uncritically. Diagnostic systems provide standard, coherent sets of guidelines which in turn sit neatly with organizational quality assurance processes. So, for example, a hospital administrator can see what percentage of patients diagnosed with **depression** experience a significant decline in symptoms following six weeks of cognitive behavioural therapy (see Chapter 19) at a given clinic. This requires an initial diagnosis of depression.

This may not be all bad. Pragmatically, diagnosis can help clinicians target treatments that are likely to be helpful to particular patients and allocate limited resources where they can do most good. However, most clinical psychologists do not accept that patients fall neatly into diagnostic categories, and some reject the whole idea of diagnosis (Hyman, 2010). The alternative way of looking at individuals who seek help for psychological symptoms is that they may be better seen as unique individuals responding personally to a unique set of circumstances rather than a case with a medical condition.

Both the DSM and ICD take the view that two primary criteria for abnormality are required before diagnosis of a mental disorder is warranted: (a) *psychological dysfunction*; and (b) *personal distress* or *impairment in functioning*. This is reflected in the structure of DSM diagnoses. Each diagnosis has one or more parts which lists symptoms (dysfunctions) and a later part which requires that symptoms cause significant distress or impairment in functioning. In practice, as we have seen, other criteria such as statistical abnormality and deviation from social norms can be involved in diagnosis because they make up some of the symptoms.

The DSM System

The DSM-5 dominates diagnosis in the USA and is sometimes used in the UK and Western Europe. It includes the categories shown in Table 18.1.

A change in DSM-5 has been to classify as far as possible according to the origins of disorders rather than by superficially similar symptoms (ie, nosology better reflects aetiology). Thus OCD has been separated from anxiety disorders and bipolar from depressive disorders. However, this has been based largely on biological

TABLE 18.1 **DSM categories of mental disorders**

Category	Examples
Neurodevelopmental disorders	Intellectual disability (intellectual developmental disorder) Autistic spectrum disorder Attention-deficit/hyperactivity disorder Tourette's disorder
Schizophrenia spectrum and other psychotic disorders	Delusional disorder Schizophrenia Schizotypal (personality) disorder
Bipolar and related disorders	Bipolar I disorder Bipolar II disorder Cyclothymic disorder
Depressive disorders	Major depressive disorder Persistent depressive disorder (dysthymia) Disruptive mood dysregulation disorder Premenstrual dysphoric disorder
Anxiety disorders	Separation anxiety disorder Specific phobia Social anxiety disorder (social phobia) Panic disorder Generalized anxiety disorder
Obsessive-compulsive and related disorders	Obsessive-compulsive disorder Hoarding disorder Trichotillomania (hair-pulling disorder)
Trauma- and stressor-related disorders	Reactive attachment disorder Disinhibited social engagement disorder Post-traumatic stress disorder
Dissociative disorders	Dissociative identity disorder Dissociative amnesia Depersonalization/derealization disorder
Somatic symptom and related disorders	Somatic symptom disorder Illness anxiety disorder Conversion disorder
Feeding and eating disorders	Anorexia nervosa Bulimia nervosa Binge-eating disorder
Elimination disorders	Enuresis Encopresis
Sleep-wake disorders	Insomnia disorder Hypersomnolence disorder Narcolepsy Restless legs syndrome

TABLE 18.1 **Continued**

Category	Examples
Sexual dysfunctions	Erectile disorder
	Female orgasmic disorder
	Premature (early) ejaculation
Gender dysphoria	Gender dysphoria
Disruptive, impulse-control, and conduct disorders	Oppositional defiant disorder
	Intermittent explosive disorder
	Conduct disorder
	Antisocial personality disorder
	Pyromania
	Kleptomania
Substance-related and addictive disorders	Alcohol use disorder
	Opioid withdrawal
Neurocognitive disorders	Neurocognitive disorder due to Alzheimer's disease
	Vascular neurocognitive disorder
Personality disorders	Schizoid personality disorder
	Borderline personality disorder
	Histrionic personality disorder
	Narcissistic personality disorder
Paraphilic disorders	Voyeuristic disorder
	Exhibitionistic disorder
	Sexual sadism disorder
	Paedophilic disorder
Other mental disorders	Other specified mental disorder
Medication induced movement disorders and other adverse effects of medication	Tardive dyskinesia
	Antidepressant discontinuation syndrome
Other conditions that may be a focus of clinical attention	Abuse and neglect
	Housing and economic problems
Conditions for further study	Persistent complex bereavement disorder
	Caffeine use disorder
	Internet gaming disorder

research, and the biomedical assumption that changes in brain function associated with mental disorder are the *cause* of said disorder remains controversial.

DSM-5 comes with a set of standard interview questions called SCID-5 (structured clinical interview questions for DSM-5). The rationale is that if diagnosing psychiatrists and psychologists use standard questions they are more likely to arrive at the same diagnosis for the same patients (ie, they should have good inter-rater reliability (see Chapter 15)).

DSM-5 also introduced a cross-cutting symptom measure in order to identify areas to investigate further and as a way to track patient improvement and deterioration. This involves a 23-item questionnaire asking patients to rate themselves between none (0) and severe (4) for how much they have been bothered by a range of symptoms representing depression, anxiety, anger, sleep disruption, suicidality, personality, and substance use. The cross-cutting measure includes items like 'Little interest or

❯ KEY IDEAS *Diagnostic and Statistical Manual of Mental Disorders* (DSM) This is the manual published by the American Psychiatric Association which classifies, describes, and presents diagnostic criteria for psychological disorders.

pleasure in doing things?' and 'Feeling more irritated, grouchy, or angry than usual?', with responses measured on a 0–4 scale from 'Not at all' to 'Nearly every day'.

The ICD System

The other major international classification system is the World Health Organization's ICD, now in its 11th edition. The ICD system has many similarities with the DSM. Its major categories are shown in Table 18.2.

TABLE 18.2 ICD major categories of mental disorders. These disorders can be found under category 06 of the ICD–11; mental behavioural or neurodevelopmental disorders, with the exception of Sleep–wake disorders, which can be found under category 07, and Sexual dysfunctions and Gender incongruence, which can be found under category 17, conditions relating to sexual health.

Category	Examples
Neurodevelopmental disorders	Disorders of intellectual development Autism spectrum disorder Attention deficit hyperactivity disorder Tic disorders
Schizophrenia spectrum and other psychotic disorders	Delusional disorder Schizophrenia Schizotypal disorder
Catatonia	Catatonia induced by psychoactive substances, including medications
Mood disorders	Bipolar or related disorders Depressive disorders
Anxiety or fear-related disorders	Separation anxiety disorder Specific phobia Social anxiety disorder Panic disorder Generalized anxiety disorder
Obsessive-compulsive or related disorders	Obsessive-compulsive disorder Hoarding disorder Olfactory reference disorder
Disorders specifically associated with stress	Reactive attachment disorder Disinhibited social engagement disorder Post-traumatic stress disorder Prolonged grief disorder
Dissociative disorders	Dissociative identity disorder Dissociative amnesia Depersonalization/derealization disorder Possession trance disorder
Feeding or eating disorders	Anorexia nervosa Bulimia nervosa Binge-eating disorder

TABLE 18.1 **Continued**

Category	Examples
Elimination disorders	Enuresis Encopresis
Disorders of bodily distress or bodily experience	Bodily distress disorder Body integrity disorder
Substance-related and addictive disorders	Disorders due to substance use Disorders due to addictive behaviours
Impulse-control disorders	Intermittent explosive disorder Pyromania Kleptomania Compulsive sexual behaviour disorder
Disruptive behaviour or dissocial disorders	Oppositional defiant disorder Conduct-dissocial disorder
Personality disorders and related traits	Personality disorder
Paraphilic disorders	Voyeuristic disorder Exhibitionistic disorder Coercive sexual sadism disorder Paedophilic disorder
Factitious disorders	Factitious disorder imposed on self Factitious disorder imposed on another
Neurocognitive disorders	Delirium Mild neurocognitive disorder Amnestic disorder Dementia due to Alzheimer's disease Vascular dementia
Mental or behavioural disorders associated with pregnancy, childbirth, or puerperium	Postpartum depression Mental or behavioural disorders associated with pregnancy, childbirth, or the puerperium, with psychotic symptoms
Sleep-wake disorders	Insomnia disorders Hypersomnolence disorders Narcolepsy Restless legs syndrome
Sexual dysfunctions	Male erectile dysfunction Female orgasmic disorder Male early ejaculation
Gender incongruence	Gender incongruence of adolescence or adulthood Gender incongruence of childhood

Although many of the ICD categories are very similar to those of the DSM, there are some key differences between the two. Unlike DSM, ICD is intended for global use, therefore it includes some disorders not usually seen in Western Europe or the USA. An example is *possession trance disorder*. The ICD does not come with standard diagnostic interviews like the DSM, but instead has the CDDG (clinical description and diagnosis guidelines). These are deliberately less prescriptive, allowing greater discretion on the part of the diagnosing psychiatrist or psychologist (First et al, 2015).

THINKING CRITICALLY

ICD diagnostic guidance is deliberately less prescriptive than that constructed for the DSM. Critically consider the implications this may have for the reliability and validity of diagnosis.

HINT: reliability is the consistency of diagnosis. For example, how likely are two psychologists to give the same patient the same diagnosis? Validity is the extent to which the diagnosis is *real*; does it, for example, predict what treatments will help the patient? A degree of reliability is essential for validity; however, very narrow guidelines can improve reliability at the expense of validity.

CRITICAL PERSPECTIVES ON CLASSIFICATION AND DIAGNOSIS

It is generally acknowledged among psychologists working in mental health that diagnostic systems like DSM-5 and ICD-11 are imperfect. There are also some well-developed critical positions.

The Myth of Mental Illness View

> *If you talk to God, you are praying. If God talks to you, you have schizophrenia.*
>
> —Thomas Szasz

> **KEY IDEAS** myth of mental illness vs the medical model **The myth of mental illness** view is a radical view of psychological disorder pioneered by Thomas Szasz which proposes that 'mental illness' is really a metaphor for problems in living and does not refer to actual illness or disease processes. **The medical model** is the general term used to describe views of psychological disorder which frame them in a medical context. Unlike the myth of mental illness view, medical models view psychological disorders as actual illnesses with specific causes and which necessitate treatment with psychotherapy, medication, or some other process.

In 1961, psychiatrist Thomas Szasz surprised (and annoyed) his profession by proposing that diagnoses of 'mental illness' were little more than social judgements about people's unusual behaviour, made in the guise and language of medical science. According to this **myth of mental illness view**, mental 'illnesses' do not exist in the sense that physical illnesses exist. This is because medical illnesses involve some sort of demonstrable, structural change and malfunction of a part of the body—broken bone, infected tissue, growth of a tumour, and so forth (termed *lesions* by Szasz). Apart from a very small number of conditions (which Szasz exempted from his critique), no one has yet been able to identify specific anatomical or biochemical 'lesions' in the brain that are specific to particular psychological disorders and are always present when the illness is present. Szasz concluded that terms such as 'psychological disorder' or 'mental illness' were little more than metaphors to describe what amount to 'problems in living'. Indeed, for the half-century before his death in 2012, Szasz denounced the **medical model** of mental illness, which views psychological problems as similar to physical illnesses, claiming that the model was grossly misleading and damaging to the individual and society (Szasz, 2007).

However, Szasz's ideas are sometimes inaccurately portrayed. He did not propose that people don't 'really' experience severe psychological distress, nor was he proposing that such people shouldn't be treated for their mental pain with psychotherapy or drugs. Szasz emphasized that people should have the right to be given any sort of treatment for their symptoms they deemed fit (including illegal or dangerous treatments). He was primarily concerned with the problem of individuals being detained in psychiatric institutions against their will, merely on the basis of a psychiatrist's diagnosis of mental illness—a legal procedure known in the UK as **sectioning** (after sections 2–5 of the 1983 and 2007 Mental Health Acts). Szasz was also concerned about possible negative social and psychological consequences to a person of merely being labelled with a mental illness diagnosis (Szasz, 2007; eg, Goffman, 1961; Jamison, 2006).

Szasz initially expressed his ideas during a time when **involuntary commitments** to mental institutions (his most important objection) were far more common than they are now. Indeed, since the development of psychiatric medications and the advent of *managed care*—the trend has been to do everything possible to keep patients *out* of mental institutions. This kind of policy is known as *deinstitutionalization*, and in the UK was operationalized in the form of *Care in the Community*. Deinstitutionalization is meant to serve the dual purpose of reducing costs and allowing patients to attempt to live productive lives.

Nonetheless, some of Szasz's ideas are insightful. They emphasize the simple truth that beliefs about what does or does not constitute a psychological disorder inevitably contain strong elements of social judgement and are generally not as straightforward as judgements about physical disorders. Szasz also correctly observed that being labelled with a mental illness can sometimes have far-reaching negative consequences for a person. Despite widespread public education about mental health, psychiatric illnesses create a **stigma**, a sort of 'mark' of shame or disgrace. A stigma due to mental illness can follow a person throughout his or her life (Goffman, 1961; Jamison, 2006).

> ❯ **KEY IDEAS** sectioning (involuntary commitment) This takes place when a person is detained in a psychiatric facility. Proceedings to section someone in this way may be brought by either your closest relative or an approved mental health professional. Initial detention (section 2) is for assessment. If it is deemed necessary to detain you for treatment this is covered by a further procedure (section 3). Section 4 is for emergency detention to prevent harm to self or others and section 5 is used to prevent voluntary patients leaving hospital against medical advice.

> ❯ **KEY IDEAS** stigma This is a social 'badge' or mark of shame or disgrace resulting from a person's behaviour or membership in a disapproved or discriminated-against group. Social stigma traditionally has been a problem for those diagnosed with psychological disorders.

THINKING CREATIVELY

The stigma attached to mental disorder can, indeed, be a problem. However, not all mental disorders carry the same level of stigma. Patients with schizophrenia are often seen as dangerous and unpredictable. Drug addicts are seen as similarly dangerous and unpredictable *and* responsible for their condition and so experience the most stigma (Corrigan, Kuwabara, and O'Schaughnessy, 2009). Based on these findings, how might psychologists go about reducing the stigma of mental disorder?

Modern Critical Psychiatry Perspectives

Szasz represents the *anti-psychiatry* movement of the 1960s; however, there is still a loose coalition of academics from psychiatry, psychology, and sociology who express grave reservations about a number of aspects of psychiatric practice including diagnosis. These are collectively referred to as the critical psychiatry movement. Timimi (2013) summarizes a number of arguments against diagnosis:

- With the exception of post-traumatic stress disorder, there is still no consistent link between the nosology (classification) of mental disorder and its aetiology. Logically this means that diagnosis in mental health is not comparable to that in physical health.

- Validity of diagnosis is poor because there is a lack of objective markers to reliably distinguish patients suffering from a given disorder from others. In the absence of such markers each diagnosis *reifies* the idea of that mental illness.

Reification is the process whereby a subjective idea is treated as if it were a concrete fact.

- Reliability of diagnosis is still not good—often different diagnosing professionals reach different conclusions about the same patient.

- Although psychological and biological treatments do help patients, most of their benefit comes from common factors in all therapies that are helpful to anyone in distress (eg, attentive listening—see Frank, 1973). So, just because a particular therapy is helpful following a particular diagnosis this does not make the diagnosis any more real.

- There is evidence to suggest that rejecting a diagnosis and searching for personal meaning in symptoms is associated with better chance of recovery.

Note that *all* of these criticisms have counter-arguments. However, taken together they do suggest problems with the process of diagnosis. Wright (2014) has offered a broader challenge to all mental health professionals working within the medical model. Wright suggests that, given that income inequality has a massive impact on mental health and that income inequality is actively maintained for the benefit of a rich minority, rather than diagnosing and treating individual patients, mental health professionals would do more good by devoting their working lives to tackling inequalities.

Clinical Psychologists' Call for a Paradigm Shift

In 2013 the British Psychological Society's Division of Clinical Psychology (DCP) took the dramatic step of publicly calling for a shift away from the medicalization of psychological distress (Awenat et al, 2013). The tone of the report is mild and its arguments nuanced, acknowledging the benefits of ICD and DSM in terms of structuring research and delivery of services as well as aiding in public understanding of mental health and the administration of benefits. Nonetheless, the message of the report is bold, reflecting perspectives from the critical psychiatry movement.

The BPS report identifies two main problems with psychiatric diagnosis. The first is conceptual. Diagnosis has limited reliability and validity, and individual judgements are much more a matter of interpretation than objective judgement. Medical diagnosis also reflects a mainly biological understanding of mental health, which in turn underplays its psychological and social aspects. In particular, diagnosis obscures the understanding of the influence of personal history and social, family, and cultural context on the individual experience of a patient. Finally, diagnosis may discriminate; for example, on the basis of ethnicity, gender, and sexuality. Thus, certain diagnoses such as depression are more likely in women and others such as schizophrenia are more common in minority ethnic groups.

The other core problem with diagnosis is its impact on the users of mental health services. Individuals with psychiatric diagnoses frequently experience self-stigma and discrimination. Their own experiences (eg, domestic abuse) are often devalued, being regarded as 'trigger events' to underlying conditions and their personal significance to the patient being undervalued. Patients are likely to be disempowered by diagnosis, with solutions being imposed by professionals, often including unwanted medication.

The DCP report concludes that the current system of medical diagnosis for mental health problems should be replaced by a multi-factor system that, rather than labelling patients, sees their current experience and behaviour in wider context and acknowledges psychological and social causes as well as biological.

THINKING CRITICALLY

As you can see, there is quite a clash between the way the dominant medical establishment sees classification and diagnosis of mental disorder and the views of many clinical psychologists and other critical voices. Consider the following:

1 How serious and how justified are the criticisms of classification and diagnosis?

2 Why might the mainstream system be so biased in favour of the biomedical model?

3 What limitations can you see in the anti-psychiatry views?

4 Based on what you know so far, where do you stand?

READ THIS

If you would like to know more about the development of diagnostic systems you might like to start with this paper:

Suris, A., Holliday, R., and North, C.S. (2016). The evolution of the classification of psychiatric disorders. *Behavioural Sciences*, **6**, 1–10.

To get to grips with the current systems there's nothing like the ICD and DSM themselves. The ICD is published free online here:

https://icd.who.int/dev11/l-m/en#/http%3a%2f%2fid.who.int%2ficd%2fentity%2f1582741816
    The DSM is available in various printed formats.

APA (2013). *Desk Reference to the DSM-5*. Washington: American Psychiatric Publishing.

For some critical perspectives you might like to start with the BPS position statement:

Awenat, F., Berger, M., Coles, S., Dooley, C., Foster, S., Hannah, J., Hemmingfield, J., Johnstone, L., Nadirshaw, Z., Wainright, T., and Whomsley, S. (2013). Classification of behaviour and experience in relation to functional psychiatric diagnoses: Time for a paradigm shift. Leicester: BPS.

Thomas Szasz has recently updated his critique, and this is well worth a read:

Szasz, T. (2011). The myth of mental illness: 50 years later. *Psychiatric Bulletin*, **35**, 179–82.

MAJOR MENTAL DISORDERS AND PERSONALITY DISORDERS

The remainder of this chapter is devoted to describing some of the major mental disorders. Having outlined some serious criticisms of classification and diagnosis, it is important to acknowledge the logical inconsistency of now describing mental disorders as if they were uncontested facts. Currently, however, there is no better way to illustrate the range of ways mental disorder manifests. In addition it is important to understand mental disorders as separate entities as this is the dominant model of understanding mental disorder in mental health systems.

ANXIETY DISORDERS

Anxiety is an unpleasant feeling of tension, physiological arousal (eg, increased heart rate), and apprehension or worry that greets us when we anticipate some sort of threat (Barlow, 2002a). Anxiety is *future-oriented* because an anxious person is

> **KEY IDEAS** anxiety Anxiety is an unpleasant feeling of apprehension and worry experienced in anticipation of some sort of threat. Anxiety includes cognitive, emotional, physiological, and behavioural components. Anxiety tends to be *future-oriented*, in that it is typically experienced in response to anticipation of a future threat, rather than in response to an immediate threat, which is the domain of *fear*.

apprehensive about something that may happen in the immediate or distant future. Anxiety is not the same as *fear*, which is a present-oriented emotion, and is evoked by threats that are *already* occurring (Barlow, Brown, and Craske, 1994). Although fear is present in certain anxiety disorders (eg, *panic disorder* and *phobia*), it is not characteristic of most anxiety disorders.

Clinical anxiety can be extremely intense, irrational, and uncontrollable. It disrupts many or all aspects of the sufferer's life (Beard, Weisberg, and Keller, 2010). Severe anxiety not only disrupts a person's life, it may shorten it. A high level of anxiety is strongly associated with increased risk of death due to coronary heart disease (Hamer, Malloy, and Stamatakis, 2008). Depending on the particular condition, up to twice as many women as men suffer from anxiety disorders (Craske, 2003).

> **KEY IDEAS** comorbidity
> **Comorbidity** is the co-occurrence of more than one disorder.

Anxiety disorders have a high likelihood of coexisting or overlapping with one another and with other types of disorders, a problem called **comorbidity**. More than 50% of patients who receive a diagnosis of anxiety disorder are diagnosed with two or more such disorders (Brown et al, 2001). Anxiety is also very closely linked with **depression**—at least 50% of those people diagnosed with an anxiety disorder are also diagnosed with depression, and for those with multiple anxiety disorders the figure for comorbid depression may be much higher (Miyazaki, Aihide, and Nomura, 2010). Unfortunately, comorbidity in anxiety disorders lowers the likelihood of recovery (Bruce et al, 2005).

Generalized Anxiety Disorder

I'm constantly juggling images of doom—even in my sleep.

—Jen

> **KEY IDEAS** generalized anxiety disorder (GAD) GAD is characterized by ceaseless, pervasive, and uncontrollable worry and apprehension about the future. Worry in GAD is often irrational, and results in physical symptoms such as muscle tension as well as irritability, sleep difficulty, and difficulty concentrating.

Generalized anxiety disorder (GAD) can be thought of as the 'basic' anxiety disorder, in a way defining the essential experience of anxiety. People who suffer from generalized anxiety are driven by uncontrollable worry and apprehension about the future. They fret continuously about almost anything and everything. Unlike rational worrying, which can be useful (though unpleasant) as long as it leads to problem-solving and as long as it can be turned off, the worrying of GAD patients is often irrational and does not help them solve their problems. GAD sufferers may experience irritability, difficulty concentrating, and muscle tension throughout the day, and sleep may also be disturbed. The condition usually becomes chronic, and many sufferers never experience full relief from their symptoms (van der Heiden et al, 2011).

Diagnostic criteria for GAD

Diagnosis under the DSM-5 (APA, 2013) requires the following:

A Excessive anxiety and worry (apprehensive expectation), occurring more days than not for at least 6 months, about a number of events or activities (such as work or school performance).

B The individual finds it difficult to control the worry.

C The anxiety and worry are associated with three (or more) of the following six symptoms (with at least some symptoms having been present for more days than not for the past 6 months): Note: Only one item required in children.

  1 Restlessness, feeling keyed up or on edge.

  2 Being easily fatigued.

  3 Difficulty concentrating or mind going blank.

4 Irritability.

5 Muscle tension.

6 Sleep disturbance (difficulty falling or staying asleep, or restless, unsatisfying sleep).

D The anxiety, worry, or physical symptoms cause clinically significant distress or impairment in social, occupational, or other important areas of functioning. (American Psychiatric Association, 2013)

It is interesting to compare this to the ICD-11 criteria. Note that the ICD criteria are set out in a discursive style and avoid specifying time spans and particular combinations of symptoms:

> Generalized anxiety disorder is characterized by marked symptoms of anxiety that persist for at least several months, for more days than not, manifested by either general apprehension (ie, 'free-floating anxiety') or excessive worry focused on multiple everyday events, most often concerning family, health, finances, and school or work, together with additional symptoms such as muscular tension or motor restlessness, sympathetic autonomic over-activity (ie, high arousal), subjective experience of nervousness, difficulty maintaining concentration, irritability, or sleep disturbance. The symptoms result in significant distress or significant impairment in personal, family, social, educational, occupational, or other important areas of functioning. (World Health Organization, 2018)

Phobias

Eventually I had to move back to the city. I know it sounds stupid but there was just too many spiders out there and I couldn't really handle it.

—LaShan

When you see someone with a bleeding cut, do you feel faint and want to flee the room? Have you avoided camping in the woods or even visiting the countryside because you are deathly afraid of snakes or spiders? Do you forgo visiting relatives abroad because you are so terrified of flying? Fears such as these—irrational, powerful, highly specific, and disruptive—are known as **specific phobias**. Whereas *fear* is a normal response to realistic danger, *phobia* is an abnormal response to unrealistic perception of danger. Most people have a mild form of phobic response to one thing or another, but specific phobias severe enough to be diagnosed can sometimes cause serious problems. Phobias are the most common of the anxiety disorders (Kessler et al, 2005), but they are frequently the least disabling because most of them are narrowly focused on specific objects and situations that generally can be avoided.

As discussed in Chapter 7, there are certain phobias that are typical in human beings, probably as a result of our human evolutionary history: fear of heights, small spaces, the dark; snakes, spiders, small rodents; and the sight of blood (Darwin, 1877; LoBue and DeLoache, 2008). Although these 'evolutionary' phobias are the most common, the list of documented phobias is extraordinarily long and varied. Human beings are fabulously creative when it comes to being terrified. Consider: fear of flowers (*anthophobia*), fear of infinity (*apeirophobia*), fear of beautiful women (*caligynophobia*), fear of gravity (*barophobia*), fear of teenagers (*ephibephobia*) . . . the list of potential phobias is exceedingly long—about as long as the list of Greek nouns (Maser, 1985)!

> **KEY IDEAS** specific phobia
> **Specific phobia** is a powerful but irrational fear of a specific object, animal, or situation. The most common phobias are often those for which evolutionary roots are suspected (eg, fear of the dark or heights, fear of spiders or snakes, fear of the sight of blood, etc).

Panic Disorder

I just can't go through that again.

—Jonathan

❯ KEY IDEAS panic attack and panic disorder **A panic attack** is a brief period—generally peaking at about ten minutes—within which a person experiences overwhelming anxiety focused upon unexplainable, terrifying physical sensations. Panic attacks are not uncommon in the population and do not necessarily signify psychological disorder. **Panic disorder** is an anxiety disorder characterized by intense anxiety over the prospect of experiencing a panic attack.

A **panic attack** is one of the most frightening experiences a person can undergo short of an actual catastrophe. The classic type of panic attack is entirely unexpected—it seems to arrive 'out of the blue'. We say 'seems to arrive' because careful inquiry often determines that the attack actually had a specific trigger—for example, being in an anxiety-provoking situation or having recently experienced one (Kessler et al, 2006). Panic attacks may be as brief as a minute or last as long as an hour or even longer, although the average panic attack reaches a peak at about ten minutes and then subsides.

The experience of a panic attack is one of overwhelming terror. You may feel unable to breathe and experience an intense need to flee. Perspiration may flow as your heart pounds in your ears, your chest tightens, and you feel that you are losing all control. Things often seem unreal during an attack, and sufferers may conclude that they are having a heart attack, dying, or losing their minds.

However, it would be wrong to confuse panic *attacks* with panic *disorder*. Large numbers of people who never develop a psychological disorder have had one or more panic attacks (Craske et al, 2010). As much as the experience is unpleasant, they do not develop intense anxiety over the prospect of experiencing another one. This is the essence of **panic disorder**: the sufferer feels overwhelmingly *anxious* about the prospect of experiencing the *fear* engendered by a panic attack. Thus, those with panic disorder have had one or (usually more) panic attacks and do everything they can to avoid another one (Barlow, 2002b; Craske et al, 2010).

Causes of Anxiety Disorders

Although there are many theories of the origins of specific psychological disorders, it is widely agreed that anxiety results from a blend of biological, social-environmental, psychological, and life experience factors. This is not to say that every case requires all these factors. You may come across these factors in the form of *theories* or *explanations* for anxiety (and other mental disorders). However, the idea that mental disorder has a single cause, such as poor relationships with one's parents, conditioning experiences, or genetic abnormality has been largely abandoned by most psychologists.

Biological factors

Twin studies (see Chapter 5 for a discussion) have yielded heritability estimates of 30–50% for anxiety disorders (Scaini et al, 2014). It thus appears that some people are more prone than others to developing anxiety disorders as a function of their genetic make-up. A large scale meta-analysis (in which the results of previous studies are combined and analysed together) comparing the whole genome (called genome-wide association studies or GWAS) in sufferers and non-sufferers of anxiety disorders by Otowa et al (2016) revealed a number of genetic variations significantly more common in anxiety patients. However, the links between these genetic variations and vulnerability to anxiety remain unclear.

Research into neural correlates (ie, distinctive patterns of measurable activity in the brain; eg, regional activity or neurotransmitter levels) of anxiety disorders has shown some variations between brain function in patients with anxiety disorders compared with controls. For example, Whittman et al (2014) found stronger activation in the lateral ventral striatum and insula of agoraphobic patients when shown pictures designed to stimulate anxiety in agoraphobics. However, there is no suggestion that dysfunction in these areas is a *cause* of agoraphobia. It may simply be that activation in these areas is a response to the personal relevance of those stimuli to phobic individuals. So if you are afraid of spiders it will probably come as no surprise to see that your brain has a distinctive response on seeing one!

Conditioning experiences

We already looked at the classic work of Watson and Rayner in conditioning a fear response in a baby (see Chapter 7). Reservations about the conduct of this study aside, there are numerous other studies demonstrating that anxiety responses can be conditioned. A more interesting question is whether anxiety patients have simply been unlucky in their experiences or whether some people are more vulnerable to acquiring conditioned anxiety responses than others.

There is some evidence for the idea that some people are more vulnerable than others to acquiring anxiety responses in the form of studies comparing anxiety patients with controls in their tendency to become conditioned to respond to safety cues. A review and meta-analysis of 44 studies (Duits et al, 2015) concluded that anxiety patients reliably show more anxiety in response to safety cues, indicating either impaired ability to inhibit fear or a tendency to generalize fear-response across stimuli. Either way there appears to be an increased vulnerability to fear conditioning in anxiety patients.

Early relationships

It appears that early experience in the family context can also increase vulnerability to developing anxiety disorders. Mistreatment and quality of infant attachment to the primary carer have been particular foci of research. Schimmenti and Bifulco (2013) interviewed 160 high-risk adolescents and young adults in London, assessing them for anxiety as well as asking about their attachment quality, experiences of parenting style, and childhood abuse. Analysis of findings suggested that cold, critical parenting was associated with anxious-ambivalent attachment style which in turn predicted later problems with anxiety. Bender et al (2015) suggest that insecure attachment leads to anxiety problems because children learn to self-regulate emotions through the development of secure attachments. According to this argument insecure attachment leads to failure to self-regulate and it is this which directly causes anxiety problems.

 THINKING CRITICALLY

The Schimmenti and Bifulco study is retrospective in design. It measures attachment and childhood experience by interviewing adults about what they recall about early experiences.

Consider the following:
1 Most studies linking adult characteristics to infant attachment are retrospective. What is the major limitation of all retrospective studies like this? To what extent does this limit the credibility of attachment theory?

THINKING CREATIVELY

The alternative to retrospective studies is to conduct prospective studies. How might you go about designing a prospective study to investigate the link between childhood experience and adult anxiety problems?

Cognitive factors

Sufferers of anxiety disorders tend to selectively attend to negative stimuli (Bar-Haim et al, 2007). There appear to be two elements to this selective attention (Rusaizky, Basanovic, and McLeod, 2014). The first is the tendency to give preferential attention to anxiety-provoking stimuli and the second is an impaired ability to disengage attention. So, for example, if you are the kind of person who looks at their calendar and focuses on the one event you are worried about—and then can't stop thinking about it—you may be at increased risk of anxiety problems.

Worry is also a cognitive feature of people who are vulnerable to anxiety disorders. Specifically, the tendency for **rumination** is associated with anxiety. Rumination can be defined as a negative, repetitive style of thinking about present and past symptoms, loss, and failure (Nolen-Hoeksema, Wisco, and Lyubomirsky, 2008). Ruscio et al (2015) found that students with a diagnosis of generalized anxiety disorder (or major depression or both) were more likely to ruminate on minor daily stressful events than were matched controls.

It is not hard to see that selectively attending to stressful events and fear-provoking stimuli, having difficulty in disengaging attention from them, and then ruminating about them afterwards would make anyone highly anxious. However, these cognitive explanations really only explain the development of anxiety symptoms—they do not explain where those cognitive vulnerabilities come from in the first place.

> **KEY IDEAS** rumination
> **Rumination** is a characteristic of anxiety. It involves thinking for long periods in repetitive and negative ways about events and symptoms.

Barlow's triple vulnerability theory

The **triple vulnerability theory** of anxiety disorders was devised by David Barlow (Barlow, 2002a; see Figure 18.1). According to Barlow's integrated model, anxiety disorders result from the interaction of: (a) *generalized biological vulnerability*, or any aspect of a person's genetic inheritance that predisposes him or her to be more sensitive to anxiety-provoking situations; (b) *generalized psychological vulnerability*, or general cognitive characteristics or beliefs that make a person vulnerable to anxiety—for example, believing that the world is an unpredictable and dangerous place over which one has little control; and (c) *specific psychological vulnerability*, highly specific beliefs learned over the course of one's life that are related to the symptoms of a *specific* anxiety disorder.

For example, some children are raised by parents who are highly concerned about how they are perceived by other people, and who may impart alarmist messages about the negative consequences of embarrassing or humiliating oneself in front of others. These children may carry such beliefs with them into adulthood. Consider what might happen if such a child also were to have inherited a generalized biological vulnerability and acquired a generalized psychological vulnerability towards anxiety. Under conditions of stress, the embarrassment/humiliation beliefs the child had adopted become *specific* psychological vulnerabilities. The end result of the interaction of all these vulnerabilities may be the blossoming of social phobia (social anxiety disorder).

> **KEY IDEAS** triple vulnerability theory **Triple vulnerability theory** is an integrated model of anxiety disorders created by David Barlow. According to the triple vulnerability theory, anxiety disorders result from the interaction of three factors: generalized biological vulnerability, generalized psychological vulnerability, and specific psychological vulnerability.

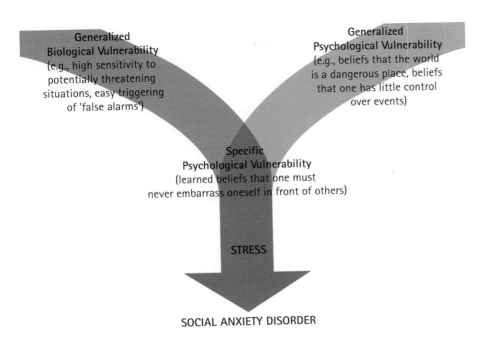

FIGURE 18.1 Barlow's triple vulnerability theory.

DEPRESSIVE DISORDERS

When I got into bed last night, the thought suddenly occurred to me that I did not deserve to sleep next to you. I didn't even deserve to sleep in our bed. I thought, I ought to go and sleep at the foot of the children's bed, like a dog. When I woke up this morning and was feeding the kids their breakfast, I thought, I don't even deserve to eat.

—From a note left to his wife by Rafael,
a patient suffering from major depressive disorder

Mood is the quality of subjective emotional feeling that one is experiencing at any given time. Like emotions, moods can function properly, or they can dysfunction—sometimes causing extremely severe problems in living. The most common dysfunction in mood is **depression**, a state characterized by exaggerated and prolonged feelings of sadness, hopelessness, grief, guilt, and low feelings of self-worth. In DSM-5 depressive disorders are a category in their own right. In ICD-11 they fall under mood disorders, along with bipolar disorder—what used to be called manic depression.

Depressive disorders are the leading cause of disability in every continent of the world other than Africa (where HIV/AIDS is the leading cause) (Üstün et al, 2004). Although often considered only to affect mental health, depression has serious effects on physical health and is associated with numerous medical conditions. Indeed, depression is associated with a reduction in overall health to a greater extent than asthma, angina (a non-fatal heart condition), arthritis, and diabetes. When depression co-occurs with any of these conditions, the result is even more profound (Moussavi et al, 2007).

Although depression and anxiety are not the same, they do co-occur extremely frequently. However, while only approximately 50% of those with an anxiety disorder

> **KEY IDEAS** depression
> **Depression** is a mood state characterized by sadness, low energy, fatigue, regret, or guilt, feelings of low self-worth, hopelessness, and helplessness.

also suffer from depression, almost all patients with depression suffer from symptoms of anxiety—and the majority could likely be diagnosed with a DSM anxiety disorder (T.A. Brown et al, 2001). The frequent comorbidity of anxiety and depression shouldn't be surprising, because they share many (though not all) of the same symptoms.

Major Depressive Disorder

Consider the note reprinted at the start of this section. The author of the note, whose name is Rafael, had been suffering from *major depressive disorder* for over eight months when he wrote it. By that time, his feelings of guilt, worthlessness, grief, and hopelessness were so entrenched that he could not see the absurdity of his statements. They were honest descriptions of his thoughts and emotions. Rafael's symptoms were manifested physically as well as emotionally. He had lost 9 pounds and had trouble sleeping more than a few hours per night, usually waking long before the sun rose. A professional musician, he had lost interest in playing his instrument and could no longer work. Five months into the depression he had tried to stab himself to death and had been saved only by emergency surgery.

Major depressive disorder (major depression) is potentially the most severe form of depression (although there is considerable variation in the severity of symptoms), and, with the exception of the phobias, is the most commonly diagnosed of all psychological disorders (Kessler, Chiu, Demler, and Walters, 2005)). However, most patients experience only mild to moderate symptoms (Kessler, Merikangas, and Wang, 2007).

As with anxiety disorders, many more women than men are diagnosed with major depression and, as depicted in Figure 18.2, increasing numbers of people seem to be experiencing depression over their lifetimes. A person born during the years 1925–45 is much less likely to report ever having had symptoms of clinical depression than

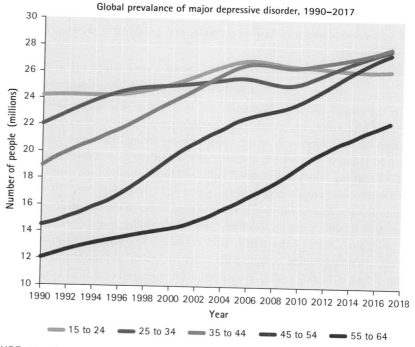

FIGURE 18.2 **Is depression becoming more common?**

Source: Global Burden of Disease Collaborative Network. Global Burden of Disease Study 2017 (GBD 2017) Results. Seattle, United States: Institute for Health Metrics and Evaluation (IHME), 2018. Available from http://ghdx.healthdata.org/gbd-results-tool

someone born during the years 1945–65; and that person in turn is much less likely to report having ever had depressive symptoms than a person born during the years 1965–85.

THINKING CRITICALLY

Psychology deals a lot in statistics. However, it is crucial that we do not take statistics at face value. Our ability to interpret and challenge statistics as well as produce them is a core skill of being a psychologist. Looking at Figure 18.2, these figures appear to show an increase in rates of depression. However, what factors other than a real increase might explain these figures?

Diagnostic criteria for major depression

Diagnosis under DSM-5 requires the following:

A Five (or more) of the following symptoms have been present during the same 2-week period and represent a change from previous functioning; at least one of the symptoms is either (1) depressed mood or (2) loss of interest or pleasure.

1 Depressed mood most of the day, nearly every day, as indicated by either subjective report (eg feels sad, empty, hopeless) or observation made by others (eg appears tearful). (Note: In children and adolescents, can be irritable mood.)

2 Markedly diminished interest or pleasure in all, or almost all, activities most of the day, nearly every day (as indicated by either subjective account or observation.)

3 Significant weight loss when not dieting or weight gain (eg a change of more than 5% of body weight in a month), or decrease or increase in appetite nearly every day. (Note: In children, consider failure to make expected weight gain.)

4 Insomnia or hypersomnia nearly every day.

5 Psychomotor agitation or retardation (ie increased or decreased motor activity) nearly every day (observable by others, not merely subjective feelings of restlessness or being slowed down).

6 Fatigue or loss of energy nearly every day.

7 Feelings of worthlessness or excessive or inappropriate guilt (which may be delusional) nearly every day (not merely self-reproach or guilt about being sick).

8 Diminished ability to think or concentrate, or indecisiveness, nearly every day (either by subjective account or as observed by others).

9 Recurrent thoughts of death (not just fear of dying), recurrent suicidal ideation without a specific plan, or a suicide attempt or a specific plan for committing suicide.

B The symptoms cause clinically significant distress or impairment in social, occupational, or other important areas of functioning.

C The episode is not attributable to the physiological effects of a substance or to another medical condition.'

The following diagnostic guidance comes from the ICD-11.

> Recurrent depressive disorder, current episode severe, without psychotic symptoms is diagnosed when the definitional requirements for Recurrent depressive disorder have been met and the current depressive episode is severe, but there are delusions or hallucinations during the episode. A depressive episode is characterized by a period of almost daily depressed mood or diminished interest in activities lasting at least two weeks accompanied by other symptoms such as difficulty concentrating, feelings of worthlessness or excessive or inappropriate guilt, hopelessness, recurrent thoughts of death or suicide, changes in appetite or sleep, psychomotor agitation or retardation, and reduced energy or fatigue. In a severe depressive episode, either many symptoms are present to a marked degree or a smaller number of severe symptoms that include a significant risk of suicide are present. The individual is unable to continue with work, social, or domestic activities, except to a very limited degree.

Other Forms of Depression

DSM and ICD systems recognize a range of other forms of depression.

- Persistent depressive disorder (called dysthymic disorder in ICD-11) is a long-term (diagnosis requires at least two years for adults, one for children and adolescents) variety of depression. Symptoms are sometimes—but not necessarily—milder than those experienced in an episode of major depression but they last a lot longer.

- Premenstrual dysphoric disorder, commonly called premenstrual syndrome or PMS, is diagnosed when depressive symptoms occur in most menstrual cycles for a year and not independent of the menstrual cycle—this would be more likely to be diagnosed as persistent depressive disorder. Symptoms must be severe enough to interfere with daily life for diagnosis.

- A new disorder has been added to DSM-5. This is disruptive mood dysregulation disorder. It refers to childhood temper tantrums. This has proved controversial, with some commentators seeing it as the medicalization of normal childhood behaviour. The argument for its inclusion in DSM is that this is a diagnosis only given when the irritability is severe and frequent enough to interfere with the child's daily life. Diagnosis is only made after the age of 6 years, so the disorder is not simply based on toddler tantrums.

 THINKING CRITICALLY

Some from the critical psychiatry movement have pointed out that new disorders that are treatable by drugs have made their way into DSM-5, whilst others such as Asperger syndrome, which are not generally treated medically, have been left out.

Consider the following:

1 What vested interests might benefit from this shift towards selectively recognizing drug-treatable conditions?

2 Not everyone accepts this cynical view of the DSM-5. What might be the counter-arguments? Think about the examples of disruptive mood dysregulation and Asperger's. What might be legitimate reasons for these changes? HINT: think about the aim in constructing DSM-5 to better align the nosology and aetiology of mental disorder.

Causes of Depressive Disorders

As with most psychological disorders, causes of depression are not known with certainty. However, it is clear that depression can have multiple causes (Lau and Eley, 2010). Often, though not necessarily, depression can be a response to **loss events**; however, there are a range of factors that make some people and not others respond to life events with depression.

Biological factors

Depression runs in families, and studies in **behavioural genetics** strongly suggest that part of the story of depression is genetic vulnerability (Lau and Eley, 2010). Although there is no gene or set of genes that *cause* a person to suffer depression, genetic inheritance can make a person more likely to respond to adversity by developing depression. The idea that a genetic predisposition towards an illness can become activated under certain conditions, but not activated in the absence of these conditions, is known as the **diathesis stress model** (Monroe and Simons, 1991).

What are the conditions or experiences that can trigger depression in genetically vulnerable individuals? Experiences of stress are strongly linked to the onset of depression, and certain types of stressors may be more likely than others to trigger depression. These tend to be experiences involving loss of important relationships, loss of status, and humiliation (Horwitz and Wakefield, 2007). Romantic rejection often involves both loss of a relationship *and* humiliation, and this may be why depression frequently follows divorces and romantic break-ups.

Recently, genetic research in depression has become more sophisticated as researchers have begun to focus on the interplay of genetics and environments (Lau and Eley, 2010). Specifically, researchers are asking two relatively new questions:

1 If depression results from a genetic vulnerability combined with certain life experiences or environments, why do certain people—but not others—tend to have these environmental experiences? For example, do some people experience more losses and/or humiliations because of an additional vulnerability beyond those that directly predispose them to depression?

2 Why do certain people have these experiences but never become depressed?

The first question—'Why do certain people tend to have the type of negative or stressful experiences that trigger depression?'—refers to gene-environment correlation, also discussed in Chapter 5 (Kendler and Baker, 2007). Gene-environment correlations describe ways that a person's genetic make-up can help create his or her environment. For example, a person with a genetic predisposition to engage in stormy relationships characterized by high levels of conflict—a predisposition often shared by the person's parents and siblings—may grow up in a stormy household and then be exposed to stormy relationships in adulthood. Stormy relationships are stressful, and therefore, in predisposing him or her to engage in conflict the person's genetic make-up has helped to create a stressful environment. The person is not simply a product of this environment, he or she contributes to it.

The second question—'Why do certain people have negative or stressful experiences but never become depressed?'—refers to gene-environment interactions, as described in Chapter 5. Some research has implicated a region along the 5-HTT gene known as 5-HTTLPR in the relationship between stress and depression—that is, as an explanation for why stress triggers depression in some people but not others

> **KEY IDEAS** loss events **Loss events** are life events involving short- or long-term loss of an attachment figure. Short-term losses include hospitalization, while long-term loss events occur in bereavement and family reordering. Loss events, particularly those occurring in childhood, are important because they are associated with later depression.

> **KEY IDEAS** diathesis stress model This is a model of psychological disorder which proposes that mental illness is most likely to be found in a person who has both genetic vulnerability to the condition *and* exposure to life experiences which contribute to the onset of the illness.

(Wankurl, Wüst, and Otte, 2010). The 5-HTT gene comes in two forms or **alleles**: a short allele and a long allele. If the research turns out to be correct—and it has been challenged frequently—those people who inherit the short version will be more likely to respond to stress by becoming depressed.

An additional biological factor implicated in depression is neurochemistry. You may have heard that depression is due to a 'chemical imbalance in the brain', referring in particular to low levels of the neurotransmitter serotonin. However, the idea that depression is caused by a neurotransmitter 'imbalance' is at best greatly oversimplified and misleading (France, Lysaker, and Robinson, 2007).

The first problem is that, while some depressed people do show unusual neurotransmitter balances, others (probably the majority) do not (France et al, 2007). Furthermore, when balances are unusual they are sometimes found in a direction opposite to the expected one—for example, more rather than less availability of the neurotransmitter (Barton et al, 2008).

More to the point, when healthy volunteers have their levels of serotonin or norepinephrine intentionally lowered in research studies (eg, through dietary restrictions or by other means), they do not become depressed. Similarly, when drugs which boost the availability of these neurotransmitters are administered to depressed patients, the drugs frequently do not work—or if they do, it often takes many weeks or even months for any therapeutic effect to be felt. In other words, alterations of neurotransmitter levels in themselves do not alter mood (Delgado, 2000; Hindmarch, 2001; Booij et al, 2002).

DEBUNKING: THE TREATMENT-CAUSATION FALLACY

A common argument in favour of a biochemical explanation for depression has been the fact that antidepressant drugs alter neurotransmitter levels and sometimes also reduce symptoms of depression. Common sense suggests that if drugs raise noradrenaline and/or serotonin levels and simultaneously relieve symptoms then low levels of those chemicals must have been the origin of the symptoms in the first place.

However, this is flawed logic. If I suffer social anxiety and use alcohol to give myself confidence would this mean that social anxiety is caused by lack of alcohol? If I break my leg and put it in plaster to heal, my broken leg was probably not caused by lack of plaster! To suggest that the effect of antidepressants demonstrates a chemical basis for depression is essentially the same argument.

This logical error is called the treatment-causation fallacy and it is important because there is a range of biological and psychological treatments for all mental health problems, each of which is based on a particular theoretical understanding of mental disorder. The fallacy is not unique to biological explanations. Those arguing for the value of any theoretical model of mental disorder can call upon evidence for the effectiveness of 'their' treatment and by implication their theoretical model, but the effectiveness of a treatment is *never* strong support for a theoretical explanation.

The role of early life events

There is considerable evidence showing a link between early negative experience and later depression. In particular, experience of childhood abuse makes people more vulnerable. Braithwaite et al (2017) reviewed studies and concluded that the maltreatment–depression link is a robust one (ie, the evidence is consistent across studies). They were also interested in mediating variables—what factors followed the abuse and impacted directly on depression. It appears that abuse makes it harder for children to form post-abuse relationships that would serve as a buffer against depression. Another mediating variable seems to be cognitive style; abuse leads to negative cognition which in turn leaves the individual more prone to depression.

Chesmore et al (2017) looked at the relationships of abuse and attachment with depression in 493 9–11-year-old children in foster care. They concluded that attachment quality to both biological and foster parents predicted likelihood of depression, independently of each other and independently of the influence of early abuse—this also predicted depression. This has an important practical application—it demonstrates the importance of professionals, in particular social workers, working to improve the quality of attachment to both biological and foster parents in order to improve the mental health of looked-after children.

Learned depressive behaviour

During the 1960s, psychologist Martin Seligman found that if rodents and dogs were given unpleasant but not dangerous electric shocks, they were able to continue to function as long as they were taught a way to escape from the shocks. Under these conditions, they continued to work to avoid the shocks, and continued to behave relatively normally. However, if these animals were given no way to avoid the shocks, they began to behave in a helpless manner and endured the shocks and did not even attempt to take advantage of avenues of escape that were subsequently offered. They had 'given up' in a way that reminded Seligman and his colleagues of human depression. Seligman termed this response **learned helplessness** (Seligman, 1975). Seligman proposed that if human beings come to believe, for whatever reason, that they have no control over the negative events of their lives, they may experience learned helplessness and suffer depression.

The role of cognitive vulnerability

Vulnerability to depression has also been linked to *cognition*—how we think about ourselves, our lives, and our world (Gotlib and Joorman, 2010). Psychologists have shown that depressed people exhibit cognitive biases in virtually all aspects of cognition—memory, perception, attention, and interpretation of events. In other words, our own habitual patterns of thinking, processing information, and responding to various events in our lives can be important stressors in themselves. Two major theories have greatly expanded our understanding of these cognitive underpinnings of depression: Lyn Abramson and Lauren Alloy's *hopelessness theory* (Abramson, Alloy, and Metalsky, 1995) and Aaron Beck's theory of the *negative cognitive triad* (Beck, Rush, Shaw, and Emery, 1987).

Lyn Abramson and Lauren Alloy refined Seligman's ideas about learned helplessness to focus on the cognitive factor of *hopelessness* rather than the behavioural factor of helplessness (Abramson et al, 1995). According to this 'revised' theory, generally known as **hopelessness theory**, learned helplessness is not enough to explain depression, because a sense of helplessness is equally present in anxiety. According to Abramson and Alloy, the factor that causes helplessness to lead to depression rather than anxiety is *hopelessness*—the idea that things can never get better.

How does hopelessness arise? Abramson and Alloy identified a negative cognitive style which creates vulnerability to the hopelessness of depression (Alloy et al,

❯ **KEY IDEAS** learned helplessness This is Martin Seligman's term to describe the passivity and resignation which an animal may experience after coming to believe that it is unable to control or halt an aversive event. **Learned helplessness** then interferes with the animal's ability to recognize when it is in fact able to halt or control the event. Seligman originally theorized that learned helplessness lies at the root of depressive disorders.

❯ **KEY IDEAS** hopelessness theory This is a revision of learned helplessness theory created by Lyn Abramson and Lauren Alloy. Hopelessness theory proposes that a negative cognitive style leads to depression. This negative cognitive style includes three aspects: (a) attributing negative events to internal causes; (b) considering causes of negative events to be stable and global; and (c) anticipating severe negative consequences from negative events.

2006). According to Abramson and Alloy, the cognitive style most likely to lead to depression has three characteristics:

- Negative events are attributed to *internal* causes and personal failings ('It's all my fault—I'm just stupid').

- Causes of negative events are thought to be *stable* and *global*—that is, they are likely to endure, be repeated in the future, and apply not only to the matter at hand but also to a great many other types of situations ('I'll probably fail the next test too. I guess I'm just not cut out for academic work').

- Severe *negative consequences* are anticipated to follow from negative events ('I'll probably get kicked out of school altogether').

These ideas are highly compatible, if not overlapping, with Aaron Beck's view of depression as resulting from a **negative cognitive triad** depicted in Figure 18.3 (Beck et al, 1987). According to Beck, depression can result from irrational cognitive 'errors'—chronic patterns of thinking that create vulnerability to depression and revolve around three aspects of existence (hence the term 'triad'). The negative cognitive triad includes irrational beliefs about:

- *The self.* Erroneous beliefs about the self include feelings that one is worthless, a failure, a bad or evil person.

- *The world.* Erroneous beliefs about the world include ideas that the world is uniformly a joyless, cold, uncontrollable, and unforgiving place.

- *The future.* Erroneous beliefs about the future focus on predictions of hopelessness and doom.

According to Beck's cognitive model, thoughts such as these may actually precipitate the neurohormonal and other biological events that lead to major depression.

Having a negative cognitive style not only makes one vulnerable to depression, it also increases the chances of experiencing stressful and depressing events in much the same way that genetic make-up can help shape the environment in gene-environment correlations (Safford et al, 2007). Consider a very simple example—the stress of romantic disappointments. If 'misery loves company but company does not love misery', a person who holds the kinds of beliefs described in the negative cognitive triad and hopelessness models is unlikely to have much success as a romantic partner. Even people who are very loving, compassionate, and supportive tend to grow tired of continual hopelessness and negativity in their interactions with their partner. This in turn leads to more failed relationships and even more negativity.

> KEY IDEAS cognitive triad
This is Aaron Beck's term to describe a set of irrational, chronic, and erroneous beliefs about the 'triad' of the self, the world, and the future.

FIGURE 18.3 **The cognitive triad.** According to cognitive therapy founder Aaron Beck, depression results from habitual patterns of irrational, erroneous negative thoughts about the self, the world, and the future (Beck et al, 1987).

Source: arka38/Shutterstock.com.

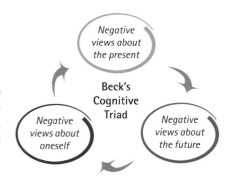

Feminist perspectives

One finding in the field of abnormal psychology that is—at first—puzzling is that rates of depression in women are almost always substantially higher than those for men. As depicted in Figure 18.4, across a range of cultures and throughout the life span, beginning in mid-adolescence, women are on average twice as likely as men to suffer from depression (Hyde, Mezulis, and Abramson, 2008). What is responsible for this lopsided ratio? Although there may be biological and cognitive factors involved (Hyde et al, 2008), there is also a strong case for saying that women experience more adverse experiences as a function of social injustice.

Discrimination against women begins early in their lives, meaning that girls experience more of the instances of humiliation, low status, and diminution of relationships that are associated with later depression. Girls are approximately twice as likely as boys to suffer sexual abuse in childhood. This pattern of victimization is maintained through **adolescence** to adulthood, where women make up the vast majority of victims of physical assault (Koss, 1994). Ouelette-Morin et al (2015) found that, once other life events were accounted for, experience of partner violence in the previous ten years doubled women's probability of a diagnosis of depression. Domestic abuse alone thus accounts for a significant number of cases of depression in women.

A further factor that may relate to higher rates of depression in women is socially sanctioned responses to stress, in which men tend to externalize (act out) where women tend to internalize stress resulting in anxiety and depression (Cochrane, 1995). Support for this explanation of depression comes from statistics showing that the lower rates of depression in men are matched by higher rates of drug abuse and violent crime in men (Rogers and Pilgrim, 1996).

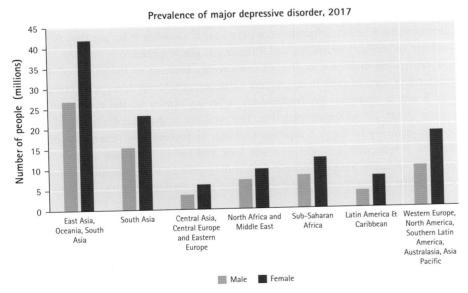

FIGURE 18.4 **Sex differences in lifetime rates of depression.**

Source: Global Burden of Disease Collaborative Network. Global Burden of Disease Study 2017 (GBD, 2017) Results. Seattle, United States: Institute for Health Metrics and Evaluation (IHME), 2018. Available from http://ghdx.healthdata.org/gbd-results-tool

Depression and Suicide

Psychological disorders are not only unpleasant to experience—they are dangerous as well because suicide is a serious risk for sufferers. Around 6,000 people commit suicide each year in the United Kingdom (about 800,000 throughout the world), and of these, over 90% would probably be diagnosed with a mental disorder (World Health Organization, 2011a, 2011b). Depression is the most common mental disorder associated with suicide. In fact suffering from major depression is the single most statistically significant risk factor for suicide apart from a previous suicide attempt (Schneider, Müller, and Philipp, 2001), with between 56% and 87% of those attempting suicide believed to be suffering major depression (Rihmer, 2007).

Although the general suicide risk for persons with depression is nowhere near as high as psychologists once believed, for certain individuals the risk is quite high. Rates of suicide are highest for those who have been hospitalized with extremely severe depression, who experienced their first depression episode at an earlier age, whose depressions are longer lasting, and who show little response to **antidepressants** (Perroud et al, 2010).

SCHIZOPHRENIA

> *When I was 18, 19, 22, my brain was just clogged all the time—non-stop voices. I couldn't figure out what was going on. There was a lot of confusion inside me, this flood of voices, often contradicting each other, often telling me stuff that would happen in the future, and then it would happen, voices insulting me, telling me what to do.*
>
> —John Frusciante, Red Hot Chili Peppers
> (The Voice Collective, accessed 2018)

John Frusciante might not have got a diagnosis of schizophrenia, but the quote above illustrates the experience of hearing voices. In psychology there is much disagreement on whether schizophrenia exists or, if so, what it is, but that the symptoms are incredibly distressing and disabling is not disputed.

If depression attracts a degree of controversy because of the range of different perspectives used to explain it, the very *existence* of schizophrenia is a battleground! This is not to minimize the tremendous suffering caused by the symptoms we are talking about. No one questions this. The problem is that the diagnosis of schizophrenia involves so many symptoms that can be present in different combinations that one person with a diagnosis might look and feel nothing like another. There is far more variation between people with a diagnosis of schizophrenia than between people with and without it, and this would be a problem for the validity of any diagnosis.

One way to square this circle is to think of **schizophrenia** as a *group* of related **psychotic disorders** characterized by severely distorted perception and experience of reality, disorganized thought and speech, and inappropriate emotions or emotional responses. It is psychotic disorders that are probably most commonly associated in the public mind with mental illness or 'madness', even though these conditions actually characterize a tiny minority of people with psychological disorders, and an even smaller minority of the general population. No more than 1% of the population at most will suffer from schizophrenia during their lifetimes (Pogue-Geile and Yokley, 2010).

> **KEY IDEAS** schizophrenia and psychotic disorders **Schizophrenia** is a group of related psychotic conditions characterized by severely distorted perception and experience of reality, disorganized thought and speech, and inappropriate emotions and emotional responses. A **psychotic disorder** is any disorder that includes extremely severe distortion in thinking and perception, where a person's ability to grasp reality and respond rationally is badly impaired.

DEBUNKING

Schizophrenia is often described by lay people as 'split personality'. They are in fact getting confused with *dissociative identity disorder* (DID) or 'multiple personality'. The word *schizophrenia* loosely translates as 'split mind'; this is probably responsible for the confusion. Note, however, that DID is an entirely separate issue, and that schizophrenia does not involve multiple personalities.

Another myth is that, because the behaviour of those who suffer from schizophrenia is unusual and unpredictable, people with schizophrenia are dangerous. These stereotypes may recently have grown more prevalent as a result of sensational media coverage of incidents involving a very small number of violent patients. However, violence among patients with a diagnosis of schizophrenia is actually very unusual. The vast majority are isolated, withdrawn, and pose no threat to anyone, even when symptomatic (Elbogen and Johnson, 2009), which in some individuals is for a small proportion of the time. I (Matt) had no concerns leaving my children in the care of a friend with a diagnosis of schizophrenia when they were younger.

A final myth we'd like to flag up at this point is that anyone who experiences hallucinations—a classic symptom of schizophrenia—is 'mentally ill' or would benefit from a diagnosis. Hearing voices is a classic symptom of schizophrenia but also quite a common sensory experience for people who in every other sense lead an entirely normal life. Famous voice-hearers who never entered the psychiatric system include Ghandi and Freud. Moreover, voice-hearing is much less likely to be experienced as distressing and a sign of mental disorder in non-Western cultures (Luhrmann et al, 2014).

Aspects of schizophrenia are often present in childhood, although obvious signs are typically seen, and the illness diagnosed, in adolescence or early adulthood. Symptoms generally remain in some form on and off throughout the lifespan, although many people with schizophrenia recover enough to lead normal lives at least for periods of time—sometimes substantial periods of time (Messias et al, 2007). However, the typical outcome for people diagnosed with schizophrenia is often worse than for the other disorders discussed in this chapter, and homelessness frequently goes hand in hand with schizophrenia. Suicide, while less common in schizophrenia than often supposed, does end the life of many (Jobe and Harrow, 2010).

Diagnostic Criteria for Schizophrenia

Diagnosis under DSM-5 requires the following:

A Two (or more) of the following, each present for a significant portion of time during a 1-month period (or less if successfully treated). At least one of these must be (1), (2), or (3):

1 Delusions.

2 Hallucinations.

3 Disorganized speech (eg, frequent derailment or incoherence).

4 Grossly disorganized or catatonic behavior.

5 Negative symptoms (ie, diminished emotional expression or avolition).

B For a significant portion of the time since the onset of the disturbance, level of functioning in one or more major areas, such as work, interpersonal relations, or self-care, is markedly below the level achieved prior to the onset (or when the onset is in childhood or adolescence, there is failure to achieve expected level of interpersonal, academic, or occupational functioning).

> **KEY IDEAS** prodromal and residual phases Schizophrenia typically remits then returns, often though not necessarily as patients stop taking medication. The **prodromal** phase precedes the main onset of symptoms and the **residual** phase follows them. Symptoms in these phases include milder cognitive distortions, depression, and sleep disturbance. Awareness of prodromal phase symptoms is important as they are easier to treat than a full-blown episode of schizophrenia and starting or altering medication may prevent a full episode.

C Continuous signs of the disturbance persist for at least 6 months. This 6-month period must include at least 1 month of symptoms (or less if successfully treated) that meet Criterion A (ie, active-phase symptoms) and may include periods of prodromal or residual symptoms. During these **prodromal** or **residual** periods, the signs of the disturbance may be manifested by only negative symptoms or by two or more symptoms listed in Criterion A present in an attenuated form (eg, odd beliefs, unusual perceptual experiences).

In ICD-11 schizophrenia is described as follows:

Schizophrenia is characterized by disturbances in multiple mental modalities, including thinking (eg, delusions, disorganization in the form of thought), perception (eg, hallucinations), self-experience (eg, the experience that one's feelings, impulses, thoughts, or behaviour are under the control of an external force), cognition (eg, impaired attention, verbal memory, and social cognition), volition (eg, loss of motivation), and **affect** (eg, blunted emotional expression). Psychomotor disturbances, including catatonia, may be present. Persistent delusions, persistent hallucinations, thought disorder, and experiences of influence, passivity, or control are considered core symptoms. Symptoms must have persisted for at least one month in order for a diagnosis of schizophrenia to be assigned.

Positive and negative symptoms

Symptoms experienced by those with schizophrenia are generally divided into two categories: *positive symptoms* and *negative symptoms*. As they are used here, 'positive' and 'negative' do not mean 'good' and 'bad'. **Positive symptoms** are those in which something is *added* to the person's behaviour that should *not* be there, such as *hallucinations* and *delusions*. **Negative symptoms** are those suggesting that something which *should* be there is lacking. This usually refers to appropriate emotional responses, facial expressions, or the ability to speak normally.

The most common positive symptoms of schizophrenia are *hallucinations* and *delusions*. Hallucinations are false sensory experiences, such as hearing voices or 'seeing things' that aren't there. Delusions are incorrect and grossly distorted thoughts and beliefs, not widely shared by other members of one's culture. Following are some common delusions:

> **KEY IDEAS** positive and negative symptoms **Positive symptoms** of schizophrenia include the *addition* of something to a person's behaviour which is not expected of a mentally healthy person. These are the more obvious symptoms of schizophrenia, such as delusions, hallucinations, and disorganized use of language. **Negative symptoms** are the less obvious symptoms of schizophrenia, which include the *absence* of characteristics which are expected of a mentally healthy person. Negative symptoms include flat affect, anhedonia, alogia, and avolition.

- *Delusions of persecution*—the idea that people are plotting to do one harm.

- *Delusions of grandeur*—the belief that one is a person of importance and accomplishment, such as a US president or even a holy person such as Jesus Christ or Buddha.

- *Delusions of reference*—the tendency to interpret various public messages as though they were intended for one personally. For example, a simple headline in a newspaper may be thought to be a coded message from the CIA warning one personally of an imminent attack from space aliens or a terrorist group. A radio announcer's use of the word 'you' to refer to all listeners may be interpreted as referring only to the schizophrenic personally.

Negative symptoms are qualities that are 'conspicuous by their absence'. At least 25% of those with schizophrenia display negative symptoms (Malla et al, 2002). There are four basic types of negative symptoms:

- *Alogia* ('poverty of speech') refers to a difficulty in replying appropriately to questions. Schizophrenics with alogia may not reply to questions at all or may reply with only a single word or brief phrase, and often not logically responsive to the question.

- *Anhedonia* or difficulty experiencing pleasure in normal daily activities. Anhedonia is also frequently present in depression, and in fact there is significant overlap of negative symptoms in depression and schizophrenia (Walker et al, 2004).

- *Avolition* or difficulty making decisions or initiating or continuing activities. Avolition is similar to the more common word *apathy*.

- *Flat affect* or inappropriately emotionless expression even in the midst of highly emotional conversation or events. A person with flat affect may be seething or weeping inside, but you would not know it. Thus, flat affect does not mean that the person with schizophrenia is not experiencing emotion (Kring and Caponigro, 2010).

Although positive symptoms of schizophrenia such as hallucinations and delusions are certainly the most dramatic aspects of the illness—and the ones most commonly thought of when the term *schizophrenia* is used—they are often of less critical importance in the lives of most schizophrenics than negative symptoms. For example, Roger Brown and Richard Herrnstein (cited by Carson, 1996, p 1133) describe a meeting of Schizophrenics Anonymous which they attended:

> The members each seemed to come alone, trailing in and out of the night, with almost no group acknowledgement of the successive arrivals. . . . [The group's leader that night] began with an optimistic testimony about how things were going with him, designed in part to buck up the others. Some of them also spoke hopefully; others were silent and stared at the floor throughout. I gradually felt hope draining out of the group as they began to talk of their inability to hold jobs, of living on welfare, of finding themselves overwhelmed by simple demands. Nothing bizarre was said or done; there was rather a pervasive sense of inadequacy, of lives in which each day was a dreadful trial. Doughnuts and coffee were served, and then each one, still alone, trailed off into the Cambridge night. (1996, p 1133)

Many with a diagnosis of schizophrenia manage to live fulfilling and happy lives in spite of their illness. Tom Harrell, diagnosed in 1967 with paranoid schizophrenia, is considered one of the finest jazz trumpeters of his generation and has released over 20 CDs as leader of his own group, and mathematician John Nash, subject of the film *A Beautiful Mind* won a Nobel Prize. Rufus May, shown in Figure 18.5, one of Britain's most original and inspiring psychologists who specializes in schizophrenia treatment received a diagnosis himself at the age of 18.

Causes of Schizophrenia

The search for a single, direct cause of schizophrenia has been puzzling and frustrating, made harder by the fact that different—or even the same—symptoms may have different origins, and that there is a serious question mark around the idea that schizophrenia is a single condition. In order to remain theoretically neutral, where possible we will refer to 'symptoms of schizophrenia' and 'diagnosis of schizophrenia'.

Genetic risk

Regardless of whether we accept the existence of a biological illness called schizophrenia, there is substantial evidence to show that some people are more vulnerable than others to developing the symptoms of schizophrenia, and that this vulnerability

FIGURE 18.5 **Rufus May, a British psychologist with a diagnosis of schizophrenia.**

Source: © Rufus May.

is at least in part a function of their genetic make-up. Numerous studies have demonstrated clearly that the closer the degree of genetic relatedness a person holds to a family member with a diagnosis of schizophrenia, the greater is the risk of that person developing the symptoms himself or herself (Gottesman, 1991). Figure 18.6 dramatically demonstrates how the risk of being diagnosed with schizophrenia increases in an orderly, linear fashion according to the degree of genetic relatedness between relatives.

While behavioural genetics studies such as those just described have confirmed that a link exists between genes and schizophrenia, recent studies in molecular genetics have attempted to identify possible candidate genes responsible for vulnerability to schizophrenia (Duan, Sanders, and Gejman, 2010). However, over the years many apparently exciting findings of links to specific genes in schizophrenia have turned out to be false leads. Very recent studies that have only been made possible due to the mapping of the human genome have demonstrated why these false leads may be occurring—it may be the case that scores, hundreds, or even thousands of genes are potential contributors to the risk of schizophrenia, and that these genes are common variations, not rare sets of genes. While each genetic variant exerts only a small effect, combined together they confer a powerful vulnerability to developing symptoms (International Schizophrenia Consortium, 2009). In a huge study of data from 37,000 patients and 113,000 controls (Ripke et al, 2014), 108 separate genetic variations all increased the risk of a diagnosis of schizophrenia.

To make things even more complicated, it seems that these genes interact in particular ways—turning each other on and off in the manner described in Chapter 5.

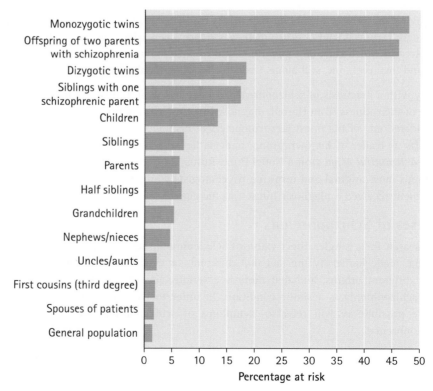

FIGURE 18.6 **Risk of developing schizophrenia by degree of genetic relatedness.**
Source: Data from Gottesman, 1991; figure from Barlow and Durand, 2009, p 481.

Given the massively complex nature of schizophrenia, this complexity of genetic activity should not be unexpected. Indeed, very recent genome-wide analysis suggests the possibility that looking for specific genes responsible for specific psychological disorders may be misguided for a simple reason: the same complex genetic interactions may be responsible for numerous psychological symptoms of disorder (Cross-Disorder Group of the Psychiatric Genomics Consortium, 2013).

Therefore, a number of researchers are taking a new approach to locating genetic markers of schizophrenia. This new approach is known as *endophenotyping* (Braff, Schork, and Gottesman, 2007). An **endophenotype** is any single characteristic or symptom that is present in people with a specific psychological disorder and is also present at a high rate in close genetic relatives who do not have the disorder. In other words, an endophenotype is part of what is heritable about a disorder—although it is not the disorder itself. Unlike a complex set of symptoms, such as those of schizophrenia, the endophenotype is simple and straightforward enough to lend itself to genetic analysis.

For example, Raquel Gur and her colleagues administered a battery of *neurocognitive* tests to a group of multigenerational families, each of which had some members with diagnoses of schizophrenia. They administered the same tests to a comparison sample of multigenerational families with no schizophrenic members (Gur et al, 2007). A neurocognitive test is any test that taps a cognitive skill closely linked to particular regions of the brain and assumed to have a genetic component. The tests included assessments of attention, verbal memory, memory for faces, spatial memory, ability to recognize emotion in facial expressions, and so forth—all skills that have been shown to be deficient in people with schizophrenia (Braff et al, 2007).

Gur and her colleagues found that people with a diagnosis did show deficits in these neurocognitive skills but so did their relatives who did *not* have symptoms—or at least did not have a diagnosis. On the other hand, these deficits were not seen in the comparison group of families with no diagnosed members. This strongly suggests that these deficits are part of what is inherited in schizophrenia, qualifying them as endophenotypes. Because these characteristics are relatively straightforward, they will lend themselves to molecular genetic analysis in the future (Gur et al, 2007).

A not very scientific—but still fascinating—insight into the cognitive symptoms of schizophrenia comes from the work of artist Louis Wain. Wain is best known for his pictures of cats. During a phase when Wain was descending into psychosis he drew the same cat a number of times (see Figure 18.7). In the first it is entirely cat-like but it is barely recognizable as a feline by the sixth picture.

Neurodevelopmental factors

While behaviour genetic, molecular genetic, and endophenotyping studies all establish the importance of genetics in the development of schizophrenia, there is much more than genes to the story. One of the most promising attempts to explain non-genetic components of schizophrenia involves *neurodevelopmental* factors. A **neurodevelopmental** factor is one that affects the brain but which is not genetic in origin; instead, it is rooted in events that occur after the moment of conception. Originally this meant that the focus for researchers would be prenatal events—experiences of the foetus while in the womb. However, as the nature of early brain development became better understood, neurodevelopmental researchers in schizophrenia have expanded their work to include events in adolescence (Walker et al, 2010).

> **KEY IDEAS** endophenotype
> This is a characteristic or symptom of a disorder that is present in people with that disorder and also is present to a greater degree than would be expected by chance in close genetic relatives of the person with the disorder. Endophenotypes are considered to reflect what is heritable about a given disorder but, unlike most disorders, are considered simple and straightforward enough to lend themselves to genetic analysis.

> **KEY IDEAS** neurodevelopmental factors Any factor which affects the brain but does not have a genetic origin can be thought of as neurodevelopmental. Neurodevelopmental events may occur prior to birth, at birth, or after birth.

FIGURE 18.7 The changes in Louis Wain's cat pictures as his symptoms of schizophrenia worsened.
Source: Louis Wain.

Scientists conducting research on neurodevelopmental factors in schizophrenia argue that while sets of genes might predispose a person to schizophrenia, without certain types of experiences occurring during early development—either prenatally, at birth, or during adolescence—schizophrenia will not develop. According to this hypothesis, prenatal, birth, or adolescent experiences can cause subtle forms of damage in the frontal and temporal lobes (forebrain) which result in disruption of brain development. However, this damage does not become apparent until late adolescence or early adulthood, when it shows up as symptoms of schizophrenia (Conklin and Iocono, 2002).

WHAT'S HOT? SCHIZOPHRENIA AND ADOLESCENT CANNABIS USE

There has been considerable publicity over the last decade around research suggesting a link between the adolescent experience of cannabis and a subsequent diagnosis of schizophrenia. As is usually the case when research leads to a moral panic, the argument in the media has become over-simplified. So what does research really tell us?

In the early 2000s a number of researchers reported robust statistical associations between cannabis use and both immediate psychotic symptoms (eg, Amar and Potvin, 2007) and the probability of later receiving a diagnosis of schizophrenia (eg, Rey and Tennant, 2002). However, the debate soon became more nuanced. Could, for example, the statistics be explained by confounding variables such as urban living or poverty that might increase risk of both cannabis use and schizophrenia? A study by Fergusson, Horwood, and Ridder (2005) that controlled for a wide range of confounds ranging from family functioning and history of mental health problems to socio-economic status and parental education and drug use suggested not. Another possibility was that adolescents self-medicated with cannabis to control early symptoms. Again, research suggested that this could not account completely for the association between cannabis use and schizophrenia (see, eg, Van Os et al, 2002).

More recent research has suggested that the cannabis-schizophrenia effect varies according to age of cannabis use. Roncero et al (2017) reviewed studies and concluded that starting cannabis use early in adolescence increased risk by 2.5–4 times more than later. Studies in this review varied in the age they classed as 'early' from 14 to 18 years. Interestingly, most studies have not distinguished between early and late onset of cannabis use, so there is actually much less information around than you might expect on the relationship between cannabis use in late adolescence and early adulthood and schizophrenia.

It also appears from recent research that cannabis is neither necessary nor sufficient to influence the development of schizophrenia symptoms, but that instead it interacts with other vulnerabilities such as genetic make-up. Thus Estrada et al (2011) reported that those that started cannabis use before 14 *and* had a particular variation on the COMT gene were particularly vulnerable.

Finally, not all cannabis is the same. Cannabis contains two major psychoactive components. THC (tetrahydrocannabinol) is the one associated with psychosis. The other, CBD (cannabidiol) is actually an anti-psychotic (Morgan and Curran, 2008). One reason why the schizophrenia-cannabis link has emerged in the last 20 years is that modern and trendy strains of cannabis have far more THC and less CBD than was the case in the past.

Cognitive factors

We have already seen that there are neurocognitive factors in the development of the symptoms of schizophrenia. This raises the interesting question of whether we should think of cognitive abilities closely associated with the functioning of particular brain systems as psychological or biological. One answer is that in this context any distinction between 'cognitive' and 'biological' is a **false dichotomy**—cognitive deficits can be attributed to abnormal neural development.

> **KEY IDEAS** false dichotomies
A **false dichotomy** is a distinction between two concepts that, at least in some situations, is meaningless because the two concepts are so hard to separate.

However, this is not to say that our understanding of the experience we call schizophrenia has not been enriched by pure cognitive perspectives. For example, Frith (1992) has distinguished between two types of thought dysfunction that underlie symptoms:

KEY IDEAS metarepresentation and central control These are both cognitive abilities that may underlie symptoms of schizophrenia. **Metarepresentation** is the awareness of our own thought, emotion, motives, etc. Failure in metarepresentation could lead to the experience of voice-hearing. **Central control** is the ability to suppress automatic cognition. Failure in central control could result in symptoms like clanging.

- **Metarepresentation** is the cognitive ability to perceive one's own thoughts, emotions, motives, and goals—in short to know what is going on in our own mind. A problem with metarepresentation could account for symptoms like voice-hearing because it might prevent the individual recognizing thoughts as his or her own and experience them as other voices.

- **Central control** is the ability to suppress automatic processes and make deliberate decisions instead. Symptoms like disorganized speech and thought disorder could result if the central control system fails to suppress automatic thoughts and speech. This could explain why some patients appear to talk to themselves or lose track of what they are saying—they cannot suppress the urge to speak thoughts out loud or suppress associations arising from individual words. The latter is called *clanging*.

Although this approach lacks a neurological basis it is extremely useful in understanding the *experience* of suffering the symptoms of schizophrenia.

Early experience and later symptoms

Early theories of schizophrenia sought to identify single causes within the social environment. Fromm-Reichmann (1948) proposed the idea of the **schizophrenogenic mother**, characterized by cold, controlling, and rejecting behaviour, which in turn created a secretive and anxious family climate. Instead of focusing on a family member, Bateson (1972) explained schizophrenia as the result of a communication style within the family. Specifically, according to Bateson, children exposed to the **double bind** are at risk of developing schizophrenia. Double binds occur when rules and expectations are unclear and people live in fear of doing the wrong thing. However, attempts to clarify rules and expectations are punished.

Theories like these are clinically derived—based on patients' accounts of their childhood experiences. Research has generally failed to support the specifics of either theory, and both lay the blame for schizophrenia at the door of sufferers' families, making contemporary clinicians wince (Harrington, 2012). However, and this is critical, research *does* suggest strong links between early trauma and the quality of early relationships and later diagnosis of schizophrenia. Studies have, for example, suggested a link between schizophrenia and child abuse. Harley et al (2010) reported that experience of abuse increased the probability of receiving a diagnosis of schizophrenia by 2.6 times—this increased to 20.9 times when combined with **cannabis** use. This link is partially contested by the findings of Sidelio et al (2015), who found that it was only the combination of physical or sexual abuse and early cannabis use that increased the risk of a schizophrenia diagnosis.

Attachment status also appears to be associated with schizophrenia, with a disproportionate number of patients reporting insecure attachment (Berry et al, 2007). However, it is unclear whether insecure attachment makes people more vulnerable, or rather secure attachment is associated with greater resilience to other risk factors (Davidsen et al, 2015). It is also unclear whether attachment is specifically linked to schizophrenia or to mental health problems in general, although it is tempting to support Bentall and Fernyhough (2008), who propose that hallucinations and

THINKING CRITICALLY

Bentall and Fernyhough (2008) are interested in understanding the personal meaning of delusions and hallucinations for people experiencing these symptoms, linking symptoms to their life experiences. This is a fascinating idea and is potentially very useful in psychological therapies for the treatment of symptoms of schizophrenia. However, gathering the kind of evidence that would support such links (eg, reliable links between life experiences and the contents of hallucinations) is methodologically very difficult indeed.

More hard-nosed psychologists would say that this kind of idea does not live up to the standards of good science because it is resistant to testing. On the other hand many clinical psychologists find these ideas of great use when working with patients. Where do you stand?

paranoia can be understood as cognitive and emotional reactions to early relationship problems.

Leaving aside family theories of schizophrenia for a moment, looking at the links between early experience and later symptoms of schizophrenia brings us back to the problem of where to draw a psychological-biological distinction. This is because the effects of early experience can be explained in biological as well as psychological terms; for example, with respect to epigenetics (see Chapter 5 for a discussion). It could thus be that bad attachment experiences or the trauma of abuse trigger the expression of genes that increase the risk of later symptoms. Equally we can speak in psychological terms of cognitive characteristics or attachment consequences. Neither is wrong, they just represent different levels of explanation.

PERSONALITY DISORDERS

Personality disorders are pervasive, chronic patterns of dysfunctional thinking, feeling, and relating to the world that generally begin in adolescence and last throughout a person's life. According to the DSM-5, those with personality disorders suffer impairments in at least two of the following areas of personality functioning:

- *Identity*: A person's sense of being a unique individual with clear boundaries between his or her self and others, a stable sense of self-esteem, and ability to self-evaluate.

- *Self-direction*: The ability to pursue meaningful goals and reflect upon one's behaviour.

- *Empathy*: Being able to understsand and appreciate others' experiences and motivations and to tolerate differing perspectives.

- *Intimacy*: The ability to form close, long-lasting connections with others.

In spite of the potential seriousness of the symptoms of personality disorders, they do not typically result in the same degree of distress or impairment and dysfunction caused by the major mental disorders. Thus, they are sometimes referred to as 'madness without loss of reason' (see Figure 18.8). Nevertheless, in keeping with the fact that personality disorders are chronic and begin early in life, they are usually more difficult to treat than the other major mental disorders.

There are ten personality disorder diagnoses in the DSM-5, plus a category that could include any disorder with mixed or unique traits, known as *trait-specific*

> **KEY IDEAS** personality disorder(s) **Personality disorder(s)** are pervasive, chronic patterns of inner experience and behaviour which generally begin in adolescence, are inflexible, and are expressed throughout many areas of a person's life. These patterns cause distress and/or impairment.

FIGURE 18.8 Personality disorders: 'madness without loss of reason'. The 1999 film *Girl, Interrupted*, directed by James Mangold, dramatized the true story of Susanna Keysen, an adolescent girl who was hospitalized with a diagnosis of *borderline personality disorder*. Those diagnosed with BPD are frightened of abandonment, impulsive, unstable in their sense of self; tend to make suicidal threats or engage in self-mutilation; are plagued by feelings of emptiness; and involve themselves in stormy relationships where they may alternate between idealizing and severely devaluing their partner. Despite Keysen's hospitalization, most people with personality disorders are not impaired to the same degree as those with clinical disorders. Pictured here are Winona Ryder as Keysen and Angelina Jolie as a fellow patient.
Source: Corbis.

personality disorder. Table 18.3 describes the ten basic disorders very briefly, and I will then describe three of them in greater detail. However, please remember that having some of the symptoms of any of the personality disorders—or even *all* of the symptoms of one or more of them—does *not* mean you have the disorder. In order for personality disorder to be diagnosed, these symptoms must seriously interfere with your ordinary life. In other words, personality disorders are extreme variations on normal human traits (Svrakic, Lecic-Tosevski, and Divac-Jovanovic, 2009).

One additional, perhaps more important, note of warning: personality disorders are among the most controversial of DSM diagnoses (Widiger, 2011). One problem is that these disorders are almost always diagnosed under the DSM system by picking and choosing from the menu offered (eg, 'borderline personality disorder with features of avoidant and narcissistic personality disorders'). It is actually rare for a person to be diagnosed with only one personality disorder (Clarkin, 2008). Given that so many symptoms of personality disorder are routinely diagnosed at once, and the same symptoms may show up in several diagnoses, many theorists now believe that the separate categories of personality disorder created by the DSM do not accurately reflect the way these disorders exist in nature, or the way most people actually experience them (Clarkin, 2008). This highlights a weakness in the DSM classification, and it is interesting that ICD has approached the notion of personality disorder quite differently.

TABLE 18.3 **The ten personality disorders of DSM-5**

Personality Disorder	Brief Description
Antisocial personality disorder	Violation of the rights of others; lack of empathy; reckless and impulsive; callous; lack of remorse; deceitfulness; often criminal behaviour, aggression, and violence; substance abuse
Avoidant personality disorder	Feelings of inadequacy, low self-esteem, extreme sensitivity to criticism, restricts social activities, fear of being shamed
Borderline personality disorder	Rollercoaster emotions and relationships, unstable self-image, lack of control over impulses, fear of abandonment, tendency to self-harm, feelings of emptiness, neediness, and mistrust
Dependent personality disorder	Passive and unassertive, needs to be taken care of and seeks constant reassurance, difficulty making independent decisions
Histrionic personality disorder	Attention-seeking behaviour, accompanied by exaggerated and excessive emotional expression. Often displays seductiveness and suggestibility, and frequently changes opinions
Narcissistic personality disorder	Self-absorbed, with a need to be admired, lack of empathy with others, beliefs that one is 'special' and the rules do not apply, seemingly high self-esteem that is actually easily crushed
Obsessive-compulsive personality disorder	Excessively focused on control, order, and perfection; lack of flexibility and openness to new experiences
Paranoid personality disorder	Suspicious and mistrustful of others, easily offended, hyper-vigilant (always on the lookout)
Schizoid personality disorder	Avoidance of emotional connection and intimacy, difficulty expressing emotions, detached from pleasure
Schizotypal personality disorder	Avoidance of social relationships, discomfort being around people, eccentric appearance and behaviour

Personality Disorder in ICD-11

Until ICD-10 the ICD system classified different types of personality disorder; however, in ICD-11 there has been a radical shift. Instead of different types of personality disorder, ICD-11 simply identifies one diagnostic category—personality disorder. This has the following diagnostic guidance:

Personality disorder is characterized by a relatively enduring and pervasive disturbance in how individuals experience and interpret themselves, others, and the world that results in maladaptive patterns of cognition, emotional experience, emotional expression, and behaviour. These maladaptive patterns are relatively inflexible and are associated with significant problems in psychosocial functioning that are particularly evident in interpersonal relationships. The disturbance is manifest across a range of personal and social situations (ie, is not limited to specific relationships or situations). Personality disorder is of long duration, typically lasting at least several years. Most commonly, it has its first manifestations in adolescence and is clearly evident in young adult life. (ICD-11)

Within this three levels of severity are recognized: mild, moderate, and severe. In addition five patterns of maladaptive functioning can be diagnosed:

- *negative affectivity*: the tendency to experience excessive negative emotions out of proportion to events
- *disinhibition*: the tendency to act unwisely and impulsively
- *detachment*: the tendency to remain emotionally detached from others
- *dissociality*: the tendency to disregard the rights and feelings of others
- *anankastia*: the tendency for perfectionism and conformity
- *borderline pattern*: unstable emotional state and intense and unstable interpersonal relationships

THINKING CRITICALLY

DSM-5 and ICD-11 have taken quite different approaches to the classification and diagnosis of personality disorder(s). What do you think might be the potential advantages of each? You might like to consider the reliability and validity of each approach and whether they have different implications for treatment.

IN REVIEW

- We can trace back much of our current understanding of mental disorder to the ancient Greeks, in whose writings we find reference to some of the same controversies we struggle with nowadays.

- In current practice there are a number of ways to identify a person's state as abnormal, including statistical abnormality, dysfunction, distress, impairment, and deviation from social norms. To a greater or lesser extent these are used in the process of diagnosis.

- Most psychologists use systems like the DSM or ICD for diagnosis, but they do not necessarily agree with the diagnostic categories or even the practice of diagnosis.

- The DSM-5 and ICD-11 categorize each psychological disorder according to its quality, symptoms, severity, course, and other phenomena.

- There are a number of serious criticisms of diagnosis, and British clinical psychologists recently called for a complete overhaul and a shift away from medical diagnosis.

ANXIETY DISORDERS

- Generalized anxiety disorder (GAD) defines the basic experience of anxiety: a feeling of tension, physiological arousal, and apprehension or worry about events that have not yet occurred.

- Phobias are powerful, disruptive, irrational fears. Specific phobias refer to a specific feared object, animal, or situation.

- Panic disorder consists of powerful anxiety over the possibility of experiencing a panic attack.

- Anxiety disorders result from combinations of causes, including genetic vulnerability, conditioning experiences, cognitive vulnerability, and early relationships

DEPRESSION

- Depressive disorders are characterized by sadness, hopelessness, helplessness, grief, guilt, and low feelings of self-worth.

- Major depressive disorder is the most commonly diagnosed psychological disorder. Virtually all patients with depression also suffer from anxiety. Many people suffer from chronic, persistent depression, and some are treatment-resistant.

- Genotypes, in combination with environmental factors, can predispose a person to become depressed.

- Depression is probably not due to a 'chemical imbalance', although many sorts of biochemical changes may be associated with depression.

- Hopelessness theory and Beck's theory of negative cognitive triad describe cognitive vulnerabilities that can trigger depression given conducive sets of circumstance.

- Early life experiences including abuse and insecure attachment make depression much more likely.

- Women have much higher rates of depression and anxiety than men. There are some compelling feminist explanations for these figures.

SCHIZOPHRENIA

- Schizophrenia affects very few people, but it is the most common psychotic disorder (ie, a disorder characterized by severely impaired ability to grasp reality and respond rationally). Its symptoms can be divided into two categories: positive symptoms (eg, hallucinations and delusions) and negative symptoms (eg, lack of appropriate emotional responses, facial expressions, or normal speech).

- Schizophrenia has a strong genetic component, and neurodevelopmental factors may also play a role in its development.

- Elements in the biological environment, such as smoking THC-rich cannabis (skunk) in adolescence, increase the risk of schizophrenia, probably by influencing gene expression in the developing brain.

- There are distinct cognitive elements to schizophrenia, and symptoms can be explained cognitively.

- There has been a large body of research into possible early experience and later schizophrenia. Early trauma and poor early relationships are associated with risk of schizophrenia; however, theories linking more specific parenting or family behaviours are generally unsupported.

PERSONALITY DISORDERS

- Personality disorders are pervasive, chronic patterns of dysfunctional thinking and relating to the world. The personality disorders tend to be relatively stable through the lifespan and thus are fairly resistant to treatment. However, compared with other psychological disorders, they result in a milder degree of impairment and dysfunction.

Those with personality disorder suffer impairment in at least two of the following areas: identity, self-direction, empathy, and intimacy.

There are ten basic personality disorders according to the DSM-5. ICD-11 has diverged from DSM by identifying a single personality disorder and classifying individual cases according to severity and patterns of dysfunction.

TEST YOURSELF

1 Trepanning was used on the basis that it would help get rid of both demons and blood. True ☐ False ☐

2 An aim of DSM-5 was to better align nosology and aetiology. True ☐ False ☐

3 The use of standard diagnostic measures aims to improve inter-rater reliability. True ☐ False ☐

4 Positive symptoms of schizophrenia are so-called because they are pleasant experiences. True ☐ False ☐

5 Which of the following terms describes the classification of mental disorder?

   a) Aetiology

   b) Nosology

   c) Neurology

   d) Psychology

6 In the diagnosis of which of the following disorders does statistical abnormality play an important role?

   a) Depression

   b) Schizophrenia

   c) Intellectual deficit disorder

   d) General anxiety disorder

7 Which of the following is not part of Barlow's triple vulnerability theory?

   a) General biological vulnerability

   b) General psychological vulnerability

   c) Construct validity

   d) Inter-rater reliability

8 Which of the following is true of the comorbidity of anxiety disorders?

   a) Anxiety disorders rarely co-occur with depression

   b) Comorbid anxiety disorders are easier to treat

   c) Most cases of anxiety co-occur with other disorders

   d Anxiety disorders have distinct sets of symptoms which do not overlap

9 Explain why the British Psychological Society's 2013 report by clinical psychologists was critical of psychiatric diagnosis.

10 Explain why the existence of schizophrenia is controversial amongst psychologists.

 Visit the online resources that accompany this book: www.oup.com/uk/jarvis-okami1e

CHAPTER 19

MENTAL HEALTH TREATMENT

LEARNING OUTCOMES

By the end of this chapter you should be able to:

- Understand the nature of psychological therapy and the distinctive elements of a range of psychological therapies, including psychodynamic, behavioural, cognitive-behavioural, client-centred, and systemic

- Discuss some of the issues in outcome research, including the equivalence paradox and the tension between effectiveness and efficacy research

- Take a view on the place of a range of psychological therapies in tackling the symptoms of mental disorder and psychological distress

- Analyse issues associated with particular psychological therapies, including the cost-effectiveness of psychoanalytic therapies, the small range of techniques and small evidence base for client-centred therapy, and allegations of hype around cognitive behavioural therapy (CBT)

- Understand the limitations of psychological therapies and the risks of harm attached to their use, with particular reference to potentially harmful psychological therapies (PHPs)

- Know the range of pharmacological treatments used to alleviate psychological symptoms

- Discuss the controversies surrounding pharmacological treatment for psychological distress and mental disorder, including the file drawer problem and ghostwriting

What do J.K. Rowling, Ellen DeGeneres, Kesha, Brad Pitt, and Katy Perry have in common? Apart from the obvious success and celebrity status, another thing is their experience of psychological therapy; their enthusiasm for it and their willingness to talk about it. For Kesha it was about anxiety and an eating disorder. For Pitt therapy was for help rebuilding his life after divorce. For Ellen Degeneres it was for depression resulting from repeated experiences of homophobia.

There is a profound social stigma attached to seeking therapy, with cultural values like the British 'stiff upper lip' preventing many in distress from seeking help. However, in recent years this has begun to change, with influential figures as diverse as Prince Harry and Michelle Obama encouraging people in distress to seek therapeutic help. In 2017, in a stark contrast to traditional British attitudes towards mental health and therapy, Katy Perry live-streamed a therapy session in which she discussed suicidal feelings.

WHAT IS PSYCHOLOGICAL THERAPY?

There are many situations where we make use of social interaction with others to make ourselves feel better. In fact our day-to-day mood can be quite dependent on our recent social interactions. So what defines a formal psychological therapy as opposed to sharing a listening ear or a pep talk with a friend or family member? Is the experience of talking to a qualified therapist very much different from talking one's problems over with a friend, family member, or religious advisor?

When a psychotherapist works with a **client** a unique healing relationship is formed. Prior to the twentieth century this type of relationship did not exist. Confidential discussions between individuals and respected relatives, friends, teachers, mentors, priests, rabbis, and imams occurred in times of trouble and stress, but these relationships differed substantially from that of the modern psychological therapy relationship in at least five ways:

1   *In therapy the focus is entirely on the client's needs and problems.* Efforts are made to ensure that the therapists' needs and problems do not enter into the relationship. Nor should the process be influenced by any external agendas like adherence to religious dogma or prioritizing the wishes of the wider family or community.

2   *The process of therapy is formal, with an agreement about the aims and scope of the therapy.* Often, though not necessarily, the therapist is paid, either by the client directly, by a public health organization, or through private health insurance. There is generally an agreed boundary that the client and therapist have a strictly professional relationship and do not work or socialize together.

3   *The therapy relationship takes place in a structured setting.* Typically this setting is the therapist's consulting room, although therapy may also be conducted by telephone or even computer under certain circumstances (Andrews et al, 2010).

4   *Each meeting between the therapist and the patient or client is scheduled and time-limited.* A typical session lasts 50–60 minutes and occurs once, twice, or sometimes three times weekly. This varies considerably, however, according to the style of therapy.

5   *The therapy relationship is expected to terminate.* The quality of most other personal relationships is judged by their longevity. However, therapy is different: unless the client is so damaged as to need lifelong support the aim is usually to help them move on with their life.

> KEY IDEAS patients and clients
The recipients of therapies are referred to as patients or clients, depending on the context of the therapy and the professional background and theoretical orientation of the therapist. The term 'patient' is most strongly associated with medical contexts and more traditional attitudes. 'Client' is most strongly associated with more liberal attitudes and theoretical models that emphasize equal-status partnership between client and therapist.

Alleviation of the symptoms of mental disorder is one reason to have psychological therapy, but this is not its only function. Some people enter therapy because they are suffering psychologically as a normal consequence of a distressing event, such as the death of a loved one or the break-up of an important relationship (Horwitz and Wakefield, 2007). People may also seek therapy when they are facing or contemplating a turning point in life—a career change, for example, or a divorce. They use therapy to clarify and explore their thoughts and feelings about this impending change. Others have found themselves mired in self-defeating habits and patterns of relating to others, and are looking for help in making changes in their general approach to life.

Styles of Psychological Therapy

In Chapter 18 we looked at the range of factors believed to be involved in mental disorder. Each of these is associated with a particular theoretical model of mental health and mental disorder. So when we emphasize cognitive aspects of disorders like anxiety or depression we are adopting a cognitive model of the condition. If we emphasize the role of learned behaviour we are adopting a behavioural model and so on. No one nowadays believes in single causes for most symptoms and disorders, so adopting a cognitive model does not mean you reject the existence of other aspects to the disorder, just that your understanding is primarily cognitive. As a therapist you would be trained in one or more models of psychological therapy, and you would both understand mental health through that model and use the therapeutic techniques that go along with that model. The combination of theoretical understanding and techniques is known as the therapist's **orientation**. By the close of the twentieth century, at least 400 different types of psychological therapy had been created.

In addition to reflecting different theoretical orientations and perspectives about the causes of mental disorders and psychological distress, styles of therapy also reflect differences in philosophy about the therapist–client relationship. For example, *psychoanalysis* historically has characterized the analyst as a mentally sound 'doctor' treating 'patients' who are, at least in comparison, less than mentally sound. *Behaviour therapists* see themselves as something closer to a teacher and the client as a student whose task it is to substitute adaptive patterns of behaviour for maladaptive patterns. *Cognitive therapists* see the therapist–client relationship as that of two collaborators on relatively equal footing, using 'hypothesis-testing' techniques to correct irrational or inaccurate beliefs that might be triggering the client's emotional pain or dysfunction.

Table 19.1 lists and briefly describes the styles of therapy we will explore (see 'Models of psychological therapy').

> KEY IDEAS therapeutic orientation Therapists are trained in one or more models of therapy, and they both understand psychological distress and mental disorder through that model and practise the techniques that go with it. Some therapists stick strictly to their model while others are more eclectic, drawing on different ideas when they are useful.

Who Are the Therapists?

Most psychological therapists receive extensive training, and many (but not all) have advanced degrees in medicine, psychology, social work, or a related field. The psychology occupations requiring the most rigorous education in therapy are *clinical psychology* and *counselling psychology*, both of which require a doctoral level qualification as well as a certain number of hours performing psychological therapy under the supervision of an experienced therapist. Training in certain styles of clinical or counselling psychology may also require that the student experience at least some psychotherapy himself or herself.

There are many controversies around therapeutic professions. Who should be allowed to call themselves a therapist? Is a core profession necessary or should anyone be allowed to train in a psychological therapy? A particularly interesting question for psychologists concerns whether there are advantages to choosing a therapist who is also a psychologist. Therapy is largely an art depending on intuition and **empathy**, so why would we expect a trained scientist to be better at it?

Of course, being a psychologist no more grants one magical healing powers than it makes us expert parents or detectives, and it would be deeply wrong to suggest that non-psychologist therapists are any less skilled in their therapy practice. However, from our (admittedly biased!) perspective there are some possible advantages to seeking a psychologist for therapy. As well as being trained to a reliably high standard in at least one model of therapy, a clinical or counselling psychologist will have more than a passing knowledge of other therapies. This allows them to choose techniques according to their own strengths and the needs of clients. Psychologists will also be aware of techniques that can do more harm than good under particular circumstances, so they are less likely than some to do something anti-therapeutic. Perhaps most importantly, psychologists are committed to evidence-based therapies and techniques.

READ THIS

For a general introduction to the nature of psychological therapies you might like to start with the guidance from the National Health Service and Royal College of Psychiatrists. You can find this here:

https://www.nhs.uk/conditions/psychotherapy/

http://www.rcpsych.ac.uk/healthadvice/treatmentsandwellbeing/psychotherapies.aspx

For something a bit more advanced try this:

Naismith, J. and Grant, S. (2007). *Seminars in the Psychotherapies.* London: Royal College of Psychiatrists.

TABLE 19.1 **Psychological therapies at a glance**

Therapy	Theoretical Perspective	Key Concepts
Psychoanalysis	Psychodynamic	Disorder/distress caused by unresolved childhood issues and conflicted and unconscious impulses; long-term, intensive analysis; sometimes on a daily basis; analyst as interpreter and neutral observer; insight necessary for healing.
Psychodynamic therapy	Psychodynamic	Disorder/distress often caused by unresolved childhood experiences and conflicted and unconscious impulses; therapy usually, but not always, long-term; insight necessary for healing.
Behaviour therapy	Behaviourist	Disorder/distress caused by learned, maladaptive behaviours; therapy systematic and short-term; therapist as teacher; client learns to substitute adaptive behaviours for maladaptive behaviours; insight unnecessary for healing.
Rational emotive behaviour therapy (REBT)	Cognitive	Disorders and psychological suffering caused by irrational and absolutist beliefs (the ABC model); therapy usually relatively short-term; therapist as blunt challenger of such beliefs; altering the beliefs alleviates the emotional suffering.
Cognitive and cognitive behaviour therapy (CT/CBT)	Cognitive	Disorders and psychological suffering caused or worsened by distorted patterns of thinking biased against the self and resultant behaviours; therapy designed to be short-term; therapist as 'scientist-collaborator' with client, testing client's beliefs against evidence; changing the way one thinks changes how one feels.
Client-centred therapy	Humanistic	Disorders and psychological suffering caused by lack of unconditional positive regard, genuineness, and acceptance from others; therapy usually long-term; therapist as an empathic, caring person, allowing the client to direct therapy and offering unconditional acceptance.
Systemic therapy	Family systems and social constructionist	The family or group is considered an organic unit or 'system' wherein members interact dynamically. No one person is singled out for treatment—rather, the entire family or group is the 'client' even if one member is seen alone.
Integrative therapy	Multiple sources	Probably more common than any of the others; techniques tailored to individual client; 'use what works!' is key.

MODELS OF PSYCHOLOGICAL THERAPY

As stated earlier, styles of therapy differ because psychologists differ in their beliefs about the causes of psychological distress and the sorts of client–therapist relationships that are most conducive to recovery. Although there are literally hundreds of therapy styles in existence, a few may be singled out as the most influential over the past half-century: *psychoanalysis, psychodynamic psychotherapy, behaviour therapy, cognitive therapies, client-centred therapy,* and *systemic therapy.*

PSYCHODYNAMIC THERAPIES

We will begin our discussion of common forms of psychotherapy with the psychodynamic varieties. As discussed in Chapter 2, the very first organized form of psychotherapy was psychoanalysis, created by Sigmund Freud (1856–1939).

Classical Psychoanalysis

Psychoanalysis as practised by Freud and his followers is often referred to as *classical psychoanalysis*. It is based on Freud's notion that psychological problems are caused by intrapsychic conflict—tension within a person's own mind between mental forces that are at odds with one another. These conflicts are thought to be primarily *unconscious*—that is, the person is unaware of their existence. According to Freud, such conflicts typically involve 'forbidden' sexual or aggressive desires and impulses often rooted in childhood experiences. It is the job of psychoanalysis to uncover such conflicts so that they can be realistically faced and resolved. Thus, the goal of classical psychoanalysis is insight, or accurate self-knowledge. To obtain insight, however, the patient must overcome his or her own *resistance* to this knowledge—a resistance based on fear and anxiety about facing unpleasant truths.

Psychoanalytic theory has evolved substantially since Freud's day, particularly in Europe, and few modern analysts consider themselves to be direct followers of Freud. Far more popular than classical Freudian analysis is analysis based on **object relations theory**. Object relations theorists do acknowledge a debt to Freud, and they continue to stress the importance of intrapsychic conflict, **transference** of the properties of early relationships on to later relationships, and many other psychoanalytic concepts. However, they do not focus on sex and aggression as the basis for these conflicts, and they place much more importance than Freud did on the quality of a person's early relationships with important others (see Jarvis, 2004, for a review).

Classical psychoanalysis, whether informed by Freudian or object relations theory, is the most intensive and ambitious psychological therapy, taking place four to five times a week over a period of years. It aims not simply to reduce symptoms or alleviate distress but to rebuild the personality from the ground up, making the patient a more resilient and well-balanced person.

Therapeutic techniques

Techniques of classical psychoanalysis are mostly interpretive; the therapist—known as the psychoanalyst—listens and periodically offers his or her view of dreams, resistance, transference, etc. They include **dream interpretation**, where patients' dreams are interpreted by the analyst with assistance from the patients' own **free associations** to the dream material. In free association, the patient—typically lying in a relaxed position on a couch or seated in a comfortable armchair—relates to the

> ❭ **KEY IDEAS** transference
> One of the principles on which psychoanalysis and to a lesser extent other psychodynamic therapies depend is **transference,** in which the properties of early relationships *transfer* on to later relationships. By developing a transference relationship with a therapist a patient can develop insight into how they relate to others and the origins of these patterns.

> ❭ **KEY IDEAS** object relations theory **Object relations theory** is the collective term for a set of ideas developed by post-Freudian psychoanalysts in the mid-twentieth century. The central idea of object relations theory is that our interpersonal behaviour and mental health is strongly influenced by mental representations of significant relationships; in particular, early ones.

> ❭ **KEY IDEAS** free association and dream interpretation Two key techniques of classical psychoanalysis are free association and dream interpretation. In **free association** the patient relaxes and says whatever comes to mind. **Dream interpretation** involves the psychoanalyst offering interpretations of the hidden meanings of patient dreams.

FIGURE 19.1 The analyst's couch. Traditionally, psychoanalysts allowed their patients to recline for greater relaxation and often seated themselves behind their patients to allow *transference* to develop. Modern psychoanalysts do not necessarily adhere to these practices.

Source: iStock.com/jacoblund.

psychoanalyst all thoughts and ideas that go through his or her mind when thinking about dream imagery or describing important events and relationships of his or her childhood. The purpose of free association is to allow unconscious material to be expressed without censorship from the patient's conscious mind.

The role of the psychoanalyst is that of a neutral observer and interpreter. The psychoanalyst may avoid eye contact while the patient is free-associating, and may even remain out of sight, seated in a chair behind the patient (see Figure 19.1). The reason for this emotionally cool approach is that the psychoanalyst wants transference to develop so that it may be analysed. Transference refers to the psychoanalytic belief that patients in therapy may *transfer* their feelings about their spouse, parent, or other important people in their lives (even themselves) onto the therapist. By analysing this transference, the therapist hopes to encourage insight in the patient. This process must proceed unimpeded by the actual personality and other characteristics of the analyst. Thus, the analyst remains a blank figure, waiting to be 'coloured in' by the patient.

Classical psychoanalysis is known for its rigid boundaries. Whilst all respectable therapists are boundaried in terms of sticking to timings and their professional role, psychoanalysis goes further and sees these boundaries as inherently therapeutic. Boundaried contact with a therapist in psychoanalysis represents to the unconscious mind of the patient the sense of security derived in early relationships and so forms a 'holding environment', literally mimicking the sense of being held as a baby (Jarvis, 2004).

 THINKING PRACTICALLY

A male patient with a difficult relationship with his mother and a history of failed romantic relationships with women is in therapy with a female analyst. He is very sensitive and thinks she is critical of him. When this is pointed out he is half an hour late for the next session. He then has a dream in which he is told off by a woman who looks a bit like a cross between his mother and therapist.

What interpretations might the therapist offer to this patient? Think about transference, resistance, and dreamwork. What might the patient learn about himself from these interpretations and how useful might they be?

Psychoanalytic Psychotherapy

During the twentieth century many therapists moved away from the tightly pre-scribed techniques of psychoanalysis. The result is termed modern **psychoanalytic (or psychodynamic) psychotherapy** (Shedler, 2010). The term *psychodynamic* implies the idea of multiple unconscious influences. Thus, psychodynamic therapists accept many of the principles of psychoanalytic theory of the mind and behaviour, but have discarded the technique of psychoanalysis itself as a form of therapy. Shedler (2010) has compiled a list of features that differentiate the techniques of psychody-namic therapy from many other types of therapy. Among these features are:

1 Focusing on helping the client to express emotion

2 Exploring situations where the client tries to avoid distressing thoughts or feel-ings in therapy

3 Identifying recurring psychological themes in the client's inner world and life experiences

4 Discussing past experiences—often long-past childhood experiences

5 Focusing on the client's relationships with other people

6 Focusing on the relationship between the client and therapist

7 Exploring the client's fantasy life and dreams

Brief Dynamic Therapy

Like psychoanalysis, psychoanalytic psychotherapy is generally expected to take time, often years. However, in keeping with the general movement towards devising briefer types of psychotherapeutic treatment, during the 1980s and 1990s short-term versions of psychodynamic therapy were developed and are being used now with increasing frequency (Dewan, Weerasekera, and Stormon, 2009).

These brief dynamic therapies (or BDTs) share the psychodynamic emphasis on exploring feelings and their origins, but are more modest in aim than the long-term therapies; for example, looking to reduce a symptom or resolve a current life problem. Techniques to achieve insight are more direct in order to make the process faster; for example, educating someone about how they relate to others rather than waiting for a transference relationship to build and interpret that in order to produce the same insight.

Issues in the Use of Psychodynamic Therapies

The major issue concerning the traditional long-term psychodynamic therapies is the time commitment and its resultant expense and disruption to the life of the patient. When you factor in travel time, having therapy several times a week is very disruptive to work and social life. Although the situation is different in each country, it is gener-ally hard to obtain publicly funded long-term psychotherapy, and the costs of going to a private therapist can add up to many thousands of pounds or euros. For some people this may well be worthwhile and affordable, but for most of us it is worth looking into cheaper and less disruptive options for therapy before committing to long-term psychotherapy. Of course, this criticism does not apply to the brief dynamic therapies.

Effectiveness and appropriateness

For many years there was also a question mark over the **effectiveness** of this kind of therapy. Hans Eysenck (1952) published a highly influential review that claimed to demonstrate that there was no evidence to show that psychoanalysis and

❯ KEY IDEAS classical psychoanalysis and psychoanalytic psychotherapy **Classical psychoanalysis** is a particularly intensive and long-term therapy, in which therapists usually stick to tightly prescribed interpretive techniques. **Psychodynamic psychotherapy** is based on principles originating in psychoanalysis. Psychodynamic theorists share psychoanalytic beliefs that unconscious emotional and motivational processes exert important effects on a person, that the origins of personality are in childhood, and that human beings create symbolic mental representations of the self and important personal relationships. However, therapy is usually less intensive and long-term, and therapists are often less rigid in their technique.

psychoanalytic therapy benefited patients at all. He claimed that his selected papers showed an average recovery rate of 66%—about the same as we would expect with no treatment. This review is still sometimes cited uncritically in textbooks but this probably says more about anti-psychodynamic bias within psychology than it does the effectiveness of the therapy. Actually, the Eysenck review cherry-picked studies that supported Eysenck's views—including poorly conducted ones. In addition, Eysenck only recognized therapy conditions as producing improvements if there was complete remission of symptoms in a short time frame. However, any improvement over a much longer period was counted as improvement in no treatment conditions. Later analysis of Eysenck's data revealed significant improvement of 83% of psychotherapy patients as compared with 30–40% of those in no treatment (Bergin and Garfield, 1978).

THINKING CREATIVELY

If you were going to conduct a review of studies examining the impact of psychoanalysis or any other therapy, how could you do your best to avoid bias? Think about how you could choose studies to include and what sort of evidence for impact you might look for. Look at the shortcomings of the Eysenck review to give you some ideas.

❯ **KEY IDEAS** evidence-based practice In its broadest sense, any professional practice taking account of research findings can be said to be evidence-based. Psychologists generally take the evidence base for the way they practice very seriously, and this is something that marks out psychologists from some other professions that involve therapy. In the therapy world evidence-based practice generally refers to choosing models of therapy—and sometimes particular techniques— that have been validated by research.

Since the 1980s and 1990s there has been considerable emphasis on **evidence-based practice** in public health care systems like the UK's National Health Service. In the current context of evidence-based health care considerable research has been carried out on the effectiveness of psychodynamic therapies. There is no longer any serious doubt that, used appropriately, psychodynamic therapies can be effective. A meta-analysis of studies of long-term psychoanalytic psychotherapy by Leichsenring, Rabung, and Leibing (2004) found an overall before and after treatment effect size of 1.39, increasing to 1.57 at long-term follow-up. Effect size represents the number of standard deviations a treatment moves the average patient through the population. An effect size of 1 would move a patient from the bottom 5% of the population, say for mood, to the bottom third, or from the bottom third to average. To put this into context, anything over 0.8 is considered a large effect. This compares favourably with reported effect sizes for other treatments, suggesting that these therapies are effective for patients.

So what about the benefits of the additional time spent undergoing psychoanalysis? A study by Knekt et al (2011) compared the effect of psychoanalysis, psychoanalytic therapy, and brief psychodynamic therapy. Patients in psychoanalysis took the longest to improve but had the best outcomes in long-term follow-up. Whether long-term psychotherapies—in particular, psychoanalysis—are cost-effective is a more complex question (Lazar, 2010), and this is reflected in the caution shown towards them in public health clinical guidance; for example, the advice about recommended therapies published in Britain by the National Institute for Health and Clinical Excellence (NICE).

Much of the recent research has focused on brief psychodynamic therapy (BDT). The evidence has generally been very supportive of the effectiveness of this kind of therapy. Broadly, the effectiveness of BDT appears to be equivalent to that of more commonly used **cognitive behavioural therapy (CBT)**, although there also appear to be subtle differences in effects depending on the patient group and how outcome is measured.

THINKING CRITICALLY

One thing that complicates comparing the effectiveness of psychodynamic therapies with others is that, whereas cognitive and behavioural therapies typically have a specific goal to focus on, such as the reduction of a symptom, the direction and outcome of psychodynamic therapies is more uncertain. Take the case of Mr A, reported by Pate and Gabbard (2003). Mr A sought help for his adult baby syndrome because he wanted to marry and have children. He (rightly) believed that his habit of defecating and masturbating in a nappy and sleeping in a nursery might be off-putting to potential partners. At the end of therapy Mr A concluded that he was happy as an adult baby and did not wish to change his behaviour.

Should we consider this a successful outcome? Consider both for and against arguments.

BEHAVIOURAL THERAPIES

Behaviour therapy was created in direct opposition to psychoanalytic and psychodynamic therapy. It is based on the behaviourists' and social learning theorists' views that psychological disorders represent learned patterns of *maladaptive* (counterproductive) behaviours. According to behaviour therapists, all the insight in the world is useless if it does not help to reshape behaviour by substituting *adaptive* (productive, desired) behaviours and associations for those that are maladaptive. Although discussions of thoughts, feelings, and past events may enter into behaviour therapy, its focus is on present, observable, changeable behaviour. Above all, the behaviour therapist is a *teacher*—taking an active role in therapy, helping the client to learn tested techniques to change learned patterns of unwanted behaviour. Behaviour therapies are often termed *behaviour modification* because they use classical and operant conditioning techniques (see Chapter 7) to modify the client's unwanted behaviours.

The founder of behaviour therapy was Mary Cover Jones (1896–1987), a student of John Watson, the founder of the behaviourist movement in psychology. Although Jones later rejected many of the behaviourists' views in favour of an approach that focused on the uniqueness of the individual (Rutherford, 2000), her successful attempt to 'extinguish' (remove) the fear of furry animals in a 3-year-old boy named Peter is the first recorded use of behaviour therapy techniques (M.C. Jones, 1924a, 1924b). Jones accomplished this feat by bringing a rabbit increasingly close to Peter over time, but pairing each exposure with a piece of Peter's favourite candy. In this way she used **classical conditioning** to help Peter develop pleasurable associations with rabbits.

Exposure Therapies

Jones' research was conducted during a time when psychoanalysis was in the spotlight, and not much attention was paid to her work until several decades later when the field of behaviour therapy was officially named and founded by South African psychiatrist Joseph Wolpe (1915–97). Deeply committed to the behaviourist approach, Wolpe created a number of techniques to treat anxiety, particularly phobia, through controlled *exposure* of the phobic person to the feared object or situation.

Wolfe's best-known technique directly builds on the procedure used by Jones to treat little Peter. Known as **systematic desensitization** (Wolpe, 1982), this technique exposes the client to increasingly intense and uncomfortable mental or visual images of the

> **KEY IDEAS** behaviour therapy Techniques of therapy based on the principles of conditioning and observational learning (see Chapter 7). The point of behaviour therapy is to teach the client how to substitute adaptive patterns of behaviour for maladaptive patterns.

> **KEY IDEAS** systematic desensitization This is a behaviour therapy technique primarily used to treat phobias and certain other anxiety disorders. Systematic desensitization involves controlled, incremental exposure to phobic stimuli while simultaneously practising relaxation techniques that are incompatible with anxiety.

feared object or situation over time ('Imagine that you're walking past a room with a snake inside . . . now imagine that you're opening the door . . . now you're going inside the room . . .'). These increasingly intense images are known as the *anxiety hierarchy*.

While navigating the anxiety hierarchy, the client simultaneously engages in relaxation exercises such as *progressive muscle relaxation*—systematically tightening and then relaxing the major muscle groups throughout the body. The idea behind this practice is that relaxation is incompatible with anxiety—the two cannot be present in a person at the same time. After learning to reduce anxiety in the face of the anxiety hierarchy during treatment sessions, the client is encouraged to try the technique in the actual phobic situation. Alternatively, if feasible, the entire process can be accomplished *in vivo*—that is, using the actual phobic object during the process of systematic desensitization.

Another technique similar to systematic desensitization is **flooding**. While systematic desensitization gently and systematically turns up the heat using an anxiety hierarchy, flooding takes a more brutal approach and essentially tosses the client in at the highest possible level of the anxiety-provoking situation and holds him or her there—sometimes for hours at a time. For example, a person with a phobia of small animals might be required to sit with a lab rat on his or her lap for an hour or more. (Of course, no one is literally *required* to do this—flooding therapy is done strictly by mutual agreement.)

One basic assumption underlies both systematic desensitization and flooding: that phobias are maintained by avoidance of the feared object or situation, and that the solution is to compel the phobic person to face his or her fears directly. During exposure the person is also exposed to corrective *information* about the feared object or situation (Foa and Kozak, 1986). For example, after hours with a lab rat on his or her lap the sufferer can see clearly that the rat is harmless. An example of a successful case of exposure enhanced with information in the form of modelled relaxation comes from Newman and Adams (2004).

> **KEY IDEAS** flooding Flooding is an exposure therapy used to treat phobia and other anxiety disorders. Flooding involves non-incremental, total immersion in anxiety-producing phobic stimuli for a prolonged period with the aim of reducing the anxiety response.

RESEARCH IN FOCUS

Newman, C. and Adams, K. (2004) Dog gone good: Managing dog phobia in a teenage boy with a learning disability. *British Journal of Learning Disabilities*, **32**, 35–8.

Aim: The aim was to treat a 17-year-old boy, MV, for a phobia of dogs. MV had a moderate learning disability and mild physical disability. He had acquired his phobia after being bitten by a dog at the age of 11 years. The phobia was serious because MV would panic at the sight of a dog and sometimes ran into the road to avoid contact. MV's parents requested that his fear be reduced to a level where he could stand still in the presence of a dog.

Method: MV was trained in relaxation by means of focused breathing exercises and an anxiety hierarchy established. This is shown in Table 19.2.

Eighteen months later MV's parents again requested treatment. MV had maintained the fear reduction from the first therapy as long as dogs were on a leash; however, he still reacted badly to loose dogs. It was noticed at this point that MV's mother also appeared nervous around dogs so she was involved directly in the second treatment. The exposure procedure was repeated using a new anxiety hierarchy including dogs off the leash. MV's mother was instructed to lead him through the relaxation procedure so that the desensitization was enhanced by her modelling of a relaxed response to loose dogs.

〉

TABLE 19.2 The initial anxiety hierarchy used to treat MV

Stage in hierarchy	Description
1	Introduction of pictures and videos
2	Relaxation technique introduced
3	Dog introduced—no contact/access (dog on other side of window)
4	Access to dog provided (client stood in doorway, leashed dog in courtyard)
5	Dog brought into personal space
6	Contact with dog (petting)
7	Contact with dog (walking alongside) (stages 1–7 were at MV's home)
8	Outdoor contact with dog (at park)—with instruction to stand still and use relaxation techniques when required
9	Introduced to new dog, repeated stages 6 and 7

Results: After 26 sessions of the second round of exposure and relaxation MV was able to remain still and quiet in the presence of loose as well as leashed dogs, including unfamiliar dogs in uncontrollable situations. Twelve of the 26 sessions were at the top of the anxiety hierarchy when MV was encountering unfamiliar loose dogs in a park. At the earlier stages of the second treatment MV's mother was effective at modelling relaxation. By the end of the treatment she struggled to model the behaviour but by then MV could self-instruct rather than wait for her.

Conclusions: Systematic desensitization is effective for dog phobia. Its effectiveness can also be enhanced by the use of a model who demonstrates relaxation through the anxiety hierarchy. Results also illustrate the importance of fully exploring the phobic stimulus and constructing an adequate anxiety hierarchy.

MASTER YOUR METHODOLOGY

1   Explain ways in which clinical case studies like this are helpful to other psychologists.

2   Case studies are often said to be hard to generalize. Explain why this is so with reference to the case of MV.

3   Outcome data for this study came in the form of observations and reports from MV's mother. This is all qualitative data.

   a)   How could you supplement this with quantitative data if you wished?

   b)   What would be the advantages and limitations of gathering quantitative data from a case like this?

> **KEY IDEAS** exposure therapy
There is a range of exposure therapies, linked by the idea that only through exposure to feared stimuli can the anxiety produced by that stimuli be lessened. **Virtual reality** technology makes exposure therapy more feasible for a wider variety of problems. It appears to work at least as well as exposure to the real thing—and in some cases, better (Powers and Emmelkamp, 2008).

Although systematic desensitization and flooding are used with less frequency than in the past, they have formed the basis of contemporary **exposure therapies,** all of which are based on Wolpe's original insight that exposing a person to a feared stimulus under controlled conditions can reduce or eliminate the fear. Using streamlined techniques and new technologies such as virtual reality, clinicians have devised exposure treatments that accomplish in a single day-long session what previously took weeks to accomplish through systematic desensitization (Antony and Barlow, 2002; Sharp and Espie, 2004).

Operant Therapies

Exposure therapies are based on models taken from classical conditioning. Through these therapies, the client learns to form new associations to feared stimuli. **Operant therapies** are also based on principles of learning, but they rely on operant conditioning, in which rewards or punishments for a person's spontaneous behaviours are used to shape desired behaviours (see Chapter 7).

One such operant technique is known as **contingency management** (Higgins, Silverman, and Washio, 2011). In contingency management, a person is rewarded with tangible, desirable goods, prizes, or privileges for engaging in desired behaviours and avoiding undesirable behaviours.

An early form of contingency management was the *token economy* (Kazdin, 2001). In a token economy, inmates of an institution—be it a school, psychiatric hospital, or prison—earn chips or tokens for performing desired behaviours. The tokens may then be cashed in for snacks, books or other goods, TV privileges, visitation rights, and so forth, depending on the particular type of institution.

Issues in the Use of Behaviour Therapies

Behaviour therapies are as different in both underlying theory and technique from psychodynamic therapies as it is possible to be! It should be no surprise then that they raise different issues. There is no issue, for example, over time or expense. A behaviour therapist using a modern exposure therapy can often effect a complete cure of a simple phobia in a single extended session. This is quicker and at least as effective as alternatives (Ougrin, 2011).

Effectiveness

There is no real question mark over the effectiveness of behaviour therapies when used appropriately. Anderson et al (2013) investigated the effects of both virtual reality and *in vivo* (real-life) exposure to public speaking in order to treat social anxiety. Both treatments resulted in significant improvement as compared to change observed in patients in a waiting list condition.

Contingency management is most commonly used in the treatment of substance and behavioural **addiction**. In one recent study McDonnell et al (2017) showed that patients with serious mental disorders and **alcohol** abuse problems were three times as likely to abstain from alcohol when entered into a prize draw, for which they qualified when urine tests were negative for alcohol.

Nowadays behavioural techniques are likely to be used, not in the form of 'pure' behaviour therapies, but as one part of cognitive behaviour therapy (CBT). This has been shown to enhance the effectiveness of CBT for addiction (Christensen et al, 2016).

Ethical issues

Behavioural therapies tend to raise ethical issues. Exposure therapies necessarily involve a degree of distress as patients are exposed to distress-provoking stimuli. Token economies are difficult to set up and maintain because they require elaborate record keeping. For this reason, and also in keeping with the movement towards shortened hospital stays for psychiatric patients, new methods using the basic ideas behind token economies have been devised to treat outpatients, particularly those with substance abuse problems. These methods work by allotting prizes (or chances to win prizes) to those who have remained abstinent from the abused substance and have engaged in various productive behaviours, such as spending time with their families (Higgins, Silverman, and Heil, 2007).

THINKING CRITICALLY

Ries et al (2004) investigated whether benefits payments could be manipulated to serve as a contingency management system for people with drug and alcohol problems. In a contingency management condition abstaining participants received their benefits in larger sums with fewer visits and received a higher proportion in cash rather than in benefits. Participants in the contingency management condition misused significantly less than in the control condition.

Consider the following:

1 What ethical issues does this study raise? In what ways are programmes like this one open to abuse?

2 Although the idea of controlling vulnerable people's behaviour by managing benefits might (and should!) make us uncomfortable there are arguments for it. What are the ethical arguments in favour of programmes like this?

COGNITIVE THERAPIES

During the mid-1950s an event occurred that was to have major repercussions for the field of psychotherapy in later decades: a maverick psychoanalyst named Albert Ellis (1913–2007) grew dissatisfied with the classical psychoanalysis he was practising. He decided that remaining silent while seated on a chair behind a reclining, free-associating client on a near-daily basis was a waste of time. He tried switching to a form of psychodynamic therapy, but he didn't find that much better. In thinking about his own life, Ellis decided that it was the written works and ideas of the great philosophers of history and other authors that had helped him deal with his own problems—more successfully and easily than all the psychoanalysis he had experienced himself. He concluded that rational *thought* was the best possible cure for *emotional* distress. As Ellis later declared, '[W]hat we call emotion is nothing more than a certain kind—a biased, prejudiced kind—of thought, and that human beings can be taught to control their feelings by controlling their thoughts . . .' (Ellis, 1957, p 344). Ellis's insight marked the birth of *cognitive therapies*—treatments based on the principle that changes in thoughts and actions can produce changes in feeling.

Rational Emotive Behaviour Therapy

Based on his insights, Ellis devised a new form of therapy that ultimately came to be called **rational emotive behaviour therapy** (REBT; Ellis, 2001). According to Ellis, people grow up with illogical, absolutist, and counterproductive ideas such as, 'If I don't perform perfectly I'm a failure', 'If I don't make a lot of money I'll be unhappy', 'I can't make it on my own', and so forth. The aim of REBT is to identify and change these ideas.

> ❯ KEY IDEAS REBT Rational emotive behaviour therapy (REBT) is a form of therapy devised by Albert Ellis and based on the idea that emotional distress is rooted in illogical, absolutist, and counterproductive ideas and beliefs. REBT is *directive*—the therapist's job is to forcefully dispute the client's illogical and unrealistic beliefs.

In contrast to standard practice in most other forms of therapy, the REBT therapist can be highly confrontational and forceful. Ellis believed that his clients often needed the cold water of reality splashed in their faces. REBT therapists may bluntly dispute their clients' beliefs, as a parent might do for a confused child: 'Where is it written that life is always fair? It usually isn't, so get over that idea as quickly as you can', is an example of therapeutic advice that might be conveyed during an REBT session.

Cognitive Therapy

> **KEY IDEAS** cognitive therapy (CT) This is the therapy principally devised by Aaron Beck that suggests that when people possess underlying dysfunctional core beliefs about the self, the world, and the future, they respond to events with automatic thoughts that are self-defeating and biased against the self. These thoughts trigger negative emotional experiences and can lead to disorders such as depression and anxiety. Unlike REBT, with which it shares a cognitive approach, the cognitive therapist does not forcefully dispute the client's unrealistic beliefs but helps the client to test these beliefs in the manner of a scientist testing a hypothesis.

REBT is quite unconventional in the world of established psychotherapy, and it did not initially have a very great impact beyond Ellis's circle of followers. However, during the 1960s, a psychiatrist named Aaron Beck, influenced by Ellis's work and also by scientific research and theories that link cognition and emotion, devised what he termed **cognitive therapy (CT)** (Beck, Rush, Shaw, and Emery, 1979; Beck, 1991, 2005). Beck, like Ellis, had previously practised psychoanalysis. He noticed that people with emotional disturbances tended to experience 'automatic thoughts' that were highly unrealistic, self-defeating, and biased against themselves. For example, they may expand a single shortcoming into the categorical statement 'I never do anything right'. According to Beck, repeated 'self-talk' of this sort and automatic, biased interpretations of events are frequently the cause of psychological disturbance—or if not always the direct cause, they represent serious roadblocks to recovery.

Where do these biased interpretations of events come from? According to Beck, a person may interpret events in a distorted way when he or she possesses dysfunctional, underlying core beliefs about the self, the world, and the future—the *negative cognitive triad* we described in Chapter 18. For example, one such dysfunctional belief might be, 'If I can't succeed at something important, I'm a complete failure' (Beck, 2005).

Although Beck's basic idea is pretty similar to Ellis's views, the process of CT is quite different from that of REBT. Cognitive therapists are not confrontational, and they do not offer advice. Instead, they attempt to form a gentler 'scientific collaboration' with their clients, whereby clients' distorted beliefs are 'tested' against real-world evidence. For example, a person may feel like a complete failure yet have a devoted partner and children, earn a small fortune, and be up for winning an award that marks them out as an outstanding success in their field of work. The cognitive therapist would have the task of helping the client use these facts as evidence showing that the client is not in fact a failure.

Cognitive Behaviour Therapy

> **KEY IDEAS** cognitive behaviour therapy (CBT) This is a development of behaviour therapy that attempts to unite traditional behaviour therapy with Beck's cognitive therapy. CBT is based on the idea that cognition, emotion, and behaviour are linked in a circle of mutual influence and reinforcement. Although CBT is not identical to CT (cognitive therapy), the term *cognitive behaviour therapy* is often used to refer to either therapy.

Although CT and REBT were highly influential, after a time some behaviour therapists and their allies in the cognitive camp came to the conclusion that the link between cognition and emotion is a complicated one that needs to include both cognition and *behaviour* (Rachman, 2009). As depicted in Figure 19.2, thought, emotion, and behaviour are linked in a circle of mutual influence and reinforcement (Hollon and Beck, 1994). This perspective led to the development of **cognitive behaviour therapy** (CBT; Godfried, 2003; O'Donohue, Fisher, and Hayes, 2003).

According to cognitive therapists, **depression** can be caused, and is always worsened, by unrealistic, biased, and counterproductive ways of thinking. Cognitive therapists have identified a number of specific patterns of distorted thinking in vulnerable individuals that can lead to depression. These patterns have been identified

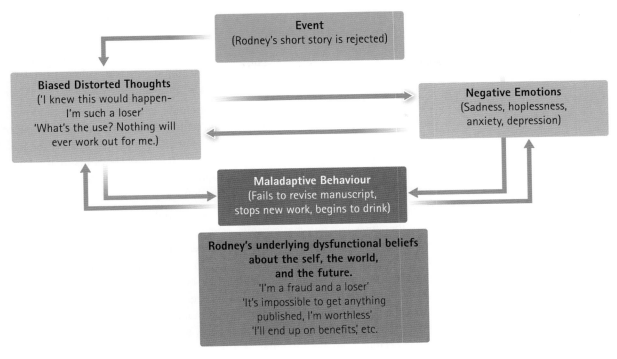

FIGURE 19.2 Cognitive-behavioural view of the origin of psychological symptoms. According to cognitive behaviour therapists, cognition, emotion, and behaviour mutually influence and reinforce one another. When a person has underlying negative beliefs about the self, the world, and the future (the negative cognitive triad), negative events can trigger cognitions that influence both emotion and behaviour. Emotion and behaviour in turn influence one another and also the probability of further negative cognitions.

Source: Zimmerman et al, 2008, p 2002.

and classified by a range of theorists so there is a degree of overlap between them. Here are a few examples:

1   *Overgeneralization.* Taking a single negative event and concluding that all events in your life will be similar. For example, you get laid off and conclude that you'll always have a hard time holding down a job.

2   *Disqualifying the positive.* Only negative experiences are meaningful—positive experiences 'don't count' for one reason or another ('Yeah, everyone who's read my poetry loves it, but they're all people who know me—of course they're going to like it. Their praise doesn't count.')

3   *Catastrophizing and minimizing.* When negative events occur (you are turned down for a promotion at work or score poorly on an important test), life on earth as you know it is over. You'll surely end up homeless. That is catastrophizing. When positive events occur (you win a prestigious scholarship to study at The Sorbonne), 'that's nice but probably nothing will probably come of it'. That is an example of minimizing—the good is not disqualified altogether but it its importance is relegated.

4   *Mind-reading.* Assuming that you know people's thoughts and motivations without evidence. For example, if your girlfriend seems withdrawn and irritable one day, you conclude that she's getting tired of you. It doesn't occur to you

that the real reason is that she only got two hours of sleep the night before and has to face a late shift at work.

5 *Magnifying.* Blowing things out of proportion. A small mistake becomes a tragic failure; a minor suggestion is interpreted as scathing criticism. Things are 'overwhelming', 'impossible', 'huge' (McKay, Davis, and Fanning, 2007).

6 *Filtering.* This takes place at the level of attention and memory. You only pay attention to, and recall, the negative, while letting the positive slip by. Consider a day when your lecturer sharply criticizes your work, you are hired for the job you've been hoping for, your romantic partner finally declares his or her love for you, and you win 100 pounds in a football pool—yet you only think about your lecturer's criticism. It's been a 'horrendous' day.

These patterns of distorted thought, as well as a number of others identified by cognitive therapists, are automatic habits. Many of us, even if we are not clinically depressed, may engage in them from time to time, but they are dysfunctional when they take over and become the dominant way in which a person thinks. To assess how prevalent someone's distorted thinking is, a cognitive behaviour therapist may ask the person to keep a 'thought journal'. This exercise not only shows the therapist how often the person engages in self-defeating thoughts, but can also help the person become aware of these habits and, over time, work on breaking them.

CBT has become extremely popular as a therapy, perhaps eclipsing CT in a number of practitioners. However, over the years the distinction between CT and CBT has been lost to some extent, because the term *cognitive behaviour therapy* is often used regardless of which type of therapy is being discussed (Beck, 2005), and many people are confused about whether a difference actually exists.

WHAT'S HOT? THIRD-WAVE CBT

The newest forms of cognitive therapy found to be useful in combating symptoms of mental disorder are known as the **third wave** of CBT. They include **mindfulness-based CBT** (MBCBT) and **acceptance and commitment therapy** (ACT).

Mindfulness-based cognitive therapy is a relatively brief (eight-week) programme that blends CBT with meditation techniques based on Buddhist practices. It was originally intended as a treatment to reduce relapse in depression, but is now used more widely. The term **mindfulness** is used inconsistently and its original form, the Buddhist concept of *Sati*, is hard to translate directly. Crudely though, mindfulness involves non-judgemental focus on both external and internal stimuli that comprise the moment. In a therapeutic context maintaining a focus on dysfunctional thinking as it occurs helps prevent disproportionate emotional reaction.

Studies have shown MBCBT to be at least as effective as other forms of cognitive therapy and antidepressant medication in treating and preventing relapse in major depression (Kuyken et al, 2008; Segal et al, 2010). There is also an emerging body of research linking MBCBT to changes in neural functioning (see, eg, Alsubale et al, 2017).

Another popular branch of third-wave CBT is **acceptance and commitment therapy** (ACT) (Hayes, 1982). Like traditional CBT, ACT is based on a cognitive understanding of symptoms. Where CT and REBT aim to challenge and alter these cognitions, ACT teaches patients to monitor and accept them, and focus on identifying what is important to them as an individual, setting goals accordingly. So if you are plagued by depressing cognitions like repetitive negative thoughts about the world, rather than challenge these thoughts you could be taught

❯

> to accept them and make plans to be happy in spite of the way you see the world. To some psychologists this is as much a behavioural therapy as a cognitive one because its emphasis is on action whilst not being swayed by cognition. Some commentators use the term 'mindfulness' to describe the self-monitoring element of ACT. In spite of their different theoretical roots ACT and MBCBT probably involve similar processes.

Issues in the Use of Cognitive Therapies

There are differences in health policy in every country—even within Europe. However, in most countries CBT and related cognitive therapies now dominate publicly funded therapeutic practice (Woelbert, 2015), and they are considered the first choice for treating a range of problems in Britain according to the National Institute for Health Care Excellence (NICE) (2009). This is not to say that cognitive therapies are above controversy or criticism, however. CBT has an impressive volume of evidence to support its effectiveness for a range of disorders, but there is considerable debate about the significance of this evidence and the claims some CBT therapists make.

For example, some CBT practitioners claim that CBT is more effective than other therapies. However, evidence in support of this particular claim is not very strong (Benish et al, 2008; Miller et al, 2008). CBT has been shown to be superior to other therapies used to treat depression only when styles of therapy poorly suited to treating depression (eg, *progressive muscle relaxation*) are included in the analysis. If only legitimate therapies appropriate for depression are considered, the statistical advantage for CBT disappears (Spielmans et al, 2007).

CBT as an empirically supported therapy

The **empirically supported therapies** movement exists to create and promote therapies whose worth can be objectively evaluated in controlled research. This is done using a method similar to that used to evaluate drugs prior to their release on the market, the *randomized controlled trial* (RCT). In randomized controlled trials, researchers statistically compare the performance of the therapy or drug against a placebo and/or a 'no-treatment' condition—a group of people who are on a waiting list and receive no treatment until after the study period is complete. In some cases a newer or less-well researched therapy is also compared against a standard treatment. Psychological therapies that demonstrate superiority over no treatment for a given disorder are known as empirically supported treatments (ESTs; Hollon, 2006).

CBT lends itself to testing by randomized controlled trials because it is usually short-term and focused on a narrow range of symptoms. To some psychologists CBT has become synonymous with empirically supported therapy. This has not gone down too well with therapists of other orientations! Psychoanalyst Jeremy Holmes (2002) summed up objections in a classic critique of CBT and defence of other therapies:

1 In the single largest study, CBT emerged as less effective than both antidepressants and other psychological therapies.

2 Little is known about the long-term outcomes for patients having different forms of therapy.

3 Although CBT fares well in **efficacy** studies—RCTs using carefully selected patients and therapists—there is less evidence of **effectiveness** in real-life settings.

> **KEY IDEAS** empirically supported therapies (EST) An EST is a therapy that has demonstrated statistically significant superiority over no treatment (and in some cases also over a placebo therapy) in a series of randomized controlled trials.

> **KEY IDEAS** efficacy **Efficacy** studies aim to be as close to a laboratory experiment as possible, controlling for extraneous variables. This means that participants are randomly allocated to conditions and both therapists and patients are carefully selected, the latter perhaps only having a single symptom and almost certainly only one diagnosis. Psychologists sometimes use the terms 'efficacy' and 'effectiveness' interchangeably to indicate how beneficial a treatment is to patients.

> **KEY IDEAS** effectiveness **Effectiveness** studies, are field studies carried out in real-life therapeutic settings using typical therapists with a range of qualifications and typical patients with a range of symptoms, complicated life problems, and sometimes multiple diagnoses. Efficacy studies are often seen as the gold standard of outcome research but what effectiveness studies lose in experimental control they make up for in realism.

4 Although CBT compares well in trials against no-treatment there is a lack of evidence for its relative efficacy compared with other therapies.

5 Changing cognition is clearly not necessary for therapeutic change, as demonstrated by ACT (see earlier in this chapter).

6 CBT has had a very effective programme of research and marketing, and this may have exaggerated its benefits.

Some of these objections (particularly 1, 2, and 4) now appear dated in the light of more recent evidence. However, the observation that CBT has been misleadingly marketed as the only empirically supported psychological therapy remains compelling.

This point was picked up by Leader (2008). Leader suggests that, much as research and evidence are valued by psychologists, when the average person reads the phrase 'research shows . . .' they stop thinking critically and accept the argument that follows. Thus CBT has largely escaped critical scrutiny. Moreover, suggests Leader, CBT plays well with the value we currently place on transparency and measurable outcome. It is thus compatible with current thinking.

THINKING CREATIVELY

The argument between CBT and psychoanalytic therapists has not become much friendlier since the Holmes critique. Drawing on the evidence base and other critiques of both approaches in this chapter put together the case for one therapy and against the other. If you are working collaboratively this would make an excellent debate.

THINKING CRITICALLY

Some CBT therapists have started to use the terms CBT and EST interchangeably. This raises a number of issues. Consider for example the following:

1 To what extent is identifying CBT alone as an EST justified, given other research discussed in this chapter?

2 In what ways could it be misleading to conflate CBT and EST and what problems could this cause?

3 CBT practitioners are justly proud of their evidence base of randomized controlled trials. Why are RCTs not practical for some therapies, say psychoanalysis?

> KEY IDEAS client-centred therapy This is the humanistic therapy founded during the late 1940s and 1950s by Carl Rogers. The goal of client-centred therapy is to promote personal growth in the client in a non-directive manner by treating the client with congruence, empathy, and unconditional positive regard.

CLIENT- OR PERSON-CENTRED THERAPY

In addition to techniques drawn from the therapies already described, many therapists use techniques of **client- or person-centred therapy (CCT or PCT)**, the therapy founded during the late 1940s and 1950s by humanist psychologist Carl Rogers and described briefly in Chapters 2 and 15 (see Figure 19.3). In response to the rather cold, mechanistic view of the behaviourists and the complex, speculative psychoanalytic theory of the time, Rogers (1951) proposed a simpler and kinder way of working. He believed that the client, not the therapist, is the expert in his or her own

FIGURE 19.3 Pure client–centred therapy is much more likely to be practised by counsellors than psychologists. Rogers' equity between client and therapist has influenced most modern therapies and therapists. In pictures it is much harder now to tell the client from the therapist!

Source: iStock.com/KatarzynaBialasiewicz.

life—and that the client must therefore be allowed to control the direction of therapy according to his or her needs. Rogers stressed the importance of the therapist extending three core conditions to the client:

- Unconditional positive regard and acceptance of the client regardless of the client's behaviour or personal characteristics.

- Empathy (ie, highly attentive listening with accurate perception of the client's emotional state).

- Congruence (ie, an honest relationship in which, rather than remaining detached from the client, the therapist reveals his or her real personality).

The client-centred therapist acts as a kind of mirror, allowing the client to clarify his or her own feelings, and helping the client to make choices congruent with his or her goals.

Although relatively few contemporary therapists adhere strictly to Rogerian therapy, his influence is enormous on therapy as a whole. It is primarily due to Rogers that the 'doctor–patient' relationship of psychoanalysis and early psychotherapy evolved into the modern 'therapist–client' relationship—a relationship based on equality of status and shared goals.

Issues in the Use of Client–Centred Therapy

Client-centred therapy is by definition benevolent and highly unlikely to cause harm. However, just *how* beneficial it is is a matter of debate because there is a very small body of research into its benefits compared with those of other therapies. In one study, Goldman, Greenberg, and Angus (2006) assessed 19 depressed patients before and after 16–20 sessions of CCT. Mean scores on the **Beck Depression Inventory (BDI)**, a standard self-report measure of depression symptoms, dropped significantly from 26.26 (moderate depression) to 9.89 (minimal symptoms). This is suggestive of significant effectiveness; however, a second group of patients were given CCT plus additional emotion-focused techniques and did even better (a drop

❯ KEY IDEAS Beck Depression Inventory The **Beck Depression Inventory** or BDI is a standard assessment tool for depression. It contains 21 items each of which can be scored 0–3 according to selection of one of four statements. The higher the score, the greater the degree of depression. A score of over 19 or 20 (depending on the BDI version) suggests moderate depression and a score of over 29 or 30 suggests severe depression. A score of under 10 or 14 depending on the version indicates minimal depressive symptoms.

from 26.21 to 4.59 on the BDI). This highlights the weakness of CCT—its lack of therapeutic techniques. We can probably all benefit from a really good listener but other therapies probably have more 'active ingredients' to offer. These will differ according to the model of therapy.

SYSTEMIC THERAPY

The systemic approach is best known for work with families; however, it can be applied to individuals, couples, work groups, and even whole organizations. The distinguishing feature of the systemic approach is that problems are seen as occurring *between* family members, or members of a team or organization, rather than within an individual. The whole family is thus treated on the basis that if the family can function better together, the mental health of individual members will improve.

Early systemic therapy was based on **family systems theory** (Bateson, 1972). In family systems theory, the family is considered an integrated, organic unit, or system, much as systems analysts view computer systems in organizations. Like a computer system, a family or any other close group is self-regulating; to maintain a kind of homeostasis in the group individuals alter their behaviour. Sometimes this can lead the individuals to act in ways that would be quite maladaptive if seen just from the individual perspective. For example, where two parents become pre-occupied with their careers, a child might develop symptoms of a mental disorder in order to refocus the attention of the family on meeting the children's needs.

> **KEY IDEAS** family systems theory This is the view that the family is an integrated, organic unit that may be analysed in somewhat the same way that systems analysts view computer systems in organizations. Symptoms in an individual can be viewed as adjustments by the system to bring about homeostasis.

A key technique of systemic therapy is circular questioning. This involves asking the same question of each group member in order to highlight differences in their perceptions. Circular questions might include asking each member to describe the same incident from their perspective, rank each member for a characteristic, or identify situations in which a problem occurs or does not occur (Carr, 2012). Brown (1997) gives the example of circular questions used in response to the statement that a mental health problem is genetic in origin. Questions could include 'who most thinks the problem is due to bad genes?' and 'when did the family begin to think the problem was caused by bad genes?' (1997, p 111). Such questions help the therapist understand what the dominant family narrative is and who individually believes it.

Following circular questioning, the systemic therapist might offer hypotheses about the origins of symptoms in the group functioning. It is important for systemic therapists to remain neutral in the face of different perspectives within a group. In order to help with this neutrality and generate a range of hypotheses, systemic therapy is conducted (budget permitting) in the presence of a reflecting team (Anderson, 1987).

Modern systemic therapy is also strongly influenced by social constructionism, with some commentators seeing this as a **paradigm shift** (see Chapter 2) in the discipline (Cantwell and Holmes, 1994). Social construction is an interpretive approach to psychology that sees meaning as constructed by our use of language and influenced by power relations. To social constructionists there can be multiple realities in a given situation; however, families have their own dominant narratives (stories), and these can narrow the range of ways in which a family can view a situation. Social constructionism is also concerned with power, both between individuals and social structures. Thus the hypotheses put forward in modern systemic therapy are likely to take account of gender and race issues within a family.

Systemic family therapy is often used in the treatment of eating disorders and schizophrenia. The early systems theorists tended to attribute the existence of these disorders to family functioning, leading to problems of parent-blaming. However, modern systemic therapists are more focused pragmatically on improving family functioning.

Issues in the Use of Systemic Therapy

In the UK, NICE recommends systemic family therapy for a range of conditions, including depression and schizophrenia. This is based on a substantial body of research showing that systemic family therapy is effective. Carr (2014a, 2014b) conducted a wide-ranging review of outcome research and concluded that systemic therapy is effective for a wide range of adult and childhood problems. However, he also identified some key limitations of the current evidence base. For example, most studies have evaluated the use of old-fashioned systems theory-based therapy, and there is much less evidence for the effectiveness of the more modern social constructionist-influenced narrative family therapy practised by most systemic therapists. In addition there is little support at present for family therapy in the treatment of personality disorder.

So, broadly, there is good empirical support for the effectiveness of systemic therapy. There are, however, other factors that affect the adoption of systemic practice. One factor is cost. Typically, systemic therapy is practised collaboratively, either with pairs of therapists or with a reflecting team observing and meeting after the session to discuss hypotheses. Although therapists often meet with clients less frequently than do practitioners of other models of therapy—say once a month—the costs of the therapy still add up. There is often tension between systemic therapists and their employers over how necessary it is to incur the extra cost of a co-therapist or reflecting team. These features of systemic therapy add considerably to its cost; however, practitioners consider them essential.

READ THIS

There is a huge range of books and articles examining different models of therapy. These are just a few, focusing on some original works from the key figures in the development of each therapy:

Freud, S. (1925). *Collected Papers Volume III Case Histories.* London: Hogarth Press.

Rogers, C.R. (1957). The necessary and sufficient conditions of therapeutic personality change. *Journal of Consulting Psychology*, **21**, 95–103.

Wolpe, J. (1973). *The Practice of Behavior Therapy*, 2nd edn. Oxford: Pergamon.

Beck, A.T. (1979) *Cognitive Therapy and the Emotional Disorders.* Madison: Penguin.

Here are a few recommendations for contemporary work. You might find these easier but we suggest strongly that you at least dip into the early work as well:

Lemma, A. (2015). *Introduction to the Practice of Psychoanalytic Psychotherapy.* Chichester: Wiley.

Beck, A.T. (2005). The current state of cognitive therapy. *Archives of General Psychiatry*, **62**, 953–9.

Wilkins, P. (2015). *Person-centred Therapy.* London: Routledge.

Carr, A. (2012). *Family Therapy.* Chichester: Wiley.

OUTCOME RESEARCH: EXAMINING THE BENEFITS OF THERAPY

Throughout this chapter we have given examples of studies which investigate the benefits of therapy. Broadly, these studies tend to show similar and positive effects for a range of therapies. However, there are many issues around the effects of therapy.

<blockquote>
❯ KEY IDEAS efficacy, RCTs, and effectiveness efficacy A treatment has good efficacy if it has been shown to be superior to a placebo in randomized controlled trials (RCTs). Because it is difficult to construct a placebo in psychotherapy, the term *efficacious* is often applied to therapies that have only shown themselves superior to no treatment. A **randomized controlled trial** is a research study used to evaluate a therapy or treatment where the research participants are randomly assigned to receive either the treatment of interest, a competing treatment, no treatment, or—if possible—a placebo treatment. An **effective** treatment is one that has shown itself to have significant utility in the 'real world' of practising clinicians treating patients in clinics, hospitals, consulting rooms, and medical offices.
</blockquote>

In 1977, Mary Smith and Gene Glass produced the first meta-analysis of the research in outcomes of psychotherapy. Recall that a meta-analysis is a statistical procedure in which researchers combine data from a large number of studies to produce statistics that can summarize the studies' overall findings. Smith and Glass found unequivocally that those participants in psychotherapy outcome research who were actually given therapy did better than those in control groups who received no treatment (see Figure 19.4). Since the work of Smith and Glass, so many studies reporting similar results have been published that psychotherapy's superiority to no treatment is considered 'proven' (or as close to as anything in psychology) and is not controversial (Wampold, 2007).

What Does 'Work' Mean? Efficacy and Effectiveness

So, then, *psychotherapy works . . .*, right? Unfortunately, the issue is a little more complicated than that. The answer to the question of whether or not psychotherapy works depends entirely on what is meant by 'works'. Many of the research studies that have demonstrated the superiority of psychotherapy over no treatment are studies of *efficacy*. The term **efficacy** has a highly specific meaning in medicine and psychology. An efficacious therapy is one that has proven itself in randomized controlled trials to be superior to no treatment—that is, superior to the simple healing effects of the passage of time (Wampold, 2001). A **randomized controlled trial (RCT)** is a research study used to evaluate a treatment where the research participants are randomly assigned to receive either the treatment of interest, no treatment, or—if possible—a placebo treatment. Some RCTs also include another group assigned to a competing treatment for comparison.

However, psychotherapy researchers take pains to differentiate the term *efficacy* from the term *effectiveness*. An **effective** treatment is one that has utility in the real world of practising psychotherapists treating distressed clients in hospitals and consulting rooms—situations which may differ in any number of ways from the world of laboratory research (Chambless and Hollon, 1998; Wampold, 2007). Many clinicians consider it important to maintain the distinction between these terms because a so-called 'empirically supported' efficacious treatment—one that is statistically superior to no treatment (or a placebo) in research studies—may not be effective in the real world.

How might a treatment be shown to be efficacious yet not be effective? First, it may be that the type of treatment a volunteer for a psychotherapy study receives from those running the study is substantially better than the typical quality of treatment received by a client in an outpatient clinical setting.

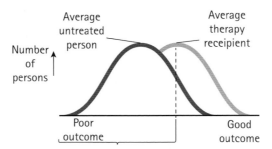

FIGURE 19.4 **Psychotherapy is superior to no treatment.** Meta-analysis of almost 500 psychotherapy outcome studies showed that the average research participant who received therapy was better off than 80% of the participants who received no treatment.

Source: Adapted from Smith, Glass, and Miller, 1980.

Second, RCT study designs may not be as appropriate for testing psychotherapies as they are for testing drug or other biology-based treatments. For example, RCTs do not take into account the simple fact that some therapists are better than others and some therapy *relationships* are better than others. Indeed, some *clients* are better than others at bringing about their own healing during therapy (Norcross and Lambert, 2011). The success or lack of success of a particular treatment might be tied more to the quality of the therapist, the client, and the therapeutic relationship than to the specific treatment (Wampold, 2009; Norcross and Wampold, 2011). Third, the type of people who volunteer for such studies may differ from those who typically seek therapy (Wampold, 2007; Baker, McFall, and Shoham, 2008).

As we have already seen in our discussions of CBT and long-term psychodynamic therapies, different therapies lend themselves to different kinds of outcome research. Behavioural therapies and CBT are almost always short-term, meaning that undertaking an RCT where you leave a control group in a waiting list does not raise major ethical problems. Moreover, these therapies are clearly focused on removing a small number of symptoms so it is straightforward to find suitable participants. Because of this CBT is easy to test in efficacy studies and there is a large body of efficacy research supporting it.

Psychodynamic and client-centred therapies, by contrast, tend not to have a pre-determined time limit and can last for years. Patients are more likely to have complex constellations of symptoms. Both practically and ethically it is much harder to set up a randomized controlled trial when you cannot easily identify key symptoms at the outset and when you don't know how long therapy will last. There is, therefore, a much smaller volume of efficacy research for the long-term exploratory therapies. However, there is a larger body of effectiveness research, particularly in Europe as opposed to the USA.

The Equivalence Paradox

Despite the large number of legitimate therapy styles available, most efficacy studies show that none of these therapies is superior to any other in general outcome (Wampold et al, 2011). Of course, it is always possible that a given person is temperamentally better suited to one style or another, and a few types of therapy are narrowly focused and intended to apply only to certain conditions. For example, *exposure therapies* are most commonly intended to treat phobias or other fearful states. However, no therapy has a better *overall* track record than other therapies. This equality of success rates among therapies has been referred to as the **equivalence paradox** or '**dodo bird verdict**', after the dodo's pronouncement at the end of a race in Lewis Carroll's *Alice in Wonderland*: 'At last, everybody has won and all shall have prizes.'

Not everyone agrees with this general finding (Lilienfeld, 2007; Olatunji and Hollon, 2010), and claims are often made that one or another form of therapy has proved superior for some particular condition. However, most evidence supports the dodo bird verdict with one extremely important qualifier: the general equality of outcome for the various therapies extends *only* to those therapies that are based on legitimate psychological principles and intended to be used for the disorder in question (Wampold, 2007; Benish et al, 2008). Innumerable forms of treatment exist that are based on pseudoscientific principles or untested ideas. Some of these treatments may lack value entirely or actually be very harmful (Barlow, 2010). Simply calling something 'therapy' does not make it therapeutic.

> **KEY IDEAS** the dodo bird verdict (equivalence paradox) This is a phrase used to sum up the 'take-home message' of outcome research in psychotherapy: no legitimate form of therapy is superior to any other in general outcome. The phrase is borrowed from an incident in Lewis Carroll's *Alice in Wonderland*, wherein a dodo bird announces of a race, 'At last, everybody has won and all shall have prizes.' This is also given the more scientific term the equivalence paradox. The dodo bird verdict applies only to legitimate forms of psychotherapy appropriate for a given condition.

Common Factors in Psychological Therapies

Despite the demonstrated efficacy (and possible effectiveness) of psychotherapy, we are left with the question of *why* it works. Each type of therapy is based on (sometimes radically) different theories of the nature and origin of psychological disorders and distress. Yet, as we have already seen, with a few specific exceptions, all legitimate forms of psychotherapy work about equally well. This 'dodo bird verdict' as regards therapy efficacy implies an important idea: *the explanation each therapy school gives for the effectiveness of its therapy may not be correct* (Blatt and Zuroff, 2005; Benish et al, 2008).

Here is an example: logically, if it were true that depression is caused by distorted and biased cognitions, as proposed by cognitive therapists, then it would be something of a mystery as to how therapies such as psychodynamic therapy—which do not address these cognitions—could possibly work. Yet, psychodynamic therapy does relieve depression (Leichsenring and Rabung, 2009; Shedler, 2010).

So how can we explain the effectiveness of such diverse therapies? One possible answer, first proposed by Saul Rosenzweig in 1936, has been elaborated on by countless theorists over the years (Frank and Frank, 1991): therapy may work not as a result of any specific 'active ingredients' of individual therapies (such as insight in psychodynamic therapies, behaviour change in behavioural therapies, and change to cognitions in CBT), but as a result of factors that appear to be shared by *all* legitimate therapies—known as **common factors**.

If it is common factors, not active ingredients, that are responsible for therapeutic change—and not everyone agrees that this is true—what are the common factors? This question cannot be answered with certainty (Kazdin, 2005). However, according to Bruce Wampold (2001), a major proponent of the common factors approach, there are probably three principal factors: **therapeutic alliance**, **therapist allegiance**, and **therapist competence**.

1 *Therapeutic alliance.* The word *alliance* implies the idea of a connection or union towards a common goal. The therapeutic alliance is built on the positive emotions and affection between therapist and client, the therapist's empathy for the client, and both parties' joint commitment to accomplish the important work of healing.

2 *Therapist allegiance. Allegiance* refers to the therapist's intellectual commitment to the specific type of therapy he or she has chosen to practise. Therapists' belief in their therapy may be transmitted to clients in a convincing 'story' about the causes of the client's distress and plan to alleviate it. This increases both parties' hope, confidence, and willingness to engage in effortful activity within therapy.

3 *Therapist competence.* Although some therapists and clients are better suited to one another than to others—and their better 'fit' produces good results—it is also true that some therapists appear to produce generally more positive outcomes regardless of the identity of their clients or what type of therapy they are providing. They are simply better at what they do (Okiishi, Lambert, Nielsen, and Ogles, 2003; Okiishi et al, 2006).

The idea of common factors may go a long way towards explaining the dodo bird verdict and findings that therapist experience and credentials do not seem to make much of a difference in therapist effectiveness overall (Tracey et al, 2014). All three common factors hypothesized as playing a major role in therapeutic success—therapeutic alliance, allegiance, and therapist competence—apply equally to all legitimate forms of therapy.

> **KEY IDEAS common factors**
These are hypothesized factors common to all legitimate forms of psychological therapy that are responsible for actual therapeutic effects. These may include:

Therapeutic alliance—hypothesized common factor of psychotherapy that refers to the positive emotions between therapist and client, the therapist's empathy for the client, and both parties' joint commitment to therapeutic work.

Therapist allegiance—the therapist's commitment to the specific type of therapy he or she has chosen to use.

Therapist competence—the degree to which a therapist tends to produce good results regardless of client or therapy techniques.

Psychological Interventions Can Cause Harm

It is no secret that therapy is not always helpful. However, the fact that therapy can sometimes be *harmful* is less often discussed and even more rarely researched (Dimidjian and Hollon, 2010). How might harm occur in psychological therapies?

First, therapy—like surgery or drug treatment—carries with it the potential for unintended side effects. Consider Jim, who worked in a career he hated for a boss who was a tyrant. As a result of therapy and the support of his therapist, he finally made the leap to quit his job and change careers. Unfortunately, Jim had three children to support, and his career aspirations did not work out as he (and his therapist) had expected. When Jim then desperately tried to find work in his old profession he was unable to do so. His family ended up on benefits. If we accept the hypothesis that none of this would have happened had it not been for therapy, then Jim's current situation could be viewed as a kind of unintended side effect of therapy.

Second, psychotherapy can instil false beliefs in clients about the nature and causes of their problems. Logically, this *must* be happening all the time. This is because psychotherapies are usually built on specific theories about the nature and causes of psychological disorders. However, these theories often contradict one another radically and cannot all be true at the same time. Someone has to be getting it wrong! To what extent this is a problem depends on the nature of the false belief. However, there have been cases where clients in therapy have come away with false memories of childhood trauma that have impacted on their family lives. See Chapter 9 for a discussion of false memories.

Third, harm in therapy can also occur as the result of simple incompetence on the part of the therapist. A therapist may be incompetent regardless of his or her training.

Potentially harmful therapies

Some legitimate 'therapeutic' techniques and perhaps whole therapies can cause harm when they are used inappropriately. An example of this is grief counselling. Studies of grief counselling in which clients self-refer because they are not coping with bereavement typically show much better outcomes than those in which participants are aggressively recruited (Hoyt and Larsen, 2010). This suggests that grief counselling *can* be helpful but that it should not be pushed on bereaved people who are already coping.

Another example of an intervention where evidence is very mixed is critical incident debriefing. The evidence probably varies according to the competence of the debriefing (Aucot and Soni, 2015), but there is a worrying body of evidence suggesting that debriefing is associated with increased rather than reduced trauma symptoms.

Other 'therapies' are not based on psychological principles or scientific evidence and have little or no support from research. These are known as potentially harmful psychological therapies (or **PHPs**; Norcross et al, 2006; Lilienfeld, 2007). As detailed in Table 19.3, PHPs have created harms ranging from simple humiliation and the worsening of disorders to the destruction of entire families and even deaths of clients.

Culturally inappropriate uses of therapy

Most psychotherapies are administered under the assumption that, with minor adjustments, they may be applied to anyone, regardless of culture, ethnicity, gender, religion, or personal philosophy. To some degree this assumption equates psychotherapy with medical treatment—rather like administering an antibiotic to treat an

TABLE 19.3 **Examples of potentially harmful therapies**

Potentially Harmful Therapies	Description	Potential Harm
Critical incident stress debriefing	3–4 hour therapy session (or sessions) conducted among people exposed to an extreme, potentially traumatic experience. Conducted within 24–72 hours of the event.	Risk of increasing post-traumatic symptoms.
Scared Straight interventions for conduct problems	Intended to frighten adolescents away from a life of crime by exposing them to the harsh realities of prison life.	Risk of worsening conduct problems.
Recovered-memory therapy	Suggestive techniques including hypnosis, medication, guided imagery in effort to release 'repressed' memories of childhood trauma.	Risk of producing false memories of trauma, false accusations of child abuse against family members, wrongful imprisonment, deterioration of family relationships.
Dissociative-identity disorder (DID)-oriented therapy	Use of suggestive interview methods and hypnosis in an effort to uncover hidden childhood traumas and contact client's 'alters'.	May induce dissociative identity disorder or induce client with DID to create additional 'alters'. (However, evidence is correlational.)
Grief counselling for normal bereavement	Counselling for those who have recently lost a loved one to death.	May increase depressive symptoms and grief.
Expressive-experiential therapies (eg, Gestalt, encounter groups)	Encourages clients to experience powerful emotions and catharsis, often in confrontation with therapist or group.	For some people, may worsen painful emotions.
Boot-camp interventions for conduct disorder	Military-style 'get tough' approach to adolescent conduct problems.	Risk of worsening conduct problems; has resulted in death.
DARE programmes (Drug Abuse Resistance Education)	Use of uniformed police officers to teach schoolchildren about risks of drugs and resistance to peer pressure regarding drug use.	May increase use of drugs, alcohol, and cigarettes.
Gay conversion therapies	Usually based on fundamentalist religious argument, attempts are made to alter a person's sexual orientation to heterosexual.	Internalization of homophobic values, resulting in reduced self-esteem.

Source: Based on Lilienfeld, 2007.

> **KEY IDEAS PHPs**
PHPs or potentially harmful psychological therapies are pseudo-scientific procedures that have been shown to risk harm to patients.

infection. However, this assumption has been challenged (Wampold, 2007), and it may well be that culturally inappropriate use of psychological therapies can do more harm than good.

Malik and Krause (2018) give two examples of behaviours that may take place in therapy and have different meanings. One is physical touch by the therapist. Although touch is not standard practice in most psychological therapies, fleeting touches are sometimes used to convey empathy, particularly in couple, group, or family therapy where the therapist is not alone with a vulnerable client. However, touch, especially by a male therapist on a female client may be perceived as grossly offensive in some cultures. Another example is sharing food. In Western Europe clients bringing food to therapy is likely to be viewed as an attempt to bribe or distract the therapist. However, in many cultures this would be considered a normal part of social interaction.

One problem with viewing therapy as a 'one-size-fits-all-more-or-less' medical treatment is the fact that individual differences in clients—for example, cultural differences—may strongly affect treatment (Van Dyk and Nefale, 2005). As Wen-Shing Tseng (2004) suggests, every person is affected by his or her own culture. Tseng emphasizes the importance of acknowledging the impact of culture for all clients, including those from the majority culture in a multicultural setting.

READ THIS

Here are some key resources for thinking about issues in the use of psychological therapies, such as effectiveness. Some of these reach quite different conclusions so get your critical thinking heads on!

Stiles, W.B., Barkham, M., Mellor-Clark, J., and Connell, J. (2008). Effectiveness of cognitive-behavioural, person-centred, and psychodynamic therapies in UK primary-care routine practice: Replication in a larger sample. *Psychological Medicine*, **38**(5), 677–88.

Hofmann, S.G., Asnaani, A., Vonk, I.J., Sawyer, A.T., and Fang, A. (2012). The efficacy of cognitive behavioral therapy: A review of meta-analyses. *Cognitive Therapy and Research*, **36**, 427–40.

Barlow, D.H. (2010). Negative effects from psychological treatments: A perspective. *American Psychologist*, **65**, 13–20.

Wampold, B.E. (2015). How important are the common factors in psychotherapy? An update. *World Psychiatry*, **14**, 270–7.

PHARMACOTHERAPY

So far in this chapter we have examined psychological approaches to helping people cope with problems and treating psychological disorders. However, over the past several decades, a second major approach to treatment has come to rival psychological approaches in prominence—the use of psychoactive medications such as **antidepressants** and other techniques that act directly on the body. For the remaining portion of the chapter we shall consider the nature of these treatments.

Psychopharmacology is the study of how drugs and other substances affect emotion, mood, and behaviour (Meyer and Quenzer, 2005). **Pharmacotherapy** is the use of drugs and other substances (eg, nutritional supplements) to treat psychological disorders and distress. Although there are a great many such *psychoactive* drugs (drugs that affect the mind), they generally fall into one of four categories of use: those used primarily to treat depression, those used for bipolar disorder, those used for anxiety, and those used for psychotic disorders such as schizophrenia.

It should be understood, however, that there is a good deal of **off-label prescribing** of these medications—prescribing a drug to treat some condition for which it was not initially intended, but for which it may have some utility (Haw and Stubbs, 2005). For example, some antidepressant drugs are commonly used off-label for conditions as varied as anxiety, sexual dysfunction, substance abuse, eating disorders, sleep problems, and personality disorders.

Anxiolytics

Drugs that treat symptoms of anxiety are known as **anxiolytics**. With a few exceptions, anxiolytic drugs currently in use generally belong to a single class of medications known as **benzodiazepines** (eg, Librium, Valium, Xanax, Klonopin, Atavan).

❯ **KEY IDEAS** pharmacotherapy This is the use of drugs and other substances to treat psychological disorders or distress. Pharmacotherapy is based on **psychopharmacology**, the study of the effects of drugs and other substances on mood, emotion, and behaviour.

❯ **KEY IDEAS** off-label prescribing **Off-label prescribing** is the practice of prescribing medication for conditions other than those for which that medication was intended in the belief that it will have some benefits for patients.

These drugs are mildly sedating and may reduce anxiety symptoms, at least in the short term, while not knocking the person off his or her feet as was the case for the *barbiturate* drugs previously used to treat anxiety.

Benzodiazepines create anxiolytic effects in part through regulation of GABA, a neurotransmitter that produces muscle relaxation and sensations of calm as it binds to specialized neuron receptors (Roy-Byrne, 2005). For more information on how this works, see 'Neurotransmitters and mental life', Chapter 4. At higher doses, benzodiazepines induce symptoms and sensations similar to drunkenness—slurred speech, giddiness, unsteady gait, and reduced inhibitions. Consequently, these drugs are often abused, and serious dependence and addiction can result (O'Brien, 2005). When dependence does result, even if it has occurred through legitimate, relatively low-dose use, it is important to withdraw from these drugs under medical supervision, because the withdrawal symptoms can be quite severe and include seizures.

Benzodiazepines have demonstrated their usefulness in treating anxiety disorders (Martin et al, 2007). However, their therapeutic effects tend to decrease over time, while unwanted side effects—including dependence, cognitive decline, and risk of accidents—increase (Barker, Greenwood, Jackson, and Crowe, 2004; Neutel, 2005). Thus, most authoritative sources suggest only short-term use lasting a few weeks or several months at most. Nonetheless, a substantial number of users take these drugs for many years or even decades.

Antidepressants

The scale of **antidepressant** drug use in the Western world may shock you if you weren't aware of it already. According to the Health and Social Care Information Centre (HSCIC) (2016), 61 million antidepressants were prescribed in the UK in 2015. This makes antidepressant drugs the fastest growing prescribed drug, up by more than 100% in ten years.

There are four principal classes of antidepressant drugs: (1) *MAO (monoamine oxidase) inhibitors*, now rarely used because of their dangers—taking them with tyramine-containing food such as cheese and drinks such as beer and red wine can cause a lethal rise in blood pressure; (2) *tricyclic antidepressants*, among the first antidepressants developed, effective but with unpleasant side effects including blurred vision, drowsiness, and impotence; (3) *selective serotonin reuptake inhibitors* (SSRIs), probably the most commonly prescribed antidepressants; and (4) so-called *third-generation antidepressants*—a catch-all category that includes antidepressants with unique chemical structures (*atypical antidepressants*) as well as the new serotonin-norepinephrine (noradrenaline) reuptake inhibitors (SNRIs).

SSRIs

SSRIs are probably the most commonly prescribed antidepressants As mentioned in 'The role of neurotransmitters', Chapter 4, SSRIs selectively block the reuptake of the neurotransmitter serotonin (meaning it is not broken down after synaptic transmission and so its level builds up), in contrast to the drugs like the early tricyclics, which act on several neurotransmitter systems at once. This selectivity was considered desirable at the time when the drugs were devised because it was believed that selecting only a single neurotransmitter system might reduce most of the side effects associated with the tricyclic drugs.

Do SSRIs have fewer troublesome side effects than earlier drugs? In short, no. As Table 19.4 shows, they just have different side effect profiles, with some side effects being more common than with tricyclics, and others less common. The SSRIs are also often rumoured to be faster acting and more effective than tricyclics. In fact, however, no one of these drugs is more effective overall than any other (Hansen et al, 2005; Rush et al, 2006).

Nevertheless, SSRIs (including drugs with brand names such as Prozac, Paxil, Celexa, Lexapro, and Zoloft) have left the tricyclics in the dust in the frequency of their prescription (Pirraglia, Stafford, and Singer, 2003). It has been suggested that drug companies aggressively market SSRIs because they hold the patents to the newer SSRI drugs, whereas the older tricyclics have been produced generically for decades. This means that they can profit far more from SSRIs.

What industry marketing has not emphasized (and often fails to mention altogether) is that SSRIs can produce withdrawal symptoms on discontinuation (Hosenbocus and Chahal, 2011). Between 35% and 50% of people attempting to discontinue taking SSRIs experience unpleasant, flu-like symptoms, including dizziness, weakness, nausea, fatigue, feelings of 'unreality', loss of balance, light-headedness, and 'electric-shock' sensations (Rosenbaum, Fava, Hoog, Ascroft, and Krebs, 1998). These symptoms may continue for weeks and are not the result of a 'rebound' of depression. This **SSRI discontinuation syndrome** may cause some individuals to continue to take these medications long after they no longer need them.

Third-generation antidepressants

Beginning in the late 1980s, a new group of antidepressants was developed that falls generally into the catch-all category **third-generation antidepressants**. The most frequently prescribed of these third-generation drugs are SNRIs (eg, brand names Effexor, Cymbalta). The SNRI drugs are based on the idea that combining selectivity for the neurotransmitter noradrenaline as well as for serotonin might produce

> **KEY IDEAS** SSRI discontinuation syndrome This is a drug withdrawal syndrome associated with the use of at least some of the SSRI and SNRI antidepressants. The syndrome may consist of flu-like symptoms, dizziness, weakness, nausea, fatigue, feelings of 'unreality', loss of balance, light-headedness, 'electric-shock' sensations, and other symptoms.

TABLE 19.4 Comparison of SSRI/SNRI and tricyclic antidepressant side effects

Class of Antidepressant	Side Effect
MORE COMMON IN SSRIs AND SNRIs (eg, Paxil, Zoloft, Prozac, Cymbalta, Effexor, Lexapro, Celexa, Serzone)	Various sexual dysfunctions (may continue after of the patient stops taking the drug) Headache Trembling Agitation Insomnia Nausea and vomiting Diarrhoea Anxiety and nervousness
MORE COMMON IN TRICYCLICS (eg, Elavil, Anafranil, Norpramin, Tofranil)	Dizziness Dry mouth Blurred vision Drowsiness Constipation and urinary difficulty Cardiovascular problems (sometimes serious) Weight gain

Sources include: National Health Service (www.clinicalanswers.nhs.uk/resource/depress.gif) and emedexpert (www.emedexpert.com).

superior results to those produced by serotonin selectivity alone (Nelson et al, 2004). The SNRIs are not more effective than other antidepressants overall (Freemantle, Anderson, and Young, 2000), and they may also produce withdrawal symptoms on discontinuation. However, they may work better for some individuals.

Antipsychotics

Introduced during the 1950s, *first-generation antipsychotics*, with brand names such as Thorazine, Mellaril, and Haldol, altered the treatment of schizophrenia and other psychotic disorders by reducing the severity of positive symptoms. As discussed in Chapter 18, positive symptoms refer to those symptoms of psychosis that involve 'something being there that should not be there'—for example, hallucinations, delusions, and general agitation. First-generation antipsychotics work primarily by restricting the availability of the neurotransmitter dopamine either by blocking dopamine receptors entirely or by inhibiting the neurotransmitter's release.

Figure 19.5 shows a marked and steady decline in the number of institutionalized patients in the United States following the introduction of first-generation antipsychotic drugs such as chlorpromazine (Thorazine) (Meyer and Quenzer, 2018).

However, the first-generation antipsychotics proved less useful than originally believed. Fewer than 50% of those taking them found substantial and/or lasting improvement (American Psychiatric Association, 2000; Meyer and Quenzer, 2005). These drugs also have very serious side effects. Patients frequently report feeling 'drugged out', overly sedated, and unable to think or concentrate. More seriously, however, the first-generation drugs (particularly if used long term) can cause tardive dyskinesia, a largely untreatable and irreversible neurological disorder. Tardive dyskinesia is characterized by repetitive, involuntary movements such as grimacing, protrusion of the tongue, lip smacking or puckering, and rapid eye blinking. Involuntary and odd movements, and twitching of the fingers, arms, legs, and torso may also occur. Tardive dyskinesia is uncomfortable to have and distressing to watch, and its potentially irreversible nature makes it a particularly unpleasant possibility

FIGURE 19.5 **Treatment of the mentally ill. Patient populations in public mental institutions in the United States increased from 1900 to 1956 before a marked and steady decline following the introduction of antipsychotic drugs such as chlorpromazine. (After Bassuk and Gerson, 1978.)**

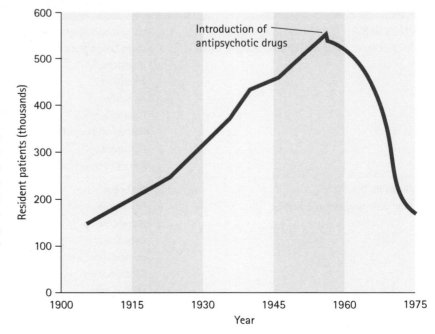

to contemplate. Indeed, in many cases it is a much more serious problem than the one for which the patient began taking the antipsychotic drug. Figure 19.6 illustrates the cumulative incidence of TD in a group of 362 chronic psychiatric patients who were maintained on antipsychotic drugs, and shows that two-thirds of those taking antipsychotics for a period of 25 years will develop TD (Meyer and Quenzer, 2018).

Because of the seriousness of such side effects, and because medical researchers wished to create more effective drugs, a new generation of antipsychotics has been developed known as **second-generation antipsychotics** (eg, Seroquel, Abilify).

Studies have found that that there is no difference in effectiveness between the first- and second-generation drugs (with the exception of clozapine, below) but several of the second-generation drugs, including clozapine and risperidone, have less risk for motor side effects which may make them more suitable for some patients.

An exception to these findings, clozapine was considered superior in the Cost Utility of the Latest Antipsychotic Drugs in Schizophrenia Study (CUtLASS) carried out in the UK in 2006. While it is not more effective in treating the positive symptoms of schizophrenia than the older drugs, clozapine has produced significant improvement in 60% of patients who have not previously responded to typical neuroleptics and there is evidence that it can alleviate some of the negative and cognitive symptoms as well as acting on anxiety and tension (Meyer and Quenzer, 2018). Nevertheless, clozapine has a wide range of serious side effects that demand careful consideration and can limit its prescription: seizures, weight gain, hypersalivation, and cardiovascular problems. More problematic still is the risk of agranulocytosis (lowered white blood cell count) which must be managed by weekly/bi-weekly blood tests.

All antipsychotics are significantly better than placebo at reducing positive symptoms and decreasing the length of time patients spend in hospital. In general, individuals may respond better to one drug than another, so patients and their psychiatrists may have to try multiple drugs before settling on the most appropriate one. Often, the most appropriate drug is the one with the least problematic side effects. Considering both the first- and second-generation antipsychotics gives patients and psychiatrists more options for finding a drug with side effects that the

> **KEY IDEAS** third-generation antidepressants These are the most recent group of antidepressants to be developed. These drugs include SNRIs as well as drugs with unique ('atypical') chemical structures and physiological mechanisms.

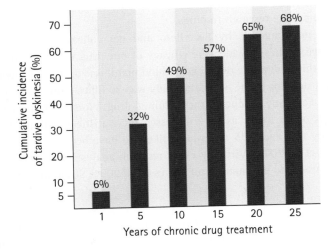

FIGURE 19.6 Cumulative incidence of tardive dyskinesia in a group of psychiatric patients on antipsychotic medication. Long-term treatment clearly increases the risk of developing TD.

Source: Reproduced with permission from Meyer and Quenzer, Psychopharmacology: drugs the brain, and behaviour. © 2018. Oxford Publishing Ltd. Reproduced with permission of the Licensor through PLSclear.

patient can tolerate. Psychiatrists will often talk about the law of thirds when giving estimates of effectiveness, that is that: one-third of patients will see dramatic reduction in their symptoms and may lead relatively 'normal' lives; one-third will show significant improvements but may experience relapses and need a return to hospital; and one-third will see little improvement in their symptoms, perhaps needing to spend extended time in hospital (Meyer and Quenzer, 2018).

Since, with the exception of clozapine, neither the first- nor the second-generation drugs improve the cognitive impairments, researchers continue to look at new approaches to drug treatment. Adjunctive treatments are also increasingly common, with therapies such as CBT sometimes used to treat persistent positive and negative symptoms in patients for whom antipsychotics are not completely effective (Rector and Beck, 2001; Morrison 2009).

Effectiveness of Pharmacotherapy

We have already seen how pharmacotherapy is rarely as successful as it claims to be.

However, the question of effectiveness of pharmacotherapy needs to be examined perhaps with even greater care—and boldness—than we gave to the same issue as regards psychotherapy. For although psychotherapy can be harmful, it is not as potentially harmful as pharmacotherapy as a general rule. In other words, the side effects of drugs are usually more worrisome than those of legitimate forms of psychotherapy.

There is another, more important reason to challenge the effectiveness of pharmacotherapy: it supports many billions of dollars of profits annually for multinational pharmaceutical corporations. Without being overly cynical, it is a matter of common sense to refrain from relying on industry pronouncements and advertisements regarding their products, or taking scientific research at face value when much of it is funded by the very companies whose products are being tested.

Recent research has documented the ways in which pharmaceutical companies powerfully influence how (and how often) their drugs are prescribed, how research on drugs' efficacy is designed and conducted, how the data is analysed and the articles written, which studies are published, and the conclusions drawn by the authors of research articles (Bekelman, Li, and Gross, 2003; Bero, Oostvogel, Bacchetti, and Lee, 2007; DeAngelis and Fontanarosa, 2008). Increasingly, numerous journalistic exposés support these research findings.

Consider a meta-analysis by Lisa Bero and her colleagues of pharmaceutical industry-funded studies in which the efficacy of one drug is compared against that of another. In this review, the researchers found that if one of the drugs was shown to be statistically superior to the other, the study was 20 times more likely to have been funded by the company producing the 'winning' drug. Worse still, if the conclusions of the authors of the study as they discussed the statistical findings favoured the drug, the study was about *35 times* more likely to have been funded by the manufacturer (Bero et al, 2007). Virtually every research analysis that has examined this question has produced the same result (Heres et al, 2006; Sismondo, 2008b).

The file drawer problem

> **KEY IDEAS** second-generation antipsychotics These are recently developed drugs designed to treat psychotic disorders such as schizophrenia, but are also used as mood stabilizers in bipolar disorder.

One reason why published research may tend to present a falsely positive picture of the efficacy of pharmacotherapy is the file drawer problem, also called **publication bias**. It is always slightly depressing as a researcher when your results don't support your hypothesis, so consciously or unconsciously it is very tempting to put negative findings aside and find another way to evidence what you believe to be true. This becomes more serious when you fear that negative findings might impact on further research grants and possibly your job! It is thus quite common to submit for publication primarily those articles that report favourable results while relegating studies producing negative results to a filing cabinet or encouraging journal editors to do so. This can be a problem for any kind of research—including outcome research for psychological therapies, but where funding from pharmaceutical companies is at stake there is additional pressure for researchers to be selective with what results they publish. Figure 19.7 shows bias in the publication of antidepressant studies reviewed by the US Food and Drug Administration.

An example of a study highlighting the dangers of publication bias comes from Eyding et al (2010). They carried out a review and meta-analysis of both published and unpublished data concerning the antidepressant reboxetine. They concluded that published studies alone were highly misleading, overestimating the efficacy of reboxetine compared with placebos by 115% and compared with SSRIs by 23%. Even more worryingly, published studies underestimated the potential harm of reboxetine, which according to the unpublished data included worsening of symptoms and withdrawal problems.

Ghostwriting

Ghostwriting is a common practice in the writing of medical articles. Often the purported authors of articles make very few or no contributions to the actual writing, and may have had little or nothing to do with the design and conduct of the study reported in the article. Nonetheless, their names appear as authors on an 'honorary' basis for political reasons, to enhance the stature of the article, or because these researchers' schedules are too tight to allow them actually to do much more than review and/or edit articles printed under their names. Ghostwriting is no secret and, while it may seem

> ❯ **KEY IDEAS** ghostwriting
> **Ghostwriting** is the practice of having professional writers write up reports of studies in articles bearing the names of researchers who did not contribute to the writing of the article and may not have been involved in the design and conduct of the study.

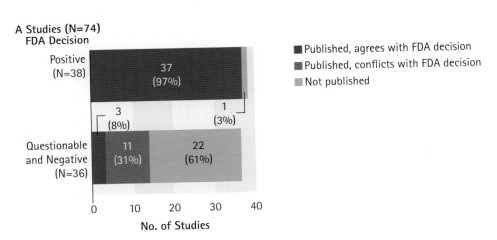

FIGURE 19.7 The file drawer problem in publication of antidepressant studies. Of the 74 studies of 12 antidepressants evaluated by the FDA, 38 showed positive results for the drug in question and 33 showed negative (or questionable) results. However, of the 38 positive studies 37 were published, and only one remained unpublished. Of the 33 negative or questionable studies, only three were published in a way that correctly identified the results as negative. Another 11 of these studies were published in a way that incorrectly interpreted the results as positive (although the FDA had deemed the results negative or questionable).

Source: Adapted from Turner et al, 2008, p 256.

strange to some, it does not necessarily compromise the quality of scientific evidence—in fact, people who are good at research are not necessarily good writers; therefore, ghostwriting can in theory improve the finished product (Healy and Cattell, 2003).

However, if ghostwriters are hired by the very corporations whose products are being tested in the research study in question, problems of bias can and do arise in the final articles (Singer, 2009). Consider the highly successful SSRI Zoloft (sertaline). By means of a lawsuit via the UK's Freedom of Information Act, researchers David Healy and Dinah Cattell gained access to a document that demonstrated the extent to which articles on Zoloft had been ghostwritten by writers hired by the manufacturer, Pfizer (Healy and Cattell, 2003). Using this document, Healy and Cattell were able to compare the characteristics of ghostwritten articles of Pfizer-funded studies of Zoloft against studies neither ghostwritten nor funded by Pfizer.

Several things distinguished the Pfizer-sponsored articles from others. First, the Pfizer-sponsored articles contained approximately twice as many authors listed per article, were on average almost three times as long, had more prestigious and prolific researchers listed as authors, and were published in more prestigious journals. Thus, these articles have likely had more impact on the field of psychiatry and medical knowledge. They were also, virtually without exception, favourable to Zoloft—overstating its true efficacy and underreporting the drug's side effects. Making up somewhere between 18% and 40% of the initial scientific research on Zoloft, Pfizer-sponsored research articles have helped to shape the way medical professionals and the public currently view the drug (Sismondo, 2007).

THINKING CREATIVELY

We have taken quite a tough line here on the evidence base for pharmacotherapy, and to be fair not everyone would agree with us. Yet, while the evidence for some commonly prescribed drugs is weak, many people do undoubtedly feel better as a result of medication. Suggest as many reasons as possible for this paradox. You can think outside the box here and consider explanations in which drugs do have genuine positive effects and alternatives.

OTHER BIOLOGICAL TREATMENTS

Although pharmaceutical remedies are the most frequently used biological treatments, there are alternative biologically based modes available for treating psychological disorders. As a general rule, however, these treatments—including **electroconvulsive therapy, electrical and magnetic brain stimulation**, and **psychosurgery**—are used when other methods have failed.

Electroconvulsive Therapy (ECT)

With the exception of psychosurgery, which consists of invasive surgical procedures on the brain (see Chapter 4), electroconvulsive therapy (ECT) is the most controversial of all treatments for psychological disorders. ECT is used principally in cases of severe depressions that have not responded to other treatments. During ECT, the patient is first anaesthetized (rendered unconscious) and given a muscle relaxant drug to prevent bone fractures during convulsions. The patient is then strapped to a table and a low-voltage electric shock is passed through the brain for a split second, causing the patient to experience an epilepsy-like seizure and subsequent convulsions.

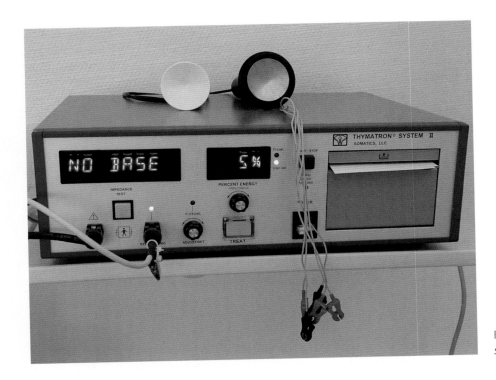

FIGURE 19.8 **ECT apparatus.**
Source: Stefan Bellini/ Wikipedia. CC0 1.0.

These convulsions last for a few minutes. The treatment is repeated each day for about 6–10 days on average. Figure 19.8 shows the apparatus used in ECT.

The distaste many people have for the idea of ECT stems partly from the versions of the technique used during the early years of its development, which can be described as somewhat barbaric. Those procedures were quite painful and were often applied by force to unwilling patients, without anaesthesia. They sometimes resulted in severe physical injury (eg, multiple bone fractures), cognitive damage, and death. There is a Frankensteinesque quality to many people's images of ECT, and the name itself is enough for people to denounce the treatment—even if the same people accept the treatment when it is described to them using a different name (Andrade and Thyagarajan, 2007).

However, ECT techniques have changed quite dramatically over the past few decades, and today ECT is considered by most psychiatric organizations and clinicians to be generally safe, with a one in 80,000 chance of death per treatment (Royal College of Psychiatrists, 2015).

One of the most interesting questions around ECT concerns how it works. Although we cannot answer this with any certainty it appears that ECT produces a number of neural changes each of which might play a role in alleviating symptoms (Singh and Kar, 2017). These include changes to regional blood flow and electrical activity in the brain, stimulation of neurotransmitter production, epigenetic stimulation of change to the number of neurons in regions of the brain. Recall from Chapter 5 that epigenetic changes take place when an environmental change affects gene expression. Any or all of these changes might impact on depressive symptoms.

> **KEY IDEAS** electroconvulsive therapy (ECT) ECT is a treatment for psychological disorders (primarily treatment-resistant depression) that consists of passing a low-voltage electrical current through a person's brain for a brief moment, resulting in seizure and convulsion. ECT is usually conducted multiple times for any given case.

Issues in the Use of ECT

As with pharmacotherapy, but even more so, opinions are often extreme regarding ECT, and it is quite easy to find two perfectly competent clinicians or researchers who will disagree radically about how well ECT actually works and whether it is safe (Fink and Taylor, 2007). It is understandable that contradictory opinions about

ECT may exist among informed scientists. Despite the fact that ECT has been studied for over 50 years, it has been suggested that the quality of the evidence is not very good relative to the quality of the outcome research in psychotherapy or even pharmacotherapy (UK ECT Review Group, 2003; Sackeim et al, 2007).

However, the evidence, such as it is, suggests several conclusions. First, the dangers of ECT are often overstated by some patient support groups and mental health activists. For example, as of this writing there is no evidence that ECT causes structural brain damage (Lisanby, 2007), and ECT is not a sadistic practice as it is sometimes portrayed. In terms of mortality, it is one of the very safest procedures performed under general anaesthetic, with accidental death being an exceptionally rare event.

On the other hand, the risks of ECT are also often *under*stated by psychiatrists and professional organizations. In particular, in addition to producing states of highly unpleasant confusion and disorientation, ECT does cause memory loss (often to a serious degree) in a substantial number of patients undergoing the treatment (Gregory-Roberts et al, 2010). Although clinicians often note some 'transient' (temporary) memory impairment, it is usually glossed over that ECT can cause long-term or even permanent memory loss (Sackeim et al, 2007; Gregory-Roberts et al, 2010).

What about the efficacy of ECT? According to the available evidence, ECT does seem to work at least as well or better than pharmacotherapy in the treatment of severe depression that has not responded to other treatment (UK ECT Review Group, 2003; Greenberg and Kellner, 2005). However, like all treatments, ECT must be viewed from a cost-benefit perspective—is the benefit worth the risk? In the case of ECT, opinions are polarized.

Magnetic Brain Stimulation: An Alternative to ECT

Since ECT was developed in Italy in the 1930s it has been gradually refined and remains a standard response to treatment-resistant depression. However, a number of alternative ways to use electrical or magnetic fields have recently been explored in order to simulate the effects of ECT with fewer risks and side effects. **Repetitive transcranial magnetic stimulation (rTMS)** involves placing an electromagnetic coil on the scalp (see Figure 19.9). The coil sends short electromagnetic pulses through the skull, gently stimulating the cerebral cortex. If you're wondering what this might feel like, it produces the sensation of someone gently knocking or tapping on your head. Some patients experience mild tension, headache, or other discomfort while undergoing rTMS. The most serious side effect is the possibility of seizure, but newer techniques have lowered this risk.

So does rTMS work? Some research has shown significant antidepressant effects for rTMS, substantially greater than that produced by mock rTMS (placebo) (George et al, 2010), and a number of recent meta-analyses have come down in favour of the technique (Berlim, Van den Eynde, and Daskalakis, 2013; Slotema et al, 2010), suggesting that it is probably about equal to ECT in efficacy.

PSYCHOSURGERY

Early techniques of psychosurgery were generally ineffective as well as extremely dangerous, resulting in brain damage, mental disability, personality change, and high rates of death. Claims have been made (some accurate, some exaggerated)

> **KEY IDEAS** repetitive transcranial magnetic stimulation (rTMS) This is a technique being developed for treatment of depression that consists of sending short electromagnetic pulses though the cerebral cortex by means of a coil placed on the scalp.

FIGURE 19.9 **A transcranial magnetic stimulation apparatus.**

Source: Phanie/Alamy Stock Photo.

that these procedures were sometimes used against people whose behaviour was disapproved rather than people who truly needed help for psychological distress (Mashour, Walker, and Martuza, 2005; Ögren and Sandlund, 2007). Early psychosurgical techniques primarily involved lobotomy procedures, which consist of cutting connections to the prefrontal cortex (or damaging it in various ways). Most societies consider such techniques barbaric, and they are frequently outlawed.

However, modern techniques of psychosurgery have evolved, although they are fairly strictly controlled and conducted at few sites around the world. These techniques are generally used only as a last resort in severe cases of neurological as well as psychological disorders including Parkinson's disease, anorexia nervosa, obsessive-compulsive disorder, and treatment-resistant depression. One such technique is known as **deep brain stimulation (DBS)**. In DBS, electrodes are implanted in various regions of the brain, and the electrodes are coupled to an external device that sends out stimulating electrical pulses (Mayberg et al, 2005). Although this procedure is promoted as being less potentially damaging than ordinary surgery, DBS *is* brain surgery, and all brain surgery carries risks (Clausen, 2010).

THE FUTURE OF TREATMENT IS PROBABLY INTEGRATIVE

Treatment for psychological disorders and distress is an enormously complex and extensive topic, and we hope that this chapter has reflected this scope and complexity. However, in separating treatments into categories either large (biological/psychological) or smaller (cognitive/psychodynamic therapies), there may be a natural tendency to assume that the various treatments compete with one another. However, recall that in Chapter 18 we discussed how understandings and treatments

> **KEY IDEAS** deep brain stimulation (DBS) A relatively new technique of psychosurgery used to treat Parkinson's disease and being tested for use in psychological disorders, particularly depression. In deep brain stimulation electrodes are implanted in various regions of the brain and coupled to an external device that sends out stimulating electrical pulses.

of mental disorders can be integrated to provide many treatment options. In these early examples, influenced by the need to balance beliefs in the religious and medical models of the time, trepanning was carried out on the rationale that either or both blood and demonic entities could be released. Fortunately we have moved on from both demonic possession and 'bad blood' but it seems that the idea of integration of rival models of the mind has finally caught on.

The question 'which is better—medication or therapy?' is often asked, and there do remain clinicians who are strongly in favour of one or the other approach. However, these extreme positions in treatment of psychological disorders are gradually fading as it becomes increasingly apparent that psychological disorders are influenced by a complex interaction of biological, psychological, and social variables. Consequently, increasing numbers of clinicians have realized that effective treatment must address the biological, psychological, and social lives of each individual. This model of treatment is known as the **integrative treatment model** (Barlow and Durand, 2005).

A simple example of integrative treatment is combining antidepressants or antipsychotics with a psychological therapy, most commonly CBT. Patients may also be prescribed an exercise regime or meditation practice and they may be advised to read books about depression (this is called bibliotherapy). The patient may also have joined a self-help group of people attempting to recover from depression. This is integrative treatment.

Within the psychological therapies there is also an increasing tendency to combine techniques or whole models of therapy. A therapist who draws on different techniques as he or she sees fit is said to be eclectic in their approach. One who systematically combines models of therapy is said to be integrative in his or her orientation. Integrative models of therapy include those between CBT and psychodynamic models. Henriques (2014) describes the rivalry between these approaches as asinine (idiotic), making therapists choose between strategies to reduce symptoms and provide insight into relationship patterns, when clearly both of these are helpful. Perhaps the best-established and validated model of cognitive-psychodynamic integration is Anthony Ryle's cognitive analytic therapy (CAT). See Ryle et al (2014) for a discussion but, briefly, CAT therapists explore both current cognitions and their link to feelings and behaviour (like CBT), but they also explore the childhood roots of these cognitions and feelings.

> **KEY IDEAS** integrative treatment model A model of treatment that reflects the reality that most current mental health treatment involves multiple modalities (eg, psychological therapy plus medication, and that within psychological therapies it is possible to systematically combine models and techniques).

READ THIS

For a range of perspectives on pharmacotherapy try these:

Arroll, B., Chin, W.Y., Martis, W., Goodyear-Smith, F., Mount, V., Kingsford, D., . . ., and MacGillivray, S. (2016). Antidepressants for treatment of depression in primary care: A systematic review and meta-analysis. *Journal of Primary Health Care*, **8**, 325–34.

Kirsch, I. (2015). Antidepressants and the placebo effect. *Zeitschrift für Psychologie*, **222**, 128–34.

Linde, K., Kriston, L., Rücker, G., Jamil, S., Schumann, I., Meissner, K., . . ., and Schneider, A. (2015). Efficacy and acceptability of pharmacological treatments for depressive disorders in primary care: Systematic review and network meta-analysis. *The Annals of Family Medicine*, **13**, 69–79.

IN REVIEW

WHAT IS THERAPY?

- Psychological therapy is a unique relationship with key characteristics that distinguish it from other relationships.

- There are a number of well-established models of psychological therapy, each with its own theoretical understanding and techniques.

- Those who practise psychological therapies are well qualified and usually, though not always, have a core profession like psychology, psychiatry, or social work behind them.

PSYCHODYNAMIC THERAPIES

- Psychoanalysis is the most intensive, long-term, and traditional form of therapy.

- Psychoanalysis is interpretive, with the analyst interpreting dreams, and most importantly the transference relationship between analyst and patient with the aim of achieving patient insight.

- Psychoanalytic psychotherapy is similar to psychoanalysis but slightly less intensive and long term, and is more flexible in its range of techniques.

- Brief psychodynamic therapy has the same basis as long-term psychotherapies but uses shortcuts to achieve insight.

- There is now a sound evidence base for psychodynamic therapies, including evidence for long-term effectiveness in real-life settings; however, questions remain over its cost-effectiveness.

BEHAVIOURAL THERAPIES

- These are based on learning theory, and aim to alter behavioural responses by classical or operant conditioning.

- Exposure therapies involve eliminating responses, most commonly to an anxiety-provoking stimulus. This can be carried out in physical or virtual reality.

- Operant therapies like contingency management use reinforcement to encourage desired behaviour.

- Behaviour therapies are effective at eliminating single symptoms but they raise difficult ethical issues at times because of the distress involved in some treatments and the power the therapist has over patients.

COGNITIVE THERAPIES

- These are based on the idea that cognition is closely linked to emotion and behaviour and can form the basis of psychological intervention.

- In REBT the therapist identifies and vigorously challenges patterns of irrational or unproductive thinking.

- In CT the therapist is less confrontational and uses scientific testing to demonstrate the irrationality of negative patient cognitions.

- Most cognitive therapists now practise CBT, a blend of techniques from REBT and CT with behavioural techniques like exposure.

- Third-wave CBT uses mindfulness techniques to teach patients to accept and move on from cognitions rather than change them.

CBT is the most recommended psychological treatment according to NICE and has a large evidence base; however, CBT has sometimes been conflated with EST, empirically supported therapy, when actually several therapies are equally well supported.

CLIENT-CENTRED THERAPY

Rogers proposed a simpler and kinder view of human nature and a correspondingly simple and warm set of therapeutic techniques.

Client-centred therapy makes use of the core conditions of empathy, congruence, and unconditional positive regard to foster personal growth in clients. These ideas have been incorporated into most modern therapies.

Client-centred therapy is probably of some help to clients but it has a small evidence base and there is evidence that its usefulness is limited by its limited range of techniques.

SYSTEMIC THERAPY

This is most commonly carried out with families and is distinguished by its view of problems as existing between members of groups like families rather than in the individual.

Systemic therapy uses techniques like circular questioning to highlight differences in the way different family members see situations.

Modern systemic therapists also look at ways in which individuals subscribe to the dominant narratives of the family.

Systemic family therapy is supported by NICE and there is good evidence for its effectiveness; however, the use of co-therapists and reflecting teams make systemic therapy expensive in comparison with brief individual therapies like CBT.

OUTCOME RESEARCH

Research has shown that, broadly, psychological therapies do have positive effects on patients/clients.

There is a tension between effectiveness and efficacy as models of outcome research, and different therapies lend themselves more to one or the other as well as to different kinds of patient and symptoms.

Overall, however, in spite of their very different understanding of the mind and different techniques, there is no clear advantage to any one form of therapy. This is called the equivalence paradox.

One answer to the equivalence paradox is the notion of common factors. The idea is that the benefits of therapy are due to elements common to all therapies.

Some 'therapies' and 'therapeutic techniques' are likely to be harmful. An example is critical incident debriefing.

Therapy also exists in a cultural context, and one reason for therapeutic failure is the mismatch between therapeutic technique and the cultural values of and/or pressures on the client.

PHARMACOTHERAPY

A number of drugs are used to treat psychological symptoms, including anxiolytics, antidepressants, and antipsychotics.

- These may be effective in reducing symptoms but are associated with unpleasant side effects.

- There is a serious problem of establishing how effective drugs like these are because of non-publication of negative results and exaggerated marketing by drug companies.

- Alternative biological treatments include ECT, TMS, and psychosurgery. These appear to be moderately effective where other treatments have failed; however, they tend to carry risks and side effects.

TEST YOURSELF

1 Therapy sessions are normally scheduled and time-limited. True ☐ False ☐

2 Systemic therapists see individuals, couples, and families. True ☐ False ☐

3 There is little or no evidence to support the effectiveness of psychoanalysis. True ☐ False ☐

4 ECT causes epigenetic changes to the nature and number of neurons. True ☐ False ☐

5 Therapists who draw on techniques from a range of different therapies as and when they are useful are best described as

   a) Syncretic

   b) Eclectic

   c) Empathic

   d) Integrative

6 Which of the following models of therapy would be best described as focusing on changing patterns of thinking?

   a) Psychodynamic

   b) Cognitive

   c) Behavioural

   d) Humanistic

7 Which of the following behavioural therapies makes use of operant conditioning?

   a) Systematic desensitization

   b) Flooding

   c) Contingency management

   d) Aversion

8 Which type of antidepressants can cause fatal rises in blood pressure if taken with tyramine?

   a) MAO-inhibitors

   b) SSRIs

   c) Tricyclics

   d) Third-generation antidepressants

9 Compare the issues associated with psychodynamic and behavioural therapies. You might wish to consider effectiveness, appropriateness for particular conditions, and ethical issues.

10 Explain why many researchers think the effectiveness of drug treatment (pharmacotherapy) has been exaggerated in published literature.

 Visit the online resources that accompany this book: www.oup.com/uk/jarvis-okami1e

PART 6

SOCIAL PSYCHOLOGY

CHAPTER 20

SOCIAL COGNITION

LEARNING OUTCOMES

By the end of this chapter you should be able to:

- Define social psychology and social cognition
- Assess the importance of cognitive biases, including self-serving bias and positive illusions, in self-perception
- Evaluate research into self-control and self-regulation with particular regard to the 'marshmallow study'
- Consider the appropriateness of the 'strength' metaphor as used by Baumeister in his model of self-control
- Explain what is meant by attribution, including the distinction between situational and dispositional attributions and between personal and impersonal attributions
- Discuss the roles of correspondent inferences and covariation in the attribution process
- Debate the evidence base for the existence and universality of the fundamental attribution error and for the actor-observer bias
- Outline the tripartite model of attitude components and factors affecting attitude strength, including valence, expertise, and accessibility
- Critically consider both the utilitarian and symbolic functions of attitudes
- Discuss the relationship between attitudes and behaviour with particular reference to the notion of cognitive dissonance

Social psychology is the study of the influence of social situations on the individual—and the influence of the individual on social situations (Ruscher and Hammer, 2004). To understand the relationship between the individual and social situations we have to understand how the individual perceives, judges, and thinks about himself or herself and others. This is the realm of **social cognition**.

Social psychology is the lens through which psychologists view the social individual by himself or herself, as well as in pairs of two, in groups of ten, and in crowds of 20 and 20 million. These social interactions are the focus of the final chapters in this book. In this chapter we consider the social self on its own—the face each of us presents to himself or herself and to the world. Specifically, we will look at how individuals manage their own perceptions of themselves, guarding against negative self-judgements and attempting to maintain feelings of self-worth. We also look

> ❯ KEY IDEAS social psychology and social cognition **Social psychology** is the scientific study of the influence of social situations on individuals, and the influence of individuals on social situations. Social psychologists often focus on the idea of the self and study the social individual alone, in interpersonal situations, and in groups. **Social cognition** is a collective term for the mental processes involved in the individuals' perception of and judgements about themselves, others, and social situations.

at the ways in which we explain the actions of others and how and why we have **attitudes** and how they shape our interactions with others.

In subsequent chapters we shall look at the self as it relates to others in interpersonal interactions, the effects others have on us, and how conflict may arise between groups, sometimes leading to catastrophic **aggression**. We shall also explore those situations in which people may inexplicably sacrifice their time, efforts, and even risk their lives for others—seemingly with no expectation of personal benefit.

THE SELF IN SOCIAL CONTEXT

The 'self' crops up at various points in this book. For example, we explore self-esteem in the personality chapter and self-efficacy in relation to motivation. In this section we are really interested in the social self (ie, how our self-perception affects the ways in which we relate to and interact with others). So, if social psychology is in part the study of the influence of social situations on the individual, exactly who *is* the individual inside the social situation? In answering this question, social psychologists often focus on the idea of the **self**—each person's subjective awareness of, and ideas about, his or her own individual nature, characteristics, and very existence (Markus and Kitayama, 2010). What sort of person am I? What do I believe? What are my strengths and weaknesses? What should others expect of me and what do I truly want for myself? To which groups do I belong? How do I compare with others, or with myself in former times? The experience of the self can be seen as a bridge between the social world and the inner world of each person (Leary, 2007).

Because the self is constantly making self-evaluations, it must be able to defend against its own negative judgements. Psychological tools by which the self engages in 'self-defence' are amazingly diverse and numerous (Tesser et al, 2000). It appears that our desire for accurate information about ourselves takes second place to the desire to feel good about ourselves—to protect feelings of self-worth (Pyszczynski et al, 2004).

> **KEY IDEAS** the self Each person has an awareness of, and ideas about, his or her own individual nature, characteristics, and existence. This is known as our **self**.

Cognitive Biases

A cognitive bias is any systematic distortion in thinking, memory, and perception. A person experiencing cognitive bias will have a predictable tendency to arrive at certain conclusions over others, to see things one way rather than another, recall certain types of events but forget others, and so forth. Cognitive biases are powerful 'self-defence' weapons. There are a number of specific cognitive biases identified by social psychologists, and we shall examine two: the *self-serving bias* and *positive illusions*.

Self-serving bias

Although humans have the capacity for accurate perception and judgements of themselves and their world, they also appear to be prone to making certain types of systematic, pervasive errors of thinking and perceiving. Suppose you are living with one other person, either as housemates or as a romantic partner. If you and your partner were asked what percentage of the housework and other domestic chores you each perform during the week, how do you think you would respond? If each partner's answer were an accurate estimate of his or her contribution, adding the figures together would logically obtain the sum of 100% (your dishwashing + partner's dishwashing = 100% of dishwashing). In reality, however, when people are actually asked such questions, their answers rarely total 100%. The obvious explanation for this is that each partner will *overestimate* the amount of time or effort he or she spends performing these behaviours, resulting in a total estimate exceeding 100% (Ross and Sicoly, 1979). The same phenomenon occurs when members of a work group or a sports or debating team estimate the percentage they each contribute toward the overall group effort (Gilovich and Savitsky, 1999).

THINKING CRITICALLY

Our choice of phrasing 'the obvious explanation for this . . .' was deliberate because we should always be cautious about assuming that effects are the result of particular causes. What other factors apart from self-serving bias (see below) might help explain why collective time/effort estimates total more than 100%?

This is known as the **self-serving bias**, the tendency to make various sorts of judgement errors—always in your own favour. The self-serving bias comes in three main forms:

1 *Overestimating your own contributions*. Thus, the 'greater than 100%' effect just described.

2 *Overestimating your positive attributes relative to others—seeing yourself as 'better than average'*. As one commentator put it, 'The one thing that unites all human beings, regardless of age, gender, religion, economic status or ethnic background, is that deep down inside we all believe that we are above average drivers' (Barry, cited by Myers, 2002, p 95; see Figure 20.1). Obviously, not everyone can be above average, otherwise 'above average' would *be* average! People also tend to believe themselves to be smarter, more athletic, more attractive, more ethical, and less prejudiced than others.

3 *Attributing your successes and good deeds to your own efforts or characteristics, and your bad deeds and failures to circumstances, bad luck, or other people*. When you do well on a test, or get a good mark in an exam, do you attribute it to simple luck or to the lecturer's brilliant teaching or unchallenging grading—or do you take credit for your hard work and knowledge? If you're like most of us, it will be the latter. But what if you get a rubbish mark? Do you again take responsibility? Do you say things like, 'I didn't study', 'I'm rubbish at stats', or 'I'm not a very good student in general'? Such responses are less likely. Far more common are: 'The lecturer was useless', 'The questions were on stuff we hadn't done', 'The marks are totally arbitrary', 'I had the flu', and so forth. (Sound at all familiar?)

Interestingly, self-serving bias appears to be much weaker in **adolescence** as compared with adulthood. Rodman, Power, and Somerville (2017) tested this in an experiment in which adolescents and adults received peer rejection. Adults externalized the peer rejection—they blamed the rejection on those judging them—whereas the adolescents internalized the rejection, blaming themselves. It seems that the adolescents had not developed the tendency for self-serving bias.

> **❯ KEY IDEAS** self-serving bias
> The tendency to make systematic judgement errors in one's favour is called **self-serving bias**. This involves overestimating one's contributions, overestimating one's positive attributes relative to those of others, and attributing successes and good deeds to one's own efforts but failures and bad deeds to circumstances, bad luck, or other people.

FIGURE 20.1 **The self-serving bias.** How well do you drive? People tend to believe they are better than average drivers (and also smarter, more attractive, and more ethical than others).

Source: luckybusiness © 123RF.com.

Positive illusions about the self

Would you say that a large part of good mental health is being able to perceive things as they actually are? This certainly has been an important part of most traditional definitions of mental health favoured by psychologists and psychiatrists as well as film makers, novelists, and the rest of the general public (Gana, Alaphilippe, and Bailly, 2004). A stereotype of a mentally ill person is someone who believes things that are patently false (eg, 'I am Kurt Cobain'), or hearing or seeing things that are not there (eg, 'hearing voices'). However, less extreme forms of inaccurate perception of reality—biases they termed *positive illusions*—may suggest good mental health.

Taylor and Brown (1994) termed these biases **positive illusions** because they are not only designed to present the self to itself in a positive (but unrealistic) way, but also because they appear to benefit the individual possessing them. Positive illusions can be defined as false beliefs with beneficial consequences (McKay and Dennett, 2009). According to Taylor and Brown, those with positive illusions experience more positive moods and feelings of well-being than other people and are more motivated and persistent.

> ❯ KEY IDEAS positive illusions
> **Positive illusions** are systematic biases and illusions that not only are self-serving by presenting the self in a positive way, but also are associated with positive mental health and other consequences for the person possessing them. Positive illusions include uncritically positive views of the self, illusions of control, and unrealistic optimism.

THINKING CREATIVELY

You will sometimes come across bold statements like 'those with positive illusions experience more positive moods . . . . How could you go about testing this hypothesis? Think about how you might measure positive illusions and establish a relationship between these and moods. Think as well about suitable measures of outcome. How might you establish the reliability and validity of your measures?

Like the self-serving bias described earlier, positive illusions come in three types:

1   *Uncritically positive views of the self.* For example, Taylor and Brown (1994) cite extensive research that shows that people's ratings of their own personalities are more positive than the evaluations of unbiased raters who observe them interacting with others. Well-adjusted individuals also tend to recall their performance on various tasks as better than it actually was, and to think they have improved in abilities they value even when they actually have not improved at all.

2   *Illusions of control.* Most people believe they have more control over events in their lives than is actually the case. In particular, people greatly underestimate the ever-present factor of *chance*, and will explain events in terms of their own skill that could not possibly be due to skill. For example, people often believe that they are more likely to win the lottery if they personally purchase the ticket (Wortman, 1975).

3   *Unrealistic optimism.* When researchers surveyed 137 American couples applying for marriage licences, and asked them to estimate the percentage of marriages that end in divorce, they correctly (for the late 1980s to early 1990s, at any rate) estimated that 50% of marriages failed. However, when they were asked to estimate the probability that *their own* marriage would fail, most of them answered *0%* (Baker and Emery, 1993; see Figure 20.2). Unless they were a particularly unrepresentative sample around half of them were wrong!

These findings reflect yet another persistent positive illusion of human beings—the tendency to view the future with unrealistic optimism. Indeed, the vast majority of the world's population, living in the vast majority of countries of the world, express optimism about their lives (Gallagher and Lopez, 2009). Given the awful events on the world stage—as well as personal tragedies experienced by so many people—it is

FIGURE 20.2 Unrealistic optimism. Despite being aware that around 50% of marriages fail, most participants in Baker and Emery's research estimated the probability of their own marriage failing at 0%.

Source: iStock.com/Neustockimages.

reasonable to ask whether all this optimism is warranted. Nonetheless, it does appear to foster good mental and physical health.

Positive illusions may benefit romantic and marital relations as well. In a three-year longitudinal study of newly-weds, those couples who viewed each other in an unrealistically idealized light at the start of their marriage were *more* likely to remain loving and *less* likely to divorce during the period of the study (Murray et al, 2011; see Figure 20.3).

THINKING CRITICALLY

The Murray et al (2011) study of idealization and marriage involved 193 American couples, 89% white, with incomes ranging from $40,000 to $70,000. Consider the following:

1   How well might Murray et al's findings generalize to other populations?

2   What advantages are there to having a fairly homogeneous sample in a study like this?

However, the idea that positive illusions are associated with mental health is not universally accepted (Colvin and Block, 1994). For example, some argue that unrealistic optimism can translate into artificially inflated self-esteem. People with unrealistic or unstable levels of self-esteem sometimes run into interpersonal problems; others may perceive them negatively because they tend to be overly defensive or even hostile when criticized (Kernis, Lakey, and Heppner, 2008). It may be that there is an optimal level, or margin, for positive illusions. If these illusions distort the truth to too great an extent, they may have unhappy consequences or may be associated with reduced mental health (Baumeister, 1989).

A large meta-analysis by Dufner et al (2018) involving data from 299 samples totalling 127,000 participants assessed the relationships between self-serving bias and a range of variables. Self-serving bias was positively associated with psychological adjustment, and this effect did not appear to be moderated by age, gender, or culture.

THINKING PRACTICALLY

Samuel Johnson famously said that 'the excesses of hope must be expiated by pain; and expectations improperly indulged, must end in disappointment'. Apply research into positive illusions to evaluate Johnson's statement.

> **KEY IDEAS** social comparison theory **Social comparison theory** is really a group of theories initially formulated by Leon Festinger that describe how and why people may compare themselves to others to rationally evaluate themselves or enhance their self-concepts and defend against negative self-judgements.

Social Comparison

Self-evaluation does not occur only through bias and positive illusion. People may also compare themselves to others for purposes of self-evaluation. Unfortunately, while these comparisons may enhance a person's self-esteem, they may also trash it unmercifully, depending on a number of factors. Theories exploring the ways in which people make social comparisons, their reasons for doing so, and the consequences of comparison judgements are known collectively as **social comparison theory**.

FIGURE 20.3 **Are you under any illusions about your romantic partner? It might be best to keep them.** Some theories propose that unrealistically idealizing your spouse or romantic partner is a recipe for disastrous disillusionment down the line. However, psychologists researching positive illusions have found that married couples and romantic partners who unrealistically idealize one another stay in love longer and have more satisfying relationships. Individuals in these relationships may even come to see themselves as their partners see them (Murray et al, 2011).
Monkey Business Images/Shutterstock.com.

The originator of social comparison theory, social psychologist Leon Festinger (1954), initially believed that people generally make comparisons with other people who are similar to them. The purpose of these comparisons, according to Festinger, is the *self-evaluative* motive—you use them to rationally evaluate your own abilities and clarify your opinions and beliefs. When you compare your grades with those of others on your course, you may be motivated by self-evaluative concerns. The same motive may be at work when you compare your opinions against those of others in your group or nation published in opinion polls.

However, there are two other reasons for making social comparisons: self-enhancement and self-defence. Researchers during the 1980s observed that people do not always compare themselves to similar others. Sometimes they choose to compare themselves with those who are *dissimilar*—specifically, *less* capable, *less* fortunate, *less* healthy, wealthy, or wise. The purpose of these kinds of comparisons is to boost one's own feelings of self-worth. Making a comparison with another person who is in a *downward* relation to you may lead to a sense of superiority, safety, competence, and well-being (Wills, 1981). According to this theory of downward comparison, comparing oneself with a person better off or more capable—that is, making an *upward* comparison—invariably makes a person feel inferior.

Although these ideas were insightful, newer research suggests that the story may be a little more complicated: both upward and downward comparisons 'have their ups and downs' (Suls, Martin, and Wheeler, 2002). For example, upward comparisons may not generate unhappiness and lowered self-esteem in all cases, as previously

FIGURE 20.4 Social comparison theory. While people generally make comparisons to others who are similar to them, sometimes they compare themselves with those in a superior category to achieve goals by using upward targets as models.
Source: Oliver Gutfleisch/imageBROKER/Shutterstock.

believed. People may sometimes compare themselves with those in a superior position to them to *boost* their self-esteem by putting themselves in the same category as those who are more competent or fortunate ('My voice is a bit like Hannah Reid's'), or increase their motivation to achieve goals by using upward targets as models: 'Damn, Rag n Bone Man's good! I'm going to work at this until I can do it like he does!' (Johnson and Stapel, 2010; see Figure 20.4). In the same way, a downward comparison may not always improve things. By bringing to mind those in an inferior relationship, a person may also be reminded that it is entirely possible for the same fate to befall him or her (Suls et al, 2002).

CHANGING THE SELF

Suppose for a moment that your self-evaluation produces an unpleasant result—regardless of your best use of bias, positive illusion, and social comparison, to enhance self-esteem. For example, you might find yourself no longer able to ignore real problems resulting from self-defeating behaviours such as overeating, binge drinking, or smoking? Or what if it should become undeniably clear that procrastination is causing problems at work, or poor choices in romantic partners are repeatedly ending in disaster? If negative self-judgements continue over a prolonged period and attempts to maintain self-esteem and self-worth are unsuccessful, the self may engage in the difficult work of *self-change*. As we shall see, however, self-change can be challenging.

Self-Regulation and Self-Control

If you've attempted to change something about yourself you don't like, and most of us do at some point, it will likely come as no surprise to you that an important factor in successful change is often *self-control*. **Self-control** involves resisting

FIGURE 20.5 **Resisting the temptation of a delicious dessert when you are trying to lose weight is an example of self-control.**

Source: Monkey Business Images/ Shutterstock.com.

temptation or impulse; in a sense, it is laying aside a powerful, immediate desire, response, or goal in the service of more important, overriding long-term goals (McCullough and Willoughby, 2009). Self-control is a specific aspect of the more general concept *self-regulation.* **Self-regulation** includes all of the ways that the self monitors and exerts control over its responses so as to accomplish goals and live up to personal standards (Baumeister and Vohs, 2004). Saying 'No thanks' if you are trying to lose weight and you are offered a tasty dessert is an example of self-control (see Figure 20.5); deciding to continue to do all the things over a period of time that are likely to produce weight loss, such as dieting and exercise, is an example of self-regulation.

As you may have observed, people differ in a general way in their ability to be self-controlled. A person able to exert self-control when the chocolate box is passed around is also likely to be someone who is able to remain at home to practise her musical instrument when her friends have gone to see a film, hold her tongue when someone says something inappropriate, and stay sober on a hen night (Baumeister et al, 2006). Because self-control appears to be fairly stable across situations like these we can think of it as a personality trait.

Self-control is not merely associated with success at changing bad habits or resisting various sorts of temptations. As Steven Pinker observes, few other traits predict a healthy and happy life as well as self-control does (Pinker, 2011). In a famous series of experiments, Walter Mischel and his colleagues gave pre-school children a difficult choice: they could eat a small treat now, or, if they could resist eating it for 15 minutes, they would be allowed to eat more (see Figure 20.6). We can look at the original 'marshmallow study' in detail in our *Research in focus* feature (ironically the original study didn't involve marshmallows at all).

❯ **KEY IDEAS** self-control and self-regulation **Self-regulation** is a collective term for the ways that the self monitors and exerts control over its responses so as to accomplish goals and live up to personal standards. **Self-control** is the aspect of self-regulation which involves suppressing a powerful immediate desire or goal in the service of a more important overriding long-term goal. Self-control typically involves resisting temptation.

RESEARCH IN FOCUS

Mischel, W. and Ebbesen, E.B. (1970). Attention and delay of gratification. *Journal of Personality and Social Psychology*, **16**, 329–37.

Aim: The aim of the study was to investigate the role of cognitive processes on children's ability to delay gratification. More specifically, to test whether having small immediate rewards and larger delayed rewards in view affected children's tendency to wait for the larger reward. It was predicted that children would find it hardest to delay gratification when neither the immediate nor the delayed reward was visible.

Method: Participants were 16 girls and 16 boys with a median age of 4 years 6 months, selected from the Stanford University nursery. Four males and four females were randomly assigned to each of four conditions. In all conditions experimenters led each child to a small room containing a table, two chairs, and a few toys. On the table were a small snack of two pretzels (a savoury snack) and a second, larger snack consisting of five pretzels and two biscuits. The experimenter told the child that they would leave the room and that the child could eat the small snack immediately or have the larger snack if they sat still and waited for the experimenter to return. At this point the experimenter was informed which condition they were administering. In one condition both small and large snacks were left visible. In two further conditions each snack was concealed with an upturned cake tin and in the final condition both snacks were covered. The experimenter then left the room, returning either after 15 minutes or when the child ate the small snack, whichever was sooner. The dependent variable, time of delayed gratification, was measured from the experimenter leaving. Observers recorded the children's behaviour.

Results: The opposite of the predicted outcome was found. None of the children managed to wait 15 minutes for the large snack (mean waiting time = 1.03 minutes) when both were visible whereas 75% waited the full 15 minutes (mean waiting time = 11.29 minutes) when neither was visible. Only 25% delayed gratification for 15 minutes when one snack was visible, regardless of which snack it was. These differences were statistically significant. Children who successfully delayed gratification tended to distract themselves; for example, by playing or singing whilst sitting still.

Conclusion: Counter to stereotypes, many of the children are able to delay gratification provided they do not have to look at rewards. The visibility of rewards exerts a powerful influence on the ability to delay gratification. Successful delay of gratification is associated with successful distraction but this is inhibited by the presence of visible rewards.

MASTER YOUR METHODOLOGY

1 This study primarily gathered quantitative data. Explain how the gathering of supplementary qualitative data (the observations of children) enhanced the results.

2 The experimenters were informed which condition they were administering after they had completed the initial phase of the procedure to avoid demand characteristics. Explain what demand characteristics are and why they can be a problem in experimental research.

3 The experiment involved a between-groups design. Explain the advantages and disadvantages of this design and suggest why it might have been used in this study.

FIGURE 20.6 The marshmallow study. Ironically the original study method didn't involve marshmallows at all!

Source: Adam Fenster/University of Rochester.

THINKING CRITICALLY

Refer back to our critical thinking about studies toolkit (Chapter 1). Work your way through these questions to evaluate the 'marshmallow study'.

Although these studies provided interesting results at the time about individual differences in self-control, the real worth of these studies was not apparent for many years. Mischel and his colleagues were interested in what the ability to delay gratification in early childhood might predict about later life, and the researchers followed the original children for the next 40 years, checking in on them periodically. They found that those who were able to wait out the 15 minutes obtained higher SAT scores in high school and went on to higher academic achievements, had better emotional and cognitive functioning in adolescence, higher levels of self-esteem, less illicit drug use, and better stress-coping skills (Mischel et al, 2011). However, not all recent attempts to replicate these classic findings have succeeded. For example, Watts, Duncan, and Quan (2018) found only very light advantages in adolescence for treat-resisting children. These recent findings represent an example of psychology's 'replication crisis'.

THINKING CRITICALLY

The findings of the marshmallow study are currently being questioned in the context of the 'replication crisis' in psychology. Explain why it might be that reviews of earlier published findings consistently find support for the marshmallow effect but current replications do not.

The Strength Model of Self-Control

If—rather like intelligence—self-control is associated with so many positive life outcomes, the question becomes whether it can be taught or purposely acquired in childhood. Roy Baumeister approached this question first by suggesting a model of self-control that likens it to a muscle (Baumeister et al, 2006). Consider the metaphors we use to describe self-control: will*power*, *exercising* the will, *force* of will, *strength* of will. We *force* ourselves to say 'no' to the chocolate mousse, and use *effort* to control our tempers (Pinker, 2011). According to Baumeister's **strength model** of self-control, self-control exists in a limited quantity that differs among people, just as people differ in physical strength. Sustained efforts at self-control can exceed a person's capacity, and the 'self-control muscle' may become fatigued—just as would happen to the upper body and arms after too many repetitions at the bench press. At that point, the ability to exert self-control will weaken, and further efforts may fail.

There is evidence now to support this idea (Baumeister et al, 2006; Hagger et al, 2010). Baumeister and his colleagues have demonstrated repeatedly that the strenuous exercise of self-control in one situation will cause a reduction in the ability to do so in a subsequent situation. For example, hungry participants forced to sit in a room where the smell of fresh-baked chocolate chip cookies hangs in the air—but who are required to refrain from sampling the cookies—expend much less time and effort attempting to solve difficult puzzles subsequently than participants who were allowed to eat the cookies (Baumeister et al, 1998). A large number of similar situations were concocted by these researchers, with alternative explanations cleverly controlled for.

Some biological evidence further supports the muscle metaphor of self-control. Just as blood glucose is depleted when a person engages in muscular exercise, blood glucose also drops during tasks demanding the exercise of will—and people who experience this drop in blood glucose can revive their willpower for subsequent tasks by drinking sugar-sweetened liquid (Gailliot et al, 2007)!

Baumeister and colleagues reasoned that if the muscle metaphor really held, a person ought to be able to 'exercise' the will systematically over time and build up self-control 'muscle' through the strengthening of relevant neural connections, resulting in increases in the strength of willpower across the board. For example, adhering strictly to a diet ought to make it easier to maintain an aerobic exercise regimen or refrain from watching as much television. So research participants were asked to spend several weeks or months performing willpower exercises on a regular basis—for example, using their left hand (if they are right-handed) for tasks such as tooth brushing or operating a computer mouse, keeping detailed food diaries, keeping to money management plans, avoiding swearing, and so on. These participants were then given willpower-draining tasks similar to those used in the original experiments. Not only was the exercise group much less vulnerable to depletion of the will in the lab, but also their newly built-up willpower was also evident in events of their daily lives. They smoked and drank less, were more responsible in their finances, improved their study habits, watched less television, and experienced other admirable changes.

READ THIS

Although it is important to remain critical—especially given the current replication issues around some of his ideas—it is well worth reading some Roy Baumeister:

Baumeister, R.F. (ed) (1999). *The Self in Social Psychology*. Psychology Press.

Baumeister, R.F. (1982). A self-presentational view of social phenomena. *Psychological Bulletin*, **9**, 3-26.

Baumeister, R.F., Vohs, K.D., and Tice, D.M. (2007). The strength model of self-control. *Current Directions in Psychological Science*, **16**(6), 351-5.

Other key texts include Festinger's exposition of social comparison and Taylor and Brown's study of positive illusions:

Festinger, L. (1954). A theory of social comparison processes. *Human Relations*, **7**, 117–40.

Taylor, S.E. and Brown, J.D. (1994). Positive illusions revisited: Separating fact from fiction. *Psychological Bulletin*, **116**, 21–7.

ATTRIBUTION

Although evaluation of the self is often of paramount importance to a person, in navigating the social world, people also are concerned with *explaining* their own behaviour and the behaviour of other people. Take the following situation. As you walk down the street, you pass a man talking to himself audibly, uttering a string of angry swearwords (see Figure 20.7). He could be having a really bad day or he could be exhibiting signs of a bad mood, irritable personality, or perhaps a mental disorder. Whatever we decide about his behaviour we are *attributing* it to something—either an aspect of the man's disposition (ie, his individual nature) or his circumstances.

This process of **attribution** occurs whenever we explain behaviour—ours or someone else's—in terms of causes that refer to characteristics of the person (*dispositional cause*) or to the situation (*situational cause*). Note that disposition is not the same as personality. Whereas 'personality' is generally used specifically to mean individual characteristics that are consistent over time, 'disposition' refers to any factors internal to the individual, both short- and long-term, including personality, mood, and attitudes. So if someone's actions are attributed to his or her mood this is a dispositional attribution even if this mood is very unusual for the individual (Heider, 1958).

Deciding that the swearing man is an irritable person, mentally ill, or in a particularly bad mood all emphasize dispositional causes for his behaviour. Deciding that something annoying must have just happened to him emphasizes situational causes. A second class of attributions categorize a person's actions as either *personal* (intentional) or *impersonal* (unintentional), according to whether we believe the person

> **KEY IDEAS** attribution
> **Attribution** is the process of explaining behaviour in terms of characteristics of the person (whether short- or long-term), the situation, or an interaction between the two; or in terms of whether a behaviour is intentional or unintentional.

FIGURE 20.7 Is this man just having a bad day or does he have an irritable personality? Attribution occurs whenever we explain behaviour in terms of dispositional or situational causes.
Source: iStock.com/Anouchka.

chose to engage in the behaviour or if the behaviour was in some way unintended or not under the person's control (Heider, 1958). This distinction is important because, as Heider believed, we are much more interested in explaining the reasons behind deliberate actions (Malle, 2010).

When people are given enough time, information, and motivation, they often make very accurate attributions about the causes of their own and others' behaviour (E.E. Jones, 1990). However, all of these are often in short supply. The ability to make accurate snap judgements is therefore equally or more important, and although human beings are sometimes good at this, in certain ways we may be biased against accuracy.

Correspondent Inferences

Jones and Davis (1965) developed Heider's ideas, picking up on the idea that we are motivated to try to make judgements about people's disposition based on their actions. Specifically they aimed to identify the circumstances in which we can infer that someone's actions correspond to his or her disposition (ie, make a correspondent inference). Put more simply, they were interested in when we can make a judgement about a person based on his or her behaviour. To Jones and Davis the key to understanding disposition was intention. They identified three criteria that have to be met before we can attribute actions to intentions.

1 The actor must be aware of the consequences of his or her actions. The key to judging disposition is intention; if the actor does not know the consequences, we cannot judge what his or her intentions were.

2 He or she must be capable of performing the action. People only carry out an action if they are capable of it. Failure to do something because we *can't* do it does not provide the same information about intentions as making a choice not to do it.

3 He or she must be acting deliberately. An accident might help us suggest that the actor is careless or distracted but provides no information about his or her *intentions*.

> KEY IDEAS correspondent inferences A correspondent inference takes place when we infer that an action corresponds to the actor's intentions and hence we can make a judgement about his or her disposition. We can only make correspondent inferences when the actor is aware of consequences, capable of acting or not acting and acts deliberately rather than accidentally.

Take the following example. If an industrial accident takes place when someone fails to press an off-button and this results in machinery injuring someone we tend to want to blame him or her. However, we should only make a judgement about this person if: (a) he or she knew not pushing the button would result in injury; (b) he or she could reach and press the button in time; and (c) knowing the consequences and having the means to press the button he or she *chose* not to do so. Only if all these criteria are met should we judge that he or she intended to allow the injury and only then should we look to judge his or her disposition.

A number of factors influence our ability make **correspondent inferences**. Our inferences become less valid where the actor's behaviours are constrained by circumstances, are highly socially desirable, or simply meet the social expectations for the situation. In addition actions that do not have particular effects are not a suitable basis to judge intention upon. So someone humming quietly to himself or herself has no distinctive impact on anyone else and so is irrelevant to forming judgements.

The Covariation Principle

Where Jones and Davis were concerned with attributions based on a single piece of behaviour seen out of context, Kelley (1973) developed a model of attribution based on the idea that much of the time we have additional information available to us. In particular, Kelley identified three sources of evidence.

1 **Consensus** is high when most people would behave in the same way in the same situation. High consensus indicates a situational cause for behaviour whilst low consensus suggests a dispositional cause.

2 **Consistency** is high when the person regularly behaves in the same way when in that kind of situation. High consistency suggests a dispositional cause for the behaviour whereas low consistency suggests situational influence.

3 **Distinctiveness** is high when the person only behaves in a particular way in a particular situation and low when he or she behaves that way regardless of circumstances. Low distinctiveness suggests a dispositional cause and high distinctiveness a situational cause.

To return to our example of the angry man described at the start of this section, if we had additional information about his past behaviour and current circumstances we would not have to rely on correspondent inferences but could make more valid attributions based on how his behaviour covaries with his previous actions and those of others. If, for example, he had just been conned out of his life savings then consensus would be high because most people would respond angrily in that situation. If we knew he was normally a placid, gentle character then distinctiveness would also be high. If we had previously seen him respond differently to injustice or aggression then consistency would be low. These would all be indicators that his behaviour was a normal response to his situation rather than a product of his irritable personality or bad mood. If on the other hand we knew that he was often angry and that on this occasion his response had been triggered by a mild inconvenience—say Waitrose (substitute your local posh supermarket) had run out of ripe avocados—then we would probably make a dispositional attribution.

The Fundamental Attribution Error

It is very difficult to explain to small children (and sometimes adults) that weather presenters are describing and predicting the weather (situation) and are not responsible for it (disposition)! Similarly, children and some adults struggle to accept that an actor portraying a mean or scary character on film might actually be a loving and gentle person off-camera. This effect can be so extreme that actors playing particularly unpleasant characters are occasionally attacked by the public. We seem to be born with a tendency to make the **fundamental attribution error (FAE)**, the tendency to attribute other people's behaviour to their dispositions, while ignoring or underestimating the possibility that behaviour may be influenced by situational factors (L. Ross, 1977).

The FAE (also known as the *correspondence bias*) was demonstrated in a classic study (Jones and Harris, 1967). Undergraduate participants were asked to read a speech supposedly written by a fellow student presenting a view either favouring or opposing a famous world leader of the day. One group was told that the student had chosen his or her position freely. Another group was told that the student had been specifically instructed which position to take. The participants were asked to assess the student's true attitude towards the world leader. Surprisingly, whether the student had supposedly been instructed to take a particular position made little difference in these assessments. If the speech was favourable, the participants assumed that the writer's attitude was favourable regardless of whether or not they were told that the writer had been required to take a particular position. This demonstrated our tendency to make dispositional attributions even when the evidence exists for the importance of the situation. This underlies the major weakness of both

> **KEY IDEAS the fundamental attribution error (FAE)** The FAE is the tendency to attribute other people's behaviour to those individuals' dispositions, while ignoring or underestimating the possibility that situational factors may have played an important or determining role.

correspondent inference and covariation as explanations for attribution. Although we can and do make use of the information highlighted in these models it can be overridden by biases like the FAE.

So why might the fundamental attribution error occur? Gilbert and Malone (1995) made an attempt at analysing the FAE in depth. According to Gilbert and Malone, when an observation of behaviour is made, information about possible situational influences is often invisible to the observer. All we see is a sunny, well-scrubbed, smiling restaurant waiter—we don't see the fact that he just got a letter of offer that morning from his chosen university to study psychology (see Figure 20.8). Thus, we conclude that he is an energetic, fastidious, cheerful person by nature. Had we come in the day before we might very well have seen his usual grumpy and scruffy self.

If an immediate attribution is required, it is easier and makes sense to attribute people's behaviour to internal, dispositional causes. Gilbert and Malone propose that this tendency evolved over time because, although it may sometimes result in error, the survival advantages of being able to make rapid attributions outweigh the downside of sometimes being wrong.

Challenges to the FAE

The first major challenge to the FAE came from cross-cultural researchers who found that the FAE was much weaker and sometimes non-existent when tested among East Asians such as Chinese, Koreans, and Japanese—thus seeding doubt that the FAE was truly universal. If the FAE is not universal, the evolutionary explanation offered by Gilbert and Malone is thrown into doubt (Masuda and Kitayama, 2004).

The next challenge came from a startling article by Sabini et al (2001). This article strongly argued that social psychologists working with the FAE have for several

FIGURE 20.8 The fundamental attribution error is the tendency to attribute other people's behaviour to those individuals' dispositions, while ignoring or underestimating the possibility that situation factors may have played an important or determining role. We assume this waiter is cheerful by nature, when actually he just got a letter of offer from his chosen university!

Source: Robert Kneschke/Shutterstock.

decades misunderstood the implications of their own research. Sabini and his colleagues set out to show that people do *not* have a general tendency to underestimate the importance of situational factors in explaining people's behaviour. Indeed, Sabini and colleagues argue that although dispositions and situations exist, it is not logically possible to separate dispositional from situational causes of behaviour.

Consider Jones and Harris's 'famous world leader' experiment just described. Social psychologists have interpreted this as evidence that people ignore situational factors in explaining others' behaviour (the writer was specifically told which position to take), relying instead on dispositional explanations (the writer really believed in his or her position).

However, Sabini and his colleagues point out that, rather than overestimating the importance of dispositional factors over situational factors, the participants may simply have been comparing the relative importance of *two dispositional factors*: the first being beliefs about the world leader, and the second being the simple desire to avoid embarrassment and save face. According to Sabini and colleagues, the desire to avoid embarrassment is a far more powerful *dispositional* motive among Americans than social psychologists generally suppose (R.S. Miller, 1995). People who write essays taking positions they were instructed to take (but in which they do not believe) may merely be attempting to avoid the embarrassment of confronting the experimenter because they are sensitive to embarrassment. This is a dispositional explanation, not a 'situational' explanation. Thus, the participants in the world leader study may have concluded, perhaps erroneously, that beliefs about the world leader were a more important dispositional factor than the desire to avoid embarrassment (another dispositional factor).

The problem is that every 'situational' cause must simultaneously imply the presence of a 'dispositional' cause and vice versa. Indeed, 'dispositions' and 'situations' are so intricately interwoven that many psychologists believe it is useless to try to separate them (Krueger and Funder, 2004). Consider a normally law-abiding teenage boy who, for one reason or another, ends up hanging out with peers who like to drink, shoplift, and steal cars. The boy finds himself committing these very acts. Have situational factors—the presence of a charismatic peer leader, for example, or pressure to conform to group standards—overwhelmed the boy's dispositional factors of honesty and moral sense? It may be just as logical to say that *some* dispositional factors—the desire to be accepted by peers and avoid rejection—were stronger than *other* dispositional factors, including honesty and moral sense.

It may also be very hard to determine where a 'situation' ends and a 'person' begins. Consider a university lecture in a large lecture theatre. Is this the same 'situation' for the professor and the students? Is it the same situation for a student there to learn about globalization and world economy as for a student there to flirt with the woman who usually sits in the twelfth row aisle seat (Sabini et al, 2001a)? To some extent, the situation is determined by the person and the person by the situation.

Bauman and Skitka (2010) took a different approach and, instead of challenging the logic of the person/situation distinction in the FAE, pointed out that the vast majority of research studies on this cognitive bias were conducted on convenient samples of university students. They examined a nationally representative sample of American adults and found that only about half showed evidence of the FAE at all. Thus, the FAE—if we accept its logic—may only exist as an interesting bias in some individuals, such as college students.

The Actor–Observer Bias

The fundamental attribution error coin has a flip side known as the **actor–observer bias**. It gets its name from the idea that people hold a separate bias depending on whether they are the *actor* in a situation (biased towards situational explanations) or the *observer* (biased towards dispositional explanations, as in the FAE). Actor–observer bias occurs primarily when a person makes an attribution for his or her *own* behaviour. Think about it: when another driver cuts in front of you, he or she is a 'drunken pig' or a 'menace on the road', but when you do the same thing to someone else, you're just late for your appointment. According to social psychologists working with the actor–observer bias, in judging our own behaviour we tend to be biased in favour of situational attributions because we are acutely aware of the many ways that circumstances alter our behaviour (Jones and Nisbett, 1971).

However, as with FAE, the importance of the actor–observer bias has been challenged in recent years (Malle et al, 2007). In an extensive meta-analysis of decades of research on the actor–observer bias, Malle has shown that this bias is found only inconsistently, and only when certain types of research methods are used— primarily those in which participants must choose between specific situational and dispositional explanations listed on questionnaires rather than being allowed to offer their own freely chosen explanations for their behaviour. Moreover, when the actor–observer bias does appear in these limited circumstances, it generally does so only when people are making attributions for their own *negative* behaviours (recall the 'menace on the road' example). Indeed, when we are attempting to explain our *positive* behaviours, we are all too willing to attribute them to our own marvellous dispositions as part of the self-serving bias described earlier.

READ THIS

The classic references in the area of attribution relate to the main theories:

Heider, F. (1944). Social perception and phenomenal causality. *Psychological Review*, 51(6), 358–74.

Jones, E.E. and Davis, K.E. (1965). From acts to dispositions the attribution process in person perception. In *Advances in Experimental Social Psychology* (Vol 2, pp 219–66). New York: Academic Press.

Kelley, H.H. (1967). Attribution theory in social psychology. In D. Levine (ed), *Nebraska Symposium on Motivation* (Vol 15, pp 192–238). Lincoln, NE: University of Nebraska Press.

For a modern review try this:

Shaver, K.G. (2016). *An Introduction to Attribution Processes.* London: Routledge.

ATTITUDES

A further aspect of cognition that we need to look at in order to really understand the relationship between individual cognition and social interaction is attitudes. An attitude can be defined as 'a summary evaluation of an object of thought' (Vogel and Wanke, 2016, p 2). An 'object of thought' simply means anything we can think about. This can be as concrete as chocolate or as abstract as a musical genre or political ideology. By 'summary evaluation' we mean an overall positive or negative judgement about the object of thought. So we might like chocolate and punk but dislike kale and jazz.

Components of Attitudes

Using terms like 'like' and 'dislike' simplifies the idea of attitudes but these terms are not entirely helpful because we still have to unpick what we mean by them. A distinction between three elements of attitudes first made by Allport (1935) is still widely used today. These attitude components are as follows:

- The **cognitive component** (ie, what we think about something)
- The **affective (emotional) component** (ie, what we feel about it)
- The **conative (behavioural) component** (ie, how we act towards it)

So if we hold anti-racist attitudes (we do) we *think* racism is unfair and unjustifiable, we *feel* disgust and anger towards those showing racist tendencies, and we act in non-discriminatory ways and (hopefully) challenge racism where we see it. This **tripartite model** (shown in Figure 20.9) is generally a helpful tool for thinking about attitudes but don't fall into the trap of thinking that the three components always have a neat fit. How emotive a particular issue is to us personally will vary widely from person to person and subject to subject. So racism might make us really angry, whilst other pressing social issues like climate change might have similar cognitive components but be less emotive. We might choose to go on a protest against racism rather than one against non-renewable energy sources more because it is local and convenient than because of a difference in our cognitions or emotions around those issues. The behavioural component of attitudes is also profoundly affected by the situation, so we might be less inclined to challenge racism when surrounded by a group of large fascists and less likely to protest against non-renewable energy when an oil company is considering setting up in our town and creating much-needed jobs.

Attitude Strength

The most obvious way in which our attitudes vary is in their emotional intensity or **valence** (Bassili, 2018). Some things arouse much stronger emotional responses than others. However, there is more to **attitude strength** than simply their valence.

> **KEY IDEAS** the tripartite model of attitudes The **tripartite model** is Allport's model of attitudes as having three components; the **cognitive (thinking) component**, the **affective (emotional) component**, and the **conative (behavioural) component**. According to this model we can think of attitudes as comprising opinions, emotional responses, and behaviours.

> **KEY IDEAS** attitude strength The term **attitude strength** is on one level self-explanatory—how strongly we hold an attitude. However, various factors affect attitude strength including its **valence**, meaning the intensiveness of its positivity or negativity, **expertise**—how much we know about the subject, and **accessibility**—how automatically we respond to something based on our attitude.

FIGURE 20.9 **The tripartite model of attitudes. Our attitudes about a particular issue include our thoughts about it, how we feel about it, and how we act towards it.**
Source: iStock.com/PabloMendo.

Attitude strength can also be based on cognitive factors such as **expertise**. So an environmental scientist who knows a lot more about the effects of non-renewables on climate change and the impact of climate change on the environment is likely to have stronger pro-renewables attitudes.

A further component of attitude strength is **accessibility**. This is the speed and automaticity with which an attitude comes to mind when we encounter something. It seems that some attitudes are evoked faster and more automatically than others, meaning we can have more than one response to the same object or situation. So we might initially think 'yum' in response to chocolate but then think about its fattening qualities! Similarly we might momentarily respond positively to a sexually provocative image before deciding that it objectifies the pictured sex and adopting a negative attitude towards it.

THINKING PRACTICALLY

Identify the cognitive, affective, and behavioural components of your attitudes towards the following:

1 Conservative politics

2 Dance music

3 Roast potatoes

Now compare your attitudes to these in terms of their valence, expertise, and accessibility.

Functions of Attitudes

So we know something about what attitudes *are*. Perhaps the next logical question is *why* do we have them? Broadly there are two categories of attitude function, one more basic and the other concerning 'higher' psychological needs.

Utilitarian functions

Attitudes make the world safer and easier to understand. Having an automatic good-bad response to everything we encounter allows us to make quick approach-avoidance choices that protect us from dangerous situations—and also situations that are likely to be unenjoyable. Say we have a choice of visiting two art exhibitions featuring very different artistic genres; having a pre-existing attitude to these genres allows us to make a quick and fairly valid choice about which we would be more likely to enjoy (Blascovich et al, 1993).

Symbolic functions

Attitudes also serve more complex psychological needs such as social identity. So Apple users typically have a particularly strong positive attitude to Apple products, not simply so that they can quickly identify and choose them, but also because they gain self-esteem from being an Apple user (Homburg, Wieseker, and Hoyer, 2009). One does not simply *use* Apple products, one tends to *be* an *Apple user*. Apple users are widely seen as people of wealth, success, good taste, and sophisticated understanding of ICT, hence identifying oneself as an Apple user and **identity signalling** by public use of Apple products carries with it benefits to self-esteem (Giroux and Grohmann, 2016).

Other social categories like 'feminist' or 'socialist' that are based on attitudes to social issues also identify us as 'on the side of the angels' and similarly convey status and self-esteem. They may also solidify our membership of social groups. Whenever we express an attitude by sharing a political meme on social media and receive likes we are both reinforcing our membership of the social category of the politics expressed and receiving social rewards for expressing the correct attitudes, boosting our self-esteem (Burrow and Rainone, 2017). It also appears that **virtue signalling** by expressing socially appropriate attitudes can boost status within a group (Massey-Abernathy and Haseltine, 2018).

Attitudes and Behaviour

Sometimes the comparisons we make for self-evaluation are not between ourselves and other people, but between our attitudes and our behaviour. Much of the time the relationship between the cognitive and affective components to our attitudes and our behaviours is straightforward. We don't gamble (behavioural) because we know the odds in gambling are stacked outrageously in favour of the house (cognitive) and this annoys us (affective). We believe that drinking **alcohol** in moderation has health benefits (cognitive) and we enjoy the physical and psychological effects (affective) so we drink (behavioural).

Sometimes, however, attitudes and behaviour (or to put it another way, the cognitive, emotional, and behavioural components of our attitudes) clash. Social comparison theorist Leon Festinger (1957) proposed an influential theory to highlight the sort of tension or anxiety people often feel when their freely chosen behaviour contradicts their attitudes in some way. He called this uncomfortable state **cognitive dissonance** because a person's behaviour and attitudes are not in harmony.

According to cognitive dissonance theory, for these uncomfortable feelings to resolve, something has to give:

a) the attitude has to change, or

b) the behaviour has to cease, or

c) beliefs about the discrepancy between them have to change.

For example, you might have a negative attitude towards those with different politics to yourself and behave by either avoiding or arguing with such people. You then meet someone whose views are radically opposed to your own and find them to be warm and gracious in personality—and you find yourself being friendly. You are likely to experience cognitive dissonance and resolve it by either changing your attitude towards people with those politics, stop being friendly, or change your beliefs about the need to avoid or argue with those with whom you disagree politically.

Although not all experiences of discrepancy between attitude and behaviour result in attempts to resolve cognitive dissonance (Cooper and Fazio, 1984), the theory has continued to provide a rich source of hypotheses for social psychology research (Harmon-Jones and Harmon-Jones, 2007).

❯ KEY IDEAS identity signalling and virtue signalling These are related ideas that have become important in the recent social-psychological research into social media use. **Identity signalling** involves revealing membership of social groups; for example, through social media posts or more concrete media like badges and logos. **Virtue signalling** involves displaying pro-social attitudes, again through online posts or traditional media.

❯ KEY IDEAS cognitive dissonance **Cognitive dissonance** is the anxiety or tension that arises when people behave in ways that run contrary to their attitudes. People may resolve cognitive dissonance by changing their attitudes to bring them in line with their behaviour, ceasing the behaviour, or changing their beliefs about the discrepancy between their attitudes and behaviour.

IN REVIEW

THE SELF IN SOCIAL CONTEXT

• How we perceive ourselves exerts an influence on our social behaviour. Our self-perceptions are not accurate but are shaped by self-defence.

We are, for example, prone to self-serving bias, making judgements that we overestimate our contributions to tasks, overestimate our positive attributes, and take credit for successes but make excuses for our failures.

We also tend to experience positive illusions in the form of uncritically positive self-views, illusions of control, and unrealistic optimism.

We make social comparisons for a number of reasons, including self-evaluation, self-enhancement, and self-defence.

CHANGING THE SELF

Self-evaluation can lead us to wish to engage in a process of self-change, often involving development of self-regulation.

An important aspect of self-regulation is self-control. Self-control means resistance to an impulse to satisfy an immediate goal or need.

Studies like Mischel's 'marshmallow' experiments have demonstrated that even young children have some capacity for self-control, and that self-control predicts positive outcomes.

Baumeister has proposed a 'strength' model of self-control, in which self-control functions like muscular strength, becoming fatigued after exertion and developing with practice.

ATTRIBUTION

Another important aspect of social cognition involves explaining others'—and on occasion our own—actions. This is called attribution. The most basic distinction is between attributing actions to the situation and to the disposition of the actor.

Where we have only access to a single incident we can make use of correspondent inferences to judge the actor's intentions. This makes use of what we know about awareness of consequences, ability to carry out the action, and the deliberate nature of the action.

Where we have further information about how the individual usually behaves in similar and different situations and about how others tend to behave in the situation we can use covariation to make attributions.

Where someone consistently displays a behaviour over time and in different situations and where this differs from the behaviour typical of others we are more likely to make dispositional attributions.

There is some evidence for the fundamental attribution error—the idea that we tend to overestimate the importance of disposition as opposed to the situation. However, this is controversial and there is evidence to suggest that the reverse is true when making attributions about our own actions.

ATTITUDES

Attitudes can be described as 'summary evaluations' of both concrete and abstract concepts. Attitudes have cognitive, emotional, and behavioural aspects.

Attitudes vary in strength. Attitude strength is affected by its emotional intensity, expertise in the subject of the attitude, and by its accessibility, how fast and automatically it is activated.

Attitudes serve a range of psychological purposes. Utilitarian functions are concerned with simplifying responses to the world and keeping the person safe. Symbolic functions serve more complex needs like social identity and signalling of group membership and virtues.

Sometimes attitudes correspond closely with our actions. However, they do not always do so and this can result in cognitive dissonance, which can be resolved by changing the attitude, changing the behaviour, or changing beliefs about the behaviour that corresponds to the attitude.

TEST YOURSELF

1 People generally rate themselves more positively than do others. True ☐ False ☐

2 Self-control involves all the ways in which we self-monitor and exert impulse control. True ☐ False ☐

3 We are more likely to attribute our own behaviour to dispositional factors. True ☐ False ☐

4 Virtue signalling means publicly signalling pro-social attitudes. True ☐ False ☐

5 Which of the following is not an example of self-serving bias?

   a) Overestimating own contributions

   b) Overestimating own weaknesses

   c) Overestimating own positive attributes

   d) Attributing successes to own attributes

6 Which of the following treats was used in the original 'marshmallow' study?

   a) Pretzels

   b) Marshmallows

   c) Cake

   d) Chocolate

7 Attributing an action to deliberate choice is which type of attribution

   a) Internal

   b) External

   c) Personal

   d) Impersonal

8 Which of the following is **not** used in the covariation process of attribution?

   a) Consistency

   b) Distinctiveness

   c) Consensus

   d) Capability

9 Explain challenges to the fundamental attribution error.

10 Explain one example of cognitive dissonance.

 Visit the online resources that accompany this book: www.oup.com/uk/jarvis–okami1e

CHAPTER 21

SOCIAL INFLUENCE AND ATTRACTION

LEARNING OUTCOMES

By the end of this chapter you should be able to:

- Evaluate classic and contemporary research into social facilitation and inhibition
- Discuss research into conformity with particular regard to the classic work of Solomon Asch
- Distinguish between informational and normative influence and consider the role of informational conformity on extremism and social division
- Assess the risks posed to decision-makers by the phenomenon of groupthink
- Describe and evaluate research into destructive obedience including the classic studies of Stanley Milgram
- Critically consider our understanding of destructive obedience in the light of modern re-analysis and replication of destructive obedience research including that concerning individual differences
- Appreciate the importance of social identity and social identity theory in European social psychology
- Reinterpret findings of classic studies in social psychology such as those of Asch and Milgram in the light of social identity theory
- Understand the role of positive assortment, propinquity, attractiveness, and self-presentation in attractiveness
- Discuss different approaches to love and relationship formation

We are very much a social species. We are constantly aware of and influenced by other people and much of our waking attention is focused on those around us and the quality of our relationships with other people. 'This is evidenced by the hours most of us spend on social media and the strong association between time spent with colleagues on social media and work satisfaction' (Robertson and Kee, 2017). As we established in Chapter 11, the desire for human attachments is a fundamental human motivator (Leary and Baumeister, 2017), and social isolation is strongly associated with problems in physical and mental health, with one study estimating that lack of social contact equates to smoking 15 cigarettes per day in its detrimental influence on health (Holt-Lunstad, 2010).

It is tempting to uncritically accept catchy headline figures like that produced by Holt-Lunstad about the equivalence of social isolation and a 15 cigarette-a-day habit. However, as psychologists we don't have that luxury. If you are up for a challenge go to the Holt-Lunstad paper and examine the methodology. Form your own view about the validity of the 15-a-day figure. HINT: this is not a trick question—we don't necessarily have a strong view—it is about what *you* think!

> KEY IDEAS social facilitation and the iPhone effect **Social facilitation** takes place when performance is enhanced by the presence of other people. This includes the effects of mere presence of others as well as competition and cooperation. Social facilitation does not necessarily require physical presence, thus the presence of a mobile phone enhances the quality of social interaction (the **iPhone effect**).

SOCIAL FACILITATION AND INHIBITION

Perhaps the simplest influence other people have on us is exerted by their presence. Much of the time we perform tasks more effectively in the presence of others. As far back as the 1890s Norman Triplett noticed that speed-cyclists tended to clock faster times when together than when cycling alone. He carried out a famous experiment in which children wound up a fishing reel faster in pairs than alone Triplett, 1898). This phenomenon of **social facilitation** affects many behaviours. For example, we eat more in groups than alone and more in larger than smaller groups Herman, 2016). Performance in a range of sport and exercise activities is better in groups than alone (Irwin, Kerr, and Feltz, 2012; see Figure 21.1).

THINKING CRITICALLY

Triplett's experiment is probably the first ever social psychology experiment and was in some ways a very clever piece of research. Accordingly it is often discussed uncritically in introductory psychology. However, Triplett did not have access to inferential statistics as they had not been developed at the time. When Strube (2005) subjected Triplett's raw data to modern analysis, differences between solo and group performances did not emerge as statistically significant. Explain what is meant by this and why it is important.

FIGURE 21.1 Social facilitation. We perform tasks better in the presence of others. For example, we cycle faster when cycling with others than when we cycle alone, as Norman Triplett noticed in the 1890s, leading to what was probably the first social psychology experiment.
Source: iStock.com/jgcoutts.

Interestingly it appears that 'presence' does not necessarily mean *physical* presence. Marker and Staianer (2015) found that both cooperation and competition with others online improved performance in exergaming, computer-based aerobic physical exercise. Misra et al (2014) demonstrated that the quality of conversation between **dyads** was greater when a mobile device was visible on a table. This has become known as the **iPhone effect**.

THINKING CREATIVELY

The iPhone effect is a relatively new idea in social psychology and the body of research into it is quite small. Formulate a hypothesis concerned with the iPhone effect. Your hypothesis might, for example, be concerned with electronic devices other than iPhones or with the range of activities on which performance is enhanced by the presence of a mobile device.

> **KEY IDEAS** social inhibition
Social inhibition takes place when we are less likely to engage in a social behaviour in the presence of others. This affects helping behaviour, emotional expression, and disapproved-of behaviours. These may have different explanations; for example, diffusion of responsibility may be important in inhibiting helping behaviour.

Less well known but also powerful in some cases is the **social inhibition effect**. This is defined as 'the tendency for behaviours that are exhibited when one is alone to be minimized in the presence of others' (McCarty and Karau, 2017, p 165). So helping behaviour, emotional expression, and any behaviour likely to be met with disapproval is subject to social inhibition. A range of factors appear to underlie social inhibition, including evaluation apprehension (worrying about what others will think of us), diffusion of responsibility (we feel less obligated to act when others share the responsibility for doing so), and ambiguity (we worry more about misjudging a situation when others are watching).

CONFORMITY

We often like to think of ourselves as non-conformist, but actually we all tend to modify our behaviours and attitudes in line with the norms of those around us. Solomon Asch (1955) conducted a classic experiment into group **conformity**. We can look in detail at Asch's study in our *Research in focus* feature.

RESEARCH IN FOCUS

Asch, S.E. (1955). Opinions and social pressure. *Scientific* American, **193**, 31–5.

Aim: To test the idea that people would conform to a majority opinion even when that opinion was clearly wrong. This was in the context of previous studies showing the tendency for conformity in ambiguous situations.

Method: Participants were a volunteer sample of 123 male students recruited from four American universities. Each participant was given a limited brief that they were taking part in a psychology experiment. Each individually joined a group of 6–8 young men sitting around a table. These were **confederates**. The group was then told they were taking part in a study of visual perception and given a task in which they matched the length of a line with one of

> three options (see Figure 21.2). In each trial each group member answered in turn with the **naive participant** last. In a control condition the confederates always identified the correct line. In the experimental condition the confederates all identified the correct line in the first two trials then all identified an incorrect line in the third. Each participant took part in 18 trials. The experimental condition contained a number of variations including different group size, presence of a truthful confederate, and an initially truthful confederate who appeared to conform to the majority during the procedure.

Results: In the control condition participants correctly identified the line 98% of the time. In the standard experimental condition accuracy fell to 63.2%. This means that participants conformed over a third of the time. Rates of conformity dropped when the group was very small. In the presence of the truthful confederate 75% responded correctly. The presence of a gradually conforming confederate had no effect on the outcomes of the standard experimental condition.

Conclusion: The majority of people do not conform to blatantly incorrect opinions; however, a sizable minority do so. This was a source of concern to Asch, who was interested in conformity in the context of the participation of ordinary Germans in the Holocaust. He put it thus: 'That we have found the tendency to conformity in our society so strong that reasonably intelligent and well-meaning young people are willing to call white black is a matter of concern' (1955, p 5).

MASTER YOUR METHODOLOGY

1 The experiment was carried out in a university seminar room, which can be seen as a natural environment for university students. Explain why the study can be said to have good ecological validity and why this is important.

2 Often, carrying out experiments in natural surroundings can lead to a loss of experimental control. Explain why that may not be a serious issue in this study.

3 Although it can be said to have a good balance of ecological validity and experimental control, Asch's procedure can be said to lack mundane realism. Explain what is meant by mundane realism and why it is important.

THINKING CRITICALLY

Look back to our critical thinking toolkit (Chapter 1). What strengths and weaknesses can you see in relation to this study?

Under what sorts of circumstances will people blindly follow group direction? In the mid-twentieth century, Deutsch and Gerard (1955) identified two types of motivation and influence to conform: *informational* and *normative*. Informational motivations and influences are not based on the fear of looking foolish or wanting to be liked, but rather on a rational desire to seek realistic information about some situation from the group and adjust behaviour accordingly. As an example, suppose you were sitting in a cinema enjoying a film along with 100 or more other people. If you were to smell smoke, observe the rest of the audience heading for an exit,

> **KEY IDEAS** confederates and naive participants Some social psychology experiments involve placing participants in social situations where other people know what is happening but they do not. Participants who do not know what is taking place are called **naive participants**. Others present who do know and are in on the details of the experiment are called **confederates**.

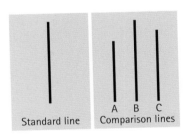

FIGURE 21.2 Which of the three lines on the right is approximately the same length as that standard line? If you choose B, you'd be (more or less obviously) correct. But what do you think it would take to get you to answer 'A'? Five shots of tequila and misplacement of your contact lenses? In fact, all that has been necessary for thousands of intelligent, sober university students to answer 'A' is the mere fact that *all the other people around them* answer 'A'. They have been willing to lie about their beliefs, even when those beliefs are obviously correct, simply to avoid embarrassment and loss of face (Sabini et al, 2001a).

> **KEY IDEAS** conformity

Conformity is the tendency of people to bring their behaviour, attitudes, and/or beliefs in line with group norms and pressures. The motivation to conform may be informational, based on a rational desire to seek realistic information of some situation from a group; or the motivation may be normative, based on a person's desire to obtain approval from the group or avoid embarrassment.

and decide to follow along after them, you would be experiencing the informational motivation to conform. On the other hand, normative motivations and influences reflect the desire to obtain approval from the group or avoid embarrassment—as in the case of participants in the Asch experiment who conformed to an obviously incorrect group opinion.

Normative influence to conform is particularly powerful. It does not merely cause people to say things they know are false. It can cause people to use drugs, refuse to offer aid to strangers in need, or commit cruel acts in times of war. It also often goes undetected by the person being influenced (Nolan et al, 2008). Nolan and her colleagues conducted two studies which demonstrated that people are often unaware of normative influences in their lives. In their first study, Nolan and colleagues surveyed a randomly selected group of Californians about their energy conservation activities and reasons for conserving energy. The most important reasons given by survey respondents for their own motivations to conserve energy were to 'benefit society' and 'protect the environment'. The least important reason given was 'because other people are doing it'.

However, Nolan also asked respondents whether they agreed with various statements about saving energy: 'Does it benefit society?', 'Does it protect the environment?', 'Are other Californians doing it?', and so forth. These answers were then correlated with the survey respondents' *actual* self-reported conservation efforts (eg, turning off electric lights in the home when not in use, conservative use of air conditioners). The best predictor of a person's actual self-reported conservation efforts was how strongly he or she believed that other people were doing it! As the correlation between 'other people doing it' and energy conservation behaviour was twice as strong as that for the next strongest pairing ('benefit to society').

In the second of their two studies, Nolan and her colleagues went beyond correlations and used an experimental design to test the importance of unconscious normative influence. They randomly divided a sample of California households into four groups and used different sorts of appeals to each group to conserve energy, conveyed in flyers attached to their doors. In three of the groups they used appeals such as saving money, benefiting society, and protecting the environment. For the fourth group, they simply conveyed the information that the majority of the respondent's neighbours were conserving energy. (A fifth, the control group, received neutral information about how to conserve energy.) Those who received the 'your neighbours are all doing it' flyer consumed the least energy in the short term and long term.

Modern studies support the existence of informational as well as normative influence (ie, that people are influenced in their beliefs by the beliefs of those around them). Informational influence is probably most important where there is no obviously correct opinion. You may have watched shows involving judgements by a panel of judges. Examples include *The X Factor* and *Strictly Come Dancing*. Ever wondered how strongly each judge is influenced by the views the others have expressed? Boen et al (2006) may provide some answers. Twenty-seven participant judges were split into panels of up to five and asked to assess 30 videotaped skipping performances. In an experimental condition the judges knew about each other's judgements. In a control condition they could not hear each other's scores. When participants were aware of each others' judgements there was significantly more agreement, suggesting that they were influenced by the information in others' judgements.

WHAT'S HOT? INFORMATIONAL INFLUENCE ON SOCIAL MEDIA: THE ECHO CHAMBER EFFECT

Many of the topics discussed on social media—politics, religion, conspiracy theories, and the like—are subject to strong and varied opinion. They are in other words ambiguous, and it should therefore come as no surprise that they are subject to informational influence. So far so good, but what happens when a blend of self-selection of 'friendly' sources (**congeniality bias**) and social media algorithms that filter out countering views and create **filter bubbles** mean that we are overwhelmingly exposed to opinions we already agree with? This is the **echo chamber effect** and it is widely believed to contribute to social division and political extremism as we increasingly conform to attitudes and beliefs of those in our social networks (Iyengar and Hahn, 2009). The echo chamber effect was documented in respect of conventional online mass media in the early 2000s (Sunstein, 2001), but has been the subject of increased concern in the age of social media (Flaxman, Goel, and Rao, 2016).

There is mixed evidence to support the idea that social media exposes people to echo chambers. Flaxman, Goel, and Rao (2016) tracked the browsing histories of 50,000 Americans using *Bing* and *Internet Explorer* and found that people generally favoured news sources that matched their own political ideology. However, they also found that search engines offered people the chance to explore different views, thus the echo chamber effect was only partially supported. Stronger support for the existence of echo chambers comes from studies looking at clustering of friendship groups around similar ideologies. In one study Bakshy, Messing, and Adamic (2015) examined the politics of ten million American Facebook users and found that users who described their politics on their profile had an average of around 80% of friends with similar views; 76% of the news stories shared by liberals and 65% of those shared by conservatives were aligned with their politics. Thus friends were largely though not entirely exposed to news that supported their views.

> **KEY IDEAS** the echo chamber effect, congeniality bias, and filter bubbles The **echo chamber effect** takes place when we are exposed to a biased selection of opinions that echo our own, reinforcing our views and perhaps making them more extreme. Two main factors contribute to the effect: **congeniality bias** is our tendency to select sources of information that appear friendly because they express views like our own. **Filter bubbles** result when social media algorithms eliminate opinions different from our own and give us the impression that our views are non-controversial.

THINKING CRITICALLY

The Flaxman, Goel, and Rao study followed American Internet users who favoured the *Internet Explorer* browser and used the *Bing* search engine. Explain why generalizability might be a serious problem for this study.

A particularly worrying aspect of the informational influence of social media concerns the spread of fake news. Fake news is spread significantly faster via social media than by other news sources (Silverman, 2016) thus once planted in the social media environment it can exert disproportionate influence on users. Allcott and Gentzkow (2017) estimated that pro-Trump fake news stories were shared 38 million times and read 760 million times in the run-up to the 2016 American election, possibly exerting a significant influence on voters.

And therein lies the biggest problem with echo chamber research. It is straightforward to demonstrate that people cluster into groups that agree with one another and share congruent news stories and posts with each other. It is much less straightforward to uncover the extent to which all this influences people to conform to the attitudes and behaviours of their group, given that they already expressed similar attitudes when they affiliated with their friendship and political networks. There is evidence consistent with such effects; for example, showing that both Brexit and the Trump election victory were predicted by social media trends but not by polls or reputable news coverage (El-Bermawy, 2016), but this is not strong evidence.

THINKING CRITICALLY

In an ideal world every question psychologists would like to answer could be addressed by controlled experiments that would provide clear causal links between independent and dependent variables. In reality, however, many of the most important questions cannot be addressed in this way and require some imagination when it comes to what evidence we bring to bear. A good example of this is the hypothesis that social media echo chambers exert an informational influence on attitudes and behaviour. The kind of evidence that appears to support this hypothesis is based on retrospective analysis of one-off events, the outcomes of which are affected by many variables. So is this good science? You'll have to make your own mind up, but certainly be cautious about uncritically accepting ideas like echo chambers without examining the evidence base.

Groupthink: Conformity in Group Decision-Making

> **KEY IDEAS** groupthink
> **Groupthink** is a way of thinking and behaving in groups whereby decisions are made not as a result of rational considerations and weighing of evidence, but as a result of group members not wanting to adversely affect group morale, make waves, or appear disloyal to leaders. The frequent end result of groupthink is the adoption of highly flawed plans and policies.

A particularly dangerous type of conformity behaviour is known as **groupthink** (Janis, 1989, 2007). Irving Janis originally borrowed this term from the George Orwell novel *1984* to describe situations where counterproductive or even disastrous and tragic group decisions are made not from rational considerations but as a result of group members not wanting to adversely affect group morale, make waves, or appear disloyal to the group leader.

The term *groupthink* was first applied in social psychology to the grossly flawed plan authorized by President John F. Kennedy and the CIA in 1961 to destroy Fidel Castro's newly formed communist government by invading Cuba at the Bay of Pigs with a ragtag army of Cuban exiles (see Figure 21.3). Because of the influence of groupthink, the possible consequences of this invasion were not carefully considered. Those who had previously fulfilled the important role of 'devil's advocate' in Kennedy's cabinet—challenging assumptions to determine their soundness or

FIGURE 21.3 **Groupthink.** The term was first applied in social psychology to the grossly flawed plan authorized by President John F. Kennedy and the CIA for the Bay of Pigs invasion, a catastrophic failure due to challengers being silenced.

Source: World History Archive/Alamy Stock Photo.

considering how a plan might fail as well as how it might succeed—were silenced by unspoken pressure to support the president and maintain morale. The result was catastrophe for all involved—the invaders were easily defeated, hundreds of people lost their lives, and the reputation of the United States suffered.

Groupthink can be discerned lurking behind numerous other historical decisions that have led to fiascos. The decision to invade Iraq in 2003 by the Bush administration and the Blair government may be seen as an example of groupthink in a couple of ways. First, decision-makers apparently grossly overestimated the probability that former Iraqi dictator Saddam Hussein was hiding arsenals of 'weapons of mass destruction'. Second, they mistakenly anticipated that Western forces would be greeted with open arms by most Iraqi citizens on the ground (Mackenzie, 2006). Instead, no such weapons were found, and most Iraqis resented the presence of US troops. Table 21.1 summarizes common symptoms of groupthink.

Groupthink breeds and is fed by overconfidence, and effective leaders recognize the dangers of such unrealistic group decision-making. Following the Bay of Pigs, President Kennedy instituted a series of 'checks and balances' to insure that decision-making would be more productive in the future. Based on these policies, Janis (1989) proposed a number of safeguards against groupthink, including the use of impartial, outside advisors; leaders refraining from taking a strong stand on a given issue at the outset of discussions; and the assigning to certain individuals the role of 'devil's advocate' to identify potential problems with a given proposal.

READ THIS

There's nothing like going back to the original material—like Asch's research:

Asch, S.E. (1955). Opinions and social pressure. *Scientific American*, **193**, 31–5.

For a more contemporary review of conformity research you could start with this:

Jetten, J. and Hornsey, M.J. (2015). The line between conformity and resistance. *The Psychologist*, **28**, 72–5.

For a good review of groupthink research try this:

Rose, J.D. (2011). Diverse perspectives on the groupthink theory–a literary review. *Emerging Leadership Journeys*, **4**, 37–57.

TABLE 21.1 **Six symptoms of groupthink**

Symptom	Description
Collective rationalization	Everyone in the group shares the same faulty explanations for why a particular strategy or tactic is necessary, or why an apparent 'red flag' warning of weakness in a plan should be ignored.
Pressure to conform	There is spoken or unspoken pressure among members to agree to a particular plan—often the plan supported by the leader.
Illusion of invulnerability	The possibility that a plan may fail is not considered.
Illusion of moral correctness	The group never questions the rightness of its actions (eg, 'God is on our side').
Bias towards out-group members	Those on the outside of the group who disagree or who may be outright enemies are underestimated in strength or intelligence, considered weak, 'evil', or otherwise inferior.
Illusion of unanimous consensus	Because of pressure to conform, there may appear to be unanimous consensus at meetings—while individual members may still harbour many private doubts and disagreements.

OBEDIENCE

❯ KEY IDEAS destructive obedience Obedience involves following a direct order. This is distinct from conforming to the actions of a group and can be distinguished from compliance to requests or suggestions.
Destructive obedience means to follow orders to deliberately harm another person or people.

We are taught at school to believe that obedience is a good thing. Indeed it is hard to imagine that humans could live together in large, complex societies without some obedience to those in authority. You might then be surprised to find that social psychologists have focused on obedience as a *bad* thing. Of course, we are not encouraging you to tell your tutor to get lost next time you are asked to complete an essay or attend a practical session! We are talking about the phenomenon of **destructive obedience**, in which people obey orders to harm others.

In 2004 a man describing himself as 'Officer Scott' called a McDonalds restaurant and ordered staff to detain and strip-search an employee suspected of theft as the police had no one available to attend. The assistant manager called her fiancé who proceeded to obey telephone orders from 'Officer Scott' to physically and sexually assault the victim. The victim suffered post-traumatic stress and depression and the 'prank' caller was sentenced to five years in jail. What is remarkable here is the degree of obedience to a stranger whose orders violated both moral codes and workplace rules. The incident has since been depicted in the 2012 film *Compliance*.

Following the unprecedented destructive obedience that facilitated the Holocaust social psychologists began to investigate the phenomenon of destructive obedience. At the same time as Nazi war criminal Adolph Eichmann was on trial psychologist Stanley Milgram (1961) carried out the first of a series of studies that demonstrated destructive obedience in the laboratory. We can look in detail at Milgram's initial study in our *Research in focus* feature.

RESEARCH IN FOCUS

Milgram, S. (1963). Behavioural study of obedience. *Journal of Abnormal and Social Psychology*, **67**, 371–8.

Aim: To test the phenomenon of destructive obedience under controlled conditions. Specifically to investigate people's willingness to inflict painful and dangerous electric shocks on a helpless stranger when ordered to do so by an experimenter.

Method: 40 male volunteers aged 20–50 took part in the procedure. They were paid $4.50 for participating. On arriving at Yale University they were introduced to a confederate who they believed to be a fellow participant. They were briefed that they would be taking part in an experiment on the effect of motivation on learning. The confederate took the role of learner and the real participant the teacher. The learner was strapped down and connected to a shock machine, which was demonstrated by giving the participant a mildly painful shock (see Figure 21.4). The learner was positioned behind a screen in the same room so that the teacher could hear but not see him (see Figure 21.5). The teacher then tested the learner on their learning of a set of word pairs. Each time the learner got an item wrong the teacher's task was to administer a shock. Shocks apparently increased by 15 V each time, up to a maximum of 450 V, although in fact the learner did not receive real shocks. The learner responded to the 'shocks' with shouts of pain and pleas to 'get me out of here'. These responses were pre-recorded so that each participant would have exactly the same experience. Following the complaint that he had a bad heart the learner went silent at 300 V. The experimenter then ordered the participants to continue administering the shocks. If participants protested at this they received a series of verbal prods to encourage them. When they ceased to obey or the maximum shock level was reached the participants were debriefed and introduced to the confederate. The dependent variable was the maximum level of shock administered. Qualitative data was also gathered in the form of what participants said and observations of their non-verbal behaviour.

Results: 100% of participants gave at least 300 V and 65% gave the full 450 V. Participants showed signs of stress: sweating, trembling, crying, or laughing nervously. However, this quickly improved once they had made the decision to disobey.

Conclusions: People are surprisingly obedient to destructive orders, obeying orders from a figure in authority even when this clearly violated their moral codes. This means that ordinary people are capable of committing atrocities under the influence of authority. However, violating their moral code puts people under severe stress—Milgram later called this *moral strain*. Participants obeyed not through lack of morality but because they perceived little alternative.

MASTER YOUR METHODOLOGY

1 Milgram's study collected both quantitative and qualitative data. Explain why the inclusion of qualitative data was important to Milgram's conclusions.

2 Milgram described his study as an experiment; however, most contemporary psychologists do not. Explain the technical features of an experiment and why Milgram's study fails to conform to them.

3 Milgram took care to make features of his procedure correspond to those of real-life situations in which atrocities take place. For example, the experimenter wore a lab coat to simulate the uniform often worn by authority figures. The ascending level of shocks represented the gradual increase in brutality of real-life destructive orders. Assess how successful these measures were at making the procedure life-like.

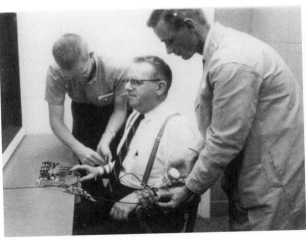 

FIGURE 21.4 AND FIGURE 21.5 Milgram's behavioural study of obedience. These photos show the 'learner' (a confederate) being strapped in the chair and wired to electrodes (left) and a 'teacher' (a participant) during the experiment.

Source: From the film Obedience © 1968 by Stanley Milgram, copyright renewed 1993 by Alexandra Milgram and distributed by Alexander Street Press.

THINKING PRACTICALLY

C.P. Snow (1961) said that 'more hideous crimes have been committed in the name of obedience than have ever been committed in the name of rebellion'. Explain and evaluate this statement making use of the concept of destructive obedience.

Milgram wanted to know under what circumstances seemingly ordinary people could be persuaded by authority figures to injure or even torture other human beings. Coming after revelations of the atrocities of Nazi Germany during World War II and Stalin's Soviet Union of the 1930s and 1940s, these questions seemed particularly important. Important questions as these are, not everyone was entirely pleased with Milgram for his study. Although Milgram and his study are now held in very high esteem by many, and his findings are among the most widely discussed in all of psychology (Blass, 2009), it may surprise you to learn that this research almost ruined Milgram's career—and it also helped to trigger major changes in ethical guidelines for psychologists. Much can be—and has been—said and argued about the Milgram studies. The ethics of the studies and the reasons for the high rates of obedience Milgram found have been debated for more than 50 years.

THINKING CRITICALLY

Milgram started his studies before there were clear and unambiguous sets of ethical guidelines as there are now. However, it is interesting to see how his procedure would have fared against modern criteria. Using the British Psychological Society's Code of Ethical Conduct, https://www.bps.org.uk/news-and-policy/bps-code-ethics-and-conduct and the Code of Human Research Ethics, www.bps.org.uk/sites/bps.org.uk/files/Policy%20-%20Files/BPS%20Code%20of%20Human%20Research%20Ethics.pdf assess the ethics of Milgram's research.

Some critics have argued that participants in Milgram's study, rather than blindly following the orders of someone *in* authority (the experimenter), may simply have trusted that the experimenter, in the original studies purportedly a Yale University professor, was *an* authority—in other words, an *expert*. (In the days of the Milgram studies, a university professor—particularly at a school such as Yale University—was likely to be accorded a degree of unquestioned respect greater than that which exists today.) The Milgram participants may have believed his claims that the 'learner' would not be seriously harmed (Morelli, 1983).

Perhaps more important, although it is tempting to draw parallels between the behaviour of the participants in Milgram's studies and that of wartime criminals and perpetrators of genocide, to some degree these parallels rely primarily on the drama inherent in the Milgram studies and less on an accurate reading of history (Waller, 2007). Specifically, James Waller (2007, pp 111–12) points out four primary ways in which the conditions of the Milgram studies do not correspond to the actualities of mass killing and genocide:

1 The participants in the Milgram studies were assured by a strict but nonetheless apparently benevolent expert that no real harm would befall the 'learner'. The reverse is generally the case in genocide and mass killing. Perpetrators are well

aware that they are destroying human life at the behest of a person bent on torturing, maiming, and killing.

2 Milgram found that if participants were given an excuse to avoid obeying the experimenter (eg, if the experimenter left the room), they would generally avoid administering shocks. Thus, Milgram's participants apparently did not want to cause pain to the 'learner'. Unfortunately, this cannot be said for those who perpetrate genocide and mass killing. For example, while certain individuals carrying out orders to kill and torture Jews during the Nazi holocaust did avoid doing so when the opportunity presented itself, a shocking number enthusiastically committed these atrocities even when conditions would have allowed disobedience to occur. Indeed, for certain of the so-called 'Jew hunts' that occurred late in the war, 'there were so many volunteers that some of them had to be turned away' (Browning, cited by Mastroianni, 2002, p 167; Goldenhagen, 1996).

3 Milgram's participants demonstrated serious mental conflict sometimes approaching real anguish when delivering the shocks. This contrasts with the outright sadism and enjoyment of killing and torturing that are often (but, of course, not always) demonstrated by perpetrators of genocide and wartime atrocities.

4 The Milgram studies lasted approximately one hour, whereas acts of genocide and wartime atrocity occur time and again, sometimes lasting over a period of years. Thus, Milgram's participants had little time to reflect on their situation, whereas those perpetrating genocide and atrocity often have months or years.

To some degree, Milgram was aware of the limits of comparing his findings with conditions of actual genocide. He raised the question, 'Is the obedience observed in the laboratory comparable to that seen in Nazi Germany?' and answered, 'Is a match flame comparable to the Chicago fire of 1898?' (Milgram, 1974, p 175). Nonetheless, in spite of their limitations, the Milgram studies have shown clearly that individuals are willing to inflict severe, potentially dangerous pain on complete strangers at the request of an expert or authority figure (Waller, 2007).

Variations on the Basic Procedure

Following the publication of his classic study Milgram looked at the effect of altering various aspects of the experimental situation. Removing the trappings of legitimate authority reduced obedience. For example, changing the experimenter's lab coat for casual clothes dropped obedience to 20% whilst changing the venue to a run-down office block reduced it to 47.5%. The degree of participants' involvement in giving the shocks also made a substantial difference; when they had to force the learner's hand on to the shock plate obedience dropped to 30%; however, it rose to 90% when they merely had to pass on the order to a third party. The physical presence of others had the greatest impact. When two confederates refused to obey obedience dropped to 10%, whilst when the experimenter was in another room it dropped to 20%.

Haslam, Loughnan, and Perry (2014) have combined and re-analysed the data from 21 of Milgram's 23 conditions. Obedience was greater when the learner appeared more vulnerable, when the teacher was female, and when the learner and teacher interaction was less direct (eg, an intermediary administered the shocks or the learner was in another room). Obedience was less when the learner-teacher interaction was more intimate, when there was peer pressure to disobey, and when the teacher was less directive and consistent in his or her orders.

Modern Partial Replications of Milgram's Procedure

Because of the ethical implications of the Milgram procedure it is not normally run in full nowadays. Nonetheless, partial replications have provided some interesting data. Slater et al (2006) ran a very similar procedure to Milgram's except that shocks were administered to an avatar in virtual reality. In spite of the fact that participants were clearly aware that the avatar could not really feel or be harmed by the shocks the results—both in terms of the obedience and the subjective responses of 34 British participants—were similar to Milgram's. In a variation on Milgram's design a condition was implemented in which 11 participants could see the avatar throughout the procedure. In this case obedience dropped from 100% to 74%.

Burger (2009) carried out a partial replication of Milgram's procedure with 70 live American participants but in order to minimize distress he reduced the maximum shock level to 150 V—this was the point at which the learner began to protest in the Milgram procedure. Obedience rates were slightly lower than for Milgram, opening up the possibility that people are less obedient now than they were in the 1960s. However, the presence of a rebellious companion did not reduce obedience as it did for Milgram. Similar results were obtained in another partial replication by Dolinsky et al (2017). Like Burger they stopped the procedure at 150 V, at which point 90% of participants were obedient.

 THINKING CRITICALLY

It has long been considered unethical to replicate Milgram's procedure; however, Burger (2009) convinced an ethics committee to allow him to do so. One of the measures he took to meet ethical guidelines was limiting the shocks to 150 V. He also took other measures. Read about these here: https://www.psychologicalscience.org/observer/replicating-milgram To what extent do you think Burger's safeguards made it ethically acceptable to carry out the procedure? Remember we aren't looking for a particular response, just that you have an informed opinion.

Individual Differences in Obedience

Milgram is best known for researching the influence of situation on obedience and indeed his research does emphasize situation. Nonetheless, Milgram was also interested in the possible role of individual differences. Elms and Milgram (1966) administered personality tests including the Minnesota Multiphasic Personality Inventory and a test of authoritarianism to participants in the obedience experiment. High scores on the F-scale of authoritarianism (where F = propensity for fascism) were strongly associated with high levels of obedience; however, personality traits were not.

More recently Begue et al (2015) gave 66 participants who had taken part in a Milgram-type procedure in the context of a fake TV show the Big Five Mini-Markers Questionnaire which measures the five personality factors of agreeableness, conscientiousness, extraversion, neuroticism, and openness, as identified by McCrae and Costa (see Chapter 15 for a discussion). They were also assessed for political orientation (on the left-right wing spectrum) and political activism. Agreeableness, conscientiousness, and political orientation all correlated significantly with maximum shock intensity, suggesting that in fact personality is an important determinant of destructive obedience.

READ THIS

For a good overview of obedience research you can't beat a bit of Thomas Blass so you might like to start with this:

Blass, T. (1999). The Milgram paradigm after 35 years: Some things we now know about obedience to authority 1. *Journal of Applied Social Psychology*, **29**, 955–78.

It's also well worth going back to some Milgram. His research papers are quite readable so there's no reason not to start with the first and work forward to a later review:

Milgram, S. (1963). Behavioural study of obedience. *Journal of Abnormal and Social Psychology*, **67**, 371–8.

Milgram, S. (1967). The compulsion to do evil. *Patterns of Prejudice*, **1**, 3–7.

SOCIAL IDENTITY

When we think about our personal identity or sense of self it sounds by definition very personal and individual. However, in reality our identity is very much tied up with our membership of social categories and groups. This is our **social identity**. Our social identity can be a powerful influence on our social cognition and social behaviour. There are various theories that seek to explain the importance of social identity but one in particular—**social identity theory**—is particularly influential. In fact the importance of social identity theory is one of the distinguishing features of European as distinct from American social psychology (Tajfel, 1984).

The Minimal Groups Studies

Social identity theory grew out of a series of studies conducted at Bristol University by Henri Tajfel and colleagues. The idea behind '**minimal groups**' is that it is possible to artificially create new social identities through establishing categories with the most minimal and apparently meaningless differences between them. In one study Tajfel and Turner (1979) randomly divided teenagers into 'over-estimators' and 'under-estimators' apparently based on their guesses of the number of beans in a jar (see Figure 21.6). Participants were then given a series of decision-making tasks involving allocating money to one another. Even though the division between the two groups was absolutely artificial and there was no conflict or competition between the two categories, participants consistently favoured members of their own category. This is most obviously explained by the participants' adopting a social identity based on their group membership.

Social Identity Theory: The Basics

The basic assumption of social identity theory is that social categories in which we believe we belong provide us with definitions of who we are as an individual (Hogg, Terry, and White, 1995). We all subscribe to a number of social categories and every individual sees each category as having a particular level of importance. So for one person his or her political or religious affiliation might be central to his or her identity whilst for someone else his or her status of cat owner or Liverpool fan might be of primary importance. In the minimal group experiments new and arbitrary categories became important as participants were divided along their membership. Identification with social categories is an emotional experience, providing us with pride (Turner, 1991).

Social identity also provides a mechanism for self-regulation of behaviour—in other words we adapt our social behaviour in line with the stereotypical behaviours

> **KEY IDEAS** social identity Our **social identity** is the portion of our personal identity that comes from our beliefs about belonging to social groups and categories. It is believed that our social identity influences our attitudes and behaviour.

> **KEY IDEAS** minimal groups studies The **minimal groups** experimental paradigm involves creating artificial social categories and testing members' responses to members of in-groups and out-groups. The approach was developed by Henri Tajfel and colleagues in the 1970s and has produced results consistent with social identity theory.

> **KEY IDEAS** social identity theory **Social identity theory** is an explanation for a range of social-psychological phenomena based on the idea that we are influenced in attitudes and behaviour by the norms of social categories with which we identify.

FIGURE 21.6 Minimal group studies show how new social identities can be created by establishing categories with the most minimal and meaningless differences between them; for example, whether you are an 'over-estimator' or 'under-estimator' of the number of beans in this jar.
Source: iStock.com/JazzIRT.

of our social categories. This influence is context-specific, so in one situation our dog-cat preference might exert a particular influence on our attitudes and behaviour whilst in another this might be pretty much irrelevant whilst our political and/or religious affiliation comes to define our beliefs and actions.

According to social identity theory two cognitive processes underlie the influence of social identity on us. The first is categorization. This is a basic cognitive process in which we divide the world, including the social world, into categories in order to understand it. We thus divide people, including ourselves, into social categories. This means we are constantly and acutely aware of what category memberships we share with those around us and what characteristics we attribute to members of our in-groups (ie, those with whom we share membership) and our out-groups (ie, those we do not). For every in-group there is at least one corresponding out-group. So if we are a cat-owner we may see dog-owners as the most salient out-group, if we box we may see martial artists as the key out-group.

Categorization is rarely neutral (Jenkins, 2008) but rather we *evaluate* members of social categories, judging them positively or negatively based on our stereotyped beliefs about that category. This brings us to the second social-cognitive process in social identity: self-enhancement. This is our tendency to enhance our self-concept by biasing our evaluations of in-groups and out-groups in favour of in-groups. So we tend to emphasize any characteristics in which our in-group holds the advantage whilst minimizing the importance of characteristics that favour the out-group.

Also important are our beliefs about the relationship between in-groups and out-groups. These are called subjective belief structures. These include the stability, legitimacy, and permeability of groups. Subjective belief structures affect our choice of strategy when it comes to self-enhancement. Where our in-group compares badly with an out-group and the differences are stable and legitimate we tend to assess the permeability of the categories (ie, the possibility of changing category membership). If we can move into the higher-status group we are likely to do so. If, however, we are trapped in the lower-status group we may respond by changing the in-group and/or biasing our perceptions further in the in-group's favour.

Re-Interpreting Classic Social Psychology Findings in the Light of Social Identity Theory

A number of social-psychological studies have been re-interpreted in the light of social identity research. For example, the results of conformity experiments like those of Solomon Asch (see earlier in this chapter) can be explained by participants' identifying with their group of confederates. Whereas the classic explanations of conformity centre around normative and informational influence, a social identity perspective emphasizes the role of social categorization as part of the group and adoption of the norms of this new in-group (Suhay, 2015). From this perspective the gains to positive self-concept in conforming to in-group norms outweigh the risks to self-concept of being wrong.

In similar vein Haslam and Reicher (2017) have developed the **engaged follow-ership** explanation of obedience based on social identity theory. Milgram himself explained his results in terms of an agentic state in which participants defined them-selves as an instrument of others and adopted a passive role in following destructive commands. However, Haslam and Reicher point out that the least effective verbal prod used by the experimenter was 'you have no choice, you must continue' (prod 4) while the most effective prod was that encouraging participants to continue for the sake of the experiment (prod 2). Milgram's agency theory would predict that in fact prod 4 would be particularly effective. On the other hand prod 2 invites partic-ipants into the shared social category occupied by the experimenter. Once accepted, this high-status group membership encourages the adoption of the norms of that group. From a social identity perspective, far from obeying a distant authority figure Milgram's participants identified with the experimenter and adopted his or her po-sition on the procedure. Support for engaged followership comes from the fact that conditions likely to foster identification with the experimenter, such as the presence of an obedient third party led to increased obedience whilst those we would expect to lead to greater identification with the learner—such as having him or her visible and audible—led to reduced obedience.

> **KEY IDEAS** engaged followership **Engaged followership** is Haslam and Reicher's social identity-based explanation for destructive obedience as was observed in the Milgram studies. The central idea is that participants obeyed the experimenter because they identified with him or her as part of a high-status pro-research group.

READ THIS

It is always tempting to accept newer explanations in psychology, especially when they are based on influential theories. However, the engaged followership explanation for obedience has not gone unchallenged. If you are up for an intellectually challenging debate read this critique and offer a view on the debate:

Hollander, M.M. and Turowetz, J. (2018). Multiple compliant processes: A reply to Haslam and Reicher on the engaged followership explanation of 'obedience' in Milgram's experiments. *British Journal of Social Psychology*, **57**(2), 301–9.

INTERPERSONAL ATTRACTION

So far in this chapter we have been concerned with the ways we influence one another's attitudes and behaviour. There is another related aspect to social interaction: liking one another. People often find themselves drawn to others—for friendship, romance, or sex—for reasons that may not be immediately apparent to either person. The study of **attraction** is an important part of social psychology. Why are we drawn to certain people but not to others?

Positive Assortment

Relationships Expert A swears that 'opposites attract', while Expert B insists that 'birds of a feather flock together'. So who's right? Do we seek mates who are similar to ourselves? Or do we look for people whose attributes complement ours, or who are in some way *different*—perhaps for the excitement and stimulation to be found in novel things? The answer is, overwhelmingly, that we are far more likely to seek mates who are similar to ourselves. This mating tendency was originally known by social psychologists as the *matching phenomenon*, but recently psychologists increasingly are calling it by the name used by biologists—**positive assortment** (Bleske-Rechek, Remiker, and Baker, 2009).

Positive assortment has been documented for everything from intelligence to personality, attitudes and values, education, attractiveness, occupation, race, age, education, religion, politics, . . . even height, weight, finger length, and freckles (Mealey, 2000; Hur, 2003; Luo and Klohnen, 2005; Gonzaga, Campos, and Bradbury, 2007; Bleske et al, 2009)! Investigators have found not only that people tend to positively assort, but also that in general they are happier in such pairings, their relationships are more stable, there are fewer infidelities and divorces, and they even seem to raise more children to maturity than couples in 'opposites attract' relationships (Bleske-Rechek et al, 2009; see Figure 21.7).

> **KEY IDEAS** attraction
> **Attraction** is the product of the factors that draw one person towards another for friendship, sex, romance, or another sort of relationship.

> **KEY IDEAS** positive assortment (matching phenomenon) **Positive assortment** is the tendency to mate with a person who is similar to you in various characteristics. Positive assortment has been documented for attractiveness, height, weight, occupation, religion, age, race, education, political attitudes, and so forth.

FIGURE 21.7 **Positive assortment.** We tend to be choose partners who are similar to us in terms of looks, personality, education, etc, and to be happier in these relationships than in 'opposites attract' ones.
Source: iStock.com/nortonrsx.

The Mere Exposure Effect

A classic fiction plot played out in innumerable films, books, and soap operas involves people who are initially indifferent coming to fall in love as they have regular contact. One of the factors in causing the change of heart may be **propinquity**—the frequency with which people encounter each other. The effect of propinquity on attraction is captured in the idea of the **mere exposure effect** (Zajonc, 2001). Researchers have found that people come to appreciate almost anything the more times they are exposed to it, be it letters, shapes, syllables, melodies, faces—or people. According to the founder of mere exposure theory, Robert Zajonc, it is part of our evolved psychology to be cautious around unfamiliar objects and people, and to be more open to familiar stimuli and individuals (Zajonc, 1968).

But does increasing exposure actually work to increase attraction between people? Some research suggests that it does (Reis et al, 2011). In one study, researchers randomly exposed groups of male-female pairs of university students who were unknown to one another to face one another and engage in a short conversation prompted by specific questions one of the participants was to ask the other. One randomly assigned group was only given two questions, resulting in a relatively short interaction. The other group was given six questions, resulting in a much longer interaction. Those participating in the longer interactions subsequently reported higher levels of attraction to each other.

In the second study, participants were paired anonymously with an online chat partner of the same sex whom they did not know. They were told to engage in 10- to 15-minute chats (with no restriction on content) at least once a day for either 1, 2, 4, 6, or 8 days, depending on their random assignment. As predicted, partners' liking for each other increased as a function of the number of days they engaged in the chat routines.

Attractiveness: Individual or Universal?

We often hear that beauty exists merely in eye of the beholder. On the other hand, as French statesman and philosopher Michel de Montaigne maintained, is beauty a 'powerful and advantageous quality' that 'holds the first place in human relations'? Operationalized in psychology-speak, the first statement suggests that everyone is equally attractive and attraction is merely a case of matching the right people who find each other attractive together. The second statement suggests that what people find attractive is universal and so everyone will find the same people attractive.

As is often the case when we are faced by two opposing cliches the truth appears to be somewhere in between these two extremes. The notion that beauty exists only in the eye of the beholder has a long philosophical history, and belief in this maxim is helped along by the idiosyncratic nature of ideals of beauty in certain cultures. For example, in some societies, distinctive scarring or distortion of the body (eg, an elongated earlobe or lower lip) is considered beautiful. In Western European society, bodily thinness in women is treasured more than in most places—although the degree to which men in Western societies *actually* prefer extremely slender women has been greatly exaggerated, with most men preferring women in the low–normal weight range (Swami and Tovée, 2007).

Although there is variance in aesthetic taste in music and art worldwide, this variance is not as great as many people think (Voland and Grammer, 2003). Similarly, when it comes to human physical attractiveness, there is considerable agreement

> **KEY IDEAS** propinquity and the mere exposure effect **Propinquity** is the frequency with which people come into contact. The **mere exposure effect** is the human tendency to come to prefer people or things simply because they have become familiar. The founder of mere exposure theory, Robert Zajonc, hypothesizes that the mere exposure effect has evolved in human psychology because it would have enhanced our survival and reproductive success to be generally cautious around unfamiliar objects and people.

across cultures and ethnicities about what constitutes attractiveness; at a fundamental level, physical attractiveness is only partially in the eye of the beholder (Gallup and Frederick, 2010). Cultural variance does exist for specific standards in bodily adornment, decoration, or weight, and a person's standards for what is attractive may even change to some degree as he or she moves from one culture to another (Tovée et al, 2006). However, there appear to be a number of underlying facial and bodily characteristics of attractiveness on which all cultures seem to agree.

And yet we must remember that when we use words like 'agree' we are referring to consistent but not complete agreement. So the majority of people tend to prefer particular characteristics but there is no characteristic preferred by all raters. Some commentators prefer to use the term 'conventional attractiveness' because this makes clear that we are referring to something that applies to the *majority* of people but not all and that this is moderated by culture and individual differences. There is an implication in the unqualified use of the term 'attractive' that we are talking about something absolute.

Facial attractiveness

A person might be judged conventionally attractive in face but unattractive in body, or vice versa, but both men and women typically judge a person's overall attractiveness primarily by the person's facial features (Peters, Rhodes, and Simmons, 2007). Nevertheless, human faces are amazingly similar. Figure 21.8 is a photographic demonstration of a single female face evolving through a succession of very slight computer morphings to appear to depict three individuals of differing racial/ethnic ancestries. The changes necessary to indicate different racial/ethnic groups are very slight, underscoring the universality of human facial features and attractiveness.

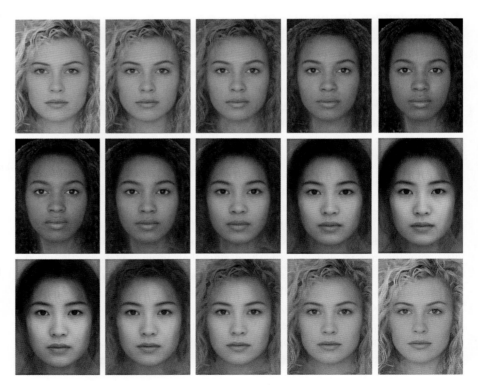

FIGURE 21.8 Human faces are amazingly similar.

Source: Reproduced with permission from B. Fink, N. Neave. et al. The biology of facial beauty. *International Journal of Cosmetic Science*, (27): 317-325 © 2005, John Wiley and Sons. [https://dental.tufts.edu/sites/default/files/pdf/The-biology-of-facial-beauty.pdf]

There appear to be four general cues to conventional facial attractiveness in both sexes: *age, symmetry, averageness*, and *exaggerated femininity and masculinity*. Age is the most obvious quality that affects facial attractiveness: younger faces are considered more attractive than older ones (Furnham, Mistry, and McClelland, 2004). Although conventional attractiveness decreases in men's faces as they age, women are perceived to lose facial attractiveness with age much more rapidly. The majority of male and female research participants agree—as do centuries of world literature and drama as well as the cash receipts of advertisers and film makers—that women's facial attractiveness peaks in young adulthood, and begins to decline soon after (Buss, 1994/2003).

Facial symmetry also appears to be important. The human face and body, like many structures in nature, is constructed to be generally symmetrical. In other words, each side of the face or body is (more or less) the mirror image of the other side. However, there are always slight fluctuations in size and shape—your right eyebrow may be very slightly higher than your left, for example, or one earlobe very slightly longer. Nature does not endow any of us with perfectly symmetrical anatomical structures. Yet some of us are lucky enough to have more symmetrical faces than others. As depicted in Figure 21.9, increasing the symmetry of a face using computer-morphing technology increases the attractiveness of the face.

Coming from an evolutionary perspective, some researchers have proposed that symmetrical features serve as a kind of 'honest advertisement' of the health of one's genes and immune system (Rhodes et al, 2007). Why would this be the case? This is very theoretical and controversial, but one idea is that it takes a strong immune system to maintain symmetry during the process of growth all the way from conception to adulthood (Thornhill and Gangestad, 2006). This is because as we develop, our bodies (and, more important, our faces) contend with innumerable potential challenges in the form of genetic mutations, parasites, infection, nutritional deficiencies, and so forth, all of which can cause minor fluctuations in symmetry (Polak, 2003).

You might think that the most attractive faces are the ones that are anything but average; in fact, the quality of averageness has an even stronger effect on judgements of attractiveness than does symmetry (Rhodes, 2006). As depicted in Figure 21.10, when a single composite photograph is created on a computer by averaging the information from a group of photographs of faces—in a sense, superimposing the faces on one another—the composite face is rated as more attractive than almost any of the individual faces (Grammer and Thornhill, 1994). In this sense the term *average* does not mean 'ordinary'; rather, it means including within it many kinds of genetic contributions.

FIGURE 21.9 Facial symmetry and attractiveness. Large numbers of experiments using computer-morphing technology have shown that increasing the symmetry of a face increases its attractiveness. Left to right: normal symmetry, high symmetry Rhodes, 2006).

Source: Image Courtesy of Gillian Rhodes.

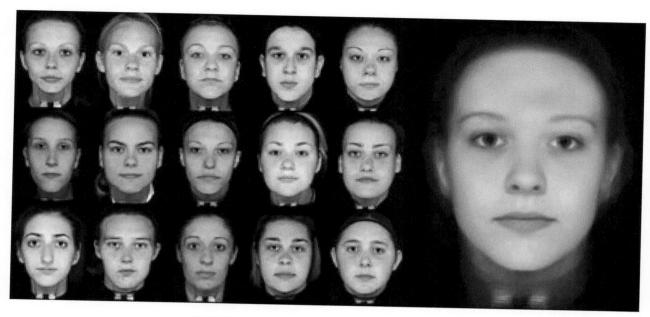

FIGURE 21.10 More average faces are more attractive. When a single face is created by averaging many faces together, the composite is generally considered more attractive than most of the individual faces. In this image, 16 women's faces were averaged to form the composite image at the right, that was judged more attractive than almost all of the individual faces.

Source: Karl Grammer (used with permission).

Why should a face that reflects many kinds of genetic contributions be attractive? Evolutionary psychologists propose that the more numerous the genetic contributions, the stronger is the person's immune system and ability to withstand disease. Like symmetry, averageness may be an 'honest advertisement' of genetic health that may be passed on to offspring (Rhodes, 2006).

The final factor in conventional attractiveness is exaggerated sexual dimorphism. Beginning in **adolescence**, men's and women's faces develop differently and typically show different characteristics, primarily as a result of differences between men and women in the average ratio of testosterone to oestrogen (Thornhill and Gangestad, 2006). As depicted in Figure 21.11, 'masculine' faces tend towards narrower and smaller eyes (relative to face size), longer and more pronounced chins, more developed brows and cheekbones, and thinner lips. 'Feminine' faces tend to have larger eyes (relative to face size), less developed brows, the appearance of high cheekbones, shorter and less pronounced chins that appear more fragile or graceful, and fuller lips. These sex differences are referred to as *sexual dimorphism* in the structure and appearance of faces.

Sexual dimorphism strongly influences the perceived attractiveness of faces, but it plays out quite differently depending on whether men's or women's faces are being rated for attractiveness—and whether men or women are doing the rating. In the case of women's attractiveness, both men and women agree overwhelmingly that attractive female faces are highly 'feminized' faces (Rhodes, 2006). An 'averaged' composite female face whose features have been further feminized is rated more attractive than a simple averaged composite female face.

When it comes to men's faces, the relationship between attractiveness and women's preferences for 'masculinity' is more complex. Women's ratings of attractiveness

FIGURE 21.11 More 'feminized', more attractive; more 'masculinized' . . . it depends. Controversial evidence suggests that both men and women agree that a more 'feminized' female face (top right) is more attractive than a less feminized face (top left). However, women's preferences may shift according to a number of factors, perhaps most importantly the phase of their reproductive cycle and their age. Women who do not use hormonal contraceptives (eg, 'the pill') find more masculinized faces (such as the three at bottom left) more appealing during the time of peak fertility. At other times, less masculinized features are preferred, such as those at bottom right.

Source: Reproduced with permission from D.I. Perrett et al (1998). Effects of sexual dimorphism on facial attractiveness. *Nature*, 394, 885. © 1998, Nature Publishing Group. http://facelab. org/bcjones/Teaching/files/PentonVoak_2003.pdf

Sources: Welling, Jones, and DeBruine, 2008, p 164; Penton-Voak et al, 2004, p 362.

of men's faces are highly dependent on *context*, and there is no consistent overall preference. For example, women's ratings respond to various cultural factors and also to whether the face is being rated as a potential short-term partner (preference for highly masculine features) or a long-term partner (preference for less masculine features; Penton-Voak, Jacobson, and Trivers, 2004).

A highly controversial line of research suggests that women's preferences for highly masculine or less masculine faces may also depend on the women's reproductive status. Women who use hormonal contraception such as birth control pills show no consistent preference; but women who do not use hormonal birth control show a consistent preference for highly masculine faces during the time of peak fertility when pregnancy is most likely. At other times, more 'feminine' male faces may be preferred (Little, Jones, and DeBruine, 2008). Moreover, girls around the ages of the **gonadarche** of puberty—when reproductive potential is low—are much more likely to prefer less masculinized male faces (think of all those devoted Justin Bieber fans!). There is also evidence to suggest that postmenopausal women are also more likely to prefer less masculinized faces (Little et al, 2010).

THINKING CREATIVELY

When research like that by Little, Jones, and DeBruine (2008) shows something sensitive and controversial, it becomes particularly important to establish whether this is a reliable (ie, consistent finding). Two approaches to this are replication and meta-analysis. Explain how you could carry out both a replication and a meta-analysis in order to test the reliability of Little, Jones, and De Bruine's findings.

Why should women's preferences for masculinized faces be highest when they are in fertile phases of their menstrual cycle and when they are of childbearing age? Evolutionary psychologists speculate that strongly masculinized faces are an 'honest advertisement' of the immune status of the man in question. This is because masculinization in facial features is an indication of higher levels of testosterone, and testosterone tends to compromise the immune system. Thus, any male who can 'afford' high levels of testosterone is a man with a potent immune system—an immune system that can be passed on to potential offspring, increasing the reproductive success of the mother and her children. At the time of peak fertility, when pregnancy is most possible, women may shift their preferences in facial features to those which promise to increase the reproductive success of potential offspring (Little et al, 2008). However, this is only a hypothesis—and it remains a controversial one.

THINKING CRITICALLY

The whole topic of attractiveness is a sensitive one because it involves a lot of generalization and stereotype and because these generalizations and stereotypes have the potential to impact negatively on our self-concept if they suggest that we are not attractive. This opens up the possibility of critical thinking at different levels. We *could* say that conducting this kind of research is irresponsible because it has more potential for harm than good. An alternative approach is to look scientifically at whether attractiveness research really predicts who will attract the man or woman of their dreams—the good news is that because of modest effect sizes and multiple additional variables attractiveness research has very limited predictive validity.

Consider the following:

1 Both these levels of critical thinking are legitimate in psychology. Which do you naturally orient towards?

2 Explain what is meant by effect size and why small effect sizes limit the applicability of psychological research to real life.

Self-Presentation

There is far more than propinquity and physical attractiveness involved in determining what people think of us and we are not helpless when it comes to making a good impression. In fact we are very concerned about the opinions of others and we do a lot to present ourselves as we would like others to see us—including but not limited to our physical attractiveness. When someone says, 'I couldn't care less what other people think of me', you can be sure that this is not the whole story. Human beings do not only care about their own evaluations of themselves—they also care greatly what other people think of them, in particular certain others (Leary, 2001).

Indeed, concerns about how others see us are among the most powerful of motives for social behaviour. Saving face, avoiding embarrassment, and appearing to be a person with valuable qualities are important human goals, even if we do not always notice that they play a part in how we behave (Sabini et al, 2001a). Consequently, we pay attention to how other people react to us and often try to control the way we appear to others. We do this to advance our own interests (ie, getting something we want) or just to make sure we are being 'ourselves' or the selves we want to be.

Monitoring and attempting to control how we appear to other people is known as *self-presentation* or **impression management** (Sadler, Hunger, and Miller, 2010.) Some situations elicit a stronger drive to manage impressions than others. At one end of the continuum are situations where we are so deeply engrossed in what we're doing that we are oblivious to other people's responses or evaluations. In those situations we are entirely unmotivated to engage in impression management. For example, we might find ourselves shedding tears at the end of a particularly compelling film and not much care how silly we look. At the other end of the continuum are situations where it is virtually impossible *not* to think about what sort of impression one is making—say, on one's first day teaching a new class or on a first date. More often than not, however, impression management activity occurs between these extremes and often below the level of conscious awareness. No matter what activity we are engaged in, we are usually unconsciously (or barely consciously) scanning the social landscape for information about how we are coming off to other people.

Leary and Kowalski (1990) describe impression management as consisting of two processes: *impression motivation* and *impression construction*. Once we are motivated actually to manage our impression—to obtain a desired goal, increase self-esteem, or alter our public identity—we have to construct the impression we wish to make. This does not imply at all that we are constructing a false identity of some sort. People often attempt to create an impression that is consistent with the person they perceive themselves to be.

The impression construction process is affected by a number of factors. One factor is self-concept—our total perception and evaluation of who we really are as individuals and social beings. We might want people to see 'who we really are' or hide it. Considering that most people's self-concept also includes a general feeling that it is immoral to blatantly lie, the self-concept usually (but, of course, not always) limits the range of possible impressions a person is comfortable making.

A person's *desired* and *undesired identity images* are also factors affecting the impression construction process. How we present ourselves is determined not only

> **KEY IDEAS** impression management The process by which people attempt to monitor and control the impressions that others form of them is called **impression management**. This consists of two components: impression motivation and impression construction.

by the person we think we are, but also by the person we would like—or not like—to be. For example, we may behave as if we already possess attributes we not only would like to have but believe we ultimately will have. This lessens the feeling of dishonesty about such a presentation and, in fact, might actually increase the chances of our ultimately fulfilling such destinies. The expression *dress for success* conveys this idea.

WHAT'S HOT? SELF-PRESENTATION IN CYBERSPACE

The Internet is enormously powerful, and it is transforming almost every aspect of our lives at a very rapid pace (Miller, 2010). Like it or not, a great deal—a *very* great deal—of self-presentation occurs over the Internet in computer-mediated communication (CMC). From chat rooms, bulletin boards and forums, texting and instant messaging, e-mail, blogging, and peer-to-peer (P2P) programs, to *social networking* sites such as Facebook, Tumblr, and Twitter, we are presenting ourselves to one another all the time. What is unique about all of this self-presentation is that it we do it without sharing the same physical space, without seeing or hearing one another, and often without even learning each other's real name, age, or sex. With the advent of wireless technology, even developing areas that lag behind the West in the numbers of people 'wired' are quickly catching up (Shyam and Bhoria, 2011).

Online dating is one form of self-presentation using computer-mediated communication that has changed in only a few years from a marginalized activity about which 'cool' people giggle to a mainstream format for meeting people and forming relationships (Finkel et al, 2012). If current trends continue it may well be that we will reach a point where over 50% of romantic couples will have met online.

Behavioural scientists disagree about the social effects of the communication over the Internet (di Gennaro and Dutton, 2007). Some researchers look to the Internet and associated electronic media as an amazing opportunity to break down racism, national borders, and narrow divisions among people, while uniting people according to deeply held values and beliefs and increasing the breadth of social networks. Others see it as portending disastrous outcomes for interpersonal relationships—creating sterile, superficial forms of exchange that promote a lack of genuineness and the breakdown of communities and extended families. These researchers predict that an entire generation of lonely individuals will emerge as a result of widespread CMC.

Although there is some evidence to support both views, in general, most evidence of CMC's negative effects was collected in the early years of online life, when relatively few people were online (Kraut et al, 1998). Newer research suggests that the Internet is less destructive to personal relationships and is associated with more positive outcomes than naysayers expected (Finkel et al, 2012).

The reasons for the contradictory findings in research on the effects of CMC may have been clarified to some extent by researchers Patti Valkenburg and Jochen Peter (2009). When they looked at the effects of CMC on adolescents, they found that it can have positive effects primarily when it is used to sustain previously existing friendships rather than to create new cyber-relationships with unseen individuals. In the period of the 1990s, when most of the negative findings emerged from research, only a small percentage of people, even in the 'developed' world, had daily access to CMC. Today, of course, it is a medium used by the overwhelming majority of adolescents and young adults in Western nations to maintain their existing friendships and family relationships.

FROM ATTRACTION TO RELATIONSHIP FORMATION

An in-depth analysis of the formation, maintenance, and failure of human relationships—in all their diverse forms—is not within the scope of this chapter but it is worth saying a little about how we move from the processes of attraction and impression management to participation in a romantic relationship. Key to this (at least in Western culture) is dating. Dating involves meeting, either in the physical or virtual world, a potential romantic/sexual partner and engaging in a carefully managed exchange of information. Dating may continue for any period of time and may or may not develop into a committed romantic relationship.

A crucial step from attraction to relationship is the first date. Mongeau, Serewicz, and Thierren (2014) questioned university students about their motives underlying a first date. The most commonly cited goals for a first date involved relationship escalation from acquaintance or friendship to romance, fun, and the reduction of uncertainty about the nature of the relationship. Some gender differences emerged, mostly along stereotypical lines, with women more likely to assess the partner for long-term relationship potential and men more likely to focus on the possibility of short-term mating (see 'Sex differences in partner variety and casual sex', Chapter 5).

Love

We typically love a number of people in different ways. In this context we are concerned with romantic love. Romantic love, like other forms, tends to reflect attachment, discussed in depth in Chapter 11. Over the course of several decades Sternberg (2013) has used three models to understand love.

A psychometric model

Early attempts to apply a scientific approach to love took a psychometric approach. Like intelligence researchers who at one time were largely concerned with the components of intelligence and who divided intelligence into varying numbers of elements, researchers into love sought to understand the components of emotional bonds. Thus Spearman (1927) conceived of love as a single factor, indivisible into smaller components, whilst at the other extreme Thomson (1939) identified a large number of components and subcomponents to love, albeit components experienced together. In between these positions Thurstone (1938) identified a smaller number of love components, most importantly trust, care, mutual respect, and affection. Sternberg and Grajek (1984) questioned 85 adults aged 18–70 about their experiences of love and factor-analysed the results. Factor analysis involves seeing what test items correlate with one another and so establishing which are related. Their results were most supportive of the Thurstone model. However, in response to criticisms of the narrowness of taking a psychometric approach to love—and influenced by his personal experiences—Sternberg (1986) went on to propose a second triangular model of love.

A triangular model

Sternberg (1986) suggested that love can be viewed as having three dimensions:

- *Intimacy*: characterized by bondedness, connectedness, and closeness. This promotes mutual support, high regard, and sharing, both in material and emotional senses.

- *Passion*: the sense of longing for union with the other, often but not necessarily tied up with sexual fulfilment. We can still experience passion in a platonic relationship or where partners have opted for celibacy in the context of romance.
- *Commitment*: in this context commitment refers to emotional (and in some cases financial) investment in the relationship as opposed to responsibility for the partner.

These vary in importance according to the longevity of the relationship. In short-term relationships or those in which prolonged dating does not lead to a monogamous relationship, passion is everything, with intimacy being largely optional and commitment not really a feature. In longer-term monogamous relationships, passion tends to decline in importance whilst intimacy and commitment increase. Sternberg (1986) is at pains to point out, however, that some kinds of relationship are designed to combine high levels of intimacy with low levels of commitment—think for example about extramarital affairs.

 THINKING CRITICALLY

Sternberg (2013) is entirely open in admitting that he drew heavily on his own experiences of romantic relationships to construct his triangular theory of love. Often psychologists are quite critical of this introspection as a basis for a theory. Explain the strengths and weaknesses of basing a psychological theory on personal experience.

Love as a story

This represents a development of rather than a replacement for the triangular model. Sternberg (1998) explained the development of love triangles from the love stories we are all exposed to. According to Sternberg we apply both stories explicitly about love and those concerning other situations to our understanding of love. We all seek in our relationships to fulfil the expectations derived from these stories. Generally, the closer the match between our personal representation of love stories and those of our partner the better the chances of relationship success. Thus Sternberg (2013) reported a +0.65 correlation between stories in stable couples and a −0.45 relationship between discrepancy in couples' stories and relationship satisfaction.

However, there is more to this than sharing similar love stories—some stories make a much better basis for a relationship than others. Healthy relationship stories include 'democratic government' in which partners share power, 'gardening' in which relationships need attention and nurture, and 'travel' in which love is seen as a journey. Perhaps less healthy are 'love as addiction' which is characterized by high levels of anxiety and control associated with an anxious attachment style and 'fantasy' in which the role of one partner is to rescue the other, whereupon they live happily ever after. Others are inherently abusive; for example, the 'horror' story in which one partner deliberately terrorizes the other and the highly controlling 'police' story in which one partner conducts surveillance on the other and bases the relationship on control strategies.

 THINKING CREATIVELY

The existence of supporting evidence is perhaps the most important criterion for evaluating the value of a psychological theory. Think about how you might look for evidence to support Sternberg's theory of love stories.

IN REVIEW

SOCIAL FACILITATION

- Social facilitation takes place when behaviour or performance is enhanced by the presence of others.
- In spite of limitations to the classic research social facilitation does appear to be a robust phenomenon.
- Under some circumstances the opposite phenomenon of social inhibition occurs.

CONFORMITY

- There are two major reasons for the existence of conformity: normative and informational influence.
- The classic conformity research by Solomon Asch demonstrated normative influence. There is supporting evidence for the importance of both normative and informational influence.
- Informational influence is important in understanding the echo chamber effect of social media as conformity to the opinions of those sharing our social media groups may make our own views more polarized and contribute to social division.
- Groupthink results from conformity to group membership during decision-making. It can lead to irrational collective decisions.

OBEDIENCE

- Destructive obedience occurs when people obey orders from authority figures to harm others. This was demonstrated in the classic studies of Stanley Milgram.
- Broadly, modern research supports Milgram's findings, but there have been a number of criticisms of his conclusions.
- Modern research has demonstrated the influence of a number of situational and individual differences on destructive obedience.

SOCIAL IDENTITY

- An emphasis on social identity as an influence on social behaviour is a feature of European social psychology.
- Social identity theory is based on the idea that even minimally different groups with no competition adopt a group identity which in turn affects their behaviour.
- The central idea of social identity theory is that we categorize ourselves and others and that to maintain a positive self-concept we emphasize the positive aspects of our in-group.
- Some of the classic social psychology studies like those of Asch and Milgram have been reinterpreted in the light of social identity theory.

ATTRACTION AND LOVE

- A number of factors influence who we are attracted to. These include positive assortment (similarity), propinquity, attractiveness, and self-presentation.
- Attraction can lead to dating and perhaps love, but there is some debate about the nature of love, with Sternberg putting forward three models.

TEST YOURSELF

1 People performing better in a sport in the presence of others is an example of social inhibition. True ☐ False ☐

2 Informational conformity becomes more important in ambiguous situations. True ☐ False ☐

3 The 'minimal' in the minimal group studies refers to the minimal differences between groups. True ☐ False ☐

4 Romantic love tends to mirror infant attachment behaviour. True ☐ False ☐

5 The impact of the presence of a communications device on face-to-face communication is known as:

a) The iPad effect

b) The iPhone effect

c) The iMac effect

d) The Android effect

6 Choosing sources of information because they appear friendly to us is best described as:

a) Conformity bias

b) Echo chamber bias

c) Filter bias

d) Congeniality bias

7 Which of the following statements that might arise in a situation of groupthink is an example of the illusion of moral correctness?

a) 'It can't go wrong'

b) 'No one is objecting'

c) 'It's in the Bible'

d) 'Only a traitor would question it'

8 Which Milgram variation led to the lowest rate of obedience?

a) Changing the venue to a run-down office block

b) Having a disobedient confederate

c) Having two disobedient confederates

d) Having a casually dressed experimenter

9 Explain the main difficulty in echo chamber research.

10 Explain one example of using social identity theory to re-interpret findings from a classic social psychology study.

 Visit the online resources that accompany this book: wwww.oup.com/uk/jarvis–okami1e

CHAPTER 22

ALTRUISM AND ANTISOCIAL BEHAVIOUR

LEARNING OUTCOMES

By the end of this chapter you should be able to:

- Understand what is meant by altruism and distinguish between proximate and ultimate causes for altruistic behaviour in humans

- Evaluate evidence for proximate factors in altruism with particular regard to the role of empathy and mirror neurons

- Consider ultimate explanations for altruism including Hamilton's theory of inclusive fitness and Trivers' theory of reciprocal altruism

- Explain bystander apathy and the real-life events that stimulated social-psychological research into the bystander effect

- Critically discuss the conclusions of field and laboratory experiments into the bystander effect

- Compare situational and dispositional explanations for high-profile failures of health professionals to show expected altruism

- Explain the nature of prejudice including the distinction between stereotypes, hostility and discrimination, and the key features of racism and sexism

- Discuss research into the role of in-group bias, implicit bias, and terror management in prejudice

- Explain the nature of aggression, including its key characteristics and the distinction between aggression and violence and between hostile and instrumental aggression

- Appreciate the differences in typical male and female aggression, with particular reference to direct and indirect aggression and consider the possible role of testosterone in sex differences

- Evaluate explanations for aggression, including the frustration-aggression hypothesis, observational learning, and the General Aggression Model

- Assess the relationship between intergroup relations and aggression, including the role of dehumanization and deindividuation in 'evil' acts perpetrated by one group on another

In Chapter 21 we uncovered some disturbing aspects of human behaviour such as our tendency for destructive obedience. In this chapter we discuss some other unfortunate human tendencies but also something of human potential for good. We'll start with the positive!

ALTRUISM: HUMAN BEINGS AT THEIR BEST

In May 2018 Professor of Psychology Timothy Hodgson of Lincoln University risked his life to save a drowning dog after leaving work—and in the process discovered that the owner was also in trouble and ended up saving him as well. He then calmly continued his journey to the pub! Incidents of selfless helping behaviour like this are not as uncommon as we might think. In natural disasters and human-made catastrophes such as terror attacks stories often emerge of people going out of their way and risking personal harm to help others in need, as in Figure 22.1. This tendency to offer or provide help to others in need without an obvious reward motive is called **altruism**.

> **KEY IDEAS** altruism **Altruism** is the offering of assistance to others without the expectation of an immediate reward.

Indeed, altruism appears to be 'in our genes', literally. Like *prosocial* emotions such as empathy and compassion, the capacity for altruism has probably evolved to be part of human psychology (Trivers, 1971, 2002). **Behavioural genetics** studies have strongly suggested that individual differences among people in their tendencies towards altruism are in part genetic in origin (Rushton, 2004), and recent research has observed a sense of fairness and willingness to share emerging in some infants as young as 15 months (Schmidt and Sommerville, 2011).

Altruism is part of a larger group of behaviours termed *prosocial* because they may promote the well-being of society as a whole. However, from a psychological perspective, altruism presents a 'problem'. Although we know that people *do* perform clearly altruistic acts, it is not always apparent *why* they do so. Why should people

FIGURE 22.1 Altruism. Why do people help others without any obvious reward motive, even when it places their own life at risk?
Source: iStock.com/cwarham.

like Timothy Hodgson offer help to complete strangers at the risk of their own safety or that of their loved ones? Why should a person contribute money to a charitable cause when that money could be used instead for his or her own family's benefit?

Proximate and Ultimate Causes of Altruism

Immediate, direct causes are known as **proximate causes**. Proximate causes of animal behaviour (including human behaviour) include not only motivations, but also physiological, biochemical, and neural processes as well as learning. Usually, when we ask, 'Why did he/she do that?' we are referring to proximate causes, and most branches of psychology (evolutionary psychology being an exception) focus on proximate explanations for behaviour. In the case of altruistic acts, psychologists interested in proximate causes are usually interested in the *motivations* for the acts (de Waal, 2008). For example, what motivated Timothy Hodgson to risk his own life to save the life of a stranger? What was he thinking and feeling?

The second type of cause for a behaviour, known as an **ultimate cause**, explains why some type of behaviour—altruism, for example—exists in the first place. In other words, ultimate explanations show how the *effects* of some behaviour would have benefited the survival and reproduction of human beings over evolutionary time and therefore evolved through natural selection (Trivers, 2002; Dickens and West, 2011). When we ask why people are altruistic, we may be interested in proximate explanations, ultimate explanations, or both.

As an example, consider honeybees, which commit altruistic acts when they sting intruders, sacrificing their lives to protect the hive. Is their motivation one of kindness and compassion towards their fellow bees and a sense of cooperative civic spirit? Probably not. It is far more likely that the motivation—a proximate cause of their altruistic act—is one of **aggression**, to injure the intruder. However, the ultimate cause of their behaviour throughout the evolutionary history of honeybees has been one of altruism—personal sacrifice that benefits others without expectation of immediate reward (de Waal, 2008).

> **KEY IDEAS** proximate causes **Proximate causes** are the immediate causes of behaviour—the trigger for something to occur. Proximate causes of behaviour include motivations; physiological, biochemical, and neural processes; and learning. Most psychologists focus on proximate explanations of behaviour.

> **KEY IDEAS** ultimate causes **Ultimate causes** of behaviour are forces that shaped the capacity or tendency for the behaviour in human beings over evolutionary time—*why*, rather than *how*, a behaviour occurs. Unlike most other psychologists, evolutionary psychologists focus primarily on ultimate explanations of behaviour.

THINKING CRITICALLY

Evolutionary assumptions about human behaviour like altruism draw upon superficially similar behaviour in other species. An example is the comparison with honeybee stinging. Explain why such comparisons are logically suspect. HINT: the answer is intuitively obvious but explaining it well is quite tricky.

Proximate causes of altruism

Some researchers suggest that the important human quality of *empathy* is the proximate explanation for many or even most altruistic acts (eg, Batson, 2010). **Empathy** is the ability to take another person's perspective, to *feel* how that person feels, understand *why* the person feels as he or she does, and often (but not always) come to share the feeling at least to some degree (Decety, Michalska, and Akitsuki, 2008).

In an interesting neuroscientific look at brain mechanisms involved in empathy, Phillip Jackson and his colleagues showed participants photographs of hands and feet in situations where they were about to be painfully cut by knives or garden shears, jammed in doors, or other predicaments we would rather not think about

> **KEY IDEAS** empathy **Empathy** is the ability to take another person's perspective, understand why the person feels as he or she does, and perhaps also come to share that feeling to some degree (although this is not a necessary component of empathy).

(Jackson et al, 2005). As shown in Figure 22.2, these photos were contrasted with photos where the hands and feet were in no danger.

Jackson et al found that areas of the brain normally activated when one experiences pain were also activated simply by viewing *someone else* about to experience pain (Decety et al, 2008). The more pain-sensitive the participants reported that they generally were, the more activation was seen in these brain areas. Jackson and colleagues' findings reflect the workings of mirror neurons, which we have described in Chapter 4. Mirror neurons are specific neurons in the brain which fire when an individual engages in a behaviour or experiences an emotion, and also fire when the individual observes someone else engaging in the same behaviour or experiencing the same emotion. Mirror neurons appear to be an important component of proximate explanations for empathy and altruism because they offer a neural mechanism by which a connection is established between one individual and another (Iacoboni, 2009).

Of course, many apparently altruistic acts can also be motivated by the desire to be thanked, to 'look good' in front of others, to increase one's own self-esteem, or

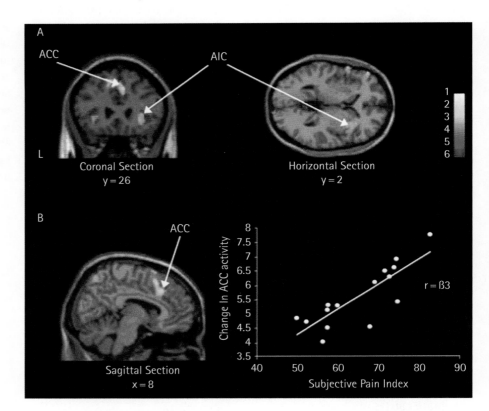

FIGURE 22.2 Sharing the pain of others: the neuroscience of empathy. When research participants were exposed to images of impending pain and injury, specific areas of the anterior cingulated cortex (ACC) and anterior insulate cortex (AIC) were activated that were not activated when viewing virtually identical images without the implication of impending pain and injury. The areas of the ACC and AIC are indicated in these images from different perspective views of the brain. The scatterplot graph shows the strong correlation between the activation of the ACC and AIC and participants' reports of their own sensitivity to pain.

Source: Reproduced with permission from Philip L. Jackson, Andrew N. Meltzoff, Jean Decety (2005). How do we perceive the pain of others? A window into the neural processes involved in empathy. *NeuroImage*, 24, 771–9.
© 2005, Elsevier. http://citeseerx.ist.psu.edu/viewdoc/download?doi=10.1.1.391.8127&rep=rep1&type=pdf

even to 'expand the boundaries of the self' by including another individual within those boundaries (Cialdini et al, 1997). Such motivations are termed *egoistic*, or self-interested. However, researchers have been able to demonstrate experimentally that egoism is not an adequate explanation for many altruistic acts. Empathy, in contrast, does seem to be at least a major motivating force (de Waal, 2008), if not the whole story (Pinker, 2011).

Ultimate explanations

If empathy is the primary proximate explanation for altruism, where does empathy come from? It is a maxim of evolutionary biology that individuals rarely act directly against their own genetic interests—that is, in a way that would compromise their reproductive success (Dawkins, 1976). If organisms acted repeatedly against their genetic interests, they would be 'out-competed' by individuals who always acted in favour of their genetic interests. Over evolutionary time, the genetic line of those acting against their interests would die out, and so would the tendency to behave in this way! Therefore, according to the logic of evolutionary theory, empathy and altruism *must* have functioned over evolutionary time in some way to increase our ancestors' success in surviving and reproducing. As Figure 22.3 shows, primate species demonstrate a range of altruistic behaviours. Two well-tested evolutionary theories explain how this might happen.

Hamilton (1964) solved this problem by demonstrating mathematically that the important thing in natural selection is not physical survival or even physical re-production—it is *gene* survival and *gene* reproduction. The resulting theory is called the **theory of inclusive fitness** because, in contrast to an exclusive focus on the survival and reproduction of an individual, it states that an organism is reproductively fit to the extent that it passes on its genetic line to new generations. For example, your genetic line survives not only in your children, but also (to a lesser

> ❯ **KEY IDEAS** theory of inclusive fitness The **theory of inclusive fitness** is Hamilton's mathematics-based evolutionary theory of altruism directed towards kin. The theory stresses the fact that natural selection operates on genes, not on individuals and their bodies. Altruistic acts directed towards genetic kin may increase a person's own evolutionary 'fitness' if the act increases the kin's survival or reproductive success. This may happen even if the individual sacrifices his or her life during the altruistic act, depending on the number of kin helped by the act or the closeness of the genetic link to the kin (eg, sacrificing your life so that one of your children or ten first-cousins may live increases your fitness more than sacrificing your life for one grandchild or ten second-cousins).

FIGURE 22.3 Primate species demonstrate a range of altruistic behaviours, including dental examination!
Source: Erna Holdorp/Shutterstock.com.

but still important extent) in your siblings, cousins, nieces, and nephews. Each child shares approximately 50% of his or her genes in common with each parent and approximately the same in common with each sibling, but approximately the same frequency of gene survival would occur in two of the parent's grandchildren (25% in each), two nieces or nephews (25% in each), or four cousins (12.5% in each).

To understand the reasoning behind Hamilton's theory, it is helpful to realize that because bodies are temporary (they always die), natural selection cannot operate to make its small incremental changes over time on individuals. It can only do so on genes, which, barring mutation, are potentially immortal. Therefore, if you were to race into a burning building to save your children, grandchildren, and a few nieces or nephews—all of whom are genetic kin—even if you were to die, by saving them you would be contributing massively to your own genetic survival. This altruistic act would ultimately serve your own genetic self-interest. However, the *motivation*— the emotions you are feeling at the time—are likely to be entirely empathetic and not at all egoistic.

Consider the story of Karen Svaerd, a Swedish tourist who ran *directly into* the oncoming tsunami wave in South East Asia on 26 December 2004, to rescue her three children, as all other people were frantically running in the opposite direction (the entire family survived, by the way). You can be sure that at that moment she was *not* thinking about the survival of her genes through her offspring, but only of her desperate love and concern for her children. Thus, empathy as an emotion may have evolved to help motivate organisms to engage in actions that assist genetic survival, even if it might mean putting their own physical survival at risk.

But what of people like Timothy Hodgson? Why is altruism also frequently directed towards complete strangers who are not our kin? Trivers (1971), whose theory of parental investment and sexual selection is discussed in Chapter 5, de-vised an ultimate explanation for altruism directed towards non-kin known as the **theory of reciprocal altruism**. The basic idea is that psychological attributes that motivate altruism, such as empathy, will evolve under conditions where altruism is expected to be reciprocated at some point in the future—either to oneself or one's kin. Recall that, according to evolutionary theory, human psychology was shaped under conditions of life in very small bands of hunters and gatherers, where many were genetically related and all knew one another. Acts of altruism were proba-bly expected to be returned. If you have a poor week of fishing, I will share my catch with you and your family; when I have a poor week, the favour will likely be returned. Each person gains more than his or her costs (Cosmides and Tooby, 1992). Under such conditions, empathy and the altruism it can inspire may have had highly positive genetic payoffs—increasing, rather than decreasing, reproduc-tive success and survival. Human beings have evolved to be altruistic, loving, and cooperative—just as we have also evolved to be selfish and aggressive when con-ditions seem to demand it.

> **KEY IDEAS** theory of reciprocal altruism The **theory of reciprocal altruism** is Robert Trivers' evolutionary theory of altruism directed towards non-kin. The theory proposes that psychological attributes that motivate altruism towards non-kin, such as empathy, will only evolve under conditions where there is some expectation that altruistic acts will be reciprocated in the future—either to oneself or one's kin.

THINKING CRITICALLY

When it comes to evaluating explanations for altruism, proximate and ultimate theories raise different issues. How do mirror neurons and reciprocal altruism compare in terms of testabil-ity and supporting evidence?

BYSTANDER APATHY

The counterpoint to altruism is bystander apathy. This takes place when we would expect people to offer assistance to those in need but in fact they fail to do so. Psychological research into bystander apathy was stimulated in the 1960s by the notorious murder of Kitty Genovese (shown in Figure 22.4). Shortly after 3:00 a.m. on 13 March 1964, a particularly horrific murder occurred in the Queens, New York City. Twenty-eight-year-old Catherine 'Kitty' Genovese, returning home from her job as bar manager, was attacked on the pavement in front of a two-story building and across the street from a ten-story apartment building. A man named Winston Moseley stabbed Kitty twice in the back and then jumped into his car and backed away from the scene. Kitty got up and tried to make her way around to the rear of the two-story building to reach her own home but was unable to make it. She collapsed in the small hallway of the building. At that point, Moseley got out of his car, found Kitty, stabbed her again multiple times, sexually assaulted her, and fled. Kitty died in the ambulance on her way to the hospital.

As it stands, it is a gruesome and tragic story of the violent end of a young life. But there are details of this crime that have given it a kind of ghastly immortality. The following is taken from the initial account in the *New York Times* on 27 March 1964:

> For more than half an hour thirty-eight respectable, law-abiding citizens in Queens watched a killer stalk and stab a woman in three separate attacks in Kew Gardens. Twice the sound of their voices and the sudden glow of their bedroom lights interrupted him and frightened him off. Each time he returned, sought her out and stabbed her again. Not one person telephoned the police during the assault; one witness called after the woman was dead. (Gansberg, 1964)

FIGURE 22.4 Kitty Genovese. The killing of Kitty Genovese in New York in 1964 initiated the study of the conditions under which bystanders will respond to pleas for help from strangers. However, for decades Genovese's killing was mythologized: beliefs that 38 neighbours stood by and refused to offer help as she was killed are entirely inaccurate.

Source: New York Daily News Archive/Getty Images.

❯ KEY IDEAS the bystander effect
The tendency for a person to be
less likely to intervene and offer
help to a stranger in an emergency
situation when others are present
is called the **bystander effect**.
Broadly, the more people present,
the less likely the bystander is to
offer aid.

The *Times* account suggested that Kitty had screamed for a full half-hour, 'Oh my God, he stabbed me! Please help me! I'm dying, I'm dying!' Yet not one of the 38 supposed witnesses to this horror so much as lifted a finger—not to go to her aid, not even to phone the police. They simply watched the crime with dispassion. The news reportage of this crime not only led to major changes in the way crimes are reported to the police (including the institution of the 911 and 999 calls), but also opened up an entire area of social psychology dealing with the conditions under which people will administer or withhold aid to strangers in need. It also helped to establish a view of modern urban life as peopled by uncaring and apathetic citizens (Manning, Levine, and Collins, 2007).

Before discussing the findings of social psychologists on what has come to be called the **bystander effect**—the tendency of people to be less likely to help strangers in need if there are other people present at the scene—it needs to be said that although the sexual assault and murder of Kitty Genovese is all too true, the story of her betrayal by 38 of her neighbours is greatly exaggerated (Manning et al, 2007). Some of the facts of this case remain in dispute, but recent research has offered the following correctives to the mythology that surrounds this crime:

- It is untrue that no one phoned the police. The police were called immediately following the first attack on Kitty Genovese (although this call did not result in immediate dispatch of police to the scene).

- Only three eyewitnesses were certain to have actually seen Kitty attacked—not 38 (and these three *do* bear responsibility for their inaction). An unknown number of people—possibly *more* than 38—did hear Kitty scream during the initial attack, however, and they have been the subject of intense criticism for their failure to investigate (Skoller, 2008). However, only one of these was reported to have heard Kitty cry that she had been stabbed.

- The three actual eyewitnesses saw Kitty get up and walk away and not return. One testified that he thought Kitty was drunk. Another thought Kitty had been struck, not stabbed. Many of those who only heard something assumed that it was a lovers' quarrel or drunken altercation (the attack took place near a neighbourhood bar). No one saw the sexual assault or the completion of the murder.

- No one watched anything for anywhere near as long as half an hour. The first attack lasted only a few moments. The second attack lasted at least several minutes, but only one neighbour could even have been in a position to see any of it.

Regardless of the degree of mythology surrounding this case, it is undeniably true that an unknown number of people chose not to help Kitty Genovese when they clearly understood (or should have understood) that she was under some sort of attack—even if the specific nature of the attack and its severity were not entirely clear. Ironically, however exaggerated, accounts of the Genovese murder prompted important research to be conducted on the conditions under which people will withhold aid to others.

What are these conditions? The initial work was done by John Darley and Bibb Latané (1968). Instead of representing 'big-city apathy' as it had been characterized, however, Darley and Latané demonstrated that the *presence of others* at a scene allows each individual to diffuse responsibility with the rationale that 'someone else is bound to take care of it'. The more people are present at a scene, the less likely any specific person is to offer aid. We can examine one of Darley and Latane's studies in detail in *Research in focus*.

RESEARCH IN FOCUS

Darley, J.M. and Latané, B. (1968). Bystander intervention in emergencies: Diffusion of responsibility. *Journal of Personality and Social Psychology*, **8**, 377–85.

Aim: To test the hypothesis that the more bystanders are present the slower and less likely people are to provide help in an emergency. Specifically, to compare the likelihood of and time taken to offer help to a stranger apparently having a fit when alone or in the presence of others. A secondary aim was to investigate the effects of individual differences such as gender and personality in bystander behaviour.

Method: 72 undergraduate psychology students (59 female, 13 male) took part in the study. Each arrived individually and was shown into a small room. They were told that they were taking part in a discussion of personal problems in university life using an intercom system to reduce embarrassment. Participants were also told that discussions were to be held in groups of two, three, or five and each person was to have two minutes to disclose his or her problems to the others. It was explained that the experimenter was not going to be listening to the discussions. The first to speak (a confederate) described his or her difficulty with epileptic seizures. The participant spoke last. When it was the first confederate's turn to speak again he or she simulated a seizure. The time the participant took to leave the room and seek help was recorded and constituted the dependent variable. Qualitative data regarding participants' reactions to the emergency was also recorded.

Results: In a group size of two 85% of participants responded before the end of the fit with a mean time of 52 seconds. In a group of three 62% responded with a mean time of 93 seconds. In a group of six only 31% responded and the mean time was 166 seconds. Analysis of variance revealed that these differences were significant at the $p < 0.01$ level. There was no difference in helping by males and females and no correlation with personality traits. Participants' reactions generally revealed concern. Those who did not offer help tended to express confusion about what to do. Those who did help expressed relief when told the victim was alright.

Conclusion: The major determinant of helping behaviour is group size, with increases in group size predicting longer response times and reduced likelihood of assistance. Individual differences does not have a major effect on helping in an emergency. However, there was no evidence of lack of care amongst participants, including those in large groups who did not help. Instead they displayed signs of confusion and indecision.

MASTER YOUR METHODOLOGY

1. Both quantitative and qualitative data were gathered in this study. Explain why having the qualitative data was helpful in drawing conclusions from the study.

2. Explain why analysis of variance was an appropriate inferential statistics test to carry out on the differences in time taken to help in three conditions of different group size.

3. There were no significant correlations between time taken to help and individual differences variables. Explain what is meant by a correlation and what inferential test might have been used to assess correlation.

THINKING CRITICALLY

Look back to our critical thinking toolkit (Chapter 1). What strengths and weaknesses can you see in relation to this study?

Psychologists also investigated bystander behaviour outside the laboratory. In a beautifully ironic study Darley and Batson (1973) invited participants to give a university talk on the Christian story of the good Samaritan, in which someone offers help to a stranger. When they arrived they were directed to a neighbouring building. On the way they passed a shabbily dressed confederate slumped on the floor. In an experimental condition the participants were told that they were late. Many people in this condition hurried past ignoring the person that appeared to need help. When questioned many said that they were so focused on getting to their talk quickly that they simply did not notice the confederate.

THINKING CRITICALLY

Field experiments in social psychology typically have good ecological validity but poor experimental control. Laboratory experiments tend to have the opposite characteristics. Explain why Darley and Batson's 'Good Samaritan' study can be said to have the strengths of both lab and field research.

Although Darley and Colleagues' early work was insightful, it was not until much later that researchers took a more comprehensive and systematic look at the bystander effect (Fischer et al, 2011). Integrating 50 years of research in a meta-analysis, Fischer and his colleagues made a more precise identification of when strangers will or will not intervene on behalf of those in need, and the results of this analysis were in some ways surprising.

The general rule that the presence of groups of bystanders in critical situations does reduce the likelihood of any single individual offering aid held true. However, surprisingly, the more dangerous the circumstance and the more clear-cut the physical danger, the *more* likely—not less likely—bystanders are to offer aid. This is probably true in part because a group of people may support one another physically, so each individual feels less fearful of intervening. Think for a moment: attempting to disarm a violent offender with five other people supporting you may seem a lot less daunting than attempting the task alone. In part it may also be true because in truly dangerous situations the need for aid to be offered is usually completely unambiguous (unlike the Genovese case), and it may be harder to rationalize failing to act ('Oh, it's probably just a lover's quarrel'). Finally, and perhaps not surprisingly, the presence of males among a group of bystanders increases the likelihood of help being offered in times of physical danger, and if the bystanders are known to one another and not strangers, the chances of aid being offered are increased still more.

WHAT'S HOT? COMPASSION DEFICIT

We have very high expectations of those who work in the caring professions to maintain very high levels of altruism towards their service users, and there is understandable shock and revulsion when professionals under chronic pressure fail to live up to these standards. The term 'compassion fatigue' has been used in discussions of burnout in therapeutic professionals to describe the effect of overexposure to trauma on the ability to maintain empathy (eg, Figley, 2002). There is currently considerable interest in this and the related concept of **compassion deficit** in the light of high-profile cases in which nurses and other healthcare staff have neglected patients on a large scale, most famously in the Mid-Staffordshire NHS Trust in England.

The debate over compassion deficit is part of the wider debate in social psychology over the influence of situation and individual differences on social behaviours. The loss of compassion that underlay the wide-scale neglect of patients in Mid-Staffordshire has been explained by some commentators as compassion deficit or even **compassion deficit disorder**, firmly locating problems in the individual staff (Darbyshire, 2014). Other commentators have used situational ideas from social psychology to explain the impact of situation on behaviour. Paley (2015) cited the Darley and Batson 'Good Samaritan' study as evidence to suggest that when people are sufficiently busy and stressed they simply do not notice individuals in need.

A further view comes from Timmins and de Vries (2015) who explain neglect using the concept of cognitive dissonance. According to this approach healthcare professionals experience dissonance when they cannot reconcile their beliefs about good care and the behaviour they constantly observe. Where the pressures of the situation make it difficult to modify behaviour, health professionals may instead have altered their beliefs about the boundaries of acceptable caring behaviour.

> **KEY IDEAS** Compassion deficit (disorder) One way to explain institution-wide neglect by health professionals is **compassion deficit**, sometimes called **compassion deficit disorder**. This is a dispositional explanation, blaming the neglect on the individual staff involved.

THINKING PRACTICALLY

In Chapter 20 we discussed the idea of situational and dispositional attributions. Explain how different commentators on neglect in healthcare have made situational and dispositional attributions.

READ THIS

For a good overview of evolutionary principles applied to human altruism you might like to start with this:

Kurzban, R., Burton-Chellew, M.N., and West, S.A. (2015). The evolution of altruism in humans. *Annual Review of Psychology*, **66**, 575–99.

For detailed accounts of particular theories try these:

Trivers, R.L. (1971). The evolution of reciprocal altruism. *The Quarterly Review of Biology*, **46**, 35–57.

Hamilton, W.D. (1963). The evolution of altruistic behavior. *The American Naturalist*, **97**, 354–6.

For a review of bystander behaviour research this provides a neat summary:

Fischer, P., Krueger, J.I., Greitemeyer, T., Vogrincic, C., Kastenmüller, A., Frey, D., and Kainbacher, M. (2011). The bystander-effect: A meta-analytic review on bystander intervention in dangerous and non-dangerous emergencies. *Psychological Bulletin*, **137**, 517–37.

PREJUDICE

The word 'prejudice' comes from the Latin *pre* (before) and *judice* (judgement). In other words prejudice is to prejudge someone before having any information about them as an individual, simply on a single, observable characteristic linked to membership of a group. A prejudice can be described as an extreme attitude. As attitudes, prejudices can be thought of in terms of their components:

- *Stereotypes*. These represent the cognitive component of our prejudices, beliefs about the characteristics of the group in question.
- *Hostility*. This is the most common emotional component of prejudice. This varies, however, according to the subject of the prejudice, and some groups such as people with disabilities are more likely to arouse pity or embarrassment than hostility.
- *Discrimination*. This is the behavioural element to prejudice, involving treating members of the target group differently and more negatively than others. Of course, we treat some people more *positively* because they share characteristics with ourselves but whether this is best seen as prejudice is a moot point.

As we saw in the discussion of attitudes in Chapter 20 the relationship between the cognitive, emotional, and behavioural aspects of prejudice is not always straightforward. This is why people sometimes express racist opinions towards recent immigrant populations (often repeated from the right-wing media), whilst actually holding great affection towards individual members of that group.

Types of Prejudices

Not all prejudices are the same. **Racism**, for example, is now widely agreed to exist on a structural level irrespective of prejudice in the minds of individuals. Although the terms *racism* and *prejudice* are sometimes used interchangeably, some theorists stress the importance of defining these terms differently. From this perspective, *racism* exists when the social institutions are structured so that certain racial or ethnic groups are systematically disadvantaged, oppressed, or violated (eg, Feagin, 2006). Thus, racism exists not only in people's minds, but also in law, policy, religion, mass media, education, and so forth. An uncomfortable truth for the white majority is that, however fair-minded people try to be as individuals, white people constantly benefit from white privilege and this advantage is at the expense of minority ethnic groups.

Sexism, prejudice against women, can also be structural as well as individual. In addition sexism is distinguished by its ambivalent nature, existing simultaneously in hostile and 'benevolent' forms (Glick and Fiske, 1996). If the term 'benevolent sexism' makes you uncomfortable you are not alone! The idea is that whereas hostile sexism involves overt negative stereotypes—for example, of women as manipulative and verbally aggressive, accompanied by corresponding anger and dislike—benevolent sexism is experienced by men as a positive set of cognitions and emotions that have negative consequences for women. For example, the stereotype that women need protection may be seen as benevolent; however, its accompanying feelings of pity and solicitude damage gender equality. The word 'benevolent' refers to the *intention* not the *consequences*.

Stereotyping and Prejudice

One hears quite a lot about *stereotypes* as though they were inherently inaccurate, irrational, or even evil. However, **stereotyping**—attributing clusters of traits to specific categories of individuals and objects—is an intrinsic property of the human mind without which we might have difficulty functioning properly or even surviving. Just imagine trying to navigate the enormous complexity of life without lumping things together that share common characteristics—we would be 'flabbergasted by every new thing we encounter' (Pinker, 2002, p 203). To some degree we *must* assume that certain things are true about objects and individuals based on the category to which they belong (Fiske and Neuberg, 1990). If you are at war, and you see a person wearing a uniform of the opposing army, you do not have time to evaluate whether he or she intends to shoot you, you have to make the assumption. That's stereotyping.

Stereotypes may or may not have a degree of validity as regards the *typical* characteristics of groups; however, applying stereotypes *to individuals* from a group is dangerous, because individuals very often don't conform to the average at all. Moreover, the information we receive about the characteristics of social groups, and from which we form our stereotypes, is sometimes grossly exaggerated. For example, consider Victorian-era stereotypes of women as being too 'hormonally driven' to succeed in professions such as medicine or law. Currently, a large proportion of lawyers and doctors are female—indeed, if current rates of women's entry into medical school continue, women will soon dominate *most* non-surgical fields of medicine (BBC, 2009). Thus, although many women do experience discomfort and other symptoms coinciding with changes in the reproductive cycle, these changes clearly have no impact on their ability to succeed as doctors and lawyers or to function at high-level jobs.

Worse still, sometimes the information we receive is 'managed' by governments or other special interests like the owners of influential media and is not merely exaggerated, but is largely inaccurate. Consider the information that American citizens received about Africans by the slave-owning class in the 1700s and 1800s, or that Germans received about its Jewish citizens from Hitler's propaganda machine in the 1930s and 1940s.

Changing stereotypes

Although stereotypes can be quite powerful, they are not all-powerful. Some evidence suggests that stereotypes are primarily applied to individuals when no specific information about that person is available. Once information about a person becomes available that contradicts stereotypes, the stereotype is often (but not always) abandoned (Madon et al, 1998). It is also interesting to note that in the decades since World War II, stereotypes about groups such as Jews and Muslims have become

> **KEY IDEAS** stereotyping
> Attributing clusters of traits to specific categories of individuals or objects is called **stereotyping**. These clusters of traits create an image or conception of the 'typical' member of the category or its stereotype. Stereotypes of social groups often contain a degree of accuracy but are also frequently misapplied. Stereotypes are misapplied when one assumes that any given individual from a group is likely to display the average characteristics of the group, or when inaccurate information about the group's average characteristics is used to construct the group stereotype in the first place.

more widespread, not *less*, in the sense that people are in greater agreement regarding the stereotypical characteristics of these and other ethnic groups. However, the *content* of the stereotypes has changed—it has become more favourable. In other words, more stereotyping is occurring, but the characteristics attributed to groups are more flattering than in the past (Madon et al, 2001).

> **KEY IDEAS** moderate bias
Moderate bias is a form of cognitive bias in which reactions to a group are shaped by a blend of positive and negative stereotypes operating on two dimensions: competence and warmth.

Cuddy et al (2007) have created a model of newer forms of ***moderate bias***—bias that is not exceedingly strong—in which positive and negative stereotyping may coexist. For example, some groups, such as people suffering intellectual disability or older people, are often considered incompetent and judged to be generally useless to society, but at the same time are expected to be sweet and warm. Other groups, such as rich people, Jews, and Asians—are thought to be highly competent and intelligent, but suspected also of being in some way sneaky, threatening, or cold (Cuddy et al, 2007; Fiske et al, 2002).

According to Fiske and Cuddy and their colleagues, stereotyping can be captured on two dimensions, *competence* and *warmth*. This allows that a group can be ranked as high on one dimension but low on the other. Apparently positive stereotypes—for example, that a group is very intelligent or wealthy—may mask negative bias if that group is simultaneously seen to lack warmth. The positive stereotype of intelligence or wealth is thus tinged with envy and resentment. Similarly, high rankings on warmth can elicit pity rather than admiration if there is a simultaneous low ranking on competence.

In-Group Bias

> **KEY IDEAS** in-group bias
In-group bias is the tendency of human beings to favour and extend loyalty to members of their own group. In-group members are generally trusted more than out-group members, and in-group bias sometimes (but not always) leads to prejudice or even hatred towards members of out-groups. In-group bias tends to be automatic, and it is triggered as soon as group identity is created.

Another human tendency that we would do well to control in the modern world, but that may have had survival value for our evolutionary ancestors, is **in-group bias**. In-group bias is the tendency to favour and extend loyalty to members of one's own group (the *in-group*) over others, termed the *out-group*. In-group bias exists universally in all societies yet studied, and has been shown in part to have a genetic basis (Lewis and Bates, 2010). We are more approving and forgiving of members of our in-group, and we donate more of our time and resources to them. We trust them more, support them in their endeavours, and will sometimes even give up our lives for them. We cheer on *our* sports team, *our* school, *our* nation, *our* ethnicity, *our* fashion style, *our* musicians.

The tendency towards in-group bias is so strong that researchers can create artificial groups by randomly assigning people to two categories by tossing a coin ('Okay, you'll be in the Reds and you'll be in the Blues'), and people will immediately show allegiance to their temporary in-group by allocating members greater cash rewards in games constructed by the researchers (eg, Tajfel and Turner, 1979). Thus, in-group bias is not only pervasive throughout the world; it also seems to appear spontaneously as soon as a group identity is created, even a relatively arbitrary group identity (Brewer, 2007). Moreover, researchers have found that different brain regions are activated when participants view faces of members of in-groups to which they have been arbitrarily assigned as opposed to equally arbitrarily assigned out-group members (Van Bavel, Packer, and Cunningham, 2008). However, although this sort of allegiance can spontaneously appear to in-groups created from random characteristics, it also needs to be said that specific types of categories—for example, race, religion, or nationality—are much more likely to result in in-group bias or show bias in a more virulent form (Lewis and Bates, 2010).

In-group bias would not be so bad if it consisted only of favouritism and loyalty towards one's in-group. Unfortunately, it often (but not always) also leads to prejudice against out-groups. People may be more suspicious of members of the out-group, consider them more potentially dangerous, disparage them in relation to members of one's in-group, and view them as 'all alike'—in contrast to members of one's in-group, who are perceived as varied in their characteristics (Quillian and Pager, 2001). Unfortunately, 'all alike' tends to refer to negative characteristics rather than positive attributes.

One of the most famous demonstrations of automatic in-group bias and prejudice against out-groups was conducted during the mid-1950s by Muzafer and Carolyn Sherif and their colleagues at a summer camp in Robbers Cave State Park in Oklahoma (Sherif, 1966). In the Robbers Cave experiment, the campers (all 11-year-old boys) were randomly assigned to two groups and allowed to give names to their groups ('Eagles' and 'Rattlers'). At first the groups were kept entirely separate—indeed, neither group knew of the other's existence. After the members of each group had spent some time creating in-group relationships and spontaneously developing hierarchies, the groups were introduced to one another and taken through a series of competitive games. During this time they developed extremely intense group rivalries that went over the line of competitive spirit and into the realm of abusive mischief (destruction of property, cruel taunting, fighting, etc).

However, Sherif and his colleagues were interested in seeing if these negative manifestations of in-group bias could be reduced by setting up situations in which the two groups had to cooperate. At first, they simply brought the groups together for friendly activities—an American Independence Day celebration, the showing of a film, and so forth. Such activities did little to reduce the group rivalries. Only when the groups had to cooperate to achieve *important* common goals—such as discovering the reason for the failure of the camp's water supply to deliver water—was rivalry reduced substantially. The groups eventually ended up in a friendly relationship.

Implicit Prejudice

Until very recently overt prejudice has been on the decline, although this has changed since the rise of right-wing populism in Europe (Bilgic and Pace, 2017) and the USA (Fernando, 2017). However, prejudice can be much more subtle than Neo-Nazis on the march. For example, even people who do not consider themselves prejudiced, and who would never endorse stereotypically negative ideas about a group, may display automatic, unconscious bias known as **implicit prejudice** (Greenwald, Oaks, and Hoffman, 2003).

Studies using the **implicit association test** (IAT) show that some people have greater difficulty rapidly associating positive words and concepts with images flashed briefly on a screen of people from specific racial/ethnic groups, genders, and ages—while negative words and concepts are more easily associated with these images (Nosek et al, 2007; see Figure 22.5). For example, in one version of the test, the participant is faced with a computer screen and two buttons, one marked 'White or pleasant' and the other marked 'Black or unpleasant'. A series of images are flashed on the screen of faces of African Americans, European Americans, pleasant words, and unpleasant words. If the image is of either an unpleasant word or an African American face, the participant presses the button 'Black or unpleasant'. If the image is of a pleasant word or a European American face, the other button is pressed. The time it takes for the person to make a judgement and press a button is recorded. The task is then reversed, with the buttons marked 'White or unpleasant' and 'Black or pleasant'. Again, the length of time it takes for participants to make their judgements

> **KEY IDEAS** implicit prejudice **Implicit prejudice** refers to automatic, unconscious bias against a group. Implicit prejudice tends to be subtle and often exists even in people who do not consider themselves prejudiced. The standard procedure for assessing implicit prejudice involves the **implicit association test** (IAT) which compares response times to positive and negative terms associated with target groups

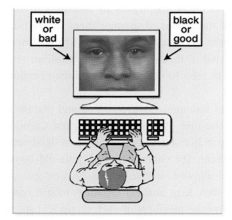

FIGURE 22.5 **The implicit association test.**

Source: Project Implicit.

is recorded. If, on average, it takes longer to press the 'Black or pleasant' than the 'White or pleasant' button—and a shorter time to press the 'Black or unpleasant' than the 'White or unpleasant' button—the participant is presumed to be biased against African Americans.

Although implicit psychology—mental activity that occurs below a person's level of awareness—is certainly a reality, and results of research using the IAT are interesting and provocative, critics have challenged the validity of tests such as the IAT and their applicability to real-world situations (Gawronski, 2009). Some claims for the applicability and accuracy of the IAT are exaggerated, and it has been shown experimentally that a person can fake responses on the IAT, at least to some degree, and remain undetected (Gawronski, 2009).

It may seem difficult to prevent implicit prejudice since people are, by definition, not conscious of it. But when individuals have been made aware of it and are highly motivated to rid themselves of it, they are able to do so, at least to an extent (Peruche and Plant, 2006). Implicit bias can also be reduced in people who have been exposed to various social influences, such as the presence of an admired member of the outgroup (Lowery, Hardin, and Sinclair, 2001). Thus, generally low levels of conscious prejudice and high motivation to remain unprejudiced may have profoundly positive effects on unconscious, implicit bias as well (Fiske, 2004).

Prejudice in the Face of Terror and Death

Human beings are unique among animals in their ability to be self-reflective and think symbolically. Among other things, this ability allows us to be aware of the awesome grandeur of being alive. Unfortunately, it also allows us to experience terror and dread in the knowledge that our lives will one day come to an end. According to terror management theory this *existential dilemma*—a problem rooted in the basic facts of human existence—has implications for understanding prejudice and intergroup conflict and violence. **Terror management theory (TMT)** proposes that much human behaviour is motivated by a need to 'manage' or reduce the terror that results from awareness of our eventual death. According to TMT, human beings accomplish terror management in two ways: (a) by strengthening beliefs in their worldview and cultural values, and (b) by increasing feelings of self-esteem. Thus, increasing beliefs that one is a 'valuable member of a meaningful universe' is the human way of transcending and defeating death by elevating oneself above

❯ KEY IDEAS terror management theory (TMT) TMT is an existential psychological theory that proposes that much human behaviour is motivated by a need to manage or reduce the terror associated with one's own mortality.

simple existence through one's personal accomplishments and adherence to a coherent worldview (Burke, Martens, and Faucher, 2010).

However, a problem arises when we encounter people with cultural values different from our own. According to terror management theory, the mere existence of different worldviews and cultural values constitutes a challenge to the absolute validity of our own—and hence, a challenge to the management of terror. To regain self-esteem and reassert belief in one's cultural values, people often resort to putting others down (in-group bias and prejudice), attempting to force others to change (the missionary strategy), or wiping them out entirely through war and genocide—the 'ultimate solution' to terror management (Hayes, Schimel, and Williams, 2008).

READ THIS

For a good general overview of the field of prejudice and discrimination you might like to start with this:

Whitley Jr, B.E. and Kite, M.E. (2016). *Psychology of Prejudice and Discrimination*. London: Routledge.

You can read more about intergroup relations and in-group bias here:

Greenwald, A.G. and Pettigrew, T.F. (2014). With malice toward none and charity for some: Ingroup favoritism enables discrimination. *American Psychologist*, **69**(7), 669–709.

For more on terror management try this:

Pyszczynski, T., Solomon, S., and Greenberg, J. (2015). Thirty years of terror management theory: From genesis to revelation. In *Advances in Experimental Social Psychology* (Vol 52, pp 1–70). Academic Press.

AGGRESSION

If bystander apathy and prejudice are amongst the less palatable *antisocial* aspects of human behaviour, what about deliberate attempts to actually cause harm to one another? The history of the world attests to the fact that, just as human beings are motivated to help one another, we are also frequently motivated to *harm* one another. **Aggression** is the general term used when an individual or group carries out an act that is intended to harm another individual or group in some way. This definition has two important qualifiers:

- For an act to constitute aggression, the aggressor must *believe* that the act is truly harmful.
- The target of the aggression must be *motivated to avoid* the behaviour (Anderson and Bushman, 2002).

Figure 22.6, by contrast, represents an activity which might appear to be an act of aggression but, when the context is considered and assessed against these two criteria, is not.

Like the social motivations, motivation to aggress has strong evolutionary roots throughout the animal world and in human history. Although it has clearly been the cause of some of the greatest tragedies in human existence, it also results in small daily miseries that may escape notice. Human aggression results in human wounds—from the death, destruction, and despair of world war and genocide to tears streaming down the face of a small child who has been ostracized from her playgroup out of cruelty.

> **KEY IDEAS** aggression
Aggression is a general term used when a person carries out an act intended to harm another in some way. However, for an act to constitute aggression, the aggressor must believe that the act is harmful, and intend it to be harmful. The target of aggression must experience it to be harmful, and be motivated to avoid the behaviour.

FIGURE 22.6 An act is only aggressive if the aggressor intends it to be harmful and if the recipient does not wish it. Technically then consensual sexual bondage and flagellation should not be considered aggressive, even if we might think it is distinctly odd behaviour!
Source: DZeta/Shutterstock.com.

Human aggression is also an enormously complex topic, one that cannot, and should not, be understood simply in psychological terms. It includes political, economic, military, philosophical, sociocultural, and historical aspects which would take many books many times the size of this one to consider adequately. However, aggression has been studied intensively from a psychological perspective, and researchers have clarified certain important aspects of the psychology of aggression.

Aggression and Violence

Violence is an aggressive act whose goal is to inflict physical injury or even death (Anderson and Bushman, 2002). All violent acts constitute aggression, because they are by definition intended to cause harm. However, not all aggressive acts are violent. For example, aggression can be *verbal* in the form of taunts, insults, cruel criticism, ostracism, or gossip. If verbal behaviour is intended to harm or denigrate a person, it can be said to constitute a form of aggression (Moore and Pepler, 2006).

On the other hand, some aggressive acts may be physical in nature, but intended to cause only minor harm, as when one child shoves another on the playground. In these cases 'violence' is too strong a term, because there is a difference not only in the *quantity* of harm intended in a shove—as compared with, say, the cluster bombing of a village—but also in the *quality* of harm intended.

WHAT'S HOT? VIOLENCE WITHOUT AGGRESSION? RITUAL VIOLENCE IN THE MOSH PIT

Social psychologists have been called upon to comment on the phenomenon of moshing. Moshing has been described as 'a form of dancing involving intense and violent physical activity; slamming into other audience members and throwing mock punches and kicks' (Kahn-Harris, 2006: p 205). Although the phenomenon has existed for longer the formal concept of 'moshing' is believed to have originated in the 1980s hardcore music scene, probably

> being first used by the band *Bad Brains*. Moshing is now associated with live performances in a range of music genres including punk, goth, metal, and alt rock.

Moshing is controversial for a number of reasons, most obviously that it appears to involve aggression and can result in injury—in one study by Milsten, Tennyson, and Weisberg (2017) around 1% of moshers required emergency medical attention. Much of the literature has painted a negative picture of moshing as 'dark leisure' (Yavuz, Holland, and Spracklen, 2018), and at the time of writing there are suggestions that moshing should be discouraged or even banned.

However, this picture disguises a complex mode of social interaction manifesting as **ritual violence**. Actually, in spite of the hectic appearance of the pit there is usually very little true aggression in the sense of deliberate attempts to harm. One participant in a study by Arnett (1996) described moshing as 'like a huge group fight, except no-one's fighting' (1996: p 83). Mosh pits have strict—if largely unwritten—rules and—considering the degree of forceful contact—injury is fairly rare. Moshing can be seen as a system of ritual violence including displays of strength and dominance, comparable perhaps to rugby or Zulu stick-fighting (Coatzee, 2002). As Lull (1987) points out, even these displays can be viewed as parodies of machismo rather than machismo itself.

Maintaining ritual and avoiding real violence takes a shared understanding of the unwritten rules of the pit. Ambrose (2013) has pointed to the importance of the 'pit lieutenant', usually a long-term fan trusted by, but not formally connected to, the band in leading dancers in good 'pit etiquette'. Pit etiquette or 'mosh pit rules' include contacting with elbows and open hands rather than fists, picking up the fallen, respecting the personal space of those on the edge of the pit and not dancing, holding up dropped items until they are claimed, not bringing drinks or cigarettes into the pit, and, most critically, not to retaliate when injured.

In some senses, the apparently violent nature of the mosh pit is incidental to understanding its psychology. Shared rituals, in particular those involving intense sensory experiences and movement, can foster increases in individual well-being (Csikszentmihalyi, 2014), whilst enduring a degree of risk and discomfort can foster a sense of group membership (Connelly et al, 2011). Like sporting and religious gatherings, attending bands and demonstrating commitment through dancing fosters a sense of *tribal* membership (Hutton, Ranse, and Munn, 2018). Epstein (2005) describes how 'an act perhaps incomprehensible to outsiders, encourages identification and cohesion amongst those who participate' (2005: p 5).

Hostile and Instrumental Aggression

Consider two incidents. In the first, a footballer kicks the legs from under a striker who receives a pass in a position from which the chances are good that he or she will score a goal. In the second a drunken man or woman carries out the same attack on someone who has danced with the aggressor's partner. In the first case, although the aggressor knowingly hurt the victim their ultimate aim was to prevent a goal being scored. This is **instrumental aggression**—aggression carried out in pursuit of another goal (Berkowitz, 1993). In the second case the ultimate aim was to inflict harm. This is **hostile aggression**.

Although the categories of *hostile* and *instrumental* aggression are useful in a general way, they are not always easy to distinguish in behaviour. These categories do not take into account the fact that motivations for aggression are often mixed,

> **KEY IDEAS** instrumental and hostile aggression **Instrumental aggression** is aggression which has an ultimate purpose other than causing harm to the victim. Instrumental aggression is often (but not always) planned, and is not necessarily accompanied by an emotion such as anger, although it may be. On the other hand, when the ultimate purpose for aggression is harming the victim, it is termed **hostile aggression**. These actions tend to be in reaction to some sort of provocation, accompanied by emotion such as anger, and are often (but not always) impulsive (Anderson and Bushman, 2002).

containing both instrumental and hostile elements (Bushman and Anderson, 2001a). For example, those engaged in violent robbery often go out of their way to hurt victims even when it is clear that they are not resisting and that the robbery will be successful.

Sex Differences in Aggression

Although both men and women are capable of the most extreme forms of aggressive behaviour, direct physical aggression is much more common in boys and men. This is particularly true when it comes to risky and deadly physical violence.

As a glaring example (illustrated in Figure 22.7), throughout the world the vast majority of murders are committed by men (most commonly against other men), and there is no known society where the level of deadly violence committed by women approaches that of men. A meta-analysis of research on real-world aggression (as opposed to laboratory experiments), conducted in ten nations on four continents, affirms that boys and men are more likely to engage in direct aggression than girls and women (Archer, 2004), particularly physical aggression. Laboratory research tells much the same story: although women can sometimes be provoked to the same degree of aggressive behaviour in the laboratory as men, men are more aggressive when *not* provoked—that is, they are more aggressive to begin with (Bettencourt and Kernahan, 1997). The size of the sex difference in real-world aggression is also much greater than that found in laboratory research (Archer, 2004).

In some other forms of aggression, however, sex differences are slight or non-existent. For example, differences between men and women in verbal aggression or *indirect aggression*—deliberately excluding or ostracizing others from a group, or speaking maliciously about another person—are very small, if they exist at all (Card et al, 2008).

So why should men be more directly aggressive and violent than women? This question once again raises the issue of *levels of analysis*, discussed earlier. Different researchers will have different ways of interpreting the 'why' in 'why are men more directly aggressive?' For example, neuroscientists and biopsychologists may interpret this question as 'Which sex differences in hormones, brain structures, brain

FIGURE 22.7 **Throughout the world the vast majority of murders are committed by men.**

Source: Reproduced with permission from United Nations Office on Drugs and Crime. Global Study on Homicide, 2014, Trends, Context, Data. https://www.unodc.org/documents/gsh/pdfs/2014_GLOBAL_HOMICIDE_BOOK_web.pdf

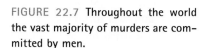

chemistry, and body build are responsible for the sex differences in aggression?' An answer rooted in hormones, brains, and bodies is an answer which addresses the most proximate mechanisms which cause the differences in aggression. In a sense, answers rooted in proximate mechanisms tell the 'how' side of the story, explaining *how* sex differences in aggression are triggered and play out.

However, other researchers are interested in those factors which might have caused men and women to differ in their hormones, brains, and bodies in the first place—the *ultimate* causes of the sex difference in aggression (Archer, 2009). Such answers are rooted in the evolutionary history of human males and females and they tell the 'why' side of the story. It is important to realize that ultimate and proximate explanations do not contradict one another. Instead, they are both needed to fully understand important questions such as the origin of sex differences in aggression (Scott-Phillips, Dickens, and West, 2011).

One of the most frequently suggested immediate, direct (proximate) causes of the sex difference in aggression is the sex difference in levels of the steroid (sex) hormone *testosterone* (Book, Starzyk, and Quinsey, 2001). Men secrete, on average, 8–10 times the amount of testosterone produced by women, the exact amount primarily being dependent upon genetic factors (Dabbs, 2000). Some researchers hypothesize that testosterone assists men in accomplishing those things necessary to attract a mate (eg, charm, resourcefulness, bravery, sexuality, dominance over other men), but simultaneously hinders those qualities necessary for parenting and long-term bonds by increasing restlessness, interest in multiple sex partners, competitiveness, anger, and aggression (Storey et al, 2000).

Of all the 'crimes' attributed to testosterone, aggression is clearly the worst. But does testosterone actually increase aggression in men? The bulk of the research does suggest that some sort of link between testosterone and aggression exists (Archer, 2004, 2006). However, the nature of this link is not straightforward. For example, there is no increase in aggression in boys at the onset of puberty when testosterone levels sharply rise; in fact, there may be a decrease in aggression (Archer, 2004, 2006). Moreover, injecting volunteers with doses of testosterone does not increase their aggression (O'Connor, Archer, and Wu, 2004). And yet, the connection between aggression and testosterone in non-human animals is well established. Moreover, when studies of humans are considered together, the majority of them do find at least some sort of link—particularly in men—even if this link is inconsistent and difficult to predict.

Archer (2004, 2006) has carefully examined the available research as well as conducting his own studies, and advanced a hypothesis regarding the connection between testosterone and aggression in humans that would account for the inconsistency in findings. Archer's idea, known as the *challenge hypothesis*, is based on research on aggression and testosterone in birds. Simply stated, the hypothesis holds that the association between testosterone and aggression in men is highly dependent on age and context. For example, the initial rise in testosterone at puberty is associated with increased interest in sexuality and mating, not aggression. However, beginning in later **adolescence** and early adulthood, increases in testosterone levels are associated with contests and challenges of various sorts. Levels of testosterone rise in young men when they win contests and competitions and drop when they lose; these changes are not found in women (Schultheiss et al, 2005). Testosterone even rises and drops in male spectators watching sports competitions as their team wins or loses, and, as Figure 22.8 shows, it drops in male voters when their candidate loses (Beehner et al, 2009)!

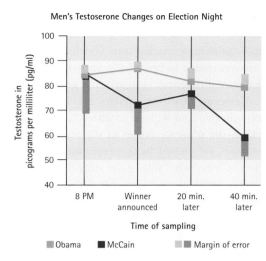

FIGURE 22.8 **McCain voters' testosterone levels drop on election night.** Testosterone was measured in the saliva of samples of male and female voters on election night in the United States, 4 November 2008, when Barack Obama was elected over John McCain. In male voters supporting John McCain, a drop in testosterone was noted immediately upon announcement of President Obama's victory, and a more dramatic drop was noted 40 minutes later. No such effect was found for women.

Source: Data from Stanton et al, 2009

In the animal world, contests and challenges among males are frequently experienced in the context of mate competition, and they usually involve aggression. Thus, testosterone becomes associated with aggression in men when they move into later adolescence and adulthood, a time of establishing serious mating relationships. However, rather than 'causing' aggression, testosterone may simply facilitate it—that is, rising in response to aggression or situations calling for aggression (Sapolsky, 1997).

Although the challenge hypothesis does *fit* the available research on testosterone and aggression in men fairly well—and there is much evidence in its favour in non-human species, particularly birds—the hypothesis has not been subject to direct tests in humans.

THINKING CREATIVELY

There is currently a lack of experimental research testing the challenge hypothesis. How might you go about testing challenge hypothesis experimentally? Consider the setting, participant design, measurement of the dependent variable, and how you might manipulate the independent variable.

> **KEY IDEAS** reformulated frustration-aggression hypothesis This is Leonard Berkowitz's revision of an earlier theory which stated that all aggression is in response to the frustration of a goal. According to the **reformulated frustration-aggression hypothesis**, frustration is only one of many types of unpleasant events that could lead to aggression. The theory holds that aggression occurs when an unpleasant event (eg, provocation by another person, extreme noise) may trigger feelings, images, and memories associated with the physiological changes that ordinarily accompany threat and danger.

Factors Triggering Aggression

Psychologists have been attempting to isolate the psychological causes of aggression ever since the time of Freud. An important early theory, known as the *frustration-aggression hypothesis* (Dollard et al, 1939), stated that aggression occurs primarily (or even exclusively) when a person is frustrated in attaining an important goal. According to this idea, frustration leads to anger which leads to aggression. If you've ever learned to play a musical instrument, been repeatedly unable to master a passage, and felt ready to smash the instrument to the ground, you were providing support for the frustration-aggression hypothesis.

However, it soon became apparent to researchers that many acts of aggression are not preceded by frustration of a goal, and the theory was then revised by Leonard Berkowitz in 1989. According to this **reformulated frustration-aggression hypothesis**, anger and consequent aggression can arise from virtually any form of unpleasant event—including frustration but also including various forms of provocation by other people or even unpleasant environmental stimuli such as loud noises and extreme temperatures. According to the theory, aggression will occur when the unpleasant event triggers feelings, images, or memories associated with the physiological changes that normally occur during conditions of threat and danger, including increased heart rate and respiration.

Because Berkowitz's reformulated theory stresses the power of cognitive associations to produce anger and subsequent aggression, it is sometimes called the *cognitive neoassociation model* of aggression (Berkowitz, 1993). Although Berkowitz's theory was an advance over the original frustration-aggression hypothesis, it failed to explain instrumental aggression and other forms of aggression apparently not accompanied by strong emotions such as anger.

Other attempts to explain how aggression occurs have focused on how aggression may be *learned* through exposure to social models that promote aggression, such as violent media or aggressive individuals present in one's environment (discussed fully in Chapter 7). Like the reformulated frustration-aggression hypothesis, however, this *social learning* model only provides part of the story and cannot account for all psychological aspects of aggression. If social learning were entirely responsible for aggression, all people exposed to aggressive models would themselves become aggressive, and this is clearly not the case.

Recognizing the many contributions of various theories of the psychological causes of aggression—but also acknowledging their limitations—Craig Anderson has integrated various perspectives into a single model he hoped would offer a more powerful explanation (DeWall and Anderson, 2011). This model is known as the **general aggression model**, or GAM. According to this model, aggression will (or will not) occur in any given situation as a result of a complex interaction among four factors:

- *Personal characteristics* (eg, a person's traits, sex, beliefs, and attitudes).
- *Characteristics of the specific situation* (eg, provocation, incentives to aggression, frustration of a goal).
- *Emotions, thoughts, and biological arousal levels* which result from the interaction of characteristics of the person and environment.
- *Decision-making processes* (how the person sizes up the situation and decides to act).

As an example, people who come to the table with already heightened levels of aggressive tendencies often have a cognitive bias towards interpreting other people's actions as having some sort of hostile motive, even when no such motive exists ('That @#$%! brushed up against me *on purpose*!'; Bushman and Anderson, 2002). This is a *personal characteristic* (#1 in the preceding list) that might be brought to a situation. Consider such a person on an extremely hot day in a cafe with no air conditioning. He tries to make a call on his mobile phone, but cannot get a connection because he is unlucky enough to subscribe to a mobile network with poor coverage in the area (#2 in the list, *characteristics of the specific situation*). Someone then accidentally brushes up against him as he is trying to get the phone to work. He is already physiologically aroused with frustration and feeling a fair amount of anger at the phone. He is also uncomfortable from the heat and has a bias towards interpreting ambiguous interactions as being hostile (#3 in the list, *emotions, thoughts, and arousal levels*). He then may decide to act impulsively and aggress against the

> **KEY IDEAS** the GAM The **general aggression model (GAM)** is Anderson and Bushman's theory of aggression which holds that whether aggression does or does not occur in any interaction is dependent upon a complex interaction between four factors: personal characteristics; characteristics of the situation; emotions, thoughts, and biological arousal levels; and decision-making processes.

offender by shoving him—or he may give thought and refrain from aggression (#4, *decision-making processes*).

Justifying Aggression

One final observation needs to be made about aggression, whether committed against individuals or entire peoples: aggressors almost always believe that they are in the right, and they do not apply the same moral judgements to themselves in regard to aggression and other destructive acts (such as betrayals) that they apply to others (Pinker, 2011; Tavris and Aronson, 2007). This is an example of self-serving bias (see 'The self in social context', Chapter 21, for a discussion). This human tendency to let oneself off the moral hook makes aggression a particularly dangerous motivated behaviour. It means that aggression can be difficult to inhibit once it begins to build up steam.

The notion that certain people—like over-the-top villains in film thrillers—are simply evil, know they are evil, and commit aggressive and other destructive acts with full knowledge that they are morally wrong is probably misguided (Trivers, 2010, 2011). As Pinker (2011) points out, many of the most notorious villains of history—not to mention perpetrators of ordinary day-to-day violence and aggression—are 'deeply moral' in the sense that they believe what they are doing in some way rights previous wrongs done to them or to their loved ones, their nation, their neighbourhood, their religion, or to mankind in general. In other words, aggressive and violent people may *truly* believe—at least consciously—that their actions are just; they are not merely hypocritically claiming justification, all the while knowing that they are really in the wrong (Pinker, 2011).

Consider the differences in perspective between members of two sides in a violent conflict, each of whom may use similar tactics, but each of whom claims that the other side is composed of 'terrorists' whereas their own side is composed of 'freedom fighters'. Steven Pinker (2011) fleshes this idea out by describing two ways each for viewing a series of well-known armed conflicts. For example, take these two perspectives on the Crusades:

1 The Crusades were an explosion of religious idealism that may have had a few excesses, but left the world better off for its promotion of cultural exchange.

or:

2 The Crusades were yet another vicious attack on Jewish communities and a brutal invasion of Muslim lands and subjugation of Muslims by Christian extremists.

Yet, some researchers have suggested that despite aggressors' conscious certainty that they are on the moral high road, there may be a lower level of consciousness at which they may be aware of their own hypocrisy (Trivers, 2011; Valdesolo and DeSteno, 2008). For example, Valdesolo and DeSteno (2008) had research participants help plan a study in which half of the group would get a simple task involving a brief survey and viewing of photographs, while the other half would engage in a gruelling 45 minutes of solving logic and maths problems. When given the opportunity to assign themselves to one task or the other, participants were highly inclined to assign themselves to the easy task. This may not be particularly unexpected, but when questioned in detail about the fairness of the procedures they used, those who assigned themselves to the easy task were adamant that their procedures had been fair. Of course, those receiving the short end of the stick disagreed!

Yet, when these participants, who had been so kind in their own self-evaluations, were asked to evaluate the behaviour of *others*, what do you suppose happened? When these others were described as having chosen the easy road for themselves, they were condemned in harsh terms. Obviously, participants in this research had different standards for judging their own actions as compared with that of other people.

However, Valdesolo and DeSteno wanted to discover whether these 'moral hypocrites', who seemed oblivious to the blatant unfairness of their procedures, really did understand at some level that they had been in the wrong. Therefore, they repeated the entire study with a second group of participants who, following their self-serving assignments of themselves to the easier task (or observing other participants doing the same) were asked to evaluate their procedures and those of others, as the first group had done. However, these participants were asked to make their evaluations under conditions of heavy 'cognitive load'—a distracting task requiring them to keep seven digits in memory while answering questions about the experience flashed on a computer.

As Figure 22.9 shows, the result was that participants who had assigned themselves to the easy task evaluated their own behaviour equally harshly to that of others who also had chosen the easy task. Keeping these digits in memory had the effect of 'tying up' cognitive resources they would otherwise have been able to apply to convincing themselves and everyone else they had been justified. The moral 'blinkers' had been removed, suggesting that those who behave in an aggressive

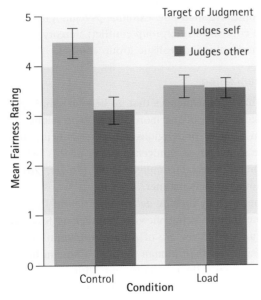

FIGURE 22.9 Moral hypocrites may know 'deep down' that they are wrong. When researchers manipulated participants into making self-serving, blatantly unfair decisions, most insisted nevertheless that they had been just. But when these same individuals observed others behaving in the same self-serving manner, they sharply condemned the others' actions as unfair. This 'moral hypocrisy' is depicted in the graph on the left, labelled 'control'. Yet when a second group made evaluations of their own and others' behaviour under conditions with a heavy 'cognitive load' consisting of a distracting memory task, the moral hypocrisy was not evident, and people judged themselves as severely as they judged others. At some level, moral hypocrites might realize that they are wrong and engage in various cognitive strategies to avoid confronting the truth.

or hurtful manner and seem to believe in the rightness of their actions may have a hidden level of self-awareness that might somehow be reachable. As Steven Pinker states: 'It may take ridicule, it may take argument, it may take time, it may take being distracted, but people have the means to recognize that they are not always in the right' (2011, p 492). This may be encouraging news.

Intergroup Conflict and Aggression

> *Kill the pig! Cut his throat! Kill the pig! Bash him in!*
>
> —William Golding, from *Lord of the Flies*, Chapter 7

If you read William Golding's *Lord of the Flies* at school, you may recall its grim vision of human nature as linked inescapably to murderous and barbarous aggression and conflict between groups. Much of the history of the world since the dawn of civilization would seem to bear out this pessimistic view. What causes the seemingly never-ending pattern of prejudice, conflict, aggression, and violence between groups? This is the question addressed by much research and theory in social psychology. Indeed, **intergroup conflict**—the social psychological term to describe non-harmonious relations among groups—has been called 'the problem of the century' by Susan Fiske (2004) because it has been the root cause of many millions of deaths and unimaginable human suffering resulting from aggression and violence.

However, it is in the context of intergroup conflict that aggression can reach the heights of violent expression in war and genocide—the deliberate attempt to exterminate an entire people. We shall now examine psychological factors that often lead to aggression in the context of intergroup conflict: stereotyping, prejudice, in-group bias, obedience to authority, and realistic group conflict.

The role of dehumanization

In-group bias may have consequences that go beyond simple prejudice and institutional racism. Consider some of the more severe expressions of human aggression often termed *evil* in a moral or religious context: genocide, torture, rape, wars of aggression, and the slaughter of innocents. Some of this behaviour can seem not merely horrifying but literally incomprehensible (Pinker, 2011). How can human beings treat one another in this manner?

One part of the puzzle may include *dehumanization* of the out-group. Dehumanization refers to one human being viewing another as less than human in some way—as a beast or animal. In the era of American plantation slavery, Black people were legally considered less than human (60% of a human being, to be exact), and this view was used to justify their enslavement. Hitler portrayed the Jewish people as less than human to justify genocide against them.

How does dehumanization occur? This is no doubt a complex process that includes socioeconomic as well as psychological variables. However, one factor that appears to be present frequently when dehumanization occurs is the emotion of *disgust* at the out-group. Disgust is one of the basic human emotions (see Chapter 15 for a discussion). Disgust probably evolved to help protect human beings from disease-causing organisms present in faeces, rotting food, and other such organic products that universally evoke disgust (Oaten, Stevenson, and Case, 2009).

However, according to psychologist Paul Rozin, disgust has evolved in human culture over the centuries to include objects that threaten not the health of the body but the *purity of the soul*. We are therefore disgusted at things that remind us of our

> **KEY IDEAS** intergroup conflict
> **Intergroup conflict** can be described as non-harmonious relations between groups. This can vary considerably in magnitude, from mutual avoidance and antilocution (verbal criticism and attack) to **genocide,** the deliberate and systematic attempt to exterminate a population.

animal nature and the fragility of our mortality—festering wounds, amputations, and so forth. Because humans often view other animals as lower forms of life bereft of souls, being reminded of our animal nature may cause us to feel debased, dirty, or polluted. This serves as a threat to the purity of our souls (Rozin et al, 1999, 2009).

According to Rozin and his colleagues, disgust has strayed even farther from its origins to include moral and social disgust. Depending on the culture or the individual, acts such as abuse of the helpless (children, elderly, animals), murder, rape, genocide, mutilation of corpses, corporate greed, and the notion of human cloning may be considered just as disgusting as rotting meat. Such acts violate the spiritual integrity of the human being, rather than the bodily integrity—they are harmful to the soul. We respond to them with revulsion, just as we do to bodily wounds and deformities.

In general, this expansion of disgust into the moral arena may serve an important socialization function, helping to enforce standards of morality. However, disgust for despised out-groups and individuals has been used as a weapon throughout history, when people assign to despised groups the characteristics associated with ordinarily disgusting objects—for example, filth, odour, sliminess, and decay (Nussbaum, 2001). The characterization of certain groups as disgusting is one step towards their dehumanization and the legitimizing of genocide (Bloom, 2004).

But why describe a despised group as disgusting rather than merely dangerous? According to Bloom (2004), it is because disgust originated as a response to bodies, not souls—it is fundamentally a bodily emotion. If a person is characterized as a body only, without a soul, that person lacks moral worth; we are not obligated to extend empathy and compassion to that person. Throughout history, many despots, propagandists, and warmongers have understood that disgust can be used to get people to commit horrendous atrocities by 'robbing' the victims of their souls in the minds of the perpetrators.

Deindividuation in Groups: Human Beings at their Worst

The bystander effect is fed by people's tendency to feel more anonymous and less accountable for their behaviour in groups. It has been suggested that this feeling may sometimes lead to **deindividuation**—a lessening of self-awareness or identity when in a group, leading to reduced concern with how your behaviour will be evaluated by others. Under such conditions a person might behave in ways he or she normally would not. If a real phenomenon, deindividuation may have disastrous consequences if it occurs in interaction with a social role that puts one in a position of power over other individuals—for example, the role of prison guard or soldier.

Consider the Stanford prison experiment, conducted (though never completed) by Philip Zimbardo at Stanford University in California (Zimbardo, 1973). Zimbardo and his colleagues wished to examine changes in individual behaviour that might accompany changes in social roles—the various roles one is expected to play in the course of one's life such as mother, doctor, soldier, student, and so forth. They created a role-play situation in which undergraduate students were randomly assigned to be 'prisoners' or 'guards' in a highly realistic prison situation that even included being 'arrested' by actual police and 'charged' prior to imprisonment.

The experiment was supposed to run for two weeks, but by the end of only six days it had to be closed down. Why? The majority of the students had taken on attributes of their roles to such a degree that their behaviour became virtually indistinguishable from that of actual prisoners and guards under deindividuating

> **KEY IDEAS** deindividuation
Deindividuation involves a reduction in self-awareness or personal identity within a group, leading to increased feelings of anonymity and reduced concern for how one's behaviour will be evaluated by others in the group.

conditions. The guards became increasingly sadistic, treating the prisoners with cruelty that would not be allowed with animals. The prisoners, for their part, had become so traumatized that their behaviour was servile; they thought only of escape and experienced genuine hatred for the guards.

It should be emphasized that the guards had been randomly assigned to their position, and were no different psychologically from the group that had been randomly assigned to be prisoners. According to Zimbardo, the Stanford experiment demonstrated that such situations often emerge, not because of 'a few bad apples' but because 'the barrel itself is rotten' (Zimbardo, 2007).

According to other researchers, however, the situation appears to be somewhat more complex than Zimbardo allows (Carnahan and McFarland, 2007). For example, although the Stanford students were randomly assigned to be prisoners and guards, all the participants had knowingly volunteered for an experiment in prison life. Carnahan and McFarland (2007) have shown that students willing to volunteer for a study of prison life such as the Zimbardo study may be more psychologically predisposed than ordinary students towards personality traits associated with aggressiveness, authoritarianism, narcissism (inflated ideas of the self), and dominance; they may also be lower on positive traits such as altruism and empathy. It may be that factors of the prison situation interacted with the personality factors of the volunteers to create the abuses that arose during Zimbardo's study.

READ THIS

The following article provides an overview of aggression research:

Warburton, W.A. and Anderson, C.A. (2015). Aggression, social psychology of. *International Encyclopedia of the Social and Behavioral Sciences*, 373–80.

For something specifically on the biopsychology of aggression this is an accessible start:

Carré, J.M. and Olmstead, N.A. (2015). Social neuroendocrinology of human aggression: examining the role of competition-induced testosterone dynamics. *Neuroscience*, **286**, 171–86.

If you are particularly interested in aggression at the intergroup level you might like to read more about dehumanization:

Haslam, N. (2006). Dehumanization: An integrative review. *Personality and Social Psychology Review*, **10**, 252–64.

IN REVIEW

ALTRUISM

- Humans have the tendency to unpredictably offer help to those in need, including strangers.
- The proximate causes of empathy appear to be related to empathy. Contemporary research suggests that empathy has a neurological basis involving mirror neurons.
- Altruism also requires an ultimate explanation. One such explanation involves inclusive fitness, the idea that we instinctively favour those with similar genetic make-up in order to promote the survival of our genes to future generations.

An alternative ultimate explanation involves reciprocal altruism. This occurs when people assist one another knowing that this is likely to be reciprocated when the actor needs help in the future.

BYSTANDER APATHY

Research into bystander behaviour was stimulated by the high-profile murder of Kitty Genovese, in which a number of neighbours reportedly failed to intervene.

Although Genovese case was widely misreported, the principle that people in larger numbers are less likely to intervene to offer help has been upheld by experimental research.

The probability of bystander apathy also increases where the situation is ambiguous and where those needing help are strangers, and decreases where there is physical danger and when males are present.

Recent high-profile mass instances of bystander apathy by health professionals towards patients have spawned the term 'compassion deficit' describing the disposition of the carers. There are, however, situational explanations for this behaviour.

PREJUDICE

A prejudice is an extreme attitude with cognitive, affective, and behavioural components. Prejudices can have structural as well as individual forms and can be hostile or benevolent in their intent.

Stereotyping is an inevitable cognitive process but can have serious consequences for the target groups involved. Stereotypes can include positive and negative characteristics and can be thought of as having two dimensions, competence and warmth.

Humans have a tendency for bias in favour of their own social categories and against members of different social categories. This is exacerbated by competition and can be tackled by the pursuit of shared goals.

Even those who reject group stereotypes and deny conscious bias may have implicit prejudice, unconscious bias towards particular social categories. However the standard tool for measuring implicit bias, the IAT, is controversial.

There may be an existential aspect to prejudice as we boost our own self-esteem and cultural identity at the expense of others in order to help manage the terror of our own mortality.

AGGRESSION

Aggression involves the attempt to harm another person by carrying out an act in the knowledge that it will be harmful and against the wishes of the person.

There are important distinctions between aggression and violence, between hostile and instrumental aggression and between real and ritual violence.

There are sex differences in aggression, with males responsible for more direct or physical aggression than females.

There are a range of factors affecting aggression including frustration and observational learning. The general aggression model takes into account a range of external factors, including frustration and provocation, and internal factors such as personality, sex, and decision-making.

- In keeping with what we know about self-serving bias, it appears that people find ways to justify their aggression.

- Intergroup conflict accounts for much large-scale aggression. This is characterized by dehumanization and deindividuation.

TEST YOURSELF

1   Altruism is an example of prosocial behaviour. True ☐ False ☐

2   Mirror neurons provide an ultimate explanation for empathy. True ☐ False ☐

3   Women are more verbally aggressive than men. True ☐ False ☐

4   The GAM includes both dispositional and situational factors. True ☐ False ☐

5   Which of the following circumstances makes helping behaviour more likely?

   a) Having more people present

   b) Helping is dangerous

   c) Compassion fatigue

   d) The situation is ambiguous

6   Which of the following is an element of prejudice?

   a) Stereotypes

   b) Hostility

   c) Discrimination

   d) All the above

7   Which of the following best describes moshing?

   a) Ritual violence

   b) Physical violence

   c) Hostile aggression

   d) Instrumental aggression

8   In the GAM which of the following is a personal characteristic?

   a) Provocation

   b) Frustration

   c) Incentives

   d) Attitudes

9   Explain the role of dehumanization in intergroup conflict.

10 Explain the difference between the original and reformulated frustration-aggression hypotheses.

 Visit the online resources that accompany this book: www.oup.com/uk/jarvis-okami1e

GLOSSARY

Absolute threshold The minimum intensity of a stimulus necessary for it to be detected by the appropriate sense organ 50% of the time.

Academic psychology Psychology literature written for psychologists and psychology students. Its aim is to provide an account of psychology closely based closely on referenced psychological theory and research.

Accommodation Piaget's term for the process whereby a person significantly alters his or her schema to incorporate new information or experiences. This may involve the creation of a new schema.

Accurate empathy Rogers' term to describe the quality of communication between two people where each person genuinely listens to the other's words, hears the words, perceives the intention accurately, and withholds judgement.

Acquisition In classical conditioning, the process of acquiring a conditioned response. Also a generic atheoretical term for developing a response.

Active gene-environment correlation A correlation between environment and genotype that results from active choices made by an organism.

Actor-observer bias The cognitive bias towards attributing our own behaviour primarily to situational factors, but others' behaviour to dispositional factors.

Adaptations Characteristics of organisms that have evolved over evolutionary time because they confer reproductive or survival advantages. Adaptations arise as a result of small, incremental changes in the genome of organisms over many generations, and they represent solutions to specific challenges and pressures faced recurrently by the organism.

Addiction A term used to describe drug dependence. Originally, the term included withdrawal, tolerance, and craving as necessary components, but currently, addiction has no agreed definition.

Additive principle The principle stating that adding an extrinsic motive to an existing intrinsic motive will increase the overall level of motivation.

Adolescence Literally 'becoming adult'. Adolescence includes cultural as well as biological dimensions. Adolescence begins at age 10, according to the World Health Organization, but the end of adolescence is highly dependent on sociocultural factors.

Adrenarche The maturation of the adrenal glands from about age 10. This is an aspect of puberty and is associated with the development of secondary sexual characteristics.

Aetiology A medical term which means the causes of illness and disease.

Affect A general feeling state which provides the 'raw material' from which emotions and moods are created. Affect differs along two dimensions: valence (positive–negative) and activation or arousal (high–low).

Afferent information Information that is transmitted from sense organs (eg, from the eye through the optic nerve to the brain). This is the basis of traditional theories of perception—afferent information is processed for meaning in the brain.

Affordance Gibson's term to explain how information about objects in the ambient optic array allows us to classify objects according how we will interact with them without reference to prior knowledge about their purpose. This is an important element of the direct theory of perception.

Aggression A general term used when a person carries out an act intended to harm another in some way. However, for an act to constitute aggression, the aggressor must believe that the act is harmful, and intend it to be harmful, and the target of aggression must experience it to be harmful, and be motivated to avoid the behaviour.

Agonist Any substance that mimics the action of a neurotransmitter and binds to the neurotransmitter receptor.

Alcohol *See* **Ethanol**.

Alleles Alleles are the different forms a particular gene might take; for example, a gene might have a long or short allele. Genetic differences among people occur not because they have different genes but because people inherit unique combinations of alleles.

Altered state of consciousness A temporary but radical change in the overall pattern of a person's normal subjective experience. This can be the result of drugs, sensory deprivation, and perhaps—though this is controversial—hypnosis.

Altruism The offering of assistance to others without the expectation of an immediate reward.

Alzheimer's disease A neurodegenerative disease characterized by increasingly severe memory loss, confusion, difficulty speaking or comprehending speech, and difficulty with self-care. Alzheimer's disease is the most common type of dementia.

Ambient optic array Gibson's term for the array of visual information available to us at any given moment as we view a scene. Gibson's theory is based on the idea that there is an enormous amount of information in this array and that this allows us to perceive objects and events without higher-level cognitive processing.

Ambivalence The experience of conflicting emotions or motivations—what we might call 'being in two minds' about something. The word comes from *ambi*, meaning 'equal' as in ambidextrous and valence, which refers to the strength of emotions.

Amphetamines A family of stimulant drugs that exert their effects primarily by increasing levels of norepinephrine, serotonin, and dopamine in the brain.

Amplitude The intensity of a sound or light output source expressed in the height of light or sound waves.

Anger A basic emotion involving high levels of physiological arousal and a sense of antagonism towards something or someone.

Anomalistic psychology A broad field looking at the full range of anomalous (ie, unusual and hard to explain) human experiences. These range from ghost-sightings through to religious ecstasy to near-death experiences.

Antagonist Any substance that blocks the receptors of a particular neurotransmitter, decreasing the availability and effects of the neurotransmitter.

Antidepressant Any drug or other substance whose primary purpose is the treatment of depression.

Antisocial personality The characteristics commonly called psychopathy (although there is debate about the extent to which the two are interchangeable), recognized as a mental disorder in major diagnostic systems. The antisocial personality is impulsive, irresponsible, and lacking in empathy.

Anxiolytics Any drug or other substance the primary use of which is the treatment of anxiety. The most common class of anxiolytic drugs is the benzodiazepines. These drugs are mildly sedating and may reduce anxiety symptoms, at least in the short term.

Apex dreams The most intense, bizarre, non-rational, and hallucinatory dreaming. Although apex dreams are uncommon they tend to be well remembered.

Applied psychology A set of professions that employ techniques based on psychological theory and research in order to benefit people in a particular context such as education or the work place.

Assimilation Piaget's term to describe the process whereby a person processes a new experience by fitting it into a pre-existing schema.

Assortative mating Assortative mating takes place when parents similar in genetically influenced characteristics tend to mate. This leads to more genetically similar children and inflates the apparent heritability of characteristics.

Attachment A two-way emotional bond between two people characterized by proximity-seeking, separation distress, and reunion pleasure.

Attachment disorders *See* **Atypical attachment**.

Attachment theory A broad collection of ideas from different psychologists, sharing the idea that the qualities of the child's first attachment relationship are stable and generalize to later attachments.

Attitude strength On one level this is self-explanatory—how strongly we hold an attitude. However, various factors affect attitude strength including its valence, meaning the intensiveness of its positivity or negativity, expertise—how much we know about the subject, and accessibility—how automatically we respond to something based on our attitude.

Attitudes Our summary evaluations about both concrete and abstract ideas, in other words how much we like them.

Attraction The product of the factors that draw one person towards another for friendship, sex, romance, or other sort of relationship.

Attribution Attribution is the process of explaining behaviour in terms of characteristics of the person (whether short- or long-term), the situation, or an interaction between the two; or in terms of whether a behaviour is intentional or unintentional.

Atypical attachment There is no clear distinction between an atypical attachment and an attachment disorder. Both are patterns of attachment behaviour that fall outside the range of normal variations in attachment.

Audition The technical term for the sense of hearing.

Auditory cortex The portion of the temporal lobe responsible for interpreting transduced auditory signals.

Auditory nerve The auditory nerve conducts transduced auditory signals to the thalamus, to then be relayed to the auditory cortex.

Auditory receptors Specialized neurons that are embedded in the surface of the basilar membrane. They respond to vibration and pass this information along the auditory nerve to the brain which interprets this as sound.

Average expectable environment An environment provided by parents that falls within normal parameters, as opposed to a particular good or bad environment. Whilst no psychologists question the effects of particularly good or bad parenting there is debate about the effects of parenting that falls within the average expectable environment on development.

Basic emotions Emotions that appear to be universal, innate, and distinct. Each basic emotion is associated with basic emotions. Psychologists are not in agreement as to the number of basic emotions, which specific emotions are basic, or even if the concept itself is valid.

Basic virtue A positive personality characteristic. In Erikson's theory there are eight basic virtues, each acquired at a particular age as the result of successfully managing a developmental stage.

Basilar membrane A collection of stiff fibres housed within the cochlear of the inner ear. The basilar membrane contains the hair cells that act as auditory receptors.

BDI *See* **Beck depression inventory.**

Beck depression inventory (BDI) A standard assessment tool for depression. It contains 21 items each of which can be scored 0–3 according to selection of one of four statements. The higher the score the greater the degree of depression. A score of over 19 or 20 (depending on the version) indicates moderate depression.

Behaviour therapy Techniques of therapy based on the principles of conditioning and observational learning. The point of behaviour therapy is to teach the client how to substitute adaptive patterns of behaviour for maladaptive patterns. However, the term is not used consistently, with some authors using it just to refer to therapies based on classical condition.

Behavioural genetics The study of the influence of genes and environments on individual differences in behaviour. Behaviour geneticists measure the differences in some trait among a sample of people and attempt to quantify the portion of these differences that is due to genes and the portion that is due to environment.

Behavioural neuroscience The branch of neuroscience that studies the neural basis of behaviour. Behavioural neuroscientists study the entire nervous system and may use non-human as well as human animals for study.

Between-groups design An experimental design in which participants take part in only one of the conditions. Sometimes called an unrelated or independent measures design.

Big Five A trait model of personality consisting of five trait dimensions or factors within which all other 'lower-order' traits can be found. The five factors are openness to experience, conscientiousness, extraversion, agreeableness, and neuroticism (OCEAN). The five personality factors are based on the lexical hypothesis, the idea that the most important personality traits are those best represented in human languages.

Binocular cues Cues for depth perception that necessitate both eyes—specifically retinal disparity and convergence.

Biological preparedness *See* **Preparedness.**

Birth defect *See* **Congenital malformation.**

Blind experiment An experiment in which the research participants are unaware of which level of the independent variable they have been assigned to and/or are unaware of the nature of the researcher's hypothesis.

Blind spot An area formed by the optic disc that contains neither rods nor cones.

Brain lateralization *See* **Hemispheric specialization.**

Brainwaves Characteristic electrical brain activity of various frequencies termed alpha, beta, theta, and delta. Each of these is associated with different states of consciousness.

Brightness constancy The aspect of perceptual constancy that allows us to perceive an object as the same brightness regardless of the available illumination.

Broad sense heritability Published heritability figures, including those calculated using Falconer's formula, usually represent broad sense heritability, which includes both pure genetic influence and that of gene-environment interaction. This produces a higher figure than narrow sense heritability, which represents the 'pure' influence of genetic make-up alone.

Bystander effect The tendency for a person to be less likely to intervene and offer help to a stranger in an emergency situation when others are present. Broadly, the more people present, the less likely the bystander is to offer aid.

Cannabis (marijuana) A mildly psychedelic drug derived from the leaves of *cannabis sativa*, a flowering plant originally indigenous to Asia. Cannabis is usually smoked, either in powdered leaf form or in a gum called hash or hashish.

Cannon–Bard theory of emotion The idea that during the perception of an event, sensory impulses are first relayed to the thalamus. From there they are relayed to the autonomic nervous system and the cerebral cortex at about the same time, rather than to the autonomic nervous system first and second to the cerebral cortex, as proposed in the James–Lange theory.

Case study A descriptive research method in which the researcher gathers detailed information about a single individual, group, family, or organization in order to better understand a particular set of circumstances.

Catharsis Derived from the Greek word for cleansing, catharsis refers to the relief one may experience by expressing emotion.

CBT *See* **Cognitive behaviour therapy**.

Cell body Also called the soma, this is the bulb-like end of the neuron containing the cell nucleus. Energy for the neuron is generated here, and waste is eliminated.

Central control The ability to suppress automatic cognition, including automatic thoughts and speech.

Failure in central control could result in symptoms like clanging and this may underlie symptoms of schizophrenia.

Central nervous system (CNS) The brain and spinal cord. This organizes and interprets the information received from the peripheral nervous system (PNS) and sends commands back to the PNS to take actions or make adjustments to bodily functions.

Central pattern generators Circuits of neurons that generate routine, rhythmic movements and are controlled entirely by the spine with no input from the brain.

Cerebellum The second largest structure in the central nervous system, located in the hindbrain. The cerebellum coordinates sensory inputs and affects balance by assisting visual-spatial perception. It is also involved at least to some degree in attention, learning, and memory, and appropriate expression of emotion.

Cerebral cortex The outer layer of the hemispheres of the forebrain. It interprets raw sensory information, initiates voluntary movement, and is home to higher cognitive processes.

Change blindness The inability to detect changes in a scene following a brief distraction.

Characteristic adaptations Adams' term to describe aspects of personality such as goals, values, beliefs, social roles, and plans for the future. According to Adams, characteristic adaptations change substantially over the lifespan.

Child-to-parent effects Child-to-parent effects occur when the behaviour of a child alters the way the parent behaves towards the child—including the parent's overall parenting style (eg, authoritative, authoritarian, or permissive).

Chromosomes Rod-shaped bodies, present in every human cell, made up of strands of DNA wound around proteins called histones.

Circadian pacemaker This is believed to function as a 'master control' for a person's various circadian cycles, consisting of a group of neurons forming the suprachiasmatic nuclei of the hypothalamus.

Circadian rhythm Any biochemical, physiological, or behavioural cycle that takes place on an approximately 24-hour schedule. The name comes from *circa* (around) and *dia* (day). We don't require accurate internal clocks to maintain circadian rhythms—they are regularly reset by environmental cues such as dark and daylight.

Classical conditioning A type of associative learning discovered by Ivan Pavlov. It occurs when an innate response known as the unconditioned response (UCR) is triggered by a neutral stimulus as a result of repeated pairings of the neutral stimulus with an unconditioned stimulus (UCS). The UCS is a stimulus that would naturally trigger the reflexive response without a conditioning procedure.

Classical psychoanalysis A particularly intensive and long-term therapy, in which therapists usually stick to tightly prescribed interpretive techniques, including interpretation of dreams and transference.

Client-centred therapy The humanistic therapy founded during the late 1940s and 1950s by Carl Rogers. The goal of client-centred therapy is to promote personal growth in the client in a non-directive manner by treating the client with congruence, empathy, and unconditional positive regard.

Clients 'Client' is sometimes used to refer to a recipient of therapy and is most strongly associated with more liberal attitudes and theoretical models that emphasize an equal-status partnership between client and therapist. *See also* **Patient**.

CNS *See* **Central nervous system**.

Comorbidity The co-occurrence of more than one disorder.

Cocaine An alkaloid of the coca plant in concentrated form. Taken recreationally cocaine produces an intense high and is highly addictive. However, cocaine also has medical applications as a painkiller.

Cochlea The cochlea is a pea-sized, tube-like structure of the inner ear filled with fluid and curled into the shape of a snail. The cochlea is the central component of the inner ear.

Cognitive behaviour therapy (CBT) A therapy that attempts to unite traditional behaviour therapy with Beck's cognitive therapy. CBT is based on the idea that cognition, emotion, and behaviour are linked in a circle of mutual influence. Although CBT is not identical to CT (cognitive therapy), the term cognitive behaviour therapy is often used to refer to either therapy.

Cognitive behaviourism Cognitive behaviourism argues, as in radical behaviourism, that behaviour is acquired according to a set of rules and can be analysed using concepts of reinforcement and punishment, but they disagree that this analysis must necessarily exclude cognition. Cognitive behaviourists pioneered the concepts of cognitive maps and latent learning.

Cognitive dissonance The anxiety or tension that arises when people behave in ways that run contrary to their attitudes. People may resolve cognitive dissonance by changing their attitudes to bring them in line with their behaviour; ceasing the behaviour; or changing their beliefs about the discrepancy between their attitudes and behaviour.

Cognitive maps A mental representation of the structure, location, or attributes of some phenomenon.

Cognitive neuroscience Cognitive neuroscience deals with the relationship between the nervous system and cognition and emotion.

Cognitive therapy (CT) CT is based on the idea that when people possess underlying dysfunctional core beliefs about the self, the world, and the future, they respond to events with automatic thoughts that trigger negative emotional experiences, leading to depression and anxiety. The cognitive therapist helps the client to test these beliefs.

Cognitive triad Aaron Beck's term to describe a set of irrational, chronic, and erroneous beliefs about the 'triad' of the self, the world, and the future.

Cognitive–motivational–relational theory of emotion The theory proposed by Richard Lazarus, stating that autonomic nervous system arousal occurs not directly, as stated in the James–Lange and two-factor theories, but only after the thought or event has been appraised so that the meaning of the event is interpreted by the person. In this theory, cognition always comes first.

Colour constancy The aspect of perceptual constancy that allows us to perceive an object as the same colour regardless of the amount or type of illumination.

Common factors Hypothesized factors common to all legitimate forms of psychological therapy that are responsible for actual therapeutic effects and may include therapeutic alliance, therapist allegiance, and therapist competence.

Compassion deficit (disorder) A dispositional explanation for institution-wide neglect by health professionals, blaming the neglect on the individual staff involved.

Concurrent validity One way to assess the quality of a psychological measure. When a test produces similar results to a concurrent test; that is, an existing test believed to measure what we are interested in—indicated by a correlation of close to 1—this means that the test has good concurrent validity.

Conditions of worth According to Rogers, conditions of worth are the conditions a person must fulfil to obtain love and approval from important people in his or her life. These conditions only exist within relationships which lack unconditional positive regard.

Cones Photoreceptors specialized for day vision, colour vision, and capturing fine detail. Cones are concentrated in a small region near the centre of the retina called the fovea; images focused here provide the clearest images and sharpest focus.

Confederates Those present in social psychology experiment who are in on the details of the experiment, alongside those who do not know what is taking place (naïve participants).

Conformity The tendency of people to alter behaviour, attitudes, and beliefs in line with group norms. The motivation to conform may be informational, based on a rational desire to seek realistic information of some situation from a group; normative, based on a person's desire to obtain approval from the group or avoid embarrassment.

Confounding variable In an experiment, any variable that exerts a measurable effect on the dependent variable without the knowledge of the experimenter is called a confounding variable or confound. Sometimes used more strictly to mean a variable that co-varies with the independent variable.

Congeniality bias The tendency to select sources of information that appear friendly because they express views like our own.

Congenital malformation (birth defect) Any physical abnormality or defect present at birth. Congenital malformations may result from genetic causes or prenatal events, including exposure to radiation, drugs and alcohol, or maternal illness. A teratogen is any harmful substance, bacteria, or virus that can be transferred through the placenta to the developing foetus.

Congruence Rogers' term to describe an environment of development where those surrounding the developing person are genuine—that is, truly being themselves and not presenting a self that reflects the values and wishes of others.

Consciousness No definition of consciousness has been agreed upon, but John Searle's 'common sense' definition includes three components: qualitativeness, subjectivity, and unity.

Conservation The understanding that an object may retain its identity even if its appearance has changed.

Constraint The notion that an inherited characteristic is unchangeable. This is a controversial idea; for example, when applied to intelligence.

Constructivism An approach to understanding learning, particularly associated with the work of Jean Piaget. The central idea is that the individual explores the world and constructs a personal mental representation of it.

Content analysis An approach to data analysis that crosses the qualitative-quantitative divide. Qualitative data is coded quantitatively and analysed statistically.

Contiguity How close in time two events occur. According to Pavlov it is the contiguity of the neutral and unconditioned stimulus that leads to their association.

Contingency The extent to which the occurrence of one stimulus is dependent (contingent) on the occurrence of another. To Rescorla, classical conditioning occurs when the unconditioned stimulus is contingent on the neutral stimulus.

Contingency management (CM) A type of operant treatment used in various types of institutions (eg, substance abuse rehabilitation, psychiatric wards, prisons). In CM treatment a person is positively reinforced with tangible, desirable goods, prizes, or privileges for engaging in desirable behaviours and avoiding undesirable behaviours.

Continuous reinforcement Reinforcement that takes place when a behaviour is reinforced every time it occurs.

Controls In experimental design controls are the ways in which experimenters keep all variables constant other than the independent variable(s) being manipulated. Controls aim to reduce the impact of other factors on the dependent variable(s) so that it can be judged that variations in the dependent variable are the result of the manipulation of the independent variable.

Conventional morality The kind of moral judgement typical of school-age children and young adolescents, based on respect for law, social norms, and rules set by authorities.

Convergence A binocular cue to depth perception based on the fact that ocular muscles rotate eyes inward when viewing close objects.

Correlation A method of study in which two or more variables are measured to see if there is a mathematical relationship (correlation) between them. Variables are correlated when a change in one variable predicts change in another variable because the variables are associated in some way. However, this association between the variables may not be causal in nature.

Correlation coefficient A statistic which quantifies the strength and direction of correlation between two variables. The correlation coefficient ranges from −1.0 (a perfect negative correlation) to +1.0 (a perfect positive correlation). A correlation coefficient near to 0 indicates no association between the variables in question.

Correspondent inferences A correspondent inference takes place when we infer that an action corresponds to the actor's intentions and hence we can make a judgement about their disposition. We can only make correspondent inferences when the actor is aware of consequences, capable of acting or not acting, and acts deliberately rather than accidentally.

Crack (cocaine) A solid form of cocaine somewhat similar to freebase, 'cooked' from cocaine, water, and baking soda or lye. Street crack often contains other chemical components.

Critical psychology A radical approach to psychology that de-emphasizes the scientific method and instead focuses on the social influences on and social consequences of psychological concepts, looking in particular at how concepts have served the interests of socially powerful groups at the expense of more marginalized ones.

Crystallized intelligence (Gc) Cattell and Horn's term used to refer to the skills or knowledge one acquires as a result of exposure to education and culture—what one has learned.

CT *See* **Cognitive therapy.**

Cultural psychology The study of psychology as it exists in different cultures. A central assumption of cultural psychology is that culture shapes the individual mind and behaviour. Some psychologists distinguish between cultural and cross-cultural psychology, the latter being concerned with comparisons between psychological phenomena in different cultures.

Culture The total pattern of behaviour exhibited by citizens of any given society, and the total products of a given society. In psychology, culture impacts on perception, developmental patterns, social behaviour, and attitudes and even mental disorder.

Data-proof topics Some debates inspire such strong feelings in people that they are not influenced in their views by evidence. These are described as data-proof topics. Astrology is one such topic.

Database A database holds material together in one place, usually tagged for searching. Wikipedia is an example of a database.

Date rape drugs These include Rohypnol and GHB. Rohypnol (flunitrazapam) is a highly potent benzodiazepine drug used to treat severe insomnia (street name: 'roofies'). GHB (Gamma-hydroxybutyrate) is a CNS depressant drug initially marketed as a food supplement for bodybuilders. Although they have a bad name for their use in sex crimes, these drugs have medical and non-sinister recreational uses.

Day care A broad term meaning non-maternal care in childhood, including that provided by relatives, nurseries, and childminders, but not including 24-hour care as in fostering. Psychologists are particularly interested in day care for babies and toddlers and there is a lively debate about the possible positive and negative effects of day care on their development.

Deep brain stimulation (DBS) A relatively new technique of psychosurgery used to treat Parkinson's disease and being tested for use in psychological disorders, particularly depression. In deep brain stimulation electrodes are implanted in various regions of the brain and coupled to an external device that sends out stimulating electrical pulses.

Deindividuation Deindividuation involves a reduction in self-awareness or personal identity within a group, leading to increased feelings of anonymity and reduced concern for how one's behaviour will be evaluated by others in the group.

Demand characteristics The cues that allow research participants to work out the aim of the study.

For example, a researcher may speak in a different tone to participants in conditions where they expect different behaviour.

Dementia Dementia is caused by biological deterioration of the brain that most commonly occurs in older people. Symptoms include progressive cognitive decline, severe memory loss, confusion, problems with speech and comprehending others, and difficulty with self-care. There are different causes of dementia and they are associated with variations in symptoms.

Dendrites The branch-like projections of neurons that receive electrochemical stimulation from other neurons.

Dependent variable (DV) The variable being measured in an experiment to determine if the manipulation of the independent variable (IV) has had any effect.

Depolarization Depolarization takes place when there is disruption of the resting potential balance between negatively and positively charged ions within and outside the neuron. Depolarization begins the process of the firing of an action potential.

Depression A mood state characterized by sadness, low energy, fatigue, regret or guilt, feelings of low self-worth, hopelessness, and helplessness.

Depth perception The visual perceptual mechanisms that allow for the judgement of distance of objects and creates a mental '3-D' image from a 2-D retinal image.

Descriptive statistics Basic statistics which provide descriptions of a set of data, including percentage, mean, median, and mode. Some descriptive statistics are represented diagrammatically; for example, correlations and distributions.

Destructive obedience Destructive obedience means to follow orders to deliberately harm another person or people.

Developmental stages Age-related periods of development with distinct boundaries, and that reflect qualitatively different types of cognitive activity.

Diagnostic and Statistical Manual of Mental Disorders (DSM) The manual published by the American Psychiatric Association (APA) which classifies, describes, and presents diagnostic criteria for psychological disorders.

Diathesis stress model A model of psychological disorder which proposes that mental illness is most likely to be found in a person who has both genetic vulnerability to the condition and exposure to life experiences which contribute to the onset of the illness.

Discourse analysis Discourse analysis involves deconstructing text or transcripts for examples of how language has been used to construct a version of reality that suits the vested interests of powerful groups.

Discrimination Discrimination prevents you from improperly applying generalization to a new stimulus that, while similar to the original stimulus in some ways, is different in important ways.

Display rules The cultural norms and expectations that govern what is or is not a socially acceptable way to display emotion.

Dizygotic twins (Dzs) Also called fraternal twins, Dzs are twins who emerge from two ova (eggs) and share only 50% of their genes in common, on average. This genetic similarity is the same as for non-twin siblings.

DNA A complex molecule with a characteristic spiralling shape. DNA contains the genetic instructions for heredity in all living organisms.

Dodo bird verdict A phrase borrowed from *Alice in Wonderland* and used to sum up the conclusion of outcome research in psychotherapy: no legitimate form of therapy is superior to any other in general outcome. This is also called the equivalence paradox. Note that the dodo bird verdict has been challenged and applies only to legitimate therapies.

Domains of development Specific, discrete areas of cognitive development such as infant perceptual abilities, moral development, and theory of mind development.

Double-blind experiment An experiment in which neither the subject nor those interacting directly with them is aware of the exact nature of the hypotheses being tested and/or to which level of the independent variable a participant has been exposed.

Dream interpretation A key technique in classical psychoanalysis which involves the psychoanalyst offering interpretations of the hidden meanings of patient dreams.

Drive theory A theory of motivation initially proposed by Clark Hull in 1943. The central idea is that behaviour is motivated primarily by the desire to reduce unpleasant conditions of arousal which have resulted from basic physiological needs.

DSM *See* **Diagnostic and Statistical Manual of Mental Disorders.**

Dualism The philosophical view that the mind and matter (including the body) belong in separate categories and are constructed of different material.

Dynamic processes One of three central ideas in Freud's theory of personality, dynamic processes describes the idea of constant motion, energy, and conflict between component parts of the mind; for example, conflict between the instinctive id and the moral superego.

Ear canal An outer ear structure that funnels sound from outside to the eardrum or tympanic membrane.

Eardrum *See* **Tympanic membrane.**

Early adulthood In developmental psychology, a term for the developmental stage between adolescence and what many would regard as true adulthood.

Echo chamber effect The echo chamber effect takes place when we are exposed to a biased selection of opinions that echo our own, reinforcing our views and perhaps making them more extreme. *See also* **Congeniality bias** and **Filter bubbles.**

Ecstasy (MDMA) A psychedelic drug derived from amphetamines. It was popularized by the Rave scene of the late 1980s and early 90s and remains one of the favoured recreational drugs in Western Europe.

ECT *See* **Electroconvulsive therapy.**

Effect size A measure of how large and meaningful differences and correlations are.

Effectiveness Effectiveness refers to how well therapies treat real patients in real settings who, unlike most patients in efficacy studies may have a range of conditions. An effective treatment is one that has shown itself to have significant utility in the 'real world' of practising clinicians treating patients in clinics, hospitals, consulting rooms, and medical offices.

Efficacy Like effectiveness studies efficacy studies measure the effects of therapy. However, efficacy studies aim to maximize experimental control. Thus participants are randomly allocated to conditions (hence each trial is known as a random control trial or RCT). A treatment has good efficacy if it has been shown to be superior to a placebo in RCTs.

Effortful control The dimension of temperament that describes the extent to which an infant or child is able to focus or shift attention, inhibit inappropriate behaviour, and plan actions constructively. It is similar to executive functions in adults.

Ego The aspect of Freud's structural model which represents that part of the mind which operates according to the reality principle. Partly conscious, partly unconscious, the ego mediates between the demands of the real world, the blind strivings of the id, and the judgements of the superego.

Ego defence mechanisms A group of psychological mechanisms described in part by Sigmund Freud but primarily by his daughter, Anna Freud. The ego uses these mechanisms to keep threatening material from reaching awareness. The defence mechanisms include repression, denial, displacement, projection, reaction formation, and sublimation.

Electroconvulsive therapy (ECT) A treatment for psychological disorders (primarily treatment-resistant depression) that consists of passing a low-voltage electrical current through a person's brain for a brief moment, resulting in a seizure. ECT is usually conducted multiple times for any given case.

Electromagnetic radiation Energy that travels around the world in waves of variable intensity (amplitude) that are separated by varying lengths known as wavelengths.

Embodied emotion The theoretical idea that emotions are 'captured' as body memories. Each time an emotion is experienced, the sights, sounds, physiological processes, and patterns of motor activity that occur are encoded in clusters of neurons assigned to the various sensory and motor modalities of the body. The emotion is then experienced in terms of these sensory and motor centres.

Emotion A short-lived, intense psychological state with physiological elements and the subjective experience of a feeling.

Emotional intelligence The ability to identify, manage, and express one's emotions constructively and to empathize with the emotions of others. Emotional intelligence is believed to be extremely important in permitting successful social interaction.

Empathy The ability to take another person's perspective, understand why the person feels as he or she does, and perhaps also come to share that feeling to some degree (although this is not a necessary component of empathy).

Empirically supported therapies (EST) A therapy that has demonstrated statistically significant superiority over no treatment (and in some cases also over a placebo therapy) in a series of randomized clinical controlled trials.

Empiricism Originally a seventeenth-century philosophical tradition which held that the mind had no innate content—personal experience was responsible for the development of all thoughts, beliefs, and knowledge. The term 'empirical' comes from the Empiricists' belief in defining knowledge as that which can be perceived. In the nature-nurture debate the position that emphasizes experience in acquiring characteristics.

Endocrine system The collective term for the system of glands and the hormones they produce.

Endophenotype A characteristic or symptom of a disorder that is present in people with that disorder and also to a greater degree in close genetic relatives of the person with the disorder. Endophenotypes are considered to reflect what is heritable about a given disorder.

Engaged followership Haslam and Reicher's social identity-based explanation for destructive obedience as observed in the Milgram studies. The central idea is that participants obeyed the experimenter because they identified with them as part of a high status pro-research group.

Environmental insults A negative event that falls outside the normal range of experiences. Environmental insults are associated with serious negative effects on development.

Environmental mismatch Environmental mismatch occurs when a psychological adaptation is expressed in an environment different from the one in which it evolved and to which it is not suited.

Equivalence paradox *See* **Dodo bird verdict.**

EST *See* **Empirically supported therapies.**

Ethanol Commonly called alcohol, ethanol is technically just one of the alcohols, the only ingestible one. Ethanol has a powerful intoxicating effect and is the main psychoactive ingredient in alcoholic drinks.

Ethics Technically the philosophy of morality, but we use the term more loosely to mean moral issues or rules. Ethical codes are constructed in order to help professionals like psychologists stick to behaviour we broadly agree to be morally correct during research.

Evaluative conditioning A type of learning in which we learn to like or dislike something after it is paired with an unconditioned stimulus that elicits a positive or negative emotional response.

Evidence-based practice In its broadest sense, any professional practice taking account of research findings. Psychologists generally take the evidence base for the way they practice very seriously. In the context of therapy evidence-based practice generally refers to choosing models of therapy—and sometimes particular techniques—that have been validated by research.

Evolutionary psychology A multidisciplinary approach to psychology based on evolutionary principles, including but not limited to Darwin's theory of natural selection.

Executive functions Those cognitive functions involved in managing attention, planning constructive action, inhibiting inappropriate action, and remaining flexible in responding to situations.

Exposure therapy There is a range of exposure therapies, linked by the idea that only through exposure to feared stimuli can the anxiety produced by that stimuli be lessened. Exposure therapies include systematic desensitization and flooding.

External validity The extent to which the results of research generalize to real-world settings. This is a particular issue for experimental research where we often use an artificial measure of the real-life variable we are interested in.

Extinction Extinction is when a learned behaviour ceases to be performed. In classical conditioning, extinction will occur when the conditioned response ceases to be exhibited following the removal of the unconditioned stimulus.

Extraversion In temperament theory the dimension of temperament that describes the degree to which an infant or child lacks shyness, is highly active, anticipates pleasurable activities, laughs and smiles frequently, and desires closeness with others.

Extrinsic motivation A category of motivation which compels a person to engage in a behaviour for an external reward that the behaviour might bring.

Facial action coding system (FACS) Ekman's coding scheme of the facial muscle configurations which create expressions of basic emotion. An example of an expression revealed by the FACS is the Duchenne smile. This is a smile of genuine enjoyment or pleasure, characterized by contraction of the orbicularis oculi muscle surrounding the eye.

Facial feedback hypothesis The idea that the facial expression associated with a basic emotion increases the experience of that emotion; and that purposely activating the muscles which form a facial expression of basic emotion may actually result in a person experiencing the emotion itself.

FAE *See* **Fundamental attribution error.**

Falconer's formula A simple way to estimate broad sense heritability from the correlations in scores for the characteristic in MZ and DZ twin pairs. The formula is h=2(MZ correlation – DZ correlation). This provides only a crude estimate of heritability.

False dichotomies A distinction between two concepts that, at least in some situations, is meaningless because the two concepts are so hard to separate.

Family systems theory The view of the family as an integrated, organic unit that may be analysed in somewhat the same way that systems analysts view computer systems. Symptoms in an individual can be viewed as adjustments by the system to bring about homeostasis. The original theoretical basis for systemic therapies.

Filter bubble Filter bubbles result when social media algorithms eliminate opinions different from our own and give us the impression that our views are non-controversial.

First pain The initial sharp sensations at the moment of a painful stimulus.

Five-factor model *See* **Big Five.**

Fixed-interval (FI) schedule A partial reinforcement schedule that provides reinforcement for the first operant behaviour after a specific interval of time has passed.

Fixed-ratio (FR) schedule A partial reinforcement schedule that provides reinforcement after a specific number of operant behavioural responses.

Flooding An exposure therapy used to treat phobia and other anxiety disorders. Flooding involves non-incremental, total immersion in anxiety-producing phobic stimuli for a prolonged period with the aim of reducing the anxiety response.

Fluid intelligence (*Gf*) Cattell and Horn's term used to refer to largely innate analytic skills and abstract reasoning ability.

Flynn effect Named after James Flynn, the steady increase in raw scores on IQ tests that has characterized the late twentieth and early twenty-first century.

fMRI (Functional magnetic resonance imaging) The use of MRI whereby continuous images of the brain are generated while a research participant engages in specific tasks. This allows us to see changes in the brain linked to its function.

Foetal alcohol syndrome (FAS) A congenital disorder resulting from prenatal maternal alcohol use. FAS symptoms include low IQ as well as physical abnormalities such as a small head.

Fovea Small region near the centre of the retina in which cones are concentrated.

Free association A key technique in classical psychoanalysis in which the patient relaxes and says whatever comes to mind.

Freebase A method of using cocaine where the active ingredient of cocaine is isolated and smoked. Unlike cocaine in powder form (cocaine hydrochloride), freebase is not soluble in water and cannot be snorted or administered through injection.

Frequency The frequency (of sound wave) represents the number of sound waves per second, expressed as Hertz units.

Functionalism The psychological school of thought championed by William James which held that the mind could only be understood by referring to the purposes for which it was shaped through evolution.

Fundamental attribution error The tendency to attribute another person's behaviour to his or her inner dispositions and character traits while ignoring or underestimating the possibility that situational factors may have played an important or determining role.

g: *See* **General intelligence.**

GABA (*gamma*-Aminobutyric acid) A neurotransmitter that primarily works by inhibiting synaptic transmission and so reducing brain activation. This gives GABA relaxant properties. Relaxing drugs like alcohol are GABA agonists.

GAM *See* **General aggression model.**

Gate control theory A theory of pain perception that emphasizes the activity not only of pain signals from the injury site but also of pain blocking signals originating in the brain or elsewhere in the body.

Ganzfeld procedure An experimental situation designed to optimize the conditions for extra-sensory perception (ESP) to take place whilst reducing as far as possible the possibility of sensory leakage, demand characteristics, and fraud.

Gc: *See* **Crystallized intelligence.**

Gene-environment correlation Gene-environment correlation occurs when a person's environment is correlated with his or her genotype. For example, a musically gifted child (genotype) also lives in a home where music is played frequently and where musical instruments are available.

General aggression model (GAM) Anderson and Bushman's theory of aggression which holds that whether aggression does or does not occur in any interaction is dependent upon a complex interaction between four factors: personal characteristics; characteristics of the situation; emotions, thoughts, and biological arousal levels; and decision-making processes.

General intelligence (*g*) A way of referring to a person's underlying general capacity to process complex information—to perform well on a variety of mental tasks. General intelligence was initially hypothesized by Charles Spearman and is measured by general IQ tests such as the Wechsler Adult Intelligence Scale (WAIS) and Stanford–Binet Intelligence Scale.

Generalization Generalization allows you to extend an association to a new stimulus that, while different in some ways from the original stimulus to which the association was formed, is nevertheless similar in important ways.

Generalized anxiety disorder (GAD) GAD is characterized by ceaseless, pervasive, and uncontrollable worry and apprehension about the future. Worry in GAD is often irrational, and results in physical symptoms such as muscle tension as well as irritability, sleep difficulty, and difficulty concentrating.

Genes Unit of heredity. Each gene is a section of chromosome that codes for the production of a particular protein and, when activated, triggers the production of this protein.

Genotype The unique collection of alleles that contribute to specific traits in living organisms is their genotype.

Gf: *See* **Fluid intelligence.**

Ghostwriting The practice of having professional writers write up reports of studies in articles bearing the names of researchers who did not contribute to the writing of the article and may not have been involved in the design and conduct of the study.

Glands A gland is a bodily organ that synthesizes and/or releases hormones.

Glia Glia are a type of cell responsible for building the myelin sheath that surrounds the axon of some neurons, and helping to develop and maintain neuron synapses.

Goal-setting theory An important theory of motivation in applied settings devised by Edwin Locke and Gary Latham. According to goal-setting theory, work motivation and performance are enhanced when specific and difficult (but not impossible) goals are set.

Gonadarche The maturation of the sexual organs during puberty.

Good subject tendency The general desire of research participants to please the experimenter or give the experimenter what he or she 'wants'.

Grand theories of personality The term given to describe theories of personality, primarily developed during the early to mid-twentieth century, whose creators wished to address the important areas in the study of personality. The most prominent grand theories were those developed by psychoanalysts, behaviourists, and humanistic psychologists.

Groupthink A way of thinking and behaving in groups whereby decisions are made not as a result of rational considerations and weighing of evidence, but as a result of group members not wanting to adversely affect group morale, make waves, or appear disloyal to leaders. The frequent end result of groupthink is the adoption of highly flawed plans and policies.

Habituation A simple type of non-associative learning that occurs when a stimulus comes to elicit decreasing response from an organism as a result of the organism's repeated exposure to the stimulus over time. 'I got used to it' expresses the idea of habituation.

Hallucinogenic drugs Hallucinogenics include LSD (lysergic acid diethylamide), magic mushrooms (a general term used for various psilocybin-containing fungi) and mescaline, the refined hallucinogen from Peyote seeds. In high doses cannabis can have similar properties. They share the property of inducing perceptual distortions and hallucinations.

Hard problem The question of how the physical human brain is able to produce the experience of consciousness. The word 'hard' does not just mean 'difficult' but also denotes hard as in hardware—the brain.

Harmful dysfunction view A view of psychological disorder which holds that disorder exists when symptoms cause harm according to subjective social or cultural judgements, *and* there is objective evidence of dysfunction. Dysfunction is said to exist only when a psychological characteristic or mechanism is not performing the function for which it evolved through natural selection.

Hemispheric specialization (or brain lateralization) The unique specializations of the two hemispheres of the cerebral cortex. The real difference between what processing takes place in the two hemispheres has been greatly exaggerated, leading to crude oversimplifications like 'you use your left brain for x function'; however, it does appear that the two hemispheres are specialized for different types of processing.

Heritability A statistic that estimates the extent of genetic influence in the differences among a sample of people on a particular trait.

Heuristic value The usefulness of a theory as a tool to help people think about a complex issue. For example, some psychometrics used to assess learning styles or personality have very little scientific validity but are still commonly used in certain settings such as business training, because they have proved useful in helping people reflect on their characteristics.

Hindbrain A lower geographic area of the brain containing the cerebellum, medulla, pons, and reticular formation.

Homeostasis Homeostasis (literally 'to stay the same') is used to describe a steady, regulated state where various physiological processes (eg, water intake, blood sugar, body temperature) are maintained at appropriate levels.

Hopelessness theory A revision of learned helplessness theory created by Abramson and Alloy.

Hopelessness theory proposes that a negative cognitive style leads to depression. This includes three aspects: (a) attributing negative events to internal causes; (b) considering causes of negative events to be stable and global; and (c) anticipating severe negative consequences from negative events.

Hormones A chemical synthesized and/or released by a gland.

Hostile aggression Aggression which has the ultimate purpose of harming the victim. These actions tend to be in reaction to some sort of provocation, accompanied by emotion such as anger, and are often (but not always) impulsive (Anderson and Bushman, 2002).

Human genome A genome is the entire set of hereditary 'instructions,' encoded in DNA, for creating an organism. The human genome, containing the necessary genetic information to build a human, exists within every cell of every human body.

Human universal A human trait, custom, or sociocultural practice that can be seen or argued to exist in every known society. There is often a degree of controversy around human universals, either because they are not fully defined and testable ideas or because exceptions sometimes appear to exist.

Hypnagogia A dream-like state at sleep onset during which a person may or may not be aware that he or she is experiencing hallucinations or delusions. Hypnagogia may be accompanied by sleep paralysis.

Hypnosis Hypnosis is an interaction between 'hypnotist' and 'subject' involving suggestions for 'imaginative experiences'. It is hard to define hypnosis any more precisely than this because there is still a debate about whether hypnosis involves an altered state or is rather a social phenomenon.

Hypothesis A specific, testable prediction about what will happen given under certain circumstances. Hypotheses are often drawn from a theory, which is a set of interconnected ideas and statements used to explain phenomena.

IAT *See* **Implicit association test**.

Id The id is that part of Freud's structural model which represents the irrational portion of the mind which lacks moral restraint or a conception of practical realities, and cares only for satisfaction of its own cravings—seeking pleasure and avoiding unpleasure (such as pain) (the pleasure principle).

Identity signalling Identity signalling involves revealing membership of social groups; for example, through social media posts or more concrete media like badges and logos.

Impairment in functioning The concept used for diagnosis in the DSM to cover situations where a person has symptoms of a disorder but does not experience personal distress.

Impeccable trivia Psychological phenomena that are straightforward to study in a traditional scientific manner; for example, by laboratory experimentation, but which do not help us answer important questions about human nature. This criticism has, for example, been levelled at some studies of cognition.

Implicit association test (IAT) The standard procedure for assessing implicit prejudice involves the implicit association test (IAT) which compares response times to positive and negative terms associated with target groups. *See also* **Implicit prejudice**.

Implicit prejudice Automatic, unconscious bias against a group. Implicit prejudice tends to be subtle and often exists even in people who do not consider themselves prejudiced. *See also* the **Implicit association test**.

Implicit theories of intelligence The basis of Carol Dweck's theory of motivation. Individuals with an entity theory of intelligence see intelligence—and by implication academic ability—as innate and fixed whereas those with an incremental theory see it as changeable. Having an incremental theory is associated with better motivation and outcomes.

Impression management The process by which people attempt to monitor and control the impressions that others form of them. This consists of two components: impression motivation and impression construction.

Imprinting A form of learning that occurs rapidly during a critical period and which the animal is biologically prepared to acquire. Specifically, in birds, imprinting occurs when a chick hatches and imprints on the first moving object it sees.

In-group bias The tendency of human beings to favour and extend loyalty to members of their own group. In-group members are generally trusted more than out-group members, and in-group bias sometimes (but not always) leads to prejudice or even hatred towards members of out-groups. In-group bias tends to be automatic, and it is triggered as soon as group identity is created.

Inattentional blindness The inability to see highly visible objects at which one is looking directly when attention is drawn elsewhere.

Incentives Any rewarding condition that provides a motive for some behaviour. Incentives are extrinsic. Examples of incentives include financial rewards and punishment avoidance.

Independent measures design *See* **Between-groups design**.

Independent variable (IV) A variable being manipulated in an experiment to determine the possible effects on one or more dependent variables (DVs). Different experimental conditions involve differing levels of the independent variable.

Indifference of the indicator Spearman's idea that you can take a person's score on any test of mental ability and use it in a general way to predict their score on a test of any other mental ability.

Inferential statistics Advanced statistical techniques which help determine the probability that research results reflect actual relationships between variables as opposed to the effects of chance variation (significance), or which quantify the magnitude of this relationship (effect size).

Insomnia A chronic difficulty falling asleep, staying asleep, and/or being unable to obtain restful sleep.

Instinct An innate, automatic behavioural tendency that will occur reliably in all normally developed members of a species in response to a releasing stimulus, or cue, from the environment. Because of past difficulties in identifying instincts, more often than not the term fixed-action pattern is used instead of the term instinct.

Instinctive drift Instinctive drift takes place when an instinctive pattern of behaviour interferes with the operant conditioning of a behaviour. Thus although we can be conditioned to behave in a non-instinctive way these conditioned responses tend to be short-lived.

Institutionalization We use the term to mean slightly different things in different contexts, but in clinical settings we most commonly use it to refer to the effects of living full-time in an institution like a hospital or orphanage. When talking about young children the institution concerned is a hospital or orphanage.

Instrumental aggression Aggression which has an ultimate purpose other than causing harm to the victim. Instrumental aggression is often (but not always) planned, and is not necessarily accompanied by an emotion such as anger, although it may be. *See also* **Hostile aggression.**

Instrumental learning *See* **Operant conditioning.**

Integrative models Ways of understanding and treating mental disorder that combine ideas from more than one pure model. For example, modern cognitive behavioural therapy uses concepts and techniques based on behavioural and cognitive models of mental disorder.

Intellectual disability disorder Formerly known as mental retardation, intellectual disability is the modern term used in psychiatry to define someone who has difficulty in managing a culturally normal life without help as a result of low intelligence—an IQ below 70.

Intergroup conflict Non-harmonious relations between groups. This can vary considerably in magnitude, from mutual avoidance and antilocution (verbal criticism and attack) to genocide, the deliberate and systematic attempt to exterminate a population.

Intermental plane In Vygotskian theory, understanding at first exists between the child and their instructor on the intermental plane, a theoretical space between the two individuals.

Internal consistency The extent to which different elements of a complex theory hang together logically.

Internal working model A notion by attachment theorists that a child's understanding of his or her place in the world, and his or her expectations about the behaviour of others, is modelled on, or reflects, attachment relations experienced in infancy.

Intramental plane In Vygotskian theory, once understanding exists between child and instructor (ie, on the intermental plane) it can be internalized so that it exists in the mind of the child on an intramental plane (ie, within the child's mind).

Intrinsic motivation A category of motivation which leads a person to engage in a behaviour because the behaviour is rewarding for its own sake, rather than providing some sort of additional external incentive or reward.

Introspection Literally to direct one's attention to one's own mind. In the late nineteenth century,

psychologists—notably William James—used the idea of monitoring one's own thoughts and sensations whilst carrying out mental tasks as a method of research into the mind.

Involuntary commitment *See* **Sectioning.**

Ion An atomic particle that carries primarily a positive or negative electrical charge.

IQ (intelligence quotient) A statistical measure of performance on intelligence tests based upon comparisons of a person's score with the average scores of others of their age. IQ was originally conceived as a measure of children's performance. Modern IQ tests identify IQ by the position of raw test scores on a distribution representing the population.

Isolated sleep paralysis Also known as a paralysis attack, an incident of isolated sleep paralysis involves paralysis and HHEs (hypnogogic and hypnopompic experiences), typically of the presence of a malevolent intruder, pressure on the chest, or of flying/floating. Paralysis attacks are interpreted in many cultures as alien abduction or demonic attack. Most psychologists and neuroscientists see paralysis attacks as a dysfunction of REM sleep.

James–Lange theory of emotion A theory of emotion that states that thoughts or the perception of events trigger directly autonomic nervous system changes; awareness of these changes reaches the cerebral cortex; and only then is there an experience of emotion.

JND *See* **Just noticeable difference.**

Just noticeable difference (JND) The smallest difference between two stimuli that can be detected by the appropriate sense organ at least 50% of the time.

Latent learning Learning that occurs without obvious reinforcement, and that is not apparent in behaviour.

Law of effect Thorndike's discovery that behaviours which lead to a satisfying state of affairs are 'stamped in', while behaviours that lead to an unsatisfying or annoying state of affairs are 'stamped out'. The law of effect formed the basis for B.F. Skinner's discoveries of operant conditioning principles.

Learned helplessness Seligman's term to describe the passivity and resignation which an animal may experience after coming to believe that it is unable to control or halt an aversive event. Seligman originally theorized that learned helpless lies at the root of depressive disorders.

Learning A fundamental way that organisms change. Learning is difficult to define precisely, but it involves relatively enduring change in knowledge and/or behaviour resulting from specific experiences.

Lexical hypothesis The idea that the most important personality traits are those best represented in human languages.

Libido In Freudian theory, a fund of psychic 'energy', or life force with which we are born. This life force has an erotic foundation, although its effects need not be explicitly sexual in nature nor bear only upon sexual life.

Lifespan perspective The perspective in developmental psychology that emphasizes the importance of studying human development throughout life, rather than focusing exclusively on infancy and childhood (as has often been the case in developmental psychology).

Limbic system A group of large structures and smaller nuclei that regulate mood, emotion, memory, and basic drives. It includes at least the hypothalamus, hippocampus, amygdala, basal ganglia, and nucleus accumbens.

Logical inference The cognitive processes by which we draw conclusions from information, including apparently very limited information. Some experiences that we might attribute to extra-sensory perception (ESP) are actually the result of logical inference. Rather than mysteriously perceiving external information we suddenly 'know' things because we have inferred them from existing information.

Long-term mating A committed, ongoing sexual relationship.

Loss events Life events involving short- or long-term loss of an attachment figure. Short-term losses include hospitalization, while long-term loss events occur in bereavement and family reordering. Loss events, particularly those occurring in childhood, are important because they are associated with later depression.

Lottery question A research paradigm used to investigate motives for working, in which people are asked whether they would continue to work if they won the lottery and no longer needed to work for financial security.

Lucid dreams A type of apex dream where the dreamer becomes aware that he or she is dreaming. In some cases the lucid dreamer can exert a degree of control over the dream narrative.

Lurking variable In correlational research a variable that influences two or more measured variables, creating the false impression that there are causal relationships between them.

Magnetic resonance imaging *See* MRI.

Magnetoencephalography *See* MEG.

Malleability The extent to which a characteristic, such as intelligence, can be altered by a change in environment. This can be seen as the opposite of constraint.

Matching phenomenon *See* **Positive assortment**.

Mean A descriptive statistic measuring the numerical average in a set of data.

Mean-level stability A measure of personality stability over time based upon comparison of the mean score for each individual trait among a sample as a whole from one measurement period to the next.

Mechanoreceptors Sensory receptors embedded in the skin that play a role in tactition.

Median An alternative measure of central tendency (technically only the mean should be referred to as the average) which reports the score above and below which an equal number of the participants has scored—that is, the 'middle' score.

Medical model The general term used to describe views of psychological disorder which frame them in a medical context. Unlike the myth of mental illness view, medical models view psychological disorders as actual illnesses with specific causes which necessitate treatment with psychotherapy, medication, or some other process.

MEG (Magnetoencephalography) A brain imaging technology by which recordings are made of magnetic fields generated by neural activity.

Menopause The cessation of a woman's menstrual cycles.

Mere exposure effect The human tendency to come to prefer people or things simply because they have become familiar.

Metarepresentation The awareness of our own thought, emotion, motives, etc. Failure in metarepresentation could lead to the experience of voice hearing and this may underlie symptoms of schizophrenia.

Microsleeps Brief and barely perceptible and involuntary periods of sleep lasting between 3 and 15 seconds. Microsleeps provide relief from fatigue but pose safety risks.

Midbrain A small, lower geographic area of the brain containing the inferior and superior colliculi, among other structures.

Mindset Used generically the term 'mindset' denotes a set of beliefs and assumptions that predispose an individual to make particular decisions or interpret situations in a particular way. Currently the major application of this idea is in Carol Dweck's growth mindset, the result of having an incremental theory of intelligence.

Minimal groups studies The minimal groups experimental paradigm involves creating artificial social categories and testing members' responses to members of in-groups and out-groups based on these categories. The approach was developed by Henri Tajfel and colleagues in the 1970s and has produced results consistent with social identity theory.

Minnesota Multiphasic Personality Inventory (MMPI) The first and most frequently used objective test of personality. It has shown particular validity in distinguishing between abnormal personality traits indicating mental health problems, and, to a lesser extent, validity in distinguishing normal personality traits.

Mirror neurons Neurons that fire both when an animal performs an action and when the animal observes another performing the same action. Mirror neurons are associated with imitation of others' behaviour, and comprehension of others' thoughts, intentions, and emotions.

Mode A measure of central tendency representing the most frequently occurring score in a set of data.

Modelling Demonstrating a behaviour, deliberately or accidentally. Observational learning takes place when an observer imitates the behaviour of an individual..

Modelling theory An early and simple view of observational learning in which individuals acquire behaviour simply by imitating those they admire.

Moderate bias A form of cognitive bias in which reactions to a group are shaped by a blend of positive and negative stereotypes operating on two dimensions; competence and warmth.

Modular model The modular model of the mind sees it as a large collection of components (modules), each of which provides solutions only to specific types of problems.

Molecular genetics Molecular geneticists attempt to identify specific genetic variations responsible for differences among people in particular traits.

Monocular cues Depth or distance cues that can operate even when only one eye is available. Specifically: relative size, texture gradient, linear perspective, interposition, atmospheric influence, and position on the horizon.

Monozygotic twins Twins who emerge from a single ovum (egg) and share 100% of their genes in common, although differing experiences may lead to different gene expression and thus a different phenotype.

Mood A feeling state that is typically less intense than an emotion, but which may last for a much longer time.

Motivations Mental states which cause people to engage in purposive behaviour (ie, behaviour directed towards achieving some goal or satisfying a need or desire). Motivations initiate actions, direct them towards the desired goal, and help the person sustain the necessary effort to attain the goal.

MRI (magnetic resonance imaging) A brain imaging technique that uses radio waves and protons within a magnetic field to produce detailed images of the brain or other neural tissue. Structural MRI gives us a detailed image; for example, of the brain. Functional MRI allows us to track blood flow in the brain, a proxy measure of brain activity.

Müller-Lyer illusion A visual illusion where two lines of identical length appear to be of unequal length.

Myth of mental illness A radical view of psychological disorder pioneered by Thomas Szasz which proposes that 'mental illness' is really a metaphor for problems in living and does not refer to actual illness or disease processes.

Naïve participants Participants present in an experimental setting who do not know what is taking place. Others present who do know and are in on the details of the experiment are called confederates.

Narcolepsy A chronic disruption of the sleep homeostat and sleep cycle. Those suffering from narcolepsy may feel the irresistible urge to sleep at any time, generally falling directly into REM sleep.

Narrow band theories Theories of personality which seek to address a particular aspect of personality rather than trying to explain personality in its entirety. An example of a narrow band personality theory is Zuckerman's sensation seeking.

National IQ The controversial idea by Richard Lynn that there are real differences in intelligence between the populations of different countries.

Nativism The view that at least some human abilities and tendencies are innate. It is often contrasted with empiricism in 'nature-nurture' debates.

Natural experiments A situation that occurs naturally, but that creates conditions that represent two or more levels of the independent variable, allowing conclusions about cause and effect to be drawn. Behavioural genetics makes use of natural experiments in the form of twin and adoption studies.

Natural selection Charles Darwin's theory of how the most important types of evolutionary events occur. Organisms with particular adaptations to their environment are more likely to survive and breed, hence those adaptations are passed on to future generations and the species is said to have evolved.

Needs A need is an internal state of physiological and/or psychological tension or discomfort that motivates a person to perform some action. This tension can be physiological, as in hunger, thirst or cold, emotional as in loneliness, or more cognitive, as in concern over future financial security.

Negative correlation Negative correlation occurs when an increase in one variable is associated (correlated) with a decrease in the other variable.

Negative emotionality The dimension of temperament that describes the degree to which an infant or child is easily frustrated, fearful, uncomfortable, sad, or difficult to soothe.

Negative reinforcement Takes place when a behaviour is reinforced through the removal of something that results in increasing the likelihood of the behaviour. Generally it is something aversive or unpleasant that is removed in negative reinforcement.

Negative symptoms (schizophrenia) The less obvious symptoms of schizophrenia, which include the absence of characteristics which are expected of a mentally healthy person. Negative symptoms include flat affect, anhedonia, alogia, and avolition.

Neurodevelopmental factors Factors which affect the brain but do not have a genetic origin. Neurodevelopmental events may occur prior to birth, at birth, of or after birth.

Neuron The cell types that transmit information throughout the nervous system. They convey information by firing or not firing. This is a binary system, rather like the 1s and 0s used by computers. There are three main types of neuron; motor neurons, sensory neurons, and interneurons.

Neurotransmitter A chemical substance that carries neural signals from one neuron to another across a neuronal synapse. There are a number of different neurotransmitters each associated with regulating particular aspects of brain and nervous system function.

Neutral stimulus A stimulus that has no natural relationship to an innate response it nonetheless eventually comes to elicit through classical conditioning. For example, a tone has no natural relationship to the human eye-blink response, but a person can be conditioned to blink when hearing a tone if the tone has been repeatedly paired with puffs of air blown at the eye.

Night terrors A parasomnia consisting of episodes during which the sleeper may suddenly sit up in bed screaming in fear, flail, or run as though pursued by a terrifying attacker. Night terrors resemble severe nightmares but are physiologically quite different.

Nociception The component of the sense of touch that registers pain.

Noise In signal detection theory, the idea of noise is an acknowledgement that detection of sensory stimuli may be affected by the occurrence of other, competing stimuli, or by varying psychological states of the perceiver.

Non-rapid eye movement *See* **NREM**.

Non-shared environment The term given to the unique biological and psychological environmental factors and experiences encountered by each developing child but not encountered by other children in the home. For example, a childhood illness, a traumatic experience, a different set of friends, and so forth.

Normal distribution A bell-shaped pattern of scores of any human characteristic across a population, in which most scores cluster around the mean and in which very few people score very high or low.

Nosology A medical term which means to the classification of illness and disease.

NREM (non-rapid eye movement) Non-rapid-eye-movement (NREM) refers to sleep stages 2–4, characterized by cognitive activity, ordinary dreaming, and reduced brain and nervous system activity relative to REM.

Nurture assumption The term used by Judith Rich Harris to refer to widespread beliefs that parents are the primary socializers of children and that the behaviour of parents has a profound impact on the personalities and behaviour of their children as adolescents and adults.

Object permanence A child's understanding that objects continue to exist even if they are no longer in view. In Piaget's theory this develops after a few months of life; however, research by Rene Baillargeon and colleagues suggests that much younger infants possess object permanence.

Object relations theory The collective term for a set of ideas developed by post-Freudian psychoanalysts in the mid-twentieth century. The central idea of object relations theory is that our interpersonal behaviour and mental health is strongly influenced by mental representations of significant relationships, in particular early ones.

Observational learning Learning through the observation of others. Mechanisms of observational learning include modelling and vicarious reinforcement.

Occipital lobe The rearmost cerebral cortex lobe containing the primary visual cortex (V1) and visual association areas.

Oedipus complex Freud's belief that children in the phallic stage (age 3 or 4 through age 5 or 6) experience powerful desires for the opposite-sex parent, while wishing to eliminate the same-sex parent who is perceived as a rival. In Freudian theory the resolution of this conflict is a key element of child development.

Off-label prescribing The practice of prescribing medication for conditions other than those for which that medication was intended in the belief that it will have some benefits for patients.

Ontology The branch of philosophy devoted to the nature of reality. This is critical to qualitative research because many qualitative researchers take an interpretive view of reality in contrast to the mainstream scientific position that there is an objective reality and the aim of research is to find ways to observe this.

Operant chamber B.F. Skinner's apparatus designed to study operant learning in animals. The chamber includes a container of food pellets, designed so that the pellets will be delivered to the animal when it presses down on a lever near its food tray. The cage is placed within a soundproof, temperature controlled, ventilated chamber.

Operant conditioning A form of learning in which the consequences of a behaviour affect the probability that the behaviour will be repeated in the future.

Operant learning *See* **Operant conditioning**.

Operant therapies A category of behaviour therapy based on principles of operant conditioning, in which rewards or punishments for a person's spontaneous behaviours are used to shape desired behaviours.

Operational definition A precise definition of a variable in terms that can be utilized for a research study.

Opiates A category of drug. They include: opium, the dried nectar of the common *Papaver somniferum* (poppy) flower containing a number of alkaloids including morphine. Morphine is an alkaloid of opium used as a potent painkiller. Alkaloids are any compounds with drug-like effects found naturally in a plant.

Opponent process theory The theory of colour vision that proposes that because certain wavelengths of light cannot be combined in an additive process, colours are created in colour vision by mixing in three opposing pairs: blue vs yellow, red vs green, and black vs white.

Optic array information The totality of visual information in the ambient optic array. This is the basis of direct theory of perception.

Optic disc The area where the optic nerve leaves the retina.

Optic nerve The optic nerve carries neural signals from the back of the retina to the central nervous system.

Optimal arousal theory The idea that people are motivated to achieve and maintain an optimal level of arousal. This could mean reducing levels of arousal from unpleasantly high levels but it could also mean increasing levels of arousal from unpleasantly low levels, as in states of boredom.

Ordinary dreaming The most common form of dreams, depicting relatively realistic activities and recognizable characters.

Ossicles Three tiny bones of the middle ear that amplify the vibrations that will be interpreted as sound. The bones are called the hammer, anvil, and stirrup.

Outer ear The outer structure of the ear, consisting primarily of the pinna and ear canal.

Overdose A lethal or nonlethal but toxic dose of a drug. Real overdoses are rare—most so-called overdoses are actually the result of mixing opioids with other psychoactive drugs.

Panic attack A brief period—generally peaking at about 10 minutes—within which a person experiences overwhelming anxiety focused upon unexplainable, terrifying physical sensations. Panic attacks are not uncommon in the population and do not necessarily signify psychological disorder.

Panic disorder An anxiety disorder characterized by intense anxiety over the prospect of experiencing a panic attack.

Paralysis attack *See* **Isolated sleep paralysis**.

Parapsychology Part of the wider field of anomalistic psychology. Parapsychology focuses on those anomalous experiences that lend themselves to scientific study under controlled conditions; for example, extra-sensory perception.

Parasomnias A group of sleep disorders characterized by unusual or bizarre physical behaviours, perceptions, dreams, or emotions during sleep.

Parasympathetic nervous system The division of the autonomic nervous system that returns the body to resting state following arousal and maintains that resting state.

Parental investment Proposed by Robert Trivers in 1972, this is an evolutionary theory which explains various sex differences in a range of species as resulting from unequal minimal levels of parental investment in reproduction between males and females.

Parietal lobe The parietal lobe is the lobe of the cerebral cortex containing the somatosensory cortex and somatosensory association areas.

Parsimony In science, the principle that if there is more than one competing explanation for some phenomenon, each plausible, scientists like to choose the simpler of the explanations. This is because simpler explanations contain fewer assumptions that might be incorrect. The principle of parsimony is also known as Occam's razor.

Partial correlation The correlation coefficient that remains between two variables once additional variables have been calculated out.

Partial reinforcement Partial reinforcement takes place when a behaviour is reinforced periodically rather than continuously. Partial reinforcement can be determined by the passage of time (an interval schedule) or the number of times an organism performs a behaviour (a ratio schedule).

Participant bias Participant bias takes place when participants realize the aim of the study and modify their behaviour accordingly.

Patients Like 'client' the term 'patient' is sometimes used to refer to a recipient of therapy and is most strongly associated with medical contexts and more traditional attitudes towards the professional–patient relationship. *See also* **Client**.

Pavlovian conditioning *See* **Classical conditioning**.

Perception A collective term for the processes by which the brain organizes and interprets sensory signals.

Perceptual constancy The ability to perceive an object as itself regardless of changes in angle of viewing, distance, or illumination.

Perceptual set The collective term for all our expectations, biases, and preconceptions that we bring to bear when making sense of a visual scene. Perceptual set means that what we perceive may differ quite starkly from what is actually there.

Perimenopause The perimenopause is the period leading up to the menopause when menopausal symptoms begin.

Peripheral nervous system The cranial and spinal nerves that allow communication to take place between the brain and body. The PNS consists of two divisions: the somatic nervous system, which controls voluntary movement and handles sensory information; and the autonomic nervous system, which regulates activities that are mostly out of voluntary control.

Person–situation controversy A major debate within personality psychology beginning during the 1960s in the work of Walter Mischel. The debate contrasted the views of those who believed traits were of primary importance in determining behaviour and those who believed that situations—not traits—determine behaviour.

Personality disorder(s) Pervasive, chronic patterns of dysfunctional thinking, feeling, and relating to the world that generally begin in adolescence and last throughout a person's life. These patterns cause distress and/or impairment.

Personality traits *See* **Traits.**

Pharmacotherapy In psychiatry, the use of drugs to treat psychological disorders or distress. Pharmacotherapy is based on psychopharmacology.

Photoreceptors Specialized neurons dedicated to capturing light in order to initiate transduction.

PHPs *See* **Potentially harmful psychological therapies.**

Pineal gland Situated in the brain the pineal gland releases the hormone melatonin which is important in regulating the sleep/wake cycle.

Pinna The visible structure of the outer ear that collects sounds and orients us to the placement of their source.

Pitch The 'highness' or 'lowness' of a sound, dependent on its frequency.

Pituitary gland Situated in the brain the pituitary gland secretes a variety of hormones and triggers other glands to secrete their hormones. This helps regulate blood pressure, body growth, aspects of pregnancy, childbirth and lactation, and the functioning of sex and reproductive organs.

Plasticity The brain's ability to change in response to learning, practice, and sensory input; and the ability of specialized regions of the brain to adapt if necessary to perform tasks for which they are not ordinarily used, for example following brain injury.

Polarization Polarization takes place when the resting potential balance between primarily negatively charged ions within a neuron and positively charged ions outside is altered so that the neuron contains more negative ions as compared to outside the cell.

Popular psychology Popular psychology, or 'pop' psychology, has a basis in psychological theory but is written for the layperson and is typically intended to provide the reader with insight into their experiences and perhaps a degree of therapeutic value.

Population The larger group of interest to a researcher, from which he or she will draw a smaller sample for the purposes of conducting a research study.

Positive assortment The tendency to mate with a person who is similar to you in various characteristics. Positive assortment has been documented for attractiveness, height, weight, occupation, religion, age, race, education, political attitudes, and so forth.

Positive correlation A positive correlation occurs when an increase in one variable is associated with an increase in the other variable.

Positive illusions Systematic biases and illusions that not only are self-serving by presenting the self in a positive way, but also are associated with positive mental health and other consequences for the person possessing them. Positive illusions include uncritically positive views of the self, illusions of control, and unrealistic optimism.

Positive reinforcement Positive reinforcement occurs when a behaviour is reinforced through the addition or presentation of something that increases the likelihood that the behaviour will be repeated. Generally it is something pleasant or rewarding that is added or presented.

Positive self-regard Rogers' term to describe feelings of self-worth and self-esteem, and being loved and accepted. According to Rogers, positive self-regard is dependent upon experiences of unconditional positive regard from others.

Positive symptoms (schizophrenia) In the context of schizophrenia positive symptoms denote the addition of something to a person's behaviour which is not expected of a mentally healthy person. These are the more obvious symptoms of schizophrenia, such as delusions, hallucinations, and disorganized use of language. *See also* **Schizophrenia.**

Post-synaptic neuron The 'receiving' neuron in neuronal communication.

Postconventional morality Moral judgement based on abstract principles and personal beliefs. In cognitive developmental theories of moral development this is typically seen in late adolescence or adulthood, although not all individuals ever achieve this advanced moral state.

Potentially harmful psychological therapies (PHPs) Pseudo-scientific procedures that have been shown to risk harm to patients.

Practical intelligence A concept hypothesized by Sternberg to describe the ability to come up with efficient solutions to everyday problems. It is roughly equivalent to the idea of 'common sense'.

Pre-synaptic neuron The 'sending' neuron in neuronal communication.

Preconventional morality Moral judgement based on the prospect of reward or punishment. In cognitive developmental theories of moral development this type of moral judgement is associated with younger children.

Preoperational stage Piaget's developmental stage lasting from approximately age 2 to 7. It is characterized by development of the symbolic capacity of the child's mind and egocentrism.

Preparedness The evolved tendency to acquire conditioned responses to stimuli that have had survival relevance in our evolutionary past more easily than to stimuli that are irrelevant to survival or were absent until recently.

Prequelae Things that precede something. In the case of attachment formation, prequelae include maternal sensitivity, as emphasized in attachment theory, but also probably also temperament and aspects of social context.

Primary reinforcers Intrinsically reinforcing because they are essential for the survival or reproduction of the organism (examples: food, water, sex, air, shelter, etc).

Primary sources Primary sources are where theory and research are first published, most commonly academic journals. It is essential that you begin to use primary sources and work towards relying on primary sources for your understanding of psychology.

Prodromal phase In schizophrenia that stage preceding the main onset of symptoms. Symptoms in this phase include milder cognitive distortions, depression, and sleep disturbance. Awareness of prodromal phase symptoms is important as they are easier to treat than a full-blown episode of schizophrenia and starting or altering medication may prevent a full episode. *See also* **Schizophrenia**.

Propinquity The frequency with which people come into contact.

Prospective studies Most studies linking early events and their sequelae are carried out retrospectively (ie, looking back after the sequelae are apparent). By contrast, prospective studies involve following people up after a significant early event like developing an attachment type and seeing how they develop.

Proximate causes The immediate causes of behaviour—the trigger for something to occur. Proximate causes of behaviour include motivations; physiological, biochemical, and neural processes; and learning. Most psychologists focus on proximate explanations of behaviour.

Pseudoscience Non-science performed for non-scientific goals, but with the superficial appearance of science.

Psychiatry Psychiatry overlaps with psychology in the area of mental disorder, but psychiatrists are medical doctors and their formal training does not cover the full breadth of human mind and behaviour.

Psychoactive drug Any substance with properties that affect mental life or consciousness in some way. Many psychoactive substances have a non-medical or recreational use.

Psychodynamic psychotherapy A therapy based on principles originating in psychoanalysis. Psychodynamic theorists share psychoanalytic beliefs in unconscious emotional and motivational processes and that the origins of personality and symptoms are in childhood experience. However, therapy is usually less intensive and long-term than in psychoanalysis, and therapists are often less rigid in their technique.

Psychological adaptation A mental characteristic that evolved through natural selection to provide solutions to specific types of problems encountered over evolutionary time by our human ancestors.

Psychological dysfunction Any breakdown in mental functioning—cognitive, emotional, or behavioural. The boundaries between 'functional' and 'dysfunctional' are often fuzzy, however, and there is wide disagreement as to how to characterize these boundaries.

Psychological thinking Thinking like a psychologist. This includes scientific reasoning but is broader as psychologists can often benefit from stepping back from an immediate issue and looking at wider issues such as historical influence and practical value.

Psychopharmacology The study of the effects of drugs on mood, emotion, and behaviour.

Psychophysics The scientific study of the relationship between sensation and perception.

Psychotic disorder Any disorder that includes extremely severe distortion in thinking and perception, where a person's ability to grasp reality and respond rationally is badly impaired.

Psychoticism In the context of personality theory Eysenck defined psychoticism as tough-mindedness. To be high in psychoticism involves being low in empathy and high in aggression. In Eysenck's theory high levels of psychoticism are associated with vulnerability to psychosis; however, the symptoms of psychosis and psychoticism are very different.

Punishment Punishment takes place when the consequence of a behaviour decreases the likelihood that it will continue or be repeated in the future.

Purposive behaviour Behaviour directed towards achieving some goal or satisfying a need or desire. *See also* Motivations.

Qualitative age-related change In the context of cognitive development, qualitative age-related change refers to the idea that we become capable of understanding different things as opposed to simply more things at different ages.

Qualitative analysis The analysis of non-mathematical data. The simplest form of qualitative analysis is thematic analysis in which key themes are identified in a section of text, which might be existing written text or a transcribed interview.

Qualitativeness In consciousness research, the feature of consciousness which suggests that something is conscious only if it 'feels like something'.

Quantitative age-related change Quantitative age-related change occurs whenever people can do more with increasing age; for example, in cognition where individuals start to know and understand more concepts.

Racism The simplest definition of racism is individual prejudice against members of other ethnic groups. However, it is now widely acknowledged that racism exists on a wider structural level, and that members of minority ethnic groups experience social disadvantage in many ways regardless of the intentions of individuals in the ethnic majority.

Radical behaviourism B.F. Skinner's version of behaviourism. Radical behaviourists propose that all behaviour can be analysed empirically by examining the reinforcements and punishments which follow the behaviour. This became known as radical behaviourism because of Skinner's insistence that psychology could never be a science of mind, but only a science of behaviour.

Random assignment When each participant has an equal chance of being assigned to any of the conditions of the experiment (ie, any of the levels of the independent variable) they are said to be randomly assigned.

Randomized controlled trial (RCT) A research study used to evaluate a therapy or treatment where the research participants are randomly assigned to receive either the treatment of interest, a competing treatment, no treatment, or—if possible—a placebo treatment.

Rank-order stability A measure of personality stability based upon the pattern of rank order of traits (from high to low) for each person in a sample from one measurement period to the next.

Rapid eye movement *See* REM.

Rational emotive behaviour therapy (REBT) A form of cognitive therapy devised by Albert Ellis based on the idea that emotional distress is rooted in illogical, absolutist, and counterproductive ideas and beliefs. REBT is directive—the therapist's job is to forcefully dispute the client's illogical and unrealistic beliefs.

Rationalism The philosophical movement founded by René Descartes which held that beliefs should be formed through the use of reason, rather than relying upon personal experience or the pronouncements of authorities.

RCT *See* **Randomized controlled trial.**

Reactive gene-environment correlation Reactive gene-environment correlation is when an organism's genotype evokes responses in others, creating an environment that shares characteristics with that genotype.

REBT *See* **Rational-emotive behaviour therapy.**

Red-green colour blindness Red-green colour blindness takes place when M- and L-cones are equally sensitive to red and green, making differentiation of these colours impossible.

Reformulated frustration-aggression hypothesis Berkowitz's revision of the earlier frustration-aggression hypothesis which stated that all aggression is in response to the frustration of a goal. According to the reformulated frustration-aggression hypothesis, frustration is one of many types of unpleasant events that could lead to aggression.

Reinforcement Reinforcement takes place when the consequence of a behaviour increases the likelihood that the behaviour will continue or be repeated in the future.

Related design *See* **Within-groups design.**

Reliability Literally consistency. A reliable test should consistently give the same result if the same person is tested and retested. *See also* **Test-retest reliability** and **Inter-rater reliability.**

REM (rapid eye movement) The fifth stage of sleep characterized by high levels of brain and nervous system activity and intensely vivid, hallucinatory dreaming.

REM-sleep behaviour disorder (RBD) A parasomnia where the sleeper is missing the muscle paralysis component of REM sleep and acts out confrontational and violent dreams.

Repeated measures design *See* **Within-groups design.**

Repetitive transcranial magnetic stimulation (rTMS) A technique being developed for treatment of depression that consists of sending short electromagnetic pulses though the cerebral cortex by means of a coil placed on the scalp.

Repression A particularly important and perhaps the most basic ego defence mechanism identified by Freud, where an unacceptable wish, thought, or impulse is removed from conscious awareness. Repression is thus a possible mechanism for forgetting, but this is a controversial idea.

Research methods This term is used differently in different contexts, but it is used here to refer to general strategies that may be used for conducting research.

Residual phase In the context of schizophrenia this follows the main onset of symptoms. Symptoms in this phase include milder cognitive distortions, depression, and sleep disturbance. *See also* **Schizophrenia.**

Response bias In signal detection theory, response bias refers to the fact that a person may be biased in favour of, or against, the detection of a stimulus.

Retinal disparity A binocular cue to depth perception based on the fact that each eye takes in a slightly different, but overlapping, view.

Reuptake Takes place when the neurotransmitter is reabsorbed by the presynaptic neuron after binding of the neurotransmitter to receptor sites in the post-synaptic neuron.

RNA A chemical compound found in each cell nucleus and cytoplasm. RNA carries out the job of constructing protein from 'instructions' contained in genes.

Rods Photoreceptors specialized to allow night vision and vision in low light.

Rorschach test A well-known projective personality and mental health test originally devised by Hermann Rorschach in 1921. The test consists of a standard set of five colour and five black-and-white symmetrical inkblots. The test-taker is then asked to describe what they see in each blot and to identify the specific areas of the blot from which the image is constructed.

rTMS *See* **Repetitive transcranial magnetic stimulation.**

Rumination A characteristic of anxiety. It involves thinking for long periods in repetitive and negative ways about events and symptoms.

Safety ratio The safety ratio of a drug is a statistic expressing its potential toxicity in terms of the dose one would need to take to cause death.

Sample The relatively small group of individuals selected to represent a larger group—the population from which the sample is drawn.

Scaffolding The processes by which an expert instructor assists a learner in mastering complex learning that they cannot yet master on their own. As a child progresses, the level of scaffolding required declines. *See also* **Zone of Proximal Development.**

Scepticism A philosophical approach or point of view based on the scientific method which proposes that compelling evidence of a claim should be presented before one comes to believe in the claim. The sceptic is not negative or cynical about new ideas but they require a high standard of evidence before they accept them.

Schemas Mental structures or cognitive models that represents some aspect of the world and how it works.

Schizophrenia A condition or group of related psychotic conditions characterized by severely distorted perception and experience of reality, disorganized thought and speech, and inappropriate emotions and emotional responses.

Science The study of the natural world assuming the philosophical position that there are facts to be discovered, and aiming to make the methods of testing themas objective as possible. Scientists accept that our current understanding will change over time as more information is discovered and maintain an attitude of open-mindedness whilst requiring high standards of evidence.

Scientific thinking The logical process of thinking about how to generate and evaluate evidence for an idea, remaining as objective and unbiased as is humanly possible.

Scientism The extent to which a topic conforms to stereotypes of science. Because it uses high-tech tools and deals with biology—a classic 'hard' science—brain science is stereotypically scientific and so may be judged as more scientific than it really is.

SCRUFFY targets SCRUFFY targets have emerged as a reaction against the alleged overuse of SMART targets. The acronym stands for Student-led, Creative, Unspecified, Fun For Youngsters.

Search engine A tool for tagging and searching for online information. A search engine looks for items that have been tagged for particular search terms. It may search the whole Internet (like Google) or selected websites.

Second pain In contrast to first pain, second pain is the generally longer lasting, less localized, and more unpleasant pain sensations, conducted along the slower C-fibres.

Second-generation antipsychotics Recently developed drugs designed to treat psychotic disorders such as schizophrenia, but are also used as mood stabilizers in bipolar disorder.

Secondary reinforcers Secondary reinforcers are not directly related to survival and reproductive success but can nonetheless prove to be just as powerful as primary reinforcers. That is because the organism has previously been conditioned to associate them with primary reinforcers. Money and status are excellent examples.

Sectioning Sectioning (or involuntary commitment) takes place when a person is detained in a psychiatric facility. Proceedings to section someone in this way may be brought by either your closest relative or an approved mental health professional. Initial detention (section 2) is for assessment. This may be followed by further detention if deemed necessary.

Selective serotonin reuptake inhibitors (SSRIs) A type of antidepressant drug that has been around since the 1980s. They block the reuptake of the neurotransmitter serotonin, while having relatively little effect on other neurotransmitters—in contrast to the tricyclics and MAO inhibitors.

Self Each person's subjective awareness of, and ideas about, his or her own individual nature, characteristics, and very existence.

Self-control The aspect of self-regulation which involves suppressing a powerful immediate desire or goal in the service of a more important overriding long-term goal. Self-control typically involves resisting temptation.

Self-efficacy Albert Bandura's term to describe one's beliefs about one's ability to accomplish a specific task. Self-efficacy is task-specific, and a person high in self-efficacy on one task can be quite low on another.

Self-esteem A person's emotional assessment or evaluation of their self-worth. Put more simply, how much we like ourselves. Self-esteem is usually consistent and global but it can vary according to situation. Of particular concern is fragile or defensive self-esteem. This tends to be high until challenged but is easily threatened.

Self-narratives Internal 'narratives of the self' which evolve through the lifespan. Self-narratives are stories and myths people tell themselves about events in their lives and personal characteristics which reflect their current understanding of their place in the world and the meaning of their life.

Self-regulation A collective term for the ways that the self monitors and exerts control over its responses so as to accomplish goals and live up to personal standards.

Self-serving bias The tendency to make systematic judgement errors in one's favour. This involves overestimating one's contributions, overestimating one's positive attributes relative to those of others, and attributing successes and good deeds to one's own efforts but failures and bad deeds to circumstances, bad luck, or other people.

Sensation The receiving of raw physical, electromagnetic, or chemical energy through the sense organs. Sensation precedes but is not the same as perception, the process by which we make sense of the energy picked up by the sense organs.

Sensation seeking The tendency to seek out 'varied, novel, complex, and intense sensations and experiences, and the willingness to take physical, social, legal, and financial risks for the sake of such experience' (Zuckerman, 1994, p 27).

Sensorimotor stage Piaget's first developmental stage lasting from birth to approximately age 2. It is characterized by unthinking responses to internal and external stimuli and events.

Sensory adaptation The tendency for one's sensitivity to stimuli to be lessened over time during continuous exposure.

Sequelae Those things that come after something; for example, psychological characteristics developing after the development of an attachment type in infancy. Because the causal relationships between events and their sequelae are unclear it is preferable to say 'sequelae' rather than 'consequences'.

Shape constancy The aspect of perceptual constancy that allows us to perceive an object as the same shape regardless of the angle from which we view it.

Shaping *See* **Shaping by successive approximation**.

Shaping by successive approximation Successive reinforcement of those operant behaviours that come increasingly closer to the behaviour one ultimately wishes to reinforce.

Short-term mating Sexual behaviour that is casual in nature and not part of a committed relationship.

Signal detection theory A theory that attempts to explain how stimuli are detected by factoring in the variables of human judgement and bias.

Size constancy The aspect of perceptual constancy that allows us to perceive an object as the same size regardless of the size of its image on our retina.

Skinner box *See* **Operant chamber**.

Sleep cycle The repeating pattern of Stages 2–5 sleep that recurs four to six times throughout the night following sleep onset (Sleep Stage 1).

Sleep mentation Cognition that takes place during sleep, including thinking, imagery, and narrative dreams.

Sleep thinking (cognitive activity) Rational, directed thought occurring during NREM sleep.

Sleepwalking *See* **Somnambulism**.

SMART targets Highly structured targets based on the work of Doran (1981), designed to be maximally motivating by being specific, measurable, assignable, realistic, and time-related.

Social cognition The collective term for the mental processes involved in the individual's perception of and judgements about themselves, others, and social situations.

Social comparison theory A group of theories initially formulated by Leon Festinger that describe how and why people may compare themselves to others to rationally evaluate themselves or enhance their self-concepts and defend against negative self-judgements.

Social constructionism A collection of approaches to psychology, which share the assumption that knowledge is highly context specific, and created through discourse.

Social constructivism The Vygotsky–Bruner model of cognitive development in which a child constructs an increasingly complex mental representation of the world with the help of expert others through a process of interaction.

Social facilitation Social facilitation takes place when performance is enhanced by the presence of other people. This includes the effects of mere presence of others as well as competition and cooperation. Social facilitation does not necessarily require physical presence, thus the presence of a mobile phone enhances the quality of social interaction (the iPhone effect).

Social identity The portion of our personal identity that comes from our beliefs about belonging to social groups and categories. It is believed that our social identity influences our attitudes and behaviour.

Social identity theory An explanation for a range of social-psychological phenomena based on the idea that we are influenced in attitudes and behaviour by the norms of social categories with which we identify.

Social inhibition Social inhibition takes place when we are less likely to engage in a social behaviour in the presence of others. This affects helping behaviour, emotional expression, and disapproved-of behaviours. These may have different explanations; for example, diffusion of responsibility may be important in inhibiting helping behaviour.

Social intuitionism A term from positive psychologist Jonathan Haidt's theory of moral judgement. The theory proposes that moral judgements are more often than not the result of intuition and emotion rather than reasoning. Reasoning tends to occur after the fact to explain to oneself or others why one has arrived at a particular moral judgement.

Society An enduring and cooperating group whose members have developed institutions and organized patterns of interaction.

Sociocognitive theory of hypnosis A theory that explains hypnotic effects in terms other than 'altered states'—generally emphasizing the subject's social role in the hypnotic interaction.

Sociocultural perspective A general approach to psychology that focuses on the ways society and culture influence behaviour.

Sociometer theory Sociometer theory posits that self-esteem provides us with feedback about how socially accepted we are.

Sociometric status Crudely, sociometric status means popularity. However, this is not a single scale from popular to unpopular. Children can also be categorized by popularity (eg, popular, rejected, neglected, controversial, or average in popularity).

Soma *See* **Cell body.**

Somatosensory area A region of the cortex where tactile sensations are perceived.

Somatosensory cortex The somatosensory cortex processes sensory information about heat, cold, pain, and posture.

Somnambulism Commonly called sleepwalking, a parasomnia characterized by wandering, often aimlessly, during late-REM sleep.

Specific phobia A powerful but irrational fear of a specific object, animal, or situation. The most common phobias are often those for which evolutionary roots are suspected (eg, fear of the dark or heights, fear of spiders or snakes, fear of the sight of blood, etc).

Spinal cord A thin, tubular bundle of nerve tracts contained in the vertebrae of the spinal column. It comprises grey matter—cell bodies, unmyelinated axons, dendrites, and glia—along with white matter—axons with myelin sheaths.

Spinal reflexes Automatic motor actions in response to stimulation. They bypass the brain entirely and are controlled by the spinal cord.

Split-brain surgery Surgical procedures used to treat epilepsy, where the corpus callosum is severed or partially severed. The modern callosotomy procedure severs a relatively small area of tissue and has replaced the more destructive commissurotomy.

SSRI *See* **Selective serotonin reuptake inhibitors.**

SSRI discontinuation syndrome A drug withdrawal syndrome associated with the use of at least some of the SSRI and SNRI antidepressants. The syndrome may consist of flu-like symptoms, dizziness, weakness, nausea, fatigue, feelings of 'unreality', loss of balance, light-headedness, 'electric-shock' sensations, and other symptoms.

Stage of concrete operations Piaget's developmental stage lasting from approximately age 7 to 11 or 12. It is characterized by mastery of tasks involving the application of logic.

Stage of formal operations Piaget's developmental stage beginning at age 11 or 12, and characterized by the ability to apply systematic logic to abstract concepts and to think hypothetically and sceptically.

Stages of psychosexual development Freud believed that children pass through five developmental stages of psychosexual development. For healthy personality to develop, the child must successfully complete the tasks and resolve the conflicts which typically occur at each stage. Fixation at any particular stage may result in adult neurosis or distortion of personality. The stages are termed oral, anal, phallic (Oedipal), latency, and genital.

Stages of sleep There are five stages of sleep, including a period of sleep onset, three periods of NREM, and one of REM sleep. Each stage is associated with characteristic brainwave activity, and the stages are played out during the night in a repeating pattern (the sleep cycle).

Stanford–Binet intelligence scale The IQ test created by Alfred Binet. The purpose of the test was to predict academic performance so that children of deficient ability could be identified and placed in special remedial programmes. The test has been revised four times over its 100-year history.

States States are not stable but depend on the situation, thus we all have anxious states but only some of us are consistently anxious and are said to be high in the trait of anxiety.

Statistical significance A figure generated from inferential statistics that allows us to understand the probability that one's research results reflect actual relationships among variables and are not due to chance factors alone.

Stereotyping The attribution of particular characteristics to members of a group or category based on their membership of that group or category. Although it is often said that stereotypes contain a grain of truth, research has generally not supported the accuracy of national stereotypes.

Stigma A social 'badge' or mark of shame or disgrace resulting from a person's behaviour or membership in a disapproved or discriminated-against group. Social stigma traditionally has been a problem for those diagnosed with psychological disorders.

Strange Situation A controlled observation procedure designed to create mild anxiety in order to measure the key elements of attachment: proximity-seeking, separation distress (and stranger anxiety), and response to reunion. Based on infant behaviour in the Strange Situation, mobile babies and toddlers can be classified with an attachment type.

Strength model of self-control Baumeister's strength model of self-control uses muscular strength as a metaphor to understand self-control. According to this approach self control works like our muscles, varying between individuals and subject to fatigue and training effects.

Structural model Freud's structural model of personality encompasses the instinctive id, the logical ego, and the moral superego. To Freud these appear at different stages of psychosexual development.

Subjectivity In the context of consciousness research, the idea that consciousness can only be experienced by an individual being and cannot exist independently of them.

Subliminal perception Subliminal perception occurs when a stimulus is perceived unconsciously (implicitly). This can occur when it is below the absolute threshold or is presented too briefly to reach conscious awareness.

Superego In Freud's structural model, the individual's conscience, and the origin of human morality. The superego observes the work of the ego and passes judgement on it—punishing the psyche with guilt or shame for wrongdoing, and pointing in the direction of ideal behaviour.

Superordinate traits Hans Eysenck's term for the two basic trait dimensions within which all possible lower-order traits could be found. The superordinate trait dimensions are extraversion–introversion and emotional instability–emotional stability.

Suprachiasmatic nuclei (SCN) A group of neurons of the hypothalamus that constitute the circadian pacemaker.

Survey research A research method used to obtain self-reported data about people's experiences, attitudes, feelings, and on occasion, their behaviour in contexts where it would be impractical to observe them.

Sympathetic nervous system The division of the autonomic nervous system that mobilizes the body for arousal, particularly in response to a threat of some sort, but also in response to certain other conditions.

Synapse The juncture of the presynaptic and postsynaptic neuron.

Synaptic gap The miniscule space over which neurons pass their neurotransmitters, from the terminal of the presynaptic neuron to the dendrites of the postsynaptic neuron.

Synaptic receptors The openings that are embedded in the dendrites of neurons to which neurotransmitters bind during the process of neuronal communication.

Systematic desensitization A behaviour therapy technique primarily used to treat phobias and certain other anxiety disorders. Systematic desensitization involves controlled, incremental exposure to phobic stimuli while simultaneously practising relaxation techniques that are incompatible with anxiety.

Tactition The touch component of the sense of touch. *See also* **Thermoception** and **Nociception**.

Temperament Each infant's relatively consistent behavioural characteristics, what we would call personality in an older child. Mary Rothbart has classified temperament within three dimensions: effortful control, negative emotionality, and extraversion. Temperament emerges as a result of genetic and other biological factors as well as environmental factors, but most theorists stress the importance of biology.

Temporal lobe The lobe of the cerebral cortex containing the auditory cortex, auditory association areas, and Wernicke's area.

Terminal The small bulb-like structure at the end of neuron axons that contains the vesicles from which neurotransmitters are released.

Terror management theory (TMT) TMT is an existential psychological theory that proposes that much human behaviour is motivated by a need to manage or reduce the terror associated with one's own mortality.

Test-retest reliability A way to assess the quality of a psychological measure. If people take a test twice and get similar results this is indicated by a test-retest correlation coefficient of close to 1. Lower scores indicate that people's scores when they take the test twice are less consistent and hence the test is not reliable.

Thematic analysis Perhaps the simplest form of qualitative analysis, it involves coding blocks of text or transcript for themes.

Thematic apperception test (TAT) A projective personality test first devised during the 1930s by Henry Murray and Christiana Morgan. In the TAT the test-taker is presented with 31 emotionally loaded but ambiguous drawings and asked to tell the 'story' of the drawings. According to proponents of the test, in doing so the test-taker reveals important motives, drives, conflicts, and emotions.

Theory A set of interconnected ideas and statements used to explain phenomena.

Theory of inclusive fitness A theory of altruism directed towards kin, which stresses that natural selection operates on genes, not on individuals and their bodies. Altruistic acts directed towards genetic kin may increase a person's own evolutionary 'fitness' if the act increases the kin's survival or reproductive success.

Theory of mind The cognitive ability to interpret what is going on in the minds of others. We are said to have a theory of mind when we hold a belief (ie, a theory) about what thoughts, feelings, and intentions are going on in someone else's mind.

Theory of reciprocal altruism Robert Trivers' evolutionary theory of altruism directed towards non-kin. The theory proposes that psychological attributes that motivate altruism towards non-kin, such as empathy, will only evolve under conditions where there is some expectation that altruistic acts will be reciprocated in the future—either to oneself or one's kin.

Therapeutic alliance An hypothesized common factor of psychotherapy that refers to the positive emotions between therapist and client, the therapist's empathy for the client, and both parties' joint commitment to therapeutic work.

Therapeutic orientation The combination of theoretical understandings and techniques through which therapists understand and treat psychological distress and mental disorder. Some therapists stick strictly to their model while others are more eclectic, drawing on different ideas when they are useful.

Therapist allegiance A hypothesized common factor of psychotherapy that refers to the therapist's commitment to the specific type of therapy he or she has chosen to use.

Therapist competence A hypothesized common factor of psychotherapy that refers to the degree to which a therapist tends to produce good results regardless of client or therapy techniques.

Thermoception The component of the sense of touch that registers temperature.

Thermoreceptors Sensory receptors embedded in the skin that register temperature.

Third-generation antidepressants The most recent group of antidepressants to be developed. These drugs include serotonin-norepinephrine reuptake inhibitors (SNRIs) as well as drugs with unique ('atypical') chemical structures and physiological mechanisms.

Three-stratum theory An empirically based theory of intelligence devised by John B. Carroll that blends the idea of *g* with Horn and Cattell's *Gf-Gc* theory and the idea that intelligence includes multiple cognitive abilities. *See also* **Fluid intelligence** and **Crystallized intelligence.**

TMT *See* **Terror management theory.**

Total sleep deprivation Going entirely without sleep for 24 hours or more.

Touch The principal sense that obtains sensory information from the skin. It is comprised of three subsenses: tactition, thermoception, and nociception.

Trait-situation behaviour profile The unique, stable behaviour patterns created by the interaction of a person's traits with specific situations. Trait-situation behaviour profiles are like 'if . . . then . . . else [otherwise]' statements in computer language. Trait-situation behaviour profiles account for the fact that people may appear to display different traits depending upon the situation.

Traits Stable, enduring personality attributes and motives for behaviour. Traits may generally be described using adjectives (eg, extraverted, conscientious, cheerful, honest, compassionate). Traits are limited in number, and each person differs in the degree to which they display any particular trait.

Transduction The conversion of raw physical or chemical energy into sensory signals.

Transference One of the principles on which psychoanalysis and, to a lesser extent, other psychodynamic therapies depends. It is the process in which the properties of early relationships transfer on to later relationships. By developing a transference relationship with a therapist a patient can develop insight into how they relate to others and the origins of these patterns.

Triarchic theory of successful intelligence Robert J. Sternberg's theory that intelligence consists of three distinct types: analytic intelligence, creative intelligence, and practical intelligence.

Trichromatic theory of colour The trichromatic theory of colour explains how all colours are created through the additive mixture of blue, green, and red. Trichromacy results because S-, M-, and L-cones in the retina are particularly sensitive to short, medium, or long wavelengths—which correspond to the perception of blue, green, and red.

Tripartite model of attitudes Allport's model of attitudes as having three components; the cognitive (thinking) component, the affective (emotional) component, and the conative (behavioural) component. According to this model we can think of attitudes as comprising opinions, emotional responses, and behaviours.

Triple vulnerability theory An integrated model of anxiety disorders created by David Barlow. According to the triple vulnerability theory, anxiety disorders result from the interaction of three factors: generalized biological vulnerability, generalized psychological vulnerability, and specific psychological vulnerability.

True experiment A research study where the experimenter satisfies all criteria necessary for causality to be inferred in the research results. These include random assignment to conditions, manipulation of variables, use of control conditions, and control over confounding variables.

Two-factor theory of emotion Schacter and Singer's theory of emotion that argues that thoughts or perceptions of events directly trigger autonomic nervous system arousal (as per James and Lange) but that emotion will emerge only after a cognitive label is attached to the arousal to explain it.

Tympanic membrane (eardrum) A membrane stretched across the end of the ear canal which vibrates in response to sound waves and marks the border between the outer and middle ear.

Ultimate causes Forces that shaped the capacity or tendency for the behaviour in human beings over evolutionary time—why, rather than how, a behaviour occurs. Unlike most other psychologists, evolutionary psychologists focus primarily on ultimate explanations of behaviour.

Unconditional positive regard Rogers' term to describe the essential quality of relationships in which the love and approval a person receives from important others is given freely and is not dependent upon particular behaviour.

Uncontrollable reinforcers A reinforcer which happens to occur after behaviour but which is not causally related to it. It increases the likelihood of the behaviour being repeated but not because it actually resulted from the behaviour.

Undermining effect The undermining effect takes place when, in direct contradiction to the additive principle, introducing an extrinsic motive in addition to an intrinsic motive reduces intrinsic motivation. This may happen, for example, when an athlete or musician turns professional or secures a lucrative contract.

Unity In consciousness studies, the idea that consciousness is always a single, unified experience.

Unrelated design *See* **Between-groups design.**

Variable-interval (VI) schedule A partial reinforcement schedule that provides reinforcement at unpredictable time intervals.

Variable-ratio (VR) schedule A partial reinforcement schedule that provides each reinforcement after an unpredictable number of behavioural responses.

Verbal intelligence A measure of our cognitive abilities concerned with handling words.

Vicarious conditioning Learning through observing the rewarding or punishing consequences of other people's behaviour. In vicarious reinforcement the model is seen being rewarded for the behaviour, in which case this behaviour is more likely to be imitated.

Virtue signalling Displaying pro-social attitudes. The term has become popular in relation to social media use but there are also offline strategies; for example, wearing charity wristbands.

Visual cortex The area at the back of the brain that receives and interprets visual neural signals from the eyes.

Wavelength A measure of the lengths between electromagnetic waves.

Weber's law A mathematical expression of the idea that for any given stimulus, the just noticeable difference (JND) is always proportionate to the level of the standard stimulus.

Wechsler Adult Intelligence Scale (WAIS©-III) A standardized test of intelligence designed by David G. Wechsler. This was the first IQ test to include testing of adults.

Williams syndrome A developmental disorder characterized by rich verbal and social interaction but low scores on non-verbal IQ.

Within-groups design An experimental design in which participants take part in all conditions.

Zone of Proximal Development (ZPD) In social constructivist theory of learning the conceptual gap between the complexity of learning that a learner can master on their own and the complexity of learning which they can potentially master with the help of an expert instructor.

REFERENCES

A class of one (1997). Transcript of *NewsHour with Jim Lehrer*. Retrieved from http://www.pbs.org/newshour/bb/race_relations/jan-june97/bridges_2-18.html on 2 January 2008.

Ableson, R. P. (1995). *Statistics as Principled Argument*. Hillsdale, NJ. Lawrence Erlbaum Associates.

Abma, J. C., Martinez, G. M., Mosher, W. D., and Dawson, B. S. (2004). Teenagers in the United States. Sexual activity, contraceptive use, and childbearing, 2002. *Vital Health Statistics*, 23. Washington, DC. National Center for Health Statistics.

Abramov, I. and Gordon, J. (1994). Color appearance. On seeing red—or yellow, or green, or blue. *Annual Review of Psychology*, 45, 451–85.

Abramson, L. Y., Alloy, L. B., and Metalsky, J. I. (1995). Hopelessness depression. In J. N. Buchanan and M. E. P. Seligman (eds), *Explanatory Style* (pp 113–34). Hillsdale, NJ. Lawrence Erlbaum Associates.

Abramson, P. R. (1992). Adios. A farewell address. *Journal of Sex Research*, 29, 449–50.

Achermann, P. (2004). The two-process model of sleep regulation revisited. *Aviation, Space, and Environmental Medicine*, 75(Suppl 1), A37–43.

Acker, C. J. (2002). *Creating the American Junkie. Addiction Research in the Classic Era of Narcotic Control*. Baltimore, MD. Johns Hopkins University Press.

Ackerman, J. M., Nocera, C. C., and Bargh, J. A. (2010). Incidental haptic sensations influence social judgments and decision. *Science*, 328, 1712–15.

Adamec, R. E., Burton, P., Shallow, T., and Budgell, J. (1999). NMDA receptors mediate lasting increases in anxiety-like behaviour produced by the stress of predator exposure—implications for anxiety associated with post-traumatic stress disorder. *Physiology and Behavior*, 65, 723–37.

Adams, G. and Plaut, V. C. (2003). The cultural grounding of personal relationship. Friendship in North American and West African worlds. *Personal Relationships*, 10, 333–47.

Adams, R. and Laursen, B. (2001). The organization and dynamics of adolescent conflict with parents and friends. *Journal of Marriage and the Family*, 63, 97–110.

Adolphs, R., Tranel, D., and Buchanan, T. W. (2005). Amygdala damage impairs emotional memory for gist but not details of complex stimuli. *Nature Neuroscience*, 8, 512–18.

Adolphs, R., Tranel, D., and Damasio, A. R. (1998). The human amygdala in social judgment. *Nature*, 393, 470–4.

Ahn, H. and Wampold, B. E. (2001). Where oh where are the specific ingredients? A meta-analysis of component studies in counseling and psychotherapy. *Journal of Counseling Psychology*, 48, 251–7.

Ainsworth, M. D. S., Blehar, M., Waters, E., and Wall, S. (1978). *Patterns of Attachment*. Hillsdale, NJ. Lawrence Erlbaum Associates.

Akiskal, H. S. and Benazzi, F. (2003). Family history validation of the bipolar nature of depressive mixed states. *Journal of Affective Disorders. Special Issue. Validating the Bipolar Spectrum*, 73(1–2), 113–22.

Alcock, J. (2001). *The Triumph of Sociobiology*. New York, NY. Oxford University Press.

Alcock, J. (2009). *Animal Behavior*. Sunderland, MA. Sinauer.

Alcock, J. E. (2003). Give the null hypothesis a chance. Reasons to remain doubtful about the existence of psi. *Journal of Consciousness Studies*, 10(6–7), 29–50.

Alegria, M., Woo, M., Cao, Z., Torres, M., Meng, X.-L., et al (2007). Prevalence and correlates of eating disorders in Latinos in the United States. *International Journal of Eating Disorders*, 40(Suppl), S15–S21.

Alexander, G. M. and Hines, M. (2002). Sex differences in response to children's toys in nonhuman primates (*Cercopithecus aethiops sabaeus*). *Evolution and Human Behavior*, 23, 467–79.

Alexander, G. M., Wilcox, R., and Woods, R. (2009). Sex differences in infants' visual interest in toys. *Archives of Sexual Behavior*, 38, 427–33.

Alexander, K. W., Quas, J. A., Goodman, G. S., Ghetti, S., Edelstein, R. S., et al (2005). Traumatic impact predicts long-term memory for documented child sexual abuse. *Psychological Science*, 16(1), 33–40.

Allcott, H. and Gentzkow, M. (2017). Social media and fake news in the 2016 election. *Journal of Economic Perspectives*, 31(2), 211–36.

Allen, K. (2003). Are pets a healthy pleasure? The influence of pets on blood pressure. *Current Directions in Psychological Science*, 12, 236–9.

Allen, K., Blascovich, K., and Mendes, W. B. (2002). Cardiovascular reactivity and the presence of pets, friends, and spouses. The truth about cats and dogs. *Psychosomatic Medicine*, 64, 727–39.

Allen, K., Shykoff, B. E., and Izzo, J. L. (2001). Pet ownership, but not ACE inhibitor therapy blunts home blood pressure responses to mental stress. *Hypertension*, 38, 815–20.

Allen, L. S. and Gorski, R. A. (1992). Sexual orientation and the size of the anterior commissure in the human brain. *Proceedings of the National Academy of Sciences of the United States of America*, 89, 7199–202.

Allik, J. and McCrae, R. R. (2004). Toward a geography of personality traits. Patterns of profiles across 36 cultures. *Journal of Cross-Cultural Psychology*, 35, 13–28.

Allik, J., Realo, A., Mõttus, R., Borkenau, P., Kuppens, P., et al (2010). How people see others is different from how people see themselves. A replicable pattern across cultures. *Journal of Personality and Social Psychology*, 99, 870–82.

Allison, S. T., Mackie, D. M., Muller, M. M., and Worth L. T. (1993). Sequential correspondence biases and perceptions of change. The Castro studies revisited. *Personality and Social Psychology Bulletin*, 19, 151–7.

Allman, W. F. (1995). *Stone Age present. How Evolution Has Shaped Modern Life—From Sex, Violence and Language, to Emotions, Morals, and Communities*. New York, NY. Touchstone.

Alloy, L. B., Abramson, L. Y., Whitehouse, W. G., Hogan, M. E., Panzarella, C., et al (2006). Prospective incidence of first onsets and recurrences of depression in individuals at high and low cognitive risk for depression. *Journal of Abnormal Psychology*, 115, 145–56.

Allport, G. (1954). *The Nature of Prejudice*. Reading, MA. Addison-Wesley.

Allport, G. W. (1955). *Becoming*. New Haven, CT. Yale University Press.

Allport, G. W. and Odbert, H. S. (1936). Trait names. A psycholexical study. *Psychological Monographs*, 47(1, Whole No 211).

Almas, A. N., Degnan, K. A., Nelson, C. A., Zeanah, C. H., and Fox, N. A. (2016). IQ at age 12 following a history of institutional care. Findings from the Bucharest Early Intervention Project. *Developmental Psychology*, 52(11), 1858.

Almeida, J., Molnar, B. E., Kawachi, I., and Subramanian, S. V. (2009). Ethnicity and nativity status as determinants of perceived social support. Testing the concept of familism. *Social Science and Medicine*, 68, 1852–8.

Aloia, M. S., Arnedt, J. T., Davis, J. D., Riggs, R. L., and Byrd, D. (2004). Neuropsychological sequelae of obstructive sleep apnea-hypopnea syndrome. A critical review. *Journal of the International Neuropsychological Society*, 10, 772–85.

Alsubaie, M., Abbott, R., Dunn, B., Dickens, C., Keil, T. F., et al (2017). Mechanisms of action in mindfulness-based cognitive therapy (MBCT) and mindfulness-based stress reduction (MBSR) in people with physical and/or psychological conditions. A systematic review. *Clinical Psychology Review*, 55, 74–91.

Alva, N. (2007). Inattentional blindness, change blindness, and consciousness. In M. Velmans and S. Schneider (eds), *The Blackwell Companion to Consciousness* (pp 504–11). Malden, MA. Blackwell.

Amato, P. R., Patterson, S., and Beattie, B. (2015). Single-parent households and children's educational achievement. A state-level analysis. *Social Science Research*, 53, 191–202.

Ambady, N. (2010). The perils of pondering. Intuition and thin slice judgments. *Psychological Inquiry*, 21, 271–8.

Ambady, N. and Rosenthal, R. (1993). Half a minute. Predicting teacher evaluations from thin slices of nonverbal behavior and physical attractiveness. *Journal of Personality and Social Psychology*, 64, 431–41.

Amedi, A., Merebet, L. B., Camproden, J., Bermphol, F., Fox, S., et al (2008). Neural and behavioral correlates of drawing in an early blind painter. A case study. *Brain Research*, 1242, 252–62.

American Academy of Pediatrics. (2001). Media violence. *Pediatrics*, 108, 1222–6.

American Psychiatric Association (2000) *Diagnostic and Statistical Manual of Mental Disorders, Text Revision—DSM IV-TR*. Washington, DC. American Psychiatric Association.

American Psychiatric Association (2000). *Practice Guidelines for the Treatment of Psychiatric Disorders. Compendium 2000*. Washington, DC. American Psychiatric Association.

American Psychiatric Association (2013). *Diagnostic and Statistical Manual of Mental Disorders* (5th edn). Washington, DC. American Psychiatric Association.

American Psychiatric Association (2013). *Diagnostic and Statistical Manual of the American Psychiatric Association* (5th edn). Washington, DC. American Psychiatric Association.

American Psychiatric Association (2013). Highlights of changes from DSM-IV-TR to DSM-5. Retrieved from www.psychiatry.org on 26 February 2013.

American Psychiatric Association Task Force (2001). *Practice of Electroconvulsive Therapy. Recommendations for Treatment, Training, and Privileging* (2nd edn). Washington, DC. American Psychiatric Press.

American Psychological Association (2005). New definition. Hypnosis. Retrieved from www.apa.org/divisions/div30/define_hypnosis.htm.

American Psychological Association Research Office (2003). *Where Are New Psychologists Going? Employment, Debt, and Salary Data*. Washington, DC. American Psychological Association.

American Trucking Associations (2013). Professional truck drivers. Retrieved from http://www.truckline.com/About/Industry/Pages/ProfessionalTruckDrivers.aspx on 15 February 2013.

Amsterdam, J. D., Li, Y., Soeller, I., Rockwell, K., Mao, J. J., et al (2009). A randomized, double-blind, placebo-controlled trial of oral *matricaria recutita* (chamomile) extract therapy for generalized anxiety disorder. *Journal of Clinical Psychopharmacology*, 29, 378–82.

Andersen, P., Morris, R. G. M., Amaral, D. G., Bliss, T. V. P., and O'Keefe, J. (2007). *The Hippocampus Book*. London. Oxford University Press.

Anderson, B. J. (2011). Plasticity of gray matter volume. The cellular and synaptic plasticity that underlies volumetric change. *Developmental Psychobiology*, 53, 456–65.

Anderson, C. A. (2008). Belief perseverance. In R. Baumeister and K. D. Vohs (eds), *Encyclopedia of Social Psychology* (pp 109–10). Thousand Oaks, CA. Sage Publications.

Anderson, C. A., Berkowitz, L., Donnerstein, E., Huesmann, L. R., Johnson, J. D., et al (2003). The influence of media violence on youth. *Psychological Science in the Public Interest*, 4, 81–110.

Anderson, C. A. and Bushman, B. J. (2002). Human aggression. *Annual Review of Psychology*, 53, 27–51.

Anderson, C. A. and Murphy, C. R. (2003). Violent video games and aggressive behavior in young women. *Aggressive Behavior*, 29, 423–9.

Anderson, C. A., Shibuya, A., Ihori, N., Swing, E. L., Bushman, B. J., et al (2010). Violent video game effects on aggression, empathy, and prosocial behavior in Eastern and Western countries. A meta-analytic review. *Psychological Bulletin*, 136, 151–73.

Anderson, I. M. (2001). Meta-analytical studies on new antidepressants. *British Medical Bulletin*, 57, 161–78.

Anderson, J. W., Liu, C., and Kryscio, R. J. (2008). Blood pressure response to transcendental meditation. A meta-analysis. *American Journal of Hypertension*, 21, 310–316.

Anderson, M. C. (2003). Rethinking interference theory. Executive control and the mechanisms of forgetting. *Journal of Memory and Language*, 49, 415–45.

Anderson, P. L., Price, M., Edwards, S. M., Obasaju, M. A., Schmertz, S. K., et al (2013). Virtual reality exposure therapy for social anxiety disorder. A randomized controlled trial. *Journal of Consulting and Clinical Psychology*, 81(5), 751.

Anderson, S. R. (2004). *How Many Languages Are There in the World?* Washington, DC. The Linguistic Society of America. Retrieved from http://www.lsadc.org/pdf_files/howmany.pdf on 24 November 2005.

Anderson, S. R. and Lightfoot, D. W. (1999). The human language faculty as an organ. *Annual Review of Physiology*, 62, 697–722.

Anderson-Fye, E. P. and Becker, A. E. (2003). Cross-cultural aspects of eating disorders. In J. K. Thompson (ed), *Handbook of Eating Disorders and Obesity* (pp 565–89). Hoboken, NJ. John Wiley.

Andersson, B-E. (1992). Effects of day care on cognitive and socioemotional competence of thirteen-year-old Swedish schoolchildren. *Child Development*, 63(1), 20–36.

Andersson, B. E. (1996). Children's development related to day-care, type of family and other home factors. *European Child and Adolescent Psychiatry*, 5, 73–5.

Andrade, C. and Thyagarajan, S. (2007). The influence of name on the acceptability of ECT. The importance of political correctness. *Journal of ECT*, 23, 75–7.

Andrews, F. M. and Withey, S. B. (1976). *Well-being. Americans' Perceptions of Life Quality*. New York, NY. Plenum Press.

Andrews, G., Cuijpers, P., Craske, M. G., McEvoy, P., and Titov, N. (2010). Computer therapy for the anxiety and depressive disorders is effective, acceptable, and practical health care. A meta-analysis. *PLoS One*, 5, e13196. Retrieved from http://www.plosone.org/article/info%3Adoi%2F10.1371%2Fjournal.pone.0013196 on 4 April 2011.

Angst, J. and Sellaro, R. (2000). Historical perspectives and natural history of bipolar disorder. *Biological Psychiatry*, 48, 445–57.

Angulo, M. C., Kozlov, A. S., Charpak, S., and Audinat, E. (2004). Gultamate released from glial cells synchronizes neuronal activity in the hippocampus. *The Journal of Neuroscience*, 24, 6920–7.

Anrep, G. V. (1920). Pitch discrimination in the dog. *Journal of Physiology*, 53, 367–85.

Anthony, J. C., Warner, L. A., and Kessler, R. C. (1994). Comparative epidemiology of dependence on tobacco, alcohol, controlled substances, and inhalants. Basic findings from the National Comorbidity Survey. *Experimental and Clinical Psychopharmacology*, 2, 244–68.

Antony, M. M. and Barlow, D. H. (2002). Specific phobias. In D. H. Barlow (ed), *Anxiety and its Disorders. The Nature and Treatment of Anxiety and Panic* (2nd edn, pp 380–418). New York, NY. Guilford Press.

Apatow, J., Robertson, S., and Townsend, C. (Producers), and Apatow, J. (Director) (2005). *The 40-Year-Old Virgin* [motion picture]. New York, NY. Universal Studios.

Apergis, N. and Georgellis, Y. (2015). Does happiness converge? *Journal of Happiness Studies*, 16(1), 67–76.

Archer, J. (2004). Sex differences in aggression in real-world settings. A meta-analytic review. *Review of General Psychology*, 8, 291–232.

Archer, J. (2006). Testosterone and human aggression. An evaluation of the challenge hypothesis. *Neuroscience and Biobehavioral Reviews*, 30, 319–45.

Archer, J. (2009). Does sexual selection explain human sex differences in aggression? *Behavioral and Brain Sciences*, 32, 249–311.

Arkes, H. R. and Tetlock, P. E. (2004). Attributions of implicit prejudice, or 'would Jesse Jackson "fail" the Implicit Association Test?' *Psychological Inquiry*, 15, 257–78.

Arnett, J. (1992). Reckless behavior in adolescence. A developmental perspective. *Developmental Review*, 12, 339–73.

Arnett, J. (2008). The neglected 95%. Why American psychology needs to become less American. *American Psychologist*, 63, 602–14.

Arnett, J. (2010). Oh, grow up! Generational grumbling and the new life stage of emerging adulthood—commentary on Trzesniewski and Donnellan (2010). *Perspectives on Psychological Science*, 5, 89–92.

Arnett, J. J. (1996). *Metal Heads: Heavy Metal Music and Adolescent Alienation*. Boulder. Westview Press.

Arnold, M. L. (2000). Stage, sequence, and sequels. Changing conceptions of morality, post-Kohlberg. *Educational Psychology Review*, 12, 365–83.

Aron, A., Fisher, H., Mashek, D. J., Strong, G., Haifang, L., et al (2005). Reward, motivation, and emotion systems associated with early stage intense romantic love. *Journal of Neurophysiology*, 94, 327–37.

Aron, A., Fisher, H., Mashek, D. J., Strong, G., Li, H., et al (2005). Reward, motivation, and emotion systems associated with early stage romantic love. *Journal of Neurophysiology*, 94(1), 327–37.

Aronow, E., Reznikoff, M., and Moreland, K. (1995). The Rorschach. Projective technique or psychometric test? *Journal of Personality Assessment*, 64, 213–28.

Arslan, R. and Penke, L. (2015). Zeroing in on the genetics of intelligence. *Journal of Intelligence*, 3(2), 41–5.

Arvey, R. D., Harpaz, I., and Liao, H. (2004). Work centrality and post-award work behavior of lottery winners. *The Journal of Psychology*, 138(5), 404–20.

Asch, S. E. (1956). Studies of independence and conformity. A minority of one against a unanimous majority. *Psychological Monographs*, 70, No 416.

Ashton, H. and Hassan, Z. (2006). Best evidence topic report. Intranasal naloxone in suspected opioid overdose. *Emergency Medicine Journal*, 23, 221–3.

Aslin, R. N. (2007). What's in a look? *Developmental Science*, 10, 48–53.

Astington, J. W. (1998). Theory of mind goes to school. *Educational Leadership*, 56(3), 46–8.

Atkins, D. C. and Christensen, A. (2001). Is professional training worth the bother? The impact of psychotherapy training on client outcome. *Australian Psychologist*, 36, 122–30.

Atkinson, R. C. and Shiffrin, R. M. (1968). Human memory. A proposed system and its control processes. In K. W. Spence and J. T. Spence (eds), *The Psychology of Learning and Motivation* (Vol 2, pp 89–195). New York, NY. Academic Press.

Atran, S. (2003). Genesis of suicide terrorism. *Science*, 299, 1534–9.

Attiullah, N., Eisen, J., and Rasmussen, S. A. (2000). Clinical features of obsessive-compulsive disorder. *Psychiatric Clinics of North America*, 23, 469–91.

Aubrey, J. S. (2004). Sex and punishment. An examination of sexual consequences and the sexual double standard in teen programming. *Sex Roles*, 50, 505–14.

Auer, E. T., Jr, Bernstein, L. E., Sungkarat, W., and Singh, M. (2007). Vibrotactile activation of the auditory cortices in deaf versus hearing adults. *Neuroreport*, 18, 645–8.

Austin, J. H. (1998). *Zen and the Brain. Toward an Understanding of Meditation and Consciousness*. Cambridge, MA. MIT Press.

Auty, S. and Lewis, C. (2004). Exploring children's choice. The reminder effect of product placement. *Psychology and Marketing*, 21, 697–713.

Auyeung, B., Baron-Cohen, S., Ashwin, E., Knickmeyer, R., Taylor, K., et al (2009). Fetal testosterone predicts sexually differentiated childhood behavior in girls and boys. *Psychological Science*, 20, 144–8.

Averill, J. R. (1982). *Anger and Aggression. An Essay on Emotion*. New York, NY. Springer-Verlag.

Avis, N. E., Stellato R., Crawford S., Bromberger, J., Ganz, P., et al (2001). Is there a menopausal syndrome? Menopause status and symptoms across ethnic groups. *Social Science and Medicine*, 52, 345–56.

Awenat, F., Coles, S., Dooley, C., Foster, S., Hanna, J., et al (2013). *Classification of*

Behaviour and Experience in Relation to Functional Psychiatric Diagnoses: Time for a Paradigm Shift. DCP Position Statement. Leicester. BPS.

Ayers, M. S. and Reder, L. M. (1998). A theoretical review of the misinformation effect. Predictions from an activation-based memory model. *Psychonomic Bulletin and Review*, 5(1), 1–21.

Azevedo, F. A., Carvalho, L. R., Grinberg, L. T., Farfel, J. M., Ferretti, R. E., et al (2009). Equal numbers of neuronal and nonneuronal cells make the human brain an isometrically scaled-up primate brain. *Journal of Comparative Neurology*, 513(5), 532–41.

Azrin, N. H., Holz, W. C., and Hake, D. F. (1963). Fixed-ratio punishment. *Journal of the Experimental Analysis of Behavior*, 6, 141–8.

Baars, B. J. (2005). Subjective experience is probably not limited to humans. The evidence from neurobiology and behavior. *Consciousness and Cognition. An International Journal*, 14(1), 7–21.

Babyak, M., Blumenthal, J. A., Herman, S., Khatri, P., Doraiswamy, M., et al (2000). Exercise treatment for major depression. Maintenance of therapeutic benefit at 10 months. *Psychosomatic Medicine*, 62, 633–8.

Back, M. D., Stopfer, J. M., Vazire, S., Gaddis, S., Schmukle, S. C., et al (2010). Facebook profiles reflect actual personality, not self-idealization. *Psychological Science*, 21, 372–4.

Baddeley, A. D. (1997). *Human Memory. Theory and Practice* (rev edn). East Sussex, UK. Psychology Press.

Baddeley, A. D. (2007). *Working Memory, Thought, and Action*. New York, NY. Oxford University Press.

Baddeley, A. D. (2012). Working memory. Theories, models, and controversies. *Annual Review of Psychology*, 63, 1–29.

Baddeley, A. D., Eysenck, M. W., and Anderson, M. C. (2009). *Memory*. New York, NY. Psychology Press.

Bae, Y., Choy, S., Geddes, C., Sable, J., and Snyder, T. (2000). Trends in educational equity of girls and women. *Education Statistics Quarterly*, 2, 115–20.

Bagai, K. (2010). Obstructive sleep apnea, stroke, and cardiovascular diseases. *Neurologist*, 16, 329–39.

Baggott, M., Jerome, L., and Stuart, R. (2001/2005). 3, 4-methylenedioxy-methamphetamine (MDMA). A review of the English-language scientific and medical literature (2005 update). Multidisciplinary Association for Psychedelic Studies. Retrieved from http://www.maps.org/research/mdma/protocol/litreview.html on 27 January 2006.

Bahrami, B., Lavie, N., and Rees, G. (2007). Attentional load modulates responses of human primary visual cortex to invisible stimuli. *Current Biology*, 20, 509–13.

Bahrick, H. P. (2000). Long-term maintenance of knowledge. In E. Tulving and F. I. M. Craik (eds), *The Oxford Handbook of Memory* (pp 347–62). New York, NY. Oxford University Press.

Bahrick, H. P. (2005). The long-term neglect of long-term memory. Reasons and remedies. In A. F. Healy (ed), *Experimental Cognitive Psychology and its Applications. Decade of Behavior* (pp 89–100). Washington, DC. American Psychological Association.

Bailey, J. M., Dunne, M. P., and Martin, N. G. (2000). Genetic and environmental influences on sexual orientation and its correlates in an Australian twin sample. *Journal of Personality and Social Psychology*, 78, 524–36.

Baillargeon, R. (2002). The acquisition of physical knowledge in infancy. A summary in eight lessons. In U. Goswami (ed), *Blackwell Handbook of Child Cognitive Development* (pp 47–83). Oxford, UK. Blackwell.

Baillargeon, R., Spelke, E. S., and Wasserman, S. (1985). Object permanence in five-month-old infants. *Cognition*, 20, 191–208.

Baker, L. A. and Emery, R. E. (1993). When every relationship is above average. Perceptions and expectations of divorce at the time of marriage. *Law and Human Behavior*, 17, 439–50.

Baker, M. (2016). Is there a reproducibility crisis? A *Nature* survey lifts the lid on how researchers view the crisis rocking science and what they think will help. *Nature*, 533(7604), 452–5.

Baker, T. B., McFall, R. M., and Shoham, V. (2008). Current status and future prospects of clinical psychology. Toward a scientifically principled approach to mental and behavioral health care. *Psychological Science in the Public Interest*, 9, 67–103.

Bakshy, E., Messing, S., and Adamic, L. A. (2015). Exposure to ideologically diverse news and opinion on Facebook. *Science*, 348(6239), 1130–2.

Balsam, K. F., Beauchaine, T. P., Rothblum, E. D., and Solomon, S. E. (2008). Three-year follow-up of same-sex couples who had civil unions in Vermont, same-sex couples not in civil unions, and heterosexual married couples. *Developmental Psychology*, 44, 102–16.

Baltes, P. B. (1987). Theoretical propositions of life-span developmental psychology. On the dynamics between growth and decline. *Developmental Psychology*, 23, 611–26.

Baltes, P. B., Lindenberger, U., and Staudinger, U. M. (2006). Life span theory in developmental psychology. In R. M. Lerner and W. Damon (eds), *Handbook of Child Psychology* (6th edn, Vol 1). *Theoretical Models of Human Development* (pp 569–664). Hoboken, NJ. John Wiley and Sons.

Baltes, P. B., Staudinger, U. M., and Lindenberger, U. (1999). Lifespan psychology. Theory and application to intellectual functioning. *Annual Review of Psychology*, 50, 471–507.

Bambico, F. R., Nguyen, N-T., Katz, N., and Gobbi, G. (2010). Chronic exposure to cannabinoids during adolescence but not during adulthood impairs emotional behaviour and monoaminergic neurotransmission. *Neurobiology of Disease*, 37, 641–55.

Bandura, A. (1965). Influence of models' reinforcement contingencies on the acquisition of imitative behaviors. *Journal of Personality and Social Psychology*, 1, 589–95.

Bandura, A. (1973). *Aggression. A Social Learning Theory Analysis*. Englewood Cliffs, NJ. Prentice Hall.

Bandura, A. (1977). *Social Learning Theory*. Englewood Cliffs, NJ. Prentice-Hall.

Bandura, A. (1983). Psychological mechanisms of aggression. In R. G. Geen and E. Donnerstein (eds), *Aggression. Theories, Research, and Implications for Policy* (pp 11–40). New York, NY. Academic Press.

Bandura, A. (1986). *Social Foundations of Thought and Action. A Social Cognitive Theory*. Englewood Cliffs, NJ. Prentice-Hall.

Bandura, A. (2000). Self-efficacy. The foundation of agency. In W. J. Perrig and A. Grob (eds), *Control of Human Behavior, Mental Processes and Consciousness* (pp 17–33). Mahwah, NJ. Lawrence Erlbaum Associates.

Bandura, A. (2001). Social cognitive theory. An agentic perspective. *Annual Review of Psychology*, 52, 1–26.

Bandura, A. (2002). Social cognitive theory in cultural context. *Applied Psychology. An International Review*, 51, 269–90.

Bandura, A. (2007). Much ado over a faulty conception of perceived self-efficacy grounded in faulty experimentation. *Journal of Social and Clinical Psychology*, 26, 641–58.

Bandura, A., Ross, D., and Ross, S. A. (1961). Transmission of aggressions through imitation of aggressive models. *Journal of Abnormal and Social Psychology*, 63, 575–82.

Bandura, A., Ross, D., and Ross, S. A. (1963). Imitation of film-mediated aggressive models. *Journal of Abnormal and Social Psychology*, 66, 3–11.

Banerjee, R. and Lintern, V. (2000). Boys will be boys. The effect of social evaluation concerns on gender-typing. *Social Development*, 9(3), 397–408.

Banse, R. (2004). Adult attachment and marital satisfaction. Evidence for dyadic configuration effects. *Journal of Social and Personal Relationships*, 21(2), 273–82.

Bar-Haim, Y., Ziv, T., Lamy, D., and Hodes, R. M. (2006). Nature and nurture in own-race face processing. *Psychological Science*, 17, 159–63.

Barber, T. X. (1979). Suggested 'hypnotic' behavior. The trances paradigm versus an alternative paradigm. In E. Fromm and R. E. Shor (eds), *Hypnosis. Developments in Research and New Perspectives* (pp 217–71). Chicago, IL. Aldine.

Barber, T. X. and Calverley, D. S. (1965). Empirical evidence for a theory of 'hypnotic' behaviour. Effects on suggestibility of five variables typically included in hypnotic induction procedures. *Journal of Consulting Psychology*, 29, 98–107.

Barclay, L. (2005, November). Advertisements for SSRIs may be misleading. *Medscape Medical News*. Retrieved from www.medscape.com/viewarticle/516262 on 18 May 2008.

Barel, E., Van Ijzendoorn, M. H., Sagi-Schwartz, A., and Bakermans-Kranenburg, M. (2010). Surviving the holocaust. A meta-analysis of the long-term sequelae of a genocide. *Psychological Bulletin*, 136, 677–98.

Bargh, J. A. and McKenna, K. Y. A. (2004). The Internet and social life. *Annual Review of Psychology*, 55, 573–90.

Barker, M. J., Greenwood, K. M., Jackson, M., and Crowe, S. F. (2004). Cognitive effects of long-term benzodiazepine use. A meta-analysis. *CNS Drugs*, 18, 37–48.

Barkow, J. H. (1989). *Darwin, Sex, and Status. Biosocial Approaches to Mind and Culture.* Toronto, Canada. University of Toronto Press.

Barkow, J. H. (2006). *Missing the Revolution. Darwinism for Social Scientists.* Oxford, UK. Oxford University Press.

Barkow, J. H., Cosmides, L., and Tooby, J. (eds) (1992). *The Adapted Mind. Evolutionary Psychology and the Generation of Culture.* New York, NY. Oxford University Press.

Barlow, D. H. (ed) (2002a). *Anxiety and its Disorders. The Nature and Treatment of Anxiety and Panic* (2nd edn). New York, NY. Guilford Press.

Barlow, D. H. (2002b). The phenomenon of panic. In D. H. Barlow (ed), *Anxiety and its Disorders. The Nature and Treatment of Anxiety and Panic* (2nd edn). New York, NY. Guilford Press.

Barlow, D. H. (2010). Negative effects from psychological treatments. A perspective. *American Psychologist*, 65, 13–20.

Barlow, D. H., Brown, T. A., and Craske, M. G. (1994). Definitions of panic attacks and panic disorder in DSM-IV. Implications for research. *Journal of Abnormal Psychology*, 103, 553–4.

Barlow, D. H. and Craske, M. G. (2007). *Mastery of Your Anxiety and Panic* (4th edn). Albany, NY. Oxford University Press.

Barlow, D. H. and Durand, M. V. (2005). *Abnormal Psychology* (4th edn). Belmont, CA. Thomson/Wadsworth.

Barlow, D. H. and Durand, V. M. (2009). *Abnormal Psychology. An Integrative Approach* (5th edn). Belmont, CA. Wadsworth/Cengage.

Barner, D., Li, P., and Snedeker, J. (2010). Words as windows to thought. The case of object representation. *Current Directions in Psychological Science*, 19, 195–200.

Barnes, V. A., Treiber, F. A., and Davis, H. (2001). Impact of transcendental meditation on cardiovascular function during acute stress in adolescents with high normal blood pressure. *Journal of Psychosomatic Research*, 51, 597–605.

Barnett, S. M. (2007). Complex questions rarely have simple answers. *Psychological Science in the Public Interest*, 8(1), i–ii.

Baron-Cohen, S., Leslie, A. M., and Firth, U. (1985). Does the autistic child have a 'theory of mind'? *Cognition*, 21, 37–46.

Barot, S. K., Chung, A., Kim, J. J., and Bernstein, I. L. (2009). Functional imaging of stimulus convergence in amygdalar neurons during Pavlovian fear conditioning. *PLoS One*, 4(7). Retrieved from www.plosone.org on 10 October 2009.

Barrett, H. C. (2005). Adaptations to predators and prey. In D. M. Buss (ed), *The Handbook of Evolutionary Psychology* (pp 200–23). Hoboken, NJ. John Wiley and Sons.

Barrett, L. F. (2006). Are emotions natural kinds? *Perspectives on Psychological Science*, 1, 28–58.

Barrett, L. F., Gross, J., Christensen, T. C., and Benvenuto, M. (2001). Knowing what you're feeling and knowing what to do about it. Mapping the relation between emotion differentiation and emotion regulation. *Cognition and Emotion*, 15, 713–24.

Barrett, L. F. and Lindquist, K. (2008). The embodiment of emotion. In G. R. Semin and E. R. Smith (eds), *Embodied Grounding. Social Cognitive, Affective, and Neuroscientific Approaches.* New York, NY. Cambridge University Press.

Barrett, L. F., Mesquita, B., Ochsner, K. N., and Gross, J. J. (2007). The experience of emotion. *Annual Review of Psychology*, 58, 373–403.

Barrière, G., Leblond, H., Provencher, J., and Rossignol, S. (2008). Prominent role of the spinal central pattern generator in the recovery of locomotion after partial spinal cord injuries. *Journal of Neuroscience*, 28, 3976–87.

Barsky, A. J., Saintfort, R., Rogers, M. P., and Borus, J. F. (2002). Nonspecific medication side effects and the nocebo phenomenon. *JAMA*, 287, 622–7.

Bartel, K., Scheeren, R., and Gradisar, M. (2018). Altering adolescents' pre-bedtime phone use to achieve better sleep health. *Health Communication*, 1–7.

Bartels, A. and Zeki, S. (1998). The theory of multistage integration in the visual brain. *Proceedings of the Royal Society B*, 265, 2327–32.

Bartels, A. and Zeki, S. (2000). The neural basis of romantic love. *NeuroReport*, 11, 3829–34.

Bartels, A. and Zeki, S. (2004). The neural correlates of maternal and romantic love. *NeuroImage*, 12, 1155–66.

Barton, D. A., Esler, M. D., Dawwod, T., Lambert, E. A., Haikerwal, D., et al (2008). Elevated brain serotonin turnover in patients with depression. *Archives of General Psychiatry*, 65, 38–46.

Bartz, J. A., Zaki, J., Bolger, N., Hollander, E., Ludwig, N. N., et al (2010). Oxytocin selectively improves empathic understanding. *Psychological Science*, 21, 1426–8.

Bateman, A. J. (1948). Intrasexual selection. *Drosophila. Heredity, 2*, 349–38.

Bateman, R. L., III. (2002). *No Gun Ri. A Military History of the Korean War Incident*. Mechanicsburg, PA. Stackpole Books.

Bateup, H. S., Booth, A., Shirtcliff, E., and Granger, D. A. (2002). Testosterone, cortisol and women's competition. *Evolution and Human Behavior*, 23, 181–92.

Batson, C. D. (2010). Empathy-induced altruistic motivation. In M. Mikulincer, and P. R. Shaver (eds), *Prosocial Motives, Emotions, and Behavior. The Better Angels of our Nature* (pp 15–34). Washington, DC. American Psychological Association.

Batson, C. D., Ahmad, N., Yin, J., Bedell, S. J., Johnson. J. W., et al (1999). Two threats to the common good. Self-interested egoism and empathy-induced altruism. *Personality and Social Psychology Bulletin*, 25(1), 3–16.

Batty, G. D., Wennerstad, K. M., Davey Smith, G., Gunnell, D., Deary, I. J., et al (2009). IQ in late adolescence/early adulthood and mortality by middle age. Cohort study of one million Swedish men. *Epidemiology*, 20, 100–9.

Bauman, C. W. and Skitka, L. J. (2010). Making attributions for behaviors. The prevalence of correspondence bias in the general population. *Basic and Applied Social Psychology*, 32, 269–77.

Baumann, M., Clark, R., Budzynski, A., Partilla, J., Blough, B., et al (2005). N-substituted piperazines abused by humans mimic the molecular mechanism of 3, 4-methlenedioxymethamphetamine (MDMA or 'Ecstasy'). *Neuro Psychopharmacology*, 39, 550–60.

Baumeister, R. F. (1989). The optimal margin of illusion. *Journal of Social and Clinical Psychology*, 8, 176–89.

Baumeister, R. F. (1997). *Evil. Inside Human Violence and Cruelty*. New York, NY. W. H. Freeman.

Baumeister, R. F., Bratslavsky, E., Finkenauer, C., and Vohs, K. D. (2001). Bad is stronger than good. *Review of General Psychology*, 5, 323–70.

Baumeister, R. F., Bratslavsky, E., Muraven, M., and Tice, D. M. (1998). Ego depletion. Is the active self a limited resource? *Journal of Personality and Social Psychology*, 24, 1252–65.

Baumeister, R. F. and Bushman, B. J. (2008). *Social Psychology and Human Nature*. Belmont, CA. Thomson/Wadsworth.

Baumeister, R. F., Bushman, B. J., and Campbell, W. K. (2000). Self-esteem, narcissism, and aggression. Does violence result from low-self-esteem or from threatened egotism? *Current Directions in Psychological Science*, 9, 26–9.

Baumeister, R. F., Campbell, J. D., Krueger, J. L., and Vohs, K. D. (2003). Does high self-esteem cause better performance, interpersonal success, happiness, or healthier lifestyles? *Psychological Science in the Public Interest*, 4(1), 1–44.

Baumeister, R. F., Dale, K., and Sommer, K. L. (1998). Freudian defense mechanisms and empirical findings in modern social psychology. Reaction formation, projection, displacement, undoing, isolation, sublimation, and denial. *Journal of Personality*, 66, 1081–124.

Baumeister, R. F. and Dhavale, D. (2001). Two sides of romantic rejection. In M. R. Leary (ed), *Interpersonal Rejection* (pp 55–71). New York, NY. Oxford University Press.

Baumeister, R. F., Gailliot, M., DeWall, C. N., and Oaten, M. (2006). Self-regulation and personality. How interventions increase regulatory success, and how depletion moderates the effects of traits on behavior. *Journal of Personality*, 74, 1773–801.

Baumeister, R. F. and Leary, M. R. (1995). The need to belong. Desire for interpersonal attachments as a fundamental human motivation. *Psychological Bulletin*, 117, 497–529.

Baumeister, R. F., Smart, L., and Boden, J. M. (1996). Relation of threatened egotism to violence and aggression. The dark side of high self-esteem. *Psychological Review*, 103, 5–33.

Baumeister, R. F. and Tice, D. M. (2001). *The Social Dimension of Sex*. Boston, MA. Allyn and Bacon.

Baumeister, R. F. and Vohs, K. D. (2004). Self-regulation. In C. Peterson and M. E. P. Seligman (eds), *Character Strengths and Virtues. A Handbook and Classification* (pp 499–516). Washington, DC/New York, NY. American Psychological Association/Oxford University Press.

Baumeister, R. F., Vohs, K. D., DeWall, C. N., and Zhang, L. (2007). How emotion shapes behavior. Feedback, anticipation, and reflection, rather than direct causation. *Personality and Social Psychology Review*, 11, 167–203.

Baumeister, R. F., Vohs, K. D., and Tice, D. M. (2007). The strength model of self-control. *Current Directions in Psychological Science*, 16, 351–5.

Baumrind, D. (1964). Some thought on ethics of research. After reading Milgram's 'Behavioral study of obedience'. *American Psychologist*, 19, 421–3.

Baumrind, D. (1967). Child care practices anteceding three patterns of preschool behavior. *Genetic Psychology Monographs*, 75, 43–88.

Baumrind, D. (1987). A developmental perspective on adolescent risk taking in contemporary America. In C. E. Irwin, Jr (ed), *Adolescent Social Behavior and Health* (pp 93–125). San Francisco, CA. Jossey-Bass.

Baumrind, D. (1996). The discipline controversy revisited. *Family Relations*, 45, 405–14.

Bavelier, D., Dye, M. W. G., and Hauser, P. C. (2006). Do deaf individuals see better? *Trends in Cognitive Sciences*, 10, 512–18.

Baxter, M. G. and Murray, E. A. (2002). The amygdala and reward. *Nature Reviews Neuroscience*, 3, 563–73.

BBC News. (2009, 2 June). Female medics to outnumber male. Retrieved on 18 March 2013 from http://news.bbc.co.uk/2/hi/health/8077083.stm

Beard, C., Weisberg, R. B., and Keller, M. (2010). Health-related quality of life across the anxiety disorders. Findings from a sample of primary care patients. *Journal of Anxiety Disorders*, 24, 559–64.

Bechara, A., Damasio, H., Tranel, D., and Damasio, A. R. (1997). Deciding advantageously before knowing the advantageous strategy. *Science*, 275, 1293–5.

Bechtoldt, H., Norcross, J. C., Wyckoff, L. A., Pokrywa, M. L., and Campbell, L. F. (2001). Theoretical orientations and employment settings of clinical and counseling psychologists. A comparative study. *The Clinical Psychologist*, 54(1), 3–6.

Beck, A. T. (1991). Cognitive therapy. A 30-year retrospective. *American Psychologist*, 46, 368–75.

Beck, A. T. (1999). *Prisoners of Hate. The Cognitive Basis of Anger, Hostility, and Violence*. New York, NY. Harper-Collins.

Beck, A. T. (2005). The current state of cognitive therapy. *Archives of General Psychiatry*, 62, 953–9.

Beck, A. T., Emery, G., and Greenberg, R. L. (2005). *Anxiety Disorders and Phobias. A Cognitive Perspective.* New York, NY. Basic Books.

Beck, A. T., Rush, A. J., Shaw, B. F., and Emery, G. (1987). *Cognitive Therapy of Depression.* New York, NY. The Guilford Press.

Beck, D. M. (2010). The appeal of the brain in the popular press. *Perspectives on Psychological Science*, 5, 762–6.

Becker, P. M. (2006). Insomnia. Prevalence, impact, pathogenesis, differential diagnosis, and evaluation. *Psychiatric Clinics of North America*, 29, 855–70.

Beckner, V., Vella, L., Howard, I., and Mohr, D. C. (2007). Alliance in two telephone-administered treatments. Relationship with depression and health outcomes. *Journal of Consulting and Clinical Psychology*, 75, 508–12.

Beeman, M. J. and Chiarello, C. (1998). Complementary right- and left-hemisphere language comprehension. *Current Directions in Psychological Science*, 7, 2–8.

Beer, J. M., Arnold, R. D., and Loehlin, J. C. (1998). Genetic and environmental influences on MMPI factor scales. Joint model fitting to twin and adoption data. *Journal of Personality and Social Psychology*, 74, 818–27.

Beggs, J. M., Brown, T. H., Byrne, J. H., Crow, T., LeDoux, J. E., et al (1999). Learning and memory. Basic mechanisms. In M. J. Zigmond, F. E. Bloom, S. C. Landis, J. L. Roberts, and L. R. Squire (eds), *Fundamentals of Neuroscience* (pp 1411–54). San Diego, CA. Academic Press.

Bègue, L., Beauvois, J. L., Courbet, D., Oberlé, D., Lepage, J., et al (2015). Personality predicts obedience in a Milgram paradigm. *Journal of Personality*, 83(3), 299–306.

Bejerot, S. (2003). Psychosurgery for obsessive-compulsive disorder—Concerns remain. *Acta Psychiatrica Scandanavia*, 107, 241–3.

Bekelman, J., Li, Y., and Gross, C. (2003). Scope and impact of financial conflicts of interest in biomedical research. A systematic review. *JAMA*, 289, 454–65.

Belcher, A. J., Laurenceau, J-P., Siegel, S. D., Graber, E. C., Cohen, L. H., et al (2011). Daily support in couples coping with early stage breast cancer. Maintaining intimacy during adversity. *Health Psychology*, 30, 665–73.

Bell, E. C., Willson, M. C., Wilman, A. H., Dave, S., and Silverstone, P. H. (2006). Males and females differ in brain activation during cognitive tasks. *Neuroimage*, 30, 529–38.

Belle, D. (1991). Gender differences in the social moderators of stress. In A. Monat and R. S. Lazarus (eds), *Stress and Coping. An Anthology* (3rd edn, pp 258–74). New York, NY. Columbia University Press.

Belsky, J. (1999). Modern evolutionary theory and patterns of attachment. In J. Cassidy and P. R. Shaver (eds), *Handbook of Attachment. Theory, Research, and Clinical Applications* (pp 141–61). New York, NY. The Guilford Press.

Belsky, J. (2001). Developmental risks (still) associated with early child care. *Journal of Child Psychology and Psychiatry*, 42, 845–59.

Belsky, J. (2009). Classroom composition, childcare history, and social development. Are childcare effects disappearing or spreading? *Social Development*, 18, 230–8.

Bem, D. J. (2011). Feeling the future. Experimental evidence for anomalous retroactive influences on cognition and affect. *Journal of Personality and Social Psychology*, 100, 407–25.

Bem, S. L. (1974). The measurement of psychological androgyny. *Journal of Consulting and Clinical Psychology*, 42, 151–62.

Bemporad, J. R. (1996). Self-starvation through the ages. Reflections on the prehistory of anorexia nervosa. *International Journal of Eating Disorders*, 19, 217–37.

Benbow, C. P., Lubinski, D., Shea, D. L., and Eft ekhari-Sanjani, H. (2000). Sex differences in mathematical reasoning ability. Their status 20 years later. *Psychological Science*, 11, 474–80.

Bender, P. K., Sømhovd, M., Pons, F., Reinholdt-Dunne, M. L., and Esbjørn, B. H. (2015). The impact of attachment security and emotion dysregulation on anxiety in children and adolescents. *Emotional and Behavioural Difficulties*, 20(2), 189–204.

Benenson, J. F., Liroff, E. R., Pascal, S. J., and Cioppa, G. D. (1997). Propulsion. A behavioural expression of masculinity. *British Journal of Developmental Psychology*, 15(1), 37–50.

Benish, S. G., Imel, Z. E., and Wampold, B. E. (2008). Relative efficacy of bona fide psychotherapies for treating posttraumatic stress disorder. A meta-analysis of direct comparisons. *Clinical Psychology Review*, 28, 746–58.

Bennett, C. M., Miller, M. B., and Wolford, G. L. (2009). Neural correlates of interspecies perspective taking in the post-mortem Atlantic Salmon. An argument for multiple comparisons correction. *Neuroimage*, 47(Suppl 1), S125.

Bennett, R. J. (1998). Taking the sting out of the whip. Reactions to consistent punishment for unethical behavior. *Journal of Experimental Psychology. Applied*, 4, 248–62.

Benson, H. (1983). The relaxation response. Its subjective and objective historical precedents and physiology. *Trends in Neurosciences*, 6, 281–4.

Bentall, R. P. and Fernyhough, C. (2008). Social predictors of psychotic experiences. Specificity and psychological mechanisms. *Schizophrenia Bulletin*, 34(6), 1012–20.

Berenbaum, S. A. and Hines, M. (1992). Early androgens are related to childhood sex-typed toy preferences. *Psychological Science*, 3, 203–6.

Bergan-Gander, R. and von Kürthy, H. (2006). Sexual orientation and occupation. Gay men and women's lived experiences of occupational participation. *British Journal of Occupational Therapy*, 69(9), 402–8.

Berger, A., Tzur, G., and Posner, M. I. (2006). Infant brains detect arithmetic errors. *Proceedings of the National Academy of Sciences. Psychology*, 103, 12649–53.

Berger, A. S. (1993). *Dying and Death in Law and Medicine. A Forensic Primer for Health and Legal Professionals.* Westport, CT. Praeger.

Berglund, A. and Rosenqvist, G. (2003). Sex role reversal in pipefish. *Advances in the Study of Behavior*, 32, 131–17.

Berkowitz, L. (1989). Frustration-aggression hypothesis. Examination and reformulation. *Psychological Bulletin*, 106, 59–73.

Berkowitz, L. (1993). Pain and aggression. Some findings and implications. *Motivation and Emotion*, 17, 277–93.

Berkowitz, L. and Harmon-Jones, E. (2004a). Toward an understanding of the determinants of anger. *Emotion*, 4, 107–130.

Berlim, M. T., Van den Eynde, F., and Daskalakis, Z. J. (2013). Clinically meaningful efficacy and acceptability of low-frequency repetitive transcranial magnetic stimulation (rTMS) for treating primary major depression. A meta-analysis of randomized, double-blind and sham-controlled trials. *Neuropsychopharmacology*, 38, 543–51.

Berman, S., O'Neill, J., Fears, S., Bartzokis, G., and London, E. D. (2008). Abuses of amphetamines and structural abnormalities in brain. *Addiction Reviews*, 1141, 195–220.

Bernhard, H., Fischbacher, U., and Fehr, E. (2006). Parochial altruism in humans. *Nature*, 442, 912–15.

Bernhardt, P. C., Dabbs, J. M., Fielden, J. A., and Lutter, C. D. (1998). Testosterone changes during vicarious experiences of winning and losing among fans at sporting events. *Physiology and Behavior*, 65, 59–62.

Bernstein, D. M. and Loftus, E. F. (2009). How to tell if a particular memory is true or false. *Perspectives on Psychological Science*, 4, 370–4.

Bernstein, D. P., Iscan, C., and Maser, J. (2007). Opinions of personality disorder experts regarding the DSM-IV personality disorders classification system. *Journal of Personality Disorders*, 21, 536–51.

Bernstein, D. P. and Useda, J. D. (2007). Paranoid personality disorder. In W. T. O'Donohue, K. A. Fowler, and S. O. Lilienfeld (eds), *Personality Disorders. Toward the DSM-V* (pp 41–63). Thousand Oaks, CA. Sage Publications

Bero, L., Oostvogel, F., Bacchetti, P., and Lee, K. (2007). Factors associated with findings of published trials of drug-drug comparisons. Why some statins appear more efficacious than others. *PLoS Medicine*, 4. Retrieved from http://www.plosmedicine.org/article/info:doi/10.1371/journal.pmed.0040184 on 7 June 2008.

Berry, C. M. and Sackett, P. R. (2009). Individual differences in course choice result in underestimation of the validity of college admissions systems. *Psychological Science*, 20, 822–30.

Berry, K., Wearden, A., and Barrowclough, C. (2007). Adult attachment styles and psychosis. An investigation of associations between general attachment styles and attachment relationships with specific others. *Social Psychiatry and Psychiatric Epidemiology*, 42(12), 972–6.

Berscheid, E. (2010). Love in the fourth dimension. *Annual Review of Psychology*, 61, 1–25.

Best, D. L. (2004). Gender roles in childhood and adolescence. In U. P. Gielen and J. Roopnarine (eds), *Childhood and Adolescence. Cross-cultural Perspectives and Applications. Advances in Applied Developmental Psychology* (pp 199–228). Westport, CT. Praeger Publishers.

Best, J. (1990). *Threatened Children. Rhetoric and Concern about Child-victims*. Chicago, IL. University of Chicago Press.

Bettencourt, A. A. and Kernahan, C. (1997). A meta-analysis of aggression in the presence of violent cues. Effects of gender differences and aversive provocations. *Aggressive Behavior*, 23, 447–56.

Beutler, L. E. (2002). The dodo bird is extinct. *Clinical Psychology. Science and Practice*, 9, 30–4.

Bhattacharya, R., Unadkat, A., and Connan, F. (2010). Cultural perspectives on eating disorders. In R. Bhattacharya, S. Cross, and D. Bhugra (eds), *Clinical Topics in Cultural Psychiatry* (pp 232–43). London. Royal College of Psychiatrists.

Bickman, L. (1999). Practice makes perfect and other myths about mental health services. *American Psychologist*, 54, 965–78.

Bigler, R. S. (1997). Conceptual and methodological issues in the measurement of children's sex typing. *Psychology of Women Quarterly*, 21, 53–69.

Bishara, S. and Kaplan, S. (2018). The relationship of locus of control and metacognitive knowledge of math with math achievements. *International Journal of Disability, Development and Education*, 65(6), 631–48.

Biswas-Diener, R., Vittersø, J., and Diener, E. (2005). Most people are pretty happy, but there is cultural variation. The Inughuit, the Amish, and the Maasai. *Journal of Happiness Studies*, 6, 205–26.

Blackmore, S. (2004). *Consciousness. An Introduction*. New York, NY. Oxford University Press.

Blackmore, S. (2005). *Consciousness. A Very Short Introduction*. New York, NY. Oxford University Press.

Blackmore, S. J. (1990, 22 September). The lure of the paranormal. *New Scientist*, 62–5.

Blair-West, G. and Mellsop, G. (2001). Major depression. Does a gender-based down-rating of suicide risk challenge its diagnostic validity? *Australian and New Zealand Journal of Psychiatry*, 35, 322–8.

Blanchard, D. C. and Blanchard, R. J. (1972). Innate and conditioned reactions to threat in rats with amygdaloid lesions. *Journal of Comparative and Physiological Psychology*, 81, 281–90.

Blanchard, R. (2008). Review and theory of handedness, birth order, and homosexuality in men. *Laterality.*

Asymmetries of Body, Brain and Cognition, 13, 51–70.

Blanchard, R., Cantor, J. M., Bogaert, A. F., Breedlove, S, M., and Ellis, L. (2006). Interaction of fraternal birth order and handedness in the development of male homosexuality. *Hormones and Behavior*, 49, 405–14.

Blanchflower, D. G. and Oswald, A. J. (2008). Is well-being U-shaped over the life cycle? *Social Science and Medicine*, 66, 1733–49.

Blanke, O., Landis, T., Mermoud, C., Spinelli, L., and Safran, A. B. (2003). Direction-selective motion blindness after unilateral posterior brain damage. *European Journal of Neuroscience*, 18, 709–22.

Blass, T. (1999). The Milgram paradigm after 35 years. Some things we now know about obedience. *Journal of Applied Social Psychology*, 29, 955–78.

Blass, T. (2009). *The Man who Shocked the World. The Life and Legacy of Stanley Milgram*. New York, NY. Basic Books.

Blatt, S. J. and Zuroff, D. C. (2005). Empirical evaluation of the assumptions in identifying evidence based treatments in mental health. *Clinical Psychology Review*, 25, 459–86.

Blavivas, A. J., Patel, R., Hom, D., Antigua, K., and Ashtyani, H. (2007). Quantifying microsleep to help assess subjective sleepiness. *Sleep Medicine*, 8, 156–9.

Bleske-Rechek, A., Remiker, M. W., and Baker, J. P. (2009). Similar from the start. Assortment in young adult dating couples and its link to relationship stability over time. *Individual Differences Research*, 7, 142–58.

Bloom, M. (2005). *Dying to Kill. The Allure of Suicide Terrorism*. New York, NY. Columbia University Press.

Bloom, P. (2004). *Descartes' Baby. How the Science of Child Development Explains What Makes Us Human*. New York, NY. Basic Books.

Bloom, P. (2010, 3 May). The moral life of babies. *New York Times*. Retrieved from http://www.nytimes.com/2010/05/09/magazine/09babies-t.html?pagewanted=all on 2 June 2010.

Blumstein, S. E. and Amso, D. (2013). Dynamic functional organization of language. Insights from functional neuroimaging. *Perspectives on Psychological Science*, 8, 44–8.

Boduroglu, A., Shah, P., and Nisbett, R. E. (2009). Cultural differences in allocation of attention in visual information processing. *Journal of Cross-Cultural Psychology*, 40(3), 349–60.

Boe, E. E. and Church, R. M. (1967). Permanent effects of punishment during extinction. *Journal of Comparative and Physiological Psychology*, 63, 486–92.

Boen, F., Auweele, Y. V., Claes, E., Feys, J., and De Cuyper, B. (2006). The impact of open feedback on conformity among judges in rope skipping. *Psychology of Sport and Exercise*, 7(6), 577–90.

Bogaert, A. F. (2006). Biological versus non-biological older brothers and men's sexual orientation. *Proceedings of the National Academy of Sciences*, 103, 10771–4.

Boland, R. J. and Keller, M. B. (2009). Course and outcome of depression. In I. H. Gotlib and C. L. Hammen (eds), *Handbook of Depression* (2nd edn, pp 23–43). New York, NY. Guilford.

Bolles, R. C. (1970). Species-specific defense reactions and avoidance learning. *Psychological Review*, 77, 32–48.

Bonanno, G. A. (2005). Resilience in the face of potential trauma. *Current Directions in Psychological Science*, 14, 135–8.

Bonanno, G. A., Brewin, C. R., Kaniasty, K., and La Greca, A. M. (2010). Weighing the costs of disaster. Consequences, risks, and resilience in individuals, families, and communities. *Psychological Science in the Public Interest*, 11, 1–49.

Bonanno, G. A., Galea, S., Bucciarelli, A., and Vlahov, D. (2006). Psychological resilience after disaster. New York City in the aftermath of the September 11th terrorist attack. *Psychological Science*, 17, 181–6.

Bonanno, G. A. and Mancini, A. D. (2008). The human capacity to thrive in the face of potential trauma. *Pediatrics*, 121, 369–75.

Bonanno, G. A., Westphal, M., and Mancini, A. D. (2011). Resilience to loss and potential trauma. *Annual Review of Clinical Psychology*, 7, 511–35.

Bond, C. F., Jr and DePaulo, B. M. (2006). Accuracy of deception judgments. *Personality and Social Psychology Review*, 10, 214–34.

Bond, C. F., Jr and DePaulo, B. M. (2008). Individual differences in judging deception. Accuracy and bias. *Psychological Bulletin*, 134, 477–92.

Bonnie, R. J. and Whitebread, C. H. (1999). *The Marijuana Conviction. A History of Marijuana Prohibition in the United States*. New York, NY. Lindesmith Center.

Bono, G., McCullough, M. E., and Root, L. M. (2008). Forgiveness, feeling connected to others, and well-being. Two longitudinal studies. *Personality and Social Psychology Bulletin*, 182–95.

Booij, A. J. W., Van der Does, C., Benkelfat, J. D., Bremner, P. J., et al (2002). Predictors of mood response to acute tryptophan depletion. A reanalysis. *Neuropsychopharmacology*, 27, 852–61.

Book, A. S., Starzyk, K. B., and Quinsey, V. L. (2001). The relationship between testosterone and aggression. A meta-analysis. *Aggression and Violent Behavior. A Review Journal*, 6, 579–99.

Booth, M. (1999). *Opium. A History*. New York, NY. St. Martin's Griffin.

Bootzin, R. R. and Epstein, D. R. (2011). Understanding and treating insomnia. *Annual Review of Clinical Psychology*, 7, 435–58.

Borch-Jacobsen, M. (1997). Sybil. The making of a disease. An interview with Dr Herbert Spiegel. *New York Review of Books*, 44, 60–4.

Borg, J., Andrée, B., Soderstrom, H., and Farde, L. (2003). The serotonin system and spiritual experiences. *American Journal of Psychiatry*, 160(11), 1965–9.

Borkenau, P., Mauer, N., Riemann, R., Spinath, F. M., and Angleitner, A. (2004). Think slices of behavior as cues of personality and intelligence. *Journal of Personality and Social Psychology*, 86, 599–614.

Borkenau, P., Riemann, R., Spinath, F. M., and Angleitner, A. (2006). Genetic and environmental influences on Person X Situation profiles. *Journal of Personality*, 74, 1451–79.

Bornstein, M. H., Hahn, C.-S., Bell, C., Haynes, O. M., Slater, A., et al (2006). Stability in cognition across early childhood. A developmental cascade. *Psychological Science*, 17, 151–8.

Boroditsky, L. (2009). How does language shape the way we think? In M. Brockman (ed), *What's Next. Dispatches on the Future of Science*. New York, NY. Random House.

Bothmer, E. von. (2006). What the nose doesn't know. *Scientific American*, 17, 62–27.

Botwin, M., Buss, D. M., and Shackelford, T. K. (1997). Personality and mate preferences. Five factors in mate selection and marital satisfaction. *Journal of Personality*, 65, 107–36.

Bouchard, T. J. (2004). Genetic influence on human psychological traits. *Current Directions in Psychological Science*, 13, 148–51.

Bouchard, T. J., Jr (1996a). Behavior genetic studies of intelligence, yesterday, and today. The long journey from plausibility to proof. *Journal of Biosocial Science*, 28, 527–55.

Bouchard, T. J., Jr (1996b). IQ similarity in twins reared apart. Findings and responses to critics. In R. Sternberg and C. Grigorenko (eds), *Intelligence. Heredity and Environment* (pp 126–60). New York, NY. Cambridge University Press.

Bouchard, T. J., Jr, Lykken, D. T., McGue, M., Segal, N. L., and Tellegen, A. (1990). Sources of human psychological differences. The Minnesota study of twins reared apart. *Science*, 250, 223–8.

Bouchard, T. J. Jr, Segal, N. L., Tellegen, A., McGue, M., Keyes, M., et al (2004). Genetic influences on social attitudes. Another challenge to psychology from behavior genetics. In L. F. DiLalla (ed), *Behavior Genetics Principles. Perspectives in Development, Personality, and Psychopathology. Decade of Behavior* (pp 89–104). Washington, DC. American Psychological Association.

Bouton, M. E. (1991). Context and retrieval in extinction and in other examples of interference in simple associative learning. In L. Dachowski and F. Flaherty (eds), *Current Topics in Animal Learning. Brain, Emotion, and Cognition* (pp 25–53). Hillsdale, NJ. Lawrence Erlbaum Associates.

Bouton, M. E. and King, D. A. (1983). Contextual control of the extinction of conditioned fear. Tests for the associative value of the context. *Journal of Experimental Psychology. Animal Behavior Processes*, 9, 248–65.

Bowen, M. (1978). *Family Therapy in Clinical Practice*. Northvale, NJ. Jason Aronson, Inc.

Bower, J. M. and Parsons, L. (2003). Rethinking the lesser brain. *Scientific American*, 289, 50–7.

Bowers, J. S., Mattys, S. L., and Gage, S. H. (2009). Preserved implicit knowledge of a forgotten childhood language. *Psychological Science*, 20, 1064–9.

Bowlby, J. (1988). *A Secure Base. Parent-child Attachment and Healthy Human Development*. New York, NY. Basic Books.

Boyce, C. J., Brown, D. A., and Moore, S. C. (2010). Money and happiness. Rank of income, not income, affects life satisfaction. *Psychological Science*, 21, 471–5.

Brabender, V. (2002). *Introduction to Group Therapy*. New York, NY. Wiley.

Bradley, R., Conklin, C. Z., and Westen, D. (2007). Borderline personality disorder. In W. T. O'Donohue, K. A. Fowler, and S. O. Lilienfeld (eds), *Personality Disorders. Toward the DSM-V* (pp 167–201). Thousand Oaks, CA. Sage Publications.

Brådvik, L., Hulenvik, P., Frank, A., Medvedeo, A., and Berglund, M. (2007). Self-reported and observed heroin overdoses in Malmoe. *Journal of Substance Use*, 12, 119–26.

Brådvik, L., Mattisson, C., Bogren, M., and Nettelbladt, P. (2008). Long-term suicide risk of depression in the Lundby cohort 1947–1997. Severity and gender. *Acta Psychiatrica Scandinavia*, 117, 185–91.

Braff, D., Schork, N. J., and Gottesman, I. I. (2007). Endophenotyping schizophrenia. *American Journal of Psychiatry*, 164, 705–7.

Braithwaite, E. C., O'Connor, R. M., Degli-Esposti, M., Luke, N., and Bowes, L. (2017). Modifiable predictors of depression following childhood maltreatment. A systematic review and meta-analysis. *Translational Psychiatry*, 7(7), e1162.

Brass, M. and Haggard, P. (2007). To do or not to do. The neural signature of self-control. *The Journal of Neuroscience*, 27, 9141–5.

Braun, J., Kahn, R. S., Froehlich, T., Auinger, P., and Langphear, B. P. (2006). Exposures to environmental toxicants and attention deficit hyperactivity disorder in U.S. children. *Environmental Health Perspectives*. Retrieved from http://www.ehponline.org/members/2006/9478/9478.pdf on 8 October 2006.

Brawley, L. R. and Rodgers, W. M. (1993). Social-psychological aspects of fitness promotion. In P. Seraganian (ed), *Exercise Psychology. The Influence of Physical Exercise on Psychological Processes* (pp 254–98). New York, NY. Wiley.

Bray, N. J. (2008). Gene expression in the etiology of schizophrenia. *Schizophrenia Bulletin*, 34, 412–18.

Brecher, E. M. (1972). The 'heroin overdose' mystery and other occupational hazards of addiction. In E. M. Brecher and the editors of *Consumer Reports Magazine, The Consumers Union Report on Licit and Illicit Drugs*. Retrieved http://www.druglibrary.org/schaffer/Library/studies/cu/cu12.htm on 12 November 2008.

Breland, K. and Breland, M. (1961). The misbehavior of organisms. *American Psychologist*, 16, 681–4.

Brenneis, C. B. (2000). Evaluating the evidence. Can we find authenticated recovered memory? *Journal of the American Psychoanalytic Association*, 17(1), 61–77.

Brewer, M. B. (2007). The importance of being *We*. Human nature and intergroup relations. *American Psychologist*, 62, 728–38.

Brewer, N. and Wells, G. L. (2006). The confidence-accuracy relationship in eyewitness identification. Effects of lineup instructions, foil similarity and target-absent base rates. *Journal of Experimental Psychology. Applied*, 12, 11–30.

Brewer, N. and Wells, G. L. (2011). Eyewitness identification. *Current Directions in Psychological Science*, 20, 24–27.

Brick, C. and Lewis, G. J. (2016). Unearthing the 'green' personality. Core traits predict environmentally friendly behavior. *Environment and Behavior*, 48(5), 635–58.

Brigham, J. C., Bennett, B. L., Meissner, C. A., and Mitchell, T. L. (2007). The influence of race on eyewitness memory. In R. C. L. Lindsay, D. F. Ross, J. D. Read, and M. P. Read (eds), *The Handbook of Eyewitness Psychology. Vol. 2. Memory for People* (pp 257–81). Mahwah, NJ. Lawrence Erlbaum Associates.

Britt, R. R. (2005). The odds of dying. *Live Science*. Retrieved from http://www.livescience.com/3780-odds-dying.html on 26 May.

Brizendine, L. (2006). *The Female Brain*. New York, NY. Morgan Road Books.

Brody, N. (2003a). Construct validation of the Sternberg triarchic abilities test. Comment and reanalysis. *Intelligence*, 31, 319–29.

Brody, N. (2003b). What Sternberg should have concluded. *Intelligence*, 31, 339–42.

Brody, N. and Ehrlichman, H. (1998). *Personality Psychology. Science of Individuality*. Englewood Cliffs, NJ. Prentice-Hall.

Brondolo, E., Brady ver Halen, N., Pencille, M., Beatty, D., and Contrada, R. J. (2009). Coping with racism. A selective review of the literature and a theoretical and methodological critique. *Journal of Behavioral Medicine*, 32, 64–88.

Brouwers, S. A., van Hemert, D. A., Breugelmans, S. M., and van de Vijver, F. J. R. (2004). A historical analysis of empirical studies published in *Journal of Cross-Cultural Psychology* 1970–2004. *Journal of Cross-Cultural Psychology*, 35, 251–62.

Brown, A. S. (1991). A review of the tip-of-the-tongue experience. *Psychological Bulletin*, 109, 204–23.

Brown, A. S. (2006). Prenatal infection as a risk factor for schizophrenia. *Schizophrenia Bulletin*, 32, 200–2.

Brown, A. S., Schaefer, C. A., Quesenberry, C. P., Jr, Shen, L., and Susser, E. S. (2006). No evidence of relation between maternal exposure to herpes simplex virus type 2 and risk of schizophrenia? *American Journal of Psychiatry*, 163, 2178–80.

Brown, A. S., Schaefer, C. A., Wyatt, R. J., Goetz, R., Begg, M. D., et al (2000). Maternal exposure to respiratory infections and adult schizophrenia spectrum disorders. A prospective birth cohort study. *Schizophrenia Bulletin*, 26, 287–95.

Brown, A. S. and Susser, E. S. (2002). In utero infections and adult schizophrenia. *Mental Retardation and Developmental Disabilities Research Reviews*, 8, 51–57.

Brown, B. B. and Klute, C. (2006). Friendships, cliques, and crowds. In G. R. Adams and M. D. Berzonsky (eds), *Blackwell Handbook of Adolescence* (pp 330–48). Oxford, UK. Blackwell Publishing.

Brown, D. E. (1991). *Human Universals*. New York, NY. McGraw-Hill.

Brown, J. B. (2007/2008, December/January). Psychedelic healing? *Scientific American Mind*, 67–71.

Brown, L. V. (ed) (2007). *Psychology of Motivation*. Hauppauge, NY. Nova Science.

Brown, R. and Kulik, J. (1977). Flashbulb memories. *Cognition*, 5, 73–99.

Brown, R. and McNeil, D. (1966). The 'tip of the tongue' phenomenon. *Journal of Verbal Learning and Verbal Behavior*, 5, 325–37.

Brown, S. L., Nesse, R. M., Vinokur, A. D., and Smith, D. M. (2003). Providing social support may be more beneficial than receiving it. Results from a prospective study of mortality. *Psychological Science*, 14, 320–7.

Brown, T. A., Campbell, L. A., Lehman, C. L., Grisham, J. R., and Mancill, R. B. (2001). Current and lifetime comorbidity of the DSM-IV anxiety and mood disorders in a large clinical sample. *Journal of Abnormal Psychology*, 110, 585–99.

Brown, W. A. (2002). Are antidepressants as ineffective as they look? *Prevention and Treatment*, 5. Retrieved from http://journals.apa.org/prevention/volume5/pre0050026c.html on 8 August 2005.

Browne, K. D. and Hamilton-Giachritsis, C. (2005). The influence of violent media on children and adolescents. A public-health perspective. *The Lancet*, 365, 702–10.

Brownell, K. D. and Rodin, J. (1994). The dieting maelstrom. Is it possible and advisable to lose weight? *American Psychologist*, 49, 781–91.

Brownlee, S. (2005, 1 August). Inside the teen brain. Mysteries of the teen years. *U.S. News and World Report*. Retrieved from http://www.usnews.com/usnews/culture/articles/990809/archive_001644.htm on 30 January 2013.

Broyles, S. J. (2006). Paranoia over subliminal advertising. What's the big uproar this time? *Journal of Consumer Marketing*, 23, 312–13.

Bruce, D., Wilcox-O'Hearn, L. A., Robinson, J. A., Phillips-Grant, K., Francis, L., et al (2005). Fragment memories mark the end of childhood amnesia. *Memory and Cognition*, 33, 567–76.

Bruce, S. E., Yonkers, K. A., Otto, M. W., Eisen, J. L., Weisberg, R. B., et al (2005). Influence of psychiatric comorbidity on recovery and recurrence in generalized anxiety disorder, social phobia, and panic disorder. A 12-year prospective study. *American Journal of Psychiatry*, 162, 1179–87.

Bruck, M. and Ceci, S. J. (1997). The suggestibility of small children. *Current Directions in Psychological Science*, 6, 75–9.

Bruck, M. and Ceci, S. J. (1999). The suggestibility of children's memory. *Annual Review of Psychology*, 50, 419–39.

Bruck, M., Ceci, S. J., Francoeur, E., and Renick, A. (1995). Anatomically detailed dolls do not facilitate preschoolers' reports of a pediatric examination involving genital touching. *Journal of Experimental Psychology. Applied*, 1, 95–109.

Brügger-Anderson, T., Pönitz, V., Snapinn, S., Dickstein, K.; for the OPTIMAAL study group. (2008). Moderate alcohol consumption is associated with reduced long-term cardiovascular risk in patients following a complicated acute myocardial infarction. *International Journal of Cardiology*. Advance publication retrieved from http://www.sciencedirect.com on 13 November 2008.

Brulé, G. and Veenhoven, R. (2017). The '10 excess' phenomenon in responses to survey questions on happiness. *Social Indicators Research*, 131(2), 853–70.

Brydon, L., Magid, K., and Steptoe, A. (2006). Platelets, coronary heart disease, and stress. *Brain, Behavior, and Immunity*, 20, 113–19.

Buccino, G., Binkofski, F., and Riggio, L. (2004). The mirror neuron system and action recognition. *Brain and Language*, 89(2), 370–6.

Buckley, C. (2007, 3 January). Man is rescued by stranger on subway tracks. *New York Times*. Retrieved from http://www.nytimes.com/2007/01/03/nyregion/03life.html on 6 January 2007.

Buckner, R. L. (2010). The role of the hippocampus in prediction and imagination. *Annual Review of Psychology*, 61, 27–48.

Budney, A. J. and Wiley, J. (2001). Can marijuana use lead to marijuana dependence? In M. E. Carroll and B. J. Overmier (eds), *Animal Research and Human Health. Advancing Human Welfare through Behavioral Science* (pp 115–26). Washington, DC. American Psychological Association.

Buhle, J. T., Stevens, B. L., Friedman, J. J., and Wager, T. D. (2012). Distraction and placebo. Two separate routes to pain control. *Psychological Science*, 23, 246–53.

Bulik, C. M. (2005). Exploring the gene-environment nexus in eating disorders. *Journal of Psychiatry and Neuroscience*, 30, 335–9.

Bulik, C. M., Thornton, L. M., Root, T. L., Pisetsky, E. M., Lichtenstein, P., et al (2010). Understanding the relation between anorexia nervosa and bulimia nervoist in a Swedish national twin sample. *Biological Psychiatry*, 67, 71–7.

Bulkeley, K. and Kahan, T. L. (2008). The impact of September 11 on dreaming. *Consciousness and Cognition*, 17, 1248–56.

Burger, J. M. (2009). Replicating Milgram. Would people still obey? *American Psychologist*, 64, 1–11.

Burk, W. J. and Laursen, B. (2005). Adolescent perceptions of friendship and their associations with individual adjustment. *International Journal of Behavioral Development*, 29(2), 156–64.

Burke, B. L., Martens, A., and Faucher, E. H. (2010). Two decades of terror management theory. A meta-analysis of mortality salience research. *Personality and Social Psychology Review*, 14, 155–95.

Burke, D. (2014). Why isn't everyone an evolutionary psychologist?. *Frontiers in Psychology*, 5(910), 1–8.

Burki, T. (2010). Healing the mental scars of combat. *The Lancet*, 376, 1727–8.

Burlingame, G. M. and Baldwin, S. (2011). Group therapy. In J. C. Norcross, G. R. Vandenbos, and D. K. Freedheim (eds), *History of Psychotherapy. Continuity and Change* (2nd edn, pp 505–15). Washington, DC. American Psychological Association.

Burman, E. (2016) *Deconstructing Developmental Psychology*. London. Routledge.

Burnham, C. A. and Davis, K. G. (1969). The nine-dot problem. Beyond perceptual organization. *Psychonomic Science*, 17, 321–3.

Burns, D. (1999). *Feeling Good* (rev edn). New York, NY. Avon Books.

Burns, J. E. (2003). What is beyond the edge of the known world? *Journal of Consciousness Studies*, 10(6–7), 7–28.

Burroughs, W. S. (1959). *Naked Lunch*. New York, NY. Grove Press.

Burrow, A. L. and Rainone, N. (2017). How many likes did I get? Purpose moderates links between positive social media feedback and self-esteem. *Journal of Experimental Social Psychology*, 69, 232–6.

Bushman, B. J. (2002). Does venting anger feed or extinguish the flame? Catharsis, rumination, distraction, anger, and aggressive responding. *Personality and Social Psychology Bulletin*, 28, 724–31.

Bushman, B. J. and Anderson, C. A. (2001). Media violence and the American public. Scientific facts versus media misinformation. *American Psychologist*, 477–89.

Bushman, B. J., and Anderson, C. A. (2001a). Is it time to pull the plug on the hostile versus instrumental aggression dichotomy? *Psychological Review*, 108, 273–9.

Bushman, B. J. and Anderson, C. A. (2001b). Media violence and the American public. Scientific facts versus media misinformation. *American Psychologist*, 56, 477–89.

Bushman, B. J., Baumeister, R. F., and Stack, A. D. (1999). Catharsis, aggression, and persuasive influence. Self-fulfilling or self-defeating prophecies. *Journal of Personality and Social Psychology*, 76, 367–76.

Bushman, B. J., Baumeister, R. F., Thomaes, S., Ryu, E., Begeer, S., et al (2009). Looking again, and harder, for a link between low self-esteem and aggression. *Journal of Personality*, 77, 427–46.

Bushman, B. M. and Anderson, C. A. (2002). Violent video games and hostile expectations. A test of the General Aggression Model. *Personality and Social Psychology Bulletin*, 28, 1679–86.

Bushnell, I. W. R. (2001). Mother's face recognition in newborn infants. Leaning and memory. *Infant and Child Development*, 10(1–2), 67–74.

Busigny, T., Joubert, S., Flician, O., Ceccaldi, M., and Rossion, B. (2010). Holistic perception of the individual face is specific and necessary. Evidence from a study of acquired prosopagnosia. *Neuropsychologia*, 48, 4057–92.

Buss, A. H. and Plomin, R. (1984). *Temperament. Early Developing Personality Traits*. Hillsdale, NJ. Lawrence Erlbaum Associates.

Buss, D. M. (1989). Sex differences in human mate preferences. Evolutionary hypotheses testing in 37 cultures. *Behavioral and Brain Sciences*, 12, 1–49.

Buss, D. M. (2003). *The Evolution of Desire*. New York, NY. Basic Books. (Original work published 1994.)

Buss, D. M. (2009). The great struggles of life. Darwin and the emergence of evolutionary psychology. *American Psychologist*, 64, 140–8.

Buss, D. M. (2009). How can evolutionary psychology successfully explain personality and individual differences? *Perspectives on Psychological Science*, 4, 359–66.

Buss, D. M. (2009a). The great struggles of life. Darwin and the emergence of evolutionary psychology. *American Psychologist*, 64, 140–8.

Buss, D. M. (2009b). How can evolutionary psychology successfully explain personality and individual differences. *Perspectives on Psychological Science*, 4, 359–66.

Buss, D. M. (ed) (2005). *The Handbook of Evolutionary Psychology*. Hoboken, NJ. John Wiley and Sons.

Bussey, K. and Bandura, A. (1999). Social cognitive theory of gender development and differentiation. *Psychological Review*, 106, 676–713.

Buysse, D. J., Germain, A., and Moul, D. E. (2005). Diagnosis, epidemiology, and consequences of insomnia. *Primary Psychiatry*, 12, 37–44.

Buysse, D. J., Grunstein, R., Horne, J., and Lavie, P. (2010). Can improvement in sleep positively impact on health? *Sleep Medicine Reviews*, 14, 405–10.

Byers, E. S., Henderson, J., and Hobson, K. M. (2009). University students' definitions of sexual abstinence and having sex. *Archives of Sexual Behavior*, 38, 665–74.

Byne, W., Tobet, S., Mattiace, L. A., Lasco, M. S., Kemether, E., et al (2001). The interstitial nuclei of the human anterior hypothalamus. An investigation of variation with sex, sexual orientation, and HIV status. *Hormones and Behavior*, 40, 86–92.

Byrne, B. et al (2007). Longitudinal twin study of early literacy development. Preschool through Grade 1. *Reading and Writing*, 20, 77–102.

C'de Baca, J. and Wilbourne, P. (2004). Quantum change. Ten years later. *Journal of Clinical Psychology*, 60, 531–41.

Cabeza, R. and Moscovitch, M. (2013). Memory systems, processing modes, and components. Functional Neuroimaging evidence. *Perspectives on Psychological Science*, 8, 49–55.

Cacabelos, R., Fernandez-Novoa, L., Lombardi, V., Kubota, Y., and Takeda, M. (2005). Molecular genetics of Alzheimer's disease and aging. *Methods and Findings of Experimental Clinical Pharmacology*, 27(Suppl A), 1–573.

Cacioppo, J. T. (2004). Common sense, intuition, and theory in personality and social psychology. *Personality and Social Psychology Review*, 8, 114–22.

Cacioppo, J. T., Hawkley, L. C., and Berntson, G. G. (2003). The anatomy of loneliness. *Current Directions in Psychological Science*, 12, 71–4.

Cadar, D., Hackett, R. A., Mischie, M., Llewellyn, D. J., Batty, G. D., et al (2017). Association of physical activity as a distinctive feature of clustering of lifestyle behaviours with dementia risk. Evidence from the English Longitudinal Study of Ageing. *The Lancet*, 390, S29.

Cadinu, M., Maass, A., Rosabianca, A., and Kiesner, J. (2005). Why do women under-perform under stereotype threat? Evidence for the role of negative thinking. *Psychological Science*, 16, 572–8.

Cahill, L. (2006). Why sex matters for neuroscience. *Nature Reviews Neuroscience*, 7, 477–84.

Calder, A. J., Lawrence, A. D., and Young, A. W. (2001). Neuropsychology of fear and loathing. *Nature Reviews. Neuroscience*, 2, 352–63.

Calhoon, H. M., McKeigue, P. M., and Davey Smith, G. (2003). Problems of reporting genetic associations with complex outcomes. *Lancet*, 361, 865–72.

Callaghan, T., Rochat, P., Lillard, A., Claux, M. L., Odden, H., et al (2005). Synchrony in the onset of mental-state reasoning. Evidence from five cultures. *Psychological Science*, 16, 378–84.

Cameron, J. J., Wilson, A. E., and Ross, M. (2004). Autobiographical memory and self-assessment. In D. R. Beike, J. M. Lambinen, and D. A. Behrend (eds), *The Self and Memory. Studies in Self and Identity* (pp 207–26). New York, NY. Psychology Press.

Cameron, P. and Biber, H. (1973). Sexual thought throughout the lifespan. *Gerontologist*, 13, 144–7.

Campbell, A. (2004). Female competition. Causes, constraints, content, and contexts. *Journal of Sex Research*, 41(1), 16–26.

Campbell, A., Shirley, L., Heywood, C., and Crook, C. (2000). Infants' visual preference for sex-congruent babies, children, toys and activities. A longitudinal study. *British Journal of Developmental Psychology*, 18(4), 479–98.

Campbell, D. T. (1965). Ethnocentric and other altruistic motives. In D. Levine (ed), *Nebraska Symposium on Motivation* (Vol 13). Lincoln, NE. University of Nebraska Press.

Campbell, E. G., Weissman, J. S., Shringhaus, S., Rao, S. R., Moy, B., et al (2007). Institutional academic-industry relationships. *JAMA*, 298, 1779–86.

Campbell-Sills, L. and Stein, M. B. (2005). Justifying the diagnostic status of social phobia. A reply to Wakefield, Horwitz, and Schmitz. *Canadian Journal of Psychiatry*, 50, 320–3.

Camperio-Ciani, A., Corna, F., and Capiluppi, C. (2004). Evidence for maternally inherited factors favouring male homosexuality and promoting female fecundity. *Proceedings of the Royal Society (England)*, 271, 2217–21.

Campfield, L. A., Smith, F. J., Rosenbaum, M., and Hirsch, J. (1996). Human eating. Evidence for a physiological basis using a modified paradigm. *Neuroscience and Biobehavioral Review*, 20, 133–7.

Cannon, W. B. (1929a). *Bodily Changes in Pain, Hunger, Fear and Rage. An Account of Recent Researches into the Functions of Emotional Excitement*. New York, NY. D. Appleton.

Cannon, W. B. (1929b). Organization for physiological homeostasis. *Physiological Reviews*, 9, 399–431.

Cantor, P. (1975). The effects of youthful suicide on the family. *Psychiatric Opinion*, 12, 6–11.

Capaldi, D. M. (1996). The reliability of retrospective report for timing first sexual intercourse for adolescent males. *Journal of Adolescent Research*, 11, 375–87.

Capell, M. B. and Sahliyeh, S. (2007). Suicide terrorism. Is religion the critical factor? *Security Journal*, 20, 267–83.

Caplan, J. B. and Caplan, P. J. (2005). The perseverative search for sex differences in mathematics ability. In A. M. Gallagher and J. C. Kaufman (eds), *Gender Differences in Mathematics* (pp 25–47). Cambridge, UK. Cambridge University Press.

Caprara, G. V., Vecchione, M., Alessandri, G., Gerbino, M., and Barbaranelli, C. (2011). The contribution of personality traits and self-efficacy beliefs to academic achievement. A longitudinal study. *British Journal of Educational Psychology*, 81, 78–96.

Card, N. A., Stucky, B. D., Sawalani, G. M., and Little, T. D. (2008). Direct and indirect aggression during childhood and adolescence. A meta-analytic review of gender differences, intercorrelations, and relations to maladjustment. *Child Development*, 79, 1185–229.

Cardeña, E. (2018). The experimental evidence for parapsychological phenomena. A review. *The American Psychologist*, 73(5), 663–77.

Carey, B. (2008, 18 December). Psychiatrists revising the book of human troubles. *New York Times*, p A1.

Carey, T. J., Moul, D. E., Pilkonis, P., Germain, A., and Buysse, D. J. (2005). Focusing on the experience of insomnia. *Behavioral and Sleep Medicine*, 3, 73–86.

Carnahan, T. and McFarland, S. (2007). Revisiting the Stanford Prison Experiment. Could participant self-selection have led to the cruelty? *Personality and Social Psychology Bulletin*, 33, 603–14.

Carr, A. (2012). *Family Therapy. Concepts, Process and Practice*. John Wiley and Sons.

Carr, A. (2014). The evidence base for couple therapy, family therapy and systemic interventions for adult-focused problems. *Journal of Family Therapy*, 36(2), 158–94.

Carr, A. (2014). The evidence base for family therapy and systemic interventions for child-focused problems. *Journal of Family Therapy*, 36(2), 107–57.

Carraher, T. N., Carraher, D. W., and Schliemann, A. D. (1985). Mathematics in the streets and in schools. *British Journal of Developmental Psychology*, 3(1), 21–9.

Carreiras, M., Lopez, J., Rivero, F., and Corina, D. (2005). Linguistic perception. Neural processing of a whistled language. *Nature*, 433, 31–2.

Carroll, J. B. (1993). *Human Cognitive Abilities. A Survey of Factor-analytic Studies*. New York, NY. Cambridge University Press.

Carroll, J. B. (1997). Psychometrics, intelligence, and public perception. *Intelligence*, 24(1), 25–52.

Carson, R. C. (1996). Aristotle, Galileo, and the *DSM* taxonomy. The case of schizophrenia. *Journal of Consulting and Clinical Psychology*, 64, 1133–9.

Carter, C. S. (2004). Oxytocin and the prairie vole. A love story. In J. T. Cacioppo and G. G. Berntson (eds), *Essays in Social Neuroscience* (pp 53–63). Cambridge, MA. MIT Press.

Cartwright, R. (1996). Dreams and adaptation to divorce. In D. Barrtett (ed), *Trauma and Dreams* (pp 178–85). Cambridge, MA. Harvard University Press.

Cartwright, R. (2005). Dreaming as a mood regulation system. In M. Kryger, T. Roth, and W. Dement (eds), *Principles and Practice of Sleep Medicine* (4th edn, pp 565–72). Philadelphia, PA. W. B. Saunders.

Cartwright, R., Agargun, M. Y., Kirkby, J., and Friedman, J. K. (2006). Relation of dreams to waking concerns. *Psychiatry Research*, 141, 261–70.

Casey, M. B., Nuttall, R. L., Pezaris, E., and Ben-bow, C. P. (1995). The influence of spatial ability on gender differences in mathematics college entrance test scores across diverse samples. *Developmental Psychology*, 31, 697–705.

Cash, T. F. (1995). *What Do You See When You Look in the Mirror? Helping Yourself to a Positive Body Image*. Des Plaines, IL. Bantam Dell Pub Group.

Caspi, A. (2000). The child is father of the man. Personality continuities from childhood to adulthood. *Journal of Personality and Social Psychology*, 78, 158–72.

Caspi, A., Roberts, B. W., and Shiner, R. L. (2005). Personality development. Stability and change. *Annual Review of Psychology*, 56, 453–84.

Caspi, A., Sugden, K., Moffitt, T. E., Taylor, A., Craig, I. W., et al (2003). Influence of life stress on depression. Moderation by a polymorphism in the 5-HTT gene. *Science*, 301, 386–9.

Caspit, J. T., Harrington, H., Moffitt, T. E., Milne, B. J., and Poulton, R. (2006). Socially isolated children 20 years later. Risk of cardiovascular disease. *Archives of Pediatric and Adolescent Medicine*, 160, 805–11.

Cassel, W., Roebers, C., and Bjorklund, D. (1996). Developmental patterns of eyewitness responses to repeated and increasingly suggestive questions. *Journal of Experimental Child Psychology*, 61, 116–33.

Cassin, S. E. and von Ranson, K. M. (2005). Personality and eating disorders. A decade in review. *Clinical Psychology Review*, 25, 895–916.

Cataneo, L. and Rozzolatti, G. (2009). The mirror neuron system. *Archives of Neurology*, 66, 557–60.

Catapano, F., Perris, F., Fabrazzo, M., Cliffi, V., Giacco, D., et al (2010). Obsessive-compulsive disorder with poor insight. A three-year prospective study. *Progress in Neuro-Psychopharmacology and Biological Psychiatry*, 34, 323–30.

Cautin, R. L. (2009a). The founding of the Association for Psychological Science. Part 1. Dialectical tensions within organized psychology. *Perspectives on Psychological Science*, 4, 211–23.

Cautin, R. L. (2009b). The founding of the Association for Psychological Science. Part 2. The tipping point and early years. *Perspectives on Psychological Science*, 4, 224–35.

Cavalieri, P. (2004). *Animal Question. Why Nonhuman Animals Deserve Human Rights*. New York, NY. Oxford University Press.

Cavalieri, P. (2006). The animal debate. A reexamination. In P. Singer (ed), *In Defense of Animals. The Second Wave* (pp 54–68). Malden, MA. Blackwell Publishing.

Cavanagh, J. T. O., Carson, A. J., Sharpe, M., and Lawrie, S. M. (2003). Psychological autopsy studies of suicide. A systematic review. *Psychological Medicine*, 33, 395–405.

Cave, C. B. and Squire, L. R. (1992). Intact verbal and nonverbal short-term memory following damage to the human hippocampus. *Hippocampus*, 2, 151–63.

CBS News. (11 February 2009). Whiz kid, 13, to graduate college. Retrieved from http://www.cbsnews.com/

stories/2003/04/21/tech/main550399.shtml on 2 September 2011.

Ceci, S. J. and Bruck, M. (1995). *Jeopardy in the Courtroom. A Scientific Analysis of Children's Testimony.* Washington, DC. American Psychological Association.

Ceci, S. J., Loftus, E. W., Leichtman, M., and Bruck, M. (1994). The possible role of source misattributions in the creation of false beliefs among preschoolers. *International Journal of Clinical and Experimental Hypnosis*, 42, 304–20.

Ceci, S. J. and Williams, W. M. (1997). Schooling, intelligence, and income. *American Psychologist*, 52, 1051–8.

Ceci, S. J. and Williams, W. M. (2010). Sex differences in math-intensive fields. *Current Directions in Psychological Science*, 19, 275–9.

Ceci, S. J., Williams, W. M., and Barnett, S. M. (2009). Women's underrepresentation in science. Sociocultural and biological considerations. *Psychological Bulletin*, 135, 218–61.

Cecil, H., Bogart, L. M., Wagstaff, D. A., Pinkerton, S. D., and Abramson, P. R. (2002). Classifying a person as a sex partner. The impact of contextual factors. *Psychology and Health. An International Journal*, 17, 221–34.

Centers for Disease Control. (1998, 22 May). *Morbidity and Mortality Weekly Report*, 47. Retrieved from http://www.cdc.gov/mmwr/PDF/wk/mm4719.pdf on 16 March 2011.

Centers for Disease Control. (2005a). Annual smoking-attributable mortality, years of potential life lost, and productivity losses–United States, 1997–2001. *Morbidity and Mortality Weekly Report*, 54, 625–8.

Centers for Disease Control. (2005b). Cigarette smoking among adults. United States, 2003. *Morbidity and Mortality Weekly Report*, 54, 509–13.

Centers for Disease Control. (2012, January). Binge drinking. Nationwide problem, local solutions. *CDC Vital Signs*. Retrieved from http://www.cdc.gov/VitalSigns/pdf/2012-01-vitalsigns.pdf on 22 January 2012.

Cepeda, N. J., Vul, E., Rohrer, D., Wixted, J. T., and Pashler, H. (2008). Spacing effects in learning. A temporal ridgeline of optimal retention. *Psychological Science*, 19, 1095–102.

Cerasoli, C. P., Nicklin, J. M., and Ford, M. T. (2014). Intrinsic motivation and extrinsic incentives jointly predict performance. A 40-year meta-analysis. *Psychological Bulletin*, 140(4), 980.

Cervilla, J. A., Molina, E., Rivera, M., Torres-González, F., Bellón, J. A., et al (2007). The risk for depression conferred by stressful life events is modified by variation at the serotonin transporter 5HTTLPR genotype. Evidence from the Spanish PREDICT-Gene cohort. *Molecular Psychiatry*, 12, 748–55.

Cervone, D. and Shoda, Y. (1999). Beyond traits in the study of personality coherence. *Current Directions in Psychological Science*, 8(1), 27–32.

Chabris, C. F. and Glickman, M. E. (2006). Sex differences in intellectual performance. Analysis of a large cohort of competitive chess players. *Psychological Science*, 17, 1040–6.

Chabris, C. and Simons, D. (2010). *The Invisible Gorilla.* New York, NY. Crown.

Chabris, C. F., Weinberger, A., Fontaine, M, and Simons, D. J. (2011). You do not talk about Fight Club if you do not notice Fight Club. Inattentional blindness for a simulated real-world assault. *i-Perception*, 2, 150–3.

Chalmers, D. J. (1995). Facing up to the problem of consciousness. *Journal of Consciousness Studies*, 3, 200–19.

Chambers, J. R. and Widschitl, P. D. (2004). Biases in social comparative judgments. The role of non-motivated factors in above-average and comparative-optimism effects. *Psychological Bulletin*, 130, 813–38.

Chambless, D. L. and Hollon, S. D. (1998). Defining empirically supported therapies. *Journal of Counseling and Clinical Psychology*, 66, 7–18.

Champagne, F. A. and Mashoodh, R. (2009). Genes in context. Gene-environment interplay and the origins of individual differences in behavior. *Current Directions in Psychological Science*, 18, 127–31.

Chan, W. Y. M., Leung, H. T., Westbrook, R. F., and McNally, G. P. (2010). Effects of recent exposure to a conditioned stimulus on extinction of Pavlovian conditioning. *Learning and Memory*, 17, 512–21.

Chandler, R. (1992). *Farewell, My Lovely.* New York, NY. Vintage. (Original work published 1940.)

Chang, L., Alicata, D., Ernst, T., and Volkow, N. (2007). Structural and metabolic brain changes in the striatum associated with methamphetamine abuse. *Addiction*, 102(Suppl 1), 16–32.

Chang, S., Newell, J., and Salmon, C. T. (2009). Product placement in entertainment media. Proposing business process models. *International Journal of Advertising*, 28, 783–806.

Chang, W., Wong, W., and Teo, G. (2000). The socially oriented and individually oriented achievement motivation of Singaporean and Chinese students. *Journal of Psychology in Chinese Studies*, 1, 39–63.

Chapman, L. A., Wade, S. L., Walz, N. C., Taylor, H. G., Stancin, T., et al (2010). Clinically significant behavior problems during the initial 18 months following early childhood traumatic brain injury. *Rehabilitation Psychology*, 55, 48–57.

Charland-Verville, V., Bruno, M. A., Bahri, M. A., Demertzi, A., Desseilles, M., et al (2013). Brain dead yet mind alive. A positron emission tomography case study of brain metabolism in Cotard's syndrome. *Cortex*, 49(7), 1997–9.

Chassin, L., Hussong, A., Barrera, M., Jr, Molina, B., Trim, R., et al (2004). Adolescent substance use. In R. Lerner and L. Steinberg (eds), *Handbook of Adolescent Psychology* (2nd edn, pp 665–96). New York, NY. John Wiley.

Chassin, L., Presson, C., Rose, J., Sherman, S., and Prost, J. (2002). Parental smoking cessation and adolescent smoking. *Journal of Pediatric Psychology*, 27, 485–96.

Chavira, D. A., Stein, M. B., and Malcarne, V. L. (2002). Scrutinizing the relationship between shyness and social phobia. *Journal of Anxiety Disorders*, 16, 595–8.

Chesmore, A. A., Weiler, L. M., Trump, L. J., Landers, A. L., and Taussig, H. N. (2017). Maltreated children in out-of-home care. The relation between attachment quality and internalizing symptoms. *Journal of Child and Family Studies*, 26(2), 381–92.

Cheung, F. and Lucas, R. E. (2016). Income inequality is associated with stronger social comparison effects. The effect of relative income on life satisfaction. *Journal of Personality and Social Psychology*, 110(2), 332.

Cheyne, J. A. (2005). Sleep paralysis episode frequency and number, types, and structure of associated hallucinations. *Journal of Sleep Research*, 14, 319–24.

Chiappe, D. and MacDonald, K. (2005). The evolution of domain-general mechanisms in intelligence and learning. *The Journal of General Psychology*, 132(10), 5–40.

Chida, Y. and Steptoe, A. (2008). Positive psychological well-being and mortality. A quantitative review of prospective observational studies. *Psychosomatic Medicine*, 70, 741–56.

Childress, A. R., Mozley, P. D., McElgin, W., Fitzgerald, J., Reivich, M., et al (1999). Limbic activation during cue-induced cocaine craving. *American Journal of Psychiatry*, 156(1), 11–18.

Chivers, M. L. and Bailey, M. (2005). A sex difference in features that elicit genital response. *Biological Psychology*, 70, 115–120.

Chivers, M. L., Rieger, G., Latty, E., and Bailey, J. M. (2004). A sex difference in the specificity of sexual arousal. *Psychological Science*, 15, 736–44.

Chivers, M. L., Seto, M. C., Lalumière, M. L., Laan, E., and Grimbos, T. (2010). Agreement of self-reported and genital measures of sexual arousal in men and women. A meta-analysis. *Archives of Sexual Behavior*, 39, 5–56.

Choi, H. and Smith, S. M. (2005). Incubation and the resolution of tip-of-the-tongue states. *Journal of General Psychology*, 132, 365–76.

Choi, I., Dalal, R., Kim-Prieto, C., and Park, H. (2003). Culture and judgment of causal relevance. *Journal of Personality and Social Psychology*, 84, 46–59.

Choi, I. and Nisbett, R. E. (1998). Situational salience and cultural differences in the correspondence bias and the actor-observer bias. *Personality and Social Psychology Bulletin*, 24, 949–60.

Choi, I., Nisbett, R. E., and Norenzayan, A. (1999). Causal attribution across cultures. Variation and universality. *Psychological Bulletin*, 125, 47–63.

Chomsky, N. (1965). *Aspects of the Theory of Syntax*. Cambridge, MA. MIT Press.

Chomsky, N. (1972). *Language and Mind* (enlarged edn). New York, NY. Harcourt Brace Jovanovich.

Chomsky, N. (1975). *Reflections on Language*. New York, NY. Harcourt Brace Jovanovich.

Chomsky, N. (1980). Rules and representations. *Behavioral and Brain Sciences*, 3, 1–61.

Christakis, D. A., Zimmerman, F. J., DiGiuseppe, D. L., and McCarty, C. A. (2004). Early television exposure and subsequent attentional problems in children. *Pediatrics*, 113, 708–13.

Christensen, A. and Heavey, C. L. (1999). Interventions for couples. *Annual Review of Psychology*, 50, 165–90.

Christensen, A. and Jacobson, N. S. (1994). Who (or what) can do psychotherapy. The status and challenge of nonprofessional therapies. *Psychological Science*, 5, 9–13.

Christensen, A. and Jacobson, N. S. (2000). *Reconcilable Differences*. New York, NY. Guilford.

Christiansen, S. L. and Palkovitz, R. (1998). Exploring Erikson's psychosocial theory of development. Generativity and its relationship to parental identity, intimacy, and involvement with others. *Journal of Men's Studies*, 7, 133–56.

Christianson, S. A. (ed) (1992). *The Handbook of Emotion and Memory. Research and Theory*. Hillsdale, NJ. Lawrence Erlbaum Associates.

Chua, H. F., Boland, J. E., and Nisbett, R. E. (2005). Cultural variation in eye movements during scene perception. *Proceedings of the National Academy of Sciences*, 102, 12629–33.

Church, T. A. (2010). Current perspectives in the study of personality across cultures. *Perspectives on Psychological Science*, 5, 441–9.

Cialdini, R. B., Brown, S. L., Lewis, B. P., Luce, C., and Neuberg, S. L. (1997). Reinterpreting the empathy–altruism relationship. When one into one equals oneness. *Journal of Personality and Social Psychology*, 73, 481–94.

Cicchetti, D. and Rogosch, F. A. (1996). Equifinality and multifinality in developmental psychopathology. *Development and Psychopathology*, 8, 597–600.

Cirelli, C. and Tononi, G. (2008). Is sleep essential? *PLoS Biology*, 6, 1605–11. Retrieved from www.plosbiology.org on 27 October 2008.

Clabaugh, A. and Morling, B. (2004). Stereotype accuracy of ballet and modern dancers. *Journal of Social Psychology*, 144, 31–48.

Clark, R. D. (1990). The impact of AIDS on gender differences in willingness to engage in casual sex. *Journal of Applied Social Psychology*, 20(Part 2), 771–82.

Clark, R. D. and Hatfield, E. (1989). Gender differences in receptivity to sexual offers. *Journal of Psychology and Human Sexuality*, 2, 39–55.

Clark, R. E. and Squire, L. R. (1998). Classical conditioning and brain systems. The role of awareness. *Science*, 280, 77–81.

Clarkin, J. F. (2008). Clinical approaches to Axis II comorbidity. Commentary. *Journal of Clinical Psychology. In Session*, 64, 222–30.

Clausen, J. (2010). Ethical brain stimulation. Neuroethics of deep brain stimulation in research and clinical practice. *European Journal of Neuroscience*, 32, 1152–62.

Clements, A. M., Rimrodt, S. L., Abel, J. R., Blankner, J. G., Mostofsky, S. H., et al (2006). Sex differences in cerebral laterality of language and visuaspatial processing. *Brain and Language*, 98, 150–8.

CNN Access (2004, 21 May). Researcher. It's not bad apples, it's the barrel. Retrieved from http://www.cnn.com/2004/US/05/21/zimbardo.access/on 30 May 2004.

Coan, J. A., Schaefer, H. S., and Davidson, R. J. (2006). Lending a hand. Social regulation of the neural response to threat. *Psychological Science*, 17, 1032–9.

Cobb, H. C., Reeve, R. E., Shealy, C. N., Norcross, J. C., Schare, M. L., et al (2004). Overlap among clinical, counseling, and school psychology. Implications for the profession and combined-integrated training. *Journal of Clinical Psychology*, 60, 939–55.

Coelho, H. F., Canter, P. H., and Ernst, E. (2007). Mindfulness-based cognitive therapy. Evaluating current evidence and informing future research. *Journal of Consulting and Clinical Psychology*, 75, 1000–5.

Coetzee, M-H. (2002). Zulu stick fighting. A socio-historical overview. *Journal of Alternative Perspectives on the Martial Arts and Sciences*. http://www.americancrisis.us/docs/2013_06_23_081249_0_zulu_stick_fighting_by_mariheleen_coetzee.pdf accessed 9 January 2016.

Cohen, E. (2007, 9 July). CDC. Antidepressants most prescribed drugs in the U.S. *CNN.com/health*. Retrieved from http://www.cnn.com/2007/HEALTH/07/09/antidepressants/index.html on 5 June 2008.

Cohen, G. (1990). Recognition and retrieval of proper names. Age differences in the fan effect. *European Journal of Cognitive Psychology*, 2, 193–204.

Cohen, L. (1995). The pleasures of castration. In P. R. Abramson and S. D. Pinkerton (eds), *Sexual Nature, Sexual Culture* (pp 276–304). Chicago, IL. University of Chicago Press.

Cohen, L. B. and Marks, K. S. (2002). How infants process addition and subtraction events. *Developmental Science*, 5, 186–201.

Cohen, P. (2007, 25 November). Freud is widely taught at universities except in the psychology department. *New York Times*. Retrieved on 25 November 2007 from www.nytimes.com

Cohen, P. J. (2009). Medical marijuana. The conflict between scientific evidence and political ideology, part. Part one of two. *Journal of Pain and Palliative Care Pharmacotherapy*, 23, 4–25.

Cohen, S. (1996). Psychological stress, immunity and upper respiratory infections. *Current Directions in Psychological Science*, 5, 86–90.

Cohen, S., Alper, C. M., Doyle, W. J., Adler, N., Treanor, J. J., et al (2008). Objective and subjective socioeconomic status and susceptibility to the common cold. *Health Psychology*, 27, 268–74.

Cohen, S., Frank, E., Doyle, W. J., Skoner, D. P., Rabin, B. S., et al (1998). Types of stressors that increase susceptibility to the common cold in healthy adults. *Health Psychology*, 17, 214–23.

Cohen, S., Janicki-Deverts, D., and Miller, G. E. (2007). Psychological stress and disease. *Journal of the American Medical Association*, 298, 1685–7.

Cohen-Kettenis, P. T. (2005). Gender change in 46,XY persons with 5∝-reductase-2 Deficiency and 17/β-Hydroxysteroid Dehydrogenase-3 Deficiency. *Archives of Sexual Behavior*, 34, 399–410.

Coie, J. D. and Dodge, K. A. (1983). Continuities and changes in children's social status. A five-year longitudinal study. *Merrill-Palmer Quarterly (1982–)*, 261–82.

Coie, J. D., Dodge, K. A., and Coppotelli, H. (1982). Dimensions and types of social status. A cross-age perspective. *Developmental psychology*, 18(4), 557.

Colapinto, J. (2000). *As Nature Made Him. The Boy Who Was Raised as a Girl*. New York, NY. Harper Collins.

Cole, J., Sumnall, H., and Grob, C. (2002a). Sorted. Ecstasy. *The Psychologist*, 15, 464–7.

Cole, J., Sumnall, H., and Grob, C. (2002b). Where are the casualties? *The Psychologist*, 15, 474.

Coleman, M. R., Rodd, J. M., Davis, M. H., Johnsrude, I. S., Menon, D. K., et al (2007). Do vegetative patients retain aspects of language comprehension? Evidence from f|MRI. *Brain*, 130, 2494–507.

Coles, C. D. (1993). Saying 'goodbye' to the 'crack baby'. *Neurotoxicology and Teratology*, 15, 290–2.

Coles, R. and Ford, G. (1995). *The Story of Ruby Bridges*. New York, NY. Scholastic Press.

Coles, R. and Stokes, G. (1985). *Sex and the American Teenager*. New York, NY. Harper-Collins.

Collaer, M. L. and Hines, M. (1995). Human behavioral sex differences. A role for gonadal hormones during early development? *Psychological Bulletin*, 118(1), 55–107.

Collins, M. P. and Dunn, L. F. (2005). The effects of meditation and visual imagery on an immune system disorder. Dermatomyositis. *Journal of Alternative and Complementary Medicine*, 11, 275–84.

Collins, N. L. and Miller, L. C. (1994). Self-disclosure and liking. A meta-analytic review. *Psychological Bulletin*, 82, 407–75.

Collins, W. A. and Laursen, B. (2004). Parent–adolescent relationships and influences. In R. M. Lerner and L. Sternberg (eds), *Handbook of Adolescent Psychology* (2nd edn, pp 331–61). Hoboken, NJ. John Wiley and Sons.

Collins, W. A., Maccoby, E. E., Steinberg, L., Hetherington, E. M., and Bornstein, M. H. (2000). Contemporary research on parenting. The case for nature and nurture. *American Psychologist*, 55, 218–32.

Collins, W. A., Maccoby, E. E., Steinberg, L., Hetherington, M. E., and Bornstein, M. H. (2000). The case for nature and nurture. *American Psychologist*, 55, 218–32.

Collins, W. A., Welsh, D. P., and Furman, W. (2009). Adolescent romantic relationships. *Annual Review of Psychology*, 60, 631–52.

Coltheart, M. (2006). What has functional neuroimaging told us about the mind (so far)? *Cortex. A Journal Devoted to the Study of the Nervous System and Behavior*, 42, 323–31.

Coltheart, M. (2013). How can functional neuroimaging inform cognitive theories? *Perspectives on Psychological Science*, 8, 98–103.

Colvin, C.R. and Block, J. (1994). Do positive illusions foster mental health? An examination of the Taylor and Brown formulation. *Psychological Bulletin*, 116, 3–20.

Commentaries to Sabini et al, 2001a. (2001). *Psychological Inquiry*, 12, 16–40.

Compton, W. M., Thomas, Y. F., Stinson, F. S., and Grant, B. F. (2007). Prevalence, correlates, disability, and comorbidity of DSM-IV drug abuse and dependence in the United States. *Archives of General Psychiatry*, 64, 566–76.

Confer, J. C., Easton, J. A., Fleischman, D. S., Goetz, C. D., Lewis, D. M., et al (2010). Evolutionary psychology. Controversies, questions, prospects, and limitations. *American Psychologist*, 65(2), 110.

Congressional Public Health Summit. (26 July 2000). Joint statement on the impact of entertainment violence on children. Retrieved from http://www.aap.org/advocacy/releases/jstmtevc.htm on 14 October 2005.

Conklin, H. M. and Iacono, W. G. (2002). Schizophrenia. A neurodevelopmental perspective. *Current Directions in Psychological Science*, 11(1), 33–7.

Conner, K. R., Duberstein, P. R., Conwell, Y., Seidlitz, L., and Caine, E. D. (2001). Psychological vulnerability to completed suicide. A review of empirical studies. *Suicide and Life-Threatening Behavior*, 31, 367–85.

Conroy, R. T. and Mills, J. N. (1970). *Human Circadian Rhythms*. London. Churchill.

Contrada, R. J., Ashmore, R. D., Gary, M. L., Coups, E., Egeth, J. D., et al (2000). Ethnicity-related sources of stress and their effects on well-being. *Current Directions in Psychological Science*, 9, 136–9.

Cooper, E. F. (2005). *Missing and exploited children. Overview and policy concerns*. Congressional Research Service, Library of Congress. Retrieved from http://www.usembassy.it/pdf/other/RL31655.pdf on 5 November 2005.

Cooper, J. and Fazio, R. H. (1984). A new look at dissonance theory. In L. Berkowitz (ed), *Advances in Experimental Social Psychology* (Vol 17, pp 229–67). New York, NY. Academic Press.

Cooper, S. A., Joshi, A. C., Seenan, P. J., Hadley, D. M., Muir, K. W., et al (2012). Akinetopsia. Acute presentation and evidence for persisting defect in motion vision. *Journal of Neurology, Neurosurgery, and Psychiatry*, 83, 229–30.

Corballis, P. M., Funnell, M. G., and Gazzaniga, M. S. (2002). Hemispheric asymmetries for simple visual judgments in the split brain. *Neuropsychologia*, 40, 401–10.

Coren, S. (1998). Sleep deprivation, psychosis and mental efficiency. *Psychiatric Times*, 15. Retrieved from http://www.psychiatrictimes.com/p980301b.html on 7 January 2006

Coren, S. (2009). Sleep health and its assessment and management in physical therapy practice. The evidence. *Physiotherapy Theory and Practice*, 25, 442–52.

Cornwell, D. and Hobbs, S. (1976, 18 March). The strange saga of Little Albert. *New Society*, 602–4.

Correll, J., Park, B., Judd, C. M., and Wittenbrink, B. (2002). The police officer's dilemma. Using ethnicity to disambiguate potentially threatening individuals. *Journal of Personality and Social Psychology*, 83, 1314–29.

Cosgrove, K. P., Mazure, C. M., and Staley, J. K. (2007). Evolving knowledge of sex differences in brain structure, function, and chemistry. *Biological Psychiatry*, 62, 847–55.

Cosmides, L. and Tooby, J. (1987). From evolution to behavior. Evolutionary psychology as the missing link. In J. Dupre (ed), *The Latest on the Best. Essays on Evolution and Optimality* (pp 277–306). Cambridge, MA. MIT Press.

Cosmides, L. and Tooby, J. (1992). Cognitive adaptations for social exchange. In J. Barkow, L. Cosmides, and J. Tooby (eds), *The Adapted Mind* (pp 163–228). New York, NY. Oxford University Press.

Cosmides, L. and Tooby, J. (2000). Evolutionary psychology and the emotions. In M. Lewis and J. M. Haviland-Jones (eds), *Handbook of Emotions* (2nd edn, pp 91–115). New York, NY. Guilford Press.

Cosmides, L. and Tooby, J. (2005). Neurocognitive adaptations designed for social exchange. In D. M. Buss (ed), *The Handbook of Evolutionary Psychology* (pp 584–627). Hoboken, NJ. John Wiley and Sons.

Cosmides, L. and Tooby, J. (2008). Beyond intuition and instinct blindness. Toward an evolutionarily rigorous cognitive science. In J. E. Adler and J. L. Rips (eds), *Reasoning. Studies of Human Inference and its Foundations* (pp 843–65). New York, NY. Cambridge University Press.

Costa, P. T., Jr, Terracciano, A., and McCrae, R. R. (2001). Gender differences in personality traits across cultures. Robust and surprising findings. *Journal of Personality and Social Psychology*, 81, 322–31.

Costello, D. M., Dierker, L. C., Jones, B. L., and Rose, J. S. (2008). Trajectories of smoking from adolescence to early adulthood and their psychosocial risk factors. *Health Psychology*, 27, 811–18.

Cotard, J. (1880). *From the Hypochondriac Delirium in a Serious Form Of Anxious Melancholy, Memory Read to the Medico-Psychological Society in the Session of June 28, 1880, by Dr. Jules Cotard.* Donnaud.

Coulthard, E., Parton, A., and Husain, M. (2007). The modular architecture of the neglect syndrome. Implications for action control in visual neglect. *Neuropsychologia*, 45, 1982–4.

Courtney, K. E. and Polich, J. (2009). Binge drinking in young adults. Data, definitions, and determinants. *Psychological Bulletin*, 135, 142–56.

Covington, M. V. (2000). Intrinsic versus extrinsic motivation in schools. A reconciliation. *Current Directions in Psychological Science*, 9(1), 22–5.

Cowan, N. (2001). The magical number 4 in short-term memory. A reconsideration of mental storage capacity. *Behavioral and Brain Sciences*, 24, 87–185.

Cowan, N. (2005). *Working Memory Capacity.* Hove, UK. Psychology Press.

Cowan, N. (2010). The magical mystery four. How is working memory capacity limited, and why? *Current Directions in Psychological Science*, 19, 51–7.

Cox, M. J. and Paley, B. (2003). Understanding families as systems. *Current Directions in Psychological Science*, 15, 193–6.

Coyne, J. C. (1976). Depression and the response of others. *Journal of Abnormal Psychology*, 85, 186–93.

Craig, J. C. and Rollman, G. B. (1999). Somesthesis. *Annual Review of Psychology*, 50, 305–31.

Craik, F. I. M. (2002). Levels of processing. Past, present . . . and future? *Memory*, 10, 305–18.

Craik, F. I. M. and Brown, S. C. (2000). Memory. Coding processes. In A. E. Kazdin (ed), *Encyclopedia of Psychology* (Vol 5, pp 162–6). Washington, DC. American Psychological Association.

Craik, F. I. M. and Lockhart, R. S. (1972). Levels of processing. A framework for memory research. *Journal of Verbal Learning and Verbal Behavior*, 11, 671–84.

Craik, F. I. M. and Lockhart, R. S. (2009). Levels of processing and Zinchenko's approach to memory research. *Cultural-Historical Psychology*, 2, 14–18.

Craik, F. I. M. and Tulving, E. (1975) Depth of processing and retention of words in episodic memory. *Journal of Experimental Psychology*, 104, 268–94.

Crandall, C. S., Eshleman, A., and O'Brien, L. (2002). Social norms and the expression and suppression of prejudice. The struggle for internalization. *Journal of Personality and Social Psychology*, 82(3), 359.

Crano, W. D. and Prislin, R. (2006). Attitudes and persuasion. *Annual Review of Psychology*, 57, 345–74.

Craske, M. G. (2003). *Origins of Phobias and Anxiety Disorders. Why More Women than Men?* Oxford, UK. Elsevier.

Craske, M. G., Kircanski, K., Epstein, A., Wittchen, H,-U., Pine, D. S., et al (2010). Panic disorder. A review of DSM-IV panic disorder and proposals for DSM-V. *Depression and Anxiety*, 27, 93–112.

Craske, M. G. and Waters, A. M. (2005). Panic disorder, phobias, and generalized anxiety disorder. *Annual Review of Clinical Psychology*, 1, 197–225.

Cray, L., Woods, N. F., and Mitchell, E. S. (2010). *Menopause. The Journal of The North American Menopause Society*, 17, 972–7.

Cregger, M. E. and Rogers, W. A. (1998). Memory for activities for young, young-old, and old adults. *Experimental Aging Research*, 24, 195–201.

Crews, F. C. (1996). The verdict on Freud. *Psychological Science*, 7, 63–7.

Crews, F. C. (1995). *Memory Wars. Freud's Legacy in Dispute.* New York, NY. New York Review of Books.

Crews, F. C. (2007). *Follies of the Wise. Dissenting Essays.* Emeryville, CA. Shoemaker and Hoard.

Crews, F. C. (2017). *Freud. The Making of an Illusion.* Profile Books.

Crick, F. C. and Koch, C. (2007). A neurobiological framework for consciousness. In M. Velmans and S. Schneider (eds), *The Blackwell Companion to Consciousness* (pp 567–79). Malden, MA. Blackwell Publishing.

Critser, G. (2003). *Fat Land. How Americans became the Fattest People in the World.* Boston, MA. Houghton Mifflin Company.

Crocker, J. and Park, L. E. (2004). The costly pursuit of self-esteem. *Psychological Bulletin*, 130, 392–414.

Cross, E. M. and Burke, D. M. (2004). Do alternative names block young and older adults' retrieval of proper names? *Brain and Language*, 89, 174–81.

Cross-Disorder Group of the Psychiatric Genomics Consortium (2013). Identification of risk loci with shared effects on five major psychiatric disorders. A genome-wide analysis. *The Lancet.* Retrieved from http://proxy.library.upenn.edu:2135/science/article/pii/S0140673612621291 on 17 March 2013.

Crouter, A. C. and Booth, A. (eds) (2006). *Romance and Sex in Adolescence and Emerging Adulthood. Risks and Opportunities.* Mahwah, NJ. Lawrence Erlbaum Associates.

Crowder, R. G. (1993). Short-term memory. Where do we stand? *Memory and Cognition*, 21, 142–5.

Csikszentmihályi, M. (1990). The domain of creativity. In M. A. Runco and R. S. Albert (eds), *Theories of Creativity* (pp 190–212). Thousand Oaks, CA. Sage Publications.

Csikszentmihalyi, M., Abuhamdeh, S., and Nakamura J. (2005). Flow. In A. J. Elliot and C. S. Dweck (eds), *Handbook of Competence and Motivation* (pp 598–698). New York, NY. Guilford Publications.

Csikszentmihalyi, M., Abuhamdeh, S., and Nakamura, J. (2014). Flow. In *Flow and the Foundations of Positive Psychology* (pp 227–38). Springer, Dordrecht.

Cubed, M. (2002). *The National Economic Impacts of the Child Care Sector*. National Child Care Association. Retrieved from www.nccanet.org on 3 April 2006.

Cuddy, A. J. C., Fiske, S., and Glick, P. (2007). The BIAS map. Behaviors from inter-group affect and stereotypes. *Journal of Personality and Social Psychology*, 92, 631–48.

Cullen, M. J., Hardison, C. M., and Sackett, P. R. (2004). Using SAT-grade and ability-job performance relationships to test predictions derived from stereotype threat theory. *Journal of Applied Psychology*, 89, 220–30.

Curry, S. J., Mermelstein, R. J., and Sporer, A. K. (2009). Therapy for specific problems. Youth tobacco cessation. *Annual Review of Psychology*, 60, 229–55.

D'Agostino, A. and Limosani, I. (2010). Hypnagogic hallucinations and sleep paralysis. In M. Goswami, S. R. Pandi-Perumal, and M. J. Thorpy (eds), *Narcolepsy. A Clinical Guide* (pp 87–97). Totowa, NJ. Humana Press.

Dabbs, J. M. (2000). *Heroes, Rogues, and Lovers. Testosterone and Behavior*. New York, NY. McGraw Hill.

Dagan, Y. and Doljansky, J. T. (2006). Cognitive performance during sustained wakefulness. A low dose of caffeine is equally effective as modafinil in alleviating the nocturnal cognitive decline. *Chronobiology International*, 23, 973–83.

Dahl, G. and DellaVigna, S. (2008, January). Does movie violence increase violent crime? Presented at the annual meeting of the American Economic Association, New Orleans, LA. Pre-publication version retrieved from http://www.aeaweb.org/ annual_mtg_papers/2008/2008_124.pdf on 14 November 2008.

Dahl, R. E. and Spear, L. P. (eds) (2004). *Adolescent Brain Development. Vulnerabilities and Opportunities*. New York, NY. New York Academy of Sciences.

Dal Cin, S., Gibson, B., Zanna, M. P., Shumate, R., and Fong, G. T. (2007). Smoking in movies, implicit associations of smoking with the self, and intentions to smoke. *Psychological Science*, 18, 559–63.

Dalenberg, C., Loewenstein, R., Spiegel, D., Brewin, C., Lanius, R., et al (2007). Scientific study of the dissociative disorders. *Psychotherapy and Psychosomatics*, 76, 400–1.

Daly, M. and Wilson, M. (1988). *Homicide*. New York, NY. Aldine de Gruyter.

Damasio, A. R. (1994). *Descartes' Error. Emotion, Reason and the Human Brain*. New York, NY. Grosset/Putnam.

Damasio, A. R. (2010). *The Self Comes to Mind. Constructing the Conscious Brain*. New York, NY. Pantheon/Random House.

Danelli, L., Cossu, G., Berlingeri, M., Bottini, G., Sberna, M., et al (2013). Is a lone right hemisphere enough? Neurolinguistic architecture in a case with a very early left hemispherectomy. *Neurocase*, 19(3), 209–31.

Dar-Nimrod, I. and Heine, S. J. (2006). Exposure to scientific theories affects women's math performance. *Science*, 314, 435.

Darbyshire, P. (2014). Character assassination? Response to John Paley, 'social psychology and the compassion deficit'. *Nurse Education Today*, 34(6), 887–9.

Darke, S. and Zador, D. (1996). Fatal heroin 'overdose'. A review. *Addiction*, 91, 1765–72.

Darke, S. and Zador, D. (2000). Heroin-related deaths in New South Wales, Australia, 1992–1996. *Drug and Alcohol Dependence*, 60, 141–50.

Darley, J. M. (1995). Constructive and destructive obedience. A taxonomy of principal–agent relationships. *Journal of Social Issues*, 51, 125–54.

Darley, J. M. and Latané, B. (1968). Bystander intervention in emergencies. Diffusion of responsibility. *Journal of Personality and Social Psychology*, 8, 377–83.

Darwin, C. (1859/2003). *On the Origin of Species*. Edited by Joseph Carroll. Ontario, Canada. Broadview Texts.

Darwin, C. (1871/1874). *The Descent of Man and Selection in Relation to Sex* (2nd edn). London. John Murray. Retrieved from http://darwin-online.org.uk/ converted/pdf/1874_Descent_F944.pdf on 28 January 2013.

Darwin, C. (1877). A biographical sketch of an infant. *Mind*, 2, 285–94.

Darwin, C. J., Turvey, M. T., and Crowder, R. G. (1972). An auditory analogue of the Sperling partial report procedure. Evidence for brief auditory storage. *Cognitive Psychology*, 3, 255–67.

Das, E. H. H., deWit, J. B. F., and Stroebe, W. (2003). Fear appeals motivate acceptance of action recommendations. Evidence for a positive bias in the processing of persuasive messages. *Personality and Social Psychology Bulletin*, 29, 650–64.

David, B. and Turner, J. C. (2001). Majority and minority influence. A single process self-categorization analysis. In C. K. W. De Dreu and N. K. De Vries (eds), *Group Consensus and Minority Influence. Implications for Innovation* (pp 92–121). Malden, MA. Blackwell.

Davidsen, K. A., Harder, S., MacBeth, A., Lundy, J. M., and Gumley, A. (2015). Mother–infant interaction in schizophrenia. Transmitting risk or resilience? A systematic review of the literature. *Social Psychiatry and Psychiatric Epidemiology*, 50(12), 1785–98.

Davidson, R. J., Kabat-Zinn, J., Schumacher, J., Rosenkranz, M., Muller, D., et al (2003). Alterations in brain and immune function produced by mindfulness meditation. *Psychosomatic Medicine*, 65, 564–70.

Davies, A. P. C. and Shackelford, T. K. (2006). An evolutionary perspective on gender similarities and differences. *American Psychologist*, 61, 640–1.

Davies, I. R. L., Sowden, P. T., Jerrett, D. T., Jerrett, T., and Corbett, G. G. (1998). A cross-cultural study of English and Setswanta speakers on a colour triads task. A test of the Sapir-Whorf hypothesis. *British Journal of Psychology*, 89, 1–15.

Davies, M. F. (1997). Belief persistence after evidential discrediting. The impact of generated versus provided explanations on the likelihood of discredited outcomes. *Journal of Experimental Social Psychology*, 33, 561–578.

Davis, N., Gross, J., and Hayne, H. (2008). Defining the boundary of childhood amnesia. *Memory*, 16, 465–44.

Davis, O. S. P., Haworth, C. M. A., and Plomin, R. (2009). Dramatic increase in heritability of cognitive development from early to middle childhood. An 8-year longitudinal study of 8,700 pairs of twins. *Psychological Science*, 20, 1301–8.

Davis, R., Rizwani, W., Banerjee, S., Kovacs, M., Haura, E., et al (2009). Nicotine promotes tumor growth and metastasis in mouse models of lung cancer. *PLoS One*, 4, e7524. Retrieved from www.plosone.org on 8 February 2013.

Dawes, R. M. (1994). *House of Cards*. New York, NY. The Free Press.

Dawes, R. M. (1996). *House of Cards. Psychology and Psychotherapy Built on Myth*. New York, NY. Free Press.

Dawes, R. M. (2001). *Everyday Irrationality. How Pseudoscientists, Lunatics, and the Rest of Us Fail to Think Rationally*. Boulder, CO. Westview Press.

Dawes, R. M., Faust, D., and Meehl, P. E. (1989). Clinical vs. actuarial judgment. *Science*, 243, 1668–74.

Dawkins, R. (1976). *The Selfish Gene*. Oxford, UK. Oxford University Press.

Dawkins, R. (1989). *The Selfish Gene* (rev edn). New York, NY. Oxford University Press.

Dawood, K., Bailey, M. J., and Martin, N. G. (2009). Genetic and environmental influences on sexual orientation. In Y.-K. Kim (ed), *Handbook of Behavior Genetics* (pp 269–79). New York, NY. Springer Science Media.

Dawson, T. L. (2002). New tools, new insights. Kohlberg's moral judgment stages revisited. *International Journal of Behavioral Development*, 26, 154–66.

Day, N. L. and Richardson, G. A. (1993). Cocaine use and crack babies. Science, the media, and miscommunication. *Neurotoxicology and Teratology*, 15, 293–4.

de Graaf, H. and Rademakers, J. (2006). Sexual development of prepubertal children. *Journal of Psychology and Human Sexuality*, 18, 1–21.

de Waal, F. B. M. (2008). Putting the altruism back into altruism. The evolution of empathy. *Annual Review of Psychology*, 59, 279–300.

Deacon, B. J. and Baird, G. L. (2009). The chemical imbalance explanation of depression. Reducing blame at what cost? *Journal of Social and Clinical Psychology*, 28, 415–35.

Dean, G. (1987). Does astrology need to be true? Part 2. *Skeptical Inquirer*, 11, 257–73.

Dean, G., Mather, A., and Kelly, I. W. (eds). (1996). Astrology. In *The Encyclopedia of the Paranormal* (pp 47–99). Amherst, NY. Prometheus Books.

DeAngelis, C. D. and Fontanarosa, P. B. (2008). The adverse effects of industry influence. *JAMA*, 299, 1833–5.

Deary, I. J. (2012). Intelligence. *Annual Review of Psychology*, 63, 453–82.

Deary, I. J., Batty, D. G., Pattie, A., and Gale, C. R. (2008). More intelligent more dependable children live longer. A 55-year longitudinal study of a representative sample of the Scottish Nation. *Psychological Science*, 19, 831–7.

Deary, I. J., Penke, L., and Johnson, W. (2010). The neuroscience of human intelligence differences. *Nature Reviews Neuroscience*, 11, 201–11.

Deary, I. J., Strand, S., Smith, P., and Fernandes, C. (2007). Intelligence and educational achievement. *Intelligence*, 35, 13–21.

Deary, I. J., Weiss, A., and Batty, G. D. (2010). Intelligence, personality, and health outcomes. *Psychological Science in the Public Interest*, 11, 53–79.

Deary, I. J., Whiteman, M. C., Whalley, L. J., Fox, H. C., and Starr, J. M. (2004). The impact of childhood intelligence on later life. Following up the Scottish mental surveys of 1932 and 1947. *Journal of Personality and Social Psychology*, 86(1), 130–47.

DeCasper, A. J. and Spence, M. J. (1986). Prenatal maternal speech influences newborns' perception of speech sounds. *Infant Behavior and Development*, 9, 133–50.

Decety, J. and Jackson, P. L. (2006). A social-neuroscience perspective on empathy. *Current Directions in Psychological Science*, 15, 54–8.

Decety, J., Michalska, J. L., and Akitsuki, Y. (2008). What caused the pain? An fMRI investigation of empathy and intentionality in children. *Neuropsychologia*, 46, 2607–14.

Decety, J., Michalska, K., and Akitsuki, Y. (2008). Who caused the pain? An fMRI investigation of empathy and intentionality in children. *Neuropsychologia*, 46, 2607–14.

Deci, E. L. (1975). *Intrinsic Motivation*. New York, NY. Plenum.

Deci, E. L., and Ryan, R. M. (2000). The 'what' and 'why' of goal pursuits. Human needs and the self-determination of behavior. *Psychological Inquiry*, 11, 227–68.

Deepest Desires (2002). In Natasha Bondy (Dir), *Human Instinct* (television documentary series). London. BBC/The Learning Channel.

Degenhardt, L., Hall, W., and Lynskey, M. (2001). The relationship between cannabis use, depression and anxiety among Australian adults. Findings from the national survey of mental health and well-being. *Social Psychiatry and Psychiatric Epidemiology*, 36, 219–27.

Del Vecchio, T. and O'Leary, K. D. (2004). Effectiveness of anger treatments for specific anger problems. A meta-analytic review. *Clinical Psychology Review*, 24(1), 15–34.

Delgado, P. L. (2000). Depression. The case for a monoamine deficiency. *Journal of Clinical Psychiatry*, 61(Suppl 6), 7–10.

Dement, W. C. and Kleitman, N. (1957). The relation of eye movements during sleep to dream activity. An objective method for the study of dreaming. *Journal of Experimental Psychology*, 53, 339–46.

Dennett, D. C. *Consciousness Explained*. (1991). Boston, MA. Little, Brown and Company.

Dennis, W. (1941) Infant development under conditions of restricted practice and of minimum social stimulation. *Genetic Psychology Monographs*, 23, 143–91.

DePaulo, B. M. (2004). The many faces of lies. In A. G. Miller (ed), *The Social Psychology of Good and Evil* (pp 303–26). New York, NY. Guilford Press.

DePaulo, B. M. and Kashy, D. A. (1998). Everyday lies in close and casual relationships. *Journal of Personality and Social Psychology*, 74, 63–79.

DePaulo, B. M., Kashy, D. A., Kirkendol, S. E., Wyer, M. M., and Epstein, J. A. (1996). Lying in everyday life. *Journal of Personality and Social Psychology*, 70, 979–95.

DePaulo, B. M., Lindsay, J. L., Malone, B. E., Muhlenbruck, L., Charlton, K., et al (2003). Cues to deception. *Psychological Bulletin*, 129, 74–118.

DeRubeis, R. J., Hollon, S. D., Amsterdam, J. D., Shelton, R. C., Young, P. R., et al (2005). Cognitive therapy vs. medications in the treatment of moderate to severe depression. *Archives of General Psychiatry*, 62, 409–16.

Deutsch, M. and Gerard, H. B. (1955). A study of normative and informational social influences upon individual judgment. *Journal of Abnormal and Social Psychology*, 51, 629–36.

Devilbiss, D. M. and Berridge, C. W. (2008). Cognition-enhancing doses of methylphenidate preferentially increase prefrontal cortex neuronal responsiveness. *Biological Psychiatry*, 64, 626–35.

Dewa, L. H., Hassan, L., Shaw, J. J., and Senior, J. (2017). Trouble sleeping inside. A cross-sectional study of the prevalence and associated risk factors of insomnia in adult prison populations in England. *Sleep Medicine*, 32, 129–36.

DeWall, C. N. and Anderson, C. A. (2011). The general aggression model. In P. R. Shaver and M. Mikulincer (eds), *Human Aggression and Violence. Causes, Manifestations, and Consequences* (pp 15–33). Washington, DC. American Psychological Association.

DeWall, C. N., MacDonald, G., Webster, G. D., Masten, C. L., Baumeister, R. F., et al (2010). Acetaminophen reduces social pain. Behavioral and neural evidence. *Psychological Science, OnlineFirst*. Retrieved from http://pss.sagepub.com on 30 June 2010.

Dewan, M., Weerasekera, P., and Stormon, L. (2009). Techniques of brief psychodynamic psychotherapy. In G. O. Gabbard (ed), *Textbook of Psychotherapeutic Treatments* (pp 69–96). Arlington, VA. American Psychiatric Publishing.

Di Gennaro, C. and Dutton, W. H. (2007). Reconfiguring friendships. Social relationships and the Internet. *Information, Communication and Society*, 10, 591–618.

Diamond, L. M. (2000a). Sexual identity, attractions, and behavior among young sexual-minority women over a two-year period. *Developmental Psychology*, 36, 241–50.

Diamond, L. M. (2000b). Explaining diversity in the development of same-sex sexuality among young women. *Journal of Social Issues*, 56, 297–313.

Diamond, L. M. (2003). What does sexual orientation orient? A biobehavioral model distinguishing romantic love and sexual desire. *Psychological Review*, 110(1), 173–92.

Diamond, L. M (2004). Emerging perspectives on distinctions between romantic love and sexual desire. *Current Directions in Psychological Science*, 13, 116–19.

Diamond, L. M. (2005). A new view of lesbian subtypes. Stable versus fluid identity trajectories over an 8-year period. *Psychology of Women Quarterly*, 29, 119–28.

Diamond, L. M. (2008). *Sexual Fluidity. Understanding Women's Love and Desire.* Cambridge, MA. Harvard University Press.

Diamond, M. and Sigmundson, K. H. (1999). Sex reassignment at birth. In S. J. Ceci and W. M. Williams (eds), *The Nature-nurture Debate. The Essential Readings. Essential Readings in Developmental Psychology* (pp 55–75). Malden, MA. Blackwell Publishing.

Dick, D. M. (2011). Gene-environment interaction in psychological traits and disorder. *Annual Review of Psychology*, 7, 383–409.

Dickens, C. (1838). *The Adventures of Oliver Twist. A Parish Boy's Progress.* London. Richard Bentley.

Diekman, A. B., Eagly, A. H., and Kulesa, P. (2002). Accuracy and bias in stereotypes about the social and political attitudes of women and men. *Journal of Experimental and Social Psychology*, 38, 268–82.

Diener, E. (2000). Subjective well-being. The science of happiness and a proposal for a national index. *American Psychologist*, 55, 34–43.

Diener, E. (2009). Positive psychology. Past, present and future. In J. S. Lopez and C. R. Snyder (eds), *Oxford Handbook of Positive Psychology* (2nd edn, pp 7–11). New York, NY. Oxford University Press.

Diener, E., Lucas, R. E., and Scollon, C. N. (2006). Beyond the hedonic treadmill. Revising the adaptation theory of well-being. *American Psychologist*, 61, 305–14.

Diener, E., Ng, W., Harter, J., and Arora, R. (2010). Wealth and happiness across the world. Material prosperity predicts life evaluation, whereas psychosocial prosperity predicts positive feeling. *Journal of Personality and Social Psychology*, 99, 52–61.

Diener, E. and Seligman, M. E. P. (2002). Very happy people. *Psychological Science*, 13, 81–4.

Diener, E. and Seligman, M. E. P. (2004). Beyond money. Toward and economy of well-being. *Psychological Science in the Public Interest*, 5(1), 1–31.

Diener, E., Suh, E., Lucas, R. E., and Smith, H. L. (1999). Subjective well-being. Three decades of progress. *Psychological Bulletin*, 125, 276–302.

Diener, E., Tay, L., and Myers, D. G. (2011). The religion paradox. If religion makes people happy, why are so many dropping out? *Journal of Personality and Social Psychology*, 101, 1278–90.

Dietz, P., Jolley, D., Fry, C., and Bammer, G. (2005). Transient changes in behaviour lead to heroin overdose. Results from a case-crossover study of non-fatal overdose. *Addiction*, 100, 636–42.

Diflorio, A. and Jones, I. (2010). Is sex important? Gender differences in bipolar disorder. *International Review of Psychiatry*, 22, 437–42.

DiFranza, J. R., Aligne, C. A., and Weitzman, M. (2004). Prenatal and postnatal environmental tobacco smoke exposure and children's health. *Pediatrics*, 113(4, Suppl), 1007–15.

Dijk, D-J. and Archer, S. N. (2009). Circadian and homeostatic regulation of human sleep and cognitive performance and its modulation by PERIOD 3. *Sleep Medicine Clinics*, 4, 111–25.

Diliberti, N., Bordi, P. L., Conklin, M. T., Roe, L. S., and Rolls, B. J. (2004). Increased portion size leads to increased energy intake in a restaurant meal. *Obesity Review*, 12, 562–8.

Dimberg, U., Thunberg, M., and Elmehed, K. (2000). Unconscious facial reactions to emotional facial expressions. *Psychological Science*, 11(1), 86–9.

Dimidjian, S. and Hollon, S. D. (2010). How would we know if psychotherapy were harmful? *American Psychologist*, 65, 21–33.

Dobbs, D. (2006). A revealing reflection. *Scientific American Mind*, 17, 22–7.

Doghramji, P. P. (2004). Recognizing sleep disorders in a primary care setting. *Journal of Clinical Psychiatry*, 65(Suppl 16), 23–26.

Doherty, R. W., Hatfield, E., Thompson, K., and Choo, P. (1994). Cultural and ethnic influences on love and attachment. *Personal Relationships*, 1, 391–8.

Doliński, D., Grzyb, T., Folwarczny, M., Grzybała, P., Krzyszycha, K., et al (2017). Would you deliver an electric shock in 2015? Obedience in the experimental paradigm developed by Stanley Milgram in the 50 years following the original studies. *Social Psychological and Personality Science*, 8(8), 927–33.

Dollard, J., Doob, L., Miller, N., Mowrer, O., and Sears, R. (1939). *Frustration and Aggression.* New Haven, CT. Yale University Press.

Dollard, J. and Miller, N. (1941). *Social Learning and Imitation.* New Haven, CT. Yale University Press.

Domes, G., Heinrichs, M., Michel, A., Berger, C., and Herpertz, S. C. (2007). Oxytocin improves 'mind-reading' in humans. *Biological Psychiatry*, 61, 731–3.

Domhoff, G. W. (1996). *Finding Meaning in Dreams. A Quantitative Approach.* New York, NY. Plenum Press.

Domhoff, G. W. (2003). *The Scientific Study of Dreams. Neural Networks, Cognitive Development, and Content Analysis.* Washington, DC. American Psychological Association.

Domhoff, G. W. (2010). Dream content is continuous with waking thought, based on preoccupations, concerns, and interests. *Journal of Clinical Sleep Medicine*, 5, 203–15.

Domjan, M. (2002). *Principles of Learning and Behavior* (5th edn). Belmont, CA. Wadsworth.

Domjan, M. (2005). Pavlovian conditioning. A functional perspective. *Annual Review of Psychology*, 56, 179–206.

Domjan, M., Cusato, B., and Krause, M. (2004). Learning with arbitrary versus ecological conditioned stimuli. Evidence from sexual conditioning. *Psychonomic Bulletin and Review*, 11, 232–46.

Donnellan, M. B. and Lucas, R. E. (2008). Age differences in the Big Five across the life span. Evidence from two national samples. *Psychology of Aging*, 23, 558–66.

Doran, G. T. (1981). There's a SMART way to write management's goals and objectives. *Management Review*, 70(11), 35–6.

Dorus, E., Dorus, W., and Rechtschaffen, A. (1971). The incidence of novelty in dreams. *Archives of General Psychiatry*, 25, 364–8.

Doss, B. D., Rhoades, G. K., Stanley, S. M., and Markman, H. M. (2009). The effect of the transition to parenthood on relationship quality. An 8-year prospective study. *Journal of Personality and Social Psychology*, 96, 601–19.

Douglas, I. J., and Smeeth, L. (2008). Exposure to antipsychotics and risk of stroke. Self controlled case series study. *BMJ*, 337. Retrieved from http://www.bmj.com/content/337/bmj.a1227 on 22 December 2008.

Dovidio, J. F. and Gaertner, S. L. (1996). Affirmative action, unintentional racial biases, and intergroup relations. *Journal of Social Issues*, 52(4), 51–75.

Drug Abuse Warning Network (DAWN). (2003a). *Area Profiles of Drug-related Mortality.* U.S. Department of Health and Human Services. Retrieved from http://dawninfo.samhsa.gov/files/ME_report_2003_Front.pdf on 31 January 2006.

Drug Abuse Warning Network (DAWN). (2003b). *Interim National Estimates of Drug-related Emergency Department Visits.* U.S. Department of Health and Human Services. Retrieved from http://dawninfo.samhsa.gov/files/DAWN_ED_Interim2003.pdf on 31 January 2006.

Drug Abuse Warning Network (DAWN). (August, 2003c). *Marijuana-related Emergency Department Visits by Youth. The DAWN Report.* Retrieved from http://dawninfo.samhsa.gov/old_dawn/pubs_94_02/shortreports/files/DAWN_marijuana_tdr.pdf on 15 March 2011.

Drug Abuse Warning Network (DAWN). (2004). *National Estimates of Drug-related Emergency Department Visits.* Rockville, MD. Substance Abuse and Mental Health Services Administration. Retrieved from https://dawninfo.samhsa.gov/files/DAWN2k4ED.htm on 11 November 2006.

Drug Abuse Warning Network (DAWN). (2006). *Emergency Department Visits Involving Dextromethorphan. The New Dawn Report.* Retrieved from https://dawninfo.samhsa.gov/files/TNDR10DXM.htm on 22 November 2006.

Drug Abuse Warning Network (DAWN). (2010). *Drug Abuse Warning Network, 2007. National Estimates of Drug-related Emergency Department Visits.* Rockville, MD. Substance Abuse and Mental Health Services Administration.

du Feu, M. and Fergusson, K. (2003). Sensory impairment and mental health. *Advances in Psychiatric Treatment*, 9, 95–103.

Duan, J., Sanders, A. R., and Gejman, P. V. (2010). Genome-wide approaches to schizophrenia. *Brain Research Bulletin*, 83, 93–102.

Duckworth, A. L. and Seligman, M. E. P. (2005). Self-discipline outdoes IQ in predicting academic performance of adolescents. *Psychological Science*, 16, 939–44.

Duclos, S. E., Laird, J. D., Schneider, E., Sexter, M., Stern, L., et al (1989). Emotion-specific effects of facial expressions and postures on emotional experience. *Journal of Personality and Social Psychology*, 57, 100–8.

Duffy, R. D. and Sedlacek, W. E. (2007). The work values of first year college students. Exploring group differences. *The Career Development Quarterly*, 55, 359–64.

Dufner, M., Gebauer, J. E., Sedikides, C., and Denissen, J. J. (2019). Self-enhancement and psychological adjustment. A meta-analytic review. *Personality and Social Psychology Review*, 23(1), 48–72.

Dugatkin, L. A. (1997). *Cooperation Among Animals. An Evolutionary Perspective.* New York, NY. Oxford University Press.

Dugatkin, L. A. (2006). *The Altruism Equation. Seven Scientists Search for the Origins of Goodness.* Princeton, NJ. Princeton University Press.

Duits, P., Cath, D. C., Lissek, S., Hox, J. J., Hamm, A. O., et al (2015). Updated meta-analysis of classical fear conditioning in the anxiety disorders. *Depression and Anxiety*, 32(4), 239–53.

Dunbar, R. I. (2008). Cognitive constraints on the structure and dynamics of social networks. *Group Dynamics. Theory, Research, and Practice*, 12(1), 7.

Dunlosky, J., Rawson, K. A., Marsh, E. J., Nathan, M. J., and Washington, D. T. (2013). Improving students' learning with effective learning techniques. Promising directions from cognitive and educational psychology. *Psychological Science in the Public Interest*, 14, 1–58.

Dunn, E. V., Aknin, L. B., and Norton, M. I. (2008). Spending money on others promotes happiness. *Science*, 319, 1687–8.

Dunn, J. and Plomin, R. (1990). *Separate Lives. Why Siblings Are so Different.* New York, NY. Basic Books.

Dunne, M. P., Bailey, J. M., Kirk, K. M., and Martin, N. G. (2000). The subtlety of sex-atypicality. *Archives of Sexual Behavior*, 29, 549–65.

Durand, M. V. (2006). Night terrors. In J. E. Fisher, and W. T. O'Donohue (eds), *Practitioner's Guide to Evidence-based Psychotherapy* (pp 654–9). New York, NY. Springer.

Duschinsky, R., Greco, M., and Solomon, J. (2015). The politics of attachment. Lines of flight with Bowlby, Deleuze and Guattari. *Theory, Culture and Society*, 32(7–8), 173–95.

Duster, T. (1972). *The Legislation of Morality. Law, Drugs, and Moral Judgment.* New York, NY. Free Press.

Dwairy, M. (1999). Toward psycho-cultural approach in middle-eastern societies. *Clinical Psychology Review*, 19, 909–15.

Dweck, C. S. (2010). Even geniuses work hard. *Educational Leadership*, 68(1), 16–20.

Dweck, C. S. and Leggett, E. L. (2000). A social-cognitive approach to motivation and personality. In E. T. Higgins and A. W. Kruglanski (eds), Motivational Science.

Social and Personality Perspectives (pp 394–415). Philadelphia, PA. Psychology Press.

Dye, J. L. (2008). *Fertility of American Women. 2006.* Washington, DC. U.S. Census Bureau. Retrieved from www.census.gov on 22 November 2008.

Dykas, M. J. and Cassidy, J. (2011). Attachment and the processing of social information across the life span. Theory and evidence. *Psychological Bulletin,* 137, 19–46.

Eagle, M. N. (1959). The effects of subliminal stimuli of aggressive content upon conscious cognition. *Journal of Personality,* 23, 578–600.

Eagly, A. H. (1995). The science and politics of comparing women and men. *American Psychologist,* 50, 145–58.

Eagly, A. H., Mladinic, A., and Otto, S. (1991). Are women evaluated more favorably than men? An analysis of attitudes, beliefs, and emotions. *Psychology of Women Quarterly,* 15, 203–16.

Eagly, A. H. and Wood, W. (1999). The origins of sex differences in human behavior. Evolved dispositions versus social roles. *American Psychologist,* 54, 408–23.

Eagly, A. H. and Wood, W. (2009). Sexual selection does not provide an adequate theory of sex differences in aggression. *Behavioral and Brain Sciences,* 32, 276–7.

Eaker, E. D., Sullivan, L. M., Kelly-Hayes, M., D'Agostino, R. B., Sr, and Benjamin, E. J. (2004). Anger and hostility predict the development of atrial fibrillation in men in the Framingham Offspring Study. *Circulation,* 109, 1267–71.

Eals, M. and Silverman, I. (1994). The hunter-gatherer theory of spatial sex differences. Proximate factors mediating the female advantage in recall of object arrays. *Ethology and Sociobiology,* 15, 95–105.

Eaton, D. K., Kann, L., Kinchen, S., Ross, J., Hawkins, J., et al (2006). Youth risk behavior surveillance. United States, 2005. *MMWR Surveillance Summaries,* 55, 1–108.

Eaton, W. W., Anthony, J. C., Gallo, J., Cai, G., Tien, A., et al (1997). Natural history of diagnostic interview schedule/DSM-IV major depression. The Baltimore Epidemiologic Catchment Area follow-up. *Archives of General Psychiatry,* 54, 993–9.

Ebbinghaus, D. L. (1964). *Memory. A Contribution to Experimental Psychology.*

New York, NY. Dover. (Original work published 1885.)

Edwards, R. R., Campbell, C., Jamison, R. N., and Wiech, K. (2009). The neurobiological underpinnings of coping with pain. *Current Directions in Psychological Science,* 18, 237–41.

Eich, E. (1989). Theoretical issues in state dependent memory. In H. L. Roediger and F. I. M. Craik (eds), *Varieties of Memory and Consciousness. Essays in Honor of Endel Tulving* (pp 331–54). Hillsdale, NJ. Erlbaum.

Eich, E., Macaulay, D., Loewenstein, R. J., and Dihle, P. H. (1997). Memory, amnesia, and dissociative identity disorder. *Psychological Science,* 8, 157–73.

Eisen, J. L. and Rasmussen, S. A. (1993). Obsessive compulsive disorder with psychotic features. *Journal of Clinical Psychiatry,* 54, 373–9.

Eisenberger, N. I. (2012). Broken hearts and broken bones. A neural perspective on the similarities between social and physical pain. *Current Directions in Psychological Science,* 21, 42–7.

Eisenberger, N. I., Lieberman, M. D., and Williams, K. D. (2003). Does rejection hurt? An fMRI study of social exclusion. *Science,* 302, 290–2.

Ekman, P. (1972). Universals and cultural differences in facial expressions of emotion. In J. Cole (ed), *Nebraska Symposium on Motivation 1971* (Vol 19, pp 207–83). Lincoln, NE. University of Nebraska Press.

Ekman, P. (1994). Strong evidence for universals in facial expressions. A reply to Russell's mistaken critique. *Psychological Bulletin,* 115, 268–87.

Ekman, P. (2003). *Emotions Revealed.* New York, NY. Times Books.

Ekman, P. and Cordaro, D. (2011). What is meant by calling emotions basic. *Emotion Review,* 3, 364–70.

Ekman, P., Davidson, R. J., Ricard, M., and Alan Wallace, B. (2005). Buddhist and psychological perspectives on emotions and well-being. *Current Directions in Psychological Science,* 14, 59–63.

Ekman, P. and Friesen, W. V. (1975). *Unmasking the Face.* Englewood Cliffs, NJ. Prentice-Hall.

Ekman, P. and Friesen, W. V. (1978). *Facial Action Coding System. A Technique for Measurement of Facial Movement.* Palo Alto, CA. Consulting Psychologists Press.

Ekman, P. and Rosenberg, E. L. (eds) (2005). *What the Face Reveals. Basic*

and Applied Studies of Spontaneous Expression Using the Facial Action Coding System. New York, NY. Oxford University Press.

El-Bermawy, M. M. (2016). Your filter bubble is destroying democracy. *Wired,* 18 November.

El-Mallakh, R. S. and Karippot, A. (2005). Antidepressant-associated chronic irritable dysphoria (acid) in bipolar disorder. A case series. *Journal of Affective Disorders Special Issue. Bipolar Depression. Focus on Phenomenology,* 84(2–3), 267–72.

Elbogen, E. B. and Johnson, S. C. (2009). The intricate link between violence and mental disorder. Results from the National Epidemiologic Survey on Alcohol and Related Conditions. *Archives of General Psychiatry,* 66, 152–61.

Elder, G. H. and Clipp, E. C. (1988). Wartime losses and social bonding. Influence across 40 years in men's lives. *Psychiatry,* 51, 177–98.

Elfenbein, H. A. and Ambady, N. (2002). On the universality and cultural specificity of emotion recognition. A meta-analysis. *Psychological Bulletin,* 128, 203–35.

Elfenbein, H. A. and Ambady, N. (2003). Universals and cultural differences in recognizing emotions. *Current Directions in Psychological Science,* 12, 159–64.

Eligion, J. (2009, 7 February). New efforts focus on exonerating prisoners in cases without DNA evidence. *New York Times.* Retrieved from http://www.nytimes.com/2009/02/08/nyregion/08exonerate.html?pagewanted=all&_r=0 on 24 June 2010.

Ellenbogen, J. M., Hu, P. T., Payne, J. D., Titone, D., and Walker, M. P. (2007). Human relational memory requires time and sleep. *Proceedings of the National Academy of Sciences,* 104, 7723–8.

Elliot, A. J. and Church, M. A. (1997). A hierarchal model of approach and avoidance achievement motivation. *Journal of Personality and Social Psychology,* 72, 218–32.

Elliot, A. J. and Dweck, C. S. (2005). Competence and motivation. Competence as the core of achievement motivation. In A. Elliot and C. Dweck (eds), *Handbook of Competence and Motivation* (pp 3–12). New York, NY. Guilford Publications.

Ellis, A. (1957). Outcome of employing three techniques of psychotherapy. *Journal of Consulting and Clinical Psychology,* 13, 344–50.

Ellis, A. (2001). *Overcoming Destructive Beliefs, Feelings, and Behaviors. New*

Directions for Rational-emotive Behavior Therapy. New York, NY. Prometheus.

Ellis, B. J. and Symons, D. (1990). Sex differences in sexual fantasy. An evolutionary psychological approach. *Journal of Sex Research*, 27, 527–55.

Elman, J. L. (2001). Connectionism and language acquisition. In M. Tomasello and E. Bates (eds), *Language Development. The Essential Readings* (pp 295–306). Malden, MA. Blackwell Publishing.

Elman, J. L. (2005). Connectionist models of cognitive development. Where next? *Trends in Cognitive Sciences*, 9, 112–17.

Elms, A. C. and Milgram, S. (1966). Personality characteristics associated with obedience and defiance toward authoritative command. *Journal of Experimental Research in Personality*, 1(4), 282–9.

Elsdon-Baker, F. (2015). Creating creationists. The influence of 'issues framing' on our understanding of public perceptions of clash narratives between evolutionary science and belief. *Public Understanding of Science*, 24(4), 422–39.

Else-Quest, N., Hyde, J., Goldsmith, H., and Van Hulle, C. (2006). Gender differences in temperament. A meta-analysis. *Psychological Bulletin*, 132, 33–72.

ElSohly, M. A. (2001). Drug-facilitated sexual assault. *Southern Medical Journal*, 94, 655–6.

Elston, G. N. (2003). Cortex, cognition and the cell. New insights into the pyramidal neuron and prefrontal function. *Cerebral Cortex*, 13, 1124–38.

Elwin, V. (1968). *The Kingdom of the Young.* Bombay. Oxford University Press.

Emanuele, E., Politi, P., Bianchi, M., Minoretti, P., Bertona, M., et al (2006). Raised plasma nerve growth factor levels associated with early-stage romantic love. *Psychoneuroendocrinology*, 31, 288–94.

Enard, W., Przeworski, M., Fisher, S. E., Lai, C. S., Wiebe, V., et al (2002). Molecular evolution of *FOXP*, a gene involved in speech and language. *Nature*, 418, 869–72.

Endleman, R. (1989). *Love and Sex in Twelve Cultures.* New York, NY. Psyche Press.

Ennis, R. H. (1975). Children's ability to handle Piaget's propositional logic. A conceptual critique. *Review of Educational Research*, 45, 1–41.

Epley, N., Savitsky, K., and Gilovich, T. (2002). Empathy neglect. Reconciling the spotlight effect and the correspondence bias. *Journal of Personality and Social Psychology*, 83, 300–12.

Epstein, S. (1979). The stability of behavior. I. On predicting most of the people much of the time. *Journal of Personality and Social Psychology*, 37, 1097–126.

Epstein, S. (2010). Demystifying intuition. What it is, what it does, and how it does it. *Psychological Inquiry*, 21, 295–312.

Erikson, E. H. (1963). *Childhood and Society* (2nd edn). New York, NY. Norton.

Erikson, E. H. (1968). *Identity. Youth and Crisis.* New York, NY. Norton.

Erikson, E. H. (1982). *The Life Cycle Completed. A Review.* New York, NY. Norton.

Erwin, P. (2013). *Friendship in Childhood and Adolescence.* London, Routledge.

Esch, H. E., Zhang, S., Srinivasan, M. V., and Tautz, J. (2001). Honeybee dances communicate distances measured by optic flow. *Nature*, 411, 581–3.

Eshbaugh, E. M. and Gute, G. (2008). Hookups and sexual regret among college women. *The Journal of Social Psychology*, 148, 77–89.

Eskine, K. J., Kacinik, N. A., and Prinz, J. J. (2011). A bad taste in the mouth. Gustatory disgust influences moral judgment. *Psychological Science*, 22, 295–9.

Espie, C. A. (2002). Insomnia. Conceptual issues in the development persistence, and treatment of sleep disorder in adults. *Annual Review of Psychology*, 53, 215–43.

Espy, A., Fang, H., Johnson, C., Wiebe, S. A., Stopp, C., et al (2011). Prenatal tobacco exposure. Developmental outcomes in the neonatal period. *Developmental Psychology*, 47, 153–69.

Estrada, G., Fatjó-Vilas, M., Muñoz, M. J., Pulido, G., Miñano, M. J., et al (2011). Cannabis use and age at onset of psychosis. Further evidence of interaction with COMT Val158Met polymorphism. *Acta Psychiatrica Scandinavica*, 123(6), 485–92.

European Monitoring Centre for Drugs and Drug Addiction (2003). *Report on the Risk Assessment of PMMA in the Framework of the Joint Action on New Synthetic Drugs.* Lisbon, Portugal. Retrieved from www.emcdda.europa.eu/on 3 February 2006.

Evans, C. S. and Evans, L. (1999). Chicken food calls are functionally referential. *Animal Behaviour*, 58, 307–19.

Evans, D. (2001). *Emotion. The Science of Sentiment.* New York, NY. Oxford University Press.

Evans, D. (2003). *Placebo. The Belief Effect.* London. Harper Collins.

Evans, G. W. and Kantrowitz, E. (2002). Socioeconomic status and health. The potential role of environmental risk exposure. *Annual Review of Public Health*, 23, 303–31.

Evans, N. and Levinson, S. C. (2009). The myth of language universals. Language diversity and its importance for cognitive science. *Behavioral and Brain Sciences*, 32, 429–92.

Evenson, R. J. and Simon, R. W. (2005). Clarifying the relationship between parenthood and depression. *Journal of Health and Social Behavior*, 46, 341–58.

Exechieli, E. (2003). Beyond sustainable development. Education for gross national happiness in Bhutan (Master's thesis). Retrieved on 14 September 2009, from http://www.stanford.edu/dept/SUSE/ICE/monograph

Exner, J. E. (2003). *The Rorschach. A Comprehensive System. Vol 1. Basic Foundations and Principles Of Interpretation* (4th edn). Hoboken, NJ. Wiley.

Eyler, F. D., Behnke, M., Garvan, C. W., Woods, N. S., Wobie, K., et al (2001). Newborn evaluations of toxicity and withdrawal related to prenatal cocaine exposure. *Neurotoxicology and Teratology*, 23, 399–411.

Eysenck, H. J. (1958). A short questionnaire for the measurement of two dimensions of personality. *Journal of Applied Psychology*, 42, 14–17.

Eysenck, H. J. and Nias, D. K. B. (1982). *Astrology. Science or Superstition?* London. Penguin Books.

Eysenck, H. J. and Wilson, G. D. (1973). *The Experimental Study of Freudian Theories.* London. Methuen.

Eysenck, S. B. G. and Eysenck, H. J. (1963). The validity of questionnaire and rating assessments of extraversion and neuroticism, and their factorial stability. *British Journal of Psychology*, 54, 51–62.

Ezzati, M. and Lopez, A. D. (2003). Estimates of global mortality attributable to smoking in 2000. *Lancet*, 362, 847–52.

Faraone, S. V. (2004). Genetics of adult attention-deficit/hyperactivity disorder. *Psychiatric Clinics of North America*, 27, 303–21.

Farrell, J. (1996). *Freud's Paranoid Quest.* New York, NY. New York University Press.

Farthing, G. W. (1992). *The Psychology of Consciousness*. Englewood Cliffs, NJ. Prentice Hall.

Faust, D. (2007). Decision research can increase the accuracy of clinical judgment and thereby improve patient care. In S. O. Lilienfeld and W. T. O'Donohue (eds), *The Great Ideas of Clinical Science. 17 Principles that Every Mental Health Professional Should Understand* (pp 49–76). New York, NY. Routledge.

Fausto-Sterling, A. (2000). *Sexing the Body*. New York, NY. Basic Books.

Feagin, J. R. (2006). *Systemic Racism. A Theory of Oppression*. New York, NY. Routledge.

Federal Drug Administration (2011). Executive summary prepared for the January 27–28, 2011 meeting of the Neurological Devices Panel to discuss the classification of electroconvulsive therapy devices (ECT). Retrieved from www.fda.gov on 6 April 2011.

Fehr, R., Glefand, M. J., and Nag, M. (2010). The road to forgiveness. A meta-analytic synthesis of its situational and dispositional correlates. *Psychological Bulletin*, 136, 894–914.

Fein, S. (2001). Beyond the fundamental attribution era? *Psychological Inquiry*, 12, 16–46.

Feingold, A. (1994). Gender differences in personality. A meta-analysis. *Psychological Bulletin*, 116, 429–56.

Feinstein, J. S., Adolphs, R., Damasio, A., and Tranel, D. (2011). The human amygdala and the induction and experience of fear. *Current Biology*, 21, 34–8.

Feldman, L. A. (1995). Valence focus and arousal focus. Individual differences in the structure of affective experience. *Journal of Personality and Social Psychology*, 69(1), 153–66.

Feldman, R., Weller, A., Zagoory-Sharon, O., and Levine, A. (2007). Evidence for a neuroendocrinological foundation of human affiliation. Plasma oxytocin levels across pregnancy and the postpartum period predict mother–infant bonding. *Psychological Science*, 18, 965–70.

Feng, J., Spence, I., and Pratt, J. (2007). Playing an action video game reduces gender differences in spatial cognition. *Psychological Science*, 18, 850–5.

Ferguson, C. J. (2010). Media violence effects and violent crime. Good science or moral panic? In C. J. Ferguson (ed), *Violent crime. Clinical and Social Implications* (pp 37–56). Thousand Oaks, CA. Sage Publications.

Ferguson, C. J. (2010). A meta-analysis of normal and disordered personality across the life span. *Journal of Personality and Social Psychology*, 98, 659–67.

Ferguson, C. J. and Heene, M. (2012). A vast graveyard of undead theories. Publication bias and psychological science's aversion to the null. *Perspectives on Psychological Science*, 7, 555–61.

Ferguson, C. J. and Kilburn, J. (2010). Much ado about nothing. The misestimation and overinterpretation of violent video game effects in Eastern and Western countries. Comment on Anderson et al (2010). *Psychological Bulletin*, 136, 174–8.

Ferguson, C. J., Rueda, S. M., Cruz, A. M., Ferguson, D. E., Fritz, S., et al (2008). Violent video games and aggression. Causal relationship or byproduct of family violence and intrinsic violence motivation? *Criminal Justice and Behavior*, 35, 311–32.

Ferguson, C. J., San Miguel, C., and Hartley, R. D. (2009). A multivariate analysis of youth violence and aggression. The influence of family, peers, depression, and media violence. *The Journal of Pediatrics*, 155, 904–8.

Fergusson, D. M., Horwood, J. L., and Ridder, E. M. (2005). Show me the child at seven II. Childhood intelligence and later outcomes in adolescence and young adulthood. *Journal of Child Psychology and Psychiatry*, 46, 850–8.

Fernald, A. (2004). Auditory development in infancy. In G. Beemner and A. Fogel (eds), *Blackwell Handbook of Infant Development* (pp 35–70). Malden, MA. Blackwell Publishing.

Ferrari, P. F., Rozzi, S., and Fogassi, L. (2005). Mirror neurons responding to observation of actions made with tools in monkey ventral premotor cortex. *Journal of Cognitive Neuroscience*, 17, 212–26.

Ferrari, P. F., Visalberghi, E., Paukner, A., Fogassi, L., Ruggiero, A., et al (2006). Neonatal imitation in rhesus macaques. *PLoS Biology*, 9. Retrieved from www.plosbiology.org on 11 September 2006.

Ferreira, M. P. and Willoughby, D. (2008). Alcohol consumption. The good, the bad, and the indifferent. *Applied Physiology, Nutrition, and Metabolism*, 33, 12–20.

Ferri, C. P., Prince, M., Brayne, C., Brodaty, H., Fratiglioni, L., et al (2005). Global prevalence of dementia. A Delphi consensus study. *Lancet*, 366, 2112–17.

Ferrie, J. E., Shipley, M. J., Cappuccio, F. P., Brunner, E., Miller, M. A., et al (2007).

A prospective study of change in sleep duration. Associations with mortality in the Whitehall II cohort. *Sleep. Journal of Sleep and Sleep Disorders Research*, 30, 1659–66.

Festinger, L. (1954). A theory of social comparison processes. *Human Relations*, 7, 117–40.

Festinger, L. (1957). *A Theory of Cognitive Dissonance*. Stanford, CA. Stanford University Press.

Festinger, L., Schacter, S., and Back, K. (1950). *Social Pressures in Informal Groups. A Study of Human Factors in Housing*. Palo Alto, CA. Stanford University Press.

Fieder, M. and Huber, S. (2007). Parental age difference and offspring count in humans. *Biology Letters*. Retrieved from www.journals.royalsoc.ac.uk on 3 September 2007.

Fiedler, K. and Bluemke, M. (2005). Faking the IAT. Aided and unaided response control on the implicit association tests. *Basic and Applied Social Psychology*, 27, 307–16.

Field, E. F. and Pellis, S. M. (2008). The brain as the engine of sex differences in the organization of movement in rats. *Archives of Sexual Behavior*, 37, 30–42.

Field, T. (2009). Exercise. In T. Field (ed), *Complementary and Alternative Therapies Research* (pp 73–9). Washington, DC. American Psychological Association.

Field, T. M. (2001). *Touch*. Cambridge, MA. MIT Press.

Field, T. M., Woodson, R., Greenberg, R., and Cohen, D. (1982). Discrimination and imitation of facial expressions by neonates. *Science*, 218, 179–81.

Field, T. M., Woodson, R. W., Greenberg, R., and Cohen, C. (1982). Discrimination and imitation of facial expressions by neonates. *Science*, 218, 179–81.

Fincham, F. D., Hall, J., and Beech, S. R. H. (2006). Forgiveness in marriage. Current status and future directions. *Family Relations*, 55, 415–47.

Fine, C. (2010). From scanner to sound bite. Issues in interpreting and reporting sex differences in the brain. *Current Directions in Psychological Science*, 22, 417–28.

Fineberg, N. A., Sharma, P., Sivakumaran, T., Sahakian, B., and Chamberlain, S. (2007). Does obsessive-compulsive personality disorder belong within the obsessive-compulsive spectrum? *CNS Spectrums*, 12, 467–75, 477–82.

Finer, L. B. (2007). Trends in premarital sex in the United States, 1954–2003. *Public Health Reports*, 122, 73–122.

Finger, S. (1994). History of neuropsychology. In D. Zaidel (ed), *Neuropsychology* (pp 1–28). San Diego, CA. Academic Press.

Fink, B., Neave, N., Manning, J., and Grammer, K. (2006). Facial symmetry and judgements of attractiveness, health and personality. *Personality and Individual Differences*, 41, 491–9.

Fink, M. and Taylor, M. A. (2007). Electroconvulsive therapy. Evidence and challenges. *JAMA*, 298, 330–2.

Finke, J. (2003). The traditional music and cultures of Kenya. Retrieved from http://www.bluegecko.org/kenya/on 2 June 2007.

Finkel, E. J., Eastwick, P. W., Karney, B. R., Reis, H. T., and Sprecher, S. (2012). Online dating. A critical analysis from the perspective of psychological science. *Psychological Science in the Public Interest*, 13, 3–66.

Finkelstein, E. A., Fiebelkorn, I. C., and Wang, G. (2003). National medical spending attributable to overweight and obesity. How much, and who's paying. *Health Affairs*, 3, 219–26.

Finkelstein, E. A. and Zuckerman, L. (2008). *The Fattening of America. How the Economy Makes Us Fat, if it Matters, and What to Do About it*. Hoboken, NJ. John Wiley and Sons.

First, M. B., Reed, G. M., Hyman, S. E., and Saxena, S. (2015). The development of the ICD-11 clinical descriptions and diagnostic guidelines for mental and behavioural disorders. *World Psychiatry*, 14(1), 82–90.

Fischer, K. W. and Bidell, T. R. (1998). Dynamic development of psychological structures in action and thought. In R. M. Lerner (ed), *Handbook of Child Psychology. Vol 1. Theoretical Models of Human Development* (5th edn, pp 467–561). Hoboken, NJ. John Wiley and Sons.

Fischer, P., Greitemeyer, T., and Frey, D. (2007). Ego depletion and positive illusions. Does the construction of positivity require regulatory resources? *Personality and Social Psychology Bulletin*, 33, 1306–21.

Fischer, P., Krueger, J. I., Greitmeyer, T., Vogrincic, C., Kastenmüller, A., et al (2011). The bystander effect. A meta-analytic review on bystander intervention in dangerous and non-dangerous emergencies. *Psychological Bulletin*, 137, 517–37.

Fisher, H. (2004). *Why We Love. The Nature and Chemistry of Romantic Love*. New York, NY. Henry Holt and Company.

Fisher, L., Ames, E. W., Chisholm, K., and Savoie, L. (1997). Problems reported by parents of Romanian orphans adopted to British Columbia. *International Journal of Behavioral Development*, 20(1), 67–82.

Fisher, R. A. (1925). *Statistical Methods for Research Workers*. Edinburgh, UK. Oliver and Boyd.

Fisher, S. and Greenberg, R. (1996). *Freud Scientifically Appraised*. New York, NY. John Wiley and Sons.

Fisk, J. E. and Montgomery, C. (2008). Real-world memory and executive processes in cannabis users and non-users. *Journal of Psychopharmacology*, 22, 727–36.

Fiske, S. (2004). What we know now about bias and intergroup conflict, the problem of the century. In J. B. Ruscher and E. Y. Hammer (eds), *Current Directions in Social Psychology* (pp 124–31). Upper Saddle River, NJ. Pearson.

Fiske, S. T., Cuddy, A. J., Glick, P., and Xu, J. (2002). A model of (often mixed) stereotype content. Competence and warmth respectively follow from perceived status and competition. *Journal of Personality and Social Psychology*, 49, 65–85.

Fiske, S. T., Harris, L., and Cuddy, A. J. C. (2004). Why ordinary people torture enemy prisoners. *Science*, 306, 1482–3.

Fiske, S. T. and Neuberg, S. L. (1990). A continuum model of impression formation from category-based to individuating processes. Influences of information and motivation on attention and interpretation. In M. P. Zanna (ed), *Advances in Experimental Social Psychology* (Vol 3, pp 1–74). San Diego, CA. Academic Press.

Fiske, S. T. and Yamamoto, M. (2005). Coping with rejection. Core social motives across cultures. In K. D. Williams, J. P. Forgas, and W. von Hippel (eds), *The Social Outcast. Ostracism, Social Exclusion, Rejection, and Bullying* (pp 185–98). New York, NY. Psychology Press.

Flanagan, K. S., Vanden Hoek, K. K., Ranter, J. M., and Reich, H. A. (2012). The potential of forgiveness as a response for coping with negative peer experiences. *Journal of Adolescence*, 35, 1215–23.

Flavell, J. H. (1996). Piaget's legacy. *Psychological Science*, 7, 200–3.

Flavell, J. H., Miller, P. H., and Miller, S. A. (1993). *Cognitive Development*. Englewood Cliffs, NJ. Prentice-Hall.

Flaxman, S., Goel, S., and Rao, J. M. (2016). Filter bubbles, echo chambers, and online news consumption. *Public Opinion Quarterly*, 80(S1), 298–320.

Fleeson, W. (2004). Moving personality beyond the person-situation debate. The challenge and the opportunity of within-person variability. *Current Directions in Psychological Science*, 13, 83–7.

Fleishman, D. A., Wilson, R. S., Gabrieli, J. D. E., Bienias, J. L., and Bennett, D. A. (2004). A longitudinal study of implicit and explicit memory in old persons. *Psychology and Aging*, 19, 617–25.

Flieller, A. (1999). Comparison of the development of formal thought in adolescent cohorts aged 10 to 15 years (1967–1996 and 1972–1993). *Developmental Psychology*, 35, 1048–58.

Floyd, R. L., O'Connor, M. J., Sokol, R. J., Bertrand, J., and Cordero, J. F. (2005). Recognition and prevention of fetal alcohol syndrome. *Obstetrics and Gynecology*, 106, 1059–64.

Flynn, J. R. (2009). Requiem for nutrition as the cause of IQ gains. Raven's gains in Britain 1938–2008. *Economics and Human Biology*, 7(1), 18–27.

Foa, E. B. and Kozak, M. J. (1986). Emotional processing of fear. Exposure to corrective information. *Psychological Bulletin*, 99, 20–35.

Fodor, J. A. (1968). *Psychological Explanation. An Introduction to the Philosophy of Psychology*. New York, NY. Random House.

Fodor, J. A. (1983). *The Modularity of Mind. An Essay on Faculty Psychology*. Cambridge, MA. MIT Press.

Fogassi, L., Ferrari, P. F., Gesierich, B., Rozzi, S., Cherisi, F., et al (2005). Parietal lobe. From action organization to intention understanding. *Science*, 308, 662–7.

Folkman, S. and Moskowitz, J. T. (2004). Coping. Pitfalls and promise. *Annual Review of Psychology*, 55, 745–74.

Ford, C. S. and Beach, F. A. (1951). *Patterns of Sexual Behavior*. New York, NY. Harper and Paul B. Hoeber.

Foree, D. D. and LoLordo, V. M. (1973). Attention in the pigeon. Differential effects of food-getting versus shock-avoidance procedures. *Journal of Comparative and Physiological Psychology*, 85, 551–8.

Forgas, J. P., Williams, K. D., and Laham, S. M. (eds) (2005). *Social Motivation. Conscious and Unconscious Processes*. New York, NY. Cambridge University Press.

Forster, B. and Corballis, M. C. (2000). Interhemispheric transfer of colour and shape information in the presence and absence of the corpus callosum. *Neuropsychologia*, 38(1), 32–45.

Fosse, R., Stickgold, R., and Hobson, J. A. (2004). Thinking and hallucinating. Reciprocal changes in sleep. *Psychophysiology*, 41, 298–305.

Foulkes, D. (1962). Dream reports from different stages of sleep. *Journal of Abnormal and Social Psychology*, 65, 14–25.

Fountoulakis K. N. and Möller H. J. (2011). Efficacy of antidepressants. A reanalysis and re-interpretation of the Kirsch data. *International Journal of Neuropsychopharmacology*, 14, 405–12.

Fournier, J. C., DeRubeis, R. J., Hollon, D. D., Dimidjian, S., Amsterdam, J. D., et al (2010). Antidepressant drug effects and depression severity. A patient level meta-analysis. *JAMA*, 303, 47–53.

Fox, A. (2011). The origins of drunkenness. In A. Fox, and M. MacAvoy (eds), *Expressions of Drunkenness (Four Hundred Rabbits)* (pp 53–119). New York, NY. Routledge/Taylor and Francis Group.

Fox, A. and MacAvoy, M. (eds) (2011). *Expressions of Drunkenness (Four Hundred Rabbits)*. New York, NY. Routledge/Taylor and Francis Group.

Fox, N. A., Hane, A. A., and Pine, D. S. (2007). Plasticity for affective neuro-circuitry. How the environment affects gene expression. *Current Directions in Psychological Science*, 16, 1–5.

France, C. M., Lysaker, P. H., and Robinson, R. P. (2007). The 'chemical imbalance' explanation for depression. Origins, lay endorsement, and clinical implications. *Professional Psychology. Research and Practice*, 38, 411–20.

Francis, A. J. and Widiger, T. (2012). Psychiatric diagnosis. Lessons from the DSM-IV past and cautions for the DSM-5 future. *Annual Review of Clinical Psychology*, 8, 109–30.

Frank, D. A., Augustyn, M., Knight, W., Pell, T., and Zuckerman, B. (2001). Growth, development, and behavior in early childhood following prenatal cocaine exposure. A systematic review. *JAMA*, 285, 1613–25.

Frank, D. A., Rose-Jacobs, R., Beeghly, M., Wilbur, M., Bellinger, D., et al (2005). Level of prenatal cocaine exposure and 48-month IQ. Importance of preschool enrichment. *Neurotoxicology and Teratology*, 27(1), 15–28.

Frank, J. D. and Frank, J. B. (1991). *Persuasion and Healing. A Comparative Study of Psychotherapy* (3rd edn). Baltimore, MD. Johns Hopkins University Press.

Frank, R. (1999). *Luxury Fever*. Princeton, NJ. Princeton University Press.

Frayser, S. (1985). *Varieties of Sexual Experience*. New Haven, CT. HRAF.

Frayser, S. G. (1994). Defining normal childhood sexuality. An anthropological approach. *Annual Review of Sex Research*, 5, 173–217.

Freedman, J. L. (2002). *Media Violence and its Effects on Aggression*. Toronto. University of Toronto Press.

Freedman, M. L. and Martin, R. C. (2001). Dissociable components of short-term memory and their relation to long-term learning. *Cognitive Neuropsychology*, 18, 193–226.

Freedman, N. D., Park, Y., Abnet, C. C., Hollenbeck, A. R., and Sinha, R. (2012). Association of coffee drinking with total and cause-specific mortality. *New England Journal of Medicine*, 366, 1891–1904.

Freedman, S. and Enright, R. D. (1996). Forgiveness as an intervention goal with incest survivors. *Journal of Consulting and Clinical Psychology*, 64, 938–92.

Freeman, C. E. (2005). *Trends in Educational Equity for Girls and Women. 2004.* (NCES 2005–016). Washington, DC. U.S. Government Printing Office.

Freemantle, N., Anderson, I. M., and Young, P. (2000). Predictive value of pharmacological activity for the relative efficacy of antidepressant drugs. Meta-regression analysis. *British Journal of Psychiatry*, 177, 292–302.

French, S. E. and Chavez, N. R. (2010). The relationship of ethnicity-related stressors and Latino ethnic identity and well-being. *Hispanic Journal of Behavioral Sciences*, 32, 410–28.

Frenda, S. J., Nichols, R. M., and Loftus, E. F. (2011). Current issues and advances in misinformation research. *Current Directions in Psychological Science*, 20, 20–3.

Freud, A. (1966). *The Ego and Mechanisms of Defense*. New York, NY. International Universities Press. (Original work published 1936.)

Freud, S. (1900). *The Interpretation of Dreams*. London. Hogarth Press.

Freud, S. (1905). *Three Essays on Sexuality*. London. Hogarth Press.

Freud, S. (1914). *The Psychopathology of Everyday Life*. London. Hogarth Press.

Freud, S. (1918). From the History of Infantile Neuroses (Wolf Man). In P. Gay (ed), *The Freud Reader*. London. Vintage Classics.

Freud, S. (1962). *The Ego and the Id*. New York, NY. Norton. (Original work published 1923.)

Freud, S. (1991). Some psychical consequences of the anatomical differences between the sexes. In A. Richards (ed), *Penguin Freud Library, Vol 7. On Sexuality* (pp 323–43). Harmondsworth, UK. Penguin.

Freud, S. and Breuer, J. (1895). *Studien über hysterie* (pp 75–312). Leipzig, Germany/Vienna, Austria. Deuticke.

Freund, A. M. and Blanchard-Fields, F. (2014). Age-related differences in altruism across adulthood. Making personal financial gain versus contributing to the public good. *Developmental Psychology*, 50(4), 1125.

Freund, K. (1974). Male homosexuality. An analysis of the pattern. In J. L. A. Loraine (ed), *Understanding Homosexuality. Its Biological and Psychological Bases*. New York, NY. Elsevier.

Frick, A. and Johnston, D. (2005). Plasticity of dendritic excitability. *Journal of Neurobiology*, 65, 100–15.

Fried, I., Mukamel, R., and Kreiman, G. (2011). Internally generated preactivation of single neurons in human medial frontal cortex predicts volition. *Neuron*, 69(3), 548–62.

Friedan, T. R. and Blakeman, D. E. (2005). The dirty dozen. 12 myths that undermine tobacco control. *American Journal of Public Health*, 95, 1500–6.

Friedman, H. S. and Miller-Herringer, T. (1991). Nonverbal display of emotion in public and in private. Self-monitoring, personality, and expressive cues. *Journal of Personality and Social Psychology*, 61, 766–75.

Friedman, M. and Ulmer, D. (1984). *Treating Type-A Behavior—and Your Heart*. New York, NY. Knopf.

Friedmann, E., Barker, S., and Allen, K. (2011). Physiological correlates and possible health care savings of pet ownership. In P. McCardles, S. McCune, J. A. Griffin, and Maholmes, V. (eds), *How Animals Affect Us* (pp 163–82). Washington, DC. American Psychological Association.

Friedrich, W. N., Whiteside, S. P., and Talley, N. J. (2004). Noncoercive sexual contact with similarly aged individuals. What is the impact? *Journal of Interpersonal Violence*, 19, 1075–84.

Frieman, J. (2002). *Learning and Adaptive Behavior*. Belmont, CA. Wadsworth.

Fromm-Reichmann, F. (1948). Intensive psychotherapy of manic-depressives. *Stereotactic and Functional Neurosurgery*, 9(3–4), 158–65.

Froufe, M. and Schwartz, C. (2001). Subliminal messages for increasing self-esteem. *The Spanish Journal of Psychology*, 4, 19–25.

Fuertes, M., Santos, P. L. D., Beeghly, M., and Tronick, E. (2006). More than maternal sensitivity shapes attachment. Infant coping and temperament. *Annals of the New York Academy of Sciences*, 1094(1), 292–6.

Fujita, F. and Diener, E. (2005). Life satisfaction set point. Stability and change. *Journal of Personality and Social Psychology*, 88(1), 158–64.

Fukuda, K., Ogilvie, R.D., Chilcott, L., Vendittelli, A.M., and Takeuchie, T. (1998). The prevalence of sleep paralysis among Canadian and Japanese college students. *Dreaming*, 8, 59–66.

Funder, D. C. (2001). Personality. *Annual Review of Psychology*, 52, 197–221.

Funder, D. C. (2001). The really, really fundamental attribution error. *Psychological Inquiry*, 12, 21–3.

Funder, D. C. (2009). Persons, behaviors, and situations. An agenda for personality psychology in the postwar era. *Journal of Research in Personality*, 43, 120–6.

Furman, W. and Buhrmester, D. (1992). Age and sex in perceptions of networks of personal relationships. *Child Development*, 63, 103–15.

Furnham, A., Mistry, D., and McClelland, A. (2004). The influence of age of the face and the waist to hip ratio on judgments of female attractiveness and traits. *Personality and Individual Differences*, 36, 1171–85.

Furnham, A., Rinaldelli-Tabaton, E., and Chamorro-Premuzic, T. (2011). Personality and intelligence predict arts and science school results in 16 year olds. *Psychologia*, 54(1), 39–51.

Furr, R. M. (2009). Profile analysis in person-situation integration. *Journal of Research in Personality*, 43, 196–207.

Furstenberg, F. F., Jr, Kennedy, S., McLoyd, V. C., Rumbaut, R. G., and Settersten, R. A., Jr (2004). Growing up is harder to do. *Contexts*, 3, 33–41.

Gable, R. S. (2004a). Acute toxic effects of club drugs. *Journal of Psychoactive Drugs*, 36(1), 303–13.

Gable, R. S. (2004b). Comparison of acute lethal toxicity of commonly abused psychoactive substances. *Addiction*, 99, 686–96.

Gable, R. S. (2006). Acute toxicity of drugs versus regulatory status. In J. M. Fish (ed), *Drugs and Society. U.S. Public Policy* (pp 149–62). Lanham, MD. Rowman and Littlefield.

Gable, S. L. and Haidt, J. (2005). What (and why) is positive psychology? *Review of General Psychology*, 9, 103–10.

Gabler, S., Bovenschen, I., Lang, K., Zimmermann, J., Nowacki, K., et al (2014). Foster children's attachment security and behavior problems in the first six months of placement. Associations with foster parents' stress and sensitivity. *Attachment and Human Development*, 16(5), 479–98.

Gagné, F. (2010). Motivation within the DMGT 2.0 framework. *High Ability Studies*, 21(2), 81–99.

Gailliot, M. T. and Baumeister, R. F. (2007). Self-esteem, belongingness, and worldview validation. Does belongingness exert a unique influence upon self-esteem? *Journal of Research in Personality*, 41, 327–45.

Gailliot, M. T., Baumeister, R. F., Schmeichel, B. J., DeWall, C. N., Maner, J. K., et al (2007). Self-control relies on glucose as a limited energy source. Willpower is more than a metaphor. *Journal of Personality and Social Psychology*, 92, 325–36.

Gais, S., Lucas, B., and Bom, J. (2006). Sleep after learning aids memory recall. *Learning and Memory*, 13, 259–62.

Galea, L. A. M. and Kimura, D. (1993). Sex differences in route learning. *Personality and Individual Differences*, 14, 53–65.

Galea, S., Brewin, C. R., Gruber, M., Jones, R. T., King, D. W., et al (2007). Exposure to hurricane-related stressors and mental illness after Hurricane Katrina. *Archives of General Psychiatry*, 64, 1427–34.

Gallagher, A., Levin, J., and Cahalan, C. (2002). GRE Research. Cognitive patterns of gender differences in mathematics admissions test. *ETS Report 02–19*. Princeton, NJ. Educational Testing Service.

Gallagher, M. W. and Lopez, S. J. (2009, May). Optimism is universal? Exploring demographic predictors of optimism in a representative sample of the world. Poster presented at the 21st annual convention of the Association for Psychological Science, San Francisco, CA.

Gallese, V. (2001). The 'shared manifold' hypothesis. From mirror neurons to empathy. *Journal of Consciousness Studies*, 8(5–6), 33–50.

Gallese, V. (2005). 'Being like me'. Self-other identity, mirror neurons, and empathy. In S. Hurley and N. Chater (eds), *Perspectives on Imitation. From Neuroscience to Social Science. Vol 1. Mechanisms of Imitation and Imitation in Animals* (pp 101–18). Cambridge, MA. MIT Press.

Gallese, V., Gernsbacher, M. A., Heyes, C., Hickok, G., and Iacoboni, M. (2011). Mirror neuron forum. *Perspectives on Psychological Science*, 6, 369–407.

Gallistel, C. R. (2000) The replacement of general-purpose learning models with adaptively specialized learning modules. In M. S. Gazzaniga (ed), *The New Cognitive Neurosciences* (pp 1179–91). Cambridge, MA. MIT Press.

Gallup Poll (2009, 11 February). On Darwin's birthday, only 4 in 10 believe in evolution. Retrieved from http://www.gallup.com/poll on 4 March 2011.

Gallup Poll (2010, 30 July). U.S. drinking rate edges up slightly to 25-year high. Retrieved from www.gallup.com on 16 March 2011.

Gallup, G. G., Jr and Frederick, D. A. (2010). The science of sex appeal. An evolutionary perspective. *Review of General Psychology*, 14, 240–50.

Gami, A. S., Howard, D. E., Olson, E. J., and Somers, V. K. (2005). Day-night pattern of sudden death in obstructive sleep apnea. *New England Journal of Medicine*, 352, 1206–14.

Gana, K., Alaphilippe, D., and Bailly, N. (2004). Positive illusions and mental and physical health in later life. *Aging and Mental Health*, 8, 58–64.

Gandhi, B. and Oakley, D. A. (2005). Does 'hypnosis' by any other name smell as sweet? The efficacy of 'hypnotic' inductions depends on the label 'hypnosis'. *Consciousness and Cognition*, 14, 304–15.

Gangestad, S. W. and Scheyd, G. J. (2005). The evolution of human physical attractiveness. *Annual Review of Anthropology*, 34, 523–48.

Gangestad, S. W. and Simpson, J. A. (2000). The evolution of human mating. Trade-offs and strategic pluralism. *Behavioral and Brain Sciences*, 23, 573–644.

Ganis, G., Thompson, W. L., and Kosslyn, S. M. (2004). Brain areas underlying visual mental imagery and visual perception. An fMRI study. *Cognitive Brain Research*, 20, 226–41.

Gansberg, M. (1964, 27 March). 37 who saw murder didn't call the police. *New York Times*. Retrieved from http://select. nytimes.com/gst/abstract.html?res= F10B16FB3A5C147A93C5AB1788D85 F408685F9 on 17 March 2013.

Garb, H. N. (1999). Call for a moratorium on the use of the Rorschach inkblot test in clinical and forensic settings. *Assessment*, 6, 313–17.

Garb, H. N. (2005). Clinical judgment and decision making. *Annual Review of Clinical Psychology*, 55, 3.1–3.23.

Garb, H. N., Florio, C. M., and Grove, W. M. (1998). The validity of the Rorschach and the Minnesota Multiphasic Personality Inventory. Results from meta-analyses. *Psychological Science*, 9, 402–4.

Garb, H. N., Wood, J. M., Lilinfeld, S. O., and Nezworski, M. T. (2005). Roots of the Rorschach controversy. *Clinical Psychology Review*, 25, 97–118.

Garcia, J. (1981). Tilting at the paper mills of Academe. *American Psychologist*, 36, 149–58.

Garcia, J., Brett, L. P., and Rusiniak, K. W. (1989). Limits of Darwinian conditioning. In S. B. Klein and R. R. Mowrer (eds), *Contemporary Learning Theories. Instrumental Conditioning Theory and the Impact of Biological Constraints on Learning* (pp 181–203). Hillsdale, NJ. Lawrence Erlbaum Associates.

Garcia, J. and Koelling, R. A. (1966) Relation of cue to consequence in avoidance learning. *Psychonomic Science*, 4, 123–4.

Gardiner, J. M., Brandt, K. R., Baddeley, A. D., Vargha-Khadem, F., and Mishkin, M. (2008). Charting the acquisition of semantic knowledge in a case of developmental amnesia. *Neuropsychologia*, 46, 2865–8.

Gardner, H. (1983). *Frames of Mind. The Theory of Multiple Intelligences*. New York, NY. Basic Books.

Gardner, H. (2006). *Multiple Intelligences. New Horizons* (rev edn). New York, NY. Basic Books.

Gardner, H. (2008). *A Multiplicity of Intelligences*. In P. Mariën and J. Abutalebi (eds), *Neuropsychological Research. A Review* (pp 17–23). New York, NY. Psychology Press.

Gardner, M. and Steinberg, L. (2005). Peer influence on risk taking, risk preference, and risky decision making in adolescence and adulthood. An experimental study. *Developmental Psychology*, 41, 625–35.

Gardner, R.A. and Gardner, B.T. (1969). Teaching sign language to a chimpanzee. *Science*, 165, 664–72

Gardner, W. L., Pickett, C. L., and Brewer, M. B. (2000). Social exclusion and selective memory. How the need to belong influences memory of social events. *Personality and Social Psychology Bulletin*, 26, 486–96.

Garlipp, P. (2008). Koro—a culture-bound phenomenon. Intracultural psychiatric implications. *German Journal of Psychiatry*. Retrieved from http://www. gjpsy.uni-goettingen.de/ on 17 May 2008.

Garlow, S. J., Purselle, D., and Heninger, M. (2005). Ethnic differences in patterns of suicide across the life cycle. *American Journal of Psychiatry*, 162, 319–23.

Garske, J. P. and Anderson, T. (2003). Toward a science of psychotherapy research. Present status and evaluation. In S. O. Lilienfeld, S. J. Lynn, and J. M. Lohr (eds), *Science and Pseudoscience in Clinical Psychology* (pp 145–75). New York, NY. The Guilford Press.

Gaser, C. and Schlaug, G. (2003). Brain structures differ between musicians and non-musicians. *The Journal of Neuroscience*, 23, 9240–5.

Gatchel, R. J., Peng, Y. B., Peters, M. L., Fuchs, P. N., and Turk, D. C. (2007). The biopsychosocial approach to chronic pain. Scientific advances and future directions. *Psychological Bulletin*, 133, 581–624.

Gawronski, B. (2009). Ten frequently asked questions about implicit measures and their frequently supposed, but not entirely correct answers. *Canadian Psychology*, 50, 141–50.

Gawronski, B., LeBel, E. P., and Peters, K. R. (2007). What do implicit measures tell us? *Perspectives on Psychological Science*, 2, 181–93.

Gay, Peter (ed) (1995). *The Freud Reader*. London. Vintage Classics.

Gazzaniga, M. S. (2005). Forty-five years of split-brain research and still going strong. *Nature Reviews Neuroscience*, 6, 653–9.

Gazzaniga, M. S. (2010). Neuroscience and the correct level of explanation for understanding mind. An extraterrestrial roams through some neuroscience laboratories and concludes earthlings are not grasping how best to understand the mind-brain interface. *Trends in Cognitive Sciences*, 14, 291–2.

Gazzaniga, M. S., Bizzi, E., Chalupa, L. M., Grafton, S. T., Heatherton, T., et al (eds) (2009). *The Cognitive Neurosciences* (4th edn). Cambridge, MA. MIT Press.

Gazzaniga, M. S., Ivry, R. B., and Mangun, G. R. (2002). *Cognitive Neuroscience. The Biology of the Mind* (2nd edn). New York, NY. Norton.

Gazzaniga, M. S., Ivry, R. B., and Mangun, G. R. (2008). *Cognitive Neuroscience. The Biology of the Mind* (3rd edn). New York, NY. Norton.

Gazzaniga, M. S. and Smylie, C. S. (1984). Dissociation of language and cognition. A psychological profile of two disconnected right hemispheres. *Brain*, 107, 145–53.

Ge, X., Donnellan, M. B., and Harper, L. (2003). Are we finally ready to move beyond 'nature vs. nurture'? In A. C. Crouter and A. Booth (eds), *Children's Influence on Family Dynamics* (pp 37–48). Hillsdale, NJ. Lawrence Erlbaum Associates.

Geary, D. C. (2007). An evolutionary perspective on sex differences in mathematics and the sciences. In S. J. Ceci and W. Williams (eds), *Are Sex Differences in Cognition Responsible for the Under-representation of Women in Scientific Careers?* (pp 173–88). Washington, DC. American Psychological Association.

Geary, D. C. (2010). *Male, Female. The Evolution of Human Sex Differences* (2nd edn). Washington, DC. American Psychological Association.

Gebauer, J. E., Sedikides, C., and Neberich, W. (2012). Religiosity, social self-esteem, and psychological adjustment. On the cross-cultural specificity of the psychological benefits of religiosity. *Psychological Science*, 23, 158–60.

Geddes, J. R., Burgess, S., Hawton, K., Jamison, K., and Goodwin, G. M. (2004). Long-term lithium therapy for bipolar disorder. Systematic review and meta-analysis of randomized controlled trials. *American Journal of Psychiatry*, 161, 217–22.

Gelbard-Sagiv, H., Mukamel, R., Harel, M., Malach, R., and Fried, I. (2008). Internally generated reactivation of single neurons in human hippocampus during free recall. *Science*, 322, 96–101.

Gelfand, M. J. and Diener, E. (2010). Culture and psychological science. Introduction to the special section. *Perspectives on Psychological Science*, 5, 390.

Gelman, R. (1972). The nature and development of early number concepts. In H. W. Reese (ed), *Advances in Child Development and Behavior* (pp 115–67). New York, NY. Academic Press.

George, L. K. and Larson, D. B. (2002). Explaining the relationships between religious involvement and health. *Psychological Inquiry*, 13, 190–200.

George, M. S., Lisanby, S. H., Avery, D., McDonald, W. M., Durkalski, V., et al (2010). Daily left prefrontal transcranial magnetic stimulation therapy for major depressive disorder. A sham-controlled randomized trial. *Archives of General Psychiatry*, 67, 507–16.

Geraerts, E., Arnold, M. M., Lindsay, D. S., Merckelbach, H., Jelicic, M., et al (2006). Forgetting of prior remembering in persons reporting recovered memories of childhood sexual abuse. *Psychological Science*, 17, 1002–8.

Geraerts, E., Bernstein, D. M., Merekelbach, H., Linders, C., Raymaerkers, L., et al (2008). Lasting false beliefs and their behavioral consequences. *Psychological Science*, 19, 749–53.

Geraerts, E., Lindsay, D. S., Merckelbach, H., Jelicic, M., Raymaekers, L., et al (2009). Cognitive mechanisms underlying recovered-memory experiences of childhood sexual abuse. *Psychological Science*, 20, 91–8.

Geraerts, E., Schooler, J., Merckelbach, H., Jelicic, M. J., Hauer, B. J. A., et al (2007). The reality of recovered memories. Corroborating continuous and discontinuous memories of childhood sexual abuse. *Psychological Science*, 18, 564–8.

Gershoff, E. T. (2002). Corporal punishment by parents and associated child behaviors and experiences. A meta-analytic and theoretical review. *Psychological Bulletin*, 4, 539–79.

Ghera, M. M., Hane, A. A., Malesa, E. M., and Fox, N. A. (2006). The role of infant soothability in the relation between infant negativity and maternal sensitivity. *Infant Behavior and Development*, 29, 289–93.

Gibbons, R. D., Hendricks, C., Hur, K., Marcus, S. M., Bhaumik, D. K., et al (2007). Relationship between antidepressants and suicide attempts. An analysis of the Veterans Health Administration data sets. *American Journal of Psychiatry*, 164, 1044–9.

Gibson, E. J. (1997). *An Ecological Psychologist's Prolegomena for Perceptual Development. A Functional Approach*. Oxford, UK. Oxford University Press.

Gibson, E. J. and Walk, R. D. (1960). The 'visual cliff'. *Scientific American*, 202, 67–71.

Gibson, J. J. (1950). The perception of visual surfaces. *The American Journal of Psychology*, 63(3), 367–84.

Gibson, J. J. (1978). The ecological approach to the visual perception of pictures. *Leonardo*, 11(3), 227–35.

Gibson, J. J. (1979). *The Ecological Approach to Visual Perception*. Boston, MA.

Gibson, J. J. (2002). A theory of direct visual perception. In A. Noe and E. Thompson (eds.). *Vision and Mind. Selected Readings in the Philosophy of Perception* (pp 77–90). Cambridge, MA. MIT Press.

Giedd, J. N. (2004). Structural magnetic resonance imaging of the adolescent brain. *Annals of the New York Academy of Sciences*, 1021, 77–85.

Giedd, J. N. (2008). The teen brain. Insights from neuroimaging. *Journal of Adolescent Health*, 42, 335–43.

Gigerenzer, G., Gaissmaier, W., Kurz-Mileke, E., Schwartz, L. M., and Woloshin, S. (2008). Helping doctors and patients make sense of health statistics. *Psychological Science in the Public Interest*, 8, 53–96.

Gilbert, D. T. and Malone, P. S. (1995). The correspondence bias. *Psychological Bulletin*, 117, 21–38.

Gilbert, P., McEwan, K., Catarino, F., Baião, R., and Palmeira, L. (2014). Fears of happiness and compassion in relationship with depression, alexithymia, and attachment security in a depressed sample. *British Journal of Clinical Psychology*, 53(2), 228–44.

Gilestro, G. F., Tononi, G., and Cirelli, C. (2009). Widespread changes in synaptic markers as a function of sleep and wakefulness in *drosphila*. *Science*, 324, 109–12.

Gillham, J. Reivich, K., Jaycox, L., and Seligman, M. E. P. (1995). Prevention of depressive symptoms in schoolchildren. Two-year follow-up. *Psychological Science*, 6, 343–51.

Gilovich, T., Griffin, D., and Kahneman, D. (2002). *Heuristics and Biases. The Psychology of Intuitive Judgment*. New York, NY. Cambridge University Press.

Gilovich, T., Medvec, V. H., and Savitsky, K. (1999). The spotlight effect in social judgment. An egocentric bias in estimates of the salience of one's own actions and appearance. *Journal of Personality and Social Psychology*, 78, 211–22.

Gilovich, T. and Savitsky, K. (1999). The spotlight effect and the illusion of transparency. Egocentric assessments of how we are seen by others. *Current Directions in Psychological Science*, 8, 165–8.

Gilovich, T., Vallone, R., and Tversky, A. (1985). The hot hand in basketball. On the misperception of random sequences. *Cognitive Psychology*, 17, 295–314.

Gilpin, E. A., White, M. M., Messer, K., and Pierce, J. P. (2007). Receptivity to tobacco advertising and promotions among young adolescents as a predictor of established smoking in young adulthood. *American Journal of Public Health*, 97, 1489–95.

Giltay, E. J., Geleijnse, J. M., Zitman, F. G., Hoekstra, T., and Shouten, E. (2004). Dispositional optimism and all-cause and cardiovascular mortality in a prospective cohort of elderly Dutch men and women. *Archives of General Psychiatry*, 61(11), 1126–35.

Giner-Sorolla, R. (2012). Science or art? How aesthetic standards grease the way through the publication bottleneck but undermine science. *Perspectives on Psychological Science*, 7, 562–72.

Giroux, M. and Grohmann, B. (2016). Activating multiple facets of the self. Identity-signaling and brand personality. In *Celebrating America's Pastimes. Baseball, Hot Dogs, Apple Pie and Marketing?* (pp 323–4). New York, NY. Springer, Cham.

Giuffra, L. A. and Risch, N. (1994). Diminished recall and the cohort effect of major depression. A simulation study. *Psychological Medicine*, 24, 375–83.

Glanzer, M. and Cunitz, A. R. (1966). Two storage mechanisms in free recall. *Journal of Verbal Learning and Verbal Behavior*, 5, 351–60.

Gleaves, D. H. (1996). The sociocognitive model of dissociative identity disorder. A reexamination of the evidence. *Psychological Bulletin*, 120, 42–59.

Glick, P., Gottesman, D., and Jolton, J. (1989). The fault is not in the stars. Susceptibility of skeptics and believers in astrology to the Barnum effect. *Personality and Social Psychology Bulletin*, 15, 572–83.

Glicksohn, J. (1990). Belief in the paranormal and subjective paranormal experience. *Personality and Individual Differences*, 11, 675–83.

Glickstein, M. (2003). The cerebellum and its disorders. *New England Journal of Medicine*, 348, 180–1.

Gobet, F. (2005). Chunking models of expertise. Implications for education. *Applied Cognitive Psychology*, 19, 183–204.

Gobet, F., Land, P. C. R., Croker, S., Cheng, P. C.-H., Jones, G., et al (2001). Chunking mechanisms in human learning. *Trends in Cognitive Science*, 5, 236–43.

Godden, D. R., and Baddeley, A. D. (1975). Context-dependent memory in two natural environments. On land and underwater. *British Journal of Psychology*, 66, 325–31.

Godfried, M. R. (2003). Cognitive-behavior therapy. Reflections on the evolution of a therapeutic orientation. *Cognitive Therapy and Research*, 27, 53–69.

Goetz, J. L., Keltner, D., and Simon-Thomas, E. (2010). Compassion. An evolutionary analysis and empirical review. *Psychological Bulletin*, 136, 351–74.

Goetz, M. C., Goetz, P. W., and Robinson, M. D. (2007). What's the use of being happy? Mood states, useful objects, and repetition priming effects. *Emotion*, 7, 675–9.

Goff, L. M. and Roediger, H. L. (1998). Imagination inflation for action events. Repeated imaginings leads to illusory recollections. *Memory and Cognition*, 26(1), 20–33.

Goffman, E. (1959). *The Presentation of Self in Everyday Life*. Garden City, NY. Doubleday Anchor.

Goffman, E. (1961). *Asylums*. Garden City, NY. Doubleday.

Gogtay, N., Giedd, J. N., Lusk, L., Hayashi, K. M., Greenstein, D., et al (2004). Dynamic mapping of human cortical development during childhood through early adulthood. *Proceedings of the National Academy of Sciences, USA*, 101, 8174–9.

Goh, J. O. and Park, D. C. (2009). Culture sculpts the perceptual brain. *Progress in Brain Research*, 178, 95–111.

Goh, J. O, Tan, J. C, and Park, D. C. (2009). Culture modulates eye-movements to visual novelty. *PLoS One*, 4, e8238. Retrieved from http://www.plosone.org/article/info%3Adoi%2F10.1371%2Fjournal.pone.0008238 on 31 January 2013.

Goldberg, D., Privett, M., Ustun, B., Simon, G., and Linden, M. (1998). The effects of detection and treatment on the outcome of major depression in primary care. A naturalistic study in 15 cities. *British Journal of General Practice*, 48, 1840–4.

Goldberg, J. E., Harrow, M., and Grossman, L. S. (1995). Course and outcome in bipolar affective disorder. A longitudinal follow-up study. *American Journal of Psychiatry*, 152, 379–84.

Goldberg, L. R. (1990) An alternative description of personality. The big five factor structure. *Journal of Personality and Social Psychology*, 59, 1216–29.

Goldberg, S. (1993). *Why Men Rule. A Theory of Male Dominance*. Chicago, IL. Open Court.

Goldenhagen, D. (1996). *Hitler's Willing Executioners. Ordinary Germans and Holocaust*. New York, NY. Knopf.

Goldman, R. N., Greenberg, L. S., and Angus, L. (2006). The effects of adding emotion-focused interventions to the client-centered relationship conditions in the treatment of depression. *Psychotherapy Research*, 16(5), 537–49.

Goldstein, A. G., Chance, J. E., and Schneller, G. R. (1989). Frequency of eyewitness identification in criminal cases. A survey of prosecutors. *Bulletin of the Psychonomic Society*, 27, 71–4.

Goldstein, E. B. (2005). *Cognitive Psychology. Connecting Mind, Research, and Everyday Experience*. Belmont, CA. Wadsworth/Thomson Learning.

Goldstein, E. B. (2010). *Sensation and Perception* (8th edn). Belmont, CA. Wadsworth/Cengage.

Goldstein, J. M., Seidman, L. J., Horton, N. J., Makris, N., Kennedy, D. N., et al (2001). Normal sexual dimorphism of the adult brain assessed by *in vivo* magnetic resonance imaging. *Cerebral Cortex*, 11, 490–7.

Goldwurm, G. F., Bielli, D., Corsale, B., and Marchi, S. (2006). Optimism training. Methodology and results. *Homeostasis in Health and Disease*, 44, 27–33.

Goleman, D. (1995). *Emotional Intelligence*. New York, NY. Bantam Books.

Gonzaga, G. C., Campos, B., and Bradbury, T. (2007). Similarity, convergence, and relationship satisfaction in dating and married couples. *Journal of Personality and Social Psychology*, 93, 34–48.

Gonzaga, G. C., Turner, R. A., Keltner, D., Campos, B., and Altemus, M. (2006). Romantic love and sexual desire in close relationships. *Emotion*, 6, 163–79.

Goodwin, F. K. and Goldstein, M. A. (2003). Optimizing lithium treatment in bipolar disorder. A review of the literature and clinical recommendations. *Journal of Psychiatric Practice*, 9, 333–43.

Gorman, D. M. and Derzon, J. H. (2002). Behavioral traits and marijuana use and abuse. A meta-analysis of longitudinal studies. *Addictive Behaviors*, 27, 193–206.

Gotlib, I. H. and Joorman, J. (2010). Cognition and depression. Current status and future directions. *Annual Review of Clinical Psychology*, 6, 285–312.

Gottesman, I. I. (1991). *Schizophrenia Genesis. The Origins of Madness*. New York, NY. W. H. Freeman.

Gottesman, I. I. and Bertelsen, A. (1989). Confirming unexpressed genotypes for schizophrenia. Risks in the offspring of Fischer's Danish identical and fraternal discordant twins. *Archives of General Psychiatry*, 46, 867–72.

Gottfredson, L. S. (1997). Mainstream science on intelligence. An editorial with 52 signatories, history, and bibliography. *Intelligence*, 24, 13–23.

Gottfredson, L. S. (2003). Dissecting practical intelligence theory. Its claims and evidence. *Intelligence*, 31, 343–97.

Gottfredson, L. S. and Deary, I. J. (2004). Intelligence predicts health and longevity, but why? *Current Directions in Psychological Science*, 13(1), 1–4.

Gottlieb, D. J., Punjabi, N. M., Newman, A. B., Resnick, H. E., et al (2005). Association of sleep time with diabetes mellitus and impaired glucose tolerance. *Archives of Internal Medicine*, 165, 863–8.

Gould, K. S., Hirvonen, K., Koefoed, V. F., Røed, B. K., Sallinen, M., et al (2009). Effects of 60 hours of total sleep deprivation on two methods of high-speed ship navigation. *Ergonomics*, 52, 1469–86.

Gould, M. S., Greenberg, M. P. H., Velting, D. M., and Shaffer, D. (2003). Youth suicide risk and preventive interventions. A review of the past 10 years. *Journal of the American Academy of Child and Adolescent Psychiatry*, 42, 386–405.

Gould, S. J. (1981, May). Evolution as fact and theory. *Discover*, May, 34–7.

Gould, S. J. (1997, 12 June). Darwinian fundamentalism. *The New York Review of Books*, KLIV(10), 24–7.

Gourevitch, P. and Morris, E. (2008, 24 March). Exposure. The woman behind the camera at Abu Ghraib. *The New Yorker*. Retrieved from www.thenewyorker.com on 8 June 2008.

Gouzoulis-Mayfrank, E. and Daumann, J. (2006). Neurotoxicity of methylene-dioxyamphetamines (MDMA; ecstasy) in humans. How strong is the evidence for persistent brain damage? *Addiction*, 101, 348–61.

Grabe, S., Ward, L. M., and Hyde, J. S. (2008). The role of the media in body image concerns among women. A meta-analysis of experimental and correlational studies. *Psychological Bulletin*, 134, 460–76.

Grabill, K., Merlo, L., Duke, D., Harford, K.-L., Keeley, M. L., et al (2008). Assessment of obsessive-compulsive disorder. A review. *Journal of Anxiety Disorders*, 22, 1–17.

Grabowski, T. J., Damasio, H., Eichorn, G. R., and Tranel, D. (2003). Effects of gender on blood flow correlates of naming concrete entities. *Neuroimage*, 20, 940–54.

Graham, C. A. (2010). The DSM criteria for female orgasmic disorder. *Archives of Sexual Behavior*, 39, 256–70.

Graham, J., Nosek, B. A., Haidt, J., Iyer, R., Koleva, S., et al (2011). Mapping the moral domain. *Journal of Personality and Social Psychology*, 101, 366–85.

Graham, J. E., Christian, L. M., and Kiecolt-Glaser, J. K. (2006). Marriage, health, and immune function. In S. R. Beach, M. Z. Wamboldt, N. J. Kaslow, R. E. Heyman, et al (eds), *Relational Processes and DSM-V. Neuroscience, Assessment, Prevention, and Treatment* (pp 61–76). Washington, DC. American Psychiatric Association.

Grammer, K. and Thornhill, R. (1994). Human facial attractiveness and sexual selection. The role of averageness and symmetry. *Journal of Comparative Psychology*, 108, 233–42.

Grant, A. (2006). Johnston gears up to launch center for learning and memory. Institute for Cellular and Molecular Biology. Retrieved from http://www.icmb.utexas.edu/Profile/Profile_Daniel_johnston.asp on 15 May 2007.

Grant, I., Gonzalez, R., Carey, C. L., Natarajan, L., and Wolfson, T. (2003). Non-acute (residual) neurocognitive effects of cannabis use. A meta-analytic study. *Journal of the International Neuropsychological Society*, 9, 679–89.

Graziano, M. S. A., Taylor, C. S. R., and Moore, T. (2002). Complex movements evoked by microstimulation of precentral cortex. *Neuron*, 34, 841–51.

Greeenwald, A. G. and Nosek, B. A. (2001). Health of the implicit association test at age 3. *Zeitschrift für Experimentelle Psychologie*, 48, 85–93.

Greenberg, A. S. and Bailey, J. M. (1994). The irrelevance of the medical model of mental illness to law and ethics. *International Journal of Law and Psychiatry*, 17, 153–73.

Greenberg, J. (2008). Understanding the vital human quest for self-esteem. *Perspectives on Psychological Science*, 3, 48–55.

Greenberg, M. S., Westcott, D. R., and Bailey, S. E. (1998). When believing is seeing. The effect of scripts on eyewitness memory. *Law and Human Behavior*, 22, 685–94.

Greenberg, R. M. and Kellner, C. H. (2005). Electroconvulsive therapy. A selected review. *American Journal of Psychiatry*, 13, 268–81.

Greenwald, A. G., Oakes, M. A., and Hoffman, H. G. (2003). Targets of discrimination. Effects of race on responses to weapons holders. *Journal of Experimental Social Psychology*, 39, 399–405.

Greenwald, A. G., Spangenberg, E. R., Pratkanis, A. R., and Eskenazi, J. (1991). Double-blind tests of subliminal self-help audiotapes. *Psychological Science*, 2, 119–22.

Gregor, T. (1995). Sexuality and the experience of love. In P. R. Abramson and S. D. Pinkerton (eds), *Sexual Nature, Sexual Culture* (pp 330–50). Chicago, IL. University of Chicago Press.

Gregory, R. L. (1973). A discussion of G. H. Fisher's 'Towards a new explanation for the geometrical illusions. apparent depth or contour proximity?' and the inappropriate constancy scaling theory. *British Journal of Psychology*, 64, 623–6.

Gregory, R. L. (1997). *Eye and Brain. The Psychology of Seeing* (5th edn). Princeton, NJ. Princeton University Press.

Gregory-Roberts, E. M., Naismith, S. L., Cullen, K. M., and Hickie, I. B. (2010). Electroconvulsive therapy-induced persistent retrograde amnesia. Could it be minimized by ketamine or other pharmacological approaches? *Journal of Affective Disorders*, 126(1–2), 39–45.

Greider, K. (1995, July/August). Crackpot ideas. *Mother Jones*. Retrieved from http://www.come-over.to/FAS/crackbaby.htm on 28 January 2006.

Greven, C. U., Harlaar, N., Kovas, Y., Chamorro-Premuzic, T., and Plomin, R. (2009). More than just IQ. School achievement is predicted by self-perceived abilities—but for genetic rather than environmental reasons. *Psychological Science*, 20, 753–62.

Griffiths, R. R., Richards, W. A., Johnson, M., McCann, U., and Jesse, U. (2008). Mystical-type experiences occasioned by psilocybin mediate the attribution of personal meaning and spiritual significance 14 months later. *Journal of Psychopharmacology*, 22, 621–32.

Griffiths, R. R., Richards, W. A., McCann, U. D., and Jesse, R. (2006). Psilocybin can occasion mystical-type experiences having substantial and sustained personal meaning and spiritual significance. *Psychopharmacology*, 187, 268–83.

Grigorenko, E. L., Sternberg, R. J., and Strauss, S. (2006). Practical intelligence and elementary school teacher effectiveness in the United States and Israel. Measuring the predictive power of tacit knowledge. *Thinking Skills and Creativity*, 1, 14–33.

Grimland, M., Apter, A., and Kerkhof, A. (2006). The phenomenon of suicide bombing. A review of psychological and nonpsychological factors. *Crisis*, 27, 107–18.

Grimshaw, G. M., Adelstein, A., Bryden, M., and MacKinnon, G. E. (1998). First-language acquisition in adolescence. Evidence for a critical period for verbal language development. *Brain and Language*, 63, 237–55.

Grinspoon, L. and Bakalar, J. B. (1995). Marihuana as medicine. A plea for reconsideration. *JAMA*, 273, 1875–6.

Grissom, R. J. (1996). The magical number .7 plus or minus .2. Meta-meta-analysis of the probability of superior outcome in comparisons involving therapy, placebo, and control. *Journal of Consulting and Clinical Psychology*, 64, 973–82.

Groh, A. M., Fearon, R. P., Bakermans-Kranenburg, M. J., Van Ijzendoorn, M. H., Steele, R. D., et al (2014). The significance of attachment security for children's social competence with peers. A meta-analytic study. *Attachment and Human Development*, 16(2), 103–36.

Groome, D. (2016). Astrology. In *Parapsychology* (pp 129–43). Hove, UK. Psychology Press.

Gross, S. R. (2008). Convicting the innocent. *Annual Review of Law and Social Science*, 4, 173–92.

Grosser, B. I., Monti-Bloch, L., Jennings-White, C., and Berliner, D. L. (2000). Behavioral and electrophysiological effects of androstadienone, a human pheromone. *Psychoneuroendocrinology*, 25, 289–99.

Grow, J. M., Park, J. S., and Han, Z. (2006). 'Your life is waiting!' Symbolic meanings in direct-to-consumer antidepressant advertising. *Journal of Communication Inquiry*, 30, 163–88.

Gschwandtner, A., Jewell, S. L., and Kambhampati, U. S. (2016). *On the Relationship between Lifestyle and Happiness in the UK* (No 1613). London. School of Economics Discussion Papers.

Guillery, R. W., Feig, S. L., and Lozsádi, D. A. (1998). Paying attention to the thalamic reticular nucleus. *Trends in Neurosciences*, 21, 28–32.

Gumley, A. I., Taylor, H. E. F., Schwannauer, M., and MacBeth, A. (2014). A systematic review of attachment and psychosis. Measurement, construct validity and outcomes. *Acta Psychiatrica Scandinavica*, 129(4), 257–74.

Gump, B. B. and Kulik, J. A. (1997). Stress, affiliation, and emotional contagion. *Journal of Personality and Social Psychology*, 72, 305–19.

Gunaratana, H. (1991). *Mindfulness in Plain English*. Boston, MA. Wisdom Publications.

Gunnar, M. and Quevedo, K. (2007). The neurobiology of stress and development. *Annual Review of Psychology*, 58, 145–73.

Gupta, B. D., Jani, C. B., and Shah, P. H. (2001). Fatal 'bhang' poisoning. *Medicine, Science, and Law*, 41, 349–52.

Gur, R. E., Nimgaonkar, V. L., Almasy, L., Calkins, M. E., Ragland, J. D., et al (2007). Neurocognitive endophenotypes in a multiplex multigenerational family study of schizophrenia. *American Journal of Psychiatry*, 164, 813–19.

Gurung, R. A. R. (2005). How do students really study (and does it matter)? *Teaching of Psychology*, 4, 239–41.

Habek, D., Habek, J. C., Ivanisevic, M., and Djelmis, J. (2002). Fetal tobacco syndrome and perinatal outcome. *Fetal Diagnosis and Therapy*, 17, 367–71.

Habel, U., Windischberger, C., Derntl, B., Robinson, S., and Kryspin-Exner, I. (2007). Amygdala activation and facial expressions. Explicit emotion discrimination versus implicit emotion processing. *Neuropsychologia*, 45, 2369–77.

Haddad, P. and Anderson, I. (2007). Recognizing and managing antidepressant discontinuation syndromes. *Advances in Psychiatric Treatment*, 13, 447–57.

Hadley, C. B. and MacKay, D. G. (2006). Does emotion help or hinder immediate memory? Arousal versus priority-binding mechanism. *Journal of Experimental Psychology. Learning, Memory and Cognition*, 32, 7988.

Hadwin, A. F. and Winne, P. H. (1996). Study strategies have meager support. A review with recommendations for implementation. *Journal of Higher Education*, 67, 692–715.

Hadwin, A. F., Winne, P. H., Stockley, D. B., Nesbit, J. C., Woszczyna, C., et al (2001). Context moderates students' self-reports about how they study. *Journal of Educational Psychology*, 93, 477–87.

Hagell, A., Coleman, J., and Brooks, F. (2017). *Key Data on Adolescence 2013*. London. Association for Young People's Health. (You might find chapter 6, which deals with well-being and mental health particularly interesting in the light of the notion of adolescence as a time of storm and stress.)

Hagen, M. A. (2003). Faith in the model and resistance to research. *Clinical Psychology. Science and Practice*, 10, 344–8.

Hagerty, M. R. (1999). Testing Maslow's hierarchy of needs. National quality-of-life across time. *Social Indicators Research*, 46, 249–71.

Hagger, M. S., Wood, C., Stiff, C., and Chatzisarantis, N. L. D. (2010). Ego depletion and the strength model of self-control. A meta-analysis. *Psychological Bulletin*, 136, 495–525.

Haidt, J. (2001). The emotional dog and its rational tail. A social intuitionist approach to moral judgment. *Psychological Review*, 108, 814–34.

Haidt, J. (2007). The new synthesis in moral psychology. *Science*, 316, 998–1002.

Haidt, J. (2008). Morality. *Perspectives in Psychological Science*, 3, 65–72.

Haidt, J. and Bjorklund, F. (2008). Social intuitionists answer six questions about morality. In W. Sinnott-Armstrong (ed), *Moral Psychology. Vol 2. The Cognitive Science of Morality* (pp 181–217). Cambridge, MA. MIT Press.

Haidt, J. and Graham, J. (2007). When morality opposes justice. Conservatives have moral intuitions that liberals may not recognize. *Social Justice Research*, 20. Retrieved from http://faculty.virginia.edu/haidtlab/articles/ on 21 November 2008.

Haidt, J. and Kesebir, S. (2010). Morality. In S. T. Fiske, D. T. Gilbert, and G. Lindzey (eds), *The Handbook of Social Psychology* (5th edn, pp 797–832). Hoboken, NJ. John Wiley and Sons.

Halberstadt, J., Winkielman, P., Niedenthal, P. M., and Dalle, N. (2009). Emotional conception. How embodied emotion concepts guide perception and facial action. *Psychological Science*, 20, 1254–61.

Hall, C. S. and Van de Castle, R. (1966). *The Content Analysis of Dreams*. New York, NY. Appleton-Century-Crofts.

Hall, J. A. and Carter, J. D. (1999). Gender-stereotype accuracy as an individual difference. *Journal of Personality and Social Psychology*, 77, 350–9.

Hall, M. (2005, 15 January). Mat man meets tsunami heroes. *The Guernsey Press and Star*. Retrieved from www.thisisguernsey.com/news on 21 January 2005.

Haller, M. and Hadler, M. (2006). How social relations and structures can produce happiness and unhappiness. A comparative analysis. *Social Indicators Research*, 75, 196–216.

Hallmayer, J., Faraco, J., Lin, L., Hesselson, S., Winkelmann, J., et al (2009). Narcolepsy is strongly associated with the T-cell receptor alpha locus. *Nature Genetics*, 41, 708–11.

Halpern, D. F. (2003) *Thought and Knowledge. An Introduction to Critical Thinking*. Mahwah, NJ. Erlbaum.

Halpern, D. F. (2004). A cognitive-process taxonomy for sex differences in cognitive abilities. *Current Directions in Psychological Science*, 13, 135–9.

Halpern, D. F. (2007a). The nature and nurture of critical thinking. In R. J. Sternberg, H. Roediger, and D. F. Halpern (eds), *Critical Thinking in Psychology* (pp 1–14). New York, NY. Cambridge University Press.

Halpern, D. F. (2007b). *Critical Thinking in Psychology*. New York, NY. Cambridge University Press.

Halpern, D. F., Benbow, C. P., Geary, D. C., Gur, R. C., Hyde, J. S., et al (2007). The science of sex differences in science and mathematics. *Psychological Science in the Public Interest*, 8(1), 1–51.

Halpern, D. F., Benbow, C. P., Geary, D. C., Gur, R. C., Hyde, J. S., et al (2007/2008, December/January). Sex, math, and scientific achievement. Why do men dominate the fields of science, engineering, and mathematics? *Scientific American Mind*, 45–49.

Halsey, R. and Chapanis, A. (1951) On the number of absolutely identifiable spectral hues. *Journal of the Optical Society of America*, 41, 1057–8.

Hamann, S. (2009). The human amygdale and memory. In P. J. Whalen, and E. A. Phelps (eds), *The Human Amygdale* (pp 177–203). New York, NY. Guilford Press.

Hamer, M., Molloy, G. J., and Stamatakis, E. (2008). Psychological distress as a risk factor for cardiovascular events. *Journal of the American College of Cardiology*, 52, 2156–62.

Hamer, M., Taylor, A., and Steptoe, A. (2006). The effect of acute aerobic exercise on stress-related blood pressure responses. A systematic review and meta-analysis. *Biological Psychology*, 71, 183–90.

Hamilton, W. D. (1964). The genetical evolution of social behavior. *Journal of Theoretical Biology*, 7, 1–52.

Hammen, C. (1991). Generation of stress in the course of unipolar depression. *Journal of Abnormal Psychology*, 100, 555–61.

Hammen, C. (2005). Stress and depression. *Annual Review of Clinical Psychology*, 55, 11.1–11.27.

Hampson, S. E. and Goldberg, L. R. (2006). A first large cohort study of personality trait stability over the 40 years between elementary school and midlife. *Journal of Personality and Social Psychology*, 91, 763–70.

Hancock, J. T., Thom-Santelli, J., and Ritchie, T. (2004). Deception and design. The impact of communication technology on lying behavior. *CHI Letters*, 6, 129–34.

Handlin, L., Hydbring-Sandberg, E., Nilsson, A., Eidebäck, M., Jansson, A., et al (2011). Short-term interaction between dogs and their owners. Effects on oxytocin, cortisol, insulin, and heart rate—an exploratory study. *Anthrozoös*, 24, 301–15.

Hanington, L., Ramchandani, P., and Stein, A. (2010). Parental depression and child temperament. Assessing child to parent effects in a longitudinal population study. *Infant Behavior and Development*, 33, 88–95.

Hankin, B. L. and Abramson, L. (2002). Measuring cognitive vulnerability to depression in adolescence. Reliability, validity, and gender differences. *Journal of Clinical Child and Adolescent Psychology*, 31, 491–504.

Hannan, C. K. (2006). Neuroscience and the impact of brain plasticity on Braille reading. *Journal of Visual Impairment and Blindness*, 100, 397–413.

Hansen, R. A., Gartlehner, G., Lohr, K. N., Gaynes, B. N., and Carey, T. S. (2005). Efficacy and safety of second-generation antidepressants in the treatment of major depressive disorder. *Annals of Internal Medicine*, 143, 415–26.

Harden, K. P., Hill, J. E., Turkheimer, E., and Emery, R. E. (2008). Gene-environment correlation and interaction in peer effects on adolescent alcohol and tobacco use. *Behavior Genetics*, 38, 339–47.

Hardman, J. G., Limbird, L. E., and Gilman, A. G. (2001). *The Pharmacological Basis of Therapeutics* (10th edn). New York, NY. McGraw Hill.

Hargrove, D. S. (2009). Psychotherapy based on Bowen family systems theory. In J. H. Bray and M. Stanton (eds), *The Wiley-Blackwell Handbook of Family Psychology* (pp 286–99). Malden, MA. Wiley-Blackwell.

Harley, E. W. Y., Boardman, J., and Craig, T. (2010). Sexual problems in schizophrenia. Prevalence and characteristics. A cross sectional survey. *Social Psychiatry and Psychiatric Epidemiology*, 45(7), 759–66.

Harlow, H. F. (1953). Learning by Rhesus monkeys on the basis of manipulation-exploration motives. *Science*, 117, 466–7.

Harlow, H. F. (1958). The nature of love. *American Psychologist*, 13, 573–685.

Harlow, H. F., Harlow, M. K., and Meyer, D. R. (1950). Learning motivated by a manipulative drive. *Journal of Experimental Psychology*, 40, 228–34.

Harlow, H, F. and Zimmerman, R. R. (1959). Affectional responses in the infant monkey. *Science*, 130, 421–32.

Harmon-Jones, E. and Harmon-Jones, C. (2007). Cognitive dissonance theory after 50 years of development. *Zeitschrift für Sozialpsychologie*, 38, 7–16.

Harmon-Jones, E. A. and Harmon-Jones, C. (2007). Anger. Causes and components. In T. A. Cavell and K. T. Malcolm (eds), *Anger, Aggression and Interventions for Interpersonal Violence* (pp 99–117). Mahwah, NJ. Lawrence Erlbaum Associates.

Harrington, A. (2012). The fall of the schizophrenogenic mother. *The Lancet*, 379(9823), 1292–3.

Harris, B. (1979). Whatever happened to Little Albert? *American Psychologist*, 34, 151–60.

Harris, B. (2011). Letting go of Little Albert. Disciplinary memory, history, and the uses of myth. *Journal of the History of the Behavioral Sciences*, 47, 1–17.

Harris, G. (2008, 22 November). Drugmakers paid radio host $1.3 million for lectures. *New York Times*. Retrieved from http://query.nytimes.com/gst/fullpage.html?res=9806EEDC153DF931A15752C1A96E9C8B63 on 2 May 2009.

Harris, G. (2009, 1 September). Document details plan to promote costly drug. *New York Times*. Retrieved from http://www.nytimes.com/2009/09/02/business/02drug.html on 30 June 2010.

Harris, G. and Carey, B. (2008, 8 June). Researchers fail to reveal full drug pay. *New York Times*. Retrieved from http://www.nytimes.com/2008/06/08/us/08conflict.html?pagewanted=all&_r=0 on 8 June 2008.

Harris, J. A. (1999). Review and methodological considerations in research on testosterone and aggression. *Aggression and Violent Behavior*, 4, 273–91.

Harris, J. R. (1995). Where is the children's environment? A group socialization theory of development. *Psychological Review*, 102, 458–89.

Harris, J. R. (1998). *The Nurture Assumption. Why Children Turn out the Way They Do.* New York, NY. Free Press.

Harris, J. R. (2006). *No Two Alike. Human Nature and Human Individuality.* New York, NY. Norton.

Harris, J. R. (2009). Attachment theory underestimates the child. *Behavioral and Brain Sciences*, 32, 30.

Harris, K. and Campbell, E.A. (1999) The plans in unplanned pregnancy. Secondary gain and the partnership. *British Journal of Medical Psychology*, 72, 105–20.

Harris, L. T. and Fiske, S. T. (2007). Social groups that elicit disgust are differentially processed in mPFC. *Social Cognitive and Affective Neuroscience*, 2, 45–51.

Harris, S. (2012). *Free Will.* New York, NY. Free Press.

Harris Poll (2008). Widely held attitudes to different generations. Retrieved on 15 May 2010 from http://www.harrisinteractive.com/NEWS/allnewsbydate.asp?NewsID=1328

Harrison, Y. and Horne, J. A. (2000). The impact of sleep deprivation on decision making. A review. *Journal of Experimental Psychology. Applied*, 6, 236–49.

Harrow, M., Grossman, L.S., Jobe, T. H., and Herbener, E.S. (2005). Do patients with schizophrenia ever show periods of recovery? A 15-year multi-follow-up study. *Schizophrenia Bulletin*, 31, 723–34.

Hartmann, E. (2000). The waking-to-dreaming continuum and the effects of emotion. *Behavioral and Brain Sciences*, 23, 947–50.

Hartwig, M. and Bond, C. F., Jr (2011). Why do lie-catchers fail? A lens model meta-analysis of human lie judgments. *Psychological Bulletin*, 137, 643–59.

Harvey, A. G. (2008). Insomnia, psychiatric disorders, and the transdiagnostic perspective. *Current Directions in Psychological Science*, 17, 299–303.

Hashibe, M., Morgenstern, H., Cui, Y., Tashkin, D. P., Zhang, Z-F., et al (2006). Marijuana use and the risk of lung and upper aerodigestive tract cancers. Results of a population-based case-control study. *Cancer Epidemiological Biomarkers Preview*, 15. Retrieved from http://cebp.aacrjournals.org/content/15/10/1829.long on 24 June 2010.

Haslam, N. and Giosan, C. (2002). The lay concept of 'mental disorder' among American undergraduates. *Journal of Clinical Psychology*, 58, 479–85.

Haslam, N., Loughnan, S., and Perry, G. (2014). Meta-Milgram. An empirical synthesis of the obedience experiments. *PLoS One*, 9(4), e93927.

Haslam, S. A. and Reicher, S. D. (2017). 50 years of 'obedience to authority'. From blind conformity to engaged followership. *Annual Review of Law and Social Science*, 13, 59–78.

Hassabis, D., Kumaran, D., Vann, S., and McGuire, E. A. (2007). Patients with hippocampal amnesia cannot imagine new experiences. *PNAS*, 104, 1726–31.

Hassan, N. (2001, 9 November). An arsenal of believers. Talking to the 'human bombs.' *The New Yorker*, 19 November. Retrieved from http://www.newyorker.com/fact/content/?011119fa_FACT1 on 27 September 2005.

Hassett, J. M., Siebert, E. R., and Wallen, K. (2008). Sex differences in rhesus monkey toy preferences parallel those of children. *Hormones and Behavior*, 54, 359–64.

Hatch, S. L. and Dohrenwend, B. P. (2007). Distribution of traumatic and other stressful life events by race/ethnicity, gender, SES and age. A review of the research. *American Journal of Community Psychology*, 40, 313–32.

Hatfield, E. and Rapson, R. L. (2005). *Love and Sex. Cross-cultural Perspectives*. Lanham, MD. University Press of America.

Haugaard, J. J. and Tilly, C. (1988). Characteristics predicting children's responses to sexual encounters with other children. *Child Abuse and Neglect*, 12, 209–18.

Hauser, M., Cushman, F., Young, L., Jin, K-X., and Mikhail J. (2007). A dissociation between moral judgments and justifications. *Mind and Language*, 22, 1–21.

Hauser, M. D., Chomsky, N., and Fitch, W. T. (2002). The faculty of language. What is it, who has it, and how did it evolve? *Science*, 298, 1569–79.

Havel, P. J. (2001). Peripheral signals conveying metabolic information to the brain. Short-term and long-term regulation of food intake and energy homeostasis. *Experimental Biology and Medicine*, 226, 963–97.

Haw, C. and Stubbs, J. (2005). A survey of the off-label use of mood stabilizers in a large psychiatric hospital. *Journal of Psychopharmacology*, 19(4), 402–7.

Hawkins, D. N. and Booth, A. (2005). Unhappily ever after. Effects of long-term, low-quality marriages on well-being. *Social Forces*, 84(1), 452–71.

Hawkley, L. C. and Cacioppo, J. T. (2007). Aging and loneliness. Downhill quickly? *Current Directions in Psychological Science*, 16, 187–91.

Hawkley, L. C. and Cacioppo, J. T. (2010). Loneliness matters. A theoretical and empirical review of consequences and mechanisms. *Annals of Behavioral Medicine*, 40, 218–27.

Hawley, C. A., Ward, A. B., Magnay, A. R., and Long, J. (2004). Outcome following childhood head injury. A population study. *The Journal of Neurology, Neurosurgery, and Psychiatry*, 75, 737–42.

Haworth, C. M. A. and Plomin, R. (2010). Quantitative genetics in the era of molecular genetics. *Journal of the American Academy of Child and Adolescent Psychiatry*, 49, 783–93.

Haworth, C. M. A., Wright, M. J., Luciano, M., Martin, N. G., de Geus, E. J. C., et al (2010). The heritability of general cognitive ability increases linearly from childhood to young adulthood. *Molecular Psychiatry*, 15, 1112–20.

Hayes, J., Schimel, J., and Williams, T. J. (2008). Fighting death with death. The buffering effects of learning that worldview violators have died. *Psychological Science*, 19, 501–7.

Haynes, J. D. (2011). Decoding and predicting intentions. *Annals of the New York Academy of Sciences*, 1224, 9–21.

Hazan, C. and Shaver, P. R. (1994). Attachment as an organizational framework for research on close relationships. *Psychological Inquiry*, 5, 1–22.

Hazan, C. and Zeifman, D. (1999). Pair-bonds as attachments. Evaluating the evidence. In J. Cassidy and P. R. Shaver (eds), *Handbook of Attachment Theory and Research* (pp 336–54). New York, NY. Guilford.

Headley, B. and Grabka, M. (2011). Health correlates and possible health care savings of pet ownership. Results from national surveys. In P. McCardles, S. McCune, J. A. Griffin, and V. Maholmes (eds), *How Animals Affect Us* (pp 153–62). Washington, DC. American Psychological Association.

Health and Social Care Information Centre (HSCIC) (2016). Health and Social Care Information Centre (HSCIC) *Annual Report and Accounts 2016–17*. Leeds. NHS.

Healy, D. and Cattell, D. (2003). Interface between authorship, industry, and science in the domain of therapeutics. *British Journal of Psychiatry*, 183, 22–7.

Heaps, C. M. and Nash, M. (2001). Comparing recollective experience in true and false autobiographical memories. *Journal of Experimental Psychology. Learning, Memory, and Cognition*, 27, 920–30.

Heath, D. B. (1995). An anthropological view of alcohol and culture in international perspective. In D. B. Heath (ed), *International Handbook on Alcohol and Culture* (pp 328–47). Westport, CT. Greenwood Press.

Heatherton, T. E. and Sargent, J. D. (2009). Does watching smoking in movies promote teenage smoking? *Current Directions in Psychological Science*, 18, 63–7.

Hebb, D. O. (1955). Drives and the C. N. S. (central nervous system). *Psychological Review*, 62, 243–54.

Hedges, D. W., Woon, F. L., and Hoopes, S. P. (2009). Caffeine-induced psychosis. *CNS Spectrums*, 14, 127–9.

Hedges, L. V. and Nowell, A. (1995). Sex differences in mental scores, variability, and numbers of high-scoring individuals. *Science*, 269, 41–5.

Heider, F. (1958). *The Psychology of Interpersonal Relations*. New York, NY. Wiley.

Heine, S. J. (2005). Constructing good selves in Japan and North America. In R. M. Sorrentino, D. Cohen, J. M. Olson, and M. P. Zanna (eds), *Culture and Social Behavior. The Tenth Ontario Symposium* (pp 115–43). Hillsdale, NJ. Lawrence Erlbaum Associates.

Heine, S. J. and Norenzayan, A. (2006). Toward a psychological science for a cultural species. *Perspectives on Psychological Science*, 1, 251–69.

Heine, S. J., Kitayama, S., Lehman, D. R., Takata, T., Ide, E., et al (2001).

Divergent consequences of success and failure in Japan and North America. An investigation of self-improving motivations and malleable selves. *Journal of Personality and Social Psychology*, 81, 599–615.

Heinrich, L. M. and Gullone, E. (2006). The clinical significance of loneliness. A literature review. *Clinical Psychology Review*, 26, 695–718.

Heishman, S. J., Kozlowski, L. T., and Henningfield, J. E. (1997). Nicotine addiction. Implications for public health policy. *Journal of Social Issues*, 53, 13–33.

Helson, R., Jones, C., and Kwan, V. (2002). Personality change over 40 years of adulthood. Hierarchical linear modeling analyses of two longitudinal samples. *Journal of Personality and Social Psychology*, 83(3), 752–66.

Helson, R. C. and Soto, C. J. (2005). Up and down in middle age. Monotonic and non-monotonic changes in roles, status, and personality. *Journal of Personality and Social Psychology*, 89, 194–204.

Hendrick, C. and Hendrick, S. (2006). Styles of romantic love. In R. J. Sternberg and K. Weis (eds), *The New Psychology of Romantic Love* (pp 149–70). New Haven, CT. Yale University Press.

Hennessey, B. A. and Amabile, T. M. (2010). Creativity. *Annual Review of Psychology*, 61, 569–98.

Henninger, P. (1992). Conditional handedness. Handedness changes in multiple personality disordered subject reflect shift in hemispheric dominance. *Consciousness and Cognition*, 1, 265–87.

Henrich, J., Heine, S. J., and Norenzayan, A. (2010). The weirdest people in the world? *Behavioral and Brain Sciences*, 33, 61–83.

Henry, D. B., Schoeny, M. E., Deptula, D. P., and Slavick, J. T. (2007). Peer selection and socialization effects on adolescent intercourse without a condom and attitudes about the costs of sex. *Child Development*, 78, 825–38.

Henry, J. A., Oldfield, W. L. G., and Kon, O. M. (2003). Comparing cannabis with tobacco. *British Medical Journal*, 326, 942–3.

Henwood, K. (2014). Qualitative research. *Encyclopedia of Critical Psychology*, 1611–14.

Hepper, P. G. (1991). An examination of fetal learning before and after birth. *Irish Journal of Psychology*, 12, 95–107.

Herculano-Houzel, S. and Lent, R. (2005). Isotropic fractionator. A simple, rapid method for the quantification of total cell and neuron numbers in the brain. *The Journal of Neuroscience*, 25, 2518–21.

Herdt, G. and McClintock, M. K. (2000). The magical age of 10. *Archives of Sexual Behavior*, 29, 587–606.

Heres, S., Davis, J., Maino, K., Jetzinger, E., Kissling, W., et al (2006). Why olanzapne beats risperidone, risperidone beats quetiapine, and quetiapine beats olanzapine. An exploratory analysis of head-to-head comparison studies of second-generation antipsychotics. *American Journal of Psychiatry*, 163, 1645.

Herlitz, A. and Rehnman, J. (2008). Sex differences in episodic memory. *Current Directions in Psychological Science*, 17, 52–6.

Herman, R. A. and Wallen, K. (2007). Cognitive performance in rhesus monkeys varies by sex and prenatal androgen exposure. *Hormones and Behavior*, 51, 496–507.

Herrmann, D., Raybeck, D., and Gruneberg, M. (2002). *Improving Memory and Study Skills. Advances in Theory and Practice*. Seattle, WA. Hogrefe and Huber Publishers.

Hersh, S. M. (2004, 10 May). Torture at Abu Ghraib. *The New Yorker*. Retrieved from http://www.newyorker.com/archive/2004/05/10/040510fa_fact?currentPage=1 on 25 May 2011.

Hertenstein, M. J. (2002). Touch. Its communicative functions in infancy. *Human Development*, 45, 70–94.

Hertenstein, M. J., Keltner, D., App, B., Bulleit, B. A., and Jaskolka, A. R. (2006). Touch communicates distinct emotions. *Emotion*, 6, 528–33.

Hertwig, R. and Gigerenzer, G. (1999). The 'conjunction fallacy' revisited. How intelligent inferences look like reasoning errors. *Journal of Behavioral Decision Making*, 12, 275–305.

Hertzog, C., Kramer, A. F., Wilson, R. S., and Lindenberger, U. (2009). Enrichment effects on adult cognitive development. *Psychological Sciences in the Public Interest*, 9, 1–65.

Herxheimer, A. and Waterhouse, J. (2003). The prevention and treatment of jet lag. *British Medical Journal*, 326, 296–7.

Herzog, H. (2011). The impact of pets on human health and psychological well-being. Fact, fiction, or hypothesis? *Current Directions in Psychological Science*, 20, 236–9.

Hespos, S., Ferry, A. L., and Rips, L. J. (2009). Five-month-old infants have different expectations for solids and liquids. *Psychological Science*, 20, 603–11.

Hespos, S. J., and Spelke, E. S. (2004). Conceptual precursors to language. *Nature*, 430, 453–6.

Hewitt, R. (2013). Is natural best? *The Guardian*, 31 August.

Hiby, E. F., Rooney, N. J., and Bradshaw, J. W. S. (2004). Dog training methods. Their use, effectiveness, and interaction with behaviour and welfare. *Animal Welfare*, 13, 63–9.

Hickle, I. (2007). Is depression overdiagnosed? No. *British Medical Journal*, 335, 329.

Hicks, R. A., Fernandez, C., and Pellegrini, R. J. (2001). The changing sleep habits of university students. An update. *Perceptual and Motor Skills*, 93, 648.

Higgins, S. T., Silverman, K., and Heil, S. H. (eds) (2007). *Contingency Management in Substance Abuse Treatment*. New York, NY. Guilford.

Higgins, S. T., Silverman, K., and Washio, Y. (2011). Contingency management. In M. Galanter and H. D. Kleber (eds), *Psychotherapy for the Treatment of Substance Abuse* (pp 193–218). Arlington, VA. American Psychiatric Publishing.

Hilgard, E. R. (1986). *Divided Consciousness. Multiple Controls in Human Thought and Action*. New York, NY. Wiley.

Hiller, J. (2005). Gender differences in sexual motivation. *Journal of Men's Health and Gender*, 2, 339–45.

Hinde, R. A., Perret-Clermont, A. N., and Hinde, J. S. (1985). *Social Relationships and Cognitive Development*. New York, NY. Oxford University Press.

Hindmarch, I. (2001). Expanding the horizons of depression. Beyond the monoamine hypothesis. *Human Psychopharmacology. Clinical and Experimental*, 16, 203–18.

Hines, M. (2004). *Brain Gender*. New York, NY. Oxford University Press.

Hines, M. (2006). Prenatal testosterone and gender-related behaviour. *European Journal of Endocrinology*, 155(S1), 115–21.

Hines, M. (2008). Monkeys, girls, boys and toys. A confirmation letter regarding 'Sex differences in toy preferences. Striking parallels between monkeys and humans'. *Hormones and Behavior*, 54, 478–479.

Hirst, W., Phelps, E. A., Buckner, R. L., Budson, A. E., Cuc, A., et al (2009). Long-term memory for the terrorist attack of September 11. Flashbulb memories, event memories, and factors that influence their retention. *Journal of Experimental Psychology*, 138(2), 161–76.

Hobson, C. J. and Delunas, L. (2001). National norms and life-event frequencies for the Revised Social Readjustment Rating Scale. *International Journal of Stress Management*, 8, 299–314.

Hobson, C. J., Kamen, J., Szostek, J., Nethercut, C. M., Tiedmann, J. W., et al (1998). Stressful life events. A revision and update of the Social Readjustment Scale. *International Journal of Stress Management*, 5(1), 1–23.

Hobson, J. A. (2002). *Dreaming. An Introduction to the Science of Sleep*. New York, NY. Oxford University Press.

Hobson, J. A., Pace-Schott, E. F., and Stickgold, R. (2000). Dreaming and the brain. Toward a cognitive neuroscience of conscious states. *Behavioral and Brain Sciences*, 23, 793–1121.

Hochberg, L. R. (2008). Turning thought into action. *New England Journal of Medicine*, 359, 1175–7.

Hochberg, L. R., Serruya, M. D., Friehs, G. M., Mukand, J. A., Saleh, M., et al (2006). Neuronal ensemble control of prosthetic devices by a human with tetraplegia. *Nature*, 442, 164–71.

Hodgkinson, G. P., Langan-Fox, J., and Sadler-Smith, E. (2008). Intuition. A fundamental bridging construct in the behavioral sciences. *British Journal of Psychology*, 99, 1–27.

Hoek, H. W. and van Hoeken, D. (2003). Review of the prevalence and incidence of eating disorders. *International Journal of Eating Disorders*, 34, 383–96.

Hoekstra, R. A., Bartels, M., and Boomsma, D. I. (2007). Longitudinal genetic study of verbal and nonverbal IQ from early childhood to young adulthood. *Learning and Individual Differences*, 17, 97–114.

Hoeve, M., Stams, G. J. J., Van der Put, C. E., Dubas, J. S., Van der Laan, P. H., et al (2012). A meta-analysis of attachment to parents and delinquency. *Journal of Abnormal Child Psychology*, 40(5), 771–85.

Hofer, A., Siedentopf, C. M., Ischebeck, A., Rettenbacher, M. A., Verius, M., et al (2007). Sex differences in brain activation patterns during processing of positively and negatively valenced emotional words. *Psychological Medicine*, 37, 109–19.

Hoffman, A. (1970). The discovery of LSD and subsequent investigations of naturally occurring hallucinogens. In F. J. Ayd, Jr, and B. Blackwell (eds), *Discoveries in Biological Psychiatry* (pp 91–106). New York, NY. J. B. Lippincott. Excerpt retrieved from http://www.psychedelic-library.org/hofmann.htm on 9 September 2006.

Hofman, S. G. and Barlow, D. H. (2002). Social phobia (social anxiety disorder). In D. H. Barlow (ed), *Anxiety and its Disorders. The Nature and Treatment of Anxiety and Panic* (2nd edn). New York, NY. Guilford Press.

Hofstede, G. H. (2001). *Culture's Consequences. Comparing Values, Behaviors, Institutions and Organizations across Nations* (2nd edn). Thousand Oaks, CA. Sage Publications.

Hofstede, G. H. and McCrae, R. R. (2004). Personality and culture revisited. Linking traits and dimensions of culture. *Cross-Cultural Research*, 38, 52–88.

Hogan, R. and Foster, J. (2016). Rethinking personality. *International Journal of Personality Psychology*, 2(1), 37–43.

Hoge, E. A., Austin, E. D., and Pollack, M. H. (2007). Resilience. Research evidence and conceptual considerations for post-traumatic stress disorder. *Depression and Anxiety*, 24, 139–52.

Hollis, K. L. (1997). Contemporary research on Pavolovian conditioning. A 'new' functional analysis. *American Psychologist*, 52, 956–65.

Hollis, K. L., Pharr, V. L., Dumas, M. J., Britton, G. B., and Field, J. (1997). Classical conditioning provides paternity advantage for territorial male blue gouramis (*Trichogsater trichopterus*). *Journal of Comparative Psychology*, 111, 219–25.

Hollon, S. D. (2006). Randomized clinical trials. In J. C. Norcross, L. E. Beutler, and R. F. Levant (eds), *Evidence-based Practices in Mental Health. Debate and Dialogue on the Fundamental Questions* (pp 96–105). Washington, DC. American Psychological Association.

Hollon, S. D. and Beck, A. T. (1994). Cognitive and cognitive-behavioral therapies. In A. E. Bergin and S. L. Garfield (eds), *Handbook of Psychotherapy and Behavior Change* (4th edn, pp 428–66). New York, NY. Wiley.

Hollon, S. D., Jarrett, R. B., Nierenberg, A. A., Thase, M. E., Trivedi, M., et al (2005). Psychotherapy and medication in the treatment of adult and geriatric depression. Which monotherapy or combined treatment? *Journal of Clinical Psychiatry*, 66, 455–68.

Hollon, S. D., Stewart, M. O., and Strunk, D. (2006). Enduring effects for cognitive behavior therapy in the treatment of depression and anxiety. *Annual Review of Psychology*, 57, 285–315.

Holmans, P., Weissman, M. M., Zubenko, G. S., Scheftner, W. A., Crowe. R. R., et al (2007). Genetics of recurrent early-onset major depression. Final genome scan report. *American Journal of Psychiatry*, 164, 248–58.

Holmes, J., Neighbour, R., Tarrier, N., Hinshelwood, R. D., and Bolsover, N. (2002). All you need is cognitive behaviour therapy? Commentary. Benevolent scepticism is just what the doctor ordered. Commentary. Yes, cognitive behaviour therapy may well be all you need. Commentary. Symptoms or relationships. Commentary. The 'evidence' is weaker than claimed. *BMJ*, 324(7332), 288–94.

Holmes, T. H. and Rahe, R. H. (1967). The Social Readjustment Rating Scale. *Journal of Psychosomatic Research*, 11, 213–18.

Holsboer, F. and Ising, M. (2010). Stress hormone regulation. Biological role and translation into therapy. *Annual Review of Psychology*, 61, 81–109.

Holt-Lunstad, J., Birmingham, W., and Jones, B. Q. (2008). Is there something unique about marriage? The relative impact of marital status, relationship quality, and network social support on ambulatory blood pressure and mental health. *Annals of Behavioral Medicine*, 35, 239–44.

Holt-Lunstad, J., Smith, T. B., and Layton, J. B. (2010). Social relationships and mortality risk. A meta-analytic review. *PLoS Medicine*, 7(7), e1000316.

Hoogland, A. I. (2015). Continuity of change. The dynamic of beliefs, values, and the aging experience. *Journal of Aging Studies*, 32, 32–9.

Horn, J. L. (1991). Measurement of intellectual capabilities. A review of theory. In K. S. McGrew, J. K. Werder, and R. W. Woodcock (eds), *WJ-R Technical Manual*. Allen, TX. DLM.

Horn, J. L. and Cattell, R. B. (1966). Refinement and test of the theory of fluid and crystallized general intelligence. *Journal of Educational Psychology*, 57, 253–70.

Horton, J. X. and Trobe, J. D. (1999). Akinetopsia from nefazodone toxicity. *American Journal of Ophthalmology*, 128, 530–1.

Horwitz, A. V., Videon, R. M., Schmitz, M. F., and Davis, D. (2003). Rethinking twins and environments. Possible social sources for assumed genetic influences in twin research. *Journal of Health and Social Behavior*, 44, 111–29.

Horwitz, A. V. and Wakefield, J. C. (2006). The epidemic in mental illness. Clinical fact or survey artifact? *Contexts*, 5, 19–23.

Horwitz, A. V. and Wakefield, J. C. (2007). *The Loss of Sadness. How Psychiatry Transformed Normal Sorrow into Depressive Disorder*. New York, NY. Oxford University Press.

Horwitz, A. V. and Wakefield, J. C. (2012). *All We Have to Fear. Psychiatry's Transformation of Natural Anxieties into Mental Disorders*. New York, NY. Oxford University Press.

Hosenbocus, S. and Chahal, R. (2011). SSRIs and SNRIs. A review of the discontinuation syndrome in children and adolescents. *Journal of the Canadian Academy of Child and Adolescent Psychiatry*, 20, 60–7.

Hoss, R. A. and Langlois, J. H. (2003). Infants prefer attractive faces. In O. Pascalis, and A. M. Slater (eds), *The Development of Face Processing in Infancy and Early Childhood. Current Perspectives* (pp 27–38). Hauppauge, NY. Nova Science Publishers.

Hotchkiss, A. K., Ostby, J. S., Vandenbergh, J. G., and Gray, L. E. (2003). An environmental antiandrodgen, vinclozolin, alters the organization of play behavior. *Physiology and Behavior*, 79, 151–6.

Hounsfield, G. N. (1973). Computerised transverse axial scanning (tomography). Part 1. Description of system. *British Journal of Radiology*, 46, 1016–22.

House, J. S., Landis, K. R., and Umberson, D. (1988). Social relationships and health. *Science*, 241, 540–5.

Houts, A. C. (2001). The diagnostic and statistical manual's new white coat and circularity of plausible dysfunctions. Response to Wakefield, Part 1. *Behaviour Research and Therapy*, 39, 315–45.

Hróbjartsson, A. and Gøtzsche, P. C. (2001). Is the placebo powerless?—An analysis of clinical trials comparing placebo with no treatment. *The New England Journal of Medicine*, 21, 1594–1602.

Hróbjartsson, A. and Gøtzsche, P. C. (2004). Is the placebo powerless? Update of a systematic review with 52 new randomized trials comparing placebo with no treatment. *Journal of Internal Medicine*, 256, 91–100.

Hróbjartsson, A. and Gøtzsche, P. C. (2007). Powerful spin on conclusion in Wampold and colleagues' reanalysis of placebo vs. no-treatment trials despite similar results as in original review. *Journal of Clinical Psychology*, 63, 373–7.

Hsu, B., Kessler, C., Knapke, K., Diefenbach, P., and Elias, J. P. (1994). Gender differences in sexual fantasy and behavior in a college population. A ten-year replication. *Journal of Sex and Marital Therapy*, 20, 103–18

Hu, G., Wilcox, H., Wissow, L. S., and Baker, S. P. (2008). Mid-life suicide. *American Journal of Preventative Medicine*, 35, 589–93.

Hu, P., Stylos-Allan, M., and Walker, M. P. (2006). Sleep facilitates consolidation of emotional declarative memory. *Psychological Science*, 17, 891–8.

Hubel, D. H. (1995). *Eye, Brain, and Vision*. New York, NY. Scientific American Library.

Hubel D. H. and Wiesel, T. N. (1970). The period of susceptibility to the physiological effects of unilateral eye closure in kittens. *Journal of Physiology*, 206, 419–36.

Hudson, J. I., Hiripi, E., Pope, H. G., Jr, and Kessler, R. C. (2007). The prevalence and correlates of eating disorders in the National Comorbidity Survey Replication. *Biological Psychiatry*, 61, 348–58.

Huedo-Medina, T. B., Johnson, B. T., and Kirsch, I. (2012). Kirsch et al's (2008) calculations are correct. Reconsidering Fountoulakis and Möller's re-analysis of the Kirsch data. *International Journal of Neuropsychopharmacology*, 15, 1193–8.

Huesmann, L. R. (2007). The impact of electronic media violence. Scientific theory and research. *Journal of Adolescent Health*, 41(Suppl), S6–S13.

Huesmann, L. R. and Taylor, L. D. (2006). The role of media violence in violent behavior. *Annual Review of Public Health*, 27, 393–415.

Hughes, C. C. (1998). The glossary of 'culture-bound syndromes' in DSM-IV. A critique. *Transcultural Psychiatry*, 35, 413–21.

Hughes, M., Morrison, K., and Asada, K. J. K. (2005). What's love got to do with it? Exploring the impact of maintenance rules, love attitudes, and network support on friends with benefits relationships. *Western Journal of Communication*, 69, 49–66.

Hull, C. L. (1943). *Principles of Behavior*. New Haven, CT. Yale University Press.

Hulme, O., Friston, K. F., and Zeki, S. (2009). Neural correlates of stimulus reportability. *Journal of Cognitive Neuroscience*, 21, 1602–10.

Human Genome Project Information (2008, 19 September). How many genes are in the human genome? Retrieved from http://www.ornl.gov/sci/techresources/Human_Genome/faq/genenumber.shtml on 28 January 2013.

Hummelen, B., Wilberg, T., Pedersen, G., and Karterud, S. (2007). The quality of the DSM-IV obsessive-compulsive personality disorder construct as a prototype category. *Journal of Nervous and Mental Disease*, 196, 446–55.

Hunsley, J., Lee, C. M., and Wood, J. M. (2003). Controversial and questionable assessment techniques. In S. O. Lilienfeld, S. J. Lynn, and J. M. Lohr (eds), *Science and Pseudoscience in Clinical Psychology* (pp 39–76). New York, NY. The Guilford Press.

Hunt, M. (1993). *The Story of Psychology*. New York, NY. Doubleday.

Hunt, M. (2009). *The Story of Psychology*. Garden City, NY. Doubleday Anchor.

Hupka, R. B., Lenton, A. P., and Hutchison, K. A. (1999). Universal development of emotion categories in natural language. *Journal of Personality and Social Psychology*, 77, 247–78.

Hur, Y. (2003). Assortative mating for personality traits, educational level, religious affiliation, height, weight, and body mass index in parents of a Korean twin sample. *Twin Research*, 6, 467–70.

Husain, M. and Rorden, C. (2003). Non-spatially lateralized mechanisms in hemispatial neglect. *Nature Reviews. Neuroscience*, 4, 26–36.

Hutton, A., Ranse, J., and Munn, M. B. (2018). Developing public health initiatives through understanding motivations of the audience at mass-gathering events. *Prehospital and Disaster Medicine*, 33(2), 191–6.

Huxley, A. F. (1959) Ion movements during nerve activity. *Annals of New York Academy of Sciences*, 81, 221–46.

Huxley, R. R. (2000). Nausea and vomiting in early pregnancy. Its role in placental development. *Obstetrics and Gynecology*, 95, 779–82.

Huynh, N. N. and McIntyre, R. S. (2008). What are the implications of the STAR*D trial for primary care? A review and synthesis. *The Primary Care Companion* *to the Journal of Clinical Psychiatry*, 10, 91–6.

Hyde, J. S. (2005). The gender similarities hypothesis. *American Psychologist*, 60, 581–92.

Hyde, J. S. (2006). The gender similarities hypothesis. *American Psychologist*, 60, 581–92.

Hyde, J. S., Mezulis, A. H., and Abramson, L. Y. (2008). The ABCs of depression. Integrating affective, biological and cognitive models to explain the emergence of the gender difference in depression. *Psychological Review*, 115, 291–313.

Hyde, K. L., Lerch, J., Norton, A., Forgeard, M., Winner, E., et al (2009). Musical training shapes structural brain development. *The Journal of Neuroscience*, 29, 2019–25.

Hyman, I. E., Jr, Husband, T. H., and Billings, F. J. (1995). False memories of childhood experiences. *Applied Cognitive Psychology*, 9, 181–97.

Hyman, R. (1989). *The Elusive Quarry. A Scientific Appraisal of Psychical Research*. New York, NY. Prometheus Books.

Hyman, S. E. (2010). The diagnosis of mental disorders. The problem of reification. *Annual Review of Clinical Psychology*, 6, 155–79.

Iascoboni, M. (2009). Imitation, empathy, and motor neurons. *Annual Review of Psychology*, 60, 653–70.

Iacoboni, M. (2009). Imitation, empathy, and mirror neurons. *Annual Review of Psychology*, 60, 653–70.

Iacoboni, M., Molnar-Szakacs, I., Gallese, V., Buccino, G., Mazziotta, J. C., et al (2005). Grasping the intentions of others with one's own mirror neuron system. *PLoS Biology*, 3. Retrieved from www.plos.org on 1 May 2007.

Ikonomidou, C., Bittigau, P., Ishimaru, M. J., Wozniak, D. F., Koch, C., et al (2000). Ethanol-induced apoptotic neurode-generation and fetal alcohol syndrome. *Science*, 287, 1056–60.

Infante, M. and Benca, R. (2005). Treatment of insomnia. *Primary Psychiatry*, 12, 47–56.

Inglehart, R., Basanez, M., Diez-Medrano, J., Halman, L., and Luijkx, R. (2004). *Human Beliefs and Values. A Cross-cultural Sourcebook Based on the 1999–2002 Values Surveys*. Mexico City, Mexico. Siglo XXI.

Inglehart, R., Foa, R. Peterson, C., and Welzel, C. (2008). Development,

freedom, and rising happiness. A global perspective (1981–2007). *Perspectives on Psychological Science*, 3, 264–85.

Innocence Project (2013). *Annual Report*. New York, NY. Innocence Project.

International Schizophrenia Consortium. Purcell, S. M., Wray, N. R., Stone, J. L., Visscher, P. M., O'Donovan. M. C., et al (2009). Common polygenic variation contributes to risk of schizophrenia and bipolar disorder. *Nature*, 460, 748–52.

Ioannidis, J. P. A. (2005). Why most published research findings are false. *PLoS Medicine*, 2. Retrieved from http://medicine.plosjournals.org/archive on 14 March 2007.

Iranzo, A., Santamaria, J., and Tolosa, E. (2009). The clinical and pathophysiological relevance of REM sleep behavior disorder in neurodegenerative diseases. *Sleep Medicine Review*, 13, 385–401.

Israel, G. E. and Tarver, D. E. (2001). *Transgender Care. Recommended Guidelines, Practical Information and Personal Accounts*. Philadelphia, PA. Temple University Press.

Ito, M., Horst, H., Bittanti, M., Boyd, D., Herr-Stephenson, B., et al (2008). *Living and Learning with New Media. Summary of Findings from the Digital Youth Project*. The MacArthur Foundation. Retrieved from http://digitalyouth.ischool.berkeley.edu/files/report/digitalyouth-WhitePaper.pdf on 14 December 2008.

Iverson, L. (2003). Comparing cannabis with tobacco. Arithmetic does not add up. *British Medical Journal*, 327, 165.

Izard, C. E. (1990). Facial expressions and the regulation of emotion. *Journal of Personality and Social Psychology*, 58, 487–98.

Izard, C. E. (2007). Basic emotions, natural kinds, emotion schemas, and a new paradigm. *Perspectives in Psychological Science*, 2, 260–80.

Izard, C. E. (2009). Emotion theory and research. Highlights, unanswered questions, and emerging issues. *Annual Review of Psychology*, 60, 1–25.

Izard, C. E. (2011). Forms and functions of emotion. Matters of emotion-cognition interactions. *Emotion Review*, 3, 371–8.

Jackendoff, R. (1994). *Patterns in the Mind. Language and Human Nature*. New York, NY. Basic Books.

Jackson, B., Gucciardi, D. F., Lonsdale, C., Whipp, P. R., and Dimmock, J. A. (2014).

'I think they believe in me'. The predictive effects of teammate- and classmate-focused relation-inferred self-efficacy in sport and physical activity settings. *Journal of Sport and Exercise Psychology*, 36(5), 486–505.

Jackson, J. W. (1993). Realistic group conflict theory. A review and evaluation of the theoretical and empirical literature. *Psychological Record*, 43, 395–413.

Jackson, P. L., Meltzoff, A. N., and Decety, J. (2005). How do we perceive the pain of others? A window into the neural processes involved in empathy. *NeuroImage*, 24, 771–9.

Jackson, P. L., Rainville, P., and Decety, J. (2006). Empathy examined through the neural mechanisms involved in imagining how I feel versus how you feel pain. An event-related fMRI study. *Neuropsychologia*, 44, 752–61.

Jacob, S. Kinnunen, J. S., Metz, J., Cooper, M., and McClintock, M. K. (2001). Sustained human chemosignal unconsciously alters brain function. *Neuroreport*, 12, 2391–4.

Jacobellis v. Ohio, 378 U.S. 184 (1964).

Jacobi, C., Hayward, C., de Zwaan, M., Kraemer, H. C., and Agras, S. (2004). Coming to terms with risk factors for eating disorders. Application of risk terminology and suggestions for a general taxonomy. *Psychological Bulletin*, 130, 19–65.

Jacobs, A., Carpenter, J., Donnelly, J., Klapproth, J. F., Gertel, A., et al (2005). The involvement of professional medical writers in medical publications. Results of a Delphi study. *Current Medical Research and Opinion*, 21, 311–16.

Jacobsen, H., Ivarsson, T., Wentzel-Larsen, T., Smith, L., and Moe, V. (2014). Attachment security in young foster children. Continuity from 2 to 3 years of age. *Attachment and Human Development*, 16(1), 42–57.

Jacobson, N. S. and Addis, M. E. (1993). Couples therapy. What do we know and where are we going? *Journal of Consulting and Clinical Psychology*, 61, 85–93.

Jacobson, N. S. and Christensen, A. (1996b). Studying the effectiveness of psychotherapy. How well can clinical trials do the job? *American Psychologist*, 51, 1031–9.

Jacobson, N. S. and Truax, P. (1991). Clinical significance. A statistical approach to defining meaningful change in psychotherapy research. *Journal of Consulting and Clinical Psychology*, 59(1), 12–19.

Jadva, V., Hines, M., and Golombok, S. (2010). Infants' preferences for toys, colors, and shapes. Sex differences and similarities. *Archives of Sexual Behavior*, 39, 1261–73.

James, L. E. (2006). Specific effects of aging on proper name retrieval. Now you see them, now you don't. *The Journals of Gerontology, Series B. Psychological Sciences and Social Sciences*, 61B, P180–3.

James, W. (1890/1981). *Principles of Psychology* (Vols 1 and 2). Cambridge, MA. Harvard University Press.

James, W. (1981). *The Principles of Psychology* (Vol 2). Cambridge, MA. Harvard University Press. (Original work published 1890.)

Jamison, K. R. (1996a). *Touched with Fire. Manic Depressive Illness and the Artistic Temperament*. New York, NY. Free Press.

Jamison, K. R. (1996b). *An Unquiet Mind*. New York, NY. Alfred A. Knopf.

Jamison, K. R. (2006). The many stigmas of mental illness. *The Lancet*, 367, 533–4.

Janis, I. L. (1989). *Crucial Decisions. Leadership in Policy-making and Crisis Management*. New York, NY. Free Press.

Janis, I. L. (2007). Groupthink. In R. P. Vecchio (ed), *Leadership. Understanding the Dynamics of Power and Influence In Organizations* (pp 163–76). Notre Dame, IN. University of Notre Dame Press.

Jankowiak, W. R. and Fisher, E. F. (1992). A cross-cultural perspective on romantic love. *Ethnology*, 31, 149–55.

Jaramillo Jaramillo, L. M., Castrillón Díaz, L. T., and López Caro, L. B. (2013). Teaching learners to set smart goals to increase their self-efficacy (Master's thesis, Universidad de La Sabana).

Jarrett, C. (2013) *Scanning a Brain that Believes it is Dead*. BPS Research Digest, 21 May 2013.

Jarvis, M. (2004). *Psychodynamic Psychology. Classical Theory and Contemporary Research*. London. Cengage Learning EMEA.

Jarvis, M. (2011) *Teaching 14–19 Psychology*. London. Routledge.

Jaynes, J. (1976). *The Origin of Consciousness in the Breakdown of the Bicameral Mind*. Boston. Houghton Mifflin.

Jeffers, S. (2003). Physics and claims for anomalous effects related to consciousness. *Journal of Consciousness Studies*, 10(6–7), 135–52.

Jensen, A. R. (1998). *The g Factor*. Westport, CT. Praeger.

Ji, R.-R., Kohno, T., Moore, K. A., and Woolf, C. J. (2003). Central sensitization and LTP. Do pain and memory share similar mechanisms? *Trends in Neurosciences*, 26, 696–705.

Jobe, T. H. and Harrow, M. (2005). Long-term outcome of patients with schizophrenia. A review. *Canadian Journal of Psychiatry*, 50, 892–900.

Jobe, T. H. and Harrow, M. (2010). Schizophrenia course, long-term outcome, recovery, and prognosis. *Current Directions in Psychological Science*, 19, 220–5.

Johanson, C., Roehrs, T., Schuh, K. and Warbasse, L. (1999). The effects of cocaine on mood and sleep in cocaine dependent males. *Experimental and Clinical Psychopharmacology*, 7, 1–9.

Johnson, C. S. and Stapel, D. A. (2010). Harnessing social comparisons. When and how upward comparisons influence goal pursuit. *Basic and Applied Social Psychology*, 32, 234–42.

Johnson, S. C., Dweck, C. S., and Chen, F. S. (2007). Evidence for infants' internal working models of attachment. *Psychological Science*, 18, 501–2.

Johnson, W. and Bouchard, T. J., Jr (2005). The structure of human intelligence. It is verbal, perceptual, and image rotation (VPR), not fluid and crystallized. *Intelligence*, 33, 393–416.

Johnson, W., Bouchard, T. J., Jr, Krueger, R. F., McGue, M., and Gottesman, I. I. (2004). Just one *g*. Consistent results from three test batteries. *Intelligence*, 32(1), 95–107.

Johnson, W. and Krueger, R. F. (2006). How money buys happiness. Genetic and environmental processes linking finances and life satisfaction. *Journal of Personality and Social Psychology*, 90, 680–91.

Johnson, W., McGue, M., and Iacono, W. G. (2006). Genetic and environmental influences on academic achievement. *Developmental Psychology*, 42, 514–32.

Johnson, W., te Nijenhuis, J., and Bouchard, T. J., Jr (2008). Still just 1 *g*. Consistent results from five test batteries. *Intelligence*, 36, 81–95.

Johnson, W., Turkheimer, E., Gottesman, I. I., and Buchard, J. Jr (2009). Beyond heritability. Twin studies in behavioral research. *Current Directions in Psychological Science*, 18, 217–20.

Johnston, L. D., O'Malley, P. M., Bachman, J. G., and Schulenberg, J. E. (2012). *Monitoring the Future National Results on Adolescent Drug Use. Overview of Key Findings, 2011*. Ann Arbor. Institute for Social Research, the University of Michigan. Retrieved from www.monitoringthefuture.org on 3 February 2012.

Johnston, R. E. (1998). Pheromones, the vomeronasal system, and communication. From hormonal responses to individual recognition. *Annals of the New York Academy of Sciences*, 855, 333–48.

Johnston, V. S., Hagel, R., Franklin, M., Fink, B., and Grammer, K. (2001). Male facial attractiveness. Evidence for hormone-mediated adaptive design. *Evolution and Human Behavior*, 22, 251–67.

Joiner, T. E., Jr (1996). Depression and rejection. *Communication Research*, 23, 451–71.

Jones, D. (1996). *Physical Attractiveness and the Theory of Sexual Selection*. Ann Arbor, MI. Museum of Anthropology, University of Michigan.

Jones, E. E. (1990). *Interpersonal Perception*. New York, NY. W. H. Freeman.

Jones, E. E. and Harris, V. A. (1967). The attribution of attitudes. *Journal of Experimental Social Psychology, 3(1)*, 1–24.

Jones, E. E., and Nisbett, R. E. (1971). *The Actor and the Observer. Divergent Perceptions of the Causes of Behavior*. New York, NY. Basic Books.

Jones, E. E. and Pittman, T. S. (1982). Toward a general theory of strategic self-presentation. In J. Suls (ed), *Psychological Perspectives on the Self* (Vol 1, pp 231–62). Hillsdale, NJ. Lawrence Erlbaum Associates.

Jones, G. (2003). Testing two cognitive theories of insight. *Journal of Experimental Psychology. Learning, Memory, and Cognition*, 29, 1017–27.

Jones, G. (2005). Echolocation. *Current Biology*, 15, R484–8.

Jones, M. C. (1924a). A laboratory study of fear. The case of Peter. *Pedagogical Seminary*, 31, 308–15.

Jones, M. C. (1924b). The elimination of children's fears. *Journal of Experimental Psychology*, 7, 382–90.

Jones, P. B., Barnes, T. R., Davies, L., Dunn, G., Lloyd, H., et al (2006). Randomized controlled trial of the effect on quality of life of second- vs. first-generation antipsychotic drugs in schizophrenia. Cost Utility of the Latest Antipsychotic Drugs in Schizophrenia Study (CUtLASS 1). *Archives of General Psychiatry*, 63, 1079–87.

Jones, T. (2002, 13 January). Bringing up genius. *The Washington Post*, W7.

Jonides, J., Lewis, R. L., Nee, D. E., Lustig, C. A., Berman, M. G., et al (2008). The mind and brain of short-term memory. *Annual Review of Psychology*, 59, 193–224.

Jordahl, T. and Lohman, B. J. (2009). A bioecological analysis of risk and protective factors associated with early sexual intercourse of young adolescents. *Child Youth Services Review*, 31, 12–82.

Josephson, W. L. (1987). Television violence and children aggression. Testing the priming, social script, and disinhibition predictions. *Journal of Personality and Social Psychology*, 53, 882–90.

Judd, D. and Kelly, K. (1939). Method of designating colors. *Journal of Research of the National Bureau of Standards*, 23, 355.

Juliano, L. M. and Griffiths, R. R. (2004). A critical review of caffeine withdrawal. Empirical validation of symptoms and signs, incidence, severity, and associated features. *Psychopharmacology*, 176(1), 1–29.

Jung-Beeman, M., Bowden, E. M., Haber-man, J., Frymiare, J. L., Arambel-Liu, S., et al (2004). Neural activity when people solve verbal problems with insight. *PLoS Biology*, 2. Retrieved from http://biology. plosjournals.org on 17 November 2005.

Jussim, L., Cain, T. R., Crawford, J. T., Harber, K., and Cohen, F. (2009). The unbearable accuracy of stereotypes. In T. D. Nelson (ed), *Handbook of Prejudice, Stereotyping, and Discrimination* (pp 199–227). New York, NY. Psychology Press.

Kagan, J. (1994). *Galen's Prophecy. Temperament in Human Nature*. New York, NY. Basic Books.

Kagan, J. (2003). Biology, context and developmental inquiry. *Annual Review of Psychology*, 54, 1–23.

Kahn-Harris, K. (2006). *Extreme Metal. Music and Culture on the Edge*. Berg.

Kahneman, D. (2011). *Thinking, Fast and Slow*. New York, NY. Farrar, Straus, and Giroux.

Kahneman, D., Krueger, A. B., Schkade, D., Schwarz, N., and Stone, A. A. (2004). Would you be happier if you were richer? A focusing illusion. *Science*, 312, 1908–10.

Kaiser, P. and Boynton, R. (1996) *Color Vision*. Washington, DC. Optical Society of America.

Kakigi, R., Nakata, H., Inui, K., Hiroe, N., Nagata, O., et al (2005). Intracerebral pain processing in a yoga master who claims not to feel pain during meditation. *European Journal of Pain*, 9, 581–9.

Kalin, N. H., Shelton, S. E., Davidson, R. J., and Kelley, A. E. (2001). The primate amygdala mediates acute fear but not the behavioral and physiological components of anxious temperament. *Journal of Neuroscience*, 21, 2067–74.

Kammrath, L. K., Menoza-Denton, R., and Mischel, W. (2005). Incorporating *If . . . then . . .* personality signatures in person perception. Beyond the person-situation dichotomy. *Journal of Personality and Social Psychology*, 88, 605–18.

Kandel, E. (2000). Cellular mechanisms of learning and the biological basis of individuality. In E. Kandel, J. H. Schwartz, and T. M. Jessell (eds), *Principles of Neural Sciences* (pp 1247–57). New York, NY. McGraw-Hill.

Kane, J. M. (2004). Tardive dyskinesia rates with atypical antipsychotics in adults. Prevalence and incidence. *Journal of Clinical Psychiatry*, 65(Suppl 9), 16–20.

Kanfer, R. (1990). Motivation theory and industrial and organizational psychology. In M. D. Dunnette and L. M Hough (eds), *Handbook of Industrial and Organizational Psychology Vol 1* (2nd edn, pp 75–170). Palo Alto, CA. Consulting Psychologists Press.

Kanwisher, N. (2006). What's in a face? *Science*, 311, 617–18.

Kanwisher, N. and Yovel, G. (2006). The fusiform face area. A cortical region specialized for the perception of faces. *Philosophical Transactions of the Royal Society B*, 361, 2109–28.

Kaplan, C. A. and Simon, H. A. (1990). In search of insight. *Cognitive Psychology*, 22, 374–419.

Kaplan, R. M. (2006). Overdiagnosis and pseudodisease. Too much of a 'good thing?' In F. Porzsolt and R. M. Kaplan (eds), *Optimizing Health. Improving the Value of Healthcare* (pp 87–91). New York, NY. Springer.

Kaplan, R. M. and Kronick, R. G. (2006). Marital status and longevity in the United States population. *Journal of Epidemiology and Community Health*, 60, 760–5.

Kaptchuk, T. J., Friedlander, E., Kelley, J. M., Sanchez, M. N., Kokkotou, E., et al (2010). Placebos without deception. A randomized controlled trial in irritable bowel syndrome. *PLoS One*, 5, e15591. Retrieved from www.plosone.org on 26 October 2011.

Karch, W., Stephens, B. C., and Nazareno, G. V. (2001). GHB. Club drug or confusing artifact? *American Journal of Forensic Medicine and Pathology*, 22, 266–9.

Kasser, T. and Ryan, R. (1996). Further examining the American dream. Differential correlates of intrinsic and extrinsic goals. *Personality and Social Psychology Bulletin*, 22, 280–7.

Kassim, S. H. (2008). The role of religion in the generation of suicide bombers. *Brief Treatment and Crisis Intervention*, 8, 204–8.

Kast, B. (2001). Decisions, decisions . . . *Nature*, 411, 126–8.

Kastenbaum, R. (2000). *The Psychology of Death* (3rd edn). New York, NY. Springer.

Katzman, M. A., Hermans, K. M. E., van Hoeken, D., and Hoek, H. W. (2004). 'Not your typical island woman'. Anorexia nervosa is reported only in subcultures in Curaçao. *Culture, Medicine, and Psychiatry*, 28, 463–92.

Kazdin, A. E. (2001). *Behavior Modification in Applied Settings* (6th edn). Belmont, CA. Wadsworth.

Kazdin, A. E. (2005). Treatment outcomes, common factors, and continued neglect of mechanisms of change. *Clinical Psychology. Science and Practice*, 12, 184–8.

Kazdin, A. E. and Blase, S. L. (2011). Rebooting psychotherapy research and practice to reduce the burden of mental illness. *Perspectives on Psychological Science*, 6, 21–37.

Keefe, F. J. and France, C. R. (1999). Pain. Biopsychosocial mechanisms and management. *Current Directions in Psychological Science*, 8, 137–41.

Keel, P. K., Brown, T. A., Holland, L. A., and Bodell, L. P. (2012). Empirical classification of eating disorders. *Annual Review of Clinical Psychology*, 8, 381–404.

Keesey, R. E. and Hirvonen, M. D. (1997). Body weight set-points. Determination and adjustment. *Journal of Nutrition*, 127, 1875S–83S.

Kelemen, W. L. and Creeley, C. E. (2003). State-dependent memory effects using caffeine and placebo do not extend to metamemory. *Journal of General Psychology*, 130(1), 70–86.

Keller, H. (2013). Attachment and culture. *Journal of Cross-Cultural Psychology*, 44(2), 175–94.

Kellog, S. H., Burns, M., Coleman, P., Stitzer, M., Wale, J. B., et al (2005). Something of value. The introduction of contingency management interventions into the New York City Health and Hospital Addiction Treatment Service. *Journal of Substance Abuse Treatment*, 28(1), 57–65.

Kelly, D. J., Quinn, P. C., Slater, A. M., Lee, K., Ge, L., et al (2007). The other-race effect develops during infancy. Evidence of perceptual narrowing. *Psychological Science*, 18, 1084–9.

Kelly, D. J., Quinn, P. C., Slater, A. M., Lee, K., Gibson, A., et al (2005). Three-month-olds, but not newborns, prefer own-race faces. *Developmental Science*, 8, F31–6.

Kelly, I. W. (1997). Modern astrology. A critique. *Psychological Reports*, 81, 1035–66.

Kelly, I. W. (1998).Why astrology doesn't work. *Psychological Reports*, 82, 527–46.

Kendler, K. S. (1996). Parenting. A genetic-epidemiologic perspective. *American Journal of Psychiatry*, 153, 11–20.

Kendler, K. S. and Baker, J. H. (2007). Genetic influences on measures of the environment. A systematic review. *Psychological Medicine*, 37, 615–26.

Kendler, K. S., Eaves, L. J., Loken, E. K., Pedersen, N. L., Middeldorp, C. M., et al (2011). The impact of environmental experiences on symptoms of anxiety and depression across the life span. *Psychological Science*, 22, 1343–52.

Kendler, K. S., Hettema, J. M., Butera, M. A., Gardner, C. O., and Prescott, C. A. (2003). Life event dimensions of loss, humiliation, entrapment, and danger in the prediction of onsets of major depression and generalized anxiety. *Archives of General Psychiatry*, 60, 789–96.

Kendler, K. S., Thornton, L. M., Gilman, S. E., and Kessler, R. C. (2000). Sexual orientation in a U.S. national sample of twin and nontwin sibling pairs. *The American Journal of Psychiatry*, 157, 1843–6.

Kennedy, J. E. (2001). Why is psi so elusive? A review and proposed model. *Journal of Consciousness Studies*, 65, 219–46.

Kennedy, J. M. and Juricevic, I. (2006). Foreshortening, convergence, and drawings of a blind adult. *Perception*, 35, 847–51.

Kenrick, D. T., Griskevicius, V., Neuberg, S. L., and Schaller, M. (2010). Renovating the pyramid of needs. Contemporary extensions built upon ancient foundations. *Perspectives on Psychological Science*, 5, 292–314.

Kenrick, D. T. and Li, N. (2000). The Darwin is in the details. *American Psychologist*, 55, 1060–1.

Kenrick, D. T., Li, N. P., and Butner, J. (2003). Dynamical evolutionary psychology. Individual decision-rules and emergent social norms. *Psychological Review*, 110(1), 3–28.

Kenrick, D. T., Neuberg, S. L., Griskevicius, V., Becker, D. V., and Schaller, M. (2010). Goal-driven cognition and functional behavior. The fundamental-motives framework. *Current Directions in Psychological Science*, 19, 63–67.

Kentros, C. (2006). Hippocampal place cells. The 'where' of episodic memory. *Hippocampus*, 16, 743–54.

Kerr, D., Kelly, A-M., Dietze, P., Damien, J., and Barger, B. (2009). Randomized controlled trial comparing the effectiveness and safety of intranasal and intramuscular naloxone for the treatment of suspected heroin overdose. *Addiction*, 104, 2067–74.

Kerr, M. and Stattin, H. (2003). Parenting adolescents. Action or reaction? In A. C. Crouter and A. Booth (eds), *Children's Influence on Family Dynamics* (pp 121–51). Mahwah, NJ. Erlbaum.

Kerrnis, M. H., Lakey, C. E., and Heppner, W. L. (2008). Secure versus fragile high self-esteem as a predictor of verbal defensiveness. Converging findings across three different markers. *Journal of Personality*, 76, 477–512.

Kessel, N. (1965). Self-poisoning, Part I. *British Medical Journal*, 2, 1265–70.

Kessler, R. C. (1997). The effects of stressful life events on depression. *Annual Review of Psychology*, 48, 191–214.

Kessler, R. C., Berglund, P., Demler, O., Jin, R., Koretz, D., et al (2003). The epidemiology of major depressive disorder. Results from the National Comorbidity Survey Replication (NCS-R). *JAMA*, 289, 3095–105.

Kessler, R. C., Birnbaum, H., Demler, O., Falloon, I. R., Gagnon, E., et al (2005). The prevalence and correlates of non-affective psychosis in the National Comorbidity Survey Replication. *Biological Psychiatry*, 58, 668–76.

Kessler, R. C., Chiu, W. T., Demler, O., and Walters, E. E. (2005). Prevalence, severity, and comorbidity of 12-month DSM-IV disorders in the National Comorbidity Survey Replication. *Archives of General Psychiatry*, 62, 617–709.

Kessler, R. C., Chiu, W. T., Jin, R., Ruscio, A. M., Shear, K., et al (2006). The epidemiology of panic attacks, panic disorder, and agoraphobia in the National Comorbidity Survey Replication. *Archives of General Psychiatry*, 63, 415–24.

Kessler, R. C., Merikangas, K. R., and Wang, P. S. (2007). Prevalence, comorbidity, and service utilization for mood disorders in the United States at the beginning of the 21st century. *Annual Review of Clinical Psychology*, 3, 137–58.

Kessler, R. C., Mickelson, K. D., and Zhao, S. (1997). Patterns and correlates of self-help group membership in the United States. *Social Policy*, 27, 27–46.

Kessler, R. C. and Wang, P. S. (2009). The epidemiology of depression. In I. G. Gotlib and C. L. Hammen (eds), *Handbook of Depression* (2nd edn, pp 5–22). New York, NY. Guilford

Keys, A. Brozek, J., Henschel, A., Mickelsen, O., and Taylor, H. L. (1950). *The Biology of Starvation*. Minneapolis. University of Minnesota Press.

Khan, A., Faucett, J., Lichtenberg, P., Kirsch, L., and Brown, W. A. (2012). A systematic review of comparative efficacy of treatments and controls for depression. *PLoS One*, 7, e41778. Retrieved from www.plosone.org on 10 March 2013.

Khatwani, K. (2003). *Theories of Love and Loss. A New Conception of Mourning* (Abstract only). Berkeley, CA. The Wright Institute. Retrieved from *Dissertation Abstracts International. Section B. Sciences and Engineering*, 64(3-B).

Kiecolt-Glaser, J.K. and Newton, T. L. (2001). Marriage and health. His and hers. *Psychological Bulletin*, 127, 472–503.

Kihlstrom, J. F. (1998). Dissociations and dissociation theory in hypnosis. Comment on Kirsch and Lynn (1998). *Psychological Bulletin*, 123, 186–91.

Kihlstrom, J. F. (2005). Dissociative disorders. *Annual Review of Clinical Psychology*, 1, 227–53.

Kihlstrom, J. F. (2005). Is hypnosis an altered state of consciousness or *what*? Comment. *Contemporary Hypnosis*, 22, 34–8.

Kihlstrom, J. F. (2008). The domain of hypnosis, revisited. In M. R. Nash and A. J. Barnier (eds), *The Oxford Handbook of Hypnosis. Theory, Research, and Practice* (pp 21–52). New York, NY. Oxford University Press.

Killgore, W. D., Killgore, D. B., Day, L. M., Li, C., Kamimori, G. H., et al (2007). The effects of 53 hours sleep deprivation on moral judgment. *Sleep*, 30, 345–52.

Kim, J-N. and Shadlen, M. N. (1999). Neural correlates of a decision in the dorsolateral prefrontal cortex of the macaque. *Nature Neuroscience*, 2, 176–85.

Kimura, D. (1992). Sex differences in the brain. *Scientific American*, 267, 118–25.

Kimura, D. (2004). Human sex differences in cognition. Fact, not predicament. *Sexualities, Evolution, and Gender*, 6, 45–53.

King, A. and Crewe, I. (2014). *The Blunders of Our Governments*. Oneworld Publications.

King, E. B., Knight, J. L., and Hebl, M. R. (2010). The influence of economic conditions on aspects of stigmatization. *Journal of Social Issues*, 66, 446–60.

King, L. A. and Corkery, J. M. (2010). An index of fatal toxicity for drugs of misuse. *Human Psychopharmacology*, 25, 162–6.

King, L. A. and Napa, C. K. (1998). What makes a life good? *Journal of Personality and Social Psychology*, 75, 156–65.

King, S. A., and Moreggi, D. (2007). Internet self-help and support groups. The pros and cons of text-based mutual aid. In J. Gackenbach (ed), *Psychology and the Internet. Intrapersonal, Interpersonal, and Transpersonal Implications* (2nd edn), pp 221–44). San Diego, CA. Academic Press.

Kinsey, A. C., Pomeroy, W. B., and Martin, C. E. (1948). *Sexual Behavior in the Human Male*. Philadelphia, PA. Saunders.

Kinsey, A. C., Pomeroy, W. B., Martin C. E., and Gebhard, P. H. (1953). *Sexual Behavior in the Human Female*. Philadelphia, PA. Saunders.

Kirkpatrick, M. G., Lee, R., Wardle, M. C., Jacob, S., and De Wit, H. (2014). Effects of MDMA and intranasal oxytocin on social and emotional processing. *Neuropsychopharmacology*, 39, 1654–63.

Kirsch, I. (2002). Yes, there *is* a placebo effect, but is there a powerful antidepressant drug effect? *Prevention and Treatment*, 5. Retrieved from http://journals.apa.org/prevention/volume5 on 7 January 2005.

Kirsch, I. (2005). Empirical resolution of the altered state debate. *Contemporary Hypnosis*, 22, 18–23.

Kirsch, I. (2005). Medication and suggestion in the treatment of depression. *Contemporary Hypnosis*, 22, 59–66.

Kirsch, I., Deacon, B. J., Huedo-Medina, T. B., Scoboria, A., Moore, T. J., et al (2008). Initial severity and antidepressant benefits. A meta-analysis of data submitted to the Food and Drug Administration. *PLoS Medicine*, 5,

0260–8. Retrieved from http://www.plosmedicine.org/article/info:doi/10.1371/journal.pmed.0050045 on 2 March 2008.

Kirsch, I. and Lynn, S. J. (1995). The altered state of hypnosis. Changes in the theoretical landscape. *American Psychologist*, 50, 846–58.

Kirsch, I., Mazzoni, G., and Montgomery, G. H. (2007). Remembrance of hypnosis past. *American Journal of Clinical Hypnosis*, 49, 171–8.

Kirsch, I., Moore, T. J., Scoboria, A., and Nicholls, S. (2002). The emperor's new drugs. An analysis of antidepressant medication data submitted to the U.S. Food and Drug Administration. *Prevention and Treatment*, 5. Retrieved from http://journals.apa.org/prevention/volume5/toc-jul15-02.htm on 5 July 2005.

Kisilevsky, B. S., Hains, S. M., Brown, C. A., Lee, C. T., Cowperthwaite, B., et al (2009). Fetal sensitivity to properties of maternal speech and language. *Infant Behavior and Development*, 32, 59–71.

Kisilevsky, B. S., Hains, S. M., Lee, K., Xie, X., Huang, H., et al (2003). Effects of experience on fetal voice recognition. *Psychological Science*, 14, 220–4.

Kissileff, H. R., Pi-Sunyer, F. X., Thornton, J., and Smith, G. P. (1981). C-terminal octapeptide of cholecystokinin decreases food intake in man. *American Journal of Clinical Nutrition*, 34, 154–60.

Klaczynski, P. A. (2001). Analytic and heuristic processing influences on adolescent reasoning and decision making. *Child Development*, 72, 844–61.

Klaczynski, P. A. and Narasimham, G. (1998). Development of scientific reasoning biases. Cognitive versus ego-protective explanations. *Developmental Psychology*, 34, 175–87.

Kleider, H. M., Pezdek, K., Goldinger, S. D., and Kirk, A. (2008). Schema-driven source misattribution errors. Remembering the expected from a witnessed event. *Applied Cognitive Psychology*, 22, 1–20.

Klein, D. N. (2010). Chronic depression. Diagnosis and classification. *Current Directions in Psychological Science*, 19, 96–100.

Klein, E. D. and Zentall, T. R. (2003). Imitation and affordance learning by pigeons (*Columba livia*). *Journal of Comparative Psychology*, 117, 414–19.

Klein, S. B. (2012). The self and science. Is it time for a new approach to the study of human experience? *Current Directions in Psychological Science*, 21, 253–7.

Kleinke, C. L., Peterson, T. R., and Rutledge, T. R. (1998). Effects of self-generated facial expressions on mood. *Journal of Personality and Social Psychology*, 74, 272–9.

Kleinschmidt, A. and Cohen, L. (2006). The neural bases of prosopagnosia and pure alexia. Recent insights from functional neuroimaging. *Current Opinion in Neurology*, 19, 386–91.

Klimstra, T. A., Hale, W. W., III, Raaijmakers, Q. A. W., Branje, S. J. T., and Meeus, W. H. J. (2009). Maturation of personality in adolescence. *Journal of Personality and Social Psychology*, 96, 679–89.

Kluger, A. N. and Tikochinsky, J. (2001). The error of accepting the 'theoretical' null hypothesis. The rise, fall, and resurrection of commonsense hypotheses in psychology. *Psychological Bulletin*, 127, 408–21.

Klump, K. L., Burt, A. S., McGue, M., and Iacono, W. G. (2007). Changes in genetic and environmental influences on disordered eating across adolescence. A longitudinal twin study. *Archives of General Psychiatry*, 64, 1409–15.

Knekt, P., Lindfors, O., Renlund, C., Sares-Jäske, L., Laaksonen, M. A., et al (2011). Use of auxiliary psychiatric treatment during a 5-year follow-up among patients receiving short- or long-term psychotherapy. *Journal of Affective Disorders*, 135(1-3), 221–30.

Knickmeyer, R. C., Wheelwright, S., Taylor, K., Raggatt, P., Hackett, G., et al (2005). Gender-typed play and amniotic testosterone. *Developmental Psychology*, 41, 517–28.

Knight, D. C., Cheng, D. T., Smith, C. N., Stein, E. A., and Helmstetter, F. J. (2004). Neural substrates mediating human delay and trace conditioning. *The Journal of Neuroscience*, 24, 1187–95.

Knoblich, G., Ohlsson, S., Haider, H., and Rhenius, D. (1999). Constraint relaxation and chunk decomposition in insight problem solving. *Journal of Experimental Psychology. Learning, Memory, and Cognition*, 25, 1534–55.

Knowlton, B. J., Mangels, J. A., and Squire, L. R. (1996). A neostriatal habit learning system in humans. *Science*, 273, 1399–1402.

Koball, H. L., Moiduddin, E., Henderson, J., Goesling, B., and Besculides, M. (2010). What do we know about the link between marriage and health? *Journal of Family Issues*, 31, 1019–40.

Kochanek, K. D., Murphy S. L., Anderson, R. N., and Scott, C. (2004). Deaths. Final data for 2002 National Vital Statistics Reports, 53(5), DHHS Publication No. (PHS) 2005–1120. Hyattsville, MD. National Center for Health Statistics. Retrieved from http://www.cdc.gov/nchs/data/nvsr/nvsr53/nvsr53_05.pdf on 22 May 2008.

Koh, A. S. and Ross, L. K. (2006). Mental health issues. A comparison of lesbian, bisexual and heterosexual women. *Journal of homosexuality*, 51(1), 33–57.

Kohl, J. V., Atzmuller, M., Fink, B., and Grammer, K. (2007). Human pheromones. Integrating neuroendocrinology and ethology. *Activitas Nervosa Superior*, 49, 123–35.

Kohlberg, L. (1963). The development of children's orientations toward a moral order. Sequence in the development of moral thought. *Vita Humana*, 6, 11–33.

Kohler, E., Keysers, C., Umiltà, M. A., Fogassi, L., Gallese, V., et al (2002). Hearing sounds, understanding actions. Action representation in mirror neurons. *Science*, 297, 846–8.

Kolata, G. (2003). *Ultimate Fitness. The Quest for Truth about Exercise and Health*. New York, NY. Farrar, Straus, and Giroux.

Komar, V., Melamid, A., and Wypijewski, J. (1999). *Painting by Numbers. Komar and Melamid's Scientific Guide to Art*. Berkeley, CA. University of California Press.

Komura, Y., Tamura, R., Uwano, T., Nishiko, H., Kaga, K., et al (2001). Retrospective and prospective coding for predicted reward in the sensory thalamus. *Nature*, 412, 546–9.

Koob, G. F. and Le Moal, M. (2008). Addiction and the brain antireward system. *Annual Review of Psychology*, 59, 29–53.

Koppenaal, L. and Glanzer, M. (1990). An examination of the continuous distractor task and the 'long-term recency effect.' *Memory and Cognition*, 18, 183–95.

Koriat, A., Goldsmith, M., and Pansky, A. (2000). Toward a psychology of memory accuracy. *Annual Review of Psychology*, 51, 481–537.

Korman, A. K. (1974). *The Psychology of Motivation*. Englewood Cliffs, NJ. Prentice-Hall.

Kosfeld, M., Heinrichs, M., Zak, P. J., Fischbacher, U., Fehr, E., et al (2005). Oxytocin increases trust in humans. *Nature*, 435, 673–6.

Kosslyn, S. M., Thompson, W. L., and Ganis, G. (2006). *The Case for Mental Imagery*. New York, NY. Oxford University Press.

Kotler, J. A., Wright, J. C., and Huston, A. C. (2001). Television use in families with children. In J. Bryant and J. A. Bryant (eds), *Television and the American Family* (2nd edn, pp 33–48). Mahwah, NJ. Lawrence Erlbaum Associates.

Kotzalidis, G. D., Patrizi, B., Caltagirone, S. S., Koukopoulos, A., Savoja, V., et al (2007). The adult SSRI/SNRI withdrawal syndrome. A clinically heterogeneous entity. *Clinical Neuropsychiatry. Journal of Treatment Evaluation*, 4, 1–75.

Kounios, J., Frymiare, J. L., Bowden, E. M., Fleck, J. I., Subramaniam, K., et al (2006). The prepared mind. Brain activity prior to problem presentation predicts subsequent solution by sudden insight. *Psychological Science*, 17, 882–90.

Kounious, J. and Beeman, M. (2009). The *Aha!* Moment. The cognitive neuroscience of insight. *Current Directions in Psychological Science*, 18, 210–16.

Kraut, R., Brynin, M., and Kessler, S. (eds). (2006). *Computers, Phones, and the Internet. Domesticating Information Technology*. New York, NY. Oxford University Press.

Kraut, R., Patterson, M., Lundmark, V., Kiesler, S., Mukopadhyay, T., et al (1998). Internet paradox. A social technology that reduces social involvement and psychological well-being? *American Psychologist*, 53, 1017–31.

Kravitz, R. L., Epstein, R. M., Feldman, M. D., Franz, C. E., Azari, F., et al (2005). Influence of patients' requests for direct-to-consumer advertised antidepressants. A randomized controlled trial. *JAMA*, 293, 1995–2002.

Krebs, D. (2005). The evolution of morality. In D. M. Buss (ed), *The Handbook of Evolutionary Psychology* (pp 747–71). Hoboken, NJ. John Wiley and Sons.

Krebs, D. L. and Denton, K. (2005). Toward a more pragmatic approach to morality. A critical evaluation of Kohlberg's model. *Psychological Review*, 112, 629–49.

Kreppner, J. M., Rutter, M., Beckett, C., Castle, J., Colvert, E., et al (2007). Normality and impairment following profound early institutional deprivation. A longitudinal follow-up into early adolescence. *Developmental Psychology*, 43, 931–46.

Kring, A. M. and Caponigro, J. M. (2010). Emotion in schizophrenia. Where feeling meets thinking. *Current Directions in Psychological Science*, 19, 255–9.

Kringelbach, M. L. and Berridge, K. C. (2009). Towards a functional neuroanatomy of pleasure and happiness.

Trends in Cognitive Sciences, 13(11), 479–87.

Krueger, A. B. and Maleckova, J. (2003). Education, poverty and terrorism. Is there a causal connection? *Journal of Economic Perspectives*, 17, 119–44.

Krueger, J. I. and Funder, D. C. (2004). Towards a balanced social psychology. Causes, consequences and cures for the problem-seeking approach to social behavior and cognition. *Behavioral and Brain Sciences*, 27, 313–76.

Krueger, J. I., Vohs, K. D., and Baumeister, R. F. (2008). Is the allure of self-esteem a mirage after all? *American Psychologist*, 63, 64–5.

Krueger, R. F. and Johnson, W. (2008). Behavioral genetics and personality. In L. A. Pervin, O. P. John, and R. W. Robins (eds), *Handbook of Personality. Theory and Research* (3rd edn, pp 287–310). New York, NY. Guilford.

Krueger, R. F. and Markon, K. E. (2006). Understanding psychopathology. Melding behavior genetics, personality, and quantitative psychology to develop an empirically based model. *Current Directions in Psychological Science*, 15, 113–17.

Krueger, R. F., South, S., Johnson, W., and Iacono, W. (2008). The heritability of personality is not always 50%. Gene-environment interactions and correlations between personality and parenting. *Journal of Personality*, 76, 1485–1521.

Kruger, J. and Gilovich, T. (1999). 'Naïve cynicism' in everyday theories of responsibility assessment. On biased assumptions of bias. *Journal of Personality and Social Psychology*, 76, 743–53.

Kruglanski, A. W., Chen, X., Deschesne, M., Fishman, S., and Orehek, E. (2009). Fully committed. Suicide bombers' motivation and the quest for personal significance. *Political Psychology*, 30, 331–57.

Krull, D. S. and Silvera, D. H. (2013). The stereotyping of science. Superficial details influence perceptions of what is scientific. *Journal of Applied Social Psychology*, 43(8), 1660–7.

Krützen, M., Mann, J., Heithaus, M. R., Connor, R. C., Bejder, L, et al (2005). Cultural transmission of tool use in bottlenose dolphins. *Proceedings of the National Academy of Sciences*, 102, 8939–43.

Kubik, A., Zatloukal, P., Dolezal, J., Syllabova, L., Kara, J., et al (2008). A case-control study of lifestyle and lung cancer associations by histological types. *Neoplasma*, 55, 192–9.

Kübler-Ross, E. (1969). *On Death and Dying*. New York, NY. Macmillan.

Kubzansky, L. D., Martin, L. T., and Buka, S. L. (2009). Early manifestations of personality and adult health. A life course perspective. *Health Psychology*, 28, 364–72.

Kubzansky, L. D., Wright, R. J., Cohen, S., Weiss, S., Rosner, B., et al (2002). Breathing easy. A prospective study of optimism and pulmonary function in the normative aging study. *Annals of Behavioral Medicine*, 24, 345–53.

Kugelberg, F. C., Holmgren, A., Eklund, A., and Jones, A. W. (2010). Forensic toxicology findings in deaths involving gamma-hydroxybutyrate. *International Journal of Legal Medicine*, 124, 1–6.

Kuhl, B. A., Dudukovic, N. M., Kahn, I., and Wagner, A. D. (2007). Decreased demands on cognitive control reveal the neural processing benefits of forgetting. *Nature Neuroscience*, 10, 908–14.

Kuhn, D. (2006). Do cognitive changes accompany developments in the adolescent brain? *Perspectives in Psychological Science*, 1(1), 59–67.

Kuhn, T. S. (1970). *The Structure of Scientific Revolutions* (2nd edn). Chicago, IL. University of Chicago Press.

Kuncel, N. R. and Hezlett, S. A. (2010). Fact and fiction in cognitive ability testing for admissions and hiring decisions. *Current Directions in Psychological Science*, 19, 339–45.

Kuntsche, E., Kuntsche, S., Thrul, J., and Gmel, G. (2017). Binge drinking. Health impact, prevalence, correlates and interventions. *Psychology and Health*, 32(8), 976–1017.

Kuroshima, H., Kuwahata, H., and Fujita, K. (2008). Learning from others' mistakes in capuchin monkeys (*cebus paella*). *Animal Cognition*, 11, 599–609.

Kuyken, W., Byford, S., Taylor, R. S., Watkins, E., Holden, E., et al (2008). Mindfulness-based cognitive therapy to prevent relapse in recurrent depression. *Journal of Consulting and Clinical Psychology*, 76, 966–78.

Kuyken, W., Watkins, E., Holden, E., White, K., Taylor, R. S., et al (2010). How does mindfulness-based cognitive therapy work? *Behaviour Research and Therapy*, 48, 1105–12.

Kyle, S. D., Espie, C. A., and Morgan, K. (2010). . . . Not just a minor thing, it is something major, which stops you from functioning daily.' Quality of life and daytime functioning in insomnia. *Behavioral Sleep Medicine*, 8, 123–40.

LaBerge, S., DeGracia, D. J., Kunzendorf, R. G., and Wallace, B. (2000). Varieties of lucid dreaming experience. In, S. LaBerge, D. J. DeGracia, R. G. Kunzendorf, and B. Wallace (eds), *Individual Differences in Conscious Experience* (pp 269–307). Amsterdam. John Benjamins.

Lacasse, J. R. and Leo, J. (2005). Serotonin and depression. A disconnect between the advertisements and the scientific literature. *PLoS Medicine*, 2, 1211–16.

Lacey, P. (2010) Smart and scruffy targets. *The SLD Experience*, 57, 16–21.

Lachman, M. E. (ed) (2001). *Handbook of Midlife Development*. New York, NY. Wiley.

Lachman, M. E. (2004). Development in midlife. *Annual Review of Psychology*, 55, 305–31.

Laird, J. D. (1974). Self-attribution of emotion. The effects of expressive behavior on the quality of emotional experience. *Journal of Personality and Social Psychology*, 29, 475–86.

Laird, J. D. (1984). The real role of facial response in the experience of emotion. A reply to Tourangeau and Ellsworth, et al. *Journal of Personality and Social Psychology*, 47, 909–17.

Lake, R. I., Eaves, L. J., Maes, H. H., Heath, A. C., and Martin, N. G. (2000). Further evidence against the environmental transmission of individual differences in neuroticism from a collaborative study of 45,850 twins and relatives on two continents. *Behavior Genetics*, 30, 223–33.

Lalonde, J. K., Hudson, J. I., Gigante, R. A., and Pope, H. G., Jr (2001). Canadian and American psychiatrists' attitudes toward dissociative disorders diagnoses. *Canadian Journal of Psychiatry*, 46, 407–12.

Lamb, S. and Coakley, M. (1993). Normal childhood sexual play and games. Differentiating play from abuse. *Child Abuse and Neglect*, 17, 515–26.

Lamb, T. and Yang, J. E. (2000). Could different directions of infant stepping be controlled by the same locomotor central pattern generator? *Journal of Neurophysiology*, 83, 2814–24.

Lambert, M. J. (2005). Early response in psychotherapy. Further evidence for the importance of common factors rather than 'placebo effects'. *Journal of Clinical Psychology*, 61, 855–69.

Lampinen, J. M., Faries, J. M., Neuschatz, J. S., and Toglia, M. P. (2000). Recollections of things schematic. The influence of scripts on recollective experience. *Applied Cognitive Psychology*, 14, 543–54.

Lampropoulos, G. K. and Spengler, P. M. (2005). Helping and change without traditional therapy. Commonalities and opportunities. *Counselling Psychology Quarterly*, 18, 47–59.

Landau, J. D. (2002). Teaching tips. Understanding and preventing plagiarism. *Teaching Psychology*. Association for Psychological Science. Retrieved from http://www.psychologicalscience.org/teaching/tips/tips_0403.cfm on 26 May 2011.

Landau, J. D., Druen, P. B., and Arcuri, J. A. (2002). Methods for helping students to avoid plagiarism. *Teaching of Psychology*, 29, 112–15.

Langfeldt, T. (1990). Early childhood and juvenile sexuality, development and problems. In M. E. Perry (ed), *Handbook of Sexology. Vol 7. Childhood and Adolescent Sexology* (pp 179–200). New York, NY. Elsevier Science.

Langlois, J., Kalakanis, L., Rubenstein, A. J., Larson, A., Hallam, M., et al (2000). Maxims or myths of beauty? A meta-analytic and theoretical review. *Psychological Bulletin*, 126, 390–423.

Langlois, J. H. and Roggman, L. A. (1990). Attractive faces are only average. *Psychological Science*, 1, 115–21.

Langström, N., Rahman, Q., Carlström, E., and Lichtenstein, P. (2008). Genetic and environmental effects on same-sex sexual behavior. A population study of twins in Sweden. *Archives of Sexual Behavior*. Advance of publication version retrieved from www.springerlink.com on 12 December 2008.

Larsen, C. C., Bonde, L. L., Bogdanovic, N., Laursen, H., Graem, N., et al (2006). Total number of cells in the human newborn telencephalic wall. *Neuroscience*, 139, 999–1003.

Larsen, E. J. and Witham, L. (1998). Leading scientists still reject God. *Nature*, 394, 313.

Larsen, R., Kasimatis, M., and Frey, K. (1992). Facilitating the furrowed brow. An unobtrusive test of the facial feedback hypothesis applied to unpleasant affect. *Cognition and Emotion*, 6, 321–38.

Larson, R. and Verma, S. (1999). How children and adolescents spend time across cultural settings of the world. Work, play and developmental opportunities. *Psychological Bulletin*, 125, 701–36.

Larson, R. W., Moneta, G., Richards, M. H., and Wilson, S. (2002). Continuity, stability, and change in daily emotional experience across adolescence. *Child Development*, 73, 1151–65.

Larsson, I., Svedin, C.-G., and Friedrich, W. N. (2000). Differences and similarities in sexual behaviour among preschoolers in Sweden and USA. *Nordic Journal of Psychiatry*, 54, 251–7.

Latham, G. P. and Pinder, C. C. (2005). Work motivation theory and research at the dawn of the twenty-first century. *Annual Review of Psychology*, 56, 485–516.

Latham, G. P., Stajkovic, A. D., and Locke, E. A. (2010). The relevance and viability of subconscious goals in the workplace. *Journal of Management*, 36, 234–55.

Lau, J. Y. F. and Eley, T. C. (2010). The genetics of mood disorders. *Annual Review of Clinical Psychology*, 6, 313–37.

Lauderdale, D. S., Knutson, K. L., Yan, L. L., Rathouz, P. J., Hulley, S. B., et al (2006). Objectively measured sleep characteristics among early-middle-aged adults. *American Journal of Epidemiology*, 164(1), 5–16.

Laugerette, F., Passilly-Degrace, P., Patris, B., Niot, I., Febbraio, M., et al (2005). CD36 involvement in orosensory detection of dietary lipids, spontaneous fat preference, and digestive secretions. *The Journal of Clinical Investigation*, 115, 3177–84.

Laumann, E. O., Gagnon, J. H., Michael, R. T., and Michaels, S. (1994). *The Social Organization of Sexuality*. Chicago, IL. The University of Chicago.

Laumann, E. O., Nicolosi, A., Glasser, D. B., Paik, A., Gingell, C., et al (2005). Sexual problems among women and men aged 40–80 years. Prevalence and correlates identified in the Global Study of Sexual Attitudes and Behaviors. *International Journal of Impotence Research*, 17, 38–57.

Laurenceau, J.-P., Feldman Barrett, L., and Pietromonaco, P. R. (1998). Intimacy as an interpersonal process. The importance of self-disclosure, partner disclosure, and perceived partner responsiveness in interpersonal exchanges. *Journal of Personality and Social Psychology*, 74, 1238–51.

Laurenceau, J.-P. and Kleinman, B. (2006). Intimacy in personal relationships. In A. L. Bangelisti and D. Perlman (eds),

The Cambridge Handbook of Personal Relationships (pp 637–53). New York, NY. Cambridge University Press.

Lavie, P. (2001). Sleep-wake as a biological rhythm. *Annual Review of Psychology*, 52, 277–303.

Law, K. L., Stroud, L. R., LaGasse, L. L., Niarura, R., Liu, J., et al (2003). Smoking during pregnancy and newborn neurobehavior. *Pediatrics*, 111, 1318–23.

Law-Smith, M. J., Perrett, D. I., Jones, B. C., Cornwell, R. E., Moore, F. R., et al (2006). Facial appearance is a cue to oestrogen levels in women. *Proceedings of the Royal Society B. Biological Sciences*, 273, 135–40.

Lawford, H., Pratt, M. W., Hunsberger, B., and Pancer, M. S. (2005). Adolescent generativity. A longitudinal study of two possible contexts for learning concern for future generations. *Journal of Research on Adolescence*, 15, 261–73.

Lawler, K. A., Younger, J. Y., Piferi, R. A., Billington, E., Jobe, R., et al (2003). A change of heart. Cardiovascular correlates of forgiveness in response to interpersonal conflict. *Journal of Behavioral Medicine*, 26, 373–93.

Layard, R., Mayraz, G., and Nickell, S. (2008). The marginal utility of income. *Journal of Public Economics*, 92(8–9), 1846–57.

Lazar, S. G. (ed) (2010). *Psychotherapy Is Worth It. A Comprehensive Review of its Cost-effectiveness*. Arlington, VA. American Psychiatric Publishing Inc.

Lazar, S. W., Kerr, C. E., Wasserman, R. H., Gray, J. R., Greve, D. N., et al (2005). Meditation experience is associated with increased cortical thickness. *Neuroreport*, 28, 1893–7.

Lazarus, R. S. (1991a). Progress on a cognitive-motivational-relational theory of emotion. *American Psychologist*, 46, 819–84.

Lazarus, R. S. (1991b). *Emotion and Adaptation*. New York, NY. Oxford University Press.

Lazarus, R. S. (1999). *Stress and Emotion. A New Synthesis*. New York, NY. Springer.

Lazarus, R. S. (2000). Cognitive-motivational-relational theory of emotion. In Y. Hanin (ed), *Emotions in Sport* (pp 39–63). Champaign, IL. Human Kinetics.

Lazarus, R. S. and Folkman, S. (1984). *Stress, Appraisal, and Coping*. New York, NY. Springer.

Leader, D. (2008). *The New Black. Mourning, Melancholia and Depression*. London. Penguin.

Leary, M. R. (1995). *Self-presentation. Impression Management and Interpersonal Behavior*. Boulder, CO. Westview Press.

Leary, M. R. (1999). The social and psychological importance of self-esteem. In R. M. Kowalski and M. R. Leary (eds), *The Social Psychology of Emotional and Behavioral Problems. Interfaces of Social and Clinical Psychology* (pp 197–221). Washington, DC. American Psychological Association.

Leary, M. R. (2001). Living in the minds of others without knowing it. *Psychological Inquiry*, 12, 28–9.

Leary, M. R. (2004). The function of self-esteem in terror management theory and sociometer theory. Comment on Pyszczynski et al (2004). *Psychological Bulletin*, 130, 478–82.

Leary, M. R. (2007). Motivational and emotional aspects of the self. *Annual Review of Psychology*, 58, 317–44.

Leary, M. R. (2011). Does impression management have an image problem? In M. R. Leary (ed), *50 Prominent Social Psychologists Describe Their Most Unloved Work* (pp 96–100). New York, NY. Oxford University Press.

Leary, M. R. and Baumeister, R. F. (2000). The nature and function of self-esteem. Sociometer theory. In M. P. Zanna (ed), *Advances in Experimental Social Psychology* (Vol 32, pp 1–62). New York, NY. Academic Press.

Leary, M. R. and Baumeister, R. F. (2017). The need to belong. Desire for interpersonal attachments as a fundamental human motivation. In *Interpersonal Development* (pp 57–89). London. Routledge.

Leary, M. R. and Cox, C. B. (2008). Belongingness motivation. A mainspring of social action. In J. Y. Shah, and W. L. Gardner (eds), *Handbook of Motivation Science* (pp 27–40). New York, NY. Guilford Press.

Leary, M. R. and Kowalski, R. M. (1990). Impression management. A literature review and two-component model. *Psychological Bulletin*, 107(1), 34–47.

LeDoux, J. E. (1996). *The Emotional Brain. The Mysterious Underpinnings of Emotional Life*. New York, NY. Simon and Schuster.

LeDoux, J. E. (2000). Emotion circuits in the brain. *Annual Review of Neuroscience*, 23, 155–84.

LeDoux, J. E. (2007). The amygdale. *Current Biology*, 17, R868–74.

Lee, J. A. (1976). *The Colors of Love. An Exploration of the Ways of Loving* (rev edn). Ontario, Canada. New Press.

Lee, K. S. and Ono, H. (2012). Marriage, cohabitation, and happiness. A cross-national analysis of 27 countries. *Journal of Marriage and Family*, 74(5), 953–72.

Lee, S. (1995). Self starvation in context. Towards a culturally sensitive understanding of anorexia nervosa. *Social Science Medicine*, 41, 25–36.

Lee, S. (2001). Fat phobia in anorexia nervosa. Whose obsession is it? In M. Nasser, M. A. Katzman, and R. A. Gordon (eds), *Eating Disorders and Cultures in Transition* (pp 40–54). New York, NY. Taylor and Francis.

Lee, W. M. (2004). Acetaminophen and the U.S. Acute Liver Failure Study Group. Lowering the risks of hepatic failure. *Hapatology*, 41, 6–9.

Leger, D. (2016). Socioeconomic impact of insomnia. In *Insomnia* (pp 35–46). London. CRC Press.

Leher, J. (2009, 18 May). Don't! The secret of self-control. *The New Yorker*. Retrieved from http://www.newyorker.com/reporting/2009/05/18/090518fa_fact_lehrer on 29 May 2012.

Leichsenring, F., and Rabung, S. (2009). Analyzing effectivenss of long-term psychodynamic psychotherapy. In reply. *Journal of the American Medical Association*, 301, 932–3.

Leichsenring, F., Rabung, S., and Leibing, E. (2004). The efficacy of short-term psychodynamic psychotherapy in specific psychiatric disorders. A meta-analysis. *Archives of General Psychiatry*, 61, 1208–16.

Leitenberg, H. and Henning, K. (1995). Sexual fantasy. *Psychological Bulletin*, 117, 469–96.

Lemery, K. S., Goldsmith, H. H., Klinnert, M. D., and Mrazek, D. A. (1999). Developmental models of infant and childhood temperament. *Developmental Psychology*, 35, 189–204.

Lenroot, R. K. and Giedd, J. N. (2010). Sex differences in the adolescent brain. *Brain and Cognition*, 72, 46–55.

Lenski, R. E. (2000, September). *Evolution. Fact and Theory*. American Institute of Biological Sciences. Retrieved from http://www.actionbioscience.org/evolution/lenski.html on 4 March 2010.

Lenzenweger, M. F., Lane, M. C., Loranger, A. W., and Kessler, R. C. (2007). DSM-IV personality disorders in the National Comorbidity Survey Replication. *Biological Psychiatry*, 62, 553–64.

Leo, J. and Lacasse, J. R. (2008). The media and the chemical imbalance theory of depression. *Society*, 45, 35–45.

Leon, D. A., Lawlor, D. A., Clark, H., Batty, G. D., and Macintyre, S. (2009). The association of childhood intelligence with mortality in adolescence to middle age. Findings from the Aberdeen 1950s cohort study. *Intelligence*, 37, 520–8.

Leonardo, E. D. and Hen, R. (2006). Genetics of affective and anxiety disorders. *Annual Review of Psychology*, 57, 117–37.

Lepper, M. P., Greene, D., and Nisbett, R. E. (1973). Undermining children's intrinsic interest with extrinsic reward. A test of the 'overjustification' hypothesis. *Journal of Personality and Social Psychology*, 28, 129–37.

Leproult, R. and Van Cauter, E. (2010). Role of sleep and sleep loss in hormonal release and metabolism. *Endocrine Development*, 17, 11–21.

Leslie, A. M. (1994). Pretending and believing. Issues in the theory of ToMM. *Cognition*, 50(1–3), 211–38.

Leslie, A. M. (2000). 'Theory of mind' as a mechanism of selective attention. In M. Gazzaniga (ed), *The New Cognitive Neurosciences* (2nd edn, pp 135–1248). Cambridge, MA. MIT Press.

Lett, H. S., Blumenthal, J. A., Babyak, M. A., Catellier, D. J., Carney, R. M., et al (2007). Social support and prognosis in patients at increased psychosocial risk recovering from myocardial infarction. *Health Psychology*, 26, 418–27.

Leung, R. K., Toumbourou, J. W., Hemphill, S. A., and Catalano, R. F. (2016). Peer group patterns of alcohol-using behaviors among early adolescents in Victoria, Australia, and Washington State, United States. *Journal of Research on Adolescence*, 26(4), 902–17.

LeVay, S. (1991). A difference in hypothalamic structure between heterosexual and homosexual men. *Science*, 253, 1034–7.

LeVay, S. (1996). *Queer Science. The Use and Abuse of Research into Homosexuality*. Cambridge, MA. MIT Press.

Levay, S. and Valente, S. M. (2002). *Human Sexuality*. Sunderland, MA. Sinauer.

Levay, S. and Valente, S. M. (2003). *Human Sexuality*. Sunderland, MA. Sinauer.

Levenson, R. (2011). Basic emotion questions. *Emotion Review*, 3, 379–86.

Levi, D. M., Klein, S., A., and Aitsebaomo, A. P. (1985). Vernier acuity, crowding, and cortical magnification. *Vision Research*, 25, 963–77.

Levin, J., Chatters, L. M., and Taylor, R. J. (2005). Religion, health and medicine in African Americans. Implications for physicians. *Journal of the National Medical Association*, 97, 237–49.

Levine, T. R., Sato, S., Hashimoto, T., and Verma, J. (1995). Love and marriage in eleven cultures. *Journal of Cross-Cultural Psychology*, 26, 554–7.

Levinson, A. (1999). Tatiana Cooley wins title, but she still sweats the small stuff. *SouthCoast Today*. Retrieved from http://www.s-t.com/daily/02-99/02-24-99/b04li047.htm on 4 June 2006.

Levinson, D. J. (1986). A conception of adult development. *American Psychologist*, 41(1), 3–13.

Levy, B. (2009). Stereotype embodiment. A psychosocial approach to aging. *Current Directions in Psychological Science*, 18, 332–6.

Lewin, C., Wolgers, G., and Herlitz, A. (2001). Sex differences favoring women in verbal, but not in visuospatial episodic memory. *Neuropsychology*, 15, 165–73.

Lewin, K. (1935). *Dynamic Theory of Personality*. New York, NY. McGraw-Hill.

Lewinsohn, P. M., Gotlib, I. H., Lewinsohn, M., Seeley, J. R., and Allen, N. B. (1998). Gender differences in anxiety disorders and anxiety symptoms in adolescents. *Journal of Abnormal Psychology*, 107, 109–17.

Lewis, G. J. and Bates, T. C. (2010). Genetic evidence for multiple biological mechanisms underlying in-group favoritism. *Psychological Science*, 21, 1623–8.

Lewis, M. W. and Petry, N. M. (2005). Contingency management treatments that reinforce completion of goal-related activities. Participation in family activities and its association with outcomes. *Drug and Alcohol Dependence*, 79, 267–71.

Lewontin, R. C. (1981). Evolution/creation debate. A time for truth. *Bioscience*, 31, 559.

Li, X. and Liu, M. (2004). A review of the self-change attempt. *Psychological Science (China)*, 27, 104–6.

Liberles, S. D. and Buck, L. B. (2006). A second class of chemosensory receptors in the olfactory epithelium. *Nature*, 442, 645–50.

Libet, B. (1985). Unconscious cerebral initiative and the role of conscious in voluntary action. *Behavioral and Brain Science*, 8, 529–66.

Lichtenstein, S., Slovic, P., Fischhoff, B., Layman, M., and Combs, B. (1978). Judged frequency of lethal events. *Journal of Experimental Psychology*, 4, 551–78.

Lidz, J., Gleitman, H., and Gleitman, L. (2003). Understanding how input matters. Verb learning and the footprint of universal grammar. *Cognition*, 87, 151–78.

Lieberman, D. and Hatfield, E. (2006). Passionate love. Cross-cultural and evolutionary perspectives. In R. J. Sternberg and K. Weis (eds), *The New Psychology of Romantic Love* (pp 274–97). New Haven, CT. Yale University Press.

Lieberman, D., Pillsworth, E. G., and Haselton, M. G. (2011). Kin affiliation across the ovulatory cycle. Females avoid fathers when fertile. *Psychological Science*, 22, 13–18.

Lieberman, D. A. (2000). *Learning. Behavior and Cognition* (3rd edn). Belmont, CA. Wadsworth.

Lieberman, J. A., Stroup, T. S., McEvoy, J. P., Swartz, M. S., and Rosenheck, R. A. (2005). Effectiveness of antipsychotic drugs in patients with chronic schizophrenia. *New England Journal of Medicine*, 353, 1209–23.

Lieberman, M. D. (2000). Intuition. A social cognitive neuroscience approach. *Psychological Bulletin*, 126, 109–37.

Liechti, M. E. and Vollenweider, F. X. (2000). Acute psychological and physiological effects of MDMA ('ecstasy') after haloperidol pretreatment in healthy humans. *European Neuropsychopharmacology*, 10, 289–95.

Lilienfeld, S. O. (2007). Psychological treatments that cause harm. *Current Perspectives in Psychological Science*, 2, 53–70.

Lilienfeld, S. O. (2012). Public skepticism of psychology. Why many people perceive the study of human behavior as unscientific. *American Psychologist*, 67(2), 111–29.

Lilienfeld, S. O., Ammirati, R., and Landfield, K. (2009). Giving debiasing away. Can psychological research on correcting cognitive errors promote human welfare? *Perspectives on Psychological Science*, 4, 390–8.

Lilienfeld, S. O., Fowler, K. A., Lohr, J. M., and Lynn, S. J. (2005). Pseudoscience, nonscience, and nonsense in clinical psychology. Dangers and remedies. In R. H. Wright and N. A. Cummings (eds), *Destructive Trends in Mental Health. The Well-intentioned Path to Harm* (pp 187–218). New York, NY. Routledge.

Lilienfeld, S. O. and Lynn, S. J. (2003). Dissociative identity disorder. Multiple personalities, multiple controversies. In S. O. Lilienfeld, S. J. Lynn, and J. M. Lohr (eds), *Science and Pseudoscience in Clinical Psychology* (pp 109–42). New York, NY. Guilford.

Lilienfeld, S. O., Lynn, S. J., Kirsch, I., Chaves, J. F., Sarbin, T. R., et al (1999). Dissociative identity disorder and the sociocognitive model. Recalling the lessons of the past. *Psychological Bulletin*, 125, 507–23.

Lilienfeld, S. O., Lynn, S. J., and Lohr, J. M. (eds) (2003a). *Science and Pseudoscience in Clinical Psychology*. New York, NY. Guilford.

Lilienfeld, S. O., Lynn, S. J., and Lohr, J. M. (2003b). Science and pseudoscience in clinical psychology. Initial thoughts, reflections, and considerations. In S. O. Lilienfeld, S. J. Lynn, and J. M. Lohr (eds), *Science and Pseudoscience in Clinical Psychology* (pp 1–14). New York, NY. Guilford.

Lilienfeld, S. O., and Marino, L. (1999). Essentialism revisited. Evolutionary theory and the concept of mental disorder. *Journal of Abnormal Psychology*, 108, 400–11.

Liljinquist, K., Zhong, C.-B., and Galinsky, A. D. (2010). The smell of virtue. Clean scents promote reciprocity and charity. *Psychological Science*, 21, 381–3.

Lim, J. and Dinges, D. F. (2010). A meta-analysis of the impact of short-term sleep deprivation on cognitive variables. *Psychological Bulletin*, 136, 375–89.

Lin, W.-F., Mack, D., Enright, R. D., Krahn, D., and Baskin, T. W. (2004). Effects of forgiveness therapy on anger, mood, and vulnerability to substance use among inpatient substance-dependent clients. *Journal of Consulting and Clinical Psychology*, 72, 1114–21.

Lindberg, S. M., Hyde, J. S., Linn, M. C., and Petersen, J. L. (2010). New trends in gender and mathematics performance. A meta-analysis. *Psychological Bulletin*, 136, 1123–35.

Linde, K., Berner, M. M., and Kriston, L. (2008). St. John's Wort for major depression. *Cochrane Database Systematic Review*. Retrieved from http://proxy.library.upenn.edu:2170/doi/10.1002/14651858.CD000448.pub3/full on 14 July 2010.

Lindenfors, P., Nunn, C. L., and Barton, R. A. (2007). Primate brain architecture and selection in relation to sex. *BMC Biology*, 5. Retrieved from http://www.biomedcentral.com/content/pdf/1741-7007-5-20.pdf on 11 May 2007.

Lindsay, D. S., Hagen, L., Read, J. D., Wade, K. A., and Garry, M. (2004). True photographs and false memories. *Psychological Science*, 15, 149–54.

Lindwall, M., Rennemark, M., Halling, A., Berglund, J., and Hassmén, P. (2006). Depression and exercise in elderly men and women. Findings from the Swedish National Study on Aging and Care. *Journal of Aging and Physical Activity*, 15, 41–55.

Lippa, R. A. (2006). Is high sex drive associated with increased sexual attraction to both sexes? It depends on whether you are male or female. *Psychological Science*, 17(1), 46–52.

Lippa, R. A. (2007). The preferred traits of mates in a cross-national study of heterosexual and homosexual men and women. An examination of biological and cultural influences. *Archives of Sexual Behavior*, 36, 193–208.

Lippa, R. A. (2007). The relation between sex drive and sexual attraction to men and women. A cross-national study of heterosexual, bisexual, and homosexual men and women. *Archives of Sexual Behavior*, 36, 209–22.

Lippa, R. A. (2009). Sex differences in sex drive, sociosexuality, and height across 53 nations. Testing evolutionary and social structural theories. *Archives of Sexual Behavior*, 38, 631–51.

Lippa, R. A. (2010). Gender differences in personality and interests. When, where, and why? *Social and Personality Psychology Compass*, 4, 1098–110.

Lisanby, S. H. (2007). Electroconvulsive therapy for depression. *New England Journal of Medicine*, 257, 1939–45.

Liszkowski, U., Schaëfer, M., Carpenter, M., and Tomasello, M. (2009). Prelinguistic infants, but not chimpanzees, communicate about absent entities. *Psychological Science*, 20, 654–60.

Little, A. C., Jones, B. C., and DeBruine, L. M. (2008). Preferences for variation in masculinity in real male faces change

852 References

across the menstrual cycle. Women prefer
more masculine faces when they are
more fertile. *Personality and Individual
Difference*, 45, 478–82.

Little, A. C., Saxton, T. K., Roberts, S. C.,
Jones, B. C., DeBruine, L. M., et al
(2010). Women's preferences for
masculinity in male faces are highest
during reproductive age range and lower
around puberty and post-menopause.
Psychoneuroendocrinology, 35, 912–20.

Littlewood, R. (1995). Psychopathology
and personal agency. Modernity, culture
change and eating disorders in South
Asian societies. *British Journal of
Medical Psychology*, 68, 45–63.

Littlewood, R. (2004). Commentary.
Globalization, culture, body image, and
eating disorders. *Culture, Medicine and
Psychiatry*, 28, 597–602.

Liu, J., Harris, A., and Kanwisher, N.
(2010). Perception of face parts and face
configurations. An fMRI study. *Journal of
Cognitive Neuroscience*, 21, 203–11.

Liu, J., Harris, A., and Kanwisher, N.
(2010). Perception of face parts and face
configurations. An fMRI study. *Journal of
Cognitive Neuroscience*, 22, 203–11.

Livingston, W. (2017). Alcohol and other
drug use. In *Handbook of the Sociology of
Death, Grief, and Bereavement. A Guide
to Theory and Practice* (pp 224–36).
London. Routledge.

Livshits, G., Kato, B. S., Wilson, S. G., and
Spector, T. D. (2007). Linkage of genes to
total lean body mass in normal women.
*Journal of Clinical Endocrinology and
Metabolism*, 92, 3171–6.

LoBue, V. and deLoache, J. S. (2008).
Detecting the snake in the grass.
Attention to fear-relevant stimuli by
adults and young children. *Psychological
Science*, 19, 284–9.

Locke, E. A. (2005). Why emotional
intelligence is an invalid concept. *Journal
of Organizational Behavior*, 26, 425–31.

Locke, E. A. and Latham, G. P. (2002).
Building a practically useful theory
of goal-setting and task motivation.
American Psychologist, 57, 705–17.

Locke, E. A. and Latham, G. P. (2006). New
directions in goal-setting theory. *Current
Directions in Psychological Science*, 15,
265–8.

Lodi-Smith, J., Geise, A. C., Roberts, B. W.,
and Robins, R. W. (2009). Narrating
personality change. *Journal of Personality
and Social Psychology*, 96, 679–89.

Loehlin, J. C., Horn, J. M., and Willerman,
L. (1990). Heredity, environment, and
personality change. Evidence from
the Texas Adoption Project. *Journal of
Personality*, 58(1), 221–43.

Loewenstein, G. F., Weber, E. U., Hsee, C. K.,
and Welch, N. (2001). Risks as feelings.
Psychological Bulletin, 127, 267–86.

Loftus, E. F. (1996). *Eyewitness Testimony.*
Cambridge, MA. Harvard University
Press. (Original work published 1979.)

Loftus E. F. (1997). Memories for a past
that never was. *Current Directions in
Psychological Science*, 6, 60–5.

Loftus, E. F. (2003). Make-believe memories.
American Psychologist, 58, 867–73.

Loftus, E. F. (2005). Planting misinformation
in the human mind. A 30-year
investigation of the malleability of
memory. *Learning and Memory*, 12,
361–6.

Loftus, E. F. (2007). Memory distortions.
Problems solved and unsolved. In M.
Garry and H. Hayne (eds), *Do Justice and
Let the Sky Fall. Elizabeth Loftus and
her Contributions to Science, Law, and
Academic Freedom* (pp 1–14). Mahwah,
NJ. Lawrence Erlbaum Associates.

Loftus, E. F. and Bernstein, D. M. (2005).
Rich false memories. The royal road to
success. In A. F. Healy (ed), *Experimental
Cognitive Psychology and its Applications*
(pp 101–13). Washington, DC. American
Psychological Association.

Loftus, E. F. and Burns, T. E. (1982). Mental
shock can produce retrograde amnesia.
Memory and Cognition, 10(4), 318–23.

Loftus, E. F., Donders, K., Hoffman, H. G.,
and Schooler, J. W. (1989). Creating new
memories that are quickly accessed and
confidently held. *Memory and Cognition*,
17, 607–16.

Loftus, E. F. and Hoffman, H. G. (1989).
Misinformation and memory. The
creation of memory. *Journal of
Experimental Psychology. General*, 118,
100–4.

Loftus, E. F. and Ketcham, K. (1994).
*The Myth of Repressed Memory. False
Memories and Allegations of Sexual
Abuse.* New York, NY. St. Martin's Press.

Loftus, E. F., Loftus, G. R., and Messo, J.
(1987). Some facts about 'weapon focus'.
Law and Human Behavior, 11(1), 55–62.

Loftus, E. F. and Palmer, J. C. (1974).
Reconstruction of automobile destruction.
An example of the interaction between
language and memory. *Journal of Verbal
Learning and Verbal Behavior*, 13(5), 585–9.

Loftus, E. F. and Pickrell, J. E. (1995). The
formation of false memories. *Psychiatric
Annals*, 25, 720–5.

Loftus, E. F. and Zanni, G. (1975).
Eyewitness testimony. The influence of
the wording of a question. *Bulletin of the
Psychonomic Society*, 5(1), 86–8.

Logue, A. W. (1998). Evolutionary theory
and the psychology of eating. Retrieved
from http://darwin.baruch.cuny.edu/
faculty/LogueA.html on 15 May 2006.

Lohr, J. M., Olatunji, B. O., Baumeister,
R. F., and Bushman, B. J. (2007). The
psychology of anger venting and
empirically supported alternatives that do
no harm. *The Scientific Review of Mental
Health Practice*, 5, 53–64.

Lorenz, K. (1937). The companion in the
bird's world. *Auk*, 54, 245–73.

Lourenço, O. and Machado, A. (1996). In
defense of Piaget's theory. A reply to 10
common criticisms. *Psychological Review*,
103(1), 143–64.

Low, G. and Molzahn, A. E. (2007).
Predictors of quality of life in old age.
A cross-validation study. *Research in
Nursing and Health*, 30, 14–150.

Lowery, B. S., Hardin, C. D., and Sinclair,
S. (2001). Social influence on automatic
racial prejudice. *Journal of Personality
and Social Psychology*, 81, 842–55.

Lubinski, D. (2004). Introduction to the
special section on cognitive abilities. 100
years after Spearman's (1904) ' "General
intelligence", objectively determined and
measured'. *Journal of Personality and
Social Psychology*, 86(1), 96–111.

Lubinski, D., Webb, R. M., Morelock, M. J.,
and Benbow, C. P. (2001). Top 1 in
10,000. A 10-year follow-up of the
profoundly gifted. *Journal of Applied
Psychology*, 86, 718–29.

Luborsky, L., Rosenthal, R., Diguer, L.,
Andrusyna, T. P., Berman, J. S., et al
(2002). The dodo bird verdict is alive and
well—mostly. *Clinical Psychology. Science
and Practice*, 9(1), 2–12.

Lucas, R. E. (2007). Adaptation and the
set-point model of subjective well-being.
*Current Directions in Psychological
Science*, 16, 75–9.

Lucas, R. E., Clark, A. E., Georgellis, Y.,
and Diener, E. (2004). Unemployment
alters the set point for life satisfaction.
Psychological Science, 15, 8–13.

Luders, E., Toga, A. W., Lepore, N., and
Gaser, C. (2009). The underlying
anatomical correlates of long-term
meditation. *NeuroImage*, 45, 672–8.

Lumeng, J. C., Cabral, H. J., Gannon, K.,
Heeren, T., and Frank, D. A. (2007). Prenatal exposures to cocaine and alcohol
and physical growth patterns to age 8

years. *Neurotoxicology and Teratology*, 29, 446–57.

Luna, B., Garver, K., Urban, T., Lazar, N., and Sweeney, J. (2004). Maturation of cognitive processes from late childhood to adulthood. *Child Development*, 75, 1357–72.

Luo, S. and Klohnen, E. C. (2005). Assortive mating and marital quality in newlyweds. A couple centered approach. *Journal of Personality and Social Psychology*, 88, 304–26.

Lustig, R. (2006a). The 'skinny' on childhood obesity. How our Western environment starves kids' brains. *Pediatric Annals*, 36, 176.

Lustig, R. (2006b). Childhood obesity. Behavioral aberration or biochemical drive? Reinterpreting the First Law of Thermodynamics. *Nature. Clinical Practice Endocrinology and Metabolism*, 2, 447–58.

Lykken, D. and Tellegen, A. (1996). Happiness is a stochastic phenomenon. *Psychological Science*, 7, 186–9.

Lynch, M. and Walsh, B. (1998). *Genetics and Analysis of Quantitative Traits*. Sunderland, MA. Sinauer Associates.

Lynn, R. and Vanhanen, T. (2006). *IQ and Global Inequality*. Washington, DC. Washington Summit Publishers.

Lynn, S. J. and Kirsch, I. (2006). *Essentials of Clinical Hypnosis. An Evidence-based Approach*. Washington, DC. American Psychological Association.

Lynn, S. J., Lilienfeld, S. O., Merckelbach, H., Giesbrecht, T., and van der Kloet, D. (2012). Dissociation and dissociative disorders. Challenging conventional wisdom. *Current Directions in Psychological Science*, 21, 48–53.

Lynn, S. J., Lock, T., Loftus, E. F., Krackow, E., and Lilienfeld, S. O. (2003). The remembrance of things past. Problematic memory recovery techniques in psychotherapy. In S. O. Lilienfeld, S. J. Lynn, and J. M. Lohr (eds), *Science and Pseudoscience in Clinical Psychology* (pp 205–93). New York, NY. The Guilford Press.

Lynn, S. J., Locke, T., Loftus, E. F., Krackow, E., and Lilienfeld, S. O. (2003). The remembrance of things past. Problematic memory recovery techniques in psychotherapy. In S. O. Lilienfeld, S. J. Lynn, and J. M. Lohr (eds), *Science and Pseudoscience in Clinical Psychology* (pp 205–39). New York, NY. The Guilford Press.

Lynn, S. J. and Payne, D. G. (1997). Memory as the theater of the past. The psychology of false memories. *Current Directions in Psychological Science*, 6, 55.

Lynn, S. J., Vanderhoff, H., Shindler, K., and Stafford, J. (2002). Defining hypnosis as a trance vs. cooperation. Hypnotic inductions, suggestibility, and performance standards. *American Journal of Clinical Hypnosis*, 44, 231–40.

Lyons, M. J., York, T. P., Franz, C. E., Grant, M. D., Eaves, L. J., et al (2009). Genes determine stability and the environment determines change in cognitive ability during 35 years of adulthood. *Psychological Science*, 20(9), 1146–52.

Lyons-Ruth, K., Yellin, C., Melnick, S., and Atwood, G. (2003). Childhood experiences of trauma and loss have different relations to maternal unresolved and hostile-helpless states of mind on the AAI. *Attachment and Human Development*, 5(4), 330–52.

Lytton, H. and Romney, D. M. (1991). Parents' differential socialization of boys and girls. A meta-analysis. *Psychological Bulletin*, 109, 267–96.

Lyubomirsky, S. and Boehm, J. K. (2010). Human motives, happiness, and the puzzle of parenthood. Commentary on Kenrick et al (2010). *Perspectives on Psychological Science*, 5, 327–34.

Lyubomirsky, S. and Layous, K. (2013). How do simple positive activities increase well-being? *Current Directions in Psychological Science*, 22, 57–62.

Lyubomirsky, S., Sheldon, K. M., and Schkade, D. (2005). Pursuing happiness. The architecture of sustainable change. *Review of General Psychology*, 9, 11–113.

Lyubomirsky, S. and Tkach, C. (2003). The consequences of dysphoric rumination. In C. Papageorgiou and A. Wells (eds), *Rumination. Nature, Theory and Treatment of Negative Thinking in Depression* (pp 21–41). Chichester, UK. John Wiley and Sons.

MacAndrew, C. and Edgerton, R. B. (1969). *Drunken Comportment. A Social Explanation*. Chicago, IL. Aldine.

Maccari, S., Piazza, P. V., Kabbaj, M., Barbazanges, A., Simon, H., et al (1995). Adoption reverses the long-term impairment in glucocorticoid feedback induced by prenatal stress. *Journal of Neuroscience*, 15, 110–16.

Macchi Cassia, V., Turati, C., and Simion, F. (2004). Can a nonspecific bias toward top-heavy patterns explain newborns' face preference? *Psychological Science*, 15, 379–83.

Maccoby, E. E. (2002). Gender and group process. A developmental perspective. *Current Directions in Psychological Science*, 11, 54–8.

Maccoby, E. E. (2002). Parenting effects. Issues and controversies. In J. G. Borkowski, S. L. Ramey, and M. Bristol-Power (eds), *Parenting and the Child's World. Influences on Academic, Intellectual, and Social-emotional Development* (pp 35–46). Mahwah, NJ. Lawrence Erlbaum Associates.

Maccoby, E. E. and Martin, J. A. (1983). Socialization in the context of the family. Parent-child interaction. In E. M. Hetherington (vol ed) and P. H. Mussen (ed-in-chief), *Handbook of Child Psychology. Vol 4. Socialization, Personality and Social Development* (4th edn, pp 1–101). New York, NY. Wiley.

Machado, C. J., Kazama, A. M., and Bachevalier, J. (2009). Impact of amygdala, orbital frontal, or hippocampal lesions on threat avoidance and emotional reactivity in nonhuman primates. *Emotion*, 9, 147–63.

Machery, E. and Cohen, K. (2011). An evidence-based study of the evolutionary behavioral sciences. *British Journal of the Philosophy of Science*, 63, 177–226.

Maciejewski, P. K., Zhang, B., Block, S. D., and Prigerson, H. G. (2007). An empirical examination of the stage theory of grief. *Journal of the American Medical Association*, 297, 716–23.

Mack, A. (2003). Inattentional blindness. Looking without seeing. *Current Directions in Psychological Science*, 12, 180–4.

Mackenzie, D. L. (2006) (Abstract only). Group hope. An antecedent of groupthink? Dissertation Abstracts International. Section B. *The Sciences and Engineering*, 66(10-B).

MacKillop, J., Lisman, S. A., Weinstein, A., and Rosenbaum, D. (2003). Controversial treatments for alcoholism. In S. O. Lilienfeld, S. J. Lynn, and J. W. Lohr (eds), *Science and Pseudoscience in Clinical Psychology* (pp 273–306). New York, NY. Guilford.

Macleod, J., Oakes, R., Copello, A., Crome, I., Egger, M., et al (2004). Psychological and social sequelae of cannabis and other illicit drug use by young people. A systematic review of longitudinal general population studies. *The Lancet*, 363, 1579–88.

Macmillan, M. (1996). *Freud Evaluated. The Completed Arc*. Cambridge, MA. MIT Press.

MacMillan, M. (1997). *Freud Evaluated. The Completed Arc*. Cambridge, MA. MIT Press.

Macmillan, M. (2000). Restoring Phineas Gage. A 150th retrospective. *Journal of the History of the Neurosciences*, 9(1), 42–62.

Macmillan, M. and Lena, M. L. (2010). Rehabilitating Phineas Gage. *Neuropsychological Rehabilitation*, 20, 641–58.

Macmillan, N. A. and Creelman, C. D. (2005). *Detection Theory. A User's Guide* (2nd edn). Mahwah, NJ. Lawrence Erlbaum Associates.

MacNeil, T. F. and Cantor-Graae, E. (2000). Minor physical abnormalities and obstetric complications in schizophrenia. *Australian and New Zealand Journal of Psychiatry*, 34, S65.

MacNeilage, P. F., Rogers, L. J., and Vallortigara, G. (2009, July). Origins of the left and right brain. *Scientific American*, 60–7.

Macrae, C. N., Milne, A. B., and Bodenhausen, G. V. (1994). Stereotypes as energy-saving devices. A peek inside the cognitive toolbox. *Journal of Personality and Social Psychology*, 66, 37–47.

Maddux, W. W., Barden, J., Brewer, M. B., and Petty, R. E. (2005). Saying no to negativity. The effects of context and motivation to control prejudice on automatic evaluative responses. *Journal of Experimental Social Psychology*, 41(1), 19–35.

Madeley, G. (2007, 19 October). £20,000 payout for woman who falsely accused her father of rape after 'recovered memory' therapy. *Daily Mail*. Retrieved from www.dailymail.co.uk on 4 June 2008.

Madon, S., Guyll, M., Aboufadel, K., Montiel, E., Smith, A., et al (2001). Ethnic and national stereotypes. The Princeton Trilogy revisited and revised. *Personality and Social Psychology Bulletin*, 27, 996–1010.

Madon, S., Jussim, L., Keiper, S., Eccles, J., Smith, A., et al (1998). The accuracy and power of sex, social class, and ethnic stereotypes. A naturalistic study in person perception. *Personality and Social Psychology Bulletin*, 24, 1304–18.

Madrigal, A. (2008, 24 April). Wired.com readers' brain-enhancing drug regimens. *Wired*. Retrieved from www.wired.com/print/medtech/drugs/news/2008/04/smart_drugs on 10 June 2009.

Magnusson, D. (2012). The human being in society. Psychology as a scientific discipline. *European Psychologist*, 17(1), 21–7.

Maguire, E. A., Vargha-Khadem, F., and Hassabis, D. (2010). Imagining fictitious and future experiences. *Neuropsychologia*, 48, 3187–92.

Maher, B. (2008, April 9). Poll results. Look who's doping. *Nature*, 452, 674–5.

Mahoney, J. L., Stattin, H., and Lord, H. (2004). Unstructured youth recreation centre participation and antisocial behaviour development. Selection influences and the moderating role of antisocial peers. *International Journal of Behavioural Development*, 28, 553–60.

Mai, F. M. (1995). Psychiatrists' attitudes to multiple personality disorder. A questionnaire study. *Canadian Journal of Psychiatry*, 40, 154–7.

Males, M. (1996). *The Scapegoat Generation*. Monroe, ME. Common Courage Press.

Malla, A. K., Takhar, J. J., Norman, R. M., Manchanda, R., Cortese, L., et al (2002). Negative symptoms in first episode non-affective psychosis. *Acta Psychiatrica Scandinavia*, 105, 431–9.

Malle, B. F. (2006). The actor-observer asymmetry. A (surprising) meta-analysis. *Psychological Bulletin*, 132, 895–919.

Malle, B. F., Knobe, J. M., and Nelson, S. E. (2007). Actor-observer asymmetries in explanations of behavior. New answers to an old question. *Journal of Personality and Social Psychology*, 93, 491–514.

Mallozzi, V. M. (2005, April 14). One millionaire's strange cry. Tickets, Please! *New York Times*. Retrieved from www.nytimes.com on 25 April 2006.

Malotki, E. (1983). *Hopi Time. A Linguistic Analysis of Temporal Concept in the Hopi Language*. Berlin. Mouton de Gruyter.

Maltby, J., Macaskill, A., and Day, L. (2001). Failure to forgive self and others. A replication and extension of the relationship between forgiveness, personality, social desirability, and general health. *Personality and Individual Differences*, 30, 881–5.

Manber, R. (2000). Night terrors. In A. E. Kazdin (ed), *Encyclopedia of Psychology* (Vol 5, pp 444–6). Washington, DC. American Psychological Association.

Maner, J. K. and Kenrick, D. T. (2010). Evolutionary social psychology. In R. F. Baumeister and E. J. Finkel (eds), *Advanced Social Psychology. The State of the Science* (pp 613–53). New York, NY. Oxford University Press.

Manna, A., Raffone, A., Perrucci, M. G., Nardo, D., Ferretti, A., et al (2010). Neural correlates of focused attention and cognitive monitoring in meditation. *Brain Research Bulletin*, 82, 46–56.

Manning, R., Levine, M., and Collins, A. (2007). The Kitty Genovese murder and the social psychology of helping. The parable of the 38 witnesses. *American Psychologist*, 62, 555–62.

Manning, R., Levine, M., and Collins, A. (2008). The legacy of the 38 witnesses and the importance of getting history right. *American Psychologist*, 63, 562–3.

Marano, H. E. (2003, November/December). Sleep or suffer. *Psychology Today*. Retrieved from http://www.psychologytoday.com on 15 January 2006.

Marazziti, D., Akiskal, H. S., Rossi, A., and Cassano, G. B. (1999). Alteration of the platelet serotonin transporter in romantic love. *Psychological Medicine*, 29, 741–5.

Marazziti, D. and Canale, D. (2004). Hormonal changes when falling in love. *Psychoneuro-endocrinology*, 29, 931–6.

Marchalant, Y., Brothers, H. M., and Wenk, G. L. (2008). Inflammation and aging. Can endocannabinoids help? *Biomedicine and Pharmacotherapy*, 62, 212–17.

Marcus, G. (2008). *Kluge. The Haphazard Construction of the Human Mind*. New York, NY. Houghton Mifflin Company.

Marcus, G. F., Fernandes, K. J., and Johnson, S. P. (2007). Infant rule learning facilitated by speech. *Psychological Science*, 18, 387–91.

Marder, E. and Bucher, D. (2001). Central pattern generators and the control of rhythmic movements. *Current Biology*, 11, R986–96.

Marin, J. M. Carrizo, S. J., Vicente, E., and Agusti, A. G. (2005). Long-term cardiovascular outcomes in men with obstructive sleep apnoea-hypopnea with or without treatment with continuous positive airway pressure. An observational study. *Lancet*, 365, 1046–53.

Marinak, B. A. and Gambrell, L. B. (2008). Intrinsic motivation and rewards. What sustains young children's engagement with text? *Literacy Research and Instruction*, 47, 9–26.

Markham, J. A., Morris, J. R., and Juraska, J. M. (2007). Neuron number decreases in the rat ventral, but not dorsal, medial prefrontal cortex between adolescence and adulthood. *Neuroscience*, 144, 961–8.

Marks, I. M. and Nesse, R. M. (1994). Fear and fitness. An evolutionary analysis of anxiety disorders. *Ethology and Sociobiology*, 15, 247–61.

Markus, H. R. and Kitayama, S. (1998). The cultural psychology of personality.

Journal of Cross-Cultural Psychology, 29, 63–87.

Markus, H. R. and Kitayama, S. (2010). Cultures and selves. A cycle of mutual constitution. *Perspectives on Psychological Science*, 5, 420–30.

Markus, H. R., Uchida, Y., Omoregie, H., Townsend, S. S. M., and Kitayama, S. (2006). Going for the gold. Models of agency in Japanese and American contexts. *Psychological Science*, 17, 103–12.

Marland, A. L., Bachen, E. A., Cohen, S., Rabin, B., and Manuck, S. B. (2002). Stress, immune reactivity, and susceptibility to infections. *Physiology and Behavior*, 77, 711–16.

Marmer, S. S. (1998, December). Should dissociative identity disorder be considered a bona fide diagnosis? *Clinical Psychiatry News*.

Marshall, J. and Aldhous, P. (2006, 28 October). Patient groups special. Swallowing the best advice? *New Scientist*, 18–22.

Marshall-Pescini, S. and Whiten, A. (2008). Chimpanzees (pan troglodytes) and the question of cumulative culture. An experimental approach. *Animal Cognition*, 11, 449–56.

Martin, C. L. and Ruble, D. N. (2004). Children's search for gender cues. Cognitive perspectives on gender development. *Current Directions in Psychological Science*, 13, 67–70.

Martin, C. L. and Ruble, D. N. (2009). Patterns of gender development. *Annual Review of Psychology*, 61, 353–81.

Martin, C. L., Ruble, D. N., and Szkrybalo, J. (2002). Cognitive theories of early gender development. *Psychological Bulletin*, 128, 903–33.

Martin, J. L. R., Sainz-Pardo, M., Furukawa, T. A., Martín-Sánchez, E., Seoane, T., et al (2007). Benzodiazepines in generalized anxiety disorder. Heterogeneity of outcomes based on a systematic review and meta-analysis of clinical trials. *Journal of Psychopharmacology*, 21, 774–82.

Martin, L. T. and Kubzansky, L. D. (2005). Childhood cognitive performance and risk of mortality. A prospective cohort study of gifted individuals. *American Journal of Epidemiology*, 162, 887–90.

Marwick, B. (1978). The Soal-Goldney experiments with Basil Shackleton. New evidence of data manipulation. *Proceedings of the Society for Psychical Research*, 56, 250–81.

Maser, J. D. (1985). List of phobias. In A. H. Tuma and J. D. Maser (eds), *Anxiety and the Anxiety Disorders*. Hillsdale, NJ. Lawrence Erlbaum Associates.

Mashour, G. A., Walker, E. E., and Martuza, R. L. (2005). Psychosurgery. Past, present, and future. *Brain Research Reviews*, 48, 409–19.

Maslow, A. H. (1970). *Motivation and Personality* (2nd edn). New York, NY. Harper and Row.

Massey-Abernathy, A. R. and Haseltine, E. (2019). Power talk. Communication styles, vocalization rates and dominance. *Journal of Psycholinguistic Research*, 48(1), 107–16.

Master, S. L., Eisenberger, N. I., Taylor, S. E., Naliboff, B. D., Shirinyan, D., et al (2009). A picture's worth. Partner photographs reduce experimentally induced pain. *Psychological Science*, 20, 1316–18.

Masters, W. H. and Johnson, V. (1966). *Human Sexual Response*. Boston, MA. Little, Brown.

Masters, W. H., Johnson, V., and Kolodny, R. C. (1982). *Human Sexuality*. Boston, MA. Little, Brown.

Mastroeni, D., Grover, A., Delvaux, E., Whiteside, C., Coleman, P. D., et al (2011). Epigenetic mechanisms in Alzheimer's disease. *Neurobiology of Aging*, 32, 1161–80.

Mastroianni, G. R. (2002). Milgram and the holocaust. A reexamination. *Journal of Theoretical and Philosophical Psychology*, 22, 158–73.

Mastroianni, G. R. (2007). Zimbardo's apple. *Analyses of Social Issues and Public Policy*, 7, 251–4.

Masuda, T. and Kitayama, S. (2004). Perceiver-induced constraint and attitude attribution in Japan and the US. A case for the cultural dependence of the correspondence bias. *Journal of Experimental Social Psychology*, 40, 409–16.

Masuda, T. and Nisbett, R. E. (2001). Attending holistically versus analytically. Comparing the context sensitivity of Japanese and Americans. *Journal of Personality and Social Psychology*, 81, 922–34.

Mathes, E. W., King, C. A., Miller, J. K., and Reed R. M. (2002). An evolutionary perspective on the interaction of age and sex differences in short-term sexual strategies. *Psychological Reports*, 90, 949–56.

Matson, J. L. and Taras, M. E. (1989). A 20 year review of punishment and alternative methods to treat problem behaviors in developmentally delayed persons. *Research in Developmental Disabilities*, 10, 85–104.

Matsumoto, D. (1999). Culture and self. An empirical assessment of Markus and Kitayama's theory of independent and interdependent self-construal. *Asian Journal of Social Psychology*, 2, 289–310.

Matsumoto, D., Consolacion, T., Yamada, H., Suzuki, R., Franklin, B., et al (2002). American-Japanese cultural differences in judgments of emotional expressions of different intensities. *Cognition and Emotion*, 16, 721–47.

Matsumoto, D. and Ekman, P. (2004). The relationship among expressions, labels and descriptions of contempt. *Journal of Personality and Social Psychology*, 87, 529–40.

Matsumoto, D. and Hee Yoo, S. (2006). Toward a new generation of cross-cultural research. *Perspectives on Psychological Science*, 1, 234–50.

Matsumoto, D., Willingham, B., and Olide, A. (2009). Sequential dynamics of culturally moderated facial expressions of emotion. *Psychological Science*, 20, 1269–75.

Matsumoto, D., Yoo, S. H., and Nakagawa, S. (2008). Culture, emotion regulation, and adjustment. *Journal of Personality and Social Psychology*, 94, 925–37.

Matthes, J., Schemer, C., and Wirth, W. (2007). More than meets the eye. Investigating the hidden impact of brand placements in television magazines. *International Journal of Advertising*, 26, 477–503.

Matthews, K. A. and Gump, B. B. (2002). Chronic work stress and marital dissolution increase risk of posttrial mortality in men from the Multiple Risk Factor Intervention Trial. *Archives of Internal Medicine*, 162, 309–15.

Matthews, R. N., Domjan, M., Ramsey, M., and Crews, D. (2007). Learning effects on sperm competition and reproductive fitness. *Psychological Science*, 18, 758–62.

Mattson, J. and Simon, M. (1996). *The Pioneers of NMR and Magnetic Resonance in Medicine*. Ramat Gan, Israel. Bar-Ilan University Press.

Matusov, E. and Hayes, R. (2000). Sociocultural critique of Piaget and Vygotsky. *New Ideas in Psychology*, 18, 215–39.

Maurer, D., Mondloch, C. J., and Lewis, T. L. (2007). Sleeper effects. *Developmental Science*, 10(1), 40–7.

Max, J. E., Levin, H. S., Landis, J., Schachar, R., Saunders, A., et al (2005). Predictors of personality change due to traumatic brain injury in children and adolescents in the first six months after injury. *Adolescent Psychiatry*, 44, 435–42.

Max, J. E., Levin, H. S., Schachar, R. J., Landis, J., Saunders, A. E., et al (2006). Predictors of personality change due to traumatic brain injury in children and adolescents six to twenty-four months after injury. *The Journal of Neuropsychiatry and Clinical Neurosciences*, 18, 21–32.

Maxwell, K. A. (2002). Friends. The role of peer influence across adolescent risk behaviors. *Journal of Youth and Adolescence*, 31, 267–77.

Maxwell, S. E., Lau, M. Y., and Howard, G. S. (2015). Is psychology suffering from a replication crisis? What does 'failure to replicate' really mean? *American Psychologist*, 70(6), 487.

May, R. (1969). *Love and Will*. New York, NY. W. W. Norton.

May, R. (1981). *Freedom and Destiny*. New York, NY. W. W. Norton.

May, R. (1982). The problem of evil. An open letter to Carl Rogers. *Journal of Humanistic Psychology*, 22(3), 10–21.

Mayberg, H. S., Lozano, A. M., Voon, V., McNeely, H. E., Seminowicz, D., et al (2005). Deep brain stimulation for treatment-resistant depression. *Neuron*, 45, 651–60.

Mayer, J. D., Salovey, P., and Caruso, D. R. (2004). Emotional intelligence. Theory, findings, and implications. *Psychological Inquiry*, 15, 197–215.

Mayes, L. C., Granger, R. H., Bornstein, M. H., and Zuckerman, B. (1992). The problem of prenatal cocaine exposure. A rush to judgment. *JAMA*, 267, 406–8.

Mayne, T. J., Norcross, J. C., and Sayette, M. A. (2000). *Insider's Guide to Graduate Programs in Clinical and Counseling Psychology* (2000–1 edn). New York, NY. Guilford.

Mazure, A. and Booth, A. (1998). Testosterone and dominance in men. *Behavioral and Brain Sciences*, 21, 353–63.

Mazure, C. M. (1998). Life stressors as risk factors in depression. *Clinical Psychology. Science and Practice*, 5, 291–313.

Mazzoni, G., Heap, M., and Scoboria, A. (2010). Hypnosis and memory. Theory, laboratory research, and applications. In S. J. Lynn, J. W. Rhue, and I. Kirsch (eds), *Handbook of Clinical Hypnosis* (2nd edn, pp 709–41). Washington, DC. American Psychological Association.

McAdams, D. P. (1989). *Intimacy. The Need to Be Close*. New York, NY. Doubleday.

McAdams, D. P. (1992). The intimacy motive. In C. P. Smith, J. W. Atkinson, and D. C. McClelland (eds), *Motivation and Personality. Handbook of Thematic Content Analysis* (pp 224–8). New York, NY. Cambridge University Press.

McAdams, D. P. (2001). Generativity in midlife. In M. E. Lachman (ed), *Handbook of Midlife Development* (pp 395–443). New York, NY. Wiley.

McAdams, D. P. (2001). The psychology of life stories. *Review of General Psychology*, 5, 100–22.

McAdams, D. P. (2004). Generativity and the narrative ecology of family life. In M. W. Pratt and B. H. Friese (eds), *Family Stories and the Life Course. Across Time and Generations* (pp 235–57). Mahwah, NJ. Lawrence Erlbaum Associates.

McAdams, D. P., Anyidoho, N. A., Brown, C., Yi, T. H., Kaplan, B., et al (2004). Traits and stories. Links between dis-positional and narrative features of personality. *Journal of Personality*, 72, 761–84.

McAdams, D. P. and Logan, R. L. (2004). What is *generativity*? In E. de St. Aubin, D. P. McAdams, and T. Kim (eds), *The Generative Society. Caring for Future Generations* (pp 15–31). Washington, DC. American Psychological Society.

McAdams, D. P. and Olson, B. D. (2010). Personality development. Continuity and change over the life course. *Annual Review of Psychology*, 61, 517–42.

McAdams, D. P. and Pals, J. L. (2006). A new big five. Fundamental principles for an integrative science of personality. *American Psychologist*, 61, 204–17.

McAdams, D. P. and Vaillant, G. E. (1982). Intimacy motivation and psychosocial adjustment. A longitudinal study. *Journal of Personality Assessment*, 46, 586–93.

McAndrew, F. T., Akande, A., Turner, S., and Sharma, Y. (1998). A cross-cultural ranking of stressful life events in Germany, India, South Africa, and the United States. *Journal of Cross-Cultural Psychology*, 29, 717–27.

McArdle, J. J., Ferrer-Caja, E., Hamagami, F., and Woodcock, R. W. (2002). Comparative longitudinal structural analyses of the growth and decline of multiple intellectual abilities over the life span. *Developmental Psychology*, 38(1), 115–42.

McBurney D. H. (2000). *Research Methods* (5th edn). Belmont, CA. Wadsworth.

McCabe, D. L., Treviño, L. K., and Butterfield, K. D. (2001). Cheating in academic institutions. A decade of research. *Ethics and Behavior*, 11, 219–32.

McCarley, R. W. (2007). Neurobiology of REM and NREM sleep. *Sleep Medicine*, 8, 302–30.

McCarty, M. K. and Karau, S. J. (2017). Social inhibition. In *The Oxford Handbook of Social Influence* (p 165). Oxford, UK. Oxford University Press.

McClelland, D. C. (1999). How the test lives on. Extensions of the Thematic Apperception Test approach. In L. Gieser and M. I. Stein (eds), *Evocative Images. The Thematic Apperception Test and the Art of Projection* (pp 163–75). Washington, DC. American Psychological Association.

McClelland, D. C., Atkinson, J. W., Clark, R. A., and Lowell, E. L. (1953). *The Achievement Motive*. New York, NY. Appleton-Century-Crofts.

McClelland, D. C. and Koestner, R. (1992). The achievement motive. In D. C. McClelland, and R. Koestner (eds), *Motivation and Personality. Handbook of Thematic Content Analysis* (pp 143–52). New York, NY. Cambridge, UK. Cambridge University Press.

McClelland, J. L., Botvinick, M. M., Noelle, D. C., Plaut, D. C., Rogers, T. T., et al (2010). Letting structure emerge. Connectionist and dynamical systems approaches to cognition. *Trends in Cognitive Sciences*, 14, 348–56.

McClintock, M. K. (2000). Human pheromones. Primers, releasers, signalers, or modulators? In K. Wallen and J. E. Schneider (eds), *Reproduction in Context* (pp 355–420). Cambridge, MA. MIT Press.

McClintock, M. K. and Herdt, G. (1996). Rethinking puberty. The development of sexual attraction. *Current Directions in Psychological Science*, 5, 178–82.

McConnell, A. R., Brown, C. M., Shoda, T. M., Statyton, L. E., and Martin, C. E. (2011). Friends with benefits. On the positive consequences of pet ownership. *Journal of Personality and Social Psychology*, 101, 1239–52.

McCook, A. (2005). Renewed faith in ecstasy. *The Scientist*, 19. Retrieved from http://www.the-scientist.com/2005/2/28/13/1/on 30 January 2006.

McCrae, R. R. (2009). The five-factor model of personality. Consensus and controversy. In P. J. Corr and G. Mattews (eds), *The Cambridge Handbook of Personality Psychology* (pp 148–61). New York, NY. Cambridge University Press.

McCrae, R. R. and Costa, P. (1997). Personality trait structures as a human universal. *American Psychologist*, 52, 509–16.

McCrae, R. R. and Costa, P. (2013). Introduction to the empirical and theoretical status of the five-factor model of personality traits. In R. R. McCrae, and P. T. Coasta (eds), *Personality Disorders and the Five-factor Model of Personality* (3rd edn). Washington, DC. American Psychological Association.

McCrae, R. R. and Costa, P. T. (1994). The stability of personality. Observations and evaluation. *Current Directions in Psychological Science*, 3, 173–75.

McCrae, R. R. and Costa, P. T., Jr (1996). Toward a new generation of personality theories. Theoretical contexts for the five-factor model. In J. S. Wiggins (ed), *The Five-factor Model of Personality. Theoretical Perspectives* (pp 51–87). New York, NY. Guilford Press.

McCrae, R. R., Costa, P. T., Jr, Ostendorf, F., Angleitner, A., Hrebickova, M., et al (2000). Nature over nurture. Temperament, personality, and life span development. *Journal of Personality and Social Psychology*, 78, 173–86.

McCrae, R. R. and Terracciano, A. (2006). National character and personality. *Current Directions in Psychological Science*, 15, 156–61.

McCrae, R. R., Terracciano, A., and 78 members of the Personality Profiles of Culture Project. (2005). Universal features of personality traits from the observer's perspective. *Journal of Personality and Social Psychology*, 88, 547–61.

McCullough, M. E. (2000). Forgiveness as human strength. Theory, measurement, and links to well-being. *Journal of Social and Clinical Psychology*, 19(1), 43–55.

McCullough, M. E., Fincham, F. D., and Tsang, J. A. (2003). Forgiveness, forbearance, and time. The temporal unfolding of transgression-related interpersonal motivations. *Journal of Personality and Social Psychology*, 84, 540–57.

McCullough, M. E., Friedman, H. S., Enders, C. K., and Martin, L. R. (2009). Does devoutness delay death? Psychological investment in religion and its association with longevity in the Terman sample. *Journal of Personality and Social Psychology*, 97, 866–82.

McCullough, M. E. and Willoughby, B. L. B. (2009). Religion, self-regulation, and self-control. Associations, explanations, and implications. *Psychological Bulletin*, 135, 69–93.

McDougall, W. (2005). *An Introduction to Social Psychology*. Brockton, MA. Adamant Media Corporation. (Original work published 1912.)

McGarrigle, J. and Donaldson, M. (1974) Conservation accidents. *Cognition*, 3, 341–50.

McGeown, K. (2005). Life in Ceausescu's Institutions. *BBC News*. Retrieved from http://news.bbc.co.uk on 8 September 2006.

McGhee, P. (2001). *Thinking Psychologically*. London. Palgrave.

McGregor, G. (2010). Moving beyond 'Y'— the children of new times. *Discourse. Studies in the Cultural Politics of Education*, 31(3), 377–92.

McGrew, J. H. and McFall, R. M. (1990), A scientific inquiry into the validity of astrology. *Journal of Scientific Exploration*, 4, 75–84. Further details appear in *Correlation* (1992), 11, 2–10.

McGue, M., Bouchard Jr, T. J., Iacono, W. G., and Lykken, D. T. (1993). Behavioral genetics of cognitive ability. A lifespan perspective. In R. Plomin and G. E. McClearn (eds), *Nature, Nurture, and Psychology* (pp 59–76). Washington, DC. American Psychological Association.

McGuffin, P., Riley, B., and Plomin, R. (2001). Genomics and behavior. Toward behavioral genomics. *Science*, 291, 1232–49.

McHugh, P. (2008). *Try to Remember. Psychiatry's Clash over Meaning, Memory, and Mind*. New York, NY. Dana Publications.

McInstry, B. (2008). Are there too many female medical graduates? *British Medical Journal*, 336, 748–9.

McIntosh, D. N. (1996). Facial feedback hypotheses. Evidence, implications, and directions. *Motivation and Emotion. Special Issue, Part I*, 20, 121–47.

McIntyre, R. S. and Konarski, J. Z. (2005). Tolerability profiles of atypical antipsychotics in the treatment of bipolar disorder. *Journal of Clinical Psychiatry*, 66(Suppl 3), 28–36.

McKay, M., Davis, M., and Fanning, P. (2007). *Thoughts and Feelings. Taking Control of Your Moods and Your Life* (3rd edn). Oakland, CA. New Harbinger.

McKay, R. T. and Dennett, D. C. (2009). The evolution of misbelief. *Behavioral and Brain Sciences*, 32, 493–561.

McKeown, R. E., Cuffe, S. P., and Schulz, R. M. (2006). U.S. suicide rates by age group 1970–2002. An examination of recent trends. *American Journal of Public Health*, 96, 1744–51.

McKone, E., Kanwisher, N., and Duchaine, B. C. (2006). Can generic expertise explain processing for faces? *Trends in Cognitive Sciences*, 11(1), 8–15.

McNally, R. J. (2003). *Remembering Trauma*. Cambridge, MA. Harvard University Press.

McNally, R. J. and Geraerts, E. (2009). A new solution to the recovered memory debate. *Perspectives on Psychological Science*, 4, 126–34.

McWhirter, B. T. (1990). Loneliness. A review of current literature, with implications for counseling and research. *Journal of Counseling and Development*, 68, 417–22.

McWhorter, J. (1998). *Word on the Street. Debunking the Myth of a 'Pure' Standard English*. New York, NY. Basic Books.

McWhorter, J. (2003). *Doing Our Own Thing. The Degradation of Language and Music and Why We Should, Like, Care*. New York, NY. Gotham Books.

Meador, C. K. (1992). Hex death. Voodoo magic or persuasion? *Southern Medical Journal*, 85, 244–7.

Mealey, L. (2000). *Sex Differences. Developmental and Evolutionary Strategies*. San Diego, CA. Academic Press.

Mecca, A. M., Smelser, N. J., and Vasconcellos, J. (eds). (1989). *The Social Importance of Self-esteem*. Berkeley, CA. University of California Press.

Medeiros, J. A. (2006). *Cone Shape and Color Vision. Unification of Structure and Perception*. Blountsville, AL. Fifth Estate.

Meehl, P. (1990). Appraising and amending theories. *Psychological Inquiry*, 1, 108–41.

Meehl, P. E. and Rosen, A. (1955). Antecedent probability in the efficiency of psychometric signs, or cutting scores. *Psychological Bulletin*, 52, 194–216.

Mehlman, M. J. (2004). Cognition-enhancing drugs. *The Milbank Quarterly*, 82, 483–506.

Melander, H., Ahlqvist-Rastad, J., Meijer, G., and Beermann, B. (2003). Evidence b(i)ased medicine—Selective reporting from studies sponsored by pharmaceutical industry. Review of studies in new drug applications. *British Medical Journal*, 326, 1171–3.

Melanson, K. J. (2004). Food intake regulation in body weight management. A primer. *Nutrition Today*, 39, 203–13.

Melanson, K. J., Westerp-Plantenga, M. S., Campfield, L. A., and Saris, W. H. M. (1999). Blood glucose and meal patterns in time-blinded males, after aspartame, carbohydrate, and fat consumption, in relation to sweetness perception. *British Journal of Nutrition*, 82, 437–46.

Melhuish, E. C., Lloyd, E., Martin, S., and Mooney A. (1990a). Type of childcare at 18 months I. Differences in interactional experience. *Journal of Child Psychology and Psychiatry*, 31, 849–59.

Melhuish, E. C., Lloyd, E., Martin, S., and Mooney, A. (1990b) Type of childcare at 18 months II. Relations with cognitive and language development. *Journal of Child Psychology and Psychiatry*, 31, 861–70.

Meltzoff, A. N. and Moore, M. K. (1983). Newborn infants imitate adult facial gestures. *Child Development*, 54, 702–9.

Meltzoff, A. N. and Moore, M. K. (1989). Imitation in newborn infants. Exploring the range of gestures imitated and the underlying mechanisms. *Developmental Psychology*, 25, 954–62.

Melzack, R. and Casey, K. L. (1968). Sensory, motivational, and central control determinants of pain. A new conceptual model. In D. R. Kenshalo (ed), *The Skin Senses* (pp 423–43). Springfield, IL. Charles C. Thomas.

Melzack, R. and Wall, P. D. (1965). Pain mechanisms. A new theory. *Science*, 150, 971–9.

Melzack, R. and Wall, P. D. (1983). *The Challenge of Pain*. New York, NY. Basic Books.

Melzer, P. and Ebner, F. (2008). Braille, plasticity, and the mind. In J. J. Rieser, D. H. Ashmead, F. E. Ebner, and A. L. Corn (eds), *Blindness and Plasticity in Navigation and Object Perception* (pp 85–112). New York, NY. Psychology Press.

Menon, V. and Levitin, D. J. (2005). The rewards of music listening. Response and physiological connectivity of themesolimbic system. *NeuroImage*, 28, 175–84.

Meredith, P. and Noller, P. (2003). Attachment and infant difficultness in postnatal depression. *Journal of Family Issues*, 24, 668–86.

Merikangas, K. R., Akiskal, H. S., Angst, J., Greenberg, P. E., Hirschfeld, R. M. A., et al (2007). Lifetime and 12-month prevalence of bipolar spectrum disorders in the National Comorbidity Survey Replication. *Archives of General Psychiatry*, 64, 543–52.

Merlo, L. and Barnett, D. (2001). All about inkblots. *Scientific American*, 285, 13.

Merskey, H. (2004). Opium. The best remedy. *Pain Research and Management*, 9, 12.

Messer, S. B. (2001). What makes brief psychodynamic therapy time efficient. *Clinical Psychology. Science and Practice*, 8, 5–22.

Messias, E. L., Chen, C.-Y., and Eaton, W. W. (2007). Epidemiology of schizophrenia. Review of findings and myths. *Psychiatric Clinics of North America*, 30, 323–38.

Messinger, D. S., Bauer, C. R., Das, A., Seifer, R., Lester, B. M., et al (2004). The maternal lifestyle study. Cognitive motor, and behavioral outcomes of cocaine-exposed and opiate-exposed infants through three years of age. *Journal of Pediatrics*, 113, 1677–85.

Mestel, R. (2012, 19 June). Florida spear gun accident. Stories of brain injury survivors. *Los Angeles Times*. Retrieved from www.latimes.com on 6 July 2012.

Meston, C., Levin, R. J., Sipski, M. L., Hull, E. M., and Heiman, J. R. (2004). Women's orgasm. *Annual Review of Sex Research*, 15, 173–257.

Meyer, J. S. and Quenzer, L. F. (2005). *Psychopharmacology. Drugs, the Brain, and Behavior*. Sunderland, MA. Sinauer Associates.

Meyer-Bahlburg, H. F. L. (2005). Gender identity outcome in female-raised 46, XY persons with penile agenesis, cloacal exstrophy of the bladder, or penile ablation. *Archives of Sexual Behavior*, 34, 423–38.

Meyer-Bahlburg, H. F. L. (2010). From mental disorder to iatrogenic hypogonadism. Dilemmas in conceptualizing gender identity variants as psychiatric conditions. *Archives of Sexual Behavior*, 39, 461–76.

Meyer-Bahlburg, H. F. L., Dolezal, C., Baker, S. W., Carlson, A. D., Obeid, J. S., et al (2004). Prenatal androgenization affects gender-related behavior but not gender identity in 5–12-year-old girls with congenital adrenal hyperplasia. *Archives of Sexual Behavior*, 33, 97–104.

Michael, K. D., Huelsman, T. J., and Crowley, S. L. (2005). Interventions for child and adolescent depression. Do professional therapists produce better results? *Journal of Child and Family Studies*, 14, 223–36.

Mikhail, J. (2007). Universal moral grammar. Theory, evidence, and the future. *Trends in Cognitive Sciences*, 11, 143–52.

Mikolajczak, M., Gross, J. J., Lane, A., Corneille, O., de Timary, P., et al (2010). Oxytocin makes people trusting, not gullible. *Psychological Science*, 21, 1072–4.

Milgram, S. (1963). Behavioral study of obedience. *Journal of Abnormal and Social Psychology*, 67, 371–8.

Milgram, S. (1974). *Obedience to Authority. An Experimental View*. New York, NY. Harper-Collins.

Miller, C. J., Marks, D. M., Miller, S. R., Berwid, O. G., Kera, E. C., et al (2007). Television viewing and risk for attention problems in preschool children. *Journal of Pediatric Psychology*, 32, 448–52.

Miller, C. T. and Kaiser, C. R. (2001). A theoretical perspective on coping with stigma. *Journal of Social Issues*, 57(1), 73–112.

Miller, E. K. and Cohen, J. D. (2001). An integrative theory of prefrontal cortex function. *Annual Review of Neuroscience*, 24, 167–102.

Miller, G., Chen, E., and Cole, S. W. (2009). Health psychology. Developing biologically plausible models linking the social world and physical health. *Annual Review of Psychology*, 60, 501–24.

Miller, G. A. (2003). The cognitive revolution. A historical perspective. *Trends in Cognitive Sciences*, 7(3), 141–4.

Miller, G. A. (2010). Mistreating psychology in the decades of the brain. *Perspectives in Psychological Science*, 5, 716–43.

Miller, G. E. and Blackwell, E. (2006). Turning up the heat. Inflammation as a mechanism linking chronic stress, depression, and heart disease. *Current Directions in Psychological Science*, 15, 269–72.

Miller, G. F. (1999). Sexual selection for cultural displays. In R. Dunbar, C. Knight, and C. Power (eds), *The Evolution of Culture* (pp 71–91). Edinburgh, UK. Edinburgh University Press.

Miller, J. D., Scott, E. C., and Okamoto, S. (2006). Public acceptance of evolution. *Science*, 313, 765–6.

Miller, N. E. (1985). The value of behavioral research on animals. *American Psychologist*, 40, 423–40.

Miller, N. E. and Dollard, J. (1941). *Social Learning and Imitation*. New Haven, CT. Yale University Press.

Miller, P. J. E., Niehuis, S., and Huston, T. L. (2006). Positive illusions in marriage. A 13-year longitudinal study. *Personality and Social Psychology Bulletin*, 12, 1579–94.

Miller, R. S. (1995). On the nature of embarrassability. Shyness, social evaluation, and social skill. *Journal of Personality*, 63, 315–39.

Miller, S., Wampold, B., and Varhely, K. (2008). Direct comparisons of treatment modalities for youth disorders. A meta-analysis. *Psychotherapy Research*, 18, 5–14.

Miller, S. C., Kennedy, C., DeVoe, D., Hickey, M., Nelson, T., et al (2009). Examination of changes in oxytocin levels in men and women before and after interaction with a bonded dog. *Anthrozoös*, 22, 31–42.

Miller, S. D., Blackburn, T., Scholes, G., White, G. L., and Mamalis, N. (1991). Optical differences in multiple personality disorder. A second look. *Journal of Nervous and Mental Disease*, 179, 132–5.

Miller, S. L. and Maner, J. L. (2010). Scent of a woman. Men's testosterone responses to olfactory ovulation cues. *Psychological Science*, 21, 276–83.

Miller, V. (2010). The Internet and everyday life. In Y. Jewkes and M. Yar (eds), *Handbook of Internet Crime* (pp 67–87). Devon, UK. Willan Publishing.

Milner, B. (1988). Description of amnesia patient H. M. In F. E. Bloom, A. Lazerson, and L. Hofstadter (eds), *Brain, Mind, and Behavior*. New York, NY. W. H. Freeman.

Milsten, A. M., Tennyson, J., and Weisberg, S. (2017). Retrospective analysis of mosh-pit-related injuries. *Prehospital and Disaster Medicine*, 32(6), 636–41.

Minami, T., Davies, D. R., Tierney, S. C., Bettmann, J. E., McAward, S. M., et al (2009). Preliminary evidence on the effectiveness of psychological treatments delivered at a university counseling center. *Journal of Counseling Psychology*, 56, 309–20.

Minami, T., Wampold, B. E., Serlin, R. C., Hamilton, E. G., Brown, G. S., et al (2008). Benchmarking the effectiveness of psychotherapy treatment of adult depression in a managed care environment. A preliminary study. *Journal of Consulting and Clinical Psychology*, 76, 116–24.

Mischel, W. (1968). *Personality and Assessment*. New York, NY. Wiley.

Mischel, W. (1979). On the interface of cognition and personality. Beyond the person-situation debate. *American Psychologist*, 34(9), 740–54.

Mischel, W., Ayduk, O., Berman, M. G., Casey, B. M., Gotlib, I. H., et al (2011). 'Willpower' over the life span. Decomposing self-regulation. *Social Cognitive and Affective Neuroscience (SCAN)*, 6, 252–6.

Mischel, W., Ebbesen, E. B., and Zeiss, A. R. (1972). Cognitive and attentional mechanisms in delay of gratification. *Journal of Personality and Social Psychology*, 21, 204–18.

Mischel, W., Shoda, Y., and Mendoza-Denton, R. (2002). Situation-behavior profiles as a locus of consistency in personality. *Current Directions in Psychological Science*, 11, 50–4.

Mitchell, D. B. (2006). Nonconscious priming after 17 years. Invulnerable implicit memory? *Psychological Science*, 17, 925–9.

Mitchell, G. (2012). Revisiting truth or triviality. The external validity of research in the psychological laboratory. *Perspectives on Psychological Science*, 7, 109–17.

Mitchell, T. R. and Daniels, D. (2003). Motivation. In W. C. Borman, D. R. Ilgen, and R. J. Klimoski (eds), *Handbook of Psychology. Vol 12. Industrial Organizational Psychology* (pp 225–54). New York, NY. Wiley.

Mitelman, S. A., Brickman, A. M., Shihabuddin, L., Newmark, R., Chu, K. W., et al (2005). Correlations between MRI-assessed volumes of the thalamus and cortical Brodmann's areas in schizophrenia. *Schizophrenia Research*, 75, 265–81.

Mitelman, S. A., Byne, W., Kemether, E. M., Hazlett, E. A., Buchsbam, M., et al (2005). Metabolic disconnection between the mediodorsal nucleus of the thalamus and cortical Brodmann's areas of the left hemisphere in schizophrenia. *The American Journal of Psychiatry*, 162, 1733–5.

Mixon, D. (1976). Studying feignable behavior. *Representative Research in Social Psychology*, 7, 89–104.

Miyamoto, Y. and Kitayama, S. (2002). Cultural variation in correspondence bias. The critical role of attitude diagnosticity of socially constrained behavior. *Journal of Personality and Social Psychology*, 83, 1239–48.

Miyamoto, Y., Nisbett, R. E., and Masuda, T. (2006). Culture and the physical environment. Holistic versus analytic perceptual affordances. *Psychological Science*, 17, 113–19.

Miyamoto, Y., Nisbett, R. E., and Yasuda, T. (2006). Culture and the environment. *Psychological Science*, 17, 113–19.

Miyazaki, M., Aihide, Y., and Nomura, S. (2010). Diagnosis of multiple anxiety disorders predicts the concurrent co-morbidity of major depressive disorder. *Comprehensive Psychiatry*, 51, 15–18.

Mizuno, K., Mizuno, N., Shinohara, T., and Noda, M. (2004). Mother-infant skin-to-skin contact after delivery results in early recognition of own mother's milk odour. *Acta Paediatrica*, 93, 1640–5.

Mizushige, T., Inoue, K., and Fushiki, T. (2007). Why is fat so tasty? Chemical reception of fatty acid on the tongue. *Journal of Nutritional Science and Vitaminology (Tokyo)*, 53, 1–4.

Mjellem, N. and Kringlen, E. (2001). Schizophrenia, a review, with emphasis on the neurodevelopmental hypothesis. *Nordic Journal of Psychiatry*, 55, 301–9.

Mobbs, D. and Watt, C. (2011). There is nothing paranormal about near-death experiences. How neuroscience can explain seeing bright lights, meeting the dead, or being convinced you are one of them. *Trends in Cognitive Sciences*, 15(10), 447–9.

Moffatt, B. and Elliott, C. (2007). Ghostmarketing. Pharmaceutical companies and ghostwritten journal articles. *Perspectives in Biology and Medicine*, 50, 18–31.

Moffitt, T. (1993). Adolescence-limited and life-course-persistent antisocial behavior. A developmental taxonomy. *Psychological Review*, 100, 674–701.

Mohamed, S. and Ajmal, M. (2015). Multivariate analysis of binge drinking in young adult population. Data analysis of the 2007 Survey of Lifestyle, Attitude and Nutrition in Ireland. *Psychiatry and Clinical Neurosciences*, 69(8), 483–8.

Mojtabai, R. (2008). Increase in antidepressant medication in the US adult population between 1990 and 2003. *Psychotherapy and Psychosomatics*, 77, 83–92.

Mokdad, A. H., Marks, J. S., Stroup, D. F., and Gerberding, J. L. (2004). Actual causes of death in the United States, 2000. *JAMA*, 291, 1238–44.

Monahan, J. L., Murphy, S. T., and Zajonc, R. B. (2000). Subliminal mere exposure. Specific, general, and diffuse effects. *Psychological Science*, 11, 462–6.

Monahan, K. C., Steinberg, L., and Cauffman, E. (2009). Affiliation with antisocial peers, susceptibility to peer influence and antisocial behavior during the transition to adulthood. *Developmental Psychology*, 45, 1520–30.

Moncrieff, J. and Cohen, D. (2006). Do Antidepressant cure or create abnormal brain states? *PLoS Medicine*, 3, 0961–5. Retrieved from www.plos.org on 12 July 2007.

Mongeau, P. A., Serewicz, M. C. M., and Therrien, L. F. (2004). Goals for cross-sex first dates. Identification, measurement, and the influence of contextual factors. *Communication Monographs*, 71(2), 121–47.

Monohan, J. L., Murphy, S. T., and Zajonc, R. B. (2000). Subliminal mere exposure. Specific, general, and diffuse effects. *Psychological Science*, 11, 462–6.

Monroe, S. M. and Simons, A. D. (1991). Diathesis stress theories in the context of life stress research. Implications for depressive disorders. *Psychological Bulletin*, 110, 406–25.

Moon, C., Lagercrantz, H., and Kuhl, P. (2013). Language experienced *in utero* affects vowel perception after birth. A two-country study. *Acta Paediatrica*, 102, 156–60.

Moonesinghe, R., Khoury, M. J., Cecile, A., and Janssens, J. W. (2007). Most published research findings are false—but a little replication goes a long way. *PLoS Medicine*, 4. Retrieved from http://medicine.plosjournals.org on 14 March 2007.

Moor, B. G., Crone, E. A., and van der Molen, M. W. (2010). The heartbrake of social rejection. Heart rate deceleration in response to unexpected peer rejection. *Psychological Science*, 21, 1326–33.

Moore, D. S. and Johnson, S. P. (2008). Mental rotation in human infants. A sex difference. *Psychological Science*, 19, 1063–6.

Moore, D. W. (2005, 16 June). Three in four Americans believe in paranormal. *Gallup News Service*. Retrieved from http://home.sandiego.edu/~baber/logic/gallup.html on 3 March 2006.

Moore, K. A., Driscoll, A. K., and Lindberg, L. D. (1998). *A Statistical Portrait of Adolescent Sex, Contraception, and Childbearing*. Washington, DC. The National Campaign to Prevent Teen Pregnancy.

Moore, M. M. (1995). Courtship signaling and adolescents. 'Girls just wanna have fun'? *Journal of Sex Research*, 32, 319–28.

Moore, M. M. (2002). Courtship communication and perception. *Perceptual and Motor Skills*, 94(1), 97–105.

Moore, T. E. (1995). Subliminal self-help auditory tapes. An empirical test of

perceptual consequences. *Canadian Journal of Behavioural Science*, 27(1), 9–20.

Moore, T. E. and Pepler, D. J. (2006). Wounding words. Maternal verbal aggression and children's adjustment. *Journal of Family Violence*, 21, 89–93.

Morelli, M. F. (1983). Milgram's dilemma of obedience. *Metaphilosophy*, 14, 183–9.

Morgan, C. J. and Curran, H. V. (2008). Effects of cannabidiol on schizophrenia-like symptoms in people who use cannabis. *The British Journal of Psychiatry*, 192(4), 306–7.

Morgan, M. J. (2000). Ecstasy (MDMA). A review of its possible persistent psychological effects. *Psychopharmacology*, 152, 230–48.

Morgan, M. J. (2002). Throwing out the baby with the bathwater? *The Psychologist*, 15, 468–9.

Mori, K. and Mori, H. (2009). Another test of the passive facial feedback hypothesis. When your face smiles, you feel happy. *Perceptual and Motor Skills*, 109, 76–8.

Morimoto, K., Fahnestock, M., and Racine, R. J. (2004). Kindling and status epilepticus models of epilepsy. Rewiring the brain. *Progress in Neurobiology*, 73, 1–60.

Morizot, J. and Le Blanc, M. (2003). Searching for a developmental typology of personality and its relations to antisocial behaviour. A longitudinal study of an adjudicated men sample. *Criminal Behaviour and Mental Health*, 13(4), 241–77.

Morra, S., Gobbo, C., Marini, Z., and Sheese, R. (eds). (2008). *Cognitive Development. Neo-Piagetian Perspectives*. New York, NY. Taylor and Francis/Lawrence Earlbaum Associates.

Morris, E. (2008, 19 May 19). The most curious thing. *New York Times*. Retrieved from www.nytimes.com on 12 June 2008.

Morris, W. N. (1999). The mood system. In D. Kahneman, E. Diender, and N. Schwartz (eds), *Well-being. The Foundations of Hedonic Psychology* (pp 169–89). New York, NY. Russell Sage Foundation.

Morrison, A. R. (2001). Personal reflections on the 'animal-rights' phenomenon. *Perspectives in Biology and Medicine*, 44, 62–75.

Mortimer, J. T. (2003). *Working and Growing Up*. Cambridge, MA. Harvard University Press.

Morton, J. (2005). Ecstasy. Pharmacology and neurotoxicity. *Current Opinion in Pharmacology*, 5(1), 79–86.

Moruzzi, G. and Magoun, H. (1949). Brain stem reticular formation and activation of the EEG. *Electroencephalography and Clinical Neurophysiology*, 1, 455–73.

Moscovitch, M., Winocur, G., and Behrmann, M. (1997). What is special about face recognition? Nineteen experiments on a person with visual object agnosia and dyslexia but normal face recognition. *Journal of Cognitive Neuroscience*, 9, 555–604.

Mosing, M. A., Madison, G., Pedersen, N. L., Kuja-Halkola, R., and Ullén, F. (2014). Practice does not make perfect. No causal effect of music practice on music ability. *Psychological Science*, 25(9), 1795–1803.

Moss, M. (2000, 31 May). The story behind a soldier's story. *New York Times*. Retrieved from http://partners.nytimes.com/library/national/053100korea-massacre-ap.html on 12 May 2006.

Moss-Morris, R. and Petrie, K. J. (2001). Redefining medical students' disease to reduce morbidity. *Medical Education*, 35, 724–8.

Most, S. B., Scholl, B. J., Clifford, E. R., and Simons, D. J. (2005). What you see is what you set. Sustained inattentional blindness and the capture of awareness. *Psychological Review*, 112, 217–42.

Motley, M.T. (1985) 'Slips of the tongue'. *Scientific American*, 253, 116–27.

Motluk, A. (2005, 29 January). Senses special. The art of seeing without sight. *New Scientist*. Retrieved from www.newscien%20tist.com on 1 January 2006.

Moulson, M. C., Westerlund, A., Fox, N. A., Zeanah, C. H., and Nelson, C. A. (2009). The effects of early experience on face recognition. An event-related potential study of institutionalized children in Romania. *Child Development*, 80, 1039–56.

Moulton, S. T. and Kosslyn, S. M. (2009). Imagining predictions. Mental imagery as mental emulation. *Philosophical Transactions of the Royal Society B. Biological Sciences*, 364(1521), 1273–80.

Moussavi, S., Chatterji, S., Verdes, E., Tandon, A., Patel, V., et al (2007). Depression, chronic diseases, and decrements in health. Results from the World Health Surveys. *The Lancet*, 370, 851–8.

Mueller, K. L., Hoon, M. A., Erlenbach, I., Chandrashekar, J., Zuker, C. S., et al (2005). The receptors and coding logic for bitter taste. *Nature*, 434, 225–9.

Mukherjee, S. (2012, 19 April). Post-Prozac nation. The science and history of treating depression. *New York Times*.

Retrieved from http://www.nytimes.com/2012/04/22/magazine/the-science-and-history-of-treating-depression.html?pagewanted=all&_r=0 on 19 April 2012.

Mullins, M. E. (1999). Laboratory confirmation of flunitrazepam in alleged cases of date rape. *Emergency Medicine*, 6, 966–8.

Mumford, M. D. and Gustafson, S. B. (1988). Creativity syndrome. Integration, application, and innovation. *Psychological Bulletin*, 103, 27–43.

Muraven, M. and Baumeister, R. F. (2000). Self-regulation and depletion of limited resources. Does self-control resemble a muscle? *Psychological Bulletin*, 126, 237–59.

Murdoch, B. B., Jr (1962). The serial position effect in free recall. *Journal of Experimental Psychology*, 64, 482–8.

Murphy, G. E. (1998). Why women are less likely than men to commit suicide. *Comprehensive Psychiatry*, 39, 165–75.

Murphy, J. M., Horton, N. J., Laird, N. M., Monson, R. R., Sobol, A. M., et al (2004). Anxiety and depression. A 40-year perspective on relationships regarding prevalence, distribution, and comorbidity. *Acta Psychiatrica Scandinavica*, 109, 355–75.

Murphy, S. T., Monahan, J. L., and Zajonc, R. B. (1995). Additivity of nonconscious affect. Combined effects of priming and exposure. *Journal of Personality and Social Psychology*, 69, 589–602.

Murray, E. A. (2007) The amygdala, reward and emotion. *Trends in Cognitive Sciences*, 11, 489–97.

Murray, H. A. (1938). *Explorations in Personality*. Oxford, UK. Oxford University Press.

Murray, H. A. (1943). *Thematic Apperception Test Manual*. Cambridge, MA. Harvard University Press.

Murray, H. A. (1963). Studies of stressful interpersonal disputations. *American Psychologist*, 18(1), 28.

Murray, H. A. and Kluckhohn, C. (1953). *Personality in Nature, Society, and Culture*. New York, NY. Alfred Knopf.

Murray, S. A., Grant, E., Grant., A., and Kendall, M. (2003). Dying from cancer in developed and developing countries. Lessons from two qualitative interview studies of patients and their careers. *British Medical Journal*, 326, 368–72.

Murray, S. L., Griffin, D. W., Derrick, J. L., Harris, B., and Aloni, M. (2011). Tempting fate or inviting happiness? Unrealistic idealization prevents the decline of marital happiness. *Psychological Science*, 22, 619–26.

Mustanski, B. S., Bailey, J. M., and Kaspar, S. (2002). Dermatoglypics, handedness, sex, and sexual orientation. *Archives of Sexual Behavior*, 31, 113–22.

Mutch, D. M. and Clément, K. (2006). Unraveling the genetics of human obesity. *PLoS Genetics*, 2, 1956–63.

Myers, D. G. (2000). The funds, friends, and faith of happy people. *American Psychologist*, 55, 56–67.

Myers, D. G. (2002). *Intuition. Its Powers and Perils*. New Haven, CT. Yale University Press.

Myers, D. G. (2007). The powers and perils of intuition. Understanding the nature of our gut instincts. *Scientific American Mind*, 24–31June/July.

Myers, D. G. (2010). Intuitions's powers and perils. *Psychological Inquiry*, 21, 371–7.

Myers, D. G. and Diener, E. (1996, May). The pursuit of happiness. *Scientific American*, 274, 54–6.

Nagasako, E. M., Oaklander, A. L., and Dworkin, R. H. (2003). Congenital insensitivity to pain. An update. *Pain*, 101, 213–19.

Nagasawa, M., Kikusui, T., Onaka, T., and Ohta, M. (2009). Dog's gaze at its owner increases owner's urinary oxytocin during social interaction. *Hormones and Behavior*, 55, 434–41.

Nagel, T. (1974). What is it like to be a bat? *Philosophical Review*, 83, 435–50.

Nakamura, J. and Csikszentmihalyi, M. (2009). Flow theory and research. In S. J. Lopez and C. R. Snyder (eds), *Oxford Handbook of Positive Psychology* (2nd edn, pp 195–206). New York, NY. Oxford University Press.

Nanninga, R. (1996/1997). The astrotest. A tough match for astrologers. *Correlation*, 15, 14–20.

Napolitan, D. A. and Goethals, G. R. (1979). The attribution of friendliness. *Journal of Experimental Social Psychology*, 15, 105–13.

Naqvi, N. H., Rudrauf, D., Damasio, H., and Bechara, A. (2007). Damage to the insula disrupts addiction to cigarette smoking. *Science*, 315, 531–4.

Narumoto, J., Okada, T., Sadato, N., Fukui, K., and Yonekura, Y. (2001). Attention to emotion modulates fMRI activity in human right superior temporal sulcus. *Cognitive Brain Research*, 12, 225–31.

Nassar, M., Katzman, M. A., and Gordon, R. A. (eds). (2001). *Eating Disorders and Cultures in Transition*. London. Brunner-Routledge.

Nathan, D. (2011). *Sybil Exposed*. New York, NY. Free Press.

Nathan, D. and Snedeker, M. (1995). *Satan's Silence. Ritual Abuse and the Making of a Modern American Witch Hunt*. New York, NY. Basic Books.

National Center for Health Statistics (2007). *Health, United States, 2007. With chartbook on trends in the health of Americans*. Hyattsviile, MD. Centers for Disease Control. Retrieved from http://www.cdc.gov/nchs/data/hus/hus07.pdf on 6 June 2008.

National Institute on Aging (2006). Alzheimer's disease fact sheet. Retrieved from http://www.nia.nih.gov/Alzheimers/Publications/adfact.htm on 3 May 2006.

National Institutes of Mental Health (2009). Schizophrenia. Retrieved from http://www.nimh.nih.gov/health/publications/schizophrenia/schizophrenia-booket-2009.pdf on 12 March 2013.

National Institutes of Mental Health (2010). Suicide in the U.S. Statistics and Prevention. Retrieved from http://www.nimh.nih.gov/health/publications/suicide-in-the-us-statistics-and-prevention/index.shtml on 11 March 2013.

National Research Council (2010). *Gender Differences at Critical Transitions in the Careers of Science, Engineering, and Mathematics Faculty*. Washington, DC. National Academies Press.

National Science Foundation (2002). Science and technology. Public attitudes and public understanding. Indicators 2002. Retrieved from http://www.nsf.gov/statistics/seind02/c7/c7h.htm on 20 November 2007.

National Sleep Foundation (2005). *2005 Sleep in America Poll*. Retrieved from www.sleepfoundation.org on 9 January 2006.

National Sleep Foundation (2010). *2010 Sleep in America Poll*. Retrieved from www.sleepfoundation.org on 15 March 2011.

National Sleep Foundation (2011). *2011 Sleep in America Poll*. Retrieved from www.sleepfoundation.org on 15 March 2011.

Naughton, M., Mulrooney, J. B., and Leonard, B. E. (2000). A review of the role of serotonin receptors in psychiatric disorders. *Human Psychopharmacology. Clinical and Experimental*, 15, 397–415.

Nawrot, M. (2003). Disorders of motion and depth. *Neurologic Clinics*, 21, 609–29.

Naylor, E. V., Anonuccio, D. O., Litt, M., Johnson, G. E., Spogen, D. R., et al (2010). Bibliotherapy as a treatment for depression in primary care. *Journal of Clinical Psychology in Medical Settings*, 17, 258–71.

Nazroo, J. Y. (2003). The structuring of ethnic inequalities in health. Economic position, racial discrimination, and racism. *American Journal of Public Health*, 93, 277–84.

Neame, A. (2003, November). Beyond 'drink spiking'. Drug and alcohol-facilitated sexual assault. *Briefing. Australian Center for the Study of Sexual Assault*, 2. Retrieved from http://www.aifs.gov.au/acssa/pubs/briefing/b2.html on 3 February 2006.

Neath, I. (1993). Distinctiveness and serial position effects in recognition. *Memory and Cognition*, 21, 689–98.

Nee, D. E., Berman, M. G., Moore, K. S., and Jonides, J. (2008). Neuroscientific evidence about the distinction between short- and long-term memory. *Current Directions in Psychological Science*, 17, 102–6.

Neimark, E. D. (1975). Longitudinal development of formal operations thought. *Genetic Psychology Monographs*, 91, 171–225.

Neisser, U., Boodoo, G., Bouchard, T. J., Jr, Boykin, A. W., Brody, N., et al (1996). Intelligence. Knowns and unknowns. *American Psychologist*, 51, 77–101.

Nelson, C. A. (1999). Neural plasticity and human development. *Current Directions in Psychological Science*, 8, 42–5.

Nelson, C. A. (2001). The development and neural bases of face recognition. *Infant and Child Development*, 10, 3–18.

Nelson, J. C., Mazure, C. M., Jatlow, P. I., Bowers, M. B. J., and Price, L. H. (2004). Combining norepinephrine and serotonin reuptake inhibition mechanisms for treatment of depression. A double-blind, randomized study. *Biological Psychiatry*, 55(3), 296–300.

Nelson, J. C., Thase, M. E., and Khan, A. (2008). Are antidepressants effective? What's a clinician to think? *Journal of Clinical Psychiatry*, 69, 1014–15.

Nelson, K. R., Mattingly, M., Lee, S. A., and Schmitt, F. A. (2006). Does the arousal system contribute to near death experience? *Neurology*, 66(7), 1003–9.

Nelson, K. S., Kushlev, K., English, T., Dunn, E. W., and Lyubomirsky, S. (2013). In defense of parenthood. Children are associated with more joy than misery. *Psychological Science*, 24, 3–10.

Nes, R. B., Røysamb, E., Tambs, K., Harris, J. R., and Reichborn-Kjennerud, T. (2006). Subjective well-being. Genetic and environmental contributions to stability and change. *Psychological Medicine*, 65, 449–75.

Nesse, R. M. (1990). Evolutionary explanations of emotions. *Human Nature*, 1, 261–89.

Nesse, R. M. (1991). What good is feeling bad? The evolutionary benefits of psychic pain. *The Sciences*, November/December, 30–7.

Nesse, R. M. (2005). Maladaptation and natural selection. *Quarterly Review of Biology*, 80, 62–70.

Nesse, R. M. and Williams, G. C. (1994). *Why We Get Sick. The New Science of Darwinian Medicine*. New York, NY. Times Books.

Neta, M. and Whalen, P. J. (2010). The primacy of negative interpretations when resolving the valence of ambiguous facial expressions. *Psychological Science OnLine First*. Retrieved from pss.sage.com on 30 June 2010.

Neubert, D. (1999). Risk assessment and preventative hazard minimization. In H. Marquardt, S. G. Schafer, R. McClellan, and F. Welsch (eds), *Toxicology* (pp 1153–86). San Diego, CA. Academic Press.

Neuspiel, D. R. (1993). Cocaine and the fetus. Mythology of severe risk. *Neurotoxicology and Teratology*, 15, 305–6.

Neutel, X. L. (2005). The epidemiology of long-term benzodiazepine use. *International Review of Psychiatry*, 17, 189–97.

New heroes, new hope. (2005, 6 January). *People*. Retrieved from www.people.com on 1 August 2009.

New York Times. (2009, 17 May). A new trend in motherhood. Retrieved from www.nytimes.com on 13 June 2009.

Newcombe, N. S. (2002). The nativist-empiricist controversy in the context of recent research on spatial and quantitative development. *Psychological Science*, 13, 395–401.

Newman, C. and Adams, K. (2004) Dog gone good. Managing dog phobia in a teenage boy with a learning disability. *British Journal of Learning Disabilities*, 32, 35–8.

Newport, E. L. (2002). Critical periods in language development. In L. Nadel (ed), *Encyclopedia of Cognitive Science* (pp 737–40). London. Macmillan.

Newstead, S. E. (2000). Are there two different types of thinking? *Behavioral and Brain Science*, 23, 600–1.

Newton, N. and Newton, M. (1967). Psychologic aspects of lactation. *New England Journal of Medicine*, 272, 1179–96.

Nicdao, E. G., Hong, S., and Takeuchi, D. T. (2007). Prevalence and correlates of eating disorders among Asian Americans. Results from the National Latino and Asian American study. *International Journal of Eating Disorders*, 40(Suppl), S22–6.

NICHD (Early Child Care Research Network) (2001). Child-care and family predictors of preschool attachment and stability from infancy. *Developmental Psychology*, 37, 847–62.

NICHD (Early Child Care Research Network) (2003). Does amount of time spent in child care predict socioemotional adjustment during the transition to kindergarten? *Child Development*, 74, 976–1005.

NICHD (Early Child Care Research Network) (2006). Child-care effect sizes for the NICHD study of early child care and youth development. *American Psychologist*, 61, 99–116.

NICHD (Early Child Care Research Network) (2010). Testing a series of causal propositions relating time in child care to children's externalizing behavior. *Developmental Psychology*, 46, 1–17.

Nicholls, C. M. and Atherton, I. (2011). Housing first. Considering components for successful resettlement of homeless people with multiple needs. *Housing Studies*, 26(5), 767–77.

Nichols, A. L. and Maner, J. K. (2008). The good subject effect. Investigating participant demand characteristics. *Journal of General Psychology*, 135, 151–65.

Nichols, E. A., Kao, Y-C., Verfaellie, M., and Gabrieli, J. D. E. (2006). Working memory and long-term memory for faces. Evidence from fMRI and global amnesia for involvement of the medial temporal lobes. *Hippocampus*, 16, 604–16.

Nickerson, C., Schwarz, N., Diener, E., and Kahneman, D. (2003). Zeroing in on the dark side of the American dream. A closer look at the negative consequences of the goal for financial success. *Psychological Science*, 14, 531–6.

Nickerson, R. S. (1998). Confirmation bias. A ubiquitous phenomenon in many guises. *Review of General Psychology*, 2, 175–220.

Nickles, C., Brecht, D. Klinger, E., and Bursell, A. (1998). The effects of current concern- and nonconcern-related waking suggestions and nocturnal dream content. *Journal of Personality and Social Psychology*, 75, 242–55.

Niedenthal, P. M. (2007). Embodying emotion. *Science*, 316, 1002–5.

Nieh, H. (ed and co-trans) (1981). *Literature of the Hundred Flowers. Vol 1. Criticism and Polemics*. New York, NY. Columbia University Press.

Nielsen, T. A. (2000). A review of mentation in REM and NREM sleep. 'Covert' REM sleep as a possible reconciliation of two opposing models. *Behavioral and Brain Sciences*, 23, 793–1121.

Nielsen, T. A., Zadra, A. L., Simard, V., Saucier, S. and Stenstrom, P. (2003). The typical dreams of Canadian university students. *Dreaming*, 13, 211–35.

Niemiec, C. P., Ryan, R. M., and Deci, E. L. (2009). The path taken. Consequences of attaining intrinsic and extrinsic aspirations in post-college life. *Journal of Research in Personality*, 43, 291–306.

Nilsson, L. (1993). *A Child Is Born*. New York, NY. DTP/Seymour Lawrence.

Nisbett, R. E., Aronson, J., Blair, C., Dickens, W., Flynn, J., et al (2012). Intelligence. New findings and theoretical developments. *American Psychologist*, 67(2), 130.

Nisbett, R. E. and Miyamoto, Y. (2005). The influence of culture. Holistic versus analytic perception. *Trends in Cognitive Science*, 9, 467–73.

Nisbett, R. E. and Ross, L. (1980). *Human Inference. Strategies and Shortcomings of Social Judgment*. Englewood Cliffs, NJ. Prentice-Hall.

Nishida, T., Matsusaka, T., and McGrew, W. C. (2009). Emergence, propagation or disappearance of novel behavioral patterns in the habituated chimpanzees of Mahale. A review. *Primates*, 50, 23–36.

Nishimaru, H., Restrepo, C. E., Ryge, J., Yanagawa, Y., and Kiehn, O. (2005). Mammalian motor neurons corelease glutamate and acetylcholine at central synapses. *Proceedings of the National Academy of Sciences*, 102, 5245–9.

Nishitani, S., Miyamura, T., Tagawa, M., Sumi, M., Takase, R., et al (2009). The calming effect of a maternal breast milk odor on the human newborn infant. *Neuroscience Research*, 63, 66–71.

Nolan, J. M., Schultz, P. W., Cialdini, R. B., Goldstein, N. J., and Griskevicius, V. (2008). Normative social influence is underdetected. *Personality and Social Psychology Bulletin*, 34, 913–23.

Nolen-Hoeksema, S. (2001). Gender differences in depression. *Current Directions in Psychological Science*, 10, 173–6.

Nolen-Hoeksema, S. (2012). Emotion regulation and psychopathology. The role of gender. *Annual Review of Clinical Psychology*, 8, 61–87.

Nolen-Hoeksema, S., Wisco, B. E., and Lyubomirsky, S. (2008). Rethinking rumination. *Perspectives on Psychological Science*, 3, 400–24.

Nomaguchi, K. M. and Milkie, M. A. (2003). Costs and rewards of children. The effects of becoming a parent on adults' lives. *Journal of Marriage and Family*, 65, 356–74.

Norcross, J. C. (2005). A primer on psychotherapy integration. In J. C. Norcross and M. R. Goldfried (eds), *Handbook of Psychotherapy Integration* (2nd edn, pp 84–102). New York, NY. Oxford University Press.

Norcross, J. C., Koocher, G. P., and Garofalo, A. (2006). Discredited psychological treatments and tests. A Delphi poll. *Professional Psychology. Research and Practice*, 37, 512–22.

Norcross, J. C. and Lambert, M. J. (2011). Psychotherapy relationships that work II. *Psychotherapy*, 48, 4–8.

Norcross, J. C., Ratzin, A. C., and Payne, D. (1989). Ringing in the New Year. The change processes and reported outcomes of resolutions. *Addictive Behaviors*, 14, 205–12.

Norcross, J. C., Santrock, J., Campbell, L., Smith, T., Sommer, R., et al (2000). *Authoritative Guide to Self-help Resources in Mental Health*. New York, NY. Guilford Press.

Norcross, J. C. and Wampold, B. E. (2011). Evidence-based therapy relationships. Research conclusions and clinical practices. *Psychotherapy*, 48, 98–102.

Nördenstrom, A., Servin, A., Bohlin, G., Larsson, A., and Wedell, A. (2002). Sex-typed toy play behavior correlates with the degree of prenatal androgen exposure assessed by *CYP21* genotype in girls with congenital adrenal hyperplasia. *Journal of Clinical Endocrinology and Metabolism*, 87, 5119–24.

Norenzayan, A. and Heine, S. J. (2005). Psychological universals. What are they and how can we know? *Psychological Bulletin*, 131, 763–84.

Norenzayan, A. and Nisbett, R. E. (2000). Culture and causal cognition. *Current Directions in Psychological Science*, 9, 132–5.

NORML. (2013). States that have decriminalized. Retrieved from http://norml.org on 11 February 2013.

Nosek, B. A., Greenwald, A. G., and Banajji, M. R. (2007). The Implicit Association Test at age 7. Methodological and conceptual review. In J. A. Bargh (ed), *Social Psychology and the Unconscious. The Automaticity of Higher Mental Processes. Frontiers of Social Psychology* (pp 265–92). New York, NY. Psychology Press.

Nowak, M. A., Komarova, N. L., and Niyogi, P. (2001). Evolution of universal grammar. *Science*, 291, 114–18.

Nowak, M. A., Plotkin, J. B., and Jansen, V. A. A. (2000). The evolution of syntactic communication. *Nature*, 404, 495–8.

Nussbaum, M. C. (2001). *Upheavals of Thought. The Intelligence of Emotions*. New York, NY. Cambridge University Press.

Nutt, D., King, L. A., Saulsbury, W., and Blakemore, C. (2007). Development of a rational scale to assess the harm of drugs of potential misuse. *Lancet*, 369, 1047–53.

Nutt, D. J. and Sharpe, M. (2008). Uncritical positive regard? Issues in the efficacy and safety of psychotherapy. *Journal of Psychopharmacology*, 22, 3–6.

O'Brien, C. P. (2005). Benzodiazepine use, abuse, and dependence. *Journal of Clinical Psychology*, 66(Suppl 2), 28–33.

O'Brien, S. F. and Bierman, K. L. (1988). Conceptions and perceived influence of peer groups. Interviews with preadolescents and adolescents. *Child Development*, 1360–5.

O'Connor, D. B., Archer, J., and Wu, F. C. W. (2004). Effects of testosterone on mood, aggression and sexual behavior in young men. A double-blind, placebo-controlled, cross-over study. *Journal of Clinical Endocrinology and Metabolism*, 89, 2837–45.

O'Connor, T. B., Deater-Deckard, K., Fulker, D., Rutter, M., and Plomin, R. (1998). Genotype-environment correlations in late childhood and early adolescence. Antisocial behavioral problems and coercive parenting. *Developmental Psychology*, 34, 970–81.

O'Connor, T. G., Deater-Deckard, K., Fulker, D. W., Rutter, M., and Plomin, R. (1998). Genotype-environment correlations in late childhood and early adolescence. Antisocial behavioral problems and coercive parenting. *Developmental Psychology*, 34, 970–81.

O'Connor, T. G., Hawkins, N., Dunn, J., Thorpe K., Golding, J., et al (1998). Family type and depression in pregnancy. Factors mediating risk in a community sample. *Journal of Marriage and the Family*, 60, 757–70.

O'Craven, K. M. and Kanwisher, N. (2000). Mental imagery of faces and places activates corresponding stimulus-specific brain regions. *Journal of Cognitive Neuroscience*, 12, 1013–23.

O'Donohue, W., Fisher, J. E., and Hayes, S. C. (eds) (2003). *Cognitive-behavior Therapy. Applying Empirically Supported Techniques in Your Practice*. New York, NY. Wiley.

O'Donovan, A., Link, J., Dhabhar, F. S., Wolkowitz, O., Tillie, J. M., et al (2009). Pessimism correlates with leukocyte telomere shortness and elevated interleukin-6 in post-menopausal women. *Brain, Behavior, and Immunity*, 23, 446–9.

Oaten, M., Stevenson, R. J., and Case, T. I. (2009). Disgust as a disease-avoidance mechanism. *Psychological Bulletin*, 135, 303–21.

Obama, B. (1995/2007). *Dreams from My Father*. New York, NY. Crown.

Ochs, E. and Schieffelin, B. B. (1984). Language acquisition and socialization. Three developmental stories. In R. Shweder and R. LeVine (eds), *Culture Theory. Essays on Mind, Self, and Emotion* (pp 276–320). New York, NY. Cambridge University Press.

Oexman, R. D., T. L., Knotts, and Koch, J. (2002). Working while the world sleeps. A consideration of sleep and shift work design. *Employee Responsibilities and Rights Journal*, 14, 145–57.

Offer, D., Kaiz, M., Howard, K. I., and Bennett, E. S. (2000). The altering of reported experiences. *Journal of the Academy of Child and Adolescent Psychiatry*, 39, 735–42.

Office of National Statistics. (2014). *Marriages in England and Wales*. London. Office of National Statistics.

Office of National Statistics. (2017). *Employment Rate (Aged 16–64) Seasonally Adjusted*. London. Office of National Statistics.

Ofshe, R. and Watters, E. (1994). *Making Monsters. False Memories, Psychotherapy, and Sexual Hysteria*. New York, NY. Charles Scribners' Sons.

Ogilvie, R. D. (2001). The process of falling asleep. *Physiological Review*, 5, 247–70.

Ögren, K. and Sandlund, M. (2007). Lobotomy at a state mental hospital in Sweden. A survey of patients operated on during the period 1947–1958. *Nordic Journal of Psychiatry*, 61, 355–62.

Ohayon, M. M. (2002). Epidemiology of insomnia. What we know and what we still need to learn. *Sleep Medicine Review*, 6, 97–111.

Ohayon, M. M., Priest, R. G., Caulet, M., and Guilleminault, C. (1996). Hypnagogic and hypnopompic hallucinations. Pathological phenomena? *The British Journal of Psychiatry*, 169, 459–67.

Öhman, A., Carlsson, K., Lundqvist, D., and Ingvar, M. (2007). On the unconscious subcortical origin of human fear. *Physiology and Behavior*, 92, 180–5.

Öhman, A. and Mineka, S. (2003). The malicious serpent. Snakes as a prototypical stimulus for an evolved module of fear. *Current Directions in Psychological Science*, 12, 2–9.

Öhman, A. and Mineka, S. (2003). The malicious serpent. Snakes as a prototypical stimulus for an evolved module of fear. *Current Directions in Psychological Science*, 12, 5–9.

Ohnishi, T., Matsuda, H., Asada, T., Aruga, M., Hirakata, M., et al (2001). Functional anatomy of musical perception in musicians. *Cerebral Cortex*, 11, 754–60.

Oishi, S., Diener, E., and Lucas, R. E. (2007). The optimum level of well-being. Can people be too happy? *Perspectives in Psychological Science*, 2, 346–60.

Oishi, S., Diener, E. F., Lucas, R. E., and Suh, E. M. (1999). Cross-cultural variations in predictors of life satisfaction. Perspectives from needs and values. *Personality and Social Psychology Bulletin*, 25, 980–90.

Oishi, S., Kushlev, K., and Schimmack, U. (2018). Progressive taxation, income inequality, and happiness. *American Psychologist*, 73(2), 157.

Okami, P. (1992). Intolerable grievances patiently endured. Referent cognitions and group conflict as mediators of anti-Jewish sentiment among African-Americans. *Political Psychology*, 13, 727–53.

Okami, P., Olmstead, R., and Abramson, P. R. (1997). Sexual experiences in early childhood. 18-year longitudinal data from the UCLA Family Lifestyles Project. *The Journal of Sex Research*, 34, 339–47.

Okami, P. and Shackelford, T. K. (2001). Human sex differences in sexual psychology and behavior. *Annual Review of Sex Research*, 12, 186–241.

Okazaki, S. (2002). Influences of culture on Asian Americans' sexuality. *Journal of Sex Research*, 39, 34–41.

Okazaki, S. (2009). Impact of racism on ethnic minority mental health. *Perspectives on Psychological Science*, 4, 103–7.

Okie, S. (2009, 26 January). The epidemic that wasn't. *New York Times*. Retrieved from www.nytimes.com on 26 January 2009.

Okiishi, J., Lambert, M. J., Eggett, D., Nielsen, S. L., Dayton, D. D., et al (2006). An analysis of therapist treatment effects. Toward providing feedback to individual therapists on their clients' psychotherapy outcome. *Journal of Clinical Psychology*, 62, 1157–72.

Okiishi, J., Lambert, M. J., Nielsen, S. L., and Ogles, B. M. (2003). Waiting for supershrink. An empirical analysis of therapist effects. *Clinical Psychology and Psychotherapy*, 10, 361–73.

Olatunji, B. O. and Hollon, S. D. (2010). Preface. The current status of cognitive behavioral therapy for psychiatric disorders. *Psychiatric Clinics of North America*, 33, xiii–ix.

Olatunji, J., Cisler, J., and Tolin, D. F. (2007). Quality of life in the anxiety disorders. A meta-analytic review. *Clinical Psychology Review*, 27, 572–82.

Oliver, M. B., and Hyde, J. S. (1993) Gender differences in sexuality. A meta-analysis. *Psychological Bulletin*, 114, 29–51.

Olson, C. K. (2004). Media violence research and youth violence data. Why do they conflict? *Academic Psychiatry*, 28, 144–50.

Olson, J. M., Vernon, P. A., Harris, J. A., and Jang, K. L. (2001). The heritability of attitudes. A study of twins. *Journal of Personality and Social Psychology*, 80, 845–60.

Olson, L. M. and Wahab, S. (2006). American Indians and suicide. A neglected area of research. *Trauma, Violence, and Abuse*, 7, 19–33.

Ong, A. D. (2010). Pathways linking positive emotion and health in later life. *Current Directions in Psychological Science*, 19, 358–62.

Öngel, Ü. and Smith, P. B. (1994). Who are we and where are we going? *JCCP* approaches its 100th issue. *Journal of Cross-Cultural Studies*, 25, 25–53.

Open Science Collaboration. (2015). Estimating the reproducibility of psychological science. *Science*, 349(6251), aac4716.

Orcutt, H. K. (2006). The prospective relationship of interpersonal forgiveness and psychological distress symptoms among college women. *Journal of Counseling Psychology*, 53, 350–61.

Ordway, G.A., Schwartz, M., and Frazer A. (2007). *Brain Norepinephrine. Neurobiology and Therapeutics.* New York, NY. Cambridge University Press, 2007.

Orne, M. T. (1962). On the social psychology of the psychological experiment. With particular reference to demand characteristics and their implications. *American Psychologist*, 17, 776–83.

Orth, U. (2018). The family environment in early childhood has a long-term effect on self-esteem. A longitudinal study from birth to age 27 years. *Journal of Personality and Social Psychology*, 114(4), 637.

Ostler, N. (2005). *Empires of the Word.* New York, NY. HarperCollins.

Ostrom, T. M. and Sedikides, C. (1992). Out-group homogeneity effects in natural and minimal groups. *Psychological Bulletin*, 112, 536–52.

Otowa, T., Hek, K., Lee, M., Byrne, E. M., Mirza, S. S., et al (2016). Meta-analysis of genome-wide association studies of anxiety disorders. *Molecular Psychiatry*, 21(10), 1391.

Oudiette, D., Leu, S., Pottier, M., Buzare, M-A, Brion, A., et al (2009). Dreamlike mentations during sleepwalking and sleep terrors in adults. *Sleep. Journal of Sleep and Sleep Disorders Research*, 32, 1621–7.

Ougrin, D. (2011). Efficacy of exposure versus cognitive therapy in anxiety disorders. Systematic review and meta-analysis. *BMC Psychiatry*, 11(1), 200.

Owen, A. M., Coleman, M. R., Boly, M., Davis, M. H., Laureys, S., et al (2006). Detecting awareness in the vegetative state. *Science*, 313, 1402.

Owen, A. M., Coleman, M. R., Boly, M., Davis, M. H., Laureys, S., et al (2007). Using functional magnetic resonance imaging to detect covert awareness in the vegetative state. *Archives of Neurology*, 64, 1098–1102.

Owen, J. J., Rhoades, G. K., Stanley, S. M., and Fincham, F. D. (2010). 'Hooking up' among college students. Demographic and psychosocial correlates. *Archives of Sexual Behavior*, 39, 653–63.

Ozer, D. J. and Benet-Martinez, V. (2006). Personality and the prediction of consequential outcomes. *Annual Review of Psychology*, 57, 401–21.

Pack, A. I. (2006). Advances in sleep-disordered breathing. *American Journal of Respiratory and Critical Care Medicine*, 173, 7–15.

Pack, A. K. and Pawson, L. J. (2010). Neuroglial modulation in peripheral sensory systems. *The Neuroscientist*, 16, 342–8.

Packer, D. J. (2008). Identifying systematic disobedience in Milgram's obedience experiments. A meta-analytic review. *Perspectives on Psychological Science*, 3, 301–4.

Padilla-Walker, L. M. and Bean, R. A. (2009). Negative and positive peer influence. Relations to positive and negative behaviors for African American, European American, and Hispanic adolescents. *Journal of Adolescence*, 32, 323–37.

Page, M. P. A. (2006). What can't functional neuroimaging tell the cognitive psychologist? *Cortex. A Journal Devoted to the Study of the Nervous System and Behavior*, 42, 428–43.

Pagnin, D., de Queiroz, V., Pini, S., and Cassano, G. B. (2004). Efficacy of ECT in depression. A meta-analytic review. *Journal of ECT*, 20, 155–62.

Paley, J. (2015). Compassion and the fundamental attribution error. A reply to Rolfe and Gardner. *Nurse Education Today*, 35(3), 474–9.

Palmer, B. A., Pankratz, S., and Bostwick, J. M. (2005). The lifetime risk of suicide in schizophrenia. A reexamination. *Archives of General Psychiatry*, 62, 247–53.

Palmer, R. K. (2007). The pharmacology and signaling of bitter, sweet, and umami taste. *Molecular Intervention*, 7, 87–98.

Palmer, S. E. (2002). Perceptual grouping. It's later than you think. *Current Directions in Psychological Science*, 11, 101–6.

Palmert, M. R., Hayden, D. L., Mansfield, M. J., Crigler, J. F., Jr, Crowley, W. F., Jr, et al (2001). The longitudinal study of adrenal maturation during gonadal suppression. Evidence that adrenarche is a gradual process. *Journal of Clinical Endocrinology and Metabolism*, 86, 4536–42.

Paluck, E. L. and Green, D. P. (2009). Prejudice reduction. What works? A review and assessment of research and practice. *Annual Review of Psychology*, 60, 339–67.

Panksepp, J. (2005a). Affective consciousness. Core emotional feelings in animals and humans. *Consciousness and Cognition. An International Journal*, 14(1), 30–80.

Panksepp, J. (2005b). Beyond a joke. From animal laughter to human joy? *Science*, 308, 62–3.

Panksepp, J. (2007a). Criteria for basic emotions. Is DISGUST a primary 'emotion'? *Cognition and Emotion*, 21, 1819–28.

Panksepp, J. (2007b). Neurologizing the psychology of affects. How appraisal-based constructivism and basic emotion theory can coexist. *Perspectives on Psychological Science*, 2, 281–96.

Panksepp, J. and Panksep, J. B. (2000). The seven sins of evolutionary psychology. *Evolution and Cognition*, 6, 108–31.

Pantev, C., Ross, B., Fujioka, T., Trainor, L. J., Schulte, M., et al (2003). Music and learning-induced cortical plasticity. *Annals of the New York Academy of Sciences*, 999, 438–50.

Paoli, T., Palagi, E., Tacconi, G., and Tarli, S. B. (2006). Perineal swelling, intermenstrual cycle, and female sexual behavior in bonobos (*Pan paniscus*). *American Journal of Primatology*, 68, 333–47.

Pape, R. A. (2005). *Dying to Win. The Strategic Logic of Suicide Terrorism.* New York, NY. Random House.

Pappini, M. R. (2002). Pattern and process in the evolution of learning. *Psychological Review*, 109, 186–201.

Pargament, K. I. (1997). *The Psychology of Religion and Coping.* New York, NY. Guilford.

Paris, J. (2012). The rise and fall of dissociative identity disorder. *The Journal of Nervous and Mental Disease*, 200, 1076–9.

Park, D. C. and Huang, C-M. (2010). Culture wires the brain. A cognitive neuroscience perspective. *Perspectives on Psychological Science*, 5, 391–400.

Parker, G. (2007). Is depression over-diagnosed? Yes. *British Medical Journal*, 335, 328–9.

Parker, G., Gayed, A., Owen, C., Hyett, M., Hilton, T., et al (2010). Survival following an acute coronary syndrome. A pet theory put to the test. *Acta Psychiatrica Scandinavica*, 121, 65–70.

Parker, G., Roy, K., and Eyers, K. (2003). Cognitive behavior therapy for depression? Choose horses for courses. *American Journal of Psychiatry*, 160, 825–34.

Parker, I. (1999). Tracing therapeutic discourse in material culture. *British Journal of Medical Psychology*, 72(4), 577–87.

Parker, I. and Burman, E. (2008). Critical psychology. Four theses and seven misconceptions. *Hellenic Journal of Psychology*, 5(1), 99–115.

Parnia, S. and Fenwick, P. (2002). Near death experiences in cardiac arrest. Visions of a dying brain or visions of a new science of consciousness. *Resuscitation*, 52(1), 5–11.

Parrott, A. C. (1999). Does cigarette smoking *cause* stress? *American Psychologist*, 54, 817–20.

Parrott, A. C. (2002). Very real, very damaging. *The Psychologist*, 15, 472–3.

Parslow, R. A., Jorm, A. F., Christensen, H., Rodgers, B., and Jacomb, P. (2005). Pet ownership and health in older adults. Findings from a survey of 2,551 community-based Australians aged 60–64. *Gerontology*, 51(1), 40–7.

Parsons, C. E., Young, K. S., Parsons, E., Stein, A., and Kringelbach, M. L. (2012). Listening to infant distress vocalizations enhances effortful motor performance. *Acta Paediatrica*, 101(4), e189.

Pascalis, O., de Schonen, S., Morton, J., Duruelle, C., and Grenet, F. (1995). Mother's face recognition in neonates. A replication and an extension. *Infant Behavior and Development*, 18, 79–85.

Pascalis, O. and Kelly, D, J. (2009). The origins of face processing in humans. Phylogeny and ontogeny. *Perspectives on Psychological Science*, 4, 200–9.

Pascoe, E. A. and Smart Richman, L. (2009). Perceived discrimination and health. A meta-analytic review. *Psychological Bulletin*, 135, 531–54.

Pashler, H. and Wagenmakers, E-J. (2012). Editors' introduction to the special section on replicability in psychological science. A crisis of confidence? *Perspectives on Psychological Science*, 7, 528–30.

Pasterski, V. L., Geffner, M. E., Brain, C., Hindmarsh, P., and Brook, C. (2005). Prenatal hormones and postnatal socialization by parents as determinants of male-typical toy play in girls with

congenital adrenal hyperplasia. *Child Development*, 76(1), 264–78.

Pate, J. E. and Gabbard, G. O. (2003). Adult baby syndrome. *American Journal of Psychiatry*, 160(11), 1932–6.

Patihis, L., Ho, L. Y., Loftus, E. F., and Herrera, M. E. (2018). Memory experts' beliefs about repressed memory. *Memory*, 1–6.

Patterson, D. R. (2004). Treating pain with hypnosis. *Current Directions in Psychological Science*, 13, 252–60.

Paul, D. B. and Blumenthal, A. L. (1989). On the trail of Little Albert. *The Psychological Record*, 29, 547–53.

Paul, E. F. and Paul, J. (2001). *Why Animal Experimentation Matters. The Use of Animals in Medical Research*. New Brunswick, NJ. Social Philosophy and Policy Foundation.

Paul, E. L., McManus, B., and Hayes, A. (2000). 'Hookups'. Characteristics and correlates of college students' spontaneous and anonymous sexual experiences. *Journal of Sex Research*, 37, 76–88.

Paulus, P. P. and Nijstad, B. A. (eds) (2003). *Group Creativity*. New York, NY. Oxford University Press.

Pavlov, I. (1927). *Conditioned Reflexes* (G.V. Anrep, trans). London. Oxford University Press.

Payne, J. D., Stickgold, R., Swanberg, K., and Kensinger, E. A. (2008). Sleep preferentially enhances memory for emotional components of scenes. *Psychological Science*, 19, 781–8.

Pedersen, D. M. and Wheeler, J. (1983). The Müller-Lyer illusion among Navajos. *Journal of Social Psychology*, 121(1), 3–6.

Peele, S. and Grant, M. (eds) (1999). *Alcohol and Pleasure*. Philadelphia, PA. Brunner/Mazel.

Pei, F., Pettet, M. W., and Norcia, A. M. (2002). Neural correlates of object-based attention. *Journal of Vision*, 2(9), 1–1.

Pelham, B. W. and Blanton, H. (2003). *Conducting Research in Psychology. Measuring the Weight of Smoke*. Belmont, CA. Thomson/Wadsworth.

Pellegrini, A. D. and Smith, P. K. (1998). Physical activity play. The nature and function of a neglected aspect of play. *Child Development*, 69, 577–98.

Pellegrino, G. di, Fadiga, L., Fogassi, L., Gallese, V., and Rizzolatti, G. (1992). Understanding motor events. A neurophysiological study. *Experimental Brain Research*, 91, 176–80.

Pelphrey, K. A., and Morris, J. P. (2006). Brain mechanisms for interpreting the actions of others from biological motion cues. *Current Directions in Psychological Science*, 15, 136–40.

Penfield, W. and Perot, P. (1963). The brain's record of auditory and visual experience. *Brain*, 86, 595–696.

Penton-Voak, I. S., Jacobson, A., and Trivers, R. (2004). Populational differences in attractiveness judgements of male and female faces. Comparing British and Jamaican samples. *Evolution and Human Behavior*, 25, 355–77.

Peplau, L. A. (2003). Human sexuality. How do men and women differ? *Current Directions in Psychological Science*, 12, 189–92.

Pepper, G. V. and Craig Roberts, S. (2006). Rates of nausea and vomiting in pregnancy and dietary characteristics across populations. *Proceedings of the Royal Society/Series B*, 273, 2675–9.

Perfect, T. J. and Harris, L. J. (2003). Adult age differences in unconscious transference. Source confusion or identity blending? *Memory and Cognition*, 31, 570–80.

Perkins, K. K. and Wieman, C. E. (2005). The surprising impact of seat location on student performance. *The Physics Teacher*, 43, 30–3.

Perkonigg, A., Kessler, R. C., Storz, S., and Wittchen, H.-U. (2000). Traumatic events and post-traumatic stress disorder in the community. Prevalence, risk factors and comorbidity. *Acta Psychiatrica Scandinavica*, 101, 46–59.

Perner, J., Kain, W., and Barchfeld, P. (2002). Executive control and higher-order theory of mind in children at risk of ADHD. *Infant and Child Development. An International Journal of Research and Practice*, 11(2), 141–58.

Perrin, M. A., DiGrande, L., Wheeler, K., Thorpe, L., Farfel, M., et al (2007). Differences in PTSD prevalence and risk factors among World Trade Center rescue and recovery workers. *American Journal of Psychiatry*, 164, 1385–94.

Perron, B. E., Bohnert, A. S. B., Monsell, S. E., Vaughn, M. G., Epperson, M., et al (2011). Patterns and correlates of drug-related ED visits. Results from a national survey. *American Journal of Emergency Medicine*, 29, 704–10.

Perroud, N., Uher, R., Hauser, J., Rietschel, M., Henigsberg, N., et al (2010). History of suicide attempts among patients with depression in the GENDEP project.

Journal of Affective Disorders, 123, 131–7.

Pert, C. B. and Snyder, S. H. (1973). The opiate receptor. Demonstration in nervous tissue. *Science*, 179, 1011–14.

Peruche, B. M. and Plant, E.A. (2006). The implications of police officer attitudes towards criminal suspects. *Basic and Applied Social Psychology*, 28, 193–9.

Peters, M., Rhodes, G., and Simmons, L. W. (2007). Contributions of the face and body to overall attractiveness. *Animal Behaviour*, 73, 937–42.

Petersen, J. L. and Hyde, J. S. (2010). A meta-analytic review of research on gender differences in sexuality. *Psychological Bulletin*, 136, 21–38.

Peterson, C., Seligman, M. E., and Vaillant, G. E. (1988). Pessimistic explanatory style is a risk factor for physical illness. A thirty-five year longitudinal study. *Journal of Personality and Social Psychology*, 55(1), 23–37.

Peterson, C. and Seligman, M. E. P. (2004). *Character Strengths and Virtues. A Handbook and Classification.* Washington, DC. American Psychological Association.

Peterson, L. R. and Peterson, M. J. (1959). Short-term retention of individual verbal items. *Journal of Experimental Psychology*, 58, 193–8.

Petrill, S. A., Lipton, P. A., Hewitt, J. K., Plomin, R., Cherny, S. S., et al (2004). Genetic and environmental contributions to general cognitive ability through the first 16 years of life. *Developmental Psychology*, 40, 805–12.

Pettigrew, T. F. (1998). Intergroup contact theory. *Annual Review of Psychology*, 49, 65–85.

Pettigrew, T. F. and Tropp, L. R. (2006). A meta-analytic test of intergroup contact theory. *Journal of Personality and Social Psychology*, 90, 751–83.

Pezdek, K., Whetstone, T., Reynolds, K., Askari, N., and Dougherty, T. (1989). Memory for real-world scenes. The role of consistency with schema expectation. *Journal of Experimental Psychology. Learning Memory and Cognition*, 15, 587–95.

Pfrieger, F. W. (2002). Role of glia in synapse development. *Current Opinion in Neurobiology*, 12, 486–90.

Phelps, E. A. (2006). Emotion and cognition. Insights from the study of the human amygdala. *Annual Review of Psychology*, 57, 27–53.

Philo, G., Secker, J., Platt, S., Henderson, L., McLaughlin, G., et al (1994). The impact of the mass media on public images of mental illness. Media content and audience belief. *Health Education Journal*, 53(3), 271–81.

Piaget, J. (1952). *The Origins of Intelligence in Children*. New York, NY. International Universities.

Piaget, J. (1954). *The Construction of Reality in the Child*. New York, NY. Basic Books.

Pierce, J. P. (2007). Tobacco industry marketing, population-based tobacco control, and smoking behavior. *American Journal of Preventative Medicine*, 33(Suppl 6), 327–34.

Pike, K. M. and Borovoy, A. (2004). The rise of eating disorders in Japan. Issues of culture and limitations of the model of 'Westernization'. *Culture, Medicine, and Psychiatry*, 28, 493–531.

Piliavin, J. A. and Charng, H.-W. (1990). Altruism. A review of recent theory and research. *Annual Review of Sociology*, 16, 27–65.

Pilling, M. and Davies, I. R. L. (2004). Linguistic relativism and colour cognition. *British Journal of Psychology*, 95, 429–55.

Pinder, C. C. (1998). *Work Motivation in Organizational Behavior*. Upper Saddle River, NJ. Prentice Hall.

Pinel, J. P. J., Assanand, S., and Lehman, D. R. (2000). Hunger, eating, and ill health. *American Psychologist*, 55, 1105–16.

Pinker, S. (1994). *The Language Instinct*. New York, NY. William Morrow and Co.

Pinker, S. (1997). *How the Mind Works*. New York, NY. Norton.

Pinker, S. (2002). *The Blank Slate. The Modern Denial of Human Nature*. New York, NY. Viking.

Pinker, S. (2004). Clarifying the logical problem of language acquisition. *Journal of Child Language*, 31, 949–53.

Pinker, S. (2008, 13 January). The moral instinct. *New York Times*. Retrieved from http://www.nytimes.com/2008/01/13/magazine/13Psychology-t.html?pagewanted=all&_r=0 on 17 January 2008.

Pinker, S. (2011). *The Better Angels of Our Nature. Why Violence Has Declined*. New York, NY. Viking.

Pinker, S. and Jackendoff, R. (2005). The faculty of language. What's special about it? *Cognition*, 95, 201–36.

Pinker, S. and Jackendoff, R. (2009). The reality of a universal language faculty. *Behavioral and Brain Sciences*, 32, 465–6.

Pinkerman, J. E., Haynes, J. P., and Keiser, T. (1993). Characteristics of psychological practice in juvenile court clinics. *American Journal of Forensic Psychology*, 11(2), 3–12.

Pinquart, M., Feußner, C., and Ahnert, L. (2013). Meta-analytic evidence for stability in attachments from infancy to early adulthood. *Attachment and Human Development*, 15(2), 189–218.

Piper, A. and Merskey, H. (2004a). The persistence of folly. A critical examination of dissociative identity disorder. Part I. The excesses of an improbable concept. *Canadian Journal of Psychiatry*, 49, 592–600.

Piper, A. and Merskey, H. (2004b). The persistence of folly. A critical examination of dissociative identity disorder. Part II. The defence and decline of multiple personality or dissociative identity disorder. *Canadian Journal of Psychiatry*, 49, 678–83.

Pirraglia, P. A., Stafford, R. S., and Singer, D. E. (2003). Trends in prescribing of selective serotonin reuptake inhibitors and other newer antidepressant agents in adult primary care. *Primary Care Companion of Journal of Clinical Psychiatry*, 5, 153–7.

Pizarro, D., Inbar, Y., and Helion, C. (2011). On disgust and moral judgment. *Emotion Review*, 3(3), 267–8.

Plassman, B. L., Langa, K. M., Fisher, G. G., Heeringa, S. G., Weir, D. R., et al (2007). Prevalence of dementia in the United States. The aging, demographics, and memory study. *Neuroepidemiology*, 29, 125–32.

Player, M. S., King, D. E., Mainous, A. G., III, and Geesey, M. E. (2007). Psychosocial factors and progression from prehypertension to hypertension or coronary heart disease. *Annals of Family Medicine*, 5, 403–11.

Pletcher, M. J., Vittinghoff, E., Kalhan, R., Ruchman, J., Safford, M., et al (2011). Association between marijuana exposure and pulmonary function over 20 years. *JAMA*, 307, 173–81.

Plomin, R. and Caspi, A. (1999). Behavioral genetics and personality. In L. A. Pervin and O. P. John (eds), *Handbook of Personality. Theory and Research* (pp 251–76). New York, NY. Guilford Press.

Plomin, R., Corley, R., Caspi, A., Fulker, D. W., and DeFries, J. (1998). Adoption results for self-reported personality. Evidence for nonadditive genetic effects? *Journal of Personality and Social Psychology*, 75, 211–18.

Plomin, R. and Daniels, D. (1987). Why are children in the same family so different from each other? *Behavioral and Brain Sciences*, 10, 1–16.

Plomin, R. and Deary, I. J. (2015). Genetics and intelligence differences. Five special findings. *Molecular Psychiatry*, 20(1), 98.

Plomin, R., DeFries, J. C., Craig, I. W., and McGuffin, P. (eds) (2003). *Behavioral Genetics in the Postgenomic Era*. Washington, DC. American Psychological Association.

Plomin, R., DeFries, J. C., and Loehlin, J. C. (1977). Genotype-environment interaction and correlation in the analysis of human behavior. *Psychological Bulletin*, 84, 309–22.

Plomin, R., DeFries, J. C., McClearn, G. E., and McGuffin, P. (2008). *Behavioral Genetics* (5th edn). New York, NY. Worth.

Plomin, R., Fulker, D. W., Corley, R., and DeFries, J. C. (1997). Nature, nurture, and cognitive development from 1 to 16 years. *Psychological Science*, 8, 442–7.

Ploner, M., Gross, J., Timmermann, L., and Schnitzler, A. (2002). Cortical representation of first and second pain sensation in humans. *PNAS*, 99, 12444–8.

Plomin, R. and McGuffin, P. (2003). Psychopathology in the postgenomic era. *Annual Review of Psychology*, 54, 205–28.

Plomin, R. and Petrill, S. A. (1997). Genetics and intelligence. What's new? *Intelligence*, 24(1), 53–77.

Plomin, R. and Spinath, F. M. (2004). Intelligence. Genetics, genes, and genomics. *Journal of Personality and Social Psychology*, 86(1), 112–29.

Plutchik, R. (1980). A general psychoevolutionary theory of emotion. In R. Plutchik and H. Kellerman (eds), *Emotion. Theory, Research, and Experience. Vol 1. Theories of Emotion* (pp 3–33). New York, NY. Academic Press.

Plutchik, R. (2003). *Emotions and Life. Perspectives from Psychology, Biology, and Evolution*. Washington, DC. American Psychological Association.

Pogue-Geile, M. F. and Yokley, J. L. (2010). Current research on the genetic contributors to schizophrenia. *Current Directions in Schizophrenia*, 19, 214–19.

Pokoradi, A., Iversen, L., and Hannaford, P. C. (2011). Factors associated with age of onset and type of menopause in a cohort of UK women. *American Journal of Obstetrics and Gynecology*, 205, e1–13. Retrieved from www.AJOG.org on 5 September.

Polak, M. (2003). *Developmental Instability. Causes and Consequences*. New York, NY. Oxford University Press.

Polivy, J. and Herman, C. P. (2000). The false-hope syndrome. Unfulfilled expectations of self-change. *Current Directions in Psychological Science*, 9, 128–31.

Polivy, J. and Herman, C. P. (2002). Causes of eating disorders. *Annual Review of Psychology*, 53, 187–213.

Polivy, J. and Herman, C. P. (2002). If at first you don't succeed. False hopes of self-change. *American Psychologist*, 57, 677–89.

Pollick, A. S. and de Waal, F. B. M. (2007). Ape gestures and language evolution. *PNAS*, 104, 8184–9.

Pope, H. G., Jr, Barry, S., Bodkin, A., and Hudson, J. (2006). Tracking scientific interest in the dissociative disorders. A study of scientific publication output 1984–2003. *Psychotherapy and Psychosomatics*, 75, 19–24.

Pope, H. G., Jr, Oliva, P. S., Hudson, J. I., Bodkin, J. A., and Gruber, A. J. (1999). Attitudes toward DSM-IV dissociative disorders diagnoses among board-certified American Psychiatrists. *American Journal of Psychiatry*, 156, 321–3.

Pope, K. S. and Tabachnick, B. G. (1994). Therapists as patients. A national survey of psychologists' experiences, problems, and beliefs. *Professional Psychology. Research and Practice*, 25, 247–58.

Popper, K. (1959). *The Logic of Scientific Discovery*. New York, NY. Basic Books.

Popper, K. R. (1962). *Conjectures and Refutations. The Growth of Scientific Knowledge* (5th edn). New York, NY. Routledge.

Porter, S. and Peace K. A. (2007). The scars of memory. A prospective, longitudinal investigation of the consistency of traumatic and positive emotional memories in adulthood. *Psychological Science*, 18, 435–41.

Posner, M. I., Rothbart, M. K., and Sheese, B. E. (2007). Attention genes. *Developmental Science*, 10(1), 24–9.

Post, R. M. (1992). Transduction of psychosocial stress into the neurobiology of recurrent affective disorder. *American Journal of Psychiatry*, 149, 999–1010.

Post, R. M., Leverich, G. S., Altshuler, L. L., Frye, M. A., Suppes, T. M., et al (2003). An overview of recent findings of the Stanley Foundation Bipolar Network (Part I). *Bipolar Disorders*, 5, 310–19.

Povinelli, D. J. and Bering, J. M. (2002). The mentality of apes revisited. *Current Directions in Psychological Science*, 11, 115–19.

Powell, L. H., Shahabi, L., and Thoresen, C. E. (2003). Religion and spirituality. Linkages to physical health. *American Psychologist*, 58, 36–52.

Powers, M. B. and Emmelkamp, P. M. G. (2008). Virtual reality exposure therapy for anxiety. A meta-analysis. *Journal of Anxiety Disorders*, 22, 561–9.

Praissman, S. (2008). Mindfulness-based stress reduction. A literature review and clinician's guide. *Journal of the American Academy of Nurse Practice*, 20, 212–16.

Pratkanis, A. R. (1992, Spring). The cargo-cult science of subliminal persuasion. *Skeptical Inquirer*. Retrieved from www.csicop.org on 4 September 2006.

Pratkanis, A. R., Eskenazi, J., and Greenwald, A. G. (1994). What you expect is what you believe (but not necessarily what you get). A test of the effectiveness of subliminal self-help audiotapes. *Basic and Applied Social Psychology*, 15, 251–76.

Premack, D. (1971). Catching up with common sense, or two sides of a generalization. Reinforcement and punishment. In R. Glaser (ed), *The Nature of Reinforcement*. New York, NY. Academic.

Premack, D. and Woodruff, G. (1978). Does the chimpanzee have a theory of mind? *Behavioral and Brain Sciences*, 1, 512–26.

Price, D. D., Finniss, D. G., and Benedetti, F. (2008). A comprehensive review of the placebo effect. Recent advances and current thought. *Annual Review of Psychology*, 59, 565–90.

Prinz, J. (2004). Which emotions are basic? In D. Evans and P. Cruse (eds), *Emotion, Evolution, and Rationality* (pp 1–19). London. Oxford University Press

Prochaska, J. O., DiClemente, C. C., and Norcross, J. C. (1992). In search of how people change. Applications to addictive behaviors. *American Psychologist*, 47, 1102–14.

Profet, M. (1992). Pregnancy sickness as adaptation. A deterrent to maternal ingestion of teratogens. In J. H.

Barkow, L. Cosmides, and J. Tooby (eds), *The Adapted Mind. Evolutionary Psychology and the Generation of Culture* (pp 327–66). New York, NY. Oxford University Press.

Ptashne, M. and Gann, A. (2002). *Genes and Signals*. Woodbury, NY. Cold Spring Harbor Laboratory Press.

Public Agenda. (2000). Child care. Red flags. Retrieved from www.publicagenda.com on 4 April 2006.

Puldrack, R. A. (2010). Mapping mental function to brain structure. How can cognitive neuroimaging succeed? *Perspectives on Psychological Science*, 5, 753–61.

Pullum, G. K. (1991). *The Great Eskimo Vocabulary Hoax and Other Irreverent Essays on the Study of Language*. Chicago, IL. University of Chicago Press.

Putnam, F. W. and Lowenstein, R. J. (2000). Dissociative identity disorder. In B. J. Sadock and V. A. Sadock (eds), *Kaplan and Sadock's Comprehensive Textbook Psychiatry* (7th edn, Vol 1, pp 1552–64).

Putwain, D., Sander, P., and Larkin, D. (2013). Academic self-efficacy in study-related skills and behaviours. Relations with learning-related emotions and academic success. *British Journal of Educational Psychology*, 83(4), 633–50.

Pyka, M., Busse, C., Seidenbecher, C., Gundelfinger, E. D., and Faissner, A. (2011). Astrocytes are crucial for survival and maturation of embryonic hippocampal neurons in neuron-glia cell-insert coculture assay. *Synapse*, 65, 41–53.

Pylyshyn, Z. W. (2002). Mental imagery. In search of a theory. *Behavioral and Brain Sciences*, 25(2), 157–82.

Pyszczynski, T., Greenberg, J., Solomon, S., Arndt, J., and Schimel, J. (2004). Why do people need self-esteem? A theoretical and empirical review. *Psychological Bulletin*, 130, 435–68.

Quillian, L. and Pager, D. (2001). Black neighbors, higher crime? The role of racial stereotypes in evaluations of neighborhood crime. *American Journal of Sociology*, 107, 717–67.

Quinn, D. M. and Spencer, S. J. (2001). The interference of stereotype threat with women's generation of mathematical problem-solving strategies. *Journal of Social Issues*, 57(1), 55–72.

Quinn, P. C., Bhatt, R. S., Brush, D., Grimes, A., and Sharpnack, H. (2002). Development of form similarity as a Gestalt grouping principle in infancy. *Psychological Science*, 13, 320–41.

Quinn, P. C., Kelly, D. J., Lee, K., Pascalis, O., and Slater, A. M. (2008). Preference for attractive faces in infants extends beyond conspecifics. *Developmental Science*, 11, 76–83.

Quinn, P. C. and Liben, L. S. (2008). A sex difference in mental rotation in young infants. *Psychological Science*, 19, 1067–72.

Quinn, P. C. and Slater, A. (2003). Face perception at birth and beyond. In O. Pascalis and A. Slater (eds), *The Development of Face Processing in Infancy and Early Childhood. Current Perspectives* (pp 3–12). Huntington, NY. Nova Science.

Quinones-Vidal, E., Lopez-Garcia, J. J., Penaranda-Ortega, M., and Tortosa-Gil, F. (2004). The nature of social and personality psychology as reflected in JPSP, 1965–2000. *Journal of Personality and Social Psychology*, 86, 435–52.

Rabinowitz, D. (2003). *No Crueller Tyrannies. Accusation, False Witness, and Other Terrors of Our Times*. New York, NY. Free Press.

Rachman, S. (2009). Psychological treatment of anxiety. The evolution of behavior therapy. *Annual Review of Clinical Psychology*, 5, 97–119.

Rácsmany, M., Conway, M. A., and Demeter, G. (2010). Consolidation of episodic memories during sleep. Long-term effects of retrieval practice. *Psychological Science*, 21, 80–5.

Rahman, Q. (2005a). Fluctuating asymmetry, second to fourth finger length ratios and human sexual orientation. *Psychoneuroendocrinology*, 30, 382–91.

Rahman, Q. (2005b). The neurodevelopment of human sexual orientation. *Neuroscience and Biobehavioral Reviews*, 29, 1057–66.

Rahula, W. (1959). *What the Buddha Taught*. New York, NY. Grove Press.

Ram, S., Seirawan, H., Kumar S. K., and Clark, G. T. (2010). Prevalence and impact of sleep disorders and sleep habits in the United States. *Sleep and Breathing*, 14, 63–70.

Ramachandran, V. S. (1992). Filling in gaps in perception. Part 1. *Current Directions in Psychological Science*, 1, 199–205.

Ramnani, N. and Owen, A. M. (2004). The anterior prefrontal cortex. What can functional imaging tell us about function? *Nature Reviews. Neuroscience*, 5, 184–94.

Randall, S., Roehrs, T. A., and Roth, T. (2008). Over-the-counter sleep aid medications and incominia. *Primary Psychiatry*, 15, 52–8.

Rasch, B. and Born, J. (2008). Reactivation and consolidation of memory during sleep. *Current Directions in Psychological Science*, 17, 188–92.

Rasenberger, J. (2004, 8 February). Kitty, 40 years later. *New York Times*. Retrieved from http://www.nytimes.com/2004/02/08/nyregion/kitty-40-years-later.html?pagewanted=all&src=pm on 19 March 2013.

Rash, C. J., Alessi, S. M., and Petry, N. (2008). Contingency management is efficacious for cocaine abusers with prior treatment attempts. *Experimental and Clinical Psychopharmacology*, 16, 547–54.

Rasmussen, H. N., Scheier, M. F., and Greenhouse, J. B. (2009). Optimism and physical health. A meta-analytic review. *Annals of Behavior Medicine*, 37, 239–56.

Rath, T. (2007). *StrengthsFinder 2.0. A New and Upgraded Edition of The Online Test from Gallup's Now, Discover Your Strengths*. New York, NY. Gallup Press.

Rauch, S. L., Shin, L. M., and Wright, C. L. (2003) Neuroimaging studies of amygdala function in anxiety disorders. *Annals of the New York Academy of Sciences*, 985, 389–410.

Rechtschaffen, A. (1998). Current perspectives on the function of sleep. *Perspectives in Biology and Medicine*, 41, 359–90.

Reddick, T. S., Shipstead, A., Fried, D. E., Hambrick, D. Z., Kane, M. J., et al (2013). No evidence of intelligence improvement after working memory training. A randomized placebo-control study. *J. Exp. Psychol. Gen.*, 142, 359–79.

Redick, T. S. (2015). Working memory training and interpreting interactions in intelligence interventions. *Intelligence*, 50, 14–20.

Reebye, P. N., Ross, S. E., and Jamieson, K. (1999). A literature review of child-parent/caregiver attachment theory and cross-cultural practices influencing attachment. Retrieved from www.attachmentacrosscultures.org on 10 April 2006.

Reed, G. L. and Enright, R. D. (2006). The effects of forgiveness therapy on depression, anxiety, and posttraumatic stress for women after spousal emotional abuse. *Journal of Consulting and Clinical Psychology*, 74, 920–9.

Reiber, C. and Garcia, J. R. (2010). Hooking up. Gender differences, evolution, and pluralistic ignorance. *Evolutionary Psychology*, 8, 390–404.

Reich, D. A., Green, M. C., Brock, T. C., and Tetlock, P. E. (2007). Biases in research evaluation. Inflated assessment, oversight, or error-type weighting? *Journal of Experimental Social Psychology*, 43, 633–40.

Reis, H. T. and Aron, A. (2008). Love. What is it, why does it matter, and how does it operate? *Perspectives on Psychological Science*, 3, 80–6.

Reis, H. T., Maniaci, M. R., Eastwick, P. W., and Caprariello, P. A. (2011). Familiarity does indeed promote attraction in live interaction. *Journal of Personality and Social Psychology*, 101, 557–70.

Reissig, C. J., Strain, E. C., and Griffiths, R. R. (2009). Caffeinated energy drinks—a growing problem. *Drug and Alcohol Dependence*, 99, 1–10. Retrieved from www.elsevier.com on 27 October 2008.

Rejection really does hurt (2003, 18 October). *New Scientist*. Retrieved from www.newscientist.com on 14 November 2004.

Remer, T., Boye, K. R., Hartmann, M. F., and Wudy, S. A. (2005). Urinary markers of adrenarche. Reference values in healthy subjects, aged 3–18 years. *Journal of Clinical Endocrinology and Metabolism. Clinical and Experimental*, 90, 2015–21.

Rendell, L. and Whitehead, H. (2001). Culture in whales and dolphins. *Behavioral and Brain Sciences*, 24, 309–82.

Reneman, L. (2003). Designer drugs. How dangerous are they? *Journal of Neural Transmission*, 66(Suppl), 61–83.

Renk, K., Donnelly, R., McKinney, C., and Agliata, A. K. (2006). The development of gender identity. Timetables and influences. In Kam-Shing (ed), *Psychology of Gender Identity. An International Perspective* (pp 49–68). Hauppauge, NY. Nova Science Publishers.

Rescorla, R. A. (1968). Probability of shock in the presence and absence of CS in fear conditioning. *Journal of Comparative and Physiological Psychology*, 66(1), 1–5.

Rescorla, R. A. and Heth, C. D. (1975). Reinstatement of fear to an extinguished conditioned stimulus. *Journal of Experimental Psychology. Animal Behavior Processes*, 1(1), 88–96.

Reynolds, D. J,. Jr and Gifford, R. (2001). The sounds and sights of intelligence. A lens model channel analysis. *Personality and Social Psychology Bulletin*, 27, 187–200.

Reynolds, M. A., Herbenick, D. L., and Bancroft, J. H. (2003). The nature of childhood sexual experiences. Two studies 50 years apart. In J. Bancroft (ed), *Sexual Development in Childhood* (pp 134–55). Bloomington, IN. Indiana University Press.

Rhodes, G. (2006). The evolutionary psychology of facial beauty. *Annual Review of Psychology*, 57, 199–226.

Rhodes, G., Yoshikawa, S., Palermo, R., Simmons, L. W., Peters, M., et al (2007). Perceived health contributes to the attractiveness of facial symmetry, averageness, and sexual dimorphism. *Perception*, 36, 1244–52.

Richardson, J. T., Best, J., and Bromley, D. G. (eds) (1991). *The Satanism Scare*. New York, NY. Aldine de Gruyter.

Richert, A. C. and Baran, A. S. (2003). A review of common sleep disorders. *CNS Spectrums*, 8, 102–9.

Ridley, M. (2003). *The Red Queen. Sex and the Evolution of Human Nature*. New York, NY. Harper.

Rieber, R. W. (1999). Hypnosis, false memory, and multiple personality. A trinity of affinity. *History of Psychiatry*, 10(1), 3–11.

Rieber, R. W. (2006). *The Bifurcation of the Self. The History and Theory of Dissociation and its Disorders*. New York, NY. Springer.

Ries, R. K., Dyck, D. G., Short, R., Srebnik, D., Fisher, A., et al (2004). Outcomes of managing disability benefits among patients with substance dependence and severe mental illness. *Psychiatric Services*, 55, 445–7.

Rietveld, M. J., Hudziak, J. J., Bartels. M., Van Beijsterveldt, C. E. M., and Boomsma, D. I. (2004). Heritability of attention problems in children. I. Cross-sectional results from a study of twins, age 3–12 years. *Journal of Child Psychology and Psychiatry*, 45, 577–88.

Riggs, A. T., Dysken, M., Kim, S. W., and Opsahl, J. M. (1991). A review of disorders of water homeostasis in psychiatric patients. *Psychosomatics*, 32, 133–46.

Rihmer, Z. (2007). Suicide risk in mood disorders. *Current Opinion in Psychiatry*, 20, 17–22.

Ripke, S., Neale, B. M., Corvin, A., Walters, J. T., Farh, K. H., et al (2014). Biological insights from 108 schizophrenia-associated genetic loci. *Nature*, 511(7510), 421.

Ritchie, S. J., Wiseman, R., and French, C. C. (2012). Failing the future. Three unsuccessful attempts to replicate Bem's 'Retroactive Facilitation of Recall' Effect. *PLoS One*, 7(3), e33423.

Rizzolatti, G. and Fabbri-Destro, M. (2010). Mirror neurons. From discovery to autism. *Experimental Brain Research*, 200, 223–37.

Rizzolatti, G., Fadiga, L., Fogassi, L., and Gallese, V. (2002). From mirror neurons to imitation. Facts and speculations. In A. N. Meltzoff and W. Prinz (eds), *The Imitative Mind. Development, Evolution, and Brain Bases* (pp 247–66). New York, NY. Cambridge University Press.

Rizzolatti, G., Fadiga, L., Gallese, V., and Fogassi, L. (1996). Premotor cortex and the recognition of motor actions. *Cognitive Brain Research*, 3, 131–41.

Rizzolatti, G., Fogassi, L., and Gallese, V. (2006, November). Mirrors in the mind. *Scientific American*, 54–61.

Roazzi, A. and Bryant, P. (1998). The effects of symmetrical and asymmetrical social interaction on children's logical inferences. *British Journal of Developmental Psychology*, 16(2), 175–81.

Roberson, D., Davies, I., and Davidoff, J. (2002). Color categories are not universal. Replications and new evidence. In B. Saunders and J. van Brakel (eds), *Theories, Technologies, Instrumentalities of Color. Anthropological and Historiographic Perspectives* (pp 25–35). Lanham, MD. University Press of America.

Roberts, B. W. and DelVecchio, W. F. (2000). The rank-order consistency of personality traits from childhood to old age. A quantitative review of longitudinal studies. *Psychological Bulletin*, 126, 3–25.

Roberts, B. W., Kuncel, N. R., Shiner, R., Caspi, A., and Goldberg, L. R. (2007). The power of personality. The comparative validity of personality traits, socioeconomic status, and cognitive ability for predicting important life outcomes. *Perspectives in Psychological Science*, 2, 313–45.

Roberts, M. E., Tchanturia, L., and Treasure, J. L. (2010). Exploring the neurocognitive signature of poor set-shifting in anorexia and bulimia nervosa. *Journal of Psychiatric Research*, 44, 964–70.

Roberts, S. (2006, 15 October). To be married is to be outnumbered. *New York*

Times. Retrieved from www.nytimes.com on 30 May 2007.

Robertson, B. W. and Kee, K. F. (2017). Social media at work. The roles of job satisfaction, employment status, and Facebook use with co-workers. *Computers in Human Behavior*, 70, 191–6.

Robertson, J. P. and Martin, S. (2008). What do happy people do? *Social Indicators Research*, 89, 565–71.

Robins, R. W., Gosling, S. D., and Craik, K. H. (1999). An empirical analysis of trends in psychology. *American Psychologist*, 54, 117–28.

Robinson, D. J. (2005). *Disordered Personalities* (3rd edn). Port Huron, MI. Rapid Psychler Press.

Robinson, D. N. (1989). The psychology of Aristotle.

Robinson, N. M., Abbott, R. D., Berninger, V. W., and Busse, J. (1996). The structure of abilities in math-precocious young children. Gender similarities and differences. *Journal of Educational Psychology*, 88, 341–52.

Robinson, P. (1989). *Aristotle's Psychology*. New York, NY. Columbia University Press.

Robinson, P. (1989). *The Modernization of Sex*. Ithaca, NY. Cornell University Press. (Original work published 1979.)

Rodman, A. M., Powers, K. E., and Somerville, L. H. (2017). Development of self-protective biases in response to social evaluative feedback. *Proceedings of the National Academy of Sciences, USA*, 114, 13158–63.

Rodrigues, A., Assmar, E. M. L., and Jablonski, B. (2005). (English abstract only). La psicología y la invasion de Irak (Psychology and the invasion of Iraq). *Revista de Psicología Social*, 20, 387–98.

Roe, C. A. (2018). Varieties of anomalous experience. Examining the scientific evidence. *The Journal of Parapsychology*, 82(1), 77–83.

Roedigger, H. L., Agarwal, P. K., McDaniel, M. A., and McDermott, K. B. (2011). Enhanced learning in the classroom. Long-term improvements from quizzing. *Journal of Experimental Psychology. Applied*, 17, 382–95.

Roediger, H. L., III. and Gallo, D. A. (2001). Levels of processing. Some unanswered questions. In M. Naveh-Benjamin, M. Moscovitch, and H. L. Roediger III (eds), *Perspectives on Human Memory and Cognitive Aging. Essays in Honour of Fergus Craik* (pp 28–47). New York, NY. Psychology Press.

Rofé, Y. (2008). Does repression exist? Memory, pathogenic, unconscious and clinical experience. *Review of General Psychology*, 12, 63–85.

Rogers, S. (1992–1993). How a publicity blitz created the myth of subliminal advertising. *Public Relations Quarterly*, 37, 12–17.

Rohrer, D. and Pashler, H. (2007). Increasing retention without increasing study time. *Current Directions in Psychological Science*, 16, 183–6.

Rolls, B. J. (2003). The supersizing of America. Portion size and the obesity epidemic. *Nutrition Today*, 38, 42–53.

Rolls, E. T. (2006). Brain mechanisms underlying flavour and appetite. *Philosophical Transactions of the Royal Society of London, Series B. Biological Sciences*, 361, 1123–36.

Roncero, C., C Abad, A., Padilla-Mata, A., Ros-Cucurull, E., Barral, C., et al (2017). Psychotic symptoms associated with the use of dopaminergic drugs, in patients with cocaine dependence or abuse. *Current Neuropharmacology*, 15(2), 315–23.

Ronen, S. (1994). An underlying structure of motivational need taxonomies. A cross-cultural confirmation. In H. C. Triandis, M. D. Dunnette, and L. M. Hough (eds), *Handbook of Industrial and Organizational Psychology* (2nd edn, pp 241–69). Palo Alto, CA. Consulting Psychologists Press.

Room, R. (2001). Intoxication and bad behaviour. Understanding cultural differences in the link. *Social Science and Medicine*, 53, 189–98.

Roozendaal, B., McEwan, B. S., and Chattarji, S. (2009). Stress, memory, and the amygdala. *Nature Reviews. Neuroscience*, 10, 423–33.

Rosamond, W., Flegal, K., Friday, G., Furie, K., Go, A., et al (2007). Heart disease and stroke statistics—2007 update. A report from the American Heart Association Statistics Committee and Stroke Statistics Subcommittee. *Circulation*, 115, e69–e171.

Rosch-Heider, E. (1972). Universals in color naming and memory. *Journal of Experimental Psychology*, 93(1), 10–20.

Rose, D., Fleischmann, P., Wykes, T., Leese, M., and Bindman, J. (2003). Patients' perspectives on electroconvulsive therapy. Systematic review. *British Medical Journal*, 326, 1363–72.

Rose, H. and Rose, S. (2010). *Alas, Poor Darwin. Arguments Against Evolutionary Psychology*. London. Jonathan Cape.

Rose, J. S., Chassin, L., Presson, C. C., and Sherman, S. J. (1999). Peer influences on adolescent cigarette smoking. A prospective sibling analysis. *Merrill-Palmer Quarterly*, 45(1), 62–84.

Rose, S. A. and Feldman, J. F. (1995). Prediction of IQ and specific cognitive abilities at 11 years from infancy measures. *Developmental Psychology*, 31, 685–96.

Rose, T. L. and Fischer, K. W. (2009). Dynamic development. A neo-Piagetian approach. In U. Müller, J. I. Carpendale, and L. Smith (eds), *The Cambridge Companion to Piaget* (pp 400–21). New York, NY. Cambridge University Press.

Rose-Jacobs, R., Cabral, H., Posner, M. A., Epstein, J., and Frank, D. A. (2002). Do 'we just know'? Masked assessors' ability to accurately identify children with prenatal cocaine exposure. *Developmental and Behavioral Pediatrics*, 23, 340–6.

Rosen, G. M., Glasgow, R. E., and Moore, T. E. (2003). Self-help therapy. The science and business of giving psychology away. In S. O. Lilienfeld, S. J. Lynn, and J. M. Lohr (eds), *Science and Pseudoscience in Clinical Psychology* (pp 399–424). New York, NY. Guilford.

Rosenbaum, J. F., Fava, M., Hoog, S. L., Ashcroft, R. C., and Krebs, W. B. (1998). Selective serotonin inhibitor discontinuation syndrome. A randomized clinical trial. *Biological Psychiatry*, 44, 77–87.

Rosenbaum, M. (2002). Ecstasy. America's new *Reefer Madness. Journal of Psychoactive Drugs*, 34(1), 1–9.

Rosenheck, R. A., Leslie, D. L., and Doshi, J. A. (2008). Second-generation anti-psychotics. Cost-effectiveness, policy options, and political decision making. *Psychiatric Services*, 59, 515–20.

Rosenzweig, S. (1936). Some implicit common factors in diverse methods of psychotherapy. 'At last the dodo said, "Everybody has won and all must have prizes".' *American Journal of Orthopsychology*, 49, 298–304.

Roset, P. N., Farre, M., de la Torre, R., Mas, M., Menoyo, E., et al (2001). Modulation of rate of onset and intensity of drug effects reduces abuse potential in healthy males. *Drug and Alcohol Dependence*, 64, 285–98.

Ross, C. E. and Mirowsky, J. (2008). Age and the balance of emotions. *Social Science and Medicine*, 2391–400.

Ross, L. (1977) The intuitive psychologist and his short-comings. Distortions in the attribution process. In L. Berkowitz (ed), *Advances in Experimental Social Psychology* (Vol 10, pp 173–220). San Diego, CA. Academic Press.

Ross, L. (2001). Getting down to fundamentals. Lay dispositionism and the attributions of psychologists. *Psychological Inquiry*, 12, 37–40.

Ross, M. and Sicoly, F. (1979). Egocentric biases in availability and attribution. *Journal of Personality and Social Psychology*, 37, 322–36.

Ross, M. and Wilson, A. E. (2003). Autobiographical memory and conceptions of self. Getting better all the time. *Current Directions in Psychological Science*, 12, 66–9.

Rossini, E. D. and Moretti, R. J. (1997). Thematic Apperception Test (TAT) interpretation. Practice recommendations from a survey of clinical psychology doctoral programs accredited by the American Psychological Association. *Professional Psychology. Research and Practice*, 28, 393–8.

Rotenberg, V. S. (2013). 'Genes of happiness and well being' in the context of search activity concept. *Activitas Nervosa Superior*, 55(1–2), 1–14.

Rothbart, M. K. (2007). Temperament, development, and personality. *Current Directions in Psychological Science*, 16, 207–12.

Rothbart, M. K., Ahadi, S. A., Hershey, K. L., and Fisher, P. (2001). Investigations of temperament at three to seven years. The children's behavior questionnaire. *Child Development*, 72, 1394–1408.

Rothbart, M. K. and Bates, J. E. (2006). Temperament. In W. Damon, R. Lerner, and N. Eisenberg (eds), *Handbook of Child Psychology. Vol 3. Social, Emotional, and Personality Development* (6th edn, pp 99–166). New York, NY. Wiley.

Rothbart, M. K., Sheese, B. E., and Conradt, E. D. (2009). Childhood temperament. In P. J. Corr and G. Matthews (eds), *The Cambridge Handbook of Personality Psychology* (pp 177–90). New York, NY. Cambridge University Press.

Rothbaum, F. and Tsang, B. Y. (1998). Lovesongs in the U.S. and China. The nature of romantic love. *Journal of Cross-Cultural Psychology*, 29, 306–19.

Rothman, R. B. and Baumann, M. H. (2006). Balance between dopamine and serotonin release modulates behavioral effects of amphetamine-type drugs. *Annals of the*

New York Academy of Sciences, 1074, 245–60.

Rotter, J. B. (1966). Generalized expectancies of internal versus external control of reinforcements. *Psychological Monographs*, 80(1, Whole No 609).

Rowland, J. (2019) Free will and the nervous system. *Psychology Review*, 24.

Roy-Byrne, P. R. (2005). The GABA-Benzodiazepine receptor complex. Structure, function, and role in anxiety. *Journal of Clinical Psychiatry*, 66(Suppl 2), 14–20.

Royal College of Psychiatrists (1995). *Fact Sheet on ECT*. London. RCP.

Rozanski, A., Blumenthal, J. A., Davidson, K. W., Saab, P. G., and Kubzansky, L. (2005). The epidemiology, pathophysiology and management of psychosocial risk factors in cardiac practice. *Journal of the American College of Cardiology*, 45, 637–51.

Rozin, P. (1976). Psychological and cultural determinants of food choice. In T. Silverstone (ed), *Appetite and Food Intake* (pp 286–312). Berlin. Dahlem Konferenzen.

Rozin, P., Haidt, J., and McCauley, C. R. (1999). Disgust. The body and soul emotion. In T. Dalgleish and M. J. Power (eds), *Handbook of Cognition and Emotion* (pp 429–45). New York, NY. Wiley.

Rozin, P., Haidt, J., and McCauley, C. R. (2009). Disgust. The body and soul emotion in the 21st century. In B. O. Olatunji, and D. McKay (eds), *Disgust and its Disorders. Theory, Assessment, and Treatment Implications* (pp 9–29). Washington, DC. American Psychological Association.

Rubin, J. (2015). Using goal setting and task analysis to enhance task-based language learning and teaching. *Dimension*, 70, 82.

Rubin, N. (2001). Figure and ground in the brain. *Nature Neuroscience*, 4, 857–8.

Rubinow, D. R. (2006). Treatment strategies after SSRI failure—good news and bad news. *New England Journal of Medicine*, 354, 1305–7.

Ruble, D. N., Taylor, L. J., Cyphers, L., Greulich, F. K., Lurye, L. E., et al (2009). The role of gender constancy in early gender development. *Child Development*, 78, 1121–36.

Rudaizky, D., Basanovic, J., and MacLeod, C. (2014). Biased attentional engagement with, and disengagement from, negative information. Independent cognitive pathways to anxiety vulnerability? *Cognition and Emotion*, 28(2), 245–59.

Ruehlman, L. S., West, S. G., and Pasahow, R. J. (1985). Depression and evaluative schemata. *Journal of Personality*, 53, 46–92.

Ruggiero, K. M. and Taylor, D. M. (1997). Why minority group members perceive or do not perceive the discrimination that confronts them. The role of self-esteem and perceived control. *Journal of Personality and Social Psychology*, 72, 373–89.

Runco, M. A. (2004). Creativity. *Annual Review of Psychology*, 55, 657–87.

Ruscher, J. B. and Hammer, E. Y. (2004). The person in the situation. Self-protection, self-evaluation, and self-change. In J. B. Ruscher and E. Y. Hammer (eds), *Current Directions in Social Psychology* (pp 1–2). Upper Saddle-River, NJ. Pearson/Prentice Hall.

Ruscio, A. M., Brown, T. A., Chiu, W. T., Sareen, J., Stein, M. B., et al (2008). Social fears and social phobia in the United States from the National Comorbidity Survey Replication. *Psychological Medicine*, 38, 15–28.

Ruscio, A. M., Gentes, E. L., Jones, J. D., Hallion, L. S., Coleman, E. S., et al (2015). Rumination predicts heightened responding to stressful life events in major depressive disorder and generalized anxiety disorder. *Journal of Abnormal Psychology*, 124(1), 17.

Ruscio, J. (2006). *Critical Thinking in Psychology. Separating Sense from Nonsense* (2nd edn). Belmont, CA. Wadsworth.

Rush, A. J., Trivedi, M. H., Wisniewski, S. R., Stewart, J. W., Nierenberg, A. A., et al (2006). Bubropion-SR, sertraline, or venlafaxine-XR after failure of SSRIs for depression. *New England Journal of Medicine*, 354, 1231–42.

Rushton, P. J. (2004). Genetic and environmental contributions to pro-social attitudes. A twin study of social responsibility. *Proceedings of the Royal Society of London*, 271, 2583–5.

Russell, G. F. M. (1995). Anorexia nervosa through time. In G. Szmulker, C. Dare, and J. Treasure (eds), *Handbook of Eating Disorders. Theory, Treatment and Research* (pp 5–17). London. Wiley.

Russell, J. A. (2003). Core affect and the psychological construction of emotion. *Psychological Review*, 110, 145–72.

Russell, T. G., Rowe, W., and Smouse, A.D. (1991). Subliminal self-help tapes and academic achievement. An evaluation.

Journal of Counseling and Development, 69, 359–62.

Russo, M. B., Kendall, A. P., Johnson, D. E., Sing, H. C., Thorne, D. R., et al (2005). Visual perception, psychomotor performance, and complex motor performance during an overnight air refueling simulated flight. *Aviation, Space, and Environmental Medicine*, 76(Suppl 1), C92–103.

Rusting, C. L., and Nolen-Hoeksema, S. (1998). Regulating responses to anger. Effects of rumination and distraction on angry mood. *Journal of Personality and Social Psychology*, 74, 790–803.

Rutherford, A. (2000). Mary Cover Jones (1896–1987). Retrieved from http://www.psych.yorku.ca/femhop/Cover%20%20Jones.htm on 14 July 2005. (Originally published in *The Feminist Psychologist*, Vol 27, Summer 2000.)

Ruthsatz, J. and Detterman, D. K. (2003). An extraordinary memory. The case study of a musical prodigy. *Intelligence*, 31, 509–18.

Rutledge, T. and Hogan, B. E. (2002). A quantitative review of prospective evidence linking psychological factors with hypertension development. *Psychosomatic Medicine, 64,* 758–66.

Rutter, M. (2002). Nature, nurture, and development. From evangelism through science toward policy and practice. *Child Development*, 73, 1–21.

Rutter, M. (2007). Gene-environment interdependence. *Developmental Science*, 10(1), 12–18.

Rutter, M., O'Connor, T. G., and the English and Romanian Adoptees (ERA) Study Team. (2004). Are there biological programming effects for psychological development? Findings from a study of Romanian adoptees. *Developmental Psychology*, 40(1), 81–94.

Ruys, K. I. and Stapel, D. A. (2008). How to heat up from the cold. Examining the preconditions for (unconscious) mood effects. *Journal of Personality and Social Psychology*, 94, 777–91.

Ryan, R. M. and Deci, E. L. (2000). Intrinsic and extrinsic motivations. Classic definitions and new directions. *Contemporary Educational Psychology*, 25, 54–67.

Rydell, R. J., Rydell, M. T., and Boucher, K. L. (2010). The effect of negative performance stereotypes on learning. *Journal of Personality and Social Psychology*, 99, 883–96.

Ryle, G. (1949). *The Concept of Mind*. Chicago, IL. The University of Chicago Press.

Sabini, J., Siepmann, M., and Stein, J. (2001a). The really fundamental attribution error in social psychology research. *Psychological Inquiry*, 12, 1–15.

Sabini, J., Siepmann, M., and Stein, J. (2001b). Author's response to commentaries. *Psychological Inquiry*, 12, 41–8.

Sachs, G. S., Nierenberg, A. A., Calabrese, M. D., Marangell, M. D., Wisniewski, S. R., et al (2007). Effectiveness of ad-junctive antidepressant treatment for bipolar depression. *New England Journal of Medicine*, 356, 1711–22.

Sackeim, H. A., Prudic, J., Fuller, R., Keilp, J., Lavori, P. W., et al (2007). The cognitive effects of electro-convulsive therapy in community settings. *Neuropsychopharmacology*, 32, 244–54.

Sacks, O. (1985). *The Man Who Mistook His Wife for a Hat*. London. Duckworth.

Sadler, M. E., Hunger, J. M., and Miller, C. J. (2010). Personality and impression management. Mapping the Multidimensional Personality Questionnaire onto 12 self-presentation tactics. *Personality and Individual Differences*, 48, 623–8.

Sadler, T. W. (2004). *Langman's Medical Embryology* (9th edn). Philadelphia, PA. Lippincott, Williams, and Wilkins.

Sadler-Smith, E. (2008). *Inside Intuition*. Abington, UK. Routledge.

Safford, S. M., Alloy, L. B., Abramson, L. Y., and Crossfield, A. G. (2007). Negative cognitive style as a predictor of negative life events in depression-prone individuals. A test of the stress generation hypothesis. *Journal of Affective Disorders*, 99, 147–54.

Sagan, C. (1995). *The Demon-haunted World. Science as a Candle in the Dark*. New York, NY. Random House.

Sai, F. Z. (2005). The role of the mother's voice in developing mother's face preference. Evidence for intermodal perception at birth. *Infant and Child Development*, 14(1), 29–50.

Salamone, J. D. (2002). Functional significance of nucleus accumbens dopamine. Behavior, pharmacology and neurochemistry. *Behavioral Brain Research*, 137(1), 1.

Salamone, J. D. and Correa, M. (2002). Motivational views of reinforcement. Implications for understanding the behavioral functions of nucleus accumbens dopamine. *Behavioral Brain Research*, 137(1), 3–25.

Salamone, J. D., Correa, M., Farrar, A., and Mingote, S. M. (2007). Effort-related functions of nucleus accumbens dopamine and associated forebrain circuits. *Psychopharmacology*, 19, 461–82.

Salander Renberg, E. E. (1999). Parasuicide in a northern Swedish county 1989–1995 and its relation to suicide. *Archives of Suicide Research*, 5, 97–112.

Salmivalli, C., Kaukiainen, A., Kaistaniemi, L., and Lagerspetz, K. M. J. (1999). Self-evaluated self-esteem, peer-evaluated self-esteem, and defensive egotism as predictors of adolescents' participation in bullying situations. *Personality and Social Psychology Bulletin*, 25, 1268–78.

Salmon, D. P. and Bondi, M. W. (2009). Neuropsychological assessment of dementia. *Annual Review of Psychology*, 60, 257–82.

Salmon, P. (2001). Effects of physical exercise on anxiety, depression, and sensitivity to stress. A unifying theory. *Clinical Psychology Review*, 21, 33–61.

Salomons, T. V., Coan, J. A., Hunt, S. M., Backonja, M.-M., and Davidson, R. J. (2008). Voluntary facial displays of pain increase suffering in response to nociceptive stimulation. *The Journal of Pain*, 9, 443–8.

Salonia, A., Giraldi, A., Chiverrs, M. L., Georgiadis, J. R., Levin, R., et al (2010). Physiology of women's sexual function. Basic knowledge and new findings. *Journal of Sexual Medicine*, 7, 2637–60.

Salthouse, T. A. (2004). Localizing age-related individual differences in a hierarchical structure. *Intelligence*, 32, 541–61.

Salthouse, T. A. (2006). Mental exercise and mental aging. Evaluating the validity of the 'use it or lose it' hypothesis. *Perspectives on Psychological Science*, 68–87.

Salthouse, T. A. (2011). Effects of age on time-dependent cognitive change. *Psychological Science*, 22, 682–8.

Samelson, F. (1980). L. B. Watson's Little Albert, Cyril Burt's twins and the need for a critical science. *American Psychologist*, 35, 619–25.

Sandler, C. (2011). *Executive Coaching. A Psychodynamic Approach*. Maidenhead, UK. McGraw-Hill Education.

Sapolsky, R. M. (1996). Why stress is bad for your brain. *Science*, 273(5276), 749–50.

Sapolsky, R. M. (1997). *The Trouble with Testosterone. And Other Essays on the Biology of the Human Predicament.* New York, NY. Touchstone/Simon and Schuster.

Sargeant, B. L. and Mann, J. (2009). From social learning to culture. Intrapopulation variation in bottlenose dolphins. In K. N. Laland and G. Bennett (eds), *The Question of Animal Culture* (pp 152–73). Cambridge, MA. Harvard University Press.

Sargent, J. D., Stoolmiller, M., Worth, K. A., Dal Cin, S., Wills, T. A., et al (2007). Exposure to smoking depictions in movies. Its association with established adolescent smoking. *Archives of Pediatric and Adolescent Medicine*, 161, 849–56.

Sarnoff, S. K. (2001). *Sanctified Snake Oil. The Effect of Junk Science on Public Policy.* Westport, CT. Praeger Publishers.

Sato, T., Bottlender, R., Sievers, M., and Möller, H.-J. (2005). Evidence of depressive mixed states. *American Journal of Psychiatry*, 162(1), 193–4.

Satpute, A. B. and Lieberman, M. D. (2006). Integrating automatic and controlled processes into neurocognitive models of social cognition. *Brain Research*, 1079(1), 86–97.

Saudino, K. J. (2005). Behavioral genetics and child temperament. *Developmental and Behavioral Pediatrics*, 26, 214–23.

Savage, J. (2004). Does viewing violent media really cause criminal violence? A methodological review. *Aggression and Violent Behavior*, 10, 99–128.

Savage, J. and Yancey, C. (2008). The effects of media violence exposure on criminal aggression. A meta-analysis. *Criminal Justice and Behavior*, 35, 1123–36.

Savage-Rumbaugh, E. S., Shanker, S. G., and Taylor, T. J. (1998). *Apes, Language, and the Human Mind.* New York, NY. Oxford University Press.

Savic, I., Berglund, H., Gulyas, B., and Roland, P. (2001). Smelling of odorous sex hormone-like compounds causes sex-differentiated hypothalamic activations in humans. *Neuron*, 31, 661–8.

Savic, I., Berglund, H., and Lindström, P. (2005). Brain response to putative pheromones in homosexual men. *Proceedings of the National Academy of Sciences. USA*, 102, 7356–61.

Savic, I. and Lindström, P. (2008). PET and MRI show differences in cerebral asymmetry and functional connectivity between homosexual and heterosexual subjects. *Proceedings of the National Academy of Sciences*, 105, 9403–8.

Savin-Williams, R. C. (2006). Who's gay? Does it matter? *Current Directions in Psychological Science*, 15(1), 40–4.

Savin-Williams, R. C. (2008). Then and now. Recruitment, definition, diversity, and positive attributes of same-sex populations. *Developmental Psychology*, 44, 135–8.

Savin-Williams, R. C. and Ream, G. L. (2007). Prevalence and stability of sexual orientation components during adolescence and young adulthood. *Archives of Sexual Behavior*, 36, 385–94.

Savitsky, K. Epley, N., and Gilovich, T. (2001). Is it as bad as we think? Overestimating the impact of our failures, shortcomings, and mishaps. *Journal of Personality and Social Psychology*, 81, 44–56.

Savitsky, K., Gilovich, T., Berger, G., and Medvec, V. H. (2003). Is our absence as conspicuous as we think? Overestimating the salience and impact of one's absence from a group. *Journal of Experimental Social Psychology*, 39, 386–92.

Sax, L. (2002). How common is intersex? A reply to Anne Fausto-Sterling. *The Journal of Sex Research*, 39, 174–8.

Saxvig, I. W., Lundervold, A. L., Gronli, J., Ursin, R., Bjorvatn, B., et al (2008). The effect of a REM sleep deprivation procedure on different aspects of memory function in humans. *Psychophysiology*, 45, 309–17.

Sbarra, D. A. and Nietert, P. J. (2009). Divorce and death. Forty years of the Charleston Heart Study. *Psychological Science*, 20, 107–13.

Scaini, S., Belotti, R., and Ogliari, A. (2014). Genetic and environmental contributions to social anxiety across different ages. A meta-analytic approach to twin data. *Journal of Anxiety Disorders*, 28(7), 650–6.

Schachter, S. (1959). *The Psychology of Affiliation.* Stanford, CA. Stanford University Press.

Schachter, S. and Singer, J. E. (1962). Cognitive, social, and physiological determinants of emotional state. *Psychological Review*, 69, 379–99.

Schacter, D. L. (1994). Priming and multiple memory systems. Perceptual mechanisms of implicit memory. In D. L. Schacter and E. Tulving (eds), *Memory Systems* (pp 233–68). Cambridge, MA. MIT Press.

Schacter, D. L. (1996). *Searching for Memory. The Brain, the Mind, and the Past.* New York, NY. Plenum Press.

Schacter, D. L. (2001). *The Seven Sins of Memory.* Boston, MA. Houghton Mifflin Company.

Schacter, D. L. (2004). When memory sins. (2004). In J. T. Cacioppo and G. G. Berntson (eds), *Essays in Social Neuroscience* (pp 93–105). Cambridge, MA. MIT Press.

Schacter, D. L., Chiao, J. Y., and Mitchell, J. P. (2003). The seven sins of memory. Implications for self. *Annals of the New York Academy of Sciences*, 1001, 226–39.

Schad, A., Schindler, K., Schelter, B., Maiwald, T., Brandt, A., et al (2008). Application of a multivariate seizure detection and prediction method to noninvasive intracranial long-term EEG recordings. *Clinical Neurophysiology*, 119, 197–211.

Schaller, M., Neuberg, S. L., Griskevicius, V., and Kenrick, D. T. (2010). Pyramid power. A reply to commentaries. *Perspectives on Psychological Science*, 5, 335–7.

Schank, R. C. and Abelson, R. (1977). *Scripts, Plans, Goals, and Understanding.* Hillsdale, NJ. Lawrence Erlbaum Associates.

Scharfe, E. and Bartholomew, K. (1998). Do you remember? Recollections of adult attachment patterns. *Personal Relationships*, 5, 219–34.

Scheck, B., Neufeld, P., and Dwyer, J. (2000). *Actual Innocence. Five Days to Execution and Other Dispatches from the Wrongly Convicted.* New York, NY. Doubleday.

Schelach, L. and Nachson, I. (2001). Memory of Auschwitz survivors. *Applied Cognitive Psychology*, 15, 119–32.

Schenck, C. H. and Mahowald, M. W. (2005). Rapid eye movement and non-REM parasomnias. *Primary Psychiatry*, 12, 67–74.

Schenck, C. H. and Mahowald, M. W. (2010). Therapeutics for parasomnias in adults. *Sleep Medicine Clinics*, 5, 689–700.

Schenkein, J. and Montagna, P. (2006). Self-management of fatal familial insomnia. Part I. What is FFI? *Medscape General Medicine*, 8. Retrieved from www. pubmedcentral.nih.gov on 27 October 2008.

Schep, L. J., Slaughter, R. J., Vale, J. A., Beasley, M. G., and Gee, P. (2011). The clinical toxicology of the designer 'part pills' benzylpiperazine and trifluoromethyl-phenylpiperazine. *Clinical Toxicology*, 49, 131–41.

Schimmenti, A. and Bifulco, A. (2015). Linking lack of care in childhood to anxiety disorders in emerging adulthood. The role of attachment styles. *Child and Adolescent Mental Health*, 20(1), 41–8.

Schizophrenia Working Group of the Psychiatric Genomics Consortium (2014). Biological insights from 108 schizophrenia-associated genetic loci. *Nature*, 511(7510), 421.

Schlegel, A. and Barry, H. (1991). *Adolescence. An Anthropological Inquiry.* New York, NY. Free Press.

Schmader, T. (2010). Stereotype threat deconstructed. *Current Directions in Psychological Science*, 19, 14–18.

Schmahmann, J. D. (2004). Disorders of the cerebellum. Ataxia, dysmetria of thought, and the cerebellar cognitive affective syndrome. *Journal of Neuropsychiatry and Clinical Neuroscience*, 16, 367–78.

Schmeichel, B. J., Gailliot, M. T., Filardo, E.-A., McGregor, I., Gitter, S., et al (2009). Terror management theory and self-esteem revisited. The roles of implicit and explicit self-esteem in mortality salience effects. *Journal of Personality and Social Psychology*, 95, 1077–87.

Schmidt, M. F. H. and Somerville, J. A. (2011). Fairness expectations and altruistic sharing in 15-month-old human infants. *PLoS One*, 6, e23223. Retrieved from http://www.plosone.org/article/info%3Adoi%2F10.1371%2Fjournal.pone.0023223 on 15 October 2011.

Schmitt, D. P. (2003). Universal sex differences in the desire for sexual variety. Tests from 52 nations, 6 continents, and 13 islands. *Journal of Personality and Social Psychology*, 85(1), 85–104.

Schmitt, D. P. (2005). Sociosexuality from Argentina to Zimbabwe. A 48-nation study of sex, culture, and strategies of human mating. *Behavioral and Brain Sciences*, 28, 247–311.

Schmitt, D. P., Allik, J., McCrae, R. R., and Benet-Martínez, V. (2007). The geographic distribution of Big Five personality traits. Patterns and profiles of human self-description across 56 nations. *Journal of Cross-Cultural Psychology*, 38, 173–212.

Schmitt, D. P., Jonason, P. K., Byerley, G. J., Flores, S. D., Illbeck, B. E., et al (2012). A reexamination of sex differences in sexuality. New studies reveal old truths. *Current Direction in Psychological Science*, 21, 135–9.

Schmitt, D. P. and Pilcher, J. J. (2004). Evaluating evidence of psychological adaptation. How do we know one when we see one? *Psychological Science*, 15, 643–9.

Schmitt, D. P., Realo, A., Voracek, M., and Allik, J. (2008). Why can't a man be more like a woman? Sex differences in big five personality traits across 55 cultures. *Journal of Personality and Social Psychology*, 94, 168–82.

Schmitt, F. L. and Hunter, J. (2004). General mental ability in the world of work. Occupational attainment and job performance. *Journal of Personality and Social Psychology*, 86, 162–73.

Schnall, E., Wassertheil-Smoller, S., Swencionis, C., Zemon, V., Tinker, L., et al (2008). The relationship between religion and cardiovascular outcomes and all-cause mortality in the women's health initiative observational study. *Psychology and Health*. Advance online publication retrieved from http://pdfserve.informaworld.com on 17 December 2008.

Schnall, S. Haidt, J., Clore, G., and Jordan, A. (2008). Disgust as embodied moral judgment. *Personality and Social Psychology Bulletin*, 34, 1096–109.

Schneider, B., Müller, J. M., and Philipp, M. (2001). Mortality in affective disorders. *Journal of Affective Disorders*, 65, 263–74.

Schooler, J. W., Bendiksen, M., and Ambadar, Z. (1997). Taking the middle line. Can we accommodate both fabricated and recovered memories of sexual abuse? In M. A. Conway (ed), *Recovered Memories and False Memories* (pp 251–92). Oxford, UK. Oxford University Press.

Schrauf, R. W. and Sanchez, J. (2004). The preponderance of negative emotion words in the emotion lexicon. Cross-generational and cross-linguistic study. *Journal of Multilingual and Multicultural Development*, 25, 266–84.

Schreiber, F. (1973). *Sybil*. New York, NY. Warner Books.

Schulte, M. J., Ree, M. J., and Carretta, T. R. (2004). Emotional intelligence. Not much more than g and personality. *Personality and Individual Differences*, 37(5), 1059–68.

Schultheiss, O. C., Wirth, M. M., Torges, C. M., Pang, J. S, Villacorta, M. A., et al (2005). Effects of implicit power motivation on men's and women's implicit learning and testosterone changes after social victory or defeat. *Journal of Personality and Social Psychology*, 88, 174–88.

Schuman, H., Steeh, C., Bobo, L., and Kyrsan, M. (1997). *Racial Attitudes in America. Trends and Interpretations.* Cambridge, MA. Harvard University Press.

Schumm, W., R., Anderson, C. V., Brinneman, A. S. Magsanoc-Deoki, M. E., Pakhalchuk, A., et al (2006). Re-analysis of Sageman's (2004) and Pape's (2005) data predicting Al'Quaeda membership and suicide terrorism. *Psychological Reports*, 98, 915–17.

Schunk, D. H. (1996). Goal and self-evaluative influences during children's cognitive skill learning. *American Educational Research Journal*, 33, 359–82.

Schurke, B. (2000). Young children's curiosity about other people's genitals. *Journal of Psychology and Human Sexuality*, 12(1–2), 27–48.

Schwartz, B. (2015). *Why We Work*. London. Simon and Schuster.

Schwartz, B. L. (2002). *Tip-of-the-Tongue States. Phenomenology, mechanism, and Lexical Retrieval.* Mahwah, NJ. Lawrence Erlbaum Associates.

Schwartz, B. L. (2010). The effects of emotion on tip-of-the-tongue states. *Psychonomic Bulletin and Review*, 17, 82–7.

Schwartz, B. L. and Frazier, L. D. (2005). Tip-of-the-tongue states and aging. Contrasting psycholinguistic and metacognitive perspectives. *Journal of General Psychology*, 132, 377–91.

Schwartz, J. and Byrd-Bredbenner, C. (2006). Portion distortion. Typical portion sizes selected by young adults. *Journal of the American Dietary Association*, 106, 1412–18.

Schwarz, A. (2012, 10 June). The risky rise of the good-grade pill. *New York Times*. Retrieved from http://www.nytimes.com/2012/06/10/education/seeking-academic-edge-teenagers-abuse-stimulants.html?pagewanted=all&_r=0 on 12 June 2012.

Schweinart, L. J., Motie, J., Xiang, Z., Barnett, W. S., Belfield, C. R., et al (2004). *Lifetime Effects. The High/Scope Perry Preschool Study through Age 40*. Monographs of the High/Scope Educational Research Foundation, 14. Ypsilanti, MI. High/Scope Press.

Schyns, P. G., Petro, L. G., and Smith, M. L. (2009). Transmission of facial expressions of emotion co-evolved with their efficient decoding in the brain. Behavioral and brain evidence. *PLoS One*, 4. Retrieved from www.plosone.org on 15 June 2009.

Science Daily (2009, 20 December). Cannabis damages young brains more than originally thought, study finds. Retrieved from http://www.sciencedaily.com/releases/2009/12/091217115834.htm on 14 January 2009.

Scott-Ham, M. and Burton, F. C. (2005). Toxicological findings in cases of alleged drug-facilitated sexual assault in the United Kingdom over a 3-year period. *Journal of Clinical Forensic Medicine*, 12, 175–86.

Scott, D. J., Stohler, C. S., Egnatuk, C. M., Wang, H., Koeppe, R. A., et al (2008). Placebo and nocebo effects are defined by opposite opioid and dopaminergic responses. *Archives of General Psychiatry*, 65, 220–31.

Scott, W. J. (1990). PTSD in DSM-III. A case in the politics of diagnosis and disease. *Social Problems*, 37, 294–310.

Scott-Phillips, T. C., Dickins, T. E., and West, S. A. (2011). Evolutionary theory and the ultimate-proximate distinction in the human behavioral sciences. *Perspectives on Psychological Science*, 6, 38–47.

Scoville, W. and Milner, B. (1957). Loss of recent memory after bilateral hippocampal lesions. *Journal of Neurology, Neurosurgery, and Psychiatry*, 20, 11–21.

Scullin, M. H., Peters, E., Williams, W. M., and Ceci, S. J. (2000). The role of IQ and education in predicting later labor market outcomes. Implications for affirmative action. *Psychology, Policy, and Law*, 48, 943–56.

Searle, J. R. (1997). *The Mystery of Consciousness*. New York, NY. New York Review of Books.

Searle, J. R. (2000). Consciousness. *Annual Review of Neuroscience*, 23, 557–78.

Sederberg, P. B., Schulze-Bonhage, A., Madsen, J. R., Bromfield, E. B., Litt, B., et al (2007). Gamma oscillations distinguish true from false memories. *Psychological Science*, 18, 927–32.

Sedgwick, H. (2001). Visual space perception. In E. B. Goldstein (ed), *Blackwell Handbook of Perception* (pp 128–67). Oxford, UK. Blackwell.

Sedikides, C., Gaertner, L., and Toguchi, Y. (2003). Pancultural self-enhancement. *Journal of Personality and Social Psychology*, 84, 60–70.

Sedikides, C., and Gregg, A. P. (2008). Self-enhancement. Food for thought. *Perspectives on Psychological Science*, 3, 102–16.

Seeman, T. (2001). How do others get under our skin? Social relationships and health. In C. D. Ryff and B. H. Singer (eds), *Emotion, Social Relationships, and Health. Series in Affective Science* (pp 189–210). London. Oxford University Press.

Seeyave, D. M., Coleman, S., Appugliese, D., Corwyn, R. F., Bradley, R. H., et al (2009). Ability to delay gratification at age 4 years and risk of overweight at age 11 years. *Archives of Pediatric and Adolescent Medicine*, 163. Retrieved from http://archpedi.jamanetwork.com/article.aspx?articleid=381236 on 20 May 2012.

Segal, N. L. (2010). Twins. The finest natural experiment. *Personality and Individual Differences*, 49, 317–23.

Segal, Z. V., Bieling, P., Young, T., MacQueen, G., Cooke, M., et al, (2010). Antidepressant monotherapy vs. sequential pharmacotherapy and mindfulness-based cognitive therapy, or placebo, for relapse prophylaxis in recurrent depression. *Archives of General Psychiatry*, 67, 1256–64.

Segal, Z. V., Williams, J. M. G., and Teasdale, J. (2002). *Mindfulness-based Cognitive Therapy for Depression. A New Approach to Preventing Relapse*. New York, NY. Guilford.

Segall, M. H., Campbell, D. T., and Herskovits, M. J. (1966). *The Influence of Culture on Visual Perception*. Indianapolis, IN. Bobbs-Merrill.

Segerstråle, U. (2000). *Defenders of the Truth. The Battle for Science in the Sociobiology Debate and Beyond*. New York, NY. Oxford University Press.

Segerstrom, S. C. (2007). Stress, energy, and immunity. *Current Directions in Psychological Science*, 16, 326–441.

Segerstrom, S. C. and Miller, G. E. (2004). Psychological stress and the human immune system. A meta-analysis of 30 years of inquiry. *Psychological Bulletin*, 130, 601–30.

Seligman, M. E. P. (1970). On the generality of the laws of learning. *Psychological Review*, 77, 406–18.

Seligman, M. E. P. (1975). *Helplessness. On Depression, Development and Death*. San Francisco, CA. W. H. Freeman.

Seligman, M. E. P. (1990). *Learned Optimism. How to Change Your Mind and Your Life*. New York, NY. Free Press.

Seligman, M. E. P. (1995). The effectiveness of psychotherapy. The *Consumers Reports* Study. *American Psychologist*, 50, 965–74.

Seligman, M. E. P. (2002). *Authentic Happiness. Using the New Positive Psychology to Realize Your Potential for Lasting Fulfillment*. New York, NY. Free Press.

Seligman, M. E. P., Steen, T. A., Park, N., and Peterson, C. (2005). Positive psychology progress. Empirical validation of interventions. *American Psychologist*, 60, 410–21.

Seligman, M. P., Linley, P. A., and Joseph, S. (eds) (2004). *Positive Psychology in Practice*. Hoboken, NJ. John Wiley and Sons.

Selye, H. (1956). *The Stress of Life*. New York, NY. McGraw Hill.

Selz, O. (1924). *Die Gesetze der produktiven und reproduktiven Geistestätigkeit*. Berlin. Cohen.

Sengupta, S. (2003, 26 September). Facing death for adultery, Nigerian woman is acquitted. *New York Times*. Retrieved from http://www.nytimes.com/2003/09/26/world/facing-death-for-adultery-nigerian-woman-is-acquitted.html?ref=aminalawal on 12 October 2004.

Serota, K. B. and Levine, T. R. (2015). A few prolific liars. Variation in the prevalence of lying. *Journal of Language and Social Psychology*, 34(2), 138–57.

Serota, K. B., Levine, T. R., and Boster, F. J. (2010). The prevalence of lying in America. Three studies of self-reported lies. *Human Communication Research*, 36, 2–25.

Severin, L. and Wyer, M. (2000). The science and politics of the search for sex differences. Editorial. *National Women's Studies Association Journal*, 12, vii.

Seyfarth, R. M. and Cheney, D. L. (2003). Signalers and receivers in animal communication. *Annual Review of Psychology*, 54, 145–73.

Shalev, A. Y. (2002). Acute stress reactions in adults. *Biological Psychiatry*, 51, 532–43.

Shanker, S. G., Savage-Rumbaugh, E. S., and Taylor, T. J. (1999). Kanzi. A new beginning. *Animal Learning and Behavior*, 27(1), 24–5.

Sharp, C., Venta, A., Vanwoerden, S., Schramm, A., Ha, C., et al (2016). First empirical evaluation of the link between attachment, social cognition and borderline features in adolescents. *Comprehensive Psychiatry*, 64, 4–11.

Sharp, J. and Espie, C. A. (2004). Brief exposure therapy for the relief of post-traumatic stress disorder. A single case experimental design. *Behavioural and Cognitive Psychotherapy*, 32, 365–9.

Shaver, P. R., Morgan, H. J., and Wu, S. (1996). Is love a 'basic' emotion? *Personal Relationships*, 3, 81–96.

Shaver, P. R., Wu, S., and Schwartz, J. C. (1992). Cross-cultural similarities and differences in emotion and its representation. A prototype approach. In M. S. Clark (ed), *Review of Personality and Social Psychology* (Vol 13, pp 175–212). Newbury Park, CA. Sage Publications.

Shea, C. (2011, 17 November). Fraud scandal fuels debate over practices of social psychology. *The Chronicle of Higher Education*. Retrieved from www.chronicle.com on 17 November 2011.

Sheaves, B., Porcheret, K., Tsanas, A., Espie, C. A., Foster, R. G., et al (2016). Insomnia, nightmares, and chronotype as markers of risk for severe mental illness. Results from a student population. *Sleep*, 39(1), 173–81.

Shedler, J. (2010). The efficacy of psychodynamic psychotherapy. *American Psychologist*, 65, 98–109.

Sheehan, P. W. and Perry, C. W. (1976). *Methodologies of Hypnosis*. Hillsdale, NJ. Lawrence Erlbaum Associates.

Sheldon, K. M. (2004). *Optimal Human Being. An Integrated Multi-level Perspective*. Mahwah, NJ. Lawrence Erlbaum Associates.

Shen, B-J., Stroud, L. R., and Niaura, R. (2004). Ethnic differences in cardiovascular responses to laboratory stress. A comparison between Asian and White Americans. *International Journal of Behavioral Medicine*, 11, 181–6.

Shepherd, G. M. (1988). *Neurobiology* (2nd edn). New York, NY. Oxford University Press.

Sherif, M. (1966). *In Common Predicament. Social Psychology of Intergroup Conflict*. Boston, MA. Houghton Mifflin.

Sherif, M., Harvey, O. J., White, J., Hood, W. R., and Sherif, C. (1961). Intergroup conflict and cooperation. The Robbers Cave Experiment. Middletown, CT. Wesleyan University Press. (Original work published 1954).

Sherif, M. and Sherif, C. W. (1966). The rise of attitudes toward ingroup and out-group. Experimental verification. In M. Sherif and C. W. Sherif (eds), *Groups in Harmony and Tension. An Integration of Studies of Intergroup Relations*. New York, NY. Octagon Books.

Sherman, D. K. and Cohen, G. L. (2002). Accepting threatening information. Self-affirmation and the reduction of defensive biases. *Current Directions in Psychological Science*, 11, 119–23.

Shermer, M. (1997). *Why People Believe Weird Things. Pseudoscience, Superstition, and Other Confusions of Our Time*. New York, NY. W. H. Freeman.

Shermer, M. (2008). Why you should be skeptical of brain scans. *Scientific American Mind*, October/November, 67–71.

Shettleworth, S. (1975). Reinforcement and the organization of behavior in golden hamsters. Hunger, environment, and food reinforcement. *Journal of Experimental Psychology. Animal Behavior Processes*, 1, 56–87.

Shibeshi, W. A., Young-Xu, Y., and Blatt, C. M. (2007). Anxiety worsens prognosis in patients with coronary heart disease. *Journal of the American College of Cardiology*, 20, 2021–7.

Shiovitz-Ezra, S. and Ayalon, L. (2010). Situational versus chronic loneliness as risk factors for all-cause mortality. *International Psychogeriatrics*, 22, 455–62.

Shirts, B. H., Kim, J. J., Reich, S., Dickerson, F. B., Yolken, R. H., et al (2007). Polymorphisms in MICB are associated with human herpes virus seropositivity and schizophrenia risk. *Schizophrenia Research*, 94, 342–53.

Shook, N. J. and Fazio, R. H. (2009). Interracial roommate relationships. An experimental field test of the contact hypothesis. *Psychological Science*, 19, 717–23.

Shurkin, J. N. (2009, November/December). Decoding dementia. *Scientific American Mind*, 56–63.

Shuwairi, S. M., Albert, M. K., and Johnson, S. P. (2007). Discrimination of possible and impossible objects in infancy. *Psychological Science*, 18, 303–7.

Shweder, R. A., Mahapatra, M., and Miller, J. G. (1990). Culture and moral development. In J. W. Stigler, R. A. Sweder, and G. Herdt (eds), *Cultural Psychology. Essays on Comparative Human Development* (pp 130–204). Cambridge, MA. Cambridge University Press.

Shweder, R. A., Much, N. C., Mahapatra, M., and Park, L. (1997). The 'big three' of morality (autonomy, community, divinity) and the 'big three' explanations of suffering. In A. Brandt and P. Rozin (eds), *Morality and Health* (pp 119–69). New York, NY. Routledge.

Shyam, R. and Bhoria, A. (2011). Information technology (Internet). Effects on social participation and well-being of users. *Journal of the Indian Academy of Applied Psychology*, 37, 157–62.

Sideli, L., Fisher, H. L., Murray, R. M., Sallis, H., Russo, M., et al (2018). Interaction between cannabis consumption and childhood abuse in psychotic disorders. Preliminary findings on the role of different patterns of cannabis use. *Early Intervention in Psychiatry*, 12(2), 135–42.

Sidney, S. (2003). Comparing cannabis with tobacco—again. *British Medical Journal*, 327, 635–6.

Sidtis J. J., Volpe B. T., Holtzman, J. D., Wilson, D. H., and Gazzaniga, M. S. (1981). Cognitive interaction after staged callosal section. Evidence for transfer of semantic activation. *Science*, 212, 344–6.

Siegel, R. (2005). *Intoxication. The Universal Drive for Mind-altering Substances*. Rochester, VT. Park Street Press.

Siegfried, T. (2010, 27 March). Odds are it's wrong. *Science News*, 177. Retrieved from http://www.sciencenews.org/view/feature/id/57091 on 9 May 2010.

Siegler, R. S. and Ellis, S. (1996). Piaget on childhood. *Psychological Science*, 7, 211–15.

Siev, J., Huppert, J. D., and Chambless, D. L. (2009). The dodo bird, treatment technique, and disseminating empirically supported treatments. *The Behavior Therapist*, 32, 69, 71–6.

Sigelman, C. K. and Rider, E. A. (2006). *Life-span Human Development*. Belmont, CA. Thomson/Wadsworth.

Signorielli, N., Gerbner, G., and Morgan, M. (1995). Violence on television. The cultural indicators project. *Journal of Broadcasting and Electronic Media*, 39, 278–83.

Sikich, L., Frazier, J. A., McClellan, J., Findling, R. L., Vitiello, B., et al (2008). Double-blind comparison of first- and second-generation antipsychotics in early-onset schizophrenia and schizoaffective disorder. Findings from the Treatment of Early-Onset Schizophrenia Spectrum Disorders (TEOSS) study. *American Journal of Psychiatry*, 165, 1420–31.

Silver, N. (2009, 27 December). The odds of airborne terror. Retrieved from http://www.fivethirtyeight.com/2009/12/odds-of-airborne-terror.html on 28 May 2011.

Silverman, C. (2016). This analysis shows how viral fake election news stories outperformed real news on Facebook. *BuzzFeed News*, 16.

Silverman, D. K., (2011). A clinical case of an avoidant attachment. *Psychoanalytic Psychology*, 28, 293–310.

Simmons, J. P., Nelson, L. D., and Simonsohn, U. (2011). False-positive psychology. Undisclosed flexibility in data collection and analysis allows presenting anything as significant. *Psychological Science*, 22, 1359–66.

Simons, D. J., Boot, W. R., Charness, N., Gathercole, S. E., Chabris, C. F., et al (2016). Do 'brain-training' programs work? *Psychological Science in the Public Interest*, 17(3), 103–86.

Simons, D. J. and Chabris, C. F. (1999). Gorillas in our midst. Sustained in attentional blindness for dynamic events. *Perception*, 28, 1059–74.

Simons, D. J., and Levin, D. T. (1998). Failure to detect changes to people in a real-world interaction. *Psychonomic Bulletin and Review*, 5, 644–9.

Simpson, J. A. (1987). The dissolution of romantic relationships. Factors involved in relationship stability and emotional distress. *Journal of Personality and Social Psychology*, 53, 683–92.

Simpson, J. A. Collins, W. A., Tran, S., and Haydon, K. C. (2007). Attachment and the experience and expression of emotions in romantic relationships. A developmental perspective. *Journal of Personality and Social Psychology*, 92, 355–67.

Simpson, J. A., Rholes, W. S., and Winterheld, H. A. (2010). Attachment working models twist memories of relationship events. *Psychological Science*, 21, 252–9.

Singer, N. (2009, 4 August). Medical papers by ghostwriters pushed therapy. *New York Times*. Retrieved from http://www.nytimes.com/2009/08/05/health/research/05ghost.html?pagewanted=all&_r=0 on 30 June 2010.

Singh, D. (2006). Universal allure of the hourglass figure. An evolutionary theory of female physical attractiveness. *Clinics of Plastic Surgery*, 33, 359–70.

Singh, D., Dixson, B. J., Jessop, T. S., Morgan, B., and Dixson, A. F. (2009). Cross-cultural consensus for waist-hip ratio and women's attractiveness. *Evolution and Human Behavior*, 31, 176–81.

Singh, D., and Young, R. K. (1995). Body weight, waist-to-hip ratio, breasts, and hips. Role in judgments of female attractiveness and desirability for relationships. *Ethology and Sociobiology*, 16, 483–507.

Singh, G. (2000). Gazstrointestinal complications of prescription and over-the-counter nonsteroidal anti-inflammatory drugs. A view from the ARAMIS database. *American Journal of Therapeutics*, 7, 115–21.

Sinno, S. M., and Killen, M. (2009). Moms at work and dads at home. Children's evaluations of parental roles. *Applied Developmental Science*, 13, 16–29.

Sismondo, S. (2007). Ghostmanagement. How much of the medical literature is shaped behind the scenes by the pharmaceutical industry? *PLoS Medicine*, 4, 1429–33. Retrieved from http://www.plosmedicine.org/article/info:doi/10.1371/journal.pmed.0040286 on 8 June 2008.

Sismondo, S. (2008a). How pharmaceutical industry funding affects trial outcomes. Causal structures and responses. *Social Science and Medicine*, 66, 1909–14.

Sismondo, S. (2008b). Pharmaceutical company funding and its consequences. A qualitative systematic review. *Contemporary Clinical Trials*, 29, 109–13.

Skinner, B. F. (1938). *The Behavior of Organisms. An Experimental Analysis.* New York, NY. Appleton-Century-Crofts.

Skinner, B. F. (1956). A case history in scientific method. *American Psychologist*, 11, 221–33.

Skinner, B. F. (1965). *Science and Human Behavior.* New York, NY. The Free Press.

Skinner-Buzan, D. (2004, 12 March). I was not a lab rat. *The Guardian.* Retrieved from http://www.guardian.co.uk/education/2004/mar/12/highereducation.uk on 31 May 2009.

Skoller, C. E. (2008). *Twisted Confessions.* Austin, TX. Bridgeway Books.

Skuse, D. H., Mandy, W. P., and Scourfield, J. (2005). Measuring autistic traits. Heritability, reliability, and validity of the social and communication disorders checklist. *British Journal of Psychiatry*, 187, 568–72.

Slater, L. (2004). *Opening Skinner's Box.* New York, NY. Norton.

Slater, M., Antley, A., Davison, A., Swapp, D., Guger, C., et al (2006). A virtual reprise of the Stanley Milgram obedience experiments. *PLoS One*, 1(1), e39.

Slaughter, L. (2000). Involvement of drugs in sexual assault. *Journal of Reproductive Medicine*, 45, 425–30.

Slaughter, V., Stone, V. E., and Reed, C. (2004). Perception of faces and bodies. Similar or different? *Current Directions in Psychological Science*, 13, 219–23.

Sleep. Spring cleaning for the brain? (2009, 11 April). *Science Daily.* Retrieved from www.sciencedaily.com on 19 May 2009.

Slentz, C. A., Houmard, J. A., Johnson, J. L., Bateman, L. A., Tanner, C. J., et al (2007). Inactivity, exercise training and detraining, and plasma lipoproteins. STRRIDE. A randomized, controlled study of exercise intensity and amount. *Journal of Applied Physiology*, 103, 432–42.

Slotema, C. W., Blom, J. D., Hoek, HY. W., and Sommer, I. E. (2010). *Journal of Clinical Psychiatry*, 71, 873–84.

Slovenko, R. (1994). Blaming a book. *Journal of Psychiatry and Law*, 22, 437–51.

Slutske, W. S., Moffitt, T. E., Poulton, R., and Caspi, A. (2012). Undercontrolled temperament at age 3 predicts disordered gambling at age 32. A longitudinal study of a complete birth cohort. *Psychological Science*, 23, 510–16.

Smeeding, T. and Phillips, K. R. (2002). Cross-national differences in employment and economic sufficiency. *Annals of the American Academy of Political and Social Science*, 580, 103–33.

Smetana, J. G., Campione-Barr, N., and Metzger, A. (2006). Adolescent development in interpersonal and societal contexts. *Annual Review of Psychology*, 57, 255–284.

Smetana, J. G., Schlagman, N., and Adams, P. W. (1993). Preschool children's judgments about hypothetical and actual transgressions. *Child Development*, 64, 202–14.

Smith, E. M. and Farah, M. J. (2011). Are prescription stimulants 'smart pills'? The epidemiology and cognitive neuroscience of prescription stimulant use by normal healthy individuals. *Psychological Bulletin*, 137, 717–41.

Smith, K. H. and Rogers, M. (1994). Effectiveness of subliminal messages in television commercials. Two experiments. *Journal of Applied Psychology*, 79, 866–74.

Smith, M. L., Cottrell, G. W., Gosselin, F., and Schyns, P. G. (2005). Transmitting and decoding facial expressions. *Psychological Science*, 16, 184–9.

Smith, M. L. and Glass, G. V. (1977). Meta-analysis of psychotherapy outcome studies. *American Psychologist*, 32, 752–60.

Smith, M. L., Glass, G. V., and Miller, T. I. (1980). *The Benefits of Psychotherapy*. Baltimore, MD. Johns Hopkins University Press.

Smith, S. M. (2003). The constraining effects of initial ideas. In P. Paulus and B. Nijstad (eds), *Group Creativity. Innovation through Collaboration* (pp 15–31). Oxford, UK. Oxford University Press.

Smith, T. W. (2006). *American sexual behavior. Trends, socio-demographic differences, and risk behavior*. General Social Survey Topical Report No. 15, National Opinion Research Center, Version 6.0. Retrieved from www.norc.org on 27 October 2007.

Smith, T. W. and Ruiz, J. M. (2002). Psychosocial influences on the development and course of coronary heart disease. Current status and implications for research and practice. *Journal of Consulting and Clinical Psychology*, 70, 548–68.

Snarey, J. R. (1985). Cross-cultural universality of social-moral development. A critical review of Kohlbergian research. *Psychological Bulletin*, 97, 202–32.

Sniderman, P. M. and Carmines, E. G. (1997). Reaching beyond race. *Political Science and Politics*, 30, 466–71.

Snyder, D. K., Castellani, A. M., and Whisman, M. A. (2006). Current status and future directions in couple therapy. *Annual Review of Psychology*, 57, 317–44.

So, W. W., Wong, F. Y., and DeLeon, J. (2005). Sex, HIV risks, and substance use among Asian American college students. *AIDS Education and Prevention*, 17, 457–68.

Sobel, N. and Brown, W. M. (2001). The scented brain. Pheromonal responses in humans. *Neuron*, 31, 512–14.

Social Issues Research Centre (SIRC) (2006). Culture, chemistry, and consequences. Retrieved from http://www.sirc.org/publik/drinking4.html on 4 December 2006.

Solms, M. (2000). Dreaming and REM sleep are controlled by different brain mechanisms. *Behavioral and Brain Sciences*, 23, 793–1121.

Solomon, S., Greenberg, J., and Pyszczynski, T. (2000). Pride and prejudice. Fear of death and social behavior. *Current Directions in Psychological Science*, 9, 200–4.

Sommer, V. and Vassey, P. L. (eds) (2006). *Homosexual Behaviour in Animals. An Evolutionary Perspective*. Cambridge, UK. Cambridge University Press.

Soreca, I., Frank, E., and Kupfer, D. J. (2009). The phenomenology of bipolar disorder. What drives the high rate of medical burden and determines long-term prognosis? *Depression and Anxiety*, 26, 73–82.

Soussignan, R. (2002). Duchenne smile, emotional experience and autonomic reactivity. A test of the facial feedback hypothesis. *Emotion*, 2, 52–74.

Spalding, T. W., Lyon, L. A., Steel, D. H., and Hatfield, B. D. (2004). Aerobic exercise training and cardiovascular reactivity to psychological stress in sedentary young normotensive men and women. *Psychophysiology*, 41, 552–62.

Spanos, N. P. (1991). A sociocognitive approach to hypnosis. In S. J. Lynn and J. W. Rhue (eds), *Theories of Hypnosis. Current Models and Perspectives* (pp 324–63). New York, NY. Guilford Press.

Spanos, N. P. (1996). Hypnosis. Mythology versus reality. In *Multiple Identities and False Memories. A Sociocognitive Perspective* (pp 17–28). Washington, DC. American Psychological Association.

Spanos, N. P., and Chaves, J. F. (1989). *Hypnosis. The Cognitive-behavioral Perspective*. Buffalo, NY. Prometheus.

Spear, L. P. (2000a). The adolescent brain and age-related behavioral manifestations. *Neuroscience and Biobehavioral Reviews*, 24, 417–63.

Spear, L.P. (2000b). Neurobehavioral changes in adolescence. *Current Directions in Psychological Science*, 8, 168–72.

Spearman, C. (1904). 'General intelligence', objectively determined and measured. *American Journal of Psychology*, 13, 201–93.

Spearman, C. E. (1927). *The Abilities of Man. Their Nature and Measurement*. New York, NY. Macmillan.

Speca, M., Carlson, L. E., Goodey, E., and Angen, M. (2000). A randomized, wait-list controlled clinical trial. The effect of a mindfulness meditation-based stress reduction program on mood and symptoms of stress in cancer outpatients. *Psychosomatic Medicine*, 62, 613–22.

Specht, J., Egloff, B., and Schmukle, S. (2011). Stability and change of personality across the life course. The impact of age and major life events on mean-level and rank-order stability of the Big Five. *Journal of Personality and Social Psychology*, 101, 862–82.

Spelke, E. S. (1998). Nativism, empiricism, and the origins of knowledge. *Infant Behavior and Development*, 21, 181–200.

Spelke, E. S., Phillips, A., and Woodward, A. L. (1995). Infants' knowledge of object motion and human action. In D. Sperber, D. Premack, and A. J. Premack (eds), *Causal Cognition. A Multidisciplinary Debate* (pp 44–78). New York, NY. Clarendon Press/Oxford University Press.

Sperling, G. (1960). The information available in brief visual presentations. *Psychological Monographs. General and Applied*, 74, 1–29.

Sperry, R. (1974). Lateral specialization in the surgically separated hemispheres. In F. Schmitt and F. Worden (eds), *The Neurosciences. Third Study Program* (pp 5–19). Cambridge, MA. MIT Press.

Sperry, R. (1982). Some effects of disconnecting the cerebral hemispheres. *Science*, 217, 1223–6.

Spiegel, D. (1994). Hynosis. In R. E. Hales, S. C. Yudofshy, and J. A. Talbott (eds), *The American Psychiatric Press Textbook of Psychiatry* (2nd edn, pp 1115–42). Washington, DC. American Psychiatric Association.

Spiegel, D. (2010). Hypnosis in the treatment of posttraumatic stress disorders. In S. J. Lynn, J. W. Rhue, and I. Kirsch (eds), *Handbook of Clinical Hypnosis* (2nd edn, pp 415–32). Washington, DC. American Psychological Association.

Spiegel, K., Leproult, R., and Van Cauter, E. (1999). Impact of sleep debt on metabolic and endocrine function. *The Lancet*, 354, 1435–9.

Spielmans, G. I., Pasek, L. F., and McFall, J. P. (2007). What are the active ingredients in cognitive and behavioral psychotherapy for anxious and depressed children? A meta-analytic review. *Clinical Psychology Review*, 27, 642–54.

Sprecher, S., Aron, A., Hatfield, E., Cortese, A., Potapova, E., et al (1994). Love. American style, Russian style, and Japanese style. *Personal Relationships*, 1, 349–69.

Sprecher, S., McKinney, K., and Orbuch, T. (1987). Has the double standard disappeared? An experimental test. *Social Psychology Quarterly*, 50, 24–31.

Sprinzak, E. (2000, September/October). Rational fanatics. *Foreign Policy*, 66–73.

Spurk, D., and Abele, A. E. (2014). Synchronous and time-lagged effects between occupational self-efficacy and objective and subjective career success. Findings from a four-wave and 9-year longitudinal study. *Journal of Vocational Behavior*, 84(2), 119–32.

Squier, L. H. and Domhoff, G. W. (1998). The presentation of dreaming and dreams in introductory psychology textbooks. A critical examination with suggestions for textbook authors and course instructors. *Dreaming*, 8, 149–68.

Squire, L. R. and Zola-Morgan, S. (1998). Episodic memory, semantic memory, and amnesia. *Hippocampus*, 8, 205–11.

Staff, J. and Mortimer, J. T. (2007). Educational and work strategies from adolescence to early adulthood. Consequences for educational attainment. *Social Forces*, 85, 1169–94.

Stanovich, K. E. and West, R. F. (2000). Individual differences in reasoning. Implications for the rationality debate? *Behavioral and Brain Sciences*, 23, 645–726.

Stanton, S. J., Beehner, J. C., Saini, E. K., Kuhn, C. M., and LaBar, K. S. (2009). Dominance, politics, and physiology. Voters' testosterone changes on the night of the 2008 United States presidential election. *PLoS One*, 4. Retrieved from www.plosone.org on 28 October 2009.

Starbuck, E. D. (1943). A student's impressions of James in the middle '90's [sic] [Note to students: mid-1890s]. *Psychological Review*, 50, 128–31. Retrieved from www.library.upenn.edu on 25 January 2013.

Steele, C. M. and Aronson, J. (1995). Stereotype threat and the intellectual test performance of African Americans. *Journal of Personality and Social Psychology*, 69, 797–811.

Steele, C. M. and Aronson, J. A. (2004). Stereotype threat does not live by Steele and Aronson alone. *American Psychologist*, 59(1), 47–8.

Stein, M. B., Simmons, A. N., Feinstein, J. S., and Paulus, M. P. (2007). Increased amygdala and insula activation during emotion processing in anxiety-prone subjects. *American Journal of Psychiatry*, 164, 318–27.

Stein, S. B. (1983). *Girls and Boys. The Limits of Nonsexist Childrearing.* New York, NY. Charles Scribner's Sons.

Steinberg, L. (2007). Risk taking in adolescence. New perspectives from brain and behavioral science. *Current Directions in Psychological Science*, 16, 55–9.

Steinberg, L. and Morris, A. S. (2001). Adolescent development. *Annual Review of Psychology*, 52, 83–110.

Steinmayr, R. and Spinath, B. (2009). The importance of motivation as a predictor of school achievement. *Learning and Individual Differences*, 19(1), 80–90.

Steketee, G. and Barlow, D. H. (2002). Obsessive-compulsive disorder. In D. H. Barlow (ed), *Anxiety and its Disorders. The Nature and Treatment of Anxiety and Panic* (2nd edn). New York, NY. Guilford.

Stellman, J. M., Smith, R. P., Katz, C. L., Sharma, V., Charney, D. S., et al (2008). Enduring mental health morbidity and social function impairment in World Trade Center rescue, recovery, and cleanup workers. The psychological dimension of an environmental health disaster. *Environmental Health Perspectives*, 116, 1248–53.

Stengel, E. (1952). Enquiries into attempted suicide. *Procedures of the Royal Society of Medicine*, 45, 613–20.

Stepper, S. and Strack, F. (1993). Proprioceptive determinants of emotional and nonemotional feelings. *Journal of Personality and Social Psychology*, 64, 211–20.

Steptoe, A., Dockray, S., and Wardle, J. (2009). Positive affect and psychobiological processes relevant to health. *Journal of Personality*, 77, 1747–75.

Steptoe, A., O'Donnell, K., Marmot, M., and Wardle, J. (2008). Positive affect, psychological well-being, and good sleep. *Journal of Psychosomatic Research*, 64, 409–415.

Sterling, P. (2000). ECT damage is easy to find if you look for it. *Nature*, 403, 242.

Stern, W. M., Tormos, J. M., Press, D. Z., Pearlman, C., and Pascual-Leone, A. (2007). Antidepressant effects of high and low frequency repetitive transcranial magnetic stimulation to the dorsolateral prefrontal cortex. A double-blind, randomized, placebo-controlled trial. *Journal of Neuropsychiatry and Clinical Neuroscience*, 19, 179–86.

Sternberg, R. J. (1999) A comparison of three models for teaching psychology. *Psychology Teaching Review*, 8, 37–43.

Sternberg, R. J. (2000). The holey grail of general intelligence. *Science*, 289, 399–401.

Sternberg, R. J. (2003a). Issues in the theory and measurement of successful intelligence. A reply to Brody. *Intelligence*, 31, 331–7.

Sternberg, R. J. (2003b). Our research program validating the triarchic theory of successful intelligence. Reply to Gottfredson. *Intelligence*, 31, 399–413.

Sternberg, R. J. (2003c). *Wisdom, Intelligence, and Creativity Synthesized.* New York, NY. Cambridge University Press.

Sternberg, R. J. (2005). The triarchic theory of successful intelligence. In D. P. Flanagan and P. L. Harrison (eds), *Contemporary Intellectual Assessment. Theories, Tests, and Issues* (pp 103–19). New York, NY. Guilford Press.

Sternberg, R. J. (2013). Searching for love. *Psychologist*, 26(2), 98–101.

Sternberg, R. J. and Davidson, J. E. (eds) (1995). *The Nature of Insight.* Cambridge, MA. MIT Press.

Sternberg, R. J. and Wagner, R. K. (1993). The *g*-ocentric view of intelligence and job performance is wrong. *Current Directions in Psychological Science*, 2(1), 1–5.

Sterpenich, V., D'Argembeau, A., Desseilles, M., Balteau, E., Albouy, G., et al (2006). The locus ceruleus is involved in the successful retrieval of emotional memories in humans. *Journal of Neuroscience*, 26, 7416–23.

Stevens, S. B. and Morris, T. L. (2007). College dating and social anxiety. Using the Internet as a means of connecting to others. *CyberPsychology and Behavior*, 10, 680–8.

Stickgold, R. and Walker, M. (2004). To sleep, perchance to gain creative insight? *Trends in Cognitive Sciences*, 8, 191–2.

Stone, A. A., Schwartz, J. E., Broderick, J. E., and Deaton, A. (2010). A snapshot of the age distribution of psychological well-being in the United States. *Proceedings of the National Academy of Sciences.* Pre-publication version retrieved from www.pnas.org on 2 June 2010.

Storandt, M. (2008). Cognitive deficits in the early stages of Alzheimer's disease. *Current Directions in Psychological Science*, 17, 198–202.

Storey, A. E., Walsh, C. J., Quinton, R. L, and Wynne-Edwards, K. E. (2000). Hormonal correlates of paternal responsiveness in new and expectant fathers. *Evolution and Human Behavior*, 21, 79–95.

Storm, B. C. and Angello, G. (2010). Overcoming fixation. Creative problem solving and retrieval-induced forgetting. *Psychological Science*, 21, 1263–5.

Storm, L., Tressoldi, P. E., and Di Risio, L. (2012). Meta-analysis of ESP studies, 1987–2010. Assessing the success of the forced-choice design in parapsychology. *Journal of Parapsychology*, 76(2), 243–73.

Strack, F., Martin, L. L., and Stepper, S. (1988). Inhibiting and facilitating conditions of the human smile. A non-obtrusive test of the facial feedback hypothesis. *Journal of Personality and Social Psychology*, 54, 768–77.

Strand, S., Deary, I. J., and Smith, P. (2006). Sex differences in cognitive ability test scores. A UK national picture. *British Journal of Educational Psychology*, 76, 463–80.

Strick, P. L., Dum, R. P., and Fiez, J. A. (2009). Cerebellum and nonmotor function. *Annual Review of Neuroscience*, 32, 413–34.

Stricker, L. J. and Ward, W. C. (2004). Stereotype threat, inquiring about test takers' ethnicity and gender, and standardized test performance. *Journal of Applied Social Psychology*, 34, 665–93.

Striegel-Moore, R. H. and Bulik, C. M. (2007). Risk factors for eating disorders. *American Psychologist*, 62, 181–98.

Strieker, G. and Gold, J. (2008). Integrative therapy. In J. L. Lebow (ed), *Twenty-first Century Psychotherapies. Contemporary Approaches to Theory and Practice* (pp 389–423). Hoboken, NJ. John Wiley and Sons.

Strupp, H. H. and Hadley, S. W. (1979). Specific vs. nonspecific factors in psychotherapy. A controlled study of outcome. *Archives of General Psychiatry*, 36, 1125–36.

Stutzer, A. and Frey, B. S. (2006). Does marriage make people happy, or do happy people get married? *The Journal of Socio-Economics*, 35, 326–47.

Su, R., Rounds, J., and Armstrong, P. I. (2009). Men and things, women and people. A meta-analysis of sex differences in interests. *Psychological Bulletin*, 135, 859–84.

Subotnik, R. F., Olszewski-Kubilius, P., and Worrell, F. C. (2011). Rethinking giftedness and gifted education. A proposed direction forward based on psychological science. *Psychological Science in the Public Interest*, 12, 3–54.

Subramanian, S. V., Kim, F., and Kawachi, I. (2005). Covariation in the socioeconomic determinants of self-rated health and happiness. A multivariate multilevel analysis of individuals and communities in the USA. *Journal of Community Health*, 59, 664–9.

Sue, S. and Chu, J. Y. (2003). The mental health of ethnic minority groups. Challenges posed by the Supplement to the Surgeon General's Report on Mental Health. *Culture, Medicine, and Psychiatry*, 27, 447–65.

Sufka, K. J. and Price, D. D. (2002). Gate control theory reconsidered. *Brain and Mind*, 3, 277–90.

Sugiyama, L. S. (2005). Physical attractiveness in adaptationist perspective. In D. M. Buss (ed), *Handbook of Evolutionary Psychology* (pp 292–343). Hoboken, NJ. John Wiley and Sons, Inc.

Suls, J., Martin, R., and Wheeler, L. (2002). Social comparison. Why, with whom, and with what effect? *Current Directions in Psychological Science*, 11, 159–63.

Sum, S., Mathews, M. R., Hughes, I., and Campbell, A. (2008). Internet use and loneliness in older adults. *CyberPsychology and Behavior*, 11, 208–11.

Sumathipala, A., Siribaddana, S. H., and Bhugra, D. (2004). Culture-bound syndromes. The story of dhat syndrome. *British Journal of Psychiatry*, 184, 200–9.

Sumner, W. G. (1959). *Folkways. A Study of the Sociological Importance of Usages, Manners, Customs, Mores, and Morals*. New York, NY. Blaisdell. (Original work published 1906.)

Suris, A., Holliday, R. and North, C. S. (2016). The evolution of the classification of psychiatric disorders. *Behavioural Sciences*, 6, 1–10.

Suschinsky, K. D., Lalumière, M. L., and Chivers, M. L. (2009). Sex differences in patterns of genital sexual arousal. Measurement artifacts or true phenomena? *Archives of Sexual Behavior*, 38, 559–73.

Svenningsson, P., Chergui, K. Rachleff, I. Flajolet, M., Zhang, X., et al (2006). Alterations in 5-HT receptor by p11 in depression-like states. *Science*, 311, 77–80.

Svrakic, D. M., Lecic-Tosevski, D., and Divac-Jovanovic, M. (2009). DSM axis II. Personality disorders or adaptation disorders? *Current Opinion in Psychiatry*, 22, 111–17.

Swaab, D. F., Chung, W. C. J., Kruijver, F. P. M., Hofman, M. A., and Ishunina, T. A. (2001). Structural and functional sex differences in the human hypothalamus. *Hormones and Behavior*, 40, 93–8.

Swaddle, J. P. and Reierson, G. W. (2002). Testosterone increases perceived dominance but not attractiveness of human males. *Proceedings of the Royal Society of London, Series B*, 269, 2285–9.

Swami, V., Neto, F., Tovée, M. J., and Furnham, A. (2007). Preferences for female body weight and shape in three European countries. *European Psychologist*, 12, 220–8.

Swami, V. and Tovée, M. J. (2007). Relative contribution of profile body shape and weight to judgements of women's physical attractiveness in Britain and Malaysia. *Body Image*, 4, 391–6.

Swann, W. B., Jr and Seyle, C. (2005). Personality psychology's comeback and its emerging symbiosis with social psychology. *Personality and Social Psychology Bulletin*, 31, 155–65.

Swartz, M. S., Perkins, D. O., Stroup, T. S., Davis, S. M., Capuano, G., et al (2007). Effects of antipsychotic medications on psychosocial functioning in patients with chronic schizophrenia. Findings from the NIMH CATIE study. *American Journal of Psychiatry*, 164, 428–36.

Swets, J. A., Dawes, R. M., and Monahan, J. (2000). Psychological science can improve diagnostic decisions. *Psychological Science in the Public Interest*, 1(1), 1–26.

Symons, D. (1979). *The Evolution of Human Sexuality*. New York, NY. Oxford University Press.

Symons, D. (1993). The stuff that dreams aren't made of. Why wake-state and dream-state experiences differ. *Cognition*, 47, 181–217.

Symons, D. (1995). Beauty is in the adaptations of the beholder. The evolutionary psychology of human female sexual attractiveness. In P. R. Abramson and S. D. Pinkerton (eds), *Sexual Nature, Sexual Culture* (pp 80–120). Chicago, IL. University of Chicago Press.

Symons, D. (1996). Forward. In D. Jones (ed), *Physical Attractiveness and the Theory of Sexual Selection*. Ann Arbor, MI. University of Michigan Museum of Anthropology.

Symons, D. K. and Clark, S. E. (2000). A longitudinal study of mother–child relationships and theory of mind in the preschool period. *Social Development*, 9(1), 3–23.

Sytsma, S. E. (2007). *Ethics and Intersex*. Dordrecht, Netherlands. Springer.

Szasz, T. (1961). The myth of mental illness. *American Psychologist*, 15, 113–18. New York, NY. Harper and Row.

Szasz, T. S. (2007). *The Medicalization of Everyday Life*. Syracuse, NY. University of Syracuse Press.

Szegedi, A., Kohnen, R., Dienel, M., and Kieser, M. (2005). Acute treatment of moderate to severe depression with hypericum extract WS 5570 (St. John's wort). Randomized controlled double blind non-inferiority trial versus paroxetine. *British Medical Journal*, 330, 503–7.

Szelenberger, W., Niemcewicz, S., and Dabrowska, A. J. (2005). Sleepwalking and night terrors. Psychopathological and psychophysiological correlates. *International Review of Psychiatry*, 17, 263–70.

Tager-Flusberg, H., Boshart, J., and Baron-Cohen, S. (1998). Reading the windows to the soul. Evidence of domain-specific sparing in Williams syndrome. *Journal of Cognitive Neuroscience*, 10(5), 631–9.

Taggart, G. (2015). Sustaining care. Cultivating mindful practice in early years professional development. *Early Years*, 35(4), 381–93.

Tajfel, H. and Billig, M. (1974). Familiarity and categorization in intergroup behavior. *Journal of Experimental Social Psychology*, 10, 159–70.

Tajfel, H. and Turner, J. C. (1979). An integrative theory of intergroup conflict. In W. G. Austin and S. Worchel (eds), *The Social Psychology of Intergroup Relations* (pp 33–47). Monterey, CA. Brooks/Cole.

Takeuchi, T., Miyasita, A., Inugami, M., and Yamamoto, Y. (2001). Intrinsic dreams are not produced without REM sleep mechanisms. Evidence through elicitation of sleep onset REM periods. *Journal of Sleep Research*, 10, 43–52.

Talmi, D., Grady, C. L., Goshen-Gottstein, Y., and Moscovitch, M. (2005). Neuroimaging the serial position curve. A test of single-store versus dual-store models. *Psychological Science*, 16, 716–23.

Tan, W. C., Lo, C., Jong, A., Xing, L., Fitzgerald, M. J., et al (2009). Marijuana and chronic obstructive lung disease. A population-based study. *CMAJ*, 180, 814–20.

Tang, N. K., Fiecas, M., Afolalu, E. F., and Wolke, D. (2017). Changes in sleep duration, quality, and medication use are prospectively associated with health and well-being. Analysis of the UK household longitudinal study. *Sleep*, 40(3), zsw079.

Tangney, J. P., Baumeister, R. F., and Boone, A. L. (2004). High self-control predicts good adjustment, less pathology, better grades, and interpersonal success. *Journal of Personality*, 72, 271–324.

Tanner-Smith, E. E. (2006). Pharmacological content of tablets sold as 'ecstasy'. Results from an online testing service. *Drug and Alcohol Dependence*, 83, 247–54.

Tarone, R. E., Blot, W. J., and McLaughlin, J. K. (2004). Nonselective nonaspirin nonsteroidal anti-inflammatory drugs and gastrointestinal bleeding. Relative and absolute risk estimates from recent epidemiologic studies. *American Journal of Therapy*, 11, 17–25.

Tart, C. T. (1972). States of consciousness and state-specific sciences. *Science*, 176, 1203–10.

Tasca, G. A. and Balfour, L. (2014). Attachment and eating disorders. A review of current research. *International Journal of Eating Disorders*, 47(7), 710–17.

Tavris, C. (1984). On the wisdom of counting to ten. Personal and social dangers of anger expression. *Review of Personality and Social Psychology*, 5, 170–91.

Tavris, C. (1989). *Anger. The Misunderstood Emotion*. New York, NY. Touchstone.

Tavris, C. (1992). *The Mismeasure of Women*. New York, NY. Touchstone.

Tavris, C. and Aronson, E. (2007). *Mistakes Were Made (but not by Me). How We Justify Foolish Beliefs, Bad Decisions, and Hurtful Acts*. Orlando, FL. Harcourt.

Taylor, C. R. (2009). Product placement. A hot topic gets hotter. *International Journal of Advertising*, 28, 753–6.

Taylor, J. Y., Caldwell, C. H., Baser, R. E. Faison, N., and Jackson, J. S. (2007). Prevalence of eating disorders among Blacks in the national survey of American life. *International Journal of Eating Disorders*, 40(Suppl), S10–14.

Taylor, M., Hulette, A. C., and Dishion, T. J. (2010). Longitudinal outcomes of young high-risk adolescents with imaginary companions. *Developmental Psychology*, 46, 1632–6.

Taylor, P. (ed) (2010). *The Decline of Marriage and Rise of New Families*. Pew Research Center. Retrieved from http://pewsocialtrends.org/files/2010/11/pew-social-trends-2010-families.pdf on 7 March 2011

Taylor, S. E. (1989). *Positive Illusions*. New York, NY. Basic Books.

Taylor, S. E. (1999). *Health Psychology* (4th edn). Boston, MA. McGraw-Hill.

Taylor, S. E. (2002). *The Tending Instinct. How Nurturing is Essential to Who We Are and How We Live*. New York, NY. Holt.

Taylor, S. E. (2006). Tend and befriend. Biobehavioral bases of affiliation under stress. *Current Directions in Psychological Science*, 15, 273–7.

Taylor, S. E. and Brown, J. D. (1988). Illusion and well-being. A social psychological perspective on mental health. *Psychological Bulletin*, 103, 193–210.

Taylor, S. E. and Brown, J. D. (1994). 'Illusion' of mental health does not explain positive illusions. *American Psychologist*, 49, 972–3.

Taylor, S. E. and Brown, J. D. (1994). Positive illusions revisited. Separating fact from fiction. *Psychological Bulletin*, 116, 21–7.

Taylor, S. E., Klein, L. C., Lewis, B. P., Gruenewald, T. L., Gurung, R. A. R., et al (2000). Biobehavioral responses to stress in females. Tend-and-befriend, not fight-or-flight. *Psychological Bulletin*, 107, 411–29.

Taylor, S. E., Lerner, J. S., Sherman, D. K., Sage, R. M., and McDowell, N. K. (2003). Are self-enhancing cognitions associated with healthy or unhealthy biological profiles? *Journal of Personality and Social Psychology*, 85, 605–15.

Taylor, S. E., Saphire-Bernstein, S., and Seeman, T. E. (2010). Are plasma oxytocin in women and plasma vasopressin in men biomarkers of distressed pair-bond relationships? *Psychological Science*, 21, 3–7.

Taylor, S. E., Sherman, D. K., Kim, H. S., Jarcho, J., Takagi, K., et al (2004). Culture and social support. Who seeks it and why? *Journal of Personality and Social Psychology*, 87, 354–62.

Taylor, S. E. and Stanton, A. L. (2007). Coping resources, coping processes, and mental health. *Annual Review of Clinical Psychology*, 3, 377–401.

Taylor, S. E., Welch, W. T., Kim, H. S., and Sherman, D. K. (2007). Cultural differences in the impact of social support on psychological and biological stress responses. *Psychological Science*, 18, 831–7.

Terracciano, A., Abdel-Khalak, A. M., Ádám, N., Adamovová, L., Ahn, C.-k., et al (2005). National character does not reflect mean personality trait levels in 49 cultures. *Science*, 310, 96–100.

Terracciano, A., Costa, P. T., and McCrae, R. R. (2006). Personality plasticity after age 30. *Personality and Social Psychology Bulletin*, 32, 999–1009.

Terrace, H. (1987). *Nim*. New York, NY. Columbia University Press.

Tesser, A., Crepaz, N., Collins, J., Cornell, D., and Beach, S. (2000). Confluence of self-esteem regulation mechanisms. On integrating the self-zoo. *Personality and Social Psychology Bulletin*, 26, 1476–89.

Tett, R. P. and Burnett, D. D. (2003). A personality trait-based interactionist model of job performance. *Journal of Applied Psychology*, 88, 500–17.

The Harris Poll (2003, 26 February). The religious and other beliefs of Americans. Poll #11. Retrieved from http://www.harrisinteractive.com/ harris_poll/index.asp?PID=359 on 20 November 2007.

The Innocence Project (2010). Facts on post-conviction DNA exonerations. Retrieved from http://www.innocenceproject.org/Content/Facts_on_PostConviction_DNA_Exonerations.php on 14 February 2013.

The Williams Institute (2010). Census snapshot. 1010. Retrieved from http://services.law.ucla.edu/williamsinstitute/home.html on 3 September 2010.

Theoret, H., Merabet, L., and Pascual-Leone, A. (2004). Behavioral and neuroplastic changes in the blind. Evidence for functionally relevant cross-modal interactions. *Journal of Physiology, Paris*, 98, 221–33.

Thiessen, V. and Looker, D. E. (1999). Diverse directions. Young adults' multiple transitions. In W. R. Heinz (ed), *From Education to Work. Cross-national Perspectives* (pp 46–64). New York, NY. Cambridge University Press.

Thomaes, S., Bushman, B. J., de Castro, B. O., Cohen, G. L., and Denissen, J. J. A. (2009). Reducing narcissistic aggression by buttressing self-esteem. *Psychological Science*, 20, 1536–42.

Thomas, M. (2004). *Universal Grammar in Second Language Acquisition. A History.* London. Routledge.

Thompson, C. P., Skowronski, J. J., Larsen, S. F., and Betz, A. (1996). *Autobiographical Memory. Remembering What and Remembering When*. Hillsdale, NJ. Lawrence Erlbaum Associates.

Thompson, E. M. and Morgan, E. M. (2008). 'Mostly straight' young women. Variations in sexual identity development. *Developmental Psychology*, 44, 15–21.

Thompson, R. A. and Raikes, H. A. (2003). Toward the next quarter-century. Conceptual and methodological challenges for attachment theory. *Development and Psychopathology*, 15, 691–718.

Thompson, R. F. (2005). In search of memory traces. *Annual Review of Psychology*, 56, 1–23.

Thompson, S. (1990). Putting a big thing into a little hole. Teenage girls' accounts of sexual initiation. *The Journal of Sex Research*, 27, 341–62.

Thompson, S. (1995). *Going All the Way. Teenage Girls' Tales of Sex, Romance and Pregnancy*. New York, NY. Hill and Wang.

Thorndike, E. L. (1898). Animal intelligence. An experimental study of the associative process in animals. *Psychological Review Monograph Supplement*, 2, 1–8.

Thornhill, R. and Gangestad, S. (2006). Facial sexual dimorphism, developmental stability, and susceptibility to disease in men and women. *Evolution and Human Behavior*, 27, 131–44.

Thornton, L. M., Mazzeo, S. E., and Bulik, C. M. (2011). The heritability of eating disorders. Methods and current findings. In R. A. H. Adan and W. H. Kaye (eds), *Behavioral Neurobiology of Eating Disorders. Current Topics in Behavioral Neurosciences* (pp 141–56). New York, NY. Springer-Verlag.

Thorton, A. and Young-DeMarco, L. (2001). Four decades of trends in attitudes toward family issues in the United States. The 1960s through the 1990s. *Journal of Marriage and Family*, 63, 1009–37.

Thurstone, L. (1938). Primary mental abilities. *Psychometric Monographs (No 1)*. Chicago. Chicago University Press.

Thurstone, L. L. and Thurstone, T. G. (1941). Factorial studies of intelligence. *Psychometric Monographs (No 2)*. Chicago. Chicago University Press.

Tilburt, J. C., Emanuel, E. J., Kaptchuk, T. J., Curlin, F. A., and Miller, F. G. (2008). Prescribing 'placebo treatments.' Results of national survey of US internists and rheumatologists. *BMJ*, 337. Retrieved from www.bmj.com on 17 December 2008.

Timimi, S. (2013). No more psychiatric labels. Campaign to abolish psychiatric diagnostic systems such as ICD and DSM (CAPSID). *Self and Society*, 40(4), 6–14.

Timmins, F. and de Vries, J. M. (2015). Follow the yellow brick road—the compassion deficit debate where to from here? *Journal of Clinical Nursing*, 24(19–20), 2689–94.

Tinbergen, N. (1974). *Animal Behavior*. Boston, MA. Little Brown and Co.

Tobler, P. N., Fiorello, C. D., and Schultz, W. (2005). Adaptive coding of reward value by dopamine neurons. *Science*, 307, 1642–5.

Tolman, E. C. (1923). The nature of instinct. *Psychological Bulletin*, 20, 200–18.

Tolman, E. C. (1948). Cognitive maps in rats and men. *Psychological Review*, 55, 198–208.

Tolman, E. C. and Honzik, C. H. (1930). Introduction and removal of reward and maze performance in rats. *Publications in Psychology*, 4, 257–75.

Tomasello, M. and Herrmann, E. (2010). Ape and human cognition. What's the difference? *Current Directions in Psychological Science*, 19, 3–8.

Tooby, J. and Cosmides, L. (1992). The psychological foundations of culture. In J. H. Barkow, L. Cosmides, and J. Tooby (eds), *The Adapted Mind. Evolutionary Psychology and the Generation of Culture* (pp 19–136). New York, NY. Oxford University Press.

Tooby, J. and Cosmides, L. (2005). Conceptual foundations of evolutionary psychology. In D. M. Buss (ed), *The Handbook of Evolutionary Psychology* (pp 5–67). Hoboken, NJ. John Wiley and Sons.

Toosi, N. R., Babbitt, L. G., Ambady, N., and Sommers, S. R. (2011). Dyadic interracial interactions. A meta-analysis. *Psychological Bulletin*, 138, 1–27.

Topolinski, S. and Reber, R. (2010). Gaining insight into the 'Aha' experience. *Current Directions in Psychological Science*, 19, 402–5.

Tori, C. D. and Bilmes, M. (2002). Multiculturalism and psychoanalytic psychology. The validation of a defense mechanisms measure in an Asian population. *Psychoanalytic Psychology*, 19(4), 701.

Toronchuk, J. A. and Ellis, G. F. R. (2007). Disgust. Sensory affect or primary emotional system? *Cognition and Emotion*, 21, 1799–1818.

Torralba, A. and Olivia, A. (2003). Statistics of natural image categories. *Network. Computation in Neural Systems*, 14, 391–412.

Torres, A. R., Prince, M. J., Bebbington, P. E., Bhugra, D., Brugha, T. S., et al (2006). Obsessive-compulsive disorder. Prevalence, comorbidity, impact, and help-seeking in the British National Psychiatric Morbidity Survey of 2000. *American Journal of Psychiatry*, 163, 1978–85.

Tortora, G. J. and Derrickson, B. (2006). *Principles of Anatomy and Physiology* (12th edn). New York, NY. John Wiley and Sons.

Tovée, M. J., Swami, V., Furnham, A., and Mangalparsad, R. (2006). Changing perceptions of attractiveness as observers are exposed to a different culture. *Evolution and Human Behavior*, 27, 443–56.

Townsend, E. (2007). Suicide terrorists. Are they suicidal? *Suicide and Life-Threatening Behavior*, 37, 35–49.

Townsend, J. M. and Wasserman, T. H. (2011). Sexual hookups among college students. Sex differences in emotional reactions. *Archives of Sexual Behavior*, 40, 1173–81.

Trachtenberg, J. T., Chen, B. E., Knott, G. W., Feng, G., Sanes, J. R., et al (2002). Long-term *in vivo* imaging of experience-dependent synaptic plasticity in adult cortex. *Nature*, 420, 788–94.

Traeen, B., Stigum, H., and Sørensen, D. (2002). Sexual diversity in urban Norwegians. *The Journal of Sex Research*, 39, 249–59.

Trappey, C. (1996). A meta-analysis of consumer choice and subliminal advertising. *Psychology and Marketing*, 13, 517–30.

Tremblay, A., Boule, N., Doucet, E., and Woods, S. C. (2005). Is the insulin resistance syndrome the price to be paid to achieve body weight stability? *International Journal of Obesity*, 29, 1295–8.

Tremblay-Leveau, H. and Nadel, J. (1996). Exclusion in triads. Can it serve 'meta-communicative' knowledge in 11- and 23-month-old children? *British Journal of Developmental Psychology*, 14(2), 145–58.

Trionfi, G. and Reese, E. (2009). A good story. Children with imaginary companions create richer narratives. *Child Development*, 80, 1301–13.

Trivedi, M. H., Greer, T. L., Grannemann, B. D., Chambliss, H. O., and Jordan, A. N. (2006). Exercise as an augmentation strategy for treatment of major depression. *Journal of Psychiatric Practice*, 12, 205–13.

Trivers, R. (1971). The evolution of reciprocal altruism. *Quarterly Review of Biology*, 46, 35–57.

Trivers, R. (2002). *Natural Selection and Social Theory*. Oxford, UK. Oxford University Press.

Trivers, R. (2010). Deceipt and self-deception. In P. Kappeler and J. Silk (eds), *Mind the Gap. Tracing the Origins of Human Universals* (pp 373–93). Berlin. Springer-Verlag.

Trivers, R. (2011). *The Folly of Fools. The Logic of Deceit and Self-Deception in Human Life*. New York, NY. Basic Books

Trivers, R. L. (1972). Parental investment and sexual selection. In B. Campbell (ed), *Sexual Selection and the Descent of Man, 1871–1971* (pp 136–79). Chicago, IL. Aldine.

Trottier, K., Polivy, J., and Herman, C. P. (2009). Effects of resolving to change one's own behavior. Expectations vs. experience. *Behavior Therapy*, 40, 164–70.

Trzesniewski, K. H. and Donnellan, M. B. (2010). Rethinking 'Generation Me'. A study of cohort effects from 1976–2006. *Perspectives in Psychological Science*, 5, 58–75.

Tsai, G. E., Condie, D., Wu, M.-T, and Chang, I.-W. (1999). Functional magnetic resonance imaging of personality switches in a woman with dissociative identity disorder. *Harvard Review of Psychiatry*, 7, 119–22.

Tsai, J. L. (2007). Ideal affect. Cultural causes and behavioral consequences. *Perspectives on Psychological Science*, 2, 242–59.

Tsai, J. L., Knutson, B. K., and Fung, H. H. (2006). Cultural variation in affect valuation. *Journal of Personality and Social Psychology*, 90, 288–307.

Tsai, J. L., Louie, J., Chen, E., and Uchida, Y. (2007). Learning what feelings to desire. Socialization of ideal affect through children's storybooks. *Personality and Social Psychology Bulletin*, 33, 17–30.

Tsao, D. Y., Freiwald, W. A., Tootell, R. B. H., and Livingstone, M. S. (2006). A cortical region consisting entirely of face-selective cells. *Science*, 311, 670–4.

Tse, C.-S. and Altarriba, J. (2008). Evidence against linguistic relativity in Chinese and English. A case of spatial and temporal metaphors. *Journal of Cognition and Culture*, 8, 335–57.

Tseng, W.-S. (2004). Culture and psychotherapy. Asian perspectives. *Journal of Mental Health*, 13, 151–61.

Tucker-Drob, E. M., Rhemtulla, M., Harden, K. P., Turkheimer, E., and Fask, D. (2011). Emergence of a gene × socioeconomic status interaction on infant mental ability between 10 months and 2 years. *Psychological Science*, 22, 125–33.

Tulving, E. (1972). Episodic and semantic memory. In E. Tulving and W. Donaldson (eds), *Organization of Memory* (pp 381–403). New York, NY. Academic Press.

Tulving, E. (2002). Episodic memory. From mind to brain. *Annual Review of Psychology*, 53, 1–25.

Tulving, E. and Craik, F. I. M. (eds) (2000). *The Oxford Handbook of Memory*. New York, NY. Oxford University Press.

Turati, C., Bulf, H., and Simion, F. (2008). Newborns' face recognition over changes in viewpoint. *Cognition*, 106, 1300–21.

Turati, C., Valenza, E., Leo, I., and Simion, F. (2005). Three-month-olds' visual preference for faces and its underlying visual processing mechanisms. *Journal of Experimental Child Psychology*, 90, 255–73.

Turiel, E., Killen, M., and Helwig, C. C. (1987). Morality. Its structure, function, and vagaries. In J. Kagan and S. Lamb (eds), *The Emergence of Morality in Young Children* (pp 155–243). Chicago, IL. University of Chicago Press.

Turkheimer, E., Haley, A., Waldron, M., D'Onofrio, B., and Gottesman, I. I. (2003). Socioeconomic status modifies heritability of IQ in young children. *Psychological Science*, 14, 623–8.

Turkheimer, E. and Waldron, M. (2000). Nonshared environment. A theoretical, methodological, and quantitative review. *Psychological Bulletin*, 126, 78–108.

Turner, E. H., Matthews, A. M., Linardatos, E., Tell, R. A., and Rosenthal, R. (2008). Selective publication of antidepressant trials and its influence on apparent efficacy. *New England Journal of Medicine*, 358, 252–60.

Turner, R. A., Altemus, M., Yip, D. N., Kupferman, E., Fletcher, D., et al (2002). Effects of positive and negative emotion on oxytocin, prolactin and ACTH in women. *Stress*, 5, 269–76.

Tversky, A. and Kahneman, D. (1973). Availability. A heuristic for judging frequency and probability. *Cognitive Psychology*, 5, 207–32.

Tversky, A. and Kahneman, D. (1974). Judgment under uncertainty. Heuristics and biases. *Science*, 185, 1124–31.

Tversky, A. and Kahneman, D. (2005) Judgment under uncertainty. Heuristics and biases. In A. Tversky and D. Kahneman (eds), *Negotiation, Decision Making, and Conflict Management* (Vols 1–3, pp 251–8). Northampton, MA. Edward Elgar Publishing.

Tversky, A. and Kahneman, D. (2005). *Judgment under Uncertainty. Heuristics and Biases*. North Hampton, MA. Edward Elgar Publishing.

Twenge, J. M. and Campbell, W. K. (2010). Birth cohort differences in the monitoring the future dataset and elsewhere. Further evidence for Generation Me—commentary on Trzesniewski and Donnellan (2010). *Perspectives in Psychological Science*, 5, 81–8.

Twenge, J. M., Campbell, K. W., and Freeman, E. C. (2012). Generational differences in young adults' life goals, concern for others, and civic orientation, 1966–2009. *Journal of Personality and Social Psychology*, 102, 1045–62.

U.S. Bureau of the Census (2010a, 10 November). U.S. Census Bureau reports men and women wait longer to marry. Retrieved from http://www.census.gov/newsroom/releases/archives/families_households/cb10-174.html on 2 September 2011.

U.S. Bureau of the Census (2010b). Families and living arrangements. Retrieved from http://www.census.gov/population/www/socdemo/hh-fam/cps2010.html on 2 September 2011.

U.S. Food and Drug Administration (2004). FDA Public Health Advisory, 15 October 2004. Retrieved from http://www.fda.gov/safety/medwatch/safetyinformation/safetyalertsforhumanmedicalproducts/ucm155488.htm on 30 July 2005.

U.S. National Center for Health Statistics (1995). Advance report of final divorce statistics, 1989 and 1990. *Monthly Vital Statistics Report*, 43, 1–31.

U.S. National Center for Health Statistics (2006). Births, marriages, divorces, and deaths. *National Vital Statistics Reports*, 54, 1–6.

U.S. National Center for Health Statistics (2010). Births marriages, divorces, and deaths. Provisional data for 2009. *National Vital Statistics Reports*, 58. Retrieved from http://www.cdc.gov/nchs on 8 March 2011.

U.S. National Commission on Marihuana and Drug Abuse (1972). *Marihuana. A signal of misunderstanding*. Retrieved from http://www.druglibrary.org/schaffer/Library/studies/nc/ncmenu.htm on 4 February 2006.

Uchino, B. N., Uno, D., and Holt-Lunstad, J. (1999). Social support, physiological processes and health. *Current Directions in Psychological Science*, 8, 145–8.

UK ECT Review Group (2003). Efficacy and safety of electroconvulsive therapy in depressive disorders. A systematic review and meta-analysis. *The Lancet*, 361, 799–808.

Uller, C., Carey, S., Huntley-Fenner, G., and Klatt, L. (1999). What representations might underlie infant numerical knowledge? *Cognitive Development*, 14, 1–36.

Ullian, E. M., Sapperstein, S. K., Christopherson, K. S., and Barres, B. A. (2001). Control of synapse number by glia. *Science*, 291, 657–60.

Ulrich-Lai, Y. M. and Herman, J. P. (2009). Neural regulation of endocrine and autonomic stress responses. *Nature Reviews. Neuroscience*, 10, 397–409.

Umberson, D. (1992). Gender, marital status and the social control of health behavior. *Social Science and Medicine*, 34, 907–17.

Umberson, D., Crosnoe, R., and Reczek, C. (2010). Social relationships and health behavior across the life course. *Annual Review of Sociology*, 36, 139–57.

Unger, R. K. (1979). Toward a redefinition of sex and gender. *American Psychologist*, 34, 1085–94.

United Nations Office on Drugs and Crime (2004). *United Nations World Drug Report, 2004*. Retrieved from http://www.unodc.org/unodc/world_drug_report.html on 14 April 2006.

United Nations Office on Drugs and Crime (2010). *United Nations World Drug Report, 2010. Executive Summary*. Retrieved from http://www.unodc.org/unodc/en/data-and-analysis/WDR-2010.html on 12 March 2010.

United Nations Statistics (2000). World marriage patterns 2000. Department of Economic and Social Affairs, Population Division. Retrieved from http://www.un.org/esa/population/publications on 14 May 2006.

Uosukainen, H., Tacke, U., and Winstock, A. R. (2015). Self-reported prevalence of dependence of MDMA compared to cocaine, mephedrone and ketamine among a sample of recreational poly-drug users. *International Journal of Drug Policy*, 26(1), 78–83.

Üstün, T. B., Ayuso-Mateos, J. L., Chatterji, S., Mathers, C., and Murray, C. J. L. (2004). Global burden of depressive disorders in the year 2000. *British Journal of Psychiatry*, 184, 286–392.

Utsey, S., Giesbrecht, N., Hook, J., and Stanard, P. M. (2008). Cultural, sociofamilial, and psychological resources that inhibit psychological distress in African Americans exposed to stressful life events and race-related stress. *Journal of Counseling Psychology*, 55, 49–62.

Uttal, W. R. (2001). *The New Phrenology. The Limits of Localizing Cognitive Processes in the Brain*. Cambridge, MA. MIT Press.

Uvnas-Moberg, K. (1997). Oxytocin linked antistress effects—the relaxation and growth response. *Acta Psychologica Scandanavica*, 640(Suppl), 38–42.

Vaillant, G. (2002). *Aging Well. Surprising Guideposts to a Happier Life from the Landmark Harvard Study of Adult Development*. Boston, MA. Little, Brown and Company.

Vaillant, G. E. (1977). *Adaptation to Life*. Boston, MA. Little, Brown.

Valdesolo, P. and DeSteno, D. (2008). The duality of virtue. Deconstructing the moral hypocrite. *Journal of Experimental Social Psychology*, 44, 1334–8.

Valenstein, E. S. (1998). *Blaming the Brain*. New York, NY. Free Press.

Valkenburg, P. M. and Peter, J. (2009a). The effects of instant messaging on the quality of adolescents' existing friendships. A longitudinal study. *Journal of Communication*, 59, 79–97.

Valkenburg, P. M. and Peter, J. (2009b). Social consequences of the Internet for adolescents. *Current Directions in Psychological Science*, 18, 1–5.

Valla, J. M. and Ceci, S. J. (2011). Can sex differences in science be tied to the long reach of prenatal hormones? Brain organization theory, digit ratio (2D/4D), and sex differences in preferences and cognition. *Perspectives on Psychological Science*, 6, 134–46.

Valli, K., Revonsuo, A., Palkas, O., Ismail, K. H., Ali, K. J., et al (2005). The threat simulation theory of the evolutionary function of dreaming. Evidence from the dreams of traumatized children. *Consciousness and Cognition*, 14, 188–218.

Valli, K., Strandholm, T., Sillanmaiki, L., and Revonsuo, A. (2008). Dreams are more negative than real life. Implications for the function of dreaming. *Cognition and Emotion*, 22, 833–61.

Valtin, H. (2002). 'Drink at least eight glasses of water a day'. Really? Is there scientific evidence for '8×8'? *American Journal of Physiology*, 283, R993–1004.

Van Bavel, J. J., Packer, D. J., and Cunningham, W. A. (2008). The neural substrates of in-group bias. *Psychological Science*, 19, 1131–9.

Van Berkum, J. J. A., Holleman, B., Nieuwland, M., Otten, M., and Murre, J. (2009). Right or wrong? The brain's fast response to morally objectionable statements. *Psychological Science*, 20, 1092–9.

van Bokhoven, I., van Goozen, S. H. M., van Engeland, H., Schaal, B., Arseneault, L., et al (2006). Salivary testosterone and aggression, delinquency, and social dominance in a population-based longitudinal study of adolescent males. *Hormones and Behavior*, 50, 118–25.

van den Berghe, P. L. (2009). Sexual selection and social roles. Two models or one? *Behavioral and Brain Sciences*, 32, 291–2.

van der Heiden, C., Methorst, G., Muris, P., and van der Molen, H. T. (2011). Generalized anxiety disorder. Clinical presentation, diagnostic features, and guidelines for clinical practice. *Journal of Clinical Psychology*, 67, 58–73.

van der Lely, H. K., Rosen, S., and McClelland, A. (1998). Evidence for a grammar-specific deficit in children. *Current Biology*, 8, 1253–8.

van Duinen, H., Lorist, M. M., and Zijdewind, I. (2005). The effect of caffeine on cognitive task performance and motor fatigue. *Psychopharmacology*, 180, 539–47.

Van Duuren, M., Kendell-Scott, L., and Stark, N. (2003). Early aesthetic choices. Infant preference for attractive premature infant faces. *International Journal of Behavioral Development*, 27, 212–19.

Van Dyk, G. A. J. and Nefale, M. C. (2005). The split-ego experience of Africans. Ubuntu therapy as a healing alternative. *Journal of Psychotherapy Integration*, 15(1), 48–66.

van Giezen, A. E., Arensman, E., Spinhoven, P., and Wolters, G. (2005). Consistency of memory for emotionally arousing events. A review of prospective and experimental studies. *Clinical Psychology Review*, 25, 935–53.

Vandell, D. L. (2000). Parents, peer groups, and other socializing influences. *Developmental Psychology*, 36, 699–710.

Vandell, D. L., Belsky, J., Burchinal, M., Steinberg, L., Vandergrift, N., and NICHD Early Child Care Research Network. (2010). Do effects of early child care extend to age 15 years? Results from the NICHD study of early child care and youth development. *Child development*, 81(3), 737–56.

Vandell, D. L., Wilson, K. S., and Buchanan, N. R. (1980). Peer interaction in the first year of life. An examination of its structure, content, and sensitivity to toys. *Child Development*, 481–8.

Vargas, P. T. (2008). Implicit consumer cognition. In P. C. Haugtvedt, P. M. Herr, and F. R. Kardes (eds) *Handbook of Consumer Psychology* (pp 477–504). New York, NY. Taylor and Francis Group/ Lawrence Erlbaum Associates.

Vargha-Khadem, F., Gadian, D. G., Copp, A., and Mishkin, M. (2005). *FOXP2* and the neuroanatomy of speech and language. *Nature Reviews Neuroscience*, 6, 131–8.

Vargha-Khadem, F., Gadian, D. G., Watkins, K. E., Connelly, A., Van Paesschen, W., et al (1997). Differential effects of early hippocampal pathology on episodic and semantic memory. *Science*, 277, 376–80.

Värnick, P. (2012). Suicide in the world. *International Journal of Environmental Research and Public Health*, 9, 760–71.

Varnum, M. E. W., Grossmann, I, Kitayama, S., and Nisbett, R. E. (2010). The origin of cultural differences in cognition. The social orientation hypothesis. *Current Directions in Psychological Science*, 19, 9–13.

Varvoglis, M. (1997). What is PSI? What isn't? Retrieved from http://www .parapsych.org/what_is_psi_varvoglis.htm on 12 September 2006.

Vazire, S. and Gosling, S. D. (2004). E-perceptions. Personality impressions based on personal websites. *Journal of Personality and Social Psychology*, 87, 123–32.

Vedantam, S. (2006, 12 April). Comparison of schizophrenia drugs often favors firm funding study. *Washington Post*. Retrieved from http://www. washingtonpost.com/wp-dyn/content/ article/2006/04/11/AR2006041101478. html on 8 June 2008.

Verney, S. P., Granholm, E., Marshall, S. P., Malcame, V. L., and Saccuzo, D. P. (2005). Culture fair cognitive ability assessment. Information processing and psycho-physiological approaches. *Assessment*, 12, 303–19.

Vicente, K. J. (2000). Is science an evolutionary process? Evidence from miscitations of the scientific literature. *Perspectives on Science*, 8(1), 53–69.

Vichi, M., Masocco, M., Pompili, M., Lester, D., Tatarelli, R., et al (2010). Suicide mortality in Italy from 1980 to 2002. *Psychiatry Research*, 175(1–2), 89–97.

Viglione, D. J. and Taylor, N. (2003). Empirical support for interrater reliability of Rorschach comprehensive system coding. *Journal of Clinical Psychology*, 59, 111–21.

Vineis, P., Alavanja, M., Buffler, P., Fontham, E., Franceschi, S., et al (2004). Tobacco and cancer. Recent epidemiological evidence. *Journal of the National Cancer Institute*, 96, 99–106.

Vizcarral, M. B., Balladares, E., Candia, C., Lepe, M., and Saldivia, C. (2004). Sexual behavior during childhood, as reported later, during high school years. *Psicothema*, 16(1), 58–63.

Voas, D. (2007). Ten million marriages. An astrological detective story. *Skeptical Inquirer*, 32, 53–5.

Vocisano, C., Klein, D. N., Arnow, B., Rivera, C., Blalock, J. A., et al (2004). Therapist variables that predict symptom change in psychotherapy with chronically depressed outpatients. *Psychotherapy. Theory, Research, Practice, Training*, 41, 255–65.

Vogel, G. W. (2000). Critique of current dream theories. *Behavioral and Brain Sciences*, 23, 1014–16.

Vogel, T. and Wanke, M. (2016). *Attitudes and Attitude Change*. Hove, UK. Psychology Press.

Voland, E. and Grammer, K. (eds) (2003). *Evolutionary Aesthetics*. New York, NY. Springer.

von Frisch, K. (1967). *A Biologist Remembers*. Oxford, UK. Pergamon Press.

von Hippel, W. and Trivers, R. (2011). The evolution and psychology of self-deception. *Behavioral and Brain Sciences*, 34, 1–56.

Voss, U., Holzmann, R., Tuin, I., and Hobson, A. J. (2009). Lucid dreaming. A state of consciousness with features of both waking and non-lucid dreaming. *Sleep. Journal of Sleep and Sleep Disorders Research*, 32, 1191–1200.

Vouloumanos, A. and Werker, J. F. (2007). Listening to language at birth. Evidence for a bias for speech in neonates. *Developmental Science*, 10, 159–64.

Vrij, A. (2008). *Detecting Lies and Deceit. Pitfalls and Opportunities* (2nd edn). Chichester, UK. John Wiley and Sons.

Vrij, A., Granhag, P. A., Mann, S., and Leal, S. (2011). Outsmarting the liars. Toward a cognitive lie detection approach. *Current Directions in Psychological Science*, 20, 28–32.

Vrij, A., Mann, S., Robbins, E., and Robinson, M. (2006). Police officers ability to detect deception in high stakes situations and in repeated lie detection tests. *Applied Cognitive Psychology*, 20, 741–55.

Vul, E., Harris, C., Winkielman, P., and Pashler, H. (2009). Puzzlingly high correlations in fMRI studies of emotion, personality, and social cognition. *Perspectives on Psychological Science*, 4, 274–90.

Vyazovskiy V. V., Cirelli, C., Pfister-Genskow, M., Faraguna, U., and Tononi, G. (2008). Molecular and electrophysiological evidence for net synaptic potentiation in wake and depression in sleep. *Nature Neuroscience*, 11, 200–8.

Vygotsky, L. S. (1929). The problem of the cultural development of the child. *Journal of Genetic Psychology*, 36, 415–32. Retrieved from http://www.marxists.org/archive/vygotsky/works/1929/cultural_development.htm on 29 January 2014.

Waber, R. L., Shiv, B., Carmon, Z., and Ariely, D. (2008). Commercial features of placebo and therapeutic efficacy. *JAMA*, 299, 1016–17.

Wada, Y. and Yamamoto, T. (2001). Selective impairment of facial recognition due to a haematoma restricted to the right fusiform and lateral occipital region. *Journal of Neurology and Neurosurgery in Psychiatry*, 71, 254–7.

Wadden, T. A., Brownell, K. D., and Foster, G. D. (2002). Obesity. Responding to the global epidemic. *Journal of Consulting and Clinical Psychology*, 70, 510–25.

Wadsworth, S. J., Corley, R. P., Hewitt, J. K., Plomin, R., and DeFries, J. C. (2002). Parent-offspring resemblance for reading performance at 7, 12, and 16 years of age in the Colorado Adoption Project. *Journal of Child Psychology and Psychiatry*, 43, 769–74.

Wagenmakers, E-J., Wetzels, R., Bordsboom, D., Kievit, R. and van der Maas, H. (2018). A skeptical eye on Psi. Retrieved from https://www.researchgate.net/publication/291337813_A_Skeptical_Eye_on_Psi

Wagenmakers, E-J., Wetzels, R., Bordsboom, D., and van der Maas, H. (2011). Why psychologists must change the way they analyze their data. The case of psi. Comment on Bem. *Journal of Personality and Social Psychology*, 100, 426–32.

Wagner, F. A. and Anthony, J. C. (2002). From first drug use to drug dependence; developmental periods of risk for dependence upon marijuana, cocaine, and alcohol. *Neuropsychopharmacology*, 26, 479–88.

Wagstaff, G. (1994). Hypnosis. In A. M. Colman (ed), *Companion Encyclopedia of Psychology* (Vol 2, pp 991–1006). London. Routledge.

Wagstaff, G. F. (1999). Hypnosis and forensic psychology. In I. Kirsch, A. Capafons, and E. Cardeña-Buelna (eds), *Clinical Hypnosis and Self-regulation. Cognitive-behavioral Perspectives* (pp 277–308). Washington, DC. American Psychological Association.

Wagstaff, G. F., David, D., Kirsch, I., and Lynn, S. J. (2010). The cognitive-behavioral model of hypnotherapy. In S. J. Lynn, J. W. Rhue, and I. Kirsch (eds), *Handbook of Clinical Hypnosis* (2nd edn, pp 179–208). Washington, DC. American Psychological Association.

Wahba, M. A. and Bridwell, L. G. (1976). Maslow reconsidered. A review of research on the need hierarchy theory. *Organizational Behavior and Human Performance*, 15, 212–40.

Wai, J., Cacchio, M., Putallaz, M., and Makel, M. C. (2010). Sex differences in the right tail of cognitive abilities. A 30-year examination. *Intelligence*, 38, 412–23.

Wakefield, J. C. (1992). The concept of mental disorder. On the boundary between biological facts and social values. *American Psychologist*, 47, 373–88.

Wakefield, J. C. (1999). Evolutionary versus prototype analyses of the concept of disorder. *Journal of Abnormal Psychology*, 108, 374–99.

Wakefield, J. C. (2003). Dysfunction as a factual component of disorder. Reply to Houts, Part 2. *Behaviour Research and Therapy*, 41, 969–90.

Wakefield, J. C. (2010). Taking disorder seriously. A critique of psychiatric criteria for mental disorders from the harmful-dysfunction perspective. In T. Millon, R. F. Krueger, and E. Simonsen (eds), *Contemporary Directions in Psychopathology. Scientific Foundations of the DSM-V and ICD-11* (pp 275–300). New York, NY. Guilford Press.

Wakefield, J. C., Horwitz, A. V., and Schmitz, M. F. (2005). Are we overpathologizing the socially anxious? Social phobia from a harmful dysfunction perspective. *Canadian Journal of Psychiatry*, 50, 317–19.

Wakefield, J. C., Schmitz, M. F., and Baer, J. C. (2010). Does the DSM-IV clinical significance criterion for major depression reduce false positives? Evidence from the National Comorbidity Survey Replication. *American Journal of Psychiatry*, 167, 298–304.

Wakefield, J. C., Schmitz, M. F., First, M. B., and Horwitz, A. V. (2007). Extending the bereavement exclusion for major depression to other losses. Evidence from the National Comorbidity Survey. *Archives of General Psychiatry*, 64, 433–40.

Wakeling, A. (1996). Epidemiology of anorexia nervosa. *Psychiatry Research*, 62, 3–9.

Walker, E., Kestler, L., Bollini, A., and Hochman, K. M. (2004). Schizophrenia. Etiology and course. *Annual Review of Psychology*, 55, 401–30.

Walker, E., Shapiro, D., Esterberg, M., and Trotman, H. (2010). Neurodevelopment and schizophrenia. Broadening the focus. *Current Directions in Psychological Science*, 19, 204–8.

Walker, M. P. and Stickgold, R. (2006). Sleep, memory, and plasticity. *Annual Review of Psychology*, 57, 139–66.

Walker, W. R., Vogl, R. J., and Thompson, C. P. (1997). Autobiographical memory. Unpleasantness fades faster than pleasantness over time. *Applied Cognitive Psychology. The Official Journal of the Society for Applied Research in Memory and Cognition*, 11(5), 399–413.

Wallen, K. (1996). Nature needs nurture. The influence of hormonal and social influences on the development of behavioral sex differences in rhesus monkeys. *Hormones and Behavior*, 30, 364–78.

Wallen, K. (2001). Sex and context. Hormones and primate sexual motivation. *Hormones and Behavior*, 40, 339–57.

Wallen, K. (2011). Female sexual arousal. Genital anatomy and orgasm in intercourse. *Hormones and Behavior*, 59, 780–92.

Waller, J. (2007). *Becoming Evil. How Ordinary People Commit Genocide and Mass Killing* (2nd edn). New York, NY. Oxford University Press.

Wallis, C. (2005, 9 January). The new science of happiness. *Time*, A2–68.

Walls, R. T. (2000). Vocational cognition. Accuracy of 3rd-, 6th-, 9th-, and 12th-grade students. *Journal of Vocational Behavior*, 56, 137–44.

Walton, S. (2002). *Out of It. A Cultural History of Intoxication.* New York, NY. Harmony.

Wampold, B. E. (2001). *The Great Psychotherapy Debate. Models, Methods, and Findings.* Mahwah, NJ. Lawrence Erlbaum Associates.

Wampold, B. E. (2007). Psychotherapy. The humanistic (and effective) treatment. *American Psychologist,* 62, 857–73.

Wampold, B. E. (2009). Clinical trials for the treatment of mental disorders. Two major flaws that limit interpretability. *The Canadian Journal of Psychiatry,* 54, 639–41.

Wampold, B. E. (2010). The research evidence for common factors models. A historically situated perspective. In B. L. Duncan, S. D. Miller, B. E. Wampold, and M. A. Hubble (eds), *The Heart and Soul of Change. Delivering What Works in Therapy* (2nd edn, pp 49–81). Washington DC. American Psychological Association.

Wampold, B. E., Budge, S. L., Laska, K. M., De Re, A. C., Baardseth, T. P., et al (2011). Evidence-based treatments for depression and anxiety versus treatments-as-usual. A meta-analysis of direct comparisons. *Clinical Psychology Review,* 31, 1304–12.

Wampold, B. E., Imel, Z. E., and Minami, T. (2007). The placebo effect. 'Relatively large' and 'robust' enough to survive another assault. *Journal of Clinical Psychology,* 63, 401–3.

Wampold, B. E., Minami, T., Baskin, T. W., and Tierney, S. C. (2002). Meta-(re)analysis of the effects of cognitive therapy versus 'other therapies' for depression. *Journal of Affective Disorders,* 68, 159–65.

Wampold, B. E., Minami, T., Tierney, S. C., Baskin, T. W., and Bhati, K. S. (2005). The placebo is powerful. Estimating placebo effects in medicine and psychotherapy from randomized clinical trials. *Journal of Clinical Psychology,* 63, 835–54.

Wang, S-H, Baillargeon, R., and Brueckner, L. (2004). Young infants' reasoning about hidden objects. Evidence from violation-of-expectation tasks with test trials only. *Cognition,* 93, 167–98.

Wang, Y. and Beydoun, M. A. (2007). The obesity epidemic in the United States—gender, age, socioeconomic, racial/ethnic, and geographic characteristics. A systematic review and meta-regression analysis. *Epidemiologic Reviews,* 29, 6–28.

Wankurl, M., Wüst, S., and Otte, C. (2010). Current developments and controversies.

Does the serotonin transporter gene-linked polymorphic region (5-HTTLPR) modulate the association between stress and depression? *Current Opinion in Psychiatry,* 23, 582–7.

Warner-Smith, M., Darke, S, Lynskey, M., and Hall, W. (2001). Heroin overdose. Causes and consequences. *Addiction,* 96, 1113–25.

Watkins, M. J. (2002). Limits and province of levels of processing. Considerations of a construct. *Memory,* 10, 339–43.

Watson C. P., Watt-Watson J. H., and Chipman, M. L. (2004). Chronic non-cancer pain and the long term utility of opioids. *Pain Research and Management,* 9, 19–24.

Watson, D., Suls, J., and Haig, J. (2002). Global self-esteem in relation to structural models of personality and affectivity. *Journal of Personality and Social Psychology,* 83, 185–97.

Watson, J. B. and Rayner, R. (1920). Conditioned emotional reactions. *Journal of Experimental Psychology,* 3, 1–14.

Watson, J. E., Darling, E. S., Venter, O., Maron, M., Walston, J., et al (2016). Bolder science needed now for protected areas. *Conservation Biology,* 30(2), 243–8.

Weaver, D. R. (1998). The suprachiasmatic nucleus. A 25-year retrospective. *Journal of Biological Rhythms,* 13, 100–12.

Webb, S. J., Monk, C. S., and Nelson, C. A. (2001). Mechanisms of postnatal neurobiological development. Implications for human development. *Developmental Neuropsychology,* 19, 147–71.

Webb, W. B. and Agnew, H. W. (1975). Are we chronically sleep deprived? *Bulletin of the Psychochronic Society,* 6, 47–8.

Webster, G. D., Kirkpatrick, L. S., Nezlek, J. B., Smith, C. V., and Paddock, E. L. (2007). Different slopes for different folks. Self-esteem instability and gender as moderators of the relationship between self-esteem and attitudinal aggression. *Self and Identity,* 6, 74–94.

Wechsler, D. (2014). *WISC-V. Administration and Scoring Manual.* NCS Pearson, Incorporated.

Weddington, W., Brown, B., Haertzen, C., Cone, E., Dax, E., et al (1990). Changes in mood, craving, and sleep during short-term abstinence reported by male cocaine addicts. a controlled, residential study. *Archives of General Psychiatry,* 47, 861–8.

Wei, W., Lu, H., Zhao, H., Chen, C., Dong, Q., et al (2012). Gender differences in children's arithmetic performance are accounted for by gender differences in language abilities. *Psychological Science.* Pre-publication version retrieved from http://pss.sagepub.com/content/early/2012/02/17/0956797611427168 on 4 March 2012.

Weiner, B. (1989). *Human Motivation.* Mahwah, NJ. Lawrence Erlbaum Associates.

Weiner, I. B., Spielberger, C. D., and Abeles, N. (2002). Scientific psychology and the Rorschach inkblot method. *The Clinical Psychologist,* 55, 7–12.

Weisberg, L. A., Garcia, C., and Strub, R. (1996). *Essentials of Clinical Neurology* (3rd edn). St Louis, MO. Mosby.

Weisfeld, G. E. (1999). *Evolutionary Principles of Human Adolescence.* New York, NY. Basic Books.

Weisner, T. S. and Wilson-Mitchell, J. E. (1990). Nonconventional family life-styles and sex typing in six-year-olds. *Child Development,* 61, 1915–33.

Weiss, A., Bates, T. C., and Luciano, M. (2008). Happiness is a personal(ity) thing. The genetics of personality and well-being in a representative sample. *Psychological Science,* 19, 205–10.

Welch, H. G., Schwartz, L. M., and Wologhin, S. (2011). *Overdiagnosed. Making People Sick in the Pursuit of Health.* Boston, MA. Beacon Press.

Wellman, H. M., Cross, D., and Watson, J. (2001). Meta-analysis of theory-of-mind development. The truth about false belief. *Child Development,* 72, 655–84.

Wells, G. L. and Bradfield, A. L. (1998). 'Good, you identified the suspect'. Feedback to eyewitnesses distorts their reports of the witnessing experience. *Journal of Applied Psychology,* 83, 360–76.

Wells, G. L., Malpass, R. S., Lindsay, R. C. L., Fisher, R. P., Turtle, J. W., et al (2000). From the lab to the police station. A successful application of eyewitness research. *American Psychologist,* 55, 581–98.

Wertheimer, M. (1950). Laws of organization in perceptual forms. In W. D. Ellis (ed), *A Sourcebook of Gestalt Psychology* (pp 71–81). New York, NY. Humanities Press. (Original work published 1923.)

West, K. K., Mathews, B. L., and Kerns, K. A. (2013). Mother–child attachment and cognitive performance in middle childhood. An examination of mediating mechanisms. *Early Childhood Research Quarterly*, 28(2), 259–70.

West Virginia OMCFH (Office of Maternal Child and Family Health). (2007). *Adolescent Health Profile*. Retrieved from www.wvdhhr.org on 27 October 2007.

Westen, D. (1991). Clinical assessment of object relations using the TAT. *Journal of Personality Assessment*, 56, 56–74.

Westen, D. (1998). The scientific legacy of Sigmund Freud. Toward a psychodynamically informed psychological science. *Psychological Bulletin*, 124, 333–71.

Westen, D. (2005). Implications of research in cognitive neuroscience for psychodynamic psychotherapy. In G. O. Gabbard, J. S. Beck, and J. Holmes (eds), *Oxford Textbook of Psychotherapy* (pp 443–8). New York, NY. Oxford University Press.

Westen, D. and Morrison, K. (2001). A multidimensional meta-analysis of treatments for depression, panic, and Generalized Anxiety Disorder. An empirical examination of the status of empirically supported therapies. *Journal of Consulting and Clinical Psychology*, 69, 875–99.

Westen, D., Novotny, C. M., and Thompson-Brenner, H. (2004). The empirical status of empirically supported psychotherapies. Assumptions, findings, and reporting in controlled clinical trials. *Psychological Bulletin*, 130, 631–63.

Westermann, G., Ruh, N., and Plunkett, K. (2009). Connectionist approaches to language learning. *Linguistics*, 47, 413–52.

Whalen, P. J., Davis, C. F., Oler, J. A., Kim, H., Kim, M., et al (2009). Human amygdale responses to facial expressions of emotion. In P. Whalen and E. A. Phelps (eds), *The Human Amygdale* (pp 265–88). New York, NY. Guilford Press.

Wheatley, D. (2006). St. John's Wort in depression. The patient's dilemma. *Primary Care and Community Psychiatry*, 11, 137–42.

Whitbourne, S. K., Sneed, J. R., and Sayer, A. (2009). Psychosocial development from college through midlife. A 34-year sequential study. *Developmental Psychology*, 45(5), 1328.

White, R. W. (1959). Motivation reconsidered. The concept of competence. *Psychological Review*, 66, 297–333.

Whiten, A., Goodall, J., McGrew, W. C., Nishida, T., Reynolds, V., et al (1999). Cultures in chimpanzees. *Nature*, 299, 682–5.

Whiten, A., Horner, V., and de Waal, F. B. M. (2005). Conformity to cultural norms of tool use in chimpanzees. *Nature*, 437, 737–40.

Whiten, A., Spiteri, A., Horner, V., Bonnie, C. E., Lambeth, S. P., et al (2007). Transmission of multiple traditions within and between chimpanzee groups. *Current Biology*, 17, 1–6.

Wicker, B., Keysers, C., Plailly, J., Royet, J-P., Gallese, V., et al (2003). Both of us disgusted in *my* instula. The common neural basis of seeing and feeling disgust. *Neuron*, 40, 655–64.

Widiger, T. A. (2011). A shaky future for personality disorders. *Personality Disorders. Theory, Research, and Treatment*, 2, 54–67.

Wilder, D. A. and Thompson, J. E. (1980). Intergroup contact with independent manipulations of in-group and out-group interaction. *Journal of Personality and Social Psychology*, 38, 589–603.

Wilkins, M. R. and the Working Party on Cannabis and Cannabis-Based Medicines. (2006). Cannabis and cannabis-based medicines. Potential benefits and risks to health. *Clinical Medicine*, 6, 16–18.

Willer, C. J., Speliotes, E. K., Loos, R. J. F., Li, S., Lindgren, C. M., et al (2008). Six new loci associated with body mass index highlight a neuronal influence on body weight regulation. *Nature Genetics*. Advance online publication retrieved from http://www.nature.com/ng on 17 December 2008.

Williams, G. C. (1966). *Adaptation and Natural Selection. A Critique of Some Current Evolutionary Thought*. Princeton, NJ. Princeton University Press.

Williams, J. E. and Best, D. L. (1990). *Sex and Psyche. Gender and Self Viewed Cross-culturally*. Newbury Park, CA. Sage Publications.

Williams J. W., Jr, Mulrow, C. D., Ciquette, E., Noel, P. H., Aquilar, C., et al (2000). A systematic review of newer pharmacotherapies for depression in adults. Evidence report summary. *Annals of Internal Medicine*, 132, 743–56.

Williams, K. D. (2001). *Ostracism. The Power of Silence*. New York, NY. Guilford Press.

Williams, K. D., Cheung, C. K. T., and Choi, W. (2000). CyberOstracism. Effects of being ignored over the internet. *Journal of Personality and Social Psychology*, 79, 748–62.

Williams, M., Teasdale, J., Segal, Z., and Kabat-Zinn, J. (2007). *The Mindful Way through Depression*. New York, NY. Guilford Press.

Williams, M. J., Sutherland, W. H., Whelan, A. P., McCormick, M. P., de Jong, S. A., et al (2004). Acute effect of drinking red and white wines on circulating levels of inflammation-sensitive molecules in coronary artery disease. *Metabolism*, 53, 318–23.

Williams, S. T., Ontai, L. L., and Mastergeorge, A. M. (2010). The development of peer interaction in infancy. Exploring the dyadic processes. *Social Development*, 19(2), 348–68.

Williams, W. and Ceci, S. J. (1998). *Escaping the Advice Trap*. Kansas City, MO. Andrews McMeel Publishing.

Williamson, D. A., Gleaves, D. H., and Stewart, T. M. (2005). Categorical versus dimensional models of eating disorders. An examination of the evidence. *International Journal of Eating Disorders*, 37, 1–10.

Willis, J. and Todorov, J. (2006). First impressions. Making up your mind after a 100-ms exposure to a face. *Psychological Science*, 17, 592–8.

Willis, S. L. and Schaie, K. W. (1999). Intellectual functioning in midlife. In S. L. Willis, and J. D. Reid (eds), *Life in the Middle. Psychological and Social Development in Middle Age* (pp 233–47). San Diego, CA. Academic Publishers.

Wills, T. A. (1981). Downward comparison principles in social psychology. *Psychological Bulletin*, 90, 245–71.

Wills, T. A. (1991). Social support and interpersonal relationships. In M. S. Clark (ed), *Prosocial Behavior* (pp 265–89). Newbury Park, CA. Sage.

Wilson, A. E. and Ross, M. (2001). From chump to champ. People's appraisals of their earlier and current selves. *Journal of Personality and Social Psychology*, 80, 572–84.

Wilson, A. E. and Ross, M. (2003). The identity function of autobiographical memory. Time is on our side. *Memory*, 11, 137–49.

Wilson, E. O. (1975). *Sociobiology, the New Synthesis*. Cambridge, MA. Harvard University Press.

Wilson, S. M., Saygin, A. P., Sereno, M. I., and Iacoboni, M. (2004). Listening to speech activates motor areas involved in speech production. *Nature Neuroscience*, 7, 701–2.

Wilson, T. D., DePaulo, B. M., Mook, D. G., and Klaaren, K. J. (1993). Scientists' evaluations of research. the biasing effects of the importance of the topic. *Psychological Science*, 4(5), 322–5.

Wimmer, H. and Perner, J. (1983). Beliefs about beliefs. Representation and the containing function of wrong beliefs in young children's understanding of deception. *Cognition*, 13, 103–28.

Winegard, B. M. and Deaner, R. O. (2014). Misrepresentations of evolutionary psychology in sex and gender textbooks. *Evolutionary Psychology*, 12(3), 147470491401200301.

Winkielman, P., Niedenthal, P. M., and Oberman, L. (2008). The embodied emotional mind. In G. R. Semin and E. R. Smith (eds), *Embodied Grounding. Social Cognitive, Affective, and Neuroscientific Approaches* (pp 263–88). New York, NY. Cambridge University Press.

Winman, A. (2004). Do perfume additives termed human pheromones warrant being termed pheromones? *Physiology and Behavior*, 82, 697–701.

Winne, P. H. and Nebit, J. C. (2010). The psychology of academic achievement. *Annual Review of Psychology*, 61, 653–78.

Winner, E. (1996). *Gifted Children*. New York, NY. Basic Books.

Wisniewski, S. R., Rush, A. J., Nierenberg, A. A., Gaynes, B. N., Warden, D., et al (2009). Can Phase III trial results of antidepressant medications be generalized to clinical practice? A STAR*D report. *American Journal of Psychiatry*, 166, 599–607.

Witek-Janusek, L., Albuquerque, K., Chroniak, K. R., Chroniak, C., Durazo-Arvisu. R., et al (2010). Effect of mindfulness-based stress reduction on immune function, quality of life, and coping in women newly diagnosed with early stage breast cancer. *Brain, Behavior, and Immunity*, 22, 969–81.

Witelson, S. F., Kigar, D. L., Scambougeras, A., Kideckel, D. M., Buck, B., et al (2008). Corpus callosum anatomy in right-handed homosexual and heterosexual men. *Archives of Sexual Behavior*, 37, 857–63.

Witham, L. (1997, 11 April). Many scientists see God's hand in evolution. *The Washington Times*, p A8. Retrieved from http://www.ncseweb.org on 15 October 2008. For greater detail see: http://www.ncseweb.org/resources/rncse_content/vol24/9863_polling_the_creationismevolut_12_30_1899.asp.

Witt, L. A., Burke, L. A., Barrick, M. R., and Mount, M. K. (2002). The interactive effects of conscientiousness and agreeableness on job performance. *Journal of Applied Psychology*, 87, 164–9.

Witt, L. A. and Ferris, G. R. (2003). Social skill as moderator of the conscientiousness-performance relationship. Convergent results across four studies. *Journal of Applied Psychology*, 88, 809–21.

Wittmann, A., Schlagenhauf, F., Guhn, A., Lueken, U., Gaehlsdorf, et al (2014). Anticipating agoraphobic situations. The neural correlates of panic disorder with agoraphobia. *Psychological Medicine*, 44(11), 2385–96.

Witvliet, C. V., Ludwig, T. E., and Vander Laan, K. L. (2001). Granting forgiveness or harboring grudges. Implications for emotion, physiology, and health. *Psychological Science*, 12(2), 117–23.

Witvliet, C. V. O. (2005). Unforgiveness, forgiveness, and justice. Scientific findings on feelings and physiology. In E. L. Worthington, Jr (ed), *Handbook of Forgiveness* (pp 305–19). New York, NY. Routledge.

Witvliet, C. V. O. and McCullough, M. E. (2007). Forgiveness and health. A review and theoretical exploration of emotion pathways. In S. G. Post (ed), *Altruism and Health. Perspectives from Empirical Research* (pp 259–76). Oxford, UK. Oxford University Press.

Wixted, J. T. (2004). The psychology and neuroscience of forgetting. *Annual Review of Psychology*, 55, 235–69.

Woike, B. A. and McAdams, D. P. (2001). A response to Lilienfeld, Woods, and Garb. TAT-based personality measures have considerable validity. *American Psychological Society Observer*, 14. Retrieved from http://www.psychologicalscience.org/observer/0501/pspicom%20ment.html on 5 November 2005.

Woike, B. A. and McAdams, D. P. (2001, May/June). A response to Lilienfeld, Woods, and Garb. TAT-based personality measures have considerable validity. *American Psychological Society Observer*, 14(5). Retrieved from www.psychologi-calscience.org on 29 November 2007.

Wolfe, J. M., Kluender, K. R., Levi, D. M., Bartoshuk, L. M., Herz, R. S., et al (2009). *Sensation and Perception* (2nd edn). Sunderland, MA. Sinauer.

Wolfe, M. M., Lichtenstein, D. R., and Singh, G. (1999). Gastrointestinal toxicity of nonsteroidal anti-inflammatory drugs. *New England Journal of Medicine*, 341, 1888–99.

Wolpe, J. (1982). *The Practice of Behavior Therapy* (3rd edn). New York, NY. Pergamon Press.

Woman in custody after forgetting baby. (2005, 12 March). KATV. Retrieved from http://www.katv.com/news/stories/0305/213321.html on 4 May 2005.

Wonderlich, S. A., Joiner, T. E., Keel, P. K., and Williamson, D. A. (2007). Eating disorders diagnoses. Empirical approaches to classification. *American Psychologist*, 62, 167–80.

Woo, H. and Raley, K. (2005). A small extension to 'Costs and Rewards of Children. The effects of Becoming a Parent on Adults' Lives'. *Journal of Marriage and Family*, 67, 216–21.

Wood, D., Bruner, J. S., and Ross, G. (1976). The role of tutoring in problem solving. *Journal of Child Psychology and Psychiatry*, 17(2), 89–100.

Wood, D. M., Stribley, V., Dargan, P. I., Davies, S., Holt, D. W., et al (in press). Variability in the 3, 4-methylenedioxymethamphetamine content of 'ecstasy' tablets in the U.K. *Emergency Medical Journal*, 28, 764–65.

Wood, J. V., Heimpel, S. A., and Michela, J. L. (2003). Savoring versus dampening. Self-esteem differences in regulating positive affect. *Journal of Personality and Social Psychology*, 85, 566–80.

Wood, J. V., Perunovic, W. Q. E, and Lee, J. W. (2009). Positive self-statements. Power for some, peril for others. *Psychological Science*, 20, 860–6.

Wood, J. V., Taylor, S. E., and Lichtman, R. (1985). Social comparison in adjustment to breast cancer. *Journal of Personality and Social Psychology*, 49, 1169–83.

Wood, W. (2000). Attitude change. Persuasion and social influence. *Annual Review of Psychology*, 51, 539–70.

Wood, W. and Eagly, A. H. (2002). A cross-cultural analysis of the behavior of women and men. Implications for the origins of sex differences. *Psychological Bulletin*, 128, 699–727.

Wood, W. and Eagly, A. H. (2007). Social structural origins of sex differences in human mating. In S. W. Gangestad, and J. A. Simpson (eds), *The Evolution of Mind. Fundamental Questions and Controversies* (pp 383–90). New York, NY. Guilford Press.

Woods, S. C., Chavez, M., Park, C. R., Riedy, C., Kaiyala, K., et al (1995). The evaluation of insulin as a metabolic signal controlling behavior via the brain. *Neuroscience and Biobehavioral Reviews*, 20, 139–44.

World Health Organization (2003). *WHO World Health Report*. Retrieved from http://www.who.int/whr/2003/en/whr03_en.pdf on 21 April 2008.

World Health Organization (2004). Public health problems caused by harmful use of alcohol. Retrieved from http://www.who.int/gb/ebwha/pdf_files on 1 February 2006.

World Health Organization (2005). Why is tobacco a public health priority? Retrieved from http://www.who.int/tobacco/en/on 3 February 2006.

World Health Organization (2008). *Global Database on Body Mass Index*. Retrieved from http://www.who.int/bmi/index.jsp on 19 April 2008.

World Health Organization (2008). *WHO Report on the Global Tobacco Epidemic, 2008. The MPOWER Package*. Retrieved from http://www.who.int/tobacco/mpower/mpower_report_forward_summary_2008.pdf on 12 March 2010.

World Health Organization (2011a). Suicide prevention (SUPRE). Retrieved from http://www.who.int/mental_health/prevention/suicide/suicidepre%20vent/en/on 11 March 2013.

World Health Organization (2011b). Suicide rates per 100,000 by country, year and sex (Table). Retrieved from http://www.who.int/mental_health/prevention/suicide_rates/en/index.html on 11 March 2013.

World Health Organization (2013). Distribution of suicide rates (per 100,000) by gender and age, 2000. Retrieved from http://www.who.int/mental_health/prevention/suicide/suicide_rates_chart/en/index.html on 16 March 2013.

World Health Organization, Alonso, J., Liu, Z., Evans-Lacko, S., Sadikova, E., et al (2018). Treatment gap for anxiety disorders is global. Results of the World Mental Health Surveys in 21 countries. *Depression and Anxiety*, 35(3), 195–208.

Worthingon, E. L., Jr, Witvliet, C. V. O., Pietrini, P., and Miller, A. J. (2007). Forgiveness, health, and well-being. A review of evidence for emotional versus decisional forgiveness, dispositional forgivingness, and reduced unforgiveness. *Journal of Behavioral Medicine*, 30, 291–302.

Worthington, E. L., Jr and Scherer, M. (2004). Forgiveness is an emotion-focused coping strategy that can reduce health risks and promote health resilience. Theory, review, and hypotheses. *Psychology and Health*, 19, 385–405.

Wortman, C. B. (1975). Some determinants of perceived control. *Journal of Personality and Social Psychology*, 31, 282–94.

Wright, D., Parkes, A., Strange, V., Allen, E., Bonell, C., et al (2008). The quality of young people's heterosexual relationships. A longitudinal analysis of characteristics shaping subjective experience. *Perspectives on Sexual and Reproductive Health*, 40, 226–37.

Wright, D. B., Boyd, C. E., and Tredoux, C. G. (2001). A field study of own-race bias, in South Africa and England. *Psychology, Public Policy, and Law*, 7, 119–33.

Wright, K. P., Jr, Gronfier, C., Duffy, J. F., and Czeisler, C. A. (2005). Intrinsic period and light intensity determine the phase relationship between melatonin and sleep in humans. *Journal of Biological Rhythms*, 20, 168–77.

Wright, L. (1997). *Twins. And What They Tell Us About Who We Are*. New York, NY. John Wiley and Sons.

Wudy, S., Dorr, H. G., Solleder, C., Djalali, M., and Homoki, J. (1999). Profiling steroid hormones in amniotic fluid of midpregnancy by routine stable isotope dilution/gas chromoatography-mass spectrometry. Reference values and concentrations in fetuses at risk for 21-hydroxylase deficiency. *Journal of Clinical Endocrinology and Metabolism*, 84, 2724–8.

Wyart, C., Webster, W. W., Chen, J. H., Wilson, S. R., McClary, A., et al (2007). Smelling a single component of male sweat alters levels of cortisol in women. *The Journal of Neuroscience*, 27, 1261–5.

Wynn, K. (1992). Addition and subtraction by human infants. *Nature*, 358, 749–50.

Wynne, C. D. L. (2004). *Do Animals Think?* Princeton, NJ. Princeton University Press.

Wysocki, C. J. and Preti, G. (2004). Facts, fallacies, fears, and frustrations with human pheromones. *The Anatomical Record*, 218A, 1201–11.

Xu, Y., Liu, J., and Kanwisher, N. (2005). The M170 is selective for faces, not for expertise. *Neuropsychologia*, 43, 588–97.

Yaksh, T. L. (1999). Regulation of spinal nociceptive processing. Where we went when we wandered onto the path marked by the gate. *Pain*, 6(Suppl), S149–52.

Yang, C-M., Han, H-Y., Yang, M-H., Su, W-C., and Lane, T. (2010). What subjective experiences determine the perception of falling asleep during sleep onset period? *Consciousness and Cognition*, 19, 1084–92.

Yang, Y. (2008a). Long and happy living. Trends and patterns of happy life expectancy in the U.S., 1970–2000. *Social Science Research*, 37, 1235–52.

Yang, Y. (2008b). Social inequalities in happiness in the United States, 1972 to 2004. An age-period-cohort analysis. *American Sociological Review*, 73, 204–26.

Yatham, L. (2005). Atypical antipsychotics for bipolar disorder. *Psychiatric Clinics of North America*, 28, 325–47.

Yavuz, M. S., Holland, S., and Spracklen, K. (2018). A descent into dark leisure in music. *Annals of Leisure Research*, 21(4), 391–4.

Yeo, S. (2007). First-year university science and engineering students' understanding of plagiarism. *Higher Education Research and Development*, 26, 199–216.

Yirmiya, N., Erel, O., Shaked, M., and Solomonica-Levi, D. (1998). Meta-analyses comparing theory of mind abilities of individuals with autism, individuals with mental retardation, and normally developing individuals. *Psychological Bulletin*, 124, 283–307.

Yolken, R. H. and Torrey, E. F. (2008). Are some cases of psychosis caused by microbial agents? A review of the evidence. *Molecular Psychiatry*, 13, 470–9.

Youngson, R. M. and Schott, I. (1998). *Medical Blunders*. New York, NY. New York University Press.

Yuki, M., Maddux, W. W., and Masuda, T. (2007). Are the windows to the soul same in the East and West? Cultural differences in using the eyes and mouth as cues to recognize emotions in Japan and the United States. *Journal of Experimental Social Psychology*, 43, 303–11.

Zadro, L., Williams, K. D., and Richardson, R. (2004). How low can you go? Ostracism by a computer is sufficient to lower self-reported levels of belonging, control, self-esteem, and meaningful existence. *Journal of Experimental Social Psychology*, 40, 560–7.

Zajonc, R. B. (1968). Attitudinal effects of mere exposure. *Journal of Personality and Social Psychology Monograph* , 9 (Part 2), 1–27.

Zajonc, R. B. (1984). On the primacy of affect. *American Psychologist*, 39, 117–23.

Zajonc, R. B. (2001). Mere exposure. A gateway to the subliminal. *Current Directions in Psychological Science*, 10, 224–8.

Zanarini, M. C., Frankenburg, F. R., Hennen, J., and Silk, J. R. (2004). Mental health service utilization by borderline personality disorder patients and Axis II comparison subjects followed prospectively for 6 years. *Journal of Clinical Psychiatry*, 65, 28–36.

Zeki, S. (1991). Cerebral akinetopsia (visual motion blindness). A review. *Brain*, 114(Part 2), 811–24.

Zeki, S. (2007). A theory of micro-consciousness. In M. Velmans, and S. Scheider (eds), *The Blackwell Companion to Consciousness* (pp 580–8). Malden, MA. Blackwell Publishing.

Zepelin, H., Siegel, J. M., and Tobler, I. (2005). Mammalian sleep. In M. H. Kryger, T. Roth, and W. C. Dement (eds), *Principles and Practice of Sleep Medicine* (pp 91–100). Philadelphia, PA. Elsevier/ Saunders.

Zhang, A. Y. and Snowden, L. R. (1999). Ethnic characteristics of mental disorders in five U.S. communities. *Cultural Diversity and Ethnic Minority Psychology*, 5, 134–46.

Zhang, G. and Simon, H. A. (1985). STM capacity for Chinese words and idioms. Chunking and acoustical loop hypotheses. *Memory and Cognition*, 13, 193–201.

Zhao, G. Q., Zhang, Y., Hoon, M., Chandrashekar, J., Erlenbach, I., et al (2003). The receptors for mammalian sweet and umami taste. *Cell*, 115, 255–66.

Zilbergeld, B. (1983). *The Shrinking of America. Myths of Psychological Change*. Boston, MA. Little Brown and Company.

Zimbardo, P. G. (1973). On the ethics of intervention in human psychological research. With special reference to the Stanford prison experiment. *Cognition*, 2, 243–56.

Zimbardo, P. G. (2007). *The Lucifer Effect*. New York, NY. Random House.

Zimmerman, M., McGlinchey, J. B., Chelminski, I., and Young, D. (2008). Diagnostic co-morbidity in 2300 psychiatric out-patients presenting for treatment evaluation with a semi-structured diagnostic interview. *Psychological Medicine*, 38, 199–210.

Zinbarg, R. E., Barlow, D. H., Liebowitz, M., Street, L., Broadhead, E., et al (1994). The DSM-IV field trial for mixed anxiety-depression. *American Journal of Psychiatry*, 151, 1153–62.

Zinke, K. et al (2014). Working memory training and transfer in older adults. Effects of age, baseline performance, and training gains. *Developmental Psychology*, 50(1), 304.

Zosuls, K. M., Ruble, D. M., Tamis-LeMonda, C. S., Shrout, P. E., Bornstein, M. H., et al (2009). The acquisition of gender labels in infancy. Implications for sex-typed play. *Developmental Psychology*, 45, 688–701.

Zuberbüler, K. (2003). Referential signaling in non-human primates. Cognitive precursors and limitations for the evolution of language. *Advances in the Study of Behavior*, 33, 265–307.

Zuberi, S. M. (2010). Narcolepsy in childhood. *Journal of Pediatric Neurology*, 8, 79–80.

Zuckerman, M. (1994). *Behavioral Expressions and Biosocial Bases of Sensation Seeking*. Cambridge, UK. Cambridge University Press.

Zuckerman, M. and Aluja, A. (2015). Measures of sensation seeking. In *Measures of Personality and Social Psychological Constructs* (pp 352–80). Academic Press.

Zwaan, M., Dijkstra, J. K., and Veenstra, R. (2013). Status hierarchy, attractiveness hierarchy and sex ratio. Three contextual factors explaining the status–aggression link among adolescents. *International Journal of Behavioral Development*, 37(3), 211–21.

NAME INDEX

Note: Tables and figures are indicated by an italic *t* and *f* following the page number.

SUBJECT INDEX

Note: Tables and figures are indicated by an italic *t* and *f* following the page number.

brain 98–122
  in adolescent development 460–2
  CNS and 94
  DBS and 683
  development 415
  function, and human experience 125–7
  geography of 99f
  magnetic brain stimulation and 682
  major structures of 100f
  and mind, difference between 133
  MRI of 98
  neural connections in 98
  plasticity 121–2
  sex differences in 119–21, 120f
  size, and autism 132
  social 157–8
  see also forebrain; hindbrain; midbrain
brainstem 98, 100f
brain training programmes 505–6, 505f
brain waves 187, 188, 189t
  alpha 375f, 375
  gamma 375f, 375
  insight and 374–6, 375f
  patterns 187f
  sawtooth 188, 189f, 189t
breast cancer 372f
brief dynamic therapy (BDT) 653
  effectiveness 654
brightness constancy 302, 303–4
British empiricism 35
British Psychological Society (BPS)
  academic psychology 30
  applied psychology 30
  ethical guidelines 69–70
  ethical principles 69–70
  psychological science 25
Broca's area 109f, 113
Buddhism 32–3
  anger and 590
  defence mechanisms and 535
  MBCT and 662
Buffy the Vampire Slayer (TV
    programme) 463
bulimia nervosa (BN) 610t, 612t
  self-esteem and 524
burden of proof 29
bystander apathy 749–53
bystander effect 750–2, 769

C

caffeine 203, 203f, 211–12
  addiction 211–12
  classical conditioning 245
  intoxication 212
caffeine use disorder 611t
caligynophobia 619
callosotomy 115–18
cancer
  ageing and 476–7
  breast 372f
candidate genes 501
cannabis 203, 207, 218, 219
  schizophrenia and 639, 640
Cannon–Bard theory of emotion 582, 583

career decisions 466
Care in the Community 614
caring 439, 440t
case studies 50–1, 504
  Freud's 518–19
catastrophizing 661
catatonia 612t
categorization 728
catharsis 590–1
cathexis 513
causation 56–8, 57f
causes
  dispositional 703, 707
  proximate 745–7
  situational 703, 707
  ultimate 745, 747–8
CBT *see* cognitive behaviour therapy
cell bodies 82, 83f
central control 640
central nervous system (CNS) 83, 92–5, 93f
central pattern generators 95, 95f
cerebellum 98, 99–101
cerebral cortex 102, 107–13
  lobes of 109f
cerebral hemispheres 102, 102f
  differences in function of 114t
  division of labour in 115f
  specialization of 112, 113–19, 120–1
C-fibres 290, 291f
chaining 251
challenge hypothesis 763–4
chance 378–80
  illusion of control and 695
  personality and 534–5
change blindness 307–8, 309f
characteristic adaptations 511
  personality changes and 542
chemical imbalance theory, of depression 628
child abuse
  depression and 628–9, 631
  memory manipulation and 345, 346
  repressed memory and 356, 357–8
  schizophrenia and 640
childbirth, associated mental and behaviour
    disorders 613t
child care 410–14
  mother–child attachment and 409–10
  wars 411
childhood amnesia 348
child-rearing style
  of parents 464
  peers and 464
  see also parents
children
  early separation experiences 410–16
  kidnapped 371
  LAD and 383–4
  memory manipulation in 345–6
  nursery care 6, 7, 8f
  peer relations 416–19
  shared environments and 533
  sociometric status 418–19
  working mothers 6
chimpanzees
  ASL and 390–1, 392f

culture and 169, 169f
  gestures and 393, 394f
  language and 389–94, 392f
Christianity 535, 590, 604
chromosomes 140
chunking 326, 349
cigarettes 212–14
  alcohol and 216
  in pregnancy 452–3
  see also smoking; tobacco use
circadian pacemaker 184–6, 185f
circadian rhythm 184–6
  disorder 196
circular questioning 666
clairvoyance 316, 317
clanging 640
classical conditioning 36, 37, 232–46
  biological preparedness and 241–3, 242f
  cognition and 239–40, 240f
  evolution and 241–3
  function of 234
  general process view of 241
  learning and 246
  limits of 245–7
  neural basis 244, 245f
  process 233f
classification of mental disorder 609–17
client-centred therapy (CCT) 664–6
  definition of 650t
  features of 664–5, 665f
  outcome research 669
clients 648
clinical psychologists 649
clinical psychology 30–1
  paradigm shift, call for 616
closed questions 52
closure 295, 296f
clozapine 677
CM *see* contingency management
CMC *see* computer-mediated
    communication
CNS *see* central nervous system
cocaine 206–7, 210–11, 453–4
  activation by 236, 236f
  cravings 236f
cochlea 283, 285f
codes, languages as 381–2
coercive sexual sadism disorder 613t
coffee 211–12
  classical conditioning 245
cognition
  ageing and 472–4
  anxiety disorders and 622
  classical conditioning and
    239–40, 240f
  deception and 581
  emotion and 582–7
  impeccable trivia 27
  influence of language on 386–8
  metacognition 567
  motivation and 561–6, 567
  observational learning and 262
  operant conditioning and 255–8
  schizophrenia and 639–40
  thoughts vs 363–6

response bias 273
response generalization 251
resting potential 84
restless legs syndrome 610t, 613t
retardation 487
reticular formation 101
retina 276, 277f
retinal disparity 297–8
retrieval 322–3, 322f
    cues 338
retroactive interference 349, 350f
reunion, response to 402, 404
reuptake 88
revenge 590
review articles 9
reward centres 106
rewards
    external 581–2
    nucleus accumbens and 106
rhesus monkeys 288f, 288
    undermining effect 555, 555f
ribonucleic acid (RNA) 141–2, 142f
rich false memory 353
risk factors
    for schizophrenia 640
    for suicide 632
risks, and ethical guidelines 69
risk-taking 461–2
Ritalin 211
ritual violence 761
RNA see ribonucleic acid
Robbers Cave experiment 757
rods 277–9, 278f
Rohypnol (flunitrazepam) 217–18
role models
    modelling and 259–60
    social role theory and 174
Romania 407, 414–16, 414f, 416f, 503
romantic relationships
    in adolescence 463–4
    adult development and 467–8
Rorschach test 309–10, 310f, 537f
    personality and 537
    reliability of 537
    validity of 537
rTMS see repetitive transcranial magnetic
    stimulation
rumination 590–1
    anxiety disorders and 622
rumours 29

S

sadness
    as basic emotion 576–7, 577f
    depression and 573
    smiling and 578f
safety ratio 208, 208t
salivation 233–4, 233f
Sally-Anne task 442–3, 444f
samples 52–3
    biased 53
    quota 52–3
sanctity 440, 440t
Sapir–Whorf hypothesis 386–7

saudade 577
scaffolding 434
Scared Straight interventions 672t
scatterplots 55, 56f
scepticism 26
schemas 427
    effects on memory 342–3, 343f
    emotion 565
schizoid personality disorder 611t, 643t
schizophrenia 98, 610t, 612t, 632–41
    antipsychotics for 676
    cannabis use and 639, 640
    causes of 635–41
    cognitive factors for 639–40
    Cotard syndrome 125
    definition of 633
    diagnosis 632, 633–5
    DID distinguished from 633
    early experience and later
        symptoms 640–1
    endophenotypes and 637
    genetics and 635–7, 636f
    heritability of 635–7, 636f
    negative symptoms of 634–5
    neurocognitive testing for 637
    neurodevelopmental factors for 637–9
    positive symptoms of 634, 635
    prefrontal lobotomy and 113
    prodromal phase 634
    residual phase 634
    suicide and 633
    systemic therapy and 666–7
schizophrenogenic mother 640
schizotypal disorder 608, 610t, 612t, 643t
science 3–4, 14
    applied psychology 32
    cognitive 363
    definition of 26
    inferential statistics 63
    qualitative research 67
    research questions 7
    self-correction of 28
    see also neuroscience; psychological
        science
Science 204–5
scientific integrity 69
scientific method 26
    academic psychology 27
    experiments 58, 71
    humanistic psychology 27
    scepticism 26
    stages 26f
    theories and hypotheses 42, 43
scientific reasoning 434
scientific thinking 15–16
scientism 132
Scientology 29
SCN see suprachiasmatic nuclei
scriptotherapy 591
scripts, effects on memory 342–3, 343f
SCRUFFY targets 564
search engines 9–10, 12, 13
second pain 290, 291f
second polar body 451
secondary oocyte 451, 452f

secondary reinforcers 251
secondary sources 9
second-order conditioning 235
sectioning (involuntary commitment) 615
secure attachment 404, 405, 407–9
seduction 162f
selective serotonin reuptake inhibitors
    (SSRIs) 88, 89, 674–5
    discontinuation syndrome 675
    side effects 675t
self
    acceptance 540–1
    boundaries of 747
    concept 523
    definition of 692
    positive illusions and 694–6
    sense of, and cortical arousal 125–6
    in social context 692–8
    uncritically positive views of the 695
self-actualization 557
self-change 698–703
self-concept 523
self-control 698–702, 699f
    strength model of 701–2
self-defence 692
    cognitive biases as 692–6
    social comparison theory and 697
    see also defence mechanisms
self-direction 641
self-efficacy 561–2
self-enhancement 171
    social comparison theory and 697
    social identity theory 728–9
self-esteem 171, 524–5
    aggression and 524–5
    attitudes and 710–11
    BN and 524
    defensive 525
    fragile 525
    happiness and 524
    narcissism and 525
    relationships and 525
    social comparison theory and 697–8
    violence and 524–5
self-evaluation
    cognitive dissonance and 711
    social comparison theory and 696–7
self-improvement 171
self-narratives 511
    personality changes and 542
self-presentation 737–8
self-regulation 698–701
self-reports 718
self-serving bias 692–3, 692f, 766
self-talk 680
self-transcendence 557
semantic cues 340
semantic encoding 326, 327f
semantic memory 330, 331
senior moments 472
sensation 269–70
sensation seeking 529
sense organs 96, 270, 275
senses 275
sensitive responsiveness 406, 408